COLUMBIA PROJECT ON

ASIA

IN THE · CORE CURRICULUM

ASIA IN WESTERN
AND WORLD HISTORY

Columbia Project on Asia in the Core Curriculum

ASIA: CASE STUDIES IN THE SOCIAL SCIENCES
A GUIDE FOR TEACHING
Myron L. Cohen, editor

MASTERWORKS OF ASIAN LITERATURE IN COMPARATIVE PERSPECTIVE
A GUIDE FOR TEACHING
Barbara Stoler Miller, editor

ASIA IN WESTERN AND WORLD HISTORY
A GUIDE FOR TEACHING
Ainslie T. Embree and Carol Gluck, editors

Roberta Martin
Project Director

Wm. Theodore de Bary, Ainslie T. Embree, Carol Gluck
Project Chairmen

COLUMBIA PROJECT ON

ASIA

IN THE   CORE CURRICULUM

ASIA IN WESTERN AND WORLD HISTORY

A Guide for Teaching

Edited by
Ainslie T. Embree and **Carol Gluck**

An East Gate Book

M.E. Sharpe
Armonk, New York
London, England

An East Gate Book

Library of Congress Cataloging-in-Publication Data

Asia in western and world history : a guide for
teaching / Ainslie T. Embree and Garol Gluck, editors.
p.   cm. — (Columbia project on Asia in the core curriculum)
Includes bibliographical references and index.
ISBN 1-56324-264-8 (cloth : alk. paper). —
ISBN 1-56324-265-6 (paper : alk. paper)
1. Asia—History. I. Embree, Ainslie Thomas.
II. Gluck, Carol, 1941–   . III. Series.
DS33.A86   1995
950—dc20   95-15507
CIP
Printed in the United States of America

BM (c)   10   9   8   7   6   5   4   3
BM (p)   10   9   8   7   6

Contents

I.   Asia in Western History

Introductions

Essays

IV. Themes in Asian History

Postscript

Preface

The Project on Asia in the Core Curriculum began in 1984 to support the introduction of material on Asia into the core curricula of undergraduate institutions throughout the country. Three "Guides for Teaching" are the result of dialogue between Asian specialists and colleagues specializing in the Western tradition who most often teach the introductory, general education courses in the various academic disciplines. There was no attempt to stress Asia at the expense of the West. The purpose was to identify texts, themes, and comparative concepts that would provide avenues of entry for Asian material into core courses in literature, history, and the social sciences.

The guides are entitled: *Asia in Western and World History, Masterworks of Asian Literature in Comparative Perspective,* and *Asia: Case Studies in the Social Sciences.* Each volume contains approximately forty essays by leading specialists that suggest a range of possibilities for introducing material on Asia. The essays are arranged to provide the widest choice of approaches to meet the reader's pedagogical needs. While the guides are discrete publications, they form a series that facilitates interdisciplinary teaching: An instructor who chooses, for example, to draw upon William Hauser's discussion of Tokugawa Japan in world history in this volume will also find material of interest in Donald Keene's essay on Chikamatsu's "Love Suicides at Sonezaki" (in *Masterworks of Asian Literature in Comparative Perspective),* in William W. Kelly's article on "Rural Society in Japan: Past and Present," in Theodore Bestor's discussion of "Urban Life in Japan," and in Stephen R. Smith's essay on "The Family in Japan" (in *Asian Case Studies in the Social Sciences).*

The Project on Asia in the Core Curriculum has involved over one hundred scholars from seventy-five public and private undergraduate institutions throughout the United States. It has been chaired at Columbia University by a panel composed of Wm. Theodore de Bary, Ainslie T. Embree, and Carol Gluck.

The National Endowment for the Humanities, the Henry Luce Foundation, the Panasonic Foundation, and the U.S. Department of Education have sponsored the project. We are deeply indebted to these sponsors for their continuing support.

We welcome any and all contributions to this ongoing curricular dialogue.

Roberta Martin
Project Director

Guide to the Reader

Asia in Western and World History is divided into four sections devoted to *Asia in Western History, Asia in World History, Modern Asia 1600–1900,* and *Themes in Asian History.* The first section, *Asia in Western History,* offers insights that might be integrated into courses focused on the history of Western civilization and of Western thought. The section begins with four introductory essays that set the broad stage for the relation of Asia to the West historically and geographically. The essays that follow discuss in chronological order significant aspects of the interconnections between Asian and Western history.

The second section of the volume, *Asia in World History,* begins with an introductory essay of the same title and continues with essays, again chronologically organized, that discuss major developments in world history. This section includes primary essays on developments in world history in a given time period, such as "Separate Spheres and New Links: A New Stage in World History, 1000–1500" by Peter N. Stearns, and parallel essays, such as the two that follow the Stearns' article ("The Case of China" by Michael Marmé and "The Case of Japan" by H. Paul Varley). The parallel essays elaborate upon the developments of the period in relationship to a particular Asian country or region.

The third section of the volume, *Modern Asia, 1600—1990,* includes essays on the recent histories of China, India, Japan, and Korea arranged chronologically and then by country.

The fourth section of the volume, *Themes in Asian History,* discusses important themes or historical perspectives useful in teaching the histories of South Asia, Southeast Asia, China, Japan and Korea as well as the relations of Asia and Latin American and Japan and America, and intercultural exchange between Asia and the West.

In the *Postscript*, "Summaries of the Essays" provide a brief survey of the contents of the articles and indicate chapters containing related material. These summaries are designed to assist the reader seeking to identify those essays most relevant to a particular topic or course.

A "crib-sheet" on East Asia, for use with the National Standards for World History, and timelines of Asian history are included at the end of the volume for reference.

Participants
NEH Institute
Asia in Western and World History

Beverly S. Almgren
Moore College of Art

Myrna Chase
Baruch College,
City University of New York

Daniel P. Connerton
North Adams State College

Arthur P. Dudden
Bryn Mawr College

Edward Ellsworth
Wheelock College

Theopolis Fair
La Salle University

Lorenz J. Firsching
Broome Community College

Paul E. Gill
Shippensburg College

William E. Gohlman
State University of New York
at Geneseo

Cho-yun Hsu
University of Pittsburgh

Dale E. Landon
Indiana University of Pennsylvania

Loyd E. Lee
State University of New York
at New Paltz

Steven A. Leibo
Russell Sage College

Derek S. Linton
Hobart and William
Smith Colleges

Michael Marmé
Fordham University

Davis Ross
Lehman College,
City University of New York

Arthur Schmidt
Temple University

Lillian Lewis Shiman
Nichols College

Gerald Sorin
State University of New York
at New Paltz

Margaret K. Stolee
State University of New York
at Geneseo

James S. Taylor
Wells College

Wei-ping Wu
University of Bridgeport

Ka-che Yip
University of Maryland,
Baltimore County

Introduction

Ainslie T. Embree and Carol Gluck

We began this project as curricular optimists, members of a rather large group of teachers and scholars committed to gathering materials on Asia for use in undergraduate courses. Our task, we thought, was relatively simple, since others had already done most of the work. Western civilization and world history had long been taught in colleges around the country, while Asian history and civilization had acquired an impressive pedagogical pedigree in recent years. We had only to bring the two together and align existing Asian content with existing Western and world history curricula. As long as the range of choice was broad enough to allow instructors to make selections appropriate to their needs, the deed would be done: Asia could join the world in the core curriculum.

Not quite. In the dozen years since the project started, nearly every one of our naive assumptions was demolished—fruitfully demolished but demolished nonetheless. The definition of world history changed, as schools and scholars worked to reframe the subject in suitably late twentieth-century terms. The academic debates and instructional experiments that today make world history such a dynamic field made it a moving target for curricular enterprises like ours. The canonical course in Western civ also came in for renewed controversy, not only because of the common claim that it was too Eurocentric but because, in the politicized mood of the early 1990s, some said that it was not Eurocentric enough. Meanwhile the discipline of history continued to shift its methodological weight away from politics and economics in the direction of social and cultural history. Yet much of the existing material on Asia devoted more attention to rulers and their dynasties than it did to families and their daughters.

Even the terms changed under examination. Asia, we said, was half the world, but what—or where—was "Asia"? Here the territory includes western Asia, better known as the Near or Middle East; the larger part of a supercontinental "Eurasia," which ranges from North Europe to South China; South Asia, primarily the Indian subcontinent; Southeast Asia, from Burma to the Phillippines; and East Asia, mostly China, Japan, and Korea. But such an "Asia" is clearly in the eye of the beholder, the constructed Self or Other which changes with time, place, and those who do the beholding. And so the process of constructing "Asia" and the "West" became a curricular topic in itself. In both instances the name suggests a singular, putative unity that masks the diversity of historical experience to which historyteaching is vocationally devoted. Just using the term Asia put us at risk of repeating the errors of reification that we hoped to correct.

If "Asia" seemed to grow in substantial weight, "the world" sometimes shrank to a shadow of its global self. World history, yes, but the history of whose world? The attention focused, in fact, on Eurasia—on "East" and "West" as we know it, "our" world. The southern hemisphere is barely mentioned: Africa coastally, Latin America barely and not in its pre-Columbian heights, the south Pacific not at all. But "we" of North America are not there either, the legacy of the segregation of American history from world history in the curriculum. And the genuinely globalized twentieth century in itself receives scant notice, at least in global terms, the commonalities of its historical experience divided into a few country-sized chunks. In the course of this project we learned again and again the limitations of our conceptual "world," and the lesson proved humbling and salutary at the same time.

Because the work was designed to provide usable material on Asia for integration into existing courses, we accepted the arbitrary division between Western and world history. This distinction means that the section on Western history stands firmly anchored in "the West" and includes "Asia" where it appeared on the horizon of those who stood in a similar position in the past. Whether Islamic interaction in the European world or European imperialism in the Asian world, Europe remains the focus. But Asian history is treated in its own right, not only as Europeans of the time may have construed it. The material is meant to serve the needs of a Western civ course expanded by an Asian perspective: it is the world seen from the West but with Asia in it. For the wider context of Western history itself, one has to turn to the world history section.

In world history Asia is present, literally, from the first, since the essays stand not in a single cultural spot but range across boundaries and borders, looking to see how the world was linked at different times and how different parts of the world compared in common human experiences. Indeed, in so far as world history is aggressively and ecumenically comparative, Asia's civilizations, empires, religions, and technologies frequently set the standard of comparison for other places. In world history, no time, no society is supposed to stand a priori in a privileged position; there is no one golden age, no single historical model. When China flourished in the Tang and the Song, its achievements draw attention; when the West rose to modern dominance, its story becomes the center. And ideally, the rest of the world ought not to disappear completely while those central stories are being told. In fact, it usually does, since the lust for coverage is world history's deadliest sin and has constantly to be restrained.

The wide open spaces of world history ought to have been easier than the fortress of Western civ to "infiltrate" with Asian history recounted on its own terms. But it did not turn out so here, in part because a number of the main essays presented their subjects in categories originally based on Western experience. If the definition of the neolithic revolution derives from the cereal growers of Asia Minor, then other peoples who settled down to grow rice and millet in southeast Asia or maize in Meso-America may not quite qualify as agricultural revolutionaries. This takeover of the narrative line sometimes made world history seem like western history writ global. As a result, we often found ourselves "adding Asia" to the main story, without necessarily getting inside the action and changing the categories themselves. That is why the short pieces on Asia often follow the main essay, seeming supplemental rather than integral to "the course of world history," a misleading impression that further work must correct.

Thus the guide is very much a work in progress, which does not pretend to offer a coherent framework or integrated corpus in itself. Instead, it is an assemblage of materials on Asia for teachers to browse through and choose from—a kind of curricular commonplace book. The third section, "Themes in Asian History," serves as a historical glossary, and the postscripts, too, are meant for reference use. Much is left out. Two types of "SOS" are noticeable—one, the Same-Old-Story, the march of political and intellectual history caused by the underrepresentation of social history; and two, the Same-Old-Sources, primarily documentary, largely omitting the wealth of visual objects and material culture. Primary texts, many of them literary, remain one of the most effective devices through which to incorporate Asia into history courses.

Some of these texts are mentioned here, and others can be found in the two accompanying guides on literature and social science.

Of the three guides in the series, history proved the least tractable to the process of "incorporation" of Asian content into various core curricula. Some said this was because social science seeks comparative generalities and literature reveals universals of human experience while history dwells ever in the realm of the particular. While the point is arguable, there is no doubt that specificity is history's province and that historyteaching and historywriting tend to follow the contours of language, nation, and region. "World historians" are few in number, and those who teach world history usually stretch themselves across vast areas of non-expertise to do so. Considering the difficulty, it is amazing how many teachers have newly taken the challenge to include unfamiliar material in their Western and world history offerings. We know because we worked with numbers of them in the course of this project. Similarly, historians are also working to reconceive the framework of world history in newly integrative and multiple ways. History may not be as far along in comparative perspective as social science or as "universally" accessible as literature, but the effort is clearly underway to rethink the human past. In the process, schooling and scholarship have the chance to work together, each helping the other, so that history curricula can be both sound **and** teachable at the same time.

This guide is a small part of this effort, and we thank the many people who have contributed to it: from world historians such as William McNeill and Philip Curtin who helped us with the "whole" to the specialists who provided the many "parts" on Asia and elsewhere. But most especially, our thanks go to the participants in the NEH Institute, which stretched over several years: the paper writers, the critics, and most of all, the teachers, whose names are appended here. Editorial gratitude goes to Madge Huntington, who ably guided every aspect of production, assisted by Lynette Peck and Winifred I. Olsen. The National Endowment for the Humanities, the Henry Luce Foundation, the Panasonic Foundation, and the U.S. Department of Education provided generous support. The greatest debt is to Roberta Martin, the director of the project, whose vision was matched only by her steadfastness and grace. Because of their enthusiasm, we started as optimists; because of our own limitations, we sank sometimes into despair; because of all of them and because of the challenge of history, we ended as optimists once again, knowing that others are already far beyond us in the effort to do a better job of teaching not only Asia's history but the world's.

I
Asia in Western History

ASIA IN WESTERN HISTORY

Ainslie T. Embree

The purpose of the essays in the following section is not to present material that may be useful in introducing courses on Asian civilizations or on world history in the undergraduate curriculum, but rather to look at Western history and to note the times and places where the different Asian civilizations interacted with the West in some significant fashion. What we are suggesting here, then, is not so much the incorporation of Asian material into the curriculum, but rather a work of excavation, of discovering Asia within the existing framework of courses on European or Western civilization. The purpose of the essays is the enrichment of such courses by a deepening of knowledge of the intersection between European and Asian civilizations, with the emphasis more on their context in Western history than on the history of the Asian civilizations themselves. The complexity of relationships between Europe and Asia is pointed up in the first essay by Rhoads Murphey's reminder that while Europe and Asia are one land mass, and while many of the ideas that we think of as "Western," including all the major religions, came from regions that we now label "Asia," the great centers of civilization in both Europe and Asia were separated from each other by formidable deserts, steppes, and mountains. As a number of the essays note, the oceans would eventually provide the most encompassing points of intersection.

These points of intersection, many of which are noted in Michael Marmé's "Brief Syllabus of Asia in Western History," may be conveniently grouped under four headings: Asia in Western thought; trade and commerce; imperial expansion; and war. These topics are obviously all interrelated, and many of the essays in this section touch upon more than one of them.

In regard to Asia in Western thought, something of our inten–

tion is summed up in the title of an undergraduate seminar started at Columbia College in the mid-1960's: "Asia in the Western Historical Imagination." This was essentially an exercise in intellectual history, tracing the extraordinary persistence of certain ideas about Asian society in classical Western thought from ancient Greece to the Enlightenment; later the seminar was narrowed to a focus on India, with a wider range of materials, including travelers' accounts, novels, and poetry. An experiment was also made in one section of the college's core curriculum course, "Introduction to Contemporary Civilization in the West," which is based on a reading of works regarded as significant for Western historical developments, of drawing attention to the use made by authors of references to Asia, especially India and China. This was indeed a work of "excavation" because very often editors of the texts widely used in such courses had left out passages referring to Asia, thinking they were not relevant to the authors' main arguments. In fact, such references are often very germane to points they were making about Asia presented as the Other, where societies seem to function on very different sets of presuppositions from those of the West, and it is over and against these strange societies that the authors tended to judge their own. Some of these ideas about Asian social and political life, irrespective of their validity, have an astonishing persistence in Western intellectual history, and they have shaped ideas about the nature of our own society as well as creating attitudes towards Asian countries that have undoubtedly at times influenced the political behavior of Western nations towards them.

Cho-yun Hsu gives an overview of these influences, and George Saliba deals specifically with the enormously important, but often slighted, interfusion of Islamic culture into Europe in the period before 1500. In his essay, Leonard Gordon discusses ideas about Asia in Western thought, with special reference to the interest of the Enlightenment thinkers in China. In the case of India, he notes the more pragmatic reasons for the views of British publicists. Harvey Goldman analyzes the images of Asia in the writings of three of the most powerful thinkers of the nineteenth century, Hegel, Marx, and Weber, showing the relation of these images to their theoretical systems and the ways in which their ideas have reinforced Western intellectual perceptions of Asian societies. While none of the essays in this volume deals specifically with art and religion, attention is given to these aspects of cultural interaction in the second volume in this series, *Masterworks of Asian Literature in Comparative Perspective*. In a Western civilization course, a consideration of the fascination in nineteenth-century Europe and America with Chinese and Japanese art and with Indian religion would be a natural development.

Despite, however, this interest in the cultural achievements of Asian civilizations, trade and commerce almost always provided the most widely diffused contacts between them and the Western world. A letter that King Manuel of Portugal wrote to King Ferdinand and Queen Isabella in 1499, just after he had received word of Vasco da Gama's voyage to India, echoes these interests in Asia:

"We learn that they did reach and discover India and other kingdoms and lordships bordering upon it; that they entered and navigated its sea, finding large cities, large edifices and rivers, and great populations, among whom is carried on all the trade in spices and precious stones . . . Of these they have brought a quantity."[1]

This was a reminder of how much more important the real Asia was to Europe than the faux-Indies discovered by their man, Columbus, reflecting not so much what da Gama actually saw as what dreams of Asian wealth, based on many centuries of actual contacts, had prepared them for.

Marc Van De Mieroop's essay, reaching back to the very beginnings of contacts between the areas we label Asia and Europe, focuses on developments in Europe for which Asian influence is most assured. He concludes that while many ideas originated in Asia, they were remodeled and then reexported to Asia, a process of interchange that characterizes the close interaction of the two continents. In a revision of a much misunderstood aspect of history, Morris Rossabi argues that a major contribution to such interaction was made by the Mongols, who inextricably linked Europe and Asia in their great conquests extending from China to the marchlands of eastern Europe. Derek Linton's essay follows the great changes in the intersection of Europe and Asia in the period between 1500 and 1850, and he points out that a historiography that insists upon seeing the period in terms of "seeds of empire" misses the fundamental fact that for a long time the Europeans were simply traders in Asia. Later technological developments in Europe combined, somewhat fortuitously, with political events in different areas of Asia to give them a territorial foothold, notably in India and Southeast Asia.

It was this territorial foothold that led to the great age of European imperialism in the nineteenth century. Linton's essay deals with the role of the rivalry of the European trading companies in the acquisition of empires, and Edward Malefakis in his essay emphasizes a point that is often forgotten, namely, that European influence was not decisive in any of the great Asian states prior to 1750. He then sets the age of imperial expansion into the context of European events, including the immense economic and industrial changes that took place in the eighteenth century. He concludes with an examination of the changes, both in Asia and Europe, that led to the end of the European empires.

War, as a point of intersection of Asia in Western history, does not find explicit treatment in any of our essays, but in fact it is implicit in them all. Herodotus, as Van De Mieroop points out, made a sharp distinction between Asia and Europe, and this was based partly at least on his perception of the Persian attack on the Greeks. In the nineteenth century, this was transformed into the opposition of the Asian spirit of despotism with the European love of freedom. This view surfaces very strongly in writers discussed by Gordon and Goldman. The Islamic world very early was pictured as making unceasing war on the West, not as the source of cultural transfusion that Saliba celebrates in his essay. Rossabi's Mongols got a particularly bad press as brutal hordes, threatening the West. War is also a necessary theme in the explications of trade, commerce, and imperial conquest in the essays by Linton and Malefakis. It is not until the twentieth century, however, that an Asian power, Japan, practices its own version of imperialist aggression.

The final essay, by Marilyn Young discusses this shift from a self-confident West, intruding into Asian space, to resurgent Asian powers asserting their sovereignty. She sees this as an action upon the part of conquered or near-conquered elites to regain control of their national destiny through modernization and the creation of a sense of nationalism. Looking at the Cold War in relation to Europe, America, and Asia, she concludes that "in the wake of the Cold War, historical processes of economic, social, and political change, of the shifting definitions of national identity and autonomy, of the tensions among regional rivalry, cooperation, and global integration become central to our analysis."[2] This would surely be one useful way to conclude a course in Western history that had attempted to mark its points of intersection with the civilizations of Asia.

NOTE

1. Cited in E.G. Ravenstein, ed., *The First Voyage of Vasco da Gama* (London: Hakluyt Society Publications, Old Series, No. 99, 1898), pp. 113–14
2. See M. Young, in this volume, p. 195.

THE SHAPE OF THE WORLD: EURASIA

Rhoads Murphey

Our purpose here is to enrich the student's understanding of Western civilization by pointing out its interconnections with Asia throughout history. The origins of what we call Western civilization are really in Mesopotamia, Egypt, Asia Minor (Anatolia, or Asiatic Turkey), Phoenicia (modern Syria, Lebanon, and Israel), and the Aegean. Influences on early Western civilization came also from ancient Persia, still farther east. The Greeks and the Romans had their major connections not northward (until quite late in the Roman Empire) but eastward, from where, they realized, most of the wealth and the sophisticated ideas came; all of the world religions, including Christianity, are Asian in origin.

THE EURASIAN LANDMASS

Eurasia is a single landmass. Europe is really a geographical expression and a cultural entity rather than a separate continent. Asia extends southwest to the Suez Canal and the Dardanelles. But the great classical civilizations of East and South Asia grew up far to the east, a long and difficult distance from Europe. After the decline and disappearance of classical Mesopotamia, Egypt, and Persia, and after the fall of Rome, civilization in the West grew up largely in isolation from what was going on at the other end of the Eurasian landmass. That western Europe and eastern Asia are joined together has been of lesser importance than that the center of Eurasia is occupied by the world's largest steppe and desert, surrounded at the eastern end by the world's highest mountains. These have remained formidable barriers, and the sparse and varied populations that lived in what has been called "the dead heart of Asia" often made their living by preying on travelers or raiding trade caravans. It was not a safe route.

Marco Polo and some half-dozen of his contemporaries made that journey safely because they traveled to China under the protection of the Great Khan during the reign of the Mongols, who in the thirteenth century had conquered most of Eurasia and imposed their rule on it, the Pax Tartarica, or Pax Mongolica. Unfortunately, their reign lasted only a short time—less than a century—and with its collapse the empire fell apart into rival local kingdoms and general disorder. Later travelers to the East had to go the long way around, by sea, but that route was not developed until the end of the fifteenth century, and very few people made the journey until considerably later.

CROSS-EURASIAN CONNECTIONS

Long before Marco Polo's time, the civilizations at the western and eastern ends of the Eurasian landmass had acquired their own distinctively different forms and styles. Polo brought back to Europe hard information about China for the first time. Many people read, or heard about, his travels, but not many took his account literally. But in fact the tales he told were reasonably accurate, apart from the bits about magic, which was a feature of nearly all medieval tales. It is said that when, on his deathbed, his confessor bade him to "take back all those terrible lies," Polo replied, "I have not told the half of what I saw." But although his tales were discounted, they sparked the Age of Discovery and the search for a sea route to those fabled rich civilizations in the East: India, China, the Spice Islands of Southeast Asia, and what Polo referred to as "Cipangu" (Japan), which he could only describe as hearsay. Marco Polo and his tales were widely known, and obviously many must have more than half believed them; Columbus carried with him a copy of Polo's journal. But until da Gama's voyage in 1498, from Lisbon to Calicut on the southwest coast of India, the major civilizations of Europe and Asia grew up largely in independent spheres.

Not entirely so, however. The clearest evidence of a very early Indo-European connection is probably contained in the languages of North India and of Europe. They are all descended from a common ancestor, as becomes clear by comparing words and their meanings in Sanskrit with their equivalents in modern English, German, and French, as well as in classical Greek or Latin, and with the modern languages of north India. The common ancestor language was that of the Aryans, who probably originated in what is now Iran. One group of them went east and ended up in India. Other groups went west, among them the Dorian invaders of Greece (hence the origins of classical Greek), the Hittites, who moved into what is now Turkey, and the Kassite invaders of Mesopotamia, all in the centuries around 2000 B.C.E.

INDEPENDENCE OF ASIAN CULTURAL SPHERES

After the Aryan diaspora, the civilizations of the East and the West largely developed in their own ways, but not without significant contact. As a whole, Asian civilization developed earlier, and was more advanced and varied than that of the West, which was attracted to "the riches of the Orient."

India remained in more or less unbroken contact with the West both before and after the Aryan migration. In the fourth century B.C.E., Alexander the Great invaded India and brought back much information about it. The Greeks subsequently maintained extensive trade with India, not only in goods but in ideas as well, for they recognized India as an important center of religion and philosophy. The Romans too were acquainted with India, and imported goods and medical knowledge on an even larger scale than did the Greeks. As in later centuries of East-West trade, the Westerners found it hard to come up with goods to exchange for Asian spices, cottons, silks, porcelain, and tea, products of more highly developed cultures whose people had little interest in the often cruder Western commodities. Much of what the West imported from Asia thus had to be paid for in cash, and one finds hoards of Roman coins at many sites along the west coast of India and Sri Lanka and as far east as Malaya.

Christianity was among the West's exports to India. In fact, the Church of South India, still a thriving enterprise, claims to be the oldest Christian church in the world, founded, it is said, by Thomas the Apostle (he of the doubts). India was certainly part of the Hellenic world, or of the world known to the Mediterranean people of New Testament times. Ships engaged in trade with India made the voyage from the Gulf of Suez regularly. It is not surprising, then, that Christianity reached South India very early, and remained as another link between the two worlds.

Connections to the east of India were much weaker. Cathay, as Polo called China, lay so far beyond the mountains and deserts of central Asia that no Westerners had ever been there or talked to anyone who had. Until Marco Polo's time, the West did not learn much more about it than Herodotus knew in the fifth century B.C.E., which was very little: "As far as India the country is peopled, but beyond that no one knows what sort of country it is."

At the more or less contemporaneous height of the Roman and the Han Dynasty empires, between the second century B.C.E. and the second century C.E., when both empires were reaching out in search of conquest or probing beyond their frontiers, there were some tantalizingly near misses at direct contact. The Romans ran a long campaign in central Asia from the first century B.C.E. to the first century C.E. to conquer the Parthians (Persians) of Iran. Roman legions were fighting in western Persia while the Chinese were making contact with other groups in eastern Persia. The two armies might well have met, and the two empires might have cooperated against their common enemy. If they had, it would have made a great difference in the subsequent shape of both the Chinese and Roman civilizations. In 166 C.E., a group of jugglers who turned up at the Chinese court claimed to have come from a great empire to the west ruled by someone whom the Chinese transcribed as "An-dun," presumably one of the Antonys; the dates fit. Earlier, in 42 B.C.E., the Chinese army fought with local forces near what is now Tashkent, far beyond its normal range. In their accounts of the battle the Chinese expressed curiosity about how their opponents, when hard pressed, would crowd together and hold their shields overlapping above their heads, walking away from their tight spot with spears pointing outward. This is in fact an accurate description of the Roman *testudo* (tortoise) formation. The troops were probably local auxiliaries rather than Romans, but the hand of imperial Roman training is clear.

Although the Chinese had heard tales from travelers of a great empire somewhere to the west on the shores of a great ocean, and knew that this was the destination of much of the silk China exported, they knew very little about its people or culture. The silk went west through a long series of central Asian and Near Eastern middlemen before it ended up in Rome. The Romans were equally ignorant about China; they called it Seres, the Latin word for silk. Pliny and other Roman historians complained about the drain of Roman gold to pay for Chinese silk and Indian spices and cottons.

With the fall of Rome (476 C.E.), the West lost direct touch with Persia and India, and Europe withdrew into itself. After the fall of the Han Dynasty in China (220 C.E.) and the fall of the Guptas in India (540 C.E.), Asia experienced a period similar to, but of shorter duration than the European Dark Ages. While India at this period was politically fragmented, its sophisticated culture and external trade, especially to Southeast Asia, continued to flourish. In the seventh century, China, under the Tang Dynasty, witnessed a glorious revival and the resumption of contacts westward. But for all their interest in the wider world and their welcoming of foreigners, the Chinese were able to learn very little of what Western civilization was like. They were curious enough about the foreigners who showed up at the Tang capital, near modern Xian, to sculpt and paint them with great care. But Tang China did not reestablish contact with the sources of the civilization from which these people had come. Perhaps the most important East-West communication during the millennium between the fall of the Han and Marco Polo's journey was the accidental result of a Tang military expedition into central Asia in 751 C.E. The expedition was repulsed near Samarkand by a Turkish force, which captured several Chinese. It was these captives who introduced to the West the recently developed Tang art of printing and the earlier (Han period) invention of paper. The returning expedition, however, brought back to China very little knowledge of what lay beyond the mountains and the great deserts of central Asia at the western end of Eurasia.

Indian connections with areas and cultures to the west were closer, but also more troublesome. Turks, Persians, Afghans, and other central Asian groups that had converted to Islam swept into India first as raiders and then as conquerors, beginning in the eleventh century C.E. Most of these groups brought with them an infusion of Persian culture that began to blend with older Indian culture. Under the Mughal Dynasty (c. 1526–1707), North India (the south remained beyond their control) became still more open to and maintained close touch with areas to the west and with the emerging states of Europe. Italian craftsmen worked on the Taj Mahal, and many Europeans traveled to India. The Mughal emperors were cosmopolitan figures who corresponded with European monarchs, and under their rule new ideas and techniques were exchanged with the West.

ROLE OF ASIA IN THE DEVELOPMENT OF THE WEST

Europeanists often do not adequately acknowledge the importance of Asian influences on the West. Montesquieu based his vision of the well-ordered society largely on what he had learned, via the early Jesuits, about the Chinese state. Voltaire spoke of China as having achieved the Platonic ideal, a state ruled by philosopher-kings. He and his contemporaries of the Enlightenment were astonished to learn that in China official posts were open only through competitive examination, and that only educated men had access to power. The Europeans of the Enlightenment admired China as a better governed, better ordered society than their own. Indirectly, their views of China and India influenced the American children of the Enlightenment and helped shape the Jeffersonian vision of an educated citizenry. During this period the Confucian order gained wide admiration among Europeans, who were enamored with all things Chinese: paintings, furniture, flowered wallpaper, and gardens.

Indeed, well before the Enlightenment, it was the material wealth of Asia that sparked the Age of Discoveries. There had always been a stream of trade, both overland and across central Asia and via sea by Arab vessels from India to western Asia. On the east coast of the Mediterranean, in trade bases like Tyre, Sidon, or Antioch, Asian goods were picked up by the Venetians, who distributed them to northern Europe. When the Venetians captured Constantinople on the pretext of engaging in one of the Crusades, they gained still greater access to the source of Asian goods; strategically located at the northern end of the Adriatic, Venice grew rich as the supplier to Europe. It was no accident that the Polos were Venetian merchants. It was Venetian and western and central Asian Muslim trade profits as well as Polo's tales of Cathay that inspired the voyages of Columbus, Magellan, Drake, and da Gama. In fifteenth-century Portugal Prince Henry the Navigator developed the ships and the technology to pursue this trade. The Portuguese worked hard at it for over a century, and were richly rewarded when da Gama returned to Lisbon with the first cargo of spices, sold for an immense profit, most of it in Amsterdam. When news of da Gama's return reached Venice, the ruler there declared official mourning, realizing that the Venetian trade monopoly had been broken. Portuguese profits inspired the Dutch and then the English to likewise develop their sea trade capabilities.

The birth of modern Europe, with the revival of trade and towns, the rise of an urban merchant group, and the technological revolution beginning with the Renaissance, owed something to the lure, the example, and the stimulus of trade with Asia. Europeans would not have been able to develop the sea routes and to found their colonial empires without their use of earlier Asian discoveries: gunpowder, the compass, ships with watertight compartments, multiple masts, and a sternpost rudder instead of the awkward and unseaworthy steering oar. Arab, Indian, and Chinese innovations in ship design and rig were basic to the later success of the Europeans. Although the credit frequently goes to the Arabs, mathematics, perhaps the most basic tool of all for modern science, is an Indian innovation, as are algebra (though the term is Arabic) and "Arabic" numerals. The Arabs merely transmitted them, as they did other Indian innovations, such as the concepts of zero, infinity, and the decimal system. The finest steel and cotton cloth also originated in India.

CONCLUSION: ASIA AS HALF THE WORLD

Asia accounts for between half and two-thirds of the population of the world; as far as we know, it has always been so from the beginning of recorded time. Its modern population surges, since the seventeenth century, have kept it in the position of demographic dominance which it occupied in Roman times and before. Asia also comprises two of the world's major centers of civilization, India and China, whose models spread respectively to Southeast Asia and to Korea, Vietnam, and Japan. The Mediterranean, the third major world center, has been involved with and influenced by the civilizations of Asia throughout its history. Europe's ongoing and enriching contacts with Asia are of fundamental importance to the modern world.

BRIEF SYLLABUS OF ASIA IN WESTERN HISTORY

Michael Marmé

The West did not develop in a vacuum. The Asia of which Europe was aware played a crucial role throughout, not least as the "other" whose—stereotyped—image provided the foil for the West's efforts at self-definition. Interaction and interchange with non-European civilizations enriched and reshaped Europe's cultural, material, and political heritage. A systematic presentation of Asian contributions helps students see this process historically. It breaks through the image of the inevitability of Western history, and provides an opportunity to introduce the notion that context, chronology, and process continuously shape reality. At the same time, by introducing the rest of the world as something other than the passive recipient of Western progress, the tendency toward ethnocentrism is mitigated.

NEOLITHIC REVOLUTION AND THE RISE OF CIVILIZATION IN WESTERN ASIA

The clusters of basic innovations which appear in western Asia at the dawn of history (agriculture, sedentary communities, religion, followed by the rise of city-states with all they imply—stratified societies, organized religion, administration, armies, public works, writing, law, art, technological innovation, and eventually empires) define civilization and provide the contours within which society develops from 4000 B.C.E. to the industrial revolution. The different ways these innovations were developed in Mesopotamia, in Egypt, and in Israel may be briefly sketched and their contribution to Western development summarized.

GREECE

Anatolian city-states of western Asia played a crucial role in the development of Greek literature, philosophy, and science. The Persian Wars grew directly out of the economic and political importance of these city-states and stimulated Herodotus to identify those characteristics that distinguished Greek from non-Greek.

THE HELLENISTIC ERA

The models which legitimated and organized Hellenistic kingdoms owed more to the Persian than to the Athenian empire. In western Asia and in Egypt, Hellenistic rule led to the interaction of Greek and indigenous cultural traditions, producing a hybrid culture. Alexander's expedition to India was far more important for its effect on the Western imagination than it was as an event in Indian history. Although a certain amount of trade as well as intellectual and artistic interaction with Bactria can be traced, this interchange was of limited significance for both sides.

ROMAN REPUBLIC AND EMPIRE

Rome was in many ways heir to the Hellenistic kingdoms and, through them, to the traditions of the ancient Near East. Western Asia and North Africa were economically important, and "the conquered who conquered the conquerors" were bearers of the hybrid culture of the Hellenistic age, not the cultural traditions of fifth-century B.C.E. Athens. The trade in spices with India and in silks with China provides evidence of the extent of the Roman world, although such trade was far less significant to Rome than its continued appropriation of ancient Near Eastern developments from Oriental models of rulership to Hellenistic science (Galen, Ptolemy) and Eastern mystery cults.

RISE OF CHRISTIANITY

Christianity is one of the most spectacular instances of the influence of Near Eastern (or western Asian) culture on the development of the West. Christianity's west Asian origin, its initial spread in the Judaic and Hellenistic parts of the Roman Empire, and its competition with other Eastern religions (notably the cults of Iris and of Mithra) all deserve emphasis.

BREAK-UP OF EMPIRE IN THE WEST, PERSISTENCE IN THE EAST

The Persian role in the breakup of the Roman Empire was important: The rise of the Sassanid Dynasty (226–651 C.E.) posed an organized threat on the eastern frontier (broadly speaking, what is now eastern Syria and Iraq), leading to the eastward shift of political and military power. Many of the barbarians—notably the Spartocids (source of Goths, Vandals, and other Germanic tribes), the Sarmatians, and the Hephthalites (or Huns)—who invaded the West spent long periods of time north and west of Persia; Sassanid expansionism **may** have helped trigger their movement west. The Byzantine Empire that survived in the east was largely Asian, and was heavily dependent on trade. Important sectors of that trade (the silk trade with China, the spice trade with the Indies) were at the mercy of hostile powers: Persia, under the Sassanids, and Axum at the mouth of the Red Sea. When Sassanid rulers tried to reinvigorate their kingdom, they employed Byzantine models, notably in the area of tax collection; during the sixth and early seventh centuries, they also provided refuge for pagans and heretics who had fled Byzantine persecution. Persia should thus be viewed as another avenue preserving and transmitting the classical culture of Byzantium.

THE RISE OF ISLAM: RESPONSE OF BYZANTINES AND FRANKS

Islam, the third major monotheistic movement to originate in western Asia, has striking affinities with Judaism and Christianity. The conquest of Persia, the Middle East, and North Africa by followers of Islam was facilitated by Arab tolerance for "people of the book" as well as the alienation of Monophysite and Nestorian victims of Orthodox Byzantine and Zoroastrian persecution. Originally, no attempt was made to convert the non-Arab population: the gradual nature of the process facilitated Islamic assimilation of classical culture. To provide stability, the Umayyads in Damascus (661–750 C.E.) copied Byzantine and Sassanid administration, ceremonies, and art; employed clerks who were learned in those traditions; and acted as patrons of classical learning. Western-Islamic interchange took place in the economic as well as the military and diplomatic realms. As example and as challenge, Islam fostered the revitalization of political organizations in both eastern and western Europe.

FEUDALISM AND THE CRUSADES

The Crusades should be seen as part of the continuing struggle against Islam by Spain and Sicily. The Syria/Palestine region was the site of numerous petty states, Christians were numerous, and the Byzantines periodically conquered parts of the region. It was thus relatively easy for the Franks to insert themselves into an already crowded field without provoking a dramatic response. In the event, the Crusades were more successful at providing Europe with greater knowledge of the East and stimulating demand for its products than at permanent recapture of the Holy Land. Venice consolidated its position as intermediary between the Near East and Europe, even (in 1204) encouraging the Crusaders to sack its erstwhile patron, Constantinople. Expansion of trade, with the diversion of profits to Italy, contributed to the commercial and urban revival of western Europe.

THE HIGH MIDDLE AGES

Islam was important as a conduit of classical Mediterranean culture—particularly Aristotelian thought—as well as of technical innovations from South and East Asia to Europe. Dante's *Inferno*—which places Avicenna and Averroes in the First Circle but consigns Mohammed and Ali to horrible punishments below—is illustrative of the ambivalent Western attitude.

THE CRISIS OF THE FOURTEENTH CENTURY

Although not chronologically accurate, the Mongols and Marco Polo seem so peripheral to the High Middle Ages that treatment might be deferred to the fourteenth century—when the spread of Marco Polo's "tall tales" and the diffusion of East Asian discoveries (notably gunpowder) throughout Europe began to have an impact. The Genoese were particularly eager to exploit the commercial possibilities of the Pax Mongolica. (Marco Polo's description of Kinsai [Hangzhou] is a reading worth assigning.) The brief era of direct contact did not have massive economic or intellectual repercussions for either culture, but it did fire the imaginations of traders who saw profit to be made by eliminating the Islamic and Venetian middlemen.

THE RENAISSANCE AND THE RISE OF
NATIONAL MONARCHIES

The rise of the Ottomans, in the fifteenth and sixteenth centuries the most formidable military power in Europe and the Near East, had both a military/political and an intellectual impact on the West. Their use of firearms provided the model for a new, more expensive military force more firmly under the ruler's control. Although Ottoman advances in the East and South coincided with Spain's final victory over Islam in Granada, Islam remained a threat—and an inspiration. The fall of Constantinople in 1453 played a far less crucial role in the Renaissance than was once believed, although refugees to Europe may have reinforced interest in Neoplatonism and facilitated mastery of Greek.

REFORMATION AND RELIGIOUS STRIFE

Until the late sixteenth century, religious wars between Catholics and Protestants were accompanied by the ongoing struggle—in central Europe as well as in the Mediterranean—between Islam and Christianity. Ottoman advances in North Africa threatened to make the Mediterranean a Muslim lake. The Mediterranean remained an economically important arena, both in its own right **and** as a channel of European trade with the Indies. Although in hindsight it is clear that Ottoman expansion had run its course by 1580, Ottoman military campaigns as late as the 1680s perpetuated a European sense of threat from that quarter.

AGE OF DISCOVERIES AND THE CREATION OF EMPIRES

The Iberians and the Genoese were, for their separate reasons, intent on breaking Islamic/Venetian control of trade with the East. The aim of both Portuguese and Spanish expeditions was to reach Asia—Columbus believed the islands he discovered were part of Japan. Where strong states existed, Europeans were able to occupy ports only at the sufferance of the local rulers. (Indeed, in Safavid Persia, trade with the Europeans enabled Shah Abbas to strengthen the monarch's hand internally.) Although the Portuguese quickly identified and captured most key points in the Indian Ocean, their failure to take Aden allowed Islamic traders to survive and regroup. Spanish control of the Philippines illustrates the geographic range of the European empires; the activities of the Dutch East India Company in the Indies demonstrate the ruthlessness of which Europeans were capable when interest dictated and opportunity allowed; Catholic missionary activity in China and Japan illustrates the possibilities and problems of cultural exchange not accompanied by political control.

THE "CRISIS" OF THE SEVENTEENTH CENTURY

Although examples from as far away as China can be invoked to suggest that the seventeenth-century "crisis" was a global phenomenon, the Ottoman case seems perhaps the closest parallel to that of western Europe.

THE ENLIGHTENMENT

Asia—and particularly China—played a significant role. The image of a wealthy, peaceful, and well-governed kingdom ruled by benevolent despots with the help of the "learned" appealed to many of the *philosophes*.[1]

THE FRENCH REVOLUTION AND THE NAPOLEONIC ERA

The Egyptian campaign was a way of restoring French access to the wealth of India and the East.

EUROPEAN IMPERIALISM

India under the East India Company and the Raj is the most dramatic example of the changes brought about by Europe's imperial expansion. In China, Emperor Qianlong's condescending letter to George III in 1793 or Lin Zexu's explanation of anti-opium policy in 1839 dramatize the enduring—but increasingly unsustainable—self-confidence of the Chinese. In Japan, the emperor's Charter Oath of 1868 symbolizes the determination to maintain Japanese autonomy by adopting the ways of the West. Attempts at reform in the Ottoman Empire (with Egypt treated as a separate case) illustrate the difficulties of guided reform from above.

NATIONALISM AND IMPERIALISM, 1870–1914

Japanese speed in industrializing, creating a constitutional government and joining the scramble for colonies and concessions—in 1905 defeating a "backward" Western power (Russia)—demonstrated to other Asians that the West might not forever monopolize wealth and power.

THE TWENTIETH-CENTURY CRISIS, 1914–1945

By bankrupting Europe, decimating a generation, and shattering its self-confidence, World War I transformed the position of Western imperialists in the eyes of Asians. The loss of European moral legitimacy invigorated nationalist movements in India and China. The place Japan was offered in the postwar Western club of powers proved unsatisfactory. The Depression exacerbated unresolved tensions, undermining the prospects for authoritarian modernization in China and encouraging Japan—like other "have-not" powers—to strike out on its own.

THE SOVIET UNION

The USSR was both an Asian country and an Asian power. The rationale Lenin devised for revolution in Russia made Marxism appear increasingly relevant in the unindustrialized world. Communism provided a role for educated elites, a way to reject imperialism without embracing the whole of an obviously inadequate tradition, and a model for postrevolutionary development. Not surprisingly, this model proved attractive throughout Asia, Africa, and Latin America.

DECOLONIZATION AND REVOLUTIONARY NATIONALISM

After 1945, European powers could no longer bear the burdens of empire. The political, economic, social, and cultural arrangements which replaced direct or indirect Western dominance were, however, deeply influenced by the West. One way of illustrating how truly profound were the changes Europe triggered—while underlining how ephemeral was European hegemony—is to analyze the triumphant nationalist movements in India, China, and Iran.

GREAT POWER RIVALRY IN THE NUCLEAR AGE

The waning of European power outside Europe was accompanied by the dominant role extra-European "superpowers" played within Europe. The Cold War was fought on other fronts, the future of the West at one time or another allegedly turning on events in Korea, Vietnam, or the Persian Gulf. Japan emerged as a major "Western" power.

NOTE

1. Short passages from Voltaire could be paired with brief selections from Jonathan Spence's *Emperor of China* (particularly those in which the Kangxi emperor concludes that Western science must have originated in China and that the Jesuits must surely be mistaken: no father, much less a divine one, would demand the death of his only son).

ASIAN INFLUENCES ON THE WEST

Cho-yun Hsu

NOMADIC MIGRATION IN THE EURASIAN STEPPES

EARLY NOMADIZATION

Before 2000 B.C.E. there were only small areas of cultivation in the southern part of central Asia. The remainder of the vast stretch of the Eurasian steppes was inhabited by peoples who engaged in hunting, herding, and in some rudimentary plant cultivation.

About 2000 B.C.E. nomadic pastoralism was gradually developed by the people who occupied the area between the Ural Mountains and the Caspian and Aral seas. They were the first to develop horseback riding, wheeled transportation, and the use of animals not only for meat but also for the production of dairy food.

As a result of greater mobility, this type of economy spread across a large geographic area. By 1500 B.C.E. it was widely dispersed, resulting in the emergence of secondary centers of nomadic pastoralism radiating north to Lake Baikal, west to the Black Sea, and south to the Hindu Kush.

By 1200–1100 B.C.E., the impacts of these secondary dispersions were also felt in the other regions of the Eurasian continent. Peoples speaking precursors of the Indo-European languages established states in West Asia; the Hyksos invaded Egypt; and the seafaring peoples were active in the eastern Mediterranean. The movement of Indo-European speaking groups, the "Aryans," was to change the ethnic composition of the Indian subcontinent forever. To the east, wars by Shang and Zhou China probably also established a permanent pattern of confrontation along the northern Chinese border. To the west, there was a sudden increase in migration in the area of Asia Minor and Greece among nomadic peoples who originated in central Asia; they caused disturbances along the transition zones between the steppe and the agricultural lands. Scythian bands overran all of southern Russia and penetrated even to the center of Europe.

XIONGNU EXPANSION IN THE QIN-HAN PERIOD (221 B.C.E.–220 C.E.) AND THE MASSIVE MOVEMENT OF PEOPLES

The Qin-Han dynasties embraced a vast empire that covered the entire Chinese agricultural area along the northern steppe, and stretched from eastern Siberia to central Asia. The Xiongnu were a confederation of several nomadic peoples that included ethnic groups speaking proto-Turkish, proto-Mongolian, and proto-Tungusic languages. Numerous states and tribes in the steppe region were in one way or another subjugated by the Xiongnu. The struggle between China and the Xiongnu lasted for centuries, and its effects could be felt in the West in two ways. In the mid-second century B.C.E., one of the states, known as Yue Zhi in the Chinese records, was defeated by the Xiongnu. Its people moved from their original site (in the modern Chinese province of Gansu) to settle in Bactria in western central Asia. This migration precipitated a disturbance that caused a surge of migration across the Parthian Empire, almost destroying it. All traces of Hellenism, the last vestiges of Alexander's conquest of central Asia, were completely erased. Another consequence of the struggle between China and the Xiongnu was the appearance in Europe of the Huns. In 44 B.C.E. one faction fled in defeat from Mongolia to settle in Russian Turkestan. These were the ancestors of the Huns, who in the fourth century C.E. crossed the Volga and the Don to invade Europe under the leadership of Balamir and Attila.

This movement of the Huns pressed the Goths to move further westward; the Goths sacked imperial Rome. In the footsteps of the Huns followed other Asian successors—the Avars and the Bulgarians. These groups drove the Slavic peoples to enter and finally conquer the Eastern Roman Empire, just as the Germans conquered the Roman Empire in the west.

The repercussions of this movement of nomads in East Asia were also felt in West Asia and India. The Hephthalites, descendants of the Yue Zhi, caused numerous disturbances on the border of the Sassanid Empire in Persia in the fifth century C.E.; they also invaded the Gupta Empire in India in 500. The domination of the Hephthalites lasted until 565, when they were replaced by the Tujue [T'u-chüeh] (Turks). A remnant of the Hephthalite people fled to the West and established a Mongol khanate in Hungary. Known as the Avars in Latin records, they attacked the Byzantine Empire and fought with the Germanic tribes to the west until they were overcome by Charlemagne in the early ninth century.

THE TURKIC PEOPLES AND ISLAM

At the time China was reunited under the Sui-Tang dynasties (589–907 C.E.), the masters of central Asia were new groups of nomads, the Tujue, whose name refers to a whole group of nations sharing the common language known as Turkish, and the Uigurs. The Tujue nomadic empire was perhaps the strongest one on the Eurasian steppes since the Xiongnu.

By the mid sixth century, the Turkic Empire extended eastward to Mongolia and westward to Sassanid Persia. In the seventh century, Arab Muslims rapidly ascended to prominence in Asia and the eastern Mediterranean world. The Tujue were caught in the struggles between the Chinese and the Arabs. In 751, the Chinese lost a decisive battle to the allied forces of the Tujue and the Arabs. Thus, central Asia, occupying the area between China and the West, embraced a form of Islam that included Turkic elements.

The Tujue Empire was succeeded in 744 by that of another Turkic people, the Uigurs, who remained the dominant power in central Asia until the twelfth century. This non-Arabic ethnic group was to share the mission of spreading the Islamic faith and protecting one-fourth the region in which it was practiced. The rise of the Seljuk sultanate around the eleventh century, therefore, should be viewed as reflecting both the Islamization of the Turks and the Turkicization of a large part of the Middle East, especially Anatolia and Asia Minor.

The Russian steppe, from the sixth century, had been the home of numerous groups of Asian nomads, including the Avars, the Bulgars, and the Magyars, all of whom were descendants of earlier Asian nomads from previous waves of migration. Later, various Turkic peoples arrived and dwelt side by side with the earlier settlers.

We should not overlook the fact that the Arabs, who spread

the faith of Islam as well as their military and political dominance over the entire Mediterranean basin, were also western Asians, who made great contributions to the development of Western civilization.

THE MONGOL EXPANSION AND ITS IMPACT

Genghis Khan's sweep across the Eurasian steppeland gained for him a gigantic empire. The Mongol warriors reached as far west as the Danube; their descendants ruled the Transoxiana and Russia for centuries. The Mongols left a permanent imprint on eastern European history. Genghis Khan's remote descendants also established the Mongol (Mughal) Empire in India in the early sixteenth century. In the Middle East, descendants of Genghis Khan were challenged by Tamerlane in the early fifteenth century. That the Mongols eventually embraced the Islamic faith of their former subjects is testimony to the strength of Islam.

EXCHANGE OF MATERIAL CULTURE

THE SILK ROAD

The Silk Road was not a visible highway, but actually several overland caravan routes stretching from China to the Mediterranean world. Since the Han Dynasty Chinese imperial troops guarded it as a supply line, used by its merchants and other travelers between China and the central Asian states. At its western end, the Silk Road fantailed into several lines that linked central Asia with Europe. Although silk was the principal commodity shipped to the West, other materials, such as spices, precious stones, and even livestock, were traded along the way. Silk woven in China was often rewoven or altered at stops along the way in order to accommodate Western tastes. Coins minted in the West and in central Asian states have been found in archaeological sites along the route. The financial loss to the Roman Empire due to the importation of silk and the luxurious style of living among the aristocrats were regarded by Gibbon as major factors contributing to the fall of Rome. Not all the profit from this trade, however, went to China. People all along the route took their share. The wealth gathered in central and West Asia probably financed, indirectly, the spectacular rise of nomadic empire-builders in their effort to dominate both Asia and the West, as described in the first section.

MARITIME ACTIVITIES AND THE SPREAD
OF NAUTICAL TECHNOLOGY

Before the age of exploration beginning in the late fifteenth century, the sea routes between Asia and Europe were mainly via the Indian Ocean. Since medieval times, maritime trade had been more significant than overland trade because the cargo of a single ship greatly exceeded the capacity of a caravan. Arabs, Indians, Chinese, and Southeast Asians routinely exported by ship spices, silk, porcelain, precious items, and even timber. The knowledge and techniques developed by these Asian seafarers were borrowed by their counterparts in the West and contributed to the expansion of maritime trade everywhere. While developments in cosmography and the nautical sciences were made in both East and West, the main contributions, up to the fifteenth century, came from Asia. These included the sprit sail from India, the lateen sail of the Arabs, the mariner's compass and axial sternpost rudder from China. Multiple masts were also used by Asians, and compartmentation was first developed by the Chinese, an innovation which Europeans came to appreciate only centuries later. A key element in maritime contacts between Asia and Europe was the European effort to explore new routes to Asia, which led to European expansion and the "discovery" of the New World. After the fifteenth century, monetary changes in Europe, related to a massive influx of gold and silver from America, attracted many Asian products into the European marketplace. Thus global economic interdependency took root in the form of Europe-Asia-American triangular exchanges.

BOTANICAL AND ZOOLOGICAL KNOWLEDGE

Traders and travelers introduced many exotic but also useful species of Asian fauna and flora to Europe.[1] Of course, some species were introduced to Europe at a very early date; wheat, for instance, was probably introduced from West Asia to Europe as early as the Neolithic period. A good number, however, were brought to Europe either along the overland Silk Road or later via the sea route.

OTHER CONTRIBUTIONS FROM ASIA

Asian innovations in such areas as agriculture, mathematics, mechanical engineering, and navigation, to name a few, are extraordinary.[2] In addition, European culture is indebted to Asia for such social institutions as the written examination, civil service system, censorial system, and paper currency.

EXCHANGE OF IDEAS

THE INFLUENCE OF ISLAM

The rapid rise of Islam in West Asia posed an unprecedented challenge to the Europeans in both the military and intellectual areas. The threat of Islamic invasion was felt all over the Mediterranean area as well as in the eastern region of the Byzantine Empire. It provided Europe with a compelling reason for forming a united front; indeed, the realignment of the European nations was a desperate response to the threat of Islam's expansion. The Crusades and the rise of Charlemagne may also be seen as responses to the challenge of Islam.

At the same time, Arab scholars in the medieval era served as transmitters of the Greco-Roman classical legacy, allowing Europeans to become reacquainted with their own cultural heritage. Indeed, the Renaissance in Europe was triggered by the Islamic transmission of classical learning.

CONFUCIANISM AND THE EUROPEAN ENLIGHTENMENT

The trade between Asia and Europe, in conjunction with the Jesuit missionary movement in Asia, brought to Europe a new body of knowledge about Asian civilization. Although India always had been a part of the European conception of Asia, China and Japan had remained remote and vague entities. Ironically, Portugal and Spain, the first nations that ventured into Pacific waters, benefited little from their contacts with China and Japan, which they regarded as mere "exotic" curiosities. It was the philosophers of Italy and France who were inspired by information about China's state structure, especially the organization of its civil service, to reassess their ideas of the state and of human values. They regarded Confucianism as an intellectual foundation for a new humanitarian utopia. This attitude, which informed the thinking of the philosophers of the French Enlightenment, particularly Voltaire's concept of universal history and his stress on reason, was more a reflection of the desire to establish a new order—for example, a nation-state to replace the authority of the

Christian Church and a bureaucracy to replace feudalism—rather than an effort to adopt Chinese institutions.

ORIENTALISM IN ART AND LITERATURE

Asian influence on eighteenth- and nineteenth-century European art, while not revolutionary, did accelerate such trends as naturalism, symbolism, and ornamentation that were already under way. The importation of large quantities of Chinese silk and porcelain, as well as Indian and Persian rugs and carved pieces, introduced Europe to new subjects, perspectives, and artistic patterns. Asian animals, such as the elephant, tiger, and peacock, and Asian plants, such as the peony and the willow, appeared in European painting and decoration. Indian arches and domes and Chinese pavilions and bridges began to appear in European architecture and landscapes; baroque and rococo ornamentation clearly reflected Asian influences. Ironically, European tastes influenced Asian arts; export porcelain, for example, was decorated in Chinese seaports to appeal to the European market. Likewise, the design of export furniture and featherwork, which was richly ornamented, was probably the result of dialogue between the producer and his customer.

Even in the medieval period Indian stories had been brought to the West. Boccaccio's *Decameron* included tales derived from such Indian sources as the Panchatantra, Mahabharata, and Ramayana. The Chinese legendary sage king, the Yellow Emperor, was the model for the Italian romance *Il magno Vitei*. And, to an even greater degree, Islamic elements, for example, from the great collection of Arabic stories, *The Arabian Nights*, were incorporated into the European literary repertoire. Contacts between Asia and Europe increased especially after the Jesuits introduced Asian literary sources and styles to Europe.

The non-Christian Orient inspired fantasy and romance, and its influence was evident in the literatures of Italy, France, and northern Europe in the genres of poetry, drama, and didactic prose.

CONTEMPORARY COMPETITION

THE END OF WESTERN COLONIALISM AND
THE REEMERGENCE OF ASIAN INDEPENDENCE

European colonialism reached its zenith in the twentieth century. On the eve of the Second World War, most of Asia was, in one way or another, subjugated to the West. In the aftermath of the war, European domination gave way to Asian self-determination. China had struggled throughout the past one-and-a-half centuries to resume a pivotal role in Asia, and it is once again a major power with which to be reckoned. The peoples of South Asia are organized into six independent states, and ten Southeast Asian states are independent and sovereign. Today, economic, political, and cultural relations between Asia and Europe are conducted on an internationally reciprocal basis.

REVIVAL OF ISLAMIC POWERS

Throughout the nineteenth century, the European powers, particularly France and Great Britain, had actively engaged, for their own interests, in independence movements throughout the Ottoman Empire, notably in Egypt, Morocco, and Algeria. These movements accelerated after the First World War, leading to the creation of Iraq, Syria, Saudi Arabia, Lebanon, Palestine, and Jordan. All of them struggled against foreign domination, and their geopolitically strategic location, combined with the wealth derived from petroleum resources, have ensured the newly independent Arab states a new and significant role in world affairs. At the same time, they have witnessed a revival in the Islamic faith and tradition. These factors will continue to affect Arab interaction (and confrontation) with the West.

ASIAN COMMUNISM AND ITS IMPACT ON
RELATIONS WITH THE WEST

The second half of the twentieth century was marked by the rise of Communist blocs in Eastern Europe and in East Asia, both of which were partly due to Soviet influence. China, North Korea, and the states on the Indochina peninsula all turned to communism. Communism combined with nationalism to form a powerful driving force in these Asian nations.

ASIA'S NEWLY INDUSTRIALIZED COUNTRIES
AND THE CHANGING WORLD ECONOMIC SYSTEM

The postwar rise of Japan as a major economic power was phenomenal. In more recent decades, states along the edge of the Asian continent, the newly industrialized countries (NICs), likewise recorded dramatic rates of economic growth. South Korea,

Taiwan, Hong Kong, Singapore, and most likely Thailand, Malaysia, and Indonesia, together with Japan, may form a third major economic bloc competing with those of North America and western Europe as well as act as a challenge to the communist economies in the region. Also, the interdependence resulting from a global economic system may foster the emergence of a global community of nations, in which both the East and the West will play equally significant roles.

NOTES

1. The Smithsonian Institution's National Museum of Natural History lists the following items as originating in Asia: almonds, anise, black mustard, black pepper, chestnuts, cinnamon, cloves, garlic, ginger, ginseng, lichee nuts, nutmeg, mace, opium poppy, pistachio, tea, walnut; alfalfa, barley, buckwheat, millet, oats, rice, rye, sorghum, vetch, wheat; apple, apricot, artichoke, banana, bean, beet, breadfruit, cabbage, cantaloupe, carrot, cherry, citron, coconut, cucumber, date, eggplant, fig, ginkgo, gooseberry, jujube, kumquat, leek, lemon, lentil, lettuce, lime, lotus, lupine, mango, olive, orange, onion, peach, pear, persimmon, plum, pomegranate, quince, radish, soybean, spinach, tangerine, taro, turnip; cotton, flax, hemp, jute, pandanus, palm, paper mulberry, sandalwood; camel, carp, chicken, cow, donkey, duck, goat, goldfish, goose, elephant, parrot, peacock, pig, rhino, reindeer, sheep, silkworm, water buffalo, yak.

2. It was from Asian cultures that the West borrowed the following: keystone arch, roof tile, porcelain, iron chain suspension bridge, segmented arch bridge, piston bellows, bucket-type water wheel, canal lock gates, windlass, pulley, deep drilling, use of coal-petroleum, lacquer, field terracing, fish farming, service cultures, horizontal loom, kite, spinning top, wheelbarrow, breast straps for horses, horse collars, rocket, winnowing machine, abacus, paper, printing, algebra, calculus, binary system, efficient sails, fore and aft rigging, sternpost rudder, magnetic compass, crossbow, composite bow, gunpowder.

THE BEGINNINGS OF CONTACT AND INTERDEPENDENCE: WESTERN ASIA AND THE WEST

Marc Van De Mieroop

INTRODUCTION

Before a discussion of the contacts between Europe and Asia can be undertaken, some caveats must be offered. Although Herodotus made a clear distinction between Europe and Asia, the boundaries between these two continents are not strict, and they do not always separate into two distinct cultural areas. This is especially true for the areas bordering on the Aegean Sea which are connected by the Greek islands. The west coast of Anatolia therefore often belonged in antiquity to the cultural sphere of Greece, and many scholars would regard the entirety of western Asiatic history before Islam as part of European history. As this volume treats Asia in its modern geographic definition, I will consider Mesopotamian and eastern Mediterranean history as part of western Asian history.

Contacts between Europe and Asia clearly started during European prehistory, probably as early as the Paleolithic period. A major problem in the study of these contacts is that evidence is often very limited and therefore subject to various interpretations. This problem becomes more acute when we compare the highly literate cultures of western Asia to those of prehistoric Europe. Many important developments seem earlier and better understood in Asia, but they may also have been indigenous to Europe. Scholarly opinion has wavered between support for foreign introduction and native evolution on many topics, and in this paper I have tried to select those developments on which Asian influence is almost certain.

DEVELOPMENT OF AGRICULTURE

Due to its proximity to Anatolia and the Levant, the Aegean is the locus of the earliest and most intense contacts between western Asia and Europe. A dramatic change in the way of life occurred in Greece around 7000 B.C.E. with the introduction of agriculture and the domestication of animals.

The domestication of plants and animals was a process of long duration which began in three regions of the ancient Near East: the Levant, Anatolia, and the Zagros Mountains (in present-day Iran). The process that led to full-fledged agriculture involved a slow change in the relationship between humans and their natural environment. Man's control of the food resources found in the wild involved four basic activities: (1) the selective sowing of seeds or breeding of animals, (2) crop and animal husbandry, (3) the harvesting of these food resources, and (4) the storage of seeds and maintenance of select animals to ensure an adequate reproductive source for the subsequent year. The evolution from reliance on wild resources to full dependence on agriculture took place over the period from the tenth to the sixth millennium B.C.E.

In the glacial and early postglacial periods, man lived as a hunter-gatherer. This lifestyle was nomadic, as man followed the migrations of the hunted animals and searched for wild plant resources in different areas. The nomadic lifestyle was not as strenuous as one might expect; anthropological research in regions where wild strands of cereals are available, such as south central Anatolia, shows that in three weeks a family could harvest, by hand or with stone-bladed sickles, more grain than it could eat in an entire year. There was thus no apparent need for people living in areas with abundant plant and animal life to engage in agriculture. A still not adequately resolved question is why agriculture was developed. Possible explanations have focused on climatic change and population pressure, but the data available to us are too incomplete to determine the influence of these factors on changes in lifestyle.

The first stage in the development of agriculture involved the cultivation of wild strands of cereals in areas where they did not naturally grow. As the heads of wild cereals shatter when the seed ripens, those types are difficult to harvest. When the seeds were sown by man and the plants harvested with sickles, a natural selection of nonshattering types occurred. A slow evolution took place in the type of cereals available; the wild, shattering types were replaced by domesticated, nonshattering ones.

At first, reliance on domesticated cereals was minimal. The major part of the food supply was still provided by wild resources. Such a mixed economy was that of Jericho in the Levant in the pre-pottery Neolithic A period (c. 8500–7600 B.C.E.). An abundance of wild wheat and sufficient groundwater for cultivation made a year-round settlement possible. By the end of the ninth millennium agricultural villages existed in the Levant, and during the eighth millennium the mixed type of economy spread westward into Anatolia and eastward into the valleys of the Zagros Mountains. At around 7000 B.C.E. we find the first evidence of pottery, which became widespread in the ensuing millennium.

The pace of agricultural expansion quickened in the seventh millennium, and the new technology was introduced along the eastern Mediterranean coast and on the islands; agricultural sites appeared on the Greek mainland in Thessaly and on Crete. The sites may originally have been aceramic but soon adopted the pottery styles prevalent in Anatolia. Throughout the entire region sheep herding became a major economic enterprise. Cereals and sheep, which were not native to Greece, are thought to have been introduced from southwest Asia.

Meanwhile, in the Zagros Mountains the evolution of agriculture continued, and by the sixth millennium the food economy relied entirely on domesticated species. During that millennium agriculture also spread throughout the entire Mediterranean region of Europe. Within the Zagros area agriculture advanced further with the development of irrigation techniques. In the foothills, where rainfall was only intermittently sufficient for agriculture, water was diverted from rivers to irrigate the fields. Originally the fields fanned out around the natural water resources and were irrigated by small channels, as is attested in Choga Mami, east of Baghdad, around 6000 B.C.E. This system was easily improved by replacing the small channels with longer, straight canals along the sides of which several fields could be located; this technology was subsequently exported to areas such as the Mesopotamian lowlands, where rainfall was never adequate for agriculture. At about 5500 B.C.E. the first settlers in southern Iraq appeared.

They may have originally relied on water from marshes for their irrigation, but soon developed a system of canals tapping water from the Euphrates River. The superior fertility of the land enabled massive settlement in that area, and the first urban society developed there in the period from 5500 to 3000 B.C.E.

Over the following millennia a gradual evolution from village economy to palace civilization took place in the Aegean. The famous Mycenean (c. 2000–1100 B.C.E.) and Minoan (c. 3000–1100 B.C.E.) palaces were the administrative centers of their regions and are evidence of a highly stratified and developed society. They may have been shaped by influences from the East; archaeological remains in Greece and the Greek islands from the third millennium show similarities with Anatolian culture. Yet Minoan society seems to have evolved autonomously, and the later Mycenean culture was mainly influenced by Minoan Crete. Although contacts with western Asia and Egypt existed throughout the following two millennia, elements typical of Bronze Age Greek culture were not borrowed from these areas. Neither the unfortified palaces of Minoan Crete nor the strongholds of Mycenean Greece had their predecessors in Asia. The point of departure for these cultures may thus have originated in the East, but they developed independently afterward.

DEVELOPMENT OF THE ALPHABET

After the collapse of Greek Bronze Age civilization around 1200 B.C.E., the basis for classical Greek culture was laid in the so-called Dark Age. One of the important elements of the classical civilization was the use of the alphabet, a writing system using a small number of characters, each representing one letter. The Greeks were aware that they had borrowed the alphabet from the East; they referred to their letters as Phoenician and ascribed their introduction to the legendary Cadmus. The names of the letters, for example, *alpha* and *beta*, do not make sense in Greek but are derived from Semitic words: *aleph*, "oxhead," and *beth*, "house." The early Greek letter forms show clear affiliation with the western Semitic ones, and the order of the letters in the Greek alphabet is the same as in the Aramaic and Hebrew alphabets. Modern archaeological information suggests that the Phoenician alphabet originated in the Syro-Palestinian area with the development of the proto-Canaanite script. Short inscriptions appear on potsherds and other objects dating from the seventeenth or sixteenth century B.C.E. that have been found in the Palestinian sites of Gezer, Shechem, and Lachish. They contain realistically drawn pictograms representing letters whose readings were mainly based on the acrophonic principle. Thus the drawing of a house, *beit* in Semitic languages, represented the letter *beth*.

The inspiration for this writing system probably came from Egypt, where the hieroglyphic system was an entirely pictorial script, including 104 signs to write syllables. The writing system did not indicate vowels, and most syllabic signs indicated two or three consonants with any combination of vowels. The drawing of a house, for instance, represented the consonants p and r, and could be read par, per, pur, pura, para, etc. Twenty-four of the signs, however, each indicated one consonant with any vowel; for example, na, ne, ni, nu, or n by itself were indicated with the sign derived from the drawing of a stream. These twenty-four signs represented all the consonants in the Egyptian language, and the writing system would have been alphabetic if these alone had been used. Throughout the history of the Egyptian language, however, bi- and triconsonantal signs remained in use, as did logograms, which are signs indicating an entire word. The people who developed the proto-Canaanite script may have had knowledge of this Egyptian group of signs and used it as the basis for their writing system.

The alphabetic system of the proto-Canaanite script was not the only one developed in the Syro-Palestinian area. From the city of Ugarit on the Syrian coast we have a large number of clay tablets inscribed with an alphabetic cuneiform script, dating to the fourteenth and thirteenth centuries B.C.E. The Ugaritic texts are of special interest since they form the largest group of western Semitic alphabetic inscriptions of the second millennium B.C.E., and contain examples of tablets inscribed with an abecedary, i.e., letters written in a fixed alphabetic order. This order was basically the same as that of the first millennium B.C.E. western Semitic and Greek alphabets.

The writing of the proto-Canaanite script was not standardized; due to the original pictographic nature of the letters, they could be written from right to left, left to right, vertically, or in boustrophedon (alternate lines from right to left and left to right). Out of the proto-Canaanite script developed the Phoenician script in the eleventh century, the writing of which was fixed from right to left.

When the Greeks adopted the alphabetic writing system they introduced two innovations. They used four signs which indicated consonantal sounds not existing in Greek to indicate the vowels a, e, i, and o, and they developed five new signs, three to indicate the consonants phi, chi, and psi, and two to indicate the vowels u and the long o (omega). Thus the Greek alphabetic system was the first to indicate both consonants and vowels.

There is a heated debate over the date when the Greeks borrowed the alphabet. The earliest Greek inscriptions date from the eighth century B.C.E., and many scholars believe that the writing system was received in that century. The Phoenicians at that time were very active as traders in the Mediterranean, and must have had commercial contacts with Greece. A major problem with such a late date, however, is the direction of writing. The archaic Greek inscriptions were sometimes written from left to right, sometimes from right to left, and sometimes in boustrophedon; only in the fourth century was the direction uniformly from left to right. This is in contrast with the Phoenician script, which was systematically written from right to left from the middle of the eleventh century on. This would suggest that the Greeks borrowed the Phoenician script at an earlier date. We have extremely little information about Greece in the period between the twelfth and ninth centuries. That there are no extant inscriptions from that period is not a strong argument for the absence of a Greek alphabetic writing system, however. In the Syro-Palestinian area very few inscriptions predating the eighth century are known, but the few that exist show that an alphabetic writing system was in use. Only in the eighth century did inscriptions become numerous in the Syro-Palestinian area. In Greece, likewise, inscriptions from before the eighth century may have existed but have not been found.

One might question the validity of the term *alphabet* for the western Semitic writing systems of the second and first millennia B.C.E. The scripts indicate only consonants, with their vocalization reconstructed by the reader based on knowledge of the language. In cases where the reader was unable to accurately determine the vowels to be read, e.g., when foreign names were written, the script allowed for the use of the weak consonants aleph, he, jod, and vav to indicate whether the vowel a, e, i, or u was to be read. As these indicators were not consistently used, we cannot regard them as a system of vocalization, but as an aid to the reader in cases when the vocalization was not easily determined. The development of an alphabet representing both consonants and vowels is thus to be ascribed to the Greeks, and their system probably influenced the later Hebrew and other Semitic systems where vowels are indicated with vowel points.

COINAGE

Historians of ancient Greece commonly consider coinage to have been a typical Greek institution, although it had been developed by the Anatolian Lydians in the late seventh century B.C.E., and despite the absence of any ancient Greek statement that this invention was an important innovation. Although the value of the earliest coins in electrum, gold, or silver was theoretically guaranteed by the authority that minted them, they were routinely weighed to determine whether they had been tampered with. The earliest coins were thus still primarily standardized amounts of precious metal. The use for trading purposes of metal objects (coils, rings, blocks), usually made of silver, but also of gold and lead, was an ancient Near Eastern practice attested in Babylonian texts as far back as the third millennium. Taxes and rents and the values of all sorts of commodities were expressed in amounts of silver. This shows the existence of a monetary system as early as the late third millennium. In the late eighth century in Assyria, there appeared bread-shaped objects of purified silver whose value was certified by the temples. Excavations at Zincirli in southern Turkey have produced silver ingots with standardized weights, dating to ca. 730, whose value was guaranteed by the king through an inscription. These objects played the same role in trade as did the earliest Lydian and Greek coins, and it is likely that the idea of minted coins was a development of earlier Near Eastern traditions which were known in ancient Lydia.

MONOTHEISM

It is commonly held that the religious concept of monotheism originated in western Asia in the late second or early first millennium B.C.E. Although the teachings of Ekhnaten in Egypt (fourteenth century B.C.E.) and Zoroaster in Iran (scholars disagree on the time he lived; suggestions range from the eighteenth to the sixth century B.C.E.) emphasized the power and importance of one god—Aten in Egypt and Ahura Mazda in Iran—they acknowledged the existence of other divine beings and did not claim that their preferred deity was the creator of all things. It is only in the Hebrew Bible that we find a single god and creator. That this idea was developed by the Israelites is clear, but the date of its origin is difficult to pinpoint. A major problem in the reconstruction of the Israelite religion stems from the difficulty of dating the books of the Bible. In the historical books there are many indications that polytheism was accepted in Israel. The early prophets did not refute the existence of other gods, but only reacted against the worship of foreign gods such as Baal. Even the first commandment does not explicitly deny the existence of other gods besides the god of Israel. Thus the early religion of Israel may be more correctly described as monolatrous. On the other hand, there are several passages in the Bible that emphasize the power of the God of Israel, such as the description of the creation in the first chapter of the Book of Genesis. It is likely that this emphasis on monotheism was of late date, probably after the Exile, from 587 to 539 B.C.E., when the Jews were in captivity in Babylonia, a country with entirely different religious ideas from their own. When allowed to return to Palestine, they were confronted with the major task of rebuilding the country and its capital city, Jerusalem. The idea of a sole, omnipotent deity could have been useful in rallying the people for this cause. The development of a strict monotheistic ideology might have been a result of the view that the Exile was a punishment from god for their tolerance of other deities. Monotheism is therefore of a more recent date than is generally accepted, and its development falls outside the period covered in this paper. Only when this ideology was firmly established among the Jews, and borrowed by Christians and Muslims, did it spread throughout the world.

The contributions of western Asia were thus of tremendous importance to the development of culture in Europe; indeed, many elements of European culture derived from the cultures of the ancient Near East. Ideas borrowed from the East often underwent revisions in Europe and were then reexported to Asia. Continuous exchange has shaped the development of culture in the two regions throughout history.

SELECTED REFERENCES

The Development of Agriculture:

Moore, Andrew M.T. "The Development of Neolithic Societies in the Near East," *Advances in World Archaeology* 4 (1985): 1–69. An up-to-date survey of the information available on the origins of agriculture. The author stresses the long coexistence of hunting-gathering and incipient agriculture.

Wenke, Robert J. *Patterns in Prehistory. Humankind's First Three Million Years.* New York: Oxford University Press, 1990, chapter 6: "The Origins of Agriculture," pp. 225–76. The most recent general survey of the information on this subject.

Sherratt, Andrew. "The Beginnings of Agriculture in the Near East and Europe." In *The Cambridge Encyclopedia of Archaeology*. London and New York: Cambridge University Press, 1980, pp. 102–11. A short but comprehensive overview of the main developments.

The Development of the Alphabet:

Healey, John F. *The Early Alphabet* (*Reading the Past*, vol. 4). Berkeley: University of California Press/British Museum, 1990. A well-written and beautifully illustrated survey of the early alphabetic scripts.
Gelb, I.J. *A Study of Writing.* 2d ed. Chicago: The University of Chicago Press, 1963, pp. 166–89. A discussion of the earliest alphabetic scripts and of the accuracy of the term alphabet for the Semitic writing systems of the second millennium B.C.E.
Naveh, Joseph. *Early History of the Alphabet.* Jerusalem: The Magness Press, The Hebrew University, 1982 (Leiden: E.J. Brill, dist.), pp. 1–42; 175–86. A survey of the Semitic alphabets. The second chapter describes the earliest inscriptions from the second millennium B.C.E., and the sixth chapter discusses the date of the borrowing of the alphabet by the Greeks.

Coinage:

A good discussion of Near Eastern precursors of coinage is not yet available. Daniel Snell has prepared a survey of the problem for *Civilizations of the Ancient Near East* (edited by Jack M. Sasson), New York: Charles Scribner's Sons, 1993.

Monotheism:

Ringgren, H. "Monotheism." *The Interpreter's Dictionary of the Bible.* Supplementary Volume. Nashville: Abingdon Press, 1962, pp. 602–4. The author makes a clear distinction between monotheism and monolatry in ancient Israel. Although he accepts the fact that the faith was in essence monolatrous, he tends to stress the origins of monotheism.
Smith, Morton. *Palestinian Parties and Politics That Shaped the Old Testament.* New York: Columbia University Press, 1971, chapter 2: "Religious Parties among the Israelites before 587," pp. 15–56. An insightful description of the various religious ideologies that were present in Israel and Judah in the period before the Babylonian exile.

INTERFUSION OF ASIAN AND WESTERN CULTURES: ISLAMIC CIVILIZATION AND EUROPE TO 1500

George Saliba

INTRODUCTION

The chronological limits for the interaction between Asian and Western cultures discussed in this section will range over the time span from the death of Alexander the Great (312 B.C.E.) until the European Renaissance (c. 1550 C.E.). The geographical part of Asia most concerned with this interaction during the early part of the time span was mainly western Asia, including Egypt, the African extension of western Asia, and the Syro-Palestinian Plateau. Other parts of Asia, mainly India and China, came to play a more important role during the later portion of the chronological period under discussion.

Culturally, this period should be further divided into two major intervals. The first occupies the early part of this period, in which the concern will be with the Greek legacy as it moved from the Greek mainland to the Afro-Asian city of Alexandria and the western Asian cities of Syria and Palestine, the Anatolian region, and the Mesopotamian Valley. In this period, some consideration should be given to the role played by the Sassanian Empire, first as a counterpart of the Byzantine Empire, and then as a link between central Asia, India, and China, and the cities of western Asia. The second main interval under question is the one marked by the interaction of Islam and medieval Europe, with the cultural wind now blowing mainly in the westerly direction, from the cities of western Asia and the Mediterranean to western Europe. Those two main intervals should not be perceived as being clearly demarcated by inviolable boundaries, because we know, for example, that the Islamic civilization shared the territory of western Asia with the Byzantine Empire, the treasure house of the Hellenistic legacy, for a period close to a millennium before the Byzantine Empire was finally dissolved by the invading Ottoman Turks. During this millennium of proximity, both Byzantium and Islam learned to live together in war and peace, and at times, as in the case during the invasion of the Crusades, they both suffered the same fate at the hands of the western Europeans.

HELLENISTIC TIMES: THE MELTING OF WESTERN ASIA

The empires that came to inherit the vast territories conquered by Alexander the Great, whether it was the Ptolemies of Egypt (c. 322–131 B.C.E.) or the Seleucids of western Asia (c. 322–64 B.C.E.), were anything but Greek in character. The local cultural traditions inherited by these empires were all of Asiatic origin, and sooner or later, after the transmission of ideas from the eastern native population to the western Greeks, the inherited eastern ideas came to be considered mainstream Greek traditions. One such transmission of ideas from East to West, or rather a conquest of the Greek cities by the eastern traditions of the people just conquered by Alexander the Great, can be dramatically illustrated by the origin and development of the Stoic philosophical school. The founder of the school, Zeno of Citium (340–265 B.C.E.), is traditionally regarded as a Semite of Asian origins who finally migrated to mainland Greece and established his school there. His influence was not restricted to the Greek city of Athens, where he established his school, but definitely bypassed it to include the intellectual theater of the early Roman Empire, when such famous figures as Seneca (c. 4 B.C.E.–65 C.E.) were among his disciples. During the second half of the Hellenistic period, such western Asiatic figures as Posidonius of Aphamea (in modern-day Syria) (c. 135–50 B.C.E.) left their own impact on the development of the Stoic school, by naturalizing it within the Roman empirical outlook. Similar statements can be made of Neoplatonism, a later intellectual movement, traditionally considered to have been started by Ammonius Saccas of Alexandria, but really propounded by Plotinus (205–270), who was born in Egypt and educated in Alexandria under Ammonius, but, like Zeno, finally migrated west and settled in Rome towards the middle of the third century of our era.

What these two philosophical schools represent is the ability of Asian intellectual currents to infiltrate, stimulate, and shape the thought of the western empires of the times: first the Hellenistic empires, and then the Roman Empire. The fact that both schools leaned heavily on the Greek heritage in the first place, be it the heritage of Aristotelian or Platonic philosophy, can in no way be denied. But it is also a fact that neither Stoicism nor Neoplatonism can really claim to be of pure Greek character. The Asian elements injected into each of these two schools of philosophy are of such a significant proportion that some would consider them more as "Oriental" philosophies rather than Western or Greek ones.

In another quarter, the scientific tradition during the same early chronological interval is equally impressive. Here too, the main scientific currents may have started in mainland Greece—although Greek traditions connect their major scientific figures with the lands of the East, in their terms, Egypt or Mesopotamia—but the actual flowering of Greek science took place outside mainland Greece; once more, the city of Alexandria played an important role for a period of at least half a millennium. When one thinks of Euclid (fl. 280 B.C.E.), Apollonius (fl. 230 B.C.E.), Eratosthenes (c. 273–192 B.C.E.), Ptolemy (fl. 150 C.E.), and Pappos of Alexandria (fl. 300–350), all of whom were connected with the city of Alexandria at one time or another, one is made aware of the depth of the interaction between mainland Greece and the African extension of western Asia, which is to say Egypt. All of these scientists played a major role in shaping what later came to be known as Greek science. In fact Greek astronomy, for example, is inconceivable without the work of Ptolemy, and Greek geometry is bare bone without Euclid.

Similarly, Greek medicine and pharmacology flourished outside mainland Greece as well. Although the major figure of Greek medicine, Hippocrates, was born on an island between the Asian and the European sides of the Greek world of antiquity, the later much more famous physician Galen (fl. 150 C.E.) was born in Pergamum in Asia Minor, and practiced medicine outside mainland Greece. Similarly, the father of pharmacology, Dioscorides (fl. c. 50 C.E.), was born in Anazarbos, also in Asia Minor, near the city of Tarsos in Cilicia, and very close to Asia proper.

In fact, the birthplace of these scientists is not as important as the traditions preserved in the classical sources that connect their science with that of the Asian continent, mainly Mesopotamia and Egypt. During Hellenistic times, contact with India was also established, and some exchange of ideas must have occurred along that axis. But that contact is poorly documented. In contradistinction, the astronomical works of Hipparchus and Ptolemy reveal an intimate knowledge of the astronomical tradition of Mesopotamia, and that claim has been well documented. At times whole concepts were lifted out of the Mesopotamian sources and incorporated into the Greek sources. Modern research has already revealed, for example, that the highly accurate value for the length of the mean synodic lunar month as reported by Ptolemy, on the authority of Hipparchus, is nothing but the very same exact value of the Babylonian astronomers. This is by no means the only point of contact between Greek astronomy and Babylonia, for it is not accidental that Ptolemy uses the observations of the earlier Babylonian astronomers to establish his own theories, and begins the era for his own observations with the reign of the Babylonian king Nabonassar (748 B.C.E.). On the whole, the classical traditions connecting major Greek scientific figures with the Orient, mainly western Asia, were not totally unfounded.

Other contacts which were not referred to in the classical sources must have also taken place. To continue the case of astronomy, modern research has also revealed a much larger area of contact between the Greek and the Mesopotamian civilizations; such contacts were documented only recently. In his monumental works on ancient astronomy, O. Neugebauer has already traced in great detail such varied areas of contact between Greek and Babylonian astronomy that it is now impossible to think of the development of Greek astronomy without the Babylonian antecedents. To mention only one obvious instance of indebtedness, think of the sexagesimal system (a system of numeration with base sixty rather than ten as in the decimal system), which was invented in Mesopotamia, used throughout the Greek astronomical sources, and survives until this very day in our division of time into hours, minutes, and seconds, each unit being sixty parts of the lower one. While discussing Babylonian influence on Greek astronomy, Neugebauer asserted in the chapter which he devoted to the "Origin and Transmission of Hellenistic Science" in his now classic book, *The Exact Sciences in Antiquity:* ". . . Babylonian influence is visible in two different ways in Greek astronomy: first, in contributing basic empirical material for the geometric theories which we have outlined in the preceding section; second, in a direct continuation of arithmetical methods which were used simultaneously with and independently of the geometrical methods."[1]

Before we consider the next interval in our chronological period, we should perhaps draw attention to the intervening years between the end of the second century C.E., when the best Greek scientific production began to wane, and the seventh century, when the Muslim Empire was born. This period witnessed the success of Christianity over the competing religious cults, and particularly over the prevalent Greek philosophical schools that had almost become universal during Roman times. The intellectual, moral, and religious impact of Christianity, whose roots and form were cast in the mold of the traditional monotheistic legacies of the ancient western Asian civilizations, cannot be emphasized enough, nor can it be properly appreciated when we are still living within its vigorous grip till this very day. The intellectual, moral, and religious issues raised by Christianity are still directing much of our daily behavior, and, in a sense, are far from being completely understood, because, in most instances, we still react to the discussion of these issues, or even to their impact, with uncritical emotional responses.

For the Byzantine Empire, beginning with the conversion of Constantine the Great, Christianity became the all-encompassing way of life. There was no longer any felt need for the sciences and the philosophies of pagan times. Books which did not deal with the salvation of the soul were discarded and at times even burned. As a result, the total sum of the knowledge of antiquity was on its way to perishing, due both to systematic neglect by the Byzantine intellectual class and to its reduction to elementary treatises, of the school textbook type, which contained only as much information as the study of the new faith required. In the scientific domain, for example, the net result was a general decline from the standard that was achieved by the end of the second century. By the seventh century, when Islam came into the picture, there were hardly any schoolboys in Byzantium who could still read Euclid and Ptolemy and understand their works. The Byzantine rulers, on the other hand, must have at least appreciated the importance of such works as treasures, for they preserved most of the manuscripts, which were copied from one generation to the next, and when Muslim rulers requested them they were sent to them as part of the national treasure exchange, or a royal gift category. Had it not been for such exchanges, and for such concern on the part of the Muslim rulers to acquire those manuscripts, the course of history, as it is related to the spread and development of science, would have definitely been different from what it came to be. I doubt very much if any of the Greek scientific masterpieces would have been appreciated as they are now had it not been for the care and study that these masterpieces received during the Islamic period.

Nevertheless, the conquest of the Byzantine Empire by the Christian faith was neither uniform nor immediately successful. We know of the survival of pagan doctrines throughout the empire, and we know of several attempts to suppress those pagan beliefs and practices, as was witnessed, for example, during the reign of Justinian (527–565) when he finally closed the Athenian school of philosophy, thus ending by formal action the last vestige of pagan philosophy. At other times we know of emperors themselves who went back to espouse pagan doctrines. The name of Julian the Apostate (361–363) comes immediately to mind in this regard.

But on more fundamental grounds, even when Christian faith was accepted as the faith of the empire, there was no universal agreement as to the interpretation of that faith. Here too the opposition between the East and the West became quite visible, and by the middle of the eleventh century, even the Christian Church itself, the most successfully organized body, split into two halves, the western half with allegiance to the Pope in Rome, and the eastern half having its own jurisdiction over its own territory, which was mainly the Asian domain. But the eastern half itself was neither uniform nor universally ruled by one doctrine. A sheer reference to the various schisms of the early church, from Nestorians to Jacobites to monophysites, etc., should convince even the casual reader of early church history of the seriousness and the spread of religious schisms.

The debates within the Christian Church, which went on for centuries, and are still going on, are the best illustration of the virile interaction between the East and the West over the major dogmas of the Christian faith, itself an essentially western Asiatic doctrine. But the schisms themselves, the official policies of the Byzantine Empire during its long history as the official seat of Christendom, and its official persecution or adoption of pagan doctrines, also allow us to appreciate the role played by the Sassanian Empire, just to the east of Byzantium. During that oscillating history, the Sassanian Empire became the bridge for eastern doctrines, such as Manichaeism, to migrate to the West and to the East well beyond central Asia. It also became the refuge for Western "heretics" who were no longer welcome in the Byzantine domain. Between the fourth and the seventh century we hear of various schools being totally uprooted from Byzantine territory and transplanted within the Sassanian realm. Just the reference to the Athenian school of philosophy, and the later Nestorian school of Edessa during the sixth century, should be sufficient reminders of the role of refuge played by the Sassanian Empire.

But under such conditions of actual migrations of people and ideas back and forth, one has to assume that influences on both sides would sink much deeper than one suspects. Religious as well as scientific, technological, and cultural ideas must have been felt on both sides of the boundary, and their mere presence must have been enough to direct the form and fate of the opposite side.

A much more systematic recourse to the ideas of neighboring cultures and their assimilation and reformulation was to be witnessed during the next period that we shall consider.

THE ISLAMIC PERIOD

The original spread of Islam over the territories of what used to be part of Byzantium, namely the land mass covered by modern Syria and Egypt, and over the whole domain of the Sassanian Empire, brought the nascent religion into direct contact with civilizations and regions that were only indirectly accessible before. This does not mean that there were no contacts, say, between ancient Syria and the Arabian Peninsula—the birthplace of Islam—before the advent of Islam. In fact some loan words from Greek or Latin that have been preserved even in the Koran, Islam's holy book, attest to this early contact, and to its considerable spread; significantly enough, the early generation of Muslims thought of these loan words as perfectly Arabic words.

As a civilization, Islam tended to seek answers to the problems that were facing it in whatever quarter it could find them. These problems were naturally numerous, partly because Islam was simply another competing religion following on the heels of the two quite successful monotheistic religions, Judaism and Christianity, and partly because Islam emerged from the very beginning both as a religion and as a worldly power that was bent on changing the order of the relationships among men and between man and God.

But just like the two previous monotheistic religions, to which Islam claimed to be a continuation and a culmination, it too was cast in the mold of western Asiatic religious beliefs, in contradistinction to the inner Asiatic religions of China and India. In Islam, for example, one still found, just as in Judaism and Christianity, the same ancient Semitic moral codes that protected the poor, the orphan, and the widow. But attempting to organize a worldly power based on the religious precepts of a new religion, a feat left unaccomplished by the previous two religions—notwithstanding the role played by Byzantium vis-à-vis the church—was by no means an easy task.

Without previous experience to benefit from, and without specific divine instructions as to how to proceed, the organizational predicament of Islam as a government and as a religious movement became immensely difficult. The death of the Prophet, who had managed to lead the Muslims in both his worldly and religious capacities, in the year 632 exacerbated the situation and created conditions that required immediate answers. The solution opted for was to pursue a curious mixture of purely Arabian traditions and the traditions of the subjugated population. From a consultative participatory government by men, who were chosen from among many on account of their piety, their wisdom, or their loyalty to Islam and the Prophet—as a tribal chief would have been normally chosen—Islam quickly moved to a quasi-hereditary government—in the Sassanian and Byzantine style—within the first three decades of its existence. But in the long run neither the idea of hereditary government nor that of participatory government became law, and consequently neither could establish itself firmly as the paramount doctrine throughout Islamic history. As a result, Islam left itself open to forces from outside its proper domain to give it direction in regard to the most crucial aspect of its political philosophy.

But political philosophy was not the only sphere in which this openness, and some may say vulnerability, manifested itself. In social and intellectual terms, and from the eastern side, Islam first came under the influence of Sassanian traditions, which we know had already incorporated Indian and Chinese outlooks. From the West, and by default, it became the heir to the Hellenistic tradition. Naturally, therefore, both traditions, Eastern and Western, were fused together under the auspices of the new Islamic civilization, and were recast in a new form, which was now expressed in Arabic, the new universal language of culture.

To illustrate the synthesizing power of the Islamic civilization, we take a few outstanding examples. For instance, the Indian invention of the decimal system, which we still use today, and which did not create a dramatic change in India itself, became the most important contribution that Islam reorganized and ultimately popularized by elevating it to a universal status after its introduction to medieval Europe. During this process of reorganization several factors were equally involved. From China, through the central Asian city of Samarkand, the making and use of paper, which was also limited in China itself, was taken over by Islam at the beginning of the eighth century and by the end of that century became so widespread that very early on one notes the existence of Arabic names such as the "paper maker."

By combining the invention of the decimal system, and by extension the methods of calculation, with the ready use of paper, several conditions were changed within Islam itself. First, the new and cheap technology of paper revolutionized the form and content of intellectual ideas by creating more accessible information as well as new modes of operations. Books, for example, became cheaper to own and easier to acquire. One went down to the marketplace, bought some paper from a "paper maker" store, and either copied whichever book was needed right there on the premises or commissioned someone at the store to copy the book.

Second, in terms of content, the new arithmetic of India, which was apparently carried on an erasable dust board, with its own set of rules, was reorganized before the middle of the tenth century so as to be performed with paper and pen. This not only changed the formal arrangement of the arithmetical procedures of addition, subtraction, multiplication, and division—for now they could be arranged differently since the numbers in the operation would no longer be erased—but also gave the practitioner the ability to review the operations which were already performed; this allowed one first to spot the places of errors, and then to reduce their occurrence.

Therefore, in a typical eclectic fashion resembling its approach to social and political problems, here too Islam took over an Indian invention, applied to it a Chinese technological innovation, and recast it in a new form to be delivered to the rest of the world as a new product. As a result, our modern persistence to call the Indian numerals, which are so called in Arabic, as "Arabic" numerals, and to refer to computational operations as "algorithms"— after the name of the famous Muslim mathematician and astronomer al-Khwarizmi, originally from the central Asian district of Khwarazm, who wrote on Indian arithmetic and on the new field of algebra—attest to the Islamic achievement in that regard, to our indebtedness towards that civilization, and to some of the modes of the cultural transfer of ideas from East to West.

But it would be foolish to assume that the main concern of

Islamic civilization was to accumulate ideas of other cultures and to fuse them together in new forms, although that was indeed the end result in most cases. The main concern was obviously for the self-definition and self-perpetuation of the culture itself. There was recourse to other cultures only when the need for their input was deemed essential for the proper domain of the Islamic civilization. Of course, different needs created different assimilation patterns, and produced different results.

At this point, and within the limitation of this discussion, it would be impossible to document in any detail the circumstances of each assimilated idea, invention, or new technique. However, the general development of Islamic civilization can be described in some general terms. The general trend seems to point first to the East for the initial inspiration and only later to the Hellenistic side. Acquisitions of translated texts, be they in astronomy, mathematics, medicine, or the like, came first from the regions which used to be within the domain of the Sassanian Empire, itself a bridge to India and China, or from India proper. The first astronomical texts in Islam, for example, were either direct translations of Sassanian astronomical texts or adaptations thereof. The first arithmetic was referred to as Indian arithmetic. And finally, the first medical works included translations of Indian medical texts. By the ninth century, however, the needs of the civilization required that it seek more sophisticated texts in all such fields, which used to be referred to collectively as natural philosophy. Astronomical, mathematical, and philosophical texts were then sought within the Byzantine domain, and were rendered into Arabic, the lingua franca of intellectual discourse. For reasons that are beyond this context, the Hellenistic legacy replaced the eastern tradition very quickly, but not before the organic interaction of the two traditions at the hands of Muslim intellectuals had already taken place.

To give an example of this fascinating process of interaction, we take the development of the field of trigonometry. On the one hand, through the East, specifically India, Arabic-writing scientists working within Islamic civilization were introduced to the concept of the trigonometric function which we now call the "sine" function. For various reasons, and for religious needs, this function was quickly adopted, and quickly employed in the production of all the other remaining trigonometric functions, namely the cosine, the tangent, the cotangent, the secant, and the cosecant. From the Greek Hellenistic sources, on the other hand, the astronomical texts which were translated into Arabic, chief among them the *Almagest* of the second-century Alexandrian astronomer Claudius Ptolemy, contained the inefficient trigonometric function the "chord." By the middle of the ninth century, i.e., when the translation process was still going on, Arabic-writing scientists who were commenting on the *Almagest*, paraphrasing it, or modeling their astronomical works on it all included in their text the full range of the trigonometric functions, whose origins did indeed stem from the Indian sine function. The end product was a typically eclectic Arabic science, which we now refer to as trigonometry, and whose origins could be sought in both the East, as traditionally defined, and the West, as represented by the orientalized Hellenistic tradition, but could never be found in its fully developed form in either of these two traditions.

Because of such circumstances, and on account of the purposeful and systematic attempts on the part of the Arabic-writing scientists to appropriate whatever solutions they could find to their problems, from whatever quarters they could find them, Islamic civilization became the main depository of Eastern and Western traditions, and the main melting pot where conflicting ideas collided, and where new syntheses were forged. As a result, new disciplines were created, and new approaches to old problems figured out.

These synthesizing attempts were not restricted to the two disciplines of arithmetic and trigonometry discussed above. They included, among other things, creative new applications of already existing disciplines. The strictly rigorous aspects of the Greco-Hellenistic science of logic, for example, were applied to Islamic religious problems on almost all levels, ranging from the discussion of the attributes of God to the actual interpretation of Islamic law for everyday needs. In addition, logic also invaded grammatical studies, sometimes offering new ways of conceptualization, but at times standing in direct conflict with their intent and purpose.

For all practical purposes, this pervasive eclecticism, and the systematization process that encompassed every field, created an unprecedented phenomenon in human history. First, within a period of about one hundred years, from the middle of the eighth to the middle of the ninth centuries, almost every scientific and philosophical text from either East or West was translated into Arabic, and put at the disposal of the intellectual guardians of the Islamic civilization. In the case of the western Greek texts, we have remarked above that they had been all but forgotten for more than six hundred years, even within Byzantium, where the

Greek language was still spoken. Second, varied disciplines and techniques were creatively harmonized to produce new disciplines and techniques that were typically Arabic, retaining only echoes of their previous origins.

When we now think of the geographical extent of this new melting pot, as we are at the moment calling the Islamic civilization, from the farthest reaches of the Iberian Peninsula on the Atlantic to the steppes of central Asia in the east, and as far south as India, and north as the southern rim of Europe, the Byzantine territory and the central Asian stretch, we can readily appreciate the role played by this civilization in shaping the future directions of world civilization.

To think of medieval Europe, for example, it would be impossible to predict the direction the Renaissance would have taken without the translations of the scientific and philosophical texts from Arabic, which were already cast in the Arabic garb that we have just described. But it is also impossible to conceive of such a Renaissance had it not been for those very same translations. Without this decisive contact with Arabic texts, Europe, and by extension the rest of modern civilization, would have been quite different from what they came to be.

In a marginal way, one should also remember that, contrary to common opinion, those translations were not a simple transfer from Arabic to Castilian or Latin, just as these texts were not simply transferred from Greek, Pahlevi, or Sanskrit into Arabic. But most importantly, whatever happened in medieval Europe during this period, these translations were definitely not a direct rehabilitation of Greek thought that had already belonged to Europe before, as one might nowadays read in most secondary sources on the subject. We have already stressed the Eastern elements that were fused with the inherited Greek tradition, the native Arabic additions which were necessitated by the need of the nascent religion of the new community, and the emergence of new disciplines that were not even known in classical Greek antiquity. All these speak against the common conception that cultural and scientific transfers are mere borrowings of intact objects.

On a different note, we should equally stress that the interaction between Europe and Islam was not always peaceful, nor was it always along predictable paths. During the period of the most creative transfer of Arabic knowledge to the Latin West, the Latin West was exporting to the East, specifically to the land of Islam, one wave of crusaders after another, all presumably seeking to free the "Holy Land" from the clutch of the "infidel" Muslims.

Incidentally, the last one of these crusading waves spent its energy fighting against Constantinople, the eastern seat of Christianity, and did not make it to the Holy Land. But even in the midst of this environment of hostility, prejudice, and stereotyping, cultural contacts continued unabated, and both cultures took a very deep look at one another in the process. A remarkable diary of a Syrian gentleman living during this period has survived. From it we can detect the image of a barbaric Europe swamping the eastern Mediterranean lands with a senseless war that had no clear aim or purpose. On the western side, we all know of the image of the famous Saladin, the archenemy of the Crusaders, and the one who actually broke their back, who was systematically portrayed as the enemy, but was also portrayed with a deep sense of admiration.

On the positive side, and on a more systematic level, just as in the early period of the Islamic civilization, the Latin West sought during the medieval Renaissance specific texts and ideas from the Muslim lands, and incorporated them into its own civilization. At the beginning, these texts dealt with "practical" subjects such as astrology and alchemy, but just as in the East, texts dealing with almost every branch of human knowledge were very quickly sought thereafter.

Although this process of emulating and incorporating Arabic writings and Arabic techniques had started sometime during the tenth century, it continued well into the seventeenth century. During this period, one can hardly think of a subject that had escaped the direct influence of Arabic sources. Modern European languages, in all their dialects and families, still bear witness to that massive transfer of knowledge. From the names of stars, which are still predominantly Arabic up till this very day and not Greek as they originally were; to the Arabic numerals; to the method of calculation by arranging numbers in units, tens, hundreds, etc., from right to left and not in the European style from left to right as one would have expected; to the direct borrowing of whole machines such as the Astrolabe, which was copied in structure as well as in design; and finally to the hordes of linguistic terms such as algebra, algorithm, alcohol, etc., which still betray their Arabic origin; one can ponder the extent and the depth of this interaction between western Europe and Islamic civilization. Who can now sift this massive corpus and weed out these Arabic concepts and still be able to say what is European and what is Islamic in the body that remains?

But to document this process of interfusion and interdependence is very difficult indeed. Some transfers and interactions are easier to document than others. When it is the matter of texts being translated, or water-lifting devices being appropriated, or windmills being transported across cultural boundaries—and all of these did take place—it may at times be a simple process of tracing antecedents to points of origin. But in most cases, the process of transfer is usually shrouded with mystery, and sources are sorely lacking.

To name only a few instances, we know, for example, that a magnetic spoon was used in China for purposes of divination from very early times. We also know that there are several medieval Arabic texts from the eleventh and the twelfth centuries that speak of a magnetic needle being mounted on a piece of wood or on any floating substance to use for navigation. But the period and the context during which this needle became an actual compass, to be employed solely for navigation and to give Europe the critical edge in the age of exploration, both remain vastly uncharted territories.

We also know that printing was known in China, both in its block form and in movable type. We now also know that block printing at least was very widely practiced in the lands of Islam from about the ninth until the fifteenth or sixteenth century. But we do not have the slightest clue whether such technology did indeed influence the movable type printing in fifteenth-century Europe.

Similarly, the concluding example comes from the area of astronomy. For years secondary sources have described in great detail the virtues and revolutionary character of Copernican astronomy. People have even pointed to that astronomy as signaling the new revolutionary era of Western science. But modern research conducted within the last thirty years or so has uncovered Islamic astronomical sources that contain the very same mathematical techniques and theorems used by Copernicus to construct his own geometric models, and to whose originality he lays no claim. As a result of this research, our basic understanding of Copernican astronomy is radically altered. We can now see, for example, that the description of the lunar motion as laid down by Copernicus is in every respect identical to that of Ibn al-Shāṭir of Damascus (d. 1375,) who wrote his own work some two hundred years earlier. Similarly, the description of the motions of the other planets and that of Mercury reveal striking similarities with the works of Mu'ayyad al-Din al-ᶜUrḍi (d. 1266), also of Damascus, and of Naṣir al-Din al-Ṭūsi (d. 1274) of Maragha in northwest modern Iran, both of whom wrote some three hundred years earlier than Copernicus.

We can certainly make the case that Copernican astronomy, as it was articulated in the sixteenth century, was definitely a continuation of the same kind of research that was actually conducted some three hundred years earlier in the Muslim lands. But we have no clue whatsoever whether Copernicus knew of these texts, in the sense that he actually saw them, or had them translated or summarized for him. We can affirm that it was not mere coincidence that, at so many points, very involved mathematical theorems and techniques can still be detected in the works of Copernicus and his Muslim predecessors. But we cannot describe with any level of certainty the method by which Copernicus could have reached the same results. At the moment, this is probably the most difficult area to investigate, but at the same time the most fascinating area of cultural transfer, presenting, as it does, a unique example of the intricate ways and means through which ideas migrate from one culture to another.

NOTE

1. O. Neugebauer, *The Exact Sciences in Antiquity* (Providence, RI: Brown University Press, 1957), p. 156.

SELECTED REFERENCES

Other than the references cited in the essay, refer to the general work on Hellenistic times and culture by M. Hadas, *Hellenistic Culture: Fusion and Diffusion* (New York, 1959). For the later Byzantine civilization, refer to A.A. Vasiliev, *History of the Byzantine Empire*, 2 vols. (University of Wisconsin Press, 1952). For Hellenistic intellectual history, refer to a recent readable collection of articles edited by Jonathan Barnes, Jacques Brunschwig, Myles Burnyeat, and Malcolm Schofield, *Science and Speculation: Studies in Hellenistic Theory and Practice* (Cambridge: Cambridge University Press, 1982).

For the Islamic civilization, read Marshal Hodgson, *The Venture of Islam*, 3 vols. (Chicago, 1974), if you need and enjoy reading more than 1500 pages. For a more manageable general text, refer to Fazlur Rahman, *Islam* (Doubleday, 1968).

For the interaction between Hellenism and Islam, refer to Richard Walzer, *From Greek to Arabic* (Cambridge, MA: Harvard University Press, 1962). And for the Islamic-European interaction, see Charles Homer Haskins, *Studies in the History of Medieval Science* (first published by Harvard University Press, 1924; Ungar, NY, 1967).

THE MONGOLS AND THE WEST

Morris Rossabi

INTRODUCTION

Eurasian history proper begins in the second half of the thirteenth century with the Mongols. Though their empire did not last for long—some authorities assert it survived for as little as forty years, and it certainly did not endure for much more than a century—they made a major contribution by inextricably linking Europe and Asia. The states and empires of the two continents had traded with each other as early as the first century B.C.E., and nomadic peoples from Asia such as the Xiongnu had raided and invaded European territory since the fourth century C.E. The fabled Silk Road, which wound its way from northwest China through the oases of central Asia, the towns and marketplaces of Persia, and the ports on the Mediterranean and then westward to Europe, had facilitated trade between Asia and Europe. But there had been no direct relations between Europe and East Asia and no European had set foot in China until the Mongol invasions.

The Mongol conquests ushered in an era of frequent and extended contact. Once the Mongols had achieved relative stability and order in their newly acquired domains, they neither discouraged nor impeded relations with foreigners. Though they never abandoned their claims of universal rule, they were hospitable to foreign travelers, even those whose monarchs had not submitted. They encouraged and expedited travel in the sizable section of Asia that was under their rule, though conflicts among the various Mongol khanates did, on occasion, interfere with transport and trade. There were numerous hazards to intercontinental contact—bandits, rebellions against Mongol rule, and the perils of desert and mountain travel. Yet European merchants, craftsmen, and envoys were, for the first time, permitted to journey as far as China. European monarchs and the popes exchanged letters and emissaries with the great khans; nearly all the Mongol khans promoted trade. Asian goods reached Europe along the caravan trails, and the European demand for these products eventually inspired the search for a sea route to Asia. Thus the Mongol era indirectly led to the European age of exploration of the fifteenth century, which culminated in the discovery of the sea route around the Cape of Good Hope to Asia and in the unsuccessful effort of Christopher Columbus to find a western route to the Indies. From Mongol times on, the flow of people and products from Europe to Asia increased dramatically. Developments in Asia often had reverberations in Europe and vice versa.

HISTORICAL VIEWS OF THE MONGOLS

Yet the Mongols generally have been cast in a harsh, negative light. A thirteenth-century Persian historian wrote of their "massacring, plundering, and ravaging." Describing one of their campaigns, he noted that "with one stroke a world which billowed with fertility was laid desolate, and the regions thereof became a desert, and the greater part of the living dead, and their skin and bones crumbling in the dust; and the mighty were humbled and immersed in the calamities of perdition."[1] A contemporary Armenian chronicler described the Mongols as "terrible to look at and indescribable, with large heads like a buffalo's, narrow eyes like a fledgling's, a snub nose like a cat's, projecting snouts like a dog's, narrow loins like an ant's, short legs like a hog's, and by nature with no beards at all."[2] One modern Western scholar has suggested that the Mongols introduced more brutality into Chinese court life, that they "brought violence and destruction to all aspects of China's civilization," and were "insensitive to Chinese cultural values, distrustful of Chinese influences, and inept heads of Chinese government."[3] Soviet scholars characterize the Mongols as destructive and disruptive and contend that Genghis Khan (Chinggis Khan) and his successors ruined the economies and depopulated some of the regions they subjugated.[4]

Unfortunately, the victorious Mongols themselves left scant accounts of their campaigns and of the rule and administration of their empire, since they did not develop a written language until the time of Genghis. Thirteenth-century sources are meager, and most of our knowledge of the Mongols derives from the chronicles of the peoples they conquered: the Chinese, Koreans, Armenians, Arabs, and others. It is understandable, then, that they were often depicted as brutal and tyrannical; some of the more outlandish tales of Mongol cruelty, however, must be discounted.

Some contemporary Western accounts were less hostile and perhaps more objective: since Europe, except for Russia and briefly Hungary and Poland, had not suffered from Mongol raids and invasions as had Islamic central Asia and Persia, its chroniclers did not share the antipathy toward the Mongols of many Muslim peoples and historians. Indeed, their perceptions were largely shaped by the stories about Prester John, a legendary Christian ruler in the Orient.[5] The Nestorian communities of the Middle East which had learned of the existence of coreligionists among the nomadic peoples to the east probably championed the myth of a benevolent Christian ruler. Western Christians, in turn, looked to this monarch as an ally in their Crusades against the Muslims. According to contemporary Western annalists, in the middle of the twelfth century this Christian king had defeated the Saracens and appeared willing to help the Crusaders. The king was modeled on the Mongol khan of the Karakitai state in central Asia, Yelü Tashi, who had, in fact, routed the Muslim Seljuk sultan Sanjar in 1141. Yelü Tashi was not a Christian nor did he intend to collaborate with the West, but the Western image of a sage Christian ruler based in central Asia persisted.

DEVELOPMENT OF WESTERN INTEREST IN THE MONGOL EMPIRE

More accurate and reliable information reached Europe as a result of the travels of papal emissaries in the thirteenth century. When the Mongol armies, under Batu Khan, arrived in Hungary in 1241, they aroused in Europeans fear and, simultaneously, renewed hope for an alliance against the Saracens. Pope Innocent IV (1243–54) dispatched the Franciscan John of Plano Carpini either to convert the Mongols to the Western form of Christianity and attract their support or at least to establish friendly relations. The diplomatic objectives of the mission were not fulfilled, as the Mongol khan rejected conversion and instead demanded that the European monarchs and the pope submit. Despite this discouraging response, John of Plano Carpini's embassy was invaluable because he wrote a history of the Mongols that included a detailed account of their religion, morality, clothing and food, military tactics and strategy, customs, and resources and products, which excited European interest in the

East.[6] A letter in 1248 from a Mongol commander in the Middle East to King Louis IX ("St. Louis") of France generated even greater excitement, as it called for a coalition against the Muslims. Although the death of the khan later that year ended exploration of such an alliance, in 1253 King Louis sent Friar William of Rubruck on an unofficial mission to the Mongol court. He too was unable to effect an agreement with the Mongols, but his tales of the East likewise generated interest in trade with the Orient.

The resulting growth in commerce may be attested in the detailed and precise information contained in the fourteenth-century commercial handbook compiled by Francesco Balducci Pegolotti. This Italian merchant, who himself never undertook a journey across Eurasia but instead gathered data from other traders, sketched a route from Azov in southern Russia to Hangzhou in southern China and identified various modes of travel—camel, boat, ass, or horse—from the major halting places. He provided seemingly exact figures for transport and customs duties, and advised merchants on the number of men and pack animals needed to escort a caravan. He also reassured them by reporting that "the road you travel from Tana [Azov] to Cathay is perfectly safe, whether by day or by night, according to what the merchants say who have used it."[7]

MARCO POLO AS CATALYST

Marco Polo was, without doubt, the critical intermediary in the West's increasing interest in and growing involvement with East Asia. The Venetian traveler, whose book was to be the principal source of information for Europeans on China for at least two centuries, reputedly reached the court of Kublai Khan in 1275, though some scholars have speculated that in fact he may not have reached China at all and that his knowledge of East Asia derived from conversations with Persian or Arab merchants or travelers.[8] His own exaggerated and certifiably false claims (that he was governor of Yangzhou and that his military expertise led to the Mongol victory over the Chinese in the battle of Xiangyang), as well as curious omissions from his book (he fails to mention tea and teahouses, acupuncture, Chinese writing, and foot binding), have given rise to such speculation. Yet as a leading scholar has observed, "until definite proof has been adduced that the Polo book is a world description, where the chapters on China are taken from some other, perhaps Persian, source (some expressions he uses are Persian), we must give him the benefit of the doubt and assume that he was there after all."[9]

Accompanying his father and uncle who had visited the court of the khans several years earlier, Marco arrived in China as an impressionable and alert twenty-one-year-old. Kublai Khan, who had asked the elder Polos to return with one hundred learned Christians to help him proselytize and rule, was disappointed that they had returned without the Christians he had requested but quickly became enchanted with young Marco, who was intelligent enough to have become proficient in several languages, including Persian, while traveling to China. He entrusted a variety of responsibilities to the relatively inexperienced Venetian, who later exaggerated their significance. Nonetheless, Marco traveled around China and observed much of the Mongol Empire.

What first impressed Marco and, through his descriptions, Europeans was the luxuriousness and splendor of the court. At Kublai's lavish banquets his staff could feed over 40,000 people. Lacquered bowls brimmed with meat and rice, and fine gold pitchers overflowed with kumiss, the fermented mare's milk favored by the Mongols. Jugglers, acrobats, magicians, and wrestlers from all over the known world entertained at these splendid occasions. Perhaps even more elaborate were Kublai's annual hunts, on which he was accompanied by an enormous retinue, including 10,000 falconers. Trained leopards and lynxes helped the hunters bag wild oxen, deer, and bears. Kublai was carried by four elephants on which a wooden room covered with cloths of silk and gold was balanced.

The power and prosperity of the Mongols were most clearly revealed in the palaces and buildings they constructed in Shangdu and Daidu (modern Beijing). Set in the cool plains of Inner Mongolia, Shangdu became Kublai's haven in the summer. He built a magnificent marble palace with countless rooms whose walls were adorned with paintings of animals, trees, and flowers. Xanadu, as Samuel Taylor Coleridge referred to it, was indeed a "stately pleasure dome." Parks, streams, and pavilions surrounded the palace, and roaming the grounds were special breeds of white mares and cows whose milk was reserved for the khan and his family. The plan for Daidu was similarly elaborate. The architects envisioned a city built around a square with twelve gates leading to the center, with avenues broad enough to allow horsemen to gallop nine abreast. Throughout the city would be markets displaying wares from as far away as Samarkand, Baghdad, and Riazan, and pagodas and observatories showing Tibetan, Persian, and Indian influences.

The size and organization of the Mongol domains also astounded Marco. Hangzhou, the capital of southern China conquered by Kublai's troops in 1276, had a population of at least 1.5 million. By contrast, Marco's native city of Venice, one of the commercial centers of Europe, had only 100,000 inhabitants. The Mongols also maintained an elaborate trade network, which they encouraged and facilitated through the use of paper money, an innovation that impressed Marco. The khan's seal on the paper notes guaranteed their acceptance throughout his domains. To foster commerce and to hasten the dispatch of important messages, Kublai had established postal stations twenty-five to thirty miles apart all over his territories. Each station maintained more than 300 horses, facilities for lodging, and food and supplies for men and animals. Messengers could, using the postal station system, travel 250 miles a day to deliver significant news, a remarkably efficient mail service for the thirteenth—or any other—century. The length and breadth of the Mongol domains was staggering—almost 10,000 miles from east to west and stretching from Korea to western Russia in the north and from Burma to Iraq in the south.

Marco's description of specific Chinese and Mongol innovations and inventions contributed even further to European interest. He was the first Westerner to note the use in China of coal as a heating fuel, which enabled the Chinese to take several baths a week—unheard of in Europe. He also described the production of fine porcelain, for which Europeans eventually cultivated a keen appreciation. His account of Mongol battles and victories alerted Europeans to the military prowess and tactics of this nomadic steppe people.

Marco naturally commented on the government, cults, and religions (emphasizing Kublai's leanings toward Christianity) at the Mongol court, but it was the economic information he offered that clearly had the greatest initial impact on Europeans. The opulence of the palaces, the seemingly endless variety of products, and the accessibility of Muslim and Chinese merchants whetted the appetites of European traders who believed that even with the costs of transcontinental travel they could still earn sizable profits by importing products from East Asia. They were also tantalized by the magnitude of the populations in the East, which presumably offered huge markets for Western products. This was perhaps the beginning of the dream that tens of millions of customers in East Asia craved European goods.

Marco's account encouraged not only merchants but also missionaries. His report of Kublai's interest in Christianity and of the number of Mongol and Chinese converts to Nestorianism inspired renewed efforts at proselytization. The arrival in Europe of the Nestorian prelate Rabban Sauma, who had received Kublai's blessing to travel from Beijing to visit the holy sites in Jerusalem, stirred hopes for mass conversions in the East. Upon reaching Persia, Rabban Sauma had been entrusted by the Mongol khan there with the task of forming an alliance with Christian Europe against the Islamic Mamluk Dynasty of Egypt. During his trip of 1287–88, Rabban Sauma had audiences with the Byzantine Emperor Andronicus II in Constantinople, King Philip the Fair of France in Paris, and King Edward I of England in Bordeaux, and he celebrated Easter in Rome with Pope Nicholas IV. He returned with a letter from Philip the Fair, urging the Mongol ruler of Persia to accept baptism and to permit Christians "to instruct the faithful in the teachings of the Roman Church."[10] His embassy also may have prompted the pope to dispatch John of Monte Corvino to establish the first resident mission in China. Though John was unsuccessful in his attempts to disseminate Christianity among the Mongols, he nonetheless received an appointment as archbishop of Daidu and was the precursor of later, more sustained missionary efforts.

PERSIA AS INTERMEDIARY

Though intrepid Western merchants and missionaries traveled across Eurasia to China, much of the Mongol and East Asian impact on Europe was transmitted through Muslim intermediaries. Persian merchants within the Mongol domains were the principal conveyors of Chinese goods to the Byzantines and Europeans, and Westerners were often exposed to East Asian innovations and influences through these traders. Chinese painting and porcelains became well known in Persia, where they strongly influenced the genre of miniature painting and Islamic ceramics. Chinese medical techniques and beliefs were introduced in Persia and were apparently so appealing that the great historian Rashīd al-Dīn was able to compile an encyclopedia of Chinese medicine. To be sure, Persian astronomy and financial administration influenced China, but Persia's principal contribution was its role in the transmission of Chinese advances to the West.[11]

SUMMARY

In sum, the Mongol era witnessed the first personal encounters between Europeans and East Asians. European merchants and missionaries returned to their native lands with accounts of their travels to China, dispelling some of the myths about the East while introducing new ones. They also stimulated an appetite for products from the East, leading eventually to the age of European maritime exploration whose primary aim was to discover a sea route to Asia. Ironically, this search had an unexpected but critical result: as one scholar has noted, "when Columbus left Spain to discover a sea route to the East Indies and to Cathay, land of the Great Khan, he had a copy of Marco Polo's book on board his ship. And so it came that instead of achieving a renewed contact between the Far East and the West a new world was discovered."[12]

NOTES

1. 'Alā-ad Dīn 'Ata-Malik Juvaini, *The History of the World Conqueror,* trans. John Andrew Boyle (Manchester: Manchester University Press, 1958), I:152.

2. Robert F. Blake and Richard Frye, trans. and eds., "History of the Nation of the Archers (The Mongols) by Grigor of Akanc," *Harvard Journal of Asiatic Studies* 12 (1949):3–4.

3. F.W. Mote, "The Growth of Chinese Despotism: A Critique of Wittfogel's Theory of Oriental Despotism as Applied to China," *Oriens Extremus* 8 (1961):17.

4. S.L. Tikhvinskii, ed., *Tataro-mongoly v Azii i Evrope* (Moscow: Nauka, 1970), pp. 11–14; Paul Hyer, "The Re-evaluation of Chinggis Khan: Its Role in the Sino-Soviet Dispute," *Asian Survey* 6 (1966):696–98.

5. On the Prester John legend, see Vsevolod Slessarev, *Prester John: The Letter and the Legend* (Minneapolis: University of Minnesota Press, 1959); George Lary, *The Medieval Alexander,* ed. D.J.A. Ross (Cambridge: Cambridge University Press, 1956); Leonardo Olschki, *Marco Polo's Asia* (Berkeley: University of California Press, 1960), pp. 381–91; and the recent eccentric work by L.N. Gumilev, *Searches for an Imaginary Kingdom: The Legend of the Kingdom of Prester John,* trans. R.E.F. Smith (Cambridge: Cambridge University Press, 1987).

6. The most accessible translations of the accounts of the religious emissaries to the Mongols are found in Christopher Dawson, ed., *Mission to Asia* (New York: Harper & Row, 1966); a fine description and analysis of these missions is Igor de Rachewiltz, *Papal Envoys to the Great Khans* (London: Faber & Faber, 1971).

7. Henry Yule, *Cathay and the Way Thither* (Taipei: Ch'eng-wen Publishing Co., 1966 reprint), III:152.

8. The best translation of Marco Polo's text is A.C. Moule and Paul Pelliot, *Marco Polo: The Description of the World,* 2 vols. (London: George Routledge & Sons, Ltd., 1938).

9. Herbert Franke, "Sino-Western Contacts under the Mongol Empire," *Journal of the Royal Asiatic Society, Hong Kong Branch* 6 (1966):54.

10. de Rachewiltz, *Papal Envoys to the Great Khans,* p. 159. See also Morris Rossabi, *Voyager from Xanadu* (New York: Kodansha, 1992).

11. On the Persian contribution to Yuan (Mongol) China, see Morris Rossabi, "The Muslims in the Early Yuan Dynasty," in *China under Mongol Rule,* ed. John D. Langlois, Jr. (Princeton: Princeton University Press, 1981), pp. 277–91.

12. Franke, "Sino-Western Contacts under the Mongol Empire," p. 71.

ASIA AND THE WEST IN THE NEW WORLD ECONOMY— THE LIMITED THALASSOCRACIES: THE PORTUGUESE AND THE DUTCH IN ASIA, 1498–1700

Derek S. Linton

INTRODUCTION

According to the distinguished Indian historian K.M. Panikkar, the arrival of Vasco da Gama at Calicut in 1498 inaugurated an era of Western dominance that would last until the end of the Second World War.[1] Such a claim, characteristic of the historiographical school that detected "the seeds of empire" in all European contact, is overly teleological.[2] Initially the Europeans lacked the means to create an Asian empire. The ability of the Portuguese and their successors, the Spanish, Dutch, and English, to establish direct trade relations with Asia and sustain a permanent foothold in India and the Far East depended upon the accelerating development of European shipbuilding, navigational techniques, and naval gunnery.[3]

While enjoying a significant advantage on the seas, the European interlopers were far from invincible, as evidenced by the loss of two of six Portuguese warships in a sharp and bloody engagement with the Chinese imperial navy in 1522, or Portuguese encounters with the navy of Acheh in northern Sumatra in the 1580s.[4] European sea power in Asian waters owed more to the indifference of the rulers of the land-based empires in India and China than to technical superiority. Local rulers were largely unconcerned with mercantile matters that generated relatively little revenue in comparison with agricultural taxation. Moreover, their courts were far from the sea, and, in the case of China, earlier involvement with maritime affairs had been expensive and politically unsettling. Thus they deemed imitating the Europeans and arming naval vessels not worth the trouble.[5] Nor in general were the Europeans a major military threat. To be sure, a handful of ill-informed Spanish conquistadors in the Philippines might idly dream of conquering China,[6] but until the early nineteenth century Europeans were in no position to challenge major Asian empires on land. After all, not only could most Asian powers field considerably larger armies, but several (Mughals, Malacca) possessed substantial batteries of cannon as well. To grasp the narrowly circumscribed limits of European military technology and power projection, one need only recall that throughout much of the "Age of Discovery" the Hapsburg monarchy was faced with serious pressure from the janissary armies of the Ottoman Empire.

Far from immediately heralding a new era of European hegemony, it would be more accurate to speak of an initial Age of Partnership.[7] The foundation of this partnership relied in part on coercion; the acts of real and symbolic violence committed by both the Portuguese and the Dutch often make it difficult to distinguish between trade, piracy, and protection rackets. But to gain a foothold the Europeans depended on the assistance of Asian navigators, informants, sailors, and merchants. To survive and thrive they would necessarily become entangled in a host of alliances, formal and tacit, with native rulers and enmeshed in long-term contracts and associations with primary producers and merchant communities. In many instances the European trade "empires" would become almost autonomous entities, deriving more of their profits from the local country trade than from long-distance exchange with the metropolitan center. Over time their bonds to Europe would weaken, their orientation becoming more Asian than European.

Although the Portuguese presence modified to some degree the organization and scope of trade between India and the West, the direct sea route to India would initially have a far more profound impact on Europe itself than on Asia. While the traditional caravan routes that had long transported spices, silks, jewels, porcelain, and other luxury goods from Asia to the Levant and from there to Venice died slowly, the existence of an alternative and direct route would ultimately contribute to shifting the preponderance of economic activity and trade from the Mediterranean to the Atlantic ports. In part because of the European discovery of the

New World, Venice and Genoa would yield to Lisbon, Antwerp, Amsterdam, and London. To carry on the high-profit but risky Asian trade, with its longer time frame, European merchants would invent and invest in new forms of enterprise, like the joint stock East India trading companies. Mounting demand for Asian commodities would spur Europeans to seek new sources of wealth to finance this trade, especially gold and silver, and impel them to develop new products or redesign traditional ones to accommodate the tastes of Asian clienteles. Moreover, in order to ensure the supply of goods, European merchants would rapidly become proficient in finding niches in the highly reticulated intra-Asian trade. To stanch the outflow of bullion and to meet this literally insatiable European demand for Asian products, enterprising European merchants would eventually search for import substitutes, the domestic manufacture of porcelain and lacquered furniture or the printing of calico being obvious cases. Asian trade would be a critical influence on the growth of merchant capitalism. Subsequent import substitution would stimulate European industry. But it would be the relative poverty of Europe, the desire to gain access to and tap the fantastic wealth of Asia rather than Europe's capacity for imperial conquest that would launch Europeans on a long career of exploration, direct trade, military exploits, and missionary activity in Asia.

If we are to ascribe epochal significance to the rounding of the Cape of Good Hope, as did Panikkar or even Adam Smith in the *Wealth of Nations*, it is because this voyage directly united distant parts of the world. Subsequently the maritime activities of the Portuguese, Dutch, and Spanish initiated the creation of a universal market.[8] This initially loosely knit world economy would predate European empires in Asia by centuries, and a more robust and much metamorphized world economy would survive their collapse.

THE PORTUGUESE TRADE NETWORK IN ASIA

Accounting for the surprising ascendance of Portugal, a somewhat minor medieval state, to a global maritime power has occasioned historical revision in recent decades. Probably the most common strategy has been to deny the secondary status of Portugal in the Middle Ages. Braudel, synthesizing such reinterpretations, argued that Portugal had been pivotal to European trade networks since the end of the thirteenth century, a crucial link between the Italian city-states and England, Flanders, and the Baltic. He and other historians have asserted that already by the end of the fourteenth century, Portugal was a proto-mercantile state, "equivalent to Venice and the Terrafirma combined," a state in which the landed aristocracy was eclipsed or being transformed into a service nobility, a state in which merchants, often Genoese or Florentines, in alliance with the crown played a considerable role.[9] While not overlooking the importance of Italian merchant communities, Immanuel Wallerstein has argued with greater plausibility that the original impulse for Portuguese expansion in the Atlantic in the fifteenth century issued from the land hunger of second sons and declining seignorial revenues of the Portuguese aristocracy. Even in 1500 Portugal was a predominantly poor agrarian society of lords and peasants with a population approaching one million. While northern European nobilities were involved in endemic internal or intra-European warfare, the strength of the Portuguese state and its geographical position made outward thrust into North Africa and the Atlantic the favored solution to the "crisis of feudalism." In this venture, the interests of nobles, merchants, and the monarchy coincided. To the question "Why Portugal?" Wallerstein replied, "Because she alone of European states maximized will and possibility."[10]

The story of Portugal's fifteenth-century exploration of and expansion into the Atlantic and along the African coast is well known. Motivated by prospects of profitable trade, rich agricultural land, and Christian allies against the Muslims and sponsored by such monarchs as Henry the Navigator, John II, and Manuel, the "Grocer King," Portuguese explorers colonized the islands of the Atlantic, including the Azores, Cape Verde Islands, and São Thomé, where they started sugar plantations, and established forts and warehouses along the west African coast.[11] This Atlantic prelude would have several consequences for Portugal's subsequent approach to Asia. First, in trading along the African coast, the Portuguese bypassed the Muslim-organized trans-Saharan caravan trade in gold, ivory, and slaves. Their success in this endeavor certainly suggested the enticing possibility of circumventing the Mameluke and Ottoman stranglehold on the Levantine spice trade by discovering a direct sea route to the East. Second, it led to the construction of better oceangoing vessels and enabled the Portuguese to refine their nautical skills and navigational techniques. Third, the Portuguese erected much of the institutional framework for trade that they would later transfer to Asia. The crown-merchant nexus and chain of forts and factories essential for the African trade would soon become characteristic features of the Portuguese trade "empire" in Asia. Thus when Dias rounded the Cape of Good Hope in 1487, demonstrating the feasibility of a sea route to the Indies, Portugal was well positioned to embark upon direct and permanent trade with the East.

A decade later, King Manuel charged da Gama with the tasks of reaching India by sea, probing the prospects for spice trade, and allying with Christian rulers.[12] Da Gama acquitted the first of these tasks on May 20, 1498, when he anchored north of Calicut, the major spice port on the Malabar Coast. Thus Portuguese seamen had begun the arduous process of mastering the winds and waters of the Indian Ocean. Despite the visit to Calicut by Pero de Covilham at the behest of John II a decade earlier, da Gama and his crew were appallingly ignorant about customs and conditions on the Malabar Coast. So convinced were they of the presence of Christian rulers beyond the Islamic world that they mistook a Hindu temple for a Christian church. The gifts they brought for the samorin, or sea raj, of Calicut were ridiculed as inappropriate for the ruler of one of the world's great ports. More fateful than Portuguese ignorance, however, was the strong presence of Islamic merchants, who conducted the Calicut/Red Sea spice trade and who apparently feared Portuguese intrusion. The religious and economic antagonisms of the Middle Eastern merchants and the Portuguese led to a number of skirmishes, guaranteeing that future Portuguese forays to the Indian coast would not always be peaceable.

The refusal of the samorin to ban Islamic traders led the Portuguese court to attempt to procure a monopoly of the spice trade in the Indian Ocean and to build forts and maintain a permanent Indian Ocean fleet to secure it, thus laying the basis for the militarization and politicization of Indian Ocean trade. Already on his second voyage, in 1502, da Gama began constructing forts on the Malabar Coast. The grand geopolitical strategy of the Portuguese crown to monopolize the spice trade, a strategy that presupposed considerable knowledge about Asian spice production and trade routes, culminated under the second viceroy Alfonso de Albuquerque between 1509 and 1515.[13] The capture of Goa by this ruthless conquistador gave the Portuguese a superb port strategically placed between the trading centers of Malabar and Gujarat from which to monitor the west coast of India. Retaining this port depended on the cooperation of the local Hindus against their former Muslim overlords and on wars in the interior which diverted the powerful ruler of Bijapur, Ismael Adil Shah, and his predominantly Turkish forces. Moreover, Albuquerque's brutal slaughter of 6,000 Muslims after the second capture of the island of Goa undoubtedly terrorized the indigenous population. Equally important for the spice trade was Albuquerque's stunning conquest and sack of Malacca, which in the early sixteenth century was the largest, wealthiest and most significant entrepot linking India and the Far East.[14] While the superior military coordination of the Portuguese was certainly decisive in their victory over the sultan's elephant-mounted cavalry and numerically superior artillery, here too local support was essential. Not only did the Portuguese supplement their forces with Indian mercenaries, but they obtained crucial aid from local Chinese merchants who objected to the sultan's oppressive rule and corrupt justice. But despite Albuquerque's successes in setting up forts and even in taking over Hormuz at the head of the Persian Gulf, his failure to seize Aden or establish some other fort on the Red Sea meant that one waterway essential for the Levantine spice trade eluded Portugal's grasp, and as a result, its aspirations to obtain a total monopoly over the spice trade would never be fully realized. Moreover, Portuguese control over the Moluccan spice trade was weak, and they faced continual opposition from the rulers of Acheh and the sultan of Ternate, who destroyed the Portuguese fort there in 1574. Before its sphere of influence in the East could be solidified, the Portuguese would also have to counter claims from the Spanish, who had established a foothold in the Philippines.

Nonetheless the fortified Portuguese trade network that emerged in the Da Gama/Albuquerque era and continued to expand over the next half-century attained impressive dimensions. It included over fifty forts and factories stretching from east Africa to Macao and Nagasaki, with significant presence in the Moluccas and Sri Lanka as well as the Malabar Coast of India. Even at its height, the Portuguese and half-Portuguese population in Asia, almost all male, reached at most 16,000, and the recruitment of adequate numbers of Portuguese soldiers and sailors consistently proved difficult.[15] Hence officials were often forced to rely on natives. The trade network remained centered on the west coast of India, with its administrative capital in Goa, where a complex Luso-Indian society formed, and its major ports at Cochin, Goa, and Diu.[16]

Essentially this trade network performed three functions. First, it supplied the Portuguese crown with large amounts of pepper and other spices and drugs, from which the monarch garnered a significant part of his income. Second, in order to ensure that the crown exercised a monopoly over the European pepper and spice trade, it tried to prevent spices from reaching the Levant and Venice. Third, the royally governed territories or Estado da India imposed duties on mercantile trade along the west coast of India.[17] In addition, of course, numerous Portuguese merchants, officials, and adventurers acquired riches in the local carrying trade or engaged in various forms of what Max Weber would call booty capitalism: plundering, extortion, piracy, slaving, smuggling, and mercenary soldiering for Asian rulers.[18] The extensive Portuguese trade in fabrics between the Coromandel Coast, the Bay of Bengal and Malacca, for example, was almost exclusively private. To carry out each of these functions the Portuguese developed various mechanisms of trade and mercantile control, which also affected the volume and composition of the flow of commodities not only between Asia and Europe but also along the western Indian coast.

Most important from the viewpoint of the Portuguese crown was the annual royal pepper fleet. During the first three decades of the sixteenth century an average of more than six ships departed annually from the Malabar Coast and returned to Lisbon with cargoes whose combined weight averaged over 1.46 million kilos.[19] The spices were sold at the Casa da India, largely at set rates, to the Antwerp pepper syndicate.[20] Usually as much as 80 percent was ordinary pepper, which was valued as a meat preservative and for its ostensible medicinal properties. In response to European demand, pepper production on the Malabar Coast may have more than doubled during the sixteenth century.[21] Shipments invariably included substantial quantities of other spices as well: ginger, cloves, cardamon, cinnamon, mace, and nutmeg, some of which were brought to the Malabar Coast from Malacca or Sri Lanka for transshipment.[22] In fact, as the century progressed, the proportion of pepper declined in relation to rarer and more expensive Moluccan spices. In addition, such items as sandalwood, sealing wax, indigo, brazil wood, Chinese silk, porcelain, rubies, incense, musk, and even some Indian slaves and an occasional elephant figured in the cargoes of the Portuguese fleet.

The Portuguese monarchy could expect enormous profits from such voyages. In the 1520s a quintal of pepper (c. 120 lbs.) purchased for 2.5 cruzados in India fetched 30 to 40 cruzados in Portugal.[23] Albuquerque estimated that between 1510 and 1520 the crown derived close to half of its revenue from Asian trade. The French economic historian Pierre Chaunu has estimated that the value of the Portuguese royal spice trade equaled almost 7,500 tons of silver, whereas the total value of the ship-borne Mediterranean grain trade was 9,000 tons of silver. The Goa/Lisbon spice trade was very big business indeed.[24]

Related to the royal monopoly in Portugal was the Estado da India's efforts to monopolize the Asian spice trade, especially in pepper, and make certain that little spice reached the Venetians and other Mediterranean rivals from the Levant. Although this monopoly was never complete, for much of the sixteenth century it was highly effective. C.H. Wake concludes that throughout most of the first half of the sixteenth century as well as during the 1570s and 1580s Portugal provided about 75 percent of Europe's pepper and probably a larger percentage of its other spices.[25] By slightly undersupplying the market in order to maintain high prices, Portugal certainly ceded a niche to Venice and other Mediterranean merchant cities which had been predominant in the fifteenth-century European spice trade. After the discovery of the Cape route, however, only when repeated disasters befell the Portuguese Indian fleet, as occurred throughout the 1550s, did the Levantine pepper and spice trade assume much importance. The Red Sea spice trade conducted by Moslem merchants revived and would suffice for the Islamic Middle East, but in relation to European spice demand it was largely a spot market.

To create their monopoly the Portuguese relied on a system of passes or cartazes for merchant ships in the Indian Ocean.[26] All merchant vessels were required to obtain from the Portuguese authorities for a nominal sum a pass listing the captain, crew, size of the ship, cargo, destination, and armaments. Native ships were forbidden to carry pepper and spices. Any ship intercepted without a pass or in violation of its terms was confiscated and its crew either killed or enslaved. Moreover, merchant vessels were required to stop at Portuguese ports on both legs of their journey to pay duties on their cargoes. This system of naval policing, later supplemented by convoys, was far from total. Much pepper was transported overland from the Malabar Coast to the Middle East, and numerous small boats skirted along the coast and slipped by the Portuguese navy into the Red Sea.[27] Moreover, such illegal trade was often overlooked for bribes by the notoriously corrupt Portuguese officials. But the policing system was still sufficient to secure Portugal's dominant position in the European pepper trade.

The duties exacted on local coastal trade, usually about 5 percent of the assessed value, made up over 60 percent of the revenues of Goa and the other Portuguese forts and factories.[28] Such duties may initially have caused a decrease in coastal trade, but the Portuguese clearly fostered some types of commerce. Most important was the import of horses from the Middle East to India. Duties from this trade alone reached 65,000 cruzados in Goa during the 1540s, and Indian rulers at war were willing to pay the Portuguese to deprive their enemies of fresh horses.[29] Although their profitable spice trade was harmed by the royal monopoly, if anything, the merchants from Gujarat, the largest and most active merchant community in Asia, whose wealth and organization could rival anything in Europe, seem to have benefited from the Portuguese presence. They expanded their dealings in such traditional items as cotton textiles, indigo, and saltpeter while raising prices to offset the Portuguese duties at Diu and Goa.[30] Moreover, Portuguese officials trading on their own account often employed Gujarati intermediaries, who became increasingly central to Asian and Middle Eastern trade throughout the sixteenth century.

This introduces a final point about the economics of the Portuguese trade network in the East. Much commerce was intra-Asian carrying trade using locally built vessels with largely Asian crews. To be sure, this trade often intersected with the long-distance Asian-European commerce, a necessity since the Portuguese and their successors had little to offer that was in demand in Asia. But the carrying trade proved so profitable that in the second half of the sixteenth century it was probably far more significant than the trade between India and Europe.[31] The pattern of trade in Portugal's outposts in China and Japan, Macao, and Nagasaki demonstrates this point. After several disastrous expeditions to China between 1517 and 1524 which completely failed because of Portuguese aggression and Ming xenophobia, official contact between Portugal and China broke off until 1557.[32] In 1557 the Portuguese finally attained recognition from regional officials for an extraterritorial but permanent foothold in Macao, recognition affirmed by the Ming court only decades later. The Portuguese population of this merchant outpost quickly grew to 900. Moreover, an earlier imperial ban on trade with Japanese pirates gave the "southern barbarians," as they were known to the Chinese and the Japanese, the prospect of dominating the trade between China and Japan, where the Portuguese had been trading spices for silver, teaching gun production, and carrying out missionary activity for a decade. A merchant ship would thus set out from Goa with a cargo of Gujarati textiles, Flemish clocks, wine, and crystal, which were traded in Malacca for spices, sandalwood, and hides, before proceeding to Macao, where these goods, as well as silver, were exchanged for silks and porcelains. In Japan, these Chinese products were sold for silver and Japanese swords and lacquerware. Thereupon the ship would return to Macao to convert the silver, which was scarce in China, into gold and copper, and to purchase pearls, ivory, and silk destined for Goa. The entire journey usually took at least two years. While such voyages brought the concessionaires much wealth and the intra-Asian trade enriched Portuguese merchants and officials in the East, they added little to the revenues of the increasingly fiscally strapped Portuguese monarchy, which failed to organize the Asian carrying trade for its own benefit. (Much the same could be said of the Spanish trans-Pacific Manila galleon trade that brought the silver of Spanish America to Manila, where it was traded for Chinese silks and porcelains.) Rather, the Asian trade network became a vast system of out-relief for impecunious nobles, royal favorites and well-connected courtiers.[33]

The diminishing importance of Asian trade as a source of royal revenues and the tendency of the Goa-centered Asian network to become autonomous contributed to the decay of the empire.[34] Some decline in revenue may also be attributable to official corruption and the need to placate regional rulers by granting free cartazes or duty-free trading privileges. But the roots of decline probably lay more in Portugal itself. From the 1520s the Portuguese monarchs ran up extraordinary debts, which required that they mortgage their Asian profits to the Antwerp pepper syndicate in advance. As was the case with the Spanish monarchy which absorbed Portugal in 1580, rather than generating a new type of post-feudal state or fostering new forms of merchant capitalism, the Portuguese crown dissipated its windfall profits in courtly extravagance and military adventures, such as the North African crusade undertaken by King Sebastian. Much of the wealth derived from trade flowed into the pockets of Portuguese merchants and officials in India or else the coffers of northern European merchant bankers like the Fuggers or Konrad Rott of Augsburg. While the Portuguese trade network retained its autonomy, the union between Spain and Portugal gave the Dutch, who were fighting for their independence against Spain, a pretext to launch an assault on Portugal's eastern trade network, thus confirming the shift in economic power from southern to northern Europe that was already well under way. The Dutch would reorganize the network according to the principles of a more rationalized merchant capitalism.

THE DUTCH EAST INDIA TEA COMPANY

Although the Portuguese possessed armed naval vessels and had access to Japanese and New World silver, their trade network was overextended and undermanned, making it extremely vulnerable both to local rulers and other European naval powers. The Dutch, with their larger navy and more maneuverable ships, their superior sea power and greater resources, ousted the Portuguese from many of their trading forts over a sixty-year period, from 1605 to 1665. Portuguese commanders received little assistance from their government, which was far more concerned with protecting its interests in Brazil. By 1665 not only Malacca (1641) and the Portuguese settlements on Sri Lanka (1658) but even Cochin, Portugal's premier port on the Malabar Coast, had fallen. Of its major outposts, only Goa and Macao remained; Portuguese continued, however, to serve as a major mercantile language in Asia into the eighteenth century.[35] The Dutch governor general at Batavia, van Diemen, would write in 1642 that

> most of the Portuguese in India look upon this region as their fatherland. They think no more of Portugal. They drive little or no trade thither, but content themselves with the interport trade of Asia, just as if they were natives thereof and had no other country.[36]

If the sixteenth century was the era of the Portuguese in Asian-European trade, the seventeenth century was to be that of the Dutch, although they were never free of European competition, specifically from the English and French.

The Dutch not only seized much of the Portuguese trade network, but adopted many of their institutions (forts and factories) and practices (passes, spice monopoly). They also introduced several innovations. The first was the establishment of the United East India Company (VOC), a novel form of merchant association, to conduct trade. Second, they moved the center of their trade network from the western coast of India to Batavia, which made the east coast of India, Japan, and especially the Indonesian archipelago of greater importance in their trade network. Third, the Dutch actually organized and limited the production of spices, in contrast to the Portuguese, who had simply concentrated on policing trade. Fourth, they systematized the intra-Asian carrying trade, largely in order to restrict the export of specie from Holland. Finally, the Dutch altered the composition of commodity exports to Europe: spices declined in importance while the share of textiles, coffee, porcelain, and a host of lesser products increased.

The United East India Company (VOC), a chartered trading company,[37] was founded in 1602 at the behest of influential political leaders to harness Asian trade to national purpose and put an end to the ferocious competition among the numerous Dutch companies that had been interloping in the Portuguese trade network for a decade. It was given a monopoly of Dutch trade east of the Cape of Good Hope and west of the Straits of Magellan, and was further endowed with the right to defend itself from attack, to negotiate treaties, and to build forts. The company was administered by a labyrinthine bureaucracy to which the wealthiest merchants belonged.

Thus from the outset the VOC fused national policy and private merchant interests. While this fusion was typical of chartered companies in the era of mercantilism, two aspects of the company were not. First was the enormousness of its initial capitalization, 6.5 million guldens. Second was the long time frame for voyages and the need to make fixed investments in warehouses, ships, and forts; instead of treating each voyage as a separate enterprise, accounts were to be settled every ten years. Rather than withdrawing their capital, investors in need of liquid funds had to sell their shares on the bourse. Thus, in practice, the United East India Company quickly became a joint stock company. However, as the economic historian Jan de Vries cautions, this should probably be interpreted as a pragmatic response to the speculative and long-term nature of Asian voyages rather than as an expression of capitalist development logic or as a precursor of industrial joint stock ventures.

In any event, the company certainly gave a massive fillip to East Indian trade. While in the sixteenth century the Portuguese sent an average of six vessels to Asia each year, in the 1610s and 1620s the VOC sent an average of more than twelve, and by the second half of the century were sending about two hundred ships each decade, half of all European vessels voyaging to the east. Tonnage rose even more rapidly than the number of ships.[38] By the end of the century the company employed 12,000 people.[39] The dividends paid on its shares were enormous, 25–30 percent during its first six years. The arrival of a VOC ship was a major event; the cargo of a ship that returned in June 1634 included:

> 326,733 1/2 Amsterdam pounds of Malacca pepper; 297,446 lb. of cloves; 292,623 lb. of saltpeter; 141,278 lb. of indigo; 483,082 lb. of sappan wood; 219,027 pieces of blue Ming ware; 52 further chests of Korean and Japanese porcelain; 75 large vases and pots containing preserved confections, much of it spiced

ginger; 660 lb. of Japanese copper; 241 pieces of fine Japanese lacquer work; 3,989 rough diamonds of large carat; 93 boxes of pearls and rubies (misc. carats); 603 bales of dressed Persian silks and grosgrains; 1,155 lb. of raw Chinese silk; 199,800 lb. of unrefined Kandy sugar.[40]

As the large amounts of Japanese and Chinese wares and of cloves indicate, the Dutch had moved the center of trade eastward, recognizing that the Moluccas were not only a source of wealth in their own right, but the crossroads of trade between India, China, and Japan. In defiance of company policy, its governor, Jan Piet Coen, seized the Javanese port of Jakarta, where in 1619 he founded Batavia as an alternative to Malacca.[41] By the mid-seventeenth century, Batavia had developed into a Dutch town, complete with city hall, sawmills, flour mills, and even a Spinhuis for female delinquents, although the town was also home to a large Chinese community.[42] It was from Batavia that "the Dutch wove the immense web of traffic and exchange which would eventually make up their empire. . . ."[43] From Batavia they made forays into Ceylon and established trade relations in Bengal and along the Coromandel Coast of India, and organized trade with China and Japan. After 1639, when the Tokugawa shogunate expelled the Portuguese for allegedly supporting a rebellion in which Japanese Christians were active, the Dutch held a European monopoly in trade with Japan, even though they were confined to the tiny island of Deshima off Nagasaki.[44]

Moreover, under Coen's direction, the company sought to secure a more complete monopoly of nonpepper spices than the Portuguese had, by eliminating trade by local merchants as well as other European powers and by restricting output. In imposing restrictions, Coen took advantage of the weak and fragmented authority of local rulers; in so doing he was a pioneer of colonialism.[45] Local headmen on the Moluccan island of Amboina were compelled to deliver their cloves exclusively to the Dutch, ostensibly in return for protection against the English and Portuguese. The entire population of the island of Banda was killed or deported as slaves in 1621, and their land with nutmeg trees handed over to Dutch colonists. Several thousand slaves were taken from Bengal and Arakan (Burma) to work the Dutch spice plantations in the Moluccas. Clove production was confined to Amboina, and after 1625 armed Dutch canoes made expeditions to other islands to chop down illicit trees. When in 1651 the inhabitants of Ceram, rebelling against these policies, killed 160

Dutch, the Dutch retaliated by forcibly resettling 12,000 Ceram-
ese on Amboina and Manipa. The Dutch soon acquired a well-de-
served notoriety for cruelty. But while their production controls
were certainly effective in monopolizing the spice trade, it is
doubtful that the profits so obtained exceeded the costs of enforcement. The brutal policy inaugurated by Coen, however, certainly paved the way for the system of sugar and coffee
plantations set up in the eighteenth century.

Coen also emphasized the importance of the intra-Asian carrying trade, and in 1619 outlined his plan for the development of a
trade network which was to extend from the Persian Gulf to
Japan.[46] Because of VOC indebtedness and its desire to minimize
the outflow of bullion, some of the specie required by this plan
had to be obtained in Asia; it was partly because they could profit
from disparities in the price of Japanese silver and Chinese gold
that the Dutch assiduously built trade relations with the two
countries. Over 15,000,000 guldens worth of silver were exported
from Japan by the Dutch during the 1640s alone; its export was
banned by the Japanese in 1668.[47]

By virtue of their monopoly of the spice trade and their privileged position in Japan, by mid-century the Dutch were able to
carve out a major role in the intra-Asian trade. Indeed, the profits
from the carrying trade may have sustained the company through
the crisis years of the 1630s and 1640s when, due to the Thirty
Years' War, plagues, and harvest failures, demand for Asian products declined precipitously.[48] (At that time there were certainly
some signs of crisis in China and Japan as well, including failed
harvests, epidemics, and economic dislocation exacerbated by bullion shortages.[49] The civil war accompanying the fall of the Ming
dynasty curtailed the export of Chinese porcelain to Europe.[50]) In
1648 the company directors considered the country trade and the
profit from it to be the soul of the company and that it "must be
looked after carefully because if the soul decays, the entire body
would be destroyed."[51] Not all the profits of the carrying trade,
however, went to the shareholders, since VOC officials were no less
corrupt than the Portuguese.[52] Nevertheless, so important was the
intra-Asian trade that its stagnation in the early eighteenth century, especially on the Coromandel Coast, which was torn by warfare, has been suggested as a major explanation, along with
excessive dividend payments, for the VOC's weakened position in
relation to the English East India Company.[53]

For many decades (approximately 1680–1730) this decline of
the carrying trade was masked by the revival of trade between the

East and Amsterdam, a revival already evident by the late 1660s. This upswing reached a peak around the turn of the century, after which trade with the East grew slowly. The value of sales of goods from the East in the Amsterdam Chamber, the chamber in which half the VOC's goods were sold, almost tripled, rising from 8.7 million guldens in 1648–50 to 17.7 million in 1668–70, and to 21 million guldens in 1698–1700.[54] Porcelain items from Japan and China, textiles and saltpeter from India, and later coffee and tea steadily displaced pepper. Whereas in 1668–70 pepper still brought in almost 30 percent of the Amsterdam Chamber's revenue, by 1698–1700 it had fallen to slightly more than 13 percent. During the same period, the value of textiles soared from under 25 percent of the revenues in Amsterdam to over 43 percent. Calicoes and muslins became mainstays of European fashion. An English politician claimed in 1681, "As ill weeds grow apace, so these manufactured goods from India met with such a kind reception from the greatest gallants to the meanest Cook Maids, nothing was thought so fit to adorn their persons as the Fabrik from India."[55] Lower food prices in Europe during the last half of the seventeenth century may have meant that sectors of Europe's urban population had greater discretionary income, enabling them to the purchase more textiles, porcelains, and luxuries.[56]

Although the lack of statistical data makes an overall assessment impossible, economic historians such as Jan de Vries have pointed to the importance of the Asian trade for European economic development:

> Consider the "demonstration effect" that non-western imports exerted on the European economy. The importation of Chinese and Japanese porcelain gave rise to imitations in Holland, where delftware was created, in Germany, where the first European porcelain was made, and in England, where by the early eighteenth century potteries enjoyed a growing mass market. Tea and coffee found an acceptance in Europe that changed social customs (and increased the demand for porcelain). . . . The importation of Indian calicoes uncovered a widespread demand that threatened the established woolens and linens industries of Europe. When England prohibited the importation of calicoes to protect its woolen industry, a domestic cotton industry arose to supply the new market. . . .[57]

English manufacturers soon pioneered new methods of textile production that could meet the Indian challenge. Increasingly the English East India Company also proved to be alert to opportunities provided by the consumer revolution of the eighteenth century. Less encumbered by a past in the spice trade, more attuned to the prospects of trading in new commodities, and already well positioned to take advantage of the disintegration of the Mughal Empire, the English would relegate the Dutch to a secondary status.

By the late seventeenth century Europeans had been present in Asia for two centuries. They had gained considerable knowledge of trade and trade routes, established close ties to Asian merchants, and indeed become an integral part of intra-Asian trade. But they by no means dominated Asian trade, and in many areas Asian wealth and productivity still probably exceeded that of Europe. Real colonialism, made possible by the exceptional fragmentation of indigenous power, was practiced only by the Dutch in the Moluccas. European trading posts like those in Nagasaki, Macao, or Hooghly could exist only if tolerated by native rulers.

But the decline of major Asian powers, especially the Mughals, the advance of industrialization in Europe—spurred in part by competition from Asian imports—and the further development of European military organization and technology would soon destabilize the balance of wealth and power. In the eighteenth century, England began to change its status from a "limited thalassocracy" to an Asian colonial power, a process that would not reach its completion until the mid-nineteenth century.

NOTES

I would like to thank William S. Atwell for having read and commented on an earlier draft of this article.

1. K.M. Panikkar, *Asia and Western Dominance: A Survey of the Vasco da Gama Epoch of Asian History 1498–1945* (London: George Allen and Unwin, Ltd., 1959), pp. 13–14.

2. Blair B. Kling and M.N. Pearson, eds., *The Age of Partnership: Europeans in Asia before Dominion* (Honolulu: University Press of Hawaii, 1979), pp. 2–4.

3. Carlo M. Cipolla, *Guns, Sails and Empires: Technological Innovation and the Early Phases of European Expansion 1400–1700* (New York: Pantheon, 1965), pp. 101–26.

4. Bailey W. Diffie and George D. Winius, *Foundations of the Portuguese Empire 1415–1580* (Minneapolis: University of Minnesota Press, 1977), pp. 385–86; C.G.F. Simkin, *The Traditional Trade of Asia* (London: Oxford University Press, 1968), p. 183.

5. M.N. Pearson, *The New Cambridge History of India*, vol. I, 1: *The Portuguese in India* (Cambridge: Cambridge University Press, 1987), pp. 53–60.

6. Joseph R. Levenson, ed., *European Expansion and the Counter-Example of Asia* (Englewood Cliffs: Prentice-Hall, 1967), p. 33.

7. Kling and Pearson, eds., *The Age of Partnership*, pp. 2–14.

8. Fernand Braudel, *The Perspective of the World: Civilization and Capitalism 15th–18th Century*, vol. 3 (New York: Harper & Row, 1984), pp. 21–5.

9. Ibid., pp. 139–43.

10. Immanuel Wallerstein, *The Modern World System: Capitalist Agriculture and the Origins of the European World Economy in the Sixteenth Century* (New York: Academic Press, 1974), pp. 46–51.

11. Diffie and Winius, *Foundations of the Portuguese Empire 1415–1580*, pp. 57–143.

12. Ibid., pp. 177–86.

13. Pearson, *The Portuguese in India*, pp. 30–31; Diffie and Winius, *Foundations of the Portuguese Empire 1415–1580*, pp. 243–71.

14. Braudel, *The Perspective of the World*, vol. 3, pp. 524–29; M.A.P. Meilink-Roelofz, *Asian Trade and European Influence in the Indonesian Archipelago between 1500 and about 1630* (The Hague: Martinus Nijhoff, 1962), pp. 36–88.

15. Pearson, *The Portuguese in India*, p. 136; C.R. Boxer, *The Dutch Seaborne Empire 1415–1825* (New York: Alfred Knopf, 1969), pp. 53–57, 129–32.

16. Pearson, *The Portuguese in India*, pp. 88–115; Maurice Collis, *The Land of the Great Image* (Reprint; New York: New Directions, 1985), pp. 30–85.

17. Pearson, *The Portuguese in India*, pp. 36–39.

18. Ibid., pp. 66–69; Collis, *The Land of the Great Image*, pp. 107–18; K.S. Mathew, *Portuguese Trade with India in the Sixteenth Century* (New Delhi: Manohar Publications, 1983), pp. 170–73.

19. Mathew, *Portuguese Trade with India in the Sixteenth Century*, pp. 121–23.

20. Diffie and Winius, *Foundations of the Portuguese Empire 1415–1580*, pp. 411–13.

21. Mathew, *Portuguese Trade with India in the Sixteenth Century*, pp. 212–14.

22. Ibid., pp. 123–41.

23. Ibid., pp. 194–99.

24. Pearson, *The Portuguese in India*, pp. 41–42.

25. C.H.H. Wake, "The Changing Pattern of Europe's Pepper and Spice Imports, ca 1400–1700," *The Journal of European Economic History* 8 (1979) 2: 361–404, pp. 394–95.

26. Pearson, *The Portuguese in India*, pp. 37–39.

27. Mathew, *Portuguese Trade with India in the Sixteenth Century*, pp. 99–100, 208–9.

28. Pearson, *The Portuguese in India*, p. 36.

29. Ibid., pp. 49–51.

30. Ibid., pp. 53–56; Philip D. Curtin, *Cross-Cultural Trade in World History* (Cambridge: Cambridge University Press, 1984), pp. 144–48.

31. Pearson, *The Portuguese in India*, p. 69.

32. Diffie and Winius, *Foundations of the Portuguese Empire 1415–1580*, pp. 380–99.

33. Pearson, *The Portuguese in India*, pp. 63–67.

34. Diffie and Winius, *Foundations of the Portuguese Empire 1415–1580*, pp. 415–35.

35. Curtin, *Cross-Cultural Trade in World History*, p. 143.

36. Boxer, *The Dutch Seaborne Empire 1415–1825*, p. 120.

37. Jan De Vries, *The Economy of Europe in an Age of Crisis, 1600–1750* (Cambridge: Cambridge University Press, 1976), pp. 130–46.

38. Peter Kriedte, *Peasants, Landlords and Merchant Capitalists: Europe and the World Economy 1500–1800* (Leamington Spa: Berg Publishers Ltd., 1983), p. 86.

39. Mark Girouard, *Cities and People: A Social and Architectural History* (New Haven: Yale University Press, 1985), pp. 159–60.

40. Simon Schama, *The Embarrassment of Riches: An Interpretation of Dutch Culture in the Golden Age* (Berkeley: University of California Press, 1988), pp. 346–47.

41. Braudel, *The Perspective of the World*, vol. 3, pp. 214–15, 530; Boxer, *The Dutch Seaborne Empire 1415–1825*, pp. 188–90.

42. Ibid., p. 236.

43. Braudel, *The Perspective of the World*, vol. 3, p. 215.

44. Holden Furber, *Rival Empires of Trade in the Orient 1600–1800* (Minneapolis: University of Minnesota Press, 1976), pp. 60–62; Om. Prakash, *The Dutch East India Company and the Economy of Bengal 1630–1720* (Princeton: Princeton University Press, 1985), pp. 120–21.

45. Boxer, *The Dutch Seaborne Empire 1415–1825*, pp. 96–100.

46. Simkin, *The Traditional Trade of Asia*, pp. 194–95; Prakash, *The Dutch East India Company and the Economy of Bengal 1630–1720*, pp. 15–23.

47. Kristof Glamann, *Dutch-Asiatic Trade 1620–1740* (Copenhagen: Danish Scientific Press, 1958), pp. 57–63.

48. C.H.H. Wake, "The Changing Pattern of Europe's Pepper and Spice Imports, ca 1400–1700," pp. 391–93.

49. William S. Atwell, "Some Observations on the 'Seventeenth Century Crisis' in China and Japan," *Journal of Asian Studies* XLV (1986) 2:223–44, pp. 223–37.

50. T. Volker, *Porcelain and the Dutch East India Company* (Leiden: E.J. Brill, 1954), pp. 50–56.

51. Prakash, *The Dutch East India Company and the Economy of Bengal 1630–1720*, p. 118.

52. Ibid., pp. 83–89.

53. Glamann, *Dutch-Asiatic Trade 1620–1740*, p. 263; Braudel, *The Perspective of the World*, vol. 3, pp. 223–32.

54. Glamann, *Dutch-Asiatic Trade 1620–1740*, p. 14.

55. Prakash, *The Dutch East India Company and the Economy of Bengal 1630–1720*, p. 201.

56. De Vries, *The Economy of Europe in an Age of Crisis, 1600–1750*, pp. 84–85.

57. Ibid., p. 146.

SELECTED REFERENCES

Atwell, William S. "Some Observations on the 'Seventeenth Century Crisis' in China and Japan." *Journal of Asian Studies* XLV (1986) 2: 223–44.

Boxer, C.R. *The Dutch Seaborne Empire 1600–1800*. New York: Alfred Knopf, 1965.

Boxer, C.R. *The Portuguese Seaborne Empire 1415–1825*. New York: Alfred Knopf, 1969.

Braudel, Fernand. *The Perspective of the World: Civilization and Capitalism 15th–18th Century*. Vol. III. New York: Harper & Row, 1984.

Chaudhuri, K.N. *Trade and Civilization in the Indian Ocean: An Economic History from the Rise of Islam to 1750*. Cambridge: Cambridge University Press, 1985.

Cipolla, Carlo M. *Before the Industrial Revolution: European Society and Economy 1000–1700*. New York: W.W. Norton Co., 1980.

Cipolla, Carlo M. *Guns, Sails and Empires: Technological Innovation and the Early Phases of European Expansion 1400–1700*. New York: Pantheon, 1965.

Collis, Maurice. *The Land of the Great Image*. Reprint. New York: New Directions, 1985.

Curtin, Philip D. *Cross-Cultural Trade in World History*. Cambridge: Cambridge University Press, 1984.

De Vries, Jan. *The Economy of Europe in an Age of Crisis, 1600–1750*. Cambridge: Cambridge University Press, 1976.

Diffie, Bailey W., and Winius, George D. *Foundations of the Portuguese Empire 1415–1580*. Minneapolis: University of Minnesota Press, 1977.

Disney, A.R. *Twilight of the Pepper Trade: Portuguese Trade in Southwest India in the Early Seventeenth Century*. Cambridge, MA: Harvard University Press, 1978.

Furber, Holden. *Rival Empires of Trade in the Orient 1600–1800*. Minneapolis: University of Minnesota Press, 1976.

Geertz, Clifford. *Agricultural Involution: The Processes of Ecological Change in Indonesia*. Berkeley: University of California Press, 1963.

Girouard, Mark. *Cities and People: A Social and Architectural History*. New Haven: Yale University Press, 1985.

Glamann, Kristof. *Dutch-Asiatic Trade 1620–1740*. Copenhagen: Danish Scientific Press, 1958.

Granzow, Uwe. *Quadrant, Kompass und Chronometer: Technische Implikationen des Euro-Asiatischen Seehandels von 1500 bis 1800*. Stuttgart: Franz Steiner Verlag, 1986.

Kling, Blair B., and Pearson, M.N., eds. *The Age of Partnership: Europeans in Asia before Dominion*. Honolulu: University Press of Hawaii, 1979.

Kriedte, Peter. *Peasants, Landlords and Merchant Capitalists: Europe and the World Economy 1500–1800*. Leamington Spa: Berg Publishers Ltd., 1983.

Lach, Donald. *Asia in the Making of Europe*. Vol. I: *The Century of Discovery*. Chicago: University of Chicago Press, 1965.

Levenson, Joseph R., ed. *European Expansion and the Counter-Example of Asia*. Englewood Cliffs: Prentice-Hall, 1967.

Mathew, K.S. *Portuguese Trade with India in the Sixteenth Century*. New Delhi: Manohar Publications, 1983.

Meilink-Roelofsz, M.A.P. *Asian Trade and European Influence in the Indonesian Archipelago between 1500 and about 1630*. The Hague: Martinus Nijhoff, 1962.

Murphey, Rhoads. *The Outsiders: The Western Experience in India and China*. Ann Arbor: University of Michigan Press, 1977.

Panikkar, K.M. *Asia and Western Dominance: A Survey of the Vasco da Gama Epoch of Asian History 1498–1945*. London: George Allen and Unwin Ltd., 1959.

Parry, J.H. *The Age of Reconnaissance: Discovery, Exploration and Settlement 1450 to 1650*. New York: Praeger Publishers, 1969.

Parry, J.H. *The Discovery of the Sea*. Berkeley: University of California Press, 1981.

Pearson, M.N. *The New Cambridge History of India*. Vol. I,1: *The Portuguese in India*. Cambridge: Cambridge University Press, 1987.

Prakash, Om. *The Dutch East India Company and the Economy of Bengal 1630–1720*. Princeton: Princeton University Press, 1985.

Schama, Simon. *The Embarrassment of Riches: An Interpretation of Dutch Culture in the Golden Age*. Berkeley: University of California Press, 1988.

Schurz, William L. *The Manila Galleon*. New York: E.P. Dutton and Co. Inc., 1959.

Simkin, C.G.F. *The Traditional Trade of Asia*. Oxford: Oxford University Press, 1968.

Smith, Adam. *The Wealth of Nations*. Reprint. New York: The Modern Library, 1937.

Souza, George B. *The Survival of Empire: Portuguese Trade and Society in China and the South China Seas, 1630–1754*. Cambridge: Cambridge University Press, 1986.

Spate, O.H.K. *The Spanish Lake*. Minneapolis: University of Minnesota Press, 1979.

Steensgaard, Niels. *The Asian Trade Revolution of the Seventeenth Century: The East India Companies and the Decline of the Caravan Trade*. Chicago: University of Chicago Press, 1974.

Vilar, Pierre. *A History of Gold and Money 1450–1920*. London: New Left Books, 1976.

Volker, T. *Porcelain and the Dutch East India Company*. Leiden: E.J. Brill, 1954.

Wake, C.H.H. "The Changing Pattern of Europe's Pepper and Spice Imports, ca 1400–1700." *The Journal of European Economic History* 8 (1979) 2: 361–404.

Wallerstein, Immanuel. *The Modern World System: Capitalist Agriculture and the Origins of the European World Economy in the Sixteenth Century*. New York: Academic Press, 1974.

Wallerstein, Immanuel. *The Modern World System II: Mercantilism and the Consolidation of the European World Economy, 1600–1750*. New York: Academic Press, 1980 (student reading).

Wilson, Charles. *The Dutch Republic*. New York: McGraw-Hill, 1968.

Wolf, Eric R. *Europe and the Peoples Without History*. Berkeley: University of California Press, 1982.

ASIA AND THE WEST IN THE NEW WORLD ORDER— FROM TRADING COMPANIES TO FREE TRADE IMPERIALISM: THE BRITISH AND THEIR RIVALS IN ASIA, 1700–1850

Derek S. Linton

INTRODUCTION

By the beginning of the eighteenth century European merchants had been trading directly in Asia for over two hundred years. The Portuguese, Spanish, Dutch, English, and French had all established permanent footholds and become recognized communities within the Asian trading world. European mercantile settlements were well ensconced in port cities like Surat, Hooghly, Cochin, Bantam, Canton, and Nagasaki. In addition, Goa, Macao, Bombay, and Batavia had been developed as European forts and factories. Mughal and Chinese officials welcomed the massive influx of gold and particularly silver brought by European commerce, since bullion was becoming vital for their steadily monetarizing revenue systems. European demand for Asian goods and the substantial European involvement in the country trade quickened economic life in Bengal, along the Malabar and Coromandel coasts of India, and in the Canton delta, redounding to the benefit of artisans, sailors, farmers, and merchants.[1]

Rulers and consumers, not to mention pirates and smugglers, also gained from the rapid growth in direct Asian trade, particularly in the late seventeenth and early eighteenth centuries. As a quid pro quo for chartering East India companies and granting them monopolies, European governments could demand loans and levy duties. Saltpeter imports from India, vital for the manufacture of gunpowder, eased the provisioning of armies.[2] While many of the goods such as precious gems, Japanese lacquerware, or Chinese porcelain graced the households of the wealthy, spices and Indian cotton goods (which by 1700 had replaced spices as the major import from the East) were used by members of all social strata. Tea drinking rapidly spread to all classes, prompting the English social reformer, Joseph Hanway, to lament in 1756, "It is the curse of the nation that the labourer and mechanic will ape the lord . . . There is a lane where beggars are often seen . . . drinking their tea. You may see labourers mending the road drinking their tea. . . ."[3] Thus the availability of a wide range of Asian products contributed to the rise of consumerism in Europe, where entrepreneurs began to manufacture such products as Delft, English, or Meissen porcelain, displacing the original imported goods in the domestic market. In particular, the development of English calico printing and, most importantly, the mechanization of the cotton textile industry were spurred by the Asian example.

Despite the mutual advantages accruing from this multifaceted long-distance commerce, trade relations between Europe and Asia were not free of problems. While Asia seemed a sinkhole for bullion, there was little demand for other European exports. At the same time, imports of Indian piece goods posed stiff competition to European textile industries.

By 1700, an estimated 10 million guldens worth of gold and silver—over a fourth of the annual output of Latin American precious metals—was wending its way around the Cape to Asia.[4] As much as 80 percent of imports from Asia were paid for in silver.

Even in the seventeenth century sophisticated mercantilists like the East India merchant Thomas Mun, arguing in terms that foreshadowed Ricardo's theory of relative advantage, cast doubt on the purely negative consequences of the specie drain.[5] For them, bullion was a commodity like any other. Because of Spanish ownership of Latin American mines, bullion could be procured more cheaply in Europe than in the East. By freely exporting specie in order to purchase and reexport Eastern goods otherwise unobtainable or more expensively produced in Europe, England would accumulate more wealth than by restricting the outflow of silver and gold. But this analysis ran counter to conventional mercantilist doctrine, which equated the wealth of states with stockpiles of precious metals. Hence throughout most of the seventeenth century European exchequers attempted, with only moderate success, to control the exit of gold and silver.

Such concerns and restrictions, however, did have substantive effects. European interloping in Asian coastal shipping, the "country trade," was undertaken in part to limit bullion exports from Europe. Trading companies hoped that multilateral intra-Asian trade would finance the purchase of Asian goods for the European market, for example, through the exchange of pepper for cotton piece goods or opium for tea. Moreover, under public pressure, they sought to augment the export of European manufactured goods to the East.[6] But apart from some woolen pieces, used as draperies or as Muslim prayer rugs, metals like copper and mercury, and such luxury goods as clocks, coral, and ivory, European companies could find little, apart from bullion, that appealed to Asian customers.

The reasons for this peculiarly lopsided structure of trade continue to be debated. According to classical trade theory, the influx of bullion to the East should have raised price levels, reducing the comparative advantage of such Indian goods as textiles. Although data on Asian prices in the seventeenth and eighteenth centuries are fragmentary, there are few indications of widespread inflationary pressures. (Limited evidence of inflation in eighteenth-century India can be imputed to war, famine and other nonmonetary causes.[7]) Two explanations have been advanced for the ability of Asian economies to absorb vast quantities of bullion without notable inflation. The first is the monetarization of Asian economies that resulted when the bullion was minted into coins, which were then funneled into domestic trade or commerce with other regions of Asia. The second claims that there was a special Asian propensity to hoard.[8] Gold in India and silver in China served as repositories of wealth and were buried in gardens or wrought into gold jewelry and ornaments used for dowries, for conspicuous display, or as insurance against calamity. While supporters of either position recognize that both monetarization and hoarding took place, proponents of the first position regard the economic behavior of Asians and Europeans as essentially similar, whereas those of the latter assert that distinctive Asian social structures and cultural values resulted in hoarding. Although the empirical evidence is far too slender to decide these issues, the debate is a potentially fruitful one for elucidating similarities and differences in European and Asian economic orientations and social structures in the early modern period.

Whatever the reasons, the capacity of Asian economies to absorb large quantities of bullion without major inflation enabled Indian cotton fabrics to retain their competitive edge until well after the onset of the industrial revolution. This was largely attributable to lower costs of production, although diversity, technical skill, and high quality also mattered. In 1736 it was estimated that wages in France were six times higher than in Bengal.[9] The East India companies were able to garner high profits in Europe by marketing an extraordinary variety of low-cost Indian piece goods: chintzes, dungarees, ginghams, diapers, percales, calicoes, and taffetas. Fabrics were sometimes sold at more than four times their procurement prices. Such imports, however, faced strong opposition from domestic textile interests; their protests prompted the English government to ban calicoes in 1700 and to introduce high tariffs on other Indian fabrics, the latter measure instituted also to raise revenue. France protected its domestic textile manufacture against Asian imports as well. Despite legislation that permitted the English East India Company to import calicoes only for reexport, large quantities of banned Indian fabrics continued to be sold illegally in England, testimony to the vitality of the trade and the consumer's preference for the attractive and high-quality Indian fabrics.

If European governments were concerned mainly about the economic consequences of Asian trade, most problematic for Asian rulers were the political and military activities of European trading companies: their demands for trading privileges, their use of naval power to blockade ports and eliminate rivals, their construction of fortified settlements. Such measures obviously infringed on the sovereignty of Asian potentates. As K.N. Chaudhuri has written of the attitudes of Mughal rulers,

> What mattered to them was the indisputable fact that the European traders were totally different from any other Asian commercial groups with which they came into contact. For one thing the corporate structures of the Companies gave them a collective strength and unity of purpose not available to the individual groups of merchants trading with or resident in the Mughal Empire. Through their command over sea power, the chartered Companies were also in position to inflict material damage to the seaborne trade of the Empire. A tacit recognition of the political reality was implicit in the treatment given by Asian rulers to the local Chiefs of the East India Company's main trading establishments. In the European travel accounts of Surat, for example, the heads of English and Dutch factories appear as the co-

equals of the Mughal ruling elite in life style and they were treated as such on the point of diplomatic status.[10]

Ever since the arrival of the Portuguese, suspicion, brutality, violence, and lawlessness invariably surrounded European enterprise in Asia. The Dutch had colonized extensively in the Moluccas and enslaved islanders; panicked by a false rumor of a planned revolt, they massacred thousands of Chinese laborers in Batavia in 1740.[11] Although it could not pose a serious military threat, the English company waged war on the Mughal Empire between 1686 and 1690. But as the Mughal historian Khafi Khan has noted, even during this war, European trade was valued too highly to consider expelling the companies.[12]

Indeed, trade was far too lucrative and beneficial for either side to contemplate a rupture. An "age of partnership," based on a dynamic equilibrium between Asian and European commercial interests, still prevailed in 1700. Close collaboration with local merchants, moneychangers, and officials was indispensable to the functioning of European mercantile companies. The country trade was still conducted with Asian crews in Asian-built cargo vessels, and in India it was often jointly financed by European, Gujarati, and Bengali merchants. Even in Bengal, which was heavily penetrated by Europeans, the companies and their servants probably carried less than half the seaborne trade.[13] Nonetheless, the foundations of a world economic system linking Europe, the Americas, and Asia had been laid by the eighteenth century.

The international division of labor and economic integration that developed between 1550 and 1750 has been aptly summarized by K.N. Chaudhuri as follows:

> American treasure helped to finance Spain's balance of indebtedness. The cost advantage enjoyed by Genoese bankers and later by the Dutch and English in the entrepot trade accumulated capital in the hands of Europe's most efficient entrepreneurs. This capital helped to finance the imports of Indian cotton textiles, Asian spices and Chinese silks and tea. Indian textiles and cowries were in turn exchanged for African slaves who produced new agricultural commodities in the New World for consumption in the Old. The circuit seems to have ended as Barbados sugar sweetened Chinese tea in porcelain cups copied from products of Ching-te-chen kilns in imperial China.[14]

With the secular upswing of the eighteenth and nineteenth

centuries, Eurasian trade relations and the international political economy underwent a series of far-reaching transformations, bringing the "age of partnership" to an end and inaugurating the era of European "free trade imperialism." Cooperative, albeit tense, trade relations gave way to trade based on unequal exchange, and colonial economic policies which fostered underdevelopment were introduced. Instead of exporting manufactured goods to Europe for bullion, many regions of Asia became exclusively exporters of raw materials, often produced on European-owned and European-managed plantations. For the first time, they also became net importers of European finished goods, thus helping to sustain the industrial revolution. Eastern wealth was channeled to European investors. These new arrangements were undergirded by the enormous expansion of European economic and military power, but would also be facilitated by changes within Asia itself as well.

Four elements conjoined to bring about these decisive transformations. First was the triumph of the English East India Company (EIC) over its Dutch and French rivals. Second was the decline of Mughal power, which opened up opportunities for European aggrandizement in the Indian subcontinent. The English East India Company was drawn by its commercial interests into the political intrigues and warfare that marked Mughal disintegration. The upshot was the British colonization of Bengal in the 1750s and 1760s, a major turning point. Third was the subsequent colonization of Bengal under the administration of the EIC, which set out to refashion the Bengali economy to meet its own needs. The institutions of the new colonial economy largely displaced native bankers and merchants, gave rise to a more commercialized agricultural system, and finally eradicated the export-oriented textile sector. Fourth was the tremendous growth of the China trade, especially the trade in tea; the English East India Company battened on the growth of the tea trade. The London–Calcutta–Canton nexus was made manifest by the trade in Bengali opium for Chinese tea, which was then shipped to England. The Opium War of 1839–42 and the resulting treaty port system showed that even the Chinese Empire was no longer invulnerable to the new economic and military might of England as the company era gave way to the age of colonialism. Ironically, the very success of the EIC contributed to its downfall. Although long waning, the company era would end definitively with the dissolution of the English East India Company following the Sepoy Mutiny of 1857.

THE PREEMINENCE OF THE ENGLISH
EAST INDIA COMPANY

By the third quarter of the eighteenth century, the English East India Company had soundly defeated its French rival and was steadily surpassing the Dutch East India Company (VOC). The reasons for its success are complex, and include organizational, economic, military, and political factors. The more streamlined business organization and simpler corporate practices of the English East India Company enabled British merchants to carve out a large niche in the Asian country trade. Also, because of the Dutch quasi-monopoly of spices, the English company was forced to deal largely in other commodities than spices. In particular, Indian textiles and Chinese tea would be the foundation of Eurasian trade starting in the late seventeenth century and a major source of the profits with which the company would erect its empire. Third, the better organization and greater wealth of the English East India Company provided the wherewithal for it to overcome its French rival during the warfare of the mid-eighteenth century. The triumph of the English East India Company would parallel the emergence of London as a port and financial center of international significance and the rise of England to great power status.

Founded by London merchants, the EIC was capitalized at about one-tenth the value of its Dutch rival, and initially it treated each voyage as an entirely independent enterprise. The Dutch virtually drove the EIC from the Spice Islands and thus compelled it to retreat to India. There it established unfortified factories at Surat and Hooghly under Mughal suzerainty, as well as at Madras on the Coromandel Coast. The company governed no Asian port of its own comparable to Goa or Batavia until 1669, when it reluctantly accepted Bombay from Charles II. Unable to enforce the sort of trade monopoly policed by the VOC, the English company permitted its servants to engage in the country trade on their own account. Although business surged in the last decades of the century, the EIC was confronted with well-organized political opposition in Parliament from merchant interlopers who demanded that its monopoly be rescinded. In the 1690s these opponents set up a rival company. As mentioned, it was also assailed by textile manufacturers who thought the company's primary role should be to export English woolens rather than to import Indian piece goods.

In 1708 the English East Indian trade was rejuvenated when

the old East India Company and the newer company of interlopers finally concluded their merger to form the United East India Company. Not only was this recast company far more heavily capitalized than either predecessor, at 3.2 million pounds; but by lending this capital to the government, which was strapped for revenue as a result of the War of the Spanish Succession, and maintaining close relations with the Bank of England, the United Company was guaranteed strong political and financial backing. Double-digit annual profits and 8 percent dividend rates soon confirmed the solidity of the United Company.[15] Moreover, its minor role in the spice trade and its concentration in India proved to be no longer liabilities but advantages.

Another advantage enjoyed by the company was a far more streamlined structure than that of its continental competitors, especially the VOC with its labyrinthine bureaucracy.[16] A twenty-four-member court of directors elected annually from stockholders presided over the company. In reality the directorate was composed of a closed, self-perpetuating oligarchy. The company divided its Asian operations into four administrative units: three in India (Bombay, Madras, and Calcutta) and the fourth in Canton. All company accounting was centralized in London. In the eighteenth century the structure of the East India Company approached Max Weber's ideal type of rational bureaucracy, with clear lines of descending authority, an upward flow of information, and strict demarcation of functional tasks.

Two company policies that distinguished it from its rivals deserve mention. First, although the company manned its ships and maintained strict control over their captains and crews, the ships themselves were rented rather than owned. This meant that at the outset the EIC required less fixed capital; it reduced the company's risks and enhanced its flexibility. But by the mid-eighteenth century the EIC was held hostage by a tightly knit London shipping interest which colluded to charge exorbitant shipping rates.[17] Second, rather than monopolizing the country trade, the company encouraged both its servants and licensed free merchants to conduct intra-Asian trade on their own account. As the historian P.J. Marshall has pointed out,

> A policy begun in weakness was eventually invested with principle. Freedom of trade, it was argued, would enable the servants to earn fortunes which cost the Company nothing, while at the same time it would turn the English settlements into thriving ports from which the Company could collect a large revenue in customs and taxation.[18]

Both of these arguments seem valid. The size and prosperity of Calcutta waxed in tandem with the growth of the British-owned private merchant fleet carrying the Indian country trade. Moreover, Marshall's case studies suggest that many East India Company officials who served in Bengal during the eighteenth century could realistically expect to retire to a country estate and live a gentleman's life in England.[19] As a result of company trade policy, British merchants were soon undercutting the VOC's Asian trade. It is clear that Dutch officials, prohibited from private trading until the 1740s, often violated the rules and cooperated closely with British merchants.[20] Certainly many EIC officials were also corrupt, but by providing a legal outlet for their voracious greed, the company restrained speculation. To some degree, it even managed to transform the private vices of its servants into public virtues advantageous to the company.

The aggressive invasion of the country trade by British private merchants helped to undermine the VOC, but probably more important was the dominant position which the EIC attained in the more dynamic sectors of Eurasian commerce, the trade in textiles and tea. In 1684 over 1.7 million pieces of fabric were imported from the East,[21] and between 1730 and 1750 annual imports often reached close to a million pieces. Moreover, in the eighteenth century more expensive and better-quality fabrics, purchased in the marketing centers or *arangs* of Bengal, accounted for as much as 80 percent of the company's sales.

Above all, however, it was tea that made the East India Company's fortune. The company's zenith coincided with what the French historian of Chinese trade, Dermigny, has appropriately entitled "the era of tea."[22] Much about the spread of tea drinking in England and on the continent remains surprisingly obscure.[23] Already in the 1650s small quantities seem to have been available for medicinal purposes, and one early London coffee house advertised it as an exotic drink. But only in the late 1660s did the East India Company import tea on a regular basis, largely from Taiwan. Two decades later, the company tried to enter direct trade with China, initially without success. Even so, by the first decade of the eighteenth century, imports already surpassed 100,000 pounds. Among the gentry tea drinking may have been part of the "civilizing process." Tea reduced the intake of liquor, and tea time presented an opportunity for sexually mixed sociability. For laborers and the poor, tea became an inexpensive and tasty medium for imbibing energy-replenishing sucrose calories and moistening their daily bread.

In 1716 the East India Company was able to secure permanent direct trade with Canton, thus ensuring itself a regular supply and laying the basis for long-term China trade. Company tea imports rose exponentially: almost 9 million pounds of tea were officially imported between 1721 and 1730, 37 million pounds between 1751 and 1760.[24] But until tariffs were lowered in the 1780s, smuggling tea was big business, and the British government acknowledged that legal tea imports probably made up as little as half the real supply.

The EIC took the lead and engrossed the lion's share of European tea imports. The Dutch originally bought tea in Batavia, but it deteriorated during the long voyage to Europe since it was shipped in bamboo cases rather than zinc-lined chests. Moreover, the VOC sold fewer varieties, since it could buy only what Chinese merchants offered. When in 1729 the VOC finally resolved to purchase directly in Canton, the English company was already firmly in place and went so far as to buy up all available green tea in order to forestall Dutch orders.[25] The belated arrival and limited role of the Dutch in Canton betokened the less venturesome approach of the VOC than that of its English rival.

GROWING INVOLVEMENT IN INDIAN POLITICS

If the EIC gradually overtook its Dutch competitor in economic performance, its victory over the French was largely political and military. Despite earlier interest in eastern trade, it was only after 1664 that Louis XIV's great finance minister Colbert launched a serious French Company of the Indies. In contrast to the VOC or the EIC, the French company was purely a state-sponsored syndicate; that its agents were often unqualified political appointees rather than merchants certainly contributed to its lackluster performance.[26] Nonetheless, by the 1680s the company had set up profitable factories in Surat, at Pondicherry on the Coromandel Coast, and in Bengal. But undercapitalization, France's schemes to colonize Madagascar, and its incessant warfare with the Dutch converged to keep the company teetering on the brink of bankruptcy. It finally went into liquidation during the War of the Spanish Succession. Reconstituted in 1725, the company flourished during the next quarter-century, when between eighteen and twenty ships departed annually for the East. Its prime source of profits was the textile trade on the Coromandel Coast, but its commerce with China also expanded steadily. Even at its height, however, the volume of French trade was probably one-fourth that of the EIC. As was often the case with the French in the seventeenth and eighteenth centuries, promising economic initiatives were soon stifled by warfare. Between 1744 and 1763 France and England were embroiled in almost continuous military operations in India. Despite some efforts by the trading companies to neutralize the East, in order to avoid costly military campaigns, national and military interests ultimately overrode mercantile concerns.[27] As a result, the French role in the East was rendered insignificant.

Two important military innovations, both of which ironically were pioneered by the French, but then used to greater advantage by the British, were introduced in Asia at this time. The first was a revolution in military organizational strategy, whereby European officers drilled uniformed armies composed of Europeans, Eurasian "topasses," and native sepoys. Armies were trained to lay down synchronized volleys of musket fire rather than fighting as aggregates of individual soldiers. The effectiveness of this strategy was demonstrated at the Battle at Adyar River, south of Madras, in 1746, where an army of French and native troops trained in musket volley defeated a force of 10,000 Indian soldiers allied with Britain.[28] By 1750, however, the British forces were following the French example. With its greater financial strength the EIC was able to recruit a larger army and defeat the French and their allies in southern India.

The second innovation was the active involvement of the European companies in Indian politics and rivalries. While English East India Company officials originally conceived of intervention exclusively as a means of protecting trade, their French counterparts sought political allies as a way of building a French empire in India. Military alliances should be concluded in return for economic and territorial concessions. It was a vision, however, that would be realized by their rivals, the British, in Bengal.

The prerequisites for interventions by the French and English companies in Indian politics were the precipitous decline of the Mughal state and the accompanying devolution of power into the hands of regionally based princes and nawabs, the latter still nominally governing for the Mughals. A variety of interpretations has evolved to account for the collapse of the Mughal Empire. According to Braudel, the perennial campaigning of the Islamic emperor Aurangzeb against the Hindu Marathas and Sikhs virtually bankrupted the empire.[29] The bloody intrigues for succession that followed his death further paralyzed the regime, and by midcentury the empire was reduced to a sort of theater state with some vestiges of authority but little real power. Its collapse was accompanied by considerable economic dislocation as the depredations of Maratha warriors, widespread banditry, and the financial demands of warfare curtailed production and trade.

To C.A. Bayly, however, the interpretation of the fall of the Mughals as a result of decadence and political anarchy is overly simple.[30] His recent work describes the various kingdoms, military adventurers, and new social groups that rushed into the vacuum left by the Mughal disintegration. Not only were these new social groups often heavily involved in commerce, but their commercial activities sometimes transcended caste distinctions. A new society, based on aristocratic landownership and merchant capitalism, began to crystalize. In many cases these commercial elites allied with the European trading companies to guarantee the stability necessary to continue trade, thus playing an active role in the process that ultimately led to the colonization of India. Gujarati merchants, for example, encouraged the English East India Company to protect trade and shipping activities; it was at their urging that in 1759 the British wrested control of the city from the impotent Mughals.

A similar process, and one with far more spectacular consequences, played itself out in Bengal, where the nawabs had been autonomous rulers for decades.[31] Appointed nawab of Bengal in 1756, Siraj-ud-Daula's excessive demands for funds from tax farmers and the great Parsi banking house of Jagat Seth turned them against him; his purge of the military and administration outraged generals and officials. When the EIC fortified Calcutta, largely against French attack, Siraj's army sacked Calcutta and drove the British out, thereby incurring the wrath of the local merchant community as well. In revenge the EIC raised an army of almost 3000 Europeans and sepoys to retake Calcutta. The company, in league with the Jagat Seths and disaffected members of the nawab's military and administrative establishment, defeated him in the battle of Plassey in 1757. But three years later, Siraj's successor was in turn replaced when he refused to cede land revenues to the company to offset its losses on military operations. It was clear that henceforth the East India Company would determine who would rule Bengal.

THE TRANSITION FROM MERCANTILISM
TO IMPERIALISM

The de facto rule of the East India Company in Bengal was legally ratified in 1765 when the Mughal emperor recognized the company as the *diwan*, or revenue agent, of the province. The company immediately reduced the nawab's army to ceremonial functions and ensured that its own mercenary troops monopolized the means of control. Thus without any initial plan or expectation of creating a colonial empire and over the objections of its directors in London, who were averse to political entanglements which diverted the company from trade, the East India Company had established itself in less than a decade as the colonial ruler of northeast India's most prosperous state. This takeover would have been utterly impossible, however, if the exactions of the new nawab had not been widely considered illegitimate and if the EIC had not received strong support among the indigenous political and commercial elite, like the house of Jagat Seth.

As colonial administrator of Bengal, the East India Company in 1767 agreed to pay the British state £400,000 annually;[32] its relationship with the British government was further institutionalized by the India Act of 1784, which set up a board of control to superintend the company's operations and finances, which were in disarray. But the privileged position of the company drew fire from Adam Smith, Edmund Burke, and Bristol and Liverpool merchants, who protested its administrative abuses and its monopoly of Indian trade. They would be effective in loosening the company's hold over the India trade in 1793 and in eliminating its monopoly of trade between India and Britain entirely through the Charter Act of 1813.[33] But throughout the period the company dominated the Bengali economy.

Its policies had several major economic repercussions. Company servants and private merchants used their newly acquired political power to encroach on sectors of the Bengali economy, such as the salt monopoly, previously reserved by the nawab.[34] The salt monopoly became a major source of income, as did opium production, which by the 1830s yielded one-seventh of the total revenue of British India.

Several other changes also had long-term significance, both economic and social. First, of course, was that the company, as diwan, collected the taxes and fees that had previously filled the nawab's treasury. This meant that it had to import very little bullion into Bengal. The stream of silver dwindled to a trickle as Bengali revenue was used to purchase Bengali goods for export and to finance the army and administration. Although Bengal still maintained a positive balance of trade, it became a net exporter of bullion, reversing the traditional pattern. Complaints of specie shortage soon followed.[35] There can be no question that the company and its servants drained wealth from Bengal to Britain, although the size of this drain and its overall impact have been subject to debate, with estimates ranging from 100 million pounds during the first fifty years of British rule to as high as ten times that amount.[36] While these funds did not in and of themselves finance British industrialization, which initially required little capital, they certainly did strengthen Britain's international financial position.

Whatever the effects, by 1789–90 British revenues from Bengal reached approximately 3 million pounds annually.[37] Whether company taxation was more burdensome to the local population than that of the Mughals remains an open question, but collection was certainly more assiduous. Already by the 1770s the company had appointed European supervisors to ensure that tax farmers and zamindars, usually large land-owning revenue collectors, delivered their contracted sums.[38] Fearing that extortion by native tax farmers was killing the golden goose, in 1793 Governor Cornwallis translated Whig notions of property and rural improvement into Bengali.[39] The Permanent Settlement Act of 1793 converted the complex revenue-collecting rights of zamindars into absolute private property. In exchange for this legal tenure, zamindars were expected to pay a fixed sum to the company collectors in perpetuity. By freezing the level of taxation and consolidating property rights, company officials believed landowners would be induced to improve their land. These expectations were largely unfulfilled, however, since land values were considerably over-assessed and zamindars were unable to meet their payments. Consequently, the Settlement Act was followed by a turnover of over 40 percent of taxable landed property in Bengal.[40] Taxation thus tended to deter agrarian improvement.

The EIC also attempted to stimulate export-oriented agriculture and agroindustry. Following the famine of 1770, which killed at least a fourth of the Bengali population and seriously damaged the silk industry, the company sedulously revived sericulture by offering rent-free land to peasants willing to cultivate mulberry trees, bringing silkworm eggs from China, and even introducing Italian silk winders to teach new techniques. During the next decade raw silk exports to England rose to 560,000 lbs. annually.[41] When the American Revolution cut off exports of indigo to England, the company advanced loans to encourage private European merchants to start indigo factories.[42] Although initially sporadic, indigo production took off in northern India after the turn of the nineteenth century due to the vast increase in demand for dyes by the English textile industry and the absence of alternative sources of supply. In 1828, at the end of the indigo boom, there were as many as 900 European-owned indigo factories in Bengal, with up to half a million employees and dependents and aggregate profits of between 1 and 2 million pounds.[43] To guarantee high profits, however, factories often coerced peasants into growing indigo and then kept them in debt peonage; it was an oppressive system that frequently precipitated riots. The company promoted other commercial crops as well, such as sugar cane—especially during the Napoleonic Wars, when the West Indies supply declined—and, increasingly, opium and cotton, which, as will be discussed below, were essential for the China trade.[44] As one writer noted in 1835, however, the increased opium production in Bengal after the mid-1820s "had enhanced the value of the land fourfold, enriched the *Zamindars*, maintained thousands of people employed in collecting and preparing the drug. . . ."[45]

While the social effects of the commercialization of Bengali agriculture continue to be debated, such observations suggest that it did conduce to some positive outcomes. Some zamindari landowners profited greatly from planting indigo, poppies, or mulberries.[46] Wages of propertyless Bengali day laborers probably rose somewhat during the late eighteenth and early nineteenth centuries. But while many peasants freely switched to cash crops in expectation of higher income, most seem to have accrued heavy debts, since advances were necessary to plant crops like sugar cane. In addition to the usual vagaries of the weather, they became vulnerable to volatile price fluctuations associated with distant events such as the Napoleonic Wars or the slumps in England between 1826 and 1935. The revenue demands of the EIC, shortages of bullion, and international market conditions led to serious depression in some rural regions during the 1830s.[47]

The most serious consequence of company economic policy, however, concerned the fate of Indian textile manufacture in the early colonial era. In a word, British colonialism destroyed the vibrant export textile sector and deindustrialized India.[48] By the last half of the eighteenth century Bengali textile manufacture was facing serious difficulties as a direct result of company policy. Although general demand for Indian piece goods remained high in Europe, prices were stable or fell in the 1770s and 1780s. To maintain its profits, the company had to obtain its supplies at low cost; it did so by eliminating competitors and imposing onerous constraints on weavers.[49] First, despite company lip service to open trade, its agents prevented Dutch, French, or private merchants from buying in the *arangs*, thus creating a monopsony. Second, before advancing weavers the cash necessary to buy yarn, the company compelled them to sign contracts granting it exclusive rights over their output. In principle, weavers were exempt from various forms of taxation, one of the few benefits of the trade. But in the 1770s and 1780s, as company revenue demands mounted, weavers began to be subjected to heavy taxation by the zamindars.[50] As a result, many weavers simply abandoned their trades and returned exclusively to farming, which was rendered an increasingly viable option since the situation of agricultural workers had improved somewhat as a result of the higher land/labor ratio after the famines of 1770 and 1787. Thus company policy had the unintended consequences of harming the export-oriented textile trade and inhibiting structural adaptation.

British policy and the mechanization of the English cotton industry would complete what company policy had begun. As described by Braudel, the growth of the cotton industry in England was itself a response to the challenge of Indian production:

> The cotton revolution, first in England, but very soon all over Europe, began by imitating Indian industry, went on to take revenge by catching up with it, and finally outstripped it. The aim was to produce fabrics of comparable quality at cheaper prices. The only way to do this was to introduce machines— which alone could effectively compete with Indian textile workers. That had to wait for Arkwright's water frame (1769) and Crompton's mule (1775–8) which made it possible to produce yarn as fine and strong as the Indian product, one that could be used for weaving fabric entirely out of cotton. From now on, the market for Indian cottons would be challenged by the developing English industry—and it was a very large market indeed, covering England and the British Isles, Europe . . . , the coast of Africa where black slaves were exchanged for lengths of cotton, and the huge market of colonial America, not to mention Turkey and the Levant—or India itself. Cotton was always produced primarily for export: in 1800 it represented a quarter of all British exports; by 1850 this had risen to fifty per cent.[51]

Although Braudel does not mention it, the timing of English mechanization can be plausibly linked to the inability of the EIC to maintain the supply of Indian piece goods during the disruptive warfare of the 1750s and 1760s. In the late 1750s prizes were offered in England for inventions to increase yarn production, thus giving incentives to inventors like Arkwright.[52] In the mid-1760s British entrepreneurs, like the calico printing shop of Robert Peel, one of the key figures in the industrial revolution, stepped into the market temporarily undersupplied by the EIC.[53]

Beginning in 1813, when a new company charter opened India to the free trade of British merchants, English manufacturers were able to export cotton fabric to the land that originally produced it: they carried calico to Calicut. Indian exports to Great Britain and the European continent had already fallen by over a third, however, during the Napoleonic Wars due to high tariffs in Britain (between 35 and 66 percent ad valorem for various types of cloth) and the French exclusion of British reexports.[54] England's infant cotton industry thrived under these high tariffs. During the commercial boom which lasted from 1815, the year the Napoleonic Wars ended, until 1827–28, the export of Indian piece goods to Europe effectively ceased as cheaper English cottons supplanted them. English cottons also drove Indian piece goods from the American and Asian markets. Moreover, aided by low tariffs of 2.5 percent ad valorem on British imports, English fabrics and yarn soon invaded the Bengali market, and by 1817 the Bengali imports of English piece goods surpassed exports to England. Within fifteen years over £2 million worth of cotton goods was being imported annually. Although these imports probably covered less than 10 percent of Indian domestic demand, the growth of the Indian market for English cotton exports "did much to alleviate the generally gloomy trading conditions of the period from the later 1820s to the mid-1840s."[55] During this period export-oriented spinners, weavers, and dyers in India were ruined and immiserated as surely as were the handloom weavers of England. Once-flourishing weaving towns like Dacca decayed into insignificance. Reported the governor general in Calcutta in 1832,

> Cotton piece goods, for so many ages the staple manufacture of India seem thus forever lost. . . . The sympathy of the Court is deeply excited by the Report of the Board of Trade exhibiting the gloomy picture of the effects of the commercial revolution, productive of so much suffering to numerous classes in India, and hardly to be paralleled in the history of commerce.[56]

Although EIC and British policy destroyed its manufacturing base for foreign trade, in the first half of the nineteenth century Bengal continued to run a positive external trade balance thanks to its agricultural exports, e.g., opium, indigo, and raw cotton. Internal trade in grain continued to flow along the Ganges and its tributaries. And what became of the Bengali merchant communities and merchant capital that had been so crucial for the British takeover? Native merchants retained their hold on inland trade and money-lending, though even intra-Indian trade seems to have been somewhat hampered by tolls until they were abolished in 1835.[57] Some merchants purchased zamindar land or urban real estate, and others switched to retailing imports, as opportunities for investment and involvement in foreign trade dried up.[58]

After the 1780s, when company servants were forbidden to trade directly on their own account, their investments were placed with agency houses, usually owned and operated by Scotsmen. Such houses soon became multiple-purpose financial institutions combining banking and brokerage activities.[59] They owned ships, invested in indigo and sugar factories, financed and insured the intra-Asian country trade, exchanged currencies, and made loans at high interest. Their close association with the indigo industry, however, made them extremely sensitive to gluts, as evidenced by the collapse of several leading Calcutta agency houses in 1833. In periods of tight money they sometimes received advances from the EIC. With their access to company funds, its servants, and private British merchants and their affiliations with London banks, the agency houses gradually displaced the native agents who had previously been indispensable in acquiring goods for trading, lending money, and overseeing the private finances of company servants. After Plassey such agents had numbered among the wealthiest men in Calcutta.[60] For some indigenous financiers, like the once powerful house of Jagat Seth, the British conquest was the beginning of the end. By the 1790s, forced to compete with the agency houses in its foreign exchange operations, Jagat Seth was in serious decline. A handful of Bengalis were able to become junior partners in European agency houses or even to start houses of their own along European lines, but for most the increasing dominance of foreign trade by British firms meant an introversion of capital into local or regional trade and a loss of status from a position of partnership with British mercantile interests to one of subordination.

This subordination was particularly evident in Calcutta, where even the wealthiest Indian merchants and landlords lived in the congested native section, or Black Town.[61] Perhaps as symbols of their intermediate position, their houses sometimes combined courtyards and other traditional elements with external features adopted from the Europeans, like Corinthian columns. The several thousand European residents—company officials, judges, lawyers, and free merchants—were concentrated in White Town, in the Chowringhee District, where, pampered by hosts of Indian servants, they recreated the life style of the English gentry. The British lived in detached villas with verandas which had the "appearance of Grecian temples."[62] Along Fort William's Esplanade, which constituted the geographic and social center of European life, were arrayed the official buildings of the British administration. From the 1780s, when company officials were increasingly joined by their families, the British shopped in European emporia like Dring's or the Lall Bazaar, which sold everything from pickled herring to pianofortes. The reformation of manners and morals and the spread of evangelical Christianity—Tory reactions against the French Revolution—that were sweeping society in England were also evident among the British in Calcutta. Not only were heavy drinking and gambling, which had been notorious among company officials, frowned upon, but the keeping of Indian concubines was no longer tolerated.[63] Although segregation was far from complete, relations were increasingly those between master and servant, not partners and equals.

The dawn of the nineteenth century also brought tightened political control, founded on an imperialist ideology and infused with modern racist sentiments.[64] To a great extent, this change was prompted by Britain's experience in the Napoleonic Wars. Fearing that the rulers of Mysore and the Maratha confederation, who were advised by French officers, would be able to build and equip armies that could oust the EIC, Governor General Lord Wellesley set about enlarging the army, adding cavalry, and planning a better-organized military supply system. By 1799 his army defeated Sultan Tipu of Mysore and was able to hold the Marathas at bay. His troops were also deployed against the French and their Dutch allies during the Napoleonic Wars in Ceylon, Java, South Africa, and Egypt. Indeed, the army in India would provide the muscle of the British Empire in Asia, Africa, and the Middle East until independence in 1947. Wellesley and his successors encouraged the collection of information and development of knowledge that would buttress British military and administrative power. They promoted the study of Indian languages, gathered intelligence on the economic and military potential of Indian rulers, and mapped the subcontinent.

By 1815, the East India Company was completing the transition from trading company to ruler of a military despotism financed from Indian revenues, which in 1819 amounted to 22 million pounds.[65] Indeed, the entire subcontinent was rapidly capitulating to British military power. Moreover, at least in Bengal, the economy was well on the way to becoming that of an underdeveloped colony, with a commercialized agricultural sector shaped by British interests. By the 1820s Bengal was an exporter of agricultural raw materials and an importer of English manufactured goods. Its textile export sector was already distressed and dying. Similar trends were apparent along the Coromandel Coast, too. International events and market conditions also affected India's economy. Revolts in Latin America in the 1830s combined with the reduction of textile exports resulted in a serious bullion shortage.

The three central problems which from a European perspective had plagued Eurasian trade in the early eighteenth century were disappearing in India: silver no longer flowed east from London to Bengal, since Indian exports were paid for with Indian funds; British traders commanded those commodities, namely, cotton textiles, that Indians wished to purchase; as a result, Indian piece goods no longer competed with European fabrics, whether in Europe or on third markets. Moreover, Indian raw materials were increasingly being substituted for silver to balance the China trade.

In China as well, the transformation of the pattern of trade would not be brought about by purely economic means. To invert Marx, it would be the heavy artillery of British gunboats, not the cheap prices of British commodities, that would batter down Chinese trade barriers.

THE CHINA TRADE

By the 1780s the structure and pattern of trade between the East India Company, by far the largest trade company operating in China, and the port of Canton had become relatively fixed.[66] The Chinese strictly regulated trade in an effort to contain the barbarians from the West. Under the Eight Regulations, foreigners were confined to their factory precincts, foreign women were denied entry, they were not permitted to winter in Canton, etc. The East India Company was compelled to deal exclusively with the *cohong*, a loose association of Chinese merchants licensed by the imperial government. While feigning indifference to foreign commerce, however, Chinese officials recognized that EIC business in Canton was an important source of income.

Although supplemented by silk, nankeen, china ware, and "drugs" such as rhubarb and camphor, tea was by far China's most important export to Europe. Exports to Great Britain, where the EIC held a monopoly, skyrocketed in the last decades of the eighteenth century as duties on tea were reduced from 100 percent to 12.5 percent by the Commutation Act of 1784, which made smuggling unprofitable, increased consumption, and actually increased government revenues. The China trade accelerated. Whereas in the 1770s fewer than ten EIC ships arrived in Canton in a season, by the end of the 1780s the number varied between twenty-five and twenty-nine.[67] EIC imports of bulk tea rose from almost 6 million lbs. in 1783 to 15 million lbs. in 1785, and would grow to an annual average of about 30 million lbs. by the 1820s.[68] By 1830 the British Exchequer was bringing in over £3 million annually from tea duties, about a tenth of its total revenue, and almost the entire profit of the EIC, perhaps £1–1.5 million, could be traced to the tea trade.

The difficulty for the EIC, of course, was paying for Chinese tea. To be sure, Chinese mandarins found European watches and mechanical toys ("singsongs") amusing; Geneva artisans even made specially designed Chinese watches.[69] But the only really important European export to China was woolens. During the 1780s the value of woolen exports to China rose to more than £400,000 annually.[70] It is doubtful, however, that this reflected a Chinese passion for wool cloth. Rather, the EIC apparently retailed these piece goods at a loss, largely to mollify British textile interests. Even so, in the 1780s, the EIC's bullion imports to Canton were sometimes double the value of the merchandise imports, at a time when Britain's war with Spain made it difficult to acquire silver coins.

Although the system worked passably well, the EIC, private traders, and other foreign merchants were dissatisfied with the drain of bullion and chafed at the galling restrictions imposed by the Chinese government. Company officials then hit upon the idea of stopping the bullion drain by financing the China trade with Indian goods.[71] They also hoped to circumvent the Canton regulations by securing a Southeast Asian port, a British equivalent to Batavia, that could serve as a naval base and an entrepot where Chinese merchants could be attracted outside the framework of the confining Canton system.[72] Such a base was actually built in northern Borneo; it soon failed, though similar notions motivated the founding of Singapore in 1819. Hopes of protecting the tea trade, ending trade restrictions, and expanding exports of English manufactured goods to China prompted the 1793 mission to Beijing of Lord Macartney, former governor of Madras. He requested, inter alia, three new ports, a warehouse in Beijing, extraterritorial merchant settlements near Chusan and Canton, and permanent ambassadorial representation.[73] The emperor peremptorily dismissed all the requests as wild ideas. In his famous response to George III, not only did he strongly reaffirm the arrangements with the Hong in Canton, he assured the king that China possessed all things, that he "set no value on objects strange or ingenious . . ." and that he had "no use for your country's manufactures."[74]

Nonetheless, both the structure and pattern of trade relations were already being loosened and would unravel completely within a few decades. The two factors working to destroy these arrangements were, first, the erosion of the company's monopoly and the concomitant growth of the free merchant community and, second, the takeoff of the opium trade.

Even before its monopoly of the China trade ended in 1833, the company had come to depend on licensed British private merchants for its system of payments in Canton.[75] This was especially true after 1813, when the India monopoly ceased. Private merchants sold Indian or Malaccan Straits goods such as cotton, opium, tin, and rattan in Canton for silver. They would then transfer their silver to the EIC for bills of exchange redeemable in London, thereby remitting their funds back to England. Increasingly this complex system of transfers became a way of laundering and recycling profits from the opium trade. Although the EIC exercised a monopoly over the production and sale of opium in Bengal and earned a substantial portion of its revenues from its opium auctions in Calcutta, to preserve its official status, the company refrained from selling the illegal narcotic in China. Private merchants, however, who were shut out of the tea trade by the EIC monopoly could sell opium to the Chinese. From this situation arose a symbiotic arrangement between private merchants and the EIC based on the transfers of opium, silver, and tea.

Opium was the key to the entire trade relationship, as it was the only commodity for which the Chinese had a sure and rapidly rising demand. Chinese opium consumption had probably been climbing since the seventeenth century, when it began to be smoked with tobacco, initially introduced by Europeans from South America. A Qing edict of 1729 criminalized opium, and in the early nineteenth century only about 4,000 chests each weighing 140 lbs. were imported annually into China, largely via Macao.[76] Despite periodic crackdowns by Chinese officials, consumption grew exponentially throughout the 1820s and 1830s. In 1836 more than 1,800 tons of opium worth over £3.6 million poured into China, making it the world's single most valuable trading commodity.[77] As a result of the opium trade, for the first time in history China's trade balance showed a deficit, with perhaps £7.6 million worth of silver leaving China between 1828 and 1836.[78] From an official Chinese perspective, the outflow of silver destroyed the reason for engaging in foreign trade. Moreover, Chinese officials estimated that 1 percent of China's entire population and perhaps 20 percent of its high officials and wealthy gentry were addicts.[79] As in India, in the 1830s foreign trade was eroding China's monetary system, resulting in higher prices for the silver with which peasants were required to pay taxes and therefore adding to rural unrest. Worse still, the opium trade was being foisted on China by foreigners and was pursued through bribery, corruption, and gangsterism.[80] In 1838 the Chinese government embarked on a major campaign to extirpate drug trafficking, whether by native Chinese or foreigners, a policy that clashed with the financial interests of increasingly aggressive British merchants.

Manchester manufacturers and private British merchants had lobbied in the late 1820s and early 1830s to end the monopoly of the China trade by the EIC, which they accused of failing to further the interests of British manufacturers and of passively complying with the restrictive Canton system.[81] The end of the EIC monopoly in 1834, however, did not bring about the desired benefits, and the same coalition continued to pressure the British government to open up Chinese trade. Imperial Commissioner Lin Zexu's campaign to crush the opium trade served as a golden opportunity to pursue such an aim. Lin's seizure of merchants' opium and his attempts to force the British merchant community to agree to stop the contraband trade heightened tensions, and the refusal of the British to hand over a sailor who had murdered a Chinese peasant triggered hostilities.[82] British merchants charged that the Chinese seizure of opium was a deadly insult to the British flag, and that China's failure to accept free trade and to deal with other nations as equals constituted grounds for war. Lord Palmerston, the prime minister, was easily persuaded to send an expeditionary force. The flag followed trade; free trade demanded war.

With their overwhelming naval superiority and more accurate guns, the British easily won the war in 1842.[83] Indeed it was the first war in which iron steamers, "fire wheel boats" to the Chinese, were used extensively. On land, too, the ill-prepared Chinese army displayed little military prowess against the Indian sepoys. In the late summer of 1842 the humiliating Treaty of Nanjing was concluded, with the imperial regime agreeing to pay an indemnity of over £4 million, ceding Hong Kong island, opening the ports of Canton, Amoy, Foochow, Ningpo, and Shanghai to free trade and consular representation, and setting up a uniform system of low tariffs.[84]

The Treaty resulted in an enormous expansion in the volume of trade. Chinese tea exports spiralled from 66 million lbs. to 109 million between 1845 and 1855, while silk exports rose almost sixfold. Over the same period, opium imports almost doubled to 60,000 chests. The commodities traded, however, remained unaffected by the war. Whether because of immutable tastes or lack of purchasing power, the Chinese showed little interest in Western manufactured goods. Moreover, Chinese officials were dilatory in reforming the tariff system as demanded by the British. With its centralized government, integrated economy, long tradition of cultural unity, and sense of superiority, China proved far less cooperative and more resistant to Western demands, and its economy more impervious to Western goods, than had been the case in India.[85]

But, despite the widening military, technological, and economic gap between Europe and Asia, even at mid-century there were very decided limits to Western power. Western penetration had always depended to some degree on Asian political weakness and economic receptivity. Although they had succeeded in battering down the old trading system, the British were not entirely successful in their efforts to introduce a satisfactory replacement. The treaty ports existed as foreign excrescences, and were never organically linked with the Chinese domestic economy.

Nonetheless, the British had dismantled the old system. Whatever the illusions of Chinese officialdom, the British were no ordinary barbarians. Their military superiority, still largely naval and organizational, and their economic dynamism had enabled them to conquer and colonize India and to embarrass the Chinese empire. Many Chinese tea and silk producers had become dependent on European demand. Whether under EIC rule in Bengal or under the rule of the Dutch in the East Indies, Asian peasants had become suppliers of unprocessed agricultural products—tea, coffee, cotton, spices, raw silk, and sugar—for the delectation of Europeans while Asian elites increasingly consumed imported European manufactured goods.

The vital importance of Asian empire and trade was widely recognized in Britain even during the 1850s and 1860s, the high era of laissez-faire, when European tariffs reached their lowest point in the nineteenth century. By 1860, 13.5 percent of Britain's imports came from Asia and 16.4 percent of its exports were destined for Asian markets. Asia was as important to British trade as was the United States.[86] While Britain and the Netherlands were the only colonial powers in Asia by mid-century, and most other European nations purchased their Asian goods from these two, some continental industries, like the silk industry of France, drew their raw materials from the Far East. Liberal free traders cheered Palmerston's use of naval power to maintain open trade relations in China in 1857–58. Peter Harnetty has argued that the proponents of free trade known as the Manchester school of free trade economics vigorously supported imperial economic development in India in mid-century.

> In this period, the Indian economy appeared to the Lancashire cotton interests as an ideal complement to Great Britain's economy: India would provide both raw materials for British industry and a vast market for British manufactures. Commercial penetration of India required a planned program of public works and significant investment by the state.[87]

Even Cobden, the apostle of free trade, ruefully admitted, "If you talk to our Lancashire friends they argue that unless we occupied India there would be no trade with that country, or that someone else would monopolize it, forgetting that this is the old protectionist theory which they formerly used to ridicule."[88] The notion of empire harmonized readily with the free trade demands of merchants opposed to trading companies and those of manufacturers for export markets in the East. Moreover, in the Royal Navy and Indian army, Britain commanded effective instruments for ensuring unequal economic relations.

CONCLUSION

Thus between 1700 and 1850 trade and political relations between Europe and Asia were dramatically transformed. Europeans had conquered India, the East Indies, and Ceylon by the mid-nineteenth century, and were able to dictate the conditions of trade to China.

To be sure, even in 1700 Europeans enjoyed some significant advantages when operating in the Asian trading world. First, they had access to large quantities of silver, which enabled them to establish themselves in the Asian trading world. Second, because European governments and mercantile companies sought to decrease bullion flows to the East, trading companies were encouraged to find other ways of financing their exports to Europe. They thus intruded in the intra-Asian country trade,[89] acquiring extensive knowledge of Asian trade networks and commodities in the process. Although European merchants often cooperated closely with their Asian counterparts, in the long run, their position in the country trade would allow them to displace much native shipping and underwrite much of their European trade with profits from Asian goods. Third, Europeans possessed superior ships and naval armaments; naval technology was one of the few areas in which Europeans had any significant advantage. This advantage increased slowly but steadily between 1500 and 1850, largely pushed forward by political rivalries in Europe among Great Britain, France, and the Netherlands. Because naval activities appeared to be of marginal importance to the land-based empires of China or Mughal India, there was little incentive to imitate the Westerners. This meant that powerful Asian rulers conceded to the Europeans uncontested control over seaborne trade. This points to the fourth decisive advantage of the Europeans. At least in northwest Europe, a far closer relation existed between mercantile interests and the state than was the case in Asia. John Fairbank has written that Qing policy on overseas trade "usually handicapped rather than aided the Chinese merchant. . . . Peking seems to have been fearful of overseas commercial expansion on the part of Chinese merchants."[90] There were, of course, distinctions within Europe as well. It was notably the Dutch and English rather than the French or Portuguese that fared best in Asia. In the latter cases, trade was largely subordinate to political ends, whereas in the former two, trading companies retained considerable autonomy while counting on military support from their governments, which in turn could count on financial backing from the monopolistic trading companies. It was Holland and England, where absolutism failed to develop and where the relation between state power and mercantilism was symbiotic rather than fused, that ultimately prevailed in Asia. Finally, the merchant companies themselves, with their records and bureaucracies, gave the Europeans great advantage in Asian trade. They had a broader vision than smaller family associations of Armenian or Gujarati merchants could have. With their wealthy and powerful stockholders they could bring pressure to bear on their domestic governments; with their larger and better armed ships they could obtain concessions from Asian rulers.

Several further changes within both Europe and Asia were necessary, however, before Europeans could move from partnership to empire. First, European dominance would have been impossible without the political disintegration of Asian powers and without the cooperation of native collaborators. It was the fragmentation of native rule that enabled the Dutch to colonize the Spice Islands of the East Indies in the seventeenth century, just as it was the collapse of the Mughals that enabled the EIC to evolve from a purely trading company to a colonial power. The decline of Mughal power was in no respect caused by the EIC, but the company proved to be the major beneficiary and legatee. Indigenous merchant and banking communities turned to it for protection from the depredations of contending native rulers and to restore order and stabilize trade. The resources of the EIC and the French enabled them to operate as political and military entrepreneurs in the complex internecine struggles that accompanied Mughal decline. It should be noted, however, that the political involvement of the EIC which led to the colonization of Bengal was opposed by the company's directors in London, who sought to avoid the expense and dangers of warfare. Regular profits, not colonization, was their aim.

The takeover of Bengal had fateful consequences, however. Most importantly, it provided the EIC with revenues to construct a major subimperialist system in India, with a European-style army, one of the largest in the world, that would be instrumental in Britain's conquest of all India and the expansion of its power elsewhere in Asia. Second, the company's economic policies led to the commercialization of agriculture and the decline of export-oriented textile manufacture in India. Henceforth, India became a source of raw materials, and its commercial crops provided the means for financing the British tea trade. Third, the new position of the EIC in Bengal emboldened the attack of free traders on company privileges. From a protracted parliamentary struggle that lasted from the 1780s to the 1830s, the free traders would emerge triumphant. With less capital and in need of quicker profits in an increasingly competitive environment, the free traders were less inclined to function within the traditional rules and framework of Asian trade. Instead they energetically pressed for governmental action to open up Asian economies to European goods and for ending restrictions on trade. Thus the free merchants played a primary role in the Chinese opium trade and in lobbying the government to end the restrictive Canton system.

In this they were aided by a more militant campaign to foster British exports, a campaign launched by Midlands textile interests in the context of the slump of the 1830s and the agitation for greater middle-class political representation. Textile interests had, of course, been intimately engaged with Asian trade policy since the end of the seventeenth century, with English manufacturers fighting for protectionist measures against Indian calicoes and urging the EIC to sell more woolens in Asia. Similar lobbying was to be found in France and the Dutch Republic. After the Napoleonic Wars, the Midlands cotton lords pushed to establish export markets in India and China. Having developed the potential to export cheaply in a protectionist cocoon, they would demand free trade in Asia, to be enforced if necessary by British gunboats and Indian sepoys. The new interest constellation of independent merchants and manufacturers eventually introduced the imperialism of free trade, first manifest in the Opium War from 1839–42. Ironically, this new imperialism depended on and would be superimposed over the former monopoly system of the EIC. Company sepoys and ships opened Chinese markets to British textiles. By the mid-nineteenth century, however, the company era was over. The age of silver exports had yielded to the age of iron gunboats. European technology, warfare, manufacture, and commercial policy were beginning to have revolutionary effects on much of Asia. The basis for this free trade imperialism depended as much on processes unleashed within Asia as within Europe; it would be of far shorter duration than the confident and triumphant merchants could have guessed at the dawn of the Victorian age.

NOTES

I would like to thank William S. Atwell for having read and commented on an earlier draft of this typescript.

1. K.N. Chaudhuri, *The Trading World of Asia and the English East India Company 1660–1760* (Cambridge: Cambridge University Press, 1978), pp. 15–18; P.J. Marshall, "Bengal: The British Beachhead: East India 1740–1828," in *The New Cambridge History of India*, vol. II.2 (Cambridge: Cambridge University Press, 1987), pp. 65–66; Eric R. Wolf, *Europe and the People Without History* (Berkeley: University of California Press, 1982), pp. 255–57.

2. K.N. Chaudhuri, "Foreign Trade and the Balance of Payments (1757–1947)," in *The Cambridge Economic History of India*, ed. Dharma Kumar, vol. II (Cambridge: Cambridge University Press, 1983), pp. 336–41.

3. Sidney Mintz, *Sweetness and Power: The Place of Sugar in Modern History* (New York: Penguin Books, 1985), p. 117.

4. Charles P. Kindleberger, *Spenders and Hoarders: The World Distribution of American Silver 1550–1750* (Singapore: Institute of Southeast Asian Studies, 1989), pp. 15–17.

5. Ibid., pp. 38–39.

6. Chaudhuri, *The Trading World of Asia*, pp. 216–23.

7. Ibid., pp. 153–89.

8. Charles P. Kindleberger, *Spenders and Hoarders*, pp. 77–80.

9. Chaudhuri, *The Trading World of Asia*, pp. 157, 237–40.

10. Ibid., p. 109.

11. C.G.F. Simkin, *The Traditional Trade of Asia* (Oxford: Oxford University Press, 1968), p. 233.

12. Chaudhuri, *The Trading World of Asia*, p. 120.

13. Tapan Raychaudhuri, "The Mid-Eighteenth-Century Background," in *The Cambridge Economic History of India*, ed. Dharma Kumar, vol. II (Cambridge: Cambridge University Press, 1983), p. 25.

14. K.N. Chaudhuri, "World Silver Flows and Monetary Factors as a Force of International Economic Integration 1658–1758," in *The Emergence of a World Economy 1500–1914*, ed. Wolfram Fischer et al. (Wiesbaden: Franz Steiner Verlag, 1986), p. 76.

15. Holden Furber, *Rival Empires of Trade in the Orient* (Minneapolis: University of Minnesota Press, 1976), pp. 101, 193–94; Chaudhuri, *The Trading World of Asia*, pp. 436–45.

16. Furber, *Rival Empires*, pp. 191–92, 198–201; Chaudhuri, *The Trading World of Asia*, pp. 25–33.

17. Furber, *Rival Empires*, pp. 195–98.

18. P.J. Marshall, *East Indian Fortunes: The British in Bengal in the Eighteenth Century* (Oxford: Oxford University Press, 1976), p. 20.

19. Ibid., pp. 228–31.

20. Furber, *Rival Empires*, pp. 275–76.

21. Chaudhuri, *The Trading World of Asia*, pp. 281–99, 547–48.

22. Louis Dermigny, *La Chine et l'Occident: Le Commerce a Canton au XVIIIe Siecle 1719–1833*, L'Ere du Thé et des Dettes Chinoises, Tome II (Paris: Université de Paris, 1964).

23. Mintz, *Sweetness and Power*, pp. 110–17, 141–43.

24. Chaudhuri, *The Trading World of Asia*, p. 388.

25. Ibid., pp. 390–91; Furber, *Rival Empires*, pp. 244–45.

26. Ibid., pp. 205–11.

27. Ibid., pp. 146–57.

28. Geoffrey Parker, *The Military Revolution: Military Innovation and the Rise of the West, 1500–1800* (Cambridge: Cambridge University Press, 1988), pp. 130–35.

29. Fernand Braudel, *The Perspective of the World: Civilization and Capitalism*, vol. 3 (New York: Harper & Row, 1984), pp. 512–18.

30. C.A. Bayly, "Indian Society and the Making of the British Empire," in *New Cambridge History of India*, vol. II.1 (Cambridge: Cambridge University Press, 1988), pp. 9–14.

31. P.J. Marshall, "Bengal: The British Beachhead: East India 1740–1828," in *The New Cambridge History of India*, vol. II.2 (Cambridge: Cambridge University Press, 1987), pp. 74–92.

32. Adam Smith, *The Wealth of Nations* (Reprint, New York: Modern Library, 1937), pp. 707–12.

33. Furber, *Rival Empires*, p. 183; P.J. Marshall, "Bengal: The British Beachhead," p. 99.

34. Marshall, *East Indian Fortunes*, pp. 106–28, 140–43; "Bengal: The British Beachhead," p. 102.

35. Chaudhuri, "Foreign Trade and the Balance of Payments," pp. 814–15.

36. Neil Charlesworth, *British Rule and the Indian Economy 1800–1914*, Studies in Economic and Social History (London: Macmillan Press, 1982), pp. 52–54; Ralph Davis, *The Industrial Revolution and British Overseas Trade* (Leicester: Leicester University Press, 1979), pp. 55–56.

37. Marshall, "Bengal: The British Beachhead," p. 123.

38. Ibid., pp. 116–22.

39. Bayly, "Indian Society and the Making of the British Empire," pp. 65–66.

40. Marshall, "Bengal: The British Beachhead," pp. 144–46.

41. H.R. Ghosal, *Economic Transition in the Bengal Presidency* (Calcutta: Firma K.L. Mukhopadhyay, 1966), p. 41; S. Bhattacharya, "Regional Economy (1757–1857): Eastern India," in *The Cambridge Economic History of India*, ed. Dharma Kumar, vol. II (Cambridge: Cambridge University Press, 1983), pp. 319–20.

42. Ghosal, *Economic Transition in the Bengal Presidency*, pp. 72–87; S. Bhattacharya, "Regional Economy (1757–1857): Eastern India," pp. 316–18.

43. Michael Greenberg, *British Trade and the Opening of China* (Cambridge: Cambridge University Press, 1969), pp. 34–35.

44. Bhattacharya, "Regional Economy (1757–1857): Eastern India," pp. 321–24.

45. Greenberg, *British Trade and the Opening of China*, p. 105.

46. Bhattacharya, "Regional Economy (1757–1857): Eastern India," pp. 324–29; Marshall, "Bengal: The British Beachhead," pp. 169–72.

47. Bayly, "Indian Society and the Making of the British Empire," pp. 123–26.

48. Charlesworth, *British Rule and the Indian Economy*, pp. 32–35.

49. Hameeda Hossain, *The Company Weavers of Bengal* (Delhi: Oxford University Press, 1988), pp. 116–22.

50. Ibid., pp. 133–39.

51. Braudel, *The Perspective of the World*, p. 572.

52. Phyllis Deane, *The First Industrial Revolution* (Cambridge: Cambridge University Press, 1965), p. 86.

53. E.J. Hobsbawm, *Industry and Empire* (Middlesex: Penguin Books, 1968), pp. 62–63.

54. Ghosal, *Economic Transition in the Bengal Presidency*, pp. 26–33.

55. Davis, *The Industrial Revolution and British Overseas Trade*, p. 19.

56. Ghosal, *Economic Transition in the Bengal Presidency*, p. 33.

57. Ibid., pp. 178–81.

58. Bhattacharya, "Regional Economy (1757–1857): Eastern India," pp. 289–95; Marshall, "Bengal: British Beachhead," pp. 166–67; Bayly, "Indian Society and the Making of the British Empire," pp. 72–73.

59. S.B. Singh, *European Agency Houses in Bengal (1783–1833)* (Calcutta: Firma K.L. Mukhopadhyay, 1966), pp. 17–33.

60. P.J. Marshall, "Masters and Banians in Eighteenth Century Calcutta," in *The Age of Partnership: Europeans in Asia before Dominion*, ed. Blair B. Kling and M.N. Pearson (Honolulu: University of Hawaii Press, 1979), pp. 194–209.

61. Mark Girouard, *Cities and People* (New Haven: Yale University

Press, 1985), p. 239; Bayly, "Indian Society and the Making of the British Empire," pp. 71–76.

62. Ibid., pp. 244–45.

63. Bayly, "Indian Society and the Making of the British Empire," p. 83.

64. Ibid., pp. 79–89.

65. Ibid., p. 116.

66. Greenberg, *British Trade and the Opening of China*, pp. 44–58.

67. Earl H. Pritchard, *Anglo-Chinese Relations in the Seventeenth and Eighteenth Centuries* (New York: Octagon Books, 1970), pp. 155–58.

68. Greenberg, *British Trade and the Opening of China*, pp. 3–4.

69. Ibid., pp. 22–23; David S. Landes, *Revolution in Time* (Cambridge, MA: Harvard University Press, 1983), p. 268.

70. Earl H. Pritchard, *Anglo-Chinese Relations*, pp. 164–65.

71. Greenberg, *British Trade and the Opening of China*, p. 9.

72. Rhoads Murphey, *The Outsiders: The Western Experience in India and China* (Ann Arbor: The University of Michigan Press, 1977), pp. 88–97.

73. Pritchard, *Anglo-Chinese Relations*, pp. 180–83.

74. Franz Schurmann and Orville Schell, eds., *Imperial China: The Decline of the Last Dynasty and the Origins of Modern China, the 18th and 19th Centuries, The China Reader*, vol. 1 (New York: Random House, 1967), pp. 107–8.

75. Greenberg, *British Trade and the Opening of China*, pp. 10–17; Frederic Wakeman, "The Canton Trade and the Opium War," in *The Cambridge History of China*, ed. John K. Fairbank, vol. 10 (Cambridge: Cambridge University Press, 1978), pp. 166–71.

76. Greenberg, *British Trade and the Opening of China*, pp. 109–12; Wakeman, "The Canton Trade and the Opium War," pp. 171–72.

77. Greenberg, *British Trade and the Opening of China*, pp. 104–5; Wakeman, "The Canton Trade and the Opium War," p. 178.

78. Ibid., p. 173.

79. Ibid., pp. 178–79.

80. Ibid., pp. 178–85.

81. Greenberg, *British Trade and the Opening of China*, pp. 179–95.

82. Wakeman, "The Canton Trade and the Opium War," pp. 185–95.

83. Ibid., pp. 195–208; Daniel R. Headrick, *The Tools of Empire: Technology and European Imperialism in the Nineteenth Century* (New York: Oxford University Press, 1981), pp. 43–54.

84. Simkin, *The Traditional Trade of Asia*, p. 273.

85. Murphey, *The Outsiders*, p. 102.

86. D.K. Fieldhouse, *Economics and Empire* (Ithaca: Cornell University Press, 1973), pp. 151–53.

87. Peter Harnetty, *Imperialism and Free Trade: Lancashire and India in the Mid-Nineteenth Century* (Vancouver: University of British Columbia, 1972), p. 124.

88. Ibid., p. 124.

89. Chaudhuri, *The Trading World of Asia*, pp. 191–92.

90. John K. Fairbank, "The Creation of the Treaty System," in *The Cambridge History of China*, ed. John K. Fairbank, vol. 10 (Cambridge: Cambridge University Press, 1978), p. 52.

SELECTED REFERENCES

Attman, Artur. *American Bullion in the European World Trade 1600–1800.* Göteborg: Kungl. Vetenskaps-och Vitterhets Samhället, 1986.

Bayly, C.A. "Indian Society and the Making of the British Empire." In *New Cambridge History of India.* Vol. II.1. Cambridge: Cambridge University Press, 1988.

Bhattacharya, S. "Regional Economy (1757–1857): Eastern India." In *The Cambridge Economic History of India,* edited by Dharma Kumar. Vol. II. Cambridge: Cambridge University Press, 1983.

Braudel, Fernand. *The Perspective of the World: Civilization and Capitalism.* Vol. 3. New York: Harper & Row, 1984.

Charlesworth, Neil. *British Rule and the Indian Economy 1800–1914.* Studies in Economic and Social History. London: Macmillan Press, 1982.

Chaudhuri, K.N. "Foreign Trade and the Balance of Payments (1757–1947)." In *The Cambridge Economic History of India,* edited by Dharma Kumar. Vol. II. Cambridge: Cambridge University Press, 1983.

Chaudhuri, K.N. *The Trading World of Asia and the English East India Company 1660–1760.* Cambridge: Cambridge University Press, 1978.

Chaudhuri, K.N. "World Silver Flows and Monetary Factors as a Force of International Economic Integration 1658–1758." In *The Emergence of a World Economy 1500–1914,* edited by Wolfram Fischer et al. Wiesbaden: Franz Steiner Verlag, 1986.

Curtin, Phillip D. *Cross-Cultural Trade in World History.* Cambridge: Cambridge University Press, 1984.

Davis, Ralph. *The Industrial Revolution and British Overseas Trade.* Leicester: Leicester University Press, 1979.

Deane, Phyllis. *The First Industrial Revolution.* Cambridge: Cambridge University Press, 1965.

Dermigny, Louis. *La Chine et l'Occident: Le Commerce a Canton au XVIIIe Siecle 1719–1833. L'Ere du Thé et des Dettes Chinoises.* Tome II. Paris: Université de Paris, 1964.

Fairbank, John K. "The Creation of the Treaty System." In *The Cambridge History of China,* edited by John K. Fairbank. Vol. 10. Cambridge: Cambridge University Press, 1978.

Fairbank, John K. *The Great Chinese Revolution.* New York: Harper & Row, 1987.

Fairbank, John K. *Trade and Diplomacy on the China Coast.* Cambridge, MA: Harvard University Press, 1953.

Fieldhouse, D.K. *Economics and Empire.* Ithaca: Cornell University Press, 1973.

Furber, Holden. *Rival Empires of Trade in the Orient.* Minneapolis: University of Minnesota Press, 1976.

Geertz, Clifford. *Agricultural Involution.* Berkeley: University of California Press, 1963.

Ghosal, H.R. *Economic Transition in the Bengal Presidency.* Calcutta: Firma K.L. Mukhopadhyay, 1966.

Girouard, Mark. *Cities and People.* New Haven: Yale University Press, 1985.

Greenberg, Michael. *British Trade and the Opening of China.* Cambridge: Cambridge University Press, 1969.

Harnetty, Peter. *Imperialism and Free Trade: Lancashire and India in the Mid-Nineteenth Century.* Vancouver: University of British Columbia, 1972.

Headrick, Daniel R. *The Tools of Empire: Technology and European Imperialism in the Nineteenth Century.* New York: Oxford University Press, 1981.

Hobsbawm, E.J. *Industry and Empire.* Middlesex: Penguin Books, 1968.

Hossain, Hameeda. *The Company Weavers of Bengal.* Delhi: Oxford University Press, 1988.

Kindleberger, Charles P. *Spenders and Hoarders: The World Distribution of American Silver 1550–1750.* Singapore: Institute of Southeast Asian Studies, 1989.

Landes, David S. *Revolution in Time.* Cambridge, MA: Harvard University Press, 1983.

Louis, William Roger. *Imperialism: The Robinson and Gallagher Controversy.* New York: New Viewpoints, 1976.

Marshall, P.J. "Bengal: The British Beachhead: East India 1740–1828." In *The New Cambridge History of India.* Vol. II.2. Cambridge: Cambridge University Press, 1987.

Marshall, P.J. "Masters and Banians in Eighteenth Century Calcutta." In *The Age of Partnership: Europeans in Asia before Dominion,* edited by Blair B. Kling and M.N. Pearson. Honolulu: University of Hawaii Press, 1979.

Marshall, P.J. *East Indian Fortunes: The British in Bengal in the Eighteenth Century.* Oxford: Oxford University Press, 1976.

Mathias, Peter. *The First Industrial Nation.* London: Methuen, 1983.

Mintz, Sidney. *Sweetness and Power: The Place of Sugar in Modern History.* New York: Penguin Books, 1985.

Murphey, Rhoads. *The Outsiders: The Western Experience in India and China.* Ann Arbor: The University of Michigan Press, 1977.

Osborne, Milton. *Southeast Asia: An Illustrated Introductory History.* Sydney: Allen and Unwin, 1985.

Parker, Geoffrey. *The Military Revolution: Military Innovation and the Rise of the West, 1500–1800.* Cambridge: Cambridge University Press, 1988.

Pritchard, Earl H. *Anglo-Chinese Relations in the Seventeenth and Eighteenth Centuries.* New York: Octagon Books, 1970.

Raychaudhuri, Tapan. "The Mid-Eighteenth-Century Background." In *The Cambridge Economic History of India,* edited by Dharma Kumar. Vol. II. Cambridge: Cambridge University Press, 1983.

Schurmann, Franz, and Schell, Orville, eds. *Imperial China: The Decline of the Last Dynasty and the Origins of Modern China, the 18th and 19th Centuries. The China Reader,* vol. 1. New York: Random House, 1967.

Simkin, C.G.F. *The Traditional Trade of Asia.* Oxford: Oxford University Press, 1968.

Singh, S.B. *European Agency Houses in Bengal (1783–1833).* Calcutta: Firma K.L. Mukhopadhyay, 1966.

Smith, Adam. *The Wealth of Nations.* Reprint. New York: Modern Library, 1937.

Wakeman, Frederic. "The Canton Trade and the Opium War." In *The Cambridge History of China*, edited by John K. Fairbank. Vol. 10. Cambridge: Cambridge University Press, 1978.

Wolf, Eric R. *Europe and the People Without History*. Berkeley: University of California Press, 1982.

Asia in Western History: Essays

ASIA IN WESTERN THOUGHT

SOME SUGGESTED READINGS

Leonard A. Gordon

The study of Asia in Western thought may be considered in the context of the sociology of knowledge. It is thus relevant to consider the sources of the images and motivations underlying the development of a body of knowledge to compare the views of those having direct experience with those of armchair theorists, of specialists with nonspecialists; to inquire about whether there are any significant differences between popular images and official or scholarly images of Asia. Further, one might look for changes in perception over time, by country, and among groups within a society. For example, it is useful to know whether those having a direct interest view Asia differently from those having no such interest. A consideration of the practical consequences in terms of official policy and attitudes, if any, that have resulted from these images might also be instructive.

For the purposes of understanding Western traditions, it is useful to consider Western ideas and understanding of Asia in the context of Western cultural and intellectual development. Conversely, one might consider the impact which Western ideas about Asia have had on Asia itself, i.e., how have the people of India, China, or Japan responded to Western attitudes about them.

This selection of readings, with comments so brief that they necessarily omit context, is offered here to present widespread Western views of Asia as a whole, with emphasis on India and China. A similar outline might focus on, for example, Japan and Southeast Asia or consider the impact of Asian art on Western thought and culture, and the like.

THE ANCIENT WORLD

A. Herodotus (484–c. 420s B.C.E.; see *The Persian Wars*, III. 89–117; IV. 1–82; VI. 101–4, 135–36). Presents the idea of extremes, i.e., the farther away a country is from Europe, the bigger, the more populous, and the more affluent it is. India is far away. Describes the strangeness of "barbaric" Asian hordes and their grandiose architectural style, notes that they lack the individuality of Europeans, a theme which continues into the present.

Refers to northwest India and the valley of the Indus, and mentions their satrapies, their little despotisms. Tells of the Scythians and their mythical history. Writes not from direct observation, and presents what became the stereotypical view of nomadic Asians.

B. Hippocrates (5th c. B.C.E.; in *Airs Waters Places*.) Claims that because the climate in Asia is more uniform than in Europe, the Asian temperament is likewise more uniform. As a result, the Asians are feeble and lazy, are not martial, and are lacking in spirit. Asian culture is stagnant. The unchanging East is another theme that endured in the Western mind.

C. Aristotle (384–322 B.C.E.; see *Politics*, VIII 7). Claims that Asians are more willing to accept despotism than Westerners. Greece is the mean between Europe and Asia. Asia is less civilized than Greece. Climate influences culture: Asia is hot, while Europe is cold or temperate. Asians have skill and intelligence, but not spirit; the Greeks have all three.

D. Strabo (64 B.C.E.–21 C.E.; see *The Geography of Strabo*, Bk. 2, Chaps. 5, 18–26; Bk. 15, Chap. 1). Describes groups in Arabia and India, and declares European culture more developed. Peoples and their cultures can be compared. Irregularity is evidence of independence and cultural development. Draws on the account of Megasthenes, who was sent to Magadha in the fourth century B.C.E. as Greek ambassador to India. Relates fabulous tales, but in general is more skeptical than Herodotus.

E. Arrian (100 C.E.–?; see *Indica*). Mainly an account of Alexander's invasion. Draws on Megasthenes. Notes that India was often invaded and its people taught by outsiders. Tells of the seven castes and says Indians have no slaves. He says they tell no falsehoods, in contrast to the view of many Westerners, who have claimed that Asians, particularly Indians, are lacking in veracity.

THE MIDDLE AGES

In a map of the City of God, the world is depicted as a circle, with Jerusalem at the center; Asia appears in the top half of the circle and Europe and Africa below. This was a common depiction at that time. (See Donald E. Lach. *Asia in the Making of Europe*. Vol. 1: *The Century of Discovery*, bk. 1. Chicago: University of Chicago Press, 1965, p. 23.)

Marco Polo (1254?–1324?; see *The Travels of Marco Polo*, sections on China and India and also Southeast Asia). This account by the most famous traveler to the East brings in a romantic element, describing great riches and enormous cities, as well as notable battles. His book kept alive through many centuries the European notions of the East as a source of riches.

RENAISSANCE AND EARLY MODERN, FOURTEENTH TO SEVENTEENTH CENTURIES

A period of renewed contact between Asia and Europe. Europeans continued to have a vague and often fantastic image of Asia, due in part to the tales of Marco Polo. With the fifteenth-century voyages of discovery, a new and growing body of information became available. By the seventeenth century, Europeans were receiving a more complex, differentiated, and thus more accurate picture of Asia and its subareas (South, Southeast, and East Asia), although old images did not disappear.

A. Matthew Ricci (1552–1610; see Louis J. Gallagher, ed., *China in the Sixteenth Century: The Journals of Matthew Ricci*. New York: Random House, 1953; Jonathan Spence. *The Memory Palace of Matteo Ricci*. New York: Penguin Books, 1985). In seeking to convert the Chinese to Christianity, Ricci, a Jesuit, searched for a more "native" approach (adapting indigenous customs), in contrast to that of the Dominicans and Franciscans, who insisted that missionaries must use Latin, and refused to compromise by accepting ancestor worship or reverence for Confucius. The Jesuits, charged with adopting Chinese customs, became involved in the "rites controversy." This referred to the sanction by the Jesuits of Chinese ancestor worship as a civil rite and therefore permissible to Christians. Other Christians objected to this step by the Jesuits, insisting that they were sanctioning pagan rituals. This involved whether Christians could sanction ceremonies or rites involving Chinese elements mixed with Christian ones. In raising the issue of the universality of Christianity, Ricci anticipated claims of universality of Western ideologies and values, including science, democracy, technology, Marxism, etc.

B. Jean Bodin (1529?–1596; see *Six Books of a Commonweale*. Bk. II, Chap. 2). In discussing antiquity, he claims that Asians were barbaric compared to the Greeks. In later times the people of Europe proved to be prouder and more belligerent than those of Asia. Cites despotic monarchies as a feature of Asia.

C. Shakespeare's India: *A Midsummer Night's Dream* (1594–95?), Act II, Scene 1:

> Puck: A lovely boy, stolen from an Indian king;
> She never had so sweet a changeling . . .
>
> Titania: Why are thou here,
> Come from the farthest steep of India?
> . . .
> The fairy land buys not the child of me.
> His mother was a votaress of my order:
> And, in the spiced Indian air, by night,
> Full often hath she gossip'd by my side,
> . . .
> To fetch me trifles, and return again,
> As fro a voyage, rich with merchandise.

Locates India in a distant, mythic fairy world, where there are votaries of fairy queens; refers to the luxuries (spices), and even a "lovely boy," an Indian prince, that may be obtained there.

D. Francois Bernier (1620–1688; see *Travels in the Mogul Empire A.D. 1656–1668*). A first-hand description of Hindustan, not armchair reporting based on the works of others; gives a detailed and lively description of India, though it is vitiated by his antipathy to its religious customs and by his sweeping and inaccurate generalizations about the economy, administration, and laws.

THE AGE OF ENLIGHTENMENT

Connections with Asia continued to grow in this period, with increasing commerce, exploration, and "discovery" of the world beyond Europe. Europeans applied their more accurate knowledge of Asia in criticisms of European institutions, religion, laws, and customs, and in an effort to understand human nature.

Asian and other non-European cultures and particularly religions were juxtaposed to their Western counterparts. Some writers looked sympathetically, even idealistically, on non-European cultures; Voltaire especially sought to show that wisdom was possible without Christianity. Montesquieu, in his comparative schema of governments, focused on Asian despotism, as had writers in antiquity.

A. Montesquieu (1689–1755; see *The Spirit of the Laws* [1748], Bk. III; Bk. IV, Chap. 3; Bk. VIII, Chap. 19; Bk. XVII; Bk. XVIII, Chaps. 1–6; Bk. XIX, Chaps. 1–20). Analyzes three types of polities: republic, monarchy, and despotism. Examples of the republic, which is characterized by public virtue, are Greece, Rome, Switzerland. The essential characteristic of the monarchy is honor; the monarch rules by law and the role of aristocracy is vital. Monarchies are mainly European (England is the prime example) and are viewed as moderate. It is in Europe that the spirit of freedom, which springs from Germanic and other sources, is to be found. Despotism, in contrast, is rule by fear; a single ruler holds the reins of power and changes direction as caprice or whim moves him.

Montesquieu, too, brings in the geographic element; associates vast plains and warm climate with servility and despotism; large populations in vast areas are terrorized and kept in line by despots. In contrast, the European landscape invites moderation, freedom, honor, and virtue.

On the other hand, cites admirable qualities of China, particularly the orderly manners of its vast population and its well-drained lands. India also has lenient laws. Both of these nations must, according to his schema, be despotic, although his data often contradict this.

In an earlier work, *The Persian Letters*, c. 1721–22, Montesquieu uses the examples of Persia, the Orient, and Asia, to criticize French society and institutions as well as to criticize the non-West. His is thus a more relativistic understanding of the world. Tries to give accurate information on some of these Asiatic areas based on his reading.

B. Voltaire (1694–1778; see *Essai sur les moeurs* [Ancient and Modern History], c. 1762, Chaps. 1–3, 121, 127–29; and article on China in *Philosophical Dictionary*). Criticizes other universal histories for ignoring the East. In this tour of the globe from east to west, acknowledges European debt to Asia, which he refers to as the "nursery of the arts": Europeans were barbarians when the fertile East developed its civilization.

In China he finds a vast, unchanging empire enduring for 4,000 years. Notes that Chinese silk, porcelain, glass were imported and later imitated by Europe. Contrasts Chinese civilization with that of Europe: "Nature seems to have bestowed on this species of men, so different from the Europeans, organs sufficient to discover all at once, what was necessary to their happiness, but incapable to proceed further; we, on the other hand, were tardy in our discoveries; but then we have speedily brought everything to perfection." In explaining their lack of progress, he mentions the difficulty of the Chinese language and respect for parental and governmental authorities and their veneration of the past, although he is extremely respectful of Chinese religion and morality and offers an admiring description of the Chinese sage.

Mentions India's moral tales, and its contribution of chess and arithmetic. Westerners trade their precious metals for India's precious commodities. Indian law is generally wholesome, but ridiculous customs, e.g., sati, and widespread superstitions abound. The Indians, too, made early achievements and then went into stagnation and decline. Explains that this is due to the Indian climate, which is conducive to effeminacy and indolence. Mentions temperate and frugal Brahmins who can be admired, but they too have degenerated over time and lost their ancient purity.

In other works, e.g., *Candide*, c. 1750, Voltaire takes a global, relativistic view of the world to criticize the West as well as the customs of other areas. Cites differences among religions and societies in other parts of Europe, the Middle East, North Africa, and the Americas.

VIEWS OF INDIA UNDER THE BRITISH RAJ

From the mid-eighteenth century onward, as the British became increasingly involved in and finally ruled India, the body of Western literature on India swelled. Two British approaches to India have been identified: the first is the sympathetic, Orientalist approach, and the second is the critical, reformist, Westernizing approach.

From the late eighteenth century on there were the Orientalists who wanted to understand Asian cultural traditions and introduce them to the West (see, e.g., selections from William Jones in P.J. Marshall, ed. *The British Discovery of Hinduism in the Eigh-*

teenth Century. Cambridge: Cambridge University Press, 1970, pp. 196–290). These early Orientalists in the late eighteenth and early nineteenth centuries believed that a revival of India's golden age was possible under British rule. They were followed in this idea by the Romantics, the Theosophists at the end of the nineteenth century, and then by "Orientalized" Westerners like Christopher Isherwood and others in the twentieth century who found the West lacking.

The other approach—paternalistic and often hostile—was taken by Western reformers who may or may not have had direct contact with India. Important among them was Charles Grant, who succeeded in 1813 in reforming the charter of the East India Company so that evangelical Christian missionaries could come into British India. Another was James Mill (1773–1836), who in his *The History of British India* (1817) wrote that Brahmins were the "most audacious . . . and most unskillful fabricators, with whom the annals of fable have yet made us acquainted." Mill and many other reformers were influenced by age-old stereotypes: that Asian rule was characterized by absolute monarchies, that Asian religions consisted of wild legends, and that their customs were depraved, or ridiculous. Another reformer, Thomas Macaulay, maintains in "Minute on Education" (1835) that there is little of value in the traditions and literature of the East and that English and Western learning is what these societies most needed.

AN ORIENTAL RENAISSANCE? ASIA IN NINETEENTH-CENTURY GERMAN THOUGHT

A. On German thinkers and other late eighteenth- and early nineteenth-century Orientalists, see A. Leslie Willson, *A Mythical Image: The Ideal of India in German Romanticism.* Durham: Duke University Press, 1964; and Raymond Schwab, *The Oriental Renaissance. Europe's Rediscovery of India and the East 1680–1880.* New York: Columbia University Press, 1984.

B. Johann Gottfried von Herder (1744–1803; see *Outlines of a Philosophy of the History of Mankind.* 1784–91. Vol. 2, Bk. XI). Expresses reverence and admiration for India and sees the Orient as the place of the childhood of mankind and where language first developed. Admires the wisdom of the Brahmans, but criticizes the Hindus for their spirit of resignation, and for such customs as sati.

C. Arthur Schopenhauer (1788–1860; see *The World as Will and Idea.* 3 vols. London: Trübner, 1883–86; translated from the German in which the first volume appeared in 1819) found Indian thought, especially in the Vedas and Upanishads, a source of personal consolation, and believed that Indian wisdom would change Europe.

D. Georg Wilhelm Friedrich Hegel (1770–1831) in the sections on the Orient in *The Philosophy of History* specified a lack of subjectivity and moral conscience in China, in contrast to the West, from the Greeks to the Prussians. He said that in China the emperor commands and all men obey. There is equality without civil freedom. The people are hampered by superstition and lack a spiritual religion.

Describes India as being static; a region of fantasy and sensibility but with a degradation of the divine because all were raised to the level of divine. The people were guided by an inner morality but followed trivial observances. They had no history, no self-consciousness. The society was characterized by diversity and rigid separation. There was no ethical code, and the goal of their religion was union with nothingness. Politically, there was no true state and hence no civil freedom. Hegel also comments on the prevalence of arbitrary despotism in this part of the Orient.

E. Karl Marx (1818–83; see "The British in India," June 10, 1853; "The Future Results of the British Rule in India," July 22, 1853; "The Revolt in India," July 17, 1857, and many other articles, available in a variety of collections).

Up to the time of Western contact, India was stuck in traditional patterns, with despotic government and unchanging villages. The British introduced tremendous changes, setting in motion the processes of modernization in India while at the same time exploiting India for their own purposes. Mentions the stultifying quality of village life in India as elsewhere; the people need an energetic bourgeoisie to move their society off dead center.

EARLY TWENTIETH CENTURY

A. The Marxist tradition: V. I. Lenin (1870–1924; see *The National-Liberation Movement in the East.* Moscow: Foreign Languages Publishing House, 1962. A collection of articles on the Middle East and Asia, 1900–1923).

In view of the isolated nature of the Russian Revolution and abortive communist revolutions in Europe, predicts that revolution may occur in Asia and colonial areas before it occurs in advanced Europe. Focuses on nationalist-cum-revolutionary movements in Asia.

B. Max Weber (1864 –1920; see H.H. Gerth and C. Wright Mills, eds. *From Max Weber: Essays in Sociology.* New York: Oxford University Press, 1958; also Weber's studies of comparative religion, *The Religion of China.* Glencoe, IL: Free Press, 1951; and *The Religion of India.* Glencoe, IL: Free Press, 1958).
Undertakes an extensive survey of China and India as part of his study of religion, economy, and society, in order to place his theory of the Protestant ethic and the spirit of capitalism in a global framework. Points to lack of economic development in China and India as compared to the modern West, and offers explanations of this difference in development.

OTHER MODERN VIEWS

There is a great range of views regarding Asia, some still attempting to prove the backwardness and static nature of the East, and others, the wisdom and advanced thought of Asia. Classic comparative studies and monographs, and commonly used textbooks provide widely divergent characterizations of Asia; novels set in Asia may also be of interest.
Karl Wittfogel. *Oriental Despotism.* New Haven: Yale University Press, 1957. Tries to show the prevalence in Asia of extensive, bureaucratic systems controlling large populations. Wrote this study of Asian systems against the backdrop of Stalinist Russia.

Joseph Needham. *Science and Civilization in China.* Cambridge: Cambridge University Press, 1954. 6 volumes (and abridged edition, 1978). Documents scientific outlook and developments throughout Chinese history to show that in early times, science was more advanced in China than in the West.

Christopher Isherwood, ed. *Vedanta for the Western World.* New York: Viking Press, 1960. Writers in this collection argue that a new teaching is needed for a sterile and materialistic age dominated by the West. Although they refer to this wisdom as Vedanta and imply that it is Indian in origin, they argue that it is composed of truths to be found in all religions and can be utilized universally.

William McNeill. *The Rise of the West.* Chicago: University of Chicago Press, 1963. Tries to explain the dominance of the West in modern times, touching on all areas of the world.

Arnold Toynbee. *Civilization on Trial; The World and the West.*

New York: Meridian, 1958. Charts the changing position of the West relative to the rest of the world. Though his long view of the rise and fall of civilizations gives him some caution, he sees the West and its outlook as dominant.

Jawaharlal Nehru. *Glimpses of World History*. London: John Day, 1939. The great modern leader, Western educated and aware of Western views of India, argues that Asia has been as great as Europe, if not greater. Describes the rise and fall of Asia, attributing this mainly to economic causes. Although he brings in the cultural achievements of Asia, he does not place his discussion in the context of a dichotomy between the spiritual East and materialist West. Calls upon India and China to overcome their material backwardness.

Barrington Moore. *The Social Origins of Dictatorship and Democracy in the Modern World*. Boston: Beacon Press, 1966. A stimulating, if uneven, comparative treatment of the United States, Great Britain, France, Japan, China, and India.

André Malraux. *Man's Fate* (La Condition Humaine). New York: Random House, 1934. Powerful novel of Western and Chinese revolutionaries and their adversaries, set in China of the 1920s.

E.M. Forster. *A Passage to India*. New York: Harcourt Brace, 1959 [1924]. In India under the Raj, a minor, mystifying incident blossoms into a cause célèbre. The main theme may be the difficulty of friendship and communication between Indians and Westerners and the powerful tensions just below the surface calm of British India.

Paul Kennedy. *The Rise and Fall of the Great Powers*. New York: Vintage Books, 1987. A stimulating analysis of the strengths (as well as weaknesses) of the great powers and the relations among them since 1500. His inclusion of China and Japan among those powers makes for an interesting and revised Western view of these two Asian countries at the end of the 1980s.

Asia in Western History: Essays

ASIA IN WESTERN THOUGHT

ASIA IN ENLIGHTENMENT AND EARLY BRITISH IMPERIAL VIEWS

Leonard A. Gordon

SYNOPSIS

Enlightenment thinkers, having inherited stereotypes of Asia passed down from antiquity, also had access to a growing body of information about the East from travelers, missionaries, and traders. This essay examines the comparative political schema of Montesquieu, who characterized Asia as the home of despotism, and then the universal historical sketch of Voltaire, who placed the creative childhood of the human race in China and India. Both used Asia to gain perspective on the West, but found that the West of their time had advanced ahead of Asia.

Then the focus shifts to early British imperial views of India, mainly those of sympathetic Orientalists like Sir William Jones and hostile reformers influenced by evangelicalism and utilitarianism. Jones and subsequent Western scholars made a positive contribution to the study of Indian traditions and linked Sanskrit and languages derived from it to the Indo-European linguistic family. Charles Grant, James Mill, and Thomas Macaulay were among those who held that the people of India were in dire need of Western reforming measures.

All of these trends (using Asia or parts of it in grand schemes, sympathetic scholarship, and hostile condemnations) have continued into the twentieth century as Asians have also made great strides in retrieving and evaluating their own traditions.

I.

In the long history of relations between Europe and Asia, many historians have maintained that from the late 1400s, there was a new beginning. With the voyages of discovery, Europeans gradually began to gain more knowledge about Asia, which they incorporated into the existing body of information and prejudices. Ideas of the strange and fabulous East in the works of writers such as Herodotus, Hippocrates, Aristotle, Strabo, and Arrian, and the reports of the medieval traveler Marco Polo that some called "ridiculous," existed side by side with later reports of merchants, travelers, adventurers, and missionaries.

The objective of this essay is to examine briefly some of the views put forth by Europeans in the eighteenth and early nineteenth centuries and to consider some of the ways in which writers at the time used the versions of Asia that came to their attention. Before looking into some of these texts, it is necessary, however, to mention some difficulties of "knowing" Asia or Asians, and even of understanding the writers who have tried to do so.

Beyond the basic problems for Westerners of learning difficult foreign languages and understanding cultural frameworks which may be very different from their own, another kind of question has been raised by critical analysts of society—from Marx to Gramsci to Michel Foucault to Edward Said—about the process of knowing. In Said's *Orientalism*, a historical and critical investigation of Western scholarship on the Islamic East from the late eighteenth century, Said maintained that the Orient as described by Westerners was their own creation, limited by their narrow understanding of the "other" involved as well as by their own political agendas. Western writers have portrayed the Islamic others as inferior and deficient, particularly when contrasted with Europeans, who represented dynamic and rapidly developing society. Following Gramsci, Said maintained that "cultural hegemony" was at work in their writings, which ". . . were shot through with doctrines of European superiority, various kinds of racism, imperialism, and the like, dogmatic views of 'the Oriental' as a kind of ideal and unchanging abstraction."[1]

Following in the steps of Said, but with a mind of his own and with his own grievances to spell out in the field of South Asian studies, Ronald B. Inden has written "Orientalist Constructions of India" and *Imagining India*. Inden is more directly concerned than Said with epistemological questions related to the cultural ones about "knowing" India. He, too, talks of the hegemonic context, but for Western versions of India, rather than the Islamic world, since the later eighteenth century. To greatly simplify his argument, Inden holds that Western writers have in their "knowing" of India also measured it by a single standard, i.e., "the Euro-American manifestation of human nature's unitary essence—rational, scientific thought and the institutions of liberal capitalism and democracy."[2] The static state of India is explained by reference to the "irrational (but rationalizable) institution of 'caste' and the Indological religion that accompanies it, Hinduism." Human agency and individual action, as well as political institutions as they exist in the West, are lacking, says Inden, in descriptions of South Asia. He objects to the societal and cultural explanations for South Asia's inferiority and to the unitary view of human nature which they evince.

Inden mentions a number of what he calls "hegemonic texts," totalizing views of India from James Mill to Vincent Smith to A.L. Basham, which put forth the kinds of views he condemns. But he takes his argument one step further. He insists that the sympathetic views of such writers as William Jones, Max Muller, and A.L. Basham are really the linked complements of the negative views of the harsh writers like the evangelicals and utilitarians. Both groups include the same "facts" about India, but evaluate them differently. Thus, non-violence can appear as cowardice to some Western writers and as noble to some others, but still refers to the same cultural traits of weak and divided India. He strains, I think, to locate all in the Orientalist camp. Inden wants an end to Western hegemonic relations to India, wants a view of human nature more diverse and tentative than so far used to confront the subtleties of India, and a revival of South Asians describing themselves without Western frameworks to guide them.

There is much in the writing of Said and Inden about knowing and knowers of the East that is persuasive. There is no doubt that Western values since antiquity and Western hegemony in recent centuries have shaped efforts to learn about "the other" in all non-European parts of the world. Furthermore, as Inden suggests, middle-class, usually white, scholars become entangled in similar difficulties learning about others in their own societies. What I would suggest, however, is that as we analyze views of Asia held by earlier writers, we also try to understand the social context in which they were writing, for they frequently utilized information about Asia, itself shaped by Western preconceptions, for their own particular purposes; this was certainly true of many of the Enlightenment and early British writers. Furthermore, it is necessary to understand how the objectives of Western writers on Asia have evolved over time.

II.

Writers from Aristotle in the fourth century B.C.E. to Montesquieu in the first half of the eighteenth century referred to the territories from the Levant eastward as Asia, the East, the Orient, lumping diverse areas together as one. Viewing Asia as a vast landmass with a hot climate, and its people as deficient in a vital quality, Aristotle made it an example of subject populations and despotic rulers.

Within the century in which Aristotle lived, Megasthenes was sent to India in an official position in the wake of the invasion of Alexander the Great. Although it has been lost, his description of rivers, castes, and civic administration of India was quoted by later writers, including Strabo and Arrian. While ancient writers had access to this descriptive account of India, they tended to focus their attention on the peoples of nearer rather than farther Asia, and purveyed fantastic stories of distant "barbaric" peoples to incredulous Westerners. Nevertheless, elements of these stories were passed on for a thousand years, until 1200 C.E., when intrepid travelers, notably Marco Polo, but also other traders and missionaries, began to visit South and East Asia.

Once the age of exploration and the commercial revolution began, new sources of information became available in the West. By 1550, a good deal of new knowledge of China, Japan, and India was made available in Europe, particularly through the reports of merchants and travelers, and the letters of Jesuit missionaries. From the sixteenth century, writers including Montaigne, Bodin, and Le Roy began to face the implications of these new cultural worlds. Donald Lach has summed up part of his investigations in this way:

> A growing consciousness of the tumultuous variety in the world was accompanied by a sturdy sense of tolerance for diversity, even in religion. . . . The historians . . . sought self-consciously to examine the implications of the discovery of the world. . . . In his *Method* Bodin identified history as a discipline which should be secular rather than religious and should focus on the study of all human societies and institutions. He accounted for diversity by reference to climate and geography. But within diversity he perceived unity in the problems common to all societies: governmental institutions, religion, emigration, and colonization.

> . . . Le Roy and La Popeliniere were impressed by the interrelat-
> edness of the world and by the effects of events in distant places
> on Europe itself. Both clearly understood that Europe had much
> to learn in practical and intellectual matters from the high civili-
> zations of Asia.[3]

Through the following centuries, European travelers, traders,
and missionaries continued to describe Asia, or parts thereof, for
their countrymen at home. One of the more influential of these
writers, at least about India, was François Bernier, a physician
and adventurous traveler who spent most of the years 1656 to
1668 in Mughal India. What reports—even those of sophisticated
writers like Bernier—make clear is that every traveler carried his
mental baggage of preconceptions and values with him and questioned them only grudgingly.

Bernier drew a vivid picture of the war of succession, finally
won by Aurangzeb, in the Mughal Empire of Hindustan. He described, from the Christian viewpoint, the court life and religious
practices of India, but his overall assessment of the country was
colored by his understanding that the emperor owned all the land
and that there was no private property. This, he insisted, led to
despotism, barbarous customs, and the economic desolation of
India. He compared Mughal India, under the sway of tyrants, to
an idealized France, where anyone might hold land and all men
were under the rule of law, so that the poorest subjects could
obtain redress of their grievances. Such a rule of law, he asserted,
did not exist in India, where each man was out for himself and
there was no concern for others and no peaceful economic or
political life. Though he gives a detailed and lively description of
India, it is vitiated by his antipathy to its religious customs and
by his sweeping and inaccurate generalizations about the economy, administration, and laws.[4]

French writers of the Enlightenment had access to Bernier's
account as well as earlier writings, which had been pouring forth
from European printing presses since 1550. But old stereotypes,
e.g., European freedom and Asian despotism, were not easily
given up or questioned. In *The Persian Letters*, for example, Baron
de Montesquieu helped shape a genre subsequently popular in
the eighteenth century. It consisted of letters written by "Persian"
visitors to Europe satirizing and criticizing French institutions.
Although Montesquieu read a number of contemporary sources
about Persia, his object was not to know Persia, but to criticize his
own country and civilization. He ridiculed the church, the decay

of the monarchy under Louis XIV, and the lax and wicked morals of aristocratic French society. However, in *The Persian Letters*, Montesquieu offered criticism of both sides: he criticized the France he knew firsthand and the Persia he knew from the accounts of travelers. He indicted Islam, the treatment of women in Persia, and hypocrisy in both Europe and Persia. The result is a more relativistic view of the world and an acknowledgement of the existence of other civilizations beyond that of Europe. Making a fictional foreign observer the mouthpiece of his criticisms of European institutions and customs allowed him to be more scathing than he might ordinarily have been. This literary device was utilized by other writers of the eighteenth century, including Voltaire, Diderot, and Oliver Goldsmith, to criticize the West. The foreigner who represents the author's voice and point of view thus appears more humane and sensible than the culture he is describing. It is a device that opens the door to cultural relativism and undercuts authority and tradition at home.

Enlightenment thinkers were profoundly concerned with the bases of government, the shaping of an ideal political order, and the protection of basic liberties. In his massive comparative study *The Spirit of the Laws* (1748), Montesquieu wrote that the physical and moral environments shaped governments. He classified governments into three types, the republic, the monarchy, and despotism, to each of which he linked a basic principle necessary for political stability. In the republic (Greece, Rome, Switzerland), this was public virtue; this quality was rare or difficult to maintain, the stability of a republic was fragile. In a monarchy (several European states), honor or prestige was the crucial principle: the monarch ruled by law, but another body, such as the aristocracy, was necessary to restrain and guide the monarch in moderation. Montesquieu was primarily concerned with the decline of monarchy and the fate of liberty in France. What he feared most was despotism, the arbitrary, lawless rule of one over all. Where was this third type to be found?

In Asia, notably in China, Montesquieu reasoned that vastness and hot climate invited despotism. Asian despots terrorized the servile masses; they held sway through fear and ruled by caprice. The huge populations of China and India were due in part to the fertility of the women. Although he pointed to some positive characteristics of these Asiatic despotisms—effective irrigation systems in China and lenient laws in India—these scarcely mitigated his negative vision of Asia, a grim and gruesome world with slaving masses and despots of unlimited power. Although some of his own data contradict it, he retained his vision of Asia in order to provide a sharp contrast to humane, well-functioning England. Montesquieu's *The Spirit of the Laws* is a way station on the Western route from Aristotle's ancient despotisms in Asia to Wittfogel's *Oriental Despotism*, this last reached by way of Marx.

The bleak picture of Asia described by Montesquieu did not go unquestioned. François Quesnay, as leader of the physiocrats in eighteenth-century France, gave first place in the economy to agriculture. Opposing selfish merchants and mercantilism, he called for a single tax on the net output of the land.[5] In looking around for a stable, flourishing polity in which agriculture was the basis of the economy and such a tax was the main source of governmental revenues, he hit upon imperial China. Contradicting Montesquieu, Quesnay argued that, rather than a capricious despot, the Chinese emperor was more a constitutional monarch, governing according to natural law to which he himself was subject. The Chinese emperor thus became an acceptable model of the "enlightened despot" to many philosophes who were often more concerned with the liberty of the educated few than with the political participation of the masses. An enlightened ruler, presumably instructed by men such as themselves, would suit their purposes.

Quesnay's lengthy and not uncritical description of China, based primarily on missionary sources, was widely read. The esteem accorded to scholars and the centrality of education in China won abundant praise from the physiocrat, as did the importance placed on agriculture and the security of property. Although unhappy with reports of Chinese dishonesty in trade and with some religious practices, he strode forth to combat Montesquieu's views, calling them a "jumble of ideas."[6]

While Quesnay attacked Montesquieu on the nature of the Chinese government and expressed concern for political and economic institutions, Voltaire was involved with putting China to other uses. A prolific, versatile, and hugely popular author, Voltaire was more concerned with religious, cultural, and historical matters than with political organization.

Voltaire was a fervent enemy of the Catholic church and of orthodox Christianity in general; he was deeply interested in ancient, complex alternatives to Christian chronology, pretensions, and wisdom. In his *Philosophical Dictionary* and elsewhere, he frequently cited Chinese sages or Brahmin pundits. The antiquity of Chinese and Indian civilization was of decisive concern to him, for if either or both of these non-Western civilizations predated the Mosaic teaching and the chronology of the Old Testament and offered a non-Christian wisdom he could offer to the West, he would best his Christian opponents. That neither the Chinese nor the Indians had been instructed by the ancient Hebrews was of great importance to him.

China and India were given priority of place in Voltaire's world history, *Essai sur les moeurs* (translated as *Ancient and Modern History*), in which he claimed that the West had learned from the genius of the East and should not neglect it; Europeans were still barbarians at the time Eastern civilization was blossoming. On China, he wrote:

> Nature seems to have bestowed on this species of men, so different from the Europeans, organs sufficient to discover all at once, what was necessary to their happiness, but incapable to proceed further; we, on the other hand, were tardy in our discoveries; but then we have speedily brought everything to perfection.[7]

He depicted a vast, unchanging Chinese empire that had early on reached great heights, and then remained more or less static for 4000 years. Like Quesnay, he said that despotism in China was not thoroughly autocratic, but restrained, concerned for the public welfare, and open to the complaints of citizens. He attributed China's lack of growth to the difficulty of its language and its veneration of authority and the past.[8]

Voltaire praised Confucian morality and insisted that the Chinese were neither atheists nor idolaters, but worshiped the Supreme Being. The wisdom of Confucian teachings drew his praise, but he had no praise for Buddhism, an import from India which, according to his understanding, involved superstition, idolatry, and materialism. Confucian teachings, which provided public and private morality and respect for the ruler, parents, and teachers, were an alternative to Christian teachings.[9]

While not as attractive as China, India was also to be respected for its antiquity and its contributions to civilization:

> The Indians being at all times a trading and industrious people, were necessarily subjected to a regular police . . . [and] must have enjoyed the protection of wholesome laws, without which the arts are never cultivated. . . . Since the time of that monarch [Alexander], the Indians have enjoyed their liberty, plunged into an excess of effeminacy, occasioned by the heat of their climate and the richness of their soil.[10]

India gave to the world its moral fables, chess, arithmetic, and many precious commodities. But according to Voltaire, India had degenerated into a world of superstition; the practice of sati particularly drew his ire. He rejected Bernier's description of India as a land of princes and slaves, but did believe that, like China, India was no longer the positive creative force in the world that it had once been. The light of reason now shone elsewhere; Voltaire and his fellow philosophes, above all, held the torch.

Nevertheless, by giving prominence to Asia and recognizing Asian contributions to the vast construction of human civilization, Voltaire offered a much more detailed picture than did European "universal" historians of the sixteenth and seventeenth centuries. He considered the possibility that human history began in India and that the ancient Egyptians learned from the Indians.[11] Now Asian civilizations, China and India, in particular, were "on the map" of Western versions of world history, just as sixteenth-century cartographers gave Asia a more accurate place in their depiction of the world. Voltaire, as arrogant and Eurocentric as he may have been, thus helped reshape world historical writing. Enlightenment writers gave Asia and Asians an important role in comparative and historical schemas for understanding cultures synchronically and through time. Some of them studied Asian languages, cultures, and texts, and began to place Asian traditions into more accurate relationship with those of the West.

III.

While French philosophes were engaged with comparative politics and universal history, British merchants and soldiers were involved in conquering India. Over a period of about one hundred years, the British gradually conquered large parts of South Asia and arranged for indirect rule in other areas. They extended their control from coastal areas inward. Under the regulating acts passed in the second half of the eighteenth century, they blocked out three presidencies, Bengal, Bombay, and Madras, with the capital of British India in Calcutta.

Many efforts had been made by Europeans since the sixteenth century to obtain, read, and understand Indian texts. However, with British rule Europeans gathered many more manuscripts, developed their knowledge of Indian languages, and wrote treatises on Indian religion, law, mythology, and languages.

The first governor-general, Warren Hastings, had risen in the East India Company service to preeminence in India, but was besieged by dissatisfied groups at home, by enemies in his own council, and by antagonists among the Indians. However, throughout his term as governor-general Hastings was an ardent patron of research into things Indian. At the same time that he saw the utility of learning about the native population by examining their culture, beliefs, and texts, he also firmly supported those who were curious about Indian religious texts. Not all of his colleagues had a practical outlook on the usefulness of this "Orientalism"; dictionaries of Sanskrit or Bengali, they argued, might be useful in a revenue court, but their compilation might lead into hitherto unknown realms. But Hastings encouraged Charles Wilkins to make the first important translation from Sanskrit into English, a version of the *Bhagavad Gītā*. In his letter to the chairman of the East India Company in 1784, recommending Wilkins' work, Hastings wrote,

> Every accumulation of knowledge, and especially such as is obtained by social communication with people over whom we exercise a dominion founded on the right of conquest, is useful to the state: it is the gain of humanity: in the specific instance which I have stated, it attracts and conciliates distant affections; it lessens the weight of the chain by which the natives are held in subjection; and it imprints on the hearts of our own country-men the sense and obligation of benevolence. Even in England, this effect of it is greatly wanting. It is not very long since the inhabitants of India were considered by many, as creatures scarce elevated above the degree of savage life; nor, I fear, is that prejudice yet wholly eradicated, though surely abated. Every instance which brings their real character home to observation will impress us with a more generous sense of feeling for their natural rights, and teach us to estimate them by the measure of our own. But such instances can only be obtained in their writings: and these will survive when the British dominion in India shall have long ceased to exist, and when the sources which it once yielded of wealth and power are lost to remembrance.[12]

Hastings saw the instrumental uses of religious and legal texts to help keep order among the population, but was never blind to the other, non-utilitarian uses of scholarly investigations.

In 1768, Alexander Dow, another East India Company servant, published "A Dissertation concerning the Customs, Manners, Language, Religion and Philosophy of the Hindoos," which also attracted a considerable readership. Dow tried to distinguish between a pure and a corrupted Hinduism.[13] Though he found many "ridiculous" and "puerile" customs, he also wrote that

> The Brahmins, contrary to the ideas formed of them in the west, invariably believe in the unity, eternity, omniscience and omnip-

otence of God: that the polytheism of which they have been accused, is no more than a symbolical worship of the divine attributes, which they divide into three principal classes. Under the name of Brimha [Brahma], they worship the wisdom and creative power of God; under the appellation of Bishen [Vishnu], his providential and preserving quality; and under that of Shibah [Śiva], that attribute which tends to destroy.[14]

Like other early British writers on Hinduism, Dow was searching for equivalents of Christian beliefs and concepts, and thus stretched Hindu terms and ideas to make them fit. Though he had limited competence in Indian languages, he recognized the richness, complexity, and antiquity of Hindu belief and practice. The achievements of Nathaniel Brassey Halhed, Charles Wilkins, and William Jones were of a higher order, for their linguistic skills allowed them to penetrate further into original sources.

In the introduction to *A Code of Gentoo Laws* (1776), Halhed noted that he was confuting the common European notion that Hindus had few written laws. Indeed, he noted that

the world does not now contain annals of more indisputable antiquity than those delivered down by the ancient Bramins.
Collateral proofs of this antiquity may be drawn from every page of the present Code of Laws, in its wonderful correspondence with many parts of the Institutes of Moses, one of the first of known legislators; from whom we cannot possibly find grounds to suppose the Hindoos received the smallest article of their religion or jurisprudence, though it is not utterly impossible, that the doctrines of Hindostan might have been early transplanted into Egypt, and thus have become familiar to Moses.[15]

Like many orthodox Christians and deists, Halhed compared the chronology of the ancient Hebrews with that of ancient Hindus to see which might be earlier. He also compared the laws of each people and held them up to the clear light of eighteenth-century reason. He found many similarities and some differences, but was, in general, impressed with the range and humanity of Hindu laws.

In his introduction to the translation of the *Bhagavad Gītā*, Wilkins differentiated between pure and vulgar Hinduism. He tried to make sense of the beliefs of Hindus, noting that they in fact really believed "in one God, an universal spirit," but that the Brahmins conducted all kinds of rude ceremonies to make their bread.[16]

The translation and even the glowing praise by Hastings did not go unnoticed. This translation of a major Hindu religious text, along with Jones's translation of Kalidasa's charming play *Shakuntala* (also *Śakuntalā*), was an important stimulus to the interest in ancient Indian culture that was gathering momentum at the end of the eighteenth century.

In this birth of Western studies of India, William Jones played a major role. Before his Indian career (1783–94), Jones had gained respect as a scholar of languages, Persian in particular, and had trained for the law. Having secured an appointment as a judge in Bengal in 1783, Jones became the driving force of a group of Oriental scholars in Calcutta. The Asiatic Society was formed with the patronage of the governor-general and was to be modeled on the Royal Society.[17]

Shortly after his arrival in Calcutta, Jones began to learn Sanskrit. In studying Hindu, Roman, and Greek gods, he found seemingly endless similarities among them and wrote that,

> we shall perhaps agree at last . . . that Egyptians, Indians, Greeks and Italians proceeded originally from one central place, and that the same people carried their religion and sciences into China and Japan; may we not add, even to Mexico and Peru?[18]

But it was regarding the origins of large groupings of languages that Jones made an even more vital suggestion. In "On the Hindus," an essay for the Society's publication *Asiatick Researches*, he wrote:

> The Sanscrit language, whatever be its antiquity, is of a wonderful structure; more perfect than the Greek, more copious than the Latin, and more exquisitely refined than either, yet bearing to both of them a stronger affinity, both in the roots of verbs and in the forms of grammar, than could possibly have been produced by accident; so strong indeed, that no philologer could examine them all three, without believing them to have sprung from some common source, which, perhaps, no longer exists. . . .[19]

Though links had been suggested by others and the task of confirming his insight was to be done by later students, Jones's views gained wide acceptance in Europe. He had extended the family of European languages into the Indo-European family of languages, and established a linguistic connection between the peoples of India and Europe.

Following Jones, many Europeans and Asians made significant contributions to the understanding of the development and basic elements of Asian languages. They compiled dictionaries and wrote grammars (using, by the bye, the writings of ancient grammarians of India like Panani). Through their work, Europeans and Asians have jointly built up a considerable field of linguistic, cultural, and religious studies.

IV.

During the same period when East India Company servants and other Europeans were beginning to explore Indian culture in a more searching and sympathetic fashion, an opposing view of Indian civilization was also being formulated. This view, one hostile to Indian achievements, society, and religion, was propounded by Europeans labeled evangelicals and utilitarians. Their view has been enormously influential, particularly among those British concerned with Indian affairs. They must be described briefly here because of their wide currency from the late eighteenth century through the period of the British Raj. Charles Grant may be taken to represent the views of evangelicals on India; among the utilitarians, there is no doubt that the most widely read scholar was James Mill.

Grant's years in India spanned 1768 to 1790, when he returned to Great Britain, but he remained influential in Indian affairs until his death in 1823. Throughout his later career, he argued that India was one of the most decadent societies on the face of the earth; fundamental reform was needed and should be spearheaded by Christian missionaries backed by the East India Company. In a tract written in 1792 and reprinted in 1797, 1813, and 1833, he wrote,

> Despotism is not only the principle of the government of Hindostan, but an original, fundamental, and irreversible principle in the very frame of society. The law . . . rests entirely on the following fundamental position: . . . that certain classes or race of the society are in their elementary principles, in the matter from which they were formed, absolutely of a higher nature, of a superior order in the scale of being, to certain other classes. . . . Now the evils that flow from such an arrangement are infinite . . . here the chain of servitude is indissoluble and eternal. Though the highest orders be guilty of the most flagitious wickedness, pervert the use of power, become weak, arrogant and oppressive, the frame of society can suffer no change. . . . The lowest rank . . . is doomed to perpetual abasement and unlimited subjection. . . . This whole fabric is the work of a crafty and imperious priest-

hood, who feigned a divine revelation and appointment, to invest their own order, in perpetuity, with the most absolute empire over the civil state of the Hindoos, as well as over their minds.[20]

The utilitarian writer James Mill painted an even direr picture of human corruption. Though writing from a more secular point of view, Mill focused on some of the same evils as had Grant, and called the Brahmins the "most audacious . . . and most unskillful fabricators, with whom the annals of fable have yet made us acquainted."[21] His description of Hinduism is no less severe:

> In the conception of it no coherence, wisdom, or beauty, ever appears: all is disorder, caprice, passion, contest, portents, prodigies, violence, and deformity. . . . Flattery, founded upon a base apprehension of the divine character, ingrafts upon a mean superstition.[22]

Mill focused on what he saw as the absurdity, depravity, and obscenity of Hindu ceremonies. Like Grant, Mill felt he had to refute any kind words that Sir William Jones had to say about Hinduism and Indian society.[23]

Though Mill had never been to India, Grant had. So the long-time resident and the armchair theorist presented many of the same analyses and evaluations. They were participants in a new age of unabashed British power in India. Grant and Mill, along with Edmund Burke, were legitimizers of the British role and voices calling for fundamental reform; it was time to remake India in the British image.[24] As the relative failure to convert Indians to Christianity became evident, what Stokes called "authoritarian utilitarianism" blended with old-style paternalism became the order of the day.[25]

Thomas Macaulay, a novice in India, and innocent of any knowledge of Indian language, played an important role in the decision to make English the medium of instruction in higher education throughout India. He wrote in his 1835 "Minute on Education":

> We have a fund to be employed as government shall direct for the intellectual improvement of the people of this country. . . . I have never found one among them [the Orientalists] who could deny that a single shelf of a good European library was worth the whole native literature of India and Arabia. . . . The claims of our own language it is hardly necessary to recapitulate. It stands preeminent even among the languages of the West. . . . it is possible to make natives of this country thoroughly good En-

glish scholars; and that to this end our efforts ought to be directed. . . . We must at present do our best to form a class who may be interpreters between us and the millions whom we govern; a class of persons, Indian in blood and color, but English in taste, in opinions, in morals, and in intellect.[26]

The elite of India were henceforward educated through the medium of English, but they continued to use and develop their own languages and practice their own religion. The British could partly mold India in their own way, but their efforts had unforeseen consequences as nationalism grew apace from the late nineteenth century to the British departure in 1947.

V.

Following the pioneering work of Halhed, Wilkins, and Jones in Calcutta, and others like the Frenchman A.H. Anquetil-Duperron, who translated Zoroastrian texts and the Upanishads from Persian to French, in the late eighteenth century, a great expansion of Asian studies took place in France, Germany, and Britain throughout the nineteenth century. Raymond Schwab has assessed the significance of this development as follows:

Only after 1771 does the world become truly round; half the intellectual map is no longer a blank. In other words, this is not a second Renaissance but the first, belatedly reaching its logical culmination . . . little by little a widening historical vision expanded the horizon of creative thinkers. . . . Henceforth the world would be one where Sanskrit and linguistics, even for those unaware of them, would have changed the images peopling time and space. . . . [T]he orientalists . . . brought back a view of humanity different from that of the gold-hunters and the slave merchants. . . . All notions concerning revelation and civilization would be reexamined. . . . [T]he continent of the Hindus, the Chinese, and the Sumerians regained—with all the grandeur of its metaphysical tradition . . . with all the weight of its intellectual seniority, which we had unveiled—the power to question us. . . . Asia suddenly began to seem again an equal in modern controversies.[27]

Schwab's enthusiasm and focus on European scholars and writers on the Orient should not lead us to forget the realities of empire building during the nineteenth century. Though the writings of the Orientalists suggest greater Western understanding and appreciation of other civilizations, this was still an age of ruthless conquest and blatant racism. The British were not deterred in the Opium War by the wisdom of Confucius or in the conquest of Burma by the message of Buddha. Nor did the French, for all their chairs of Asian languages, behave any less cruelly in Cambodia and Vietnam in the nineteenth and twenti-eth centuries. Were these imperial conquests and the growth of Oriental studies in the West two parts of the same process? They were no doubt related, for the outward movement of the Europeans allowed the more scholarly and reflective among them the opportunity to study Asian (and African) cultures, history, and languages. While some may have served the cause of imperialism, others have enhanced understanding—among Westerners and, indeed, among Asians themselves—of Asian cultures through their scholarship; in certain instances they have preserved ancient artifacts of Asian civilizations that would otherwise have been lost. Is the invaluable Sanskrit-to-English dictionary of M. Monier-Williams a product only of Western ethnocentrism? Are we to discard all the work done by Western Orientalists because of the imperialist attitudes and racism that infect a certain measure of it? Or should we build upon their efforts, taking what is positive and useful in con-structing a more multicentered, subtle, and complex under-standing of Asian civilizations as well as our own?

During the Indian nationalist movement, the Bengali poet Rabindranath Tagore said that for a long time India had "lost interest in itself." He blamed British imperialism, but he also put some responsibility on the shoulders of his countrymen:

> If we had only kept ourselves acquainted with our country, that would have been something,—but so lazy are we, we know next to nothing about her. The foreigner writes our history, we trans-late it; the foreigner discovers our grammar, we cram it. If we want to know what there is next door, we have to look into Hunter. We gather no facts first hand,—neither about men, nor commerce, nor even agriculture. And yet, with such crass indif-ference on our own part, we are not ashamed to prate about the duties of others towards our country.[28]

In recent decades, the people of India, as well as other formerly colonial peoples, have taken up the task of studying and preserv-ing their cultures. While it is important that they take the lead in this endeavor as much as possible, others—scholars from the West or elsewhere—should not be excluded because of the preju-dices that colored so much of Oriental scholarship in the past. Studies of Asia can benefit from the different perspectives that Asian and non-Asian scholars each bring to their work.

NOTES

1. Edward Said, *Orientalism*, p. 8. This remark is framed in a question in the original. But Said wants us to see that many of these characteristics are present in Orientalist works.

2. Ronald Inden, "Orientalist Constructions of India," *Modern Asian Studies*, No. 3, 1986, 402 and his *Imagining India* (Oxford: Basil Blackwell, 1990), passim.

3. See Donald F. Lach, *Asia in the Making of Europe*, II, Book Two, p. 319.

4. François Bernier, *Travels in the Mogul Empire* A.D. *1656–1668*. The 1914 edition contains numerous letters by Bernier to his countrymen as well as the main narrative of the war of succession. These briefer letters, e.g., the one to Colbert, are, perforce, more schematic and didactic than the longer account.

5. The basic source of my information on Quesnay is Lewis A. Maverick, *China: A Model for Europe* (San Antonio: Paul Anderson, 1946), 2 vols. bound as one. The first sketches the context for Quesnay's views and the second part is a translation of Quesnay's *Le Despotisme de la Chine*, Paris, 1767.

6. Maverick, *China*, Part II, p. 247.

7. Voltaire, *The Works of Voltaire*, Vol. XIII, pp. 28–29.

8. Voltaire, *Works*, XIII, 29ff; XV, Part 2, pp. 171–73.

9. Voltaire, *Works*, XIII, pp. 32–38.

10. Ibid., pp. 39–42.

11. Voltaire, *Works*, XV, Part 2, pp. 175–92.

12. Warren Hastings, "Letter to Nathaniel Smith," from *The Bhagvat-Geeta*, in *The British Discovery of Hinduism in the Eighteenth Century*, ed. P.J. Marshall (Cambridge: Cambridge University Press, 1970), p. 189. Throughout this section, I have relied on Marshall's excellent introduction and his selection of texts.

13. Alexander Dow, "A Dissertation concerning the Customs, Manners, Language, Religion and Philosophy of the Hindoos," in Marshall, *British Discovery*, p. 127.

14. Ibid., p. 138.

15. Nathaniel Brassey Halhed, "The Translator's Preface," to *A Code of Gentoo Laws*, in Marshall, *British Discovery*, p. 162.

16. Charles Wilkins, "The Translator's Preface," to *The Bhagvat Geeta*, in Marshall, *British Discovery*, p. 194.

17. On Jones and the founding and legacies of the Asiatic Society, see S.N. Mukherjee, *Sir William Jones: A Study in Eighteenth-Century British Attitudes to India*, chaps. 5 and 7.

18. William Jones, "On the Gods of Greece, Italy, and India," in Marshall, *British Discovery*, p. 239.

19. Jones, "On the Hindus," p. 252.

20. Charles Grant, "Observations on the State of Society among the Asiatic Subjects of Great Britain, particularly with respect to Morals, and on the means of Improving It. Written chiefly in the Year 1792." *Parliamentary Papers*, 1812–13, X, Paper 282, pp. 34–35. See Ainslie T. Embree's analysis in *Charles Grant and British Rule in India*, pp. 141–50.

21. James Mill, *The History of British India*, Vol. I, p. 117.

22. Mill, *History*, I, pp. 267–68.
23. Ibid., p. 292.
24. Ross J.S. Hoffman and Paul Levack, eds. *Burke's Politics*, 233ff.
25. On the influences of the evangelicals and the utilitarians, see Eric Stokes, *The English Utilitarians and India* (Oxford: Clarendon Press, 1959).
26. Thomas Babington Macaulay, "Minute on Education," reprinted in Wm. Theodore de Bary, ed., *Sources of Indian Tradition*, Vol. II, pp. 44–49.
27. Raymond Schwab, *The Oriental Renaissance*, pp. 16–19.
28. Rabindranath Tagore, "The Way to Get It Done," in *Greater India*, p. 45.

SELECTED REFERENCES

Primary Sources

Balzac, Honoré. *Louis Lambert* [1832].
Bernier, François. *Travels in the Mogul Empire A.D. 1656–1668* [1670]. Translated by Archibald Constable (1891). Vincent Smith, ed. Oxford: Oxford University Press, 1914.
Burke, Edmund. *Burke's Politics*. Edited by J.S. Hoffman and Paul Levack. New York: Knopf, 1959.
Diderot, Denis. "The Encyclopedia," and "Supplement to Bougainville's 'Voyage.' " In *Rameau's Nephew and Other Works*. Translated by Jacques Barzun and Ralph H. Bowen. Garden City, NY: Doubleday, 1956.
Goldsmith, Oliver. "The Citizen of the World" [1760–1774]. In *The Works of Oliver Goldsmith*. Vol. II. London: John Murray, 1854.
Grant, Charles. "Observations on the State of Society among the Asiatic Subjects of Great Britain, particularly with respect to Morals; and on the means of Improving It," [1792]. In *Parliamentary Papers*, 1812–13, X, Paper 282, pp. 1–112.
Jones, William. "On the Gods of Greece, Italy, and India," "On the Hindus," "On the Chronology of the Hindus" [1789–90]. In *The British Discovery of Hinduism in the Eighteenth Century*, edited by P.J. Marshall. Cambridge: Cambridge University Press, 1970. [Also contains articles by J.Z. Holwell, Alexander Dow, Nathaniel B. Halhed, Warren Hastings, and Charles Wilkins]
Kalidasa. *Shakuntala.* 1789. Translated by William Jones. A modern translation appears in Miller, Barbara Stoler, ed. *Theater of Memory.* New York: Columbia University Press, 1984.
Macaulay, Thomas. "Minute on Education" [1935]. In *The Sources of Indian Tradition*, edited by W.T. de Bary. New York: Columbia University Press, 1958.
Macaulay, Thomas. "Lord Clive" [1840]. "Warren Hastings" [1841]. In *Critical, Historical, and Miscellaneous Essays.* Vols. II and III. Boston: Houghton Mifflin, 1860.
Mill, James. *The History of British India* [1817]. Edited by Horace Mayman Wilson (1858). Reprint. New York: Chelsea House, 1968.
Montesquieu. *Persian Letters* [1721]. Translated by J. Robert Loy. New York: Meridian, 1961.
Montesquieu. *The Spirit of the Laws* [1748]. Translated by Thomas Nugent. New York: Hafner, 1959.

Polo, Marco. *The Travels* [1298?]. Translated by Ronald Latham. New York: Penguin Books, 1958.

Quesnay, François. "Despotism in China" [1767]. In *China: A Model for Europe*, translated and edited by Lewis A. Maverick. Vol. II. San Antonio: Paul Anderson, 1946.

Voltaire. *Ancient and Modern History [Essai sur les Moeurs]*, [1756]. In *The Works of Voltaire*. Vols. XIII, XIV, XV. New York: St. Hubert Guild, 1901.

Voltaire. *Philosophical Dictionary.* Edited by Peter Gay. New York: Harcourt, Brace and World, 1962.

Secondary Works

Adas, Michael. *Machines as the Measure of Men. Science, Technology, and Ideologies of Western Dominance.* Ithaca, NY: Cornell University Press, 1989.

Bearce, George. *British Attitudes towards India, 1784–1858.* London: Oxford University Press, 1961.

Chaudhuri, Nirad C. *Scholar Extraordinary. The Life of Professor the Rt. Hon. Friedrich Max Muller, P.C.* London: Chatto and Windus, 1974.

Clive, John. *Macaulay. The Shaping of the Historian.* Cambridge, MA: Harvard University Press, 1973.

Embree, Ainslie T. *Charles Grant and British Rule in India.* New York: Columbia University Press, 1962.

Inden, Ronald. "Orientalist Constructions of India." *Modern Asian Studies*, 20, 3 (1986):401–46.

Inden, Ronald. *Imagining India.* Oxford: Basil Blackwell, 1990.

Iyer, Raghavan, ed. *The Glass Curtain between Asia and Europe.* Oxford: Oxford University Press, 1965.

Kopf, David. *British Orientalism and the Bengal Renaissance.* Calcutta: Firma KLM, 1969.

Lach, Donald F. *Asia in the Making of Europe.* Vol. I, Books One and Two, Chicago: University of Chicago Press, 1965; Vol. II, Books One, Two, and Three, 1977.

Manuel, Frank E. *The Eighteenth Century Confronts the Gods.* Cambridge, MA: Harvard University Press, 1959.

Marshall, P.J. *The Impeachment of Warren Hastings.* Oxford: Oxford University Press, 1965.

Marshall, P.J., and Williams, Glyndwr. *The Great Map of Mankind.* London: J.M. Dent, 1982.

Mason, Philip. *The Men Who Ruled India*, 2 vols. London: J. Cape, 1953.

Mukherji, S.N. *Sir William Jones: A Study in Eighteenth-Century British Attitudes to India.* Cambridge: Cambridge University Press, 1968.

Said, Edward. *Orientalism.* New York: Pantheon, 1978.

Schwab, Raymond. *The Oriental Renaissance.* New York: Columbia University Press, 1984.

Spence, Jonathan. *The Memory Palace of Matteo Ricci.* New York: Penguin Books, 1985.

Steadman, John M. *The Myth of Asia.* New York: Simon and Schuster, 1969.

Stokes, Eric. *The English Utilitarians and India.* Oxford: Clarendon Press, 1959.

Willson, A. Leslie. *A Mythical Image: The Ideal of India in German Romanticism.* Durham: Duke University Press, 1964.

ASIA IN WESTERN THOUGHT

IMAGES OF THE OTHER: ASIA IN NINETEENTH-CENTURY WESTERN THOUGHT—HEGEL, MARX, AND WEBER

Harvey Goldman

SYNOPSIS

This essay examines the works of Hegel, Marx, and Weber as a fruitful source for understanding Western intellectual representations of Asia. Hegel strove to integrate the "East" as a stage of the development of "spirit" culminating in the modern Germanic Protestant world. Marx, though condemning the cruelties of the West's colonial exploitation of Asia, nonetheless also integrated the East into a theory of development, believing that the advance of capitalism into Asia would rescue the East from the backwardness of its culture. Weber, on the other hand, did not try to fit Asia into a theory of stages of historical progress, but he still viewed it from the perspective of its capacity to produce an analogue to the "Occidental personality" that had helped make the West what it was. Despite the rich and imaginative portraits of Asia in the work of these thinkers, they each put Asia into a Eurocentric scheme and agenda of their own that forced them to oversimplify and reduce many aspects of Asian culture and society.

To what extent the intellectual and cultural encounter with Asia affected nineteenth-century European thought and culture is difficult to measure, as are the relations between such thought and both popular views of Asia and the development of Western society and culture.[1] The experience of Asia clearly influenced, and was strongly influenced by, European economies and their political and military policies. It also influenced the arts in every form and inspired a scholarly engagement with the "Orient" in all of its manifestations, though that engagement was not without serious distortion.[2] England and France were pioneers, not only in colonialism, but in making available Asian texts of all kinds, as well as generating studies of Asian religious, social, and political life more generally. Yet it was Germany, through the intensity of its engagement and the profundity of its thinkers and writers, that was the home of the "renaissance" of Oriental studies, especially of India, and of much of the greatest and most influential philosophical and social thought of the century.

Our concern here is the representation or "construction" of the Orient in the works of a few of the great thinkers that Germany and the West produced then: G.W.F. Hegel (1770–1831), the last great philosophical system builder, whose work was the culmination of the Western philosophical tradition since Plato; Karl Marx (1818–1883), Hegel's most powerful critic, who produced a materialist interpretation of history that sought to comprehend all societies from the ground up; and Max Weber (1864–1920), the founder of modern social science, who recognized the importance to Occidental self-understanding of a serious encounter with Asian culture in all its forms.

Despite the great differences between them, Hegel, Marx, and Weber had enormous influence, not only in the West but in Asia. Indeed, their works are a fruitful vehicle for understanding Western conceptions more generally, for as we learn from recent anthropological thought, the way a culture represents the "other" of a different culture involves not simply translating the reality of that other but imposing a meaning as well. More to the point, "every version of an 'other,' wherever found, is also the construction of a 'self.' "[3] Thus, while representations by Western thinkers of the "other" of Asia reveal crucial aspects of European understanding of the Orient, they also illuminate the larger theoretical schemes of these thinkers, and, through them, some of the West's more important and characteristic "discourses" as well.

A number of cultural and social facts influenced the West's experience of Asia. First was the European view of the ancient Greeks, whose understanding of "Asia" was mediated by the Persian wars and later by the conquest of parts of Asia to the Indus valley by Alexander the Great. Herodotus, for example, visited Persia and Egypt, and left impressive accounts of their culture and life. At the same time, he interpreted the Persian wars as a struggle between East and West and as the preservation of ancient freedoms from mass enslavement by an Asian emperor. Though Greek freedoms were themselves built on slavery; though Asian "enslavement" tolerated the greatest diversity of cultural, religious, and ethnic groups; and though Eastern religious elements undoubtedly influenced the religious mysteries of Greece and Rome, these facts were deemed of lesser account than the important elements of philosophy, politics, and culture that Hellas had bequeathed to the West by its victory. Second were the complicated attitudes toward the Islamic peoples, which Catholic Europe had seen as barbarians in control of the "Holy Lands." It had been forgotten that Arabic culture had flourished and preserved and translated ancient Greek texts at a time when Westerners outside of the church could no longer even write their names. Third was the fact of Turkish power in the eastern Mediterranean and the "underbelly" of Europe, which, despite European naval and military strength, was an uncomfortable reminder of Europe's vulnerability to "incursions" from Asia. Fourth, and most importantly, were the greater and greater exploratory, colonial, and imperial ventures undertaken in East and South Asia, which produced not only new sources for the encounter with Asian culture but also embroiled the European powers in worldwide conflicts, exploitation, and domination. European perceptions were also linked to the fear, among a number of thinkers, that the West and its economic system would lapse into crisis, rigidify, and lose its dynamism in a social organization that would cripple individual development. Thus, the overdeveloped bureaucratization of Egypt, the immobility and lack of movement of China, the horrors of the caste system of India: each of these images of Asia had enormous negative symbolic power in the imagination of Europeans. Yet, before the time of the domination of capitalism and its extension to all sectors of life, the Orient was viewed as a source of principles for wise rule and balanced social order, as well as for religious wisdom. Intellectuals like Leibniz, Schopenhauer, and the Physiocrats were much more open than later figures to learning about Asian social order and learning from the wisdom they believed resided in the East. Apart from the case of Adam Smith, the fear of stasis and rigidity became widespread only with the extension of capitalism and the development of romanticism, when evils of all kinds were projected onto Asia, although the reverse idealization of Asia occurred as well.

In nineteenth-century Europe, there were as many vantage

points on Asia as there were thinkers, each one motivated by a different need to use, appropriate, or understand the East. At the same time, the thinkers we are considering here all steeped themselves in the literature on Asia. Hegel sought to integrate the East into a picture of "spiritual" development and the development of freedom, taking as his vantage point what he regarded as the achievements of modern Protestantism and the Germanic world. For him, Asia, Greece, Rome, and the Protestant German world were sequential stages in the unfolding and development of "spirit" in history. Thus, Hegel could grasp Asian culture only in terms of its relation to a spirit whose culmination and fulfillment he found in the West. Marx, on the other hand, focused on Western social and economic "foundations," and examined the East both historically—in terms of its "old" modes of production that were being surpassed by the modern capitalist mode—and politically—criticizing the barbaric exploitation of the East by the colonial powers of the West. While recognizing the cruelties of the capitalist mode of production as it expanded over the earth, he still believed that capitalism furthered the general advance of humankind. Asian culture—backward, enslaved, and riddled with mystical and primitive religion—needed the liberation and modernization that capitalism could bring, despite the destruction it also brought. In this way, Marx hoped to find a silver lining in the dark cloud of imperialism. Yet he never really condoned the violent destruction of the old patterns of life. Weber, who did greater justice to the integrity, value, and many-sidedness of Asian experience than the others, did not try to fit the East into similar lines of development. He was interested, rather, in what a culture equips men and women for, what it encourages and what it prevents. Nonetheless, Weber evaluated Asia through the optic of his notion of the "Occidental personality," to discover whether in Asia there were sources of innovation and inner-worldly character strength and mastery comparable to those that had appeared in the West at the time of the birth of capitalism. Because of this, he could not provide a rounded picture of Asian culture and its genuine difference.[4]

HEGEL AND THE ORIENTAL SPIRIT

Hegel's obvious attempt to undermine the esteem in which Asian culture was held during the nineteenth-century "renaissance" of Oriental studies suggests that he feared the potentially corrupting influence of Asian culture on Western thought and mores. He claimed, for example, that the much-vaunted "knowledge" of the Indians and Egyptians was shown each day to be emptier than formerly believed,[5] and that it would have been better for their reputation had Chinese philosophers like Confucius never been translated.[6] Some people even believed that there was as much "social virtue and morality" in Asia as in the Christian states, which, if true, would cast doubt on the idea of progress in history. But this, said Hegel, is an error created by the "forms" of the East, which are so enchanting that we overlook the dreadful "content" of Asian culture.[7] For a man who believed that the unfolding of "spirit" meant the development of the self-consciousness of freedom and that the Germano-Christian world was the highest stage of this unfolding, any Western attitude that went beyond purely historical respect for Asian notions of truth and the good must have seemed a profound and dangerous step backward. Indeed, though Hegel argued that religion is one of the modes of absolute spirit, he was cautious in his attitude toward Asian religion.

> It still must not be forgotten that religion may take a form leading to the harshest bondage in the fetters of superstition and man's degraded subservience to animals. . . . This phenomenon may at least make it evident that we ought not to speak of religion at all in general terms and that we really need a power to protect us from it in some of its forms and to espouse against them the rights of reason and self-consciousness.[8]

Thus to Hegel it is not religion in general but Western religion, principally Christianity—and, in particular, Protestantism—that is the vehicle through which absolute spirit reveals itself.

For Hegel, reality as it is does not show us the truth of things. It is thought that discovers truth, and thought is more real than its objects. Reality thus lies not in appearance but in the thought that comprehends it. The divine Idea—a conception Hegel takes from Plato—is the truth of history and the foundation of reality; spirit, which can be discovered by thought, is the motive force of history, embodied in concrete phases of historical development. The Idea is, in fact, the concept of "spiritual self-consciousness" that world history develops, the potential which spirit makes actual. Spirit is the Idea "brought down from formal ideality to full embodiment in human experience."[9] Indeed, spirit and the course of its development is the substance of history and of all reality. Thus, world history is the exhibition of spirit striving to attain knowledge of its own nature. But since, for Hegel, "freedom" in every sense is the sole truth of spirit, world history represents phases in the progress of the self-consciousness of freedom. The "self-actualization" of spirit is the focus of philosophy, which comprehends history, and truth lies in the entirety of the development of spirit and not in any single phase.

It is into this framework of the unfolding of spirit that Hegel strives to fit Asia in his *Philosophy of History*. In Asia "arose the light of spirit, and therefore the history of the world," but it is only "Hither" Asia (Persia, Syria, Asia Minor, etc.), and not "Farther" Asia (China, India)—that is, the world of Caucasians, who act in history, rather than Mongols, who are stationary—that originated all religious and political principles. Even so, only Europe has been the theater of the real development of these principles.

Hegel used two principal metaphors to express the relation of East and West. The first metaphor is that of a man whose first sight is the sun, which rises in the East and sets in the West. For Hegel, the "history of the World travels from East to West, for Europe is absolutely the end of history, Asia the beginning." The initial reaction of a formerly sightless man on seeing the rising sun for the first time is astonishment and forgetfulness of self and individuality. This is the experience of the East, overpowered by and suffused with emerging spirit. But once the sun has risen, astonishment subsides, and the individual begins to perceive objects and then proceeds to contemplate his own inner being and, ultimately, the relation between the two. Contemplation is then left behind for activity, and by the end of day, the person has erected a building from his own "inner sun." In the evening, the person contemplates his creation and esteems it higher than the original and physical sun. This is the experience of the West, of Greece, Rome, and Germanic Christianity, where humankind has developed a conscious and free relation to spirit. "If we hold this image fast in mind, we shall find it symbolizing the course of history, the day's work of Spirit."[10]

The second metaphor is that of human development from childhood, which is the East, to old age, which is the West. In this metaphor, the East is the home of unreflective consciousness, where individuality and subjective freedom are unknown. This is "the childhood of history," and all are subject to a supreme being like children obeying parents, with undifferentiated identities. Not surprisingly, the model of the Chinese world for Hegel is the family relation. But the move west, to Hither Asia, takes humankind beyond the repose and trustingness of the child and into a boisterous and active life, the "boyhood" of history, found in Syria and Egypt, followed by "adolescence," represented by the Greek world, where individuals now truly form themselves. Rome represents the active and mature manhood of history, building objects that civilize the world. Finally, after long struggle, spirit turns inward and, through that, pacifies the external world, represented by the Christian development of the Germanic world. This is the old age of history. But unlike the old age of nature, which is weak, the old age of spirit is mature and strong, even though the "Mohammedan principle," Islam, intrudes on it. This Protestant religious teleology, sublimated into history, provides the links between all elements of spirit and of world history, and reveals "the ultimate result which the process of history is intended to accomplish."[11]

These poetic metaphors, of course, are hardly neutral in their implications for understanding Asia. Indeed, in their simple ethnocentrism and their arrangement of history in a line leading to the Hegelian present, the morning-evening and child-adult metaphors illuminate a stage of Western narcissism and its encounter with the "alien" much more than they do the experience and reality of Asia. Unfortunately, a great number of Hegel's interpretations of Asian religion, philosophy, and history are suffused with short-sighted condemnation and the inability to see anything in Asia but backwardness, immorality, lack of regard for life, and a stunted and infantilized spirit that, fortunately for history, was overcome by the West. Hegel had only praise for Alexander bringing Greek culture to Asia "in order to elevate into a Greek world this wild medley of utter barbarism, bent solely on destruction, and torn by internal dissensions, these lands entirely sunk in indolence, negation, and spiritual degeneration."[12]

Hegel believed that history must be evaluated in terms of the development of freedom.[13] From that perspective, the Oriental world did not consider the human being as such as free and believed in the freedom of only one person, the tyrant. The Greco-Roman world, where the consciousness of freedom first arose, believed that some human beings were free, and instituted democracy, followed by aristocracy. Only in the Germano-Christian world is it understood that the human being as such is free, and thus only there does the freedom of spirit constitute the essence of the world.

To Hegel, China and India lie outside the history of freedom, hence outside world history. In China, all are subject to the paternal care of the Emperor in a world with absolute equality but without freedom. Moreover, Chinese religion is linked to the state and has not risen to that stage of development known in the West, where religion means the "retirement" of the spirit into itself. True faith is only possible, to Hegel, where individuals can seclude themselves. But in China, the human being has no inherent worth or dignity and is without the power of personal decision and subjective freedom. Thus, though Chinese religion seems to be moral, it is filled with magic and superstition. Chinese art, too, is without spiritual qualities, Chinese science merely empirical and useful, not theoretical—the Chinese could not even construct a reliable calendar—and even the language is an obstacle to the development of real knowledge! Similar problems lie in jurisprudence, ethics, and philosophy. Thus, Hegel concludes, "everything which belongs to spirit—unconstrained morality, in practice and theory, heart, inward religion, science and art properly so-called— is alien to it."[14]

To Hegel, no genuine philosophical knowledge exists in the Orient, but only a religious mode of thought pervading everything. In Asian thought the individual has value only through identification with a higher "substance" or being, and so does not exist as a subject. Moral thought, as in Confucius, is commonplace, Hegel claims, and a single work of Cicero's is more comprehensive and better than all the books of Confucius taken together. The *Yi Jing* [*I Ching*] evidences no conception of universal natural or spiritual powers. Of Lao Zi (Lao Tzu), he says: "What is there to be found in all this learning?" Indian philosophy, too, he argues, lacks objectivity, and stands within Indian religion as Scholastic philosophy stood within Christian dogmatism. Thus: "The Idea has not become objective in the Indian philosophy; hence the external and objective has not been comprehended in accordance with the Idea. This is the deficiency in Orientalism."[15]

In Indian religion, which Hegel calls a religion of "fantasy," the fundamental conceptions are "baroque and wild and are horrible, repulsive, loathsome distortions." Although they recall the highest elements of the Idea, they are stunted because their fundamental spiritual nature is not understood. Everything is made divine, and human beings place themselves on the same level with the rest of nature: they do not know their nature to be higher than the nature of a spring or a tree. Thus, among the Hindus, life is despised, and human beings do not value themselves. This "perverted character of the Hindu mind" leads to the sacrifice of wives, children, and self in suicide. The people of India are, therefore, "sunk in the most complete immorality."[16]

In Hinduism, spirit resides in a dream state, and the Hindu is incapable of rational reflection. Since there is a universal deification of all finite existence, the divine is degraded. Further, the stereotyping of the caste system condemns Indians to "the most degrading spiritual serfdom." Thus, "neither morality, nor justice, nor religiosity is to be found." Instead, deceit and cunning are the fundamental character of the Hindus. India does have ties to the world—through Sanskrit and through emigration to the West—and strikes a special chord within the West as a "Land of Desire." In fact, the world longs for access to its treasures, spiritual and natural. Indeed, "it is the necessary fate of Asiatic Empire to be subjected to Europeans; and China will, some day or other, be obliged to submit to this fate." This will be an advance over Asian despotism, whose worst form is found in India. While other Asian nations know despotism, they see it as contrary to right order and are roused to resentment. But in India, no one sees despotism as abnormal, for there is no sense of personal independence. Finally, the Hindus are incapable of writing history, since that requires understanding and objectivity, and thus the comprehension of one's own existence as independent, whereas in India all fixed rational and definite conceptions of the ideal are degraded and dissolved into the Hindu spirit of dreaming and transiency.[17]

In contrast to Farther Asia, Hither Asia, the Near East, is credited with much greater spiritual advance. Indeed, Hegel calls the Persians the first historical people. Persia is the scene of development and revolution, the origin of the first great moral religion, Zoroastrianism, with neither consolidated totalities, as in China, nor anarchy and caprice, as in India. Here, each people is free. The seafaring Phoenicians free the human spirit from bondage to nature, while in Judea and Egypt, spirit is elevated further, pervading life and institutions.[18]

Islam, or what Hegel calls Mohammedanism, is, of course, a much later development and an advance over the negative and enslaving spirit of Asia. For Islam, worship of Allah was the only final aim. God is the absolute One, and before Him the human being has no interests of his own. Indeed, Islam displays a tendency toward absolute fatalism and lack of respect for life. No practical end has any intrinsic worth, and all ends must aim to bring about worship of God. Thus, Islam was restrained by nothing, enthusiastic only for abstractions. Yet the Arabs were without national or caste distinctions, and without regard for race. Whoever converted gained equality of rights with all other believers. Under Islam philosophy flourished, and scientific knowledge passed from the Arab East to the West. Still, Hegel claims, the Arabs did not actually advance philosophy because they established no principle of self-conscious reason, relying instead on revelation. Eventually, the Islamic East sank into vice like the rest of Asia. "Islam has long vanished from the stage of history at large, and has retreated into Oriental ease and repose."[19]

What can we say of Hegel's interpretative approach as a whole and of the source of its blindness to the complexity and meaning of Asian experience more generally? In the first place, the problem was not sources. Hegel was incredibly well informed, and apparently drew on all of the English, French, and German sources that had become available since the birth or rebirth of Oriental studies in the eighteenth century. He knew all of the sacred works of the East, as well as modern studies of the social and political life of Asia. Hegel's problem derives instead from his need to represent and interpret every aspect of spirit or culture, East and West, in terms of a totalizing history. Within Hegel's perspective, the East is revealed for its "contributions" to spirit (the sun has to rise somewhere; there has to be a childhood at some time), but also for its inability to develop in a Western manner, a manner vindicated by Hegel as a more advanced form of the development of spirit. Though Hegel often conceives spirit in organic metaphors of unfolding, spirit ultimately follows a unidirectional, if not linear, path.

Consider the metaphor of childhood. The East is childhood, because the Christian West, which opposes and conquers the East spiritually and politically, is taken to be adulthood. Once Western maturity is made the standard, Eastern childhood follows directly. Thus Hegel must interpret Asia **symbolically,** because Asia is not granted its own story, independent of a Eurocentric vision of history. In Hegel, there can be only one story, the story of how spirit has come to localize itself and fulfill itself in the West. If spirit is only a single flower unfolding from within itself, then there can be only one story of its life cycle. The normal diversity and richness of nature are here overthrown. Hegel's history, as the realm of spirit's "nature," is a garden with only one plant, though seen in many "moments" and "stages" of development, and Asia becomes only a part of the story of that one plant, an earlier stage, whose fullest flower is Germano-Protestant culture and society.

In a sense, Hegel is egalitarian, in that his belief in unidirectional development and in the progress of spirit leads him to find all "earlier" stages of spirit, including earlier Western ones, in some way limited, measured by what spirit can attain. Hegel has thus erected a unified edifice with places for everything in human culture, though these places are all stepping stones for the emergence of his own world. His judgments of human experience reflect the perspective of his world and system as the culmination of the Western and world-historical tradition. He did correctly see the relation of his system to the rest of the Western tradition, because the great nineteenth-century thinkers after Hegel—Marx, Kierkegaard, and Nietzsche—understood their efforts to overturn, undermine, or destroy the Hegelian system as an attack on the Western tradition generally, from its birth in Plato to its "end" in Hegel.[20]

Hegel strove to assimilate what he saw in Asia to a system that could not comprehend it adequately. Hegel could not grasp the "concept" of the alien without reduction, and he demonstrated, though unintentionally, that his notion of spirit could not penetrate to the heart of Asian life. Rather than engaging Asia in real dialogue, he looked to see if and to what extent it belonged to the same "family" from which he himself derived. Clearly, it did not. Yet that inability cannot account for Hegel's derogation and caricature of so much of Asian experience. Despite his vast knowledge and the greatness of his intellect, Hegel seems unfortunately to have shared in the racial and cultural stereotypes that pervaded Europe.

MARX AND THE ASIATIC MODE OF PRODUCTION

Marx's intellectual career was built on a critique of Hegel and of the Hegelian interpretation of history. Instead of seeing history in terms of the unfolding of spirit, Marx placed concrete material existence at the foundation of human culture, society, and politics. For Marx, religion, law, morality, and the state have no history independent of the society that has produced them, and they must be interpreted in terms of the social organization of production, whether it is the village commune, the slave society, the feudal organization of town and country, or the bourgeois mode of manufacturing and industry. Thus, though religion, law, and morality always represent in some form the "truth" of a society, it is a truth rooted in the limits and possibilities of a specific material life.

Marx was thus able to overcome much of Hegel's provincialism and ethnocentrism by grounding the development of freedom in specific modes of production, which, unlike the stages of Hegel's spirit, can appear anywhere on earth. Indeed, Marx witnessed the extension of capitalism throughout the world in the nineteenth century, as well as the direct domination and exploitation of British and French imperialism. At the same time, he saw the capitalist mode of production as the last "antagonistic" mode, that is, the last that would be based on exploitation, and thus, to Marx, we do not live at the end of history, as Hegel thought, but on the verge of it.

Yet, as a correspondent for the *New York Tribune*, Marx was also a chronicler of the travails of Asia at the hands of European colonialism. Though he analyzed the European powers' struggle over Persia, and argued that Japan's feudal organization of landed property and developed small-scale agriculture "gives a much truer picture of the European Middle Ages than all our history books,"[21] Marx focused principally on China and India as objects of European exploitation. Thus, to understand Marx's representation of Asian experience, we have to consider, first, his materialist interpretation of history; then his analysis of the nature and place of the Asiatic mode of production in the context of the uniqueness of capitalism and its preconditions; and finally, his portrait of Asia under colonial domination.[22]

Marx's materialist interpretation of history begins in his critique of Hegel's interpretations of religion, state, and, ultimately, history. Marx argued that religion cannot be viewed as a form of the appearance of absolute spirit, but that it is, rather, a sphere of illusion. In religion, humankind forgets that it is the actor and subject of history, and attributes both its suffering and control over the world to a realm of Gods who are actually human powers projected into a magical beyond. Religion thus expresses the suffering and the hopes of redemption that arise in specific conditions of oppression, yet it teaches people that they are powerless.

In the same way that religion makes God the creator of humankind, thus inverting the true relation, so too does philosophy make consciousness or spirit superior to all concrete material existence. Philosophy claims to find the source of value in the human being, but in fact it depletes individual life on behalf of an illusion, thus undermining action, for it attributes true significance to the universal of spirit, which merely finds its concretization in the particulars of life. Only by recognizing that the true condition of humankind is material, rooted in the organization of production for existence, can humankind overcome its illusions and act. According to Marx, then, we must not focus on consciousness and its development but on conscious material existence, something Hegel ignored in his picture of Asia and of history generally. Thus, in Marx, instead of a history of the stages of development of spirit, we find a history of modes of production, a history of humankind's development of its material life, which is, as spirit and reason were for Hegel, the reality behind appearances.

In *The German Ideology* Marx gives a first version of the stages of the modes of production in terms of property ownership. The first mode is tribal ownership, an extension of the natural division of labor in the family, characterized by hunting and gathering, and, at its highest stage, agriculture. The second mode is ancient communal and state ownership, produced by uniting several tribes into a city, and including at its higher stages the ownership of movable and immovable property. The third mode is feudal or estate ownership, rooted in the country rather than the town, with large manors and an enserfed small peasantry rather than the slaves held in the first two forms. The fourth form is capitalist private property ownership.

A decade later, Marx added a new mode of production, describing at least three forms of property or periods of ownership, which Eric Hobsbawm characterizes as "alternative routes" out of the primitive communal form.[23] They are the Asiatic or Oriental, the ancient (Greece and Rome), and the Germanic-feudal. Along with the modern bourgeois form, they are described by Marx elsewhere as marking "progressive epochs" in the formation of society. These four modes of production, however, do not necessarily form a chronological sequence of development, although the bourgeois form does grow out of the feudal form. They are to be understood, rather, as independent modes, analytically distinct, with their own "laws of motion" and laws of decline. Marx's understanding of Asian society is rooted in his analysis of the Asiatic mode of production.[24]

In all modes of production preceding capitalism, production aims at subsistence of the individual proprietor and his family and the satisfaction of needs, and trade only occurs with the surplus that remains after needs are met. Unlike previous modes, capitalism aims at the production of commodities for exchange and meets needs as a consequence of this production rather than as its direct aim. For the capitalist mode of production to appear, owners of money wealth and means of production, oriented to production of commodities for profit, must encounter owners of "free" labor power in the marketplace, who sell that labor power as a commodity for use by owners of money. For free laborers to emerge, people must be released from the land as their productive workplace, which implies the "dissolution of small, free landed property as well as of communal landownership resting on the oriental commune."[25] For owners of money wealth and means of production to emerge, there must be concentration of wealth and means among individuals disposed to use them for pursuit of profit in commodity production and exchange, and this, too, results from the dissolution of previous modes of production and ownership.

For Marx, the most fundamental form of landed property is found in the Asiatic or Oriental mode of production, grounded in a natural community built around families and clans. In this mode, there is no private ownership of land, and the earth is considered the property of the commune.[26] Indeed, in "most of the Asiatic landforms," Marx says, it is not unusual to find a despot above these communities, who appears as the higher or sole proprietor. In one form of the Asiatic mode, "Oriental despotism," communal agriculture requires the creation of large-scale irrigation through hydraulic works or aqueducts. The climate from the Sahara to India made artificial irrigation by canals and waterworks the very basis of Oriental agriculture. This led to regulation of agriculture by central governments, as in Egypt, India, Persia, and Arab Spain and Sicily.[27] In Oriental despotisms, the state takes the greater part of the social surplus product in its own hands as tribute. This leads to bureaucratization, whose staff are social strata maintained purely by this surplus and constituting the dominant power in society, as in China, India, and Egypt.[28] Thus, in Asia the state is landowner and sovereign at once, with no private landed property, and it can be more despotic or more democratic, depending on whether the higher power is a remote figure, a chief within the clan, or an association of patriarchs.[29]

The Asiatic mode of production is very stable, even static, resisting evolution despite "aimless movements on the political surface," and Marx gives various reasons for this: the concentration of public works in the hands of a strong state, the character of the natural economy, the absence of private property in land, and the fact that self-reproducing villages form a world unto themselves and "vegetate independently alongside one another."[30] While Asiatic states are continually dissolving and being refounded, "the key to the riddle of the unchangeability of Asiatic societies" lies in the simplicity of their productive organization, the union of small-scale agriculture with domestic industry in the household.[31] Indeed, there is no more solid foundation for stagnant Asiatic despotism than the "idyllic republics" of the Indian village. To Marx, "the breaking up of those stereotyped primitive forms was the *sine qua non* for Europeanization. . . . The destruction of their archaic industry was necessary to deprive the villages of their self-supporting character."[32]

In his discussion of European imperialism, Marx focused less on the mode of production than on the interaction of European invaders and native cultures. Indeed, Marx hoped that the disruption of China and India would help to spark revolutions there which would not only change the ancient social systems but also drain European treasuries and cause crises that would shatter the capitalist order. For Marx, the end of the "barbarous and hermetic isolation from the civilized world" of the Asian empires signaled the dissolution of the old mode of production and the social order built upon it. England was using direct political and economic power, technical superiority, and low-priced commodities to destroy the framework and forms of production of Indian society. The sickening destruction and misery inflicted on India by British plunder meant the loss of an ancient civilization and tradition and its hereditary means of subsistence, without establishing a new order.[33] Even so, Marx said, the old mode was so resistant in India and China that the English were succeeding only gradually.[34]

Still, Marx suggested, we must not lose sight of the order being undone, for the destruction of the economic basis of "these small semi-barbarian, semi-civilized communities" has produced "the only social revolution ever heard of in Asia."

> We must not forget that these idyllic village communities, inoffensive though they may appear, had always been the solid foundation of Oriental despotism, that they restrained the human mind within the smallest possible compass, making it the unresisting tool of superstition . . . and rendered murder itself a religious rite. . . . We must not forget that these little communities were contaminated by distinctions of caste and by slavery . . . that they transformed a self-developing social state into never changing natural destiny.[35]

Is this a judgment like Hegel's, or is Marx simply striving to find some good that can come from the inevitable worldwide domination of capital, despite its barbarity?

Marx's attitude toward Asia has some similarities with Hegel's. He deplores the backwardness and degradation of Asian society, along with its fixity and stagnation, because it holds the possibilities of human development in thrall, both materially and culturally. Marx does this because he situates the various modes of production in an historical order that measures them strictly in terms of their advance of human productive powers, and he understands culture only in terms of its reflection of relations of production. Still, Marx acknowledges the integrity and the historical and cultural role of the Asiatic mode as a pre-capitalist form with laws of motion of its own. Though Marx is aware of the "advance" that capitalism marks over more primitive productive modes, he is also aware of the staggering costs in human suffering, costs paid in Europe over centuries and now paid, though more painfully, over decades in Asia. Despite his conviction that Asian culture stifles human development, in his later writings Marx looked more and more for the ways in which Asiatic resistance to Western inroads, formerly disparaged as backwardness, could obstruct the cruel advances of British imperialism. He certainly defended the right and need of the dominated Asian peoples to defend themselves with all means at their disposal, and he exposed the hypocrisy of "the Christianity-canting and civilization-mongering British government" which compelled the growth of opium in Bengal and its sale in China and committed hideous atrocities in its Asian wars, while denouncing the Hindus for their barbarity.[36]

Thus, the picture of the Asian "other" in Marx is complex. On the one hand, Asian civilization is understood in terms of its own mode of production. On the other hand, that mode supported a culture and society of the most backward kind. On the one hand, Asia is a victim of the cruelties and domination of self-interested European imperialism, whose resistance to oppression Marx applauds. On the other hand, the intervention of Europe brings social revolution to Asia. From the perspective of the world economy spawned by capitalism, which advanced human productive powers but was built on exploitation, Marx saw Asian civilization as a stage which would be destroyed inevitably by Western arms, Western trade, and the universalization of the capitalist mode of production. Though this would be, in its way, an advance, it would also mean the loss of a culture that had endured for centuries. From the perspective of an enemy of capitalism and a friend of suffering humanity, Marx saw Asia in terms of the West's effort to make itself the ultimate subject and power of history, and he deplored the costs to the oppressed and defended their resistance. Marx could not confront the cultural structures of Asian society in their own terms because of his assimilation of culture and economy into his own historical system, but he was also unable to confront the cultural structures of the West on any better terms.

Marx was one of the figures of his century most critical of the exploitation of East by West. True, he dealt with the East often as a potential "trigger" for progressive Western developments rather than in terms of its own cultural logic, and he sincerely believed in progress through capitalist development. But he never saw Asians as objects of mere curiosity or scorn. Without racist feeling of any kind, Marx at least confronted the human costs of the worldwide dominion of capitalism without unambiguously endorsing the civilizing powers of the West.

WEBER AND THE STRUCTURE OF
THE ASIAN SELF

In his pursuit of categories adequate for comprehending society, Weber drew on the history and cultural order of every society he could study. Though Weber's works are filled with a knowledge of Asia, it is principally in his works on Asian religion that he provided a sustained analysis of the Orient, having read every available Western source, and revealed a rich portrait of the social and political facts of the East and of the richness, diversity, and cultural meanings to be found there. Though he did not correctly grasp all of the features of the East, he did not "Orientalize" it, several commentators to the contrary.[37] Nor did he conceal his standpoint or his agenda. Indeed, he defended the potential contribution of analyses from totally different standpoints than his own.

Weber did not strive to put Asia into an historical line of any kind. Still, his concern to understand the origins of capitalism led him to examine Asian religions and society in terms of their ability to have advanced indigenous capitalist development or prevented it. To him this meant analyzing the modes of shaping the "person" that Asian religions cultivated, to see if they contained sources of rational capitalist innovation and to evaluate their capacity for "inner-worldly" mastery of the kind generated by ascetic Protestantism. Naturally, there were many aspects of Asian culture that Weber could not appreciate from a search for analogies to the "Occidental personality." We must first understand Weber's conception of the origins of a capitalist spirit in the development of capitalism, and then consider his comparisons of Western "personality formation" with those forms found in Asia.

Weber argued that material conditions alone could not account for the emergence of capitalism in the West. Something more was required at its origins to turn capitalist enterprise into a dominant economic system, for the older "traditionalist" economic order was a formidable barrier to systematic rational innovations. What must have been present, he argued, was a new "spirit" opposed to the traditionalist spirit, a disposition in some individuals to engage in practical rational conduct at a level of intensity that could overcome older ways of pursuing profit. Now that capitalism is dominant, it can shape people to its needs, but at its origin this was not so. Thus, Weber searched for a transformative force, an agent of historical change present in the interstices between two different systems of material life. This was the "spirit of capitalism," an ethos of worldly conduct that helped nascent capitalism struggle against tradition and establish itself, which, he argued, was created by the new saints of Calvinism.

Weber then embarked on a vast comparative project to confirm the importance and uniqueness of the capitalist spirit in the development of capitalism, to see what other cultures might have given birth to capitalism, and to find out why they did not. But in *The Protestant Ethic and the Spirit of Capitalism*, Weber discovered not only the origin of the unique "spirit" of modern capitalism: he discovered as well, he believed, a source of strength that had transformed and fortified the Puritan believer into a hardened "tool" of godly purposes. Weber posited the existence and action of a new type of "character" generated in the Reformation, capable of extraordinary feats of action and innovation, carried on with great intensity and energy.[38] For modern capitalism to have developed as it did, Weber argued, a new kind of *person* must have existed, a person with special qualities and capacities for work, and an inclination for the rationalized labor that capitalism brought with it. It was Calvinism, through its notion of "calling," that created the ascetic Occidental "personality" of the Puritan entrepreneur.

To Weber, being a "personality" means having "an inner core . . . an above all regulated unity of life conduct, deriving from some central point of view of one's own," built on devotion and submissive service to an ideal whose demands must be carried out rationally.[39] Though Weber speaks occasionally of the possibility of "personality" existing elsewhere, specifically in Asia, the "occidental ideal of **actively acting** 'personality', based . . . on a center, be it religious concerning the beyond, be it inner-worldly," is unknown to, and would be disapproved of by, all the religions of Asia.[40]

Of all the world's religions, only ascetic Protestantism created the generalized motivations to seek salvation through exertion in a calling and in sanctified inner-worldly ascetic and profitable work. To Weber, only this unifying discipline, or one just like it, could produce "personality" in the truest sense, and only these personalities, perfected by and acting through a calling, ever helped to create the "spirit of capitalism." No such personalities and no such spirit could have emerged, in Weber's view, from the adaptation to the world of Confucianism, the rejection of the world of Buddhism, the magic garden and traditional vocational ethic of Hinduism, or the desire for rule of the world and feudal enjoyment of Islam.

For Weber, there were four elements that constituted the nature of personality: first, unification and systematization of life on the basis of an ultimate sacred value, usually provided by prophecy; second, ascetic conduct, based on subjugation of the natural self that faith in the value makes necessary but only strength of character makes possible; third, an orientation toward the realization or service of the value in practical action; and fourth, a channeling of human energies and purposes through the discipline of the calling. Weber set the Occidental development of "personality" against models of self and meaning in other religious cultures. The other models were not judged to be "failures" or "negative" when compared to the modern Occident; still, their shortcomings vis-à-vis the Occidental personality and its power and possibilities are manifest everywhere in Weber's work, especially from the point of view of the strength with which they endow adherents for action in the world.

According to Weber, Confucianism, the most important religion of China, does develop the "personality," but in a way totally different from the West. Confucianism was the "status ethic" of a group of officials, possessors of feudal prebends, who were secular and rationalistic. Its ideal was the "gentleman" educated in aesthetics and literature who devoted his life to the study of the classics. Chinese religious development, according to Weber, was determined by the fact that in China there was no supra-mundane God, and "a tension against the 'world' never emerged, because an ethical prophecy of a supra-mundane God posing ethical **demands** was fully missing." "**Never** has the Chinese 'soul' been revolutionized through a prophet." There was, hence, no tension between God and the natural world, between ethical demand and human failing; consequently, there was no leverage for influencing conduct through the generation of "**inner** forces that were not purely traditionally and conventionally bound." Confucian duties always consisted of expressions of piety toward living or dead relatives and ancestors, "never toward a supra-mundane God and **therefore** never toward a holy 'object' or 'idea.' " Thus, the foundation of Occidental personality was missing. "The Confucian was lacking the central rational methodology of life of the classical Puritan, religiously determined from within."[41]

The Confucian ideal was propriety and "the shaping of the self to an all-sided harmoniously balanced personality" through adaptation to the eternal order, wakeful self-control, and the repression of irrational passions. This led not to specialized service in a calling but to a preference for bureaucratic office that would permit the pursuit of well-roundedness. The refined man or gentleman was not a "tool" or a means, but an "end in himself." The Confucian personality was not shaped like the Puritan from the "inside" standing against the world but from the "outside," not from a unified core, but as adaptation to the world. Thus, Confucianism "could not let arise any striving toward unity from within, which we connect with the concept of 'personality.' "[42]

To Weber, then, Confucian personality is "negative" in comparison with Occidental personality because, first, it lacks an overarching transcendental goal, which alone can inspire the individual toward self-transformation "from within"; second, it lacks an ethical tension with the world to motivate the self to conquer itself and the world; and, finally, its ethos calls for "self-perfection" and sees the self as an "end in itself." Whatever else Confucianism accomplished, it could never lead to transformation of the social order, nor allow the development of an inner strength for overcoming the weight of the world and its traditions on behalf of goals posited or defended from within. Thus to Weber, Confucianism was an ethos of readers, not innovators, of beautiful gestures, not actors, of gentlemen, not real "personalities."

Weber saw obstacles to the emergence of personality of the modern Occidental kind in South Asia as well. Buddhism, for example, was the religion of contemplative, mendicant monks who rejected worldly life and treated their followers as laymen. Created by intellectuals, and based on the teachings of an "exemplary" prophet who rejected the world, Buddhism rejected rational purposive activity as leading away from salvation. Indeed, according to Weber, all of the mass religions of Asia accepted the world as eternally given as it was; there was thus no tension and no motive to transform the world in accordance with divine commands. In Buddhism there was no deity, no savior, no prayer, no religious grace, no eternal life, and no predestination. Buddhism sought wakeful self-control of all natural drives and a psychic state free from passion and desire. In Buddhism, as in Puritanism, salvation is a purely personal act of the single individual. Buddhism believes in karma, which Weber describes as "the universal causality of ethical recompense." Despite Buddhism's asceticism and its subjugation of self through the overcoming of desire, "it is not the 'personality,' but the meaning and value of the *single* act" which matters.[43] Thus, the inner core or center of Occidental "personality" is missing in Buddhism. Once again leverage over the world and the self that comes from an ethical prophecy with "demands" is missing.

Hinduism's "carriers," according to Weber, were originally a hereditary caste of genteel and cultured literati, the Brahmans, not unlike the Confucians, whose magical charisma rested on their possession of sacred "knowledge." For Hinduism as for Buddhism, there is an automatic functioning of the ethical process, and no consequences of actions are ever "lost" or unexperienced. At the same time, Hinduism demands ritualistic purity. It has no election by divine grace, and each individual creates his own destiny exclusively. According to Weber, Hinduism provides choice among a variety of possible holy "ends" toward which a believer may strive, and the means appropriate for the religious life depend on which end is sought. Ultimately, however, "knowledge," whether mystical or literary, is the path to the highest holiness and the means of domination over the self and the world. Thus Hinduism seeks the "meaning" and significance of the world and life, rather than leaving such issues to a supra-mundane creator. Despite the emergence of an opposition of the godly and the "worldly"—an opposition that "conditioned" the systematization of life conduct in the Occident, that is, the "ethical personality"—Weber maintained that for the Hindu an " 'inner-worldly' autonomous life methodology of occidental character was . . . not possible."[44]

The notion of salvation through acting to meet the "demands of the day," which Weber considered "the basis of all the specific occidental meaning of 'personality,' " was alien to Hinduism.[45] Nor could Asiatic thought ever associate eternal punishment and rewards with the transitory deeds of this world and the demands of an all-powerful god, despite the significance of life in this world for reincarnation. Thus, though it could be said to have a conception of personality, Hinduism could never give to life on earth the significance, and hence the tension and leverage, that the Occident found in its own notions of the beyond. Nor could the highly ritualized and ceremonial structure of religion lead to the search for a unique individual self of the Occidental type. Indeed, "all asiatic, highly developed intellectual soteriologies would reject the occidental ideal of actively acting 'personality' resting on a center."[46]

However, there was still an important place in Hinduism for "identity" through work. According to Weber, Hindu law had an "organic, traditionalistic ethic of vocation," similar to the medieval Catholic ethic but more consistent. Thus, Hinduism solved the problem of the tension between its demands and the unethical powers of this world through "the relativizing and differentiating of ethics in the form of 'organic' (as opposed to ascetic) *ethics of vocation.*"[47] There were, hence, no absolutely unethical callings in the world. Callings or castes were providentially ordained, and there were different ethical obligations and different functions for each. Further, only devotion to one's calling and remaining in it could guarantee the fulfillment of the Hindu promise of rebirth. The social theory of Hinduism thus elaborated not a universally valid ethic, but a dharma, or law, for each calling, from war to prostitution, and in this was quite opposed to the anti-specialization of Confucianism, but it had no reason to provide principles for an ethical universalism which could raise general demands on the self and the world. Indeed, what grace there was was reserved for those who performed their tasks without regard for results and without personal interest; otherwise, one becomes entangled in the world by desires for success and reaps the bitter fruits of karma. Such an organic ethic does not shape the self for world-transforming tasks undertaken through the strength of personality, but remains an ethic accommodating itself to the world and to the powers that be.

Thus, the Hindu taming of the self did not produce a center within the individual from which action could be undertaken. The self, though controlled and ascetic, was not fortified from within itself to confront the orders of the world and make them over in ethical service of a deity and its commands. Ultimately, the path of knowledge was at best a mode of "possessing" the deity or its secret, rather than of shaping a self for action and service. There is no path here to the "autonomous" life methodology associated with Occidental personality.

Weber did not live long enough to provide an analysis of Islam's orientation toward "self" and "personality" and to determine whether there were elements linking it to Judeo-Christian developments. Still, the slim evidence he provides suggests that Islam did not play a decisive role in the development of personality, despite the fact that it believed in predestination, as did Puritanism, and was partly modeled after Judaism. Islam was essentially feudal in its orientation toward life, work, and the world. It was fundamentally a religion of world-conquering warriors, a stratum of knights who were disciplined crusaders of the faith, and as a religion Islam flourished particularly in wars of faith. Later in its history, contemplative Sufism changed the orientation of popular observance and Islam's cultural orientation. But Islam was never really a religion of salvation in Weber's sense, for its character was essentially political. There was no individual quest for salvation and no mysticism, for its religious promises were for this world. Even predestination concerned events in this world. Thus ascetic control of everyday life or any "planned procedure" was completely alien to it.[48]

Considering the different elements scattered through Weber's discussions of personality, it seems that the generation of personality depends on four fundamental conditions. First, there must be a transcendental-like ultimate goal or value, which gives leverage over the world through the "tension" it creates between the believer and the world. Second, there must be a "witness" to action which is transcendent, seeing the "inner" person, rather than social, seeing the "outer." Third, there must be the possibility of salvation or redemption from death or from the meaninglessness of the world and the possibility of a sense of "certainty" about it. And fourth, there must be no ritual, magical, or external means for relieving one's burden, guilt, or despair. Together, these four conditions anchor the sense of meaning and provide a basis for action. But one or more of them is missing in every case in Asia.

For Weber, then, cognizant of the diversity and complexity of Asian society, politics, and culture, the question was whether Asian culture could have produced a personality of the Occidental type, capable of initiating as fateful a development in the East as was initiated in the West, and the answer was no. But by posing the question this way, Weber was unable to measure what Asian culture was capable of in any other terms. Actually, in this limitation, Weber resembles Hegel and Marx: he is just as blind toward other modes of being, self, and culture in Western religions as he is toward Asia. Methodologically there is some difference between his treatment of Eastern and Western religious cultures, for though Weber grounded his understanding of Protestantism on the study of religious practices more than on texts, his judgments of Asian religious experience and its shaping of the person were based almost solely on texts.[49] Thus, it is not surprising that only ascetic Protestantism emerges whole. The question did not occur to Weber whether other types of personality might generate strength, or whether personalities of the Puritan type and the developments of Western capitalism were so much more preferable than other alternatives, or whether Western forms might not exclude other, possibly richer, human possibilities. Whatever the subtlety of Weber's analyses of Asia, we cannot look to him for a complete picture, for his conviction of the contemporary West's need to generate personalities to assure its continued vitality governed and limited his understanding and appreciation of the East.

Despite the range and profundity of their discussions of Asia, neither Hegel, Marx, nor Weber was fully able to enter into "dialogue" with Asia, though Weber did so much more than the others. Each constructed an Asian "other," which was not comparable to the Western self, without questioning the imperative of comparison and the terms of their representations of the West and the East, or wondering whether the Occidental self and world could benefit and learn from a more equal and open encounter with Asia.

NOTES

1. See Raymond Schwab, *The Oriental Renaissance: Europe's Rediscovery of India and the East, 1680–1880,* trans. Gene Patterson-Black and Victor Reinking (New York: Columbia University Press, 1984). Also Donald Lach, *Asia in the Making of Europe,* vol. 1 (Chicago: University of Chicago Press, 1965).

2. See Edward Said, *Orientalism* (New York: Pantheon, 1978).

3. James Clifford, "Introduction: Partial Truths," in *Writing Culture. The Poetics and Politics of Ethnography,* eds. James Clifford and George E. Marcus (Berkeley: University of California Press, 1986), p. 23.

4. On the difference between the developed consciousness of the West and the East's penetration of the unconscious, see Heinrich Zimmer, "On the Significance of the Indian Tantric Yoga," in *Papers from the Eranos Yearbooks,* vol. 4: *Spiritual Disciplines* (New York: Pantheon Books, 1960), pp. 3–58. Also Zimmer, *The King and The Corpse. Tales of the Soul's Conquest of Evil,* ed. Joseph Campbell (New York: Pantheon Books, 1948).

5. G.W.F. Hegel, *Lectures on the Philosophy of Religion,* 3 vols., trans. Rev. E.B. Speirs and J. Burdon Sanderson, and ed. E.B. Speirs (1895; reprint ed., London: Routledge & Kegan Paul, 1962), 1: pp. 285–86.

6. Hegel, *Hegel's Lectures on the History of Philosophy,* 3 vols., trans. E.S. Haldane and Frances H. Simson (London: Routledge & Kegan Paul, 1894; 1955), 1: 121.6.

7. Hegel, *Philosophy of History,* trans. J. Sibree (New York: Dover, 1956), pp. 65–67.

8. Hegel, *Hegel's Philosophy of Right,* trans. T.M. Know (1952; reprint ed., Oxford: Oxford University Press, 1967), p. 165.

9. John Findlay, *Hegel. A Re-examination* (London, 1958; New York: Oxford University Press, 1976), p. 226.

10. Hegel, *Philosophy of History,* p. 103.

11. Hegel, *Philosophy of History,* p. 109.

12. Hegel, *Lectures on the History of Philosophy,* 2: 123.

13. Hegel, *Philosophy of Right,* pp. 216–23.

14. Hegel, *Philosophy of History,* p. 138; see also *Lectures on the Philosophy of Religion,* 1: 335–49.

15. Hegel, *Lectures on the History of Philosophy,* 1: 124, 146.

16. Hegel, *Lectures on the Philosophy of Religion,* 2: 10, 46–47; *Philosophy of History,* p. 154.

17. Hegel, *Philosophy of History*, pp. 142, 144, 147.

18. On the Near East, see Hegel, *Philosophy of History*, pp. 176–218; *Lectures on the Philosophy of Religion*, 2: 65–122.

19. Hegel, *Philosophy of History*, p. 359. See also *Lectures on the Philosophy of Religion*, 3: 143–44; *Lectures on the History of Philosophy*, 3: 26–35.

20. On Hegel and his critics, see Hannah Arendt, "Tradition and the Modern Age," in Arendt, *Between Past and Future* (New York: Viking, 1961), pp. 17–40; and Karl Löwith, *From Hegel to Nietzsche*, trans. David E. Green (1964; reprint ed., Garden City, NY: Anchor, 1967).

21. Karl Marx, *Capital*, vol. 1, trans. Ben Fowkes (New York: Vintage, 1977), p. 878n. 3.

22. See Karl Wittfogel, *Oriental Despotism: A Comparative Study of Total Power* (New Haven: Yale University Press, 1957).

23. Eric J. Hobsbawm, introduction to Karl Marx, *Pre-Capitalist Economic Formations*, trans. Jack Cohen (New York: International Publishers, 1965), pp. 32–37.

24. See George Lichtheim, "Oriental Despotism," in Lichtheim, *The Concept of Ideology and other Essays* (New York: Random House, 1967), pp. 62–93; Daniel Thorner, "Marx on India and the Asiatic Mode of Production," in Thorner, *The Shaping of Modern India* (New Delhi: Allied Publishers Private Limited, 1980), pp. 349–82; and "Asiatic Society," in *A Dictionary of Marxist Thought*, ed. Tom Bottomore, Laurence Harris, V.G. Kiernan, and Ralph Miliband (Cambridge: Harvard University Press, 1983).

25. Marx, *Grundrisse*, trans. Martin Nicolaus (New York: Vintage, 1973), p. 471.

26. Marx, *Grundrisse*, p. 473.

27. See Marx, "The British Rule in India," in Karl Marx and Friedrich Engels, *On Colonialism* (New York: International Publishers, 1972), p. 37; *Capital*, 1: 649.

28. See Marx, *Capital*, 1: 650n. 7.

29. Marx, *Capital*, vol. 3, trans. David Fernbach (New York: Vintage, 1981), p. 927.

30. Letter of Marx to Engels, 6–14–53, in Marx and Engels, *On Colonialism*, p. 315; Marx, *Capital*, 3: 927, 932. See also "The British Rule in India," p. 39.

31. Marx, *Capital*, 1: 477–79; *Capital*, 3: 451, 922; "The Anglo-Chinese Treaty," in Marx and Engels, *On Colonialism*, p. 255.

32. Letter of Marx to Engels, 6–14–53, in Marx and Engels, *On Colonialism*, pp. 315–16.

33. Marx, "The British Rule in India," in Marx and Engels, *On Colonialism*, pp. 37, 40; and *Capital*, 1: 917.

34. Marx, *Capital*, 3: 451–52.

35. Marx, "The British Rule in India," in Marx and Engels, *On Colonialism*, pp. 40–41. See also Marx, *Capital*, 1: 459–60.

36. Marx, "The Opium Trade," in Marx and Engels, *On Colonialism*, p. 219.

37. See Said, *Orientalism*, p. 259, 350. Said unfortunately bases his judgment on Maxime Rodinson, *Islam and Capitalism*, trans. Brian Pearce (London: Penguin Books, 1973). Rodinson totally misunderstands Weber and Weber's comparative project.

38. Weber, *The Protestant Ethic and the Spirit of Capitalism*, trans. Talcott Parsons (New York: Scribners, 1958), p. 69. On the Protestant ethic and on Weber's views of Asia, see Harvey Goldman, *Max Weber and Thomas Mann: Calling and the Shaping of the Self* (Berkeley: University of California Press, 1988); also Benjamin Nelson, "On Orient and Occident in Max Weber," *Social Research* 43 (1976): 114–29.

39. Weber, *Economy and Society*, ed. Guenther Roth and Claus Wittich (Berkeley: University of California Press, 1978), pp. 560–63; Weber, *The Religion of India: The Sociology of Hinduism and Buddhism*, trans. and ed. Hans H. Gerth and Don Martindale (New York: The Free Press, 1958), pp. 336–37.

40. Weber, *Religion of India*, pp. 338–39.

41. Weber, *From Max Weber*, p. 268; Weber, *Religion of China*, pp. 229, 142, 236, 243.

42. Weber, *Economy and Society*, p. 1049; *Religion of China*, pp. 156, 160, 235, 243–44. See also Thomas Metzger, *Escape from Predicament: Neo-Confucianism and China's Evolving Political Culture* (New York: Columbia University Press, 1977); Wm. Theodore de Bary, "Introduction" and "Neo-Confucian Cultivation and the Seventeenth-Century Enlightenment," in de Bary et al., *The Unfolding of Neo-Confucianism* (New York: Columbia University Press, 1975), pp. 1–36, 141–214; Mark Elvin, "Why China Failed to Create an Endogenous Industrial Capitalism: A Critique of Max Weber's Explanation," *Theory and Society* 13 (1984): 379–91.

43. Weber, *Religion of India*, pp. 206–7, 213. See also *From Max Weber*, p. 269; *Economy and Society*, pp. 627–29.

44. Weber, *Religion of India*, p. 314.

45. Weber, *Religion of India*, p. 342.

46. Weber, *Religion of India*, p. 339.

47. Weber, *Economy and Society*, pp. 598, 599.

48. Weber, *From Max Weber*, p. 269; *Economy and Society*, pp. 574, 623–27. See also Bryan Turner, *Weber and Islam: A Critical Study* (London: Routledge and Kegan Paul, 1974).

49. I owe this particular observation to Prof. Philip Oldenburg, Columbia University.

THE RISE AND FALL OF WESTERN EMPIRE IN ASIA: 1500-1975

Edward Malefakis

Western empires in Asia are far more difficult to deal with than are those in the Americas or Africa. It is hard to decide even from when to date them. In Central and South America, the Spanish empire was established extremely rapidly: in less than two decades, from Cortes' arrival in Mexico in 1519 to Pizzaro's overthrow of the Inca state in Peru in 1535, the conquest of the continent had been substantially consolidated. In Africa, the process was somewhat more prolonged, but it also was mostly concentrated into two decades, the 1880s and 1890s. Although there was a continuous Western presence in Asia from Vasco da Gama's voyage in 1498 onward, the West did not control any substantial portion of the Asian mainland until nearly three centuries later, nor would European empires truly dominate Asia as a whole until almost four centuries had passed.

The main reason for this extremely lengthy process of imperial penetration is clear. Asia, unlike Africa or the Americas, was a world of highly articulated societies, with strong state systems commanding well-organized military forces and, in many areas, with populations far denser than those of Europe. Most Asian societies were secure in their identities and traditions because of their long-established urban centers and their highly developed literary and religious cultures. Their economies for the most part either equaled or were superior to those of the West in the sixteenth and seventeenth centuries; the West could claim superiority only in maritime technology. Thus, initially Europeans limited their activities to creating a network of trading posts and fortresses on the fringes of the continent, either on islands or along sectors of the coast where the conditions described above did not prevail and where the European maritime advantage could have the greatest impact.

The Portuguese were the first to establish such an "empire" when, between 1509 and 1515, they conquered a string of outposts from Ormuz to Malacca and asserted their maritime supremacy by sweeping from the seas the Arab merchants who had previously dominated trade. They were followed by the Spaniards, who in the 1570s began to take control of the Philippine Islands. Around 1600, the English and Dutch both organized East India companies and sent ships to Asian waters. But by this time, the limits of the easily conquerable Asian territories had been reached and most of the struggle of the next half-century was not of Europeans against Asians, but of Europeans among themselves for control of the marginal coastal areas or islands belonging to their rivals. By 1650 the Dutch had gained supremacy over the English and the Portuguese. With several critical areas of the Malayan archipelago and Ceylon under their control, the Dutch established the most significant—though still very limited—European empire in Asia. Second in importance was perhaps Spain's continued dominance over the Philippines. Of lesser significance were the few possessions retained by the English, French, and Portuguese on the coast of the Indian subcontinent. By the mid-seventeenth century, after 150 years of activity, the Europeans probably had not established as strong a presence on the Asian mainland as had, for example, the Crusaders in the Middle East during the twelfth century.

The chief reason for the slightness of Western penetration has already been mentioned: the demographic, cultural, economic, and political strength of the indigenous societies throughout most of Asia. There were other reasons as well. It was easier for the English, French, and Portuguese to concentrate their activities in the Atlantic basin than to engage in more distant Asian adventures. The Spaniards maintained their presence in the Philippines more indirectly, via voyages from their colony in Mexico, than directly, from the Iberian Peninsula itself. The Dutch alone devoted most of their resources to their Asian empire, in large part because while they had been winning the early seventeenth-century struggle for control of the East Indies, they had been losing the struggle in the Atlantic basin. The Portuguese lost to the Dutch in Malacca, but won over them in Brazil; the English were driven out of Amboina, but forty years later ousted their Dutch rivals from New York.

Nor was economic enticement sufficient to warrant herculean efforts on Europe's part. The relative significance of the spice trade, which had been the single most important economic impetus to Europe's entry into Asia, was gradually reduced by the great gold and silver discoveries of the mid-sixteenth to early seventeenth centuries in South America, bonanzas that were repeated, this time with the diamonds of Brazil added, in the eighteenth century. More continuous in its effects was the sugar boom that transformed the Caribbean area and northeastern Brazil from the early seventeenth century onward. Still other activities— furs and tobacco in North America and the slave trade from Africa—further energized the economy of the Atlantic basin in the latter part of the century. As against these, spices, fine textiles, porcelain, and the few other items in which Europe traded with Asia, while valuable, were of diminishing importance. In short, Portugal, France, and England found themselves coming around to a situation similar to the one Spain had been in from the start: their American empire, with its African slave corollary, was of greater consequence to them economically and politically than was their Asian presence. Only for the Dutch, and only after the 1660s, when they were driven out of the Americas, did Asia remain of paramount concern.

For the Asians as well, until 1700, or even 1750, the European presence had been significant but secondary. Probably the least important aspect of that presence, ironically, was its most directly imperial one—the hegemony that first the Portuguese and then the Dutch achieved in the Malayan archipelago. Although this was a large area, it was in a relatively isolated corner of that immense totality known as Asia. Moreover, the Europeans by no means controlled the entire archipelago; hundreds of indigenous political or social units co-existed with them. More generally important for the Asians, perhaps, was the predominance that Europeans established in the inter-Asian oceanic carrying trade; by bringing a new level of maritime activity, the Portuguese, Dutch, and Spanish increased commerce among various parts of Asia. But this too was fairly limited and short-lived: China felt no great need for foreign trade, and Japan deliberately banned it after 1640.

An inverse correlation holds: the most significant aspects of the European presence in Asia prior to the eighteenth century were the least directly imperial ones. The continuous presence of Jesuit savants in Peking from the 1580s onward brought a flow of European thought to Ming and then Manchu court circles, although the ideas transmitted were not necessarily representative of the best Europe had to offer, nor were they received with as much seriousness as they deserved, the exotic elements in them attracting more attention than the substantial. Far and away the most important impact the West had on Asia prior to 1750 was an unconscious and indirect one. This was the introduction of American food crops, especially corn, sweet potatoes, and peanuts, into the Asian diet, which seem to have contributed to dramatic growth in the population of Manchu (Qing) China. Also significant was the New World silver with which the Europeans, lacking products that Asians wanted to purchase, paid for much of their trade. This too was an economic stimulus in China, and contributed to the prosperity that nation enjoyed during the eighteenth century.

All in all, European influence was not decisive in any of the great Asian states prior to 1750. Paradoxically, the society where, very briefly, it came closest to being critical was the one that would later prove most resistant to Western control. The possibility of a strong European presence in Japan manifested itself in the late sixteenth century both through sporadic intervention in its fierce civil wars and through the astonishingly rapid and numerous conversions to Christianity that took place. This potential was never realized, however: Japan was then at the extreme periphery of Europe's Asian interests, and the civil wars that gave Westerners an opening were suddenly ended after 1600 by the highly absolutist Tokugawa shogunate. Within four decades, Christianity had been all but eradicated in Japan and other traces of Western presence or commerce had been eliminated except for the minuscule Dutch trading outpost that was allowed to remain at Nagasaki. No similar potential for Western penetration in a major Asian society would appear for another century.

For the first quarter-millennium of the European presence in Asia, then, from 1498 to the 1750s, it is reasonable to speak of Western empires in Asia only if we remember that they were small-scale units which controlled tiny areas. Three major new sets of circumstances combined to alter this situation in the mid-eighteenth century. The most decisive perhaps was the collapse and rapid disintegration of the Mughal Empire in India, especially after the 1720s. No match for the Mughal Empire during its 180 years (1526–1707) of unity, the small European coastal enclaves suddenly acquired great importance in the new Indian political constellation of dozens of indigenous state units competing against each other and against the waning Mughal power.

Moreover, two of the European powers which maintained outposts in India, France and England, had become enormously more powerful in every way—politically, militarily, economically—than they had been when they first arrived in the early 1600s. Less internally divided by religious and political conflicts, much wealthier and more populous, they were now, for the first time, strong enough to act simultaneously in widely separated parts of the globe. This was proven during the Seven Years' War of 1756–63, the first "world war" in history, when the French and English fought one another in Europe, North America, the Caribbean, and the Philippines, as well as in India. It was in India that England's victory was most decisive, permanently weakening the French and establishing its own enclaves as the most dynamic and expansive force on the subcontinent.

The third set of circumstances was the great European economic boom of the 1730s onward, which preceded but would eventually merge into the early stages of the industrial revolution. American products were still favored, but the growth in European demand also gave new openings to Asian products, above all to Indian cottons, tea from China, and coffee from Java. The gap between the relative economic importance of the Atlantic basin and of Asia therefore diminished, and more considerable economic motivations for Western intervention in Asia appeared than had existed since the early seventeenth century.

These three factors combined to raise the possibility of an abrupt expansion of Western empire in Asia. But no such expansion occurred for another century. The massive struggle within Europe from 1793 to 1815 unleashed by the French Revolution and the Napoleonic Wars absorbed European attentions and left only one power active on the Asian scene, England. That power was satiated after 1815 with the commercial opportunities that arose because of its precocious industrialization, and with the contemporaneous opening of vast new markets in Latin America following the collapse of the Spanish and Portuguese empires there. Moreover, the English were now paradoxically becoming more convinced than any European state had been since the sixteenth century of the drawbacks of empire. To be sure, this new attitude did not prevent the constant expansion of their Indian strongholds, or their seizure of part of Burma in the 1820s. Nor did it stop them from intervening in Asian affairs when they deemed this vital to their interests. Nor, finally, did the English desist from engaging in "free trade imperialism," the achievement of their economic objectives without establishing continuous political dominion over a society. The most dramatic example of such imperialism was probably the war they launched in 1839–42 to prevent China from banning opium imports from India.

Nevertheless, it must be recognized that economic liberalism also helped prevent the English from systematically seeking to expand their empire; most of their commercial goals could be met without actually governing Asia, and no other power seriously threatened their position there (though England, with the paranoia characteristic of most great powers, sometimes suspected they did). Even in India they never had a grand plan for conquest; rather, one local pressure or temptation after another led England gradually to take over most of the center and south of the subcontinent between the 1760s and the 1830s. The northwestern regions—the Punjab and the areas bordering Afghanistan—proved more difficult, but in a series of wars in the 1840s they too were subdued.

Thus, although the signs were already clear by the 1840s, the truly effective start of Western empires in Asia, outside of India, should probably be dated from no earlier than the mid-1850s. A number of factors combined to inaugurate the new stage. Most important was the cumulative technological transformation of Europe that had been taking place, especially during the previous two decades. Industrialization had passed from an age of textiles to one of iron, with railroads, steamships, heavier cannons, and breech-loading rifles following. Moreover, industrialization had spread to continental Europe and to North America as well. New political factors were nearly as important. The French will to glory, subdued from 1815 to 1851, was revived by Napoleon III. The never-absent Russian drive eastward escalated to compensate for the check Russia had suffered in the west during the Crimean War of 1853–56. Above all, as a culmination of the gradual disintegration of Manchu rule since the turn of the century, China fell into civil war of epochal proportions with the Taiping Rebellion of 1850–64 and the several lesser regional and ethnic revolts it sparked.

What proved to be a dramatic cluster of events began with the "opening" of Japan in 1853 by the Americans under Commodore Perry, just ahead of the Russians and the English. Four years later the "Sepoy Mutiny," a volcanic succession of military mutinies, popular uprisings, and elite revolts, seriously endangered the English position on the Indian subcontinent for the first time. England not only hung on, however, but, together with France, had enough Asian resources to seize Guangzhou in China in

December 1857. In 1858 the French widened their reentry into Asia (how well Napoleon III's Crimean War alliance with Britain had paid off for him!) with an expedition to what later became Indochina. During the same year Russia took advantage of China's disarray by pressing treaty concessions in northeastern Manchuria. The decade ended with the second Anglo-French War against China, as Beijing was seized and the Summer Palace burned in 1860. Along the way, the second Anglo-Burmese War occurred in 1852–53, the "opening" of Siam took place in 1855, a brief but important Anglo-Persian conflict erupted in 1856, and the Dutch started their expansion from Java to Sumatra, the Celebes, and Borneo between 1856 and 1859. Asia had now been penetrated on all sides by several Western powers.

What was decisively begun in the 1850s would be completed in the 1880s and 1890s. Still further European technological might had been accumulated, higher standards of organization and discipline characterized Western military forces, and British control over their Indian army had been made more secure after the Sepoy Mutiny of 1857. Hence punitive actions that were already militarily simple in the 1850s had become almost absurdly easy and cheap by the 1880s. Other factors also contributed to imperial expansion. The new ideologies of social Darwinism and racism lessened the moral compunctions against colonial war that Europeans might still have been felt at mid-century. The "scramble for Africa" also stimulated imperial rivalries in Asia. Increased demand for certain Asian products (jute, tin, rubber) made it more vital to control the territories that produced them. The reversal after the 1870s of the movement toward free trade, and the growth of trade restrictions worldwide, caused each European power to place a greater premium on maintaining colonies, where its goods could not be denied entry through stiff tariffs.

Within this context of greater military strength, greater contempt for the Asians, and greater fear of potential European rivals, the British and French completed their conquests of Burma and Vietnam, respectively, in the 1880s. The absorption of Cambodia and Laos by the French, the Malayan Peninsula by the British, and the rest of the East Indies by the Dutch was mostly accomplished in the 1890s; the century ended with the scramble for territorial concessions over important portions of China by all the great powers, including a major new actor, Germany. The culmination of it all was the Boxer Rebellion of 1900. This never approached the scale of the 1857 rising in India, and did not seriously inconvenience the European powers: indeed, it merely gave them a new pretext for further demands, and resulted in Russia's occupation of Manchuria. Nevertheless, it probably reflected a considerably more unanimous anti-Western feeling among the indigenous population than had the Indian upheaval.

The establishment of Western empires in Asia was therefore quite different from what it had been in the Americas or Africa. They did not arise *ex novo* to the same extent, but had been preceded by centuries of non-imperial contact; and once established, they were far more heterogeneous and incomplete than in the other two continents. Only in Java, Burma, the more heavily populated parts of India, and Russian central Asia was as direct a political dominion established as that of the Spaniards and Portuguese in America or of several European powers in sub-Saharan Africa. In the greater part of India and in much of Southeast Asia, colonial rule was indirect, mediated by native princes who nominally retained a few attributes of sovereignty. Or, as in certain coastal regions of China, especially in the post-"Boxer" period, control was exercised on a theoretically temporary basis, under "lease" or "concession" arrangements. Finally, huge areas of Asia—Afghanistan, Persia, the Ottoman Empire, Siam, most of China—nominally retained full sovereignty, despite the extraterritorial status they were obliged to grant resident Europeans, and notwithstanding the profound influence European powers exerted over most of their policies. Japan also fell into this last category until the mid-1890s (and in some senses even until 1899, when extraterritoriality was rescinded), but it thereafter accentuated the heterogeneity of the Asian scene by establishing full independence, in reality as well as in name.

The varieties of the European experience in Asia in part reflected the immensity of the continent, which is really five continents—West, Central, South, Southeast, and East—and the differing natures of the precolonial societies. That the Europeans had been able to establish dominion over them to the extent they did reflected the huge technological gap that had become manifest by the 1840s, and the exceptional internal political instability that emasculated India during the eighteenth century and China during the nineteenth. It also reflected European ability to exploit the divisions that existed among Asians; during the long preimperial contact, Europeans gained detailed knowledge about their societies and greater access to dissident groups among them.

Some of the rivalries the Europeans exploited were of one state against another. This was especially true in the Indian subcontinent after the Mughal breakup, but also on India's northwestern fringes (Afghanistan vs. Persia vs. various northwestern Indian states) and in Southeast Asia (Burma vs. Siam vs. Cambodia vs. Vietnam, not to speak of the myriad rivalries among the states of the Malayan peninsula and archipelago). Only in East Asia—because of China's overarching hegemony so long as it remained united, and Japan's policy of isolation during the Tokugawa era—was exploitation of interstate rivalries a minor factor in the growth of European empire. More frequent still were struggles within a given state, whether religious, ethnic, regional, or social in nature. In religious divisions, the Indian subcontinent again is the preeminent example, but shares the frequency of ethnic and regional conflicts with Southeast Asia and—particularly during the great rebellions of the 1850s and 1860s—with China. Social tensions existed everywhere, some having arisen as a result of the earlier European presence: the comprador groups in Canton, and the zamindar landowners in Bengal were particular sources of tension. But most of the difficulties long antedated European contact and stemmed from the social inequalities that characterized almost all complex societies at the time, Asian perhaps even more than European.

Finally, the Europeans could create their own Asian instruments of rule. Aside from the native princes who became dependent on them and the native armies with which they often allied, the forces of coercion under direct European control ended up being composed mostly of Asians. This too was not unusual, and had its counterpart in other conquered territories. Without precedent or later parallel, however, was the Indian army, the most powerful in Asia until the Japanese army surpassed it in the 1890s and, along with the European naval forces, the chief striking force during the main stages of the conquest of Asia. A litany of the places in which the Indian army intervened (usually more than once) tells the tale: Persia, Afghanistan, Burma, Malaysia, and China in Asia; Ethiopia, Egypt, Nyasa, Sudan, and Uganda in Africa. All this for British purposes and at no cost to the British taxpayer, since the army was supported by revenues extracted from India. That this instrument could be dangerous was demonstrated by the great Sepoy Mutiny; but once that rebellion had been crushed (mostly by other Indian forces), the Indian army was honed to a high degree of reliability and utility.

The cultural impact of Western imperialism on Asia varied as much as did the specific forms of Western influence and rule. In only one region, the Philippines, did the ruling power—Spain—attempt to impose its religion and cultural values more or less completely. Despite their almost equally long presence in the Indonesian archipelago, the Dutch sought political and commercial, not cultural, hegemony. Something similar might be said for the British and French enclaves established on the coast of India in the seventeenth century. Only in the 1820s and 1830s would the British consciously set out to reform Indian culture, and even this effort, inspired by the utilitarian liberalism that waxed strong in England itself during the period, proved brief. Sati, the burning of Hindu widows on the funeral pyres of their husbands, and other antihumanitarian rituals were prohibited; the Education Act was initiated; English was made an official language. But even these measures were a far cry from the degree of cultural imperialism imposed earlier by Europeans on the Americas, for example.

Individual Westerners who gained access to Asia through imperialism were, of course, culturally more aggressive. By far the most important among them were the Christianizing missions, which existed in all Asian nations in the nineteenth century. For the most part, however, attempts to introduce Christianity were met with extreme local hostility that frequently served, especially in China and Vietnam, as a catalyst for anti-Western disturbances and then for further foreign intervention. Paradoxically, the nation that would end up becoming the most Christianized in Asia except for the Philippines was Korea, the "hermit kingdom" which had been least subject to the impact of the West, directly or indirectly.

More significant as an instrument of cultural change was the inherent appeal of Western secular culture. To some extent its attractiveness to Asians, especially the Chinese, lay in its apparent link to Western political and economic strength, but the ideals of inherent human rights and of social and political equality, the questioning of long-standing religious and secular traditions, also appealed to many Asians. Acceptance of Western values started earliest and went deepest in India, primarily due to the lengthy British presence in Bengal, but also due to the variegated nature of Hindu philosophy and its relative indifference to social and political phenomena, which helped make the new ideas more intellectually tolerable.

Newspapers, journals, institutions of higher learning, a literary movement dynamic enough to be named the Hindu Renaissance, and a notable intellectual reformer, Ram Mohun Roy, had all made their appearance in Bengal by the 1830s; in the 1850s a more adequate institutional framework of primary, secondary, and university education began to take shape. Thus, as imperialism was seriously getting under way in the rest of Asia, a Westernized elite had already arisen in Hindu India.

Its equivalent among India's Muslims would be long delayed. Both in India and elsewhere, peoples of an Islamic tradition would prove singularly resistant to Western cultural influence, whatever their ethnicity. The reasons for this are uncertain, but probably relate to the unique linkage of religious with secular life in the Islamic religion.

In China, the reasons for the failure of Western culture to penetrate more deeply stemmed primarily from the extraordinary power acquired by the elites over the centuries within the context of a cohesive Confucian worldview. Strongly blending ethical with social and political values, and bringing to the whole exceptionally detailed institutional and behavioral articulation, the Confucian mental order enjoyed a prestige that even the colossal disasters, internal and external, that befell China in the 1840s and 1850s could not entirely shake. The "self-strengthening" movements which began in the 1860s permitted only the most superficial and begrudging exploration of Western values. Chinese reluctance to change would not begin to be effectively overcome until half a century later, after China had endured new military humiliations first by the French, then by the Japanese, then (in 1900, in response to the Boxer Rebellion) by an international force which included all the European powers plus Japan. Only in 1905 did China initiate a major effort to reform education and send students abroad to study modern forms of knowledge.

Most of these students went to Japan, the recent enemy which had nevertheless gained great stature by successfully modernizing itself and by defeating a European giant, Russia, on both land and sea. Japan is the great exception in the Asian equation. Several other nations—Siam, Persia, the Ottoman Empire, Ethiopia—had been able to preserve limited independence within a colonial context. But none had managed to convert their precarious autonomy into full equality, much less to do so within the brief space of four decades. To some extent, Japanese exceptionalism is explicable by fortunate geographical and temporal circumstances. On the fringe of Asia, Japan had neither natural resources nor so large a population as to arouse serious Western covetousness. And during the fifteen years from 1853 to 1868, when Japan was still struggling toward a cohesive response to foreign intrusion, it was fortunate in that Western attentions were diverted by the Crimean War, the Indian rebellion, the wars in China, and the American Civil War.

But Japan's true uniqueness was internal. Homogeneous ethnically and culturally, it nevertheless maintained a very fruitful ambiguity in its political relationships. This ambiguity both permitted strong regional networks of power to exist within a highly centralized state and allowed an emperor who had not exercised effective rule for the better part of a millennium to retain a latent legitimacy. Ambiguity and complexity also characterized the Japanese social ethic, which combined a stress on such military values as discipline, decisive action, and fierce loyalty with an equally important emphasis on learning and a cultivated life. The sword was crossed with the chrysanthemum in a manner unparalleled in any other society, East or West. This combination proved apt for the new circumstances that confronted Japan, giving it cohesiveness without rigidity. There were moments when the synthesis was in danger of breaking down, of course, especially with the internal split among the original reformers that led to the Satsuma rebellion of 1877. But, generally speaking, triumph followed triumph in a highly systematic way.

During the 1870s and 1880s Japan focused on internal change: abolition of feudalism, creation of a modern army and navy, industrialization, promulgation of legal codes, educational reform, the appearance of a modern press, modernization of the administrative structure, adoption of a constitution. By the 1890s, it was strong enough to humiliate China in the 1894–95 Sino-Japanese War, and to induce the Western powers to accept the abolition of extraterritoriality. In the first decade of the twentieth century, Japan would deploy one of the world's most powerful navies; sign a full-scale treaty of alliance with England, the first Asian power to enter an agreement with a European power as an equal; decisively defeat Russia in the Russo-Japanese War of 1904–05; and annex Korea. Having already taken Formosa and the Pescadores from China in 1895, Japan in effect created in two decades an Asian empire almost comparable in population and resources to any of the European empires except that of England. And it joined those powers in the incipient partition of China by assuming a "lease" over the Liaodong Peninsula and by reaching agreements with Russia on "spheres of influence" in Manchuria.

Although few realized it at the time, the abrupt rise of Japan spelled the beginning of the end for European empires in Asia. This was true for two reasons. Japan's rise coincided with the unraveling of the long-lasting and highly unusual web of circumstances that had made the nineteenth by far the most peaceful century in Europe's history. Japan remained weaker on a world level than Britain, France, or Germany, but it was as strong as any of them locally once growing rivalries required the European powers to concentrate massive forces in their home continent. It was a precocious recognition of this shift in the regional and world balances of power that prompted the British to ally with Japan in 1902. Geographical proximity, shortness of supply lines, a strong one-ocean navy, the sympathy toward fellow non-Europeans that existed among many Asians—all these made Japan a formidable opponent within Asia, as Russia and later the United States would learn.

Almost as important was Japan's role in stimulating Asian nationalism. In China and in colonial Korea the stimulus was mostly negative. Perhaps humiliation by neighbors which had always been considered inferior was the straw that finally tipped the balance against the Confucian worldview that had for so long held sway in China. After China's defeat in the Sino-Japanese War of 1894–95, radicals among its intelligentsia launched the reform effort that would all too quickly be cut down by the empress dowager in 1898. But in Asia as a whole the stimulus to nationalism provided by the Japanese example was primarily positive, especially in those regions too distant from Japan to have suffered from its imperialistic policies. This was true to some extent even among the Chinese. As stated earlier, Chinese students began to flock to Japan after 1905, and the new revolutionary organizations that would eventually overthrow the Manchu dynasty were created there.

In other ways as well, 1905 was a turning point. From the beginning of the year, Russia was shaken by the fiercest revolution it had ever experienced. The Marxian socialist ideas that gathered strength during that revolution would begin to take hold elsewhere also, and in countries where they could be cross-fertilized by anticolonial sentiments. But Marxism was not a necessary ingredient in the new ferment in Asia. For example, Bengal was in upheaval throughout 1905, as antipartition protest, both popular and elite, swept the region and gave extremist elements in the Congress movement greater weight than before. Not since 1857 had British rule in India experienced such determined opposition. The year 1905 also witnessed the first major Persian revolution; together with the revolutionary events in Russia and Japan's victory in the Russo-Japanese War, this would help inspire a modernizing effort among army officers in the Ottoman Empire and lead to the Young Turk revolt of 1908.

Profound stirrings were occurring in many places. Not all of them were related to the Japanese stimulus, of course. In India, for example, nationalism had been growing since the 1880s and had already passed through a brief extremist phase in the mid-1890s. But Japan was a major catalyst. Perhaps its impact is best revealed not in Asia but in distant Greece. Militarily humiliated in a war with Turkey in 1897, politically humiliated by being forced to accept foreign control boards during the financial crisis of the early 1900s, many Greeks sought radical solutions to their plight. After 1905 the group of young politicians who advocated a drastic restructuring of their country through greater discipline, rapid industrialization, and military modernization came to be called . . . what else but "the Japanese faction"?

The process of decomposition in Europe's Asian presence begun in 1905 would be sharply accelerated between 1914 and 1918, when Europe reverted to its old traditions of internecine warfare; at war's end two imperial powers, Germany and Russia, ceased to be active in Asia. Superficially, the British and French empires seemed unaffected; indeed, they actually increased in size as the collapse of the Ottoman state enabled them to add Palestine, Syria, and Iraq to their holdings.

Nevertheless, European imperialism had suffered a severe blow from which it would never recover. Like shock victims the extent of whose injuries are not immediately apparent, France and especially England would experience a sometimes ebullient sense of confidence in the 1920s. But in the 1930s war-caused trauma set in, and the will to action was further paralyzed by the Great Depression and by the reemergence of the German danger at home. The consequence was that in Asia the European colonial powers in large part ceased to act as such during the interwar period. They no longer played any role in China, either during its civil wars of the 1920s or after the Japanese seized Manchuria in 1931 and then invaded China itself in 1937. Inertia, together with a willingness to allow greater participation by the indigenous elites in governmental affairs, also marked European colonial policies in India, the East Indies, and even Indochina.

These concessions were no longer sufficient to satisfy Asian nationalism, which had been stimulated on all sides by war-related events. Well over a million native troops and laborers returned home to India and Vietnam from the fronts in Europe, the Middle East, and East Africa to which their colonial masters had sent them. Wartime economic booms had created new elites and greater social ferment in India, and to a lesser extent in Malaysia and the Dutch East Indies. To maintain order in their colonies,

European governments had made promises of fundamental post-war changes which they were now reluctant to keep. In 1917, after the Bolshevik Revolution, Russia broke European ranks, strenuously denounced Western imperialism, and called on Eastern peoples to rise up against it. Led by Wilsonian idealism, the United States also questioned the legitimacy of imperialism and encouraged dreams of national self-determination. When few of the hopes aroused were in fact satisfied at war's end, movements of protest proliferated which led to repression and sometimes to brutality—as in the Amritsar massacre of 1919—that weakened still further whatever tenuous bonds of trust had survived between ruler and ruled.

In three Asian nations, nationalism assumed especially imposing proportions after the First World War. It was most effective in Turkey, where between 1919 and 1922 Kemal Atatürk led a revolt against the harsh European peace terms imposed by the Treaty of Sèvres. His victories prevented the Asia Minor peninsula from being politically fragmented, as the rest of the Ottoman Empire had been, and permitted him to create the first aggressively secular state in the history of Islam.

Nationalism was perhaps most widespread in China, where the chaos of the republic established by the 1911 revolution against the Manchu dynasty opened doors to every political faction. But with the collapse of Russian and German imperialism and the weakening of the English and French presence, Chinese protest became focused almost exclusively against Japan, which had taken advantage of the power vacuum in East Asia by insisting, for example, that it assume Germany's concession of Shandong province. Participation in the anti-Japanese boycott riots of 1919 would be the first major political act of future revolutionary leaders like Mao Zedong. The outbreak in Korea, known as the March 1st Incident of 1919, marked a similar watershed for anti-Japanese Korean nationalism.

The new nationalism in India was the most complex. With Gandhi's emergence as a leader during the war, it reached the masses to a greater extent than before; the tactics of non-violent civil disobedience he developed were peculiarly effective in morally disarming the British and touching world opinion. Revolutionary extremism also shed its earlier religious guise and became a more secular movement, headed by Subhas Bose. Finally, India's Muslims also began to organize more seriously under M.A. Jinnah, as much against the Hindus as the British. The result was a multisided conflict that grew steadily over the next two decades.

Everything militated against the Europeans: the new fragility of their home continent, the increasingly obvious contradiction between colonialism and the more democratic values the 1914–18 war had engendered among them, their diminished monopoly of modern knowledge and culture with the rise of new Asian elites (Tagore was the first Asian to win a Nobel Prize, in 1913), their increased dependence on such elites for the functioning of the colonial economies and administrations, the demographic balance, which after 1930 began to swing ever more decisively against them. Europe was already on the defensive when the Japanese invaded Manchuria in 1931 and inaugurated the great Asian crisis that would continue for the next two decades, and in some senses until 1975, when the United States finally accepted its loss of control over South Vietnam.

In this crisis Europeans would be relatively minor actors: their paralysis in the face of Japanese aggression against China was a prelude to their appeasement of nazism and fascism in Europe. During World War II, the Vichy government permitted the Japanese to occupy Indochina before general hostilities began, the Dutch were impotent against Japan's invasion of the East Indies in December 1941, and in Singapore in 1942 the British suffered one of the most humiliating military defeats in their long history. The British would recover some of their lost credit by their tenacious struggle against the Japanese in Burma, and by stopping the "Free India" army of Bose as it invaded Bengal in the hope of stimulating a general Indian revolt against them. But for the French and the Dutch the humiliation suffered was total and without redemption.

In the postwar era, the British never seriously contemplated trying to retain direct control of India or Burma; by 1956, after years of low-grade guerrilla conflict, they came to see the wisdom of granting independence to the Malaysian states as well. The Dutch tried to swim against the current in Indonesia, only to be forced to admit defeat in 1949. For the French, the agony of decolonization was still more costly; not until a major war had been fought and lost in Vietnam would they agree to leave in 1954. In short, from 1931 onward, the European powers wandered about the Asian stage as ghosts, still present, but in shadowy form. During World War II, their formerly hegemonic roles would be assumed by Japan and the United States; after the war was over, the Americans and Asian nationalist leaders of various kinds became the main actors.

Japan, in the attempt to create its own empire, ironically delivered the coup de grâce to Western empires everywhere in Asia, except India, by occupying them militarily. At the same time it unwittingly brought into being the conditions that eventually permitted the triumph of the Communists in China. Finally, it was because of Japan that the United States entered the Asian scene in full force.

The United States had long been present in the Pacific, longer, for example, than France or Germany: its merchants were active in the China trade of the early nineteenth century; its ships had forced Japan to open itself to foreign trade in the treaty of 1854; its navy had decisively defeated the Spanish in 1898 and taken the Philippines; its diplomats had proclaimed the "open door" policy toward China in 1900. But America's preoccupation with the settling of its own immense territory in the nineteenth century and its isolationism in the early interwar period had kept it from playing a major role in Asian affairs. Another factor was America's intoxication with economic success: as in Britain prior to the 1850s and Japan from the 1960s onward, the unspoken assumption in the United States was that economic hegemony could substitute for political. There was also the long American self-identification with the idea of freedom: just as pride in their liberalism had once made the British reluctant colonialists, so too pride in their revolutionary origins and their republicanism made the Americans want to keep their hands clean. To be sure, the American mind was as compartmentalized as the British had been earlier, but its contradictions made themselves felt mostly in Latin America, not Asia.

The United States entered Asia at first as liberator. One can easily read Machiavellian motives into its policies, but to do so would be to obscure the generous impulses that were also present, and the positive role the Americans played in Asian affairs prior to the 1960s, even within the framework of the Cold War. As a result of America's war effort from 1941 to 1945, China was saved from the Japanese, and the Japanese were saved from themselves. In the postwar era, the American occupation of Japan permitted as great a secular miracle as the Japanese themselves had performed during the Meiji Restoration and again after the 1960s. Americans set an example of decolonization in the Philippines in 1946, and helped end the war of independence in Indonesia in 1949.

No other Western power could match that record of achievement. It might even be argued that the U.S. occupation of Japan, in the swiftness and extent of its accomplishments or in the intelligence and good will which both Americans and Japanese brought to bear, represented perhaps the highest point in the centuries-long relationship between Asia and the West. Only one other forced collaboration between Asians and Westerners, India, can be compared to it in fruitfulness.

If the American presence in the 1940s and early 1950s was a high point in the Asian-Western relationship, the American experience in Vietnam in the 1960s and early 1970s was the nadir. Under the banner of anticommunism, the United States moved step by step into a disastrous war; of all the colonial struggles in the history of Asia, only that waged by the Chinese against the Japanese in 1937–45 was costlier in terms of human suffering.

Its defeat in Vietnam convinced the United States of what the Europeans had learned earlier: that the era of Western imperialism was definitively over. It had always been *contra natura*, possible only because of deep but temporary disjunctures in social and technological development. To some extent these disjunctures continued to exist, but no longer to the point where a smaller portion of humanity could so dominate a greater one.

ASIA AND THE WEST IN THE TWENTIETH-CENTURY WORLD ORDER

Marilyn B. Young

Teaching world history today brings new rewards as well as new difficulties, both arising from the radical indeterminacy of the present time. In his essay for this volume, Peter Stearns describes the period 1000 to 1500 as "waiting for the Western shoe to drop," a situation that is more often referred to as the "Rise of the West." So inexorable and powerful was this rise that for five centuries it seemed impossible that the trajectory would ever curve into a fall. But in the twentieth century, cyclical theories of history emerged among poets like Yeats as well as historians like Toynbee and Spengler, signaling unease and uncertainty about the still ascendant West. Paul Kennedy's recent and popular book, *The Rise and Fall of the Great Powers*, flatly announced what would have once been virtually unthinkable.

Still, rising and falling are orderly linear motions which often seem to repeat themselves reassuringly throughout history. Yet the world of such predictable motions has now been rudely disrupted by a new physics whose laws we have yet to learn. The postwar world offers the teacher of Western history who pays due regard to the non-Western world a unique opportunity. It is possible, now, to convey to students a genuine sense of the contingency of history, for if we no longer know where the world is going, where it came from also appears less inevitable, more circumstantial. This is of particular importance in terms of teaching non-Western history as something more than responses to events in the West.

For half a century or more, it was difficult to think of the world outside the Cold War narrative dominated by American and Soviet power. The United States was the center of a world system of political, cultural, social, and economic exchanges; the Soviet Union was the center of a much weaker but no less coherent system. Both had allies, both vied for the resources and the loyalties of the uncommitted, both employed financial and military coercion to keep order within their respective systems. Now that that story no longer describes the world, we are free to begin telling the story of the twentieth century anew, with a frank acknowledgement that we do not know where it will end.

The new story must still begin somewhere. Historians will disagree about precisely when: the fall of Singapore to the Japanese in 1942, the end of World War II in 1945, the establishment of the People's Republic of China in 1949, President Nixon's pilgrimage to the Great Wall in 1972, the American defeat in Vietnam in 1975[1] are all possibilities. The story the historian tells depends a great deal upon when it begins. But most would agree that whatever date is chosen, the relevant issues remain the same all over the world: modernization, imperialism, nationalism, war, resistance, and revolution.

It is sometimes difficult to convey the meanings of these words to students for whom nationalism means American patriotism and the only familiar revolutions are the American and possibly the French. It requires showing students the postwar world from the perspective of the colonized rather than the colonizer, and helping them to understand that the colonized were never merely passive victims of the West but, no matter how exploited and suppressed, still always active participants in their own history.

To present this other side of history is to challenge basic historical categories. The "postwar world," for instance, like the term "Far East," can now be seen to be Eurocentric: after which war? far from where? In Asia as a whole, which is not at all far from the East, there has been no single postwar period. In almost every year since 1945 there was war somewhere: in Korea or Vietnam or Cambodia; between India and China or between China and Russia or China and Vietnam.

One result of the expansion of Europe had been the consensus among the elites of the colonial or semicolonial world that the return to sovereignty depended on the internal transformation of their states. Both the colonial powers and the colonized elites agreed that what was at issue was "modernization," by which was inevitably meant "Westernization." For there could be no doubt that chronologically the West had got to modernity first. Of course there had been a premodern West, but no modern non-West existed without Western influence. Modernization also seemed to require a commitment to what the anthropologist Benedict Anderson has called the "imagined community" of the nation-state. But how could nationalism, which must draw upon a people's distinctive past, be put to the service of such a cosmopolitan project as modernization? And how would the colonial powers respond to such efforts, which paid the West the highest form of compliment by imitating its ways, but at the ironic price of demanding the withdrawal of Western power? Finally, which of the modernizing nationalist groups would inherit the newly sovereign nations? For as Tony Smith has pointed out, "civil war lurks in the heart of every movement for nationalist liberation."[2]

In Asia, only Japan was able to preempt Western technology in the service of its own national autonomy, and it accomplished this only by joining the ranks of the imperialists. In 1895, when Japan was itself still subject to unequal treaties imposed by the Western powers, it succeeded after a short, brutal war in imposing a yet more onerous treaty on China. But if victory in this first Sino-Japanese War confirmed the colonial ordering of the world, the longer, yet more brutal war which began, officially, in 1937 permanently unhinged it. For however oppressive Japanese imperialism, it claimed to act on behalf of the oppressed themselves, an Asian leader for an Asian world, a world free of the domination of the white West. These claims were not entirely spurious: while keeping its own colonies (Taiwan and Korea) tightly subordinate, the Japanese encouraged anti-Western independence movements in India, Burma, and Indonesia and fomented anti-Western sentiments everywhere from China to the Philippines.

The Pacific War was among other things a racial war and was recognized as such by the protagonists. Even if the Allies won, an Australian diplomat worried, "the Asiatic people might band together [after the war] to forward their mutual interests. . . . The idea has an attraction to the Asiatic mind and I feel it must be watched." A senior American State Department official urged the importance of defeating Japan in terms of the "prestige of the white race and particularly of the British Empire and the United States." Why be apologetic about Anglo-Saxon superiority? Churchill mused in 1943, when "we are superior."[3] In the European war it was generally accepted that the enemy was not the German people but Hitler and the Nazi regime. In Asia, the Japanese people as a whole were cast as the near subhuman enemy, and President Roosevelt, for one, wondered whether it was not their small skulls that made them such a wicked and despicable race. The racism of all the belligerents, Japan included, was not simply a matter of wartime propaganda but, as the historian John Dower has explained, the terms in which the war was fought, terms which made it a war of annihilation, a war singularly without mercy.[4]

In Tokyo, after the war, twenty-eight "Class A" Japanese civilian and military officials were indicted as war criminals, and all but two were sentenced to life imprisonment or death. With the history of Western imperialism and the American use of the atomic bomb in mind, the Indian Judge Radhabinod Pal dissented from the majority and found for the defense. After all, he argued, the crimes for which Japan was being judged were hardly crimes at the time they were committed: "According to [Mr. Justice Jackson at Nuremberg] a preparation by a nation to dominate another nation is the worst of crimes. This may be so now. But I do not see how it could be said that such an attempt or preparation was a crime before the Second World War when there was hardly a big power which was free from that taint."[5]

The Japanese conquest of the European empire in Asia meant that European reassertion of that empire after the war would be contested. Yet there was nothing inevitable about decolonization, just as there had been nothing inevitable about colonization; and in every country, decolonization was **interactive,** just as colonization had been. The organization of movements for the recovery of sovereignty was shaped by the specific history of each colony as well as by the differing responses of the colonizing country. British accommodation to Indian nationalism, for example, had at least as much to do with the nature of the Indian nationalist elite (bourgeois, nonviolent, respectful of property rights, in alliance with the powerful peasant movement led by Gandhi) as with the decision of the Labour government to grant independence. In Vietnam, by contrast, the declaration of Vietnamese independence in 1945 by a Communist-led nationalist movement was adamantly resisted by the French; only after three decades of war, first against the French, then against the Americans, was the divided country unified as an independent communist nation. Korea passed from decades of harsh colonial subjugation by the Japanese to the geopolitical division of its peninsula on opposite sides of the Cold War, a legacy that has yet to be resolved.

One dramatic way to focus the issues of modernization, imperialism, nationalism, war, resistance, and revolution is to concentrate on China, whose slide from Middle Kingdom to Third

World country marked, in reverse, the rise of the West. Chinese movements have served as models for countries as different as Vietnam (whose early twentieth-century nationalist leaders consulted with reforming Chinese nationalists like Liang Qichao) to Peru (whose late twentieth-century insurgent leaders of the "Shining Path" cast themselves as followers of Mao Zedong). For Europe, too, China had been the center: control of the markets of Cathay had been the object of European desire since Marco Polo in the thirteenth century, and Japan's twentieth-century challenge to Europe in China was a major source of the hostility that led to the Pacific War. Indeed much of late nineteenth- and twentieth-century Asian history can be studied through the lens of China's effort to reclaim sovereignty and, within the limits of an interdependent world, self-determination.

Every variety of reforming and revolutionary possibility was tested in China. Christian reformers and anarchist, socialist, communist, and even national socialist revolutionaries organized to seize control of the government in order to strengthen the state and protect the nation. To trace the course of these efforts is to recapitulate the history of twentieth-century Western political movements and their complex Asian naturalizations.

China since 1949 similarly provides a context for reviewing the full spectrum of approaches to economic development, popular mobilization, and social change. Bureaucratic capitalism, strict central planning, experiments with decentralization, the introduction of the market—the Chinese leadership has at one time or another, and sometimes simultaneously, pursued them all. Even a brief review of Chinese policies will suggest the difficulty of achieving economic prosperity and social justice in a largely poor and peasant country. We can now see how irrelevant to such a project were the categories and values of the Cold War. The democracy movement of 1989 in China,[6] for example, was hailed at the time as the latest example of America's victory over the Soviet Union. Yet the movement is far more interesting, as well as more comprehensible, if—among other possible approaches—it is placed firmly in the context of Chinese student movements of the past hundred years. More particularly, the movement was in some measure part of an ongoing dialogue with the most recent revolutionary upheaval in China, the Cultural Revolution.

Indeed, by focusing on the specific history of revolution and decolonization, the anachronistic paradigm of the Cold War can no longer be taken as a description of historical reality but rather as itself requiring interpretation. The Cold War thus joins earlier paradigms of conversion as yet another effort to integrate Asia on terms convenient to the West. In the wake of the Cold War, historical processes of economic, social, and political change, of the shifting definitions of national identity and autonomy, and of the tensions among regional rivalry, cooperation, and global integration become central to our analysis.

NOTES

1. The Paris Peace Accords were signed in 1973. The United States closed its embassy and left Saigon in 1975.
2. Tony Smith, *The Pattern of Imperialism: The United States, Great Britain and the Late-Industrializing World since 1815* (Cambridge: Cambridge University Press, 1981), p. 121.
3. Quoted in Christopher Thorne, *Allies of a Kind: The United States, Britain, and the War against Japan, 1941–1945* (New York: Oxford University Press, 1978), pp. 8, 730.
4. Of these, seven were sentenced to death, sixteen to life imprisonment, one to twenty years, and one to seven years. Two men died during the trial, and one went insane. See Misiko Hane, *Modern Japan: A Historical Survey* (Boulder, CO: Westview Press, 1986), p. 345. See also John Dower, *War without Mercy: Race and Power in the Pacific War* (New York: Pantheon, 1986).
5. *The Tokyo Judgment*, ed. B.V.A. Roling and C.F. Ruter, vol. 2 (Amsterdam: APA, University Press, 1977), p. 574.
6. The short life of this movement has yielded an enormous literature. One of the most interesting accounts is the collection of essays edited by Jeffrey Wasserstrom and Elizabeth Perry, *Popular Protest and Political Culture in Modern China: Learning from 1989* (Boulder, CO: Westview Press, 1991).

SELECTED REFERENCES

Robin Jeffrey has edited an excellent collection: *Asia—The Winning of Independence* (New York: St. Martin's Press, 1981), which includes essays by Alfred W. McCoy on the Philippines, Anthony Reid on Indonesia, David Marr on Vietnam, Lee Kam Hing on Malaya, and one on India by Jeffrey himself. Tony Smith's *The Pattern of Imperialism: The United States, Great Britain and the Late-Industrializing World since 1815* (Cambridge: Cambridge University Press, 1981) puts "The American Century" in world perspective and discusses France as well as Great Britain and the United States in the chapter on decolonization. John Dower's account of the Pacific war, *War without Mercy: Race and Power in the Pacific War* (New York: Pantheon Books, 1986) and Christopher Thorne's *Allies of a Kind: The United States, Britain, and the*

War against Japan, 1941–1945 (New York: Oxford University Press, 1978) make the racial nature of the war inescapable. Benedict Anderson's *Imagined Communities: Reflections on the Origins and Spread of Nationalism* (London: Verso, 1983) is a stimulating discussion of the roots of nationalism, and Thomas McCormick's *America's Half-Century: U.S. Foreign Policy in the Cold War* (Baltimore: John Hopkins Press, 1989) puts the post-1945 United States in a world-systems framework. Jonathan Spence has made it easy to recommend books on modern China, from his literary and intellectual history of China's revolutionaries, *The Gate of Heavenly Peace: The Chinese and Their Revolution* (New York: Viking Press, 1981), to his recent *The Search for Modern China* (New York: Norton, 1990). Two further works on nationalism and colonialism will help shift the perspective of both student and teacher: Partha Chaterjee, *Nationalist Thought and the Colonial World* (London: Zed Books, 1986) and Albert Memmi, *The Colonizer and the Colonized* (Boston: Beacon Press, 1967).

II
Asia in World History

Asia in World History

Carol Gluck

Teaching world history is both necessary and impossible. It is necessary because we know that the conventional boundaries of historical knowledge are too narrow for the world today. It is impossible because the expanse of world history across space and time is too broad for the classroom. Our curricular appetites are admirable; so, too, is our indigestion. Steering the instructional straits between the flatlands of coverage and the cliffs of coherence, we veer first one way, then the other. The lure of coverage seems to me the greater danger, materialized by the heft of most world history textbooks and the drop-a-pencil, miss-an-empire syllabi that, bowing to good global intentions, find it hard to leave anyplace or anybody out. It **is** hard, and there is no single solution to the problem of inclusion. Selection, often brutal in its excisions, is the only answer. And if it leaves much of world history on the curricular cutting-room floor, at least the story that remains may make compelling narrative sense. The bad news is that we cannot do it all in one course. The good news is that the possible principles of selection are varied enough to enable each of us to teach to our strengths and still be true, historically, to the world.

WAYS TO WORLD HISTORY

The choices of approach are expanding every year. The days of ICCINAH—that parochial wonder known as the Introductory College Course in Non-American History—are numbered.[1] Fewer of us will contend with the double negative of trying to introduce the Non-West into Non-American history. But many will seek to bring the world into courses on Western Civilization, the name itself an instance of peculiarly American nomenclature. The term does not exist in this form in Europe, where—although it is seldom taught because of the dominance of national histories—it would at least be recognized as what it is: European history, expanded to include its allegedly classical origins. Not that Western Civ courses are obsolete; on the contrary, the need for such historical grounding has grown as American secondary education has fallen away from fundamentals. But Western Civilization is no substitute for knowledge of the wider world. And the "World

History" long offered in high schools in the U.S. (also in Japan and China) amounted to European history, too, whether it moved from the Greek ecumene to the EC, from the ice age to the cold war, or, less ebulliently, from the black death to the Holocaust.

When it comes to the inclusion of Asia, the historical hazards here are by now well-marked. Classic textbook examples include the Conjunctive approach, which imperially conjoined the West and the world. In Palmer's *A History of the Modern World*, the Portuguese encircled the globe in a paragraph, ushering in what one Indian scholar sharply called "the Vasco Da Gama epoch of Asian history."[2] Then, in another paragraph, Asia produced calico, chintz, and "china" for the consumption of eighteenth-century Europe. A page or two described nineteenth-century Asia, as Europe took imperialist control over significant chunks of it—or, in the words of the text, as "European history broadened out into the history of the world." The "revolt of Asia" and "the end of colonial empires" brought the imperial narrative to its twentieth-century end, two pages each.[3] It is important to note that Palmer's classic text was nothing if not true to the temper of its times, for much of mid-century Euro-America saw "the modern world" in precisely these terms.

The Collision model presents modern Asia in an impact-response mode, reacting to the imperialist threat or civilizational stimulus of the West rather than acting in the context of its own histories. Focused on modernity, this particular Westcentrism discussed, as the famous Teng-Fairbank title put it, *China's Response to the West*, or in Reischauer's works, Japanese "responsiveness" to the "challenge of the West" in the nineteenth century.[4] Not only did these historians define modernization in Western, primarily American, terms, but the benchmark of comparative responsiveness led to the "Japan succeeded, China failed" storyline that has taken so long to unseat. Primarily a postwar U.S. phenomenon, the collision (or more gently, encounter) model suffused the English-language scholarship on modern East Asia.[5] As the founding Asianists in their fields, Reischauer and Fairbank were scarcely Eurocentric in their concerns, but like Palmer, their rendering of Asian history epitomized the thinking of their age, which still saw Asia in terms of the Western impact upon it.

Less scholarly, but more prevalent, at least in American texts, was the Narcissistic lens, which focused on Asia only when the West saw itself. In the three mentions of Japan in many a high-school textbook, Marco Polo first provides the name *Cipangu*, then Commodore Perry opens the country to commerce, and, finally, General MacArthur brings the gift of democracy. Let these past examples of Conjunction, Collision and Narcissism show that times have changed in the way we teach about Asia in the world.

Scholarly interest in world history has surged in many countries as the twentieth century winds down, leaving a legacy of globalization that seems as ineluctable as it is hard to fathom. One need not wax romantic over the global village or indulge in rhetorical globaloney to recognize the imprint of the world on the individual, local, and national futures of everyone in it. Just as the world has a future in common, the logic goes, it has a past as well. Many courses set out to convey the history of the present world, generally defining the present as "the modern." Rounding up the usual chronological suspects in this case means a line-up of the last several centuries, which because they did in fact encompass "the rise of the West" often leads to the charge of Eurocentrism. But since contesting such Eurocentrism is one of the goals of recent world history, resistance to the theme of the "westernization of the world" has generated a number of innovative approaches intended to decenter the West without denying its central role in the modern world.

The aim, according to Michael Geyer and Charles Bright, is "to present the world's pasts as history or, more likely, as a braid of intertwined histories."[6] They divide the efforts into two kinds. The first takes its lead from the "grand civilizational studies" of William H. McNeill and Marshall Hodgson and practices comparative history, usually with some macro-thematic focus, like power, empire, or technology.[7] By focusing on what are often called "major" world civilizations, of which Europe is only one—and a late one at that—the regional sweep shows Asia's prominence in earlier periods as well as the historical context for the West's later rise.[8] Scholars like Janet Abu-Lughod have transposed Wallerstein's world-systems theory from its locus in the post-1500 capitalist West to other times and other places, in her case thirteenth-century Eurasia under the Mongols.[9] K.N. Chaudhuri has written a Braudelian comparative history that covers a millennium of "economy and civilization of the Indian Ocean." His series of maps showing "the world" as it looked first with Mecca, then Delhi, Jakarta, and Peking in the center offers a graphic rendering of the civilizational space of the Indian Ocean regions he discusses.[10] The titles of these two books, *Before European Hegemony* and *Asia Before Europe*, suggest that this work is in part compensatory, employing theories developed from European experience to demonstrate that similar phenomena existed elsewhere (and earlier) in world history. But the globalizing of both historical and historiographical attention in a regionally more evenhanded manner is also a sign that civilizational analysis can escape the ethnocentrisms and essentialisms so often associated with this approach.

The second strategy identified by Geyer and Bright is what I think of as "trans-" history. They associate it with the study of movement and migration, travelers and trade, diasporas and borderlands, and link these to antecedent histories of discovery, nomads, and maritime empires. Few of these scholars call themselves world historians, and many are linked to cultural studies. They share an interest in edges, margins, and borders, which is a way to "trans-"cend the center, whether it be the dominant social class, the homogeneous nation-state, or the ideologies associated with them. By studying peoples who cross borders, like the African or Chinese diasporas, these scholars cross borders themselves and write "trans-"national history. Border-crossing has long been the forte of world history, which cares for the caravans, the connections, the conduits of people, goods, and ideas that cross continents and seas.

Such crossing also makes it feasible to "trans-"gress the conventions of national histories, received narratives, and disciplinary boundaries. A world historian such as Philip Curtain was more likely to evoke "the Atlantic" as a historical space than a historian of U.S. national history. And the newer work shows a similar aptitude in cultural politics, as in Paul Gilroy's *The Black Atlantic*.[11] The transgressive, or oppositional, aspect enables the "trans-"scholars to retrieve parts of the past ignored in the dominant narrative, such as the people who did not settle down into agriculture but continued to hunt and gather or those who did not subside into nation-states but remained pastoral peoples. Hence the remark that we need a "Nomadology, the opposite of a history." In contemporary times the movement of people—migration, diasporas, refugees, tourists—and the movement of ideas—popular culture, mutual images, information—occur on a global scale, requiring a global history.[12] The great virtue of border-crossing history lies in its ability to transcend conventional categories. Following the paths of the Chinese diaspora, for example, unlooses the concept "the Chinese" from the territorial nation-state and reveals a social, economic, and cultural story of enduring historical significance.

There are many other innovative approaches to international, transnational, interregional, comparative, and global history—the proliferation of names represents the ferment of intellectual activity.[13] New organizations like the World History Association (and its *Journal of World History*), collections of primary materials like Kishlansky's *Sources of World History*, resources on the different world regions available in university outreach centers, in print, on film and on the internet—the pedagogical infrastructure for world history, by whatever name it calls itself, is developing with great speed.[14] Indeed, few historians today remain unaffected by the late twentieth-century imperative to think across boundaries. Good national history, too, now requires a global perspective, disciplinary hybridity, and a transgressive imagination. It is the way of the world.

PEDAGOGICAL POTHOLES

It is not, however, an easy way. While scholars expand the vistas of world history and innovative courses sprout in curricular gardens, the work of shaping a syllabus has, if anything, grown more difficult. We know too little to do world history justice, but that has long been true. What is new is that we now also know too much—too much about the pitfalls and the problems that attend the teaching of something as large and complicated as world history.

If one follows the "comparative civilizations" route, for example, one has to choose which civilizations and when. At first glance it may seem sensible to highlight the regional histories at their peaks, so that the rise of Islam takes center stage from the seventh to the tenth centuries, Song China around the turn of the millennium, and Europe of the three revolutions—scientific, social, and industrial—at the onset of modern times. But in such a peaks-and-glories scheme, Ainslie Embree has reminded us that South Asia is apt to disappear once its ancient empires, religions, and social ("caste") systems have been treated, leaving India forever immured in an image of changeless "tradition."[15] In a broadly thematic chronology, it is easy enough to trace the "birth of civilization(s)" in Mesopotamia, Egypt, China, and the Indus Valley without serious chronological violation. But the consequence of adherence to chronology may be that "the vanished civilizations of Mesoamerica," as one highly rated world history textbook calls them, appear separately, and later, without conceptual links to the other civilizational "births"—if indeed they appear at all. In this particular textbook the Olmecs, Mayas, and Aztecs enter, for three pages, so that the Spanish can get on with the business of conquering them.[16]

If one rides with the nomads or sails with the seafarers, the course gains the advantage of showing the connectedness of peoples across time and space. In the works of William McNeill and in Lynda Shaffer's "Concrete Panoply of Intercultural Exchange" in this volume, the moving stream of germs, crops, spices, stirrups, warriors, bureaucrats, pilgrims and every manner of idea from Arabic numerals (Indian, actually) to the transcendental religions traverses the Afro-Eurasian land mass and crosses the great oceans.[17] The dynamic arrows of color that sweep across the maps of Eurasia in a historical atlas graphically depict the spread, not only of silk and armies, but also of Islam and Buddhism across vast distances.[18] Students always respond to Marco Polo and the Pasta Connection, the fateful Columbian exchange, the New World origin of Italian tomatoes and Irish potatoes, and the rest. But too much of this, and history becomes a shopping list. Also, too great a stress on interaction, interfusion, interchange, and interdependence—I think of this as the "inter-" approach—can sometimes give cultural diffusionism an exaggerated role. It can also repress the transformations wrought by peoples along the way, as if Chinese culture moved through Korea to Japan on a transit visa, without stopping long enough for any Korean admixture. Nor did the Arabs, as George Saliba argues here, simply "preserve" ancient Greek and Indian knowledge and then pass it on when the medieval West was "ready" for it. Instead Islamic civilization synthesized, systematized, transmuted—and then transmitted—the "lost" knowledge of the classical past.

The recent move to "trans-"history suggests looking around the edges and across the borders of the canonical "major civilizations" to find historical spaces that equally well, or sometimes better, exemplify the patterns of the human experience. In some cases regions lost to the historian's gaze can be reconstituted. As with Braudel's Mediterranean—though better, I think, without his focus on the deep structures of unchange—the Indian Ocean, the Black Sea, Eurasia under the Mongols, the "lands below the winds" in Southeast Asia, all reveal stories rich in both civilization and interchange.[19] All were effaced from conventional history by the latter-day nation state and by modern arrangements of global and regional power, which is to say, their historical presence was anachronistically rubbed out. Erasing the erasure has obvious appeal to historians at the end of a century in which nation-states not only dominated but did so violently. To study regions that were multiethnic, non-territorial entrepôts of trade and culture can seem an antidote to a hypernational present and a link to a transnational future. Certainly the study of the history of Okinawa works this way in relation to hypernational Japan: for centuries a peaceful, prosperous center of trade between north and southeast Asia, the Ryukyuan kingdom is evoked to counter the closed-off island-country identity of mainland Japan. But as with the other approaches, such a relativizing emphasis can only go so far. A world history consisting entirely of edges would be empty at its center.

Choosing the topics to include is but part of the challenge. There is also the question of the story. The grand narrative of world history is often characterized, in Peter Stearns' words, as "the study of how the world got to be what it is today."[20] But what is it today? We are unlikely to agree, the more so since the answer is different for different people in different places. Grand narratives, by their nature, tend to tell a single story and so do not easily accommodate such differences. Our awareness of this fact makes us cautious. One common choice today is the story of the integration of the globe, what one otherwise expansive world historian moderately calls "the creeping unity of mankind."[21] But even this innocuous plotline presents problems. It is tempting, for example, to assume that integration is a value in itself, and if global connectedness is a good, then well-connected societies may be privileged and eras of integration stressed. One sees this in the way post-Ming China is treated: I think of it as the Chinese Admiral syndrome.

Why, ask historians, after Admiral Zheng He traveled the vast reaches of the Southern Seas (Indian Ocean), reaching the Red Sea and the shores of Africa in the fifteenth century, did the Ming court cease the maritime expeditions? Although much scholarly ink has been spilt assessing the multiple internal reasons for this decision, the stereotypical impression is that China "withdrew" from the seas just as the Iberians were about to embark, thereby losing its chance to girdle the globe.[22] Historians offer similar judgments about the "central kingdom" complex that made the Qing emperor reject the diplomatic overture of the English king in 1793 with the oft-quoted remark that "we have never valued ingenious articles, nor do we have the slightest need of your Country's manufactures." Rather than evaluate the rebuff in the context of Qing dominance of the East Asian international order, China is judged to have missed the commercial boat in the currents swirling toward modern global trade. In both cases "anti-foreign" China is presented as having isolated itself from the main—read, proper—direction of world history.[23] In a contrasting instance, Japan receives credit for having thrown its civilizational lot in with Western-style modernity in the nineteenth-century, a turn of events that not only "integrated" Japan into the (Western) world order but also resulted in Japanese imperialism, which is integration of a less well praised sort.

These examples are not meant to dismiss the narrative of integration, only to suggest that whatever narrative one selects, similar pitfalls await. Another problem with a strong storyline is its tendency toward linearity. Nearly all history is written backward from the present, which means we know how the story comes out. It is hard not to tell the past as a straight line to the present and easier to disavow historical inevitability than it is to escape the teleology of the "us" and the "now." The yearning for progress remains strong, as if we need to feel that each historical phenomenon "adds" something to the world. World history is cumulative, as the textbooks used to put it.

From the neolithic revolution and the emergence of ancient civilization to the informational revolution and the emergence of a global economy, world historical narratives are often driven by "origins" and "revolutions." It is presented as good to be "first"—to be the "cradle" of civilization, the "inventor" of paper, the "originator" of the joint stock company (though not the founder of tyranny, the father of genocide, or the first master of ecological destruction). This sometimes becomes a civilizational jousting match: Song China was already modern in the eleventh century; Tokugawa Japan was already postmodern in the eighteenth century, or a competition for historical "firsts" that resembles the recent national scrambles to build the highest skyscraper or the longest suspension bridge. Once the "first" instance has occurred, the narrative favors acute change, as in "revolution," whether real or metaphorical, over the slower drama of settlement and stability.

This obsession with origins and change belongs, of course, to the temper of modernity. Thus world history seems to march forward, in one direction, towards "the" modern, as if there were only one such thing. It is the old Hegel Line, which many writers of Universal History shared, as Leonard Gordon and Harvey Goldman show in their essays here. For Hegel, history moved from its origins through change to its end, or fulfillment, not only through time but through space as well. Since he assigned origins to Asia and fulfillment to Europe, the East was left, famously, immobile or asleep. To contest this view in the late nineteenth- and early twentieth-century, Japanese like Fukuzawa Yukichi and Chinese like Liang Qichao argued that in the new age history would reverse direction and move instead from West to East. But though they changed the direction of history, the notion of a single history moving in a linear or dialectical way toward a single outcome—history as the moderns defined it—survived the cultural transposition intact. Americans developed their own version of the Hegel Line. Peter Stearns reports that his students learned in high school that civilization begins in Mesopotamia, moves westward first to Greece and Rome, then to France and England, and culminates (surprise) in the United States. Stearns went on to hypothesize that perhaps it then transmigrates to California and "splits off in an earth-quake and sails to Japan."[24] Students in Japan would be unlikely to see it that way, but then this El Niño image of civilization as a prevailing Westerly ought by now to be beside the point.

We no longer regard Asian civilization as the childhood of history any more than we accept the old European image of the New World savages, noble or primitive, as the embodiment of Europe's past, from which Europeans had so dazzlingly progressed. We know that there is more than one story, and yet we are seduced by the narra-tive sweep. The struggle to keep the stories multiple is sometimes a simple matter of reminding ourselves that not everyone in the world did the same thing at the same time—alright, folks, now settle down and plant seeds—and sometimes a complex task of addressing the tension between the commonality of human experience and the di-versity of the patterns in which it is historically embodied. To avoid the Toynbee teeter-totter—one civilization up, another down—it helps to keep the Unevenness Principle in mind. For even if we choose to tell an interrelated story of the world's past, at least we may do so without rounding everything and everyone off. This is especially important in recent history, since the structural uneven-ness of the world's multiple modernities is one of the salient charac-teristics of modern times.

One may multiply the narratives and still face the fact that it is the winners who write history. Morris Rossabi's rehabilitation of the Mongols in his chapter here works against the deeply etched image of the plundering hordes, an image generated in large part by the peo-ples whom the Mongols subjugated. The Mongol empire neither wrote much of its own history at the time of its flourishing nor prevailed to write—and rewrite—it at a later date. So Mongol history disappeared into pieces of other people's pasts, and the historical space of their once vast Eurasian empire fragmented into cartographic units of later times. Though they had once been conquered, the peoples who sur-vived to tell their tales became history's winners, passing on to pos-terity their own dim view of the Mongols.[25]

More serious perhaps than the kingdoms lost to winner's history is the damage done by the modern nation-state. Because nations use their history in service of identity, they tend to usurp the entire past, imprisoning centuries and sometimes millennia within recently estab-lished national boundaries. Pakistan was founded in 1947, but it traces its history back to Mohenjo-daro. Indonesia did not exist until 1945, but it has fashioned a unitary national past, primarily out of Javanese cloth. What is "India" in the earlier centuries? Or "Ukraine" and others of the aggressively national newer nations? Even in mod-ern times there is work to do in "rescuing history from the nation," as the title of a recent book on China urges.[26] For national history not only coopts the long past but also drives out present heterogeneity, so that other histories—of minorities, for example—disappear from the story. The received national narratives limit our ability to do justice to social history and cultural construction, two areas of great interest that remain underrepresented in the teaching of world history. And finally, national history obscures the connectedness that constitutes most definitions of globalization, whether in the form of deterritorialization, transnational corporations, or "global ethnoscapes."[27] In this sense, too, national histories serve world history poorly.

Add to these and other substantive and narrative problems the dilemma of historical correctness. World history is nothing if not multicultural; that is its inherent nature. But it is impossible to get everybody in, and the excisions can be invidious. Africa almost always gets short shrift, although adopting a Hodgsonesque interregional approach to the Afro-Eurasian historical space can help in the earlier periods. "Big" countries, including England and Japan, overshadow "small" ones like Brazil and Canada. Politics and war, trade and technology take over from families and gender, work and daily life. World history is mostly male, not only because patriarchy dominates but because the story so often centers on elites. One sometimes feels that the exclusion is total: that there are no people in the world, only peoples; no human beings, only humankind.

And all the peoples are mutually ethnocentric. This unedifying fact can at least be used as a decentering device. Tracing the distinction between the civilized and the barbarian, which is as old as civilization itself, shows how the definitions changed over time, how things looked different from different sides, and how these elemental constructions of the Other operated in history, for both good and ill. One can avoid the nasty—and dangerous—essentialism of the civilizational approach of Samuel Huntington by refusing to draw the wagons into a circle around one's own (superior) place.[28] Indeed, perspective is precisely what world history can teach. "Western capitalism in its totality" Marshall Sahlins reminds us, "is a truly exotic cultural scheme, as bizarre as any other." We are simply blinded by its seeming practicality to "the cunning of culture" that supports it.[29]

The politics of teaching world history presents another problem, but not one that I hope will prevail. Rhetorical care must be taken. Richard Bulliet has described the debate among the authors of a recent world history textbook over the use of the word "tribe." Arab tribes were admissible, but not so tribes in Africa or among Native Americans. The historians decided not to use the word at all, with but one exception: "The Twelve Kin-Groups of Israel" seemed awkward.[30] In regard to the politics of inclusion, most world historians have already taken their stand. In principle, everything belongs, including the United States; in practice, most things must be omitted. World history does not replace either American history or Western Civilization. It is neither the history of "the West" nor the "Non-West" but of the whole, and the whole does not always divide along such lines. In this respect the goals of world history seem clearer than the practice; the struggle for coherence lies ahead.

MACRO-MICRO MANAGING

So far the road to coherence seems to lead, roughly speaking, in two different directions: one, macro, the other, micro. The macro approach is the most familiar, taking on the world as a whole, from hominid beginnings to twentieth-century endings, across the oceans and the continents. In his much-used textbook, Stavrianos wrote "perched upon the moon" looking down on "spaceship earth." While the lunar approach strikes me as a stretch, it is possible to follow selected grand themes of metageography and megahistory, so that a narrative builds around the relation of society and the environment, the integration of the globe, or—in one impressive attempt to gender the world history survey—causes of order and disorder in different societies at different times.[31]

Several macro-narratives are imbedded in the essays in this volume. Extracting a sub-narrative that focuses on Asia in world context might yield, in caricature, an account divided into three main periods: I. The Beginning, or The Invention of Everything; II. The Middle, or the Afro-Eurasian era; III. The Modern, or the Invention of Everything Else. The name "Asia" here is an anachronism. Geographically, Asia, like Europe, is a cartographic fiction, as the authors of *The Myth of Continents* insist; the continental terrain is Eurasia.[32] Nomenclaturally, Asia did not call itself "Asia" until the mid-nineteenth century and then by incorporation of the Western name, that is, from outside. By the same token, "Europe" also defined itself against the outside infidels and Turks, and the idea of Europe only took real root after the French Revolution. Geopolitically, Asia began to think itself "Asian" in the twentieth century and not until the century's end did Asia assert its identity as "Asian" in an empowered sense—not unlike the Euro-thinking since the Second World War. Both "Asia" and "Europe," then, are ideas that developed historically, rather late, and in juxtaposition to the outside world. Not that China or France lacked a view of the world and a sense of their place in it, only that the present notions of Asia and Europe came quite late in historical time.[33]

The Beginning, or The Invention of Everything, from Homo sapiens sapiens, Paleolithic times—or wherever one decides to start—until about 300 CE, is the original period of "firsts." Special attention is given here to four of these: the Neolithic revolutions, the emergence of early civilizations, the ancient empires, and the transcendental religions. The beginnings of agriculture, long associated with cereals in Çatal Hüyuk in Anatolia—as if something like cultivation ever happened "first" in an single place—also occurred in China (millet), Southeast Asia (rice), Mesoamerica (maize) and perhaps other places. Walter Fairservis here takes the older diffusionist view, which emphasizes the Neolithic revolution in Western Asia, while Cho-yun Hsu notes that there was already a cultural "Chineseness" to late Neolithic China. Others have also identified characteristics of this Chineseness from the Neolithic to the Han, including hierarchical social distinctions, massive labor mobilization, an emphasis on ritual, an ethic of service, and so on.[34] Even Neolithic China was relatively densely peopled, and Rhoads Murphey claims that Asia always had between half and two-thirds of the world's population. (If today's global population were reduced to a village of 100 people, 57 would be Asian, 21 European, 14 from the Americas, and 8 from Africa.)

Having planted the seeds, people invented "civilization." Now that we no longer say that "history begins at Sumer," the four great riverine civilizations can be treated together: Mesopotamia on the Tigris-Euphrates; Egypt on the Nile, Harappa in the Indus valley, and Shang-Zhou China on the Yellow River. The trick here is not to let one case generate the definition of "civilization" for all. Marc Van De Mieroop credits Western Asia with the alphabet, coinage, and monotheism, and the textbook portrait that Fairservis uses clearly does derive from Sumer—writing, cities, and so on. It might be better to invert the order and begin with the Shang; or divide the class into groups and compare civilizational characteristics—anything that makes the point that people "civilized" themselves in various ways. And, by all means, include the great Mesoamerican civilizations as well. In this period Shang-Zhou China developed such abiding features as the Chinese state, its cosmology, social hierarchy, and kingship (the mandate of heaven), thus demonstrating that while early civilizations addressed common problems, they also evolved distinctive and enduring solutions.

The ancient empires, roughly 500 BCE to 300 CE, also lend themselves to comparison (and inversion): The Persian empire, Alexander's conquests, the Mauryan empire in India, Rome in the West, and the Qin-Han empire in China were all universal empires, which devised political and ideological devices to maintain coherence in what Richard Billows here calls a "supranational state." The term is anachronistic but useful, in that it evokes the empire's need to imagine itself as a far flung community—of citizens in Rome, of common culture in China. Out of the feudal disunity of the Zhou came the Chinese ideal of unity, which Hsu argues made the Han empire different from that of Rome, and which, according to Frederic Wakeman, remained a fundamental theme throughout China's history.

The emergence of the transcendental religions was related to the universal empires. Although writers here disagree about Jaspers' term, "the axial age," in the broad sweep of things—which this is—the rise of Buddhism, Jainism, Confucianism, Taoism, Greek philosophy, and (the dates are off) Zoroastrianism does point to a religious ferment in the three-quarters of the millennium before Christ. More important than chronological confluence, however, is the role these religions played in systematizing the transcendental, as Peter Awn, Julia Ching, and Willard Oxtoby argue. The later development of Judaism, Christianity, and Islam inherited this stance toward the ultimate, at the same time that monotheism resonated with the metaphorical unity demanded by imperial rule. Unlike Christianity and Islam, Confucianism, Irene Bloom shows, eschewed a revealed text and rendered the ordinary ultimate. By any standard of world historical inclusion, the great religions —and their movement across great spaces—had great significance then, as they do now.

Until this time—300 CE—apart from the emergence of early man in Africa, some attention to Sub-saharan peoples and the Mesoamerican Olmecs, most of what is conventionally considered to be "history" happened on the continent between Egypt and China. Broadly speaking, civilization was Asian. Britain, with its "pagan" stones, was a remote Roman outpost, and in northern Europe, beyond the Danube, the "barbarians" had begun to stir.

In **The Middle, the Afro-Eurasian Era**, from the fourth to the mid-fourteenth century, the narrative emphasis shifts to scenes of interfusion and the contact of cultures, or at times, the lack of it. Eurasia, the real geographical continent, became a real historical space. What William MacNeill calls the Eurasian ecumene encompassed continental trade across the silk route, the maritime economy of the Indian Ocean, and the diffusion of religion, as Buddhism moved to China and Islam across the continent. It was the millennium of "Southernization," in Lynda Shaffer's view, when, from India and elsewhere, sugar, cotton, spices, mathematics, trade routes and religions "created a prosperous south from China to the Muslim Mediterranean."[35] Richard Bulliet calls it the "Era of Asian Discovery," produced by the travelers and traders who brought the cultural capital of remote parts of Eurasia into contact that bore rich hybrid fruit. One such fruit was the efflorescence of Tang China, which S.A.M. Adshead called the world's center, and the striking "modernity" of Song China, described here by Michael Marmé and Robert Hymes as the most flourishing society in the world of its time.[36] Under the Mongols the Arabs and Marco Polo both contributed to the Southernization of distant medieval Europe, which had for centuries remained isolated in its "separate sphere."

The consequences of Eurasian cultural diffusion and flourishing development were immense. From the Tang, Chinese culture crossed the Eastern Sea to Japan, which, like Britain, lay on the periphery of civilization. Adopting Chinese writing and political practices, Japan, Korea, and Annam entered what Joshua Fogel calls the "Sinic world." The societies of Asia, in Peter Stearns' account, "constituted the developed world," from which Europe, aware of its inferiority, later sought to learn. Meanwhile Song "over-development," followed by the Mongol conquest, damped Chinese splendor. But when Europeans began to voyage, their goal was the riches of the East, and Columbus insisted to his dying day that he had sailed to India. By the seventeenth century, when Francis Bacon singled out the three discoveries that had changed the world, he did not even realize that the compass, printing, and gunpowder had all come Europe's way from Song China. Out of these and out of Europe's earlier sense of inferiority came the beginning of modern times.

The Modern, or the Invention of Everything Else, from the fifteenth century through the present, saw the West rise, in two phases, which Loyd Lee calls "the rise of an interdependent world." Because the rise was neither inevitable nor direct, it pays to attend to the complexities and contingencies of the processes of Western domination, which included the workings of that exotic cultural scheme, capitalism. The early modern phase, from 1450 to 1700, saw the globe encircled, with disastrous consequences for the "New World" but not for the old. Both Derek Linton and Edward Malefakis stress here, as Eric Wolf once did, that for almost three centuries the European merchants worked in "partnership" with local counterparts on the sea margins of India, China, and Southeast Asia.[37] Nonetheless, John Cell argues that with the beginning of the Wallersteinian "world system" in the sixteenth century, Europe began a rise to economic dominance that was powerful—although, in Cell's view, anomalous in a world order normally characterized by balance or anarchy rather than hegemony. European mercantilism was driven by a "headless" polycentric system of competitive states, a geopolitics quite different from the imperial dynasties of the Ming and Qing. For different reasons but with similar consequences, both Ming China and Tokugawa Japan turned inward, away from contact with the European commercial powers. In view of Asia's earlier centrality, I tend to think of the subsequent rise of Europe as "the revenge of the periphery."

During the second phase of this period, from the end of the 18th century, the classical form of modernity was "invented" in Europe: industrialization, the nation-state, expanded political participation, changes in social formation, first to an enlarged middle class, later to mass society, and increased integration in the world. This textbook definition of the modern derived from its first historical instance in England and France, just as the definitions of civilization had once derived from Sumer. But, like "civilization" the patterns of "modernity" would eventually be multiple; only instead of occurring, more or less, independently in different parts of the world, modernity would move out from its origins, sometimes at the barrel of a gun, until it had become, more or less, indigenized around the globe. The disagreement here between Morris David Morris and Derek Linton about the fate of India's cotton industry gives evidence that "proto-modern" developments that were already occurring indigenously sometimes clashed and sometimes meshed with the advancing modernity of the West. Such is the significance of an interdependent world.

Because the increased integration of Europe in the world took the form of the so-called New Imperialism, Asia was subjected to a challenge it could not rebuff, not only because the West came with force but also because of complicated internal factors. These ranged from the decline of the Mughal empire in India to internal rebellion in China. From the late nineteenth to the late twentieth-century, the main Asian story was the intertwined struggle to escape the yoke of the West and to gain the ground of the modern and to do so, as Madeleine Zelin writes, while still remaining Chinese—or Japanese, or Filipino. This, of course, was the main world story as well: from Turkey to Thailand, from Mexico to Iran, from Tonga to Turkestan, the modernizing imperative was everywhere. Not that every society pursued the same modernity, or even sometimes, modernity at all, but the globalization of money and power made insulation and isolation nearly impossible. The historiographical rule is to grant each society the process of its own modern condition. Japan's was short and sharp, while China experienced a "long modernization" that stretched across a century and two revolutions and has not ended yet. The West's imperialist hegemony, in contrast, lasted but a hundred years, and, as Marilyn Young points out, the cold war paradigm, too, is now an anachronism. The new world disorder presents a challenge for everyone, and Asia stands at the center of that challenge.

The macro-historical principle here is that modernity happened first in the West, but is not by virtue of that fact, Western. Just as cities are not Sumerian, Christianity is not West Asian, Islam is not Saudi Arabian, and railroads and rockets are not Euro-american—not any more, that is. They all belong to the world, and in five hundred years, the same will be said of such modern phenomena as capitalism and the nation-state. It is the unevennesses that are the problem. One glance at *The State of the World Atlas* will serve to make graphic the terrible imbalances in nearly every quarter of global life, not least the fact that the United States alone consumes two-thirds of the world's resources.[38] The macro-narrative may as well end there; the history certainly will not.

The micro-approach to world history can be more briefly discussed, since it is not much apparent in these pages, although I am partial to it myself. Instead of a meganarrative "from the muck to the stars" (in Geyer and Bright's words), one takes specific instances of history and "world-izes" them. To world-ize is both to place the specific local, regional, or national case steadfastly in a global context and also to pursue the commonalities of human experience through the lens of the local. One could teach world history entirely through the history of Japan, the Indian Ocean, the United States—or all three together. One could do the same with themes like family and work, women through the ages, subaltern cultures, modes of production, etc., as long as the themes are situated in real historical times and places. My essays on the patterns of Japan's past and Japan's modernities might, I think, be usefully broken out into world history. Certainly the world's past can be told from inside Asia and Africa just as it can from inside Europe.

As a contribution to the Columbus quincentennial of 1992, Martin Bernal, of *Black Athena* fame, taught a course at Cornell entitled "America and the World Before 1492." It unsettled received notions in a suitable fashion. In a different way, the global cultural contextualization provided in the sumptuous volume *Circa 1492* made world history out of the Columbus-discovers-America national fable.[39] In 1996 Anders Stephanson and I offered a course at Columbia entitled "Histories of the Present: Modernity and Geoculture," whose entire purpose was to subvert our ways of looking at the modern world by juxtaposing different historical "sites" ("Africa," "Europe," the Americas, India, and Japan) with our strikingly inadequate theoretical conceptions of modernity. I think a "History of the Modern World Seen Through Newfoundland" would tell the story of modern times as well as any meganarrative. And Ray Huang's book, *1587: A Year of No Significance*, can serve as the fulcrum for a unit that explores the world of imperial China.[40] The curricular imagination in this regard is unrestrained.[41] The advantage of micro-world history is its anchoring; it can be palpably concrete without losing its links to the big questions. And it helps to avoid the eighth deadly sin of coverage.

At the end, it comes back to coherence and evenhandedness. Ideally, we should be able to devise a world history course that could be taught in any country, without adaptation. It would have a strong narrative; a clear chronology; accessible primary sources; human stories; maps, visual images, films, and fiction; a sixth sense for the connectedness of things, and a generous moral tone. It might excite the imagination and incite action, perhaps even rising to the challenge of James Joyce's evocation of "History, thy rill be run unhemmed as it is uneven."

NOTES

1. For a spirited defense of Western Civilization as the only sensible remaining ICCINAH, see J.H. Hexter, "Introductory College Course in Non-American History: An Ethnocentric View" in *What Americans Should Know: Western Civilization or World History?*, Josef W. Konvitz, ed. (East Lansing: Michigan State University, 1985), pp. 179-98.

2. K.M. Panikkar, *Asia and Western Dominance* (London: Allen and Unwin, 1959), quoted in Talal Asad, "Are There Histories of Peoples Without Europe? A Review Article," *Comparative Studies in Society and History* 29, no. 3 (July 1987):595.

3. R.R. Palmer, with Joel Colton, *A History of the Modern World* (New York: Alfred A. Knopf, 1958).

4. Ssu-yü Teng and John K. Fairbank, *China's Response to the West: A Documentary Survey 1839-1923* (Cambridge: Harvard University Press, 1954); for the influential textbook for Harvard's "rice paddies" course, in its one-volume form: John K. Fairbank, Edwin O. Reischauer, and Albert M. Craig, *East Asia: Tradition and Transformation* (Boston: Houghton Mifflin, 1973); Reischauer's synthetic treatment of Japanese history (1977) remains the choice of many general readers: Edwin O. Reischauer and additions by Marius B. Jansen, *The Japanese Today: Change and Continuity* (Cambridge: Harvard University Press, 1995).

5. See Paul Cohen's critique: *Discovering History in China: American Historical Writing on the Recent Chinese Past* (New York: Columbia University Press, 1984).

6. Michael Geyer and Charles Bright, "World History in a Global Age," *American Historical Review* 100, no. 4 (October 1995): 1038-40.

7. E.g., William H. McNeill, *The Human Condition: An Ecological and Historical View* (Princeton: Princeton University Press, 1980). Marshall G.S. Hodgson, *Rethinking World History: Essays on Europe, Islam, and World History* (Cambridge: Cambridge University Press, 1990).

8. For this global approach in a textbook written by three of the leading "new" world historians, see Peter N. Stearns, Michael Adas, Stuart B. Schwartz, *World Civilizations: The Global Experience*, 2 vols. (New York: Harper Collins, 1992).

9. Janet L. Abu-Lughod, *Before European Hegemony: The World System* A.D. 1250-1350 (New York: Oxford University Press, 1989).

10. K.N. Chaudhuri, *Asia Before Europe: Economy and Civilisation of the Indian Ocean from the Rise of Islam to 1750* (Cambridge: Cambridge University Press, 1990), pp. 32-35.

11. Paul Gilroy, *The Black Atlantic: Modernity and Double Consciousness* (Cambridge: Harvard University Press, 1993).

12. See Wang Gungwu, ed., *Global History and Migrations* (Boulder, CO: Westview Press, 1997); "Nomadology," from Deleuze and Guattari, *A Thousand Plateaus*, quoted in Wang, p. 239. For the Chinese diaspora, see Anthony Reid, ed., *Sojourners and Settlers: Histories of Southeast Asia and the Chinese* (St. Leonards, N.S.W.: Asian Studies Association of Australia, and with Allen and Unwin, 1996).

13. E.g., Marshall G.S. Hodgson, "Interregional Studies as Integrating the Historical Disciplines," in Hodgson, *Rethinking World History*, pp. 288-99; Bruce Mazlish and Ralph Buultjens, *Conceptualizing Global History* (Boulder, CO: Westview Press, 1993; the project of the American Historical Association entitled "Globalizing Regional Histories," *AHA Perspectives* (April 1996):15.

14. Among other examples, Mark A. Kishlansky, ed., *Sources of World History*, 2 vols. (New York: Harper Collins, 1995).

15. Ainslie Embree made this point during the 1992 deliberations over a framework for the National Standards for World History, which I also participated in. Others made similar pleas not to perpetuate stereotypes by relegating a region to one period or theme from its history.

16. Albert M. Craig et al., *The Heritage of World Civilizations*, 2 vols. (New York: Macmillan, 1990). Its coverage of Mesoamerica notwithstanding, this text was rated among the best for coverage of Asia and is a useful reference for world history, both high-school and college level. See National Project on Asia in American Schools at Columbia University and The Association for Asian Studies, *National Review of Asia in American Textbooks in 1993* (Ann Arbor: The Association for Asian Studies, 1993).

17. For an exhaustive, sometimes exhausting, compendium, see Donald F. Lach and Edwin J. Van Kley, *Asia in the Making of Europe*, 9 vols. (Chicago: University of Chicago Press, 1965-1993).

18. E.g., Geoffrey Barraclough, ed., *The Times Concise Atlas of World History* (Maplewood, NJ: Hammond Inc., 1982).

19. E.g., Neal Ascherson, *Black Sea* (New York; Hill and Wang, 1995).

20. Peter N. Stearns, *World History: Patterns of Change and Continuity* (New York: Harper and Row, 1987), p. 3.

21. J.M. Roberts, *History of the World* (New York: Oxford University Press, 1993), p. 915.

22. For a recent popular book on the subject: Louise Levathes, *When China Ruled the Seas: The Treasure Fleet of the Dragon Throne, 1405-1433* (New York: Oxford University Press, 1994).

23. The Qianlong emperor's letter remains an excellent primary source for close discussion. For the best new work on the Macartney

Mission, which does treat it in Chinese context, see James L. Hevia, *Cherishing Men from Afar: Qing Guest Ritual and the Macartney Embassy* (Durham, NC; Duke University Press, 1996).

24. Peter N. Stearns, *Meaning over Memory; Recasting the Teaching of Culture and History* (Chapel Hill: The University of North Carolina Press, 1993), p. 77.

25. Morris Rossabi, *Khubilai Khan: His Life and Times* (Berkeley: University of California Press, 1988), pp. 1-3.

26. Prasenjit Duara, *Rescuing History from the Nation: Questioning Narratives of Modern China* (Chicago: University of Chicago Press, 1995).

27. "Global ethnoscapes": Arjun Appadurai, *Modernity at Large: Cultural Dimensions of Globalization* (Minneapolis: University of Minnesota Press, 1996). For other approaches, e.g., David Harvey, *The Condition of Postmodernity: An Enquiry into the Origins of Cultural Change* (Oxford: Basil Blackwell, 1989); Roland Robertson, *Globalization: Social Theory and Global Culture* (London: Sage Publications, 1992).

28. Samuel P. Huntington, *The Clash of Civilizations and the Remaking of World Order* (New York: Simon and Schuster, 1996).

29. Marshall Sahlins, "Goodbye to *Tristes Tropes* Ethnography in the Context of Modern World History," *Journal of Modern History* 65 (March 1993):12.

30. Richard Bulliet, speech at a workshop on "New Approaches to Global History," sponsored by The New York Council for History Education, Riverdale, NY, April 5, 1997. The textbook is Richard Bulliet et al. *The Earth and its Peoples: A Global History* (Boston: Houghton Mifflin, 1997).

31. For the older texts, L.S. Stavrianos, *A Global History: The Human Heritage* and *The World since 1500: A Global History* (Englewood Cliffs: Prentice-Hall, 1983 and 1992); the contributions of William H. McNeill, including his famous *The Rise of the West: A History of the Human Community* (Chicago: University of Chicago Press, 1963)—see also his "The Rise of the West After Twenty-five Years, *Journal of World History* 1, no. 1 (Spring 1990): 1-21; *A World History* (New York: Oxford University Press, 1967), etc.; for more recent approaches, on technology and the environment: Bulliet et al. *The Earth and Its Peoples*; for gender: Judith P. Zinsser, "And Now for Something Completely Different: Gendering the World History Survey," *AHA Perspectives* (May/June 1996): 11-12.

32. Martin W. Lewis and Kären E. Wigen, *The Myth of Continents: A Critique of Metageography* (Berkeley: University of California Press, 1997).

33. See Carol Gluck, "Asia in Time," *Journal of Asian Studies* (Nov. 1997).

34. David N. Keightley, "Early Civilization in China: Reflections on How It Became Chinese," in Paul S. Ropp, ed., *Heritage of China: Contemporary Perspectives on Chinese Civilization* (Berkeley: University of California Press, 1990). pp. 15-54.

35. Lynda Shaffer, "Southernization," *Journal of World History* 5, no. 1 (1994):15.

36. S.A.M. Adshead, *China in World History* (New York: St. Martin's Press, 1988).

37. Eric Wolf, *Europe and the Peoples without History* (Berkeley: University of California Press, 1982), pp. 232-61.

38. Michael Kidron and Ronald Segal, *The State of the World Atlas,* fifth edition (London: Penquin Books, 1995).

39. Jay A. Levinson, ed., *Circa 1492: Art in the Age of Exploration* (New Haven: Yale University Press, 1991).

40. Ray Huang, *1587: A Year of No Significance: The Ming Dynasty in Decline* (New Haven: Yale University Press, 1981).

41. Examples of older syllabi are available in Kevin Reilly, ed., *World History* (New York: Markus Wiener Publishing, 1985), more recent examples on the Web and the internet.

THE NEOLITHIC TRANSITION: HUNTING-GATHERING TO SEDENTARY VILLAGE FARMING AND PASTORALISM

Walter A. Fairservis

It is generally accepted by anthropologists that *Homo sapiens sapiens* emerged during the last stage of the Pleistocene epoch and that he inhabited Eurasia as early as 50,000 years ago. Variations developed as the species adapted to diverse environmental factors; the modern human races are the consequence.

Environmental factors, which included extremes of cold and hot climate, differences in nutrition, selective values relative to disease, and regional stresses of a hunting-gathering way of life, caused genetic changes of a complex type that stimulated cognitive capabilities. Science has not yet defined these changes, but it is clear that the human mind was stimulated to an unprecedented degree. One result was the development of speech, a symbolic way of communicating and of obtaining vicarious experiences. This contributed to the creation in the human brain of a cognitive memory bank far beyond the enactive and iconic levels characteristic of hominids in earlier Pleistocene times.

The late Pleistocene also saw the final development of the species and varieties of fauna and flora which were to characterize the landscape. These included potentially domesticable forms such as the millets, wheats, barleys, rice, and legumes, as well as goats, sheep, dogs, cattle, buffalo, onagers, and horses.

With the gradual retreat of the last great glacier in Eurasia there was a shift of the earth's climatic zones north of the equator toward their modern positions. There was also the effect on ecological zoning whereby flora and fauna characteristic of alpine terrain moved up into mountainous regions and were replaced by those of temperate zone ecologies in the lower levels, and by those of semitropical or even arid ecologies in the lowest-lying regions. As a result of these changing conditions numerous ecological niches were created, running from seashores to the crests of mountain ranges. Some of these, such as the great river basins, plains, and deserts, extended over vast areas; others, as exemplified by upland valleys, oases, marshes, and lake shores, were smaller in area.

This ecological variety created equivalent variations in the hunting-gathering way of life. For example, there developed a flint-blade tool technology which called for the use of various tools in the making of a final complex artifact. Except in Europe, where cave paintings and a variety of figurines and ornaments shed some light on socio-religious developments, the rest of Eurasia offers little extant evidence of anything other than technological and economic ways of life. The evidence suggests that hunting-gathering in small bands with rather precise seasonal movement within given regions was the norm in most parts of Asia. In Europe there were larger concentrations of people and the animal and plant resources upon which they depended. Some historians have argued for sizable tribal groups in western and southern France, evidence of which are the famous cave clusters of the Dordogne, in which were religious sanctuaries where magic hunting rituals were performed. At Dolni Vestonice in Slovakia, a Gravettian site dated about 24,000 B.C.E., there is evidence of camps near a river where hunters slaughtered numbers of young mammoths which concentrated there in winter. This meat resource, along with small mammals, fish, and edible materials such as hazelnuts, allowed for a concentration of probably at least a hundred people at each camp, and for several thousand in the region proper.

A similar situation seems to have prevailed in much of central and western Europe, differing only in emphasis upon certain food animals: reindeer, bison, horse, buffalo, etc. Indeed, where adequate studies have been made the evidence suggests that the whole spectrum of locally available plants and animals was exploited, not only for subsistence but for dyes, paint, shelter, artifacts, and probably medicinal purposes, which is typical among hunting-gathering peoples everywhere.

One hypothesis enjoying widespread support among historians is that as the last phases of the Pleistocene occurred and the variety of ecological niches appeared, some groups migrated north and eastward in search of the plants and animals upon which they had traditionally depended. Thus Ice-Age hunters of the Gravettian type may have moved into the Ukraine as the tundra-taiga biozones with which they were familiar slowly receded northward. Others have hypothesized that groups remained in the same region while gradually changing the basis of their subsistence. A more likely hypothesis is that the group's movements within a region along traditional seasonal routes made certain ecologies in a changing climate more acceptable as a new subsistence basis than others. For example, highland-lowland migration would be altered to take advantage of changing conditions that resulted in longer summers and shorter winters as long as subsistence resources necessary to a hunting-gathering way of life were available.

About 14,000 years ago *Homo sapiens sapiens* divided into groups along several general lines: those who located in increasingly marginal areas and maintained older ways of life; those who occupied regions where regular sources of subsistence were widely available; and those who were in proximity to a variety of ecological niches. The consequences were different for each group. The first group faced gradual extinction as the Pleistocene environment faded away. The second group exhibited a conservative trend, continuing an established pattern of subsistence, such as that found among the shellfish- and fish-hunter-gatherers of the Jomon of Japan or the so-called Mesolithic hunters of central and western India and the Hoabinhian of Southeast Asia. The third group—prevalent in western Asia from the Caspian Sea littoral westward to southeastern Europe and including the slopes of the Zagros Mountains, the Mediterranean littoral, and the basins of the river systems (those of both interior and exterior drainage)—developed varieties of economic dependencies. There were vole and seal hunters in the Caspian region; gazelle, deer, and onager hunters in the marginal lands fringing the growing deserts; wild cattle, boar, and deer hunters in the Anatolian highlands; goat and sheep hunters on the slopes of the Zagros; fishers along the maritime and lakeside shore. Throughout there is evidence of active gathering of wild grains, legumes, nuts, and herbs, as well as snails, tortoises, and the like. It is notable that in this region many of the groups with different subsistence emphases were in contact with each other and shared many traits. Indeed, there is evidence that obsidian, horn, seashell, and perhaps native dyes were traded across considerable distances.

It seems certain that in the process of natural selection generally, variety is a factor in stimulating change. Whether one can reduce that to a principle of challenge and response, as did the historian Toynbee, is debatable, but it is perhaps no coincidence that the first successful experiments in the domestication of plants and animals took place in western Asia in precisely the region where there was the greatest variety of subsistence emphases. We can assume that this variety was matched by differences in language, and by changes in social organization reflective of the economic exploitation of the different ecological niches. Most interesting, however, is that by and large there were no major technological innovations, although tool-making became increasingly refined (small, even tiny, blade tools were inserted into bone or wooden handles or shafts). The introduction of the bow and arrow and the use of grinding in the manufacture of artifacts were not, in this sense, revolutionary. Thus it can be argued that improvements in technology did not in themselves spur the domestication of plant and animal life and the development of sedentary village farming.

Rather, it was increased cognitive awareness together with intensified exploitation of contiguous ecological niches that constituted the key factors in the fundamental transition to agriculture, what is called the **Neolithic revolution.** R.J. Braidwood's propensity theory, which states that *Homo sapiens sapiens* was in direct contact with those plants and animals which were potentially domesticable, gains greater validity when one recognizes that change is gradual and evolutionary when it occurs in isolated groups, but that innovation or experimentation in one area can lead to rapid change spreading among groups which are in regular contact with one another.

The basis of innovation and change is therefore to be found in western Asia, where diverse groups were in contact. Domestication is a fairly complex process which requires human interference in the life cycle, and thus the behavior, of otherwise wild, or feral, species. In horticulture, this means obtaining control over seed bearing, planting, protecting, and nurturing growth. The plants are then harvested and kernels are processed into flour, which is then used to make an edible product. The plants must be artificially selected according to their ability to survive in ecologies other than their own. Similarly, animal life, particularly sheep and goats at the earliest stages of animal domestication, must develop a dependence on man for food and protection. Animals which breed in sufficient number are required to ensure a durable supply of meat, milk, and wool or fur.

There is little doubt that one consequence of the hunting-gathering way of life which characterized human history for millennia was a profound familiarity with a wide spectrum of plant and animal life. This familiarity almost certainly existed before the advent of *Homo sapiens sapiens*. The difference, however, was that in late Pleistocene and early recent times populations divided into different ecological niches contiguous to one another, intensely exploiting these niches; they also had the cognitive capability to store experience in memory and thus possessed a more sophisticated intellectual capacity than ever before. The concern now was not merely to find subsistence but to create it. Such subsistence on agriculture developed in different parts of the world. In western Asia cereals (wheat and other grains) formed the basis for the Neolithic revolution, in MesoAmerica, maize, and in East and Southeast Asia, millet and rice. The degree to which the transition to subsistence on agriculture was an indigenous development or was stimulated by diffusion from the earlier known sites in western Asia is a question of controversy. (See "Afterword.")

The site which provides the best data for understanding some aspects of the process that led to domestication of plants and animals is Çatalhüyük in central Anatolia. It is a large mound located near marshland in a basin of interior drainage which is one of the most important grain-growing areas in modern Turkey. Still only partially excavated, Çatalhüyük produced numerous occupation levels dating to a period around 6000 B.C.E. The excavators unearthed a settlement of mud-brick houses whose walls butted against one another, allowing for no alleyways or avenues. Entrance to the houses was through holes in the thatched and plastered roofs. Each house had an oven hearth and a storeroom. Dramatically, there were earthen benches around three of the walls, under which were found the skeletons of men, women, and children (the adults separated by sex). Some of the bones were stained with red ochre, and objects of daily life—necklaces and tools—were found among them. The disjointed bones indicate that the deceased were initially taken away from the settlement to have their flesh removed either by deliberate defleshing or, more likely, by local birds of prey. The cleaned bones were then interred in the houses. Most striking were a series of paint-on-plaster murals found in certain rooms, thought to be shrines. These murals show, among other things, hunting rituals carried out by males while females watch. The female role, in turn, is depicted by modeled clay breasts attached to the walls, within which are weasel or fox jaws, and by stone figurines placed in the grain bins of the storerooms, some of which show females giving birth.

This important Neolithic site provides an example for understanding some aspects of the process that led man from hunting-gathering to domestication and cereal agriculture in western Asia. The evidence strongly suggests that at Çatalhüyük males were hunters of big game and females were agriculturalists. Prior to the advent of the plow, it was with the hoe and the dibble stick that grains such as emmer wheat, einkorn, six-row naked barley, and also peas were cultivated. Males hunted onager, deer, boar, wild cattle, and sheep. Gathering, probably by both sexes, brought almond, pistachio, and acorn nuts as well as juniper and hack-berries to the early human pantry.

The murals depicting hunting rituals provide evidence of sodalities, presumed to be clans, whose membership was confined to males. Females, as ethnohistorical parallels indicate, owned the land they cultivated. In such cases matrilineal descent was critical to the social organization, in which males were pooled by females in order to ensure that those who were familiar with the hunting territories remained in residence. Moreover, the custom of burying the dead within the settlement ensured the presence of the spirits of the deceased and thus the permanency of the household.

This sexual division of labor suggests that females were the first to domesticate plants because child-rearing and household management made it necessary to gather plants in the proximity of the settlement. Harlan has demonstrated that a family of five, working for a week or so in the fields, could harvest enough wild grain in season to feed the family for a year. This does not, of course, include the process of converting the wild kernels into flour for bread-making. Clearly the raw grain is not inedible, but it is the roasting and grinding which makes grain central in a subsistence economy. Thus it was in food processing that females made the critical contribution to plant domestication, as this subsistence resource became increasingly important in the human diet after 10,000 B.C.E. It can be stated with certainty that sharp observation coupled with general experimentation led from simple imitation of the natural process (i.e., the sowing of seed by drop-off from the ripe plant and the scattering by wind) to the development of methods of planting, nurturing growth, and providing protection from birds during the harvesting season. Eventually, of course, the reaping of grain in quantity led to the need for storage, and thus the storage bin became a characteristic feature of human settlements from Anatolia to southwestern Iran, from the shores of the Levant to the slopes of the Zagros Mountains in western Iran. It is evident from this distribution that prehistoric people were carrying seed of wild grains, which are essentially upland flora, to lowlands, and were increasingly successful in developing lowland tolerance for grain growth generally.

The flocking tendency of wild goats and sheep was critical in their domestication. These animals are likewise found in upland habitats, where they gather in sizable groups. Such habitats occur on the slopes of the Zagros and Elburz mountains in Iran. In consideration of pet-making, whereby young animals are given human care which establishes dependencies in the ensuing adult, it is not unexpected that man was able to develop flocks of sheep and goats. In this development the dog was probably a necessity. This animal also grew from a dependent puppy to a tamed adult dependent on man for a degree of care, returning protection and assistance in herding the flocks. It is noteworthy that sheep flock tightly and move together, whereas goats act far more individually. It is good strategy to mix goats with sheep; the former provide a more stable flock, resistant to the panic to which sheep are prone. It is probable that early goat domestication had something to do with this factor. Sheep are grazers, providing abundant meat and wool; goats are browsers, capable of finding food in the same ecologies without interfering with the sheep.

Hunting was still a significant part of the year's activities in much of western Asia as late as 5500 B.C.E. Thus from 10,000 to 5500 B.C.E. or even later in some parts, the settlements show a mix of domesticated or semidomesticated plants and animals with those on which hunter-gatherer societies depend. Each region varies in the kinds of animals and other subsistence resources evidenced. The settlement patterns found at Çatalhüyük are repeated, although less elaborately, in other settlements: secondary burial within houses, closely clustered houses, storerooms, female figurines, small flint and grinding tools, and proximity to fields capable of grain cultivation. Clearly, settlements became increasingly permanent at this time. As far east as Baluchistan in central Asia, however, there is evidence of transhumance, the seasonal movement of flocks between uplands and lowlands. There seems little doubt that as hunting game became less an essential activity and more a matter of prestige, the seasonal following of the game to some degree ran counter to the thrust toward permanency of settlement; the sexual division of labor noted at Çatalhüyük was thus reinforced.

In sum, over a five-thousand-year (or longer) period in western

Asia human societies gradually shifted away from the utilization of a wide spectrum of plants and animals and concentrated upon a select body of plants and animals for subsistence. This transformation, which likely originated in the highland areas (what Braidwood has called the hilly flanks of the classical Fertile Crescent), was made possible by the availability of potentially domesticable plants and animals, the variation of ecologies, where innovation in one niche often spread to contiguous niches, and the cognitive capability of man to relate results of one stage to other stages in the process of invention. This cognitive development deserves comment. Jean Piaget, the eminent French pioneer in scholarship on child cognitive development, delineated stages in this process. According to his work, as advanced and modified by Jerome Bruner and others, a child moves from a one-to-one relationship to his environment as he learns through his physical senses what is hot or cold, comfortable or uncomfortable, etc., to a one-with-others relationship as he conceives of self in the context of his relations to others or, in effect, becomes aware of his social identity. The final stage is one in which the child reacts to symbols, i.e., signs relative to the surrounding environment, whether physical or social, without requiring the immediate presence of that which is signified. The cognitive evolution of hominids is roughly parallel, demonstrated by the increasing evidence of the evolution of the species from the Australopithecine stage, characterized by an essentially mammalian reaction to nature, to the *Homo erectus* stage (as exemplified by Peking man), marked by the growth and distribution of larger social groups, and finally to the symbol-using *Homo sapiens Neanderthalensis* and later the *Homo sapiens sapiens* phases associated with early human cultures. There is no doubt, in fact, that *Homo sapiens sapiens* is the most advanced in symbol utilization and development, from which derives one of civilization's most telling attributes, writing. However, in the period during which domestication was taking place, the critical symbolic activity was speech. The growing complexities of the domestication process, together with the attendant social and ideological shifts, resulted in an increase of words. That is, for every innovation a new substantive (noun) had to be used to link the initial idea to the process of creation to the final idea or product. This was generally true whenever tools were made in the remotest times, that is, the idea was expressed before the final product was created. However, with domestication the process was more complicated. It was not only a matter of naming objects, people, and phenomena, like the seasons or the rise and fall of the sun and moon. Marshak has demonstrated that this naming process was already under way in the Paleolithic, the period before the development of agriculture. But the verbalization or statement of action required a meaningful shift in cognition. For when there are two complementary objects (for example, a mortar and a pestle) and each lacks identity without the other, the relationship is expressed with a verb, to mortar, to pestle, to grind, to pound, etc. In other words, for every substantive there has to be an active verbal equivalent. Thus in the process of domestication we have both new nouns and new verbs. In the creation of verbs from nouns there is a mental stimulus in the symbolic order of a most profound kind. Thus from all the objects, known relationships between objects, and assumptions as to social organization, polity, and ideology, a sophisticated vocabulary of substantives and verbal equivalents emerges. Whatever the language that was spoken at this stage of development (possibly an agglutinative form based on root morphemes affixed to a fairly simple syntax), with domestication came greater complexity. This pressed speakers to find words to express such abstracts as next year, fertility, danger, death, and perhaps even concepts of justice and happiness.

The archaeological evidence in western Asia demonstrates that over the critical five-thousand-year period (ca. 10,000 to 5000 B.C.E.), domestication—if not always central—was nonetheless increasingly present and was beginning to reach into Europe and across the Iranian plateau toward the Indian subcontinent and to the limits of the cultivable lands of the west Turkestan region of central Asia. Thus, agriculture, once independently developed, also spread to other areas by diffusion.

From 5500 to 4000 B.C.E. significant changes were taking place in western Asia and immediately adjacent regions. It appears that while big game and thus hunting were rapidly disappearing, not only did farming increase in importance but more and more farming settlements were locating in fertile alluvial foothill country and plains. With this change also came the domestication of cattle. Wild cattle inhabit grasslands and the edges of marshes and rivers, moving seasonally according to the availability of forage. Studies indicate that cows with their young form distinct clusters, while bulls roam more individually in loose, often far-flung, groups. Bulls select certain cows in estrus periods and remain sentinel over them in times of crisis, but the protection of the young from carnivores is primarily the cow's role; the clustering of the cows in a herd is a viable defensive tactic. Cattle, like sheep, are grazers, in contrast to browsing goats. As they moved into the grasslands where good soil and water were found, farming communities were coterminous with sheep flocks; goats remained ubiquitous. Presumably, cattle were domesticated at first for the subsistence advantages of meat, hide, and horn, but later took hold as a source of milk and probably butter, as adult cows were retained in herds and bulls selected out for breeding and slaughter.

Cattle were a great boon, not only as an important food resource but also, increasingly, for their energy. Sometime after 5000 B.C.E. the plow was invented in western Asia; initially it was a simple wooden apparatus, but later more efficient stone plows were developed.

The seasonal migration of cattle herds led to the development of **pastoral societies,** whose primary dependence was upon the herds; they also engaged in cultivation of grain or obtained agricultural products via trade. The sedentary farming communities which now sprung up in the fertile lowlands had to limit the size of their herds, as cattle competed with the farmer in the use of the grassland or cultivable soils; cattle were used increasingly as draught animals, and to a lesser extent as sources of meat and milk.

The development of village farming brought other significant changes in **sedentary societies.** Social organization shifted from a tendency toward a matrilineal kinship system rooted in female possession of cultivated land (as in Çatalhüyük) to a patrilineal kinship system with property passed on from father to son or a chosen male heir. This may have been a consequence of the shift from hunting to farming as males, no longer having big game to chase, became involved in herding cattle and cultivating ever larger tracts of land. With the invention of the plow, the possibility of exploiting the land was increased, although the plow demanded greater strength from the farmer.

Wealth and power in village society increasingly depended on the possession of land or, in the case of pastoralists, cattle. The need for male heirs who would work the land led to polygyny, the practice of a man having several wives at once. In patrilocal-patrilineal societies, exogamy was practiced, whereby the wife left her birth family to live in the husband's residence. Extended families, with all the sons, their wives, and children residing with the parents in the patriarchal household, were common. In cases where the daughter remained home and her husband or husbands lived with her and a male heir was not produced, sororal contracts were arranged. Under such a contract the son of a wife's or husband's sister was designated as heir. As a result, barring disease or other local factors of mortality, population grew rather rapidly.

The central position of the eldest male as both authority and lineage leader of the family resulted in a characteristic funeral practice in western Asia. Although cemeteries were located at the outskirts of villages, the body or the skull, in some cases plastered over with a likeness of the deceased male, was buried in the floor of the house. This demonstrated respect for the dead and ensured the continuity of the lineage. Rather spectacular examples of such remains have been found at the mound of Tell-es-Sultan at Jericho in Palestine and at numerous other sites in western Asia.

The sodalities, or groupings, which bound males collectively in the hunting of animals when intensive cooperation was necessary underwent a change in response to the problems posed by sedentary life. The most critical problem was that of a father having several sons but only a limited amount of land (or cattle). If each son received a share, the property would be fractionalized. If one son, the eldest, for example, was the sole heir, he would have to provide for the other sons, a situation that often led to familial conflict. One solution was what the Chinese later called "the division of the stove" or "family division," whereby some sons established homes elsewhere at the expense of family unity. Another was the development of **familial clans,** with descendants acknowledging the original ancestor and celebrating rites using the symbols and rituals of the main family. Though other kinds of sodalities may have existed, the familial clan, whose members were often widely dispersed, was probably typical of the time. The repetitive designs painted on pottery which are found with increasing frequency as one goes from Anatolia to eastern Iran are evidence of this custom. Though some of the designs were purely ornamental and others probably religious in origin, certain of them were familial in representation. The division of extended families was then one consequence of the rise of sedentary village farming and pastoralism.

The continued focus on females in cultist practices derived from the previously central place of females in both the economy and social organization. There is evidence of cultism in which human females were central even before the earliest experiments in domestication. The famous Venuses of the Upper Paleolithic of Europe (or the possible female shamanism at Dolni Vestonice) and figures with female breasts and the sharp teeth of carnivores show females to have been central to certain cults. The depiction on a figurine from Çatalhüyük of a human birth by a female between two leopards indicates a relationship between birth and death, or at least the dangers attendant on giving birth. Significantly, no phallic symbols (common to later cultures) are known in this period in western Asia. Birth, agriculture, females, danger, death were all bound together in the symbolism of the time. Later, as the control of agriculture in the village economy passed from the female, the central theme of the female and fertility still persisted in cultist practices. Female figurines from later periods have been found in the habitation debris of villages and, though some may be dolls, their style and prevalence reinforce the idea that the ancient cults still persisted. At the famous site of Tepe Hissar in northeastern Iran, the graves of females in the cemetery contain painted pottery on which is depicted the leopard motif and stamp seals bearing designs known from far earlier times.

As can be determined from modern excavations, the western Asian village at that time comprised a number of earthen-floored brick-adobe houses separated by alleyways and usually informally arranged. Each house contained a hearth, perhaps an oven, and a storage facility. The floor plans varied; some were round while other were square or rectangular, and the rooms were of varying size and shape. Several families or households probably lived together. At almost every excavation the remains of mortars, pestles, rollers, knives, pots, beads, pins, and other artifacts of daily life have been found. Bones, seeds, and broken artifacts were apparently tossed into nearby alleyways and are occasionally found on the habitation floor, perhaps suggesting that tidiness was not a high priority. The often beautifully painted and fired pottery, the expertly woven reed mats and cloth of woven hair, as well as the order of the houses themselves, give an impression of a good life within the bounds of survival nature had laid down. Study of the skeletal remains at Çatalhüyük suggests that malaria was a factor in the mortality rate, but there is also indication that over the centuries the site was inhabited, life expectancy grew to about thirty-five years of age for males and about thirty for females. Thus natural selection resulted in a longer lifespan and an increasing adaptation to the sedentary conditions of village life. As populations grew, villages developed and spread throughout western Asia.

With the migration movement of people toward the lower hill country and grasslands, settlements sprang up in the alluvial basins of riverine territories such as that of the lower Tigris and Euphrates. On the lower Tigris, the meandering river course and the drainage streams from the nearby hills to the east provided ideal watered alluvial land for farming. In the hills, weir damming, which permitted the diversion or storage of stream flow, was already practiced by farming communities; settlement at critical points where streams conjoined was related to the capability of controlling water flow through weirs. The villages established at these conjunctions grew in importance, some of them eventually becoming the cities of Sumeria, one of the world's earliest civilizations. An important factor in this development was the gradual change in polity which intensive village farming brought about.

We can assume that in the earliest villages where agriculture was prominent, what Braidwood has called "secondary village farming," leadership was essentially a family affair under the authority of a male. As villages grew and a number of families, not always related, made up the population, village elders or those who held the family leaderships met in council to consider pan-village affairs. In situations where a number of villages were tied together by marriage and trade, as well as by common interests of defense, of access to water and other natural resources, and of the equitable distribution of subsistence resources in times of difficulty, perhaps clan representatives met to elect regional leaders. In time, with the accumulation of wealth and consequent power, leadership roles became hereditary and a familial dynastic situation arose, with attendant alliances forged among the leaders. As new settlements were established, certain village farming communities developed as nonsubsistence administrative bureaucracies to resolve questions of water and land control and to respond to the need for goods and services distribution in order to maintain authority and to keep settlements cohesive. This would eventually lead to the development of city-states, a later consequence of sedentary settlement.

Another change was the gradual diffusion of village farming and cattle pastoralism westward into what is now the Balkan area and the Danube basin and eastward toward the Indian subcontinent and eastern Asia. This was a slow movement, not a migration. It was propelled by such factors as family fission, the need for pasturage for larger herds (particularly where herd size determined wealth), prolonged periods of drought, and a need for better fields for cultivation. Most likely a desire for aggrandizement was also a factor, as human ambition in the more populous areas of western Asia sought to control lands and people for the local benefit. Though in large part a later story, the search for raw materials such as metal ore, hard stone, fine wood and semiprecious stones (like lapis, carnelian, jasper, and serpentine) also played a role. As in the biblical story of the Tower of Babel, the movement and concentration of people at this time resulted in differences in language, economic growth, style of ornamentation, and social identity. These differences, readily identifiable by modern archaeologists, are testimony to an ongoing process of change, adaptation, and diffusion.

Though the above discussion traces developments in western Asia, it must be emphasized that developments in domestication, technology, and social organization were observable in other parts of Asia and were going on at the same time in other regions as well.

At Bagor in central India there is evidence of experimentation in grain cultivation perhaps as early as 6000 B.C.E. Rice and small cattle were probably domesticated in Thailand (Ban Chiang) after 5500 B.C.E. Recent work in China by archaeologists and paleontologists has unearthed strong evidence of the indigenous development of domesticated millet (fifth millennium B.C.E.) and rice (perhaps a few centuries later). Since these two plants were basic to later Chinese agriculture, this early development suggests the indigenous foundations of Chinese civilization. Other evidence is accumulating in both Southeast Asia and China of the early domestication of such later staples of the east Asian economy as tea, mulberry, soybeans, and the water buffalo. There is little doubt that in much of Eurasia at the close of the Pleistocene, groups were experimenting with potentially domesticable plants and animals.

As early as 6000 B.C.E., settled life dependent on grain domestication and cattle transhumance was established in the Indus River plain, as evidenced at Mehrgarh in the low plain of Kachi in present-day Pakistan. It seems clear that this development was the first in the evolution of settled life on the Indian subcontinent. In China, the situation was more complex. The site of Banpo [Pan P'o] in the Wei River basin, dating to around 4000 B.C.E., represents China's earliest developed village farming community of the Yangshao culture. Its population practiced a slash-and-burn type of shifting agriculture largely dependent on the cultivation of an indigenous millet. In general, Yangshao sites are found in what K.C. Chang has referred to as China's nuclear area, which includes the alluvial plain at the conjunction of the Wei River and the Huang He (Yellow River), and the eastward region of the great North China loessic and alluvial plain, where classical Chinese civilization had its seat. The interest of sites like Banpo lies in the provocative mixture of independently developed indigenous traits and those that may well have resulted from contact and diffusion from the western Asian developments described above. Although Yangshao settlements were characterized by the mobility associated with slash-and-burn agriculture, large communities of more than eighty houses have been found. At Banpo, both ground-level and semisubterranean houses of wattle-and-daub and post construction have been identified, suggesting single-family occupancy. Grain storage bins and animal pens found in the center of these house clusters, however, also suggest communal sharing. Evidence has been found of a great longhouse, constructed at a later stage in the center of the village square. This house was partitioned into rooms, each with its own hearth.

The area around Banpo was probably forested; it is no coincidence, then, that pigs, essentially forest animals, were domesticated and became very much a part of the economy. At that time they were also widely used in Europe to reclaim forest lands.

As one might expect, in the technology of Yangshao settlements there was a prevalence of the stone axes and adzes necessary for felling trees, and the chisels and hammers, scrapers, and knives for carving wood. Also commonplace were ground stone hoes and shovels for clearing and digging fields that were to be planted. Stone, shell, bone, and antler provided the material for the necessary arrowheads, awls, beads, fishhooks, sinkers, etc., familiar to village life throughout the world. In addition, Yangshao artisans made utilitarian pottery in a variety of forms and finely painted ceramic vessels, largely used as burial objects. In cemeteries that were part of the village, the dead were laid out accompanied by objects of daily life and often by these decorated vessels. Some of these decorations represent human figures and include designs suggesting rituals, perhaps pertaining to fertility and ancestor cults.

The Yangshao type of village farming is unique to East Asia, although there are similarities to the West in the painted pottery, the domestic pig, the cultivation of grain, burial customs, etc. These similarities need not be interpreted as signs of the diffusion of ideas as such. These early Chinese sites, which are chronologically at least three thousand years later than the western Asian sites showing domestication, essentially arose independent of direct contact with areas to the west, although there may have been some contact of which we have no evidence.

Along the Chinese coast, especially to the south and along lake shores, there is increasing evidence of a people using cord-marked pottery, dependent on shellfish and netted fish, and already having a technology which enabled them to cut trees, make canoes, and hunt effectively. The suggestion is made that these people also created gardens in which they grew tubers, edible roots, and wild millets ancestral to the later cultivated types. One possible hypothesis is that the contact between these ancestral Chinese (an eastern branch of *Homo sapiens sapiens*) and the myths and techniques of western domestication resulted in the development of domestication in China's nuclear area. This is for future work to determine.

Following the Yangshao in central China, the Lungshanoid stage of developed village farming, thoroughly Chinese in character, arose and became the preamble to the civilization to come. This stage will be discussed in the next chapter.

In sum, the development of sedentary village life in Asia was the consequence of a variety of factors, including greater cognitive awareness due to the changing geographical conditions at the end of the Ice Age. The exploitation of varied but contiguous ecological niches led to the Neolithic Revolution, and to the development of pastoral sedentary agricultural societies, which were the prelude to the different indigenous civilizations that arose in the centuries to come.

AFTERWORD

In any modern presentation of ideas based on archaeological evidence, there is an inherent imprecision which is frustrating to those educated in the hard sciences. This lack of exactness arises directly out of the fact that human remains, whether physical or cultural, are preserved only randomly. Most of what had once been a way of life is lost. This is a given in archeological interpretation and is particularly so in dealing with evidence of the early human past of Eurasia.

However, modern science, represented by such fields as paleopathology, paleobotany, and paleozoology that use radiocarbon and thermoluminescence techniques of dating and apply research on geomorphological evolution and paleoclimatology, is now able to reconstruct a portion of an extinct way of life with considerable accuracy, from which the anthropologist can make assumptions about cultural behavior. Where there is no solid evidence, we are required to speculate.

What concrete evidence we do have makes it possible to sketch in, as it were, certain fundamental steps in the early history of humankind.

In the case of the revolutionary transition from hunting-gathering to sedentary village farming and pastoralism, I have argued that this first occurred in western Asia because, in a nuclear area in which potentially domesticable plants and animals were present, diverse ecologies were occupied by diverse cultural groups. A valid counterargument is that a similar situation existed elsewhere in the world, although with differing patterns and consequences. This theory of first emergence in western Asia rests upon the contention that the necessary preconditions existed there on a scale not matched elsewhere.

The growing evidence that western Asia was a meeting ground for cultural and human strains drawn from northeastern Africa, eastern Europe, and Iran demonstrates that diverse cultural influences were a precondition to the transition to settled life. Nowhere else in either Europe or Asia did such diversity exist or did an integrating process occur on a **comparable scale** in the ecological setting previously described. Whether the invention of agriculture was the act of individual genius or the consequence of numbers of people manipulating the features of local ecologies on a pragmatic and experiential basis, the fact remains that **acceptance of innovation,** not simply the innovation itself, is the critical factor. There is no doubt at all that with the close of the Pleistocene there were probably many inventions critical to settled life in areas far from western Asia, but these tended to occur in relative isolation and generally gained little acceptance at the time. Certainly it appears that a **complex** of innovations creating the conditions necessary for settled life did occur outside of the area, but at a demonstrably later time. The factor of diffusion from west to east must be given due consideration. Clearly, the combination of a high level of cognitive awareness evolving out of a sophisticated integrative prehistory and ecological and cultural diversity was responsible for the first appearance of settled village farming in Asia. Nothing in the archaeological evidence unearthed so far appears to contradict this assumption.

A second reservation can be made concerning male-female roles and how they changed with the advent of the plow. A number of societies in the world engage in labor-intensive plant cultivation without evidence of a period of female control of that cultivation. But according to an analysis of social organization by G.P. Murdock[1] based on data gathered from 250 societies in all parts of the world, that situation is rare:

"The condition which most frequently lifts [the woman's] eco-

nomic contribution to a level above that of the man is the introduction of agriculture into a society previously dependent upon
hunting and gathering. Since agriculture is usually woman's work
matrilocal residence and matrilineal descent tend to be particularly common among lower agricultural peoples" (p. 205). The
shift to patrilocal and patrilineal societies can occur "when men
supplant women as tillers of the soil, often in consequence of
harnessing their domestic animals to the plow" (p. 206). The interpretation of the remains at Çatalhüyük, as set forth on previous
pages, is not at variance with Murdock's sample. There it is very
clear that females were the agriculturists and males the hunters.

NOTE

1. G.P. Murdock, *Social Structure* (New York: Macmillan Co.,
1949), pp. 202–6.

SELECTED REFERENCES

These are a number of important writings on the transition from
hunting-gathering to sedentary village farming and pastoralism.

Allchin, Bridget, and Allchin, Raymond. *The Rise of Civilization in India &
   Pakistan.* Cambridge: Cambridge University Press, 1982. The best
   summation to date.
Braidwood, R.J. *Prehistoric Men.* Glenview, IL: Scott, Foresman, 1967. A
   substantive overview and demonstration of his hypothesis.
Braidwood, R.J., and Wiley, Gordon R. *Courses toward Urban Life.* Chi-
   cago: Aldine, 1962. Includes discussions of the New and Old Worlds.
Chung, K.C. *The Archaeology of Ancient China.* Rev. ed. New Haven: Yale
   University Press, 1971. The best work on the subject.
Childe, V. Gordon. *New Light on the Most Ancient East.* New York: F.A.
   Praeger, 1952. A classic study.
Fairservis, Walter A., Jr. *The Roots of Ancient India.* 2d ed. Chicago:
   University of Chicago Press, 1975. A review of the late prehistory up
   to the Mehrgarh work.
Fairservis, Walter A., Jr. *The Threshold of Civilization.* New York:
   Scribners, 1975. A summary of the cognitive approach.
Hole, Frank; Flanner, Kent V.; and Neely, James A. *Prehistory and
   Human Ecology of the Deh Luran Plain.* Memoirs of the Museum of
   Anthropology, no. 1. Ann Arbor: University of Michigan Press,
   1969. An important report on the interpretation of archaeological evi-
   dence as it relates to the problem; a model of its kind.
Keightley, D.N., ed. *The Origins of Chinese Civilization.* Berkeley: Univer-
   sity of California Press, 1983. An essential group of papers by leading
   experts in the field.
Lamberg-Karlovsky, C.C. Introduction to *Hunters, Farmers and Civiliza-*

tions. Old World Archaeology Readings from *Scientific American*. San Francisco: W.H. Freeman & Co., 1979. Covers Southeast Asia as well as western Asia.

Marshack, Alexander. *The Roots of Civilization*. New York: McGraw-Hill, 1972. A pioneering study of the mind of prehistoric man.

Misra, V.N., and Bellwood, Peter, eds. *Recent Advances in Indo-Pacific Prehistory*. New Delhi: Oxford University Press, 1985. Numerous important contributions in the section on "Monsoonal Lands."

Mellart, James. *The Neolithic of the Near East*. New York: Scribners, 1975. A net summation of the evidence.

Murdock, George Peter. *Social Structure*. New York: Free Press, 1949. The best ethnographic review of the subject.

PRIMARY CIVILIZATION IN ASIA

Walter A. Fairservis

Civilization, as defined by many anthropologists, is the most complex stage in the evolution of human culture. It is a stage at which symbolic behavior achieves most dramatic form in such activities as writing and art—and in which large parts of the human population are concentrated in communities or states. Characteristically, a civilization organizes the population into distinct groups based on a division of labor. These groups include not only subsistence raisers (farmers, herders) but also artisans or laborers in specialized crafts (metallurgy, weaving, goldsmithing, brickmaking, pottery) whose products are used by the larger community. Common to most civilizations are the groups (bureaucrats, soldiers, rulers) dependent on but controlling the producers of subsistence and artifacts. Religion is often pantheistic, manifested in rituals, specialized buildings, temples, temple servants. In some polities the rulers have a special relationship to the deity or deities (god-kings, priest-kings).

In general, because civilizations are built on large interacting populations, goods and services exchange is complex and often involves nonresident groups (merchants, pedagogues, wandering entertainers) who help identify a people's sense of place in the world.

A distinction is often made between primary civilizations, which develop in large part indigenously (those of Egypt, Sumeria, the Harappans, Three Dynasty China [see below page 245–248 for a discussion of Three Dynasty, or San Dai, China), and secondary civilizations, which through contact or conquest succeed the primary civilizations and develop in part out of them (Achaemenid Persia, Classical Greece and Rome, the Mauryan Empire in India).

It is the primary civilizations that developed directly out of local sedentary farming and pastoralism that concern us here, particularly the Sumerian civilization in the area between the Tigris and the Euphrates rivers known as Mesopotamia, which, along with the Egyptian, emerged around 3200 B.C.E. A half a millennium or so later similar developments occurred in the so-called nuclear areas, the Indus Valley in South Asia and the Yellow River basin in East Asia.

In making this distinction one runs into a problem of definition. For many archaeologists studying the remains of ancient cultures, it is a culture's accomplishments in technology (such as state-wide irrigation systems, metal smelting and casting, sophisticated instruments of calculation), its monuments (pyramids, temple platforms, rock-cut tombs, hard-stone sculpture), its complex achievements in chemistry, and its sophisticated system of graphic symbols (writing, iconography) that qualify it to be considered a civilization. Since these advanced achievements relate to concepts of government and belief and possibly to sophisticated levels of thought, they provide a basis for assumptions about the character of the life of the time. This view supports the material positivism that sees technology as the foundation of civilization and equates the ultimate destruction of that technical foundation with the fall of the civilization historically.

A review of the cultures of early human history demonstrates that some had achieved high levels of technological accomplishment in a number of categories. Graphic symbolism, anticipating a system of writing, for example, was widely used in southeastern Europe as early as 4000 B.C.E., and it is known that large-scale engineering endeavors were undertaken in the late fourth and third millennia B.C.E. in central Asia (Turkmenistan) and the Indo-Iranian borderlands. Comparison of these remains from cultures which had no known direct successors with those of other cultures which evolved into primary civilizations shows little difference in many aspects. Thus the seeds of civilization were not confined to those areas where civilization did eventuate. It is likely that stages in the development of civilization have been fixed rather arbitrarily by scholars on the basis of the preserved evidence, which emphasizes technology. At their early, primarily technological, stages Sumeria, Egypt, Harappa, and Three Dynasty China have been generally included as phases of the great civilizations but are more properly seen as their precursors.

Some social scientists, historians, and other scholars argue that civilization only emerges when there is higher abstract thought, manifest in scientific activity, philosophical questioning, and the institutionalization of morality and its rationalization in ethical conduct and law. While this is demonstrated in a variety of ways, there is general agreement among these scholars that engineering achievements and other pragmatic demonstrations of applied knowledge are not in themselves criteria for the presence of civilization. Nor can one cite urbanization or the development of cities as a prerequisite for civilization. It can be demonstrated that numerous cultures had cities and knew urban life but did not develop into civilizations. Indeed, civilizations characterized by generally nonurban populations are very well known, such as early Pharaonic Egypt and Shang China.

Writing, as a commonly cited criterion for civilization, provides us with a more concrete basis for settling the controversy between what some call technocracy versus humanism in determining the presence of civilization. But there are two critical phases in the use of writing: an accounting and naming phase, and a literary and history phase. It is to a consideration of these two phases that we may turn in determining the presence or absence of civilization.

Chronologically one has to look at developments in southern Mesopotamia, for it is here that the world's first civilization, the Sumerian, appeared. Southern Mesopotamia, the so-called Fertile Crescent, is a flat area dominated by the meandering Tigris River. Relatively little rain falls in the region, but the rich alluvium, watered by the Tigris and subsidiary river flow emanating from the hills to the north, makes it highly productive agriculturally. It is a stoneless land with marshes in the delta area; thus clay and reeds are the primary building materials. The wood of palm trees is available in some areas.

In the period when village farming was developing, movement into the region was characterized by settlement at critical junction points where water access (and eventual control) was ensured. These settlements became centers of agricultural activity. Centralized storage facilities also appear to have been a magnet for the growth of these centers. Temples to a particular deity were erected and eventually became the most prominent structures of the developing centers.

There is evidence, for example in Sumerian records of assemblies of elders, that the farmer-settlers were initially gathered into clans with leadership provided by distinguished lineages. In time, wealth in land and the control of water (depending on whether one's land was at the head or the base of the irrigation system) became the decisive factors in determining leadership. As populations grew, established, dependable leadership became necessary to manage a redistribution system based on centralized storage and to control intersettlement rivalries that might lead to warfare. Indeed, a number of later Sumerian epics refer to great warrior kings, like Gilgamesh, and there is abundant archaeological evidence that defensive walls were constructed around the expanding centers on the Tigris plain.

Critical to an understanding of how the Sumerian civilization arose from these centers is the fact that not only was there active intersettlement contact—belligerent, economic, and social—but there were regular interactions with peoples to the east, in what became Assyria and is now western Iran, to the north in present-day Syria, and probably as far to the west as the Levant. It was this variety of contact that provided an essential stimulus for development. The need for raw materials—stone, metal ores, wood, spices—in the resource-poor plain motivated trade and international contact. Writing, which in its proto-form had been essentially pictographic, now became more efficient. It was a highly functional system, evolving initially to respond to accounting needs arising from storage and trade activities but gradually used for literary, historical, and legal purposes. Tokens, small objects used to represent commodities and whose number and size symbolized quantity, were also used as coins to represent merchandise of various sorts for barter. The designs on the tokens were probably precursors of the signs used in the writing system itself. The orthography, highly influenced by the use of reed styluses with which marks (cunei) were impressed into clay tablets, developed into an efficient cursive system (called cuneiform), in keeping with what seems to have been a fundamental characteristic of Sumerian civilization: the search for and development of an ordered society.

The clay tablets that have so far been deciphered offer substantial evidence of a belief that man was created to serve the gods through sacrifice, entertainment, and worship rituals. But at the same time, humanity was expected to order its own affairs; it is here that Sumerian civilization comes into full fruition. Not only were the ravages of flood, drought, and plague to be dealt with, but warfare, the problems of social friction in what may be called cities, and the need for reliable standards of value in the mercantile and politico-economic world of the times had to be addressed. Institutionalized order was required in divine worship and in the regulation of human affairs. The multiethnic, multioccupational, multivalue quality of the time apparently motivated far-reaching speculation, for ethnocentric as the Sumerians appeared to be, they nonetheless were concerned that their order be rooted in some kind of universal principle rather than in one arising out of a given city or group. This principle related human order to cosmic order, one result of which was the development of codified law. The famous Code of Hammurabi, a later Babylonian king, arose out of the precedents of earlier Sumerian codes. The laws were pragmatic and efficient; they involved the services of judges and witnesses and strove to avoid the vagaries of interpretation as far as possible. They were nevertheless described as having been received from the gods, and it was regarded as the wish of the gods that they be followed. In this the kings (who achieved their position by virtue of lineage or dynastic confirmation) were the instruments of the gods and the secular advocates of legal justice. The term priest-king may be an appropriate label for them.

The Sumerians (the name is derived from the biblical reference to the Plain of Shinar or Sumer and is used by scholars to differentiate their language from other ancient Mesopotamian languages) may have been inheritors of the accomplishments of earlier settlers (the Ubadians, who may have entered the plain around 4000 B.C.E.). By 3100 B.C.E., they were the masters of the place. Their original homeland was probably the Zagros Mountains to the east, and in memory of that place it appears they created on the flat plain mountains of brick, upon which they built their temples. These temple mountains, referred to later as ziggurats, were often over fifty feet in height and extended over an area of many hundreds of feet. Perhaps the presence of these platformed places of worship represented stability in an uncertain world, for the duress of the times and the accelerating variety of contacts with other cultures led to speculation about man and the universe and a rather astonishing period of innovation. The Sumerians were accomplished architects and the first to use the brick vault, the arch, and the dome. They appear to have developed the sailboat and the four-wheeled cart (often pulled by onagers or oxen). They knew how to solder metal and rivet bronze; they perfected the plow and the potter's wheel. In addition to their accomplishments in law, the Sumerians are also credited with having been the first to establish schools and a pharmacopoeia, to collect proverbs, histories, and love songs, and to hold literary debates. Whether or not future research will confirm these "firsts," the fact is that the Sumerian worldview was innovative and speculative. It was also somewhat pessimistic. A deep-seated sense of human inadequacy in the face of the forces of nature occurs in Sumerian writing. The discovery by the hero in the Epic of Gilgamesh of his own mortality in a universe ruled by the gods is echoed in Sophocles' tragedy about Oedipus, suggesting that the origins of the classic Greek worldview may lie in part in that of the Sumerians.

The history of Sumeria is one of constant internecine combat between the numerous city-states that were the successors to the earlier settlements of the Shinar region. The Sumerians were also subject to attacks by surrounding peoples, notably the Semitic pastoralists of Wahia, numerous powerful groups from the north and west, and the Elamites, a city-oriented group to the east. Sumerian political independence was lost after 2000 B.C.E., but the culture provided the foundation for later Mesopotamian civilizations.

Egypt, located in the northern part of Africa, was part of the vast civilized ecumene which originated in the eastern Mediterranean late in the fourth millennium B.C.E. The Egyptian civilization developed from Neolithic settlements in the fertile Nile River valley. A ruler named Menes founded the first Egyptian dynasty in about 3100 B.C.E., initiating 3000 years of Egyptian dynasties. The king (Pharaoh, Per-ha, or great house) was also a deity, and the royal tombs (including the pyramids) were built to ensure material comfort in the afterlife, an important part of Egyptian religious belief.

In contrast to Mesopotamian community centers, in Egypt there were small, scattered administrative centers set in alluvial areas along the Nile and its tributaries, and much of the population remained essentially rural. The capital was first Memphis and later Thebes.

Isolation and the agricultural dependability brought by the Nile, coupled with the arduous but productive work of the Egyptian peasantry, sustained the essential good fortune of the Egyptians. Two important developments resulted: a state cult with the king-pharaoh at its center and a fundamental morality given practical form. For the first, the Pharaoh was regarded as the essential cohesive force in the state: he was born God, "Sun of Ra," the sun god, and was also the secular authority, dependent on a growing bureaucracy critical for effective administration. Here the role of morality had its most pervasive influence. There were two resources for this bureaucracy: members of a landed aristocracy, whose origins were mostly found in local chiefdoms, and the general populace, where a man of ability might technically rise from peasant beginnings to vizier. Morality was expressed in a concept called *ma'at*, which essentially meant "truth," but a wider interpretation included ideas of duty, responsibility, and the knowledge that wisdom was not confined to noblemen or the privileged.

Good family relationships were recognized as demonstrating practical morality. Administrators, at any level, were required by society's moral order to observe *ma'at* in all that they did. In later times, in fact, one would have to stand before the gods and be judged as to whether one had observed "truth" in life or not, with consequences good or bad accordingly. In this sense of responsibility for one's action, codified law (in early Egyptian civilization) was unnecessary.

Egyptian writing, called hieroglyphics ("sacred carvings" in Greek), was first used for naming and accounting and gradually for rituals in mortuary cults and temples. The capability of writing abstract concepts using hieroglyphics, concepts like idea (before action), truth, creation, etc., is immensely significant in the evolution of thought. One aspect was a developing investigation into nature considered as object. The study of anatomy and the effect of injury on the human body, the solution of problems in geometry, algebra, and trigonometry, and the concept of sidereal time were some of the results of Egyptian investigations into nature.

The Sumerian and Egyptian civilizations are in sharp contrast to one another: the former dynamic, innovative, and in general holding a pessimistic view of the cosmos; the latter stable, conservative, with an optimistic view regarding man's place in the universe. Thus out of roots in early western Asian and northern African history two essentially different civilizations arose. Geography played its role but did not determine concepts of time and space in the two civilizations. Both Sumerian law and Egyptian moral order arose out of a concern for human life and the desire to promote human character as the basis of civilization itself.

In both the Sumerian and the Egyptian cases, there was an early stage of development (i.e., Mesopotamia before the Sumerian city-states, predynastic Egypt) followed by a second stage which produced a writing system for naming and accounting as well as a level of technological innovation that supported the creation of cities or states (archaic Egypt, early dynastic Sumer [ca. 3200–2600 B.C.E.]). In both cases this was followed by a concern with abstract ideas of justice, happiness, human behavior, and universals in man's relationship to self and the cosmos; and concerns with nature epitomized by the deities and in observable natural life (Middle Kingdom Egypt, middle and late dynastic Sumer [c. 2500–2000 B.C.E.]). In my view, only when a culture has developed to this stage can it be said to constitute a civilization.

Early civilizations in India and China invite similar consideration. The earliest culture in the Indian subcontinent is known as the Harappan civilization, named for the site at Harappa in the Indus Valley in present-day Pakistan, discovered in the early 1920s. A second large "urban" site belonging to the Harappan civilization was that of Mohenjo-Daro, located on the west bank of the Indus River in northern Sind and dating to the same time as the Sumerian civilization, probably 2300–1750 B.C.E. The fact that the Harappan culture was first discovered at these two large urban-like sites prompted some scholars to refer to it as an empire or state and to posit the existence of citadels, colonies, great kings, extensive trade, peasantries, etc. Continuing research of the Harappan culture, however, has revealed over a thousand rather small sites spread over a vast territory, from the vicinity of Delhi to the Narbada River in western India, with the greater number in the Indus River valley in Pakistan. Harappan sites have also been found as far away as Baluchistan and, remarkably, Badakhshan in northeastern Afghanistan, and probably in Kashmir as well. The majority of Harappan settlements were short-lived; even Mohenjo-Daro may have been occupied for less than two hundred years. Study of these sites also reveals that they were generally functional parts of a larger whole. That is, the sites included industrial centers (with kilns, metal smelting facilities, and shell or clay working areas), seasonal cattle camps, administrative and storage centers, and large capitals along main or subsidiary rivers. One gets the impression of a dispersed but organized society made up of agricultural specialists, herders, urban craftsmen, merchants, and bureaucrats integrated in an efficient symbiotic political and economic relationship.

The artifacts of the Harappans are essentially objects used in daily life. The few small but beautifully made statues, expressive clay figurines, and some well-executed jewelry do not bespeak the range of monumental art and design associated with the artifacts found in Egypt and Mesopotamia. Most intriguing are small, square seal-like tablets cut in soft stone with pierced bosses, indicating that they were to be worn on the person. These usually are engraved with motifs of domesticated bovids, goats, or, more rarely, wild animals—tiger, elephant, buffalo, or rhinoceros. These main symbols are generally surrounded by five or six graphemes which only recently have been deciphered as references to the name and status of the individual, who was usually a clan chief, or to his occupation or role in the bureaucracy. The larger animal motifs, in turn, are references to some form of totemic clan. These are divided into moieties signified by wild and domestic animals. It is probable that these objects were worn by women as symbolic statements of the marriage contract which cemented intersettlement relationships. They are found in habitation debris, and their motifs are widespread among Harappan settlements, demonstrating pansodality relationships that were essential in keeping society cohesive as it rapidly expanded its geographic range.

The roots of the Harappan culture appear to be among Neolithic village farming groups and pastoralists. At Mehrgarh in the lowlands of eastern Baluchistan there are indications of transhumance as early as 6000 B.C.E., followed by stages of sedentism. Adjacent areas also reflect this trend, demonstrating an essential tie between upland and lowland peoples through transhumance and trade. What stands out is a process we can call "Indianization," by which the western Asian culture is substantially replaced by a style deriving from life on the Indian subcontinent, separate from the cultures to the west. The depictions of Indian flora and fauna motifs are striking. Certain ornaments and costumes on figurines, their bangles, turbans, draped cloth or dhoti-type loincloths, are distinctly Indian. Iconographic images of bangled, dais-seated chiefs, peacock-feather-bedizened females, wedding processions, the pandal, the hooved-female anthropomorphs, buffalo-horn headdresses likewise provide undeniable evidence of an indigenous subcontinental style. The Harappans contributed their own technological innovations as well. They used the lunar calendar and probably kept records of the passing months with an abacus-like device; theirs was a base-eight number system, and there is evidence that precise accounts and records were kept of grain storage and of measurements for house construction. They built large fired-brick structures, cultivated cotton, and may have domesticated the elephant and the water buffalo; they experimented with rice growing, probably had the windmill, sailed square-rigged vessels up and down river, probably engaged in coastal shipping, and used four-wheeled carts. They appear to have attempted city planning, and built excellent drainage and sewer systems.

There were apparently classes of chiefs responsible for the settlements who owed ritual and material tribute to paramount chiefs located in the urban centers (of which there are now at least five known). Wealth was counted in measures of grain and cotton and, most prestigiously, numbers of cattle. The larger herds required reliable pasturage and water, motivating movement away from cultivated fields. This pressure to seek new pasturage may have influenced the demise of the Harappan world, since even strong sodalities, interclan marriage, and hegemonies of leadership under paramount chiefs were weakened as they spread across ever greater geographic distances. Although the reasons remain unclear, Harappan civilization gradually disappeared as it was absorbed into the vast heterogeneous ethnic mosaic of the subcontinent.

One looks in vain for evidence of kingship, colleges of priests, armies, traditional arts, pantheons of deities, literatures, law codes, or even lengthy inscriptions describing cultural life. The Harappans spoke a form of early Dravidian language and used a borrowed (proto-Elamitic) ideosyllabic writing system. It did not seem to go beyond the stage of naming, accounting, and identifying objective things. The Harappans appear to have been tribe-oriented and, in terms of polity at least, organized as chiefdoms. Their gods were characteristic of tribal culture in a pastoral setting, with images of bulls, males with headdresses, females pregnant or with a child. Their social organization reflected a well-balanced, cohesive economy. The Harappans gave way before the next stage of Indian civilization, which arose during the stress of the movement of the Indo-Aryans into North India in the second millennium B.C.E. It is conceivable that Indian civilization, as expressed in the *Vedas*, the *Vedanta*, and the *Mahābhārata*, and which gave birth to Buddhism and Jainism (all before the time of Christ), was shaped by the interaction of central Asian concepts brought by the invading Indo-Aryans with the existing Harappan technological and economic achievements. Although Harappan civilization did not directly lead to subsequent developments, it may well have influenced the character of later Indian civilization.

Early civilization in China presents a quite different story. The combination of Chinese traditional historical methods and the recent emphasis in anthropology on theories about the origin of the state has strongly influenced comparisons of early Chinese civilization with other primary civilizations. In the case of China, early civilization is represented by the Three Dynasties (or San Dai), the Xia (ca. 2200–1750 B.C.E.), the Shang (ca. 1750–1100 B.C.E.), and the Zhou (ca. 1100–256 B.C.E.). Historically these were believed to have succeeded one another, but modern research suggests that they were somewhat contemporaneous. Much of this period, from approximately 1600 to 500 B.C.E., was coterminous with the Bronze Age in China, which is conventionally dated from approximately 1600 to 500 B.C.E. The Xia was centered in Henan, the early Shang in Shandong and the Zhou in Shaanxi. In the pre-Bronze Age, Neolithic village farming cultures coalesced by about 2500 B.C.E. into a general cultural panregional entity called the Longshanoid in the Yellow River valley in North China. While there were regional differences, there is much that was common throughout the area: permanency of village settlements; dependence on grain agriculture supplemented by fishing and hunting; similar tool kits (adzes, knives, sickles, many of polished stone); similarities in kinds of pottery, both handmade and, more rarely, wheel-made pottery; and similar ensembles of horn, shell, and bone objects of daily life. Some sites in Shandong are surrounded by stamped earth walls, and there are cemeteries containing both poorly and richly furnished burials, suggestive of class differentiation based on wealth. Scapulimancy was regularly practiced, and there is some evidence of fertility cults.

The Xia Dynasty until recently has been largely regarded as a mythic one, since nothing in the archaeology of North China could be specifically referred to as Xia. Now, however, the Xia is identified with the Erlitou culture in Henan. This identification indicates that early Chinese civilization largely derived from the commonalities of indigenous Neolithic culture of the Longshanoid.

More is known about the Shang and the Shang Dynasty (ca. 1750–1100 B.C.E.) because of the archaeology, especially from the excavations of Anyang, one of the Shang capitals. Evidence from other sites is rapidly accumulating.

The Shang is differentiated from the Longshanoid background by the presence of horse-drawn wheeled chariots; new forms of pottery; tools, weapons, and magnificent ritual vessels cast in bronze; cowrie shell and fine jades as exotic symbols of wealth; human sacrifice (especially in connection with an imperial funerary cult); and, above all, a developed writing system found most frequently inscribed on oracle bones, although also on bamboo and bronze. These artifacts are obviously related to wealth, power, and status. The oracle writing itself is much concerned with the affairs of the Shang state. The king's actions were prescribed by interpreting the cracks found (usually) on turtle plastrons after heating. From this kind of evidence and later Chinese written accounts of the Shang, there emerges a picture of a king concerned with ensuring the safety of his state. The state was regularly threatened by both internal disorder and alien attack. The king ensured his own status by requiring his officials to carry out administrative tasks to ensure the well-being of the Shang state. Surrounded by well-to-do officials presumed to be members of the royal clan or distinguished aristocratic clans in a hierarchically stratified society, the Shang king had a strong hand and produced ritual proofs of his power. He enhanced this power by building large palaces on platforms; by accumulating bronzes, jade, cowrie, and other valuables; and by having elaborate rituals and funerary rites performed by members of the lineage and court. The latter involved the building of pit-graves with burial chambers and the sacrifice of animals, especially dogs, as well as large numbers of humans, which presumably made up the retinue of the deceased in the afterlife.

In Anyang, the area surrounding the palaces and temples extended along both banks of the river Huan and was occupied by noblemen's residences, workshops, cemeteries, and house clusters of commoners. It was a busy, dynamic urban cluster stretching for thousands of yards, in considerable contrast to the pre-Shang villages, whose existence, often far from rivers, depended on rainfall, which allowed for the widespread distribution of grain agriculture over the northern Chinese plain. A number of Shang centers, like that of Anyang, have been identified, reinforcing the classic picture of peripatetic rulers regularly moving over their kingdom from town to town, backed up by a substantial warlike chariotry. Rural China that emerged from earlier farming villages was subject to the vagaries of despotic rulership. This picture remains true apparently until the golden age of the Zhou rulers. Was the Shang Dynasty representative of Chinese civilization? An answer is possible only by knowing the content of Shang writing. Chinese writing is based upon an ideographic system in which each character represents a word or concept. A rebus could allow for combining ideographic representation with sound symbols. Thus early Chinese writing already shows a sophistication in development that indicates it could have been used for literary purposes. In fact, the oracle writing seems to have been primarily used for the naming of the members of lineages, both ancestors and living, with reference to familial clans; identifying town names, military units, subunits with sodalities, class, rank, etc.; and divination. Indeed, one is struck by the absolutism which makes significant in public affairs only the future or success of rulers in ruling the state. The pressure on the rulers and their followers led to innovations in administration and ritual, but among a limited group. In large part the rural parts of China remained, it seems, at the Longshanoid level, parochializing, probably, what Shang cultural universalism brought to the rural world.

The Zhou Dynasty (ca. 1100–256 B.C.E.), which was established with the defeat of the Shang and which gradually dominated North China, saw the reduction of warfare, growth in population, and significant development within urban areas and across the vast countryside. It is no wonder that Confucius, a citizen of the late Zhou, referred to the accomplishments of the early Zhou rulers as constituting a golden age. The Zhou produced the theory of legitimate rule known as the Mandate of Heaven, as well as the earliest Chinese classics, including the *Book of Songs* and the *Yi Jing* [*I Ching*]. When the central Zhou government weakened and factionalism was renewed, there emerged a number of ideas and philosophical concepts about the human condition, developed by, in particular, Lao Zi [Lao Tzu], Zhuang Zi [Chuang Tzu], Mo Zi [Mo Tzu], Mencius, and Confucius, and leading to what has been referred to as China's Classic Age.

AFTERWORD: WRITING, CITIES, STATES

Few tasks are more controversial in the study of early civilizations than that of establishing the criteria which enable us to differentiate civilization from culture. There is almost universal agreement that a fundamental criterion must be **writing**; my thesis, however, is that the existence of a form of writing is not in itself sufficient ground for labeling a culture a civilization. In most cultures some form of graphic symbolism occurs: for example, the love letters of the Yukaghir in Siberia, the rock drawings of indigenous peoples in Australia and the American Southwest, the totem poles of the Haida in the Pacific Northwest, and the cave paintings in the Dordogne. Many such graphic statements are concerned with abstract ideas of love, war, trouble, happiness, and the supernatural. There are also numerous cultures where accounting or numbering is demonstrated graphically: the quipu of the Inca, the counting sticks of the Ainu, the lunar calendars of many tribal peoples. The frequent occurrence of number and references to personal identity at an early stage in the development of writing appears to be simply parallel to primitive man's already established use of graphic symbolism. It is no coincidence, then, that **all** of the writing systems of primary civilizations are derived from or remain picture writing: Egyptian, proto-Sumerian, Harappa, Shang oracular signs. Some of this picture writing has the character of a rebus. It is often found on seals or in texts identifying property or the person owning the property, or identifying the self in ritual or in the social organization.

It should be noted that although Sumerian has a preserved archaic form, there is little archaeological evidence of the proto forms of hieroglyphic Egyptian, logosyllabic Harappan, or the Shang oracular script. This is owing either to the lack of preservation of the earlier foundational "texts" or to the fact that in at least some of these examples writing sprang up rather suddenly. But whatever its origin, orthography existed because it fulfilled a functional **need**. Even the oracle bones of the Shang are archived in records setting forth kings' names, eclipses, hunting expeditions, lineages, harvests, rituals, and divinations relative to daily life. This is in the religious context of a belief in the role of ancestral deities. This archival quality is found in early Sumerian, early Egyptian, and Harappan seal texts. In all these cases there is **no** evidence of a literature, or philosophical or aesthetic expression bearing on the human condition like that which characterizes Pharaonic Egypt, later dynastic Sumer, Zhou China, or Vedic India. It can be argued that the roots of the development of a literature lay in earlier writings or in a rich oral tradition, and this is in part probably correct, but the actual appearance in a literature of concern for the human condition involves a complex shift wherein the written symbol is created to express **specifically, concretely**, and **immediately** the whole character of an idea, no matter how abstract it may be. This entails a far closer relationship of written symbol to oral speech and the development, not only of sophisticated written vocabularies, but of an ability to relate them syntactically. That development made possible the growth of concepts in science, law, religious taxonomies, technology, polity, and other aspects of the human condition, which are the essential characteristics by which early civilizations are identified.

In my view, civilization is **not urbanization.** Urbanization is the development of communities that serve specific functions for the culture at large. Characteristically, cities are concentrations of specialists (craftsmen, bureaucrats, priests, merchants, soldiers, administrators) centered around a given function (commerce, administration, religious service, military control). The interdependence of the inhabitants and the relationships built upon the exchange of goods and services within the city and extending to the nonurban food-producing communities are dynamic elements in city life. City societies tend to divide into classes according to occupation, wealth, and political power. Status is essential for the symbiotic controls of city life, and divisions of rich and poor, noble and common are often characteristic of city society. Cities have large populations which exploit the surrounding landscape and whose members are dependent upon one another. Thus coercive controls via taxes, police, rules and regulations of exchange, and protecting armies are in one way or another characteristic of cities. Urban centers have basic functions and are located geographically according to the requirements of those functions: near seaports, along rivers or trade routes, in strategic zones, or in sacred areas. Though the dynamism of city life often motivates innovation and speculation and thus stimulates the development of a civilization, urbanization is specifically concerned with human communities, which can differ widely, as demonstrated by the differences between such early cities as the royal capital of Shang, the chiefdoms of Harappa, the metropolitan centers of Sumer, and the Pharaonic city of Memphis. Indeed, cities do exist in many contexts, as is demonstrated in Kumasi, Zimbabwe, Machu Picchu, and, in central Asia, Altyn Tepe.

Another concept, that of the **state,** is also often confused with civilization. The state can be defined as a political entity, central in the rulership of a geographically defined area. States usually depend for cohesion on the ability of the governing polity to control the wealth of the state and to accrue benefits by which the ruled sustain the order of the society. In some states, like that of Pharaonic Egypt, the regularity of the Nile flood and the emphasis upon village life for the inhabitants created a fundamental economic and social stability that sustained the Egyptian state for centuries. In Sumeria and Mesopotamia, however, the multiplicity of city-states and the competition for soil, water, and other resources led to internecine struggles which, with foreign wars, created instabilities and the city-states rose and fell accordingly. This is similar to Three Dynasty China, where the military power of ruling dynasties was constantly being tested. Throughout the world, states have been created and have risen and fallen according to their military and political fortunes. Though states are often the polities of given civilizations, they do not in themselves constitute civilizations.

SELECTED REFERENCES

Adams, R.McC. *The Evolution of Urban Society.* Chicago: Aldine, 1966.
Chang, K.C. *Shang Civilization.* New Haven: Yale University Press, 1980.
Emery, W.B. *Archaic Egypt.* Baltimore: Penguin, 1961.
Fairservis, W.A. Jr. *The Fourth River.* New York: Alfred A. Knopf, 1988.
Kramer, S.N. *The Sumerians.* Chicago: University of Chicago Press, 1963.
Wheatley, Paul. *The Pivot of the Four Quarters.* Chicago: Aldine, 1971.
Wheeler, R.E.M. *The Indus Civilization.* 3d ed. Cambridge: Cambridge University Press, 1968.
Wilson, John A. *The Culture of Ancient Egypt.* Chicago: University of Chicago Press, 1951.

THE ORIGINS OF CIVILIZATION IN CHINA

Cho-yun Hsu

Professor Walter Fairservis, after investigating the appearance of civilization in Mesopotamia and the Nile Valley, suggests that early developments in these areas led to a culminative stage where writing for naming and accounting appeared, and that technological development reached a climax which created support for cities or states. He argues that such a culmination was followed by a stage of concern for and achievements involving abstract ideas of justice, happiness, human behavior, and the universals in man's relationship to self and the cosmos, as well as universals in nature, epitomized in the character deities and those observable in natural life. He thus defines this latter stage as the actual presence of a civilization.

Professor Fairservis applies this set of criteria to Chinese history and, largely adopting K.C. Chang's concept, he assigns the early days of civilization to the San Dai, or Three Dynasties (Xia-Shang-Zhou). I agree in general with Professor Fairservis on his theory of the origin of civilization and also in principle with his assignment of early civilization to the Three Dynasties. I would like to elaborate as follows:

The Neolithic background of early civilization in China should first be examined. Neolithic China covered a major area of China proper, with its peripheries stretching into Mongolia, Manchuria, and today's northwestern provinces. This extensive landmass is much larger than any single region in the three ancient civilizations of the Nile Valley, Mesopotamia, or the Indus Valley. Few barriers exist within this area which would have compartmentalized cultural development into subareas. Interaction among the local Neolithic cultures in China was thus unavoidable. In late Neolithic China, i.e., 3000–2000 B.C.E., at least five major cultural clusters flourished as contemporaries. They were located in the middle reaches of the Huang He (Yellow River), the lower reaches of the Yangzi (Yangtze) River, the middle reaches of the Yangzi River, the Shandong Peninsula and its adjacent coastal regions, and the northwest loess highland in the present provinces of Gansu (Kansu) and Shaanxi (Shensi). Beyond these regions, which can be called China proper, regional cultures in the north and northeast linked Neolithic China with regional cultures developed on the pastoral steppelands of lower Asia. In the mountainous southwest, local cultures seemed to be influenced by Chinese Neolithic culture as well as the cultures developed in Southeast Asia and the Pacific regions. These interactions among neighboring cultures should have enriched participants through contacts and exchanges, even if indirectly. On the one hand, local cultures in Neolithic China maintained distinctive characteristics which they inherited from their local traditions and, on the other hand, late-Neolithic culture throughout these five regions exhibited remarkable homogeneity. There was a certain "Chinese-ness" common to their development. If one drew a line across the map of Neolithic China, the regional culture at the west end of the line would clearly be different from that at the east end. The transition from one culture to a neighboring one was so gradual, however, that there would be little clear-cut demarcation. In other words, in late Neolithic China a very large pool of cultural "genes" existed within the territories which are called China today. This is a situation of great potential which the people of the Nile valley, Mesopotamia, and the Indus Valley did not enjoy, since their territories were much smaller.

In late-Neolithic sites in China, village communities comprised between thirty and seventy houses. Using these figures, I estimate that in each village there were about two hundred people. Throughout the entire landmass of the five clusters of regional culture there were a few thousand villages. Thus, the total population who participated in cultural interaction numbered several million. This is a much larger population than those estimated at other sites of ancient culture. Moreover, active interregional trade seems to have been conducted in this large area. It may not be coincidental that the Xia and Shang states, both of which were pivotally located in the central plains, led the development which formed the basis of early Chinese civilization. This location was advantageous for both the flow of cultural exchange and the accumulation of resources.

The people of the Xia culture, as judged by the level of development represented by the sites of the Erlitou culture, had an organized state with urban areas which were probably state capitals. They were able to cast bronze weapons and tools. Xia writing has not been found as yet. However, pottery marks have been found in both Shaanxi in the west and Shandong in the east. Many of the pottery marks resemble Shang writing, although they may be merely signs representing the names of the owners or craftsmen. The Xia culture, as represented by the Erlitou phase, which is dated around 2100 B.C.E., definitely can be regarded as a prelude of early civilization in China.

There is much better archaeological and literary documentation of the Shang culture. Remains of Shang sites, including inscriptions on oracle bones, are rich sources of information on Shang life and culture. The evolution of political and social structures during a three-century span can be well constructed by scanning the change of relationships between the Shang king and his court, between the royal domain and the subordinate states, and between man and his gods. The Shang capacity to mobilize resources, human as well as material, may be estimated by calculating the number of people enlisted in the army and the amount of labor and wealth that were required to build the royal palaces, tombs, and ceremonial buildings. Other salient guideposts include bronze and pottery ritual vessels, war chariots, and various cultural artifacts. The characters inscribed on the oracle bones testify not only to the prevalence of a sophisticated writing system, but also to the existence of a literary elite who served as recorders of human affairs and who functioned as mediums between the living and the dead—between man and the deified cosmic forces. Indeed, the Shang people had developed a culture which could boast of political states, relatively sophisticated technology, a complex social structure with urban centers, a religion based on shamanism and ancestor worship, a fairly advanced agrarian society, and an extensive network of exchange which brought materials from distant places to the Shang peoples.

These facts have been presented explicitly or implicitly by Professor Fairservis. I need to add here some observations on the spiritual aspects of the Shang people. Shang scribes diligently recorded the daily routine for all activities—which included state affairs, religious rituals and ceremonies, festivals and sacrifices—as well as data on climate and weather, and also noted everyday concerns. They incorporated both the lunar and solar cycles and the Shang sixty-day cycle into a complex calendar.

Although they routinely included the gods of natural forces in their pantheon of deities, it seems that they also observed rather objectively the movement of the sun, moon, and other celestial bodies, as well as seasonal changes. In this way they achieved a fair degree of precision in their time-keeping system. These activities and systems went far beyond simple religious motivation.

Furthermore, Shang scribes and recorders probably made serious efforts to reflect their religious practices. In the repertoire of Shang oracle bone inscription, there appear to be two distinctive schools of thought among the literary elite. One school of scribes (let us call it School A) tended to write bold-faced characters, rather free in style, and included in the list of deified and worshiped objects a great variety of people and natural forces. This type of list was far more inclusive than that which included only deceased kings and queens who were royal ancestors. Another school of scribes (School B) tended to write well-arranged characters neatly and carefully in well-regulated styles. They arranged festivals and offered sacrifices only to the royal ancestors, in accordance with a precise calendar which prescribed a sequence of such activities. These two schools dominated the professions of divination and record keeping. It seems as though society or the court switched back and forth to employ the services of both schools.

I would suggest that these two schools of scribes probably represented two different views of the relationship between man and his gods. School A provided access to a large number and type of deities which were to receive the worship of the Shang court. Their practices coincided with the atmosphere of the Shang expansion, by which numerous tribes of other local cultures were absorbed into the Shang political system. For the sake of cultural integration, the gods and/or ancestral spirits of these people had to be included in the Shang religion. Thus the Shang scribes of School A actually displayed a mentality of universalism and changed fundamentally the formerly exclusive faith of the Shang.

School B developed a different path toward a transcendental mentality. In arranging all ceremonies mechanically within the framework of their neat calendars, they seemed to care little about the will or wishes of the new members of the empire. In the Shang practice of divination, the individual deity or ancestor was to be consulted on preferences for the date of a ceremony. In the hands of the scribes of School B, all procedures became routine. They did not hesitate to delete from the Shang pantheon a number of deities that had been included by the scribes of School A. This functional approach probably reflected a mentality of rationalism, which is quite foreign to naive superstition—a hallmark of primitive religion.

The rotation of these two schools of scribes in dominating Shang religious activities may have compelled some Shang intellectuals to seriously review the basic assumptions of their original faith. In the twelfth century B.C.E., at the height of its political power, the Shang Dynasty was challenged by the minor state of Zhou, located on the relative periphery of the Chinese world. Shang intellectuals had to face the confusion and desperation of the collapse of a cultural order which they represented. This may be assumed to have provided another opportunity for the Shang intellectual to reflect and to review the old faith. I believe the experience of living through the crises of conquest and subsequent societal breakdown was a key factor in their intellectual breakthrough, which brought the Chinese mentality one step closer to the development of civilization.

This is the background to a new interpretation emerging in the Shang-Zhou juncture. The concept of the Mandate of Heaven did not appear until the Zhou people tried to legitimize their rule over the entire Chinese world by dominating the Shang. Many Shang elite did join the Zhou court to serve as scribes, recorders, and ritual experts, and may have helped the Zhou shape the concept that a universal heavenly god, who was the supreme judge of the conduct of people, could and would decide which ruler should govern. As revealed in Zhou literature, the Mandate of Heaven was bestowed upon or taken away from ruling households without preference or prejudice. The only criterion was their behavior and performance as rulers. Thus the moral judgment was made by a supreme god who held the rulers morally accountable in exercising their political authority. It was indeed a novel approach. Its sudden emergence in the early Zhou period cannot be a sheer accident. It was probably tied to the collapse of a powerful kingdom with a superior culture and to the rise of an otherwise lesser state.

These two developments, the implication of the Shang schools of scribes in their possible approaches of universalism and rationalism and the crystallization of a concept of moral accountability in the belief of the Mandate of Heaven, should be regarded as having enormous significance in the advancement of abstract ideas. These conceptual approaches were just as crucial as the redefinition of the notions of Ma'at and the Akhnaton monotheism in Egypt or the Gilgamesh quest for the meaning of immortality in Mesopotamia.

The axial-age civilization of ancient Judaism, Greek philosophy, and Christianity that arose in the eastern Mediterranean world represents great strides in the development of civilization after the Mesopotamian and Egyptian eras. Likewise, in Shang-Zhou China, preliminary transcendence also prepared the ground for the emergence of Confucianism, Daoism, and Mohism. Thus the dawning of early civilization in China occurred in the Shang-Zhou period.

SOME CONTRASTS AND COMPARISONS OF ZHOU CHINA AND ANCIENT GREECE

Cho-yun Hsu

EARLY DEVELOPMENTS

Prior to the rise of the Zhou, the central plain was dominated by the Shang people, who had developed a mature bronze culture with a writing system and organized a state that in its initial stage had been just a chiefdom and then gradually culminated in a monarchy. The Shang state was probably one of a few entities that existed along the middle and lower reaches of the Yellow River and the Yangzi (Yangtze) River drainages. By the late part of the second millennium B.C.E. the Shang appeared to have been the strongest of the contenders for dominance in that area until they were replaced by the Zhou ca. 1200 B.C.E. The early past of the Zhou is not totally clear to us. They might have been related to the Xia, who were the major competitors of the Shang. It is possible that the Xia dominated the yellow earth plain before the Shang achieved that status. Thus, in traditional Chinese historiography, the Xia, the Shang, and the Zhou are collectively called the Three Dynasties. On the other hand, according to their own legendary past, the Zhou experienced a period of several centuries during which they eventually gave up agriculture and over several generations migrated into the Wei River valley, where they left abundant archaeological remains by which we may verify their presence. Early Zhou epics depicted their migratory path along the Jing River to enter the rich Wei valley as they were pressed by the Jungdi people. Although there are only a few suggestive clues to their predynastic migration, the long-distance migration itself, in addition to the claim that they once gave up agriculture, reveals that there had been rather active movements of peoples along the transitional zone between the pastoralists in Inner Asia and the farming cultures in China. The close alliance between the Zhou and the proto-Tibetan Jiang therefore appears as a natural one.

In other words, the rise of the Zhou seems to be related to the phenomenon of large-scale movements of peoples in Inner Asia. The period of such movements probably falls within the middle of the second millennium B.C.E. The Zhou's final conquest of the Shang and other states in the central plain was the invasion by a relatively less civilized nation of a people of an already developed bronze culture.

The early history of the Greeks bears a similar hallmark. In the second millennium B.C.E., the Minoans of Crete in the Aegean Sea had developed a rich bronze culture and hieroglyphic systems known as Linear A and Linear B. The Minoans also had introduced literacy to the backward mainlanders. The Mycenaean chieftains in the middle of the second millennium ruled the south of the peninsula as the Helladic cultures pervaded practically the entire mainland of Greece. Active trading supported these Mycenaean statelets, which were ruled by regimes that built luxurious palaces. From the mid-thirteenth through the mid-twelfth centuries B.C.E., however, destruction everywhere brought these palaces to ruin. This is probably the period depicted in the Homeric epics of the *Iliad* and *Odyssey*. It also seems to be related to the widely spread activities of the Sea Peoples in Egyptian records. Throughout the late second millennium B.C.E., states in the Nile Valley, Mesopotamia, Asia Minor, and the Aegean Sea had become victims of the turbulence brought about by invaders from the north. It is against this historical backdrop that the Dorians, a group of northern migrants, established themselves as masters of the Greek world. The widespread raids attributed to the Sea Peoples in the Egyptian records reveal only one end of a long chain of reactions of massive demographic displacement.

In other words, the southward movement of the Indo-Europeans, including the arrival of the Dorians in Greece, was but one of a long chain of movements of peoples. What appeared in the ancient Greek world was the conquest by a backward people invading the more culturally advanced Minoan-Mycenaean states and, in the process, taking over the lead in the development of a Greek civilization.

The rise of the Zhou and of the ancient Greeks resembled parallel developments taking place separately in the East and the West. Yet both were related to massive demographic movement in the inner part of the Eurasian continent. What remains a puzzle is whether these disturbances caused by the migrations of peoples were related to one another, and if so, what was their common origin and what triggered the impulse that created such a long chain of reactions. At present, these are at best open questions, to which there is no ready evidence to begin to provide answers.

FORMATIONS OF STATES AND NATIONS

The Zhou's conquest of the "central plain" and its peripheries took the continuous efforts of at least three royal reigns to complete. The process was slow and gradual. As a small power located at the edge of the Chinese world, the Zhou developed a strategy of establishing garrison stations in key areas in order to control their newly subordinated peoples, some of whose ancestors could be traced back to Neolithic days. Few in number, the Zhou were able to dispatch only a small detachment of their own people to be stationed, together with others from their close alliances, notably the Jiang, at strategically crucial localities. The strength of these garrison stations was then augmented with the descendants of the Shang forces and other surrendered troops. A network of such garrison stations, which eventually formed the vassal states of Zhou feudalism, provided these individual states with a collective security. The leaders of the garrison detachments were nominally either the Zhou princes or their descendants. Non-Zhou leaders were included in the kinship network by matrimonial ties through cross-marriages between Zhou kinsmen and the cooperative elite of the non-Zhou peoples, who included descendants of the Jiang, the Shang, and ruling elements of other older eastern chiefdoms.

The Zhou king enjoyed a dual superior status of being the overall lord of the hierarchy of the Zhou feudal system and the patriarch of a vast kinship network that included initially all the upper levels of the Zhou vassal states, because the same kinship bonds and matrimonial ties were formed within each of these vassal states. Obligation to the lord was reinforced by obligations to the elders and seniors. An extension of the Zhou kinship network, therefore, incorporated the delegation of sovereignty and authority to its members at all levels of the feudal hierarchy and established familial relations at the heart of the Zhou system.

Meanwhile, the Zhou royal court successfully maintained a

strong home base in its old domain of the Wei Valley, while a second capital was settled in the east, within the former Shang heartland, to serve as the headquarters of eastern collective security. Religious ceremonies of ancestor worship, periodic visits of the vassals to the court of the lord, reconfirmation of oaths on occasions of investiture as well as conferences of alliances, and the crisscrossing of matrimonial bonds among aristocrats, all together gave the Western Zhou a solid ruling structure to sustain the stability of Zhou China rather effectively for three to four centuries. By means of this lasting tradition, the upper class of the Zhou feudal structure developed a common identity, out of which emerged an awareness of belonging to the Zhou system politically and an even stronger awareness of sharing the same culture. This identity culminated in the foundation of a nation of people, known as Hua-Xia, as against the "outsiders," who were denoted by various terms that meant "barbarians."

In the case of nation formation in ancient Greece, the process involved wave after wave of migration of archaic Greek-speaking peoples, including the Dorians and the Ionians.

By the beginning of the first millennium B.C.E. the Greeks had established themselves all over the peninsula and had formed numerous city-states. By 750–500 B.C.E. Greek traders had successfully founded trading posts throughout the eastern Mediterranean world. Some of these trading posts then evolved into colonial city-states, which were often duplicate copies of the mother city as far as political institutions and social structures were concerned.

The ties among archaic Greek city-states were by no means strong. Each polis was a sovereign political unit. However, in much of European Greece, especially in the northwest, the unit was not a polis, but rather an ethnos, roughly speaking, a nation. A village that made up an ethnos was only loosely linked in some type of federation without a given dominating center. Since the Greek migration generally started from the north, the ethnos probably predated the polis. The polis may have been a way for the migrants to distinguish themselves from the natives, and its fortified center was formed for the sake of defense. The polis was linked to other city-states through alliances of expediency, and sometimes through matrimonial ties between elites. Nevertheless, due to the weak status of the kings, who were checked by powerful councils, the royal matrimonial ties did not create the basis for a permanent network. Therefore, the Greek city-states, being so independent of each other, were not organized in a large, linked political structure like the Zhou feudal system. Greek common identity was cultural rather than political, a result of sharing the same migratory background, the same language, and some common religious faiths, such as the cults of the Delphic oracle and of Olympia. Greek national awareness became established primarily as Greeks dealt with outsiders, reaching a climax when the independent states joined to fend off the Persian invasion. The Hellenistic expansion, too, may be considered a cultural rather than a political one, since it occurred after the days of the domination of the Greek city-states.

Internally, a Greek city-state, in the early days, was divided into phylae (or tribes), which could be dated back to the age of migration before the Greeks had settled into cities. There were strong households known as gene within the city. Each genos (or clan) had many dependents who might have been descendants of the subjugated native population or earlier settlers. The names of the phylae often were the same in the different city-states. A Dorian city usually consisted of three phylae, while an Ionian city, although of less uniformity, usually consisted of phylae bearing the same names as in other Ionian cities. The pluralistic structure of the Greek city-state left few options other than to develop cooperation among these participating members. The king was therefore in a weaker position than the council, which was formed to represent the interests of these powerful households in the city. The complexity of internal divisions and stratifications of a city-state testified to its having been developed from a tribal structure superimposed upon the foundation of a subjugated aboriginal layer or several such layers, as wave after wave of migrations arrived.

The contrast between the cases of the Western Zhou and of ancient Greece is quite obvious. The Zhou established a solid home base to rule the peoples in eastern China. On the other hand, after the Greek migratory population, including the Dorians and the Ionians, entered Greece and merged with the earlier settlers, there was no power center around which the Greeks could build up a central authority such as the Zhou managed to maintain. Therefore, the Greeks were dispersed rather than attached to a feudal hierarchy. The Zhou royal house built its hierarchical edifice of distribution of power upon the foundation of a kinship structure, and Zhou feudal ethics were derived directly from a kinship-based code of conduct. All human relationships, therefore, were based on the analogy of familial relations. The Greeks, however, developed their democracy in the sovereign polis, partly on the basis of surviving tribal interests, and developed a system in which a diversity of interests of participating groups were resolved by the discussions of a council. The Shang monarchy, perhaps, had set a precedent for the Zhou to adopt its course toward a universal state, although the Greeks could easily have found similar precedents of monarchy in the oriental states in Mesopotamia. That the Greeks took a different course determined the evolution of democracy in the West. The universal state infused with familial relations of the Western Zhou and the citizens' democracy based on the open reconciliation of interests of the Greek city-states established two enduring and contrasting forms of government in the history of Western and Asian civilization.

COMPARISONS BETWEEN THE PHILOSOPHIES OF CONFUCIUS AND PLATO

Although there were significant intellectual developments in both China and Greece before the times of Confucius and Plato, respectively, Confucius has always been regarded as the most important fountainhead of the Chinese way of thinking, while Plato's role in Western intellectual history is attested to by the saying that all subsequent philosophies are merely footnotes to his thought.

Confucius (551–479 B.C.E.) was born in the Spring-and-Autumn period as the ancient order of the Western Zhou feudalism gave way to the subsequent phase, during which the former vassal states of the Zhou contended for supremacy in a multistate world. Ceaseless wars and frequent power struggles led to a prolonged time of turmoil called the Period of the Warring States. Born into a petit aristocrat's household that had suffered a drastic decline in social status, Confucius devoted his lifetime to envisioning a stable moral and political order set in contrast to the disruption of his own age. In so doing, he developed a universal value system that became the mainstay of the Chinese way of thinking.

Essentially, Confucius redefined the codes of conduct of Zhou feudal society into a set of values for all humankind. On the one hand, he lamented the fall of the ancient order that he idealized as one built upon the principle of mutual respect among members of the society, what is known as the principle of reciprocity. It was from a universal character of humaneness that an individual derived self-esteem and extended the same esteem to the respect of others. The crucial content of humaneness consisted of sincerity toward oneself as well as toward others and compassion to understand and forgive the conduct of others. In other words, Confucius regarded that all individuals possessed the sacred right of being human. Confucius thus granted to every individual the opportunity to be educated and to nurture his or her character toward perfection of human nature, without discrimination of birth or background. An ideal society, as Confucius saw it, would be a society in which each individual member asserted great effort to nurture his or her own character to the extent of being able to live harmoniously with other fellow members. There would be a sage-king who was an exemplar for the people. While each individual member of society would be held responsible for being a good person, the king would reign rather than rule. The fabric of a perfect world was based on the analogue of a perfect household. Confucius leaned toward the optimistic expectation that the goodness of individuals should be the primary concern, while the collective good would be cherished after the goodness of the individual had been achieved.

Plato (431?–327 B.C.E.) was born into a distinguished Athenian aristocratic family. He learned much from Socrates, and then went further and higher than Socrates in developing a sophisticated system of theories on morality and politics. In Plato's time, the Greek world was in a precarious condition. The incessant wars between Greek city-states and even within cities led his contemporaries to doubt that any form of government would work adequately, be it the Spartan oligarchy or the Athenian democracy. Plato, realizing that individualism had led to the death of the city of Athens, sought to find a philosopher-king who could exercise all powers of the Republic. The Republic would be authoritarian, endowed with sufficient power to create a set of unchangeable laws by means of which stability and harmony would be guaranteed. The Platonic philosopher-king would be an active ruler who designed, controlled, and sustained a good society of pure reason. Goodness of individuals, therefore, would be subordinated to the collective good. The idealized city-state would be made up of three classes. The highest would be that of the guardians, who received the benefit of education and functioned as rulers, while the other two, the auxiliary and the laborers, would not be educated or given any political power. Therefore, in the Platonic Republic the opportunity of receiving education would not be a universal right to be claimed by any citizen. The principle of division of labor in the Republic would create a stratified society, which would likely be hereditarily perpetuated.

The contrast between Confucian and Platonic premises is sharp. Ironically, however, the Confucian literati recruited to serve the government after the civil service examination was established in China during the later dynasties probably constituted an elite quite similar to the guardians in the Platonic Republic. It is also ironic that from the Athenian model of government, democracy became the preferred form of government in Western civilization and human rights the common goals of all.

In this brief essay, the Western Zhou and ancient Greece are contrasted in three aspects: the pattern of development in their initial stages; the respective processes of shaping states and forming a nation; and the fundamental premises of two great thinkers, Confucius and Plato. From even this brief a presentation, we may appreciate that distinctive conditions found in the history of different cultures and societies, which bear some resemblance and have other compatible elements, yet led to remarkable differences in their actual courses of development. Choices made by human groups as well as interpretations of such choices eventually determine the events of human history.

THE SPREAD OF POWER: EMPIRES EAST AND WEST

Richard A. Billows

SYNOPSIS

To begin with, a definition of the term **empire** is proposed, and it is suggested that the creation of long-term, viable empires required the prior attainment of a certain degree of civilization in the imperial region. Four significant factors are put forward as important, if not always absolutely necessary, prerequisites for the creation of empires. A historical summary of ancient empires in Asia follows, concentrating on the period from roughly 600 B.C.E. to 600 C.E., beginning with the observation that Asia is made up of four geographically, politically, and culturally distinct regions which need to be discussed separately. It is argued that western Asia, being closely linked to Europe and Africa, is the most important of the four regions in terms of its impact on wider world developments, as well as being the region with the most extensive and interesting development of empires. The other three regions—India, China, and northern Asia—were more isolated from the rest of the world and, with the important exception of China, did not develop important and long-lasting empires; these regions are therefore discussed more summarily. It is concluded that, though obviously exploitative, the universalist empires developed in western Asia particularly—the Persian Empire of c. 550 to 330 B.C.E. being the most influential model—provided long periods of peaceful, harmonious, and reasonably just rule to wide regions, thereby helping to create conditions fruitful for the advancement of civilization.

CONDITIONS FOR THE CREATION OF EMPIRE

1. A discussion of empires within the broad framework of "Asia in World History" naturally calls first and foremost for a definition of the term: what, for our purposes, is to constitute an empire? Any definition of such a broad and widely used concept as that of **empire** is bound to be controversial, and there is not room in the present context to reason at length concerning the definition. What is offered here, therefore, is very much a use definition, proposed only to provide a clear basis for the material on empires which follows, and by no means intended to be above criticism but rather to provide a starting point for critical examination of the problem of what constitutes an empire.

An empire, then, is an institutionalized system whereby a particular elite, often but not always of a particular national complexion, exploits the populations of wide territories comprising several formerly autonomous regions and often (even usually) including peoples of different ethnicity from the ruling elite. In return, the imperial power normally offers various forms of protection enhancing the general comfort and security of life: physical protection by military force against molestation by unruly elements within and hostile powers outside the empire; protection, even promotion, of economic activities such as farming, manufacturing, trading, etc.; protection of the established social order within the empire against subversive movements by disaffected or underprivileged elements; or protection against attempts by powerful local elites to improve their socioeconomic position at the expense of the less privileged. In addition, or alternatively, the imperial power often offers access (or demands adherence) to a "universal" ideal of some sort which is generally seen as life-enhancing, frequently, though not necessarily, taking the form of a religion.

2. It is appropriate that the discussion of early empires should follow chapters on the emergence of "civilization," for the creation of empire does seem to hinge on the prior achievement of a certain level of what we call civilization. For the purposes of this discussion, I should like to draw a distinction between culture and what I shall refer to as civilization. The latter term has its roots in the Latin word *civitas*, with its sense of a settled and to some degree urbanized community. I take civilization therefore to imply the attainment by a society of a certain level of material and organizational infrastructure within a settled way of life. Many societies with high cultural attainments—e.g., nomadic societies—are

therefore nevertheless not classed as civilizations within this meaning of the term. Four particular features of relatively advanced social organization seem worth emphasizing as prerequisites for the establishment of large and viable empires, with the proviso that not all of them need be present in any one case.

2.1. First, and most obviously, there must exist the conditions for the relatively easy and rapid mobilization and projection of military force—this naturally on the part of the conquering elite of the empire. To mobilize and project military power on a significant scale, sufficient to conquer and police an empire, clearly requires a large social and economic base. In other words, it requires that the imperial people be a large and fairly cohesive people, and that it should have reached a degree of socioeconomic organization at which a significant percentage of adult males can be spared from day-to-day economic activity—mostly farming—and made available instead for military activity.

2.2. The second prerequisite is perhaps less obvious: the existence of readily alienable wealth in the hands of the subject population. The reason for this is that empires are maintained not so much by the exercise of force as by the threat of its exercise, for military power is a limited resource and is often expended in its exercise. While one can sometimes, in the process of conquest, mount a credible threat to the lives of a people, it is impractical to maintain this threat. What normally causes people to surrender to conquest and remain peaceful thereafter is not so much a threat to their lives as to their property, i.e., to their **livelihood.** A people which has little settled (readily alienable) wealth is very hard to conquer and pacify, because its members can evade the threat of military force by escape and retaliate by guerrilla tactics. Settled wealth, however, in the form, for example, of crops, orchards, large flocks and herds, buildings, and towns, is not easily rendered invulnerable to superior military force. In consequence, relatively settled and wealthy peoples are easier to conquer and pacify than poor, scattered, nomadic or hill-dwelling peoples.

2.3. Third, and following from the above, is the development of communications—contacts, mutual knowledge, transport facilities—within a broad region of various peoples, turning it into a conquerable "world system" (or ecumene, as the Greeks referred to the eastern Mediterranean and western Asian region which formed Alexander the Great's empire). A conquering army needs knowledge of the peoples and terrain to be conquered, and the availability of passable routes for its operations. Even more so, the administrators who run the empire when conquered require an adequate communications system to be in place. Usually the requisite knowledge, routes, and overall communications systems are at least embryonically developed by the growth of intraregional trading networks, paving the way for conquering armies and governing administrators to follow.

2.4. The fourth factor commonly present in large and viable empires is an organizing/unifying/motivating principle or ideal, either among the ruling people internally or extended to many or all of the subject people(s). This can be something as simple as a sense of cultural superiority among the conquering people, as in the Greco-Macedonian empires of Alexander the Great and his successors; or it can be an ideal of settled, peaceful, and just governance, as to some extent in the Persian Empire, and as certainly developed in the Roman Empire (n.b. the famous lines of Vergil's *Aeneid* VI. 851–53: "Remember, Roman, that these shall be your arts—to rule the nations by your power and to impose the custom of peace, to treat the humbled with forbearance, and to war down the arrogant."). Often it takes the form of a more or less complex and universal ideology, frequently religious in origin. This can range from the relatively straightforward conviction that one's own god is more powerful than other gods and authorizes the winning of universal rule—as in the case of the Assyrians with their god Ashur—to such relatively idealistic goals as the incorporation of all peoples into a single social or religious structure, such as the gradual extension of Roman citizenship in the Roman Empire to cover virtually all free inhabitants by the third century C.E., or the missionary zeal of Islam in the seventh and subsequent centuries C.E. A common factor seems to be that the ideal or principle which helps to motivate, organize, or unify an empire or imperial people is generally seen as somehow life-enhancing, and thus as a positive force in human affairs worth the expending of effort and blood, and the sacrifice of individual or local autonomy.

A HISTORICAL SUMMARY

To speak or write simply of "Asia," as if this vast region constituted a single cultural-political continuum, would be a mistake. In the ancient period, as in many respects still today, Asia consists of at least four major regions largely independent of each other in terms of cultural or any other interchange. One such region is western Asia, from the Hindu Kush in the east to the Mediterranean basin in the west, and from the Black, Caspian and Aral seas in the north to the Indian Ocean in the south.

Despite the many and important contacts with the East, this region has tended to look westward and be linked more closely with the history of Europe and North Africa than with that of the rest of Asia. The other three regions are, broadly speaking, the Indian subcontinent, the region encompassed by modern China, and the region corresponding to the former Soviet Republics of northern Asia.

Of course these regions have never been entirely cut off from each other. The Hindu Kush has never been an effective barrier to entry into the plains and river valleys of northern India; tribes from the steppes and tundras of northern Asia have from time to time penetrated into China and into western Asia and Europe; the arid plains of central Asia with their sparse but fierce population did not prevent trade in luxuries along the famous Silk Road between China and western Asia; and the peripheral lands of Southeast Asia have generally been as much a meeting place as a zone of division between the Indian region and the Chinese region. All the same, the histories of these regions have generally followed separate paths, and I shall accordingly review them separately.

1. The beginnings of empire in western Asia go back to the ancient Sumerians in the third millennium B.C.E., from whom there followed a succession of empires in Mesopotamia and the surrounding regions, the most significant being perhaps the Babylonian Empire of Hammurabi in the early second millennium and the later Assyrian Empire between the ninth and seventh centuries B.C.E. The Assyrians, hence, already had a long tradition of empire behind them, and they had certainly developed universalist aspirations and titulature. The Assyrian kings claimed to rule as representatives of their god Ashur, and assumed the right to hold sway wherever they pleased—and wherever their armies could enforce their authority.

It was to this ancient Mesopotamian tradition of empire that the Persians and Medes under King Cyrus fell heir in the sixth century B.C.E. This empire began as a confederation of the Median tribes of the northern Iranian plateau with its capital at Ekbatana (near modern Hamadan). It expanded to include nearly all of the peoples of mostly Iranian stock in the regions of modern Iran and Afghanistan, and in the late seventh century played a major role in the demise of the hated Assyrian Empire. The seizure of power by the highland tribes of Persis (modern Fars) under King Cyrus, whose mother came from the Median royal family, was an internal shift in the balance of power between the Iranian tribes, rather than the creation of a new empire. The Medes continued to be part of the ruling elite of the empire, and outsiders like the Greeks continued to refer to the Persians and their empire indiscriminately as "the Medes."

The Persian takeover did, however, unleash a new period of expansionist activism, which in the half-century between about 550 and 500 B.C.E. saw all of western Asia from the Indus Valley in the east to the shores of the Black, Aegean and Mediterranean seas in the west fall under Persian sway. Though the old Median capital of Ekbatana and the old Persian centers of Pasargadae and Persepolis continued to be important, the center of gravity of this expanded empire shifted westward somewhat. The primary capital was at Susa in the territory of ancient Elam, a region whose people were apparently Iranian but which had always formed a peripheral part of the Mesopotamian region and culture. In addition, Babylon became an important administrative center, and the Akkadian language and script of Babylon became the medium of official documents. Old Persian was retained as a court language, but the most common spoken language appears to have been a form of Aramaic, the language of the Semitic tribes of most of Mesopotamia, Syria, Palestine, and the Arabian Peninsula.

The result was that the Persian Empire was heavily influenced by the Mesopotamian imperial and cultural tradition, as indicated, for example, by the royal titulature: "Great King, King of kings, King of the lands," reflecting its universalist aspirations, inherited from the Assyrian Empire. In many respects, however, the Persian Empire was a very different entity from that of the Assyrians. Where the Assyrians had been a harsh, cruel, militaristic, exacting people, the Persians instituted a rule that was relatively noninterventionist and undemanding, suggesting that their success in pacifying all of western Asia and ruling it for two centuries was due not only to their outstanding military qualities and manpower resources, important as these of course were.

The image of the Persian Empire, among Westerners at least, has tended to be dominated by its relations with the Greeks, the one great failure which eventually destroyed the empire. But the Greek view of the Persians can be very misleading: the successful refusal of the Greeks to be incorporated into the empire and their characterization of the Persians as "barbarians" say much about the Greeks but little about the Persians. Against the unfavorable Greek view, one must place the view of that other highly individual nation, the Hebrews: to the author of the second half of the Book of Isaiah, Cyrus, the Persian emperor, was the Lord's anointed and his empire the Lord's work. Similarly, the cruel and hubristic king Xerxes of Greek legend appears in the Book of Esther as the just and sympathetic Ahasuerus. The Persian Empire, in short, was generally regarded by the peoples of Asia, if not with favor, at least not with disfavor.

The reason is that the Persian administration was based on the enhancement and protection of general security and prosperity, the exaction of a relatively modest tribute, and a considerable degree of respect for local customs, especially religious customs. Local elites were fostered and given important roles in the Persian administration, encouraging them to identify their interests with those of the Persians. The Persian authorities refrained on the whole from any extensive meddling in local affairs, and the Persian nobility had developed a code of truth-saying and fair dealing which impressed even many Greeks, as can be seen from the sympathetic account Herodotos gives of Persian culture, and from Xenophon's romantic biography of Cyrus.

The degree to which the relative mildness and justice of Persian rule derived from the influence of the Zoroastrian religion is a matter of dispute. Darius, the king most responsible for creating the Persian administrative system in the closing decades of the sixth century, emphasized his relationship to the great god Ahura Mazda and his truthfulness as the justification for his (usurpatory) royal authority in his famous rock inscriptions at Behistun. Ahura Mazda is of course the great god of truth of the Zoroastrians, opposed to the evil and lying Ahriman. It may well be that Zoroastrian fervor provided the initial unifying and justifying impetus for Persian conquest, but there is certainly no evidence of missionary zeal on behalf of Zoroastrianism by the Persians, nor were the Persians themselves at all exclusive in their attachment to their god, Ahura Mazda. Many other gods were certainly worshiped at various times by various Persians, and they evinced little desire to interfere with the religious beliefs of their subject peoples.

The extraordinarily sudden fall of the Persian Empire to the Greco-Macedonian army of Alexander the Great between 334 and 330 was due not to significant disaffection against the Persians in Asia, but to the stagnation of Persian military technology and method, and indeed of technology and culture generally, after about 500 B.C.E. The superiority of the heavily armored Greek infantry to the Persian infantry had been decisively demonstrated during the Persian invasions of Greece in 490 and 480/79 B.C.E., but no lesson had been drawn from the defeats suffered at that time, and the Greeks were too disunited to follow up their victories effectively. The lesson was driven home again at the end of the fifth century, when an army of ten thousand Greek mercenaries was prevented from conquering the Persian Empire for the would-be usurper Cyrus II only by the latter's suicidally rash behavior at the battle of Cunaxa. Even so, the Persians were too entrenched in their ways by then to change, and sought to compensate for their weakness merely by hiring Greek mercenaries.

The unification of Greece by Philip of Macedon, and the creation of a professionally trained and led army, enabled Philip's son Alexander to conquer all of western Asia with an army of some forty thousand men, growing to perhaps sixty thousand at the end of his reign. Three great battles enabled him to secure western Asia as far as the Caspian Gates: the subject peoples who had been quiescent under the Persians remained equally quiescent under their new masters. It then took Alexander as long again (another three years) to conquer just Bactria and Sogdia (roughly modern Afghanistan), where the fierce Iranian tribesmen refused to accept the decision of battle and resorted to guerrilla tactics, neatly exemplifying how much easier it is to conquer a "civilized" foe than a seminomadic one.

The Greco-Macedonian Empire in western Asia was similar to the nineteenth-century European empires, then, in that it was made possible by a temporary cultural and technological military advantage enjoyed by the imperial people. The administration set up by Alexander and his Seleucid successors was by and large simply a continuation of that of the Persians, with the major difference that they encouraged urbanization by establishing a large number of Greek cities, especially in the lands west of the Tigris. The chronic disunity of the Greeks, however, soon manifested itself in their new empire, with the ultimate result that the desire for autonomy of many of the subject peoples of western Asia was revived and satisfied. By about 250 the Indian and Iranian lands in the east had separated from the Greco-Macedonian Empire, and most of Asia Minor had likewise become autonomous under local dynasts.

Attempts by the Seleucid rulers after about 220 to counter the dissolution of their empire were scotched by the rise of two new powers in the region: the Romans in the west and the Parthians in the east. The Greeks had ceased to maintain their technological advantage, and were at a disadvantage to the Parthians and Romans in terms of manpower. The Parthians, being Iranian, were able to unite against the Greeks, however precariously at times, the various tribes of the Iranian region, forming thereby a coalition too strong for the relative handful of Greek settlers in Asia. Furthermore, they had developed an army and tactics ideally suited to the population and terrain of the Iranian plateau and the plains of northern Mesopotamia. The Romans had developed in their legions a tactically flexible version of the Greek heavy infantry phalanx, and the burgeoning population of Italy in the third century B.C.E. gave them a decisive manpower advantage over all rivals in the Mediterranean basin.

The result of Parthian conquest in the east and Roman conquest in the west was that western Asia was divided between two large empires, a situation that was to prove permanent. Parthian rule was a lax affair with many ups and downs in its fortunes in the 350 plus years that it lasted until being overthrown and replaced by the more tightly organized and disciplined Persian Empire of the Sassanians in the early third century C.E. Although this dynasty from Persis (Fars) looked back to the glory days of the old Achaemenid Persian Empire and had designs on the western Asian lands which had once belonged to the Achaemenids, it never succeeded in permanently expanding its western border much further than the Parthians had, which is to say that the western boundary of Iranian power remained essentially the Euphrates Valley. The Arab conquests of the seventh century C.E. pushed this boundary back further east to the Tigris Valley, but Arab conquests to the east of the Tigris proved ephemeral, and the lands east of the Tigris Valley have remained Iranian to the present day.

Roman rule attached Asia west of the river Euphrates to a tri-continental state, comprising in addition North Africa and southern and western Europe, for nearly six hundred years. This extraordinary achievement was made possible in the first instance by a burgeoning class of peasant farmers in third-century B.C.E. Italy, which enabled Rome to survive defeat after defeat by its great western Mediterranean rival Carthage, and in the end to wear it down and win. The military machine forged in this great conflict thereupon cast down the empires of Alexander's successors like a house of cards early in the second century B.C.E. Armies of peasant farmers, however, proved unsuited to major warfare at great distances from Italy. In the late second and early first centuries B.C.E. a tremendous socioeconomic transformation took place in Italy whereby the populous peasant class was largely driven off the land, which was turned into great estates worked by slaves. In the midst of the resulting social unrest, the enormous surplus manpower thus "liberated" from economic activity found a haven in professional armies, with which Rome annexed north Africa and western Europe, and defeated attempts by the Anatolian Mithridates and the Armenian Tigranes in the early first century B.C.E. to create a great Asian empire in Anatolia and Syria/Palestine.

The military experience and glory thus obtained by these armies and their commanders were then used to overthrow the sociopolitical system in Rome, resulting in the establishment of a monarchical government by Julius Caesar, Augustus, and their heirs. These upheavals in Italy gradually exhausted the manpower on which Roman power had been based, but by the early third century C.E. Rome had granted citizenship to virtually all free inhabitants of the empire, and the whole empire thus served as the recruiting base for its armies. In the crisis caused by the Germanic and Persian invasions and succession problems in the third century C.E., for example, it was armies and leaders recruited mainly in the Balkan peninsula and in North Africa that saved the empire.

If its resources of military manpower were the foundation for the Roman Empire's existence, the extension of uniform peaceful government, and ultimately of Roman citizenship and the benefits of Roman law, provided its justification. The Romans had, indeed, developed a concept of "just war" which held that all of their conquests had been made in the course of "defensive" warfare, and hence were justified in the eyes of the gods, who consequently promoted Roman power. And like the Parthians and Sassanians, the Romans came to regard themselves as successors to the Persian Empire by the favor of the gods. A regular progression of divine favor and imperial power was established, with universal rule passing from the Assyrians to the Persians to the Macedonians, and so to the Romans. But such theoretical justifications can have had little broad appeal.

The Roman Empire of course provided the medium for the establishment of Christianity as a world religion, and for a time in the fourth and fifth centuries C.E. Christianity, its protection and promotion, came to be regarded as the justification for the empire's existence. In fact, however, Christianity if anything promoted the dissolution of the empire, as the great schisms in the Christian movement between the "orthodox" believers and "heretical" sects created bitter tensions and hostilities among different regions of the empire. Ultimately, for example, most Christians in Syria/Palestine and North Africa welcomed the Islamic Arab invaders as rulers in preference to their fellow Christians in Constantinople. Thus if the Roman Empire made it possible for Christianity to spread, the spread of Christianity made it impossible for the Roman Empire to continue. The western empire succumbed to waves of Germanic invaders in the fifth century C.E.; the eastern part, however, survived for another one thousand years as the Byzantine Empire, combining Asia Minor and the Balkan Peninsula into a Eurasian power which overcame Persian and Arab threats and survived to transmit knowledge of the ancient world to late medieval Europe, before finally succumbing to the Ottoman Turks in the fourteenth and fifteenth centuries.

2. As stated above, in the period under review, the rest of Asia was largely unaffected by what transpired in western Asia, undergoing its own historical transformations in its own times and ways. Of the other three regions I identified above, only one—China—was seriously affected by the growth of empire, at least in the ancient period (before c. 600 C.E.). China, however, was the most self-contained and cut off from outside contacts, exerting as little influence upon the outside world as the outside world influenced it. These three regions of Asia can therefore be dealt with more briefly than western Asia in the present context of world history in general and the growth of empire in particular.

2.1. The Indian subcontinent, and especially the great river valleys of the Indus and Ganges systems, had been the home of highly developed cultures from very early times, not much (if at all) later than the Sumerians and Egyptians in the west. The early history of India is, however, very obscure and shrouded in legend and myth. There does not appear to have been any significant attempt to create a large empire in the region before the appearance of Alexander the Great in the Indus Valley in 326 B.C.E. Very quickly after Alexander's death in 323, however, Chandragupta Maurya conquered most of northern India, forming a large empire from his base in the upper Ganges basin. Whether this was purely the outcome of preexisting local factors—competition for primacy between rival principalities in the Ganges basin, with the winner going on naturally to broader conquests—or whether the career of Alexander is to be seen as a catalyst and his weakening of the Indus Valley states as a precondition for Chandragupta's successful imperialism is a problem not easily solvable. Perhaps both explanations are partly true.

Chandragupta's successors added to his conquests, and the Mauryan Empire reached its height in the mid-third century

B.C.E. during the reign of his grandson Ashoka, who added the eastern coast and thus made the empire virtually coextensive with the Indian subcontinent (only the southernmost tip of India was not included). Around 260 B.C.E., Ashoka converted to Buddhism (which had originated in northern India more than 200 years earlier), and used the empire as an instrument for spreading Buddhist teachings, the dharma, as he understood them. Edicts engraved on rocks and stone pillars chronicle his benevolent policies. He is said to have established Buddhism in Sri Lanka, Kashmir, Nepal, Khotan, and Southeast Asia, but historians have found little material evidence to support these traditional claims. Not long after Ashoka's death the empire fell into disunion, and by about 187 B.C.E. the Maurya dynasty came to an end. India was again divided up into numerous states. After the eleventh century Buddhism was virtually eradicated in India, remaining an important religion—perhaps ironically—only in areas Ashoka had not ruled: Sri Lanka, Tibet, China, Burma, Japan.

The second and early first centuries B.C.E. saw a short-lived empire in northern India established by a Greek dynasty (or dynasties) which had created an independent state in Bactria and the Hindu Kush (Afghanistan) during the decline of the Seleucid Empire in western Asia. This soon decayed for lack of Greco-Macedonian manpower, however, and was destroyed in the first century B.C.E. by invasions of tribesmen from central Asia. No pan-Indian empire was again achieved for centuries, until the Gupta dynasty—again from the upper Ganges basin—succeeded in uniting much of India in the fourth century C.E., but this empire too was short-lived. Essentially the experience of India until modern times (post-1500), therefore, has been political fragmentation and cultural and religious diversity, and indeed these are still its hallmarks.

2.2. Russian central Asia is a special case in this study, since for largely geographic and climatic reasons its peoples never reached the stage of "civilization" at which—as I have argued above—empire becomes a possibility. As a result, the early stage of human history, that is, the stage at which cultures have not yet become sufficiently self-aware and literate to leave considerable historical and documentary evidence of themselves, lasted much longer in this region than in the rest of Asia, indeed virtually until modern times. The cultures that did arise in Russian central Asia were largely of nomadic type, and modern archaeological finds, such as the fifth-century B.C.E. Altaian tombs at Pazyryk with their rich nomadic artwork, have shown that they were sometimes very impressive. It would be historically unwarranted and by the definition I have proposed a misnomer to speak of empires in this region, however. Large conglomerations or confederations of nomadic tribes there sometimes were, to be sure. Examples are the Yue Zhi (Yüeh Chih) and the Xiongnu of Chinese records, the latter perhaps the same as the Hunni who later terrorized the Roman Empire. But these tribal confederations created what might properly be called empires only on the (relatively rare) occasions when they erupted from their native steppes and succeeded in conquering more settled lands to the southwest or southeast. The prime examples are the short-lived Hunnish empire of Attila in central Europe and the Mongol empire(s) of Genghis Khan and his successors. These, however, properly belong to the history of Europe, western Asia, and China, rather than to that of Russian central Asia. Only the Russian conquest in the nineteenth century succeeded in bringing empire to that vast region.

2.3. China occupies a unique place in world history, with its cultural and ethnic continuity reaching back millennia into the mists of history, for most of that time virtually cut off from the rest of the world except for its peripheral lands. As one largely unversed in Chinese history and culture, I can offer no more than some brief and general remarks here on the early Chinese empire. From about 1000 B.C.E. a number of fairly large states grew up in the valleys of the Huang He (Yellow River) and Yangzi (Yangtze) River and the intermediate lands, in what is now eastern and central China. Though the language and culture were broadly similar in these states, they were frequently at war with each other. In the fourth century B.C.E. the westernmost of them, Qin (Ch'in), came under rulers who instituted far-reaching social and economic reforms with a view to strengthening the state for warfare. The key figure seems to have been a philosopher named Shang Yang, and the reforms involved a restructuring of the system of land tenure and the creation of an efficient administrative bureaucracy. The result was a tremendous growth in the power of Qin, so that by the decade 230–221 B.C.E. its brilliant and ruthless ruler was able to conquer the other states and unite China. This Qin Empire was extremely unpopular, and did not long survive the death of its founder in 210, but after a few years of chaos the Chinese states were again united by Liu Ji, the founder of the Han Dynasty, and this unification proved permanent. Our information on all this derives from a history written only about one hundred years after the events just described by the second-century B.C.E. historian Sima Qian.

From this period on China remained, with occasional brief but chaotic interruptions, a unified empire, expanding through the centuries southward into Southeast Asia, westward into central Asia and Tibet, and northward toward the region of modern Mongolia. Its expansion had natural limits: to the north and west lay the vast and almost empty steppes and deserts of Siberia and central Asia, difficult and unrewarding to seize or occupy; to the southwest there was the impenetrable barrier of the Himalayas; to the south the small but populous countries of Southeast Asia could be culturally and economically dominated but not easily conquered, and beyond them lay the Indian Ocean; and to the east lay the vast reach of the Pacific Ocean, with only the peripheral lands of Korea and Japan in the north, again dominated culturally, and in the case of Korea, at times militarily. These barriers to expansion were also barriers of protection, however, isolating China from the rest of the world. Secure behind them China developed its own culture and its own worldview, seeing itself as the Middle Kingdom, the center of the world, with only lesser states on its periphery, and the further away they were, the less important and more barbaric they were considered.

To be sure, China had contacts with the rest of the world. One constant security problem came from the nomadic tribes of the steppes beyond China's long, open northern border. Thence the Xiongnu confederation threatened China for centuries, dealt with by warfare, diplomacy, bribery, and of course wall building. In connection with the long struggle against the Xiongnu, an embassy was sent west in the late second century B.C.E., headed by the great traveler Zhang Qian. His mission was to find the Yue Zhi, a nomadic tribe which had moved westward after defeat in war, and to persuade them to return and fight the Xiongnu again as allies of China. He reached Afghanistan shortly after the fall of the Greek kingdom there c. 130 B.C.E., and entered upper India a little later, some fifty years after the disappearance of the Mauryan Empire. Later, at the height of the Roman Empire, there was trade between that empire and China, not only along the central Asian Silk Road with Parthia as intermediary, but directly by sea. Intrepid sea captains from the eastern Roman Empire crossed the Indian Ocean, passed through the Straits of Malacca, and reached the coast of China itself. None of this was of great significance, however: a minor trade in luxury goods at best.

The basis for Chinese power, wealth, and unity was the vast agricultural productivity of the Huang He and Yangtze valleys, and the huge population sustained thereby. With proper organization and efficient administration, a large surplus population of soldiers, artists, intellectuals, and courtiers could be sustained. Administration was the key, and to take care of this there developed a bureaucracy whose members eventually came to be composed of the literati who dominated Chinese culture and invested it with the Daoism and Confucianism which summed up their intellectual and spiritual outlook. Under this system, Chinese culture reached very great heights by the early Middle Ages, but even at this time China remained largely isolated from the rest of the world. In any case, this brings us well beyond the period we are concerned with here.

CONCLUSION

The contribution of Asian universalist empires to world history, and particularly of the Persian Empire, the earliest of them and the one which had most influence both within and beyond Asia, is to have created the ideal of the supranational state, with peoples of many regions and cultures living together in at least some degree of harmony, cooperating for their mutual economic and security needs. In today's world the rather dubious European ideal of national autonomy and self-determination holds sway, and imperialism is a pejorative word, synonymous with exploitation. Ancient imperialism was of course exploitative, but it should be clear that it was a two-way street: the subject peoples received benefits as well as paid tribute, and in the better empires were gradually assimilated, ceasing to be in any meaningful sense "subject." The result was that for long periods large regions of the world were governed peacefully and knew a certain amount of stability and prosperity, in contrast to the fruit of nationalism, which has generally been strife and warfare.

SELECTED REFERENCES

Creel, H.G. *The Origins of Statecraft in China.* Chicago: University of Chicago Press, 1970.
Frye, Richard N. *A History of Ancient Iran.* Munich: Beck, 1984.
Hopkins, Keith. *Conquerors and Slaves.* Cambridge: Cambridge University Press, 1978.
Larsen, Mogens T., ed. *Power and Propaganda.* Copenhagen: Akademisk Forlag, 1979.
Postgate, J.N. *The First Empires.* Oxford: Oxford University Press, 1977.
Wesson, Robert G. *The Imperial Order.* Berkeley: University of California Press, 1967.

EMPIRE IN EAST ASIA

Cho-yun Hsu

Professor Richard Billows points out three prerequisites for the establishment of great and viable empires:

(1) The ability to mobilize and project military forces.
(2) The vulnerability of the subordinated peoples; the fear of losing their properties renders them incapable of resisting conquest.
(3) A commitment to a religious or philosophical belief—often in the form of a universal ideology—among the ruling elite which is sometimes adopted by the subject peoples.

Once a conquest is completed, the ruling elite often seeks to ensure a continuous and dependable supply of resources, human as well as material, to sustain the newly established system.

Continuous effort is required to consolidate internally and expand externally the geographical and cultural potential of the conquering state. In the case of confrontation between two or more such expanding states, the need to defend one's own territory might lead to offensive and expansion efforts. Sometimes conflicts might lead to territorial conquest, with the winner annexing the territory of the loser. Sustaining such a coalition requires both the organizational capability for mobilization and cultural-ideological claims to assimilate all the subjects within the empire.

The history of Chinese empire building will be examined within the conceptual scheme proposed by Professor Billows and further developed.

The feudal Western Zhou (the first part of the Zhou Dynasty, twelfth to eighth century B.C.E.) is a prototype of the Chinese imperial system. Its most important legacy to Chinese political culture is the concept of the Mandate of Heaven, which transcended both ethnic rule and national boundary. During the next period of the multi-state system, the Eastern Zhou Dynasty (eighth to third century B.C.E.), the expansion of individual states within the common world of Chinese culture reinforced the conviction that a single central authority should reign over all lands that shared the same cultural identity. It was the ensuing dynasties, the Qin (221–206 B.C.E.) and the Han (205 B.C.E.–C.E. 220), that unified the realm and became the model of empire building in China. The four-century history of the Han, to which the Chinese owe their national identity as a people, deserves particular attention.

The Han Empire was built upon three elements: an administrative bureaucracy, an economy built around intensive farming, and the universal ideology of Confucianism. The imperial sovereign claimed the Mandate of Heaven to legitimize his rule. By proclaiming that all people under heaven were potentially imperial subjects and that all lands were potentially imperial domains, the Han Empire sought to extend its boundaries to the far reaches of Chinese culture, thus establishing a universal empire.

Bureaucrats were recruited from all over the empire in order to ensure that regional interests would be represented. Intellectuals, an elite circle that very much overlapped with the bureaucracy, held the imperial authority accountable according to Confucian principles of "ideal governance." The responsibility of local administrators consisted of governing by teaching their subjects Confucian ethics. Thus, the reinforcement of state power with Confucian precepts further universalized the legitimacy of the Han Empire.

The rural-based Han economy combined intensive farming with marketing activities. Throughout the entire empire a gigantic, interregional network of exchange brought staple products to markets. This network of exchange linked local rural communities with towns and cities. In much the same way, human talent was circulated through a recruitment network. Even the administrative networks of provinces and counties ran parallel along these two networks. The Han Empire thus maintained a coherent structure for the mobilization of resources.

Han agriculture reached a fairly sophisticated level of intensive cultivation. Han farmers, unlike their Roman counterparts, were reluctant to move to other locations; colonialization was thus a slow and gradual process. Increases in population, however, eventually must have pressed people to move to less crowded areas beyond China proper, which consisted of the core areas in the

Yellow River drainage system. The loess plains of the Yellow River (Huang He) valley were a major destination. Whether the result of the government's attempts to relocate the population or, more likely, spurred by adverse conditions during times of war and famine, the migrations of the Han people constituted an important factor in the expansion of the empire.

Han expansion beyond China proper followed very different patterns and was pursued for very different reasons in the north and the south. The northern strategy was basically defensive, to fend off the threat posed by the Xiongnu nomadic empire along the steppe. The Han garrisons held territories beyond the Great Wall, which actually marked the transitional zone between the pastureland of the nomads and the farming land of the Chinese. The expansion toward central Asia along the Silk Road was also more a military strategy than a policy of the imperial administration.

The expansion southward was undertaken for economic reasons. Chinese settlers gradually migrated southward to lands which were originally inhabited by non-Chinese native peoples. The migrants founded their colonies along the main traffic trails, such as river valleys and lakes in the coastal regions. A branching network of colonial settlements therefore gradually formed as they extended into the Huang He drainage basin. Once the colonies were well established, the Han administration extended its influence and consolidated power. Throughout Han history, administrative control grew continuously in the regions beyond the drainage basins of the Yangtze and the Pearl River (Zhu Jiang). Eventually all main routes were absorbed by Han counties and provinces. Although there were campaigns against the natives in the south, the scale of these operations was relatively small. Therefore, during the entire process of Han expansion, the principal objective seemed to be consolidation rather than direct conquest by means of military force. The local natives, once assimilated into the Han population, then became the spearheads for further Han expansion southward.

Meanwhile, the vast land areas off the main routes and behind the mountains remained only nominally part of the Han Empire. In these areas indigenous peoples led their traditional ways of life without being Sinicized. Subsequent Chinese empires, such as the Tang, Song, and Ming, are likewise characterized by waves of expansion and then consolidation. But even today, in a sizable portion of the southwestern provinces of China, several million people of non-Han origin have yet to become fully integrated into the Chinese cultural system.

There were empires also in the vast Eurasian steppe. The first was that of the nomadic Xiongnu, contemporaneous with Han China and its most formidable challenger. The Xiongnu Empire was actually a confederation of numerous ethnic groups who were subordinated by the powerful Xiongnu Shang-yu. Among the peoples within the Xiongnu Empire there were certain kinds of fraternal relationships which were probably a common feature of the steppe culture, developed as a defense against the Han farming people with whom they were in competition. A universalism thus spread among the Eurasian steppe peoples. Varied nomadic groups organized themselves into unified entities as they expanded southward: the Xiongnu, the Wuhuan, the Ruanruan, and other cases. The most renown case is the expansion of the Mongols, who under their leader Genghis Khan temporarily subjugated all the peoples in Eurasia. Although these nomadic empires could mobilize, they did not survive their rapid expansions. As the nomadic courts moved into China and other land areas that supported people with an agrarian lifestyle, they did not develop a well-organized bureaucracy, and until Islam and Buddhism were adopted there was no sophisticated ideological system to hold their peoples together.

There was also some hybridization among the Chinese and the nomadic empires. The Tobas (386–557 C.E.), the Tartar Khitans (916–1125), the Turchids (1115–1234), the Mongols in China after Kublai Khan (1271–1368), and the Manchus (1644–1911) are examples of this phenomenon. A dualism in administration was usually adopted to rule the empire: traditional fraternal relationships bonded the members of the nomadic confederation while on the steppe, and a Chinese-style court with Chinese bureaucrats was put in place to govern the Chinese population.

The nomadic empires extended far beyond China. For example, the Mongol Empire consisted of many parts, of which China was only one. As it expanded into China, however, it followed the Chinese pattern of a continuous process of internal consolidation of the empire.

Of course, each of these nomadic empires eventually had to choose between being either more nomadic or more Chinese in nature. The Tobas opted to be completely Chinese; the Mongols withdrew from China and returned to their steppe homeland after the Chinese revolted and overthrew the Mongol overlords. The Manchus, however, chose to preserve their fraternal relationships with the Mongols and Tibetans and simultaneously underwent a rather smooth process of Sinicization to become a Chinese empire within China. That empire prevailed until the 1911 Revolution brought it to an end. Ironically, modern China inherited from the Manchu dynasty the sovereignty of both Tibet and Mongolia; the ambiguous relationship between China and these two domains is a source of controversy even today, some eighty years after the fall of the Manchu Empire.

In summary, the Chinese empires extended their cultural and political influence southward, beyond the core area. A thoroughly Confucianized bureaucracy was essential to the consolidation of the Chinese imperial system because the cultural carriers and the political power holders were initially members of the same group of cultural elites. The Chinese economy, based upon intensive farming and exchange networks, definitely facilitated the continuous dominance of the core area of China proper—the drainage areas of the Yellow and Yangzi (Yangtze) rivers. All these factors made the Chinese pattern of extending power drastically different from that of the nomadic empires of the Eurasian steppes. The Chinese pattern also differed from the Roman pattern. Rome dispersed its citizens widely to all parts of the empire to serve in its legions. The Roman world was therefore divided, and the center shifted to the peripheries. The Romans lacked, as did the Asian nomads, a well-organized bureaucracy to perpetuate the Roman order. As a result, the provinces tended to observe local and regional law rather than the potentially universal Roman law. Separation of church and state did not give the Christianized Roman world a group of cultural elites who could simultaneously Christianize and Romanize the old Roman world and weld it into a single integrated entity. But only this type of state could have withstood the centrifugal forces of the establishment of nation-states by diverse ethnic groups in western Europe. In contrast, the long survival of the Byzantine Empire may be seen as a consequence of its having followed a pattern of development which was relatively similar to the Chinese one.

SYSTEMATIZING THE TRANSCENDENTAL

THE EMERGENCE OF MAJOR RELIGIONS AND WORLD VIEWS

Peter J. Awn

One function of religion in the modern West is to set communities apart from one another, not to integrate them. Each religious world-view by definition purports to possess an essential dimension of ultimate Truth, if not all Truth itself. Other religious communities with different worldviews are often perceived, therefore, to be custodians of a lesser truth, if not completely misguided. In many parts of the modern West religious communities find themselves part of a larger society that describes itself as secular, that is, a society whose structures do not institutionalize the vision of any one religious community. Consequently, not only does each religious group feel itself separate from other religious groups, but it is also conscious of its alienation from secular society, some of whose institutions it may find morally reprehensible.

In contrast to the modern emphasis on the privatization of religion and the separation of religious communities from one another and from secular society, ancient societies envisioned a more integral world in which all powers, both human and transcendent, interacted to create political and social unity. During the third and second millennia B.C.E. this interaction took on particularly creative forms in ancient Mesopotamia, the great river basin civilization on the Tigris and Euphrates.

The Mesopotamian cosmos was alive with multifaceted, dynamic powers whose intervention was essential for the survival of society. In third-millennium Mesopotamia, powers were identified with the realities in which they manifested themselves. Nidaba, the goddess of the reeds, for example, was coextensive with the very reed shoots themselves. As Thorkild Jacobsen described, third-millennium gods were intransitive, locked within the realities whose power they represented. Thus Nidaba's power related to the building of reed huts, the cultivation of grains, and even writing, for the sharpened reed was the stylus used in the writing of cuneiform. Her influence, however, could not be felt beyond these limits.

The most important of these Mesopotamian powers were related to the atmosphere and the powers of agriculture: An (the sky), Enlil (the storm wind), Enki (the sweet waters). The entire pantheon was an interactive body with a pyramid structure of authority, often described as henotheism, that is, a high god ruling over a number of other complex divine powers. Such a structure was not rigidly determined but allowed for a limited amount of fluidity, since the actual ruler among the gods at any particular moment in Mesopotamian history was usually identified with the particular city or region that had attained political supremacy.

The second millennium points to a significant shift in the way Mesopotamians dealt with divine power. The former intransitive powers move beyond their limited purviews to more complex and abstract functions. Thus Enki, who was identified with the sweet waters and the irrigation that supported Mesopotamian agriculture, becomes as well the god of intelligence and guile. Enlil, the god of the storm winds, becomes the god of warriors and military power. Thus power in its many forms became more complex and capable of intense and intimate involvement in human society. The great myths and epics of ancient Mesopotamia reflect vividly this emerging sophistication. The creation myth, the Enuma Elish, recounts the interaction of positive and negative forces leading to the creation of the cosmos and mirrors the stages in the political evolution of Mesopotamian society. In the Gilgamesh Epic, man's struggle for immortality against all odds and his eventual acceptance of mortality is poignantly captured in the lives of the great heros Gilgamesh and Enkidu.

In the first millennium the move toward greater intimacy between human and divine becomes apparent in the growing emphasis on the role of personal gods. Each family possessed a personal deity who was passed genetically from father to son. The personal god acted as chief protector and sustainer of the individual and the family unit.

The first millennium, however, was an age of political unrest and instability in Mesopotamia. The increasing failure of the personal gods to provide security during times of crisis created an environment of religious skepticism, epitomized by texts questioning the justice and even the power of transcendent beings. This genre of "wisdom" literature is paralleled in ancient Israelite texts like the Book of Job.

The influence of Mesopotamia on emerging religious worldviews of the ancient Near East is clearly evident in a number of the holy books of the people of Israel. The Noah story and references to Rahab and Leviathan all have their roots in Mesopotamian mythology. Most significant, however, are not the textual parallels but the evolution of religious ideas that takes place in the Hebrew sources. For no longer is the high god perceived to be the strongest among a complex pantheon of positive and negative forces; he eventually is affirmed by the ancient Israelites as the only transcendent reality. All other powers are not merely impotent but nonexistent. The move from henotheism to radical monotheism is critical for the later development of the great Semitic religious traditions: Judaism, Christianity, and Islam.

We must be careful, however, not to misinterpret the significance of this transition from henotheism to monotheism. As products of a culture heavily influenced by Christianity and Judaism, we often uncritically accept the notion that monotheism is the sign of a culture's growing maturity and sophistication. Instinctively Americans understand monotheism to be a more evolved, a "higher" form of religion. In contrast, polytheistic cultures are branded as "primitive." One need only look at the traditional literature dealing with the religions of the ancient world, especially ancient India, to see how rampant this prejudice is. For any student of religion, such a value judgment in favor of monotheism has no basis in the observable data and skews one's ability to deal seriously with cultures and worldviews different from one's own.

The shifting emphasis from henotheism to monotheism evident in the ancient Near East has an analogous parallel in the evolving religious culture of ancient Greece. The *Iliad* and the *Odyssey* reflect clearly the henotheistic structures of the heroic society of second-millennium Greece. In the fifth and fourth centuries of the first millennium, however, the philosophical speculation of Plato and Aristotle represents a significant revision of the ancient worldview.

Plato's theory of forms, especially the primacy of the Form of the Good, while not an articulated monotheism, does shift the emphasis from the interaction of numerous powers to the centrality of one originating principle. So too in Aristotle's theory of the Unmoved Mover, the origin of the universe is pinpointed in one supreme reality.

On the level of religious experience, Platonism articulates a personal involvement with transcendent power, exemplified by Socrates' reliance on the voice of *theos* who guides the course of his life. So too Plato's emphasis on the contemplation of the Form of the Good highlights the centrality of the soul's unique relationship with the transcendent. It is not necessary here to summarize the extraordinary role Greek philosophy has played in the articulation of the great Semitic monotheisms. Suffice it to say that the influence of Greek thought is all-pervasive.

Mesopotamia and ancient Greece are not alone as formative influences on Semitic religion. The extraordinary richness of ancient Iranian religion, especially Zoroastrianism, was to become a prized legacy in Judaism, Christianity, and Islam. The prophet Zoroaster lived sometime between 1700 and 1500 B.C.E., although his dates are disputed. The ancient Iranian society of his time was tripartite, comprising of priests, warriors, and herdsmen. It appears that the violence of the marauding warrior class and the consequent victimization of the more sedentary population impressed on Zoroaster's mind the need for a more just society.

Zoroaster began to have visions of the Wise Lord, Ahura Mazda, who revealed himself as the supreme God of Goodness and the guardian of Asha, truth. The earliest revelations, some of which may go back to Zoroaster himself, are preserved in the collection of ancient hymns known as the Gathas, part of the Zoroastrian scripture, the Avesta.

The notion of revelation is key to understanding Semitic and ancient Iranian religions. In these revelation traditions a transcendent, omnipotent, and personal creative power breaks into the historical process to communicate ultimate truth through a chosen instrument, the prophet. It is presumed that, left to their own devices, men and women would not be able to discover this truth on their own, due either to their own finitude or to the active forces of evil in the cosmos.

The God of Goodness, Ahura Mazda, who reveals himself to Zoroaster, is not alone in cosmic isolation, for he has a twin, Angra Mainyu, who has chosen to champion not Asha, truth, but Drug, the lie. (In middle Persian, Ahura Mazda later became known as Ohrmazd and Angra Mainyu as Ahriman.) The cosmic dualism of Zoroastrianism is based on the central principle of freedom of choice. In the same way that the gods of Goodness and

Evil freely chose Asha or Drug, so too must each man or woman choose to become a warrior in the camp of either Ahura Mazda or Angra Mainyu.

The covenant myth of Zoroastrianism captures best both the centrality of freedom and the critical link between god and mankind. In the myth the beleaguered Good God turns to the souls of as yet uncreated men and women for help in his battle against the Evil God. But men and women cannot be coerced into service; they must freely choose to fight for the Good God. Without the cooperation of mankind, however, the Good God will suffer defeat at the hands of Evil. In a very real sense, the Good God needs men and women to survive. The souls of men and women choose to commit themselves to the struggle, which will entail their taking on human forms and being sent to the battleground, which is earth. In return, the Good God promises mankind eternal life in paradise.

The weapons of battle for the Zoroastrian are good thoughts, good words, and good deeds. Anything that improves quality of life is by that very fact a religious act and a strike against the power of Evil. Zoroastrian worship, which centers on the Fire Temple, affirms the goodness of all the fundamental elements of creation. And Zoroastrian society, with its highly ritualized structure and concern with purity and pollution, attempts to provide the ideal environment for the eventual victory of Good over Evil.

In the covenant myth, the Good God promises the souls of men and women that he will provide them with eternal rewards if they choose to join battle with him against Evil. Zoroastrian eschatology affirms the existence of paradise and the resurrection of the body. Even those sinners who have followed Angra Mainyu and are condemned to the fires of hell will eventually be rehabilitated through the power of goodness.

The ancient Iranian religious worldview is but one half of a broader religious and cultural movement that can be traced to the mid-second millennium. For it was at this time that the Aryan tribes moved into the Indian subcontinent, supplanting a much older civilization centered in the Indus Valley. It was in this period that the Sanskrit Vedas began to emerge, voluminous and complex texts comprising hymns, rituals, and, most important, the ritual of the fire sacrifice which was believed ultimately to control the universe. These texts are revealed truth, not in the sense that one finds in Zoroastrianism and the Semitic traditions, where revelation consists of God breaking into history, but rather a truth that is discovered by the great sages. The sacred texts of ancient India are the products of those who attained a unique level of wisdom and insight. Only religious specialists were allowed to hear and learn the Vedas, which remained for generations oral literature.

The gods of the Vedas are atmospheric gods and gods of the natural elements: Indra, the storm god and god of war; Varuna, the guardian of cosmic order, rita; Agni, the god of fire; and Soma, a divine liquid which transforms humans into beings like the gods (parallel to the sacred drink, haoma, in Zoroastrianism). The transcendent powers described in the Vedas and in later Hinduism form two categories, the powers of goodness (deva) and the forces of evil and destruction (ahura). These are the complete opposite of what one encounters in Zoroastrianism, where the ahuras are the beneficent powers, whose chief is Ahura Mazda, and the devas are evil powers derived from Angra Mainyu. (In Avestan, the spellings are daeva and ahura; in Sanskrit, the spellings are deva and asura.)

A number of key principles undergird the religious vision of ancient India. The most central is that of karma, action, which presupposes that every act one performs has a consequence. Karma represents justice in its most relentless form. Every being in the cosmos is what it is because of what it has made itself through its own actions. Essential to any understanding of karma is belief in reincarnation. The soul, or atman, which is eternal, unchanging, and immutable, migrates from existence to existence, taking on a lower or higher form depending on one's karmic state.

It is essential to keep in mind that in the ancient Indian worldview both gods and humans are on the same side of creation. All realities, human or superhuman, animal or vegetative, seek the same goal, liberation from the endless cycle of death and rebirth. Indian sages insisted that there was no one answer to the origin of the universe, if there was any answer at all. Clearly there was no belief in a monotheistic god who created the universe out of nothing.

In contrast to the Semitic notion of *creatio ex nihilo,* the ancient Indian worldview affirmed the eternality of time and repeating cycles of existence. These cycles devolve into greater states of corruption, eventually reaching a point when the cosmos is annihilated, only to reemerge in a cycle of perfection which initiates anew the process of devolution.

The struggle to liberate the atman from the round of death and rebirth requires rigorous training in yoga, meditation, and detachment from the world of change and flux. The goal of the liberated atman is to experience its true being, namely its unity with the universal substrate of existence, brahman. As the later speculative texts of Hinduism, the Upanishads, affirm, *Tat tvam asi*, "That art thou," in other words, atman and brahman are identical realities, part of a universal, unchanging, immutable unity.

In the same way that Zoroastrianism emerged from a social structure of priests, warriors, and herdsman, ancient Indian society comprised four classes or colors (varnas): Brahmans (the priestly class), Kshatriyas (the warrior class), Vaishyas (the merchant and commercial class), and Shudras (the lower class, whose occupations were often involved with ritually polluting materials). In addition, there was and still is a large group outside the recognized social structure, known as untouchables, who are shunned by all four varnas. From this basic social organization eventually evolved the more complex system of castes, comprising innumerable subsets of the traditional four classes.

In the middle of the first millennium, traditional Indian religion was challenged from within by a number of sages who criticized its overly hierarchical religious and social structure. The arhat ideal, especially, came under fire. The arhat was the exemplar of the yogi and ascetic whose rigorous physical and spiritual training had prepared him for liberation in this life. For many this ideal appeared overly elitist and totally inaccessible because of the years of training it required.

In response to these anti-Brahmanical religious movements, the emphasis in Hinduism gradually shifted to devotional religion as the means to liberation, thus opening the possibility of its attainment to all, regardless of class or caste. The text which represents most clearly this shift is the *Bhagavad Gītā*, perhaps the most influential text in all of modern Hinduism.

The individual whose critique of the Brahmanical synthesis in the mid-sixth century B.C.E. was to alter dramatically the shape of Asian religion was Shakyamuni Buddha. In contrast to the social hierarchy of traditional Hinduism and its reliance on the arhat ideal, the Buddha taught a new law or dharma, centering on the four noble truths and the eightfold path. The four classes of Hinduism as well as the ritual control of the Brahmans were rejected.

The first of the noble truths asserts that all human existence is characterized by suffering, because all is touched by impermanence. The second noble truth pinpoints the source of suffering in human craving, the desire to perpetuate the self. The cure of suffering is affirmed in the third noble truth as the cessation of craving. And the fourth noble truth outlines the eightfold path which brings about the cessation of craving and suffering.

Essential to the Buddhist path is a commitment to discipline which focuses on detachment, the development of meditation techniques, and the attainment of gnosis. In the Old Wisdom School, or Theravada Buddhism, the monk and the monastic community become the ideal social contexts in which to attain enlightenment. In fact one can say that in Theravada Buddhism the monastery represents the focal point of society. The New Wisdom School, or Mahayana Buddhism, opens the goal to all through devotion and dedication to the bodhisattva ideal. Bodhisattvas are enlightened beings who have vowed to refuse the experience of Nirvana until they have succeeded in bringing all sentient beings with them.

Another key area in which Buddhism differs from Hinduism is in its denial of the existence of the soul or atman as described in Hinduism. For the Hindu, the atman is the unchanging, eternal, spiritual core at the heart of changing beings. The effects of karma on the atman result in the continuing cycle of rebirth. Only by freeing the atman from all the effects of karma can liberation be achieved. For the Buddha, this reliance on a permanent and eternal soul was a fundamental flaw in Hinduism, for, in the Buddha's mind, all existence, material or spiritual, is characterized by flux, impermanence, and change.

In the same way that Buddhism denies the existence of a permanent, immutable, and eternal soul, so too it denies that liberation entails a return to the One that is the substrate of all existence, for such a One does not exist. Enlightenment in Buddhism leads to the attainment of Nirvana, which is totally without quality, unthinkable, and incomprehensible. Nirvana is described more easily in negative terms like "emptiness" than in any positive terms whatsoever.

The Buddhist message spread from India to China, Japan, and Southeast Asia. Ironically Buddhism, which has had and continues to play such a major role in Asia, has ceased to exist as a serious influence in India, the land of its birth.

Buddhism presents for Westerners a unique religious problem because of its refusal to affirm the existence of any supreme being analogous to the god of the Semitic traditions. Because of this, Buddhism has been perceived by some as atheistic, by others as no religion at all. Doubtless Buddhism affirms the existence of transcendent powers, because the cosmos for Buddhists is populated with thousands of gods, spirits, and bodhisattvas. Once again, however, it is essential to be aware that all of these cosmic powers are seeking the same goal as the Buddhist monk, nun, layman, or laywoman, namely, enlightenment and Nirvana. Therefore no god or group of gods is ultimate in any way.

Instead of focusing primarily on a transcendent Other, Buddhism stresses commitment to the three refuges, namely the Buddha, the dharma, and the monastic community, which are the key vehicles for the attainment of Nirvana. Nirvana, however, is not god nor should it be seen as even analogous to the god of the Semitic traditions.

As interesting as Buddhism's denial of ultimate transcendent power is the synthesis arrived at during the same time period in China. For during the sixth century B.C.E., while the Buddha's preaching was taking root in India, the great sage Confucius was active.

The religious worldviews that were articulated by the various ancient societies in Asia from the fourth through the first millennium B.C.E. remain vibrant forces in the modern world, either in forms similar to those in which they originated or as formative influences on other religions and cultures. The emergence of religious worldviews in Asia cannot be limited solely to the first four millennia B.C.E. For the end of the first millennium B.C.E. ushers in the enormous growth and expansion of the great Semitic monotheisms, especially Christianity and Islam. The limits of space, however, allow us only to acknowledge in passing their influence.

Christianity was born in Asia as an offshoot of Palestinian Judaism. The followers of the rabbi Jesus developed quickly a sense of separate identity which allowed them to preach salvation through the risen Messiah to non-Jewish communities throughout the Asian, African, and European worlds. The early Christian churches in Palestine, Anatolia, and Persia provided Christianity with a solid Asian foundation.

As the Christian community matured, developed hierarchical structures, and pursued a vigorous missionary program, it articulated with greater clarity and forcefulness its religious vision. Jesus is the son of God, born of a virgin, through whose suffering, death, and resurrection all men and women will be saved.

Christian influence in Asia, which appeared so vibrant during the first five hundred years of Christian expansion, experienced significant decline with the coming in the sixth century C.E. of the third of the great Semitic monotheisms, Islam. The prophet Muhammad was born in the Arabian city of Mecca in c. 570 C.E., where he began to receive revelations from God in the year 610. The revelations continued until his death in 632.

Islam understands itself to be the last of the great Semitic revelations and thus sees itself as the fulfillment of Judaism and Christianity. The oral revelations to Muhammad were eventually collected and preserved in the Qur'an. The heart of Islam is the affirmation of radical monotheism and the commitment to the apostleship of Muhammad. Islam shares with Judaism its reliance on a divinely revealed code of law which touches every aspect of human life.

The early history of Islam was marked by rapid expansion. Within a hundred years of the prophet's death Islam had spread east through Persia to the Indian subcontinent and west through Syria, Palestine, Egypt, and North Africa to Spain. From that time on, Islam has remained a potent religious and political force in many Asian cultures and societies.

This brief survey of emerging religious worldviews in Asia has focused primarily on the history of ideas. It is essential, however, to bear in mind that the evolution of the history of ideas in Asia is affected by numerous factors, like the politics, economy, and ecology of a particular region at a particular moment in history. Nevertheless, there is a genuine, if limited, advantage in examining the broad sweep of religious movements that have so shaped the course of Asian history.

SYSTEMATIZING THE TRANSCENDENTAL

THE *ANALECTS* OF CONFUCIUS, THEN AND NOW

Irene T. Bloom

First-time readers of the *Analects* of Confucius sometimes experience a vaguely disquieting intimation that the wisdom of the East may not travel as well as they had hoped. That the work is a classic of Chinese and of East Asian culture is indisputable; that it deserves its reputation as a classic of world culture may seem less sure. The *Analects* offers nothing resembling the exhilarating intellectual journeys of the Platonic dialogues, the robust religious dramas of the Bible, or the sublime metaphysical visions of the Upanishads. Nor does Confucius (551–479 B.C.E.), though an almost exact contemporary of Siddhartha Gotama, the historical Buddha, present a life story with a mythic shape so compelling and a central message so immediately intelligible that biographical fact fades into virtual irrelevance. For most readers Confucius emerges as an earnest and exemplary teacher, dedicated and skillful enough that there is little difficulty in seeing how in time he might gain the stature of a sage. Still, few are likely to nominate him for the title of father of a nation, savior of humankind, or world-honored one. From what we can learn of his life, he remained, like most teachers, a person of his time and place.

Confucius often comes to us with a number of tags attached as well, including one with the clear instruction that his thought is to be taken as "philosophical" rather than "religious." This instruction is commonly proffered as if it were simple fact, too obvious to require any explanation, while its very simplicity seems to ensure its firm adherence to the surface of the text. To insinuate the possibility that this categorization of the *Analects* as "philosophical" rather than "religious" is not fact but interpretation or judgment may entail a considerable challenge. One reason such an interpretation has gained currency is no doubt that the very concept of "religion" or "the religious" seems to require an element of transcendence, and it may be unclear whether this exists for Confucius, so rooted does he at first appear to be in his own time and place.

Not only do we find him using images of rootedness in his speech when he wants to indicate the source of things and the basis of their strength and stability, but the roots he speaks of seem close enough to literal roots that they hardly seem metaphorical at all: the primary value of groundedness in an agrarian society is almost palpable. The way Confucius distinguishes between root and branch, or between the fundamental and the peripheral, suggests a deeply practical cast of mind. Yet practicality, it seems, is often practical primarily within a particular cultural context and, often enough, is no special concern of religion—at least, not of religion as it opens outward toward universality. Inspiration **is** a religious concern, but if inspiration is taken to mean, literally, the infusion or internalization of a spirit, then Confucius may be found too human-centered, too spiritually self-contained, to allow for that. Ritual, conjoined with art, is another common and often compelling feature of religious life. But in his discussions of ritual Confucius may appear fixated on externals, and never more so than when he speaks of how the details of ordinary life are to be disposed—what clothing shall be made of, how food shall be served, how mats shall be arranged, or how sacrifices shall be offered.[1] Allowing that in the details of our own lives we are far removed from Confucius, as we may be in our estimations of the relevance of "external" detail, he may seem the less religious and the more remote.

If it happens, then, that the practicality of Confucius is not **our** practicality, and if we cannot identify with—or even identify—his source of "inspiration," he may tend to recede from our sphere of sympathetic comprehension. Separated from him by time and by culture, and mindful of his absorption in an ordinary life that no longer resembles in obvious ways the ordinary lives we ourselves lead, we may wonder about the connections between his world and ours and what our world may have to learn from his. Help may be needed in hearing the human heartbeat.

The personality of Confucius, in other words, is crucial: this was true for his contemporaries, and it is no less true for ours. This is what the *Analects* is really about. One may begin to come close to this personality in attending to the nature of the *Analects* as a text. The English word "analects" (from the Greek, *analekta*) means "a selection," and the Chinese title *Lun-yu* may be translated as "conversations." The text was, of course, not written by Confucius; it is known that the selection of conversations was compiled by later followers, perhaps as much as a century after his lifetime. The twenty short chapters of the *Analects* represent a record, or, more aptly, a recollection, of conversations that transpired between Confucius and his disciples, or between Confucius and the rulers of several of the feudal states that he visited during the peripatetic phase of his teaching career.[2] There are also descriptions of Confucius, brief and telling accounts of the way he appeared as a personality to those who were most intimately acquainted with him. The conversations are all exchanges that might actually have occurred in real time, and several of the disciples emerge in them as individual personalities who receive differing responses from Confucius according to his assessment of their personal development—a personalized tuition. Given the nature of the text, the descriptions are multi-perspectival, and it is particularly interesting to notice that, while the disciples often seem to suggest that the Master is elusive, slightly beyond their comprehension, even mysterious in his moral capacities, Confucius himself appears modest and unassuming. He assures his disciples that he hides nothing from them. Notably inclined to self-deprecation, he is yet unfailingly dignified.

Most of the conversations recollected in the *Analects* focus on the practicalities of interpersonal relationships, personal cultivation in the context of those relationships, and the relation of personal cultivation on the part of rulers and ministers to the conduct of government. The fact that the source, the subjects, and the tone of the work are all quite human clearly sets the *Analects* apart from many of the classics that are reliably recognized as religious. Unlike the Bible or the Qur'an, it does not purport to be a revealed text. Chinese literature, in fact, claims no "revealed" or divinely inspired texts even remotely comparable to the Bible or the Qur'an, nor does it recognize a distinction comparable to that in the Hindu tradition between the Vedic literature recognized as sruti (texts believed to have been "heard" or revealed, deriving from a supra-human source) and the post-Vedic literature designated as smrti (texts thought to be "remembered," implying a human origin). While the text of the *Analects* was subject over the course of centuries to a wide range of interpretations, based on different ideas about what Confucius actually meant by what he is recorded to have said, never in the history of the tradition would there be cause for controversy between fundamentalists and proponents of a metaphorical interpretation of the text. Conventional miracles not infrequently beget controversies, and this is a text without miracles of a conventional sort. Confucius may even be described as adopting a perspective of ordinariness—an ordinariness that can be thought of as characteristically Chinese in the sense that it entails a conscious focus on the present life and a sympathetic acceptance of ordinary humanity.

Just how ordinary the perspective of Confucius was may be illustrated by comparing any one of a number of conversations recorded in the *Analects* with equally famous conversations in the classic Indian collection known as the Upanishads. In Book 6 of the *Chandogya Upanishad,* for example, there is a conversation about learning between the sage Uddalaka and his already highly tutored, if not yet wise, son Svetaketu. Svetaketu has spent a dozen years studying the Vedas with a teacher and has returned, "conceited, priding himself on his learning, and obdurate." The discussion in which his father engages him involves a reflection by the father, intended for the edification of the son, on the nature of Being. It opens with the father questioning the son about what he has learned under the guidance of his teacher:

> Did you also ask about that teaching by which what had not been heard of is heard; what had not been thought of, is thought of; and what had not been known, is known?[3]

In other words, asks the father, did you advance to the teaching that concerns itself with **ultimate** questions? Svetaketu evidently has not gotten that far and requires some continuing education from his father. The ensuing discussion moves slowly but unswervingly toward a particular perspective on the nature of a higher truth, of an ultimate reality involving the identity of the soul (atman) with the world-soul (brahman).

Given the worldliness of Confucius, we typically find ourselves in the *Analects* on ground that is less elevated and more like the ordinary earth. The opening passage, for example, is likewise concerned with learning:

> The Master said, To learn and at due times to repeat what one has learned, is that not after all a pleasure? That friends should come to one from afar, is this not after all delightful? To remain unsoured even though one's merits are unrecognized by others, is that not after all what is expected of a noble person (junzi) [chun-tzu]?[4]

The times having been out of joint, Confucius was consistently thwarted in his hope for an opportunity to prove himself
in the service of a humane ruler, or a ruler whom he might
encourage in the direction of humaneness. That he never attained a high official position must have been a continuing
source of regret for him. Yet here, at the outset of the text, he
expresses an affirmative spirit, alluding to the pleasures of
learning, the joy of being with friends, the resolution to remain
unembittered in the face of life's disappointments. His concern
is not with ultimate reality, but with a proximate or quotidian
reality—with taking satisfaction in what is available, making
the best of one's abilities, benefiting from one's interactions
with others. His concern is not with a person who is twice-born,
but with a person presumed to have one lifetime only—the
junzi, the "noble person" or "gentleman" whose nobility Confucius understands to be based on character rather than on
birth.

In fact, there are several exchanges recorded in the *Analects*
that might almost suggest the situation of Uddalaka and
Svetaketu **in reverse:** when disciples come to Confucius with
what, for the.n, are **ultimate** questions—questions having to do
with knowledge, with what lies beyond death, and with the requirements of serving the spirits of the deceased—Confucius
firmly deflects their questions. "Devote yourself to what you must
rightly do for the people, and respect spirits," he advises, "but
keep them at a distance."[5] And "Before you have learned to serve
human beings, how can you serve spirits?"[6] "Until you know
about the living, how are you to know about the dead?"[7] In other
words, concern yourself with the people and the life around you;
transfer your focus of attention from matters that are ultimately
beyond you to those that are fully within your ken, and not just
within your ken but within your ordinary experience. At just the
point that Uddalaka tries to draw his son away from the mun-
danely obvious and into the immensity of metaphysical reflection,
Confucius seeks to redirect his disciples away from what he considers ultimately unknowable and into the immediacies of ethical
action.

The questions posed by the disciples bear on the relation between the living and the dead, the responsibilities of the living to
the dead, and the possible influence of the dead over the living—
issues of immense importance in the religious life of every ancient
culture. Confucius' responses have been understood to signal an
emergence from what Arthur Waley aptly described as an "au-

guristic-sacrificial"[8] mentality and a movement toward values that are this-worldly and moral. Were the living to devote themselves primarily to consulting and appeasing the spirits of deceased ancestors? Or should the focus of human concern be on the quality of human interactions and the capacity of the living to act as moral agents responsible for the conduct of human affairs? The former view and practice had been central to the religious life of the earlier Shang period; the latter view was becoming prevalent at the time of Confucius and is emblematic of his thought. There was in China's "axial age," and above all in the advocacy of Confucius, a transfer of attention from an invisible world to the visible one, from prognostication to "virtue," and from external controls over human affairs to the significant possibility of self-control on the part of living individuals.

Confucius did not argue for abandoning the belief in spirits or the sense of connectedness between the living and the dead. Is there nonetheless evidence that would suggest that this "axial-age" movement should be understood to involve the replacement of sacred concerns with secular ones, a shift from a "religious" to a "philosophical" approach to human existence? Before reaching the conclusion that Confucius's concerns were **not** religious, or that he dismissed religious attitudes in favor of secular ones, consideration should be given to an alternative possibility: just as there is a religious background to the questions posed by his disciples, there is, by implication, a kind of religious message in his response. Encouraging reflection on this possibility has the advantage of affording an opportunity for a deeper examination of the criteria of "the religious" and the implications of transcendence.

It is clear that in the course of the transfer of attention from other-worldly to this-worldly concerns—this great "axial-age" movement associated with Confucius—the scope of human competence was enlarged and the sense of personal responsibility deepened. The Upanishadic questions, "Who am I?" and "How do I relate to the totality of Being?" were somehow less urgent and compelling in the Chinese context than in the Indian.[9] The fundamental questions for Confucius and his later followers were more along the lines of: "What must I do?" and "What is there in me that enables me to do it?" Rather than a metaphysics of the person, such as Uddalaka gradually reveals to Svetaketu, Confucius's exchanges with his disciples have to do almost entirely with ethical conduct. The concerns are how a human being can be expected to act and to **inter**act with others and which personal resources need to be cultivated in order to make such conduct possible. Confucius apparently has little to reveal; rather, he seems to remind his hearers of what he expects them already to have learned from their ordinary life experience. Where Uddalaka seems consummately tender in the education of his son,[10] Confucius appears firmly resolved in the presence of his disciples, and resolve seems to be fundamental to the *junzi*'s project.

The concept of a *junzi*, often translated as "noble person" or "gentleman,"[11] was evolving in the time of Confucius and coming to be understood to require a developed moral nobility rather than simply an inherited social nobility. A prepared reader of the *Analects* may discover a kind of tension in virtually any of the text's references to the *junzi*. On the one hand, the term has a more egalitarian implication than it could have had in earlier usage because in the Confucian perspective anyone can, in principle, become a *junzi*; on the other hand, one who aspires to become a *junzi* faces stringent moral requirements that apply no less to attitude and motivation than to behavior. Among the kinds of conduct that Confucius associated with moral nobility, and evidently expected of the *junzi*, perhaps the three most important are filial devotion (*xiao*), humaneness (*ren*), and courtesy or ritual propriety (*li*). The moral vocabulary of Confucius is by no means exhausted in these three, but these are central, expressing in three distinct modes the Confucian awareness of and concern with human interrelatedness.

Even a brief examination of each of them should make clear that what contemporary Western readers of the *Analects* invariably encounter as **ideas** are, from the perspective of Confucius and his followers, also **practices.** That is to say, *xiao*, *ren*, and *li*, among other Confucian concerns, are not merely concepts but modes of behavior that are understood to have a bearing on what a human being will be like as a person, within as well as without. Embedded in these thoughts are not simply behavioral rules or standards but expectations about what the practitioner of these virtues should be like as a personality.

Xiao, or filial devotion,[12] is moral behavior with a built-in time line, as it were, from cradle to grave, and even beyond. Typically, *xiao* is associated with the responsibility incumbent upon a child for the care of parents, and, indeed, the Chinese graph for *xiao* shows a son beneath an old man, suggesting both support and hierarchy. Evidently, *xiao* had its roots in the most ancient practices of ancestor veneration in early Chinese religious practice and in the most ancient concerns for biological continuity of life. However, in the *Analects*, as in many later Confucian sources, *xiao* also implies the care that parents give children at the beginning of life, with the support of parents by children later in life being understood as the reciprocal of the nurturing the parents have already provided. Given the moral amplitude involved in the Confucian notion of reciprocity, filial duty takes on what might be called a spiritual dimension. Confucius is concerned that the care of parents by children should not be merely a matter of seeing to their physical needs, without the proper spirit, demeanor, and involvement. A number of his statements indicate that he takes the style and spirit of a son's mourning for his parents after their death and his ability to carry on the will or intention of his deceased father to be the most crucial indicator of the son's own moral character. Obviously, it is important for the well being of the parents that they should be served in a spirit of caring that goes beyond the pro forma satisfaction of an obligation. It is also important for the child who is caring for the parent because it is through this care that one develops and expresses one's own personality.

The same can be said in the case of *ren*, the most explicitly interactive of virtues. In some translations of the *Analects ren* has been translated as "benevolence"[13] or "Goodness,"[14] but there is much to recommend "humaneness," which serves to bring out the connection between *ren* as a virtue and another word, also pronounced *ren*, meaning simply "human" or "human being." More than being merely homophones, the two words are cognates. The graph for "human being" in Chinese is "a summary picture of a walking man."[15] The graph for "humaneness" or "humanity" has an added component: alongside the walking person is the number "two," suggesting a human being in company with others or "humanity towards another."[16]

At the beginning of the *Analects* Confucius is quoted as saying that *ren* is rooted (literally) in *xiao*, or filial devotion, suggesting its source in that complex blend of duty, affection, reciprocity, and longing. Despite being repeatedly questioned by his disciples about *ren*, he generally declines their requests to characterize it or to identify a particular person as an exemplar of this virtue. However, at one point he responds to a question by saying, "As for humaneness—you want to establish yourself; then help others to establish themselves. You want to develop yourself; then help others to develop themselves. Being able to recognize oneself in others, one is on the way to being humane."[17] What this translation rather freely renders as "being able to recognize oneself in others," is, literally, "being able to take what is near and grasp the

analogy." The idea is that one begins with an immediate awareness of one's own desires and, recognizing the similarity between
oneself and others, forms an assessment of the needs and wants of
the other. Motivated by a sense of reciprocity or mutuality, one
responds empathetically; in so doing, one is "on the way" to being
humane. That is, one can at least be sure of moving in the right
direction, and direction is everything. Humaneness in some ways
resembles what, in other traditions, has been represented as the
"golden rule," but, again, Confucian humaneness is not so much a
concept or a precept as it is an engagement or a practice. Through
being engaged in the practice of humaneness one responds appropriately to others and, once again, also refines one's own personality.

If filial devotion has its origins in the sense of relatedness that
derives from biological inheritance and continuity, and humaneness involves an extension of that sense of relatedness, working
outward from the familial source toward a larger community, ritual (*li*) represents the structure, discipline, or order through
which the sense of human relatedness is expressed, perpetuated,
and celebrated. The graph for *li*, or ritual, is composed of a radical
element indicating "prognostication" or "presaging" alongside an
element designating a ritual vessel. The graph unmistakably suggests that the ritual of the later Zhou period had its roots in the
most archaic strata of Chinese religious culture and represented
an outgrowth of the practices referred to above as the "auguristic-
sacrificial" mode. In the thought and practice of Confucius and
his followers, who were known as the most ardent and devoted
ritualists,[18] the *li* seem to take on new significance, yet without
being dissociated from their origins in antiquity. In fact, it is the
connection with the past to which Confucius constantly recurs in
his comments about the value of *li.*

Rites are understood by Confucius as a link with the past, a
time-honored means of celebrating the momentous occasions as
well as the ordinary events of human life. Along with the transfer
of attention to the world of the living that is so striking a feature
of China's "axial age," rites are subtly transmuted. Increasingly
associated with reverence, respect, courtesy, and what might be
called "good form," ritual practice comes to be understood not so
much as a means of propitiating the spirits of the deceased as of
expressing the role of living individuals in a biological continuum
of life and in the human community. Rites are seen to ensure
balance and dignity in human interactions and to allow individuals to give appropriate expression to their feelings in morally con-
siderate ways. Again, as in the case of filial devotion and

humaneness, ritual practice is understood to be conducive to the cultivation of particular moral attitudes within the self. When Confucius speaks of humaneness in terms of "mastering one's self and returning to ritual,"[19] he seems clearly to have something of this sort in mind. Rites, for him, serve both to develop and to express a recognition of one's own humanity along with that of others. No less than a discipline, ritual represents a formative experience.

Having considered these three concerns of Confucius—each of which can be construed as highly contextualized both in conception and in practice—the question remains whether there is something in the profession of this teacher that suggests a religious dimension or that implies an element of transcendence. This way of posing the question would be misleading, however, were it to imply that "the religious" is an aspect of life rather than its very fabric or that transcendence requires a being or power remote from the human realm which must be experienced by human beings through grace or the gift of revelation. A distinction between "secular" and "sacred" is not made by Confucius,[20] who seems, rather, to focus on the ultimacy of the ordinary. His counsel about "devoting oneself to what one must rightly do for the people," "serving human beings," and "knowing the living" may be understood to reflect "ultimate concerns"[21] not only because these represent all that we know on earth, but because human beings are recognized to be part of an order that is highly interactive. The service that an individual performs in the world, even in seemingly limited contexts, is found to have an influence in a much larger frame, with private melding into public as reliably as the more obvious converse. Filial devotion practiced within one's own family, for example, has ramifications in a far wider sphere.[22]

Confucius may not be "inspired" in the literal sense of the Latinate English word, but he has an abiding faith in Heaven. The concept of the Mandate of Heaven (or the ordinance of Heaven) that had emerged in the early Zhou period, with a largely political significance,[23] finds its way into his later reflections on his own life in a passage that may well qualify as the world's shortest autobiography:

> At fifteen, I committed myself to learning. At thirty I established myself. At forty I no longer had doubts. At fifty I knew the ordinance of Heaven. At sixty I could hear and comply. At seventy I could follow my heart's desires without transgressing the appropriate limits.[24]

This brief life history turns, of course, on Confucius' understanding of the ordinance of Heaven and his gradual but steady progress in accepting it. The order that prevails in the wider world is found to operate in an individual life as well, and, while it appears to be just **that**—an order rather than a deity—it is a beneficent order and a source of life, support, and even a certain austere comfort. At the same time, Heaven is also the source of what is beyond human understanding, including such inexplicable events as the dire illness or untimely death of a blameless and worthy person.[25] Yet for some reason there is barely any tension generated by the complexity of Heaven's role, no soul-searing search for an answer to the problem of suffering such as is found in the biblical Book of Job. By the time the Book of Job concludes, a powerful if painful message has been delivered concerning the vastness of God's universe and the inadequacy of human understanding to fathoming God's design—the incomprehensibility of God. Speaking out of the whirlwind, God has conveyed this message to Job in a magnificent poem.

The Confucian intuition is different. Heaven, according to Confucius, does **not** speak. "The four seasons pursue their course, and all things are born," he observes, "yet what words does Heaven speak?"[26] The way the question is posed suggests that he understands Heaven as a natural order rather than a supernatural power. Yet despite the muteness of Heaven, and the fact that its ways too cannot always be comprehended, human beings are not distanced from Heaven as Job is distanced from his God. Confucius has the confidence that Heaven produced (or, "gave birth to") the virtue or power that is in him,[27] a sign, it would seem, of its protection as well as its validation of his efforts,[28] even if those efforts are not always availing in an immediate or obvious way.

"Heaven alone is great,"[29] he says in words hardly less evocative of awe and admiration than those pronounced by a prophet who lived more than a millennium later, in a culture remote from his, in declaring his submission to his God. Elsewhere Confucius is recorded as saying that, "The noble person is in awe of three things: he is in awe of the ordinance of Heaven, in awe of great persons, and in awe of the words of the sages."[30] This statement might appear to contradict the one recorded in the previous quotation, but there may be no contradiction here because the three objects of awe are so obviously co-implicated: great persons are great and sages are sages because of their ability to model themselves on Heaven[31] and their mindfulness of its ordinance.

Heaven, then, is a natural order in the world, one that favors moral action. Confucius recognizes, however, that it will not always be given to human beings to understand Heaven's functioning, a recognition that shows up in his conversations and observations in a distinctive and often poignant interplay of confidence and resignation. Nor can there be any expectation that the reward for right conduct or punishment for its opposite will be immediately apparent within the lifetime of particular individuals: Heaven's ordinance is expressed within a longer and larger frame. Does such a view allow for the possibility of transcendence, and, if so, is the conception of transcendence found here one that would permit some significant comparison with the conceptions found in other world religions?

The question has been actively debated among Western students of East Asia at least since the time of Max Weber's reflections on the religion of China the better part of a century ago,[32] and, however much depth and scope we may be able to achieve in our discussions, it is unlikely to be readily or easily resolved. But if the possibility of transcendence **is** recognized as part of the Confucian vision, it is clearly not transcendence of the world itself, but transcendence of any sense of incoherence in the world and transcendence of any sense of separation from the forces that energize the world and the order that governs it. The transcendent is not **other** in the sense that God is generally understood to be **other** in the monotheistic religions of the West; rather, it may be found in a more encompassing reality—in the wholeness of things in the world and the connectedness among them across time. Though the human family seems already in the thought of Confucius to be on the way to becoming a model of this connectedness, the Confucian view of the universe is not essentially anthropocentric.[33] Still, human beings are felt to have a home in the natural order and assurance of the ultimate significance, and even resonance, of moral action. There is something remarkably subtle about this view, and something immensely powerful as well, a subtlety and a power that seem to inhere less in the ideas than in the personality of this very worldly teacher.

NOTES

1. See especially *Analects*, ch. 10.
2. See, for example, *Analects* 12:11, 13:15, 13:16, 13:18, 14:22, and 15:1.
3. *Chandogya Upanishad* 6:1; translation by Robert Ernest Hume, in

The Thirteen Principal Upanishads (Madras: Oxford University Press, 1962) p. 240.

4. *Analects*, 1:1; translation adapted from Arthur Waley, *The Analects of Confucius* (New York: Vintage Press) p. 83.

5. *Analects*, 6:20.

6. *Analects*, 11:11.

7. Ibid.

8. Arthur Waley, *The Way and Its Power: A Study of the Tao Te Ching and Its Place in Chinese Thought* (London: George Allen and Unwin, 1965), p. 21.

9. Caution might favor a more guarded statement to the effect that these questions were not primary ones in the Confucian tradition. A plausible argument might be made that a closer analogy to those central Upanishadic questions can be found in the Taoist tradition, but this is a complex issue that goes beyond the scope of the present essay.

10. I am grateful to my colleague Eric Huberman, who informs me that where R.E. Hume has Uddalaka repeatedly addressing Svetaketu as "my dear," he is translating the Sanskrit epithet *somya*, suggesting gentleness, tenderness, and pliability. Is Uddalaka responding to or perhaps evoking in Svetaketu qualities opposite to the ones his son has recently been displaying in his arrogance and high-minded pride in his Vedic learning?

11. It should be noted that, whereas the translation of *junzi* as "gentleman" is very common, the Chinese term itself is ungendered. It originally meant "the child of a lord," referring to the person's elite social origins, with the nobility gradually coming to be understood under Confucian influence as primarily moral rather than social. In purely etymological terms, a *junzi* could be female as well as male, though this was relatively uncommon.

12. See especially 1:2, 1:6–7, 1:9, 1:11, 2:5–8, 2:20–21, 12:11, and 17:21.

13. This is the preferred translation of D.C. Lau in his translation of the *Analects* (Harmondsworth: Penguin, 1979).

14. The preferred translation of Arthur Waley in *The Analects of Confucius* (London: George Allen and Unwin, 1938; reprinted New York: Vintage, nd).

15. Bernhard Karlgren, *Analytic Dictionary of Chinese and Sino-Japanese* (Paris: Librairie Orientaliste Paul Geuthner, 1923; New York: Dover reprint, 1974), p. 271.

16. Ibid.

17. *Analects*, 6:28.

18. It is only in the West that the followers of Confucius are known as "Confucians," no doubt following the Western habit of naming religions after their founders. In Chinese, followers of the "Confucian" tradition are known as *ru*—ritualists.

19. *Analects*, 12:1.

20. The philosopher Herbert Fingarette entitled his lively and stimulating book on the role of ritual in the thought of Confucius, *Confucius: The Secular as Sacred* (New York: Harper & Row, 1972). However, if my interpretation is correct, we would be unjustified in assuming that a "secular" realm was invested with "sacred" significance. Rather, the dis-

tinction between secular and sacred (or, morally speaking, between the claims of Caesar and the claims of God) was absent in the Confucian context and probably in the wider world of thought in ancient China.

21. Borrowing the famous phrase of Paul Tillich.

22. See, for example, *Analects*, 2:21.

23. The concept of the Mandate of Heaven *(tian-ming)* is found in the classic known as the *Book of History (Shu-jing)*. In that context the implication is that Heaven decreed the overthrow of the Shang dynasty by the Zhou people owing to the corruption of the Shang, as seen in its cruel abuse of the people. The Zhou is favored by Heaven, and accorded the Mandate, on the condition that it rule with appropriate regard to the interests of the people.

24. *Analects*, 2:4.

25. *Analects*, 11:8

26. *Analects*, 17:19.

27. *Analects*, 7:22.

28. See also *Analects*, 9:5, 14:37, and 14:38, where Confucius professes confidence in an order far more potent than a menacing adversary.

29. *Analects*, 8:19.

30. *Analects*, 16:8.

31. *Analects*, 8:19.

32. See Max Weber, *The Religion of China, Confucianism and Taoism*, translated by Hans H. Gerth (New York: The Free Press, 1951).

33. By this I mean that Confucius and his followers do not see the universe as having been created **for** human beings, nor is human dominion over the natural world taken for granted as a feature of the natural order.

SYSTEMATIZING THE TRANSCENDENTAL

RELIGIONS AND WORLD VIEWS IN ASIAN AND WORLD HISTORY

Julia Ching and Willard G. Oxtoby

The twentieth century has witnessed two world wars as well as the rise and decline of fascism and communism. It would appear that we have—in this context, fortunately—failed to produce an ideology of an enduring nature. However, several of the major world religious traditions which emerged in the past, appear to have functioned over large spans of space and time as guiding ideologies. Indeed, their parallels and certain near-simultaneous developments have been a topic of fascination to historians.

Looking back some two and a half millennia, we shall first reflect on the so-called axial age. This term was used by the German philosopher Karl Jaspers, who spoke of an epoch in antiquity as a turning point in world history, an age that produced the great civilizations of ancient Greece, Israel, India, and China. It was this epoch that witnessed the sudden outburst of intellectual and spiritual energy all over the then-known world. Strictly speaking, this was the sixth century B.C.E., which witnessed such individuals as the prophetic writer Deutero-Isaiah in Israel, Zoroaster among the Persians, the philosopher and mystic Pythagoras among the Greeks, the sage Confucius in China, and the religious founder called the Buddha in India.

Reflecting on this list, we should point out that these individuals played different world-historical roles. Deutero-Isaiah (the Second Isaiah) was basically an anonymous figure who acquired his name from the incorporation of his chapters into the Book of

Isaiah, the largest prophetic book in the Hebrew Bible, in which scholars have discerned composite authorship. He worked among the exilic Jewish community in Babylon and regarded Cyrus the Great of Persia, the community's liberator, as God's agent. But the obscurity of this figure as a historical person is such that it is difficult to ascribe too much influence to him. Pythagoras is almost in the same league, since reliable information about him comes down mainly from Aristotle. Zoroaster eventually exercised great influence through the religion that bears his name, even though the prophet's dates and home region remain a subject of scholarly dispute, the successive ancient Persian empires differ in their explicit mention of him, and the religion today has a small following. Confucius and the Buddha, however, are a different story. Confucius's name is associated with an entire cultural tradition transcending national boundaries, while the Buddha gave rise to a world religion that rivals Christianity in the extent and depth of its influence over many populations. While Confucius definitely belonged to the sixth century B.C.E., the Buddha's dates remain uncertain; he belonged either to the sixth or to the fifth century B.C.E.

It is possible to accept the concept of an axial age and give it a more flexible time period, expanding it backward to the eighth century B.C.E. to include earlier Hebrew prophets, and to make room for Zoroaster in case his dates were earlier, and also pushing it forward to the fifth century B.C.E. to include the very important Greek philosophers Socrates and Plato. It is much harder, indeed impossible, to bend the concept further to include the figure of Jesus, who came six hundred years later, and that other prophet, considered by the believers of Islam to be the greatest of prophets, Muhammad, who belonged to the seventh century C.E. And indeed, Karl Jaspers himself calls four persons "paradigmatic individuals" for their impact on later ages, even though they did not all belong to the same century. He was speaking of Socrates, the Buddha, Confucius, and Jesus. The other Chinese wise man, Lao Zi [Lao Tzu], belonged to another class, that of "intellectual visionaries"—ranking after Plato and Augustine, who are called "seminal thinkers." After these come certain intellectual "disturbers" like Descartes and Hume and then the "creative orderers" like Thomas Aquinas (1225?–74) and the Chinese philosopher Zhu Xi [Chu Hsi], who preceded him (1130–1200).

The axial age was marked not just by individuals, but also by entire spiritual and intellectual elites, people belonging to classes such as the prophets and priests of Israel, the philosophers and teachers (Sophists) of Greece, the Chinese literati, the Hindu brahmans, the Buddhist sangha, and, much later, the Islamic ulama. They emerged in an age of new visions, and differed from the magical and ritual specialists of an earlier time. Their influence radiated to develop new civilizations. Indeed, the whole concept of the axial age has fascinated many people. Novels have been written imagining persons who traversed the world, meeting and talking with one after another of the great thinkers and religious leaders whom we presume to have functioned in isolated cultures. Jack Finegan's *Wanderer Upon Earth* (1956) tells the story of the travels of a certain Yaush, a sixth-century B.C.E. Israelite, whom Finegan sends all the way to China, while Gore Vidal's *Creation* (1981) gives the tale of Cyrus Spitama, Zoroaster's grandson, who lived a century later, traveled just as extensively, and talked to numerous wise men all over the civilized world.

As mentioned, the great figures of the axial age were prophets, sages, religious founders. Their beliefs were diverse, but their influences over civilizations were arguably parallel. The great prophets, whether in Israel, in Iran, or later in Arabia, are the teachers of the great monotheistic faiths, with their belief in one God guiding world history, giving meaning and value to all, and holding all accountable for their actions. To the extent that Christianity arose out of a Jewish milieu, we may speak of it too as a religion belonging to the family of West Asian monotheistic religions including Judaism, Zoroastrianism, and the later Islam.

In our own times, however, monotheism has come under criticism by scholars who define it as a political ideology linked with the notion of divine kingship, associated with military conquests and empires, and often leading to totalitarianism. Our definition of empire entails the control by one people of others' regions, putting these under military occupation and assuring access to supplies of food and raw materials. In this sense, the ancient Hebrews never founded an empire; Zoroastrianism might have provided the initial unifying impetus for Persian conquest (550–500 B.C.E.) in West Asia, but the extent of its influence remains a matter of dispute, as Richard A. Billows points out in this volume. Alexander the Great in his turn wrested much of West Asia from the Persians, after which he had himself divinized in Egypt (331 B.C.E.)—hardly an act of monotheistic faith. Constantine, in spite of the vision of conquests in the sign of the cross (312 C.E.) attributed to him, inherited the Roman Empire at a time when political decline had already set in, due in part to divisive conflicts among regions and beliefs, including the struggle among Christians between what in retrospect are termed orthodoxy and heresies. In the third century B.C.E., Ashoka, the protector of Buddhism, expanded the Mauryan Empire, but his belief was hardly monotheistic and his conquests did not last long, while Confucian China (which we can hardly describe as promulgating monotheism), as Professor Cho-yun Hsu's chapter explains, expanded more through population settlements than through conquests. In our own day, modern Japan attempted to carve an empire out of conquests. And while it made use of State Shinto to do so, it could hardly expect such an ethnopolitical ideology to convert subject peoples.

Another question has to do with why religions have staked out their territories where they are now. We think of the Roman Empire becoming Christian, and being taken over by a faith that came from Palestine. This happened in large part because the great apostle Paul of Tarsus, coming himself from Asia Minor, went back there with the zeal of a new convert, and followed the trade routes in the Roman Empire. The *Pax Romana* facilitated the spread of Christianity, which would eventually define Western civilization. The religion of the Buddha went north and east to China, Korea, Japan, and Southeast Asia, where it exercised a great historical influence, but never an overweening one like that of Christianity in Europe. In other words, one could hardly call East Asia predominantly Buddhist (even during the seventh to ninth centuries, when Buddhism was at a climax of influence) the way one could call medieval and postmedieval Europe Christian. Today, Buddhist influence is still more visible in those parts of Southeast Asia where Theravada Buddhism dominates and monks are still numerous—Sri Lanka, Burma, Thailand, Laos, and Cambodia—than it is in the Mahayana Buddhist traditions of East Asia.

The believers of Islam were more an exception than a rule in their zeal in propagating a monotheistic religion. In the first hundred years after the Hijra (622 C.E.), Arab Muslims took over formerly Roman and Christian North Africa and pushed into Spain. They were turned back at Tours, in France, by Charles Martel (732). Arab Muslims also went east to conquer Persia, and the religion would spread to the Turkic peoples of central Asia, who would eventually dominate the Arabs. The Turks, in their turn, took over Byzantine terrain and continued their thrust into Europe but were stopped at the gates of Vienna by a combined European army under the command of the Polish John Sobieski (1683). After the twelfth century, India became exposed to Islam, as did Indonesia subsequently, as well as sub-Saharan Africa. Its cultural influences over the vast regions were not uniform. While the Arabic language quickly replaced the Latin vernacular in North Africa and Greek in the eastern Mediterranean, it did not take similar hold in Persia. The pattern of conversion was not as thorough further east, where for centuries Muslims would rule northern India but remain a minority in its large population. And beyond the lands to which Islam spread by conquest, traders would carry and promote Islam: to China, to Indonesia—today the country with the world's largest Muslim population—and by sea to the coast of East Africa and by land to the interior of West Africa. Nevertheless, non-European domination of continental Europe, whether by the earlier Huns under Attila or by the Muslims (Arab or Turkish), was prevented time and again only by a few strategic battles. The thirteenth-century Mongols with their Golden Horde also threatened Europe, taking over Kiev (1240) and defeating German and Hungarian troops on the battlefield, before a sudden withdrawal (1242) toward the steppes of South Russia. But the Mongol conquests were made before the Mongols themselves had even decided on a religion of choice. This was to be Tantric or Tibetan Buddhism, at least for some time and for some of them. Others converted later to Islam, influenced in part by the people over whom they ruled, such as happened in Persia.

The **religious** problem with monotheistic religions is their tendency to make exclusive claims for truth. Peter Awn is right to say in this volume that religions in Western societies have been separating people into different communities. This has been the experience with Judaism, Christianity, and Islam—the Abrahamic religions of Semitic origin, with their separate claims to definitive divine revelation. In India, Islam introduced the idea that only its God is the true God to a Hindu population that was not accustomed to making an exclusive choice among divinities, a distinction between "true" gods and "idols." Christian missionaries did the same in East Asia, where the Confucian, Daoist, and Buddhist traditions, in spite of conflicts over interests, have always been nonexclusive. Even today, a Jew, a Christian, or a Muslim finds it difficult to understand why a Chinese or a Japanese might belong to more than one "religious tradition" at the same time. Indeed, contemporary Japan appears far from "religious" to an occasional visitor. Yet responses to questionnaires have indicated that there are more religious believers in Japan than the entire population put together—since some people claim adherence to more than one religion.

To reflect further on Asia and religion, we might wonder why an Indian religion like Buddhism would find more hospitable terrain in China than in its own homeland. Presumably, Ashoka's military thrusts prepared the ground for the spread of the religion northward as well as eastward. Political disunity was India's historical experience more than political unity, and disunity fragmented religious influence. Presumably also, Buddhism's anticaste stance made the religion less acceptable in longer terms. Jainism, the other egalitarian and much more ascetical religion, had a founder in Vardhamana (Mahavira), who was roughly the historical Buddha's contemporary (i.e., he too belonged either to the sixth or the fifth century B.C.E.). It did take root in India, but at the cost of remaining very small (about two million adherents today) and making concessions to the caste system.

Another question that may arise in our minds has to do with why China has not influenced India the way India influenced China through Buddhism. To explain the spread of Buddhism in China, we might say that China's political unity and ethnic and cultural cohesion had been initially a hindrance and eventually a help. Buddhist scriptures needed only to be translated into one written language to be propagated everywhere in the country. Buddhism, however, became acceptable to the Chinese only because it adapted to Chinese cultural influences, to the point of radically transforming—some would say nearly losing—its own identity and, as mentioned earlier, influencing Chinese civilization in its turn but never "defining" it. But even as an empire, China represented a country of settlers who were generally loath to expand by military conquests—except under the nonethnic Chinese rulers like the Mongols and Manchus. Confucianism (and Daoism) spread to Korea, Japan, and Vietnam more through China's moral and cultural influence than through any military adventure. The same happened with the spread of Buddhism in East Asia.

In a sense, also, India's long periods of political disunity, and its "introverted" caste system, helped to protect the subcontinent from receiving strong cultural influences from the outside. The British period (mid-eighteenth to mid-twentieth century) introduced Western influence without fundamentally changing Indian religiosity. That Western-educated Indian, Mahatma Gandhi, eventually challenged British might with his eclectic religious vision of love and nonviolence. And while he did not start a religion, his spiritual influence extended far beyond his native land. He was also unable to prevent the division of British India along communal lines into two countries, the other being the two-part Muslim Pakistan, whose eastern region subsequently became independent as Bangladesh.

India and China eventually made their impact each in a different cultural circle. Their earlier historical meeting ground was central Asia, through which Buddhism went into China. But central Asia—including northern Pakistan and today's Afghanistan—eventually fell to Islam, which also found its way into North India. In later times, mainland Southeast Asia was the fertile ground for mixed or so-called Indo-Chinese influences, even as Islam also penetrated Malaysia, as did Christianity the Philippines. Of the great Asian civilizations, China's was comparatively speaking the most isolated and the longest lasting. Certainly, it was not removed from outside influences, but it was able in the longer run to indigenize nonethnic peoples who dominated the country from time to time. Nevertheless, in our own days, on account of Western and Marxist onslaughts, a cultural rupture has occurred with the past, the extent of which is still difficult to measure. And then, just as China's own culture has encountered a serious crisis, we hear of claims that the Confucian work ethic has been pushing forward Asian Pacific economies.

For many decades, the West has witnessed the growth of secularism in its own society while presuming the triumph of atheism in Communist lands. The recent unraveling of the erstwhile Soviet Union and its former satellite nations was instructive in more than one way. We are learning the strength of both religion and nationalism after four to seven decades of suppression. Prescinding from value judgments, we should point out the usefulness of understanding the forces that have been unleashed. Among other things, religion was passed on from generation to generation, for all of seven decades, through family and village influences, especially in Muslim central Asia. It outlasted Communist ideology.

Moreover, even earlier, we had learned that a religious revival of sorts had been going on in Communist China after the death of Mao Zedong (1976), that is, very soon after the devastating Cultural Revolution (1966–76). There too, both the traditional religions and Western Christianity, the religion introduced by missionaries, have continued to demonstrate surprising strength, through popular attendance at temples, churches, and rituals and through numerous reports of conversions. At the same time, the dominance of political ideology—Chinese Marxism—appears to be assured only by political decree and military support. Whither China, and whither Chinese civilization, remain open questions.

THE ERA OF ASIAN DISCOVERY: TRADE AND THE CONTACT OF CULTURES

Richard W. Bulliet

INTRODUCTION

No historian questions the fact that in premodern times the great majority of the population in every civilized society lived as agriculturalists or otherwise devoted their working lives to the production of basic foods. Yet every historian likewise grants a special place to the role of movement and trade in civilization. Implicit in assigning this privileged place to the history of trade and cultural contact is the notion that change is of particular interest and that throughout history a great deal of change has been externally generated.

At the practical level, the history of premodern trade and cultural contact consists in large part of lists of imported or exported products, techniques, and ideas and accounts of the impact they had on one or another people. Many important cultural contacts of this sort precede the written record. Most easily documented are the material ones. The chicken was domesticated from a Southeast Asian jungle fowl; but the story of its spread around the world is largely unknown, and the linkages between widely separated regions where chickens with black skins are used in religious rituals remain conjectural. Domesticated wheat and barley reached northern China from the Middle East, but the story of who carried the seeds and planted the first crops is lost, and there is no way of telling whether the impact of the plowing, sowing, and reaping cycle on sexual division of labor and notions of the calendar was as important for the Chinese as some historians have asserted it was for people in the Middle East.

How certain products became known to distant people in remotest time must remain obscure, but the evidence of long-distance exchange is abundant. Obsidian from volcanic islands in the Mediterranean, lapis lazuli from northeastern Afghanistan, ivory and mangrove wood from East Africa, bananas from the East Indies, and frankincense and myrrh from southern Arabia all became known to peoples in geographically remote locations before the development of writing in the regions concerned.

In early modern times people's fascination with new things from distant lands is much better recorded, and it is apparent that it was compounded partly of utility and potential for economic exploitation and partly of love of novelty. The products brought back from the New World by European explorers—tobacco, potatoes, turkeys, chocolate, etc.—not only spread rapidly, but excited the interest of the lettered classes as well. The spread of coffee from its first use in southern Arabia in the fourteenth century to the Ottoman Empire, and thence to Europe, is well known, as is the parallel development among the Ottomans and in Europe of a craze for coffee houses. Another history traces the tulip from a central Asian wildflower to an Ottoman and, by way of the Ottoman Empire, a Dutch obsession in the eighteenth century.

The scientific age saw the appearance of the Napoleonic *Société impériale d'acclimatation*, devoted to experimenting with new plants and animals from all parts of the world. In one enterprise, the society planned and carried out an experimental introduction of camels to northeastern Brazil which ended in total failure. Not long afterward the U.S. Department of War imported camels into Texas, with similar results; and Australian contractors did the same with greater success, thus providing the seed of today's wild camel population on that continent.

The reason for citing these examples from so many times and climes is to point out that humans have always been interested in novelty, and no one period or region can be singled out for this characteristic. What is important to periods of unusual material or cultural interchange, therefore, is change in facilitation: how goods, techniques, and ideas move, political or military constraints on movement, inducements for people to undertake distant journeys, ability of markets to reward novelty, and so forth.

The period from about the third century C.E. to the building of the pan-Asian Mongol Empire of the thirteenth century seems to have witnessed, in Asia, a degree of human movement resulting in material and cultural exchange unprecedented in the historical record before that time. The importance of this period is often lost sight of when it is compared with the subsequent age of European exploration, but this is partly a matter of Eurocentrism.

In the realm of products, the earlier period saw the dissemination from and through Asia of citrus fruits, sugarcane, apricots, rice, and a wide variety of spices and aromatics, including camphor, cinnamon, clove, pepper, and nutmeg. In this light, it would be difficult to argue that the impact of New World products on diet has been more important.

Techniques that spread from and through Asia during the period in question were of equal historical importance: the stirrup, with its logical accompaniment the mounted lancer; papermaking; printing; distillation and other chemical processes; efficient horse harnessing that enabled farmers to put more land to the plow without increasing the input of labor; and silk making.

Ideas, however, may have been the most important commodity in cultural exchange, for 300–1200 C.E. was the world's most important period of religious proselytization. Buddhism, Islam, Christianity, and Manichaeism all spread through Asia, carrying with them attitudes toward ethics, aesthetics, asceticism, mysticism, and religious law and governance that greatly influenced all subsequent history.

One way to look at this extraordinary era of cultural contact and exchange is through the facilitating factors referred to earlier. The factors we will focus upon will be movements of peoples, organization of trade, urbanism, and finally religious expansion.

MOVEMENT OF PEOPLES

The beginning of the era under investigation coincides with the collapse of Roman authority in western Europe and North Africa, the end of Parthian imperial rule in Mesopotamia and Iran, and the fall of the Han Empire in China. The strong and prosperous Gupta Dynasty in India came to power around 320 C.E. as these other empires were failing, but it had collapsed by the end of the following century, leaving no major imperial successor state.

Great political upheavals have far-reaching effects. The story of Germanic and later Scandinavian reshaping of the political map of western Europe through military action and popular migration is well known. But these geopolitical perturbations linked to the fall of Rome helped upset population distributions all the way across central Asia, just as did the collapse of the Han at the other end of the continent.

The Huns, who reached Europe from lands far to the east and

may have been related to the Xiongnu adversaries of the Han of China's northern frontier, are well known, but there is a broad transformation that takes place in central Asia that is more general. Central Asia is normally thought of as a land of nomadic horse pastoralists, but it was inhabited originally by people who raised cattle and sheep and goats but did not have domestic horses. When horses became common as a domestic animal, they were highly valued and assimilated into a preexisting symbol system in which celestial gods, and the godliness of worldly kings who claimed divine association, were represented by wheeled vehicles. Carts, wagons, or wheels are often found in the most elaborate tombs of this period. The product of this assimilation was the war chariot, a noble vehicle of enormous symbolic significance and much more modest battlefield potential.

The war chariot is a recurrent theme in Middle Eastern, Indian, North African, and Chinese imagery of the first millennium B.C.E. Its widespread occurrence is taken as an indicator of the impact this central Asian development had on surrounding lands. On the battlefield, the chariot became obsolete fairly soon, though generals in Roman triumphs continued to ride in chariots because of their symbolic importance. The survival of the chariot cult in the West is best seen in the unusual cachet of chariot racing well into the Byzantine period. The Chinese replaced the religiously significant two-horse, yoke-based harnessing system with the much more efficient one-horse, horse-collar-based system and retained the vehicle mostly for upper-class transportation.

The most striking change in the horse and chariot pattern, however, occurred in its homeland, central Asia. Horseback riding, though known from the earliest period of domestication, had been comparatively insignificant during the era of the war chariot. During the latter half of the first millennium B.C.E., however, it emerged as the dominant mode of utilization. The Indo-European Scythians, or Sakae, continued to bury wheeled vehicles ceremonially, but they rode horses in battle. The stirrup is first attested in northern Afghanistan in the first century or so C.E. in territory inhabited by an Indo-European people who had migrated there from Gansu Province in northwestern China because of political conflicts with other central Asian peoples, notably the Xiongnu.

In the immediately following centuries, evidence of a vehicle cult in central Asia dies out, the efficient but symbolically insignificant Chinese-style horse harness is adopted for ordinary carts, and horse pastoralism becomes synonymous with the military use of mounted archers. At the same time, there is a massive and progressive change in the identity of the populations of central Asia. The peoples who spoke Indo-European languages generally disappear or become relegated to urban nodes within a general population of Turko-Mongolian-speaking pastoralists. Attila's Turko-Mongol Huns are the exception in the fifth century C.E., but their related descendants have become the rule by the thirteenth century when Genghis Khan appears on the scene.

It can be seen in the foregoing example that population changes, which often appear in history as the inscrutable replacement of one unfamiliar name by another, can occasionally be correlated with large-scale changes in economic structure, social organization, and symbol systems.

ORGANIZATION OF TRADE

Movements of people, however, do not produce the same kinds of cultural exchange produced by trade. For example, migrating people are often not agriculturalists. They may not travel with seeds in their pockets. This is not an absolute rule because the prehistoric spread of bananas, coconuts, and certain plants producing edible tubers and rhizomes from Southeast Asia to Africa in the west and throughout the Pacific islands in the east almost certainly came through human migration. This is attested in Africa by the survival to the present day of an Indonesian language as the common tongue of the people of Madagascar off the southeast coast. Clearly, however, the pastoralists of central Asia did not bring Chinese lemon trees and silkworms with them during their migrations. Yet this does not mean that their movements were not connected with the burgeoning of Asian trade in the pre-Mongol era. Again we will use a particular example to illustrate the interconnectedness of the factors favoring cultural exchange.

The Silk Road ran from Mesopotamia, across the Zagros Mountains of western Iran, over or around the eastern end of the Iranian Elburz Mountains, across the deserts that separate the Murghab, Amu Darya (Oxus), and Syr Darya (Jaxartes) rivers in Turkmenistan and Uzbekistan, over the Pamir Mountains to the inland drainage basin of the Tarim River, past Lop Nor and other saline lakes below sea level at the eastern end of the Tarim basin (Xinjiang), and finally through the corridor between mountain ranges known as Gansu Province onto the North China plain. Traversing this immense distance at the twenty-mile-per-day rate of a typical caravan was a matter of months, and the perils of river, desert, and mountain crossings were compounded by the continual danger of pillage, whether by nomads, bandits, or some ruler's soldiery.

How and when did this extraordinary route come into being? The latter question is more or less answerable. Evidence clearly points to the Parthian and Han empires as the western and eastern termini and to the first couple of centuries B.C.E. as the time. But the interchange seems not to have been extensive at that time. Perhaps some intrepid explorer-traders took untold risks to initiate the contacts, or perhaps they arose more easily from the connections between central Asian Indo-European tribes linking the Parthians themselves, who originated as pastoralists in northeastern Iran, across the entire route to the Indo-European Yue Zhi of Gansu.

More important than the source of the initial contact was the growth of the route. During the outward-looking rule of China's Tang dynasty (seventh–ninth century C.E.), sophisticated people in northeastern Iran developed such a taste for expensive, imported Chinese pottery that they began to imitate it in great quantity for sale to people who could not afford the real thing. And in northern China there was a vogue for beautiful pottery figurines of camels laden with caravan goods or ridden by obviously non-Chinese merchants, musicians, or entertainers. Non-Chinese camel figurines found in Mesopotamia carry loads that duplicate the distinctive appearance of the loads on the Chinese figurines. So it is clear that by the time of the rise of Islam in the seventh century, contact across the Silk Road not only was extensive, but had affected the material and aesthetic cultures on both ends.

We get only glimpses of what happened in between to facilitate the transformation of a route of occasional contact into a major artery of international trade capable of surviving until fatally challenged by European-dominated maritime trade in the seventeenth century. Firsthand accounts of central Asia caravan trading in the twentieth century by Owen Lattimore and others testify to the complexity of organization required to assemble and move hundreds or thousands of animals, scores of drivers, tons of merchandise specially packed to conform to the weight and balance characteristics of pack camels, and the supplies needed to keep beast and human alive during months of travel in the bitter cold of a central Asian winter.

Camels afford us one glimpse of how this system came into being. The two-humped or Bactrian camel was native to central Asia and Iran and was used as a domestic animal from at least the third millennium B.C.E. onward. The one-humped camel was native to Saudi Arabia. Physically the two species share resistance to thirst and to hunger, which probably explains the survival of both of these comparatively defenseless species in regions too arid or barren to support many predators. They differ, however, in their resistance to heat. The two-humped camel has a long, shaggy coat during the winter and molts in the spring; one-humped breeds have much less hair in their torrid native climate of Arabia.

It is reasonable to assume that two-humped pack camels were used from the beginning by travelers along the Silk Road. Once they got to Mesopotamia, however, they must have suffered terribly from summer heat. Yet summer was the most likely time of arrival because the several-month journey from northern China usually began in the fall, when the camels were in best condition after a summer of grazing.

Of course, it must have been evident to traders that Mesopotamia had its own camel, the one-humped animal herded in great numbers by Arabs along the Euphrates desert frontier. But the one-humped camel obviously could not take the cold of a central Asian winter. Not surprisingly, some people experimented with interbreeding one- and two-humped camels. The earliest evidence of this comes from the first century B.C.E. after the Silk Road had been opened up.

The offspring of such mixed parentage exhibit what is known as hybrid vigor; that is, they share characteristics of both parents but are stronger than either. The hybrid was called a *bukht* and was the ideal animal for the Silk Road and other cold-weather caravan areas such as Iran, Anatolia, and Afghanistan. The problem was that the *bukht*, though fertile, produced offspring that were either runts, if the mate was another *bukht*, or ordinary one- or two-humped camels depending upon the species of the other parent. In short, the ideal caravan camel had to be steadily manufactured like a car or a truck. There could never be any herds of *bukhts* producing more of their kind, and caravaneers could not simply buy *bukht* replacement animals from the nearest nomadic tribe since there was no particular reason for the tribe to have any for its own purposes.

The Silk Road, and lesser caravan routes in the same period, thus gave rise to an animal husbandry industry. The ideal pattern was to have a herd of female animals of one species and a single carefully selected male of the other. In a region with abundant two-humped camels, the male would be one-humped, and vice versa in one-humped territories.

Most of the evidence for the extensive breeding of *bukhts* comes from the Islamic period, which makes it plausible that the Arab conquests of the seventh century accelerated the process of livestock change. Moreover, Tang dynasty figurines rarely show the *bukht*, which may indicate that the industry was devoted mostly to providing animals for the part of the Silk Road west of the Pamir Mountains.

These qualifications do not lessen the illustrative value of the history of the *bukht*. Discovering an overland route to China, however it occurred, was doubtless an important feat; but the conversion of that contact into a major trade artery took a good deal of ingenuity, investment, and organizational skill. The same would be true of the equally complex system of coastal trading by sailing *dhow* that saw Arab, Iranian, Indian, and Indonesian traders dealing in a wide array of products from East African mangrove poles and ivory, to Persian Gulf pearls, to Indian cloth, to East Indian spices. The exotic products may dominate the story, but letters written in Judeo-Arabic by Jewish traders from Cairo about transactions in Malaysia or Indonesia, or Hindu inscriptions left by Indian traders in caves near Lar on the road into the interior from the Persian Gulf coast in southeastern Iran, provide hints as to the complexity of the human network undergirding any major trade artery.

Indian Ocean *dhow* trading, like the trans-Asian overland trade, was an industry based upon an elaborate infrastructure developed over a long period of time. It proved durable and flexible for centuries and provided an unparalleled conduit for cultural exchange. European maritime trading eventually ruined both trading systems, though this seems not to have happened until the Dutch and the British discovered the commercial device of the joint stock company in the seventeenth century. Even then, the Indian Ocean system may have provided a rudimentary model for European ideas about controlling trade on an international basis, just as the Silk Road may have provided a template for the Eurasian empire established by Genghis Khan and his descendants in the thirteenth century.

The question remains, however, why so much investment was made in something as superficially implausible as the prospect of an overland connection between China and Mesopotamia, or in something as risky as sailing a small boatload of valuable spices all the way from Sumatra to the Red Sea. For part of the answer we will turn to the role of urbanism as a factor in facilitating the growth of trade and cultural exchange.

URBANISM

Trade depends upon markets. A dispersed rural population of farmers or pastoralists provides a poor market for goods imported from long distances. Before the days of the mail-order catalogue, distribution networks were generally poor, and monetization was frequently absent. Royal or aristocratic courts, on the other hand, could provide a market for high-priced goods; but it was a market of limited size that might easily be saturated. Important trade networks cannot thrive on royal patronage alone.

Cities were the most important concomitant of long-distance trade in the period under consideration. When cities were large and flourishing, they not only provided facilities for marketing imported goods, but they served as manufacturing centers for exportable goods. And the economic vitality stemming in part from this active trade generated the wealth that made urban populations the most important consumers of imported goods.

With regard to China, large cities appear early in history and are a fairly constant phenomenon. In India the opposite seems to be the case, although the archaeological record may be weak in this respect because of perishable materials being used for construction. Further west, Mesopotamia and the Levant are consistently famous for their city-centered polities from the third millennium B.C.E. onward, but the Iranian and Afghan plateaus and highlands and the central Asian steppes and river valleys developed cities rather later and on a smaller scale.

During the period under examination, Asian urbanism significantly increased in China with the consolidation of Tang dynasty rule in the seventh century, immediately followed, in the tenth century, by the Song Dynasty, which presided over a remarkable period of economic and demographic growth. In western Asia, the collapse of Roman authority in the west moved the center of gravity of the late Hellenistic world to the Middle East. Antioch, in Syria, and Constantinople became large and prosperous. They and a number of secondary cities constituted major markets for imported goods. The replacement in the third century of the Parthians by the Sassanians had a similar effect in Mesopotamia and southwestern Iran. Despite the rivalry between the Byzantine and Persian empires, their collective wealth and urbanism greatly stimulated trade and contact with lands further to the east.

A second phase of urbanism was even more important and far-reaching. This occurred under the aegis of Islam between the eighth and eleventh centuries. The Iranian plateau, where under the Sassanids cities had seldom amounted to more than fortress-centered communities of a few thousand, witnessed the growth of several cities with populations in the 100,000 range: Nishapur, Rayy, Isfahan, and possibly others. Similar urban growth took place in central Asia, with Marv, Bukhara, Samarkand, and Balkh becoming significantly larger than they had been.

In the absence of evidence indicating a general demographic surge parallel to that of Song China, the source of this Islamic urbanism is somewhat mysterious. A strong argument can be made, however, for rural-urban migration being a concomitant of increasing conversion to Islam. The Arabs, who conquered an enormous empire stretching from Spain to the Indus Valley by the year 711, chose to concentrate their limited manpower by governing from garrison centers. Taxes and war booty came into these centers in great quantity, and Islamic religious activities were almost exclusively carried out there. Early converts to Islam, who faced ostracism if they were living in predominantly Christian, Zoroastrian, or Jewish communities, often migrated to these Arab military and administrative centers. These centers quickly took on urban characteristics or, if situated in preexisting cities, saw their populations multiply.

Associated with the conversion factor that impelled new Muslims toward the growing Muslim cities was the attractive power of the economic and cultural florescence these cities manifested. Largely unconfined by inherited urban traditions and tastes, Muslim city dwellers developed many new forms and styles of manufactures. Money was abundant, and a distinctively new urban consumer market stimulated extensive increases in trade both within the Islamic caliphate and with other Asian lands. Chinese, Indian, and Southeast Asian products, though often known in western Asia in pre-Islamic times, became increasingly sought after, both through maritime connections that saw the growth of a large Arab trading community in China and across the Silk Road.

One might note, following the discussion earlier of the interconnectedness of the various elements facilitating trade and cultural contact, that the Indo–European-speaking peoples of central Asia who had gradually been supplanted, as pastoralists, by Turko-Mongol peoples during the first half-millennium C.E. became concentrated in cities. There they became especially active in the fostering of trade and organization of caravans. Down to the present day, Persian, an Indo-European language, is readily understood in the marketplace of Bukhara, a major city in Turkic Uzbekistan.

While it is difficult to quantify the impact of Islamic and Song urbanism on trade, there is no questioning the obvious relationship between cultural contact and the growth of cities as consuming and producing centers and as nodes for the organization of trade during the period under consideration. The fact that Islam plays a significant role in this development leads to our fourth and final topic in contact facilitation, namely, religious expansion.

RELIGIOUS EXPANSION

It is surely no coincidence that four different religions went through periods of remarkable geographic expansion during the period in question. It is hard to imagine this expansion taking place without well-developed routes of communications and reliable support for travelers. On the other hand, traveling missionaries, pilgrims, converts, and pious laymen unquestionably accentuated the cultural importance of these routes by their transmission of religiously based ideas from one religion to another. It would be difficult to cite a parallel period in world history when so many different and even conflicting religious ideas were vying for prominence over such an enormous geographical area.

Buddhism is older than Christianity, Manichaeism, and Islam, but it remained largely confined to the Indian subcontinent for several centuries after the Buddha's death around 500 B.C.E. The first notable missionaries in China worked in the second century C.E. and arrived there over the Silk Road. One important early translator of sacred texts was himself a Parthian. The new religion reached Burma and other parts of Southeast Asia in the fifth and sixth centuries C.E., and Tibet in the seventh century.

The best-known route of Buddhist expansion is the one across central Asia. Chinese pilgrims returned to northern India by this route to search out sacred texts and visit the original centers of the faith. Accounts written by Fa Xian, who visited India in 400 C.E., and Xuanzang, who traversed the same route in the seventh century, attest to the important position Buddhism had by then achieved throughout central Asia. In time Buddhism had a profound impact upon the societies and cultures of China, Japan, and Southeast Asia, but that is beyond the scope of our current discussion.

Christianity is known, of course, as a proselytizing religion; but except for the apparent early establishment of a Christian community in India, expansion eastward from the Fertile Crescent and Anatolia was not robust prior to the rise of the Sassanid

Empire in the third century C.E. While Christianity never did become dominant in eastern lands, it certainly gained many adherents in Iran and took advantage of the Silk Road to extend itself all the way to the Chinese frontier. Nestorian Christianity was a cultural force to be reckoned with in central Asia by the time of the Mongol Empire.

Mani founded the religion named for him in Mesopotamia in the fourth century C.E. His dualistic doctrine was derivative from the Zoroastrianism of the Sassanids and was eventually judged to be heretical. The Manichaeans were severely persecuted in Iran and survived by sending missionaries to distant lands. St. Augustine in North Africa was a Manichaean in his youth, but a more important area of growth was central Asia, with which the Silk Road afforded easy communication.

Islam, however, outdid all of the other religions in geographic expansion. The story of the Arab conquests is well known, as is the further military expansion into India after 1000 C.E. that laid the foundation of the large Muslim communities of India and Pakistan. Less well studied is the expansion of Islam into regions beyond the reach of Muslim armies. Muslim communities arose in central Asia, China, Bengal, and, somewhat later, Indonesia without prior military conquest or political absorption. The Turks of central Asia, for example, play a major role in the history of the Islamic Middle East after the year 1000, but they enter Middle Eastern history at least nominally as Muslims. How their conversion took place remains unknown, though many scholars have vaguely speculated that they were converted by traders or wandering holy men.

In the case of Islam, there is evidence to support the theory that the key factor in gradual Islamization was communications. By and large, people did not convert to Islam until they had heard something about it in a familiar language. The proselytizing success of Islam, therefore, which is all the more striking in the absence of any organized missionary endeavor, is a testimony to the richness and density of the Asian communications networks, both overland and maritime.

The myriad ways in which religious expansion effected transfers of ideas and institutions among the various lands of Asia are beyond what can be discussed in a brief paper. Suffice it to say that Europe, isolated on the far western extremity of the Eurasian landmass and enjoying comparatively little contact with lands on the south side of the Mediterranean throughout the period in question, both profited and suffered from the relative lack of intellectual and cultural stimulus that the expansion of differing religions and philosophies brought to those parts of Asia that were tied into the great communications systems of the Silk Road and the Indian Ocean. On the positive side, Europe was able to develop its own distinctive medieval Christian civilization without significant challenge or widespread awareness of the arguably richer alternatives available elsewhere. But on the negative side, it suffered from a comparative intellectual stagnation that suddenly became apparent with the translation into Latin of Arabic philosophical and scientific works and the resulting explosion of new ideas and attitudes at the end of our period.

CONCLUSION

We have focused in this essay upon four factors facilitating the unusual degree of cultural exchange throughout Asia in the period 300–1200 C.E. Though separated in our analysis, these factors were in many ways interconnected. This was the era of Asian discovery. By this we mean the discovery not of new lands but of the material, technological, religious, and philosophical traditions that had matured in comparative isolation in different parts of Asia during the preceding centuries. And the discoverers were not conquistadors or explorers. They were the thousands of people who walked for months beside their camels across the steppes and mountains of central Asia or sat for weeks beneath a lateen sail on a fragile sailing *dhow* as it scudded before the monsoon across the Indian Ocean and the South China Sea.

Travel was slow and dangerous. Traders and other travelers expected to be away from their homelands and families for many months and even years. They knew that they might well die before they saw their homes again. When we read accounts of arduous journeys by more modern European travelers, we think of them as intrepid individuals pitting their individual stamina and will power, in the best European tradition, against the perilous unknown. But during the era of Asian discovery such perils were commonplace, and the determination of the individual was buttressed by the strength of religious community and the interdependence of people traversing the same route. The goods and ideas they carried overshadow their personal lives, but it should never be assumed that what they did was easy or that cultural contacts across vast distances just happen.

SELECTED REFERENCES

Bulliet, Richard W. *The Camel and the Wheel.* Cambridge, MA: Harvard University Press, 1975.

Ibn Battuta. *Travels in Asia and Africa, 1325–1354.* Translated by H.A.R. Gibb. London: Routledge and Kegan Paul, 1929.

Lattimore, Owen. *The Desert Road to Turkestan.* Boston: Little, Brown, and Co., 1929.

Schafer, Edward. *The Golden Peaches of Samarkand.* Berkeley: University of California Press, 1963.

Villiers, Alan. *Sons of Sinbad.* New York: Scribners, 1969.

CHINA, 300–1200

Michael Marmé

Between 300 and 1200 C.E., the Middle Kingdom was embattled. Except for the relatively brief Sui and early Tang (589–755), parts of North China—the original home of Chinese civilization—were in the hands of Turkic or Sino-Turkic "barbarians." Relative to the dynasties of earlier and later periods, as well as to the challenges they faced, native dynasties were weak and ineffectual. Such political weakness facilitated institutional change, cultural innovation, and economic growth—not least since the existing system was clearly not working as it should. The Qin-Han empires (221 B.C.E.–220 C.E.) had provided Chinese of subsequent ages with a model of the way the world should be. The ruler's ethnic identity was less important than that he, as a true Son of Heaven, control the Middle Kingdom. Possession of the Mandate of Heaven enabled such a ruler to link mankind to the cosmos. If all was right with the world, barbarians would enter the Middle Kingdom only on Chinese terms and only so that they might "come and be transformed." For most of the period of trade and the contact of cultures, none of this was true.

No historian should exaggerate the ease of cultural contact or the enthusiasm for it in generations past. The Silk Road existed from Han times. By Tang at the latest, Arab traders were calling regularly at Fujian ports (in South China) and, by Southern Song (1127–1279), the Chinese government was encouraging its subjects to engage in **overseas trade.** A number of factors conspired to limit the economic, and especially the cultural, impact of such exchange, however. China's internal market was huge, its isolation (by land **and** sea) from other high civilizations real. Under these conditions, trade was and would remain overwhelmingly internal. When foreign merchants came to China, they were restricted to certain areas, were permitted to trade in certain markets, lived under their own headmen, and ran their affairs according to their own laws. Although it is reasonable to assume that enterprising individuals attempted to circumvent such barriers, differences in language, dress, and physical appearance facilitated control. Even when the authorities urged Chinese to trade overseas, Chinese junks were required to return to the port from which they sailed. Government monopolies of certain products and restrictions on certain exports were maintained. This was, in short, an administered trade, one intended to supplement rather than to supplant the tribute system. Although weak states were less able than strong ones to limit the impact of such transactions, the organization of the trade, language barriers, and limited volume made this a picturesque but minor conduit of change for China.

More important were the **invasions**—a string of military victories which began with the destruction of the Western Jin in the early fourth century and ended with the Manchu conquest in the seventeenth. The boundary between steppe and sown fields is especially stark in East Asia, and steppe nomads (unlike desert nomads) do not develop symbiotic relationships with sedentary peoples. Thus, absent a vigorous dynasty whose leaders believed the best defense was offense (Han, Tang, Ming, Qing), China's northern regions were particularly prone to attack. The dynasties which ruled North China from 317 to 581; the Tang's Uighur allies and Sino-Turkic generals, who dominated North China from 755 to the consolidation of Song power in 960; the Liao and Xi-xia, with whom the Song were forced to deal as equals and to whom they were forced to pay tribute; and the Jin, rulers of North China from 1127 to 1234, were all barbarian regimes. The success of these invaders called into question the legitimacy of the ruling Chinese dynasty, as based on having the Mandate of Heaven, prompting both military response and institutional reform.

Chinese interest in Buddhism was largely attributable to the crisis of confidence which resulted. Both the message (Buddhism) and the avenue of transmission (the Silk Road) had long been in existence, yet Buddhism became a significant intellectual and cultural force in China only after 300 C.E. The barriers to Chinese appropriation of Buddhism were formidable. Above and beyond the friction of distance were the daunting difficulties involved in translating Buddhist scripture into Chinese. In addition to the very real problems of language, these works were rooted in a mental universe profoundly unlike anything that existed in Chinese. Neither concepts nor imagery had obvious resonance in pre-Buddhist Chinese culture; social and cultural realities were radically different. In ways subtle and obvious, Buddhism was reshaped in the process of transmission. The cultural crisis that barbarian rule in the heartland of civilization triggered in the Chinese elite was crucial in gaining an audience for this message. And, had elite interest in the new religion not been paralleled by official support, Buddhism in China—like Christianity in the West—would have remained the property of an intellectual elite.

Sui and early Tang deserve stress in any survey of world history. Important in their own right, the contrast with conditions in Europe in these centuries is a vivid reminder that the West was not always "number one." Particularly noteworthy are Tang success in extending military control and civil administration over large parts of central Asia as well as over all China; the creation of the Grand Canal; the size and regular design of Changan; the glories of Tang high culture. Also important was the dynasty's peaceful and military contact with areas outside China: the Tang in these centuries exported paper to the Middle East, Buddhism and Chinese high culture to Japan. Emphasizing the difference between this aristocratic, Buddhist culture of the Tang and the preimperial Confucian culture of classical Chinese civilization helps to undermine any residual notions of an "unchanging East."

The period's most famous event, the revolt of the high Tang's most powerful general, the Sogdian-Turkic An Lushan (755), did not bring down the dynasty. Yet it shook the Tang to its foundations. The following changes may be traced, directly or indirectly, to the crisis:

1) the shift from conscript armies—their crack troops and horses obtained from the steppe—to mercenary ones;
2) the shift from taxes levied on individual households (sparking government attempts to provide households with an economic base: the "equal field" system) to taxes levied on land (the "two tax" system introduced in 780);
3) the decline of the great families and the emergence of a far larger group of locally prominent landlords (shidafu);
4) the increasing importance—thanks in large part to the development of printing from the late eighth century and the wider literacy it made possible—of recruitment by competitive exam;
5) the shift from government by aristocracy (typical of the 280–755 era) to government by scholar-official (typical of Song and after); and
6) the consequent transformation of emperor from first among equals to autocrat—a transformation influenced in style but not in substance by barbarian rule.

Changes in the tax system eliminated barriers to a free market in land. Weakening of the central power and collapse of the aristocracy reduced status discrimination against merchants, restrictions on domestic commerce, and the regimentation of urban life. The implications of these changes for Chinese culture and society would not be fully realized for centuries.

The Song (960–1279) emperors deliberately attempted to limit the threat military men could pose to central power. Yet, if they were profoundly dedicated to civilian control, Song Chinese were not pacifists. The boom economy of the central plain—still the center of Chinese civilization—was in part due to the rapid expansion of iron and steel production (much of it intended for military use), and the Song took the lead in finding military applications for gunpowder. The Song faced foreign as well as domestic challenges: the barbarian Liao controlled part of the area within the Great Wall. In 1004, the Song was forced to conclude a peace treaty in which the Liao were addressed as equals and the Chinese agreed to pay annual tribute. When the Xi-xia kingdom emerged in the northwest (1038), the Middle Kingdom's access to the Silk Road and to war horses was cut off. War led to fiscal crisis, fiscal crisis to reform (Wang Anshi, in power 1068–1076, 1078–1085), reform to factionalism, factionalism to paralysis, paralysis to defeat (Jin conquest of North China, 1127).

The southward migration of Chinese began long before 300 C.E., and since Sui times, the Grand Canal had permitted the capital to move southern surpluses north. Had it not been for the pressures of war, misrule, and ecological collapse in North China during the twelfth century, the center of population would probably have continued to drift gradually south. In fact, political and military developments accelerated this process. The implications for the subsequent history of China were profound. The south was better watered than the north and enjoyed a longer growing season. Once the necessary, back-breaking investments in water control had been made, a given number of peasants in southern China could produce far larger and more dependable surpluses than they could in the north. (The officially sponsored introduction of early-ripening and upland strains of rice from Southeast Asia of course played a role in this.) These surpluses made possible a population explosion (from the 60 million or so Chinese of Han through Tang to 120 million circa 1200). More people and more wealth led to a dramatic rise in urbanization and commercialization. Moreover, the shift from dryland to wet-rice agriculture had profound social implications in the countryside. The optimal size of a wet-rice field proves to be a sixth of an acre or less; labor demands are intense at planting and harvest, relatively modest at other times; and the cultivator's skill affects yields dramatically. Under such conditions, production will be most efficiently organized at the family level; a landlord-tenant nexus will prove more efficient than either manorialism or managerial landlordism; and the substantial amount of surplus labor in the off-season will encourage development of peasant handicrafts and "petty commodity production."

In light of these characteristics of wet-rice agriculture, Francesca Bray has argued that, although the diffusion of Chinese farming techniques contributed to the agricultural revolution in dryland farming in early modern Europe, "the relations of production in wet-rice cultivation have an internal dynamism that enables them to sustain not only significant increases in agricultural productivity, but also rapid economic diversification, without undergoing historical change."[1] Unlike Mark Elvin's hypothesis of a "high-level equilibrium trap," which holds that population and resources were so balanced from the Song on that technological innovation in China henceforth produced sharply diminishing returns, this formulation can incorporate the dynamism of subsequent periods.[2] These were centuries of qualitative change as well as quantitative growth. As a result, late imperial Chinese confronted novel forces as well as the eternally uneven, hence always unsettling, effects of growth. By 1200, however, barbarian pressure and Southeast Asian strains of rice had put the Middle Kingdom on a particular path, in which hundreds of thousands of peasant households, their skill and dedication crucial to wringing the maximum out of paddy fields, consolidated their position as the basic units of consumption **and** production. Combined with China's remarkably efficient system of nested markets, such households were able to exploit areas of comparative advantage and to use their surplus labor—the old, the young, and the underemployed cannot be laid off by the household "firm," and hence to the household their labor is a free good—to produce commodities for the market.

For centuries after the medieval economic revolution, these changes afforded the Chinese people the world's highest standard of living. This wealth underwrote the political integration of the Middle Kingdom, the glories of its high culture, the cultivated lifestyle of its elites, the widespread ability of the general population to realize its basic cultural norms (among them, to have numerous descendants). Yet the system was so successful at producing growth (increase in output) that it proved a substantial barrier to further development (increase in output per capita). There was, after all, nothing magical about the transition from the preindustrial/tributary to the industrial/capitalist order. At base, it involved a reorganization of economy—and society—to use available resources more efficiently. The dryland agriculture of the West was both inefficient and technologically backward. Those who controlled society's surpluses had means, motive, and opportunity (in part, thanks to the diffusion of East Asian techniques) to reorganize and rationalize that key sector. This triggered the agricultural (and ultimately the industrial) revolutions of the eighteenth and nineteenth centuries. The post-Song Chinese peasant household, intensively exploiting both its irrigated microholding and the labor of its members, integrated with and responsive to a quite sophisticated system of markets, was an extremely efficient producer. By driving down real wages and driving up rents, the dense populations in China's most advanced areas tended to shift wealth from the population at large to the society's elites. And, while the Chinese remained more than willing to borrow useful innovations from without (as with the New World foodcrops), innovations which would offer the Chinese peasant household higher returns per acre were few. Thus, if China's medieval economic revolution made possible the full elaboration of a preindustrial peasant-based society, its very strengths reduced means, motive, and opportunity for an agricultural revolution like the one which occurred in Western Europe in the early modern era. In this sense, it excluded the possibility that Song innovations, remarkable as they were, would lead to transition from a preindustrial/tributary to an industrial/capitalist order. [*For additional discussion of the Song Dynasty, see the essays "The Case of China," by Michael Marmé, and "Song China," by Robert Hymes.*]

NOTES

1. Francesca Bray in Joseph Needham, ed., *Science and Civilization in China*, vol. 6, part 2: *Agriculture* (Cambridge: Cambridge University Press, 1984), p. 616; see also Philip C.C. Huang, *The Peasant Family and Rural Development in the Yangzi Delta, 1350–1988* (Stanford: Stanford University Press, 1990), and Michel Cartier, "Aux origines de l'agriculture intensive du Bas Yangzi (note critique)," *Annales E. S. C.* 46.5 (Septembre–Octobre 1991): 1009–1019.

2. Mark Elvin, *The Pattern of the Chinese Past* (Stanford: Stanford University Press, 1973).

SONG CHINA, 960–1279

Robert Hymes

That the Song Dynasty was a turning point not only in Chinese but in world history is an idea with a considerable pedigree. The Japanese scholar whose work most promoted the study of the Song both in Japan and later in the West, Naitō Torajirō, saw Song China as the world's first "modern" society.[1] More recently William McNeill has argued that China in the Song became the first country in the world to demonstrate the growth-producing capacities of a (relatively) unrestricted private commercial economy.[2] One of the most widely read books on China, Mark Elvin's *Pattern of the Chinese Past,* regards the Song as the peak of China's development, both economically and technologically; and his notion of the "high-level equilibrium trap" proposes to explain why China declined or stagnated in the centuries that followed.[3] A leading economic historian of modern China, writing in 1992, finds "modern economic growth" in the Song, and never again in China until the twentieth century.[4] These are modern witnesses; but anticipatory support for such claims had been offered unwittingly centuries ago by Francis Bacon, who proposed that the three inventions most crucial to the transformation of his own European world were printing, gunpowder, and the mariner's compass.[5] We now know, as Bacon did not, that all three were first used on a broad scale in Song China. And to these three one may add Marco Polo's marvel, government-issued paper money; Joseph Needham's marker of bureaucratic modernity, the written examination in school and in civil service;[6] and perhaps even Sydney Mintz's sinister engines of cheap energy for the working class: caffeine and cane sugar as mass consumption goods.[7] Does "modernity," then, begin with the Song?

World-historical claims aside, all historians of China would now recognize that the changes of the Song reshaped Chinese society in ways still important in the nineteenth and twentieth centuries.

Many ways of living and acting that Westerners now see as most thoroughly "Chinese," or even as characteristically East Asian, did not appear before the Song. The Chinese, we know, are rice eaters and tea drinkers; but most Chinese in the Tang and before ate wheat or millet and drank wine, in that respect looking perhaps more "Western" than "Eastern"; rice and tea became the dominant food and drink in the Song.[8] China's population, we know, is huge, and tends to "explode"; its first explosion occurred in the Song. The Chinese, we know, are "Confucians"; but the kind of Confucianism that served as government orthodoxy throughout late imperial times was a Song reinvention. Chinese women, we may know, bound their feet; but they did not bind them until the Song.[9] Even the "Chinese" roof with its turned-up corners is by origin a **Song** Chinese roof.[10]

What happened here? It is worth considering what has caught the attention of so many observers. The broad outlines of the changes of China's "middle period" (for many of the processes I will place in Song began during the preceding Tang Dynasty) are clear. First, Chinese society simply grew much bigger. Massive migrations southward, together with indigenous southern population growth, for the first time shifted the center of population from the North China plain, the traditional heartland of Chinese civilization, to the wet and fertile lands south of the Yangzi (Yangtze) River. The movement may have been a response to the mainly North-Chinese wars of the last half of Tang and the succeeding brief time of disunion (the so-called Five Dynasties); to the economic opportunities that South China offered after the Grand Canal (built in the Sui Dynasty in the late sixth century) connected the Yangzi Valley with the capital region and other northern markets; to the long-term drying of North China; or to all of these. In any case the filling of the south both generated and depended upon the rise of wet-rice agriculture as the main source of food for southern and (via interregional trade) increasingly even for northern city dwellers. Tea, also a southern crop, changed from an exotic medicinal or luxury potation to the standard drink of the population at large. (Here is Mintz's caffeine.) Rice is famously labor-intensive and can support a larger population per unit area than wheat or other dry crops; once a sufficient threshold of density was reached in South China to support rice culture across a broad area, a dramatic upsurge in population was a natural consequence. It is possible that both the boiling of water associated with tea making and the relative shift away from alcohol consumed in wine also had health consequences that encouraged population growth. From the fifty or sixty million that had been a typical population of China for the ten preceding centuries or so, the numbers swelled to a hundred million at the end of Northern Song (ca. 1100) and perhaps 120 million or more by the thirteenth century. Though wars, plagues, or natural disasters would cause periodic short-term declines, sometimes dramatic, in the centuries that followed, the long-term upward trend that China's population embarked upon in the Song has continued, with a further steepening in the eighteenth century, to the present day. From this time on China was and remained by far the most populous political unit in the world, with producing and consuming capacities that repeatedly affected the commercial patterns and balance of trade of the Indian Ocean, the Islamic world, and even Europe in ways largely favorable to China through as late as the eighteenth century.

Song population growth was urbanizing growth: Chinese cities grew disproportionately and were from then until the nineteenth century typically the largest in the world.[11] Cities thrive on commerce; and the commercial growth of the Song is the second striking fact of the period, recognized even by contemporaries, who commented on the growth of private wealth and mercantile fortunes and sometimes worried out loud about the movement of common people out of farming and into trade or manufacturing. The older Tang market system, which had strictly confined trade to cities, and within cities to specific sites and hours, utterly broke down as urban commerce spread throughout cities and into extramural mercantile quarters.[12] Over long distances, large cities and whole regions of dense population came to depend on ship-borne bulk trade in staple goods, especially rice.[13] Over shorter distances, trade penetrated the countryside, drawing farmers into new periodic market centers and rapidly proliferating market towns.[14] In the late eleventh century a variety of new money taxes under Wang Anshi's [Wang An-shih] reform administration probably reinforced this movement of the rural population into the monetary and marketing economy. The quantity of money in circulation increased vastly in Song: in the first half of the eleventh century government issue of copper coin rose by several orders of magnitude over a few decades without major inflationary consequences, suggesting remarkable expansive capacity in the commercial economy. In the same century the government began issuing the world's first official paper currency. In its turn this would generate the world's first paper-money inflation, which recurred several times in Song and most dramatically under the succeeding Yuan Dynasty. Yet even with the expansion of official money, new or expanding private media of exchange flourished: silver and gold, though never officially minted by the government, became (in a process well underway in the Tang) standard currency for larger transactions. The conversion to money of metals that had earlier been favorite materials for the household utensils of the wealthy gave added impetus—since substitutes had to be found—to a newly thriving and expanding domestic porcelain industry; while copper moved easily and fluidly (though often illegally) back and forth between the coinage supply and a commercial industry in bronze images, depending on the value of coin at the moment.

Porcelain manufacture, which, as Margaret Medley has shown, underwent at some larger centers a process of standardization for mass domestic consumption as well as prodigious technical advances, was only one of the "new" industries of the Song.[15] Robert Hartwell's work demonstrated that iron and steel production, stimulated by government military needs and by private demand for cooking utensils and agricultural tools, and facilitated by canals connecting the major production centers to the capital market, expanded to levels unequaled in Europe before the eighteenth century.[16] Production sites became virtual industrial centers employing thousands of workers, and Hartwell argues that Song iron and steel technology rested, for the first time in world history, on the use of coke. Silk manufactories in cities and monastic centers similarly employed large numbers of workers in producing cloth to standardized patterns for regional or national markets. Textile production in other fibers, especially hemp, ramie, and by the end of the dynasty increasingly cotton, was centered in the individual rural household, employing largely female labor to supplement agricultural or other family income. The iron and steel industries and the larger porcelain or silk manufactories, in fact, were surely untypical of Song industry in their degree of concentration and the permanence of their labor force: across the countryside, small kilns and potteries, oil presses, wine-making shops, paper-making concerns, and similar small enterprises drew on rural labor largely in the agricultural off-season. In the villages, "peasants" themselves (for the term may grow less appropriate from this period on) underwent a division of labor and specialization at the household-to-household level: in stories and anecdotes of rural life of this period one meets the broommaker, the fish cook, the innkeeper, the petty diviner, the drug seller, the cloth trader, or indeed the landless day laborer almost as often as the farmer himself. Song officials who produced famine-relief surveys of rural areas assumed in drawing up their forms that households with little or no land—and these were the majority of Song households in the south—would always engage in some nonfarming activity at least as a sideline.[17] This trade-mediated multiplication of sources of income in countryside and town alike may justify applying the term "proto-industrial," drawn from recent reconsiderations of the European rural experience, to Song and post-Song China.

Commercialization affected rural social hierarchies as well. How relations between landowner and direct producer changed in Song is a question that has spawned a scholarly industry.[18] The "Tokyo school" in Japanese scholarship proposed a dominant model of Song "manors" resting on a dependent and subordinate servile tenantry, yet oriented toward production for the market. This model gained currency in the West partly owing to Mark Elvin, though a careful reading of Elvin will show that he recognizes the variety and complexity of Song tenancy and landholding.[19] One must always remember that the landlord-tenant relationship did not exhaust or epitomize Song rural social structure: both a vast population of small owner-cultivators and a considerable pool of hired laborers were key players. But the solution to the Song "land problem" that now has probably the greatest scholarly following is that tenancy practices and tenant statuses varied greatly, but systematically, from region to region, with more extended contiguous holdings, managerial landlords, and more servile or land-bound forms of tenancy in more sparsely settled regions, and fragmentation of holdings, a trend toward absentee landownership, and less servile, more purely economic tenant-landlord relations where population was denser and cities closer.[20] This locates what Naitō and the "Kyoto school" of Japanese scholarship have seen as characteristically "modern" forms in just the regions that one naturally thinks of as the core of Song change, especially the lower Yangzi region and the surrounding southeast. The temptation is then strong simply to array the regions of Song China along a scale of modernity and treat areas of servile tenancy and large unified estates as relatively "backward" and so not "typical." But this may miss the real relations of different regions within a single commercial system. For there is evidence for a **tightening** of servile status, supported by specific government decree, in these less populated regions during the course of the Song; and we know that certain of these regions—Hunan-Hubei and parts of Jiangxi in particular—increasingly become rice bowls for the populations of more densely settled regions in the latter half of the Song. Attempts to bind tenants to the land and to enlist the state as enforcer (where tenants might otherwise seek to open their own lands and work for themselves) may then represent a response by landlords in land-rich, relatively labor-short areas precisely to the rich commercial opportunities offered by markets far downriver in the Yangzi delta and points south. In densely settled regions the relative shortage of land and abundance of labor would tend to keep tenants on the land without force and so would allow freer formal tenure relations, since the market itself would favor the landlord—indeed, in the southeast in the later Song one finds landlords evicting tenants in search of a higher rent, not trying to attach them to the land or to themselves. We may see, then, not "more modern" and "less modern" regions but regions whose landowners, owing to different conditions of the land and labor markets, responded in appropriately different ways to a unified "modern" development: the commercialization of land and labor and the rise of a national market in rice. If this picture works, then in China commercialization yielded **both** "freer" **and** "more servile" tenures, precisely as in Europe the development of a continentwide market in grains favored both "modern" contractual tenancies in the more densely populated western countries and a "refeudalization" of tenures in the east. How the need to conceive and absorb both the resulting situations within a single political and especially a single legal system made the Song Chinese picture different from the European is a question worth considering: it may, for instance, have kept alive a degree of intraregional variation that would otherwise be hard to explain.

At the other extreme of social hierarchy, too, the Song brought change, broad enough for some observers to speak of a "new class" of "gentry" or "scholar-officials" that rose to replace the "aristocracy" of Tang and before. Caution is very much in order here: our picture of Tang and earlier periods as aristocratic may be growing less secure; how much genealogical continuity there was between Tang and Song elites is probably unknowable; and the nature, degree of mobility, and relation to state and officeholding of the "new" Song elite remain among the livelier issues in the field.[21] It may be safest to put things this way: in Song the Chinese elite—the pool from which government officials were drawn, the educated stratum, the circle of the locally powerful or notable—grew much **larger,** even proportionately, than it had ever been before. In this, too, commercialization played a critical part, along with perhaps the most vital of Bacon's inventions, the printed book. New sources of wealth—meaning not only commerce as such but the richer opportunities offered by commercial agriculture as well—made it easier to get rich, or as rich as one needed to be to refine one's style of life and educate one's sons; and that was probably not as rich as it had once been, now that printing made access to a commercially distributed, ever-expanding, more or less public trove of knowledge, speculation, literary art, religious writing, news, official secrets, and gossip far cheaper and more readily available than it had ever been before, in China or anywhere in the world.[22] The famous civil service examination system, founded in Sui-Tang but first expanded to constitute a normal route to an official career in Song, made it in turn easier than before to convert wealth, education, or other local prominence, **once achieved,** into official position (always administering a locality other than one's own) and government-sanctioned status.[23] As existing elites reproduced and overreproduced themselves[24] and as literacy spread, the group that could consider itself socially and educationally qualified for the exams grew far larger than the supply of degrees and offices could possibly begin to accommodate, and this meant that high status in a broader social sense never became dependent on official standing. But the success of the Song state in inducing local elites to devote a considerable effort, in the face of ever more overwhelming statistical odds, to the pursuit of centrally granted civil-service degrees is a striking and deeply important phenomenon. It is perhaps one of the truest and historically most lasting achievements of that state—on which more below.

It is all this change—but particularly change in the economic sphere—that has provoked the sorts of claims for the Song with which we began, and with those claims a question that, explicitly, covertly, or sometimes by being ignored, continues to haunt the field: **what happened** to this Song "revolution"? The question really means: what **didn't** happen; and the answer it assumes is: what happened in the West, industrialization, **our** "modernity." That the question is presentist, presupposes that change is linear, assumes that Western patterns represent what ought to happen, treats East as odd and West as normal, and so on—all easy enough to argue, and hard to disagree with—has not made it go away; it has shaped a great deal of work on later periods in China as well as on the Song. Indeed, at least heuristically, it may yet be a legitimate enough question, for it is hard to deny that much of what happened in Song looks extraordinarily reminiscent (or rather, anticipatory) of what happened in Europe's Renaissance and commercial revolution. It also seems clear that China in the Song, and for some centuries afterward, was the wealthiest and, in economic and technological terms (though here again linear models creep in), the most highly developed society in the world. It is not utterly unreasonable to ask why it did not remain so. Was there a reversal or an interruption of Song "advances," and why?

This is not an easy question, but it is useful to consider the range of answers it has called forth. Broadly, the answers divide into those that deny the premise (or, along the lines just suggested, the legitimacy of the question) and those that accept it. Consider the first strategy first. One may argue that there is no reversal: what had begun in Song did not end at all, or at least not for good. This is now the burden, explicit or implicit, of most work on social and economic change in the Ming-Qing transition and the high Qing. Scholars now often describe the seventeenth and eighteenth centuries in China in terms eerily like the received account of the Song: commercialization, urbanization, increasing literacy, transformation of elites, "economic and social revolution," and so on. Such work may tend in the end not to reject our question—what didn't happen and why not?—but simply to move it forward in time; for this, see the appropriate essays in this volume [see Zelin, "China's Economy in Comparative Perspective, 1500 Onward," in this volume]. Few workers in the field so far have tried to compare, or otherwise to sort out the relation between, two such similar and seemingly repetitive "revolutions," or to solve the problem of what at least looks like hiatus, retrogression, or stagnation in between, especially in the first half of the Ming. One who has tried, William Rowe, speaks explicitly of the "first and second commercial revolutions," and suggests that the second was an advance upon the first largely in its "routinization" and generalization of an interregional trade in staple goods that in Song times was still largely ad hoc, "to make up temporary or accidental shortfalls."[25] From the perspective of a specialist in Song this solution will not fly—both Ch'än Han-sheng some years ago and Hugh Clark more recently have shown from different angles the highly regular, routinized, and nationwide character of Song long-distance trade in grain and other staple goods, especially in the later years of the dynasty—but it stands out as an important attempt at a synoptic vision of major change in the last millennium of Chinese history. The exploration of the Ming-Qing "revolution" has been crucial, however, for showing that we probably need to treat a high and perhaps increasing degree of commercialization, with its extensive social consequences, as a more or less persistent condition of post-Tang China. This is a critical recognition for comparisons with Europe and for our picture of world history as a whole.

Persistent commercialization in China suggests another approach to our question (in effect another way of denying its premise), an approach recently taken by Philip Huang: this is to attack the question at the root by denying the assumed link, in European history and elsewhere, between commercialization and industrialization (or modernization). In effect one argues: there was no reversal, but linear development; but the nature and direction of that development have been misperceived from the outset. Huang argues that in China the commercialization of agriculture acted in fact to preserve the small peasant owner-or-tenant household, built around multiple laboring adult members, as the fundamental productive unit in the agricultural market, and that the nature of that unit, and the way it adjusted to and took advantage of commercial opportunities and multiplying outlets for labor, served over the long run to **reduce** the returns per person-hour of labor, extend the needed work year, and so tie the worker ever more closely to the household economy. Huang calls the process "involutionary growth."[26] He begins his story only with the Ming and has nothing to say explicitly about whether his picture would apply to Song as well, but he certainly makes available an answer to the question for Song: that Chinese commercialization, given the nature of the productive unit and its interface with the larger economy, was not in the first place the sort of process that could have generated larger-scale industrializing transformations along European lines. In this connection, if Elvin's extensive, managerial manors could be shown to be the typical or predominant form of commercial agriculture in the Song, one could build an argument for Song exceptionalism; but the Song evidence at this point tends very much the other way. Huang's argument itself, however, remains highly controversial.[27]

Another approach, perhaps logically similar to Huang's in suggesting that China was from the start moving along a different track, has been to argue that China's urbanization took a different form from Western models, a form less conducive to further transformation and subsequent industrialization. Gilbert Rozman, basing himself on comparative studies of China and Japan, has proposed separate Chinese and Japanese models of urbanization: a Japanese form focused tightly on the largest city at the top, with a highly integrated descending hierarchy of centers below and with relatively less nucleation and urbanization at the lower levels; and a Chinese form in which growth concentrates more heavily at the bottom of the scale, in the multiplication and swelling of smaller marketing centers, while integration is looser and growth at the top of the urban scale (after a certain point) is less striking.[28] Rozman's work is based not in Song, but entirely in late imperial materials from the Qing. There is a ray of light here for those who want to hold onto the Song as a special period, however, for there is reason to think that the pattern of Song urban growth, especially in the first half of the dynasty, more closely resembled Japanese than later Chinese patterns.[29]

All these arguments deny, or can be used to deny, the notion of a break or reversal in economic and social change as something that needs explaining. Where instead the premise of the question is accepted—that something happened in Song that did not last— a similarly wide range of positions emerges. Scholars who have taken note of Song developments but whose own work has centered in things Western have often argued that something in traditional Chinese culture or institutions ultimately and unshakably hostile to dramatic social or economic change is responsible: that promising beginnings were in the end choked off, say, by the institutionalized power of the Confucian tradition and its bias against commerce and self-interest. McNeill argues something very like this, holding that the considerable but still partial or temporary freeing of the power of market relations in Song provided an example and impetus to the rest of the world but could not break through the stronger bonds of anticommercial tradition and policy in China itself until this century.[30] Such arguments now gain far less support within the China field than outside it, on the one hand because deeper study of Confucian and Neo-Confucian ideas has shown the complexity, variety, and changeability of "traditional" Chinese attitudes toward trade, self-interest, and innovation; and on the other hand because the field as a whole no longer sees the traditional Chinese state as the all-encompassing, all-containing force it was once imagined to be. Indeed, the consensus of the field may now be that the Chinese state, especially in late imperial times, was weak in rather consequential ways, and especially weak at the interface between its lowest bureaucratic levels and local society.[31] Arguments such as that of Etienne Balazs that the state in China was a proto-totalitarian force that crushed all independent power sources, including private wealth and enterprise, have thus fallen by the wayside.[32] Much more influential in recent discussions is Mark Elvin's work, often summarized by his notion of the "high-level equilibrium trap" but in fact combining several factors in an argument of some complexity. For Elvin there was a true "turning point" in the fourteenth century, such that renewed economic growth in the sixteenth and seventeenth centuries was of a very different and less dynamic kind than before; and factors in this change were a filling up of internal frontiers for expansion, reduction in overseas trade and foreign contacts, a shift in ideas (note: not the force of "traditional" ideas, but a **shift,** an innovative movement) away from investigation of nature and toward introspection, and—when commerce and growth did revive—a sort of "disadvantage of forwardness," by which a relatively high degree of development and a relative lack of transport and trade bottlenecks both reduced incentives for and increased the expense of innovation and invention. No element of Elvin's argument has escaped criticism, and probably no part of it is now accepted by all in the field, but it has supplied a powerful model to which research can respond and so has shaped the terms of discussion.

Other arguments rest more on historical contingency and less on system. The Mongols, whose final conquest of South China in 1279 brought the Song to an end, have come in for much blame, probably generally ill-founded, since there is reason to think their Yuan dynasty strengthened foreign trade and with it a domestic economy that may have been faltering toward the end of Song; certainly Marco Polo's observations and those of other Europeans do not suggest economic stagnation or retrogression. McNeill's suggestion, in his earlier work on world disease patterns, that the Pax Mongolica allowed the transmission of bubonic plague from east to west, with its implication that the so-called Black Death may have had as great an impact on China as on Europe, should probably be taken more seriously and deserves much more attention than China scholars have given it: the apparent catastrophic decline shown by early Ming census figures might thus prove more real than many scholars have supposed.[33] But while this might explain the apparent long stagnation between two "revolutions" already touched on, it would not explain, as Elvin has tried to, why the second should have had a different character than the first. A different and more nuanced recent argument for the interruption of Song change goes as follows: that "pressures of defense forced the state to cannibalize the very economy that it had done so much to expand, [via] a squeeze on the commercial economy, loss of control over monetary policy, and runaway surtaxes; this exacerbated an incipient demographic crisis in the twelfth and thirteenth centuries that can be seen in rising rent prices and the increasing parcelization of land, [constituting an] 'economic crisis of the thirteenth century.'"[34] One gains a sense of the rather detailed exploration of Song economic history that may be required to understand whether and how "progressive" change came to a halt. And all this still would leave unanswered the question of the relation of Song to later changes.

The notion of Song change as something uniquely promising, of promise unfulfilled, is in sum quite problematic, perhaps now more clearly so than it once seemed. We simply understand too poorly the nature of the Song changes, of seemingly similar or continuous developments that came after, and of the relation between them. The period nonetheless stands out, again, as perhaps a height of Chinese wealth and economic power in relation to the rest of the world. Chinese themselves have sometimes looked back at the Song state in shame over its willingness to pay annual "tribute" to "barbarian" neighbor states to keep them at peace, and at its loss of North China to the Jurchen in 1127 and final conquest by the Mongols in 1279. But the Song government's payments to the northern states amounted to about 1 percent of its annual military budget, and in turn helped to prime the pump of a trade that was enormously imbalanced in the Song's favor. As to the Mongols, that the Southern Song was able to hold out for forty years against an enemy that up to that time had conquered quickly wherever it had exerted sustained effort, and that the final conquest was achieved with naval and artillery technology borrowed from the Song, suggests military strength more than weakness. For the first and last time in imperial Chinese history before the nineteenth century, a Chinese state acted within a multistate system of rough military equals, and did so with skill and flexibility, engaging in sophisticated diplomacy and concluding treaties that assumed formal equality of partners. There is an unappreciated success story here.

Yet to turn to the state, which has not much occupied our attention so far, raises issues important for any comparison of Europe and Asia and for any notion of Song "modernity." A critical feature of European developments in the last several centuries, after all, has been the building of nation-states, entailing the extension of state power deeper and deeper into the everyday lives of subjects, the bureaucratization both of internal state structures and of state-subject relations, and so on; and this—not commercialization and industrialization alone—is a significant part of our broad notion of "modernity." But it is in precisely this sphere that

Song Chinese developments may most differ from European. Bureaucracy was very old in China, and the Song state appears to be not only an effectively centralized bureaucracy but a very large and powerful state in comparison to its Western contemporaries. But in its direction of change it may represent a key point in a trend virtually opposite to the line Western states, or those that have survived, have traced. As G. William Skinner has argued, as China's population rose and as its economy grew larger and more complex over the last thousand years, the Chinese state stayed essentially the same size.[35] Far from extending itself more deeply into local society or strengthening its direct contact with its subjects' lives, the Chinese state, by not expanding its personnel or increasing its numbers of administrative centers, in effect grew farther from its local base; and its apparatus both of local control and of revenue extraction, it can be argued, grew proportionately less effective. Local government was not further bureaucratized but grew to depend more and more on quasi-formal and informal arrangements between state and local elites or among local elites themselves. The contrast with the bureaucratizing *han* governments of Tokugawa Japan is as striking, and may ultimately be as consequential, as the difference from Europe. Now if this picture is roughly accurate, the Song may again represent a certain "turning point": for it is in Song that population and economy first begin to grow dramatically, and it is in Song that something like an attempt at "state building" is made, in response to the fiscal pressures created by the military threat of hostile neighbors as well as to the general economic changes of the time; and the attempt fails, perhaps once and for all. The attempt is the famous "New Laws" administration of Wang Anshi and his reform-party successors.[36] Wang not only tried to expand channels of revenue and the apparatus of local order, but explicitly argued that the state must enlarge itself, and in effect absorb into an expanding bureaucracy the growing wealthy and educated elite. The ultimate defeat of his party, and its discrediting by the fall of North China, effectively marked a halt to all Song attempts to "grow the state" to match the growth of society and economy. The Neo-Confucianism of Zhu Xi [Chu Hsi] that gained wide support among the elite in the period that followed—far from being a mere "inward turn" toward self-cultivation and metaphysics—in important part expresses and ratifies the resulting new relation of state and elite, by locating gentlemanly virtue and status in a life outside of office and by transplanting the world-reforming impulses of earlier Song political thinking into a context of individual, private, and local action.[37] No state-building project as ambitious as Wang's would be tried again, and no ideas as state-centered as his would again gain a wide following, before the late nineteenth and twentieth centuries. The case cannot be fully argued here; but if the penetrating, bureaucratizing, standardizing, and homogenizing state is a major feature of "modernity," and if state power itself has played an important role in processes of industrialization, then in the political sphere the Song may mark the beginnings of a specifically Chinese direction of change that is something different from "modern."

NOTES

1. For Naitō of the "Kyoto School" of Japanese scholarship on China, see Joshua A. Fogel, *Politics and Sinology: The Case of Naitō Konan (1866–1934)* (Cambridge, MA: Harvard Council on East Asian Studies, 1984), and Hisayuki Miyakawa, "An Outline of the Naitō Hypothesis and Its Effects on Japanese Studies of China," *Far East Quarterly* 14.4 (1955): 533–52.

2. William McNeill, *The Pursuit of Power: Technology, Armed Force, and Society since A.D. 1000* (Chicago: The University of Chicago Press, 1982), pp. 24–62.

3. Mark Elvin, *The Pattern of the Chinese Past* (Stanford: Stanford University Press, 1973).

4. Albert Feuerwerker, "Presidential Address: Questions About China's Early Modern Economic History That I Wish I Could Answer," *Journal of Asian Studies* 51.4 (November 1992), pp. 765–66.

5. Bacon said "the magnet," but counted it important specifically for its use in navigation. Bacon, *Novum Organum*, bk. 1, aphorism 129, cited in Joseph Needham, "Science and China's Influence on the World," in *The Legacy of China*, ed. Raymond Dawson (Oxford: Oxford University Press, 1964), p. 242.

6. Written civil service examinations were not a Song invention but were expanded by the Song government to be the primary means to a career. On their possible transmission westward during Song, see Joseph Needham, "China and the Origin of Qualifying Examinations in Medicine," in Needham, *Clerks and Craftsmen in China and the West* (Cambridge: Cambridge University Press, 1970), pp. 379–96.

7. Sidney W. Mintz, *Sweetness and Power: The Place of Sugar in Modern History* (New York: Penguin Books, 1985). On sugarcane and cane sugar in the Song, see Michael Freeman, in *Food in Chinese Culture*, ed. K.C. Chang (New Haven: Yale University Press, 1977), p. 147.

8. Michael Freeman, "Sung," pp. 145–48.

9. I am indebted here to ongoing work by Patricia Ebrey, as yet unpublished.

10. Michael Sullivan, *A Short History of Chinese Art* (Berkeley: University of California Press, 1967), p. 173.

11. G.W. Skinner, "Introduction: Urban Development in Imperial China," in Skinner, ed., *The City in Late Imperial China* (Stanford: Stanford University Press, 1977), pp. 29–31.

12. Katō Shigeshi, "On the *hang* or Association of Merchants in

China, with Special Reference to the Institution in the T'ang and Sung Periods," *Memoirs of the Research Department of the Toyo Bunko* 9 (1936): 45–83.

13. See for example Hugh Clark, *Community, Trade, and Networks: Southern Fujian Province from the Third to the Thirteenth Century* (Cambridge: Cambridge University Press, 1991), pp. 146–48.

14. Shiba Yoshinobu and Yamane Yukio, *Markets in China during the Sung, Ming, and Ch'ing Periods* (Honolulu: University of Hawaii Press, 1967).

15. Margaret Medley, *The Chinese Potter: A Practical History of Chinese Ceramics* (New York: Scribners, 1976).

16. Robert Hartwell, "Markets, Technology, and the Structure of Enterprise in the Development of the Eleventh-Century Chinese Iron and Steel Industry," *Journal of Economic Development* 26 (1966): 29–58.

17. See for example Elvin, *Pattern*, p. 70.

18. See Peter Golas, "Rural China in the Song," *Journal of Asian Studies* 39.2 (1980): 291–325.

19. Elvin, *Pattern*, pp. 69–83.

20. This view was first articulated by Yanagida Setsuko in work published in Japanese. See Golas, op. cit. It is elaborated and refined in Joseph P. McDermott, "Charting Blank Spaces and Disputed Regions: The Problem of Sung Land Tenure," *Journal of Asian Studies* 44.1 (1984): 13–41.

21. Among important recent work on these issues, see David Johnson, *The Medieval Chinese Oligarchy* (Boulder, CO: Westview Press, 1977), and "The Last Years of a Great Clan: The Li Family of Chao Chün in Late T'ang and Early Sung," *Harvard Journal of Asiatic Studies* 37.1 (1977): 5–102; Patricia B. Ebrey, *The Aristocratic Families of Early Imperial China: A Case Study of the Po-ling Ts'ui Family* (Cambridge: Cambridge University Press, 1978) and *Family and Property in Sung China: Yuan Ts'ai's Precepts for Social Life* (Princeton: Princeton University Press, 1984); Robert Hymes, *Statesmen and Gentlemen: The Local Elite of Fu-chou, Chiang-hsi, in Northern and Southern Sung* (Cambridge: Cambridge University Press, 1986); Beverly Jo Bossler, "Powerful Relations and Relations of Power: Family and Society in Sung China, 960–1279," Diss. UC Berkeley, 1991.

22. Song printing remains understudied. See Denis Twitchett, *Printing and Publishing in Medieval China* (New York: Frederic C. Beil, 1983).

23. That the exams by themselves conferred status or that mobility of low-status people upward through the exams was common now appears less plausible than it once did. See Hymes, op. cit., *Statesmen and Gentlemen*, ch. 1.

24. Cf. Stevan Harrell, "The Rich Get Children," in *Family and Population in East Asian History*, ed. Susan B. Hanley and Arthur P. Wolf (Stanford: Stanford University Press, 1985), pp. 81–109.

25. William Rowe, "Approaches to Modern Chinese Social History," in *Reliving the Past: The Worlds of Social History*, ed. Olivier Zunz (Chapel Hill: University of North Carolina Press, 1985), p. 273.

26. Philip Huang, "The Paradigmatic Crisis in Chinese Studies: Paradoxes in Social and Economic History," *Modern China* 17, no. 3 (July 1991), pp. 299–341, and *The Peasant Family and Rural Development in the Yangzi Delta, 1350–1988* (Stanford: Stanford University Press, 1990).

27. See for example the exchange between Huang and Ramon Myers: Ramon H. Myers, "How Did the Modern Chinese Economy Develop?—A Review Article," and Philip Huang, "A Reply to Ramon Myers," *Journal of Asian Studies* 50, no. 3 (August 1991), pp. 604–33; and compare Albert Feuerwerker's remarks on Huang's model in Feuerwerker, op. cit.

28. Gilbert Rozman, *Urban Networks in Ch'ing China and Tokugawa Japan* (Princeton: Princeton University Press, 1973).

29. Chao Kang, *Man and Land in China: An Economic Analysis* (Stanford: Stanford University Press, 1986).

30. McNeill, *The Pursuit of Power*, pp. 24–62.

31. See for example Ray Huang, *Taxation and Governmental Finance in Sixteenth-Century Ming China* (Cambridge: Cambridge University Press, 1974), pp. 306–23.

32. Etienne Balazs, "China as a Permanently Bureaucratic Society," in Balazs, *Chinese Civilization and Bureaucracy* (New Haven: Yale University Press, 1964), pp. 13–27.

33. William H. McNeill, *Plagues and Peoples,* ch. 4: "The Impact of the Mongol Empire on Shifting Disease Balances, 1200–1500" (Magnolia, MA: Peter Smith Publications, 1992), pp. 132–75; Ping-ti Ho, *Studies on the Population of China, 1368–1953* (Cambridge, MA: Harvard University Press, 1959), pp. 3–23.

34. Paul Smith, personal communication based on work in progress.

35. As indeed it had done for the thousand years before. But the stability is less striking where population and general social complexity were not, as in the Song, rapidly expanding. G.W. Skinner, op. cit., pp. 19–25.

36. For a fuller version of this argument, see Robert Hymes and Conrad Schirokauer, *Ordering the World: Approaches to State and Society in Song China* (Berkeley: University of California Press, 1993), ch. 1: "Introduction." For Wang Anshi's reforms, see James T.C. Liu, *Reform in Sung China: Wang An-shih (1021–1086) and His New Policies* (Cambridge, MA: Harvard University Press, 1959), and more recently, the very important articles by Paul Smith and Peter Bol in Hymes and Schirokauer, *Ordering the World.*

37. On Neo-Confucianism and its development by Zhu Xi [Chu Hsi], see Wm. Theodore de Bary, "A Reappraisal of Neo-Confucianism," in *Studies in Chinese Thought,* ed. Arthur Wright (Chicago: University of Chicago Press, 1953), pp. 81–111; and more recently, Peter Bol, *"This Culture of Ours": Intellectual Transitions in T'ang and Sung China* (Stanford: Stanford University Press, 1992), and Hoyt Tillman, *Confucian Discourse and Chu Hsi's Ascendancy* (Honolulu: University of Hawaii Press, 1992). For the social-political view of Zhu Xi's Neo-Confucianism offered here, see also Hymes and Schirokauer, *Ordering the World,* "Introduction."

Asia in World History: Essays

JAPAN, 550–838

H. Paul Varley

From the mid-sixth through the mid-ninth century Japan engaged in a remarkable process of cultural borrowing from abroad, primarily from China but also from Korea. What made the borrowing remarkable was both its scale and the fact that it was undertaken voluntarily.

China in the late sixth and early seventh centuries was in a dynamic stage of reunification under the Sui (589–618) and Tang (618–907) dynasties after three centuries of disunity. A reunited China presented a potent model for emulation by its neighbors, but it posed no overt threat to the Japanese in their archipelago more than a hundred miles off the Asian continent. No Chinese (or Korean) forces crossed the sea to conquer or invade Japan: nothing was forced upon the Japanese at gunpoint or by zealous missionaries. On the contrary, the Japanese continued (as they had from the fourth century) to send their own military expeditions to fight for territorial interests in Korea until the late seventh century, and they went to great effort to organize and dispatch cultural missions to China, four to the Sui between 600 and 614 and fifteen to the Tang from 630 until 838.

Fundamental to the process of cultural borrowing during this age was the effort to fashion Japan into a centralized, bureaucratic state like China. In the terminology of John Hall (taken from Max Weber), Japan sought to transform itself from a loosely organized "familial state," whose ruling aristocracy was divided into territorially based, extended family units, or clans, called *uji*, into a Chinese-style "imperial-bureaucratic state." This transformation in the seventh and eighth centuries entailed elevation of the status of the ruling clan's head, who was little more than *primus inter pares* among the clan leaders, to the exalted position of *tennō*, or emperor; nationalization of the country's rice lands, which provided the Japanese with their basic foodstuff, and redistribution of these lands on an equal-field basis to cultivators (the equal-field system, taken from the practice of Tang China, was implemented as part of Japan's famous Taika Reform of 645–46); institution of a rationalized structure of central governing offices and a network of provincial offices, both to be staffed by ministers selected according to merit (the organization of the offices of the new imperial-bureaucratic state was set forth in the Taihō Code of 702); and construction of a major urban center as a capital city, which from 710 was Nara.

Underlying the Chinese concept of an imperial-bureaucratic state was **Confucianism,** which called for government by ethical men and which was in the process during this age of being firmly institutionalized in Song China as a ruling ideology through the examination system for a bureaucracy of scholar-officials. Idealistic reformers in Japan conceived that their state, like China, would become a meritocracy, with colleges in the capital and the provinces to provide training, primarily in the Confucian classics, that would enable students to pass state-run examinations and thereby gain appointment to ministerial positions. In fact, the examination system as it was established in Japan merely allowed students who were successful in testing to enter the bureaucracy at its lowest level, promising them little advancement in their future careers. And within a few centuries, the system fell entirely into disuse. Despite the formal construction of an imperial-bureaucratic state, Japan's ruling elite—descendants of the leadership of the old clans of the central provinces—remained powerfully entrenched as a hereditary aristocracy whose status was determined not by merit but by birth.

Probably the most powerful force in the cultural borrowing from the Asian continent during this age was **Buddhism,** which to one degree or another affected nearly every aspect of Japanese life. Buddhism brought wonders of art and architecture to Japan, and introduced an attitude toward life—seeing it in terms of suffering in a world of impermanence and ceaseless flux, from which all beings sought release through enlightenment or salvation—that profoundly altered the sentiments and beliefs of the Japanese. It became established, through temples great and small, as a major institutional component of the Japanese state, and it exerted its influence upon such diverse fields as education, medicine, literature, history writing, and even governance.

Buddhism did not, however, soon become the dominant religion of Japan. Although it was quickly embraced by members of the ruling elite, several centuries passed before it penetrated all classes of Japanese society to secure a mass following; and it never fully displaced the indigenous beliefs of Shinto. Indeed, Shinto, although it was partly merged with Buddhism, retained its own vitality both as a little tradition—that is, as a set of folk beliefs focusing on localistic and particularistic deities (kami)— and as a great tradition in its connection to the imperial institution, which was based on mythic claims of descent from the sun goddess.

One of the most important things the Japanese borrowed from China during this age was the Chinese writing system. Until the early Heian period (794–1185), the Japanese for the most part simply wrote in Chinese. From about early Heian times, however, they evolved a syllabary (a set of symbols to reproduce the syllables of their language) called kana, and from then to the present Japanese has been written primarily in the form of a mixture of Chinese characters and kana. Use of Chinese characters has been, along with Confucianism and Buddhism, one of the great unifying forces in East Asian civilization.

The Nara period, 710–84, was a time of glorious attainment. Nara, the capital located near Kyoto in central Japan, became an impressive city with a population of perhaps 200,000. Modeled on the Tang capital of Changan (although on a smaller scale), it was the seat of a far more centralized state than Japan had ever known. Physically, as we can judge from the many structures— mostly Buddhist temples and Shinto shrines—that survive today, Nara possessed great beauty and was a worthy symbol of a land that had taken giant strides toward higher civilization on the Chinese model.

Outwardly, the court government of the Nara period functioned like the imperial-bureaucratic institution it was intended to be. But politics at the Nara court comprised essentially a succession of **disputes among familial entities**, most prominently the imperial family—represented both by emperors and empresses and by power-seeking princes—and the Fujiwara, a ministerial clan that had been on the rise since the Taika Reform of the seventh century. The Fujiwara were the ultimate victors of these political wars, but they did not consolidate their primacy at court until the ninth century, after the capital was transferred to Heian, or Kyoto, some twenty-eight miles north of Nara. Emergence of the Fujiwara as imperial regents in the late ninth century represented, in John Hall's scheme, reversion from the imperial-bureaucratic state to the earlier, familial form of state.

The chief tool used by the Fujiwara in their steady ascent to power at court in the Nara period and the early Heian period

(794–1185) was marriage into the imperial family. In reign after reign, Fujiwara women were married to emperors and their male issue were designated crown princes or emperors-to-be. Typically, the Fujiwara regent was the grandfather or other close relative of the emperor.

Reversion in the political realm to a familial form of state dominated by the Fujiwara was accompanied, in the economic realm, by the decline of the equal-field system of land distribution and the establishment of private estates *(shōen)*. Granted various immunities from taxation and intrusion by government officials, rice lands were gradually gathered into estates, whose holders were noble families (including the Fujiwara), members of the imperial family, and Buddhist and Shinto religious institutions. The full evolution of the estate system required several centuries: by the late eleventh and early twelfth centuries, rice lands throughout the country were organized into estates.

The move of the capital to Heian in 794 was undertaken for several possible reasons: greater open space; better water facilities (for consumption and for river travel to the sea); and direct access to land routes to the eastern and northern provinces. It is also likely that the court wished to distance itself from the Buddhist temples of Nara, whose priests had frequently meddled in politics. Temples soon proliferated in Heian as well, but priests were not again allowed to participate directly in government affairs.

Japan's long period of cultural borrowing from China ended with the dispatch of its last mission to the Tang in 838. The decline of the Tang Dynasty (it fell in 907) made travel to China unsafe. But more fundamentally, the Japanese no longer felt the need to borrow from the great Middle Kingdom. Viewing Japan in the late ninth century, we can see that, although it had absorbed much from the continent, it had by no means become a replica in miniature of China. Abandonment of the core aspects of the imperial-bureaucratic state structure (including the examination system and equal-field system) was perhaps the most conspicuous indication that Japanese cultural borrowing had, in the long run, been selective. Indeed, from at least the beginning of the Heian period, Japan developed institutionally—e.g., in the establishment of the Fujiwara regency—in a way totally independent from Chinese influence.

Cultural selectivity was apparent in other areas as well. One of the most important was literature, where the late ninth century witnessed the "triumph of the *waka*": that is, the firm and lasting adoption, after periods of flourishing of poetry written in Chinese, of the native thirty-one-syllable *waka* as the dominant, indeed virtually exclusive, medium of poetic expression. *Waka* poetry became the "queen of the arts," the supreme repository of the aesthetic tastes and social values of the Heian courtiers as they crafted their high culture in the tenth and early eleventh centuries. Lady Murasaki's *The Tale of Genji*, the world's first novel and the great masterpiece of Japanese literature, exemplifies the success of Japanese as the language of literature. Deeply indebted to China, Heian court culture was unique in its own right and became one of the supreme achievements of Japanese civilization.

Decline of the equal-field system brought, in the late eighth century, abandonment of military conscription, which had been part of the labor levy made under the system and had been used by the court to recruit and station units of soldiers (*gundan*) throughout the country. In 792, two years before its move to Heian, the court directed district magistrates in the provinces (a district was a subdivision of a province) to organize militias to maintain order locally. Although the court used mercenary armies in the first years of the Heian period to expand its authority in the eastern and northern provinces, thereafter it maintained no regular military force. Rather, it sought various ways to use members of the emerging warrior or samurai class to maintain order and deal with disputes in the provinces.

As the court, in making the transition to the Heian period, relinquished its direct control over the military arm of government, it also gradually allowed administration of the provinces in general to devolve into local hands. For example, although most provincial governors were selected from among the courtier class, they increasingly remained in the capital and allowed surrogates, often vice-governors who were local men (and frequently samurai), to manage the provincial governments.

The emergence of the provincial samurai class set the stage for the evolution—in a process that required several centuries— of John Hall's third state model of premodern Japan: **the feudal state.** Even as the courtier elite of Heian rose to its most splendid heights culturally in the tenth and early eleventh centuries, the provinces steadily came under the management of samurai headed by their own arms-bearing elite. Although this new elite and its followers by and large faithfully served the court in various provincial and even central governmental posts throughout the Heian period, it was destined eventually to supplant the courtiers as the country's real rulers and to establish the feudal form of state that lasted in Japan from the late twelfth until the late nineteenth century.

INDIA, 100 B.C.E.–1500

*Hermann Kulke and Dietmar Rothermund**

There is evidence of trade and cultural interchange between the Indian subcontinent and the ancient civilizations of the Mesopotamia region during the period of the Indus civilization and then later, during the Mauryan Empire, with Iran. [*See Embree, "South Asian History: A Cursory Review."*] Trade between India and the Mediterranean world is much better documented, however, during the Roman Empire. Somewhat later, there were many cultural and trading contacts with China and Southeast Asia. Some of these contacts are explored in the following essay by Professors Hermann Kulke and Dietmar Rothermund of the Sudasien-Institut at Heidelberg, Germany, which is taken from their work, *A History of India* (Delhi: Manohar, 1986), pp. 105–8, 152–61.

INTERNATIONAL TRADE AND THE ROMAN CONNECTION

An important aspect of early Indian history was the flourishing trade with Rome, especially in the first two centuries of the empire. In addition to earlier Greek reports, the Roman references to the trade with India provided the information on which the European image of India was based. The European discovery of India in the late medieval period by people like Marco Polo was in effect only a rediscovery of that miraculous country which was known to the ancient writers but had been cut off by the Arabs from direct contact with the West for several centuries. Hegel commented on the trade with India in his *Philosophy of History:* "The quest for India is a moving force of our whole history. Since ancient times all nations have directed their wishes and desires to that miraculous country whose treasures they coveted. These treasures were the most precious on earth: Treasures of nature,

---

*Reprinted with permission of the authors.

pearls, diamonds, incense, the essence of roses, elephants, lions etc. and also the treasures of wisdom. It has always been of great significance for universal history by which route these treasures found their way to the West, the fate of nations has been influenced by this."[1]

For India itself the trade with the West flourished most in ancient times. But when India's trade with Rome declined in the third and fourth centuries C.E., India, and especially South India, turned to Southeast Asia, where Indian influence became much more important than the vague impression which India had made on the nations of the West.

Indian trade with the countries around the Mediterranean goes back far before the Common Era. This early trade was probably conducted by isolated seafaring adventurers, and it was only under Emperor Augustus (30 B.C.E. to 14 C.E.) that it suddenly attained much greater dimensions. The Roman annexation of Egypt opened up the trade route through the Red Sea. Furthermore, after a century of civil war, Rome experienced a period of greater prosperity which increased demand for the luxury goods of the East, a demand which could not be met by means of the old cumbersome method of coastal shipping. Hippalus' discovery early in the first century C.E. that the monsoon could take a ship straight across the Arabian Sea in about a fortnight shortened the trade route and greatly eased access to the goods of the East. In subsequent years there was a great spurt of trading activity which was paralleled only many centuries later by the renewed European trade with India after Vasco da Gama's voyage of 1498.

A comparison of Strabo's geography, which was written at the time of Augustus (edited and amended between 17 and 23 C.E.), with the *Periplus of the Erythraean Sea*, which was written by an anonymous Greek merchant in the second half of the first century C.E., shows a great increase in Roman trade with India. Strabo was more interested in North India and in the ports between the mouth of the Indus and present Bombay, and he reported next to nothing about South India, Sri Lanka, and the east coast of India. The author of the *Periplus*, who probably visited India personally, described in detail the ports of the Malabar coast. When Ptolemy wrote his geography around 150 C.E., Roman knowledge of India had increased even more. He wrote about the east coast of India and also had a vague idea of Southeast Asia, especially about "Chryse," the "Golden Country" (*suvarnabhūmi*), as the countries of Southeast Asia had been known to the Indians since the first centuries C.E.

The most important port of the Malabar coast was Muziris

(Cranganore near Cochin) in the kingdom of Cerobothra (Chera-putra), which "abounds in ships sent there with cargoes from Arabia and by the Greeks." The *Periplus* reported on Roman trade with Malabar:

> They send large ships to the market-towns on account of the great quantity and bulk of pepper and malabathrum [cinnamon]. There are imported here, in the first place, a great quantity of coin; topaz, thin clothing, not much; figured linens, antimony, coral, crude glass, copper, tin, lead, wine, not much, but as much as at Barygaza [Broach]; realgar and orpiment; and wheat enough for the sailors, for this is not dealt in by the merchants there. There is exported pepper, which is produced in quantity in only one region near these markets, a district called Cottonora [north Malabar?]. Besides this there are exported great quantities of fine pearls, ivory, silk cloth, spikenard from the Ganges, malabathrum from the places in the interior, trans-parent stones of all kinds, diamonds and sapphires, and tortoise shell; that from Chryse Island, and that taken among the is-lands along the coast of Damirica [Tamil Nadu]. They make the voyage to this place in favorable season who set out from Egypt about the month of July, that is Epiphi.[2]

This provides evidence for a great volume of trade in both direc-tions, and also indicates that the South Indian ports served as entrepôts for silk from China, oil from the Gangetic plains, which was brought by Indian traders all the way to the tip of South India, and also precious stones from Southeast Asia. But, as far as the Eastern trade was concerned, the Coromandel Coast to the south of present Madras soon eclipsed the Malabar Coast. To the north of Cape Comorin (Kanya Kumari) was the kingdom of the Pandyas, where prisoners were made to dive for precious pearls in the ocean. Still further north there was a region called Argaru, which was perhaps the early Chola kingdom with its capital, Ura-iyur. The important ports of this coast were Kamara (Karikal), Poduka (Pondichery) and Sopatma (Supatama). Many centuries later European trading factories were put up near these places: the Danes established Tranquebar near Karikal, the French Pon-dichery, and the British opted for Madras, which was close to Supatama.

The British archaeologist Sir Mortimer Wheeler discovered in 1945 the remnants of an ancient port near the fishing village Arikamedu about two miles south of Pondichery. The great num-ber of Roman items found there seems to indicate that this was Poduka of the *Periplus*, called "New Town" (Puducceri) in Tamil.

Brick foundations of large halls and terraces were found, also cisterns and fortifications. Shards of Roman ceramics were identified as red polish ware which could be traced to Arezzo in Italy, where it was produced between 30 B.C.E. and 45 C.E. The finds of Arikamedu conjure up the image of a flourishing port like Kaveripatnam as described in an epic poem of the Sangam era:

> The sun shone over the open terraces, over the warehouses near the harbour and over the turrets with windows like eyes of deer. In different places of Puhar the onlooker's attention was caught by the sight of the abodes of Yavanas, whose prosperity never waned. At the harbour were to be seen sailors from many lands, but to all appearances they live as one community.[3]

This Kaveripatnam situated at the mouth of the Kaveri was probably identical with the emporium of Khaberis described by Ptolemy.

The trade with Rome brought large numbers of Roman gold coins to South India. In contrast with the Kushanas, who melted down all Roman coins and reissued them in their own name, the rulers of South India did not do this but simply defaced the coins. A sharp cut across the face of the Roman emperor indicated that his sovereignty was not recognized but his coins were welcome and would be accepted according to their own intrinsic value. Just as in later periods, the Indians imported very few goods but were eager to get precious metals, so the quest for Roman gold was the driving force of India's international trade in ancient times. The *Periplus* recorded this influx of coins and a text of the Sangam era also highlights this: "The beautifully built ships of the Yavanas came with gold and returned with pepper, and Muziris resounded with the noise."[4] Thus it is no accident that the largest number of Roman gold hoards have been found in the hinterland of Muziris. In the area around Coimbatore, through which the trade route from the Malabar coast led into the interior of South India, and on the east coast, eleven rich hoards of gold and silver Roman coins of the first century C.E. were found. Perhaps they were the savings of pepper planters and merchants or the loot of highwaymen who may have made this important trade route their special target.

THE TRANSMISSION OF INDIAN CULTURE TO SOUTHEAST ASIA

The transmission of Indian culture to distant parts of central Asia, China, Japan, and especially Southeast Asia is certainly one of the greatest achievements of Indian history or even of the history of mankind. None of the other great civilizations—not even the Hellenic—had been able to achieve a similar success without military conquest. In this brief survey of India's history, there is no room for an adequate discussion of the development of the "Indianized" states of Southeast Asia, which can boast of such magnificent temple cities as Pagan (Burma; constructed from 1044 to 1287 C.E.), Angkor (Cambodia; constructed from 889 to c. 1300 C.E.), and the Borobudur (Java; early ninth century C.E.). Though they were influenced by Indian culture, they are nevertheless part and parcel of the history of those respective countries. Here we will limit our observations to some fundamental problems concerning the transmission of Indian culture to the vast region of Southeast Asia.

Historians have formulated several theories regarding the transmission of Indian culture to Southeast Asia: (1) the "Kshatriya" theory; (2) the "Vaishya" theory; (3) the "Brahman" theory. The Kshatriya theory states that Indian warriors colonized Southeast Asia; this proposition has now been rejected by most scholars, although it was very prominent some time ago. The Vaishya theory attributes the spread of Indian culture to traders; it is certainly much more plausible than the Kshatriya theory, but does not seem to explain the large number of Sanskrit loan words in Southeast Asian languages. The Brahman hypothesis credits Brahmans with the transmission of Indian culture; this would account for the prevalence of these loan words, but may have to be amplified by some reference to the Buddhists as well as to the traders.

We shall return to these theories, but first we shall try to understand the rise and fall of the Kshatriya theory, which owed its origin to the Indian freedom movement. Indian historians, smarting under the stigma of their own colonial subjection, tried to compensate for this by showing that at least in ancient times Indians had been strong enough to establish colonies of their own. In 1926, the Greater India Society was established in Calcutta, and in subsequent years the renowned Indian historian R.C. Majumdar published his series of studies, *Ancient Indian Colonies in the Far East.* This school held that Indian kings and warriors had established such colonies, and the Sanskrit names of Southeast Asian rulers seemed to provide ample supporting evidence. At least this hypothesis stimulated further research, though it also alienated those intellectuals of Southeast Asia who rejected the idea of having once been colonized by a "Greater India." As research progressed, it was found that there was very little proof of any direct Indian political influence in those states of Southeast Asia. Furthermore, it was demonstrated that Southeast Asian rulers had adopted Sanskrit names themselves—thus such names could not be adduced as evidence for the presence of Indian kings.

The Vaishya theory, in contrast, emphasized a much more important element of the Indian connection with Southeast Asia. Trade had indeed been the driving force behind all these early contacts. Inscriptions also showed that guilds of Indian merchants had established outposts in many parts of Southeast Asia. Some of their inscriptions were written in languages such as Tamil. If such merchants had been the chief agents of the transmission of Indian culture, then all their languages should have made an impact on those of Southeast Asia. But this was not so: Sanskrit and, to some extent, Pali words predominated as loan words in Southeast Asian languages. The traders certainly provided an important transmission belt for all kinds of cultural influences. Nevertheless, they did not play the crucial role which some scholars have attributed to them. One of the most important arguments against the Vaishya theory is that some of the earliest traces of Indianized states in Southeast Asia are found not in the coastal areas usually frequented by the traders, but in mountainous, interior areas.

The Brahman theory is in keeping with what we have shown with regard to the almost contemporary spread of Hindu culture in southern and central India. There Brahmans and Buddhist and Jain monks played the major role in transmitting cultural values and symbols, and in disseminating the style of Hindu kingship. In addition to being religious specialists, the Brahmans also knew the Sanskrit codes regarding law (*dharmaśāstra*), the art of government (*arthaśāstra*), and art and architecture (*śilpaśāstra*). They could thus serve as "development planners" in many different fields and were accordingly welcome to Southeast Asian rulers who may have just emerged from what we earlier described as first- and second-phase state formation.

THE DYNAMICS OF CULTURAL BORROWING

What was the role of the people of Southeast Asia in this process of cultural borrowing? Were they merely passive recipients of a culture bestowed upon them by the Indians? Or did they actively participate in this transfer? The passive thesis was originally emphasized by Indian advocates of the "Greater India" idea, as well as by European scholars who belonged to the elite of the colonial powers then dominant in Southeast Asia. The concept of an earlier "Indianization" of Southeast Asia seemed to provide a close parallel with the later "Europeanization" under colonial rule. The first trenchant criticism of this point of view came from the young Dutch scholar J.C. van Leur.

Van Leur highlighted the great skill and courage of Indonesian seafarers and emphasized the fact that Indonesian rulers themselves had invited Indian Brahmans and had thus taken a very active role in the process of cultural borrowing. Van Leur's book on Indonesian trade and society was published posthumously, in 1955.[4] In the meantime, further research has vindicated his point of view.

The Indian influence is no longer regarded as the prime cause of cultural development; rather, it was a consequence of a development which was already in progress in Southeast Asia. Early Indonesian inscriptions show that there was a considerable development of agriculture, craftsmanship, regional trade, and social differentiation before Indian influence made itself felt. However, indigenous tribal organization was egalitarian and prevented the emergence of higher forms of political organization. The introduction of such forms required at least a rudimentary form of administration and a kind of legitimation of these new governmental forms which would make them, in the initial stages, acceptable to the people. It was at this point that chieftains and clan heads required Brahmin assistance. Although trade might have helped to spread the necessary information, the initiative came from those indigenous rulers. The invited Brahmans were isolated from the rural people and kept in touch only with their patrons. In this way the royal style emerged in Southeast Asia just as it had done in India.

A good example of this kind of development is provided by the earliest Sanskrit inscriptions found in Indonesia. Several inscriptions from around 400 C.E. on large megaliths mention a ruler whose name, Kundunga, shows not the slightest trace of Sanskrit influence. His son assumed a Sanskrit name, Ashvavarman, and founded a dynasty (*vaṃśa*). His grandson, Mulavarman, the author of the inscriptions, celebrated great sacrifices and gave valuable presents to the Brahmans. Of the latter it is explicitly stated that "they had come here"—most likely from India. After being consecrated by the Brahmans, Mulavarman subjected the neighboring rulers and made them "tribute givers" (*kara-dā*). Thus these inscriptions suggest the history of the rise of an early Indonesian dynasty. It seems that the dynasty had been founded by a son of a clan chiefly independently of the Brahmans, who on their arrival consecrated the ruler of the **third** generation. With this kind of moral support and the new administrative knowledge, the ruler could subject his neighbors and obtain tribute from them.

The process paralleled the rise of kingdoms in India, but in its initial stages it was not necessarily due to Indian influence. Around the middle of the first millennium C.E. several such small states seem to have arisen in this way in Southeast Asia. They have left only a few inscriptions and some ruins of temples; most of them were obviously very short-lived. There must have been a great deal of competition, with many petty rajas vying with each other and all wishing to be recognized as maharajas entitled to all the Indian paraphernalia of kingship. Indian influence increased in this way, and in the second half of the first millennium C.E. a hectic activity of temple erection could be observed on Java and in Cambodia, where the first larger realms had come into existence.

Though it is now generally accepted that Southeast Asian rulers played an active role in this process of state formation, we cannot entirely rule out the occasional direct contribution of Indian adventurers who proceeded to the East. The most important example of this kind is the early history of Funan at the mouth of the Mekong. Chinese sources report the tale of a Brahman, Kaundinya, who was inspired by a divine dream to go to Funan. There he vanquished the local Naga princess by means of his holy bow and married her, thus founding the first dynasty of Funan in the late first century C.E. There is a similar legend in connection with the rise of the Pallava Dynasty, and this may indicate that Kaundinya came from South India, where the Kaundinyas were known as a famous Brahman lineage. A Chinese source of the fourth century C.E. describes an Indian usurper of the throne of Funan; his name is given as Chu Chan-t'an (Zhu Zhantan). "Chu" always indicates a person of Indian origin and "Chan-t'an" could have been a transliteration of the title "Chandana," which can be traced to the Indo-Scythians of northern India. Presumably a member of that dynasty went to Southeast Asia after having been defeated by Samundragupta. In the beginning of the fifth century C.E. another Kaundinya arrived in Funan, and of him it is said in the Chinese annals:

> He was originally a Brahman from India. There a supernatu-
> ral voice told him: 'You must go to Funan.' Kaundinya rejoiced
> in his heart. In the South he arrived at P'an-p'an. The people of

Funan appeared to him; the whole kingdom rose up with joy, went before him and chose him king. He changed all the laws to conform to the system of India.[5]

This report on the second Kaundinya is the most explicit reference to an Indian ruler who introduced his laws in Southeast Asia. In the same period we notice a general wave of Indian influence in Southeast Asia, for which the earliest Sanskrit inscriptions of Indonesia—discussed above—also provide striking evidence. We must, however, note that even in this case of early Funan there was no military intervention. Kaundinya had obviously stayed for some time at P'an-p'an at the Isthmus of Siam, then under the control of Funan, and he was later invited by the notables of the court of Funan to ascend the throne at a time of political unrest.

THE CONTRIBUTION OF THE BUDDHIST MONKS

So far we have discussed the contribution of Brahmins to the early transmission of Indian culture to Southeast Asia. Buddhist monks, however, were at least as important in this respect. Two characteristic features of Buddhism enabled it to make a specific impact on Southeast Asia: first, Buddhists were imbued with a strong missionary zeal; and, second, they ignored the caste system and did not emphasize the idea of ritual purity. By his teaching as well as by the organization of his monastic order (sangha), Gautama Buddha had given rise to this missionary zeal, which had then been fostered by Ashoka's dispatch of Buddhist missionaries to western Asia, Greece, central Asia, Sri Lanka and Burma.

Buddhism's freedom from ritual restrictions and the spirit of the unity of all adherents enabled Buddhist monks to establish contact with people abroad, as well as to welcome them in India when they came to visit the sacred places of Buddhism. Chinese sources record 162 visits to India of Chinese Buddhist monks for the period from the fifth to the eighth century C.E. Many more may have traveled without having left a trace in such official records. This was an amazing international scholarly exchange program for that day and age.

In the early centuries C.E. the center of Buddhist scholarship was the University of Taxila (near the present city of Islamabad), but in the fifth century C.E., when the University of Nalanda was founded not far from Bodh Gaya, Bihar, the center of Buddhist scholarship shifted to eastern India. This university always had a large contingent of students from Southeast Asia. There they spent many years close to the holy places of Buddhism, copying and translating texts before returning home. Nalanda was a center of Mahayana Buddhism, which became of increasing importance in Southeast Asia. King Balaputra of Shrivijaya established a monastery for students of his realm at Nalanda around 860 C.E., which was then endowed with land grants by King Devepala of Bengal. But the Sumatran empire of Shrivijaya had acquired a good reputation in its own right among Buddhist scholars and from the late seventh century C.E. attracted resident Chinese and Indian monks. The Chinese monk I-tsing visited Shrivijaya's capital for six months in 671 C.E. in order to learn Sanskrit grammar. He then proceeded to India, where he spent 14 years, and on his return journey he stayed another four years at Palembang so that he could translate the many texts which he had collected. In this period he went to China for a few months in 689 to recruit assistants for his great translation project (completed in 695). On his return to China he explicitly recommended that other Chinese Buddhists proceeding to India break journey in Shrivijaya, where a thousand monks lived by the same rules as those prevailing in India. In subsequent years many Chinese Buddhists conscientiously followed this advice.

Prominent Indian Buddhist scholars similarly made a point of visiting Shrivijaya. Towards the end of the seventh century C.E. Dharmapala of Nalanda is supposed to have visited Suvarnadvipa (Java and Sumatra). In the beginning of the eighth century C.E. the South Indian monk Vajrabodhi spent five months in Shrivijaya on his way to China. He and his disciple, Amoghvajra, whom he met in Java, are credited with having introduced Buddhist Tantrism to China. Atisha, who later became known as the great reformer of Tibetan Buddhism, is said to have studied for twelve years in Suvarnadvipa in the early eleventh century C.E. The high standard of Buddhist learning which prevailed in Indonesia for many centuries was one of the important preconditions for that great work of art, the Borobudur, whose many reliefs are a pictorial compendium of Buddhist lore, a tribute both to the craftsmanship of Indonesian artists and to the knowledge of Indonesian Buddhist scholars.

THE LINK BETWEEN SOUTHEAST ASIA AND SOUTH INDIA

Indian historians have conducted a heated debate for many decades about the relative merits of different Indian regions with regard to the spread of Indian influence in Southeast Asia. Nowadays there seems to be a consensus that, at least as far as the early centuries of the Common Era are concerned, South India—and especially Tamil Nadu—deserves the greatest credit for this achievement. In subsequent periods, however, several regional shifts as well as parallel influences emanating from various centers can be noticed. The influence of Tamil Nadu was very strong as far as the earliest inscriptions in Southeast Asia are concerned, showing as they do the influence of the script prevalent in the Pallava kingdom. The oldest Buddhist sculpture in Southeast Asia—the famous bronze Buddha of Celebes—shows the marks of the Buddhist sculptures of Amaravati (Coastal Andhra) of the third to the fifth centuries C.E. Early Hindu sculptures of western Java and of the Isthmus of Siam seem to have been guided by the Pallava style of the seventh and eighth centuries C.E. Early Southeast Asian temple architecture similarly shows the influence of the Pallava and Chola styles, especially on Java and in Cambodia.

The influence of the North Indian Gupta style also made itself felt from the fifth century C.E. onward. The center of this school was Sarnath, near Varanasi (Benares), where Buddha preached his first sermon. Sarnath produced the classical Buddha image, which influenced the art of Burma and Thailand, as well as that of Funan at the mouth of the Mekong. The art of the Shailendra dynasty of Java in the eighth and ninth centuries—of which the Borobudur is the most famous monument—was obviously influenced by what is termed the Late Gupta style of western central India, as manifested in the great cave temples of Ajanta and Ellora. An inscription at the Plaosan temple in central Java (c. 800 C.E.) explicitly refers to the "constant flow of the people from Gurjaradesha [Gujarat and adjacent regions]"—due to which this temple had been built. Indeed, the temple's sculptures show a striking similarity with those of the late Buddhist caves of Ajanta and Ellora.

In later centuries Southeast Asia was more and more influenced by the scholars of the University of Nalanda and the style of the Pala dynasty, the last of the great Indian dynasties which bestowed royal patronage on Buddhism. The influence of Mahayana Buddhism prevailing in Bihar and Bengal under the Palas was so strong at the court of the Shailendras of Java that a Buddhist monk from "Gaudi" (Bengal), with the typical Bengali name of Kumara Ghosh, became rajguru of the Shailendra king and in this capacity consecrated a statue of Manjushri in the royal temple of the Shailendras in 782. Bengal, eastern Bihar, and Orissa were at that time centers of cultural influence. These regions were in constant contact with Southeast Asia, whose painters and sculptors reflected the style of eastern India in their works. Typical of this aesthetic was the special arrangement of figures surrounding the central figure: this type of arrangement can be found both in Indonesian sculptures and in the temple paintings of Pagan (Burma) during this period.

In the same era South Indian influence emerged once more under the Chola Dynasty. Maritime trade was of major import- ance to the Cholas, who thereby also increased their cultural influences. The occasional military interventions of the Cholas did not detract from this peaceful cultural intercourse. On the north- ern coast of Sumatra the old port of Dilli, near Medan, had great Buddha sculptures evincing a local variation of the Chola style; indeed, a magnificent statue of the Hindu god Ganesha, in the pure Chola style, has recently been found at the same place. Close to the famous temple of Padang Lawas, central Sumatra, small but very impressive Chola-style bronze sculptures of a four- armed Lokanath and of Tara have been found. These sculptures are now in the museum of Jakarta. They are dated at 1039 C.E., and a brief inscription containing Old Malay words in addition to Sanskrit words—but no Tamil words—proves that the figures were not imported from India but were produced locally.

Nevertheless, Chola relations with Southeast Asia were by no means a one-way street. It is presumed that the imperial cult of the Cholas, centered on their enormous temples, was directly influenced by the grand style of Angkor. The great tank at Gangaikondacholapuram was perhaps conceived by the Chola ruler in the same spirit as that which moved the Cambodian rulers who ordered the construction of the famous Barays (tanks) of Angkor, which are considered to be a special indication of royal merit.

In the late thirteenth century Pagan (Burma) was once more exposed to a strong current of direct Indian influence emanating from Bengal, at that time conquered by Islamic rulers. Nalanda had been destroyed by the end of the twelfth century, and large groups of monks in search of a new home flocked to Pagan and also to the Buddhist centers of Tibet. The beautiful paintings in the temples of Minnanthu in the eastern part of the city of Pagan may have been due to them.

Islamic conquest cut off the holy places of Buddhism. A millen- nium of intensive contacts between India and Southeast Asia had come to an end. There was another factor, however, which must be mentioned in this context. In 1190 Chapata, a Buddhist monk from Pagan, returned to that city after having spent ten years in Sri Lanka. In Burma he founded a branch of the Theravada school of Buddhism, established on the strict rules of the Mahavihara monastery of Sri Lanka. This led to a schism in the Burmese Buddhist order which had been established at Pagan by Shin Arahan about 150 years earlier. Shin Arahan was a follower of the South Indian school of Buddhism, which had its center at Kanchipuram. Chapata's reform prevailed and by the thirteenth and fourteenth centuries Burma, Thailand, and Cambodia had adopted Theravada Buddhism of the Sri Lanka school. In Cambodia this shift from Mahayana to Theravada Buddhism seems to have been part of a sociocultural revolution. Under the last great king of Angkor, Jayavarman VII (1181–1218), royal Mahayana Buddhism had become associated in the eyes of the people with the enormous burden which the king imposed upon them in order to build the Buddhist temples of Angkor Thom (e.g., the gigantic Bayon).

Even in Indonesia, however, where Tantrist Buddhism with an admixture of Shaivism prevailed at the courts of rulers all the way from Sumatra down to Bali, direct Indian influence rapidly receded in the thirteenth century. This was only partly due to the intervention of Islam in India, its other cause being an upsurge of Javanese art which confined the influence of Indian art to the statues of deified kings erected after the death of the ruler. The outer walls of the temples were covered with Javanese reliefs which evince a great similarity to the Javanese shadowplay (*wayang kulit*). The Chandi Jago (thirteenth century) and the temples of Panantaran (fourteenth century) show this new Javanese style very well. It has remained the dominant style of Bali art up to the present time. A similar trend toward the assertion of indigenous styles can also be found in the Theravada Buddhist countries. The content of the scenes depicted is still derived from Hindu mythology or Buddhist legends, but the presentation clearly incorporates the respective national style.

THE IMPACT OF ISLAM

After conquests in India by Muslim rulers, Islam also spread to Southeast Asia via the maritime trade routes which connected India with the spice islands of the East. We find the first traces of Islam in Atjeh (north Sumatra) at the end of the thirteenth century and in Malaya in the early fourteenth century. In the fifteenth century Islam penetrated the interiors of the respective countries, whereas it had hitherto been mostly confined to the coasts. Just as rulers at an earlier stage of Southeast Asian history had found it convenient to adopt an Indian religion, they now found the Islamic creed helpful in many respects.

India once more became an important transmitter of cultural influences under the new dispensation. The oldest tombstones of Muslim rulers and traders in Southeast Asia point to an influence from western India, mainly Gujarat, whose traders played a major role in the spice trade from Indonesia via India to the ports of western Asia. But Muslim traders of the Coromandel coast were also active in this connection. In 1445 Tamil Muslim traders even staged a coup at Malacca, installing a sultan of their choice. In this way they greatly enhanced their influence in an area of great strategic importance. However, a few decades later the Portuguese conqueror of Goa, Albuquerque, captured Malacca with nineteen ships and eight hundred Portuguese soldiers. Thus, after a millennium of intensive intercourse, the era of European influence started for India and Southeast Asia at about the same time.

NOTES

1. G.W.F. Hegel, *Vorlesungen über die Philosophie der Geschichte* (Stuttgart: Reclam, 1961), pp. 215ff.
2. W.H. Schoff, trans., *The Periplus of the Erythraean Sea* (London: Longmans, Green, 1912), pp. 44ff.
3. Quoted in R.E.M. Wheeler, *Rome Beyond the Imperial Frontiers* (London: Bell, 1954), p. 133.
4. J.C. van Leur, *Indonesian Trade and Society* (The Hague: W. Van Hoeve, 1955).
5. P. Pelliot, "Le Fou-nan," *Bulletin de l'école française d'extréme-orient* 3 (1903): 269.

SEPARATE SPHERES AND NEW LINKS: A NEW STAGE IN WORLD HISTORY, 1000–1500

Peter N. Stearns

INTRODUCTION

This essay focuses on two interrelated challenges in teaching and conceptualizing world history during a crucial half-millennium: first, how to deal with the time period itself as anything besides a grab bag of facts or a waiting room between dramatic developments like the rise of Islam and the rise of the West. And second, how to maintain a geographical balance that will retain appropriate, though in no sense disproportionate, focus on the civilization of Asia during this time. It is unquestionably easy, particularly for world history teachers reluctantly lured away from a Western civilization tradition, to dismiss China after its classical age with a fleeting more-of-the-same tag, while neglecting India altogether—leaving India's history disconnected—between its formative centuries through the Guptas and the return of "coherence" under British domination. Ultimately, geographical balance and thematic emphasis must intertwine to create a picture of the period in which Asian civilizations, and connections among them, receive both due emphasis and essential continuity.

The twin challenges can be met, but not without some serious attention and more than the usual dollop of creative imagination in spinning out coherent frameworks. There is no need, in addressing the challenges, to introduce great ranges of underutilized facts—some conventional coverage might indeed be pruned. The task is mainly conceptual in highlighting a few keynotes of the period, and Asia's central place in it, that not only make the era teachable, but give it some claim to central importance in the larger sweep of world history.

THE CONCEPTUAL CHALLENGE: SEEKING COHERENCE

The period between 1000 and 1500 is one of the most difficult to teach in the entire span of world history. Earlier periods are sustained by the advent of agriculture and the invention of civilization itself, illustrated then by the river-valley examples, and followed by the flowering of the great classical civilizations, happily few enough in number to permit some comparisons. The next period, after the fall or adjustment of the classical empires, when West-based images of decline and darkness or Eurasian emphases on interaction predominated, is more problematic, although the rise of Islam and the spread of new belief systems now give this period some coherence and analytical vigor. But what after 1000? Islam remains a dominant force but soon in its Arab version loses some of its organizing power as the caliphate declines and earlier cultural diversity comes under new attack in the Middle East. The theme of conversion from animism to some form of monotheism continues to apply in certain instances, as in the spread of Islam to the Middle Eastern countryside and to the elites in the Sudanic kingdoms of Africa, but the basic thrust has already been established despite the importance of the individual new cases. What gives thematic coherence to the next five centuries?

The question follows from the need to establish world history as a framework that goes beyond a somewhat random collection of separate histories. A great deal went on, in various parts of the world, in the centuries after 1000 C.E. The issue is how to make some sense of the mass of detail, how to identify some larger patterns, as can be done for earlier periods around mechanisms such as the spread of agricultural technology, the rise of civilization and then the classical empires, or the larger trend of shifting belief structures toward one of the great world religious systems. The goal is always elusive, in that not all societies neatly fit the predominant patterns (China, to cite an obvious case, needs special handling in the world religions unit, though through Buddhism the transcendental theme accurately if distinctively relates China to larger world developments). Nevertheless, an ability to conceptualize world history in terms of patterns, to make chronological breaks more than haphazard pauses for breath, is one of the real challenges in teaching an effective world history course, where goals other than maximum possible memorization are sought; indeed, the challenge has been great enough to propel world history into the realm of active scholarly research.

One of the obvious candidates for thematic priority for the half-millennium after 1000 is, simply, the **spread and proliferation of civilization.** Roots of the phenomenon lie earlier, to be sure. But it is in this period that the Sudanic kingdoms and Zimbabwe blossom in Africa, along with Arabized settlements down the eastern coast. Civilization in sub-Saharan Africa moves from fascinating but rather isolated pockets to the mainstream of contact and interaction. The period falls a bit late to catch the most dynamic Mayan period in Central America, but it is a fairly good point to deal with the later manifestations of Amerindian civilizations in this region and with the Inca rise in the Andes. Still more recent antecedents prepare discussion of the flowering of Kievan Russia and the development of feudal Japan. The migrations of new peoples and the establishment of new kingdoms in Southeast Asia, along with the impact of Islam in part of the region, brings the spread or elaboration of civilization theme to yet another part of the world. So does the increasing inclusion of Scandinavia and northern Germany in the Western orbit. Some historians would even point to the migration of Polynesian peoples as another example of the same phenomenon. Because of contact with areas of more established civilization (the cases of Russia, northern Europe, Japan) or an ability to build on earlier but often more purely regional civilizations (the Americas, sub-Saharan Africa) or simply new migration and exploration, civilization developed far more outcroppings around 1000 than had been the case before. Tracing these outcroppings is unquestionably one of the major tasks of a world history that deals seriously with the period.

Yet this focus, while valid, has obvious drawbacks as a main theme. It is centrifugal. It risks so much attention to individual cases that any sense of larger coherence is lost. The civilizations are of greatly different types, from cultures without writing (Benin, Polynesia, the Incas) to established centers of literate culture, from empires to fragmented regional monarchies. General definitions almost always miss the mark. Some historians have even proposed using the fragmentation theme as the basic labeling device for the period, and without much question coherence is harder to come by than in earlier eras. Yet, while the proliferation-of-civilizations idea has merit, and must be introduced, it need not be taken to the point of world-historical anarchy. Several foci can supplement the proliferation device to introduce some larger order.

THE GEOGRAPHICAL CHALLENGE:
THE CALL OF THE WEST

One of the difficulties encountered in teaching world history during this period is what might be called waiting for the Western shoe to drop. We all know that the West is about to "rise" by the fifteenth century. Here will be a clear focus for world history (though this simplification, too, must be qualified); small wonder that even responsibly nonethnocentric historians, from a Western-history background, may be tempted to race through this period mainly to explain how and why the West got going. Less responsible world historians indeed continue to label the period "medieval," as if all civilizations can be defined by the West's growing pains.

It is certainly legitimate, as part of civilizational coverage after 1000, to note the growing political, economic, and intellectual sophistication of western Europe during its High Middle Ages, along with important changes in social structure including a loosening of serfdom and the rise of a merchant class. The West's outreach into the wider world, through new trading and cultural contacts around the Mediterranean and through the Crusades, form an important part of this survey and prepare for some rebalancing of the relative strengths of different civilizations compared to the previous period. Even knowing what was to happen after 1500, however, it is important to keep the sketch of Western transformation relatively modest, making it clear that this civilization remained a partial backwater in the overall civilizational map. Various comparative devices can help drive this point home without distracting from the theme of important Western change. Russia, like the West, was in a period of development (and until about 1100 superior to the West in metalworking technology) that would yield important fruit later on. The proud emergence of strengthened feudal monarchies in the West, though unquestionably significant and promising some further change, allowed the West to reach approximately the same level of political sophistication as the major African kingdoms in the period.

It is also true that as the West entered wider world contacts after 1000 C.E., it did so primarily as borrower—of goods that it could not produce itself, of ideas that it had forgotten or failed to develop. The very **inferiority of the West** in the world was indeed to help motivate the West to deal with pressing resultant problems, notably an adverse balance of payments situation with Asia that helped whet the Western appetite both for new trade routes—

sought from the thirteenth century onward, though long abortively—and for gold. The ability to react constructively and aggressively to problems caused by inferiority constituted no small Western talent, as things turned out, but the inferiority itself was the dominant fact of the half-millennium before outright Western expansion.

Identifying qualifications of the Western-transformation theme, however, through comparison and careful analysis of ongoing inferiority in commercial and cultural exchange serves mainly to improve the presentation of Western history itself; it only begins the process of broadening into a genuine world history for the period. And it must be admitted that students can easily dismiss evidence of Western inferiority as, at best, an interesting curiosity, a prelude to the rise of "their own" civilization to the superior position that (they sometimes rather desperately hope) it can still maintain. Caveats are useful, but they can only go so far.

The obvious geographical starting point for coverage of the period is not the West at all, despite its ascending importance, but the civilizations of Asia. With due acknowledgement of the Byzantine Empire as a partially European society, and of the important North African and Spanish extensions of West Asian Islam, the **key centers of the world were solidly Asian.** The Indian Ocean remained the world's leading international waterway, enhanced by the extension of trade to East Africa. China was the world's most solidly organized political unit, its leading rival Byzantium and the caliphate. China also remained the world's leading center of technological innovation and, for the fascinating moment under the early Ming, its leading trading power. Despite important oscillations in fortune, China, India, and the Middle East remained the most dynamic commercial centers, with the most highly developed urban cultures and the greatest overall wealth—as early Western visitors would readily attest. Asia was, by all relevant measurements, the center of the world through the centuries following 1000 C.E. Its relative prominence was in many ways even greater than during the Classical era, when Greece and then Rome had constituted clearer rival claimants. Asia's central importance was indeed the source of the Western disadvantages already discussed and the stimulus to the West's zeal for more effective contacts and compensatory trading stakes. Any treatment of world history for the half-millennium thus logically begins with the key Asian societies, and only after their characteristics and evolution are firmly established moves on to the other continents.

It is possible, indeed, to sketch a "development" model for this period that can be usefully compared to more familiar models used later in a world history course. The great Asian societies constituted the developed world, in terms of wealth, commercial sophistication, and political skills in controlling large territories. Societies that came into new contact with Asia, such as those of western Europe or the Sudanic kingdoms beginning with Mali, readily perceived the relevance of Asian superiority and tried to figure out a combination of imitation and compensation that might bring them closer to the same levels. The process was less full-blown than the development challenges the West would later pose to the rest of the world, but it has some similarities worth exploring in order to structure a basic comparative framework that begins, accurately, with Asian world leadership.

CHANGE AND CONTINUITY

In addition to the proliferation-of-civilization theme, as a first but inadequate way of conceptualizing the period after 1000, and to a balance-of-power statement that begins with Asian superiority, three other, overlapping conceptual schemes provide a framework for more specific developments during the five-century span.

The first focuses on Asia itself, and may usefully have been applied in covering the immediately preceding centuries. The historian's basic questions about change and continuity apply readily to the key Asian centers. Most world history courses, of necessity, focus initially on establishing the basic themes of each civilization and, it is hoped, on instilling some comparative sense, as between Chinese and Mediterranean political and intellectual emphases or differences in the role of merchants and technology. By the time a course reaches 1000 C.E., students should be ready for a richer analytical diet, while maintaining consideration of the earlier comparative framework. They are ready, in sum, to pay more coherent attention to the issue of change over time, and not simply in terms of obvious signposts such as Rome's fall or the destruction of the Gupta Empire.

Attention to **a more nuanced approach to change and continuity** is particularly essential for the established Asian civilizations, though it also entails an analytical style that abler students can learn to apply to other cases, even to other history courses. The fact is that, having mastered some essentials about India or China, many students will try to simplify their lot by returning to these staples for as long as possible. They will eagerly seize on the claim—correct to a point—that China tended to preserve or revive key features of the imperial, bureaucratic, and Confucian legacies, or that two durable features of Indian history involve Hinduism and caste. What is needed, clearly, is a carefully presented understanding that even a relatively stable civilization, where continuities are indeed considerable, undergoes more than superficial change, and that this was also true well before the flurries and alarms of the recent, modern centuries.

Introducing students to changes in China's bureaucratic tradition, toward a refinement of the scholar-gentry model, and to innovative uses of Confucianism by Zhu Xi [Chu Hsi] constitutes a vital corrective both to Chinese history as it evolved after 1000 C.E. and to a larger sense of historical analysis. Still more important is consideration of the increasingly vibrant urban economy and culture created by the Song dynasty as a significant new theme in Chinese history, though one that was successfully integrated into the political and cultural framework.

India can be handled in similar terms, though here the new political landscape and the challenge of Islam call attention to change more readily than is the case with China. India's continued religious evolution, its emendations of the caste system, maintain the overall emphasis on looking to a combination of innovation and tradition as a "normal" historical framework.

The obvious point, in launching substantive consideration of the 1000–1500 period, is that several civilization areas—Byzantium and Islam as well as India and China—had well-established traditional structures which were not, however, stagnant. Use of the change/continuity framework simultaneously calls attention to the primary importance of the Asian civilizations, to major developments in the five-century span, and to a vital analytical approach of even greater potential scope.

EXPANSION OF THE CIVILIZED WORLD AND THE CONCEPT OF ZONES

After an initial, Asia-centered segment, unified through the change/continuity lens, the next conceptual task in covering world history 1000–1500 involves making sense of the proliferation-of-civilization theme. Here, attention widens from an Asian base but continues to utilize this base in several ways.

For while each of the new civilizations or culture areas deserves attention, a larger conceptual framework can restrain the fragmentation process. The fact is that **three major civilizational zones** emerged in this period, and understanding the generic features of each prepares for more specific coverage. The most important civilizations combined well-established traditions and sophisticated commercial and political forms with ongoing innovation—the Asian plus Byzantine cases already described. A second set of civilizations developed in areas where civilization itself was novel but where contacts developed with the more powerful centers, such that a variety of techniques and ideas could be borrowed. Political systems were less elaborate, economies less developed than in the first zone—these were areas of less wealth and more decentralized political structures. Through borrowing, however, a world religion and other relatively advanced cultural forms could gain ground fairly quickly, while Asian-originated technologies—papermaking is an interesting case in point for the period—could be imitated. Here is a framework in which newer centers of Asian civilization—Japan and parts of Southeast Asia—can be discussed along with western Europe, Russia, and (at a slight remove in terms of extent of contact) the Sudanic kingdoms. All constitute cases in which borrowing speeded development but in which distinct prior traditions and the sheer novelty of civilization produced values and institutions separate from those of the advanced centers.

Finally, some civilizations developed entirely separately from the first two zones, sharing neither ideas nor more fundamental biological contacts. The Amerindian civilizations constitute the most important instance of this third zone, but Polynesia also fits, and so to a degree do some of the more isolated centers of African advance such as Zimbabwe or Benin. These cultures are important, and their characteristics must be sketched; but they by definition impose a case-by-case approach.

Southeast Asia, the fringe areas of East Asia, plus northern and western Europe and parts of sub-Saharan Africa are a different matter, allowing some common treatment in terms of what could be borrowed from the more established centers, when and why the borrowing took place, and how the results mixed with regional traditions such as European or Japanese feudalism. The common treatment in turn permits some overall comparisons between these new centers and the older civilization areas or among the new centers themselves—as in comparing Japan's relationship to China with Russia's to the Byzantine Empire. Distinctive features in each case must still be noted, but random fragmentation is minimized. Finally, the West's important surge can be seen as part of a common process of civilization's extension where certain shortcuts were possible through imitation and dissemination from the older centers in creative combination with regional features.

The zonal approach is of necessity generalized. Specifics on the individual cases can and should be introduced as time permits. The fact remains, however, that by 1000 C.E. new patterns of imitation and dissemination had developed, worthy of attention in their own right and providing a focused comparative framework for societies too often compartmentalized in separate sections of a textbook or a lecture series. Zone features can also be utilized in explaining subsequent developments in world history, including reactions to the West, again to help focus a comparative approach. Finally, attention to the new kinds of contacts developing in the Asian–European–African world leads to the most important single development in world history in the centuries after 1000 C.E.: the enhancement of intercivilizational contacts on a variety of fronts.

A WORLD NETWORK

Various world historians have argued that by the year 1000, though with some preparation in the immediately preceding centuries based particularly on the expansion of Arab Islam and attendant trading networks, a regular chain of linkages had developed among the major civilizations in the world, particularly in Asia and eastern Europe but extending to western Europe and important parts of Africa, sub-Saharan as well as Mediterranean. Putting the same point another way: by 1000, intercivilizational contacts had shifted from being largely tangential to the development of major regions to playing a central role, and from being sporadic (an invasion, a particular cultural effusion) to being fairly consistent. Levels of trade and of cultural and technological exchange had expanded notably from the patterns of the classical world, where contacts, while interesting, were either a luxury (the silk trade) or occasional and unusual (the Hellenistic-Indian moment).

No single, sharp point denotes **the emergence of a world network,** and obviously major portions of the globe were still entirely omitted, as the zonal analysis already suggests. The spread of major religions—Buddhism, Islam, and Christianity, plus Hinduism in a few cases—beyond their "home" region had presaged more regular and significant interactions among civilizations of the three Old World continents, with Asian initiatives characteristically playing a leading role. A focus on the nature and impact of intercivilizational contacts between 1000 and 1500 C.E. highlights the most important world-historical development of the period, beyond the sheer spread of civilizations, which the extending contacts in fact help explain. The increasing involvement particularly of Southeast Asia, and to a lesser degree Japan and the various regions of northern and western Europe, in the commercial and cultural exchange process constituted a key ingredient of the whole process of heightened interaction.

Not only is a grasp of the emergence of a world network, even in its first, somewhat halting phase, vital in describing the period itself as more than a disparate factual melange; it also prepares students to perceive a phenomenon larger, older, and more significant than the more familiar "world united through the West" approach that will become tempting after 1500.

The world-network theme can be partially explained and illustrated by giving particular focus to the nomadic movements that so frequently linked the major Asian civilizations during these centuries—the expansion of the Turkic peoples, touching all three of the major Asian centers, and then the Mongol surge. Here, after all, were ingredients of recurrent political change and commercial rebalancing throughout much of Asia, stretching into eastern Europe as well. Here also were vital sources of intercivilizational contact, from the spread of paper to the Middle East via Turkic soldiers the Arabs encountered on China's western borders, to the wider opportunity for dissemination of Chinese and southern Asian products and technologies during the Mongol heyday.

A focus on the Mongol Empire, as part of the process of international dissemination, and on its immediate consequences into the fifteenth century, including the Ottoman conquests and the commercial expansion and withdrawal of the early Ming, indeed logically draws consideration of this period to a close. The Eurasian–North African world was closer in 1500, in some respects, than it would be for another five centuries—certainly closer to equality in technological levels than for a long time before and after, as a result of the series of exchanges, flowing primarily from Asia and capped by the communications possible under Mongol rule. At the same time another set of exchanges was about to begin, primarily though by no means exclusively under European sponsorship, that would build on the world network established after 1000 C.E.

CONCLUSION

Exploration of the period 1000–1500 in terms of a skein of major themes: proliferation of civilizations, the preeminence and evolution of the leading Asian centers, and a set of civilizational zones based on relationships to the expanding network of international contacts, provides both balance and coherence, though with some undeniable but pedagogically manageable complexity. It was neither surprising nor novel that the world encompassed several major currents of development. Reliance on the major themes, with expansions on individual regions or topics within the framework they set, offers another advantage, beyond the entry provided into a complex half-millennium whose coverage is often needlessly fragmented. An approach to the subsequent period is suggested that can go beyond the rise-of-the-West label that students seize on all too readily. Change would come after 1500, of course, including a rebalancing of which the West was the major beneficiary. Exchanges in the previous period ironically helped prepare this shift. But world history after 1500 would continue to witness diverse manifestations of the heightened level of international exchange, with Asia affected, for example by new foodstuffs, along with Europe. Asian civilizations, several reformed in new empires, would continue a pattern of change building on tradition. The early modern world, in other words, was by no means a world entirely transformed, precisely because of the possibility of building on the patterns set during the previous centuries. While the West's rise (and that of Russia) was dramatic, its study must be balanced by a recognition of other, ongoing themes, including Asian strengths and continuities and the elaboration of international contacts undergirding the efflorescence of any particular society.

The world by 1500 might, indeed, be tentatively compared to the world in the later twentieth century, in an analogy that spurs analysis of both points in time. A growing series of international contacts, capped by a short century of far-flung empires (the Mongol holdings of the fourteenth century, the European of the nineteenth), yielded to a time of rebalancing, with the predominant powers of the previous period challenged by new and undeniably more dynamic upstarts. Ironically, the challenger of 1500 became by the later twentieth century the challenged, and a leading source of renewed dynamism came from Asia's rim. Grasp of the world linkages established during the centuries before 1500, with their implications for relations among leading civilizations and those of a second zone in contact with the leaders but capable of distinctive formulations, may aid in understanding the complex results of the modern world linkages that rose on the earlier foundations. Here is a final means of utilizing the central features of the premodern world network and the attendant transformations of Asia and its neighbor civilizations, and of grasping their crucial position in the larger evolution of world history.

SELECTED REFERENCES

For a more elaborate discussion of world history periodization, see Peter N. Stearns, "Periodization in World History Teaching: Identifying the Big Changes," *History Teacher* (1987): 561–80. William McNeil is noteworthy for his specificity about 1000–1500, as a world history span, and about the network or ecumene concept; see *The Rise of the West* (Chicago: University of Chicago Press, 1970) and *A World History*, 3d ed. (New York: Oxford University Press, 1979).

General perspectives on the period from an Asian vantage point are less numerous than one might hope, if only because of the pronounced area studies focus that has led both to major research advances and to a certain narrowness of focus. An important recent study is K.N. Chaudhuri, *Trade and Civilization in the Indian Ocean: An Economic History from the Rise of Islam to 1750* (Cambridge: Cambridge University Press, 1985). See also Jerry H. Bentley, *Old World Encounters: Cross-Cultural Contacts and Exchanges in Pre-Modern Times* (New York: Oxford University Press, 1993). Other cross-cutting studies include Luc Kwanten, *Imperial Nomads: A History of Central Asia 500–1500* (Philadelphia: University of Pennsylvania Press, 1979) and Jonathan Spence, *The Memory Palace of Matteo Ricci* (New York: Viking Penguin, 1984). For a discussion of recent monographic work on China in the period, including Ming trade policies, see Harriet Zurndorfer, "The 'New' Social and Economic History of China (1000–1800)," *International Review of Social History* 32 (1988): 148–201.

On other key areas and topics: Marshall G.S. Hodgson, *The Expansion of Islam in the Middle Periods*, vol. 2, *The Venture of Islam* (Chicago: University of Chicago Press, 1964); S.M. Ikram, *Muslim Civilization in India* (New York: Columbia University Press, 1964); R.C. Majumdar, *The History and Culture of the Indian People*, vol. 6, *The Delhi Sultanate* (Bombay: Bharatiya Vidya Bhavan, 1980); John W. Hall and T. Toyoda, *Japan in the Muromachi Age* (Berkeley: University of California Press, 1977).

THE CASE OF CHINA, 1000–1500

Michael Marmé

Any account of China between 1000 and 1500 must begin with the superlatives. Especially when compared with the petty kingdoms and internecine struggles of Europe, Song China (960–1279) had much of which to boast: a centralized bureaucratic empire, the world's largest standing army, an expanding population, huge cities, an active commerce, thriving manufactures, breakthroughs in the arts of peace (printing) and war (gunpowder), an increasingly open social order.

Impressive as they are, to those who lived between 1000 and 1500 such achievements were either the source of problems or problematic in themselves. Barbarian kingdoms on the northern border were a constant reminder that China did not inspire the awe it should in All under Heaven. Nor was the empire able to mobilize the resources needed to enforce its claims. Economic expansion and demographic growth were accompanied by a southward shift in China's economic, political, and cultural center of gravity. In the process, the original locus of Chinese culture was eclipsed, the nature of its peasant agriculture transformed (as wet-rice culture became dominant). Change always produces losers as well as winners, but, under such conditions, it is not surprising that both were left with a nagging sense of insecurity. Simultaneously, printing increased access to canonical texts and literacy expanded. Although half those qualified to hold office in Song had benefited from some form of special privilege, the empire's social, cultural, and political elite (the scholar-officials) were acutely aware of the competitive pressures inherent in an examination system. They needed a new understanding of reality, one which would provide both a guide to proper action and a legitimating rationale for their social position.

The intellectual departure we know as Neo-Confucianism was a response to this crisis. The Confucian classics were "Confucian" only in a limited sense. Master Kong Fuzi (Confucius, 551–479 B.C.E.) edited the texts, and his disciples devoted themselves to transmitting them to subsequent generations. But these texts— the *Book of Changes,* the *Book of Songs,* the *Book of Documents,* the *Book of Rites,* and the *Spring and Autumn Annals*—were the definitive source of high culture, the ultimate repository of wisdom, for **all** educated Chinese. If things were out of joint, this was not (many believed) attributable to this or that error of policy. It was the result of a contemporary failure to grasp the true meaning of the classics and to apply that meaning to current situations. Some, like the classicist/reformer Wang Anshi [Wang An-Shih] (1021–1086), tried to impose past forms on present realities. Others, believing that changes in government and society in the intervening centuries doomed so literal an approach, sought to penetrate the innermost meaning of the classics. Inspired by Buddhism, they believed that the classics, properly understood, would reveal both the metaphysical principles which underlay reality and a guide to proper action. Those who pursued "true learning" (instead of studying just to gain place and power, wealth and status through success in the exams) knew that study and moral cultivation were the necessary basis for bringing order to the state and peace to the world. It was the main twelfth-century exponent of this "school of principle," Zhu Xi [Chu Hsi] (1130–1200), who made the Confucian *Analects,* the *Mencius,* and two chapters from the *Book of Rites* (*The Great Learning* and *The Doctrine of the Mean*) the equals of, and keys to understanding, the classics.

Although the Southern Song posthumously honored Zhu and his Northern Song predecessors, affairs were not rectified. The thirteenth century was a kind of golden age: China's population reached 120 million, its internal and overseas commerce expanded, its cities (especially the "temporary capital" of Hangzhou) were loci of a vibrant urban culture. All this was undergirded and made possible by the intensive and highly productive riziculture of the area's paddy fields and the excellence of its water-borne transport networks. Productivity rose, specialization flourished, and the use of money increased. In many areas, peasants chronically underemployed in the off-season turned to handicrafts, the processing of agricultural products, and temporary work outside the village. As a result, the total fund of goods and services available to Chinese society increased dramatically and the basic parameters for China's development in subsequent centuries were established.

Yet the Song failed to reconquer the north. Its internal divisions—over ideology, over personnel policies, over land and taxes, over military and foreign affairs—were so great that they could only be accommodated, not overcome. Gunpowder and the navy enabled the Song to resist first the Jin (1127–1234), then the Mongols. (Only the Mamelukes, the Egyptian warrior caste, were more successful at resisting the latter.) Once the Mongols learned to fight on water, however, the Song was compelled to mobilize all available resources. This alienated important segments of the population—large landlords and wealthy merchants ultimately preferred barbarian rule to higher taxes and unending war. The Southern Song (1127–1279) was as much victim of its unresolved internal contradictions as of Mongol onslaught.

The Mongols were not the unmitigated disaster of legend; they were a mitigated disaster, and a national humiliation. By the time the Mongols conquered southern China, violence had become a means to an end rather than an end in itself. Their aim was systematically to exploit, not simply to plunder and destroy, the sedentary societies they conquered. For this reason, Mongol conquest was not as great a catastrophe in East as in West Asia. Nonetheless, from the establishment of the Yuan Dynasty in 1279 until its fall in 1368, barbarians ruled all of China for the first time. Unlike many of their predecessors, the Mongols resisted sinicization. Mongol rulers had no brief against Confucianism: regarding it as a religion, they registered some 18,000 households (14,000 in South China) as its hereditary "priesthood." In the early fourteenth century, they even revived the examination system. Although they made very limited use of it, they established a definitive standard by imposing Zhu Xi's commentaries as orthodoxy. The conquered Chinese never conquered their Mongol conquerors, however. Within China, positions of power and influence went first to Mongols, then to central Asians, then to northern Chinese (who had lived under barbarian rule since 1127). Southern Chinese, who had monopolized key positions since the collapse of the northern aristocracy in Tang, were relegated to a limited number of scholar/advisor posts. Mongol rule remained true to its nomadic origins: decentralized, collegial, the military intervening in (and frequently overruling) the civil sphere. A great deal of power devolved into the hands of the scholar-official's perennial bête noire, the clerk. At least in some localities, this system managed to keep the peace, collect taxes, and maintain essential public works. Yet, even when Mongol rule did not make matters worse, it failed to resolve problems which had baffled the

Song. On balance, the Mongols indeed seem to have been a model of "how not to govern China."[1]

The Mongols did create an Asian world network, a network which played an important role in transmitting Chinese science and technology as well as knowledge about China (through Marco Polo) to the West. The Chinese received relatively little in return: some Islamic advances in medicine, astronomy, and calendrical science. We do not, and will probably never, know if the volume of trade under the Mongols equaled the volume of trade under the Song. It is clear that much of it within China and almost all of it between China and western Eurasia was in Moslem *ortaqh* (merchant associations), rather than in Chinese hands. By the early fourteenth century, the Mongol Empire had in any case dissolved into four mutually suspicious pieces. The Asian world network of the Mongols was thus a short-lived achievement. Whether as the result of epidemic disease, climatic change, or misrule, the Chinese population plummeted (to between 60 and 90 million) in the fourteenth century. Chronic problems became acute crises. The Mongols, unable to suppress a wave of peasant rebellions, were driven out.

Some strains within the Neo-Confucian movement saw a benevolent despotism as **the** way to solve the Middle Kingdom's ongoing problems. China's reduced population was concentrated within two hundred miles of the new capital (Nanjing) in the south, an area with excellent water-borne transport and communications. Barbarian rule, socioeconomic crisis, and civil war had weakened or discredited most of society's organic institutions. The victorious claimant of the Dragon Throne, the peasant Zhu Yuanzhang (Ming Hongwu, reigned 1368–1398, establishing the Ming Dynasty [1368–1644]), needed little urging to make the most of the opportunity thus afforded to remold society. He grouped households into units of ten (the *lijia* system), extracting tax and corvée on the basis of remarkably comprehensive land and population registers. Having centralized the administrative structure, he then abolished the post of prime minister, using terror to subordinate the bureaucracy to his will. After some experimentation with other methods, triennial exams in the Five Classics and Four Books (as understood by Zhu Xi and his followers) at the prefectural, provincial, and central levels became the primary method of recruiting that bureaucracy. By severely restricting the protection (*yin*) privilege and by abolishing Confucian household status, the first Ming emperor completed the shift from aristocracy to meritocracy. In the process, he made the gap between emperor and bureaucrat a chasm.

The first Ming emperor's vision of the world was essentially static and defensive. By limiting the sphere of government activity, by using labor service or hereditary occupational groups (notably soldiers) to perform many public functions, and by keeping all reins of power in imperial hands, proper order could be achieved within. Without, the preferred course was peaceful—if wary—co-existence. His son, the Yongle emperor (reigned 1403–1424), pursued a much more aggressive foreign policy. He launched military expeditions into Inner Asia and northern Vietnam; moved the capital to Beijing in the north, the better to watch the northern border; and dispatched the eunuch Zheng He [Cheng Ho] on his famous voyages to the South Seas. Yongle's motives were clearly mixed: having just usurped the throne from his nephew, the desire to have as many tributaries as possible come to acknowledge him as a true Son of Heaven (thus validating his claim to the throne in the eyes of politically conscious Chinese) must have been especially strong.

The Zheng He voyages have understandably captured the imagination of historians. A forceful emperor dispatching subordinates to distant lands had ample precedent (most notably, Zhang Qian's journeys to the west after 139 B.C.E.), however. And Zheng He was not venturing into uncharted waters: his expeditions were a new departure only for the government, not for the Chinese traders.[2] Indeed, "in 1404 [the Yongle emperor] decreed that all seafaring ships in private ownership be converted to have flat bows, so as to eliminate their ability for distant voyages."[3] Legally or not, Chinese had engaged in overseas trade before 1403. They continued to do so after 1433. Although few went as far as the east coast of Africa, regular interchange with Japan, Korea, and Southeast Asia continued. The decision to discontinue official voyages was, however, important. It signaled the end of China as the dominant East Asian naval power, although not the beginning of China as hermit nation.

In part, the decision was a triumph of the first Ming emperor's vision over that of the second. In part, it was a victory of the "outer court" (scholar-officials) over the "inner court" (the emperor and his eunuchs). In theory, the Son of Heaven, aided by those who had demonstrated a correct—that is, Neo-Confucian—understanding of the classics, mediated between the cosmos and mankind. In practice, Confucian bureaucrats ruled in the emperor's name. For the first time since the Tang, China was not just economically more prosperous and culturally more advanced than its neighbors. It was, in its own eyes and in those of others, truly the

Middle Kingdom. It was in Ming times (1368–1644) that inexpensive books, widespread literacy, and reliance on examinations made the bureaucracy a career open to talent. It was in Ming that the rise of secure tenancy relationships and the decline of semi-free agricultural labor occurred. Although parts of China were highly commercialized in the fourteenth century, the range of products expanded from agricultural staples and luxuries to articles of mass consumption (like cotton cloth) in Ming. Simultaneously, the geographical areas and the social groups wholly or largely dependent on the market increased. Thus, even before New World silver and New World food crops were introduced, intensifying the process, low taxes, competent administration, and internal peace encouraged demographic expansion (to 150–200 million circa 1600) and economic growth.

These developments had not ushered in the millennium. When (in 1514–1516) the Portuguese forged a new link between the separate spheres of Europe and China, most Chinese lived uncomfortably close to bare subsistence. Subjects of the Ming, like those of all other preindustrial societies, were largely at the mercy of the elements. As the population grew, the poor multiplied in absolute numbers and relative poverty (if not in relative numbers and absolute poverty). The static assumptions of the Ming fisc ill suited a time of economic growth and increasing commercialization, population increase, and mass migration. Public resources were limited. And the ingenuity of the haves in shifting burdens to the have-nots made attempts to augment those resources practically difficult and potentially explosive. The ambitious faced intensified competition in the examination halls. As those who succeeded increasingly came from (and came to depend on) commercial wealth, the bases of elite status were redefined. In response, there were attempts both to streamline the tax system (the Single Whip reform implemented at varying times and to varying degrees on a prefecture-by-prefecture basis over the sixteenth century) and to organize society outside—and independently—of the state. There was also a growing conviction that Song thinkers had failed to grasp the perennial truths contained in the classics. The Ming thinker Wang Yangming (1472–1529) argued that, by reversing the classical relationship between moral cultivation and intellectual attainment, Zhu Xi had made the unity of thought and action, of self-realization and sage rule, an unattainable goal. Personal fulfillment and social order alike, Wang Yangming argued, hinged on rectifying this error.

On its own terms, the China of 1500 was a great success. It

was recognized as such by its neighbors: the Koreans, the Japanese, the Vietnamese, and the Manchus borrowed extensively from the Ming. In wealth and in scale, it dwarfed Europe. Few Ming Chinese would have denied that their society had its problems. All remained certain that solutions to those problems lay in a proper understanding of the Middle Kingdom's own traditions. This was a formula neither for stagnation nor for complacency: in almost every respect, changes outweigh continuities in Chinese experience between 1000 and 1500. Friction of distance ensured that China would be loosely connected (at best) to the emerging world network. But, even if this had not been true, the Chinese of 1500—or of 1750—would have seen little attraction in the call of the barbarian West.

NOTES

1. Elizabeth Endicott-West, "Imperial Governance in Yuan Times," *Harvard Journal of Asiatic Studies* 46 (1986): 549.

2. Zheng He was a Muslim. When ethnicity failed, he was able to draw on the expertise of fellow believers. Since Arabs had been crisscrossing the seas between Africa and the Indies for centuries, Zheng He's ability to reach the east coast of Africa is less amazing than is usually implied.

3. Ray Huang, "Administrative Statistics in *Ming T'ai-tsung shi-lu*: An Illustration of Chinese Bureaucratism as Criticized by Dr. Needham," *Ming Studies* 16 (Spring 1983): 49.

THE CASE OF JAPAN, 1000–1500

H. Paul Varley

The eleventh century witnessed both a culmination and a turning point in Japanese civilization. Ancient court life and culture, the products of the courtier class that served the emperor in the capital city of Kyoto, reached their zenith about the time of Imperial Regent Fujiwara no Michinaga and the writing of *The Tale of Genji* in the first years of the century. In the century's second half, the samurai or warrior class that had been evolving in the provinces from earlier in the Heian period (794–1185) began to play a more prominent role in national affairs and to take the first major steps that led within a century to its emergence as the new ruling class of the country.

The courtiers, the traditional ruling elite, had by 1000 become a largely insular group residing predominantly in Kyoto and maintaining only limited contacts with the outside world. Official relations with China had been terminated after the last mission to the Tang in 838, although the court continued to receive goods from and knowledge of China through the private trade that flourished in Kyushu ports. Within Japan, the courtiers contributed little directly to the administration of the provinces. Most rice lands were, by this time, gathered into private estates from which the courtiers derived their principal income but over which they exercised only minimal management. And the provincial governments, although officially headed in most cases by courtier governors, were also primarily self-managing inasmuch as the governors usually remained in Kyoto and allowed their assigned provinces to be administered by local people serving as vice-governors and lesser officials.

It should not be thought, however, that the court simply neglected the provinces. Remaining generally well informed about provincial affairs, the Fujiwara regents and other court ministers exerted their influence over the provinces in a variety of ways.

They were able to do this in large part because the provinces could not dispense with court authority. Even in the Kantō, which was relatively distant from the court, was blessed with fertile land, and had a growing warrior population, conditions were such that no leader could transcend local feuding to establish a significant territorial base. By custom and need, men in the Kantō—and elsewhere—continued to rely on the court's authority. They needed the court, for example, to confirm their interests in and arbitrate their disputes over land. Hence the court, although for the most part physically isolated from the provinces, was able to maintain rule over this hinterland on the basis of its traditional role as the universally recognized dispenser of highest governing authority.

The rise of a military class in the provinces and the accession of its leaders to national power in the late twelfth century brought to Japan what many scholars regard as a form of feudalism remarkably like the feudalism of western Europe during its medieval age. The principal features of this feudalism were: an economy based primarily on agriculture and a class of peasant cultivators bound to the land as serfs; a high degree of local self-sufficiency and relatively little commercial growth beyond local markets; a ruling military class whose members were joined by lord-vassal ties; and the institution of the fief, usually an interest in or holding of agricultural land that supported the vassal economically and enabled him to serve his lord as a fighting man. (The fief either was bestowed upon the vassal by the lord or was confirmed—i.e., guaranteed—by him.)

Although some scholars question the value of using the European model of feudalism in analyzing the institutions that evolved with warrior society in premodern Japan, the student of comparative history cannot help being struck by the extraordinary similarities between feudal Europe and feudal Japan. At the same time, the historian of Japan must be vigilant not to press the comparison with Europe too far and thus distort the special characteristics—the particularities—of Japanese feudalism.

Much of the study of the evolution of warrior society in Japan focuses on the growth and organization of territorially based warrior bands. Leadership of the larger bands was, by the late Heian period, held primarily by members of the Taira (or Heike) and the Minamoto (or Genji), multibranched families spread throughout the provinces whose forebears were descended from the imperial family. One branch of the Taira, which had its seat in Ise Province, became dominant at court in the 1160s and 1170s, holding courtly ranks and offices and even marrying into the imperial family. In 1180, the chieftains of several branches of the Minamoto rose in the provinces to oppose the Ise Taira, precipitating a five-year war (known as the Genpei or Minamoto-Taira War) that ended in total victory for the Minamoto.

From the larger standpoint of history, the victory over the Ise Taira was less important than the establishment during the Genpei War of a hegemony over the eight provinces of the Kantō by Minamoto no Yoritomo, who emerged as the supreme Minamoto commander. From this hegemony, Yoritomo fashioned the first military government in Japanese history. This government had its capital at Kamakura (just south of today's Tokyo), and is called by historians the Kamakura shogunate from the title of shogun (an abbreviation of *seii tai-shōgun* or "barbarian-subduing great general") that Yoritomo received from the emperor.

Although an eastern territorial regime in its origins, the Kamakura shogunate became a national government through the creation of various offices, chief among which were *jitō* (land steward) and *shugo* (constable). *Jitō* were appointed to estates (or were men already in estates who received the *jitō* designation), and *shugo* were assigned to provinces as constabulary officials, one to each province. During the next few centuries the *jitō* became the principal agents of the destruction of the estate system, as they steadily and rapaciously intruded upon and eliminated the interests of absentee estate holders (including courtiers, members of the imperial family, and religious institutions) and carved out feudal fiefs.

During most of the Kamakura period (1185–1333), the powers of the *shugo* were restricted by the shogunate to police functions and the maintenance of military guard rosters. But in the succeeding Muromachi period (1336–1573), the *shugo* evolved into territorial barons or lords known as daimyo (literally "great names"). Evolution of the daimyo and the daimyo domain through several stages is one of the main themes of Japanese institutional history from the medieval age (1185–1568) through the early modern (1568–1867) age—or, using a slightly different periodization, from the Kamakura period through the Tokugawa period (1600–1867).

The advent of the medieval age brought a great religious awakening in the form of the salvationist sects of Buddhism. Imbued with the conviction that the world had entered a degenerate "final age of the Buddhist Law *(mappō)*," Japanese of late Heian and medieval times believed themselves to be hopelessly mired in sin and incapable of helping themselves (*jiriki*) to achieve release from this world of suffering. They sought, instead, salvation through faith in the "power of another" (*tariki*). The most prominent of the salvationist sects established in the medieval age were the Pure Land (*jōdo*) sects devoted to the Buddha Amida, who promised to save all supplicants by transporting them upon death to his Pure Land paradise in the western realm of the universe. In looking beyond dark times and a debased world to a future paradise after death, the salvationist sects were another feature of medieval Japanese society that resonates strongly with medieval Europe.

A steady weakening of the estate system of landholding and of other traditional institutions of control, such as the provincial governorships, was accompanied by a marked trend toward regionalism in the fourteenth century. The Kamakura shogunate was overthrown in 1333 and, after a brief, unrealistic attempt by an emperor to "restore" imperial rule (the Kemmu Restoration, 1333–36), a new shogunate, the Ashikaga or Muromachi shogunate (1336–1573), was established in Kyoto. The court from about this time ceased to have any capacity to govern and became an institutional relic of the past, although it still possessed a legitimating symbolism that was periodically invoked by the Ashikaga shoguns and other military leaders.

Bereft not only of political power but also of most of their economic base in land, the courtiers who served the emperor's court in Kyoto became primarily the custodians of traditional culture, style, and ways. This custodial function was important because it catered to the cultural tastes of the age, which were powerfully nostalgic. The Muromachi-period Japanese looked back—as medieval Europeans looked back—to a golden age of civilization in the past. To the Japanese, the golden age was the high period of court life in mid-Heian times, primarily the late tenth and early eleventh centuries, when the Fujiwara regents were at their zenith and the *Tale of Genji* and other classics of court literature were composed.

The Muromachi shogunate was the weakest of the three shogunates—Kamakura, Muromachi, and Tokugawa—of premodern Japan. Even at its peak under the third Ashikaga shogun, Yoshimitsu, at the end of the fourteenth century and the beginning of the fifteenth century, the shogunate's enforceable authority extended only partially beyond the central and western provinces of Honshu and the island of Shikoku. The Kantō was never firmly under central Ashikaga control, and in the early fifteenth century this important region lapsed into disunion.

Meanwhile, Kyushu Island in the west remained resolutely defiant of Ashikaga control. And in the great Ōnin War of 1467–77, fought primarily in Kyoto, the Ashikaga lost most of their power even in the central provinces, as Japan slipped into a century of widespread disorder known as the age of the "country at war" (*sengoku*, 1468–1573).

Among the casualties of the Ōnin War were the *shugo* daimyo, leading vassals of the shogunate, who were either destroyed or irreparably weakened by this protracted conflict. *Shugo* daimyo is a term used by historians to refer to holders of the *shugo* or constable title who had increasingly arrogated powers to themselves and emerged as a group of territorial administrators in the first half of the Muromachi period. Most *shugo* daimyo governed domains of two or more provinces (one presided over eleven provinces). All had difficulty in controlling the local chieftains who became their vassals and in establishing sound and adequate economic bases in landholdings. A number of prominent *shugo* daimyo families fell into succession disputes in the early decades of the fifteenth century, and many *shugo* daimyo fought themselves to exhaustion in the Ōnin War. The years of the war and its aftermath saw the disintegration of nearly all the *shugo* daimyo domains.

Although an age of unprecedented disorder, the Muromachi period was also a time of brilliant cultural achievements. The Noh theater, the tea ceremony (*chanoyu*), linked verse poetry (*renga*), and monochrome ink painting (*sumie*) in the Sung-Chinese manner were only some of the artistic accomplishments of the age. Zen Buddhism, founded in Japan at the same time as the salvationist sects in the early Kamakura period, played a particularly prominent role in the molding of cultural and aesthetic tastes.

If the eleventh century was a culmination and a turning point in Japanese civilization, the late fifteenth century was both a nadir and a beginning. The country reached its nadir of disunion in the aftermath of the Ōnin War and its entry into the age of the country at war. But by at least 1500 a new class of daimyo, the *sengoku* daimyo, controlling what were for the most part newly created domains, began to emerge. Within a half-century the entire country was organized into these domains, and the stage was set for the national unification that was achieved in the late sixteenth century.

The *sengoku* daimyo, many of whom were vassals of the former *shugo* daimyo, assembled powerful armies, encouraged agricul-

THE CASE OF JAPAN, 1000–1500   395

ture, mining, and commerce, built strong castles, and promulgated codes to place their rule on a strong legal basis. Thus they created autonomous domains capable of survival in a violent, often anarchic age. From about the mid-sixteenth century, some of the more prominent *sengoku* daimyo entered into competition to unify the country. The victor in this competition was Oda Nobunaga, a daimyo from the region that today contains Nagoya. Entering Kyoto in 1568, Nobunaga began a series of campaigns that brought about a third of Japan under his control by 1582, when he was assassinated by one of his leading vassals. Another vassal, Toyotomi Hideyoshi, avenged Nobunaga's death and, succeeding to the role of unifier, brought the entire country under his dominance by 1590.

Although Nobunaga dissolved the Muromachi shogunate in 1573, neither he nor Hideyoshi established a new shogunate. Both certainly possessed the power to make themselves shoguns, but they evidently preferred to seek ruling legitimacy from other sources, including the evolving concept of *kōgi* or "public authority"—that is, authority to rule based on rulership for the benefit of the state and society as a whole. While not challenging the ultimate legitimacy of the emperor, *kōgi* established criteria for rule that concerned the ability and achievements of the ruler himself and not simply the fact that he possessed imperial approval.

The age of unification in the late sixteenth century was unusual because of the presence of Europeans in Japan for the first time. Portuguese traders arrived in 1543, and were soon followed by Christian missionaries. The Spanish came from Manila in the 1580s, and the Dutch and English reached Japan's shores in 1600. In addition to trade and Christianity, the Europeans brought guns (muskets) and cannons to Japan, and Nobunaga, Hideyoshi, and other military chieftains made effective use of these weapons in carrying out unification.

Hideyoshi, having swept away all the opposition that faced him as he completed unification between 1582 and 1590, sought to expand his military might to the Asian continent, invading Korea in 1592–93 and 1597–98. The first invasion was unsuccessful when the Japanese army, its supply lines overextended, was repulsed in northern Korea by a combination of Korean and Chinese forces, and the second invasion was terminated upon the death of Hideyoshi in 1598.

As unifier, Hideyoshi did not seek to destroy the structure of daimyo domains in order to establish a more centralized national government; rather, he strengthened the structure by rewarding the daimyo with additional lands and supporting them as territorial rulers. When Hideyoshi died in 1598, he was succeeded by an infant son, and the opportunity was presented to Tokugawa Ieyasu, the most powerful of the daimyo, to become the real successor to Hideyoshi's power. In 1600 Ieyasu, heading a coalition of primarily eastern daimyo, was victorious in the Battle of Sekigahara over a coalition of daimyo from the central and western provinces. A decisive event in Japanese history, the victory at Sekigahara enabled Ieyasu to establish the Tokugawa shogunate, which governed Japan until the Meiji Restoration of 1868.

THE RISE OF AN INTERDEPENDENT WORLD, 1500–1990

Loyd E. Lee

INTRODUCTION

A new phase of world history began in the sixteenth century when circumnavigation of the globe by explorers from Western Europe established new forms of contacts among the various cultural and political regions. These contacts eventually gave rise to an interdependent world and the origins of a distinctively modern civilization. Although the West had never been wholly isolated from Asia, after 1500 the contacts between the two expanded significantly. This story, so often told in terms of the expansion of the West and its subsequent global hegemony by the nineteenth century, should not, however, obscure the great changes that were taking place in the different regions of Asia during the same period. These changes frequently derived not from Western impact alone, but from indigenous forces working within Asian societies from the sixteenth through the nineteenth century.

The complex interactions that took place in this emerging interdependent world have generally been treated through two approaches to world history. The first stresses the concept of modernization, the second, the methods of comparative history. Both have pitfalls, created by the evaluation of Western experience as normative, but, used with care, they can nevertheless be helpful. Modernization, although often misused as a synonym for Westernization, in fact refers to such phenomena as industrialization and increased productivity, capital formation, the development of science, and the replacement of localized, peasant-based agrarian economies by complex productive systems in which food production required increasingly smaller portions of a society's energy. It is further associated with population growth, urbanization, greater popular participation in political affairs, and the development of a nation-state with a centralized, bureaucratic apparatus of control and administration. Modernization, in this understanding, is a dynamic and interactive process occurring throughout the world, which differed from region to region owing to different national patterns as well as to unequal distributions of international power.

Comparison is a second common approach to world history. By analyzing how societies are organized in different civilizations, how constituent social groups are treated, how political institutions function, how religious ideas and practices influence society, it is possible to avoid focusing on Europe as the main initiator of changes in the modern world. Comparison generates new questions and leads to new perspectives on both global and regional developments, provided that specific common elements are not overly abstracted from specific cultural contexts.

Both the modernization and the comparative approaches require a balance between the connections and interactions of the globe as a whole and the structures, evolution, and development of the different regions. Each society, state, culture, or region must retain its separate integrity, even as it is related to common experiences transcending the subunits of world history.

Whichever approach is chosen, the period from the fifteenth century to the present is often divided into three periods when treating Asia in the context of world history. The first period, roughly from 1500 to 1750, saw the world encompassed by European powers, through discoveries, explorations, and the founding and expansion of trade routes along the southern rim of Asia. These helped transform the wealth, culture, and intellectual world of West Europeans, though they had far less impact on the societies of Asia.

The second period, from the middle of the eighteenth century to the First World War, was momentous for both the West and Asia. The "long nineteenth century," as it may be called, witnessed the initial phases of the transformation produced by the industrial revolution, which resulted in a dramatic rise in productivity, communications, and transport technologies in the West. It also encompassed the political changes wrought by the American and the French revolutions. In India, Mughal rule weakened and British involvement increased. In China, internal rebellion and the external challenge of the West weakened the Qing bureaucratic state and the Confucian consensus upon which it was based. In Japan there were social, economic, and intellectual changes that first presaged and then resulted in the transformation from a feudal order to a modern state.

The third period runs from roughly 1919 to the present. The First World War saw the beginning of the end of the long period of European expansion and imperialist hegemony. A global watershed occurred in the second decade of this century with the collapse of the last great Islamic empire of the Ottomans; the strengthening of nationalist movements in India, China, and Korea; the increasing tension in Japan between the rise of ambitious national power and the social and economic changes caused by rapid modernization; the Bolshevik Revolution of 1917 in Russia; and the rise of the United States in international politics and the world economy. These developments initiated the third period of modern world history, which saw the globe reshaped in the twentieth century in what the Chinese leader Zhou Enlai called the age of "great disorder on the earth" (Zhou Enlai, 1973). Several chapters, one on European expansion and others on China, Japan, and India, look at the period from 1500 to the mid-nineteenth century. This essay takes up various aspects of imperialism, nationalism, and revolution in the late 1800s and the reshaping of the globe in the twentieth century.

THE WORLD ENCOMPASSED (1500–1750)

EUROPEAN EXPANSION IN ASIA

This period has two parts, with a break in the early 1600s. The first is the era of Portuguese and Spanish expansion, when the Portuguese established a trading empire throughout the Indian Ocean and into the seas of East Asia. The Ottoman, Safavid, and Mughal dynasties also expanded, consolidated their empires, and then, like the Iberians, begin to decline. Meanwhile, in East Asia the Manchu Qing Dynasty installed itself in China (1644) and the Tokugawa shogunate achieved dominance in Japan (1600), ushering in periods of political stability in both countries. These broad developments within Asia helped to shape its relationship to the rest of the world.

After the early seventeenth century the Netherlands, Britain, France, and Russia began more fully to organize their relations with Asia as they searched for new markets and new products.

The Dutch with their successful United East India Company re-placed the Portuguese in Asia, but by the end of the century they had become junior partners of the British, allied against the French. At the same time the Russians moved eastward, exploit-ing the fur trade for the czars' treasury and reaching the eastern coast at Okhotsk (1649). During this period both China and Japan restricted the activities of the West Europeans and the Russians within their realms and strictly limited their trade.

In spite of this intensification of activity, the direct impact on Asia of Europeans, who probably numbered about 50,000 in 1740 and 75,000 in 1800 in all of Asia, remained marginal, with com-merce still on Asian terms and with Asians carrying on most of it. British requests for greater commerce with China were rebuffed, and the Tokugawa shogunate restricted trade with Europe to one small Dutch installation on Deshima island in Nagasaki harbor after the 1640s. The exception was India, where the Mughals yielded more trade concessions to European companies after the seventeenth century.

DEVELOPMENTS IN ASIA

The main civilizational units of Asia in 1500 continued along paths laid down centuries before: Islamic states in West Asia; a prevailing Hindu culture in South Asia (though Muslims had ruled large parts of it for three hundred years); a region of pre-dominantly Buddhist culture in Southeast Asia; and a Confucian-ist East Asia. The major Asian empires still considered themselves universal states with the claim to rule the civilized world, an outlook that conflicted with emerging European conceptions of the nation-state and of its role in international relations. The histories of the Asian civilizations from 1500 to 1700 were dy-namic and innovative, though none achieved a breakthrough to sustained economic growth.

Despite challenges in the Balkans and the western Mediterra-nean, Islam was in a third period of expansion. The Turkish Ottoman Empire (1300s–1918) had continued its rise from early medieval obscurity by capturing Constantinople (1453), one of the most important events in eastern Europe in the last millennium. In the early sixteenth century the Ottomans conquered Egypt and Syria and, under Suleiman the Magnificent (1520–1566), overran Hungary, drove the Portuguese from the Red Sea, founded colo-nies in Yemen and Ethiopia, and sent a fleet with artillery to Sumatra (1558). In allying with Francis I of France against the

Hapsburgs (1536), the Ottoman Empire became a permanent party in the contest for European hegemony.

As in many multiethnic empires with large religious minorities, the Turks ruled by relying on the collaboration of local elites and reserved military supremacy to themselves. Territorially the empire expanded to limits imposed only by communications and economy, but no breakthrough to more intense interaction between the central state and subjects of its rule occurred, as it did in the maritime states of Western Europe. By the seventeenth century Ottoman power was weakened by incompetent rulers, an expanding population, and a shrinking economy deprived of income from the valuable transit trade between Asia and Europe, which now moved by sea around the Cape of Good Hope.

In India, a new Islamic dynasty, the Mughals, who traced their origin to central Asia, established itself in 1526. They conquered areas previously held by Muslim rulers as well as areas that had remained under Hindu control, creating an empire more enduring than that of any of their predecessors. By the end of the seventeenth century most of the Indian subcontinent was under their control, but by the middle of the eighteenth century internal rebellions of an indigenous people, the Marathas, defection by military governors, and invasions by Afghans and Iranians had virtually destroyed the central authority. It was at this juncture that the British East India Company took possession in the last decades of the eighteenth century of Bengal, and made it the base for the British expansion that ended only with the reorganization of the subcontinent in the Government of India Act in 1858.

In China, the Ming Dynasty (1368–1644), often described as conservative and internally oriented, discouraged overseas commerce, pursuing a defensive policy from the end of the sixteenth century against their Mongol enemies, their domestic rebels, and coastal Japanese pirates. Struck by plague, urban disturbances, and rural rebellion, the Ming Dynasty fell in 1644, succeeded by the foreign Manchu Qing Dynasty, which lasted until 1911. In the eighteenth century, a series of capable Manchu emperors closely identified with Chinese culture and raised the Confucian administrative system to new levels of efficiency. The government controlled internal revolts and pushed the frontiers of the empire west and southwest, including Tibet. With villages and towns linked together by rivers and canals, China enjoyed a varied domestic economy, with a per capita standard of living comparable to that of the rest of the world. Urbanization along the lower Yangzi (Yangtze) River, the conversion of labor services into money payments, the commercialization of management activities, the spread of literacy—all hint at "sprouts of capitalism" rising in China before the nineteenth century. By 1800, the Jesuits were gone and foreign trade was restricted to a few border outposts, most notably Canton. Although foreign trade was growing, with its large continental empire and dynamic internal market, China had little incentive to look outward.

During the period of civil wars in Japan (1467–1590), the Portuguese reached Japan, bringing guns, trade, and Christianity. Francis Xavier and other missionaries made many converts, initiating the "Christian Century," from the 1540s to the 1630s. With the unification of the realm by Tokugawa Ieyasu, who became shogun in 1603, however, foreigners found themselves increasingly restricted as part of the new regime's energetic assertion of order and stability. Foreigners were expelled in 1639, except for the Dutch and Chinese merchants in Nagasaki. The shogun suppressed Christianity and forbade Japanese to leave the country, beginning the two-century "seclusion" from the world. The "Pax Tokugawa" is associated with domestic peace, social stability, commercial development, expanded literacy, and isolation from the world in the period that historians call "early modern Japan" (1600–1868).

ASIA IN EARLY MODERN WORLD HISTORY

These developments in Asia pose interesting questions for world history. Why did Europe take the lead in establishing trade empires along Asia's coast? Answers that stress Europe's peculiar institutions and modernizing dynamics are discussed in the next section, but what is strikingly clear is that the civilizations of Asia had little motivation to discover Europe. The thriving merchants of the Indian Ocean and the South China Sea had no reason to seek a shortcut to Portugal. The riches and spices of the East were, after all, within their reach. Whatever the Ming motivation for ending the famous exploratory voyages of Zheng He (1433), there was at least no impelling commercial reason to continue them. And for Asian rulers, taxes from land and domestic trade remained far more important than international commerce. Thus, economic forces did not disturb the disposition to think of themselves as the center of civilization, without a need to push in the direction of Europe.

EUROPE ASCENDANT: NATIONALISM, IMPERIALISM, AND REVOLUTION (1750–1919)

THE TRANSFORMATION OF EUROPE

The dual industrial and democratic revolutions of the late eighteenth century, with their connections to Europe's global relations, disrupted and transformed the continent at an accelerated pace down to and beyond the First World War. Only parts of the "Neo-Europes," settled by Europeans in the Americas, Australia, and New Zealand, escaped the worst turbulence, in part because they emerged *de novo* within a new global environment. Opinions and emphases divide on the specific relations among factors such as industrialization and merchant capitalism, the dynamics of the European-centered world economy, the impact of technology, the scientific revolution, the collaboration between artisans and thinkers, as well as a host of other issues. But whatever the causes for "the rise of the West," in 1750 Europe had no obvious economic advantage over other countries, whereas by 1850 a gap had emerged that in many cases still continues to grow, as Table 1 shows.

Europe shared a population explosion with the rest of Eurasia in the mid-eighteenth century, though its rate of growth may have been faster. In the case of Britain, industrialization, and to some extent emigration, kept the problems of overpopulation within

Table 1

Per Capita Income Compared, 1750–1970
1960 dollars and prices

	Developed Countries	Third World	World
1750	182	188	187
1800	198	188	191
1860	324	174	220
1910	662	192	364
1938	856	202	433
1970	2229	308	868

Source: Paul Bairoch, "The Main Trends in National Economic Disparities Since the Industrial Revolution," p. 7 in *Disparities in Economic Development Since the Industrial Revolution,* ed. Paul Bairoch and Maurice Levy-Leboyer (New York: St. Martin's Press, 1981). He surmises that the average standard of living in Europe in 1750 was slightly lower than that of the rest of the world owing to the high level achieved by the Chinese.

bounds. Factors other than those noted above that were conducive to industrialization include a mobile wage-labor force, late marriage and lower birth rates, improved food supplies as a result of an agricultural revolution, a powerful entrepreneurial class, government policies favoring private initiative and profit making, the abolition of guild monopolies of production, the security of private property, the accumulation of surplus capital, inculcated habits of investing, patent protection for inventions, and the growth of a consumer-oriented national economy.

The easily exploitable coal fields of northeast England in proximity to iron ore deposits expedited the replacement of animal muscle with energy derived from mineral sources, an essential element in the transition from an agrarian to an industrial economy. Abundant waterways and canals reduced the costs of transport and knitted together a national market with resulting economies of scale. These in turn encouraged the invention of mechanized production of cheap cotton textiles to supply a market previously developed through the India trade. The advent of railroads slashed the costs of land transportation, reversing the age-old advantage of waterways. Railroads, steamboats, the industrialization of warfare, and instantaneous telegraphic communication thrust Britain and then western Europe far ahead of any global competitors. Rapid communications and a monopoly over their means gave Britain a special advantage, which it retained well into the twentieth century and which enabled it to assault the still agrarian empires of Asia.

Democratic revolution, the second aspect of the dual European revolutions, exemplified by the French Revolution, unleashed enormous political and social energies by linking the people and government in the form of the nation-state. Although couched in terms of universal liberty and brotherhood, the struggles for popular sovereignty also reinforced state power through the forces of nationalism. The nation-state broke the hold of decentralized intermediary powers (such as nobles, guilds, and ecclesiastical authorities) and replaced them with uniform administrative and legal structures. In turning subjects into citizens, the French Revolution freed military energies and generated the taxes to sustain them. In France, as throughout Europe, these political developments paralleled the introduction of capitalist market economies and property systems. They may also be seen as interactions between commercialized urban-centered society based on global trade and feudal or aristocratic monarchy based on land and an agrarian economy.

The results of Europe's revolutions in production and politics were felt everywhere in Asia, although not in all regions or by all classes with the same effect. The political and economic power of Europe meant that Asian rulers could not turn away from the European challenge, and as time-honored solutions failed, ancient empires tumbled. In many ways the processes resemble the revolutionary contest within France, as agrarian dynasties simultaneously contended with overpopulation, changing class structures, and the foreign challenges of money and power.

Common historiographic approaches to this era of Asian history include: a) the so-called challenge-and-response approach, where western expansion and modernization evoked an eastern response; b) the imperialist exploitation of the East by the West pursuing its own capitalist dynamics; c) the "world economy" concept, which sees the European core subordinating the non-European periphery and semiperiphery in an elaborate global division of labor; and d) the model of global interaction with multiple stimuli and responses in which power is unequally distributed, preglobal institutions continue to have effect, relations among regions are porous, and a continuum develops that ranges from absolute domination by the West through voluntary collaboration with it to armed resistance against it on the part of the peoples of Asia and elsewhere in the world.

EUROPE AND ASIA

The "long nineteenth century," which began in the 1700s and ended in 1919, divides in two around the 1860s. During the first part Britain, triumphant over global competition and on the basis of its industrialization, penetrated landed empires throughout Asia. This was followed by the so-called Pax Britannica, a long period of international peace that has come to seem characteristic of a hegemonic world order. The most intense Western imperialism, however, occurred after British preeminence declined, partly as a result of economic depression (1873-96) that saw a collapse in European agricultural prices and ended the era of free trade. During this second period of Western imperialism, the French renewed their goal of empire, Italy and Germany united into modern nation-states, while the United States reunited after a catastrophic civil war. Russia, already an Asian power, entered a period of reform and expansion after the disaster of the Crimean War in 1856. Japan, forced out of isolation by Commodore Perry's arrival in 1853, established a modern nation-state after

1868. The late nineteenth century suggests the question: Can a global economy without a hegemonic center like Britain experience both prosperity and stability? The historical record of the early twentieth century is not encouraging. Or again, can agrarian empires modernize without the experience of social revolution? Most did not. That Germany and Japan did may account for the authoritarian imperialism that characterized their subsequent history from the late nineteenth century to the mid-twentieth century.

The 1870s are the watershed between the "free trade imperialism" of the older economic expansion of the British Empire and others and the "new imperialism" of colonial acquisition. Was this new imperialism motivated primarily by internal western dynamics? Were there extra-European factors of collaboration and rebellion drawing in the West? Did imperialism benefit Europe? Asia? For Asia as a whole the per capita income declined during the nineteenth century. Was this a result of imperialism and the underdevelopment it produced? Or would population surges without Western interaction have been worse? Did the same capitalism that undermined other countries help to build the new Japan? Did the same European diplomacy that partitioned Africa delay the division of the Chinese empire? Obviously the questions are too simple, and the answers far too complex to phrase in this manner. But the point is that such questions should be asked, so that the course of history does not appear predetermined or foreclosed by a single evaluative stance. It is a fact of world history that the nineteenth century ushered in a global era of Western dominance, which played itself out in different ways in different contexts, no less in Asia than elsewhere.

DEVELOPMENTS IN ASIA

Asian rulers evolved different strategies to meet the Western challenge, employing various forms of borrowing, adaptation, and indigenous modernization. Local merchants, for example, sometimes collaborated with the Western-dominated import-export economy, and even if they were isolated from the power, they were often the wedge for expanded European intervention. In some areas, local rulers made military alliances with the foreigners against their rivals. Relations with the West did not occur only at the level of the imperialist state.

While the Ottoman Empire fissured along ethnic lines in the Middle East, in the Mughal Empire of India power devolved from the center to regional rulers. Some of these were the military governors of the imperial provinces, while others, like the Marathas, were indigenous groups who took advantage of the weakness of the central authority. It was in this situation that the British East India Company established British power in India. Widespread uprisings in 1857 (known to the British as the Sepoy Mutiny and to Indians as the first war of independence), the last serious attempt to overthrow the foreign rulers, led the British Parliament to assume direct control. While the British rulers made few direct attempts to change Indian society, their presence reached deep into Indian society through the bureaucracy, the use of the English language, legal codification, schools and colleges, railroads, printing presses, and greatly expanded internal trade. All these things helped to unite the region in new ways. Members of the old Hindu elites took a leading part in all aspects of the social and political changes of the nineteenth century, as merchants, bankers, lawyers, journalists, and college and university teachers. From their ranks came the leaders of the Indian National Congress, established in 1885, which was eventually to be the dominant force in winning India its independence. It was the first political party of its kind in Asia.

In Southeast Asia, the Dutch government turned nominal economic hegemony into territorial control (the United East India Company was abolished in 1798). In 1830 it introduced the "culture system," setting export quotas for all agricultural production. The effect was brutal, and it made the colony the only one that contributed directly to its home national treasury. The French engaged in a protracted struggle after 1858 to bring Indochina under their sway. Commercial permeation occurred throughout the region, with old monarchical cities being transformed into European-dominated merchant towns populated by large numbers of Chinese and other immigrants, or new urban cities arising to support the export trade. Europeans, by demarcating boundaries, also destroyed the complex of earlier authorities and unwittingly laid the basis for the region's modern states. Only Thailand retained its independence through this period of aggressive colonization of Southeast Asia, but in many places local resistance to the European incursions was common. The Dutch, for example, took five years to put down a rebellion in Java in the 1820s and fought three others before the end of the century. The French had to suppress several rebellions in Indochina, while the British fought for five years in Burma. The United States took three years to end Aguinaldo's Filipino revolt (1897–1902) and even longer to defeat the Moros (1898–1913).

In China and Japan the European impact in the nineteenth century was very different from what it was in India and Southeast Asia. When the Chinese court rejected proposals for equal relations between themselves and Great Britain in 1793, it felt superior to the Europeans, and probably in many respects this was true. There may have been more printed books in China at the time than in Europe; China had the world's largest internal free market; and per capita income may have matched that of much of the West. As late as 1890 China had the world's largest gross national product.

But difficulties, internal and external, hovered on the horizon. Aided by the introduction of New World food products and an extension of agriculture, the population exploded from 150 million in 1700 to 430 million in 1850. Production and commerce grew, too, though not fast enough to prevent a decline in the standard of living after 1820. Before this, an uprising, known as the White Lotus Rebellion, had broken out in 1796, and was not put down until 1805, evidence of the weakness of the imperial authority in peripheral regions of the country. External intrusion came from the West, whose merchants were demanding freer trade, and who objected to the restrictions placed on them by the Chinese authorities. The most severe problem, however, arose with Britain over the trade in opium, which traders associated with the East India Company smuggled into China from Bengal in vast quantities, posing a threat to the Chinese economy as well as leading to significant drug addiction. Chinese resistance to British demands led to the Opium War (1839–1842), which ended in a Chinese defeat. The British were permitted to trade at ports beyond Canton and were ceded the island of Hong Kong as a trading base. Other Western countries demanded, and received, trading privileges. The prestige of the imperial government was weakened by these concessions to foreign powers. The Taiping rebellion broke out in 1850, followed by the Nian rebellion in the north and uprisings among the Muslims in the northwest and southwest. An estimated 30 million of China's people died in these rebellions, about 5 percent of China's population at the time and the largest loss of life in a civil war in human history.

The worst international humiliation came in 1895, when the Japanese defeated China and imposed harsh imperialist terms of their own. Programs for economic reform, or "self-strengthening," begun in the 1860s resulted in only minor changes in China's massive continental market economy. After the defeat by the Japanese, the government took large loans from the West to pay reparations known as "indemnities" and to fund a small number of government industrialization projects. Resentment against the West led to the Boxer Rebellion in 1900, a popular uprising against foreigners to which the government gave its support. Western armies intervened and extracted further concessions from Beijing. A flurry of paper reforms followed, but the government's effectiveness continued to decline.

A nationalist movement outside official scholarly circles arose during the 1890s in maritime China. Its most prominent leader was Sun Yat-sen, and though inspired by Western democratic constitutionalism, he placed emphasis on national revival rather than individual rights. When the Qing Dynasty collapsed in the 1911 Revolution amid a military mutiny, students, businessmen, and other urban classes sought to set up a republic along Western lines. Lacking rural support and beset by factionalism, their revolution failed and power fell into the hands of General Yuan Shikai. In 1917 the republic declared war on Germany, hoping to renew its national power through an allied victory, but had also to face the rising imperialist ambitions of Japan during the First World War.

In Japan, by the 1840s, the need to come to terms with the West had been recognized by some of the samurai elite, but the Tokugawa shogunate vacillated on reforms and the reconsideration of the policy of foreign exclusion. At the time, both the Russians and the Americans were pressing for the safety of sailors along Japan's coast and the opening of trade. The Americans arrived first, in 1853, ending Japan's isolation and forcing unequal treaties upon Japan similar to those Westerners had signed with China.

In 1868 an alliance of samurai forced the national issue, ending the two and a half centuries of shogunal rule, and culminating in the Meiji Restoration of the emperor to the throne. A Charter Oath promised that "Knowledge shall be sought throughout the world in order to strengthen the foundations of imperial rule," a remarkably terse promise to adopt the best of the West in order to establish Japan's national strength. After a brief civil war and antiforeign outbreaks, the reformers carried out an ambitious program of modernization which amounted to the establishment of a modern nation-state on the European model: political centralization, abolition of the feudal domains, universal military service, a national taxation system, abolition of the hereditary class system, legal codification, compulsory education, and government sponsorship of industrialization. In comparison to China, Japan's small size, coherent ruling elite, governability, and economic, social, and demographic stability all contributed to the rapid and effective "Meiji Renovation," from 1868 to 1873. After the emergence of a generally nonviolent political opposition, the imperial government of former samurai now turned bureaucrats granted constitutional government with a parliament under the emperor. These reforms on behalf of a "wealthy nation, strong military" enabled Japan to defeat China (1895) and Russia (1905) and, finally, to end the extraterritoriality of the unequal treaties (1899).

Russia's expansion into south central and eastern Asia resumed in mid-century. Vladivostok was founded in 1860; the Trans-Siberian Railroad was built and extended into China in 1896, thus helping to provoke Japan's attack on Russia in 1904. Japan's victory in the Russo-Japanese War in 1905 sent a shock wave around the globe. Asians noted that Western powers could be defeated by Asian peoples, and Asian nationalism recognized the possibility of using the West to defeat the West. At the same time East Asia was now victim of a dual imperialism, one Western, one Japanese, as Japan annexed Korea in 1910 and exerted aggressive pressure on China during World War I.

It has also been argued that Japan modernized effectively while others did not because of the favorable timing of its entry into the European world system, that is, when Britain's hegemony was under challenge. Others stress Japanese social, ethnic, and linguistic homogeneity; traditions of obedience and obligation; the legacy of imperial rule; geographic compactness; habits of borrowing foreign institutions, earlier from China, now from the West; elite solidarity; or social cohesiveness. Some discern a historical dialectic comparable to that of western Europe from feudalism to capitalism, the Meiji Restoration acting as a surrogate bourgeois revolution from above, comparable to that of Bismarck in Prussia.

Whatever its causes in Europe, World War I proved momentous in weakening European control over Asia. The British and French schemed to mobilize Arab and other nationalisms against the Ottoman Empire. They enlisted hundreds of thousands of soldiers and laborers throughout their empires to fight and work for them, giving them a taste both of European standards of living and of European racism. The imperialist powers bought the products of Asia's farms and factories and wooed its merchants and bankers. Conversely, Asians used the Allies' plight to press their own national demands for autonomy and authority. These developments, rooted in the nineteenth century, were a foretaste of the world of the twentieth century.

Two other wartime developments also presaged the future: the entry of the United States into the war in 1917 under an anti-imperialist, free trade banner; and the Russian revolution, with the triumph of the anticapitalist and anti-imperialist Bolsheviks. Before 1917 the Western model for most Asian reformers and revolutionaries had been largely capitalism, and often parliamentary Britain. That a social revolution could result in the seizure of power in a peasant country and enable it to reassert national strength against the hegemonic West impressed nationalists and revolutionaries everywhere.

Despite the material and political importance of Asia to imperialist Europe, during this extended nineteenth century Asia in fact had less impact on European cultural and intellectual life than it had in the eighteenth century (see the essay on "Asia in Western Thought" by Leonard Gordon). Instead, the dominant view saw Asia as barbarian and backward, static and ahistorical, asleep in its age-old torpor and destined to be led by the civilized power of Europe. Some admired Asian philosophy and art, but they were a minority. Instead, this was the century of European influence upon Asia, when Asian elites and ruling classes borrowed and adapted—or resisted and excluded—the ideas and material culture of the West. The masses, too, were affected by Western thought and technology, including everything from Christianity to railroad trains. Asians now belonged to an inescapably interactive world, one they would soon seek to shape and hence forever share with Westerners, though on different terms than the nineteenth-century West had imagined.

THE GLOBE RESHAPED, 1919–1992

THE TWENTIETH CENTURY CONTEXT

The First World War, 1914–18, was a struggle among Europeans for hegemony that ended in British and French victory over Germany. But it also accelerated colonial nationalisms, brought the United States more prominently into world affairs, and established the Soviet Union as an alternative to the Western liberal, capitalist order. By the mid-twenties it seemed to most Europeans that the essentials of the old order had been restored. But that was a temporary illusion. The world Depression of the 1930s both enhanced the revisionist Axis powers and weakened the sinews of older empires. The tumble in agricultural prices impressed upon primary colonial producers their dependency on world markets and nudged national colonial politics throughout the world away from collaboration with the West toward resistance and independence.

The Second World War, 1939–1945, especially in Asia, severed the ties of imperial administration, disrupted the European domination of commerce, broke the spell of white rule, and undermined Europeans' self-confidence. The historical result was decolonization, independence, and the decline of the West in Asia. The war elevated communist Russia to a world power contending with the United States, whose economic hegemony stretched over the capitalist world. Offering alternative visions for the future of humanity, the Soviet Union and the United States engaged in a Cold War of ideological, military, and political conflict, which staked out worldwide spheres of influence. In an age of bipolarity the anticolonial nationalist movements and the independent nations that came to be known as the Third World were clients to be wooed and economic and geopolitical prizes to be gained.

By the late 1960s, the bipolar globe had begun to fracture. Asians, like others in the Third World, were not passive players in a Soviet-American scenario. Pressed by expanding economies in Europe and Asia and a war in Vietnam too costly to win, the United States could no longer wield its hegemonic power as it had in earlier decades. The Soviet Union, unable to bury capitalism abroad or deliver utopia at home, was increasingly unable to command support from communists in other countries who had their own problems and interests to look after. The superpowers also struggled to contain domestic discontent, which often widened to global ideological and political conflict. Finally, nuclear stalemate among the superpowers ironically opened a space for the secondary powers to pursue their national policies, as France, India, and China did in developing a nuclear capacity of their own.

One underlying theme of the twentieth century was thus the dissolution of European control over the world economy, the rise of the United States and the Soviet Union and their subsequent weakening in the face of a multiplicity of centers of power, and the true globalization of the world order. At the same time, the continuing industrial and postindustrial changes widened the gap between rich and poor, or between North and South, a division exacerbated by high rates of population growth and lagging development among the poor nations. The West and its developed associates still played a hegemonic role, especially in the collective domination of global communications and monopoly over technological innovation.

How the century would end could not be predicted, as the disintegration of the Soviet Union and the end of the Cold War in 1989–90 revealed. Barring nuclear, demographic, or environmental catastrophe, none of which can be ruled out, it seems probable that in the year 2000 the world will be even more globalized, nationalized, and interdependent than now. The technological advances of the nineteenth century tended to concentrate power. Those today, such as fax machines, photocopiers, computers, television, and satellites, tend to disperse and fragment power because each of these can be utilized by individuals and organized groups not easily controlled by the state. Ethnic nationalism poses challenges to the nation-state and its centralizing apparatus, which in form has spread to all the continents except Antarctica. Regionalism, as in Europe and Southeast Asia, is yet another contending force. And most difficult of all is the disparity of power and economic development that affects the entire globe, unequally and as yet insolubly.

GLOBAL DEVELOPMENTS AND THE ECLIPSE OF EUROPEAN EMPIRE

Peacemaking in 1919 Paris focused on European affairs, with five nations—Britain, France, Italy, the United States, and Japan—playing the leading roles. Woodrow Wilson, in articulating United States' participation in the war on the basis of anti-imperialism, free trade, and national self-determination, emboldened some Asians to believe that European predominance over their affairs would soon end.

The Paris Treaties and the League of Nations fell far short of Asian expectations. When news of the Versailles Treaty arrived in China on May 4, 1919, students, workers, and middle-class nationalists poured out in a great manifestation of protest and forged a mass nationalist movement, which came to be known as the May Fourth Movement. Two weeks later Kemal Atatürk announced Turkish resistance to the Paris settlement. The previous month in Amritsar, India, colonial troops had fired on demonstrators protesting British antisedition laws and the limited self-government London was willing to grant India. On March 1, 1919 Koreans rioted against Japanese colonial rule and were brutally suppressed (the March First Incident). In July Syrians demanded complete independence, but Britain handed them over to the French in accord with decisions reached in Paris. At the same time, European Jews began to emigrate to Palestine, a British mandate, a right claimed on the basis of the 1917 Balfour Declaration. While Europeans continued to decide domestic Asian issues among themselves, nationalism strengthened as Asians increasingly resisted imperialist control.

Some areas benefited during the immediate postwar years. Thailand had ended extraterritoriality and tariff exemptions for citizens of the Central Powers during the war and got other countries to agree to its abolition afterwards. The Japanese gained a permanent seat on the League of Nations' executive council and acquired some Pacific islands as mandates. Nonetheless, the rejection of racial equality in the League's charter angered the Japanese and people of color around the world. Prince Konoe Fumimaro, later to become a wartime prime minister, vowed that Japan would have to tear down the postwar status quo, which, he said, was a monument to Anglo-American economic and racial imperialism.

The United States emerged as the world's creditor nation in 1918, with a gross national product surpassing that of Europe and a pace-setting level of industrial production. Nonetheless, it turned away from international involvement. Congress erected tariff barriers and passed racially based immigration quotas that excluded Asians entirely in 1924, and the Senate voted to stay out of the League of Nations. None of this meant that the United States was not globally engaged as it sought to break into new markets, continued its proprietary actions in Latin America, and in the 1920s acquired naval parity with Britain, the world's foremost naval power.

By 1945 the United States was producing two-thirds of the world's industrial products and the dollar had become the lifeblood of the capitalist global economy. World War II had scattered American troops throughout the world and launched what came to be known as the imperial presidency in the United States. With Hiroshima, the Truman Doctrine, and the importance of strategic air power, the United States became the preeminent world power. Whereas Saudi Arabia, India, and Southeast Asia had been remote to United States' interests in 1919, Washington now considered them central. The United States' idea of a manifest destiny and a fascination with China and its supposedly limitless market, an allure extending well back to the late eighteenth century, seemed to reach its culmination now that the Pacific had become what some called an "American lake" after the defeat of Japan in 1945.

The Soviet Union had much longer involvement with Asia than the United States, but its relationship to the East in 1919 was problematic. The Soviets not only offered an example of a peasant society undergoing a national regeneration under an authoritarian revolutionary party, they also renounced czarist imperial ambitions and offered aid to anti-imperialist revolutions. That the Soviet revolution soon entailed secret police, militarization, and an absence of individual liberty mattered little to some Asians, who had not themselves enjoyed the benefits of liberalism either before or during colonialism. On the other hand, Bolshevik hostility to nationalism, especially within the borders of prewar Russia, tended to belie the pledges of Soviet internationalism.

The Soviet hope for leadership of suppressed Asians must be weighed against Asian dexterity in adding the Soviet Union and communism to their stockpile of weapons against the West. Of course, Moscow held no attraction for Asian merchants, capitalists, landlords, and those already sharing power in modernizing countries. But noncapitalist groups such as students, professionals, popular leaders, and army organizers more easily switched from admiring constitutional Britain and the United States to learning from the Soviets, or from fascist Italy and Nazi Germany on occasion. Such lessons seemed even more appropriate during the Depression, when the capitalist world languished, while the Soviet Union industrialized under Five-Year Plans and Nazi Germany achieved full employment.

Few West Europeans had anticipated the demise of empire in 1919. Indeed, the 1920s have been described as bargain basement days for imperialists in the Middle East and the Pacific. Domestic critics weighed the costs of empire against its dubious benefits, while imperial reformers felt a need to involve local leadership in administration as a way of penetrating societies more deeply and of justifying colonial rule. Advisory councils, legislatures, and economic investment schemes were put on the agenda, and sometimes into effect.

It was the combination of the world wars and nationalist movements that ultimately broke the colonial links and the imperialist mold, and with them, eventually the domestic political consensus on which empire had so long rested.

ASIA HELPS RECONSTRUCT THE WORLD

In the Middle East, state after state became independent in the interwar period or after the Second World War, with neither pan-Arabism nor a common Islamic identity able to overcome their strategic, economic, and political differences. Even violent opposition to the state of Israel failed to galvanize them into a common purpose. Those states rich in oil reserves moved center stage for strategic reasons after World War II and for financial reasons after the successes of OPEC in 1973. The effect of the oil cartel, the Iranian revolution of 1979, and other signs of resurgent Islam were felt from Africa across the world to Southeast and central Asia. Islamic fundamentalism befuddled those who had long identified secularization with modernization, and Iran exemplified the new contest between the traditional religious leadership and the Westernizing modernizers who had prevailed in earlier stages of independence.

In the early 1920s in India, Mahatma Gandhi moved to the forefront of the Indian nationalist movement, transforming Congress into a mass organization pursuing noncooperation and nonviolence in order to attain *swaraj* (self-rule). Gandhi instilled pride in being Indian, but also knew how to win Western humanitarian opinion. To gain broad support within India, during the Depression the Indian National Congress employed various measures. Among them was an appeal to those peasant farmers who were relatively well off, but at odds with large landowners on certain issues. To some extent, their interests influenced the Congress platform even though "land reform" per se was not a central issue for the Congress during those years.[1] The 1920s and 1930s saw increasing conflicts between Muslims and Hindus, between advocates of nonviolence and revolutionaries, between those who cooperated with the British and those who sought dominion status or complete independence.

During World War II the Indian Congress rejected an offer of postwar autonomy, demanding instead immediate action to permit independence. With Britain's refusal, Congress ceased to cooperate with the war effort, which led the British to arrest and imprison Congress leaders at all levels until the last year of the war.

The war helped Indian nationalists in many ways. It speeded the decline of Indian imports from Britain (69 percent in 1900, less than 20 percent in 1945). Britain had to cash in its Indian investments to finance the war, while Indians invested heavily in capital goods to manufacture war supplies. At war's end India had a very favorable balance of trade with London. The Indian Civil Service and the army had become more Indianized. Globally, British power ebbed, while that of the United States and the Soviet Union, which opposed the retention of the European colonies, soared. Finally, the election of the Labour Party to power in 1945 confirmed that independence was on London's agenda, though not in the form Congress wanted.

Independence in 1947 brought partition and communal violence, but no social revolution. Nonetheless, India became a unified state and the world's largest democracy, itself a remarkable feat given the great ethnic, linguistic, religious, and economic differences within the country that defy the once conventional judgment that modern states must be ethnic nation-states. The country has had a steady economic growth rate. Its army, Asia's largest single institution in 1945, is under civilian control. On the other hand, though famine has become rare, a population growth of 25 percent each decade eats up much of the country's new production.

Twentieth-century reconstruction of Southeast Asia has taken routes as diverse as its peoples, languages, and histories. Though separated from India in 1935, Burma was denied independence by Britain. Nationalists rallied briefly to the Japanese side in 1942, and Burma was declared "independent" by the Japanese the next year. After the war Britain offered dominion status to Burma, but in 1948 the Burmese declared complete sovereignty. Years of domestic conflict between ethnic and political factions followed, with the army seizing complete control of the country and suppressing the democratic movements that threatened their power.

Malaysia and Indonesia, both rich in a variety of ethnic and religious communities, experienced similar histories. As in Burma, the interwar period saw a growing involvement with world markets and increased penetration of society by the colonial state. Nationalism spread rapidly among the urban classes, fed by the fall of commodity prices and wages during the Depression. World War II had a different impact on Malaysia and Indonesia, which were occupied by the Japanese military, than it did on unoccupied Asia. The Japanese military administrators formed national armies among non-Chinese groups in the countries, while the Communists, anticolonialist since the 1920s and uncommitted to the wartime imperialist regimes, grew in popularity. The Dutch and British returned in 1945 to both colonies, but Malaysia (1963) and Indonesia (1950) eventually won their independence. Both countries had strong Communist movements, which were ultimately defeated. The emergence of strong, industrial nation-states depended on extensive redevelopment, which was handicapped by overpopulation, undereducation, and disadvantageous changes in the world economy. Singapore flourished, and other

Southeast Asian nations pursued the paths of economic and political development, usually in that order of priority.

The Philippines shared the region's diversity and political weaknesses. The American decision in 1936 to grant independence ten years later meant that the war itself was not the social or political watershed of decolonization that it was elsewhere. The landholding elite governed the country before and after the war, and continued to do so, while remaining an economic dependency of the United States. In subsequent decades the Philippines experienced the same troubled dialectic between economic and political development as elsewhere in Asia and the world.

Thailand, Cambodia, and Vietnam stood out as strong, nationalist states. During World War II Thailand maintained its fragile independence amidst a Japan-dominated "Greater East Asia co-prosperity sphere." In Vietnam an active communist resistance to the French dated from the 1930s. As did other colonialist powers, the French pursued a policy of economic and administrative penetration of agrarian society, but ended up mobilizing it against themselves. The Dutch bowed out of Indonesia in 1950, but the French army, stung by its 1940 defeat in Europe, tenaciously hung on in Indochina until the disastrous battle of Dienbienphu (1954). The United States, pursuing its Cold War policies, picked up where the French left off and fought the Cold War by proxy against the Communist North Vietnamese. In 1975 the independent North Vietnamese Communists overran the southern regime, having deprived it of the ability to turn from collaboration with the West to resistance against it. As in China, indigenous nationalism, Communist leadership, and peasant revolution combined to make a clean sweep. The triumphant revolution seemed initially less able to industrialize the country and attend to its overpopulation and insufficient agricultural yields than in either India or Indonesia.

Throughout this century peasant societies dominated in Asia in spite of massive urbanization. Social scientists who emphasize the specific processes by which peasants enter the modern world as critical to regime formation underscore this key theme. In addition to this factor, China's sheer mass and its potential global role give the Chinese revolution a central place in modern world history.

Though deeply imbued with a sense of being Chinese, the half billion Chinese of 1919 lacked the cohesiveness engendered by nationalism in other, smaller countries. They were, in Sun Yat-sen's telling analogy, a heap of sand. Nationalists hoping to move the country forward needed most of all to mobilize the peasantry, both to lay the basis of national self-assertion and to free China of foreign intervention.

The Guomindang (Nationalist) Party became a mass party after 1919. By that time the competing centers of power under a variety of warlords and local strongmen had all but destroyed the reality of national government. The process of building a strong party movement raced against the corrosive influence of Westernization in the port cities and against Japanese imperialism. In the 1930s these forces clashed. The European powers were stalemated by domestic weakness and imperial overextension, while the United States recoiled in Depression. This enabled Japanese expansionists to renew their drive in China, first in Manchuria in 1931 and then toward the south with the Sino-Japanese War of 1937.

The Guomindang aimed to form a broad consensus under strong leadership. Thus its new leader after Sun's death (1925), Chiang Kai-shek, launched a Northern Expedition (1926) and expelled his Communist allies from the party (1927). Forced to abandon their urban, proletarian base, the Communists in the 1930s elaborated a peasant-oriented strategy with which Chiang could not effectively compete. The Nationalists made significant progress in the 1930s in industrializing and reforming the sectors of China under their control. The Japanese, by capturing important industrial areas and the most advanced commercial areas along the eastern coastlands after 1937, drove the Nationalists into the agricultural areas of the country, which increased their reliance on landlords. The entry of the United States into the war in 1941 suggested to Chiang that Japan would be defeated from abroad and that he should save his energies for gaining victory within China.

Meanwhile the Communists, after their heroic Long March of 1934–5, mobilized peasants to their cause and broadened their military base. At the war's end they were able to take advantage of the Japanese military collapse in northeastern China, where the Nationalists were weakest. The extent of their support among Chinese peasants and urban classes may be doubted, but not that they had the stronger political movement. Chiang's Nationalists found themselves at the end of the wrong road. To the extent that they relied on foreign support, they exposed themselves to the same fate that undermined collaborating nationalists in Vietnam and elsewhere.

With Mao Zedong's declaration of the New China from the Gate of Heavenly Peace in 1949, China emerged as another model for peasant nations striving to achieve national sovereignty without following the path of collaboration within the global capitalist economy. The road of social revolution was rocky. First Mao followed the Soviet example. Forced collectivization, intervention in the Korean War, war with India and then Vietnam, the Great Leap Forward in the 1950s, the Cultural Revolution in the 1960s, the break with the Soviet Union, nuclear military capacity, and Nixon's visit in 1972 followed in quick succession as the regime lurched one way and another, often at great domestic cost. Constant, however, was the fact that the Chinese were in control of their own future. When the great Middle Kingdom emerged into world affairs in the 1970s, outsiders had now to deal with China on its own terms. The great Chinese revolution, which had begun in the late nineteenth century, seemed to be over.

In the late 1970s Mao's successor, Deng Xiaoping, broke with his predecessors' doctrinaire policies. He restored peasant households as the society's economic base, as one part of the Four Modernizations in agriculture, industry, science and technology, and the military. Decollectivization of agriculture was gradually joined by restoration of the free market and increasing private enterprise in transportation, commerce, and industry. As demonstrated by the failure of the 1989 democracy movement, political reform has not kept pace with economic reform in China.

China's history in the twentieth century demonstrated two important themes. The first was that most of Asia ran on local time, not on a schedule imposed by the West. The modern world did not start with Western intrusion nor end with decolonization. The second was that intra-Asian affairs were as important as relations between Asia and the West. Japan, for centuries the recipient of the largess of Chinese culture, became first an imperialist aggressor and then a source of economic power in the region. The booming economies of Korea, Singapore, Taiwan, and Hong Kong also altered the physiognomy of East Asia and the world much as a united India and a reassertive Islam were doing further to the west.

Japan, at the end of World War I, had expected recognition as a great power, but was frequently rebuffed by the West, both in international relations and in such race-related acts as the 1924 exclusion of Japanese from immigration to the United States. In the 1920s, parliamentary democracy strengthened, but the economy lagged, and as a highly export-dependent economy, Japan felt the Great Depression severely. A combination of right-wing terrorism, militaristic expansion, and economic crises led to the fascism of the 1930s. Japan's alliance with Germany and Italy (1940), however, had more to do with trying to cope with an unfavorable and changing international setting than with any mutual affinities between Japanese and European fascism.

Japan's aggressive war against China, which had begun in 1931 and continued as a total war since 1937, impelled Japan to wage preemptive war against the United States in 1941 in the hope of knocking the United States out so that Japan could concentrate on winning its seemingly unwinnable war in China. It was a suicidal gamble, as some of its leaders recognized, which in the end destroyed half the outcome of the original slogan of the Meiji modernization: strengthen the military. After a long war, two atomic bombs, unconditional surrender, and a seven-year Allied occupation, Japan eventually regained its hold on the other half of the Meiji slogan: enrich the country. The occupation, which was predominantly American, transferred sovereignty from the emperor to the people in a new, democratic constitution, and oversaw a series of reforms comparable, it was said, to the original "Meiji renovation." As part of its Cold War policy, the United States later shifted the emphasis of the occupation to economic recovery. Largely as a result of the Korean War, the Japanese economy revived, and Japan renewed its long-term industrial ascent based on corporate productivity and close cooperation between government and business.

In 1972 Japan normalized relations with China, becoming its best trading partner, and faced increasing competition from other exporting states such as Korea, Taiwan, Hong Kong, and Singapore. Resource-poor and with a large population, Japan continued to rely on foreign trade and its competitive advantage in a world market, with the result in the 1980s that Japan's economy had become the second largest in the world. In terms of international economic power, it had in some respects, such as its role as the world's creditor, traded places with the United States, still its closest geopolitical and economic ally.

Asia as an entity did not exist in 1500—"Asia" was a European term for the world east of the Mediterranean. The civilizations of Asia today continue their disparate traditions even as Asia becomes ever more important in the global scheme of things. Neither Europe nor its hegemonic successor, the United States, remains the sole epicenter of world affairs. No longer do trade and communications and decision making flow only to and from the West. Instead, there are many centers and complex global interrelations.

Asian societies have become deeply involved with one another, with Europe, Africa, and Latin America in ways unimaginable in 1500 or even in 1900. Each national society, though facing similar problems, has sought its own solution. Above all, the Asian nations have sought, like the rest of the world, for means to live and act within a global framework. Few believe any longer that the diverse societies of the world will converge in their domestic patterns as they modernize, but that ever-increasing interaction and interdependence is our common heritage can be doubted by none.

NOTE

1. H.C. Merillat, *Land and the Constitution in India* (New York: Columbia University Press, 1970), pp. 30–31.

SELECTED REFERENCES

The World Encompassed

Braudel, Fernand. *Civilization and Capitalism, 15th–18th Centuries* (New York: Harper and Row, 1981–1985).

Crosby, Alfred W. *Ecological Imperialism: The Biological Expansion of Europe, 900–1900* (Cambridge: Cambridge University Press, 1986).

Furber, Holden. *Rival Empires of Trade in the Orient, 1600–1800* (Minneapolis: University of Minnesota Press, 1976).

Hodgson, Marshal G.S. *The Venture of Islam; The Gunpowder Empires and Modern Times*, Vol. 3 (Chicago: University of Chicago Press, 1974).

Jones, E.L. *Growth Recurring: Economic Change in World History* (Oxford: Oxford University Press, 1988).

Jones, E.L. *The European Miracle; Environments, Economies, and Geopolitics in the History of Europe and Asia* (Cambridge: Cambridge University Press, 1981).

Kautsky, John H. *The Politics of Aristocratic Empires* (Chapel Hill: University of North Carolina Press, 1982).

McNeill, William H. *The Pursuit of Power: Technology, Armed Forces and Society Since A. D. 1000* (Chicago: University of Chicago Press, 1982).

Meilink-Roelofsz, M.A.P. *Asian Trade and European Influence in the Indonesian Archipelago Between 1500 and About 1630* (The Hague: Martinus Nijhoff, 1962).

Parker, Geoffrey. *The Military Revolution: Military Innovation and the Rise of the West, 1500–1800* (Cambridge: Cambridge University Press, 1988).

Scammel, G.V. *The World Encompassed* (Berkeley: University of California Press, 1981).

Smith, Alan K. *Creating a World Economy: Merchant Capital, Colonialism and World Trade, 1400–1825* (Boulder, CO: Westview Press, 1991).

Tilly, Charles, ed. *The Formation of National States in Western Europe* (Princeton: Princeton University Press, 1975).

Tracy, James D., ed. *The Rise of Merchant Empires: Long-Distance Trade* in the Early Modern World, 1350–1750 (Cambridge: Cambridge University Press, 1990).

Wallerstein, Immanuel. *The Modern World-System* (New York: Academic Press, 1974).

Wolf, Eric. *Europe and the People without History* (Berkeley: University of California Press, 1982, 1987).

Europe Ascendant: Nationalism, Imperialism, and Revolution

Betts, R.F. *The False Dawn: European Imperialism in the Nineteenth Century* (Minneapolis: University of Minnesota Press, 1975).

Embree, Ainslie T. *India's Search for National Identify* (New York: Alfred Knopf, 1972).

Fairbank, John King. *The Great Chinese Revolution 1800–1980* (New York: Harper and Row, 1986).

Gellner, Ernest. *Nationalism* (Ithaca, NY: Cornell University Press, 1983).

Goldstone, Jack A. *Revolution and Rebellion in the Early Modern World* (Berkeley: University of California Press, 1990).

Headrick, Daniel R. *The Tools of Empire; Technology and European Imperialism in the Nineteenth Century* (New York: Oxford University Press, 1981).

Jansen, Marius B. *Japan and Its World: Two Centuries of Change* (Princeton: Princeton University Press, 1981).

Kelly, Marjorie. *Islam: The Religious and Political Life of a World Community* (New York: Praeger, 1984).

Louis, W.R. *Imperialism; The Robinson and Gallagher Controversy* (New York: New Viewpoints, 1976).

Steinberg, David. *In Search of Southeast Asia: A Modern History* (New York: Praeger, 1971).

The Globe Reshaped

Barraclough, Geoffrey. *An Introduction to Contemporary History* (New York: Basic Books, 1965).

Betts, Raymond F. *Uncertain Dimensions; Western Overseas Empires in the Twentieth Century* (Minneapolis: University of Minnesota Press, 1985).

Bianco, Lucien. *Origins of the Chinese Revolution 1915–1949* (Stanford: Stanford University Press, 1971).

Holland, R.F. *European Decolonization 1918–1981; An Introduction* (New York: St. Martin's Press, 1985).

Laue, Theodor von. *The World Revolution and Westernization: The Twentieth Century in Global Perspective* (New York: Oxford University Press, 1988).

Porter, Bernard. *Britain, Europe and the World, 1850–1986* (London: Allen and Unwin, 1987).

THE EXPANSION OF EUROPE, 1450–1700

John W. Cell

This essay is based on the assumption, which underlay William McNeill's pioneering *The Rise of the West* (1963), and which was further articulated by Geoffrey Barraclough, *Introduction to Contemporary History* (1967), that the normal condition of world politics is neither domination by the power and culture of a single civilization, nor even the bipolar model which had become fashionable during the era of the Cold War, but international anarchy.[1] From this perspective the age of Western dominance that came to an end about the middle of the twentieth century was both transient and artificial. It therefore has to be explained.

The question of the effective beginning of the era of Western hegemony—whether 1500, 1700, or even later—will be taken up later in this essay. Before that date **a rough balance of power and influence** had been maintained for centuries among the primary civilizations of Eurasia: China, India, the Middle East, and Europe. (The Americas, as well as the interior of tropical Africa, remained almost entirely outside the area of continuous cultural interchange which McNeill has aptly called the Eurasian ecumene. North and much of West Africa, however, lay within the orbit of the power that controlled the Middle East and participated continuously in cultural interaction and diffusion.) From time to time this Eurasian balance of power had been threatened. The challenge launched by Hellenism went to the Indus Valley in northern India (now Pakistan) during the fourth century B.C.E. The expansion of Islam after 700 C.E.—reaching to Indonesia in the east and Spain in the west—was far stronger and more sustained. But though its expansion would never really cease even during the height of European ascendancy, Islam too failed to extinguish its rivals.

In the eleventh–thirteenth centuries rose the empire of the Mongols, dominating the mass of Eurasia from China right across to eastern Europe. Though best known for their barbarous cruelty—military force, after all, does tend to be the way empires are established and maintained—the Mongols succeeded in establishing an impressive degree of peace and stability, ensuring safer, more continuous trade across the land routes of central Asia than at any time before or since. Even in the thirteenth century Marco Polo's well-known adventures were by no means unique. A century later such expeditions had become commonplace. Silk, spices, and specie—the latter even then largely moving from West to East—dominated East-West trade. It needs to be emphasized that for meat-eating Europe spices were not merely a luxury. Europeans lacked both refrigeration and sufficient fodder to keep large herds alive through the winter.

The Pax Mongolia too was temporary. By the late fourteenth century it began to break up into competing khanates, the most powerful of which was that of the Ottoman Turks, who themselves were originally a Mongolian people. For European medievalists the subsequent period is one of "general crisis"—but it seems to have been equally catastrophic right across the Eurasian continent. After the warm cycle of earlier centuries, when a population explosion had taken place in Scandinavia and Greenland had become habitable, the climate turned unusually wet and cold. Crop failures were frequent, trade declined, states were disrupted by civil wars, and peasant revolts were frequent. Above all, the great pandemic of bubonic plague, the result of a closing of the world disease pool after greatly increased Eurasian communication, decimated populations.

In the late fifteenth century, again in common with other parts of Eurasia, western Europe began to recover from this general crisis. The population increased, crops improved, trade revived, and political systems somewhat consolidated. Europeans were pushing outward in all directions: in the eastern Mediterranean, in the north Atlantic, in the south Atlantic along the West African coast. But now the Ottoman Empire lay across their traditional trade routes with Asia. As Vasco da Gama explained in detail in his journal entries from the Indian port of Calicut after rounding the Cape of Good Hope in 1498, the prices of silk, precious stones, and spices were at least three to five times lower there than in the markets of western Europe.[2] The reason was not merely the carrying charges of the traders. All along the Red Sea route the Ottomans or Arab rulers were imposing customs duties.

These price differentials presented western Europeans, led by the Portuguese, with what in ecological terms would be called a potential niche: an opportunity to enrich themselves as well as to strike a blow against their Muslim, Turkish adversary. Moreover, they hoped to link up with the legendary Christian ruler, Prester John, gripping the Ottomans in a vice.

The expansion of Europe has ordinarily been explained on the basis of motives—the familiar trilogy of Gold, God, Glory—and means, that is, technology. So long as the trilogy is explained, it seems serviceable enough. *Gold:* Europeans did indeed go in quest of specie, although silver was in fact more significant than gold. But they sought raw materials of all kinds—fish, timber (especially for masts), furs, agricultural products, slaves—as well as markets for their exports. *God:* Like Islam, medieval Christianity was a militant, chauvinist, expansionist ideology. Especially for Portugal and Spain the expansion of Europe was a continuation of the Crusades. *Glory:* In European terms this means the ideology of the fierce competition of nascent nationalism, in some ways unique to Europe—Portugal vs. Spain, France vs. Holland or England. The important motives in favor of expansion do **not** include the export of surplus population. Despite the large contemporary literature on overpopulation, very few Europeans in fact went overseas until the eighteenth century.

The relevant technology was primarily naval. In the late fifteenth century Portuguese shipbuilders combined the classic Mediterranean square rig with the lateen or triangular rig which then prevailed in the Indian Ocean, producing the so-called lateen caravel. It possessed the advantages of both speed and maneuverability. Guns had spread west from China. (Contrary to popular notions, the Chinese **had** used them in military and naval warfare, not just for firecrackers.) The Portuguese introduced various improvements, the most significant being that of cutting holes in the sides of ships through which guns could be fired. Though there was also progress in mapmaking, the growth of practical knowledge can be traced most clearly in the charts sailors kept of coastal waters. Navigation across open water continued to be done by dead reckoning: setting a course by means of compass and then estimating the ship's speed and therefore its progress along it.[3]

Their once continuous and lucrative trade with Asia now effectively controlled by Arabs and the Ottoman Turks, by the late fifteenth century western Europeans had both the motives and the means to bypass land-based obstacles and reestablish direct communication with Asia, this time by sea. But the same after all was true of the Asians. One way to turn the expansion of Europe into a historical problem, to conceive of it as something that was neither normal nor inevitable and that must therefore be explained, is to ask: Why not China?[4] For China had both the means and at least for a time the resolve to expand overseas.

Several years ago Joseph Needham and Lynn White carried on an intense debate concerning the relative development of the technologies of China and western Europe down to 1500, after which both agreed Europe's went ahead.[5] The answer to that question may still be in doubt. So far as it relates to Chinese expansion, however, it is moot. In the late fourteenth and early fifteenth centuries Chinese sailors were active all along the western coasts of the Americas. Simultaneously, under the eunuch admiral Zheng He [Cheng Ho], they mounted expeditions in the Indian Ocean that reached as far as southeast Africa, voyages far outstripping those of Vasco da Gama or Columbus.

Clearly China possessed the technology to expand. It was its will that flagged. In the 1420s the Ming emperor called off the expeditions, ordering the eradication of all records pertaining to them. Meanwhile the Arabs were preoccupied by the challenge of the Ottoman Turks. The Mughals, the establishment of whose empire in India roughly coincided with the expansion of Europe by sea, were central Asians thoroughly oriented toward the land. It therefore happened that when the Europeans began to arrive in strength in Asian waters in the early sixteenth century, they had them largely to themselves.

The reasons for the Chinese decision to end overseas enterprise remain mysterious. Yet speculation about them helps to sharpen the contrast between China and Europe.

1) Economic: Like Egypt, China had originated as a hydraulic society whose economy and division of labor had concentrated on the opportunities and challenges posed by its two principal rivers, the Huang He (Yellow River) and the Yangzi (Yangtze). The canal system linking these two riverain systems had been a major imperial project for centuries—and it was largely completed at the time the overseas expeditions were being terminated. By contemporary European standards, as observed by the Venetian Marco Polo (a man accustomed to busy, cosmopolitan ports), the coastal and overseas commerce of China was impressive. Relative to the Chinese economy as a whole, however, external trade was

comparatively marginal. The striking characteristic of China was its economic self-sufficiency. Its only important need appears to have been silver, for which its appetite was huge and insatiable. If China had continued its overseas expansion, the action would certainly be explained as having been economically determined by its demand for silver. As it was, the demand was met by importations from Spanish mines in Peru via the Philippines, by tribute paid in from surrounding kingdoms, and by the general flow of specie from west to east.

2) Political: The Ming Dynasty which had overthrown the alien Mongols was native Chinese, far less tolerant of strangers than the relatively cosmopolitan regime of the khans and fearful of a resurgence of the threat from central Asia. More immediately, the decision to end overseas voyages seems to have resulted from a dispute at court between Muslim eunuchs (of whom the admiral Zheng He was one) and orthodox Confucian mandarins.[6]

3) Social and ideological: As Max Weber argued in his classic comparative study of the world's religions, the Confucian ethical system helped to maintain a profoundly conservative social structure which inhibited the development of a powerful bourgeoisie and the spirit of capitalism.[7] Power was concentrated in the bureaucracy, entry into which was determined by competitive examinations in the Confucian classics, which in turn were a powerfully reinforcing ideology for the gentry class. There was nothing in China resembling the Puritan ethic, by which Weber understood not merely Calvinism but the more general Christian belief in the godliness of the active, civically oriented life. The Chinese system did not eliminate the acquisitive spirit; it absorbed it. Although there may be something in this argument, it is also probably true that, like other ideologies, Confucianism was sufficiently broad and flexible that it could support conflicting viewpoints.[8] If the Chinese empire had wished to continue its expansion in the early fifteenth century, then sound Confucian reasons would undoubtedly have been provided for doing so.

If Weber may have placed too strong an emphasis on value systems, the fact remains that there was indeed a sharp contrast between the dynamism of Europe and the conservatism of China. The most striking evidence for this is the huge impact that was exerted on European society in this period by innovations which were originally Chinese.[9] Gunpowder revolutionized European warfare, making armored cavalry obsolete, greatly increasing the importance of infantry, enabling a common soldier to kill a lord. By severely inflating the cost of warfare, it strengthened the claims of the centralized state to exercise a monopoly of violence. Similarly, the printing press enabled both state and opposition to broadcast propaganda across entire populations. Without that instrument, which spread Luther's fiery statements across Germany within weeks or even days, it is hard to conceive of the success of the Reformation.

The key contrast, after all, is probably the simple fact that China was an empire. Having already expanded its boundaries to their natural limits, it was primarily concerned with defending them. The Chinese empire's foremost objective was to maintain its internal stability, which foreign entanglements might threaten—as they emphatically did in Europe. China possessed a central mechanism capable of weighing the costs and benefits of overseas expansion and deciding against it. Europe had no such central political authority. Indeed, "Europe" did not decide in favor of seaborne empire. The tiny state of Portugal did. Others followed.

It is also true that Europe offered little enticement to the technologically developed, self-contained, and self-confident Chinese of the Ming dynasty. It was Europe that sought the goods and riches of the East, not vice versa. Thus European dynamism was in part activated by the attractions of Asia, just as China's conservatism was in part intended to preserve the system that had conferred so much benefit and stability.

Both of the extremities of Eurasia, China and Europe, possessed the technological and organizational capacity for overseas expansion. Both began the race to reach the other end of the continent by sea, China's effort being conducted on an impressive scale. Abruptly China halted its drive. Europe's continued, accelerated—and transformed the world. Although the Chinese decision may have been made on narrowly political grounds, perhaps even so apparently inconsequential as a factional dispute at court, it evidently reflected powerful forces operating at all levels of Chinese imperial society. Similarly, an attempt to understand the underlying causes and dynamics of European expansion must go far beyond the mind of Prince Henry the Navigator.

In European historiography medievalists have argued that the roots of Western civilization were firmly planted well before 1500, that the continuity between medieval and Renaissance Europe is more impressive than the change. In terms of actual conditions and institutions, even of the quality of mind, that may well be true. In retrospect, however, it is apparent that early modern Europe (c. 1450–1700) was a society preparing to exercise world-wide hegemony. At every level important changes in degree were occurring that would ultimately add up to a change in kind.

1) Economic: It was not the scale of European economic activity that made it different from that of China or India, both of which were undoubtedly wealthier in 1500. It was the mode of organization. Again, China's economic system was based on, and intended to reinforce, the political boundaries of a land empire. Europe's economy had no such politically determined limits. Instead, in the phrase appropriated by Wallerstein, it was a world economy.[10] Although in the late fifteenth century it in fact comprised only a portion of the world—the Mediterranean, the interior of Europe and its Atlantic coast, Scandinavia, the Baltic, and European Russia—Europe's was a world economy in the sense that it possessed no such boundaries. In all of these areas Europeans were pressing outward: into the Levant, down the western coast of Africa for slaves and gold, out into the Atlantic for fish, north into Russia for timber and fur.

Europe's economy was also different by virtue of its underlying organizing principle, the system of possessive individualism which we call capitalism. Early modern capitalism was intensely, fiercely competitive, a Hobbesian world ruled by "a generall inclination of all mankind, a perpetuall and restless desire of Power after power, that ceaseth onely in Death. And the cause of this, is not alwayes that a man hopes for a more intensive delight, than he has already attained to; or that he cannot be content with a moderate power; but because he cannot assure the power and means to live well, which he hath present, without the acquisition of more."[11]

As Marx explained in *Das Kapital*, the mechanism that made capitalism run did not depend on the temperament of the individual businessman. It was structural. The businessman who did not expand both vertically and horizontally, protecting rear and flanks against competitors who were likewise expanding in self-protection, would soon cease to be a businessman. The employer who did not push workers to produce up to and beyond the customary maximum of productivity would also fail. Were European merchant-capitalists individually more acquisitive, more rapacious, or more sophisticated than Chinese merchants or Indian *bunniahs?* It seems unlikely. The difference is that they operated within a different milieu.

It was not merely that, in their effort to protect their rears and flanks, European merchant-capitalists extended the range of their activities. They were also forced to invest in technology which overturned and transformed the means of production. Whereas in 1500 the technological levels of Europe and China may still have been roughly equivalent, a century later that was certainly no longer true. In coal, iron, and many other fields the pressure generated by the fiercely competitive structure of capitalism brought forth new inventions or found new applications for old ones.

The other extremely important and virtually unique feature of early modern European capitalism was the world division of labor it imposed upon other areas which it brought into its orbit. Typically the center specialized in diversified agriculture and manufacturing, the periphery (or colonies) in extraction or cash-crop monoculture. In the interpretations of classical economists, this division of labor just happened: as the inevitable result of natural, normal market processes. In fact, economic speculation—what has been called the development of underdevelopment—was largely created artificially by the power of the European state.[12] Although the foundations of this modern world system were laid before 1700, only in the Americas, Indonesia, and southeast Africa did it become actuality; a more detailed analysis will therefore be given in the chapter "Europe and the World in an Expanding World Economy, 1700–1850." The capitalist world economy should be the heart of any course in modern world history.

2) Political: The single most important distinguishing feature of early modern Europe was therefore probably at the political level: the national state. In some ways it was a unique development. Throughout Eurasia the characteristic political form had been that of China or India: the land-based empire, extending to natural geographical limits and dedicated primarily to maintaining order, stability, and self-sufficiency within them. In the early sixteenth century it might have seemed that there was every prospect that Europe too would go in that direction, the Hapsburg, Valois, and Ottoman dynasties being the leading contenders. The continent might well have lapsed back into feudalism or, less believably, it might have been unified by a resurgent Catholic church. Instead, European power was both concentrated and divided in the medium-sized national state: England, France, Spain, the Dutch Republic.

It has been estimated that in 1500 Europe contained some sixteen hundred states or proto-states, compared with the sixteen that survived to begin the Great War in August 1914.[13] Survival depended on strategies of extraction and mobilization. Mercenary armies—the ability to mobilize peasants effectively for military service was not achieved until the French Revolution—required taxes (ordinarily confiscations in kind), which needed bureaucracies, which had to be backed by armies, which required taxes, etc., etc. This too was a fiercely competitive, Hobbesian world. Princes who did not behave according to Machiavellian canons, extracting and mobilizing ruthlessly—but not **too** ruthlessly—went to the wall, their states eaten up by stronger, more resourceful adversaries.

In the short run, against the large armies that could be raised by the land-based empires of Ming China, Mughal India, or Ottoman Turkey, Europeans were at a disadvantage—or would have been if they had been foolish enough to challenge them directly, instead of outflanking them by sea. A Flemish ambassador of the Hapsburgs at the Ottoman court in the early sixteenth century, writing at the very time when Hapsburg coffers were being enriched by Peruvian silver, foresaw a grim future: soft, pampered European troops would be no match for the hard, highly disciplined Janissaries.[14] We know that he was wrong. It was not capitalism in the abstract sense of impersonal market forces that created the world division of labor. The competitive national state system provided Europeans with the most effective mechanism of extraction and political mobilization ever invented.

3) Social and ideological: The competitive motif that emerges so clearly from an analysis of economic and political institutions is apparent in many other areas of European life and thought. It is obviously true in the shattering of the unity of medieval Christianity by the Protestant Reformation. Although rivalry between Catholics and Protestants may have been no more fierce or protracted than, say, that between the Shi'a and Sunni factions in Islam, wars of religion prevailed within and between European states during the sixteenth and seventeenth centuries. Although comparative data on world family systems are insufficient for confident generalizations, it may be that the early modern European family produced a harder, more inner-directed, more competitive, more instrumentally calculative personality than was typical of other parts of the world.[15] The journal of Christopher Columbus, for instance, shows a Renaissance European entering the Garden of Eden—and **instantly** sizing up how the garden and its inhabitants can be put to practical use. The people have no iron; they are ignorant of warfare; they can be made slaves—and therefore they will be.[16]

The competitive motif extended even into the world of thought. Europe, and only Europe, developed the so-called scientific method: a systematic, methodical scrutiny of the theories of predecessors with the goal of overturning and replacing them. As Joseph Needham has said, the same society—the same social forces—that produced capitalism also produced modern science. Where the structural competitiveness that ran through all levels of European civilization came from is a question that probably cannot be answered. It seems apparent, however, that **this** was the feature that gave Europe its restless, relentless energy, that made possible its artificial and transient but truly revolutionary domination of the world.

For most of the world in 1700 the establishment of European hegemony still lay in the future. In the early sixteenth century the Portuguese seized control of a string of strategically important bases in the straits of Hormuz, along the East African coast, and on the coast of western India: the world's first seaborne empire. Only in southeast Africa, now Mozambique, however, did their intrusions penetrate inland—and the Africans resisted them fiercely. The Dutch were more successful. In less well-organized parts of the Indian Ocean area, especially Indonesia and (though it did not amount to much at the time) in the western Cape of South Africa, they founded plantation economies based on the systematic employment of slave labor. Other Europeans followed, organized like the Dutch in joint-stock companies, the English East India Company being founded on the neat date of 1 January 1600.

For the well-organized, land-based empires of China and India, these European interlopers made little immediate difference. There on sufferance, they established themselves in forts, bribing local officials and paying due deference to mighty rulers at capitals in the interior. Europeans did not yet possess the military technology to challenge them. Even in West Africa, where the Portuguese had pioneered the trades in gold and especially in slaves, Europeans perched precariously in enclaves. Though the devastating malaria of the White Man's Grave provided a potent obstacle, the plain fact is that they lacked the power to move past African coastal powers into the interior. Apart from the fringe areas of the Indian Ocean, then, the world division of labor became a reality only in the Americas.

The European invasion of America took place essentially by accident—that is, Columbus ran into it on the mistaken assumption that the world was small enough that he could reach Asia by a voyage of only a few weeks—and long before Europe's preparation for world hegemony had been accomplished. Moreover, in the Americas Europeans came upon peoples who, unlike Asians or Africans, were militarily and biologically incapable of withstanding them.

The biological factor bears stressing.[17] Having developed in virtually complete isolation at least from the bacteriological parasites of the main Eurasian disease pool, native peoples of North and South America lacked any immunity to a wide range of epidemic diseases: smallpox, measles, TB, etc. Within a century of the Spanish conquest of Mexico the population had fallen by an estimated 75 percent. Although traditional estimates of the North American population ordinarily agreed on a figure of one million, based on the assumption that, since they were savages lacking settled agriculture, their economy could support only a sparse population, more recent assessments assume that a similar demographic catastrophe must have taken place north of the Rio Grande. These place the precontact level at eight to ten million.[18] (Which means that something comparable to the Holocaust had been wiped from the historical record by the assumptions of anthropologists!)

In the classic formula of high-school textbooks, European expansion in the Americas was governed by the motives of the various European powers: the Spanish searched for gold, the French for furs, the English for places in which to plant sturdy farmers. In fact all Europeans were after wealth, either specie directly from extraction or products that could be turned into wealth. The primary targets were therefore not so much products but concentrations of people who could be induced or forced to produce them. Hence the Spanish focus on Mexico and the western coast of South America (Peru and Chile), where—although much of it found its way to other parts of Europe, the Middle East, and eventually to Asia—the silver mines brought them spectacular riches.[19] Although the Spaniards' guns, swords, and horses gave them military superiority, disease was undoubtedly more significant in enabling them to overwhelm indigenous societies. Their ability to form alliances with some societies against others—as, for example, in Cortez's conquest of the Aztec Empire in Mexico— should also not be overlooked: a central feature of European imperialism that would be repeated elsewhere.

The approaches of the various European powers to the problem of exploitation were also similar. Until the eighteenth century none of them possessed surplus populations of their own for export. They therefore had to resort to alternatives. Where native populations could be forced to work, Europeans organized means to control them, as in the Spanish *encomienda* system. Where those indigenous populations were insufficient, or where they died off, Europeans imported slaves from Africa, as in the coastal areas of Brazil or in what would become the sugar islands of the West Indies. When trade with native peoples proved profitable—as in the French fur trade in the far north, where natives were not devastated by disease until later—Europeans relied on them to procure the products. In that case it was the natives themselves who, by extending the range and volume of their trapping, transformed the trade into a form of capitalist production. By all these means Europeans transformed the Americas into true colonies, into what Wallerstein has called peripheral areas of the European world economy.

By making available new miracle crops—especially maize, the potato, and the sweet potato—what Crosby has called the Columbian Exchange greatly enlarged the world's food supply, enabling it to support a population that would accelerate dramatically in the centuries after 1700. All continents benefited. (By the early eighteenth century, for instance, when Europeans penetrated the interior of south central Africa, they found maize already growing there in large quantities, having spread overland across the continent from West Africa.) But the Europeans, who exploited America directly, benefited first and most. The invasion of America was therefore both cause and effect of the expansion of Europe.

By 1700, it can be seen in retrospect, Europe had gone far toward preparing itself for the exercise of world hegemony. Except in the Americas and in the fringe areas of the Indian Ocean, however, actual dominance still lay in the future: perhaps not before the middle of the eighteenth century; more likely as the result of the dual revolution (French and Industrial) which would so transform European society around 1800.

NOTES

1. William H. McNeill, *The Rise of the West: A History of the Human Community* (Chicago: University of Chicago Press, 1963); Geoffrey Barraclough, *An Introduction to Contemporary History* (New York: Basic Books, 1964).

2. M.G. Ravenstein, ed., *A Journal of the First Voyage of Vasco da Gama, 1497-1499*, 1st series, vol. 99 (London: Hakluyt Society, 1898).

3. John H. Parry, *The Age of Reconnaissance* (Cleveland: World Publishing Co., 1963); Samuel Eliot Morison, *Admiral of the Ocean Sea: A Life of Christopher Columbus*, 2 vols. (Boston: Little, Brown, 1942).

4. This is the approach by Immanuel Wallerstein in his widely discussed work, *The Modern World System* (New York: Academic Press, 1974–), of which two volumes of a projected four have so far appeared.

5. Joseph Needham, "Science and Society in East and West," and Lynn White, "What Accelerated Technological Progress in the Western Middle Ages," in *Scientific Change*, ed. A.C. Crombie (New York: Basic Books, 1963).

6. On China in this period, see the excellent anthology edited by Joseph Levenson, *European Expansion and the Counter-Example of Asia* (Englewood Cliffs: Prentice-Hall, 1967). For a good general survey, see Mark Elvin, *The Pattern of the Chinese Past* (Stanford: Stanford University Press, 1973), which develops the comparative theme of the nature of land-based empires.

7. Max Weber, *The Religion of China: Confucianism and Taoism,* trans. Hans Gerth (Glencoe, IL: Free Press, 1951); *The Protestant Ethic and the Spirit of Capitalism,* trans. Talcott Parsons (London: Unwin, 1985).

8. See, for instance, the classic debate edited by E. Gale, *Discourses on Salt and Iron: A Debate on State Control of Commerce and Industry in Ancient China* (Leyden: Brill, 1931), in which Confucian arguments are used on both sides, both for and against state monopolies.

9. Eugene Rice begins his masterful survey, *The Foundations of Early Modern Europe, 1460–1559* (New York: Norton, 1970), with an account of the impact of these innovations.

10. One of the most useful features of Wallerstein's work is its extensive quotations from the ample secondary literature, especially the writings of the French Annales School and the multivolume *Cambridge Economic History of Europe*. For an excellent brief survey of the economic history of the period, see Fernand Braudel, "European Expansion and Capitalism: 1450–1650," in *Chapters in Western Civilization*, ed. Contemporary Civilization Staff of Columbia College, Columbia University, 3d ed. (New York: Columbia University Press, 1961–), 1:245–87.

11. Thomas Hobbes, *Leviathan* (1651; Oxford: Blackwell, 1955), p. 4. The argument that Hobbes's model was in fact that of unregulated capitalism is made by C.B. Macpherson, *The Political Theory of Possessive Individualism: Hobbes to Locke* (London: Oxford University Press, 1964).

12. See Andre Gunder Frank, *Capitalism and Underdevelopment in Latin America: Historical Studies of Chile and Brazil* (New York: Monthly Review, 1969).

13. This analysis draws upon that by Charles Tilly, ed., *The Formation of National States in Western Europe* (Princeton: Princeton University Press, 1975), especially the author's superb introductory essay, and the brilliant study of Perry Anderson, *Lineages of the Absolutist State* (London: New Left Books, 1974). A striking example of the difference in perspective between the world-history and internal-European perspectives would be provided by comparing these books with Sir Geoffrey Elton's essay, "Constitutional Development and Political Thought in Western Europe," in *New Cambridge Modern History* 2: 435–63 (14 vols.; Cambridge: Cambridge University Press, 1957–79). Elton begins by assuming that England, France, and Spain were characteristic of the new

monarchies, and examines the features they had in common.

14. From *The Life and Letters of Ogier Ghuhs de Busbecq*, excerpted in the fine anthology edited by J. Saunders, *The Muslim World on the Eve of Europe's Expansion* (Englewood Cliffs: Prentice-Hall, 1976).

15. See Lawrence Stone, *The Family, Sex and Marriage in England, 1500–1800* (Abr. ed.; New York: Harper & Row, 1979). It is fair to add that, even without the qualification in the sentence, Stone with good reason would probably dissociate himself from the extrapolation of his conclusions beyond England.

16. Cecil Jane, ed., *Journal of Christopher Columbus* (New York: Potter, 1960).

17. Alfred W. Crosby, *The Columbian Exchange* (Westport, CT: Greenwood, 1972), and by the same author, *Ecological Imperialism: The Biological Expansion of Europe, 900–1900* (Cambridge: Cambridge University Press, 1986).

18. Francis Jennings, *The Invasion of America: Indians, Colonialism, and the Cant of Conquest* (Chapel Hill: University of North Carolina Press, 1975).

19. A good deal of silver also went directly to China via the Philippines, thus completing the circuit of the early modern world economy.

JAPAN AND THE WEST, 1543–1640

Michael Cooper

History has often witnessed the sudden rise of a country to an extraordinary level of national vitality and expansion, and it is not always easy to account for the phenomenon. In the case of Portugal, however, several factors are obvious. After freeing themselves from Moorish domination in the thirteenth century and defending their national sovereignty against the claims of Castile in the following century, the united Portuguese were free to turn their attention abroad. Cut off from the rest of Europe by the geographical barrier of Spain, the Portuguese could expand their activities only by sea. North Africa was in the hands of the Moors, who effectively controlled the lucrative spice trade, and so the Portuguese sailed down the west coast of Africa, attempting to break the Moorish monopoly of spice and seeking the legendary Christian king Prester John. The chief geographical barrier was the southernmost tip of Africa, but once this obstacle had been circumvented by Bartholomeu Días in 1488, the Asian continent lay open to Portuguese explorers, merchants, and missionaries.[1]

Coming from a relatively poor country of meager resources and manpower, the Portuguese did not try to establish colonies by force of arms, but instead set up a chain of commercial bases—Mozambique, Ormuz, Goa, Cochin, Malacca, Macao, and, at the end of the line, Nagasaki. This chain enabled them to supply and refit their ships after the long and arduous voyages, exchange goods, and protect their shipping lanes.

News of Japan had been recorded by Marco Polo, who during his stay in China in the thirteenth century had heard of the mysterious island country called "Zipangu," where "the quantity of gold is endless . . . and abundant beyond all measure."[2] This alleged wealth aroused the interest of European explorers, who made repeated attempts to find the remote island country.[3] But it was only in 1543 that Europeans finally set foot on Japanese soil when a Chinese junk carrying three Portuguese traders was blown ashore onto the small southern island of Tanegashima.[4] News of the discovery spread quickly in East Asia and within a few years a number of Portuguese ships managed to reach Japan and establish trade relations.

It is important to note that the arrival of the first Europeans coincided with the so-called *sengoku jidai,* or warring states period, in which there was no effective central government in Japan; instead, the country was fragmented into domains governed by independent daimyo, or barons, who were constantly at war to defend and extend their territories. While this unstable state of affairs may not at first sight seem conducive to international trade, it did mean that there existed no central authority to forbid the Europeans entry into the country; if the ruler of one particular domain proved inhospitable, then the merchants could pack up and sail their ships elsewhere in search of a warmer welcome. Further, the daimyo were continually strapped for money to fund the defense and expansion of their territories, and were usually willing to deal with the European traders in order to raise capital.

There was another factor contributing to this artificial situation. As far as Japanese trade was concerned, the Portuguese merchants were essentially middlemen dealing between China and Japan. On account of the depredations of the *wakō* pirates, the Chinese government had forbidden its nationals to deal directly with Japan, and the Portuguese were quick to take advantage of this anomalous situation. There was a great demand in Japan for high-quality Chinese silk, while the Chinese on their part coveted Japanese silver. The Portuguese were able to provide ample transport facilities in their large carracks (at the time the largest ships afloat), and by exchanging Chinese silk for Japanese silver they made considerable profits (provided, of course, that their ships were not plundered by pirates or destroyed by natural hazards such as fire, storm, or shallows).[5]

Along with the Portuguese merchants arrived Catholic missionaries, who saw their chance of regaining in Asia what they had lost in Reformation Europe. The first group, led by Francis Xavier, reached Japan in 1549, and subsequent reinforcements, although relatively few in number, achieved remarkable results. Their success may be explained by the fact that many of the missionaries were educated and zealous men, that Buddhism was in a state of decline, that in a period of social instability people's thoughts turn to religion. Furthermore, the close connections between the missionaries and the Portuguese merchants with their lucrative trade did not go unobserved. Converts to Christianity were numerous, initially in the southern island of Kyushu but later also in the main island of Honshu, and these included various daimyo and influential officials. It is easy but simplistic to attribute all the conversions of powerful lords to commercial considerations, but the subsequent steadfastness of Christian daimyo such as Konishi Yukinaga and Takayama Ukon proves otherwise. Precise numbers are not available, but a figure of 300,000 Japanese Christians was recorded for the year 1614.[6]

Committed to spend the rest of their lives in the country, many of the missionaries learned to speak the language well and sent back to Europe a stream of detailed information about Japan and its people.[7] In 1603 the missionaries published in Nagasaki the *Vocabulario da Lingoa de Iapam*, a Japanese-Portuguese dictionary of colloquial Japanese containing more than 32,000 entries, and in 1608 the *Arte da Lingoa de Iapam*, a grammar of spoken Japanese.[8] Both of these works remain a valuable source of information about spoken Japanese in the early seventeenth century. Mention may also be made of the Jesuit boys' school in Kyushu, where European languages, painting, and music were taught; four of the pupils left Japan in 1582 and traveled to Rome as representatives of the Christian daimyo of Kyushu, met two popes, had two audiences with Philip II of Spain, and returned to Japan in 1590.[9]

Japanese fascination with the European *nanbanjin*, or southern barbarians (for they sailed up to Japan from the south), is apparent in contemporaneous screen paintings, usually featuring tall, long-nosed Portuguese merchants and missionaries walking through the streets of a port city (presumably Nagasaki) and the great carrack being unloaded at a wharf. This curiosity about the Europeans extended to the most powerful lords, and there are records of the three great unifiers of the country, Oda Nobunaga, Toyotomi Hideyoshi, and Tokugawa Ieyasu, spending hours talking with Japanese-speaking missionaries and questioning them about life in the fabled West.[10]

With luck, skill, and treachery, the petty daimyo Nobunaga managed to seize control of central Japan in the 1570s. Following his assassination in 1582, his lieutenant Hideyoshi extended central power down to Kyushu before he died in 1598, leaving his five-year-old son Hideyori as successor. Ieyasu gained effective control of the country after winning the Battle of Sekigahara in

1600, and for the next two and a half centuries the Tokugawa line of shogun rulers governed the country.

At the beginning of the seventeenth century, however, Tokugawa hegemony did not go unchallenged; the family had no divine right to rule the country, and there existed the possibility of a coalition of hostile daimyo rising up in arms against its authority. The shogunate tended to view with suspicion Christianity, which could conceivably act as a catalyst to unite disaffected daimyo, especially as opposition came mostly from the southern and western parts of the country, where the Christian presence was strongest. The Tokugawa, and other rulers, demanded total and unqualified obedience from their subjects, and the Christian teaching of a higher moral order and the supremacy of individual conscience was regarded as subversive of traditional social stability.

As a result, the shogunate issued a decree in 1614 expelling all missionaries from Japan; the edict was not strictly enforced, but it was an indication that the initial period of welcome extended toward the European visitors was drawing to a close. At Osaka, in 1615, Tokugawa forces overcame troops loyal to Hideyori, and Tokugawa rule was thenceforth firmly established. But ever concerned about any potential threat against its authority, the government ordered the apprehension of underground missionaries and local Christians. At the beginning of the persecution, executions served only to increase the fervor of the Christian spectators, and the authorities resorted to torture to obtain apostates rather than martyrs. By the middle of the seventeenth century, the Christian presence in Japan had been for all practical purposes eradicated, although a few communities continued to exist secretly on remote islands off Kyushu.[11]

Internal political events also had an effect on European trade, and increasing restrictions were placed on Portuguese and Spanish merchants, who, the authorities rightly suspected, were willing to shelter and succor the outlawed missionaries. The arrival of Dutch (1609) and English (1613) traders, not concerned with, and indeed hostile to, Catholic missionary activity, further strengthened the hand of the shogunate. Spanish traders were expelled from the country in 1624, and the English left voluntarily in 1623.

A minor incident in a remote part of Kyushu took on national importance in 1639 when some peasants in Shimabara rose up against the harsh treatment inflicted on them by their local lord. What started as a protest against excessive taxation took on a Christian character and became a full-scale rebellion. To the shogunate's consternation, the inexperienced Tokugawa soldiers took more than three months to overcome the samurai and peasants, many of whom were Christian, beseiged in Hara Castle.[12] This alarming incident served to increase the xenophobic fears of the government, which then expelled the Portuguese merchants and confined the Dutch traders to Deshima, an artificial islet in Nagasaki harbor. Japanese were not allowed to travel abroad, while foreigners, with the exception of some Asian and Dutch traders, were forbidden to enter the country under pain of death. This *sakoku jidai,* or period of national seclusion, was to last until the 1850s when Commodore Matthew Perry arrived in his iron ships to demand the establishment of U.S.-Japanese relations and the end of national isolation.

When the Portuguese sent an unarmed and unladed ship to Nagasaki in 1640 with a delegation to plead for resumption of trade, the local authorities, on orders from the central government, executed sixty-one of the officials and crew, and sent thirteen crew members back to Macao with the grim news.[13] Thenceforth a few Dutch merchants (and other Europeans in their employ), kept under strict surveillance, were the only Europeans allowed to remain in the country.

The period of European presence in Japan, conveniently but inaccurately called the "Christian century," is a fascinating field of study. It was the first significant encounter between Europeans and Asians on an equal footing. Elsewhere, in India, for example, European force of arms had prepared the ground for and then supported the work of Iberian merchants and missionaries. Owing to the island country's isolated location and tenuous lines of communication with the mainland, however, the Europeans in Japan were in no position to assert themselves militarily, and it was their turn to be dubbed barbarians by the populace. As a result, the visitors were obliged to conform to local laws and customs, and this may explain the wealth of detail about Japanese culture and way of life to be found in missionary records. Moreover, the Europeans' stay in Japan coincided with a tumultuous period of Japanese history, a period dominated by strong personalities battling for national supremacy; the Tokugawa emerged victorious out of this power struggle and established a regime that provided more than two centuries of peace and stability.

It may be instructive to view this European interlude as part of a cycle of Japanese foreign relations with the West. Initial enthusiasm for the West in the second half of the sixteenth century was repeated for a time after both the Meiji Restoration (1868) and the Pacific War (1945); all three occasions were marked by social upheaval and dislocation. In the first two cases, the intense Japanese interest in the West was eventually replaced by a growing sense of nationalism and a turning away from the community of nations. The warm reception of things American in the immediate postwar period has long since given way to a more critical attitude, but it is no longer possible for Japan to turn itself away from the world.

NOTES

1. An excellent account of early Portuguese exploration is provided in Donald F. Lach, *Asia in the Making of Europe*, vol. 1 (Chicago: University of Chicago Press, 1965), Bks. 1–2.

2. Marco Polo, *The Book of Ser Marco Polo*, ed. and trans. Henry Yule and Henri Cordier (London: John Murray, 1903), 2:253.

3. It is noteworthy that one of the aims of Christopher Columbus's voyages was to discover the fabled "Zipangu."

4. An exhaustive investigation as to whether the date was 1542 or 1543 is made in Georg Schurhammer, "O descobrimento do Japão pelos Portugueses no ano de 1543," in his *Orientalia* (Rome: Institutum Historicum Societatis Jesu, 1963), pp. 485–577; Schurhammer inclines toward 1543.

5. The history of the Macao–Nagasaki trade is provided in C.R. Boxer, *The Great Ship from Amacon: Annals of Macao and the Old Japan Trade, 1555–1640* (Lisbon: Centro de Estudos Históricos Ultramarinos, 1961); specific details of the Portuguese restrictions to maintain their monopoly of this commerce are supplied in Michael Cooper, "The Mechanics of the Macao-Nagasaki Trade," *Monumenta Nipponica* 27 (Winter 1972): 423–33.

6. C.R. Boxer, *The Christian Century in Japan, 1549–1615* (Berkeley: University of California Press, 1951), pp. 320–21. Higher figures, possibly accumulative, are quoted in J.F. Schütte, *Introductio ad Historiam Societatis Jesu in Japonia, 1549–1650* (Rome: Institutum Historicum Societatis Jesu, 1968), pp. 425–27.

7. See Michael Cooper, *They Came to Japan: An Anthology of European Reports on Japan, 1543–1640* (Berkeley: University of California Press, 1965), for excerpts from contemporaneous European accounts of Japanese life.

8. Details of the dictionary are given in Michael Cooper, "The *Nippo Jisho*," *Monumenta Nipponica* 31 (Winter 1976): 417–30, and "The First European-Language Dictionary of Japanese," *Transactions of the Asiatic Society of Japan* 13 (1976): 104–28; and of the grammar in Michael Cooper, *Rodrigues the Interpreter: An Early Jesuit in Japan and China* (Tokyo: Weatherhill, 1974), pp. 220–38.

9. A full account of the expedition is given in Luis Frois, *La Première Ambassade du Japon en Europe, 1582–1592*, ed. J.A. Abranches Pinto et al., Monumenta Nipponica Monograph 6 (Tokyo, 1942); a summary of the embassy's travels is supplied in Lach, pp. 688–706.

10. See, for example, Cooper, *They Came to Japan,* pp. 95–97, 111–14, and 136–38; and Cooper, *Rodrigues the Interpreter,* pp. 186–87, 192–93, and 202.

11. See Boxer, *Christian Century,* pp. 308–61, and Cooper, *Rodrigues the Interpreter,* pp. 385–95, for a general account of the persecution.

12. Boxer, *Christian Century,* pp. 375–83.

13. Cooper, *They Came to Japan,* pp. 401–3.

EUROPE AND THE WORLD IN AN EXPANDING WORLD ECONOMY, 1700–1850[1]

John W. Cell

As argued in the chapter "The Expansion of Europe, 1450–1700," the foundations of the modern world system had been laid by the middle of the seventeenth century. Except for the Americas and the fringe areas of the Indian Ocean, however, that system did not come into practical being until well after 1700. Moreover, except for their dominance at sea—though in the long run that made all the difference—it is premature to talk in terms of European world hegemony. Quite simply, early modern Europeans lacked the military resources to challenge the powerful land-based empires of Asia and the Middle East—or even the far weaker states of West Africa.

The first phase of European expansion took place in what Braudel and other economic historians have called the long sixteenth century (1450–1660).[2] By this they mean a full and completed economic cycle: beginning with the gradual emergence from the catastrophe of the late medieval crisis, to confident growth and boom dominated by price inflation, and ending with an extended depression sometimes called the general crisis of the seventeenth century. In the last half of the eighteenth century came another cycle of expansion. But this one was profoundly different. By developing their industrial techniques and modes of economic organization, above all by peripheralizing and exploiting other areas of the world, Europeans and their overseas offshoots invented means of extending the cycle indefinitely. Even though its originators have long since ceased to control it, the framework of the modern world system that began definitely to be established in the eighteenth century remains into the late twentieth century.

By rounding the Cape of Good Hope in the late 1400s, the Portuguese had identified a niche which they or other western Europeans might hope to occupy and exploit to their immense benefit. The prize seemed to be there for the taking. Contemporary observers in Venice—the primary European terminus of the Red Sea route from Asia and the Middle East—predicted that Portuguese merchants would soon effectively undercut prices to such an extent that they themselves would be ruined. In fact their fears were premature. The volume of the Red Sea trade decreased little if at all; the decline of Mediterranean Europe was gradual and protracted.[3]

Although the Portuguese swiftly seized a far-flung network of bases at strategic locations around the Indian Ocean, they lacked the resources and organizational expertise to follow up their advantage. The tiny state of Portugal was incapable of converting the world's first seaborne empire into a world economy. Nor, despite the flood of Peruvian silver into its treasury after about the 1530s, could Spain. Neither of the two Iberian countries who had led the expansion of Europe seemed to derive any lasting benefit from it. Instead the chief beneficiaries of the growth in trade and in the expansion and liquidity of currencies were northern Europeans, especially the Dutch.

The obstacles that had to be overcome in establishing a profitable and relatively stable world economy need to be emphasized. The unbelievably enormous profits which early expeditions sometimes achieved are misleading. When they did occur—and the figures might have been inflated either by zealous promoters or by envious outsiders—the explanation was that their cargoes were high-density luxury products, such as silk or precious stones, for which demand was high. A profitable world economy could not, however, be based on such items. Like the industrial revolution later, it had to concentrate on goods for popular consumption. It had to carry them in bulk and provide them at prices ordinary people could afford.

Such an enterprise required a huge fleet of merchant ships and a navy to protect them, mechanisms for raising capital and for providing insurance, sophisticated knowledge of overseas and domestic markets. Since many of the main items of Asian commerce—especially tea, coffee, and cotton—were comparatively unknown in Europe, advertising had to create demand. But perhaps the most difficult obstacle of all was acquiring enough gold and silver to carry to Asia in return for those goods. For the basic fact of the early modern world economy—a condition that did not change until the industrial revolution of the late eighteenth and early nineteenth centuries—was that Europe was manufacturing virtually nothing Asians wanted or needed.

Not the Iberians but northern Europeans—first the Dutch, followed by their English imitators—developed the sophisticated financial institutions to organize and sustain far-flung seaborne empires. Unlike the Portuguese, whose prince had claimed the Indies trade as a royal monopoly, closing it to private individuals, the Dutch Republic made overseas enterprise a national project in its long and ultimately successful struggle to maintain its independence from the Hapsburgs. The great advantage of the Dutch, as contemporary English observers were quick to note, was that they opened investment opportunities to all.

Two of their innovations deserve particular notice. The first was the stock exchange, which made it possible for potential investors to buy in at a late stage or realize early profits. Still more important was the joint-stock company, of which the Dutch East India Company was the outstanding example. The typical commercial organization of the Middle Ages had been the regulated company restricted to members of a guild of merchants who combined, ordinarily under government charter, to create a monopoly of trade with an area. English examples were the Russia or Levant companies. In contrast, the joint-stock company was open to all. Its profits were not necessarily shared out at the end of each voyage, dividends instead being voted from time to time by boards of directors, who could also decide that most of the funds needed to be reinvested or that even further calls had to be made on shareholders.[4]

The invention of the joint-stock company enabled the Dutch and their English imitators to draw capital from a broad cross section of the prosperous classes, not merely from merchants. Moreover, it was gentry and aristocrats, who were often pressed by their inability to raise rents fast enough to keep pace with inflation, who turn out to have been the readiest risk takers. All the famous companies in the history of British expansion—East India, Royal Africa, Newfoundland, Virginia, Massachusetts Bay—were of the new type. The joint-stock company enabled the promoters of overseas enterprise to ally with and draw upon the far more powerful and better-financed field of domestic capitalist agriculture. Nor did the institution merely increase the sheer volume of capital. It assured the crucial political struggle of the powerful.[5]

The integral role of the state, as well as of the propertied and prosperous classes who largely controlled it, is the essential point to be made about the dominant economic theory and practice of the period, commonly called mercantilism, for which a broader but probably more accurate term would be state-directed capitalism.[6] Several basic assumptions underlay the mercantilist approach. The first was that the stagnant economic situation of the late seventeenth and early eighteenth centuries would continue for the foreseeable future. The volume of world production and wealth being more or less constant, one country's gain would be another's loss. The second assumption, which was largely inspired by the Dutch example, was that foreign trade was probably the only area where growth was likely to occur; eventually the domestic sector might also benefit. A favorable balance of trade, from which profits might be raked off for domestic consumption, was therefore essential—hence the popular conception that mercantilists were preoccupied with accumulating bullion.

The third assumption was that trade and war were inextricably connected. To survive politically, a country had to protect its own overseas commerce while denying opportunities to competitors as much as possible. It might do so by planting colonies at strategic locations, as the English tried to do at Roanoke, as the Dutch did at the Cape, as the French did at Quebec. But the main weapon was naval. Unlike the strategy later favored by the American captain, A.T. Mahan, for whom navies existed to knock out other navies, eighteenth-century fleets were essentially defensive. Their primary role was to defend their own commercial routes, while nibbling away at those of their opponents. It was assumed that the struggle would go on indefinitely—as indeed, in what amounts to a second hundred years' war between England and France, it did. In essence, the theory and practice of mercantilism amounted to a policy of protectionism. Later derided by Adam Smith and his free-trader successors, it was probably the most appropriate economic strategy for European economies before the Industrial Revolution.

In analyzing the development and extension of the world economy in the eighteenth and early nineteenth centuries, it is helpful to think of three more or less distinct though intersecting world economies. These have already been identified in the earlier essay: the North Atlantic, the South Atlantic, and the Indian Ocean. Though to some degree common themes ran through them, each had its own boundaries and its own peculiar dynamics.

NORTH ATLANTIC

The North Atlantic system included the coastal trade of northern Europe as far as the Baltic, Scandinavia and European Russia, the North Atlantic islands of Iceland and Newfoundland, and what by the second quarter of the eighteenth century were already substantial settlement colonies on the eastern coast of North America.[7] Its main products were timber and wood by-products, fish, and fur.

In orthodox mercantilist terms the white settlement colonies produced disappointingly little that Europe wanted. Their primary cash crop was tobacco, for which European demand had to be created. Their diversified agricultural production was mainly for home consumption; and the American miracle crops (especially the potato) were bulk items that affected Europe not through trade but through their incorporation as staples in European agriculture. By the late eighteenth century the northern colonies had mainly become competitive rather than supplementary to the domestic economies of Europe. In what became the southern United States, the long-awaited cash crop took off only when the industrial revolution greatly accelerated the world demand for cotton, which in turn rigidified and expanded slavery as the region's peculiar institution.

Manned entirely by Europeans and transplanted Europeans, the fishing industry did not involve cultural interchange with the native peoples of North America. Undoubtedly more important to the European economy than all the silver of Peru, its sheer volume needs to be emphasized. It was also one of the most substantial means of linking northern and southern European economies, re-exports of fish enabling the former to pay for imports of spices from the eastern Mediterranean as well as for silver bullion from Spain. Moreover, since mortality rates were far lower than in the South Atlantic, the name of nursery of seamen was far more appropriate for the fishing than for the slaving fleets.[8]

Unlike the fishing industry, the fur trade did involve Europeans and native peoples in complex patterns of economic and cultural interchange.[9] An internal traffic already existed, with northern tribes exchanging furs for agricultural products, copper, or shells (i.e., currency) with those to the south. By linking the domestic trade to the North Atlantic world economy, Europeans greatly increased both the volume of the traffic and its range, stimulating the growth of what has been called capitalist hunting. At least at first, little or no European coercive power was involved. Nor, primarily because the longer voyages lasted beyond the incubation periods of diseases that were decimating populations in the south, were those in the far north unduly harmed in the first century or so of contact. Native Americans therefore remained in control both of acquiring the raw materials and of processing them for the market. The operative economic motive in the expanding trade was therefore that not of Europeans but of native peoples. They were trading for items—shells, beads, cloth, guns, liquor—that were valuable domestically. In the long run the terms of trade worked powerfully to the advantage of Europeans. But it should probably not be assumed that the indigenous traders were less acquisitive, less economic animals than Europeans.

In the eighteenth century Europeans for the first time began to migrate overseas in substantial numbers. Whatever their nationality, their principal destinations were England's colonies on the eastern seaboard, strengthening England in its long rivalry with France for North America. As late as 1700 an outside observer, noting its domination of the continent's two principal river networks, the Mississippi and the St. Lawrence, might well have bet on France. Though England won the Seven Years' War (1756–63), ultimately the great gainers were the colonists themselves, whose subsequent revolution might be interpreted as a successful attempt to move from the periphery of the world economy into its core. After the revolution white settlement swiftly pushed beyond the first mountain barrier, the Appalachians. Though conflicts between colonists and natives had occurred from the beginning, the struggle now accelerated. This was warfare of the most ferocious type in world history, to be repeated in Argentina, southern Africa, and Australasia: a war of removal and extermination, of Lebensraum, in which Darwin's metaphorical language was literally realized.

SOUTH ATLANTIC

The South Atlantic world economy focused on the familiar triangular trade linking Europe with the slave-producing societies of West Africa and the cash-crop plantation economies of Brazil, the West Indies, and the southern United States. The marginality of the American South must be stressed. Only 5 percent of slaves, including those who originally came to other destinations, went to the mainland colonies in North America, compared with 50 percent to Brazil and 33 percent to the Caribbean.

In some ways the West African slave trade worked surprisingly like the fur trade in North America. In Africa too slavery and an internal slave trade were already in existence. There too the irresistible pull of the world economy accelerated the volume and range of the traffic, transforming it into a form of capitalist enterprise. There too Europeans on the whole did not possess a preponderance of power, for though they obviously controlled the sea, they lacked the means as well as the will to penetrate into the interior. Disease, especially malaria, was certainly an important obstacle: the mortality rate on a short Niger expedition in the early 1840s, if computed at an annual rate, was actually more than 200 percent! But the power on the spot of the African states and city-states which controlled the traffic was probably a still more important barrier.

On the whole, then, Europeans and Africans carried on the slave trade on more or less equal terms. Africans did the raiding, mainly in the so-called middle belt 50–150 miles from the coast but often ranging far into the interior; they brought the slaves down to the coast, where European ships were waiting. They bargained shrewdly for a wide variety of goods, cowrie shells (currency), guns, cotton and other textiles, iron (scarce in Africa), and gin being the most significant. African slave dealers possessed a sophisticated understanding of market mechanisms. Knowing that the longer a European ship remained at anchor the more its crew was likely to be decimated by disease or slaves already on board would revolt, they habitually held back their human products to drive up their price. Again, it would appear that the economic instincts of Africans were little if any less pronounced than those of Europeans. The difference was not the motivations of individuals but the structure in which they operated. In the short run African traders may have got as good as they gave. In the long run the terms of trade ran strongly in favor of the manufacturing countries.

Although estimates of the volume of the Atlantic slave trade have ranged as high as 30 million, with another 20 million added for "wastage" during the trek to the coast, the interval between arrival and sale, and the infamous middle passage, the figure is now generally agreed to have been in the neighborhood of 9–11 million arrivals and a total of perhaps 13 million.[10] Lowering the total does not of course reduce the hideous enormity, say by 75 percent! But it does have some practical effect on attempts to assess the impact of the slave trade on West African societies. Clearly, the trade aided the state-making efforts of some coastal peoples, that is, the middlemen, as well as their accumulation of wealth. Because all of the region was later colonized, the political effects were ultimately abortive. And, though African traders and political leaders became wealthy, they did not accumulate capital— because capital is invested in growth-producing enterprise.

In demographic terms the results seem to have been mixed. The ecology of Africa has historically placed serious limitations on the development of agriculture and thus on the density of population, and much of the continent was underpopulated, but not the coastal and middle belts from which the large majority of slaves were drawn. There, as in parts of Europe, the slave trade may even have drawn off excess population. Again, however, there were differences. European migrants may have been hard pressed economically, but on the whole they went voluntarily. Moreover, in Africa the people were simply removed and there were no remittances. In the long run the impact was therefore undoubtedly negative.[11]

For us the moral implications of the slave trade are awesome. That, however, is **our** problem. The title of the standard book by David Brion Davis, *The Problem of Slavery in Western Culture*, is a little misleading. For centuries—in Aristotle and Greek thought generally, in medieval Christianity, even in much of the Enlightenment and the development of democracy—slavery was not a problem to the Western conscience (or to the African).[12] In fact, the mechanics of the slave trade were like those of any other commercial enterprise. It has often been assumed that since the trade was so evil it must have been sustained by extremely high profits. In fact, the average rate of profit for the eighteenth-century British slave trade turns out to have been about 10 percent— good but not **that** good.[13] As Hannah Arendt said of Adolf Eichmann, in some ways the most horrifying thing about the slave trade was its matter-of-fact, businesslike banality.

In Immanuel Wallerstein's scheme West Africa remained an external arena in the world economy of the eighteenth century. As in India, the few Europeans who lived there semipermanently remained in small forts or enclaves. Though the impact of the linking of this part of Africa to world capitalism was considerable, not until the late nineteenth century was it colonized directly—or, in Wallerstein's terminology, peripheralized.

Throughout the New World except in the northern mainland colonies—and even there slavery was well established before being largely ended during the eighteenth century—forced labor prevailed. Simultaneously free wage labor was triumphing in Western Europe itself. This apparent contradiction has been resolved in three ways:

a) Sequential: The first colonizers came from one of the least advanced parts of Europe, where slavery had never disappeared and where feudalism continued. The Portuguese were slave traders before they were colonizers, their early fifteenth-century West Africa excursions having brought back small numbers of slaves. As they moved across the Atlantic islands they were unable to persuade Portuguese laboring classes to migrate, so they resorted to African slaves. In Brazil the problem was repeated, West African slaves were plentiful, and the system was extended. Meanwhile, drawing on their own institutions, the Spanish organized the indigenous population of New Spain in the *encomienda*, parceling out large chunks of territory and the people who lived on it as feudal estates, buying slaves when necessary from the Portuguese. Picking up the slaving habit from the Portuguese, the Dutch conducted it with characteristic efficiency. The French and English copied the Dutch.

The decisive factor, however, was the establishment of sugar as the dominant cash crop of the Caribbean. The first settlement of the West Indies featured white indentured labor growing mainly tobacco. Unlike tobacco, however, sugar is produced efficiently only on a large scale, and it was hard to induce whites to do the backbreaking work. The large plantation therefore superseded the small farm, black slaves displacing free or indentured whites. Slavery spread from the coast into the interior of Brazil, and from the West Indies to South Carolina and other southern colonies.[14]

b) Racial: Long before effective contact with Africans the European and especially the northern European psyche was dominated by a color-identification syndrome which associated white with all that was good, true, and beautiful and black with evil, ugliness, and filth. When Europeans encountered Africans, they projected these associations onto them; in the black mirrors they saw despised parts of themselves. Regarding Africans as subhumans, Europeans were prepared to treat them differently from themselves or from indigenous North Americans. Hence slavery became racial and peculiar to Africans.[15]

c) Structural: Until the eighteenth century, the economic and demographic situation of western Europe was such that working classes could not be induced to go overseas in substantial numbers. The New World's indigenous people were dying off, while their familiarity with the terrain and their ability to flee to support groups made them hard to enslave. The colonizers therefore faced what became the classic problem of so-called new societies: the contradiction between huge amounts of comparatively sparsely populated territory, where land was cheap or even free, and small quantities of labor. The solution was just as ubiquitous—some variety of forced labor. If either white or red people could have been organized and controlled successfully in the colonial situation, Europeans would certainly have done so. Africans were available at an economic price, and they could be enslaved. Without them the New World simply could not have been exploited successfully. There would not have been enough people to do the work.

In the structural interpretation the emergence of slavery in the New World is no longer an anomaly in the development of capitalism but a necessity. Slavery became ubiquitous in colonies not because it was transferred from less advanced parts of Europe, nor because its victims were black, but because it was the appropriate labor system for capitalism in the periphery of the world economy.[16] The structural explanation is strengthened by the fact that, although the Portuguese may have begun the slave trade, it was the advanced, highly capitalist Dutch who systematized it. The credibility is augmented further by the simultaneous rigidification of forced labor in Russia, the so-called second serfdom, which was the way the Russian state and ruling class attacked the land-labor equation in the colonization of Poland and Lithuania. The structural interpretation is quite compatible with the sequential explanation: the one answers "why," the other "how." Moreover, so long as prejudice is distinguished from racism—which is imposed by power to the point that it takes root in social institutions and the mode of production—the structural explanation incorporates the racial argument. Racism was not so much a cause as a justification of slavery.

The African role in the invasion and exploitation of America needs to be emphasized. As late as 1800 more people of African than of European descent had migrated to the New World. Nor was the African contribution merely that of unskilled labor. Their knowledge of rice growing, for example, made slaves from particular regions highly prized.[17] They brought their culture—their religion, their music, their tales, their art, their language. And their long resistance to oppression became part of American and Latin American history, ultimately feeding back as an important force in the struggle for freedom within Africa itself.

INDIAN OCEAN

In the New World Europeans overwhelmed indigenous peoples over whom they possessed enormous military and biological advantages. In Africa they drew slaves but not much else from a continent not yet organized to produce other surplus commodities for export. In Asia, however, they encountered civilizations larger, older, and more continuous than their own that were well able to contend with them on land. Asia possessed sophisticated productive and market systems on a huge scale, with well-developed mechanisms of exchange and credit. The situations varied so widely that it is hazardous to generalize: from Malaya, where both the Dutch and the English used force to compel the production of pepper on a quota system; to China, where Europeans were permitted to trade only in Canton, and then only with officially approved merchants. There was, however, a constant factor that was the single driving force in European-Asian relations before the nineteenth century. That was the expanding volume of world trade and especially the rising European consumption of the produce of Asia.

In a famous passage in *The Wealth of Nations* Adam Smith wrote that it was "not by the importation of gold and silver that the discovery of America has enriched Europe." Instead, "by opening a new and inexhaustible market to all the commodities of Europe, it gave occasion to new divisions of labour and improvements of art, which, in the narrow circle of the ancient commerce, could never have taken place for want of a market to take off the greater part of their produce." Similarly the opening of the Cape route to the East had enabled Europeans to exchange American treasure for Asian commodities, further enriching them by increasing their division of labor. The Atlantic and Indian Ocean regions of the world economy were indeed closely linked. The imports of silver from Mexico and Peru enabled Europeans to pay for their rapidly increasing consumption of a wide variety of new Asian products—notably cotton, tea, and coffee—as well as older staples of the trade such as silks and spices.

Without the New World's treasure it is hard to see how Europeans could have established themselves economically in Asia. In its charter of 1697 the English East India Company was required to export 10 percent of its trade in the form of the produce and manufactures of England. It may be presumed that this figure was a goal not ordinarily reached in practice and that without it the company's exports to Asia might have consisted entirely of bullion. Not until after about 1720 did Asian demand for European products—notably woolens and copper—begin to rise. Even so, it was primarily their enormous profits from the imports of Asian products into Europe that increased the financial strength and stability of the Dutch and English East India companies. By 1709, for instance, the English company ranked below only the

Bank of England and the government exchequer in the scale of its operations. That year the company granted the government a loan of £3 million, the first of many. By the late eighteenth century it became hard to tell where the government's finances ended and the company's began, which is the main reason for the series of India Bills and for the emergence of India as a prime issue in British domestic politics.

From the very beginning of European activity in the Indian Ocean, trade and war were closely linked. The Portuguese, with their strongly anti-Islamic ideology, began the pattern; the more pragmatic Dutch continued it in Indonesia and Malaya, where they developed plantations based on forced labor. The English, who were also involved in Malaya, had no compunctions against using force themselves. When it came to employing it in Mughal India itself, however, they tended to be more cautious. They entrenched themselves in fortified factories near the sea from which they could be evacuated. But they also moved into well-established markets in the interior as free traders.

The English company's policy alternated between caution and aggressiveness. In the 1690s the company tried a forward policy which failed disastrously and the Mughals drove them back. Yet only the presence of the European companies enabled their profitable trade with Europe and the flow of silver to continue, so the Mughals never seriously considered driving them out altogether. For the time being the company seemed to have learned its lesson. Force, advised a famous minute, was "like extreme unction, never to be used unless in the last extremity."

In the second quarter of the eighteenth century, however, the last extremity recurred with increasing frequency. Swiftly the Mughal Empire collapsed from within, disintegrating into a series of semi-independent entities under the control of nawabs with whom alliances could be formed or who could be picked off individually. This dramatic collapse has never been fully explained, the weakness of individual rulers and peasant revolts as a result of price inflation being cited as two of the primary causes.

Although Europeans had little direct influence on the process of disintegration, they benefited from it enormously. Both the English and French East India companies formed armies of native soldiers (called sepoys) with European officers. In India's version of the Seven Years' War the English company gradually enlarged territory: sometimes conquering it, sometimes gaining it through chicanery as in the so-called Battle of Plassey (1757). By the 1760s the company had already become the strongest power in north India, much of which until a later reorganization they called Bengal, as well as in the south. In the west the insurgent Marathas offered a strong challenge which was not finally defeated until 1818.

The apparent explanation of the British triumph in India is that they must have enjoyed an overwhelming advantage in military technology. But that is probably not true. Europeans did have an advantage at sea. When sea and land power meet, however, the most likely result is standoff. Sea power can bombard or blockade a port; but land power can close off a fort's inland communications or put it under siege. The company's soldiers were Indian; ordinarily they had no particular edge over the forces of contending nawabs, let alone over the Marathas, either in size or in weapons. Instead the company's advantage was primarily organizational: drilling techniques and tactics developed on European battlefields over several centuries of continuous warfare. Indian rulers often concluded that if they were to survive, they must employ European officers.

First in its gradually expanding enclaves, then by the last quarter of the eighteenth century over much of the subcontinent, the company behaved as a sovereign power. That meant both law enforcement, including requiring Indians to observe English contract law, and exercising the power of taxation, especially the land revenue. At first the company simply took over the existing and comparatively sophisticated revenue system of the Mughals, ordinarily employing Indians as tax farmers (whom they subsequently transformed into a "traditional" aristocracy). The land revenue system became one of the two principal institutions in which the British formed working alliances with substantial portions of the Indian landed ruling class. The other was the Indian army. Without such effective collaborative relationships, the rule by a few thousand Britons over millions of Indians would be inexplicable.

The landed revenue has rightly been called a form of tribute or drain, enabling Great Britain to turn what even after the industrial revolution would remain a chronically unfavorable balance of trade into a highly favorable balance of payments. Revenue replaced trade as the basis of the company's solvency. As a monopoly primarily composed of London merchants and capitalists, the company had always drawn antagonism from outports such as Bristol (whose representative in Parliament was Edmund Burke), and it became a prime target of Adam Smith. In 1813 its commercial monopoly, which had long been evaded in practice, ended officially. Twenty years later the company was forbidden to trade at all. Henceforth, until its abolition after the great rebellion of 1857–8, it was a governing body, responsible to Parliament for its exercise of what Burke called its trust, paying its administrative costs as well as regular dividends to British shareholders out of what it could glean from the Indian taxpayer.

By the early nineteenth century India had become the center of a mighty world power, the so-called second British Empire. In a sense the whole of that empire east of Suez—from Botany Bay in Australia to the Cape of Good Hope—was a subimperialism radiating from British India. And the subimperialism itself was expanding. Eventually it would move into the Red Sea and East Africa, Malaya, and Hong Kong. The tense relations that culminated in the wars between Britain and China in the 1840s and 1850s owed much to pressure from British merchants to open the Chinese market to British exports, especially textiles. But those wars grew directly out of the company's dependence on revenue from the sale of opium—a clear illustration of the semiautonomous nature of the subimperialism centered in India.

By 1800 the division of the world into zones, for which the foundation had been laid as long ago as the sixteenth century, had already been largely accomplished. The zones were: 1) the core, comprising western Europe lately joined by the northern British colonies in North America, characterized by free labor, diversified agriculture, manufacturing, strong state formation, and a well-developed bourgeoisie; 2) the semiperiphery, comprising Russia and eastern and southern Europe, characterized by large grain estates, serfdom, comparatively weak state formation, and a laggard bourgeoisie; 3) the periphery, comprising the rest of the New World (including the American South) and much of Asia, now including India, characterized by slavery or other forms of forced labor, colonial or semicolonial status, and a bourgeoisie either weak, nonexistent, or imported.[18]

According to classical economics and many Western historians, this division of the world into economic zones just happened in the normal course of free exchange, each party producing what was best for itself. Backwardness was the result of insufficient natural resources, or of insufficient capital, or of the inability of peoples to shake off the burden of tradition in order to develop rational modes of economic behavior. In this perspective deeper contact with the advanced West provided the main hope of improvement.

According to Marxists and the so-called dependency school, the international division of labor was created artificially, imposed on the world by power. In 1500 the regions of Eurasia may have been more or less equal in wealth and living standards. Three centuries later a substantial gap had been opened, and it would widen further. Europe's living standard had improved; that in the peripheral zone had deteriorated. These two phenomena were structurally related: the development of underdevelopment. As Owen Lattimore put it, civilization had created barbarism.[19]

This structural interpretation of the developing world economy and the inequality it fostered has provided the basic framework for this essay. Yet the specific corollary of it, which sees the impoverishment of other areas of the world as having been directly and specifically responsible for the industrial revolution in England and Europe, has often been seriously overstated.[20] That interpretation is based on the assumptions (a) that eighteenth-century Europe was an underdeveloped society short of available capital for investment and (b) that profits from overseas commerce are considerably more mobile than those from domestic sources.

Both of these assumptions appear to be incorrect. Economic historians largely agree: (a) that the technology required to accomplish the first stage of the industrial revolution was relatively inexpensive; (b) that eighteenth-century England was hardly a typical underdeveloped society, but one possessing a relatively well-educated work force and an already well-developed system of production and exchange; and (c) that shortage of capital was definitely not a problem. The profits from the British slave trade over the eighteenth century have been estimated as falling between 0.11 and 1.11 percent of the total available capital.[21] Even though that figure does not include the profits from the West Indian plantations, it seems clear that the role of slavery in financing British capitalism was surprisingly modest. The capital accumulated from trade and tribute from India would have been higher, but still far less than the profits drawn from British agriculture.[22] Finally, there seems to be no truth whatever in the notion that domestic capital is inherently less venturesome than that from the overseas commercial sector.

An alternative world history perspective emphasizes not the role of overseas exploitation in British capital accumulation but the comparative analysis of England with other countries that might have industrialized but did not. Within Europe, Holland and France seem to be the principal contenders.[23] Both were sophisticated economies with enough capital, and neither had any important barriers to the adoption of available technology. France even possessed a government department specifically responsible for fostering inventions and stealing secrets of competitors. Holland had been the world's leading capitalist economy in the seventeenth century. But it lacked a vital ingredient, a home market of sufficient size. If Holland was too small, France may have been too large. Its textile industry, devoted primarily to the production of luxury goods for the upper classes of France and continental Europe, continued to be profitable. England's home market was sufficiently large, it was composed of what travelers agreed was by far the most prosperous working class in Europe—and the industrial revolution specialized in providing cheap goods for mass consumption.

Although still more hazardous, comparisons with Asia are fascinating and potentially fruitful. At the beginning of the eighteenth century China and India both possessed comparatively well-developed textile industries that were considerably larger than those of Europe. China's must have been huge, for its extremely efficient wet-rice agriculture had permitted its population to attain a high level much more quickly than in any other part of the world and China was importing little from abroad. India also possessed a vast home market, and it was the principal exporter of cotton to Europe. According to contemporary English pamphlets, its sole advantage was the low average wages paid to the producers; but the renowned quality of the product makes it probable that India also possessed a technological advantage. Asian and European textiles alike were organized in the so-called putting-out system, in which merchant-capitalists bought the raw material, paying individual spinners and weavers to process it in their homes.

It is commonly held that England's industrial revolution took place not in the older woolen industry but in cotton, which had hardly existed in 1700. But the traditional explanation that wool was burdened by government regulation and the equally restrictive power of the guilds, whereas cotton was open to penetration by entrepreneurs seems less significant than the accelerating demand for cheap cotton cloth. Although the English home and European markets led this demand, it was worldwide, for cotton was a principal product in the trade with Africa and with the growing plantation economies of the New World. In time the demand for wool in Asia would increase too; but not as much or as quickly as that for cotton in Europe and its colonies.

This greatly increased world demand placed extreme pressure on an already developed industry, to which the English and Indian systems reacted in very different ways. In England it highlighted inefficiencies in the putting-out organization, especially wastage, pilferage, considerable variation in quality, and irregular working hours. The entrepreneur who brought his workers together into factories could hope to correct such defects, cut costs, and raise margins. (The word "factory" meant trading establishment, and the first cotton factories were really warehouses where operatives worked as before, but under supervision.) The pressure of demand also stimulated capitalists to raise productivity by investing in mechanical, work-saving inventions such as the spinning jenny and the roller frame.[24] In contrast, Indian merchant-capitalists reacted to the need to raise productivity by lowering wage levels still further while increasing the number of workers. Contrary to Marx's famous aphorism about weavers' bones bleaching in the Bengal sun, the workforce therefore actually rose.[25]

Holland's small scale had set limits on its growth. France's comparatively large size had enabled relatively inefficient luxury industries to remain profitable without being reorganized or mechanized. But the scales of the economies of India and China were far larger than France's. Entrepreneurs attempting to transform Indian textiles with machinery—as eventually they did in the late nineteenth and early twentieth centuries, enabling India to resume its competitive position—would have had a far larger bill to pay than did those of England. Instead they naturally chose to play to what seemed to be their main advantage, the average low wages of the industry. Nor is it clear that the supply of the raw material would have been sufficient. If China's textile industry had expanded at the same rate as England's, it has been estimated that by 1850 the world supply of cotton would have had to be ten times greater than it was.[26]

"Industrial revolution" is in fact a shorthand term for a whole series of changes in the organization of the economy and society. It is often regarded as synonymous with the substitution of mechanical for human or animal power. Technological innovations were indeed a significant part of it. Still more significant, however, were sweeping alterations in financial and managerial organization and in attitudes toward work. In trade after trade—including those like the building trade that were not affected by machines—work processes were speeded up and rationalized with the aim of increasing productivity. Ultimately there would be enormous benefits: a rising standard of living as well as sustained growth, enabling industrialized societies to sustain far larger populations. But there were significant costs, including those Marx described as alienation. And the process happened only in some parts of the world: the core zone of the capitalist world economy.

Even though they paid higher average wages, the mechanized industries of Great Britain and the rest of the core could manufacture textiles, iron products, or pottery of higher quality and at lower cost than their competitors. With these they flooded the world, ruining handicraft after handicraft that had endured for centuries. They also exported capital, especially for railways, on which they made high returns. The result was deep economic dependency. Only a protectionist policy would have helped, and only other Western nations and Japan had the political power or the political will to enforce it. With the British in the lead, Europe developed the so-called imperialism of free trade.[27] The industrial revolution therefore widened and accelerated the already existing gap between the zones of the capitalist world economy.

Industrialization was only half of what Eric Hobsbawm has called the dual revolution of the late eighteenth and early nineteenth centuries, a wholesale systemic change that transformed an already developed society into one recognizably like our own.[28] The other half was a series of alterations in ideas and modes of political organization that we associate with the English Revolution, the Enlightenment, the American Revolution, a widespread religious awakening, and the French Revolution. Within Europe itself these ideas led toward constitutional government and democracy. Overseas, with some significant exceptions such as missionaries, Europeans were ordinarily conservatives reluctant to promote progressive social change. But they could not prevent ideas about individual freedom and equality, which after all were embedded in the New Testament, from taking root. Ultimately the Western intellectual tradition, including later accretions such as Marxism, would become a significant force in the revolt against the West.

The internal history of Europe is one of the more difficult subjects for teachers in world history courses. Some topics that are significant in European history, for example Romanticism or the details of Bismarckian diplomacy, have little or no external relevance. The industrial and the French Revolution, the American Civil War, the Russian Revolution and the world wars of the twentieth century, are all events in world as well as Western history—except that the teacher grounded in the world-historical perspective has rather different things to say about them.[29]

In practical, immediate terms the most significant external result of the changes in European ideas was the drive to abolish slavery, substituting rational and free wage labor, ending or at least largely reducing the glaring contradiction between the prevailing organizations of work in the different zones of the world economy. Abolish slavery they did: the high points being its elimination by the French National Convention in the 1790s, the ending of the British slave trade in 1807, and the abolition of slavery in the British Empire in 1833. Contemporary antislavery tracts repeatedly argued that free labor would prove to be economically more efficient than slavery. In fact the defenders of slavery were consistently the better economic prognosticators.[30] Slavery was not abolished because it had become economically inefficient or because it had become economically incompatible with capitalism, but because the European conscience had identified it as evil. Later imperialists did not return to outright slavery. But they did resort to a variety of alternatives—quota systems, depriving peasantries of land, especially taxes that had to be paid in cash—that continued forced labor in peripheral regions of the capitalist world economy.

Within Europe itself the French Revolution accelerated the development of nationalism, resulting in the world's first mass-conscript peasant army. Mass armies increased the power of the Western state enormously. During the age of the so-called New Imperialism, however, these armies were not ordinarily employed overseas. There, though Europeans enjoyed a monopoly of sea power, and though they could ordinarily bring irresistible power to bear at particular points of crisis, they remained thin on the ground. Of necessity they relied on alliances with indigenous collaborators—usually a conservative ruling class—who developed a stake in maintaining the colonial system.[31] By the late nineteenth century nationalist movements would begin to develop in the colonies. A struggle would begin, the goal of which would be to deprive the alien rulers of collaborators. That ultimately successful struggle is the central theme of world history in the twentieth century.

The bulk of the European seaborne empires would be dismantled by the end of the 1960s. Traditionally the whole of modern history from 1500 onward has been characterized as the age of Western dominance. This chapter and that on "European Expansion, 1450–1700," have suggested that, although the foundations of the capitalist world economy were certainly laid before 1700, and though Western hegemony was assured by 1800, the effective exercise of that dominance over much of the world became a reality only after 1850. How brief and transitory a phase it was. Yet it changed the world forever.

NOTES

1. The title suggested by the directors of this project was "Europe and Asia in an Expanding World Economy, 1700–1850." The change reflects my own rather profound disagreement with the implication that a bipolar

(European-Asian) approach is preferable to the world-historical framework.

2. Fernand Braudel, "European Expansion and Capitalism, 1450–1650," in *Chapters in Western Civilization*, ed. Contemporary Civilization Staff of Columbia College, Columbia University, 3d ed. (New York: Columbia University Press, 1961–), 1: 245–87.

3. Fernand Braudel, *The Mediterranean and the Mediterranean World in the Age of Philip II*, trans. S. Reynolds, 2 vols. (New York: Harper, 1972).

4. See Barry Supple, "The Nature of Enterprise," in *Cambridge Economic History of Europe*, 2d ed. (8 vols.; Cambridge: Cambridge University Press, 1966–), vol. 5, *The Economic Organization of Early Modern Europe*, ed. E. E. Rich and C. H. Wilson; Charles H. Wilson, *England's Apprenticeship, 1603–1763* (New York: St. Martin's Press, 1965); Charles R. Boxer, *The Dutch Seaborne Empire, 1600–1800* (London: Hutchinson, 1965).

5. Incidentally, the joint-stock company had an extremely significant effect on English constitutional history. Among the organizations that copied from the Dutch was the Bank of England, loans from which financed William III's wars against Louis XIV of France, thus inventing the national debt. Members of Parliament, who had invested heavily in the Bank, could no longer permit the king's government to go bankrupt. In effect, having won recognition of its power of the purse in the Revolution Settlement of 1689, Parliament lost the ability to use it as it had done repeatedly earlier in the century.

6. See Charles H. Wilson, *Mercantilism* (London: Routledge and Kegan Paul, 1958), and Joseph J. Spengler's essay on mercantilist economists in *Theories of Economic Growth*, ed. Berthold Hoselitz (Glencoe, IL: Free Press, 1960).

7. The standard work on the North Atlantic world economy is Ralph Davis, *The Rise of the Atlantic Economies* (Ithaca: Cornell University Press, 1973).

8. See Harold A. Innis, *The Cod Fisheries: The History of an International Economy* (New Haven: Yale University Press, 1940), and Gillian T. Cell, *English Enterprise in Newfoundland, 1557–1660* (Toronto: University of Toronto Press, 1969).

9. See Harold A. Innis, *The Fur Trade in Canada: An Introduction to Canadian Economic History* (Toronto: University of Toronto Press, 1956), and Francis Jennings, *The Invasion of America: Indians, Colonialism and the Cant of Conquest* (Chapel Hill: University of North Carolina Press, 1975).

10. Philip Curtin, *The Atlantic Slave Trade: A Census* (Madison: University of Wisconsin Press, 1969).

11. For an exhaustive study of a single African society, see Patrick Manning, *Slavery, Colonialism, and Economic Growth in Dahomey, 1640–1960* (Cambridge: Cambridge University Press, 1982).

12. David Brion Davis, *The Problem of Slavery in Western Culture* (Ithaca: Cornell University Press, 1966), and *The Problem of Slavery in an Age of Revolution, 1770–1823* (Ithaca: Cornell University Press, 1975).

13. Roger Anstey, *The Atlantic Slave Trade and British Abolition, 1760–1810* (Atlantic Highlands: Humanities, 1975).

14. For this interpretation see E. E. Rich, "Colonial Settlement and Its Labour Problems," in *Cambridge Economic History of Europe* 4: 308–64.

15. Winthrop D. Jordan, *White Over Black: American Attitudes Toward*

the Negro, 1550–1812 (New York: Oxford University Press, 1974).

16. Immanuel Wallerstein, *The Modern World-System* (New York: Academic Press, 1974–).

17. Peter H. Wood, *Black Majority: Negroes in Colonial South Carolina from 1670 Through the Stono Rebellion* (New York: Knopf, 1974).

18. The fact that such zones existed is recognized widely, for example, in Robert R. Palmer and Joel Colton, *History of the Modern World*, 6th ed. (New York: Knopf, 1984). But this standard textbook's explanation of why the world economy came into existence and how it worked is very different from that of Wallerstein or other exponents of the underdevelopment thesis.

19. Owen Lattimore, *Inner Asian Frontiers of China* (New York: American Geographical Society, 1940).

20. Eric E. Williams, *Capitalism and Slavery* (Chapel Hill: University of North Carolina Press, 1944).

21. Anstey, *Atlantic Slave Trade.*

22. For the Indian debate see K.N. Chaudhuri, *The Trading World of Asia and the English East India Company, 1660–1760* (Cambridge: Cambridge University Press, 1978); Irfan Habib, "Colonialization of the Indian Economy, 1757–1900," *Social Scientist* No. 32 (1973–75), and Morris D. Morris et al., *Indian Economy in the Nineteenth Century: A Symposium* (Delhi: Indian Economic and Social History Association, 1969).

23. See François Crouzet, "England and France in the Eighteenth Century: A Comparative Analysis of Two Economic Growths," in *The Causes of the Industrial Revolution in England*, ed. Ronald M. Hartwell (London: Methuen, 1967), pp. 139–74.

24. The standard work is the survey by David Landes in *Cambridge Economic History of Europe 6*, and published in book form as *The Unbound Prometheus: Technological Change and Industrial Development in Western Europe from 1750 to the Present Day* (Cambridge: Cambridge University Press, 1969). He has an extremely useful précis in *Chapters in Western Civilization 2*.

25. See Chaudhuri, *Trading World of Asia and the English East India Company.*

26. Mark Elvin, *The Pattern of the Chinese Past: A Social and Economic Interpretation* (Stanford: Stanford University Press, 1973), ch. 17.

27. Despite long and continuing controversy, the article by Ronald Robinson and John Gallagher, "The Imperialism of Free Trade," *Economic History Review* (1953), remains the best statement.

28. Eric J. Hobsbawm, *The Age of Revolution, 1789–1848* (New York: New American Library, 1962).

29. See for instance Barrington Moore, *Social Origins of Dictatorship and Democracy: Lord and Peasant in the Making of the Modern World* (London: Penguin, 1967) and *Injustice: The Social Bases of Obedience and Revolt* (Armonk, NY: M.E. Sharpe, 1978), both of which are written from a profoundly comparative, world-historical perspective.

30. Seymour Descher, *Econocide: British Slavery in the Era of Abolition* (Pittsburgh: University of Pittsburgh Press, 1977).

31. On the nature of collaboration in the colonial situation, see Ronald Robinson, "Non-European Foundations: Sketch for a Theory of Collaboration," in *Studies in the Theory of Imperialism*, ed. Roger Owen and Bob Sutcliffe (London: Longman, 1972).

CHINA AND THE WORLD, 1500–1800

William T. Rowe

In conceptualizing China's position in the world during the first phase of Western expansion, it seems no longer adequate to pose a model of Western "impact" and Chinese "response." Rather, we need to think of China's history in this era as but one part of an increasingly interconnected process of world history, one in which China, the West, and indeed much of the rest of the globe underwent changes marked by an increasing similarity one to another, as well as by a growing systemic interdependence. As Joseph Fletcher pointed out, it was precisely in this three-century period that previously compartmentalized "histories" gradually began to constitute a unified "history."[1] Politically and culturally the major civilizations were still of course quite distinctive, and diplomatically their links remained minimal. Yet these obvious facts should not blind us to the equally remarkable extent to which demographically, economically, and even socially, the early modern era witnessed common, recognizable sets of changes around the globe. Here let me begin by stressing the links and parallels in the case of China, and then return to the question of the Middle Kingdom's persistent distinctiveness.

Though the mammoth size of China's domestic economy ensured that overseas trade would never, under conditions of pre-industrial technology, constitute more than a small fraction of the empire's total volume of exchange, cross-cultural trade was hardly insignificant for China during this period, and in fact played a critical role in a variety of ways in shaping China's socioeconomic development. The beginnings of seaborne trade with the West occurred in a context of a flourishing trade within East Asia itself; crucial imports of monetary metals from Japan, and of spices and (increasingly) rice from Southeast Asia were made possible by steady demand throughout the region for Chinese silks, ceramics, carpets, and other manufactured goods.[2] Indeed, one of the most important roles that the Portuguese and Dutch carved out for themselves in East Asia during the early period of maritime expansion was as more efficient carriers for this ongoing intraregional trade.[3]

It was these same Chinese manufactures, and above all silk, that in the sixteenth and seventeenth centuries became the foundation of the maritime trade with South Asia, western Europe, and Spanish America, eventually greatly surpassing in volume the continuing overland trade to Europe via central Asia.[4] But they were not alone. The growing adoption of cotton cloth as a staple of costume by elites and commoners alike constituted a worldwide early modern revolution in taste and technology. Introduced to China from the south around 500 C.E., cotton gradually assumed importance as an item of regional trade during the medieval period; by the fifteenth century China had become one of the great cotton-growing areas of the world, and its weaving industry perhaps the most highly developed. Over the next three hundred years Chinese cotton textiles (including the famous "Nankeens") were increasingly exported to Europe and the New World. By the late eighteenth century, in fact, British merchants were exporting from Canton some 90,000 bolts of cloth per year for their home market, most produced from raw cotton which these same merchants were bringing into China from India.[5] This is a sobering consideration for anyone who would argue for a simple model of China, as a peripheral area, exchanging raw materials for finished goods of the metropolitan region.

Ultimately, of course, there was tea. The East India Company's first recorded shipment of Chinese tea to England—some 222 pounds—occurred in 1669; by the 1750s it was importing nearly 4 **million** pounds per year, and fifty years later approximately 28 million. From an unknown beverage, tea emerged as an item of consumption claiming an estimated 5 percent of the average British subject's annual income. As explained by K.N. Chaudhuri, this "astonishingly rapid assimilation of a new economic product" was intimately related to other major shifts in global commodity circulation:

> The complementarity of tea and sugar probably explains the relative decline of [Southeast Asian] pepper in [British] household budgets. Pepper was no longer a prestigious high-cost commodity; money spent on it competed with other attractive alternatives. The greater availability of sugar supplies from the West Indian plantations and the decline of its cost provided the

context in which the mass consumption of tea could become a reality. For people in the lower income groups, tea as a beverage was appealing not only for its intrinsic taste and quality, but also as a means of taking sugar.[6]

This was by no means a one-way process of a self-sufficient China exerting an impact on Europe while itself remaining aloof from outside influence, as an overly credulous reading of Qing imperial pronouncements would suggest. Overseas linkages drastically reshaped the conditions of Chinese life in this era, and did so in a manner bearing marked resemblances to their impact on Europe itself. The introduction and spread of hardy New World crops (the peanut, the sweet potato, maize) provided a hedge against famine in China, as it did in Europe, and contributed in part to the distinctly modern pattern of accelerated population growth in both civilizations.[7] (China's population may have risen from some 65 million in 1400, to 150 million in 1600, to around 300 million by 1800.) Chinese exports to Europe and the Americas were paid for in large part by enormous imports of silver from Potosi and Taxco, carried first by the Portuguese via Malacca and Macao (the Portuguese also brought into China greatly expanded Japanese silver outputs during these years), then by the Spanish via Seville and Manila.[8] The effects in China were analogous to those in Europe: an early modern "price revolution" and an accelerating monetization of the economy, beginning in the Chinese case with the **fiscal** monetization of the late Ming "Single Whip" tax reforms. In the eighteenth century, imports of New World bullion were joined by those of currency, and the reliably standardized "Mexican dollar" became a principal medium of wholesale exchange within China's own domestic economy.

Beyond population growth and monetization, this period saw a number of other basic, transformative changes in China, in part the result of greater integration into a global system, and in part simply the result of a cumulative domestic process of increasing social complexity. It was a period of great commercial intensification, in which very long-distance exchange of bulk staples such as grain and fibers first became the norm, with whole regions of the empire increasingly specializing in certain cash crops. The massive circulation of commodities was managed by overlapping diasporas of compatriot merchant groups from Shaanxi, Huizhou, Ningbo, Guangzhou, and other localities, each of which maintained permanent colonies in the empire's major commercial cities. This was accompanied by another set of changes which historians in the People's Republic like to call the "sprouts of capitalism": a greater reliance on formal business contracts, innovations in the structure of the business firm, new forms of capital accumulation including bank loans and issues of stock, a movement of commercial capital into production and an expansion of the scale of individual manufacturing enterprises, and a much greater reliance on contractually hired wage labor. The trends of personal emancipation, proletarianization, heightened geographic and occupational mobility, and urbanization which characterized this early modern period led to important cultural changes—stimulated further by the growth of the publishing industry and an increasingly popular print culture in the empire's most developed regions. For its part, the elite-official culture was marked by a set of new concerns familiar from the early modern West: a turn away from cosmology and speculative philosophy to a more empirical intellectual orientation (epitomized by the *kaozheng* or "empirical research" movement), a search for more pragmatic solutions to problems of social and economic management (often dubbed the *jingshi* or "statecraft" movement), and a subtle but broadly based reevaluation of the importance of the individual (seen, among other ways, in an increased challenging of traditionally accepted gender roles, and in a new-found moral legitimacy accorded to the profit motive).

This whole complex of changes in China was not smooth or unidirectional, but was interrupted by the severe shocks associated with the dynastic transition from Ming to Qing in the 1640s. Here too we see evidence of China's new integration into an early modern "world history," for whatever degree of credence one places in a global "general crisis" of the seventeenth century, China's political turmoil of this era does bear apparent resemblances to that in, say, Stuart England and Ottoman Turkey.[9] Climatic change—the "little ice age" and prolonged periods of subnormal rainfall—led to a devastating series of poor harvests in China, as they did elsewhere in the world. Drought and famine were followed by epidemics, notably of bubonic plague and smallpox, which likewise knew no national boundaries.[10] Compounding this problem was a sudden (though short-term) contraction of the volume of international trade. Spanish shipments of American silver to Manila, which had fueled China's burgeoning commercial economy, dropped in the 1630s to about one-third of what they had been in the preceding decade, while Japanese silver exports to China were halted altogether in 1635. The result was both economic depression and fiscal strangulation. The Ming government's maladroit response to the latter, combined with its declining military effectiveness and general demoralization, prompted devastating internal rebellions and foreign invasion. Between warfare, famine, and disease, China's population underwent a sudden and dramatic (though again short-term) decline, perhaps as much as 40 percent in the first half of the seventeenth century.[11]

What the seventeenth-century crisis did not lead to in China, in marked contrast to Europe, was a reconstitution of either the elite or the polity; China experienced neither a "crisis of the aristocracy" nor the rise of a system of mutually competitive nation-states.[12] A centralized bureaucratic empire, resting on the social base of a broad landlord-literatus stratum, was quickly and effectively reconstituted under the Manchu court. At least through the end of the eighteenth century, however, the revival of the ancient imperial system in China can in no way be taken as evidence of the degradation of an indigenous political regime under the influence of a domineering "capitalist world-system."[13] On the contrary, China under the early and mid-Qing experienced a period of unprecedented expansion, nearly doubling the amount of territory under its direct or indirect administration. This actual expansion was legitimated by an aggressively redefined political ideology of universal empire.[14] Thus, both in rhetoric and in practice, China's attitude toward the outside world in the late seventeenth and eighteenth centuries was anything but passive and defensive.

What then of the Middle Kingdom's much-vaunted isolationism in the period prior to its enforced "opening" by the West? I do not here need to recount the well-known history of the "sea bans" *(haijin)*, periodically imposed by successive imperial courts after the fourteenth century on Chinese traveling overseas or engaging in maritime commerce. It should already be clear that these did not constitute any insurmountable barrier to the conduct of significant foreign trade. I might add that the second half of the eighteenth century, an era in which the bans were being proclaimed in progressively harsher form, was also one in which the volume of that trade was reaching unprecedented levels. As Mark Elvin has noted, the sea bans were never primarily intended for control or isolation of foreigners, but rather to prevent the rise of autonomous centers of political economic power along the coast and away from the court.[15] As such, they reflected not China's weakness but on the contrary the special difficulties associated with maintaining an empire of so great a scale. Nor were the sea bans more than essentially ad hoc measures. As John Wills has demonstrated, the Chinese court had come to react to any disturbance in foreign relations first by cutting off contact, and then by attempting to bring such contact under bureaucratic control. The sea bans thus represented a conditioned pattern of pragmatic policy, rather than a basic aversion to foreign contact.

Wills also usefully cautions against making too much of "the Chinese sense of superiority to all other peoples," noting that "some kind of sense of cultural and political superiority is common to high cultures, and it remains to be shown how such a common characteristic can be used to explain the distinctiveness of the Chinese system."[16] What imperial authorities really sought to defend, he suggests, was a basic conception of ritual order and propriety. So long as this order was not challenged, "a variety of practical arrangements" could be worked out for foreign contact, such as those devised to accommodate the Portuguese and Dutch in the sixteenth and seventeenth centuries, and the English in the eighteenth. The early Qing rulers were especially adept at such improvisation, as their management of relations with Inner Asia and with the expanding Russian Empire demonstrated. Their lesser degree of creative innovation in dealing with the maritime nations was largely the product of "boredom and neglect," stemming from the fact that those nations before the nineteenth century offered China neither a significant threat nor an attractive target of opportunity, a universal empire such as Qing having less need than competitive nation-states for diplomatic alliances.[17]

Historical thinking is clearly not well served by characterizations of Qing China as an *empire immobile* (the title and theme of a well-received recent study of the famous 1793 Macartney mission).[18] Such romantic, orientalist images betray far more the ethnocentrism of their authors than that of their subjects. Nor can we be comfortable with generalizations about a growing "xenophobia" and cultural isolation, or an alleged civilization decline, of the Ming and Qing empires. As we have seen, China's integration into world history was growing, not declining, over the course of the early modern period. And into the second half of the eighteenth century one can still make a case for China as the single preeminent political entity in the world.

This changed quite rapidly during that half-century, due to a combination of factors. The first was secular: the years after 1750 saw China experiencing an increasingly adverse ratio of population to land and food supply, despite a conscientious program of agricultural expansion and intensification. The second was cyclical: the indisputably recurrent process of dynastic administrative decline. And the third was external: the unique phenomenon of the industrial revolution, which with remarkable suddenness shifted the balance of global power away from universal empires in favor of a small island nation in the North Atlantic called England.

NOTES

1. Joseph Fletcher, "Integrative History: Parallels and Interconnections in the Early Modern Period, 1500–1800," *Journal of Turkish Studies* 9.1 (1985): 37–57.

2. See for example John W. Hall, "Notes on the Early Ch'ing Copper Trade with Japan," *Harvard Journal of Asiatic Studies* 12 (1949): 444–61; Sarasin Viraphol, *Tribute and Profit: Sino-Siamese Rice Trade, 1652–1853* (Cambridge, MA: Harvard University Press, 1977); Philip D. Curtin, *Cross-Cultural Trade in World History* (Cambridge: Cambridge University Press, 1984), chap. 8.

3. C.R. Boxer, *Fidalgos in the Far East, 1550–1770* (The Hague: Martinus Nijhoff, 1948).

4. See especially William Lyle Schurz, *The Manila Galleon* (New York: E.P. Dutton, 1939), chap. 1.

5. Peng Zeyi, "Yapian zhanzheng qian Guangzhou xinxing de qingfang goneye" (The developing textile industry of Canton before the Opium War), *Lishi yanjiu* 1983.3: 109–30.

6. K.N. Chaudhuri, *The Trading World of Asia and the English East India Company, 1660–1760* (Cambridge: Cambridge University Press, 1978), p. 385.

7. Ping-ti Ho, "The Introduction of American Food Plants into China," *American Anthropologist* 57.2 (1955): 191–201.

8. Quan Hansheng, "Ming-Qing jian Meizhou baiyin de lunru Zhongguo" (Imports of American silver into China during the Ming and Qing), in his *Zhongguo jingjishi luncong* (Studies in Chinese economic history) (Hong Kong: Chinese University of Hong Kong, 1972), pp. 435–50; William Atwell, "International Bullion Flows and the Chinese Economy; *circa* 1530–1650," *Past and Present* 95 (May 1982): 68–95.

9. Jack A. Goldstone, "East and West in the Seventeenth Century: Political Crises in Stuart England, Ottoman Turkey, and Ming China," *Comparative Studies in Society and History* 30 (1988): 103–42; William Atwell, "A Seventeenth-Century 'General Crisis' in East Asia?" *Modern Asian Studies* 24.4 (1990): 661–82.

10. Anthony Reid, "The Seventeenth-Century Crisis in Southeast Asia," *Modern Asian Studies* 24.4 (1990): 639–59; Helen Dunstan, "The late Ming Epidemics: A Preliminary Survey," *Ch'ing-shih wen-t'i* 3.3 (November 1975): 9–18.

11. Mark Elvin, *The Pattern of the Chinese Past* (Stanford: Stanford University Press, 1973), p. 311; Frederic E. Wakeman, Jr., "China and the Seventeenth-Century Crisis," *Late Imperial China* 7.1 (June 1986): 5–7.

12. S.A.M. Adshead, "The Seventeenth-Century General Crisis in China," *Asian Profile* 1.2 (October 1973): 271–80.

13. This general model is a central argument of Immanual Wallerstein, *The Modern World-System* (New York: Academic Press, 1976), though Wallerstein does not specifically apply it to the China of this period.

14. This position is argued in the work of Pamela Crossley, for example in her *Orphan Warriors: Three Manchu Generations and the End of the Qing World* (Princeton: Princeton University Press, 1990), pp. 21–22.

15. Elvin, pp. 221–25.

16. John E. Wills, Jr., *Pepper, Guns, and Parleys: the Dutch East India Company and China, 1622–1681* (Cambridge, MA: Harvard University Press, 1974), p. 205.

17. Wills, *Embassies and Illusions: Dutch and Portuguese Envoys to K'ang-hsi, 1666–1687* (Cambridge, MA: Harvard University Press, 1984), pp. 179–82.

18. Alain Peyrefitte, *L'empire immobile, ou, le choc des mondes* (Paris: Fayard, 1989).

CHINA'S ECONOMY IN COMPARATIVE PERSPECTIVE, 1500 ONWARD

Madeleine Zelin

The story of China's effort to develop a modern industrial economy is one that students can follow in the news media today. The relatively slow pace of China's economic development in the nineteenth and early twentieth centuries led observers in the past to portray China as an unchanging giant. Chinese culture itself came to be seen as an obstacle to economic change, and many commentators came to believe that only the "impact of the West" could propel China into the modern world. This essay is intended to dispel these myths. Instead we shall see that in the period between 1500 and 1800 China underwent important changes, which can be called a commercial revolution. However, a number of factors, both indigenous and external, limited the development of an industrial economy both before and after the mid-nineteenth century, when the Western presence became a major force in Chinese affairs. Our discussion of these factors will be divided into two parts:

I. A comparison of Chinese and Japanese development, to counter the myth of East Asian culture as an obstacle to development.

II. An examination of China's commercial revolution and the role that the development of a complex commercial economy played in China's industrialization process.

THE CHINESE-JAPANESE COMPARISON

An early nineteenth-century Chinese official discussing problems of governance would have found a sympathetic audience among officials in Japan. In China the Qing Dynasty continued a centuries-long process during which centralizing, bureaucratic rule by officials largely selected through government examination brought order to a vast and varied empire. In Tokugawa Japan a more fragmented feudal structure left a large arena of social and economic policy making to individual daimyo domains, within a central structure headed by the Tokugawa shoguns in Edo (present-day Tokyo). Nevertheless, Confucianism formed the basis for elite education and self-definition in both countries. Loyalty to the ruler, reinforced by Confucian ideals of hierarchy and reciprocity, and quasi-religious notions of the ruler's descent from "Heaven" also played an important role in state legitimization. For the Qing Empire and the Tokugawa shogunate, the "long eighteenth century" had been one of peace, the development of political institutions, and economic growth from a largely rice-growing peasant base. However, by the 1800s both were beset, although to a different degree, by popular unrest, elite dissent, and the increasing threat of military and economic challenge from the West. In China and Japan, the experience of internal change and external confrontation wrought fundamental changes in political and social structures. These changes influenced the way in which more long-lasting economic structures served the goal of economic development.

A COMPARISON OF POLITICAL STRUCTURES

Japan's response to its nineteenth-century crisis was the abolition of Tokugawa feudalism and the establishment after the Meiji Restoration in 1868 of a new system of rule. Although couched in terms of a restoration of ancient political traditions, this imperial government necessitated a number of extraordinary changes. Among these was the centralization of political authority, the end of domain rule and the cession of domain land to the central government, the abolition of the hereditary class system, revision of the land tax, the establishment of a system of universal education, and the institution of conscription and a national army.

The legitimizing power behind this transformation was the institution of the emperor, a strong symbolic focus for national unity apart from any political structure. This period also saw a revival of the use of Shinto beliefs to reinforce loyalty to the emperor and the new regime. The fact that Confucianism and the political and social values associated with it were themselves borrowed made it possible for Japanese to Westernize, abandoning some elements of their tradition without feeling that they were abandoning their entire culture. All of these factors contributed to the dynamism with which Japan undertook the reform of its institutions in the last decades of the nineteenth century.

Following the downfall of the Tokugawa shogunate Japan was thus able to establish a vital, strong, centralized government. This feat was not accomplished without difficulty, and clearly the struggle to become a powerful, modern state led to many competing visions of the state in Japan. Nevertheless, the contrast with China can be made as one of a strong, centralized Japan emerging from feudalism, compared to a weak, fragmented China emerging from a centralized regime.

Although on the surface the Chinese political system appeared to be far more centralized than Japan's, by the turn of the nineteenth century China faced two critical problems. The agrarian bureaucracy, which China had perfected over the course of centuries, never had the resources to mobilize thoroughly the populace. Thus there always existed within the Chinese state system a contradiction between the exercise of state power and reliance on local elites to govern local people. This was exacerbated in the early nineteenth century when a series of rebellions, most notably the Taiping, forced government to cede both military and tax collecting power to local elites. Once peace was restored, the new demands of economic development, local defense, and postwar reconstruction enabled elites to carve out new domains of responsibility outside the bureaucratic structure. Thus, at the same time that Japan was developing a modern, national conscripted army, Chinese military defense came increasingly to rely on the efforts of local militia and powerful regional leaders. Central government attempts to rectify this problem with the establishment of the national New Army were consistently hampered by fiscal problems at the national level and by competing regional interests. By the twentieth century, in the period we commonly call the warlord era, this translated into political disunity as well, as the power of military strongmen was increasingly identified with political authority.

Unlike Japan, China could not easily look toward alternative foci of national unity. Whereas the emperor could be invoked as a sacred link to the Japanese people, the Manchu ruling house of Qing China was itself a non-Chinese ethnic minority. Moreover, while it was difficult for Chinese to imagine a system of rule other than that of a Confucian-based imperial regime, the notion that individual dynasties come and go was built into the dynastic system. This made the existing ruling house extremely vulnerable to political pressure and, some would argue, made it less able to undertake innovative responses to the Western threat. Finally, whereas the Japanese easily moved away from the Confucian foundations of the state and elite status, in China Confucianism and Chinese culture were synonymous. Reformers did attempt a Confucian synthesis that moved China into the modern world. And, as we will see, it is mistaken to see Confucianism per se as the key to China's underdevelopment. Nevertheless, the kind of intellectual, pedagogical, and organizational flexibility that characterized late Tokugawa Japan was not evident in China.

A COMPARISON OF ECONOMIC STRUCTURES

In addition to their very different political experiences in the nineteenth century, both the natural endowments and the political economies of China and Japan varied in important respects. Thus it was not simply a "greater willingness to change" that enabled Japan to move ahead in the area of economic development. Indeed, while scholars of China often point to Japan's abandonment of Confucian values in its quest for modernization, scholars of Japan have often linked the persistence of key Confucian values to Japan's early economic success.

Geography and infrastructures

Several factors helped stimulate the development of Japan's market economy during the Tokugawa period. Japan is a small island country, with cheap and accessible coastal water transport. The Tokugawa requirement that all feudal lords reside in Edo in alternate years stimulated the growth of trade in the Edo region and the development of communications and transport between Edo and the main production centers at Kyoto and Osaka. In many key commodities, nineteenth-century Japan already had a well-developed national market. This national market continued to expand, as the political elite was forced to encourage the sale of more goods at Osaka to get cash for residence in Edo. In addition, the interest of daimyo in increasing productivity at home was enhanced by their desire to generate a surplus to spend in Edo. This, of course, did not preclude many daimyo from going into debt and contributing to the wealth of merchants and others who acted as their creditors in the later years of the shogunate.

By contrast, China was a vast land-based empire. It had a flourishing coastal trade, and indeed, it was in large part because of this that the coastal provinces were the most prosperous and developed even before the so-called coming of the West. However, coastal trade accounted for only a small part of China's total market economy, and political factors often interfered with its development.[1] It was China's extensive network of navigable inland waterways that played the greatest role in encouraging commercialization and handicraft production in China. However, most of this riverine network lies in south China, which had the most famous centers for the production of silk, cotton cloth, porcelain, and so on. The Yellow River, the main waterway of north China, is not navigable for most of its length. In the north transportation was largely by cart or pack animal, making the cost of moving goods very high. This put a severe limitation on the market range of goods and limited the opportunities for by-employment for farming families. China's extensive mountainous terrain also made interregional trade difficult and hampered the efficient use of a large part of its land mass. Recent research has shown that Qing China had the manpower and knowledge to engage in ecologically and economically sound forest management, highly sophisticated management of mountain-based handicrafts (i.e. papermaking), the cultivation of commercial crops like tong trees and indigo and bamboo, and mineral extraction. However, in the absence of low-cost transportation, hill populations were forced to devote much of their land to the cultivation of food, particularly corn. This invariably resulted in degradation of hillside soils and serious erosion, with predictable consequences in the form of increased flooding of regions downriver. This is still a serious problem in China today.

Population

Between the seventeenth and nineteenth centuries Japan experienced near zero population growth. This was most likely due to a combination of factors. Japanese families practiced primogeniture, which required only one male heir. Japan's rigid status hierarchy also discouraged the production of surplus sons who would have no ascribed occupation. The Japanese emphasis on the survival of the "house," or corporate family, and not the line of blood kinship also diminished the impulse to repeated pregnancies until a son was born. Moreover, the greater involvement of lords in the agricultural output of their domains led to laws against abandoning taxable land, dividing land, or forming branch families. All of these factors appear to have encouraged birth control in Japan, which, as in other premodern societies, took the forms of infanticide, late marriage, and abortion.

By contrast, the seventeenth to the nineteenth century in China was a period of population growth. During these years China's population increased approximately threefold. We will discuss the effect demographic growth had on the government, on the structure of the market economy and on industrial production, on the generation of surplus wealth for industrial investment, and on the peculiar fragmentation of Chinese economic activity.

Primogeniture

Although primogeniture has already been mentioned in relation to population growth, its effect on capital accumulation and the consolidation of family fortunes is equally important. In contrast to Japan, Chinese families practiced equal inheritance. This led to the diffusion of wealth, which was then exacerbated by population growth as property was divided among larger and larger numbers of people. Although institutions like the lineage counteracted this trend to some extent, most lineage resources took the form of ritual endowments, and it is not until the late nineteenth century that this kind of corporate wealth was used to build industrial infrastructures.

Legal restrictions on economic and social activity

One of the apparent ironies of the comparative economic development experiences of China and Japan is that the society in which the traditional state placed the greatest limitations on economic activity ended up as the most developed in the modern world. It has been argued that the restrictions placed on economic actors in Tokugawa Japan left considerable room for economic expansion utilizing traditional technologies in the nineteenth century, while few such opportunities existed in China. In China, restrictions on occupational and physical mobility were never rigidly enforced. In terms of the market economy, the limitation of markets to designated times and places, the control of merchants through government-appointed guild organizations, and the hereditary registration of populations in certain occupations largely ended in the Middle Ages. The last vestiges of such a system had died out by the middle of the Ming Dynasty (1368–1644), when the decline in the usefulness of hereditary artisan and military status groups was finally recognized in law. The same can be said of the agricultural sector. Where bonded status can be documented—and such places are not numerous—this status was largely gone by the seventeenth century. At the same time, limits on the physical movement of populations were generally pro forma. Occasional efforts were made to restrict migration to border areas and mountain areas for fear that disorder would result from the limited reach of government to such areas and the potential conflicts that might arise between new settlers and aboriginal or early settling populations. Nevertheless, the history of China, particularly from the Middle Ages on, has been one of external and internal migration. The "filling up of the frontier," a major theme in the late imperial period, is of tremendous significance to social, economic, and political historians.

In Tokugawa Japan occupational, status, and geographic mobility was limited. In addition, individual daimyo restricted the development of urban centers, in general confining commercial centers to the sites of their castle towns. Until relatively recently, Japanese urbanization was characterized by few lower-level markets and a concentration of marketing activity at middle- and higher-level market towns and cities. Moreover, quite early a national market developed in Osaka, a purely commercial city, and in Edo, the shogunal capital.

China, which had no such restriction on urban development, saw the very early elaboration of a system of marketing towns arranged in a nested hierarchy of at least seven levels. If Japan's market structure was top-heavy, China's was bottom-heavy. In addition, while in China regional markets were internally well integrated, until the nineteenth century the national market in anything but luxury goods was relatively weak. Some people would argue that even in the twentieth century China could not be said to have a national market. Even those who do acknowledge its existence recognize that it is largely due to the role of Shanghai as a national collection point for most of China's foreign trade.

Similar differences can be detected in the realm of occupational and geographical mobility. Until the late nineteenth century most Japanese were expected to remain within the occupations to which they were born and under the jurisdiction of the lord who controlled their domain. This took on particular significance for Japan's ruling elite. Whereas Chinese of all classes could aspire to membership in the bureaucratic elite, Japanese who were not born into the elite had no hope of making their fortune there. This is seen by many scholars as encouraging merchant activity among the Japanese outsider classes and discouraging it among ambitious Chinese.

In fact these distinctions were less rigid for the Chinese than even this scenario would have us think. Many men of official status or background did engage in commercial activity in China. The key to underdevelopment does not lie there. Nor is it unusual in any society to find those who succeed in the commercial world taking on the attributes of the political elite. Successful merchants and industrialists in England were just as quick to buy landed estates and join the squiredom as were their Chinese counterparts. Where the difference becomes important is in the early development of commerce and lack of restrictions in China, in contrast to the late development of commerce and escape from restrictions we find among Japan's elite. The end of the Tokugawa shogunate meant the sudden end of status classification in Japan, which in turn meant that economic entrepreneurship was the only option open to many of Japan's best-educated men. Samurai, who now found themselves out of a job as well as a status, frequently turned their administrative talents and political connections to business in the fluid economic atmosphere of early Meiji. Rich peasants were freer to engage in local commercial ventures. The injection of new entrepreneurial energies contributed to the dynamism of the late nineteenth-century Japanese economy.

Agriculture

One final area in which early restrictions and later sudden release became important was agriculture. China and Japan both depended to a large extent on rice agriculture. This has numerous implications for development that can be discussed in comparison to the European experience. Most interesting are the issue of involution, and the contrast between agricultural regimes in which livestock do and do not play a part.[2] Despite the apparent similarities one might expect between China and Japan, there were considerable differences, some of which relate once again to the impact of early and late development. Among these, three stand out.

As in the case of urban development, China's political structure presented no obstacles to the spread of agricultural technology. Although there were areas in twentieth-century China, particularly in the north, that were still using relatively primitive tools, by and large the best traditional technology had already spread throughout China by 1750 and was utilized by peasants to provide China with yields that were not matched in India and Japan until modern times. In Japan, the relative isolation of the various domains from one another meant that the most advanced technology did not spread evenly. This gave Japan an "advantage of backwardness" in the nineteenth century when, during a period of low rates of population growth, traditional technologies were rapidly improved, and with them overall yields.

Land tenure and distribution in China were very complex and varied greatly depending on geographic location, type of crop, the potential for multiple cropping, status of landlord, and so on. A number of generalizations are nevertheless possible. By the nineteenth century most of China's land was being farmed in small plots tilled by individual nuclear families. About 50 percent of arable land was rented out to tenants, and through a combination of mechanisms rents tended to equal about 50 percent of the primary crop. Except in a small number of highly commercialized areas, tenure was still relatively insecure, particularly in the north. During the Qing, an increasing number of landlords moved to urban places. This high rate of absenteeism contributed to a growing trend toward tenant rent resistance and a decreasing degree of landlord involvement in production. While the state played a growing role in assisting landlords in the collection of rent, income from agricultural taxes diminished as a proportion of total state revenues.

In the Japanese case generalizations are equally dangerous. However, the literature seems to indicate the following differences, particularly in the richer heartland domains. While farms were similar in size to those in China, Japanese farmers appear to have had greater security of tenure. This encouraged long-term investment in improving the productivity of the land. In some domains there was also greater involvement of government in improving agricultural productivity, since the daimyo's income was directly dependent on the amount of rice produced within his territory.

Finally, Japanese political institutions were more conducive to the appropriation of the agricultural surplus by the state. Quite early the samurai were removed from the land and allocated stipends by the domainal government. This separation of the political elite from land ownership resulted in far less interference by the elite in tax collection than we find in China. The responsibility for payment of taxes resided in the village and not in the individual. The community decided how to collect its quota, and intracommunity pressure meant that tax evasion was virtually nil. Moreover, the ratio of population to local administrative units in Japan was much smaller, allowing greater administrative control of local populations than in China. At the same time, the improvement of agricultural productivity in nineteenth-century Japan was achieved within the context of a stable population. The surplus generated at this time provided the Japanese state with a tax base, enabling it to take a leading role in the development process.

Until the twentieth century, in both China and Japan the state depended on the land tax for the bulk of its revenues. In China, however, the rate of taxation remained quite low, between 4 and 10 percent of GNP. Despite its lower tax rates, the Chinese state had a very difficult time collecting the land tax in full. This was because, in contrast to Japan, in China the elite were often landowners, and their political power provided the means to lower their rates of taxation and to evade taxation altogether. Moreover, in China taxation was based on the individual household and on the size of its holdings. The government insisted on individual household responsibility, but did not have the administrative capacity to keep up cadastral records, resurvey land in a fluid land market, and reconstruct land and population registers following their destruction in time of war and rebellion. As a result, arrears were more or less endemic throughout the Qing period. In the wake of China's mid-nineteenth-century rebellions, the provinces themselves began holding back funds, leaving the central government seriously underfunded at a time when the costs of administration and defense and the demands of foreign powers were increasing.

IMPERIALISM AND THE ROLE OF GOVERNMENT IN INDUSTRIALIZATION

The role of the West in either stimulating or inhibiting the process of development is a major historiographic issue deserving more space than can be provided here.[3] There is no doubt, however, that the relative capacities of the Chinese and the Japanese state to deal with the West were an important factor in the economic development of each country. Both the indigenous factors cited above and the nature of the Western impact itself determined how the rulers of China and Japan responded to the challenges presented by the Western powers. Railway construction and the development of the export market in silk provide interesting examples of two aspects of this problem.

Railways played an important part in Japan's rapid industrialization in the late nineteenth century and in many ways are a symbol of the role of government in Japan's modernization process. The Japanese government recognized quite early the advantages of an integrated railway network for domestic trade. Development of that network was subsidized by the state, which made a point of relying strictly on domestic revenues for this purpose. It was largely completed by the beginning of the twentieth century. By contrast, the Chinese did not really begin railway development until the 1890s. With inadequate revenues of its own, the central government turned to foreign loans for its initial efforts at railway construction. Nationalist sentiment made the recovery of the rights to build railways a major issue in the anti-Qing movement that eventually brought about the dynasty's fall. However, domestic private investment added little to the national grid. Indeed, many of China's main trunk lines were not constructed until after 1949, and even today many areas of China are poorly served by railway transportation. One legacy of the program to build railways in late Qing China was an intensification of government debt to foreign banking consortia and the strings attached to these loans in the form of spheres of influence for the lending nations.

While China was not as successful as Japan in importing transportation technology, in the early years of Western trade China led the way in exports. China was the world's leading exporter of silk until the turn of the twentieth century, when competition from Japan began gradually to erode China's international market. Japan's success was attributed in part to governmental promotion of quality controls and the institution of modern technology in the raising of cocoons. Chinese industrial reformers attempted similar programs but found it impossible to bring under their control the literally millions of small peasant producers that fed China's modern steam filatures. Fragmentation of production and the persistence of household manufacture, one of the strengths of China's premodern economy, thus became a serious obstacle to meeting the challenge of industrial development.

In noting their different responses to the challenge of modern Western economies, it is important to remember that China and Japan also had different experiences of imperialism. China was the first to be attacked, and the Japanese reaction to the West was tempered by the Chinese experience and the knowledge that the West would take what it wanted by force. In contrast to the centralized bureaucracy that was in command in China, the decentralized political system in Tokugawa Japan allowed individual domains to experiment with things Western even before it became politically acceptable to the regime as a whole. Thus a portion of Japan's elite was prepared and familiar with Western technologies and their usefulness by the time Western pressure began to intensify during the second half of the nineteenth century. While Westerners were preoccupied with China, Japan had first the breathing space to modernize and later the opportunity to join the ranks of the imperialists in the late nineteenth century. Increasingly after 1895, Japan can be seen using Chinese resources and markets to help build its own economy. China, on the other hand, was increasingly hampered in its development by debt obligations and indemnities to foreign powers, including Japan. These came to approximately 44 percent of annual national tax revenues by the turn of the century. In the nineteenth century both China and Japan were forced to accept an unequal relationship with the West, through a series of so-called unequal treaties. However, a strong Japanese state was able to achieve revision of the terms of these by 1911, while the greatly weakened post-Qing republic was doomed to live with most of their provisions until World War II.

CHINA'S INDIGENOUS ECONOMY: THE TRAP OF EARLY DEVELOPMENT

One of the ironies of the China-Japan comparison is that China before 1600 was clearly a more "developed" country than was Japan. The sophistication of Chinese political institutions permitted centralized administration of a vast empire with a population of at least one hundred million. Chinese agricultural technology was in many respects more advanced, and the most advanced technology was certainly more evenly distributed throughout the countryside. China had a more complex and more highly developed marketing system and was more integrated into the world economy through its overland trade with central Asia and its oceangoing trade with Southeast Asia. Differential experience of imperialism and the weakening of the state go only part of the way in explaining China's subsequent lag, particularly if we can show that some of the factors at work in the 1800s are still at work in determining the structure of industrialization and resource use in China today. If we take as measures of development increasing per capita output and income, China is still a lesser developed country. Even during the 1950s, when industrial growth averaged at least 10 percent a year, per capita output remained relatively low. The early Communist experience demonstrated that investable surplus did exist. The Chinese Communist Party would never have been able to commandeer the large proportion of rural output that it did to promote industrial development had that potential surplus not been there in the pre-1949 years. Moreover, the program in the 1950s to extract rural surplus was undertaken with little increase in capital inputs to agriculture. In order to obtain a fuller picture of the factors influencing China's industrialization, it is necessary to look in greater detail at some of the structural factors influencing its pattern of economic development.

THE SMALL PEASANT ECONOMY

China's prerevolutionary rural landscape was populated in large part by individual peasant proprietors, peasants who were part tenant part proprietor, or wholly tenant households, all of whom were linked by one fact, the small size of the land they managed. The large estate managed by the owner or his agent and farmed by large tenants or rural wage laborers was exceedingly rare in early modern China. Instead, landlords typically lived off rents from numerous tenants on tiny plots, often spending their lives in towns or cities at some remove from their land. In both north and south China, this fragmentation of land management led to considerable inefficiencies, and most of the productivity gains achieved in Chinese agriculture in the early Communist period grew out of the elimination of waste by consolidating land into collective farms.

As the size of farms declined, most Chinese farmers had to rely on employment in addition to or in lieu of the growing of crops in order to make ends meet. Rural residents were generally able to find such employment because of the dense rural marketing structure that was in place in China by the eighteenth century. Opportunities to supplement household income existed in cottage industry and in a variety of seasonal jobs, in transport and peddling, and in industries such as winemaking, salt production, papermaking, and so on. Where seasonal opportunities were not readily available, we typically see the development of patterns of seasonal brigandry. Backward regions, cut off by poor transportation from the centers of economic activity, were therefore often the site of endemic problems of social control.

The rural marketing system, with its rich variety of handicrafts and other occupations, thus helped perpetuate a fragmented agricultural system. The symbiosis between the two contributed to China's slow rate of industrialization in two ways. On the one hand, the development of factory and workshop production was discouraged by the availability of a large pool of rural residents willing to work at home for below subsistence wages. On the other hand, the availability of sideline employment meant that farmers, even when unable to support their families from the plots they managed, were not driven to abandon the land as they were in other parts of the world.

BOTTOM-HEAVY MARKETING SYSTEM

One of the remarkable characteristics of China's economy from the Middle Ages on was the almost total lack of legal impediments to trade and to the growth of institutions associated with trade. This in part accounts for the development of a dense network of rural markets and the concentration of Chinese marketing in the lower levels of the marketing hierarchy. It is difficult to indicate which came first, as they are interrelated. China's small farmer economy could not have developed without the support of its network of local markets. In rural periodic markets and market towns rural dwellers could obtain credit to tide them over hard times, pay for ritual functions like weddings and funerals, and bridge the income gap that often developed between harvests. Rural markets were also a venue for the sale of rural produce and the purchase or exchange of raw materials for cottage industry. Markets also played important roles in the organization of rural social life and in the transmission of information and technology in premodern China. By the late imperial period government did little to control where such markets could be established. Low taxes and relatively few taxes on commercial goods and transactions also helped to encourage trade. Government policies such as the decision to collect taxes in cash instead of in kind also contributed to the monetization of the economy from the sixteenth century on.

G. William Skinner, a pioneer in the study of China's rural markets, has estimated that every peasant in China, save those in the most remote regions, lived within two hours' walk of a periodic market. By the nineteenth century, many of these markets met as often as every other day, and some had become permanent market towns. Moreover, through a nested hierarchy of markets above the rural periodic market, rural producers and consumers were linked to each other at least to the level of the regional metropolis, and in some cases to the emerging national market of Shanghai.

IMPLICATIONS FOR CHINESE
ECONOMIC DEVELOPMENT

Economic fragmentation

Rather than encouraging the development of large merchant/
manufacturers, China's dense and highly integrated market
structure encouraged the perpetuation of peasant household production. Peasants could get all the raw materials they needed
from peddlers or merchants at periodic markets, and could sell
their finished goods to these same men. This obviated the need for
putting out, as developed in Europe, and discouraged capital accumulation, the control of production by merchants, and the concentration of production in rural and quasi-urban workshops. It
also guaranteed that the large wholesalers who eventually dealt
with the long-distance marketing of certain goods, like textiles,
were economically remote from the actual producers of the goods
they sold.

China's large size and its integrated network of rural markets
also allowed for a high degree of flexibility in dealing with changing market conditions. If shortages emerged in one region, it was
relatively easy to find alternative sources elsewhere. Therefore we
find few examples in China of the kind of production crisis that in
some countries acted as a spur to innovation and the modernization of techniques.

The cotton textile industry provides a good example of the market mechanism at work. By the nineteenth century cotton was
grown almost everywhere in China. Rural dwellers either grew
their own or bought raw cotton in periodic markets and sold their
yarn to small merchants in exchange for cash or more cotton to
spin. Spinning wheels were homemade and involved little commitment in cash. When a family needed more money, its members
spun more. When other uses of their time were deemed more
valuable, they stopped spinning. If prices for spun yarn went up,
more people engaged in spinning yarn instead of in other employ-
ments such as weaving mats or making sandals. In other words,
the inflow and outflow of labor into this industry responded well
to the forces of supply and demand and ensured that there were
few bottlenecks in the labor market sufficient to stimulate labor-
saving innovations.

Similar claims can be made for the supply of raw cotton. For a
brief period China imported raw cotton from India to supplement
native supply. However, this was soon supplanted by increased

native production in north China, supplying weavers who were mostly in the south. The ability of this large empire to act as its own supplier and to generate most of its demand is an important contrast, not only with Japan, but also with the West. With few barriers to trade, there were fewer stimuli to innovation. Some scholars would argue that there was also no equivalent to the impulse to conquer new markets, to compete by creating new and better products, and so on, that was crucial to the development process in the West. Indeed, the distribution chain created by this marketing structure seriously muffled the impact of consumer preference on producer activity. Between the peasant producer in the village and the consumer, perhaps in a city hundreds or thousands of miles away, was the peddler who bought his cloth and sold it to a larger peddler, who sold it to a wholesaler, who sold it to a broker, who contracted with dyers and finishers and then sold it to another wholesaler, who then sold it himself to retailers or went through retail brokers who then sent it to the shops where it was bought as finished cloth. This too is seen by some scholars as inhibiting innovation and entrepreneurship in the manufacturing sector.

The structure of the market also helps explain why Western penetration of China's economy brought so few tangible results. Many scholars have debated the negative and positive influence of Western economic penetration of China. One element in this debate centers on the failure of Western trade to transform China's native economy. If Western economic institutions, as well as most Westerners, remained restricted to a small number of treaty ports, one could argue that the West did not really hurt China's economy because it remained largely detached from it. On the other hand, one could equally argue that the demonstration effect of Western technology and business methods was small. However you choose to view this issue, it is important to note that the relative imperviousness of China's native economy to the transformative influences of Western trade and manufacturing were in part due to the marketing system we have been describing. Here, tea provides a good case in point.

Tea was one of China's main exports during the early modern period. When treaty agreements made possible Western merchant residence inland, many Westerners believed they had won a privilege which would free them from Chinese merchant intermediaries and would herald the direct management of production by Western trading companies. In fact, they soon discovered that the fragmentation of the Chinese production regime and the role of the local periodic market in coordinating production and marketing meant that they would never really be able to control directly the activities of Chinese producers.

Tea in China was not produced on large plantations which could be bought or contracted to a particular trading company. Rather, it was grown by thousands and thousands of small peasant freeholders and tenants on small plots of land, and sold to Chinese agents and peddlers, who then traded it up the market hierarchy in much the same manner as cotton was traded. Even the British-American Tobacco Company, which was one of the most successful foreign companies in penetrating the Chinese market structure, ultimately ended up plugging itself into Chinese merchant networks. No foreign company could muster the manpower or the ground-level expertise to operate a direct marketing concern. The fragmentation of production also made standardization and quality controls geared toward an international market much more difficult in China than in Japan.

The fragmentation described above may be called horizontal fragmentation, the division of an industry into a multitude of independent producers. Chinese industry also experienced vertical fragmentation. It was highly unusual in China to find manufacturers who also had control of the sources of raw materials, coordinated all the processes of production, and engaged in their own marketing. Indeed, in some industries undercapitalization led to separate ownership of the physical manufacturing plant and the firm that used the plant to manufacture goods.

Poor transportation

Geography was a major obstacle to the development of an inexpensive national transportation network in China. The effect of poor transportation was to deter the movement of bulk goods like coal in a national market. Even in the twentieth century the cost of transport could double the price of coal within a few kilometers of the mine. This, and the paucity of easily harnessed water power, discouraged development of inorganic energy sources before the period of Western impact. Railways have played an important role in linking remote and more isolated regions of China to the national economy. However, as we have already seen, the introduction of railway transportation was also fraught with difficulty. Efforts at private railway investment met with only partial success, and government efforts to build railways with foreign loans contributed to the fall of the imperial regime. During the

Republican period China's railway grid doubled in length, but military considerations often superseded economic concerns in the placement of track, and political fragmentation often interfered with the integrating effects of railway construction. It is no accident that even today it is the coastal provinces, within easy reach of foreign markets, and benefiting from ease of interregional trade, that are the most advanced, both economically and in terms of the development of a cosmopolitan cultural perspective.

Low levels of capital accumulation

The domination of agriculture by small peasant farming regimes impeded capital accumulation in a number of ways. Profits from the land were low. Although peasants often paid 50 percent or more of the crop in rent, this translated into a relatively low return on investment for landlords. That land was considered an important target of investment by those with wealth in China reflected both a lack of other investment opportunities and the security that landed wealth could provide. Farmers were left with little surplus to invest in improved productivity. Although many daily use items were purchased in rural markets, overall the level of demand in the countryside remained low and could not stimulate a dramatic rise in the production of manufactured goods.

The vertical fragmentation described above also contributed to low levels of capital accumulation. Where profits were divided over long chains of production and distribution, a low marginal return at each stage was common. Equal inheritance and a relatively egalitarian social structure further hampered the concentration of wealth. Thus, while China had no shortage of surplus capital, that capital was often too dispersed to be easily combined for industrial investment.

CONCLUSION

The structural conditions which slowed China's early industrial development were exacerbated by political instability, weak central government, world depression, and war during the first half of the twentieth century. The communist government which took power after the revolution in 1949 in part solved the problem of industrial investment through a planned economy in which the state financed industrial development, in part through high levels of extraction from the agricultural sector. Western trade played almost no part in this development, and following the Sino-Soviet split of the 1960s, the Chinese economy was largely self-suffi-cient. Although much of China's modern industrial plant, partic-ularly that devoted to heavy industry, was built up in this way, policy decisions taken during the Cultural Revolution (1966–76) led to a slowing down of China's industrial growth. Emphasis was placed on the establishment of large industrial projects in inland regions, largely for strategic purposes.[4] Most of these pro-jects were built at enormous cost in regions far from China's main concentrations of population and transportation resources, were shoddily built, and required large subsidies to keep in oper-ation. At the same time, the decentralization of economic decision making undertaken during this period resulted in the disman-tling of the central planning apparatus. When it became apparent that something had to be done to restore the high rates of indus-trial growth that China had enjoyed during the early years of the PRC, two things became clear: a) reform had to include incen-tives to the rural population to increase declining rates of agri-cultural productivity under collectivization and b) it would be impossible to restore the central planning structures upon which growth during the 1950s was based.

In the end, China under Deng Xiaoping opted for a semi-free market economy after 1978, beginning with decollectivization of agriculture and the legalization of small-scale enterprise in the early 1980s. By the early 1990s private and provincial/local col-lective enterprise accounted for a larger portion of GNP than state-run industry. GNP growth rates were once again in the dou-ble-digit range, and the expanding market in consumer goods and increasing popular access to entertainment and service industries gave China an air of prosperity unknown in living memory. And for the first time since 1949 foreign trade, particularly a growing market for Chinese exports abroad, played an important part in China's economy.

Nevertheless, as China approaches the twenty-first century, many questions regarding its economic future remain. Some of them hearken back to problems which helped mold China's early modern economy in centuries past. What role will the state play in the economy of China? What will be the fate of China's state-run industries? Will the Chinese state be able to develop a system of civil and administrative law that will both foster growth and pro-tect the public interest as a larger and larger portion of GNP is outside the state? Will the state, which now depends almost en-tirely upon profits from state-run industries, be able to develop a system of taxation that will provide it with sufficient revenues to fund the social services and infrastructural investments that until recently were the responsibility of the collective sector? Will efforts at family planning succeed in preventing population growth from offsetting the benefits of China's development process? And will China be able to address persistent inequalities between rural and urban, between coastal and inland regions, and between north and south? The answers to these questions will not only help determine the economic future of the Chinese people. They will also be a critical factor in the survival of the communist state.

NOTES

1. Coastal trade was banned during the early Qing in an effort to isolate rebels on Taiwan. Pirates, who often raided the Chinese coast, also plagued the Qing rulers and led to an underutilization of coastal waters during the early Qing.

2. An interesting exercise for students is the examination of the implications of these different forms of agricultural management for the development of community, community property, agricultural cooperation, the use of household labor, and so on.

3. See Paul Cohen's discussion of this issue in *Discovering History in China* (New York: Columbia University Press, 1984.)

4. See Barry Naughton, "The Pattern and Legacy of Economic Growth in the Mao Era," in *Perspectives on Modern China: Four Anniversaries* (Armonk, NY: M. E. Sharpe, 1991) pp. 226–54.

AN APPROACH TO MODERN INDIAN ECONOMIC HISTORY

Morris David Morris

Attempts to explain India's poverty and lack of modern economic growth before 1947 generally fall into two categories. There are those, like Marx in his famous essays on India, who emphasize India's social structure, culture, and values as the barriers to economic growth and modernization. In this formulation, English imperialism is said to have fulfilled a double mission in India: one destructive, the other regenerating—the annihilation of traditional society, and the laying of the material foundations of Western society in Asia. The other more recent and now much more widely held interpretation, subscribed to by many Indian as well as by non-Indian scholars, is similar to the "dependency" theory initially developed from Latin American experience. It views the impact of the West as largely negative—limiting, distorting, or even actively destroying indigenous capacities for modern economic development.

Despite substantial differences, both interpretations assume the inevitability of a certain form of modern economic growth; it is in explaining the failure of the society to modernize and develop that they differ. In Marx's formulation—shared by other analysts in what I call the "imperialist" theory—if railroads, cotton mills, and free trade did not automatically lead to the modernization of the system, the barriers clearly had to derive from indigenous values and social structure. According to "dependency" theory, by contrast, the inevitability of modernization was frustrated in India by imperialist policies imposed directly through colonial rule and somewhat more indirectly after 1945 by the operation of international markets dominated by the monopoly power of North Atlantic economies.

I find neither of these interpretations satisfactory. Despite the intellectual power of Max Weber's formulation in *The Religion of India,* the evidence is overwhelming that, in South Asia as in China, values and social structure have not been decisive as inhibitors of rapid economic growth or modernization.

But neither do arguments that attribute India's failure to grow rapidly or to modernize dramatically to the role of British imperialism satisfy. My dissatisfaction can be summarized in a simple historical paradox, the very rapid growth of the Indian cotton textile industry. The first mill was established in 1854, and the industry grew most dramatically after 1870. By 1914, financed almost exclusively by local entrepreneurs, it was the fourth or fifth largest textile industry in the world.[1] Given the economic and political importance of the British cotton textile industry—it was Britain's most important industry through most of the nineteenth century, and as late as 1914 accounted for about 10 percent of the total manufacturing labor force and for 26 percent of Britain's total exports—it is quite puzzling that the British permitted this Indian industry ever to get a footing, much less to reach the enormous size it did. Despite British refusal to permit Indian mills to be protected by tariffs or to receive any other special assistance, Indian entrepreneurs not only increasingly challenged the British within South Asia but after the mid-1880s were driving British yarns out of Chinese markets.

From this initial paradox flows a second puzzle. If British imperialism did not (or could not) inhibit the growth of Indian competition against Britain's most important industry, why then did aggressive Indian entrepreneurs not expand into other sectors of modern industry? The answer, it seems to me, requires a more sophisticated interpretation of how the Indian economy worked under British imperialism than is usually suggested.

While economists tend to analyze social processes almost entirely in terms of market forces, to the exclusion of values, social structures, and political factors, historians of India have concerned themselves with little else, attributing all economic development and nondevelopment in India to the way the Raj exercised power. But in so doing historians ignore the fact that in the nineteenth and twentieth centuries decisions about the allocation of resources were made almost exclusively in the private sector. In no decade throughout this period did the state's share of annual GNP average more than 10 percent, and it was usually less than that. Of course, private decisions were shaped by the framework of more general official policy and by local values and social structure. But private entrepreneurs were entirely free to seek the most favorable results within the scope the system provided. If the system provided Indian businessmen after 1850 with sufficient incentives to permit the rapid growth of a cotton textile industry, why did these private entrepreneurs not find similar incentives in other sectors?

The answer is that industrialization does not occur inevitably. There are preconditions that must be satisfied if modern large-scale economic organization is to emerge in any sustainable form. It will be helpful to identify these preconditions; one should bear in mind that what is being offered is not a theory but rather a checklist of five general, interdependent requirements.

(1) **Political stability, predictability, flexibility.** What is required is a system within which relatively stable commercial conditions prevail, incentives are provided, and economic decisions can be implemented.

(2) **Increasing capital accumulations to finance large-scale investment.** This implies not only the amassing of real social surpluses but also the presence of institutions to mobilize them: banks, relevant forms of business, adequate monetary and credit mechanisms, and an underlying legal structure.

(3) **Increasing agricultural productivity.** In addition to supporting a growing **proportion** of the total population in non-agricultural activities, the growing agricultural sector provides an expanding market for industrial output and is also a source of capital.

(4) **A trained and versatile labor force.** It should be both geographically and occupationally mobile, willing and able to develop skills responsive to the changing requirements of the developing system.

(5) **Expanding market demand.** Essential to the development of a factory system with the extensive introduction of machines that greatly increase productivity is an expanding market that will make this new system profitable.

By the middle of the nineteenth century the formal conditions that favored private market activities suggested by precondition (1) were being created in India as they had been in Britain: for example, a legal and monetary system favorable to private enterprise and an increasingly reliable transport and communications network that reduced the cost of transactions on the subcontinent. Given that the formal environment of market institutions was favorable to private initiative, it must have been the specific calculations of concern to entrepreneurs—the demand for products and the supply of factors, the prices at which products could be sold and the costs of producing them—that were unfavorable. Let us examine these.

One can certainly suggest that effective demand was generally unfavorable. Although India's population was large, average per capita income was extremely low. It has been estimated that in 1870 it was no more than half and by 1913 about a third that in Japan. At least half of that income was produced in nonmonetized ways and therefore was not directly influenced by or responsive to market supply-and-demand forces. While unequal distribution contributed to creating more market demand than the low average per capita income might suggest, much of that demand existed in the great trading towns—ports and upcountry railway junctions— which were also most exposed to foreign competition. Domestic demand was heavily dependent on agricultural performance: not only did the average low per capita income in this sector offer generally limited markets for industrial products, but for climatic reasons farm output tended to be unstable. This combination of difficulties certainly dampened entrepreneurial expectations.

There were also very serious inhibitions on the supply side. In India's economically underdeveloped state, most factors of production were costly in absolute terms and, often, relative to costs abroad. All machinery had to be imported. Human capital in the form of skilled labor and technical managers was scarce and initially also had to be imported. Fuel was expensive, and so was transport. Because of the lack of adequate maintenance and repair facilities, parts inventories had to be large or allowance had to be made for long and costly shutdowns. The small modern banking system was designed to support short-term commercial transactions, largely connected with foreign trade. Longer-term needs for industrial capital had to come almost entirely from private negotiations and a very frail stock market. Thus fixed capital costs to aspiring industrialists were high and credit facilities for working capital were thin and quite unreliable. Only raw labor was cheap, and on occasion—as in the jute and cotton mill industries—it provided a substantial advantage. But cheap labor often worked against mechanization, encouraging entrepreneurs to expand existing forms of production rather than shift to techniques requiring greater capital investment. The system, of course, did not generate public or private institutions to provide a flow of literate workers or technical and managerial skills on any substantial scale.

In addition to all these objective features, entrepreneurs and investors had to keep in mind the very considerable additional uncertainties surrounding projections in underdeveloped economies. Business people in developed economies have at their disposal a formal structure of public and private facilities that reduces uncertainty, including middlemen performing specialized activities through futures markets, insurance mechanisms, and the provision of extensive price and other statistical information. They can assume that most demand, supply, and cost relationships will fit into a predictable system of expectation. But this is precisely what does not exist in newly developing countries generally and did not exist in India. Entrepreneurs had to accept not only a higher level of risk but also a much greater range of uncertainty in all their calculations. Thus, if novel enterprises were to be undertaken, they had to promise very high rates of return, which further limited the number of opportunities that entrepreneurs and investors would find attractive.

So far I have identified elements that affected the judgments of entrepreneurs, whether native or foreign. An explanation as to why Indian entrepreneurs tended to respond to different opportunities than did Europeans will be helpful. Again, the cotton textile industry is illustrative.

The cotton and jute textile industries both were started in the 1850s, the technical and financial requirements were virtually identical, and there were no overt barriers to entry in either case, yet most of the cotton mills were financed and ultimately managed by Indians, while jute mills were promoted and managed entirely by foreigners. Why did Indian entrepreneurs invest so aggressively in cotton textile mills but not in jute mills? Why did Europeans do exactly the reverse? The explanation, I suggest, is to be found in the different structures of risk and uncertainty confronting the two groups and the real differences in costs and potential profitability which these implied for native and foreign entrepreneurial groups.

The success of the jute industry was dependent on the continuous expansion of world commerce, particularly the trade in agricultural commodities that required sacking and wrapping. This required an ability to estimate fairly accurately existing and potential international demand. These foreign markets could be developed and sustained by European trading houses with extensive international contacts. Native entrepreneurs without equally efficient information networks were at a serious disadvantage.

Briefly put, Indians were at a disadvantage in the foreign trade aspect of any activity and in any venture that depended on knowledge of international demand. This was not solely a matter of monopoly discrimination by the British merchant houses, although that could have been a small part of the problem. It was mainly due to the enormous costs of building and maintaining an effective independent network of information about foreign marketing opportunities.

The same problems afflicted Indian businessmen in western India. Despite their acknowledged aggressiveness, these merchants were also largely dependent on foreigners for the expansion of their international trade. Only those merchants who were active along the trade routes in the Indian Ocean and East Asia, where for centuries Indians had traded on their own and in partnership with Europeans, were immune to these problems. This explains the ability of Bombay mill owners to rapidly displace the British in East Asian yarn markets after 1873.

Furthermore, once we recognize how difficult and costly it was to develop commercial contacts and reduce business risks to reasonable levels, we can see not only why foreigners tended to concentrate their efforts on export-oriented investments but why at the same time they tended not to invest in industries whose markets were primarily within India. Language skills and the intimate knowledge of the countryside and local cultures that was needed for buying and selling were extremely costly to acquire. Throughout the British period it was Indian merchants and agents who dominated every aspect of trade behind the great seaports. And so, as opportunities arose to satisfy internal demand with modern organization and technology, it was Indians and not foreigners who were best able to take advantage of them.

It has been frequently suggested that a vigorous protective tariff policy would have reduced foreign competition and increased the effective demand for native factory products. While the point has some validity, its significance has been exaggerated. To the extent that tariffs were justified in allowing infant industries time to learn to produce at lower costs, the argument assumes that native enterprises had natural advantages that needed only experience to be brought forth. It is true that Indian producers could count on some substantial locational advantages where transport costs often provided protection against foreign competitors. Nevertheless, industries where such advantages were important—cement, iron and steel, certain kinds of chemicals, paper—did not develop or developed very slowly. And the cotton and jute textile industries grew rapidly without any tariff protection. The expansion of jute manufacturing and the major part of the cotton textile industry that was centered in Bombay depended largely on an ability to compete in foreign markets, where protective tariffs could not have helped. Looked at in this way, the policies that would have been truly useful were those which would have increased competitiveness in foreign markets by reducing production costs and/or expanding domestic demand in India.

Viewed from the cost side, typically input costs to a firm or industry were high not just because of lack of experience but for structural reasons over which the individual entrepreneur had no effective control. Real cost reductions required action and investments in other sectors, possibly on a scale beyond the ability of private individuals. For example, reducing the costs of raw materials required the development of new industries, sharply reduced transport costs, and considerable investment in research and development. The reduction of labor costs demanded not only investment to produce highly skilled technical, administrative, and supervisory talent, but also massive educational expenditures to provide a generally literate workforce. The reduction of capital costs required (among other things) investment to improve banking and other mechanisms for the mobilization of capital and credit.

These requirements underline the distinction between social and private advantage. Many measures to reduce input costs might prove economically advantageous to the society as a whole but not to an individual entrepreneur, since the costs might be greater than any short-term benefit. For example, an employer who invested in upgrading the quality of his workers by financing their general education would face the threat of having them raided by competitors who did not incur these costs. Yet it is often just such basic investments that in the long run are indispensable for reducing factor costs on which general economic development and industrialization ultimately depend.

But costs of production are not all that have to be considered. As my final precondition suggests, no modern industrial economy can develop unless it is sustained by rising effective demand. Foreign markets may help the process, but sturdy industrial development requires the expansion of **domestic** demand. In India's case (as in that of most poor countries where the vast proportion of the workforce is in agriculture) this also required the expansion of agricultural income, particularly among the impoverished peasantry. To achieve this combination of results, it would have been necessary to undertake extensive research and development efforts to increase agricultural productivity; to create a system of credit to help small producers introduce new methods; and to establish a widely accessible educational system to enable cultivators to respond more quickly and effectively to such innovations. Every one of these requirements implies basic investments that were socially advantageous but beyond the capacity or economic advantage of individual entrepreneurs working through the market system. They imply a systematic public development approach that went well beyond simple tariff protection, and the mobilization of national energies on a scale that was well beyond the capacities of any imperialist system. In fact, experience since 1945 suggests how complex the task is even for a developing country that is independent.

In this discussion I have suggested that development does not occur inevitably but depends on the realization of certain basic preconditions. This explains why India was able to develop certain elements of modern economic life but not a full-blown modern economy.

In discussing certain vexing features of India's economic development after 1800–1850, I have also implied that one should think somewhat differently about the nature of imperialism. If one accepts Adam Smith's dictum that there is "a certain propensity in human nature . . . to truck, barter, and exchange one thing for another,"[2] it follows that foreigners in a given country are willing to do so wherever they can make money. If they have tended to concentrate their investments in export-oriented enterprises, it is not so much because imperialist countries needed to invest capital abroad in specific types of economic activities as because these were the enterprises where risk and uncertainty were lowest.

NOTES

1. For a discussion of the earlier decline of hand-loomed cotton piece goods production in India, readers are referred to the essay "From Trading Companies to Free Trade Imperialism: The British and Their Rivals in Asia, 1700–1850" by Derek Linton.

2. Adam Smith, *An Inquiry into the Nature and Causes of the Wealth of Nations*, ed. Edwin Cannon (New York: The Modern Library, 1937), p. 13.

SUGGESTED REFERENCES

For an elaboration of my formulation, with an emphasis on the theoretical argument, see my article, "South Asian Entrepreneurship and the Rashomon Effect, 1800–1947," *Explorations in Economic History* 16 (1979): 341–61. My emphasis is more factual in "The Growth of Large-Scale Industry to 1947" in *The Cambridge Economic History of India, 1757–1970*, ed. Dharma Kumar (Cambridge: Cambridge University Press, 1983). I explain the minimal role of values and social structure in the Weberian sense in "Values as an Obstacle to Economic Growth in South Asia," *Journal of Economic History* 27 (1967): 588–607. For an analysis that suggests the contradictions with which British imperialism was forced to cope, see B.R. Tomlinson, *The Political Economy of the Raj 1914–1947: The Economics of Decolonization in India* (London: The Macmillan Press Ltd., 1979). For an overview of the scholarly debate on Indian economic history during the British period, see Morris D. Morris, Toru Matsui, Bipin Chandra, and T. Raychaudhuri, *Indian Economy in the Nineteenth Century: A Symposium* (Delhi: Indian Economic and Social History Association, Delhi School of Economics, 1969). While this volume has the advantage of presenting the unreconciled views of the participants, its bibliography is by now somewhat outdated. More up-to-date bibliographic references as well as criticisms of the position advanced here can be found in a number of reviews of *The Cambridge Economic History of India*, vol. 2. See also, for example, *Modern Asian Studies* 19, pt. 3 (July 1985), particularly the essays by Colin Simmons and Rajnarayan Chandavarkar.

III
Modern Asia, 1600–1990

TOKUGAWA JAPAN, 1600–1867

William B. Hauser

THE POLITICAL CONTEXT

The Tokugawa era (1600–1867) represents a new stage in the development of Japanese society. A new form of military-bureaucratic government, the Tokugawa *bakufu*, provided a degree of centralized control and political stability previously unknown in Japan. Centered in Edo (modern Tokyo), the Tokugawa consolidated their control over the regional military power holders (daimyo) by 1651. Thereafter, the *bakufu* represented central political and military authority until the resignation of the last shogun in 1867.

Tokugawa dominance included control over the largest private domain in the realm. This included nearly 25 percent of the agricultural lands, the cities of Edo, Osaka, Kyoto, and Nagasaki, and rights to the products of the primary gold and silver mines. The Tokugawa house maintained the largest army, including 80,000 vassals and subvassals and reinforcements provided by its daimyo allies and relatives. While rarely required to display its military might after 1615, the Tokugawa house dominated both the regional daimyo and the emperor. As national hegemon, the shogun was unassailable. Further, the shogun controlled most aspects of Japan's relations with the outside world. This resulted in the exclusion after 1639 of Portuguese and Spanish traders due to their ties to Catholic missionary efforts, the violent suppression of Christianity, and the restriction of most foreign trade to the Tokugawa-controlled port of Nagasaki. After 1640, Japan's foreign relations were limited to contacts with China, Korea, the Ryukyu Islands, and Holland. Thus began Japan's long period of self-imposed national seclusion.[1]

Several policies reinforced the dominance of the Tokugawa shogun. First, Tokugawa Ieyasu, the founder of the Tokugawa house, created three branch houses to provide adoptive candidates for the office of shogun. This ensured the succession of his male heirs as hegemon. Second, the shogun controlled daimyo succession. Each new daimyo required the approval of the shogun to succeed to office. In the first fifty years of *bakufu* rule daimyo were relocated, had their lands increased or decreased, or saw their houses abolished at the whim of the shogun. This power illustrated the dominant authority of the Tokugawa house.[2]

A third support was the *sankin kōtai* system of alternate attendance. This required daimyo to maintain their immediate families and most important vassals in the shogunal capital, spend every other year in attendance on the shogun in Edo, and participate in elaborate and costly processions back and forth between Edo and their domains.[3] After vassal salaries, *sankin kōtai* expenses were the largest items in daimyo budgets and limited their ability to challenge Tokugawa authority.[4] This subordination of the daimyo to the shogun was amplified in the laws for military households (*buke shohatto*) issued by the *bakufu* in 1615 and elaborated thereafter.[5] Their intent was to maintain discipline and decorum among the daimyo and members of the samurai class.

Further reinforcing the dominant position of the Tokugawa were daimyo oaths of loyalty to the shogun. Tokugawa ideology distinguished the shogun from potential rivals and included Confucian theories of natural hierarchy and proper governance reinforced by elements of Buddhist and Shinto religion. Tokugawa Ieyasu was enshrined at Nikko, where he was worshiped as the "divine founder" of the Tokugawa house. As Herman Ooms noted, "Shogunal rule became sacralized as an incarnation of the Way of Heaven." With the deification of Ieyasu, Tokugawa political authority took on a quasi-religious character.[6]

Yet Tokugawa authority was far from absolute. While the daimyo required Tokugawa consent for succession to office, within their domains they ruled autonomously. Except for irregular service or construction obligations, daimyo incomes were not subject to Tokugawa taxes. When daimyo economic policies conflicted with *bakufu* objectives, after 1700 it was increasingly the daimyo who prevailed. Domain autonomy enabled daimyo to issue domain currencies, create commercial monopolies, and assert local economic interests. Even the required land surveys which measured the productive wealth of the domains did not always conform to Tokugawa standards and procedures. So long as the *bakufu* was not directly challenged, daimyo autonomy was respected.[7]

URBANIZATION

A major feature of Tokugawa society was urbanization. One result of the unification of Japan between 1560 and 1600 was an increase in urban centers. Regional military leaders created cities and towns to concentrate their forces in heavily fortified castles and provide the goods, war materiel, and services necessary to support their armies. This helped to separate the samurai from the commoners and break their ties to the land, making them more available for military and administrative service. Urbanization concentrated the power of the daimyo and reinforced his authority over his vassals.[8]

Three central cities—Kyoto, Osaka, and Edo—dominated urban life and culture. Kyoto was the source of aristocratic culture and high-quality craft production. Osaka was a major commercial city and served as the headquarters of *bakufu* military power in western Japan. Osaka was a center of consumption, handicraft production, and processing industries. By the mid-eighteenth century, both Osaka and Kyoto were large cities, with populations of around 400,000. Edo, the capital of the Tokugawa *bakufu*, was the largest Japanese city; with a population of over one million in 1720, it ranked among the largest cities in the world. Resident in Edo were the Tokugawa shogun and his immediate vassals, the 264 or so daimyo families, and the merchants, artisans, and service personnel required to support the needs of a great metropolis. Edo was a center of government and consumption and the axis of a commercial network in eastern Japan.[9]

Complementing the three great central cities were dozens of provincial cities and towns. They serviced the needs of the daimyo and their samurai retainers. One cause of urbanization was the removal of most samurai from the land to distinguish them functionally from farmers. Another was the attempt to separate trade and handicraft production from agriculture by concentrating merchants and artisans in urban centers. Other factors were the expansion of trade and travel between regional centers and Edo, the associated improvements in waterborne and overland transportation systems, and population growth. By the mid-eighteenth century, as much as 10 percent of the total population lived in cities of 10,000 residents or more. By the mid-Tokugawa period Japan was an integrated, preindustrial economy with well-regulated systems of shipping, banking, commodity marketing, and handicraft industrial production.[10]

SOCIAL CHANGE

In accordance with Confucian principles, Tokugawa society placed most people in one of four classes, or estates. At the top were the samurai, including the shogun and the daimyo. Next were the farmers who produced the food crops and whose taxes supported the ruling class. Then came the artisans and finally the merchants. Artisans were perceived as essential because they produced vital goods. Merchants were viewed as a necessary evil. While they distributed food and other essential goods, they profited from the labor of others and produced nothing of their own. In addition to the four classes were the emperor and the Kyoto court aristocrats, the Shinto and Buddhist clergy, certain professionals like physicians and teachers, and the outcasts—including actors, prostitutes, leather workers, grave diggers, and other suspect professions. Each class had its own function and was expected to conform to status-specific norms of behavior.[11]

Tokugawa conceptions of social hierarchy and natural order were increasingly inconsistent with social realities. While urbanization concentrated the samurai, artisans, and merchants in castle towns, this late-sixteenth- and seventeenth-century effort did not prove lasting. For one thing, Japanese cultivators were farmers, not peasants. Rather than passively adhere to legal constraints on their cropping and by-employment choices, many cultivators made household decisions which enhanced their cash incomes and responded to market forces. As the urban demand for goods increased, farmers discovered that growing crops other than rice was very profitable. While legally limited in their cropping choices, they evaded controls and used rice fields and upland fields for growing vegetables, tobacco, cotton, rapeseed, and other market-oriented crops. Over the course of the Tokugawa era, farm acreage probably doubled while population increased more slowly and leveled off after around 1720. The result was improvements in village material culture and changes in socioeconomic conditions in rural Japan.[12]

The diffusion of processing industries and trade, combined with new cropping patterns, resulted in dramatic changes in the character of village life by the late eighteenth and early nineteenth centuries. No longer isolated from the monetized economy of urban centers, villages now offered many of the same employment opportunities available in cities. Villagers engaged in craft production or trade to supplement farm incomes. The idealized Confucian class system no longer represented the social reality of villages in the vicinity of major cities like Edo, Osaka, and Kyoto or on major trade routes. Farmers worked as merchants and artisans in the off-season, and some village residents never farmed at all. Others worked for wages. By the early nineteenth century, while seasonal or permanent migration to cities and towns was still common, many landless farmers found work closer to home.[13]

Changes in village society reflected the increased monetization of the Japanese economy during the Tokugawa period. This significantly affected the lives of urban residents, including the samurai. Paid in bales of rice, samurai needed cash to buy household necessities and pay their servants. While samurai incomes remained stable for most of the Tokugawa period, their wants increased. Samurai incomes were less and less sufficient as their demands for goods and services expanded in the eighteenth and nineteenth centuries. This led to the impoverishment of many samurai and greater dependence on loans from urban merchants and bankers. Lower-income samurai turned to handicraft production or teaching to supplement their meager stipends. While legally superior to the commoners in Tokugawa cities, urban samurai experienced difficulty matching the lifestyles of the more successful merchants and artisans.[14]

Urban life changed substantially during the Tokugawa period. Cities like Osaka and Edo expanded in size as new immigrants came in search of work. Merchant and artisan houses rose and fell, property was bought and sold, and the turnover in rental property was especially dramatic. Studies of Edo and Osaka merchant houses, neighborhoods, employment patterns, and social mobility all testify to the instability of urban life. Fires, famines, natural disasters, and economic booms and busts all affected the nature of urban life in Tokugawa Japan.[15]

Demographic patterns also changed. Village data indicate that the population was relatively stable from the 1720s. Many families consciously limited their offspring to enhance the material quality of their lives. Family limitation reflected rational decision making by farmers confident that smaller households could still ensure succession and provide the labor to till their fields. In rural Japan, shrewd choices about cropping patterns, by-employments, and family size enhanced the quality of village life.[16]

POPULAR CULTURE

Urbanization and improved material conditions resulted in the emergence of a new popular culture in Tokugawa Japan. This complemented the elite culture of the samurai and the Kyoto aristocrats. Two important features of this process were improvements in printing technology and the establishment of licensed entertainment districts in major cities. The diffusion of printed books and woodblock prints revolutionized access to information. In the seventeenth century, books and prints became available in multiple copies. Readership was limited, but by the end of the century most samurai were literate and increasing numbers of merchants and artisans had access to education in private academies and temple schools.

The increased commercialization and monetization of the economy required written records. Urban and rural administration demanded literate functionaries who came from the commoner classes. Urban commoners (chōnin) had better access to education than did farmers, but wealthy village residents found ways to educate their sons so they could keep family records and serve as village leaders. By the late Tokugawa period, it is estimated that 40 or 50 percent of boys and 15 percent of girls received some schooling and had basic literacy skills. As the reading public expanded, so did the number of publishers, booksellers, and lending libraries. This greatly expanded access to information in Tokugawa Japan.[17]

Widespread literacy had dramatic social and cultural implications. Schools spread Confucian ideology throughout Tokugawa society. Many samurai and commoners engaged in Confucian scholarship, wrote classical prose and poetry, and studied science, medicine, and agronomy. Nativist scholars probed early Japanese texts in search of the essence of Japanese culture. "Dutch studies" provided limited access to Western science and geography from European books imported through Dutch traders at Nagasaki.[18] The development of popular culture was stimulated by printed collections of fiction and poetry, guidebooks, miscellanies, and instruction manuals, many with extensive illustrations. Woodblock printing enabled the diffusion of graphic art and literature to a growing public with interests in theater, style, and the "floating world" of urban entertainment. The establishment of licensed brothel districts encouraged the concentration of theaters, tea houses, restaurants, and other components of urban entertainment in specific areas of major cities. Edo, Kyoto, and Osaka each had centers of popular culture. Entertainment districts primarily catered to male needs in cities where the male population often greatly outnumbered that of women. *Bakufu* and domain officials condoned, but did not approve, the activities of the urban entertainment districts. They recognized their value for relieving social tensions.[19]

CONCLUSIONS

Japanese society in 1850 was very different from that of 1600. It was more urban and more literate, better able to provide a range of goods and services to residents of cities, towns, and villages than ever before. The self-sufficient agrarian community was displaced by villages integrated into elaborate marketing systems that gave them access to goods from a wide range of sources. Farmers could purchase books, paper and writing materials, metal tools, hair and cooking oils, specialty foods, fertilizers and seeds, and a host of other commodities in their own communities or nearby market centers. Virtually all villages were tied into some kind of trading network.

Regular shipping routes transported goods and people from coastal Hokkaido to Kyushu. Osaka commodity prices influenced the costs of goods in urban areas throughout Japan. The highways and coastal transport systems were used not only by daimyo and samurai on their processions to and from Edo, but also by merchants, peddlers, transporters, pilgrims, and pleasure seekers. Commoners traveled to cities in search of employment or just to see the sights and sell the regional specialities they carried with them. Constraints still limited the choices available to many Japanese, but they were far less inhibiting than Tokugawa-era legal codes and sumptuary edicts suggest. Farmers altered crop choices in response to market demands, engaged in trade and handicraft production as forms of village by-employment, and sent their sons and daughters to work for wages as farm laborers or in village workshops; others went to nearby or distant towns and cities.

For a preindustrial society, Japan was by 1850 highly literate, remarkably mobile, and economically integrated. Experience with wage labor, monetary transactions, handicraft industrial production, education, cash-cropping, by-employments, family limitation, and migration in search of work prepared the Japanese to respond to the demands of industrialization and political modernization after 1868. Although largely isolated from the West until

1854, Tokugawa Japan experienced significant economic and social changes which prepared the Japanese people well to serve the needs of a nation in transition after the Meiji Restoration of 1868.

NOTES

1. For a discussion of foreign relations, see Ronald P. Toby, *State and Diplomacy in Early Modern Japan* (Princeton: Princeton University Press, 1984). For Japanese reactions to European missionary activities, see George Elison, *Deus Destroyed: The Image of Christianity in Early Modern Japan* (Cambridge, MA: Harvard University Press, 1973).

2. Harold Bolitho, *Treasures Among Men: The Fudai Daimyo in Tokugawa Japan* (New Haven: Yale University Press, 1974), pp. 34–36, passim; John Whitney Hall, "The *bakuhan* system," in *The Cambridge History of Japan*, vol. 4, *Early Modern Japan* (Cambridge: Cambridge University Press, 1991), pp. 128–82; Harold Bolitho, "The *han*," in *The Cambridge History of Japan*, vol. 4, *Early Modern Japan*, pp. 183–234.

3. Toshio G. Tsukahira, *Feudal Control in Tokugawa Japan: The Sankin Kotai System* (Cambridge, MA: East Asian Research Center, Harvard University, 1966), pp. 76–80.

4. Bolitho, *Treasures Among Men*, pp. 13–14.

5. The laws for military households can be found in Wm. Theodore de Bary, ed., *Introduction to Oriental Civilizations* (New York: Columbia University Press, 1958), *Sources of Japanese Tradition*, vol. 1, pp. 326–29.

6. *Tokugawa Ideology: Early Constructs, 1570–1680* (Princeton: Princeton University Press, 1985), pp. 57, 60–61.

7. Bolitho, *Treasurers Among Men*, pp. 19–36, passim; Philip C. Brown, *Central Authority and Local Autonomy in the Formation of Early Modern Japan* (Stanford: Stanford University Press, 1993).

8. John W. Hall, "The Castle Town and Japan's Modern Urbanization," in *Studies in the Institutional History of Early Modern Japan*, ed. John W. Hall and Marius B. Jansen (Princeton: Princeton University Press, 1968), pp. 169–88.

9. See William B. Hauser, *Economic Institutional Change in Tokugawa Japan* (Cambridge: Cambridge University Press, 1974), especially Chapters 2 and 3; and "Osaka: A Commercial City in Tokugawa Japan," *Urbanism Past and Present*, no. 5 (Winter 1977–78): 23–36; James L. McClain, John M. Merriman, and Ugawa Kaoru, eds., *Edo and Paris: The State, Political Power, and Urban Life in Two Early-Modern Societies* (Ithaca: Cornell University Press, 1994).

10. Nakai Nobuhiko and James L. McClain, "Commercial Change and Urban Growth in Early Modern Japan," in *The Cambridge History of Japan*, vol. 4, *Early Modern Japan*, pp. 519–95; Gilbert Rozman, "Social Change," in *The Cambridge History of Japan*, vol. 5, *The Nineteenth Century* (1989), pp. 533–48; Katsuhisa Moriya, "Urban Networks and Information Networks," in *Tokugawa Japan: The Social and Economic Antecedents of Modern Japan*, ed. Chie Nakane and Shinzaburo Oishi, translation ed. Conrad Totman (Tokyo: Tokyo University Press, 1990), pp. 97–114.

11. John W. Hall, "Rule by Status in Tokugawa Japan," *The Journal of Japanese Studies*, vol. 1, no. 1 (Autumn 1974): 39–49.

12. See Susan B. Hanley, "Tokugawa Society: Material Culture, Standards of Living, and Life-Styles," in *The Cambridge History of Japan*, vol. 4, *Early Modern Japan*, pp. 660–705.

13. Thomas C. Smith, "Farm Family By-Employments in Preindustrial Japan," in his *Native Sources of Japanese Industrialization, 1750–1920* (Berkeley: University of California Press, 1988), pp. 71–102; William B. Hauser, "The Diffusion of Cotton Processing and Trade in the Kinai Region of Tokugawa Japan," *Journal of Asian Studies*, vol. 33, no. 4 (August 1974): 633–49.

14. See Kozo Yamamura, *A Study of Samurai Income and Entrepreneurship* (Cambridge, MA: Harvard University Press, 1974), pp. 26–48.

15. Susan B. Hanley and Kozo Yamamura, *Economic and Demographic Change in Preindustrial Japan, 1600–1868* (Princeton: Princeton University Press, 1977); Saitō Osamu, "The Changing Structure of Urban Employment and Its Effects on Migration Patterns in Eighteenth- and Nineteenth-Century Japan," in *Urbanization in History: A Process of Dynamic Interactions*, ed. A. van der Woude, J. de Vries, and A. Hayami (Oxford: Oxford University Press, 1990), pp. 205–19.

16. Hanley and Kozo Yamamura, *Economic and Demographic Change*; Thomas C. Smith, "Peasant Families and Population Control in Eighteenth-Century Japan," in *Native Sources of Japanese Industrialization*, pp. 103–32; William B. Hauser, "Some Misconceptions About the Economic History of Tokugawa Japan," *The History Teacher* 16, 4 (August 1983): 569–83.

17. See Katsuhisa Moriya, "Urban Networks and Information Networks," in *Tokugawa Japan*, ed. Nakane and Oishi, pp. 114–23.

18. Bitō Masahide, "Thought and Religion, 1550–1700," in *The Cambridge History of Japan*, vol. 4, *Early Modern Japan*, pp. 373–424; Tetsuo Najita, "History and Nature in Eighteenth-Century Tokugawa Thought," in *The Cambridge History of Japan*, vol. 4, *Early Modern Japan*, pp. 596–659.

19. Howard Hibbett, *The Floating World in Japanese Fiction* (New York: Grove Press, 1960); Donald H. Shively, "Popular Culture," in *The Cambridge History of Japan*, vol. 4, *Early Modern Japan*, pp. 706–69.

FIVE MYTHS ABOUT EARLY MODERN JAPAN

Henry D. Smith, II

The story line is a familiar one. Japan in the Tokugawa period was a small country, isolated from the rest of the world under the despotic and oppressive rule of a feudal lord known as the shogun, and hierarchically divided into the four separate classes of samurai, peasant, artisan, and merchant. Then in 1853 Commodore Matthew Perry arrived to open Japan, which responded by modernizing into a strong and prosperous modern nation-state.

This is of course a mythology, but like all mythologies it is remarkably durable, and continues to appear in only modified guise in most nonspecialist characterizations of early modern Japan. And like most mythistories, it is by no means wholly incongruent with current scholarly opinion; indeed, many of the issues that I present here as "myths" continue to be hotly debated among historians. Still, the extreme version offered above would be seen today as hopelessly one-sided. It is a version of the past that has its origins in the nineteenth century, and although it may smack of Western bias, it has in fact been promoted vigorously by many Japanese themselves, and across a wide political spectrum. Those who supported the Meiji state certainly favored such a negative estimation of the ancien regime, but so did the Marxist opponents of the twentieth-century Japanese state who saw Meiji as perpetuating the worst features of the Tokugawa order.

To dissect this mythology, let me separate out five elements in the above characterization of Tokugawa Japan as a way of placing it more effectively in the history of the West and the world.

MYTH #1: "Japan is a small country." This a useful proposition to discuss at the start of any introductory course on Japan. The correct response of course is, "it all depends." In land area, Japan is indeed small relative to the three neighbors which have had a major impact on its history at various times: China since ancient times, Russia since the later eighteenth century, and the United States since the early nineteenth century. But when compared to Korea (too often forgotten in such comparisons by Japanese themselves) or to the nation-states of Western Europe (which for reasons outlined in the next section is perhaps the best comparative framework for the early modern period), then Japan is about normal size. In terms of today's national boundaries, it is two-thirds the size of France, three-quarters that of Spain, about the same size as Germany, roughly one-quarter larger than Italy or the British Isles, and three-quarters bigger than the Korean Peninsula.

But when Japanese today claim, as they have been increasingly prone to do since the nineteenth century, that theirs is a "small" country, they more often mean that it is *semai*, densely populated and cramped for space. In the contemporary world, Japan is indeed densely populated: at 850 people per square mile, only Holland (952) and Belgium (842) are in the same league in Europe, although in an Asian context there are even denser nations, such as Bangladesh (2028), Taiwan (1478), or South Korea (1134).[1] And of course, as is always stressed, much of Japan's land area is mountainous ("only 16 percent arable" is a common formula) and inhospitable to habitation.

What about early modern times, however, when the population was only one-fourth what it is today, and far less heavily concentrated in crowded cities? Even then, it was still a dense country by comparison either with its Asian neighbors or with European nations. In about 1700, for example, Japan was about twice as densely populated as France or the British Isles. This means of course that in absolute population size as well, early modern Japan was a very large country, its 30 million people making it larger than any European nation in 1700, including France (22 million) and Russia (20 million).[2]

On a world scale, then, early modern Japan was a "small country" only in relation to its great historical neighbor China, the nation that rightfully continued to be the cornerstone of Japan's larger perception of "the world." The Indian subcontinent was much larger in population, but was not under a unified state. Russia, which emerged as the first great outside threat to Japan in the eighteenth century, was far larger in area but smaller in population, most of it a great distance away. Within a European framework, Japan was large in both area and population.

MYTH #2: "Tokugawa Japan was a feudal society." This is the most complex and intriguing issue for placing Japan in world history. In teaching about feudalism, it is necessary first to deal with the popular sense of "feudal," which whether in English or Japanese (as *hokenteki*) tends to mean anything that is old-fash-ioned, authoritarian, and hierarchical. It is what teenagers call their parents, akin to "medieval" or "primitive." It is necessary to put to one side this colloquial sense of the term before approach-ing feudalism as an analytical concept of historical change.

Feudalism as a tool of historical analysis has a complex history, and its meaning for Japan has been widely debated.[3] Without going into the details, however, it seems fair to say that most historians today would agree that if "feudalism" is defined such that it is more than a local phenomenon of western Europe, but less than a historical stage through which all societies must pass (as in most Marxist schemes), then the one non-European society that indisputably had a feudal period was Japan.[4] No other candi-date comes nearly as close, and none of Japan's East Asian neigh-bors is even a candidate (notwithstanding the voluminous literature on Chinese feudalism).

The problem, however, is one of timing. All agree that Japan reached the stage of "high feudalism" in the period from the late fifteenth to the early sixteenth century, when central authority was minimal and the nation divided into territories under the rule of military lords known as daimyo, each ruling through bands of vassal warriors who gave their loyalty in return for landed fiefs. In the decades that followed, however, the country was reunified and a new central regime finally established under the Tokugawa line after 1600. It fell short of total unifi-cation, however, with upward of three hundred lords continuing to rule their own fiefs directly, and reciprocal loyalty to the shogun the continuing basis of control.

Many modern Japanese historians, working under the influ-ence of Marxist theories of stage development, have seen the cre-ation of the Tokugawa regime as a freezing of earlier feudal patterns, or even as a "refeudalization" after the defeat of embry-onic trends toward capitalism and the absolutist state. American historians of Japan have tended rather to mobilize the oxymoronic concept of "centralized feudalism." Today most would agree that such efforts to preserve the concept of feudalism simply undercut the comparative leverage that the concept was designed to allow, since no European society was ever "refeudalized" or "frozen" for over two centuries past its feudal peak.

Unfortunately, no good alternative paradigm has yet emerged to replace feudalism as a comparative concept, but the most persuasive tool these days is an old one—the state. However "feudal" the Tokugawa regime may have appeared at the start, by the early nineteenth century it indisputably had many of the marks of a European state. Control over the daimyo was efficient and consistent, as reflected by the remarkable uniformity of methods of taxation and administration of justice among the domains. To be sure, the Tokugawa state was not "absolutist" in any European sense: there was no national army, no uniform national currency, no state bureaucracy extending to the local level. If one defines the state in terms of monopolization of the means of coercion, however, the Tokugawa regime was very state-like.[5] The one critical contrast with the states of early modern Europe was the absence of the one imperative that most drove the engine of absolutism: foreign war. Japan, in other words, was distinguished not by being feudal, but by being peaceful—an attribute that made it more Asian than European.

MYTH #3: "The Tokugawa regime was a police state." Japan may have been peaceful abroad, but what about at home? The characterization of Japan as a kind of police state appears in many of the first Western accounts of Japan in the nineteenth century, which emphasized in particular the use of spies by the Tokugawa regime—a reference to the censors, or *metsuke*, who made sure that both domain and *bakufu* officials stayed in line. Later Japanese and Western scholarship has rather devoted attention to the heavy levels of surplus extracted from the peasantry, which was often reduced to poverty and driven to revolt. There is no doubt that Japan was autocratically ruled by the samurai class, and that justice was severe. But we also have the testimony of European observers, both at the beginning and end of the era, that justice was also leveled equally, and was rarely arbitrary. Punishments were harsh and often cruel, but they were never inflicted before large and leering public crowds as in early modern Europe.

More generally, it might be proposed that the Tokugawa state was relatively passive in its exercise of coercive authority. Both in villages and cities, most administration was left to local autonomous units. To be sure, it was autonomy only at the indulgence of the state, and in no sense true self-government. Still, the state was content for the most part not to interfere. In the techniques of administration as well, the "feudal" Tokugawa regime favored checks and balances rather than overt coercion. The entire national system of daimyo domains was in fact an intricately balanced network of power, further held together by the requirement of "alternate attendance" *(sankin kōtai)* that obliged every daimyo to live in alternate years in Edo, the capital. Many official posts were held in tandem, with two officials rotating every year or half-year to obviate entrenched corruption. Responsibility was imposed on groups, and punishment for individual crimes was suffered by the group as a whole. Such techniques were common in China as well.

These notions of collective responsibility were very different from the situation in western Europe, where the state was obliged to carve out its coercive realm in the face of a growing sense of absolute property rights and individual political rights. The levels of violence to which European societies were subjected in this confrontation were probably much higher than in Japan or other East Asian societies of the seventeenth or eighteenth century. So was Japan a police state? Well-policed to be sure, and oppressive. But it was relatively even-handed oppression, and almost never despotic. Much depends on one's relative valuation of the private individual versus the community.

MYTH #4: "Tokugawa Japan was divided into four separate classes." This formula has been recited so many times that it will take a long time to overcome it. The notion is flawed in two ways. First, the division was not into socioeconomic "classes," but rather into what are better called "estates," groupings by occupation. Second, it was an ideal formula, borrowed from Chinese Neo-Confucian doctrine, that never really fit the reality of Japan (or even of China, for that matter). The basic division in Tokugawa Japan was between samurai and nonsamurai, but even here the distinction was often blurred, since mobility across the line increased with time. Moreover, the samurai estate encompassed a wide range of socioeconomic stratification, from the daimyo aristocracy on down to rowdy foot soldiers whose lot in life was little better than common coolies. It is often asserted that a samurai could cut down with impunity any commoner who insulted him. This was simply not true: any samurai exercising the right in question would be obliged to provide elaborate justification for the act, and as often as not suffer punishment for its commission.

The nonsamurai estates were similarly stratified, and the lines between them never really enforced. The primary restriction was that of residence, since farmers were in theory forbidden from moving to the cities. This was never enforced except in the most futile and sporadic ways, and mobility between city and country was rapid and increasing throughout the period. Technically, land was inalienable, but in practice land was inherited, traded, and marketed (albeit under legal constraints).

None of this is to deny that Tokugawa society was elaborately differentiated—but so were all premodern societies. A person's status and occupation were immediately apparent from appearance, with complex rules of dress and hair style. It is often alleged that such things were minutely prescribed by law, but this is incorrect: *bakufu* regulations were proscriptions rather than prescriptions, rules not about what one should wear but about what one should **not** wear. These proscriptions were rarely obeyed (and hence frequently repeated), and at any rate were far less important than the endless customary rules that emerged spontaneously in a highly status-conscious society, particularly in the cities where people constantly encountered strangers.

A final misleading feature of the "four-class" formula is the valuation implied by the hierarchy, with peasants coming just after the samurai elite, and merchants at the very bottom. It is important to remember that the hierarchy was not one of people, but of function: it was not peasants above merchants, but farming above trade. As the British historian G.B. Sansom nicely summed up the plight of peasants, Tokugawa statesmen "thought highly of agriculture, but not of agriculturalists."[6] As for merchants, they were far less denigrated as a group than the formula implies. The earliest elite merchants in Tokugawa cities were of samurai origin, and many merchant families maintained house codes and customs that closely paralleled those of samurai. Contempt for trade was far less deeply rooted in the Japanese elite than in the Chinese gentry class (and even there it was less virulent than often depicted). Rather, the relationship between samurai and merchant should be seen, as anthropologist William Kelly has argued, as one of "essential mutualism," each depending on the other and acutely aware of their reciprocal dependency.[7]

For proof of the inadequacy of the four-class stereotype, one need only look to the first years of the Meiji period, when all limitations of occupational estate were dropped and the only group to protest was a small minority of the samurai. At the same time, ex-samurai were even more numerous than merchants among the leading entrepreneurs of Meiji; so much for their contempt of trade.

MYTH #5: "Tokugawa Japan isolated itself from the rest of the world for over two centuries." This is in many ways the most pernicious of all the myths about early modern Japan. Although the Eurocentric quality of the formulation is immediately apparent, it has in fact been sustained by the Japanese themselves as much as by Westerners. The standard cliché is "self-imposed isolation," and it often goes under the Japanese term *sakoku*, translated as "closed country." This is the term, for example, applied to the series of edicts of 1633–39 that excluded the Catholic nations of Spain and Portugal from trade with Japan and forbade Japanese from traveling abroad. In the conventional historiography, Japan is seen as retreating into an isolationist shell, like a hermit crab, thereby shutting itself off from all the progressive influences available from Europe.

This whole picture has been completely revised in English-language scholarship by the work of Ronald Toby, who argues that what has been called "isolation" was in large part a restoration of normal relations by Japan with the two neighbors that had always been most important to it, China and Korea.[8] Part of the process, to be sure, involved excluding the Catholic nations of the West, but this was largely a political measure aimed at controlling the threat of aggressive and disruptive Westerners. A few simple points should be remembered. First, the concept of "isolation" or "closing" never appeared in either the minds or the words of the Tokugawa rulers. The term *sakoku* made its first appearance, rather, in the early nineteenth century in a Japanese translation of an essay by Engelbert Kaempfer, a German doctor who traveled to Japan in 1690–92 and left a remarkable description of the country. The title (too long to quote here in its entirety) begins "An Enquiry, whether it be conducive for the good of the Japanese Empire, to keep it shut up, as it is now, and not to suffer its inhabitants to have any Commerce with foreign nations, either at home or abroad."[9] The real irony is that Kaempfer's answer to the question posed in the title was a resounding "Yes!" He had nothing but admiration for the Japanese for avoiding the kind of foreign entanglements that led only to the ceaseless hatred and bloodshed that he had observed firsthand in mid-seventeenth-century Europe. Kaempfer's essay remains today one of the most remarkably perceptive accounts of Tokugawa Japan available, and is essential reading for anyone interested in the period.

But was Japan in fact all that isolated? Consider the fact that Japanese foreign trade actually increased somewhat in the wake of the alleged "closing" of the country, and continued to flourish until the end of the seventeenth century.[10] The eventual reduction of trade after 1715 was the result not of any isolationist impulse, but rather of a bullionist belief in the need to preserve the nation's precious metals for the minting of new coins rather than the payment for exports. At the same time, the cultural impact of the trade with the Dutch and Chinese at Nagasaki continued to increase. In 1721, just as total trade was being reduced, the shogun Yoshimune lifted the import ban on Chinese translations of Western books as long as they did not deal with Christianity. This marked the beginning of what by the end of the century would become a flourishing movement in Western Learning, first by way of Chinese translations and then through original Dutch texts that Japanese scholars laboriously learned to read. This Western knowledge, however imperfectly understood, had a tremendous leavening effect in Japanese intellectual life.

Stock descriptions of Tokugawa Japan depict the continuing trade through Nagasaki as a minor exception to an isolationist policy, seeing it as a "tiny loophole" or a "crack in the door." I prefer the metaphor of a relay or an "antenna" by means of which Japan received a continual flow of knowledge and information from both China and the West, as well as countless cultural objects that worked their own ways of change. It is impossible to tell the story of Tokugawa art, for example, without reference to the transformations wrought by continuing input from both Chinese paintings and Western copperplate prints. The highly developed internal network of communications in Japan by way of the *sankin kōtai* further insured that new knowledge spread rapidly to even the most remote castle towns.

Elsewhere in this volume, William Rowe has made a similar point about China, arguing that the "much-vaunted isolationism" of this era was largely limited to paper edicts, and that China's basic "attitude toward the outside world in the late seventeenth and eighteenth centuries was anything but passive and defensive." The Japanese in the same period were undeniably more restrictive than the Chinese, effectively prohibiting any Japanese from traveling abroad. But they participated in the same East Asian world order, which was "isolationist" only in comparison to the aggressive expansionism of Western Europe. We are finally brought back to the matter of war and peace. The acceptance of orderly hierarchical relations among the nations of East Asia was basically a policy of peaceful coexistence rather than isolationism. It was a state of affairs that Europe should perhaps have envied rather than challenged.

NOTES

1. The figures are for 1991, from *The World Almanac and Book of Facts 1988* (New York: Pharos Books, 1992).
2. These figures are from Colin McEvedy and Richard Jones, *Atlas of World Population History* (New York: Facts on File, 1978), and as with all premodern population figures should be taken only as rough estimates.
3. The best introduction to the issue is Peter Duus, *Feudalism in Japan* (New York: Knopf, 1969). See also Joseph Strayer, "The Tokugawa Period and Japanese Feudalism" and John W. Hall, "Feudalism in Japan—A Reassessment," in *Studies in the Institutional History of Early Modern Japan*, ed. John W. Hall and Marius B. Jansen (Princeton: Princeton University Press, 1968), pp. 3–51.
4. I find the most persuasive proponent of this view to be the British Marxist historian Perry Anderson, in his thoughtful discussion in *Lineages of the Absolutist State* (London: Verso, 1979), pp. 411–61.
5. For a recent argument along these lines, see James White, "State Growth and Popular Protest in Tokugawa Japan," *Journal of Japanese Studies* 14 (Winter 1988): 1–25.
6. George B. Sansom, *Japan: A Short Cultural History* (New York: Appleton, Century, Crofts, 1962), p. 465.
7. William W. Kelly, *Deference and Defiance in Nineteenth-Century Japan* (Princeton: Princeton University Press, 1985), p. 5.
8. Ronald P. Toby, *State and Diplomacy in Early Modern Japan: Asia in the Development of the Tokugawa Bakufu* (Princeton: Princeton University Press, 1984; paper ed., Stanford: Stanford University Press, 1991). See also Marius B. Jansen, *China in the Tokugawa World* (Cambridge, MA: Harvard University Press, 1992). For a useful short account of Toby's major arguments, see "Reopening the Question of Sakoku: Diplomacy in the Legitimation of the Tokugawa Bakufu," *Journal of Japanese Studies* 3 (Summer 1977): 323–63.
9. Engelbert Kaempfer, *The History of Japan, Together with a Description of the Kingdom of Siam, 1690–92*, trans. J.G. Scheuchzer (Glasgow: James MacLehose and Sons, 1906), pp. 301–36.
10. Robert Innes, "The Door Ajar: Japan's Foreign Trade in the Seventeenth Century," Ph.D. diss., University of Michigan, 1980.

STATE AND SOCIETY DURING THE QING DYNASTY, 1644–1911

Myron L. Cohen

Established in 1644 through the Manchu conquest, then toppled by the revolution of 1911, the Qing was the last of the imperial dynasties of traditional China. My perspective in this chapter is not chronological; rather, I focus on China's social system during Qing, and its connections with the institutions of the Chinese state. During the traditional period covered by this chapter Chinese society indeed underwent changes but these largely were quantitative, and importantly different from the qualitative changes which, beginning during the latter half of the nineteenth century, were directly linked to the defeat and penetration of that country by the Western powers.

Following anthropology's holistic approach, which seeks to pull cultural and social facts together, I treat China as having an integrated social system. This holistic approach is especially appropriate in the Chinese case, for that country's social system **was** highly integrated during Qing, the result of a long process of development, one measure of which is homogeneity in language. Because China often has been characterized as a land of many "dialects," it is important first to indicate what is meant by "Chinese" from a linguistic point of view. It commonly is accepted that two mutually unintelligible forms of speech are different languages. If mutually intelligible, they are considered to be different dialects of one language, even with obvious differences in brogue, pronunciation, accent, or items of vocabulary. Defined on the basis of these criteria, there are many Chinese languages, with Mandarin the most important. Derived from the Portuguese word for "official," the term "Mandarin" is quite apt: both before and during Qing, Mandarin indeed was the "language of officials" (*kuanhua*). Using the mutual intelligibility criterion, it also is true that Mandarin in various dialects comprised the native speech of about 70 percent of China's population during Qing (and in modern times the Beijing form of Mandarin has been made China's national language). Mandarin contrasts with other, obviously different, Chinese languages, such as Wu (Shanghai-Ningbo region), the Fujianese languages, Hakka, Cantonese, and others. Yet that such a large proportion of the Chinese spoke Mandarin is a rather striking measure of homogeneity with respect to a population of between 400 and 450 million, with Mandarin-speakers inhabiting about three-quarters of the area of agrarian China.

There were important linguistic ties between the approximately 30 percent of the Chinese not speaking Mandarin and the majority who did. First, all of the separate Chinese languages belong to the same language family and evolved from a common archaic or middle-period form of speech. Second, as is well known, they shared a common written language, one using ideographs rather than an alphabetic form of representation; a text could be read by an educated speaker of any Chinese language. Among other things, possession of a common written language meant shared access to a classical heritage involving the texts of the Confucian and other Chinese traditions, and also a shared vocabulary largely derived from these texts. Linked to these shared linguistic roots and written forms was third set of connections involving social gradations in all of the spoken Chinese languages. In contrast to everyday speech, there was a formal style of discourse to which even an illiterate farmer could switch under appropriate circumstances, such as when called to give a speech or make remarks at the wedding or funeral of a relative or acquaintance. This style was marked, among other ways, by the use of many elements of "elite" or classical vocabulary. By using this formal style of speech native speakers of different forms of Chinese might not be able to achieve full mutual intelligibility, but at least they would understand each other more, both because there were more of the older classical forms of Chinese in this mode of speech, and also because the linguistic distance between the speakers was now a matter more of pronunciation and less of vocabulary, syntax or grammar.

My discussion of linguistic and other expressions of homogeneity is with reference to the "ethnic" Chinese, for whom their own term is "Han." A preliminary definition of the Han Chinese is that they are people speaking a Chinese language and fully participating in Chinese society. This is with reference to traditional China during Qing where, as in China today, there was a small minority who were not Han Chinese, who spoke one of several languages not belonging to the Chinese language family, and who did not fully participate in the cultural, institutional, economic, or educational arrangements that otherwise integrated into Chinese society those known as the "Han." During Qing the non-Han minority—made up of many different ethnic groups—comprised roughly five percent of the Chinese empire's population, with the rest being Han.

The homogeneity of the Han Chinese with respect to social organization was even more pronounced than its linguistic manifestations. There was gender differentiation powerfully biased in favor of men as far as access to education and important political and social positions was concerned. Common to Han society throughout China were key features of family organization, including a patrilineally orientated and male-centered arrangement of marriage, authority, and social and economic roles reflecting the family's character as being as much an enterprise as a domestic group. Among the characteristic roles were those of the family head (*jiazhang*)—the senior male and the family's formal representative to the outside world—and the family manager (*dangjia*), who was in charge of family work and earnings. Although there was a clear social distinction between these two roles, in small families the father would have both; with his advancing age and increasing family size the position of family manager was frequently taken over by one of his sons. Brothers had equal rights to family property, the dominant form of ownership, but were also obligated to pool their earnings as long as the family remained intact. The distribution of this property among them was a key element in family division (*fenjia*), which also involved the setting up of separate kitchens for each of the new and now economically independent families. Han Chinese society during Qing was characterized by a high degree of premodern commercialization and commoditization, where land was commonly bought, sold, and mortgaged, and where contracts, written and oral, played an important role in village life. It was in this context that families and the family farm were distinctly entrepreneurial and market-oriented to the extent permitted by their resources. Contracts even entered into the intimacies of family relationships and conflicts in the form of the business-like partition documents that were signed by brothers about to form separate households.

A major factor behind Han social and cultural homogeneity was the close connection between national institutions and local society; indeed, local social organization cannot be understood unless the impact of certain national institutions are noted. To take the most obvious example: traditional China—even before Qing—was that rare if not unique example of a pre-modern agrarian society where the state could continually control the rural local elite and define its composition. In many other such societies the authority of a local hereditary elite would be acknowledged by the state, but not defined by it in the first instance. All other things being equal, such local elites basically inherited their positions; the state might eliminate members of the local nobility or appoint new ones only under special circumstances, there being no institutionalized succession procedure other than through inheritance. In China however, the local elite were defined most importantly through the state examinations, and these helped insure that there would be a turnover in leadership through the generations. In addition to the examination system, elite standing was marked by wealth and literacy; these, like examination degrees, could not readily be preserved through the generations, except for restricted area of southeastern China where certain families managed to maintain control of lineage corporate holdings.

The life-style which marked off a community's elite was similar in content throughout China during Qing; elite homogeneity was importantly reinforced through the examination system, which served to recruit the national bureaucracy at the same time that it selected the elite leadership of local communities. As the informal leaders of their local communities, degree-holders would have many dealings with their fellow degree-holder who was posted as their county magistrate and who, by law, had to be a native of a different province. Degree-holders from over a wide area would also often meet with each other informally in the towns and cities; they would also meet periodically at the county, prefectural, provincial, or national examination centers. These frequent interactions among the degree-holding group served to preserve and reinforce the elite life-style they shared in common.

But the impact of the bureaucracy, the examination system, and of the national culture both helped to reinforce, extended far beyond the small minority of degree-holders in and out of office. Consciousness of the bureaucratic presence was so much a part of local life that a major dimension of traditional Chinese religion itself was bureaucratized. Many of the gods of Chinese popular religion were officials, and in religious contexts they often were dealt with as one would treat ordinary officials in more mundane settings.

As an ideal, the life-style supported by the institutions of imperial government was thoroughly absorbed into the values of the population as a whole. With increases in a family's wealth and literacy, there would be an increasingly closer approximation of the elite standards: ordinary rustic attire would be replaced by a scholar's gown; weddings, funerals, and other rituals would become more elaborate; a more substantial home would be built or purchased, and an ever-expanding collection of books, scrolls and other objets d'art would be placed in its guest rooms and studies.

When the government was strapped for funds it might sell imperial degrees and (often-honorific) official posts. There always was a strong demand for such degrees, positions, and titles; they were desired by members of various social classes, including even those farmers who had acquired the means to purchase them. For example, among the poor Chinese migrating to southeast Asia in the nineteenth century there were some who did become rich, and therefore able to purchase these symbols of elite status; although some contemporary non-Chinese observers might be amused at the sight of an illiterate or minimally literate man of rural background on the streets of Singapore dressed in scholars's gown and wearing the cap and button of a degree-holder, what they were witnessing was in fact the expression of an important set of values well established even among rural farmers. It precisely was the incorporation of such values into local culture that was one of the major factors—although certainly not the only one—behind the overall cultural and social homogeneity of the Han Chinese population. But if this population's homogeneity testified to the political, economic, and cultural integration of Chinese society, there still remains the important question of the means by which this unity was achieved and maintained in a territory of subcontinental proportions and on the basis of a pre-industrial technology of communications, transport, and political control. Although agrarian China occupied the smaller part of the Qing Empire as a whole, it seems clear that given control of the former, the maintenance of the latter was not difficult to achieve; a unified agrarian China provided the wealth and the man-power for the imperial armies that extended Manchu rule into central Asia.

EMPEROR AND BUREAUCRACY

The two major components of imperial administration were the emperor and his court, on the one hand, and the bureaucracy on the other. The relationship between the two was not simple, although both were provided for in the pre-Qing Chinese political tradition and in Chinese ideology. Certainly, by the time the Manchus seized power the functions and duties of bureaucracy and of emperor were well spelled out and understood, both in a statutory sense and with respect to cultural and ideological norms and precedents. During Qing and preceding dynasties there nevertheless had been the potential for conflict between the bureaucratic and imperial centers of state power, and much of the Qing bureaucracy's organization can only be understood as reflecting the efforts of emperors to maintain their own power. An emperor was as interested in controlling the bureaucracy as he was in using it for administration.

Precisely because the bureaucracy historically and ideologically transcended any particular dynasty, it offered no justification for Manchu rule as such; yet this bureaucracy did comprise the top membership of that class of scholar-officials who received, perpetuated, and developed the ideological framework of imperial rule in general. But the idea of the mandate of heaven, and the larger cosmological framework within which it was placed, were never linked to specifications of ethnicity. For the Qing rulers, the preservation of Han-Manchu ethnic differentiation was closely linked to the maintenance of their own power. At the same time, these rulers accepted and employed for their own purposes the Han Chinese ideology and institutions of imperial rule. In fact, the ethnic and Confucian ideologies framing Qing rule were never combined into one system; if in theory the mandate of heaven pertained to any emperor or to any dynasty, for the Qing this mandate had to be protected both by the particularistic ethnic loyalties of Manchus as well as by the theoretically universalistic Confucian loyalties of Han Chinese scholar-officials. The Qing emperors were not willing to rely totally on the ideology and values of the Han Chinese they had come to rule; yet control over China was quite impossible if based solely on the ethnic sentiments of the tiny Manchu minority.

Thus the Qing rulers had to compromise between the two very different supports for their legitimacy and power. An important byproduct of this Manchu compromise was that it gave their opponents ideological ammunition with which to attack Qing legitimacy. Since the Manchu emperors themselves were unwilling to disassociate dynastic legitimacy from the ethnic identity of the ruling house, it made it all the more easier for "secret societies" and other such illegal groups to advocate Ming restorationism on the basis that the Qing ruling house was more Manchu, alien and barbarian, than it was Chinese, Confucian and imperial.

A technique of bureaucratic control developed by the Manchu emperors and their advisers was to maintain within the bureaucracy a separate Manchu identity defined on the basis of Manchu dominance. Thus an effort was made to have an equal division between Manchu and Han Chinese officials with respect to all major bureaucratic positions in Beijing. This included, at the apex of the bureaucracy, the Six Boards (Public Works, Punishments, War, Rites, Finance, Civil Appointments) each with one Manchu and one Han co-director. This pattern of ethnically-based appointment derived from the attempt to combine rule based upon ethnic dominance with that representing the institutionalization of Han Chinese Confucian patterns. In any event, such a symmetrical application of combined ethnic-bureaucratic criteria largely was confined to appointment of high-ranking positions within Beijing itself. In the rest of the country the impact of ethnic considerations could be seen in that the proportion of governors or governors-general who were Manchu was far in excess of Manchu representation within the empire's population as a whole. But at the lower county level the vast majority of the bureaucracy outside of Beijing was Han Chinese.

The major means of determining those qualified for appointment to the bureaucracy was the examination system. It probably is more accurate to say "court" rather than "emperor" as far as appointments are concerned, because imperial decisions usually were made after consultation with the Grand Council. The court would set the quotas for the regular examinations given at each level every three years, thereby limiting the number of degrees in each category to be awarded at any particular place and time. The court, by imperial edict, could also announce special examinations, the granting of which were held to acts of imperial favor. These special examinations usually were announced to commemorate auspicious events within the imperial family, such as the decennial birthday of an emperor or empress, a royal marriage, or the accession to the throne of a new emperor; they could also be given in celebration of a military triumph.

To hold examinations in years other than those called for by the traditional triennial schedule was to bestow the favor of creating more degree-holders, which meant the creation of additional opportunities for access to the highest (non-hereditary) statuses available in Chinese society. Although the emperor did not interfere with the routinized examination schedule, his periodic proclamations of extra examinations comprise but one example of his ability to manifest his own will by going beyond regular bureaucratic procedures.

The relationship between bureaucracy and emperor was acted out in ritual, and during several important annual ceremonies the emperor displayed his dependency on the bureaucracy and its ideology. For example, during the emperor's annual worship of Heaven his every move would be dictated by bureaucrats. The Board of Rites, among its other duties, was in charge of such ceremonies and some of its officials were ritual specialists.

The tensions between court and bureaucracy were linked to the fact that while the emperor had total power in theory, he in reality was subject to both ideological and practical constraints in the exercise of this power. Nevertheless, for most purposes the bureaucracy and the emperor were as one, their common aim for strong control over China having far greater weight than any tensions that might divide them. The bureaucracy conveyed vital information from society at large to the emperor, in effect acting as liaison between court and society. Court and bureaucracy together maintained centralized rule and preserved their cohesion.

The question remains as to the means by which court and bureaucracy managed to maintain centralized rule over such a large country and empire. It has been estimated that in all of China there were no more than 20,000 civil bureaucratic positions controlled from Beijing, with half of these being in the capital itself (there were also 7,000 positions for military officers in the entire country). Appointments to these positions were directly controlled by Beijing or, with Beijing's approval, specifically delegated as the responsibility of provincial governments. Far more numerous were the low-level positions, such as yamen clerks or yamen runners, appointment to which was not under direct supervision of the central government. Nevertheless, what remains impressive and of major importance for an understanding of China's social system as a whole is the fact that this small centralized bureaucracy did manage to run the entire country. Outside of the capital, about 10,000 officials governed and taxed a population of approximately 400 million (mid-nineteenth century); these people lived in approximately 1,400 counties (xian), the lowest-level government administrative units, for an average of about 250,000 in each county. Above the county, the basic administrative unit was the prefecture (fu), also under the jurisdiction of a magistrate. At a higher level, "China proper" (agrarian China) was divided into 18 provinces, each administered by a governor, with most of these provinces being grouped into units of two or three, each unit being the responsibility of a governor-general.

On the face of it, the county magistrate's assignment could not be easy; not only was a county population large, but a magistrate's term of service in any single county would be limited to two or three years. Also, some counties were enormous, there tending to be an inverse relationship between a county's population and its size. Thus the magistrate's problem either was to deal with a relatively small population spread across a huge area, or with a comparatively dense population in a smaller area. In either case, the control problem was serious in the absence of modern means of communication and coercion. The magistrate, perhaps with a few private secretaries who followed him everywhere, might have had to travel for days or weeks simply to get to his post. Given this context of often tenuous communication links, and the very small bureaucratic presence at the local level, the magistrate could only control the county under his jurisdiction by making use of the local degree-holders.

This local-level relationship between magistrate and degree-holders had several important characteristics. First, all degree-holders, no matter what their rank, were members of an elite status group; they were far more equal to each other than was a commoner to any of them. Lowest- and highest-ranking degree-holders basically were social equals; although separated by the gaps in their respective ranks, they could deal with each other as gentlemen, demonstrating reciprocal deference, chatting face-to-face, and all of this and more without the lower-ranking degree-holder having to make customary statements of inferiority. Most important, they could work together in a collegial fashion. The major social distinction was between degree-holders as a group and commoners.

In order to understand the relationship between degree-holders and society, on the one hand, and between them and government on the other, two important distinctions among the body of the degree-holders should be noted. One is as between holders of higher- and lower-ranking degrees; only the former were eligible for government appointment, which meant that the lower-ranking degree-holders remained in their home communities, where they were in the best position to enjoy their degree-provided elite status. The other distinction is as between those holders of higher degrees in or out of office, with the latter greatly outnumbering the former at any point in time. Included among the high-ranking degree-holders not in office were some simply at home waiting for appointment, some who already had retired from government service, and some at home in observance of the rule requiring an official to mourn three years upon the death of a parent, which usually meant a total of six years of home leave for statutory mourning during the course of every official's career.

Thus a region's local elite included that large majority of high-ranking degree-holders at home due to the various reasons noted above, together with the much larger number of lower degree-holders. The magistrate worked with this local elite in running the county under his jurisdiction. The higher degree-holders, the very men who might serve as officials in other parts of China, were the community leaders in their home regions. Within a community, the higher a man's degree, the more important his informal social and political position. Ranking within the community or region followed that of the degree system itself.

The magistrate's interactions with the local elite were quite formal in many contexts. Local degree-holders and the magistrate jointly initiated or managed a variety of projects involving irrigation, granaries, charitable institutions, and the like, and such projects could be specifically identified as "joint magistrate-gentry" undertakings. It was expected and understood that local degree-holders would collaborate with the magistrate in ruling their region. Another aspect of the close connection between the state and degree-holders of any rank was revealed at the annual worship (or veneration) of Confucius held in the state-run civil or Confucian temple; participation of commoners was not permitted, but the local degree-holders were there, joined by the magistrate in common veneration of the sage. To subsidize such ceremonies, or at least their own participation, degree-holders would obtain funds through their own taxation mechanisms in local society, or through contributions. In general, they frequently gained much financially from their activities in society, but except for certain degree-holders receiving small "scholars stipends," they were not paid by the magistrate.

Degree-holders were set apart as a privileged group by laws that clearly distinguished them from commoners and made them the beneficiaries of special treatment from the state. The county magistrate could not treat degree-holders in the same rough manner he would employ when dealing with commoners. Degree-holders did not have to ritually display subordination to the magistrate, such as kneeling before him; and he could not whip them or in other ways apply physical punishment, treatment he would mete out to commoners frequently enough, as during judicial inquiries or trials. Only the provincial director of education, whose duty it was to supervise the degree-holders under his jurisdiction, was able to strip a degree-holder of his rank; and only then could he be prosecuted by the magistrate as a commoner. The legally protected status of the degree-holders generally facilitated their cooperation with the local magistrate in governing local society.

Although chances were that in a particular village there would be no degree-holders at all, most villages had traditional ties with some neighboring settlements so as to form larger communities; such multi-village communities comprised a level within a hierarchy of community organization, and one would not have to go too far up that hierarchy to find degree-holders. Degree-holders were quite familiar to ordinary farmers, frequently enough on a face-to-face basis, and local lore abounded with often humorous stories about native sons who had obtained degrees. Degree-holders had deeply penetrated the popular imagination because they in fact were found throughout the country, both during Qing and earlier dynasties. It is safe to say that at a scale of community organization involving several thousand people it was almost impossible not to find degree-holders, and that in most cases they were to be encountered at even lower levels.

The local degree-holders were indispensable for ideological control. Their very power and high standing was a statement as to the desirability of examination success. The importance of the examination system was such that it largely dictated China's curriculum of studies, even at the most elementary level of schooling. It was precisely because so very few boys had any realistic chance at all even to participate in the examinations that the link between the examinations and general education was so important for ideological control. China clearly was far ahead of most traditional agrarian societies with respect both to the availability of schooling and the prevalence of literacy. Although female literacy was quite limited, it has been estimated that 40 percent of the adult male population was functionally literate, such a high rate being connected to the fact that many villages had their own schools. The purpose of these schools was not to prepare every young farm boy for the examinations, yet their curriculum indeed was that required at the beginning stage of this preparation. The use of such curricula was linked to the hope that among the students there might be the rare one with the intellect, stamina, and family circumstances who would use this education as the first stepping-stone towards acquisition of an examination degree. The instructors themselves comprised a mixture of holders of lower degrees, men who had failed in the examinations, and those still trying to pass, such that their own educations provided them

with training for the teaching of hardly anything other than exam-
ination-linked classical texts.

The important byproduct of this educational system was that
general literacy in traditional China was obtained through study
of the first few of the many texts whose mastery was required for
examination competition. Thus the village school curriculum provided an exposure to the state-supported orthodox Confucian ideology for every young boy who might attend classes even for only
one or two years.

Degree-holders also played an active role in more direct forms
of local control, for in many ways they stood between the state
and local society. The county magistrate would discuss with them
those ordinances or instructions he had received from higher levels of government, and they in turn would explain them to other
members of their local communities. The avoidance rule greatly
increased the magistrate's dependence on the local degree-holders. Because he came from another part of China, the magistrate
had to depend on these degree-holders, on his own local yamen
staff, and on reference materials such as the "local gazetteers"
(difangzhi) prepared by the local literati of particular counties or
even larger administrative units.

Mediation or settlement of disputes in their home communities
was another important activity of the degree-holders; they often
would be asked to arbitrate disputes precisely because their effectiveness was increased by the reluctance of people to antagonize
degree-holders by disregarding their suggestions. For their part,
the degree-holders were quite willing to be involved in arbitration
and other forms of dispute-resolution; both for ideological and
practical reasons they did not want conflicts within the local community to receive the public exposure consequent upon the initiation of legal proceedings in the yamen, and therefore they tried to
solve such disputes locally.

In addition to helping the magistrate control local society, the
degree-holders also represented community interests to the magistrate, such as when they would request a tax reduction or re-
mission because of drought or flooding. Thus the degree-holder
had the dual role of representing the interests of the state to their
home communities, and those of their home communities to the
state. But there was a third element involved, their own interests as
degree-holders, the expression of which took a variety of forms. For
example, there could be special organizations, such as "Confucian
study associations," open only to a region's degree-holders, thus
providing them a framework for interaction among themselves.

The three major orientations of China's degree-holding elite could also be seen in religion and ritual. First, the intimate ties between degree-holders and the state bureaucracy would be epitomized, for example, during ceremonies at the Confucian temple, where degree-holders worshipped with officials while commoners were kept out. But also there were the at least equally intimate relationships of degree-holders to their home communities as shown, among other ways, through their informal management of the local temples which were the focus of popular and community religion. Yet at the same time the degree-holders could have their own temples, such as the joint civil-military temples below the county level, or those dedicated to the god of literature (*wenchang* or *kuixing*).

In their local communities the degree-holders comprised the necessary functionaries for the initiation and on-going management of a variety of institutions and undertakings, such as temples, irrigation systems, granaries, and so forth. These degree-holders had the literacy, the local influence and the special ties with the magistrate which facilitated their undertaking such managerial tasks in local society. Their situation in their home communities thus requires correction of a misunderstanding commonly enough encountered in writings on traditional China, which is the view that the orthodox Confucian training obtained in the course of preparing for the examinations created humanists or generalists not prepared to assume the managerial responsibilities entailed by appointment to the bureaucracy. This view ignores the fact that upon obtaining even the first degree a man became deeply involved in the administration of his home community; such a man would have accumulated considerable administrative experience by the time of his becoming eligible for appointment to the state bureaucracy.

RURAL SOCIETY

Rural Chinese society was characterized by levels of local organization: as between the lowest level of the administrative system, the county, with its yamen at the county seat, and the village community there were intermediate and interconnected levels of social and community organization, and the village itself was a level of organization below which there frequently were well-defined neighborhood communities.

Villages had varying numbers of neighborhoods; each would be named, with a large variety of terms in use; for example, those in a three-neighborhood village might be known as "village head" (*zhuang tou*), "village middle" (*zhuang zhong*), and "village end" (*zhuang wei*); in a village with four neighborhoods they might be named "east," "west," "south," and "north." A village's neighborhood subdivisions were well defined, and often they were separated by gates. Each neighborhood had its own round of religious festivals, and its own earth god or *tudigong*. The neighborhood was the lowest level of multi-family community organization, and usually the next highest level would be that of the village itself. Often, the interconnection between the neighborhood and the village levels of community organization would be dramatized through religious ritual. For example, it was common for a village to have an annual village festival sponsored in rotation by each neighborhood. In a village divided into four neighborhoods, say, this meant that each year one would be responsible for organizing and supporting the opera and other activities connected with the festival. A neighborhood's responsibility for the village festival gave both it and the village as a whole strong ritual definition as social units.

More generally, this kind of ritual expressed within the most intimate community context the arrangement of society into a territorial hierarchy. In the village, hierarchy was at its most concrete; expressed not only in ritual, but also in the daily rhythm of village social life, it reinforced a more general idea of territorial hierarchy, one strong enough to be a basic element in traditional Chinese culture. This is not to suggest that village life was **the** source of this cultural orientation; rather, the indication is that the facts of social life at the neighborhood and village levels gave support to the territorial orientation and in this respect were congruent with other sources of support as from local organization at larger scales, and from the state examination and administrative systems.

While the village represented but one level of local and community organization, it was a basic unit of rural society. Villages were concentrated clusters of houses separated from each other by fields. Villages thus tended to be discrete settlements within the larger framework of rural Chinese social organization, and as such were characteristic of most of rural China. (Sichuan's Chengdu Plain, in western China, was characterized by dispersed homesteads rather than concentrated villages, but even here there were scales of local organization which organized community life and received religious expression.) Village residents were members of the village community: a man was a member because he had been born into a village family, adopted into one, or in some cases had entered one through uxorilocal marriage; a woman was a member either by dint of her birth or because of her marriage into a village family. Women usually changed village membership upon their marriage, village exogamy being common.

The multi-village face-to-face community did not represent the highest level of local organization, but it was the highest level of organization in terms of face-to-face community interaction. Therefore, it was the highest level of local organization providing a context for social familiarity between degree-holders and commoners; at higher levels of local organization, social familiarity and interaction involved the local elite but not the entire population. There were a variety of organizations and social and economic relationships that integrated the multi-village face-to-face community. Usually, one or more temples represented this larger community, and their religious activities would be coordinated with those of temples linked to particular constituent villages, with these villages often rotating sponsorship of the multi-village community festival in a manner parallel to the rotation among neighborhoods of village festival sponsorship, as described earlier; voluntary associations would take their membership from within this multi-village community; some of these communities were endogamous and thus provided a framework for kinship ties between families from different exogamous villages. The community would be named, and consciousness of its existence, and of their membership in it, would be common among its population.

Membership in a village community meant participation in the entire hierarchy of local community organization. This was vital for survival in that rural community arrangements provided the context for cooperative relationships among families, without which rural life could not have been maintained. For families with little or no land available for cultivation, community membership provided avenues of access to other local families needing to hire their labor or willing to rent them land. Otherwise, in both rural and urban China the family was the basic economic unit, and in the countryside farm management and production was in its hands. The family tried to use its own labor as much as possible and minimize reliance on non-family members. However, a family might not have enough labor for its own farm; or if it had enough labor but had diversified into nonfarm activities some family members might not be available for farm work. But the most fundamental problem was the nature of traditional agriculture's labor requirements, such that even a family with enough labor for usual farm requirements would not have enough to meet the far heavier short-term demands of the busy seasons, such as during harvest, planting, and the like. A family large enough to satisfy peak requirements with its own labor would not have been economically viable for the rest of the year, when family members would be seriously underemployed.

Families coped with the problem of labor demand periodicity by hiring extra labor, but the most desirable solution involved various forms of labor exchange and cooperation among families. These cooperative relationships reflected a mutual interdependence expressed within the framework of community organization. Community solidarity was strengthened by the combined effect of the family's independence with respect to the management of its farm and its need to cooperate with other families at critical points during the agricultural year. Thus the family was characterized both by managerial independence and by functional interdependence. The two were not contradictory, because the strength of multi-family interdependence was defined in the first instance by the important managerial independence of each family unit. The managerial independence of individual families made for their strong interdependence at the community level, and this fundamental interdependence was one of the basic foundations of community solidarity.

There were many other areas reflecting the basic interdependence of families. Because they lived together in the intimacy of a face-to-face community, families were able to enter into many kinds of relationships with each other simply on the basis of mutual trust and confidence. Within the community framework, even the frequent agreements among families that took the form of written contracts were protected in the first instance not by the state, but by the most undesirable consequences which would be suffered by any family violating them. Diffuse sanctions operated to maintain the reliability of local agreements, be they oral or in writing; in the event that a family reneged on its agreements with other community families it would come under considerable local criticism and face the possibility that its future cooperative ties within the community would be threatened. The possibility that a family might find itself isolated was a powerful sanction encouraging people to honor their commitments to their neighbors.

Variations in village leadership composition reflected what might be called the principle of relative elite standing. Within a village, elite ranking was defined according to national criteria, but as relative to the village population. Literacy, land ownership and other forms of wealth, and the maintenance of an elite life-style were all involved in the definition of the village leadership, but in the absence of any one with higher qualifications in a village consisting entirely of farm families, say, the wealthier and more literate farmers would fill the leadership positions. If there were a landlord, or indeed a degree-holder, they would hold the leading elite positions. In other words, the village leadership would be comprised of the highest-level representatives of na-tional strata that happened to be locally resident. Although the state played a vital role through the examination system in defin-ing rural elites, not all villages had degree-holders. As already noted, it was far more probable that there would be one or more degree-holders within the larger multi-village community. Thus the village in any event was deeply involved in the examination system and the leadership group it produced.

Where there were degree-holders, there was an important dif-ferentiation between formal and informal leadership and power. Informal leadership surely would be in the hands of degree-hold-ers, but generally they would not occupy formal leadership posi-tions, such as that of the designated village headman appointed by the county magistrate. This post often was filled by a wealthier property-owning farmer, who was a representative of that class supplying a stable conservative foundation for community life. Leisured members of the elite avoided taking such formal admin-istrative positions precisely because as degree-holders they were in a position of informal equality with the local magistrate. On the other hand, degree-holders, if present, commonly were involved in the nomination of the village headman and their recommendation usually received the magistrate's routine approval.

Only within the context of co-membership in a rural commu-nity (or as kin) did degree-holders and commoners have social intimacy. As members of the same local community they could have an informal relationship even though their social positions were vastly different. On the other hand, the informal relationship between degree-holders and the magistrate—who because of the law of avoidance was from another province—was a reflection of their being members of the same national legal-social class. Thus the remote, formal, administrative and hierarchical relationship between magistrate and village head was informed and mediated by the social equality of magistrate and local degree-holder on the one hand, and by the social intimacy of local degree-holder and local commoner on the other. This, basically, was the triangular relationship through which the Qing Dynasty ruled China (the

"China proper" of the Han Chinese). In this relationship, community organization and class arrangements played vital and mutually reinforcing roles.

URBAN SOCIETY

In China the city was the center of administration for its surrounding region; even at the county level, the magistrate's yamen would be in a city. In addition to its administrative functions, a city was an economic center; it was characterized by far greater economic diversity than any rural region, and by much higher population density.

The very fact that urbanity was linked to administration both ideologically and empirically sharply differentiated urbanity in the Chinese cultural context from that of the West. China's entire administrative system was urban-based; a city was the government center for a county, prefecture, or province, and then of course there was the national capital. Chinese cities had their characteristic attributes: in addition to administrative functions, they had economic diversity and specializations, a city being both the economic focus of its own hinterland and also a nodal point with respect to trade between different urban-centered regions or even at a higher national level. But given the obviously special attributes of cities it nevertheless is incorrect to assert that cities were somehow different from rural China with respect to basic principles of social organization; rather, it must be understood that these basic principles pertained to city and countryside alike.

Urban territorial organization was importantly linked to the territorial hierarchy in rural society that has already been described. At the higher levels of rural organization the nodal point of each region was a city. Moving from the village neighborhood level to those of the village, the multi-village community, and beyond, the larger regions had as their centers nonadministrative market towns of varying sizes, and above the largest sub-county scale of organization there was the county itself, with the county seat as its center. In the context of this mode of territorial organization, those involved in city life fell into four broad categories: sojourners from other parts of China — such as merchants or officials — who considered that their presence in the city was temporary; residents of the city itself; persons with residences both in the city and also in its hinterland; and hinterland residents who were in the city for business of one kind or another.

While in rural China the largest face-to-face community was a multi-village unit, the urban situation also was more complex in this respect. The largest urban face-to-face unit was smaller because city social life to a far greater extent involved relationships where there was an absence of prior social intimacy; indeed, beyond the confines of one's immediate neighborhood much social interaction was with strangers. This involvement with strangers marked an important difference between urban and rural social organization. Even in one's own neighborhood there was the constant arrival of strangers to make purchases, perform services, and so forth. While the overall scale of social interaction was much broader in the cities, the intimate face-to-face community was smaller. These rural-urban differences were quantitative rather than qualitative, because in both contexts the same basic principles of social organization were involved. If the basic economic unit of rural society was the family, the same was true of the city; rural China's characteristic family enterprise was the farm, while that of urban society was the shop.

The various regional associations found in China's cities offered interesting confirmation of the importance of territorial hierarchy as a basis of organization, and also demonstrated that this hierarchy related at its lower levels to the traditional, largely self-generated, subcounty scales of organization which articulated with the higher levels that were defined in terms of the administrative system. The urban regional associations largely but not exclusively had as their members merchants or craftsmen from different parts of China. For purposes of organizing such an association, any convenient level within this hierarchy could serve as focus. Thus, if in one city there were enough merchants from a village in another part of China to support an association, they would organize their regional grouping on the basis of their native village. But in most cases these associations were organized by merchants with reference to higher levels of the territorial hierarchy such as the county, prefecture, or province. With respect to territorial hierarchy as a cultural concept, community, multi-community, and administrative units were fitted together and had equivalent meaning; the level chosen by an organization for its focus depended on the circumstances of the urban setting in which the merchants and others found themselves.

Occupational guilds were a major component of urban social structure. In some cities there also were clan associations, which usually recruited their members on the basis of the assumption that common surname indicated shared descent from a remote ancestor. There was not necessarily a clear-cut distinction between occupational guilds and regional associations, for their respective membership criteria could overlap in a variety of interesting ways. There was a tendency for regions to have occupational specializations, such that within a city specialists in a certain line would tend to be from the same region; thus some regional associations were guilds at the same time. At the other extreme, there might be no correlation between native area and occupation, such that the members of a regional association belonged to different guilds and, for that matter, to different clan associations. This most complicated case of no overlap between occupation, region, and surname meant that a person had one set of social connections through his fellow guild members, another through the members of his regional association, and yet a third through those belonging to his clan association. Such a total lack of overlap, while possible, must have been quite rare and is noted here so as to illustrate the potential for organizational complexity provided by the application in an urban setting of basic principles of Chinese social organization. Usually there was far more overlap, and there sometimes was almost total identity, at least as between occupation and native region. In any event, as between guild, regional association, and clan there could be a great variety of combinations from the point of view of the memberships involved.

Through this organizational complexity the heterogeneous urban population was arranged into a social system that substantially reduced what otherwise would have been considerable mutual unfamiliarity. Guild organization especially extended to all elements of society: there were guilds for beggars and, at the other end of the economic scale, for bankers.

It is obvious that an urban population was far more representative of the national arrangement of social and economic classes than any rural community. The larger the city, the more complete its representation; obviously, total representation was most closely approximated in Beijing. While in the rural communities only a small number of classes were represented, the cities by definition had members of the bureaucracy, including at least one magistrate; there were higher degree-holders on leave from government posts or not in office and also a larger number of lower degree-holders; the entire range of commoners was represented, from the wealthiest merchants and artisans at one extreme, to the numerous property-less poor at the other. This representation extended to farmers as well, for Chinese cities had farm families and cultivated fields within their walls, such that in effect there was a rural-urban continuum within the city itself. Members of all classes in the cities would have at least visual contact with each other, thus contributing to the more variegated quality of urban life.

RELIGION IN STATE AND SOCIETY

Traditional China did not have a religious system analogous to that, say, of medieval Europe, where the Church provided a unified religious framework. Yet in China the arrangement of religious institutions, practices, and beliefs formed a coherent whole largely due to the state's deep involvement. The state's basic attitude was that religious rituals and beliefs could either be supportive of the imperial house and state institutions and values or antagonistic to them. Religious practices opposed to the state were held to be heterodox; those basically in correspondence with beliefs and practices encouraged by the state were orthodox. Orthodoxy and heterodoxy, as defined by the imperial state, were two components or domains with respect to which we can begin to organize the totality of Chinese religious practices. However, there also was a tradition of state tolerance of certain religions, especially Buddhism; although the state viewed Buddhism as heterodox, its large-scale suppression during the Tang Dynasty was followed by the imposition of tight controls which under Qing rule were still in effect. Thus a religion might be heterodox but nevertheless acceptable within limits. Orthodoxy likewise can be seen to have had two dimensions. Religion could be orthodox in the sense that in ideology and practice it merited state approval, and sometimes explicit state support. On the other hand, an organization might use against the state the very beliefs that the state sought to uphold. It could, for example, deny the dynasty's legitimacy through an appeal to the very same standards used by the dynasty to confirm its receipt of the Mandate of Heaven.

As far as the state was concerned, orthodoxy encompassed a wide range of beliefs, including those associated with the popular orthodoxy of the masses as well as those characteristic of the literati elite. There was within philosophical Confucianism the basis for a non-theistic view of the cosmos as constituting an order that was morally good. At the other extreme, the religious world of an illiterate farmer was filled with gods and ghosts. Thus there are a variety of contrasts when the beliefs that might be held by a top degree-holder such as a Hanlin scholar are compared with those of an illiterate village woman. But these extremes in fact represent the polar ends of a continuum. They are also hypothetical extremes because no one really knows the extent to which degree-holders did or did not believe in gods and other supernatural forces. Most probably some did not have such beliefs and many did. The matter of beliefs is a tricky business precisely because both extremes were represented within the totality of the orthodox tradition. While some Confucian writings had to be mastered by everyone preparing for the examinations, there is not one whit of evidence that such scholars, with their traditional rural or urban backgrounds, did not at least to some extent maintain their beliefs in the gods and other supernatural beings. With the understanding that the two extremes in belief, and the continuum that bridged them, could be variously represented, we can move on to consider actual religious behaviors and institutions.

In both its written and ritual expressions elite orthodox religion was rationalistic, naturalistic, and humanistic. It was this-worldly, there being no belief in immortality or spirits. Rather, spirits were given an ethical, metaphysical, or philosophical interpretation. In the state cult's Confucian temple there was not the worship of Confucius, but rather his veneration. In elite religion immortality was identified as the effect one had on the living, on the society that one left behind; it did not imply actual existence as a supernatural entity. This was in keeping with the Confucian cosmological outlook that saw the unity of man and heaven; the perspective was not completely mechanical in that a person's individual nature was held to be identical with or a manifestation of the cosmic nature. There was a moral element involved here, because it was up to man to fulfill his nature, and by doing this he both served and was in harmony with heaven. By "heaven" was really meant the cosmos, and a fundamental Confucian concept was that moral and ethical relationships among people were as much cosmic phenomena as were the stars, movement of the planets, and the like. Because all were equally natural, relationships between father and son, husband and wife, and sovereign and minister were manifestations of heaven's way.

The Confucian inclusion of matters pertaining to human ethics within the cosmic domain was the basis of the idea that heaven was an "order." Being a particular relationship between emperor and heaven, the "mandate of heaven" was part of this natural order. An emperor who did not properly carry out his duties as sovereign could disturb the proper functioning of the cosmos; if a wife did not obey her husband, or a minister his emperor, each was violating his or her own nature, which meant violating heaven. Thus while there was a cosmological perspective incorporating human relationships, it was not a perspective on the divine. Indeed, the pure Confucian perspective was natural; there was a naturalistic view of heaven and therefore of the cosmological significance of human behavior.

Elite orthodox religion was firmly based in society, and its major emphasis was on rituals that could be ethically and socially interpreted. The rites of elite religion were the negation of personal prayer; instead of an individual, emotional relationship to a deity or god, there was highly formalized, structured, and expressive ritual. Elite rites formed the basis of the state cult, by which is meant a set of institutions and practices under the supervision of the Board of Rites during Qing and earlier dynasties; the state cult was not the Board's only concern, but it was a major one. The state cult had no priesthood independent of the official bureaucracy, and all bureaucrats potentially were clergy. During state cult rites the ritual specialists were designated officials; the worshipers were the bureaucrats and other degree-holders, and one way or another all officials were required to participate in this cult. State cult institutions in Beijing were linked to worship involving the emperor himself. Other institutions throughout the country at every administrative seat served as sites for state cult rituals carried out by locally posted officials.

The most important state cult ritual was the emperor's annual sacrifice at the Temple of Heaven in Beijing. This was the key ceremonial occasion of the year, one for which all officials in the country had to prepare. The emperor's sacrifice reflected his special relationship, based on his having received heaven's mandate. During the same ritual sequence the emperor sacrificed to his own ancestors, expressing through his participation in China's kinship religion his non-divine status; he sacrificed to the emperors of previous dynasties, thereby acknowledging continuity with respect to the imperial institution itself. The emperor's entire sequence of ritual acts was directed by a member of the Board of Rites, who would instruct and guide the emperor throughout the ceremony. He would repeatedly call out for the emperor to kneel down, kowtow, and rise, according to a procedure used in elite and popular sacrificial rites throughout China. In the emperor's case, his being directed by an official symbolized, among other things, that in certain ways he was under the control of the bureaucracy and the Confucianism of which it was custodian. Another important set of rites carried out by the emperor, was to Shennong, the spirit (or god) of agriculture. This included the famous ceremony where the emperor ritually plowed the first furrow of the agricultural year, representing his being the focal connection between human society and the rest of the cosmos.

Also in the capital were two other important temples: the Confucian temple (*Wenmiao*) of the civil bureaucracy, and the military temple (*Wumiao*) of the bureaucracy's military branch. These two temples were also found at every other administrative seat of the empire, including the provincial, prefectural, and county levels; a city concurrently the administrative seat at several levels would have a separate set of temples for each. The symbolism involved in this component of the state cult did not leave much to the imagination: the two temples were perfect parallels and expressions of the bureaucratic structure, which was divided into civil and military branches. The annual rites in these temples were led by the appropriate top official at each level.

In both civil and military temples the objects of sacrifice were tablets, as was the case in all state cult rituals; a contrast was with the temples of orthodox popular religion, where the gods were represented as statues or other images rather than as inscribed tablets. But to distinguish between objects of "worship" is to make an arbitrary assumption, because a tablet in a Confucian temple might be an object either of reverence or worship, depending on the beliefs of the ritual participants involved. But in any event the rituals were the same. By allowing either for ritual or for worship within the context of one religious system, full participation was encouraged; this included a probable minority of Confucian purists and the far larger number of participants who believed in some or all of the gods. Yet they all were involved in the ritualized expression of the basic social and political values supported by the imperial state.

The civil and military temples were foci of that component of the state cult which was exclusivistic and represented the unity of an elite composed of bureaucrats and other degree-holders; this unity was manifested during state cult rituals at every administrative seat, when local degree-holders joined the posted officials in ceremonies from which commoners were barred. Because the county was the lowest level of central administration, most manifestations of elite religion below the county level were not organized within the framework of the state cult proper.

Elite religious institutions below the county level included many combined civil-military temples and also those dedicated to great men. For example, a temple could venerate and memorialize an official who had aided in the development of an area's irrigation system and brought flooding under control. Depending on the extent of elite involvement and exclusivity, such a temple might only have tablets, or there could be tablets and images; the latter's presence implied popular involvement as well. Temples to great men were encouraged by the state, whose values they upheld; local magistrates were invited to serve as co-sponsors of such temples, even though they were set up through local degree-holder initiatives. Such temples were dedicated to officials, local scholars, or to groups of people meriting reverence. They were widespread, run by the local elite, and their rites followed the pattern of those performed in the state cult temples. These temples emphasized loyalty and patriotism; their focus was on social relationships, social stability, and social control, not on matters of supernatural aid, eschatology, or supernatural meaning. The temples were this-worldly, for objects of worship were all exemplars for the present. They did not answer questions of life beyond the present, for they were not supposed to.

Another state cult temple was dedicated to the city god (*chenghuang*); unlike the civil and military temples, that of the city god represented the interpenetration of the state cult with popular religion. In his temple there was both a tablet for the city god, and also his image. The city god's dual representation was a manifestation of his temple's dual role: it was part of the state cult, but also of key significance in popular religion; indeed, the city god was one of the major elements linking the elite and popular dimensions of orthodoxy.

Within the same orthodox domain as elite religion were the popular religious activities and beliefs which under ordinary circumstances represented the major religious concerns of the Chinese people. These were the religious expressions sometimes misleadingly labelled "folk religion" or even "superstition." My approach here to the relationship between the popular and elite components of orthodox religion is to deal with the former first as it contrasted most notably with the latter, just as we earlier dealt with elite religion by emphasizing its greatest contrasts with popular beliefs and practices. Having shown the contrasts, we will be in a better position to appreciate the important areas of overlap and interconnection.

Taken as a whole, popular religious beliefs and practices formed a system, but not one resembling Western religions or church organization. Chinese popular religion was a system of beliefs evolving in constant mutual interaction with those of the elite, yet the elements in popular religion were of diverse origin: there were gods and spirits, and elements of Taoism, Buddhism, yin-yang beliefs, heaven, and of local native cults, all formed into one pattern. Popular religion was polytheistic, extremely eclectic in terms of its origins, and spontaneous. If in elite religion the objects of sacrifice were subordinate to the rituals, in popular religion the objects of sacrifice were most important.

The supernatural cosmos of popular religion was inhabited by deities and spirits and modelled upon the human world; that orthodox popular religion involved much social projection revealed it to be basically supportive of the social and political status quo. The gods and spirits of popular religion had supernatural powers, but were accessible to human beings, who could worship or plead with them. Thus elite sacrifices became popular worship and personal relationships. Popular religion first and foremost was appreciated emotionally, elite religion intellectually. The functions of popular religion ranged from the solution of mundane affairs through supernatural means to the matter of individual personal salvation. A major focus was on social and personal adjustment, whereas that of the elite was on the ethics of social and political relationships.

In popular religious belief there were four supernatural domains: in the first were the gods and spirits who dwelt on the earth in closest contact with living human beings; the second domain was that of the underworld of gods and spirits; the third was an upper world where the Jade Emperor held court; finally, there was pure Paradise or Nirvana, which was a domain of the supernatural rather different from the other three.

Many important gods were among the supernatural beings living on the earth among humans. Every household had its god of the kitchen hearth or "stove god" (*zaowang, zaochun*). Because zaowang was the household's god, family division meant that where previously there had been one kitchen hearth god, there now were as many as there were new families formed. The kitchen god's worship was completely separate from that involved in the ancestral cult; brothers, having divided and worshipping different stove gods, still shared one line of ancestors and often enough one set of ancestral tablets. At every lunar year's end there was a report to the Jade Emperor by the kitchen god on the behavior of the family or household over which it had watched during the previous year. Linked to this belief were a variety of customs; one of the most common was to put honey on the kitchen god's image, the hope being that the kitchen god would have nothing but sweet things to report.

The earth god (*tudi*) was the god of a locality or territorial community, one which guarded over every neighborhood and village; a neighborhood had a small earth god shrine, and larger shrines could be built for the earth god of a village or a multi-village community. In any event, there was a hierarchy of earth god shrines matching that of local community organization. Earth god shrines were also placed in the compounds housing the county magistrate and his government office (yamen) as well as in the compound of the Confucian temple and its attached academy. Thus the distribution of earth god shrines was another link between elite and popular religion and institutions.

At the higher reaches of the hierarchy of earth god shrines there was the city god. As noted earlier, every administrative seat had its city god, who therefore was represented at the county, prefectural, and provincial levels. Because the city god was part of the state cult, its temple was established at every administrative seat together with the Confucian (civil) and military temples. Yet the city god also occupied a pivotal position in popular religion, and therefore represented an extension of the state cult into this domain. The state provided the institutions for the elite component of orthodox religion, and by incorporating the city god into the state cult it made popular religion orthodox as well. The relationship between the earth god and the city god was the supernatural equivalent of the relationship between a village headman and the county magistrate. In its construction the city god temple was a duplicate of the county yamen, and it functioned as that yamen's spiritual equivalent. A person's death was reported by his or her family to the earth god, who in good bureaucratic fashion relayed the report to the city god. Once or twice a year the city god toured his domain, as would (at different times) his human counterpart the county magistrate. A new county magistrate had the ritual duty to report to his spiritual colleague upon taking office.

The city god also had an important connection with the underworld, this lower world of purgatory being the second domain of the supernatural in popular religion. A report of a death received from the earth god by the city god in turn was sent by the latter down to the ten magistrates or judges of hell. Each of these had his own yamen and had jurisdiction over particular sections of hell; together they comprised the top officials in hell's bureaucracy, there being subordinate officials under the command of each. Sets of ten pictures of the hell magistrates were in city god temples, confirming the connection between the city god and hades. Each illustrated a magistrate sitting at a desk with papers, files, brush, ink slab and other paraphernalia of bureaucracy; he is surrounded by members of his staff, and the dead are being brought to him for judgment or already undergoing torture by devils and demons. This purgatory derived originally from India, whence it entered China with Buddhism; but well before Qing hell had been sinicized and bureaucratized.

Accompanying the deceased to hell was his dossier, likewise transmitted by the city god. The vast majority of the dead had to pass through all ten yamens of hell; if the deceased had led a most exemplary life he was processed only in the first of these, from whence he could go right to paradise. However such quick release was believed to be quite rare, and Chinese funeral rituals were guided by the assumption that the deceased were suffering in purgatory. Indeed, very important in traditional Chinese funerals were rituals to speed up the dead person's passage through hell. The burning of paper spirit money during such funerals also involved considerable critical social projection, for the money was meant for the gods; in some funerals one kind of money was pocket money for the deceased to take through hell for his or her own expenses; another kind was for bribing the magistrates of hell so that they would expedite their processing of the deceased.

The third domain of the supernatural in popular religion was the higher world of the spirits, ruled by the Jade Emperor. In popular religion the Jade Emperor embodied the merged representations of two major elements in orthodox elite belief, the emperor himself and heaven. The Jade Emperor and his court was a projection of the imperial court into the supernatural, but at the same time the Jade Emperor also personified heaven. Ruling from his court, the Jade Emperor was believed to hold sway over the entire cosmos of heaven, earth and the underworld.

Most of the gods in China's village and other temples were present in the Jade Emperor's court. If, for example, a village had a temple to Mazu—a very popular and powerful goddess, especially in southern China—this meant that Mazu was the village community's guardian deity. The goddess was not considered to reside in the village; rather, the Mazu image was considered to represent the goddess, who was in the Jade Emperor's court and in that favorable location able to protect the village. Inhabiting the same world as humans, each earth god and city god was considered to be a separate divine being. Mazu and the other gods in the Jade Emperor's court were protective because of their power, and there was only one of each.

In sum, villagers and city residents alike were religiously involved in a cosmos where there were three spheres of the supernatural: there were the supernatural beings on earth, such as the earth god and the city god, as well as a variety of deities linked to nature, such as the dragon god or the god of locusts; under the earth were the gods of hell; while patron deities of villages and other local or occupational communities were in the Jade Emperor's court.

The Jade Emperor, and the gods in his court, were also important for the state. In addition to its sponsorship of the state cult, with its formalized Confucian ritual and beliefs, the imperial government also exercised control over a pantheon within the domain of popular religion. A local deity becoming increasingly popular in China at some point would be recognized by the state and incorporated into the imperial pantheon. One example is the goddess Mazu, by Qing also commonly known as Tianhou. As her popularity grew, she was given increasingly higher-ranking titles: she advanced to become "Heavenly Consort" (concubine), but with further increase in her local popularity the imperial court raised her rank to "Queen of Heaven" (Tianhou). There was additional state involvement in the Mazu cult, when during Qing it was ordered that Tianhou temples be built along the entire China coast, as far north as Tianjin. The state, in recognizing the cult's local importance, not only made it its own but even facilitated its spread. The incorporation of the gods of the common people into a pantheon shows, once again, how the state's involvement in and manipulation of popular religion was a major factor in forming this domain of belief into a "popular orthodoxy" supportive of state values.

The forth domain of the supernatural in popular religion was separate from the cosmos noted above, for it comprised paradise or Western Heaven which, rather than projecting the relationships among mortals on earth, constituted precisely a joyful escape from them. Here was expressed an ideal of salvation as a totally and supernaturally blissful existence, one free of the torments and insecurities of earthly life. This "Pure Land" paradise was ruled by the Amitabha Buddha. It was thought that the souls of those who had achieved perfection in real life gained admittance to this paradise directly from the first yamen of hell. In orthodox popular religion the strongest expression of salvation was with reference to this domain of Paradise. But this idea of salvation was very much modified and qualified compared to the representation of salvation in the heterodox tradition (see below).

Apart from paradise, the structure of the earthly, underworld, and heavenly domains of the supernatural realm was parallel to that of human society, including the Chinese bureaucracy. That popular religion was deeply penetrated by bureaucratic motifs testified to the institutional longevity, unity, and continuity both of the bureaucracy and of the society that had absorbed the bureaucratic model into its religious beliefs. The content of these supernatural domains also was parallel to the world of the living. The large number of gods who were divine officials could have wives and could be bribed. During a village festival the petitions read to the gods were written in the same format as that of a bureaucratic memorial or petition to a higher official or to the emperor himself. These divine officials could be controlled or placated. They could be given birthday celebrations. They could be entertained by opera, which in theory was performed in the first instance for the pleasure of the gods, not the people; but the people certainly were able to enjoy the performance, which was given opposite the temple so that the gods were in the audience. The gods could be approached directly, or indirectly by bribing their subordinates. Indeed, the demarcation between officials and gods was not clear, for living officials had a certain terrifying if not divine quality; and this lack of clarity was not discouraged by the state. Thus the city god was treated publicly as a colleague by the county magistrate, who upon taking office had to report to him. Furthermore, public pressure often forced a magistrate to perform rituals involving the local gods, whether he believed in them or not. For example, during a drought the city god's image might be put in the sun, so that he might also experience the people's suffering; or in the event of a flood the same image might be thrown into a river. The magistrate's responsibility for such rituals shows how the human and supernatural bureaucracies were melded into one, at least as far as popular perceptions were concerned.

Within orthodox state-supported religion, the ancestral cult linked elite and popular practices more thoroughly than did any other component of orthodoxy as a whole. As far as the rituals were concerned, degree-holder and commoner were often together, especially in a larger lineage village. The ancestral rites perhaps most forcefully illustrated why ritual was attractive to the state. Philosophical, religious and emotional differences even as between common farmers and the elite could be bridged through common participation in ritual; this potential or actual unifying effect made ritual attractive to the state, and fed its desire to control it. Among all sectors of the population the rites of ancestor worship involved tablets or scrolls. The ancestral tablets had basically the same format as did those used in the civil and military state cult temples and in the various state cult temples in the capital. The ancestral rites involved the communal feasting of the living and dead; offerings first given the ancestors were then consumed by the living, for the former had eaten the spirit or essence of the offerings, the latter their substance.

While co-participation of degree-holder and commoner in religious ritual was most public in the context of the ancestral cult, there remains the question as to if what was involved was worship or veneration. Although elite and commoners shared a common core of ancestral rites, these rites could be differently interpreted. From a purist Confucian elite point of view, the important thing was the sacrifice itself and not the presence of a supernatural ancestral spirit. According to this elite view sacrifice maintained human relationships that otherwise would be interrupted by death; it expressed gratitude and filial piety to the ancestors. Also, the importance of sacrifice was with respect to its effects on the living; sacrifice expressed and reinforced the unity of the kinship group and eternally maintained the father-son relationship. Such values could also be important for the masses, but for them what was involved was indeed ancestor worship. The soul was held to survive death, but Chinese popular belief had it that there was more than one soul. Although there were variations from area to area in the details of this belief in multiple souls, it generally was thought that upon death one (the *po*) entered the grave, another (the *hun*) the ancestral tablet, while the third soul (the *gui*) went to the underworld.

When ordinary Chinese villagers worshipped their ancestors, these were taken to be supernaturally present entities, as souls in the tablets, graves, or in the underworld. This Chinese belief in multiple souls led to the weakening of the ideal of salvation in orthodox popular religion. With souls fated to go in different directions, the individual did not simply worry about personal salvation after death; of equal concern was his or her continuing relationship to the living. In the grave and in the tablet the dead stayed with the living and continued to enjoy their support; and at the same time they needed the help of the living to reach paradise from the underworld. Thus the true strength of salvationist religion was manifested more in contexts outside the realm of orthodox popular religion, in forms of religious expression often taken by the state to be heterodoxy.

In orthodox popular religion the idea of personal salvation was hedged in by continuing social constraints or social obligations after death. Food and drink were served to all three souls at one point another in the rituals of popular orthodoxy. The soul in the grave was so served during the burial service, and it was believed that it enjoyed the refreshment. This soul was also given offerings during the Qingming Festival, when people would worship at their ancestors' graves, and there could be grave worship at other times as well. When offerings of food and drink were placed in front of the ancestral tablets, it was believed that the ancestors were present in the tablets and enjoying the offerings. For villagers and ordinary city residents alike, reporting events to the ancestors was thought to be actual communication with the dead. For example, it was not uncommon during family division for an additional copy of the partition contract to be prepared and then burnt in front of the ancestral tablets, thereby notifying the ancestors that the family had divided.

The third soul, or *gui* was of vital significance to popular religion as a whole. Third souls constantly needed the aid of the living to fare well and were objects of both individual and community worship. It was assumed that many of these souls were not being cared for by their descendants. These souls then became the fearsome "hungry ghosts" (*e gui*) of traditional China, who wandered about the world of the living searching to satisfy their needs. Hungary ghosts either had descendants who did not care for them or had no descendants at all. The latter circumstance often resulted from death as a bachelor or spinster who had been deprived of a spouse due to poverty, from an early death before marriage, or from a similarly premature dying off of all descendants. There was an obvious association of such deaths with events such as accidents, violence, illness or a family's economic collapse: all of these were causes of deaths that were "bad," and a bad death would be anti-Confucian because a person's responsibility to society and to his or her own ancestors was to marry and have offspring.

Hungry ghosts were creatures who in the world of the dead were torn out of the social fabric. They did not have a network of kinship ties which would both protect them and insure their proper behavior; they were strangers, hungry and dangerous. Social projection served to support kinship and community ideals and values in this context, because among the living there also were those with no acceptable social connections, who likewise were hungry and dangerous: these were the beggars and bandits in real society. The connection made between hungry ghosts among the dead and beggars and bandits among the living largely explains why the worship of these ghosts was a crucial part of community religion. Many important community festivals had as their religious core worship of hungry ghosts. The Jiao ceremony of cosmic renewal was among the most prominent of these and included Taoist masses for the dead. In such festivals, the community prayed that it would prosper in a world that was hostile, dangerous, and filled with strangers. From the local community's point of view, if their connection with the world of stability, predictability and prosperity was through the protection of their patron god or goddess, their possible exposure to the world of instability, of dangerous strangers, was represented by the hungry ghosts. The community prayed to its patron deity for prosperity and protection at the same time that it tried to placate hungry ghosts through religious means.

A substantial portion of the thousands of gods and goddesses in the popular Chinese pantheon had died violently, according to legend or historical fact. There was strength, power, and vitality associated with violent death, and also with the character of a person whose good deeds placed him or her in circumstances leading to his own destruction. Nevertheless, the issue was whether the power linked to violent death was expressed beneficially, as by the gods, or malevolently, as with hungry ghosts. In any event, these beliefs certainly reinforced the desire for male offspring, for with the exception of those destined for godhood, people without them would themselves become a hungry ghosts. The practical necessity of having a son to provide support during old age was reinforced by the religious belief that without a son one was in trouble even after death.

HETERODOXY

By "legal heterodoxy" I refer to the perspective of the imperial Chinese state as regards the organized religions of Buddhism and Taoism. A major reason for Buddhism being considered heterodox was because its pessimistic view of the cosmos — as representing a cycle of birth and rebirth from which escape through enlightenment or salvation was the religious ideal — seriously conflicted with the state Confucian view of the cosmos as morally good. Taoism was heterodox because its view of the individual's ability to directly control cosmic forces so as to achieve personal health or even immortality conflicted with state ideology which positioned the emperor as heavenly-appointed mediator between the cosmos and humanity. Yet Buddhism and Taoism were legal but kept under close supervision by the state, which through quotas and licenses restricted the number of temples and the size of the clergy. Furthermore, if in some modern Western societies there is the idea of separation of church and state, in traditional China the concern of the state was the separation of church and society. The village and other temples that were foci of community religion, or of territorial religion on an even larger scale, usually did not have clergy, but were run by local elites and informal temple management committees. On the other hand the temples, monasteries, and nunneries where the Buddhist clergy resided—usually in the countryside, but away from local communities—generally were not centers for community religion. Worshipers went to Buddhist temples as individuals or in small groups; sometimes they went to temples relatively nearby but on other occasions there were large pilgrimages to more distant sites of worship. Worshipers at Buddhist temples usually did not ask for the protection of their communities, but rather made contact with the clergy, and with the Buddha, as individuals seeking salvation or enlightenment. While these Buddhist temples attracted people from over larger areas, they did not serve to give religious definition to local communities or indeed to any territorial level of social organization. Therefore they are to be distinguished from the various village temples, city god temples, or other religious institutions embedded in and expressive of the territorial organization of Chinese society.

Although these were different systems of temples, they were related in several ways. First, while Buddhist and Taoist temples generally were located outside of communities, their clergy were called in to carry out community religious rites. But their power was minimal; they were hired only as religious specialists, paid by the village elite or its representatives, and when they had finished their work they returned to their temples. Thus if by clergy we mean specialist practitioners, then there was separation between clergy and community; but from another point of view, the clergy were the village elite, who in certain ritual contexts needed the services of hired religious practitioners. During large community festivals Taoist or Buddhist clergy would officiate in the technical sense. Even for family rites it was commonly said that for a wedding one call in a Taoist, for a funeral a Buddhist. In fact, Taoist or Buddhists could perform on either occasion; during a funeral put on by a wealthier family, there could be Buddhist monks and nuns as well as Taoist priests carrying out their respective rituals. During funerals both Buddhist and Taoist clergy were at least as busy negotiating the passage of the dead through purgatory as they were working for salvation. Thus as servants of popular religion they remained deeply involved in its cosmos, and perhaps this is one reason why they were tolerated by the imperial state.

Patron deities, oath kinship, and sworn brotherhoods were quite common in the daily life of rural and urban society, and were involved in many different kinds of organizations. These same elements loomed very prominently in the secret societies, which in terms of the values supported by the Chinese imperial state were orthodox in many respects but nevertheless held by that state to be subversive and illegal. These secret societies, common in southern China but also found elsewhere in the country, cannot be said to have denied or attacked the Confucian values espoused by the state. Indeed, they were illegal precisely because of their claim that the dynasty itself was not legitimate in terms of these very values. The secret societies asserted that the Manchu Qing rulers had usurped the Dragon Throne from China's legitimate rulers, the emperors of the Ming Dynasty. Obviously, this was a stance taken against the state, and the Manchu regime clearly was out to destroy such groups. Yet the secret societies did not challenge any of the basic elements in orthodox ideology. They did not deny the idea that there was a mandate of heaven, but only that the Manchus had received it. In a sense, the secret societies claimed that they were more authentically Confucian than was the state. Many secret societies held that this lack of Qing legitimacy was linked to the moral decay of society, and it was because of this decay that perfectly good people had to form societies so as to survive. Of obvious relevance to this perspective was the fact that the secret societies were important actors in an underworld where they could be involved in piracy, kidnapping, extortion, prostitution, and the like.

Secret societies such as the Triads had as their patron deity Guan Gong, who was also the god of the military bureaucracy. Guan Gong—a historical figure who later became a god—was patriotic, loyal, and had entered into oath brotherhood with two other famous men. The often complex initiation ceremonies of some secret societies included an oath to regard all fellow members as kinsmen, indeed as brothers; certain of the secret societies banned marriage among members' children since members already were related by dint of oath brotherhood. Secret societies were different from the acceptable voluntary associations because they were indeed secret and anti-state, frequently engaged in criminal activities, and also because a secret society could have branches distributed over a relatively large area, whereas ordinary voluntary associations usually were organized within the framework of a smaller local community.

The state identified as true heterodoxy those religious traditions which in one way or another rejected ideas central to both elite and popular orthodoxy concerning the cosmos as a moral force and the importance of maintaining cosmic order and continuity. The wrath of the state could be especially severe when notions of cosmic rejection or cosmic decline were taken up by religious sects, rather than being confined to Buddhist clergy or individual believers. One important tradition of organized rejectionistic religious heterodoxy focused on the same Western Heaven or Pure Land that was involved in orthodox popular religion. But for many of the Western Heaven cults the desirability of salvation so overwhelmed other aspects of belief that death was held to be a happy event: the important thing was to escape from the cosmos, defined by them as a source of suffering and misery. It is not surprising that many members of such cults were poor and unmarried, such that the world they lived in could readily be seen to be part of the cosmos so pessimistically described by their religion. While Western Heaven sects were at times persecuted by the Qing state, their beliefs may have appeared to be more escapist than confrontational: they did not deny the cosmos, but merely sought—at least in death—relief from suffering in it.

The state was far more hostile to the beliefs and sects of the White Lotus religion, which represented a radical counter-tradition in China, one with a long history of its own. The White Lotus focus on the inevitability of cosmic destruction represented a blatant rejection of basic concerns of orthodoxy in its elite or popular versions. Although most White Lotus followers were peaceful, or militant only when faced with government persecution, some of the larger uprisings during Qing were within the White Lotus tradition. Linked to White Lotus religious beliefs were some egalitarian tendencies. In this tradition an important role was played by the teacher-leader who revealed the truth to persons who then became believers and followers and were thus assured of salvation. The teacher-leader could be male or female, young or old, thus denying the social importance of the age and sex differences that received strong emphasis in both elite and popular orthodoxy.

Knowledge of the White Lotus tradition derives largely from their religious texts, many of which were discovered in the Qing period during government raids on White Lotus religious establishments. This tradition drew much of its content from Buddhism, but also from Taoism and other elements in the Chinese popular religion. The major deity unique to this religious tradition was the "Unbeggoten Eternal Mother," *wusheng laomu.* This figure looms large in White Lotus texts, which when used by sect teachers often were disguised to look like ordinary Buddhist sutras. Another important divine figure was the Meitraya Buddha, whose appearance on earth was linked to the idea of the kalpa *(jie)* or cosmic cycle, also derived from Buddhism. The White Lotus religion held that through eternity there will be three kalpas, and that the second kalpa was now nearing its end; only those knowing the "truth" would survive the destruction of the cosmos and with the onset of the third kalpa attain immortality in an earthly paradise.

Heterodoxy was in opposition **both** to elite and to popular orthodoxy. A contrast of heterodox ideas with some of the key elements of orthodox ideology will reveal how antithetical the two traditions were. Confucianism had as its main theme the ongoing and continuing harmony of humanity, heaven and earth. The cosmos is a continuing process, and it is everyone's duty to live in harmony with it and thereby keep it in good order. Cosmic disorder can and indeed must be corrected. In heterodoxy this enduring cosmos is replaced by kalpas of universal destruction. What for Confucianism was the non-divine Son of Heaven became for White Lotus believers a divine emperor who was the Buddha messiah. According to White Lotus beliefs the divine Meitraya Buddha is sent to earth by the Unbeggoten Eternal Mother to save her children from the universe's imminent destruction. The anticipated arrival on earth of the Meitraya Buddha introduces a political element into White Lotus belief. A villager proclaiming himself to be the Meitraya Buddha, sent by the Unbegotten Eternal Mother, will have as his goal seizure of the imperial throne so as to be in the best position to teach the truth to as many people as possible and thereby save them from the coming destruction.

In contrast to orthodox popular religion, in heterodoxy personal individual salvation was the main theme. In popular orthodoxy the idea of salvation was circumscribed because the dead continued to have social functions for the living and at the same time had to be cared for by them lest they turn into hungry ghosts; even that aspect of the soul attaining paradise had first to be processed by the bureaucracy of hell. All this was denied by the White Lotus tradition, which asserted that the Unbegotten Eternal Mother had sent (or would send) the Meitraya Buddha to earth so that all believing in the truth would attain while still alive total and eternal salvation in the new cosmos.

Orthodoxy was a religion of community, local, and other group affiliations; it was a religion of social relationships: kinship, family, village, community, administrative district, region, the imperial state and, ultimately, the cosmos as a whole. Heterodoxy was a religion of believers: the distinction was between those who did not believe, and those who did; the former would perish with the end of the universe, and the latter would be saved. This focus on belief cut across community and kinship ties. Heterodoxy was associated with the breakdown or serious weakening of that sense of security or minimal predictability which gave meaning to orthodox popular religion, and which therefore could be rendered irrelevant under circumstances of drought, famine, severe economic deprivation, and the like. To the extent that political, economic, or natural circumstances could render increasingly problematic the daily predictability of elementary security or survival, the heterodox tradition had grounds for expression and growth. If orthodoxy gave religious confirmation to the order and organization of society and the cosmos, heterodoxy testified to the power of orthodoxy precisely by denying its basic tenants.

Heterodoxy constituted a critique of a cosmic orientation that encompassed the arrangement of society; heterodoxy advocated either escape from this cosmos or its replacement by one that would include paradise on earth. Because traditional heterodox aspirations did not importantly include a practical plan for social change they offered no viable alternative to the orthodox vision of social order. With China's entrance into the modern era, however, there emerged unprecedented critiques of traditional orthodoxy expressed by the new intellectual and political elites in response to the crisis of national and cultural identity brought about by the triumphant forces of Western imperialism. These new elites also initiated a cultural and political assault upon the orthodox tradition which, unlike those launched by the older heterodoxies, did indeed succeed in destroying the political institutions with which this tradition had been associated and in severely weakening it as a religion. However, as following chapters will show, even these new elites were not ultimately successful in imposing their vision of society upon the Chinese people.

JAPAN'S MODERNITIES, 1850s-1990s

Carol Gluck

THE PERILS OF COMPARISON

"Becoming modern" is the main story in the history of nineteenth and twentieth-century Japan. Japanese historians have produced a rich literature on the nature of Japan's modernity and how it differed, for better or worse, from that of the West. Western scholars have tended to pose the question in terms of exploring "the first Asian (or non-Western) society to modernize." Both perspectives make the same point: the study of modernity is inevitably comparative. And not only in hindsight. Ever since England and France defined the modern by getting there first, most countries have had little choice but to conceive their own modernities in the conceptual frame derived from these historical examples. Germany no less than Japan looked "West" in the nineteenth century to discern the characteristics necessary to the modern. Call it even the "necessary modern," since its achievement so often appeared compulsory, if not because of imperialist threat, as in Japan's case, then by virtue of forces ranging from economic development to the allegedly irresistible march of Progress.

But necessity does not imply uniformity. The first of three common pitfalls in the study of comparative modernities is the by now well-known "models of modernization." True, nineteenth-century Japanese leaders looked, ineluctably, to what they called "Euro-America" (Ōbei) for the perquisites of "civilization" (bunmei), from police and post offices to the constitution, calendar, medicine, and modern motherhood. No sooner had they done so than they confronted the task of sorting out East from West, seeking first to identify indigenous "customs" and then working to mold Euro-American ways to Japanese form and Japanese ways to Euro-American institutions. The result, conceptually, was an East-West axis laid over the landscape of modern Japan. Words neatly divided things into Japanese painting and Western painting, Japanese clothes and Western clothes, Japanese food and Western food—phrases of daily life still in common use today. Arguments over parliamentary government, legal codes, military organization, and nearly everything else in the Meiji era (1868-1912) took the form of this dichotomized distinction.

The assertion of absolute difference between Japan and the West also served metaphorical purposes. Meiji Japanese debated the nature and extent of change by laying out the choices in polar extremes, each with strong political and cultural connotations. By conflating the Western with the modern, the one pole implied a stance for or against progress. By identifying the Japanese with tradition, the other pole posed the challenge of national identity. Like the labels conservative and liberal, or Right and Left in many countries, the polarity between East and West, or Japan and non-Japan, could be evoked to map positions on almost any issue. From the mid-1850s to the mid-1990s, this axiomatic division pervaded vernacular discourse about Japan's past, present, and future. No matter that the rhetoric continued to represent East/West as an either/or alternative long after the two could be so easily separated in real life. Every society falls captive to its own self-stereotypes, which though perpetuated in ideologies of national identity usually owe their origins to historical experience. For Japan, and so many other places, the historical experience that marked the beginning of the modern moment was the precedence, preeminence, and preponderant power of Western formations of modernity.

The analytic pitfall lies in allowing these conceptions from the historical past to continue into the historiographical present. We know now that there is no single "Euro-American" model of modern society just as there is no single process of "modernization" that leads to the same outcome in different societies. We look instead for variations on the theme of modernity, diverse patterns of modernizing process, and differences in the logic and chronologic of the modern experience, which are not susceptible to the simple labels of East or West. And we must do so, despite those in our own societies who persist in assuming that the West is the "model" and also despite those in the societies we study who insist, as they often do in Japan, that the best-dressed modernity parades in "either" Western "or" Japanese costume.

A second pitfall of comparison straddles the East-West axis

only to claim that whatever the fashion of the modern in Japan, its cut is distinctive—even unique. In Japan the declaration of exceptionalism is an old one, dating back to the assertion of cultural identity over the long centuries when China was the object of Japan's civilizational gaze. One response to the bedeviling dichotomy between Japanese and Chinese ways was to argue Japan's distinctiveness, either by virtue of its purely nativist essence or of its having achieved a superior Sino-Japanese cultural blend. Similarly, beginning in the late nineteenth and continuing to the late twentieth century, Japanese commentators posited a unique modernity, either because of its "traditional" Japanese elements—the imperial institution, the family system, the value placed on social harmony, and the like—or because of the extreme hybridity of its modern formation, which combined samurai bureaucratism with Western parliamentarism, village paternalism with industrial management, habits of island-country isolation with ventures in imperialist aggression and war, even Shinto rites of purification with the successful production of semiconductors (with "cleanliness" as the alleged link between the two).

Nationalists intoned the mantra of uniqueness throughout the modern period: intellectual advocates of "national-essence-ism" in the 1890s, chauvinistic champions of the "Japanese spirit" in the 1930s, romantic ultranationalists calling for Japan to "overcome [Western-style] modernity" in the wartime 1940s, and cultural conservatives professing the faith of "Japaneseness" from the 1970s through the 1990s. The language of exceptionalism joined with the habits of essentialism to postulate a distinctively "Japanese" culture as the reason for Japan's modern history, both its failures and its successes. Such culturalist explanations, which were nothing new, pervaded the Japanese and American media again in the 1980s. They remain, however, anathema to historical explanation, not least because of their ahistorical conceit of an immutable "culture" that marches through time unchanged.

For very different, often opposite, reasons, Japanese historians also stressed the distinctiveness of Japan's modern experience. From the Left, which produced the Marxist and left-liberal scholars who dominated the universities in the postwar period, came the view that modernity had developed in a particularly distorted form in Japan. Their argument echoed German interpretations of a "special path" to the modern, yet both German and Japanese scholars tended to see their own history as particularly particular, if not downright unique. The experience of fascism and war had greatly intensified these ideas of "deviation" from the course of world history. Yet assumptions of Japanese "difference" are nearly as old as modern social science itself, which has often treated Japan as exempt from history. In a famous footnote of 1867, Marx argued that because "Japan with its purely feudal organization of landed property and its developed small-scale agriculture, gives a much truer picture of the European Middle Ages than all our history books," it was not truly "Asiatic," thus exempting Japan from the history of Asia.[1] More common was the straightforward exemption from history in general. In 1990 Eric Hobsbawm wrote that "Japan, though patently *sui generis*, could be considered an honorary western imperial power, and thus a national and nation-alist state somewhat like its western models."[2] To say that a modern society is "in a class by itself" violates every known rule of world history. Nonetheless, Japan continues to draw this kind of remark, even from the best historians.

At the other end of the uniqueness/universality scale lies the idea of "convergence" put forward by social scientists in the U.S. after World War II. American triumphalism at mid-century fostered the assumption that the developing nations, once on track, would eventually come to look something like the United States. The American occupation of Japan also operated on this premise in its promotion of democratic reforms after 1945. When Japan became a formidable economic rival in the 1980s, some American analysts concluded that not only had the expected convergence failed to occur, but Japanese capitalism was so utterly different that it needed to be treated as a hostile force.

Now that we no longer admit a single model or pursue a univer-sal history of modernity, our stance toward Japan—and every-where else—must shift away from dichotomous comparison. All societies cannot be measured by some imagined Euro-norm, on the one hand. And on the other, no society is—in terms of its modernity—unique. The task is to place Japan in recent world history: to trace the **commonalities** as well as the **particular figurations** of its experience. In sum, Japan is an instance of the modern, no more, no less. The question is what kind of instance it is and why.

Answering this question leads to the brink of a third compara-tive pitfall, one that avoids both the frontal comparison between East and West and the seductions of uniqueness, only to tumble into a related trap. If modernity is inevitably comparative, to what should Japan be compared? China is one conventional answer. On grounds of civilizational affinity, regional proximity, and rela-tion to the nineteenth-century imperialistic West, China and

Japan have long been compared in terms of political reform, economic development, "response to the West," and the rest. All too often the result is the "Japan succeeded, China failed" storyline, which applies Western standards of the time to conclude that Meiji Japan coolly managed the transition from feudal to modern state, from peasant to industrial economy, from isolated Asian kingdom to imperialist power, while China, to put it simply, did not.

However valid the reasons for the differences between Chinese and Japanese history between 1850 and 1990, the impression given by a sweeping frontal comparison remains erroneous on two counts: First, Japan's transition appears smoother, more "successful," than it was, considering the social costs at home and the subsequent depredations of imperialism and war in Asia. Second, the course of modernity seems, once again, to be foreordained and one-tracked instead of multi-pathed and differently timed as it clearly was in China and Japan. The reverse of the comparative coin can be equally counterfeit. Compare China and Japan on the subject of revolutions (a not uncommon practice), and similar distortions arise. China's 1949 revolution is usually considered in conceptual terms derived from the French or Russian revolution, and Japan, in these terms, failed to have a revolution at all. This is true enough, but not much help in explicating the patterns of modernity in Asia.

In times past, modern Japan was compared to Russia, Turkey, and other "late-developers," a trend that subsided with the decline of modernization theory in the 1970s. More recently, Korea seemed to some a good comparison, one that works better in relation to economic development than it does with other aspects and breaks down utterly on the point of three-and-a-half harsh decades of Japanese colonial rule (1910-1945). It is suggested elsewhere in this book that Europe makes a more apt comparison for "early modern" Japan (the Tokugawa period, 1600-1868) than does China. It also holds true for the period after 1868 that France, Germany, Italy, Britain, and even the United States offer useful comparison to Japan, as long as the comparison is discriminatingly partial, not indiscriminately total. Wilhelminian Germany and Meiji Japan, for example, have much in common in matters of political and institutional change in the two newly unified nations. For ideology and citizenship during the same period, France and Japan are nationally comparable. A study of urban consumer culture in the 1920s could bring Italy, France, Germany, and Japan into comparative perspective, as would an analysis of economic reconstruction after the Second World War. And if one does engage in country-size comparison, then at least string them together: Japan and China, Japan and France, Japan and Russia, one after another. With serial comparison, multiple differences become obvious and help to shatter the comparative monolith.

The perils of frontal comparison amount to a reductive, oversimplified history that flattens modernity into a single linear narrative, which makes Europe seem more universal and Asia more special than in fact they were. Modernity everywhere shares elements in common, while the differences derive from context and conjuncture, both of which are historical products. It matters, contextually, that Japan was small and China, huge; that India was a British colony, Korea a Japanese colony, and Japan no colony at all; that social systems differed, based on class, status, or kinship; and so on. It matters, conjuncturally, that Japan established its modern nation-state in the 1870s, at the same time as Germany and Italy, along nineteenth-century European models; under imperialist but not colonial threat; on an agrarian base with side-products like raw silk that happened to find a ready world market because of a disease afflicting European silkworms; and much more. Of the two intertwined themes in the global history of modernity, "development" took precedence over "emancipation" in the Japanese story precisely because of such contexts and conjunctures. These overlapping frames consisted of historical elements large and small, structural and contingent, general and specific—and there were so many of them in each case that macro-comparisons are easily undercut.

Yet the commonalities remain. The main message of the story of modern Japan is how complicated the process, how varied the patterns, but how affected by the world, how much in the context of world history all the seemingly disparate modernities took shape. To keep this point in view requires constant border-crossing to escape the confines of a single national history, where Japan tells only its own story, without setting up a rigid macro-comparison, where Japan and China (or Russia or Germany) march in lockstep across a century, as if everything in their histories were comparable. Better to micro-compare on specific aspects, such as changes in demography, local government, women and work, and macro-suggest the generalities like industrialization, nation-state, and mass society that seemed everywhere, eventually, to comprise the modern.

THE NATIONAL MODERN (1850s-1900s)

The narrative of modern Japan nearly always begins with the Meiji Restoration of 1868. The Restoration, like the French Revolution in France, is presented as the founding event of modern times, as if something as complex as modernity could begin with such chronological precision. In fact, it is typical of the modern to announce itself as a rupture with the past: "a new age now begins." Like the French Revolution, the Meiji Restoration is both an event and a symbol, and what it symbolizes is the beginning of the national modern: the enterprise of modernity undertaken in the name of the nation-state. The fall of the Tokugawa shogunate and the "restoration" of the emperor to the throne in early 1868 itself amounted to little more than a change in political leadership, since the new Meiji government set out to rule in the emperor's name as the shogunate had done for centuries before. But the symbolic change was immense, for the nation was henceforth to be reconstructed as a unified, centralized state with every trapping of civilization as the nineteenth-century West defined it. Over the course of the next several decades, the national symbol was made substance. And in 1909 the Meiji leaders looked back, with patent satisfaction, over what they called "fifty years of new Japan."[3]

The nature of the "newness" is the historical question. But first, what was the nature of the "old"? Why did the Tokugawa shogunate "fall" after 268 years of continuous peaceful rule? The verb hints at the mechanisms of change that accounted for the seemingly rapid disappearance of the old regime and the establishment of the new imperial state. So many incremental changes had taken place in the previous century, and especially since the 1820s, that Japan in the 1860s had already outreached the order established by the early shoguns more than two centuries earlier. Commercial and proto-capitalist sectors in the economy, political innovation in the feudal domains, an entrepreneurial peasant elite, and many other developments had substantially changed Japan, without however challenging the established shogunal order. This substantive change-within-institutional-continuity comprised one important context for the abrupt changes after the Restoration. For these changes were not as abrupt as they appeared.

Commodore Perry's arrival in 1853 was a contingent event, which brought the shogunal system to crisis by posing a threat it could not deal with—the opening of the country to the international order of the imperialist West. The conjuncture of this threat with the by now hollowed-out incompetence of the shogunal bureaucracy proved to be too much for the system. But note that the initial response of court, shogunate, and feudal lords alike was to preserve order by shoring up the existing system; their goal was to rouse the shogunal bureaucracy to do a better job in dealing with the barbarians, not to throw the shogun out. When that proved impossible, overthrow became "necessary," and the shogunate "fell." Unlikely as it seems, the best comparison here may be with the American Revolution, which also initially set out to bring the King to rule his colonies more justly, and only in the course of the revolutionary ferment came to fight instead for independence. Both were conservative revolutions, which had outcomes unforeseen by their participants at the beginning of their engagement.[4] It is not the outcomes, of course, but the historical process that is similar in the two cases. But the similarity highlights the role of contingency in what is so often told as a straight-line story, as if initial intentions led, through a chainlink of cause and effect, to "pre-envisioned" historical consequences. The Meiji Restoration of 1868, while not exactly an accident, was neither planned nor contemplated until late in the restorationist day, when "events overtook" the momentum of political action. The actual form of the Restoration was determined by another contextual factor. The same abiding concern for order that had kept the shogunate in place for so long also militated against an extreme solution to the challenge of establishing a new political system. Hence the Meiji government, concerned both with preserving social order and its own authority at the same time, assumed power in the name of the emperor, newly restored to the throne to rule rather than merely to reign. This "restoration" (*ōsei fukkō*) changed the nature of the political system but did so in a manner that Harry Harootunian has called "the least radical of the secessions that contemporary history could offer."[5] The new was embedded, symbolically and institutionally, in the old, a practice long followed in Japanese political history. Through this tenacity of institutional continuity, the Meiji government pacified the country in the name of the emperor, suppressing both the rebellion of its samurai opponents and the rising peasant unrest of the late 1860s. It then went on, in the so-called Meiji Renovation (Meiji ishin), to reform the realm.

The outline of the reforms did not emerge brand-new after 1868, since portions of the Japanese elite had been aware of both Western threats and Western models since early in the century. The conceptual context for the Meiji reforms was the gradual reconception of the realm in the Western idiom, much as samurai of the seventeenth century had reconceived the early Tokugawa world in the socio-moral language of neo-Confucianism. In a sense the nineteenth-century proponents of "Western learning" were following the precedent of their Confucian predecessors in aggressively rethinking their world. Both rethinkings were profound enough to be revolutionary. Sakamoto Ryōma, the samurai swordsman and "man of spirit," formulated his "Eight-point Program" on the eve of the Restoration his assassins would prevent him from living to see. Yet his plan included nearly every provision that the new Meiji government—more of them bureaucrats than swordsmen—would undertake in establishing the new imperial state.[6] But a samurai outsider like Sakamoto owed his knack of showing up in the thick of things during the 1860s to another conjuncture of factors, including political ferment in the domains and at the court in Kyoto, a renewed shogunal interest in naval development, and an exuberant personality, which only thirty years earlier would have landed him in prison if not on the gibbet. And the international context favored the reforming plans as well, since the United States demanded trade, not territory, and though Perry paraded his black ships before Japanese shores, he did not fire their guns in pursuit of hostile conquest.

Just as the Restoration was a long time in coming, 1868 did not change things overnight. Incremental change combined with conjunctural contingency had brought the old order down, but the new order also required decades of historical process to establish. The 1870s saw the period of the Meiji "refolution"—to borrow a term that suggests a hybrid of reform and revolution, which rather aptly describes the series of government measures of "renovation," from the "return of the feudal domains" (centralization) and the abolition of the Tokugawa status system (samurai included) to the establishment of compulsory education, a conscript army, and a new taxation system.[7] The historical mechanism of these government initiatives resembled not the end, but the beginning of the Tokugawa shogunate, in that the state aggressively sought to establish a new order by pronouncing it from above. But pronouncing change is easier than making it happen: it took decades for Japan's national modernity to evolve. Historians now consider the nineteenth century as one period of extended transition, from the 1820s to the 1890s: "the long Restoration," consisting of an ever shifting mix of old and new.

In Japan as elsewhere, the dominant contextual imperative of the period was the formation of the modern nation-state in its nineteenth-century European version. This imperative affected existing nations like France and the United States as well as newly unified nations like Germany, Italy, and Japan. Meiji Japan's version of the nation-state depended as much—or more, I would

argue—on the environment of nineteenth-century world history as
it did on legacies from the long national past. Consider the emperor, for example, steeped in ancestral tradition as old as the
sun goddess but paraded in the uniform of a mustachioed genera-
lissimo worn by well-dressed European monarchs of the age. The
effect was calculated: Meiji leaders sought to make Japan a nation
like the Western nations in order to achieve revision of the unequal treaties and gain parity with the West. The comparative
point here is the determined "nationalization" that occurred in
established nations, old and new. From capitalism to language,
from politics to education, from literature to the family—the nation dominated developments in all the precincts of social experience. Nationalism, it has often been said, was the preeminent
force of nineteenth-century history, a force bequeathed in formidable forms to the proliferating nation-states of the twentieth-century. In its nineteenth-century embodiment, the Nation was
conjoined with Progress—both in capital letters—so that what was
in fact a product of a particular historical moment seemed instead
an incarnation of the universal.

The nationalizing efforts of Meiji Japanese are well known,
beginning with institutions like the emperor-system, the 1890
constitution, the education, police, and the military. They also
included identifying a national language, producing a canon of
national literature, establishing a discipline of national history,
redrawing national borders to "Japanize" the Ainu in the North
and the Ryūkyū islands (Okinawa) in the South, regendering the
role of women as mothers of children now labeled "the next
citizens" and the role of men as soldiers of the empire. Not that
"Japan" was new, but that "it" was rearticulated and reified, made
to seem inevitable, a product of destiny as well as history. As in
France, regionalism and localism were subsumed in the national
project: everyone would be "Japanese," subjects of the emperor,
citizens of the nation. This nationalizing assertion also acted as a
wedge between Japan and Asia, as Meiji Japanese practiced reverse orientalism, wielding the same blunt instrument of
civilizational superiority against China and Korea that Western
commentators had wielded against Japan. From this arrogance of
national progress came the legitimating ideologies of empire. It
sometimes seems scarcely to matter where one looks: Almost everywhere in the nineteenth-century "grammar of modernity," the
nation-state was the main subject of the historical sentence.

The national modern had two elements, the nation and modernity, always joined at the rhetorical hip. Modernity embodied

Progress, the avatar of the "new Japan." But modernity was defined in terms of its obverse, the new inevitably juxtaposed against the old. So Meiji Japan, like Victorian Britain, early Republican China, and other modern-minded places, were simultaneously engaged in an almost wholesale "invention of tradition." Sometimes, as in the early Meiji condemnation of Confucianism or the Republican Chinese "invention of the peasant," tradition was portrayed as an obstacle to modernity.[8] At other times, as in the reinvention of the Japanese emperor or the mythologizing of the Scottish kilt, tradition served as a native reservoir of cultural strength for the modern transformation. Meiji inventions of tradition ran the gamut, including everything from bonsai and sumo wrestling to the "Japanese employment system" and the romanticized rural village. In fact, scratching the surface of many widely acknowledged "Japanese traditions" soon leads, if not to wholly Meiji origins, then to Meiji reconstructions of earlier practices consecrated as timeless tradition only after they appeared in the mirror of the modern.[9]

Think, for example, of the "traditional Japanese woman," whose role as "good wife, wise mother" made the home her domain and child-rearing her responsibility. This domesticated middle-class woman, whose private life served public (national) purposes, was a production of Meiji law, ideology, and social discourse. Not only had peasant women worked in Tokugawa times, but their work was integral to the household economy. And samurai women, who did indeed "serve their husband as their lord," were not charged with the primary responsibility for child-rearing. Traditional Japanese women, it turns out, were not so very traditional. It was less the assertion of women's subservience than the belief in the crucial importance of the family to the maintenance of the social order that impelled Meiji men (and women) to tie women to the home and make motherhood their sanctified social contribution. In comparative terms, this ideology of childrearing motherhood came rather late in the Japanese history of female gendering: it was, in fact, a product not of tradition but of modernity.[10]

In the wake of the dissolution of Tokugawa class and status differences, masculinity, too, was reinvented. New institutions like the schools, the military, and the village youth groups created an "imperial male," who, like the "good wife, wise mother," was assigned a dual public and private role: disciplined imperial subject for the nation and family patriarch in the home. Practices of daily life reflected these changes. Where once household members had taken their meals on individual trays at different times, now the ideal family of the newly described middle classes was to dine together at a single table—visually portrayed as the picture of Victorian propriety—and to share the day's experiences with one another, waiting however for Father to speak first.[11] In the gendering of empire, Japan assumed the masculine role. From the denigration of pigtailed Chinese soldiers during the Sino-Japanese War of 1894-95 to the image of a weak, feminized China rescued by manly, martial Japan in the wartime propaganda films of the late 1930s, an entirely modern "tradition" of civilizational superiority was fabricated in support of Japanese imperialism.

Who made modernity and invented all these traditions? The traditional answer is the modern state. But like other traditions this answer deserves skeptical examination. Because the Meiji state first pronounced the institutional outline of modernity and later took credit for its realization, modern Japanese history often appears to have been almost entirely directed "from above." Certainly in comparison to other places, the state was strong, the elite small and coherent, and the imperial symbol ideologically potent. Some historians in China have recently expressed a kind of distanced admiration for what Western scholars used to call "the pragmatic Meiji oligarchs," who so briskly went about the business of making a modern nation-state. That they did, but they did not themselves succeed in bringing it about. In many ways society was the real protagonist of change, or at least, it was a combination of state-and-social actors who wrestled their way through the unsettling shifts in historical terrain.

In 1872, for example, the Meiji government established a national education system — on paper, but virtually without national funding. In reality, the localities built and paid for the schools, and in many places families had to pay tuition for their children as well. In some villages the elite prided themselves on their Western-style clapboard schoolbuildings, already persuaded that education was "the key to success," as the original Education Act had declared. But in other places the villagers either built no schools or protested against those that were built. And as centralized as Japan's educational system later became, it continued to depend on the localities for financial and ideological support. It has been said that by 1905 Japanese primary schooling was on "an even par with England and Sweden and behind Prussia and France by only a few percentage points."[12] If so, then the credit goes less to the Ministry of Education than to the village leaders, country schoolteachers, and peasant parents who invested in education for their own reasons and complained to the government when their needs were not met. The same holds true for the technological transformations that undergirded the industrialization of Meiji Japan. Yes, the government fostered the adoption of advanced Western technology in modern industries, but often it was the innovative techniques developed by provincial entrepreneurs to meet the demands of the domestic market that brought significant economic gain. The state "top" and the local "bottom" were linked by what one scholar calls a "social network of innovation," which dispersed new ideas widely across society, responding to regional needs along the way.[13] These social networks had been operating long before the Restoration, another instance of older structures which operated in different ways in the new historical context.

In sum, the rule of inquiry in exploring agencies of change in modern Japan ought to be: Take not the government's word for itself, but seek the social sites of action and look to local loci of negotiation. For there one can trace the indirect and contentious process by which modernity happened. Of course this rule applies in other societies as well. Perhaps the main difference derives from the persistent habit of the Japanese state—from the Tokugawa shogunate of yore to the Finance Ministry mandarins of today—of pronouncing social order by announcing its control over social, economic, and political process. In fact, the pronouncement was almost always more absolute than the control, and the processes messier and more complicated than the government would have liked. Not that the state was not strong, for it most certainly was. But to understand how its strength was exerted—and contested—one has to look beyond the assertions of absolute top-down control and ask *how* something happened. Then, even big modern stories like the "development of capitalism" or "political centralization" have to be told very differently indeed. A recent study of the Hokkaidō herring fishery from 1672 to 1947 reveals in stunning detail the multi-structural and unpredictable course of economic change that produced what the author calls "indigenous capitalism" in the "periphery" of the Tokugawa state. Context and contingency then combined in a complicated interweaving of economic, social, and institutional changes to disrupt the earlier social equilibrium that had accompanied this economic formation, transforming it into a modern, "immiserating" capitalism that eventually doomed the fishery, not because it was brutal but because it was anachronistic.[14] The point is that neither the state nor the fishers strode "purposefully" toward capitalism, and the line of "development" was anything but straight.

National modernity tells itself as too simple a story. Becoming modern is a process, and the process was uneven and unsettling to live through. Rapid institutional change of the sort that took place after the Restoration was like a tectonic shift in the ground of social existence. Some people landed on their feet, while others took years to regain their footing, and some never did. By the beginning of the twentieth century, the social consequences of modernity had become as pressing an issue as the nation-state had been in the 1870s. Not that the nation lost its centrality, but that society now had a new inspiring and troubling saliency of its own.

MODERNITY AND THE SOCIAL (1900s-1940s)

Just as the history of nineteenth-century Japan often unfolds as a march to the modern, the twentieth-century story tends to roll inexorably down the road to war. Several authors in this volume mention the fact that Japan, "the first Asian country to modernize," was also the first Asian nation to practice modern Western-style imperialism on its Asian neighbors.

The history of that imperialism is usually said to have begun with the Sino-Japanese War of 1894-5. The war brought victory over China and Japan's new imperial spoils, Formosa (Taiwan), which remained a Japanese colony until 1945, and the Liaodong Peninsula in southern Manchuria, which France, Germany, and Russia forced Japan to cede, so they could later have their own go at carving that particular slice of the Chinese melon. For the next two decades Japan continued to participate in "the Great Game" of imperialism in Asia, acquiring its claim in Manchuria after the Russo-Japanese War of 1904-05, and annexing Korea in 1910. Ever responsive to the Western players who dominated the imperial game, Japan changed its tactics after the First World War, but never its target: hegemony over Korea, Manchuria, and ultimately, China entire. To escape the "China quagmire" of the unwinnable war it had begun in 1937 and to extend its empire in the South, Japan joined the Axis and launched a preemptive strike against the United States in 1941. Pearl Harbor, which had been intended to preserve Japanese power in Asia, led instead to defeat and the end of empire— not only Japan's but those of the West as well. Its pan-Asian propaganda notwithstanding, imperial Japan did not set out to end Western colonialism in French Indochina, the Dutch East Indies, and other parts of South and Southeast Asia. Decolonization in Asia was an unintended outcome of the Second World War, which emerged from a conjuncture of nationalist

movements, civil wars, Japanese wartime occupation, the fall of
Europe to Nazi armies, the postwar rise of self-denominated "anti-
imperialist" powers like the US and the Soviet Union, and other
interrelated but not causally connected factors. During the Chinese
civil war the Communists benefited from the experience the peasants had had in making common cause against the Japanese, another unintended (and for the Guomindang, unwelcome)
consequence of the "Anti-Japanese War of Resistance," as the Chinese call World War II. We are accustomed to treating these sometimes ironic consequences of war as contingent historical outcomes.
But when it comes to the rise of Hitler or the road to Pearl Harbor,
we too often revert to the straight-line of inevitability.

The history of Japanese imperialism, from the early Meiji debates over Korea in 1873 to unconditional surrender to the Allies
in 1945, needs to be unraveled from a tightly twisted skein into its
constituent threads. These threads included divisions in domestic
politics and shifts in international context that ranged from revolution in China and Russia to US demands for disarmament in
the 1920s and war in Europe after 1939. But they also included
economic difficulties, social destabilization, the fear of social unrest, and the intellectual "revolt against the West" in culture and
ideology. Each thread has its own history. The intellectual revolt
in the 1930s, for example, arose after long decades of mapping
modernity as East or West, with the West dominant in both power
and culture.[15] In the economy, the consequences of uneven development intensified hardship in the countryside as well as in the
"dual economy" of the industrial sector during the 1920s; the
structure of the financial system contributed to the 1927 Bank
Panic; the perpetual need to restore balance in international trade
and exchange rates drove the shifting deflationary policies that
buffeted Japan's economy throughout the 1920s and resulted in
the fatefully timed decision to return to the Gold Standard just as
the World Depression hit in 1930. Yet, these individual threads
notwithstanding, it was the simultaneous conjuncture of several
factors that usually proved decisive, not only for international
relations but for domestic developments as well.

Consider 1932, the year that Japan established the puppet
state of Manchukuo in the wake of the Manchurian Incident of
September, 1931. This act of imperialist aggression initiated the
so-called Fifteen Years War in China, which continued until
Japan's defeat in 1945. 1932 also saw the "end of Taishō democracy," evidenced by the demise of party cabinets and the rise of
the military to power, ushering in the period of "Japanese fas-

cism." The immediate trigger of the shift to "national unity" cabinets was the May 15th Incident, in which the prime minister fell victim to the latest in a series of assassinations of prominent leaders by assorted factions of the radical Right. The year 1932 also marked the depth of the Depression for most Japanese, with the shattered world economy affecting everything from capital outflows to the demand for silk stockings. The combination of economic collapse, social crisis, the threat of domestic insurgency—**and** the military urgency, patriotic fervor, and international condemnation brought on by "victory" in Manchuria— made "time of emergency" (*hijōji*) the slogan of the day. Brandished not only by the government and the army, but also by the newspapers and the newer mass media of radio and newsreels, the watchword of national crisis was soon so widespread that the joke became: "Question: What time is it? Answer: The time of emergency."

But it was, of course, no joke, and the serious historical question must be: how such a confluence of domestic and international factors, each with its own history, interacted to produce the fascism, militarism, and war that characterized the rest of the 1930s. Similar questions are frequently asked of 1933 in Germany and of other societies, including the United States, which were affected by the political challenge of economic distress, social unrest, and international instability. But the Japanese story, unlike the German, for example, often concentrates on the international domain, where the contexts and conjunctures are well outlined.[16] Far less attention is paid to the social history of the 20s and 30s, which offers equally important opportunities for comparison, especially when the framework is the international history of modernity.

In brief, one might argue that the temper of modernity changed in the period between the 1890s and the 1930s. In a country like Japan, which had flung itself headlong toward the national modern in the nineteenth century, the twentieth century brought social change to the forefront of concern. Call it the unintended consequences of industrialization, the social results of the Meiji "rich nation, strong army" policies, or "the underside of modern Japan"—whatever the label, it refers to a new focus on society that emerged after the Russo-Japanese War of 1904-05.[17] Often called a "watershed" by Japanese historians, the war made Japan a full-fledged imperialist power at the same time that it accelerated—as wars so often do—the forces of social change. From country to city, field to factory, ownership to tenancy, subsistence to poverty, samurai to salaryman—these transitions created what some regarded as "social problems" requiring state remediation and others considered social opportunities for reform or revolution. In Japan as elsewhere, the demands of society grew more insistent after the Russian Revolution and World War I. During the 1920s an array of critiques of modernity sought to redefine the modern in the realm of the social. Meanwhile, labor strikes, tenant unrest, and Leftist political parties reached new crescendos of protest, urban consumer culture heralded new forms of mass society, and the state and its attendant elites sought to establish new measures of social control.

Japan shared these dilemmas of modernity with other industrialized countries and shared, too, with much of the world the international influences of socialism, communism, Wilsonianism, republicanism, democracy, and a nationalism reinvigorated by a combination of all these forces. The 1920s marked a historical moment which, like the nineteenth-century version of the nation-state, left a distinctive imprint on both the definition and experience of modernity. Struggles for political democracy, social reform, and economic stability intertwined in different forms around the world. Here again it is probably better to avoid fully frontal comparisons of the Weimar Republic and Taishō democracy, constitutionalism in Republican China and Taishō Japan, or economic "rationalization" in interwar Germany, the United States, and Japan. But it is important to recognize that these represent the contextual fact that many societies were struggling with similar problems: in particular, forms of mass society, popular political participation, and the social concomitants of economic inequities in the context of industrial capitalism. Not the beribboned monarch in regal uniform but the peasant in arrears and the worker with his wrench now symbolized the issues of "Modern Times."

The call for reform or reconstruction (*kaizō*) resounded from Left to Right in Japan after World War I. Although the history of the socialist and communist movements is usually recounted separately from that of the rise of the radical Right, it makes conjunctural sense to see them both as different responses to the same socio-economic dilemmas. Kita Ikki, the so-called ideological father of Japanese fascism, wrote his famous "Plan for the Reconstruction (*kaizō*) of Japan" in 1919, the same year that the left-liberal journal *Kaizō* was founded, and the "New Man Society" began its activities on behalf of "rational reform." Communists called for revolution; the Right called for a reprise of the Meiji Renovation (*ishin*); and the liberal Yoshino Sakuzō called for democracy in the form of *minponshugi* (people-as-the-base-ism). In the wake of the Rice Riots of 1918, social movements protested on behalf of the rights of workers, tenant-farmers, women, and outcaste groups, while suffrage groups organized to expand the right to vote.

The ferment of class and mass issues produced no single blueprint for social justice, and injustice reached new extremes as well. Two months before the May 4th Movement in China (also in 1919), the Japanese colonial regime roughly suppressed the March 1 Korean uprising for national independence. Four years later, after the Tokyo Earthquake of 1923, the government helped to foment the rumors that led to the massacre of Koreans in the capital, bringing home the social byproducts of imperialism in a particularly brutal way. Shaken by the prospect of social disorder, ranging from moderate reform to violent revolution, the elites—and the middle classes—in Japan and elsewhere responded to the threat by seeking stability. Japanese historians often express this contest between reform and repression by citing the simultaneous achievement of universal manhood suffrage and the enactment of the Peace Preservation Law in 1925, the first a victory for parliamentary democracy, the second an advance in the state apparatus of social control. In Japan the social roiling of the 1920s took place in an economy already troubled by deflation and recession. When the Great Depression occurred, the specter of unrest only increased and with it, the search for stability. In such an atmosphere, the Manchurian Incident of 1931 became a welcome opportunity for whole-nation patriotism. Even without applying the German concept of "social imperialism" to Japan, one cannot tell the story of Japan's Asian empire without reference to the social turns taken by modernity in the early decades of the twentieth century.

Urban mass society and consumer culture of the interwar years offer another set of examples of comparative modernity in twentieth-century transition. For purposes of illustration, here are three of many: First, Americanization perceived in Europe and Japan as both the boon and bane of modern times; second, the *moga* (short for *modan gaaru*, or modern girl), who like her counterpart, the New Woman in Europe, represented a socially subversive regendering of modernity; and third, the search for authenticity in a lost world of the Folk, high culture, or the past, in each case presented as a cultural critique of modern mass society.

The phenomenon identified as "Americanization" in Europe and Japan appeared in at least two concentrated historical phases, the first in the 1920s and the second in the period after World War II. The influence of the United States took diverse forms in the 1920s, including Fordism and Taylorism in industry, flappers, jazz, and Hollywood movies in popular culture, and the rationalization of household management and creation of a new women's culture. Many in the urban middle classes welcomed American influence as speedy and efficient, others as empowering and emancipatory. But in the face of their enthusiasm for American ways, most of the public talk focused instead on the negative impact of a culture its critics regarded as superficial, materialistic, and a threat to national values and the social order alike. At the end of the decade social critics in Tokyo named the threat *Amerikanizumu* and despaired of the future unless the youth (always the youth) returned to Japanese ways. But the mass production, the cult of speed, and the urge to consume that they identified as "Americanism" belonged to the very infrastructure of twentieth-century capitalism. And what so agitated Japanese, German, and other critics of American "soullessness" in the interwar years was the direction of modernity itself.

Like "Americanism" the *moga* also stood for the modern. The "modern girl," with her bobbed hair, short skirts, and open sexuality, appeared to her critics as a threat to the "traditional" Japanese woman, the "good wife, wise mother" promoted since the late 1890s. But the *moga* was not the first threat. Her predecessor was the "New Woman" (*atarashii onna*) of the 1910s, who like her Italian sister, the *donna nova*, was primarily elite, educated, and feminist—a bluestocking rather than a flapper. After the 1923 earthquake destroyed Tokyo, reconstruction brought a frenzy of new urban culture in its wake. The *moga* began to appear in the mass media, which themselves constituted another element common to emerging mass societies of the time. In some ways the media created the image of the *moga*, or at least exaggerated it, overdrawing the menace posed to society by this independent-minded modern woman striding the streets of Tokyo.[18]

In the politics of gender, women (like youth) are often made to bear the symbolic weight of social change. In some cases, as in Weimar Germany or the New Life Movement of Guomindang China, women were charged with transformative tasks in the rationalization of housework or the production of a "modern" family, although usually the conventional gender roles remained unchanged. In other cases, as in the criticism of the Japanese *moga* (and the Weimar "new woman"), their progressive ways were read by both men and many women as transgressions, which indeed they were often meant to be. Then the transgressions were re-read as a challenge to all things good, stable—and Japanese. But no matter the constructions and derisions of their critics, the militant modern girls, the "new working women" who became telephone operators and shopclerks, and the cafe waitresses of working-class Tokyo all represented women making their way through the changing social landscapes of modernity. That the terrain was confusing, and the roles fluid, showed in the sexual ambivalence embodied by the "male actors" in the all-female Takarazuka revue, the sharing of clothes and cosmetics between the *moga* and the *mobo* (the modern boy), and other inventive expressions of androgyny, including "the housewife with a mustache" of popular song. Like Paris or Berlin, interwar Tokyo developed a gender-bending culture that seemed to both its advocates and its critics to be none else but the mark of what they called *modan* (modern).[19]

A few intellectuals, like one self-proclaimed "modernologist," celebrated such contemporary "customs," but most social commentators joined the state in condemning them as heralding the demise of culture. Interwar Japan had its share of what one historian of Germany termed "reactionary modernists," and it also had critics who turned away from the modern in search of what they felt was a lost authenticity. Ethnographers, like their German counterparts, sought the authentic Folk in the rural customs of indigenous Japan. Others turned to the cultural past, to revel in old Tokugawa times, before the onslaught of Western-style civilization. In the 1930s literary romantics joined the call for a "return to Japan," developing a Japanese version of the ethnic nationalism that was becoming endemic around the world, a nationalism that resonated in their slogan of the early 1940s: "overcoming modernity."[20] But however much cultural nationalists inveighed against the West, they were themselves heir to the hybrid of East/West modernity that they condemned. And well they knew it. Indeed, they had more in common with their fellow critics of the modern (however defined) in other countries during the turbulent interwar years than they had with their Meiji forebears, whose embrace of civilization had seemed so untroubled by comparison.

Without engaging commonalities such as these, fascism (however defined) remains unfathomable. A German historian once described Nazism as "modernity's most fatal developmental possibility." Something similar might be said of Japan of the 1930s, when a conjuncture of social and economic dislocation in a context of a disintegrating political process and narrowing international horizons made excesses of aggression abroad and suppression at home seem, madly, the course to normalcy. But commonalities are only part of the story, and for Japan, the resort to authoritarianism requires its own further explanation. No Nazi party was voted to power, no masses cheered a fascist dictator, no terror silenced untold numbers by death. Thus the largest historical question to be asked of wartime Japan remains: why did the people support the state? Japanese historians have answered, essentially, that they had little choice, so powerful was the apparatus and ideology of the imperial state. One famous interpretation speaks of "fascism from above" and "a system of irresponsibility," in which no single person or office was ultimately accountable.[21]

But once the social history of the 1930s is written (surprisingly little has as yet been done), then we may better understand the process by which many different kinds of people—from above, from below, and from the side—participated in what one historian has called "total empire," the analogue of total war from which few were exempt.[22] As in the modernizing processes of Meiji, society will likely be seen to have contributed its own agencies and energies to the enterprise of empire and war, and probably for its own reasons, different ones for different people. The strong state left this legacy, too: its people so much believed in its strength that they felt powerless and, even in retrospect, did not question the mechanisms and motives of their own actions. The legacy of war also played a part. For when it was over and the nation, and much of Asia, lay in ashes, most Japanese wanted to turn away from war, away from the past, and away from what they perceived, almost immediately, as a failure of the modern.

LATE MODERNITY (1940s-1980s)

August 15, 1945, the day the emperor announced surrender and defeat, marked the end of the war in Japan. It also signaled the beginning of "the postwar" (*sengo*), a name for contemporary Japan still in use in the 1990s. Japanese commemorations of the war in 1995 bore the title "Fiftieth Anniversary of the Postwar," suggesting that the beginning of the present mattered as much as the end of the past. In Japanese history and memory, 1945 broke the twentieth century in two, severing the failure of modernity, which had culminated in catastrophic war, from the "new beginning" of postwar peace and prosperity, which redeemed the modern by redoing it. This story, so often repeated through the postwar decades, took shape immediately after the war. The war, judged unjust in itself, was also seen as a judgment on history: Japan's modernity had gone awry and had now to be set right, which was the task of the postwar reforms. Peace and democracy, the twin slogans of the Occupation, became the goals of the "new Japan."[23]

Like the Renovation that followed the Meiji Restoration, the reforms that followed the defeat would set the new apart from the old, or so it was widely felt. And like 1868, 1945 was enshrined in memory as an epochal moment. The mythistory of "becoming modern" now read: Modernity in the form of nineteenth-century civilization began with Meiji; modernity "reborn" in the form of mid-twentieth-century democracy began with "the postwar." And so the historian faces the same challenges in approaching both centuries: First, the challenge of connecting in continuous historical process what mythic memory has sundered. This means recognizing the tectonic changes that occurred during the Occupation while acknowledging the structures of continuity that affected the course of reform. Second, the challenge of resisting the official or "Japan, Inc." view that the old instantly rearranged itself according to the pronouncements of the new. This means tracing the evolution of the "postwar system" from the 1940s to the 1970s (or perhaps later) in order to see how the interactions between society and the state produced the linked social, economic, and political arrangements that Japanese came to know, and support, as "the postwar."

First, the continuities: In its stress on the chasm of 1945, Japan is in considerable comparative company. Many countries took the end of the war as a charge to embark on a new course. Germans called it "zero hour"; leaders all over Europe set their sights on "renewal"; Indonesia declared its independence from the Dutch on August 17, even before the Japanese troops left the islands; and other Asian nationalists planned for the final anti-colonial fight. Even the United States, whose "American Century" had been declared in 1941, felt the full meaning of its power, atomic and economic, only in 1945. The impact of World War II, while variable in different contexts, was profound enough a conjuncture that many national histories contain chapters that begin with 1945. Among historians of Europe the work of escaping these conventional chronologies began some years ago, when they noted the continuities across Europe's "two civil wars," as the two World Wars are sometimes called. Examining the two postwar eras, they traced evolving patterns from the 1920s to the 1950s, notably the growing interpenetration of state and economy, of public and private sectors, which came to characterize so many regimes (not excluding the United States).

Similarly, recent scholarship—and common sense—suggests that we at first consider "transwar Japan," from the 1930s through the 1950s, and then also what Hobsbawm has called the "short twentieth century," from World War I to the end of the Cold War (for Japan, 1919-1989). Scholars of Japan have now begun to trace transwar links, both long and short. One pioneering study tracked the Ministry of Trade and Industry (MITI), so often credited with directing Japan's postwar growth, between 1925 and 1975.[24] Others pointed to the more proximate legacies of war, including the structures of a command economy put in place during total mobilization in the late 30s, the continuity of bureaucratic personnel, and other prewar aspects that survived 1945 to affect the course of postwar history.[25] A 1995 Japanese work, "The 1940s System," made a similar—and still controversial—point about transwar continuities in political economy.

Some of these scholars were seeking to counter the "economic miracle" story that had long attracted attention. Indeed, the allegedly linear path to economic power in postwar Japan is like the straight-line road to war in imperial Japan: it drives out historical complexity and loses both context and conjuncture. Like Germany's "economic miracle," Japan's economic growth, while impressive, was by no means miraculous. Nor, I think, was the nature of its democracy, its long-term political stability, or its enduring pacifism. Each had its multiple determinants, which need to be both traced back in time and set in their common context. Since modernity is the theme here, let me (over)simplify in the following comparative way.

The immediate postwar period constituted another conjunctural moment in the history of modernity. For some countries, the experience of totalitarianism and total war seemed to have violated the premise and the promise of modern civilization. Like postwar Japan, they sought a better modern. For others, including the United States, victory in a just war had vindicated the value of their particular modernity. But the war had also changed its definition, raising the level of expectations of prosperity and security to new heights. Polar ideologies of democracy—one parliamentary liberal, the other state socialist (both, in the crucible of war, declared anti-fascist)—set out to modernize their parts of the postwar world in their own image. The Cold War between the United States and the Soviet Union involved a clash, not only of military might, but of modes of modernity as well. Interestingly, very few people suggested that it was time to abandon the idea and ideals of modernity and move beyond a modern that had brought such extremes of death and destruction. On the contrary, the goal in most places was either to "renew" the modern or, in many parts of the Third World, to achieve it on their own terms. For that reason I think of the period after World War II as a time of "late modernity," when conceptions of modern society were recast in mid-twentieth-century forms.

The conjuncture of late modernity suggests that Japan's postwar ambience, which is usually considered in Japanese-American terms, also had much in common with that of Europe. This commonality derived, in part, from shared aspects in Japan's earlier modern formations, both the national modern of the late nineteenth century and the social modern of the interwar period. By 1945 elements of Euro-modernity had become integral to the Japanese context. One historian of Western Europe has described the immediate postwar hopes for radical change, the calls for a renewal of democracy, the resurgence of the political Left, the remarkable "supremacy of economics," indeed of "growthmanship," which made prosperity the sign of stability at home and the instrument against Soviet expansion abroad. Now the modern state was expected to provide to the masses "full employment, stability, more production and consumption." Add "rising standards of living" and you have the American postwar program as well.[26] What had been fought for in the 1920s and in some places institutionalized in response to the Depression in the 1930s became normalized in postwar rhetoric as a kind of "standard-of-living modern."

Continuities though there were, let it not be mistaken: the changes in postwar Japan were momentous. As a result of the war and the "postwar reforms," as they are called in Japanese, society changed shape and direction. If the Meiji Renovation was a "refolution," the postwar program was probably a "revorm." To use the banner words, the leap seemed greater from "feudalism to capitalism" in the nineteenth century than from fascism and imperialism to democracy and peace after the war. This may seem odd, and in some ways it was. The alacrity with which so many Japanese turned away from empire and the imperial state is perhaps more puzzling than the rapidity of economic growth reflected in the postwar rise in GNP. Yet, seen from the vantage point of 1945, it is also understandable. Sick of war, most people on the homefront welcomed August 15 as a release and soon thereafter greeted General MacArthur's occupying forces as an "army of liberation." While the aftermath of war provided the context for change, the Occupation of Japan by the United States (with Douglas MacArthur as its Supreme Commander) was the significant contingency that determined the direction those changes would take.[27] Had Japan been partitioned into Allied zones, as Germany was, its postwar history would have been very different. Had the Soviets and the Americans divided Japan in the way they did Korea—the division itself a geopolitical legacy of Japanese colonial control—the history of postwar Asia would also have taken a different course.

Instead, the United States dominated the Allied Occupation of Japan from its beginning in August 1945 to its end in May 1952. If one compares other U.S. occupied areas, whether Germany, Austria, Korea, or Okinawa, it soon becomes clear that the Americans treated Japan as a special case. This was partly due to U.S. wartime planning, partly to Cold War concerns, and partly to the visionary eccentricities of General MacArthur. The presurrender planning to "remake" Japan into a peaceable democracy appeared benign indeed, compared to the Morgenthau Plan's proposal to strip Germany of its industrial capacity. Because the United States always considered Germany the more important enemy, the Roosevelt administration paid less attention to the Japan planning, with the ironic result that the Americans arrived in Tokyo with an ambitious blueprint for domestic reform. Some of the more idiosyncratic policies—from removing the emperor from the list of war criminals to inserting the "no-war clause" into the Constitution and proposing the free distribution of Bibles—owed much to the General himself. But the dramatic reforms of 1945-47 in fact depended on an almost alchemical collaboration between occupiers and occupied. American and Japanese voices chimed in on behalf of fundamental reform, and those Japanese who would have liked to sing a different song had little choice but to silently mouth the same words as everyone else.

The reforms touched everything from the Constitution, which the Americans wrote, to religion, education, the family, and the rights of women. Because he insisted that women be given the vote, General MacArthur was described as the Elizabeth Cady Stanton of Japan. If women's suffrage was an American idea, the land reform, often cited as one of the most successful—because enduring—reforms of the Occupation, followed proposals drawn up by the Japanese bureaucracy before the war. Yet, without the nearly absolute authority wielded by the Occupation the landlords would likely have resisted far more strenuously than they did.

Again, it was a conjuncture of factors that explains the outcome. Japan thus experienced more than the widespread "coca-colonization" that accompanied the postwar wave of Americanization around the world. The remodeling of Japanese modernity along American lines did indeed reshape institutions from the emperor-system to the school system, from parliamentary politics to property rights, from mythology to the military. But the result, as in Meiji, was a hybrid of new reforms and old practices, which soon came to appear less American than Japanese.

On the important matter of international relations, the postwar American embrace—sometimes warm, sometimes patronizing, always dominant—essentially relieved Japan of geopolitical responsibilities. Asia receded sharply and starkly from both the rhetoric and reality of Japanese foreign relations. The experience of war and atomic bombings made peace a persuasive cause, sincerely supported by the majority of Japanese over the postwar decades. Once incorporated in the U.S. Cold War framework, Japan's first task had been economic recovery, sparked finally not by Occupation policies but by the Korean War, and then, economic stability, which accompanied the dramatic growth of the 1960s. This growth took place in a largely favorable environment: the global economy was expanding, the yen was artificially stabilized, and protective and protectionist policies from the early postwar years remained in place. The manufacturing sector provided the exports, which in turn furnished capital inflows. Not only was the growth no miracle, but it flourished because of a conjuncture of domestic productivity and international receptivity, which was itself a product of postwar times.

The conventional chronology of postwar Japanese history reflected these changes in context. Like many Japanese periodizations, the postwar was divided into three parts: 1945-55, Recovery and Reconstruction (in effect, the **real** postwar era, comparable to the same period in other countries); 1955-73, the "Era of High Growth," when the economy expanded and standards of living rose; and 1973-?, the "Post-high-growth" Period, after the dollar and oil "shocks" hit Japan and the social costs of GNP-ism, from pollution to quality of life, became public issues. Since the third period was defined by what had ended—high growth—rather than what had begun, it revealed more about the prominence of the economic story in postwar consciousness than it did about the years that followed the shocks of the early seventies. Indeed, the re-rise to affluence and economic power during the 1980s suggests that "post-high-growth" was relative. But because this lengthy and eventful period still carried the postwar label, I call it "the long postwar." Certainly Japan retained this term for decades after it was abandoned in Europe, generally during the 1950s. The *real* postwar then might better be used to refer to the first decade after the war, or at most, 1945-65, when late modernity placed its stamp on the direction of change in Japan as it did in other places.

In this sense, Japanese democracy, too, bore a postwar imprint. Defined in social rather than in electoral terms, democracy came to mean equal access to material and social goods. Relieved to be released from the state at the end of the war, people soon enshrined private life at the center of social value and measured their postwar progress in terms of *seikatsu*, a word that means both livelihood and life-style. During the 1960s, prosperity joined peace and democracy to comprise the national image of what the long postwar was really about: the Japanese version of the standard-of-living modern. The so-called "55 system"—referring to one-party rule by the conservative Liberal Democratic Party from 1955 to 1993—remained in place so long largely because it seemed to preserve this middle-class status quo. In comparative terms, the "supremacy of economics" seemed more pronounced in Japan than elsewhere, at least in its displacement of electoral politics as a focus of popular interest. But, as before, politics as a form of oppositional social action flourished, from the citizens protests on environmental and nuclear issues to "contests for the workplace" and individual crusades on behalf of freedom of religion and honest history in the schools.[28] Opposition came from the Right as well, usually in the form of ideological nationalism but sometimes also in violence. But the evidence of democracy, socially defined, seemed to many Japanese to reside in the stability they had become accustomed to since the end of the war.

In some ways postwar Japan did indeed "complete the modern," at least according to its own self-definition. The massive transition of population from rural to urban occurred after the war, as did the shift from agriculture, which employed half the people in 1945 but only about 4 percent by 1990. Not only did cities, and especially megalopolitan Tokyo, grow, but the countryside was "metropolitanized," redefining its rurality as regional and its lifestyle as "middle-class."[29] Although most scholars remain skeptical of the myth of the "98 percent" of the Japanese who identified themselves as middle class, it is nonetheless true that postwar society had a larger middle than ever before, despite the many who lived below the social midpoint. Comparatively, it makes sense to think of the Japanese middle classes in the context of the middle classes of Western Europe, North America, and more recently, of Korea, Taiwan, and parts of Southeast Asia. In various national contexts the middle classes undergirded the stability, political economy, social welfare policies, and economic productivity of the postwar decades. As the typical social formation of late modernity in the capitalist economies, the middle classes, too, were a product of the particular postwar conjuncture. In many places, including Japan, the origins of the middle class lay well in the past but its "massification" did not occur until the second half of the twentieth century.

The nature—and the tensions—of this transformation appeared in each of the three social sites of daily life: home, work, and school. Often evoked as separate spheres, the social schematic depicted women in the home as mothers and caretakers of children and the elderly, men in the firm as samurai salarymen marching for the GNP, and children cramming their way toward the entrance exams that would determine their fate in an "education-credentialist society." But this separation of roles was not as neat and tidy as it sounds.

The demands on women, for example, had changed across the century. In the context of wartime mobilization in the late 1930s, being a "good wife" had become ideologically less important than being a "wise mother"—or rather, just being a mother, since the state's pronatalist policy encouraged women to "give birth and multiply." And imperial Japan had proved even more reluctant to move women into the wartime labor force than Nazi Germany, which possessed a similar "mothers-in-the-fatherland" mindset. In the postwar period, legal reform liberated women in such matters as property rights and the constitutional freedom to choose their husbands. At the same time government policies and middle-class values "produced motherhood" by tying women to the home as housewives and "education mamas" (whose overzealous exemplars were called "mama Godzillas," so relentless was their oversight of their children's study habits).[30]

But the historical fact is that Japanese women had always worked, the ideology of "good wives, wise mothers" notwithstanding. Full-time housewives did not appear in significant numbers until the 1960s, and many of them had become part-time workers again by the 1980s. Whether they were unmarried, like the BGs (business girls) of the fifties and the OLs (office ladies) of the eighties, or they were housewives returning to part-time work after raising their children, they did so for the same reason that women had always worked: to increase the family income. But because they faced continued discrimination in the workplace, they had jobs, not careers, positions but not status. And while the Equal Employment Opportunity Act of 1985 recognized the problem, it did not lead to a solution, since part-timers remained outside the benefits of the so-called lifetime employment system. Although legal measures, feminist activism, expanded education, and labor shortages combined to exert pressure on the system, change for women in the workplace came slowly and with mostly modest success. For Japanese women, and for women in many postwar societies, late modernity brought "revorm" but no "refolution" in economic and social equity. Indeed, by the 1980s the original promise of the postwar late modern—and the middle classes that supported it—was everywhere under economic, social, and political strain.

POSTMODERN TIMES? (1980s-90s)

Since the mid-nineteenth century Japanese had spoken of modernity as something to achieve, something "out there" with which Japan would "catch up." By the 1980s the standard phrase had changed: Japan, it was said, had now "caught up and overtaken" the models of modernity it had so long pursued. The expression usually meant "Western" models, the old East/West dichotomy now evoked in Japan's favor. As an economic superpower and a peaceful democracy, the nation could pride itself on its postwar accomplishments. Such was the official view, the refrain of cultural nationalists, and the slogan of the popular media. In matters of culture, the word *posuto-modan* became the cliche of the day: Japan was presented as the epitome of postmodernity. But not everyone agreed that all was well in postmodernland, and widening cracks of criticism appeared in the supposedly solid middle class. The nation was rich, but the people were poor, it was said, poor in housing, leisure time, and quality of life. Politicians responded to this plaint of "rich Japan, poor Japanese" with rhetoric such as the slogan of becoming a "lifestyle superpower." Meanwhile the world was also changing and with it, the world's demands on Japan, to which the rhetorical response since the mid-80s was the oft-repeated call for "internationalization."

In 1989, in an entirely accidental coincidence, the Shōwa emperor, Hirohito, died, and the Berlin Wall fell, both in the same year. The death of the emperor, who had came to the throne in 1926, meant the end in Japan of the long era that had included the war, the transwar, and the postwar as well. And the close of the Cold War in the West meant the end of the global geopolitical system that had provided Japan international shelter within the American imperium. Two years later the economic "bubble" burst, and Japan went into a lengthy recession. Another two years passed, and the Liberal Democratic Party "fell," much the way the Shogunate had collapsed so many years ago, without a revolution. Six prime ministers held office between 1989 and 1996, an orderly turnover that was nonetheless routinely described as political "chaos." Japanese society was aging rapidly, its elderly increasing, and its birthrate dropping. The "1.57 shock" of 1990 brought fertility well below the level required for demographic replacement. Even more shocking to some was the increasing number of younger urban women who were refusing to marry or choosing not to bear children. The Gulf War of 1991 administered an international shock to Japan's Constitution, raising the post-Cold-War question of sending uniformed troops to participate in peacekeeping operations abroad and challenging the customary practices of postwar pacifism. And the nations of Asia, now increasingly important to Japan's economic and geopolitical relations, made ever more insistent demands on the Japanese to acknowledge and apologize for their earlier acts of colonialism and wartime aggression.

After so long a period of structural "unchange," these events were perceived by many as earthshaking shifts in the historical terrain. Indeed, when the Kobe earthquake and the Tokyo subway gassing occurred within months of one another in 1995, the ground of social order seemed atremble, and people talked of the year of "unease." In the media the term *posuto-modan* had been replaced by "end-of-the-century" in order to evoke the ambience of momentous change. To many outside observers, of course, Japan of the 1990s seemed remarkably stable, even slow in the pace of its domestic change. But whether the change came fast or slow, Japan was in fact experiencing challenges similar to those confronted by many other societies. The years following 1989 will one day be viewed, no doubt, as another historical conjuncture of global import, not simply because the Cold War ended, but because so many other things were happening at the same time. The young women in Tokyo who chose not to marry, the rapid rise of the Asian economies, the distributive dilemmas in late capitalist societies — these and other aspects of the conjuncture each had a history of its own. But taken together, they seemed to signify that a different age had indeed arrived. New periodizations would be necessary. In Japan, perhaps the long postwar was finally over. Certainly something beyond the label "post-"high-growth would be needed to situate Japanese history of the 1990s.

Japan was not alone in resorting to the prefix "post-" to describe its situation, whether post-cold war, post-postwar, post-colonial, or postmodern. From the vantage point of the mid-nineties, the past in many places appeared in far clearer guise than did the future. And the largest historical question, not only in Japan but around the world, was whether the conjuncture of the 1990s heralded the "end" of modernity, or yet another phase in the complexity of its unfolding.

NOTES

1. In *Capital,* vol. 1 (New York, Vintage Books, 1977) p. 878n. See Joshua Fogel, "The Debate over the Asiatic Mode of Production in Soviet Russia, China, and Japan," *American Historical Review* 93, no. 1 (February, 1988), p.77.

2. E.J. Hobsbawm, *Nations and Nationalism Since 1780: Programme, Myth, Reality* (Cambridge: Cambridge University Press, 1990), p. 151.

3. ŌKUMA Shigenobu, comp., *Fifty Years of New Japan,* 2 vols. (London: Smith, Elder, 1909)

4. See Bernard Bailyn, *The Ideological Origins of the American Revolution* (Cambridge: Harvard University Press, 1967).

5. Harry D. Harootunian, "Ideology as Conflict," in Tetsuo NAJITA and J. Victor Koschmann, eds., *Conflict in Modern Japanese History: The Neglected Tradition* (Princeton: Princeton University Press, 1993), p. 61.

6. Marius B. Jansen, *SAKAMOTO Ryōma and the Meiji Restoration* (1961), (New York: Columbia University Press, 1994), pp. 294-296. Also, Harry D. Harootunian, *Toward Restoration* (Berkeley:University of California Press, 1991).

7. Timothy Garton Ash, referring to Poland and Hungary, in "Refolution: The Springtime of Two Nations," *London Review of Books,* September 17, 1987.

8. See Myron Cohen, "Cultural and Political Inventions in Modern China: The Case of the Chinese 'Peasant'," in TU Wei-ming, ed., *China in Transformation* (Cambridge: Harvard University Press, 1994), pp. 151-170.

9. See Stephen Vlastos, ed., *Mirror of Modernity: Invented Traditions in Modern Japan* (Berkeley: University of California Press, 1998)

10. See Gail Lee Bernstein, *Recreating Japanese Women, 1600-1945* (Berkeley: University of California Press, 1991).

11. Jordan Sand, *House and Home in Modern Japan,* forthcoming.

12. Byron K. Marshall, *Learning to Be Modern: Japanese Political Discourse on Education* (Boulder: Westview Press, 1994), p. 88.

13. Tessa Morris-Suzuki, *The Technological Transformation of Japan:*

From the Seventeenth to the Twenty-first Century (Cambridge: Cambridge University Press, 1994), pp. 71-104.

14. David L. Howell, *Capitalism from Within: Economy, Society, and the State in a Japanese Fishery* (Berkeley: University of California Press, 1995); see my review, "Give Us Herring or Give Us Death," *Times Literary Supplement* (January 26, 1996). For another contribution on the question of centralization, see Kären Wigen, *The Making of a Japanese Periphery, 1750-1920* (Berkeley: University of California Press, 1995).

15. Tetsuo NAJITA and Harry D. Harootunian, "Japanese Revolt against the West: Political and Cultural Criticism in the Twentieth Century," *The Cambridge History of Japan*, vol. 6, *The Twentieth Century*, ed., Peter Duus (Cambridge: Cambridge University Press, 1988), pp. 711-774.

16. For summaries, see Akira IRIYE, *The Origins of the Second World War in Asia and the Pacific* (New York: Longman, 1987) and Michael A. Barnhart, *Japan and the World since 1868* (London: Edward Arnold, 1995), distributed by St. Martin's Press, New York.

17. Mikiso HANE, *Peasants, Rebels, and Outcastes: The Underside of Modern Japan* (New York: Pantheon Books, 1982).

18. Miriam Silverberg, "The Modern Girl as Militant," in Gail Bernstein, ed., *Recreating Japanese Women, 1600-1945* (Berkeley: University of California Press, 1991), pp. 239-66; Barbara Hamill Satō, "The Moga Sensation: Perceptions of the Modan Gaaru in Japanese Intellectual Circles During the 1920s," *Gender & History* 5, no. 3 (Sept. 1993) 363-381.

19. Donald Roden, "Taishō Culture and the Problem of Gender Ambivalence," in J. Thomas Rimer, ed., *Culture and Identity: Japanese Intellectuals during the Interwar Years* (Princeton: Princeton University Press, 1990), pp. 37-55; Jennifer Robertson, "The Politics of Androgyny in Japan: Sexuality in the Theater and Beyond," *American Ethnologist* 19, no. 3 (August 1992): 419-442.

20. Kevin Michael Doak, *Dreams of Difference: The Japan Romantic School and the Crisis of Modernity* (Berkeley: University of California Press, 1994), prologue.

21. Masao MARUYAMA, *Thought and Behavior in Modern Japanese Politics* (Oxford:Oxford University Press, 1963).

22. Louise Young, *Japan's Total Empire: Manchuria and the Culture of Wartime Imperialism* (Berkeley: University of California Press, 1997).

23. Carol Gluck, "The Past in the Present," in Andrew Gordon, ed., *Postwar Japan as History* (Berkeley: University of California Press, 1993), pp. 64-95.

24. Chalmers Johnson, *MITI and the Japanese Miracle: The Growth of Industrial Policy, 1925-1975* (Stanford: Stanford University Press, 1982).

25. John Dower, "The Useful War" in Carol Gluck and Stephen Graubard, eds., *Showa: The Japan of Hirohito* (New York: W.W.Norton, 1992), pp. 49-70.

26. David W. Ellwood, *Rebuilding Europe: Western Europe, America and Postwar Reconstruction* (New York: Longman, 1992), pp. 1-28.

27. For U.S.-Japan relations, see my essay in this volume, "Japan and America: A Tale of Two Civilizations."

28. Andrew Gordon, "Contests for the Workplace," in *Postwar Japan as History* (Berkeley: University of California Press, 1993), pp. 373-94;

Norma Field, *In the Realm of a Dying Emperor: A Portrait of Japan at Century's End* (New York: Pantheon, 1991).

29. William W. Kelly, "Finding a Place in Metropolitan Japan: Ideologies, Institutions, and Everyday Life," in Gordon, ed., *Postwar Japan as History*, 189-238.

30. Anne Allison, "Producing Motherhood," in Anne E. Imamura, ed., *Re-imaging Japanese Women* (Berkeley: University of California Press, 1996), pp. 135-55.

MODERN CHINA, 1840–1990

Madeleine Zelin

BACKGROUND

China's political and social development from the mid-nineteenth century to the present day may best be studied in terms of China's "long modernization."[1] This approach allows a focus on the working out of large problems that have analogies in most cultures. It eschews a definition of the political moment that divides the traditional and the modern, and in doing so, avoids the tendency to define China's experience during the past 150 years in terms of impact of and response to the West.

China's path toward the modern began with the technological and commercial revolution of the Song Dynasty (960–1279). During the late imperial period of the Ming and Qing dynasties (fourteenth to nineteenth centuries) it combined territorial expansion, perfection of the bureaucratic institutions of the universal empire, absorption of non-Chinese ethnic groups, and growth of the commercial economy. By the end of the eighteenth century, Chinese authority had been extended to Taiwan, Tibet, and Xinjiang, as well as the territories now known as Manchuria and Inner Mongolia. China's internal frontier was also pushed to its limits as ethnic Chinese settlers moved to hilly and mountainous areas hitherto populated largely by non-Han peoples. Although government-sponsored maritime expeditions ceased in the fifteenth century, private Chinese merchants continued a flourishing trade with Southeast Asia and, through the Portuguese, with Japan. As early as the mid-sixteenth century, trade with the West brought a massive influx of New World silver into the Chinese economy, through private trade at Manila and later through trade at Chinese ports such as Xiamen (Amoy) and Guangzhou (Canton).

The political philosophy of the Manchu rulers who governed China during the Qing Dynasty (1644–1912) combined traditional Confucian notions of the king as sage with a relatively activist approach to the state-society relationship. While never as directly involved in the economy as their Song predecessors, the Qing took as their mission the Confucian imperative to promote the people's welfare and enable their moral transformation. Toward this end the state actively stabilized grain prices, provided famine relief, and encouraged the development of the market economy. Fiscal reform during the reign of the Yongzheng emperor (1723–35) helped address the chronic problem of local government revenue shortages in the late imperial period and enhanced the ability of local government to fund road, bridge, and ferry projects, and assist in land reclamation and flood control.

By the nineteenth century, the Qing state faced a number of domestic problems which, when combined with imperialism, precipitated China's long modernization. Cultural factors, prolonged peace, benevolent tax policies, and a growing commercial economy contributed to the expansion of the Chinese population from about 100 million in the seventeenth century to approximately 430 million in 1850. Pressure on the land meant diminishing farm size, underemployment of rural dwellers, and increasing reliance on income from cash crops and agricultural sidelines, especially in south China. Rapid population growth also challenged the capacities of the traditional bureaucracy. The technological limitations of the late imperial state, an ideological commitment to low taxation, and concern with the effects of a rising man-to-land ratio impaired government ability to increase its extractive capacity and helped to undermine the benefits of many of the activist policies of the early Qing. Unable to expand to rule a growing population, the bureaucracy of the nineteenth century was increasingly plagued by problems of corruption and inadequate mechanisms of social control. While the private economy continued to grow, particularly in regions suited to cash crops and linked to regional and international networks of trade, the state's role as a stabilizing force in the economy and as a major contributor to infrastructural development and maintenance began to decline.

At the same time, the development of peripheral regions during the preceding century began to present new problems for the Qing central state. In remote areas like Taiwan, Manchuria, the Yangzi (Yangtze) River hills, the Han River highlands, the mountains at the borders between Jiangxi and Hunan and between Sichuan, Shaanxi, and Hubei, parts of Guangxi, as well as Xinjiang and the foothills of Tibet, new settlement brought new opportunities and new strains. Immigrants to these regions were often young men, driven to the frontier by economic need. Unlike the far smaller numbers of settlers who preceded them into these regions to cultivate perennials like indigo, tea, and timber, the new arrivals often engaged in mining, the collection of furs and mountain herbs, and slash-and-burn agriculture based on recently introduced New World crops. Poor soil management in the highlands led to erosion and an increased incidence of flooding in the heartland agricultural communities downriver. The absence of stable community life and orthodox elite leadership and the heightened need for self-defense in a region which was home to aboriginal peoples and bandit gangs led to a high level of militarization at the frontier. It also provided fertile ground for the spread of religious sects and other unorthodox social organizations. The threat that these developments in remote areas presented to the central state was dramatically demonstrated by the outbreak of the White Lotus rebellion along the Sichuan-Shaanxi-Hubei border during the last years of the eighteenth century. In south China, secret societies whose political raison d'être was the ouster of the Qing and restoration of the former Ming Dynasty, also enhanced their power through control of smuggling and gambling and an increasing role in local militia organizations.

THE NINETEENTH-CENTURY CRISIS

EXTERNAL INVASION

At mid-century China was beset by the twin catastrophes of external invasion and internal rebellion that portended the end of a dynasty in traditional political theory. The traditional external threat had usually come from the north, in the form of land invasions by people of the steppe or, in the case of China's Manchu rulers, people of the forested regions northeast of the Great Wall. China's new adversary came in the form of maritime traders who for more than a century had engaged in a mutually beneficial commerce between the British East India Company and Chinese monopoly traders organized in the Thirteen Hongs. Throughout the second half of the eighteenth century that trade was based on the exchange of Chinese silk, tea, and porcelains in large part for silver obtained from the New World. During the early nineteenth century the British failure to develop a Chinese market for their own manufactures was increasingly addressed by illegal trade in opium. By the 1830s this trade had reversed the balance of payments and resulted in an outflow of silver from China.

The confrontation between China and Britain known as the Opium War (1839–42) had many causes. With the dissolution of the East India Company in 1834, pressure by British "free-traders" to open China beyond the port of Guangzhou—to which it had been confined by the Chinese in 1760—intensified. Discontent was also mounting against the traditional Chinese system of dealing with non-Chinese people, a system that institutionalized the Chinese belief in their civilization's universal cultural centrality and superiority. For the Manchu rulers of China, the desires of the British "barbarians" to ply their wares throughout China and conduct diplomatic relations on the basis of "equality" were as unacceptable as their continued violation of Chinese exhortations to cease their trade in the deadly narcotic, opium.

Far more important than the reasons for which each side went to war (about which scholars are still engaged in lively debate) were the results of the Opium War for the Chinese people and the Chinese state. The end of the Opium War marked the beginning of Western imperialism in China. Unequal treaties, imposed at the end of the war, forced China to relinquish Hong Kong, open new "Treaty Ports" to foreign trade, pay indemnities to her vanquishers, and allow foreigners to live and work on Chinese soil free of the jurisdiction of Chinese law (extraterritoriality). Over the years new wars with Western powers would expand these impositions on China's national sovereignty, culminating in the Treaty of Shimonoseki, which ended the Sino-Japanese War of 1894–95. Among other things, this treaty made Taiwan a colony of Japan and allowed foreign investors for the first time to build factories and exploit resources on Chinese soil. A direct result was the late-nineteenth-century scramble for concessions, which, in the view of many historians, left China a "semi-colony" of the West and Japan. The economic impact of imperialism has become a matter of considerable debate in China and in the West. It included the introduction of new manufacturing and communications technologies, including railways, telegraphs, steam navigation, and mechanized production of cotton and silk yarn, modern mining and metallurgy, and modern weapons technology. Western-dominated treaty ports became main centers of modern production and services. Shanghai, which had been a small town before 1842, became the largest city in China, a major center of trade, banking, and manufacture. However, opium and finished goods continued to make up the majority of foreign exports to

China, in exchange for which foreigners purchased Chinese agricultural products. The superior access of foreign manufacturers, both in China and abroad, to capital, management skills, and technology is also seen as having disadvantaged China in its struggle to compete in an industrial marketplace. Thus, China experienced a classical colonial economic relationship with the first world, even if nominal political sovereignty was maintained.

INTERNAL REBELLION

The combined impact of population growth, development of the frontier, declining effectiveness of the bureaucracy, popular discontent with a state unable to protect its people from Western pressure, as well as various local factors led to the outbreak of a number of popular movements against the state in the mid-nineteenth century. The most successful challenge to state power was that of the Taiping Heavenly Kingdom, which at its height controlled almost a third of China's national territory, much of it in the economic heartland of central China. If the Opium War is seen as a turning point in China's international and economic relations, the Taiping is often taken as the point at which state-society relations in China began to be transformed. The ability of the Qing state to survive the Taiping onslaught depended on resistance by popular militias at the local level and, to a greater extent, by large provincial armies formed by members of the upper-level Confucian elite. While neither of these new institutions directly challenged the authority of the state, elite participation in dynastic defense and in the process of postwar reconstruction helped shift the balance of power from the center to the provinces and create a new realm of elite activism outside of the bureaucracy, funded by new revenue sources developed at the local level during the Taiping War. While popular discontent during the remaining fifty-odd years of Qing rule tended to be directed largely against the foreign presence (in the form of antimissionary activity and in the famous Boxer Uprising), elite efforts to redefine Chinese politics would ultimately prove the greater threat to the power of the ancien regime.

INTELLECTUAL AND POLITICAL CHALLENGES
TO THE QING

The intellectual response to the founding of the Qing Dynasty was in many respects a withdrawal of intellectuals from the political arena. Loyalty to the Ming dynastic house and dismay at the Manchu conquest led many scholars, particularly in southern China, to eschew service in the bureaucracy. While this manifestation of Ming loyalism did not last more than a generation and never affected more than a small group of China's elite, the overall tenor of early Qing Confucian scholarship can be characterized as fundamentalist in nature, oriented toward a rediscovery of the "genuine" tradition of the pre-Song period. The relatively bookish orientation of the early Qing began to change as the problems of the late eighteenth and early nineteenth centuries prompted an increasing interest in "practical learning" and scholarship oriented toward "statecraft." A small group of scholars, largely in southern China, began to reevaluate the inherent conservatism of China's philosophical orthodoxy through a revival of the long-neglected New Text school of Confucianism. While international challenges did not cause this shift in intellectual orientation, they did contribute to its intensification and direction.

By the end of the nineteenth century a major focus of intellectual energy was the search for the means by which China could strengthen herself, both in a material sense and in terms of her position in the international family of nations. The so-called self-strengthening movement of the 1870s, 1880s, and 1890s was less a unified movement than a conglomeration of widely varying efforts. The state itself participated by modernizing China's international relations and endorsing the efforts of provincial officials and elites to develop a modern military and a modern armaments industry, and in the later years, the beginnings of a modern industrial economy. However, the real impetus for material modernization continued to come from the latter, and increasingly from private entrepreneurs. While structural factors played a major role in China's slow progress toward modernization, frustration with China's backwardness and with the intensification of imperialist attacks on Chinese sovereignty led some intellectuals to begin to question the very foundations of the imperial state system. In 1895 Sun Yat-sen undertook the first of his many attempts to organize secret society members to overthrow the Qing Dynasty. Just three years later, reformers under the leadership of Kang Youwei and his disciple, Liang Qichao, briefly succeeded in winning imperial support for a transformation of China's political system towards constitutional monarchy. Although soon thwarted by the Empress Dowager, Cexi, the Hundred Days Reforms set the agenda for reform when it was revived in early years of the twentieth century.

UNFINISHED BUSINESS IN THE
EARLY TWENTIETH CENTURY

The revolution that brought about the downfall of the Qing dynastic house and the establishment of a Republic of China in 1911 was the culmination of the forces described above. As China entered the first decade of the twentieth century, a growing portion of the elite came to accept the need for political as well as economic and military reform if China was to reassert its independence from and equality with the West and Japan. Those who saw the Manchus themselves as the obstacle to reform began to work toward revolution, although the revolutionary movement as such, epitomized in Sun Yat-sen's umbrella organization known as the Tongmenghui, never achieved sufficient organizational or military strength to bring about an end to the regime on its own. More important were the new urban provincial elites who began to work for change through Westernizing educational reform, the movement to recover economic rights from the West and Japan, and the campaign for implementation of a constitutional monarchy and greater provincial autonomy. Although the Qing Dynasty made slow progress in the direction of all three, first in the Empress Dowager's Reforms of 1901–1905, and later in the constitutional reforms promulgated in 1909, generalized popular unrest and a slow and uneven commitment to change ultimately lost the dynasty its mandate. A minor uprising in Wuhan, Hubei in October 1911 precipitated the successive withdrawal of most of China's provinces from the imperial state. Within a few months both Qing and dynastic rule were gone forever.

To many scholars the 1911 Revolution was an unfinished revolution. In strictly political terms it did not succeed in establishing a stable, unified government for all of China, and a second republican revolution was carried out for this purpose in 1926–27. It left unaddressed serious problems of economic modernization and social welfare. And it inherited and compounded questions of Chinese national identity that had begun to emerge as early as the late eighteenth century.

THE QUEST FOR NEW POLITICAL FORMS

China's quest for a new political form, beginning in the late nineteenth century, was foremost a response to Western imperialism. The fact that it grew out of the attempt of an established elite to strengthen China and facilitate its modernization says much about its outcome. The struggle for constitutional monarchy during the Qing Dynasty was an attempt to broaden the influence of provincial elites on central government decision making and to institutionalize their growing authority at home. That it was never intended to be a means to expand popular participation in the political process is attested to by the paternalistic treatment of the masses in constitutionalist literature and the highly restrictive qualifications established for the electorate.

Distrust of the ability of the masses to share in their own governance was built into constitutionalism in the form of a period of tutelage, during which time popular education would be expanded. The dynasty never had the opportunity to prove its own commitment to a broadened electorate. Subsequent governments accorded little more than lip service to the democratic ideal. The paramount desire of the provincial elites who made the 1911 revolution was to remove the Manchu ruling house and what they perceived as its obstruction of their modernizing and political ambitions. To achieve this with a minimum of bloodshed or social disruption was critical to the maintenance of their own power. It was also a key to maintaining foreign neutrality and avoiding foreign pretexts for reparations. As a result, in almost every province ultimate authority was granted to the military. Nowhere was the civilian elite successful in wresting power away from the military governors established during the first weeks of the revolution, and it is these men and their successors who became the warlords who gave the first stage of the Republican period its name.

The second republican revolution, often called the Nationalist Revolution, was in many respects more a movement of national unification than of political democratization. The Kuomintang (KMT, Guomindang) or Nationalist Party, which led this revolution in 1927, was heir to the political leadership that first tried to overthrow warlordism and expand the political arena in 1913 under the leadership of Sun Yat-sen. However, by the time it established its national capital in Nanjing, both China's circumstances and the nature of the party itself had changed. Under the tutelage of the Third International of the Communist Party (Comintern), both the Chinese Communist Party (founded in 1921) and the Guomindang were reorganized as tightly knit Leninist parties. Under the leadership of Chiang Kai-shek (Jiang Jieshi), the Guomindang first agreed to work with the communists to wipe out warlord power in China. However, once Chiang succeeded in consolidating his power in south China, he broke with the communists and proceeded to establish alliances with remaining warlord leaders that acknowledged his as the national government of China. The Guomindang government was essentially a one-party state that was held together by the relative weakness of its competitors and skillful manipulation of competing factional interests within its own camp. Also contributing to its survival was general fear that disunity would provide an opening for a communist challenge, or for the expanding power of Japan on the Chinese mainland. Although it too proposed a period of tutelage after which democracy modeled upon Sun Yat-sen's "five-power constitution" would be established, the Guomindang regime in practice was no more willing to share power than were its predecessors.

THE QUEST FOR NATIONAL IDENTITY

The China of the late imperial period was for the most part a cultural construct. It was dependent not on fixed borders, but rather on fluid demarcations between populations that were culturally Chinese and those that were in the process of cultural assimilation. Thus, during the Qing period, that territory which we now consider to be China could contain within it aboriginal peoples whose way of life was completely different from that of the Chinese and who were governed by their own leaders. The Manchu state sought to extend its bureaucratic control over these peoples after the early eighteenth century, in large part by encouraging cultural assimilation. However, repeated instances of aboriginal uprisings throughout the eighteenth and nineteenth centuries are sure signs that this effort was not a great success. At the same time, the looseness of the definition of the state under the dynastic system allowed China to insist on a definition of itself that included peoples who were only marginally within the late Qing cultural sphere.

Beginning in the nineteenth century, the strictly cultural definition of Chinese identity was challenged in a number of ways. Most immediate was the competing Western understanding of the nation-state defined not so much by culture as by national borders. For many Chinese leaders this was not as alien a concept as it might at first appear. China had always been a multiethnic entity in practice, and at least one Manchu emperor, Qianlong, had preferred to view himself as the ruler of a universal empire in which a multiplicity of culturally distinct groups could thrive and remain distinct. The growing debate among China's scholar-official class over the adoption of Western material technology, Western learning, and, later, Western political and cultural practices was intimately linked to the shifting understanding of what it meant to be Chinese. For most revolutionaries and many reformers, the survival of the Chinese political entity was paramount and could be accomplished at the expense of specific elements of China's traditional culture, including the dynastic system of rule. For others, it would have been better to see China as a political entity dissolve than to sacrifice that which was seen to be the essence of being Chinese. A middle position gained adherents during the last years of the Qing, including the famous late-nineteenth-century scholar official, Zhang Zhidong, who argued that one could adopt Western learning for practical use *(xixue weiyong)* without abandoning traditional Chinese learning as the essence of Chinese society.

The failure of China's modernization process, as measured by continued imperialist pressure and relatively slow economic growth, led many Chinese intellectuals in the early twentieth century to seek the cause of Chinese backwardness in the very culture that their predecessors had struggled to preserve in the face of Western incursion. The New Culture Movement of the nineteen teens and twenties was in part a dramatic rejection of traditional Chinese values, customs, and philosophical and educational traditions in favor of the wholesale Westernization that many hoped would allow China to emerge as an equal of the West and Japan. The preeminent role attributed to culture in achieving social, political, and economic goals helps to explain the importance that cultural transformation has had in China's modern history. In this context, the Chinese desire to be modern has continuously come up against the equally strong desire to remain Chinese. The result has been successive "cultural revolutions," exemplified by the New Culture Movement, the New Life Movement of the early 1930s, the Great Proletarian Cultural Revolution of the 1960s, and the anti-spiritual pollution campaigns of the 1970s and 1980s. Beginning in the late nineteenth century, the acceleration of Chinese migration, to Southeast Asia, the Caribbean, Great Britain, the United States, and Canada, has also raised the question of who represents Chinese culture in the contemporary world.

THE QUEST FOR ECONOMIC MODERNIZATION

Economic modernization has been a primary goal of all of the national governments that have ruled China since the downfall of the Qing. This issue is discussed in detail elsewhere in this volume. However, a number of overriding trends are worth mentioning here. There is considerable debate over the extent to which China can be said to have experienced modern economic growth, defined as sustained growth of per capita productivity accompanied by structural change of the economy as a whole. Differences in interpretation of data account for some of the disagreement, while the difficulty in obtaining reliable economic data for China account for the rest. Most scholars would agree that during the twentieth century, China experienced a modest increase in industrial plant and industrial output, with rates of growth differing in different periods. Nevertheless, industrial growth was insufficient to bring about a shift in the relative roles of the agricultural and urban sectors in the overall economy, and handicraft production continued to play a major role in overall manufacturing output down to the communist revolution. At the same time, the regional imbalances that resulted from the concentration of Chinese industry largely in coastal treaty ports continued. The greatest advances in the percentage growth of manufacturing were made during the period following the outbreak of World War I, when the West was unable to compete in Chinese markets in the way that it had before. Japanese competition, both at home, in the form of challenges to China's trade in silk with the West, and on Chinese soil, in the form of Japanese-owned mines, mills, and textile manufactories, intensified during the early twentieth century. The Japanese takeover of Manchuria in 1931–32 led to an intensification of Japanese investment which made that region one of the most important industrial centers in China.

Beginning in 1937, the disruption in the Chinese economy caused by the War of Resistance Against Japan makes it difficult to assess the contribution of the Nationalist government's policies to economic development. Without a sizable increase in nonfarm employment, the standard of living of China's growing rural population was unlikely to improve. The disruptions of war and natural disaster (brought about in part by the reduced involvement of the post-Qing state in water control and famine relief) intensified their poverty, particularly in regions that had not benefited from the growth of international trade during the past half-century. Like their counterparts in the bureaucracy of the late Qing, many Guomindang officials questioned the ability of the private sector to bring about the kind of sustained growth that would propel China into the ranks of world economic powers. Nevertheless, the Nationalist regime's limited tax base and the large percentage of government income devoted to military expenditure, foreign and domestic debt service, and the maintenance of the bureaucracy meant that few resources were available for state-directed development purposes. State investment in the development of transportation was comparable to that of the Qing and the early Republican governments, but has been criticized for its bias towards the requirements of the military. During the 1930s the German National Socialist model of state capitalism became attractive to many Guomindang officials. The state took control of the modern banking center during the Nanjing decade (1927-37) and through a variety of means, including the confiscation of Japanese-held industries after the war, came to control about a third of the modern industrial, energy, and transportation sectors by 1949. However, the contribution of state capitalism to economic development is generally considered to have been minimal, lessened by hyperinflation in Guomindang-controlled areas during and after the war. The most important contributions of this period were in the private sector, in the training of managerial and technical personnel, in the expansion and diversification of foreign trade, and in the laying of the foundations for the rapid growth of China's industrial plant in the post-1949 period.

1949 AND BEYOND

The founding of the People's Republic of China (PRC) in 1949 provided China with a new opportunity to address the issues outlined above. The radical restructuring of the Chinese political and economic systems that accompanied the communist revolution did not end their significance to the long modernization process any more than the initiation of a period of radical reform in 1978 meant that no progress toward their resolution had taken place during the previous thirty-nine years.

Under the Chinese Communist Party (CCP) the Chinese state achieved a degree of unity that had not been known in China since 1911. Political authority of the central state was once again exercised throughout the traditional provinces of China proper, as well as at the periphery in Manchuria, Inner Mongolia, and Tibet. At the same time, the state and party apparatus was extended deep into the local community to affect the everyday lives of the people in ways never conceived of under the ancien regime. The nationalization of commerce and industry, and the collectivization of agriculture, meant that employment, welfare services, housing, food supply, and so on were all controlled by agents of the state. While the revolution succeeded in removing the old elite, particularly the rural landed elite, it created a new elite with greatly expanded powers and opportunities for abuse. The quest for a mechanism that will broaden popular participation in the political process is still underway, most often operating at the margins of the state system. During the years before economic reform, this quest was often manifested in the form of mass campaigns against bureaucratization, such as that which took place during the Cultural Revolution. In more recent years it has been expressed in urban movements for democracy, such as that which gained international attention in May and early June of 1989. Where the PRC has been most successful is in the establishment of China's position in the international arena. China's ability to assert its national sovereignty during the first half of the twentieth century was limited. Most of the stipulations of the unequal treaties were not abolished until World War II, by which time Japanese political and economic control had been extended over most of east and northeast China. While the United States promoted the myth of China as a great power during the 1940s, it was only after 1949 that China achieved the political and economic strength to earn that title.

The quest for national identity has taken many forms in the communist period. Joseph Levinson has suggested that one of the attractions of communism for Chinese intellectuals in the early twentieth century was its potential for freeing China from the choice between its own cultural past and the past of the West. By joining the ranks of peoples moving toward communism, China could take on a completely new identity as a pioneer of mankind's future. Cultural transformation played an important role in state policy, with education and leisure all under state supervision and directed toward the creation of a new socialist man, oriented toward collective goals and national empowerment in the international arena. The antitraditionalism of the political and intellectual elite during the twentieth century has been seen by some scholars as widening the gap between elites and the populace. However, the efforts of the state to ban popular religious and other practices have proven far less successful than previously thought, a fact attested to by their rapid reemergence after 1978.

By the 1990s, China has become one of the world's largest and fastest-growing economies. The implications for China's political future are great. Efforts to foster economic growth during the 1980s resulted in considerable decentralization of political, as well as economic, power. For the first time in Chinese history, the majority of China's population is no longer engaged in agriculture. Private and local collective production now outstrip that of state enterprises, so that employment and the generation of wealth are no longer the monopoly of the state. With a greatly improved standard of living, access to foreign imports and information, and geographic and job mobility unheard of during the communist period, many scholars predict that China's millions will demand a much greater role in the political process in future years.

NOTE

1. See the essay "Asia in World History" by Carol Gluck.

MODERN INDIA, 1885–1990

David Lelyveld

OF CIVILIZATIONS AS NATION-STATES

The ways South Asians define their history and cultural boundaries have undergone radical changes during the past two centuries. Categories like "India" and "Hinduism" stand for complex,
shifting ideas, muddled by obscure academic arguments and
fierce political controversy. How these two terms relate to each
other, whether they fall into a neat congruence of geography and
civilization, whether they exclude "non-Hindu" from a rightful
place on the Indian map—these questions have become essential
to drawing national boundaries and creating viable national communities. Loyalties have rallied around ideas of what is indigenous and what is foreign, and the relevant evidence can often
reach back centuries or even millennia.

Many facts and ideas of South Asian history that young Indians, Pakistanis, and Bangladeshis study in school are relatively
recent discoveries and inventions. They have by no means been
perfectly assimilated into popular historical consciousness. The
question has often been raised whether the very concepts of
"India" or "Hindu civilization" are meaningful for historical analysis before recent times. Even if one accepts the history of South
Asian civilization as a worthwhile unit of study, it is clear that this
is not the story of a single seed that grew into a single tree,
however spreading and many branched.

The map we look at today with its clear boundaries of oceans
and Himalayan mountains was not, until modern times, in the
mind's eye of the land's inhabitants. In some respects the internal
formations of rivers and hills loomed as more salient obstacles to

the flow of people, symbols, goods, and technologies. South Asian civilization as a whole was never isolated from the rest of the world, even as parts of South Asia were often substantially separated from each other. It is, in fact, a civilization that has combined diverse influences from many sources both inside and outside the subcontinent.

If one can speak of an overarching problem of modern South Asian history, it has been the effort to fit a complex civilization into the standard template of the nation-state system, first as a way of liberating British India from imperial domination, and then to enable the successor states to participate and prosper in the postimperial international system. Terms like "nationalism" and "the nationalist movement" have served for more than a hundred years to describe a great variety of actions and beliefs by which Indians have sought to assert cultural identity and exercise practical power in the face of colonial domination.

Insofar as the nationalist movement had an overarching objective, it was the establishment of social order, making the parts fit into a harmonious whole, more than the achievement of social justice or economic advancement. Disorder and fragmentation have been the great anxieties addressed by the dominant ideologies of Indian history. For this reason, "nation building" was an end in itself. India still stands at a considerable distance from a fully mobilized nation-state, poised to devote the entire energies of its population to an identifiable set of goals. More realistically, India's relatively weak integration places severe limits on the impact of national policy. Whether that kind of nation-state is a prerequisite for further economic and social development is a matter for speculation. Those who seek such development must decide what obstacles stand in its way, and some would say that an ideology of social harmony is one such obstacle. But if the price of change is conflict, what social groups can or should be mobilized into conscious movements for the reallocation of power? Can India as a whole be the primary arena for such conflict? And are there forms of conflict that can lead to something other than *matsyayana*, the condition of anarchy in which the big fish devour the small?

These questions of legitimate social boundaries, domains, and methods of action do not require an overall philosophy of development or revolutionary strategy. Such issues have been played out over the last hundred years in the ordinary give and take of Indian political life as well as in the grand social movements. In the course of this history, the concept of an Indian nation-state has been set off against what came to be known as "fissiparous tendencies," the clustering of loyalties around concepts such as religious community, caste and tribe, language, and region. Movements have also arisen in the name of economic class solidarity, but they are rarely free of these "primordial" ties. In the context of new political institutions, however—voluntary associations like parties and unions, structures of government like parliaments and bureaucracies—one cannot assume a continuity with the social loyalties of the past, even when the names are the same. Major political and economic institutions, founded on principles of equality, have replaced the model of hierarchy with open competition and transformed the internal structure of groups as well as their relation to each other and to society as a whole. Fissiparous tendencies, the politics of ethnicity, are as much a creature of modern institutions as is the nation-state itself. They bespeak radical transformations. But it can also be argued that these political (and economic) realms of life do not necessarily dominate the thoughts and actions of most Indians, that they are still "encompassed" by the ideology of hierarchy. How one may judge the intersections, contradictions, or compartmentalizations of one form of society as against another depends on the questions you are asking. They are all part of the new totality that is India and the difficulty of making sense of it.

From the outset of the self-conscious movement to assert Indian national identity in response to British rule, whether one dates that from the reformation of Hinduism initiated by Ram Mohan Roy in the 1820s or the rise of voluntary associations that culminated in the founding of the Indian National Congress in 1886, there was a deep concern about the historical civilization of India and its relation to demands for institutional change. Often efforts to rediscover the past have been interpreted as a selection of bits and pieces of religion or history to fit into a European ideological matrix, exercises in apologetics designed to claim mere equivalence to the ruling culture. But it is just as possible to construct an intellectual history which asks why Indians were attracted to some features of European culture and not others: from what indigenous cultural foundations did they make their selection?

The overwhelming majority of the Indian population had only the most casual exposure, if any, to British ideas, whether political or religious. The task for a would-be nationalist leadership was to interpret the shortcomings and opportunities of the colonial situation in a way that was meaningful in indigenous terms. But this was a game the British themselves tried to play, even going so far as to argue that they were more representative of the people of India than were the English-educated Indians of the cities. If British claims were unconvincing, those made by spokesmen for Indian nationalism were often of interest to a relatively small public. The larger population, however, had its own motivations and priorities and was capable of reinterpreting, in turn, the words and actions of its supposed leaders. And increasingly in the early twentieth century, politicians in search of constituencies had to be responsive to the beliefs and demands of a wider public. One of the tasks, then, of any history of nationalism is to relate the development of modern politics to ideas and expectations about power and authority that are rooted in indigenous society and a precolonial past.

CULTURAL SELF-ASSERTION AND
THE GOALS OF NATIONALISM

The early demands made in the name of Indian nationalism, however, were by no means antagonistic to British rule, and it was to be nearly fifty years before the Indian National Congress was prepared, in 1930, to call directly for political independence. What the early movement sought was enfranchisement for Indians, as individuals and "interests," within Britain's own political system. To raise the age at which one could take the Indian Civil Service examination and to hold it in India as well as in England were primary concerns for the founders of the Congress. Representative institutions, based on a highly limited franchise, would see that Indian revenues were spent for Indian purposes. The Indian press would enjoy the same liberty of expression as its British counterpart, and tariffs would enable Indian manufacturing enterprises to compete with English ones. Each year the Congress gathered to pass such resolutions, acting on the assumption, which was not entirely misplaced, that reiteration and the support of a few hundred or a few thousand names would eventually influence government policy.

Both British officials and a second generation of nationalists, who became known as the "extremists," considered the founders of the Congress "denationalized," out of touch with both the culture and the actual life of the people. But if many of them adopted the language and lifestyle of the rulers, they remained members of families, caste, religious and territorial communities, and as lawyers—as most of them were—were continually involved in interpreting Indian institutions for British ones and vice versa. Their attachment to particular British ideals and political processes was not based simply on acculturation but on a considered judgment of what India required to win freedom. At the same time they retained a commitment to social harmony, a recognition of cultural diversity, and a belief in authority by moral example that was consistent with older Indian political ideals.

Since so much of the nationalist demand was for places in government, when the opportunity came, a good number accepted. The gradual emergence of elected representative councils—in 1884, 1909, 1919, and 1937—were responses to Indian demands. The slow opening of the civil service, higher judiciary, and military officer corps to Indians, despite later periods of noncooperation by the mainstream nationalist movement, was a goal of nationalism. Those who accepted such posts were not repudiated. When independence came, they were considered full-fledged heirs to the struggle for freedom.

The desire to achieve the advantage of political power and economic prosperity that the British themselves so convincingly represented stood in tension with the need for cultural affirmation for India. But even cultural self-definition could be dictated by British concepts. The official analysis of Indian society in legal codes, censuses, and ethnographies as well as educational and employment statistics served to demarcate potential constituencies and channels of patronage. This analysis emphasized cultural fragmentation by language, religion, and caste, all of which demonstrated to the British the unsuitability of representative government and the nation-state to Indian society.

If the "moderate" nationalists cautiously downplayed social reform or political issues that might exacerbate such divisions, there were others prepared to assert the rightful claims of a more unified cultural identity. The result was that holistic models of hierarchy and segmentation gave way to competitive ethnicity, with spokesmen for different cultural categories seeking out historical or statistical justification for special claims for the positions and patronage opened up in response to nationalist demands. A good deal of politics became a matter of gathering people under opposing banners of cultural loyalty. It was at this point that the nationalism of the urban, English-educated might come in contact with traditions of popular insurgency in the greater society.

If one looks beyond statements to social networks established or activated by the politics of nationalism, a more convincingly

"Indian" model of social loyalty may come into play. According to
one influential line of interpretation, the vivid personalities of the
nationalist movement were in a sense the segmentary leaders of
the new age. But for large sections, though by no means all, of
Indian society Mahatma Gandhi represented the culmination of
the several streams of nationalism as well as the mediator between English-oriented politics and the world of actual or potential peasant insurgency. The many pieces of Gandhi's carefully,
painfully constructed persona and their resolution into an image
of world-renouncing simplicity made him an appropriate source of
moral authority and symbol of Indian unity. But, as so often in
Indian civilization, this symbolic role did not entail power—even
the power to dictate how the symbol might be construed. "My
language is aphoristic, it lacks precision," Gandhi himself conceded. "It is therefore open to several interpretations."

"What I want to achieve,—what I have been striving and pining
to achieve these thirty years,—" Gandhi wrote in 1925, "is self-realization, to see God face to face, to attain Moksha." Self-realization as an ultimate, cosmic harmony was for Gandhi the goal not
only for himself but for India. It was to be achieved through action
in the world, but it was action founded on the persuasion of moral
example. Gandhi's leadership allowed considerable autonomy to
various political actors who identified, however loosely, with his
leadership. He sought to create a shared community of moral
concern among competing groups, whether cultural, ideological,
or economic.

The popular appeal of Gandhi's message, however, lay in its
negation of the quest for wealth and power that could be identified
not only with the British but with much of the nationalist leadership. Gandhi's radical critique not only of industrialization but of
any society founded upon principles of competition and individual
interest in favor of a utopia of localized communal harmony and
"enlightened anarchy" could appeal to a population for whom the
fruits of the modern world were so unattainable as to be the
symbols of oppression. By his own account Gandhi was less concerned with the practical attainment of such a utopia than with
the "experimental" pursuit of it, almost as a spiritual exercise.
Such experiments tolerated the role of capitalists, socialists, and
political bosses but sought to hold in and discipline the disharmo-
nious assertiveness of the population at large. By capturing the
social imagination of the discontented in the name of renunciation
and rural communitarianism, Gandhi's leadership deliberately left
local hierarchies in place. While calling for the removal of foreign

dominance, a vehicle of exploitation by world commerce and industry, Gandhi opposed the mobilization of people to demand power or positive action by the state.

The actual messages that Gandhi expressed in his tour of the rural countryside—Hindu-Muslim unity, disciplined nonviolence—could be ignored. Instead "Gandhi swaraj" became a charter for looting the rich and powerful, attacking and killing the police, and a general sense of empowerment among those previously considered passive and excluded from what was known as the nationalist movement. Gandhi had successfully mobilized the peasantry, but with results that were totally opposed to his utopian vision. It is arguable that violence and the breakdown of authority had as much to do with the departure of the British as *satyagraha*, political party organization, or the articulation of constitutional demands.

Condemnation of British exploitation, praise for features of Indian civilization, calls for reform of particular social practices—these were the major concerns of the nationalists, but not a practical working model of an independent India. It is true that at least from 1907 much of political discourse was what was called "constitutional" in the sense that it dealt with the definition of the units and procedures of government. These debates played a large part in defining the national community. Looming over constitutional questions were cultural definitions of political loyalty, most of all the question of whether Muslims constituted a separate political community. Other religious communities, notably Sikhs, coalitions of non-Brahman Hindus, untouchables, and, cutting across all of these, linguistic regions had "constitutional" demands to make. So did the princely states, largely creations of British colonialism now granted recognition as independent bargainers in any future division of power. Against all this was a vision of a unified nation-state, based on individual citizenship and popular elections, able to take a full and prominent role in the international community.

But having defined and divided up the units of political authority, what did the Indian nationalists propose to do with it? Part of the answer was, once again, cultural self-definition. Ban the killing of cows, promote the use of Hindi or Hindustani, abolish dowry and child marriage, open the temples to untouchables—there were many such, often conflicting, demands upon government to which foreign rule had been insufficiently responsive. The supporters of social reform were often at odds with the nationalists, whose first priority was national unity and self-rule. Similarly there were numerous practical interests to which government might be more responsive if it were in Indian hands. British control inevitably meant concessions, for example, to the textile interests of Lancashire at the expense of Ahmedabad. The layout of British railways served the interests of British-controlled international commerce, not domestic distribution. The international value of the rupee was determined by British monetary interests in such a way that Indian goods were at a disadvantage in world trade. There was a long-standing platform of economic policy demands which involved a conflict of Indian and British interests.

Only in the decade before independence does one find detailed statements of the goals of national independence. The prospect of actual governing power, achieved at the provincial level in 1937, as well as the failure of Gandhian civil disobedience, forced Indian political leaders to face up to the future with some concrete ideas. The world depression had created a further sense of urgency, for it showed as never before how closely bound up with the international economy India was. During these years Gandhi virtually withdrew from politics, concerning himself with localized "constructive work," the promotion of Hindustani as a national language and the rights of untouchables. But the attention of other political leaders turned to economic growth, particularly through industrialization. This concern was further stimulated by a desire to win the political support of the popular sections of society that had been brought into the political arena by Gandhi. Emphasis on economic appeal, it was hoped, could draw away support from parties, notably the Muslim League, based on cultural identity. But most of all, the concern with economic growth was necessary to the idea of what Indian national independence would mean. Poverty was part of the humiliation of foreign rule. The failure of Britain to bring prosperity to India was the surest sign of the illegitimacy of its power.

The greatest fear of the nationalist leaders, however, was not poverty, but, in Nehru's words, "fragmentation and conflict and disorder." The task of Indian nationalism, as the poet Sarojini Naidu put it, was "to set my mother's house in order." Order, making the parts fit together into a unified whole, not power or wealth, was the ideal goal of Indian nationalism as a movement. The room that left for more practical, short-term goals was a matter to be discovered in the course of an unknown future.

The partition of India and the creation of two independent nation-states, India and Pakistan, in 1947, did not calm the troubled waters of culturally defined group conflict. Since the mid-1980s, in particular, the politics of religious identity has dominated much of the Indian political scene, though scholars and politicians may disagree on the extent to which religion in any sense motivates those who act in its name. In Punjab, an armed movement partly in the name of Sikh communal autonomy blossomed into a full-fledged separatist movement modeled in part on the creation of Pakistan. When the Indian army besieged the sacred Golden Temple of Amritsar in June 1984, a cycle of violence was set off that included the assassination five months later of the prime minister, Indira Gandhi, and years of mutual terrorism by the Indian state and Sikh guerrillas. About 1989, a similar pattern of violence erupted from the long-festering problem of Kashmir, India's only Muslim majority state, the site of three wars with Pakistan and of a long-standing independence movement.

More far-reaching in recent years has been the increased strength of political movements that identify India's nationhood with Hindu symbols and, in some cases, explicitly racist concepts of Hindu and non-Hindu identity. Hindu nationalism seeks to override other sorts of division such as those of region, language, and class in a great, enthusiastic wave of cultural mobilization. As a strategy of opposition to affirmative action schemes that have sought to redress the historical deprivation of lower-status castes, the relatively higher-status, mostly Brahmin leadership of the Hindu nationalist movement has advanced a noncaste image of a reformed Hinduism in the face of non-Hindu enemies. In December 1992, the destruction of an early-sixteenth-century mosque by members of the Hindu nationalist movement in the name of a historicized divinity, Rama, set off a chain of violence in many parts of India, most particularly in Bombay, where Muslims were attacked as enemies of the nation.

Despite these terrible, but intermittent spasms of social conflict, what has saved most of India so far as one of the world's last great pluralist political formations has been something like the sort of social mechanism foreseen for the United States by Madison and de Toqueville: the great multiplicity of associations within India as a whole and the situational, transitional character of their emergence and demise. The idea of distinct, bounded groups must compete with the fact that group identities overlap, factions emerge, networks expand and contract according to the situation. Whether religion, caste, language, or class consciousness applies to a given occasion, and at what level of generality, is not a constant condition of Indian life. Much of modern Indian history has consisted of negotiating or fighting over priorities with regard to group loyalty. What prevails, usually imperfectly, at a particular time may well color future occasions, but other considerations, like control of economic resources or access to information, may realign coalitions. Unless partitions or unforgivable mass murder intervenes, and maybe even then, social alignments are open to challenge and negotiation.

If Indians are thus protected at the national level from a totalitarian uniformity, this is certainly not the case at more local levels, where the flexibility of grand systems, constitutional or metaphysical, often does not intrude very effectively and overarching authority is often unable to intervene. One price of India's "galactic" pluralism is that the resources of the central government to protect the weak, even when it is so inclined, are limited. And this is just one aspect of India's difficulty in finding and pursuing a consistent, conscious national program that might lead it to greater prosperity and social justice.

MODERN KOREA, 1860–1990

Michael E. Robinson

THE POLITICAL AND SOCIAL CONTEXT

In the mid-nineteenth century Korea was in the fifth century of its last great dynastic system. Founded in 1392 the Chosŏn (Yi) Dynasty represented a political and social system of extraordinary stability and balance. The system had survived the Japanese invasions of 1592 and 1597, the Manchu incursions of 1627 and 1636, economic downturns, peasant rebellions, and recurrent, serious internal political disputes. In the nineteenth century it faced its most serious challenges in the form of the changed international environment in East Asia, economic difficulties, and profound weakness within its own central government. In spite of these difficulties, the Chosŏn system continued into the twentieth century, only to be destroyed in the wake of Japanese colonization in 1910.

The strengths of this system belie the stereotypical views of Korean isolation, bureaucratic ineptness, economic stagnation, and military weakness that are catchphrases within the historical representation of Korea. In fact, the system's longevity testified to its internal effectiveness. Its demise in the era of high imperialism spoke more to the increased military and economic requirements demanded of the changed conditions in East Asia in the nineteenth century than to the integrity and sophistication of traditional Korean society. That the dynasty failed in this environment has led to a retrospective condemnation of the entire Chosŏn period by Korean and Western historians alike. In fact, the Chosŏn Dynasty had not been occupied by foreign powers, nor was it a dependency of China, as some accounts assert. It had maintained its autonomy by an adroit diplomatic policy of ritual subordination to the Ming and Qing rulers in return for informal guarantees of noninterference in its internal political affairs. The Chosŏn dynasty couched its relations with Japan on the basis of "neighborly" relations, and, in spite of the enmity incurred by the Hideyoshi invasions of the 1590s, it resumed relations within decades of the incursions.

Ironically, Korea's late-nineteenth-century military weakness was linked to its successful diplomacy and relatively effective border control and pirate suppression. Its strict adherence to principles of civilian rule subordinated military power to civilian bureaucrats. The Korean military was seldom used because of the dynasty's success in normalizing its foreign relations to maintain stable borders. Thus, unlike the previous dynasty (Koryo Dynasty, 918-1392), the Chosŏn Dynasty was never threatened from within by a politically ambitious military clique.

Economically, Korea was a small and relatively poor country, particularly in comparison with Japan and China. Its relatively small population (eight to ten million in the mid-nineteenth century, rising to twenty million by the 1920s) engaged primarily in subsistence agriculture. While there had been an economic expansion in the eighteenth century, its level of commercialization a century later was still low relative to Japan or the coastal regions and river basins of China. The dynasty also controlled international trade with China and Japan; this trade remained limited to high-value luxury items. Given Korea's few natural resources, a small population, circumscribed international trade, and difficult internal communications, it was not surprising that Western traders ignored Korea until the second half of the nineteenth century.

The balance and stability of Chosŏn society rested primarily in its political and social arrangements. At the top of the system sat the Chosŏn monarch, who ruled over a polity that emulated the central bureaucracy developed in China. While the Koreans adopted many Chinese-style institutions (a process that goes back to the three kingdoms period, 300-700 C.E.), they indigenized their staffing, function, and operation to Korean patterns over centuries. One central difference from China was the relative weakness of the Korean king. Unlike the Chinese emperor, the power of the Korean king was more in balance with the power and prerogatives of his bureaucrats (*yangban*).[1] The system operated to inhibit monarchical despotism while, in turn, it checked a devolution of power into the hands of the bureaucrats and out-of-office local elites. The adoption of Neo-Confucianism as state orthodoxy at the beginning of the Chosŏn period supported restraints on kingly power and legitimated elite status for all officeholders. This created intense competition among elites, both aspiring clans and traditionally powerful clans, for offices in the Chosŏn bureaucracy. The monarch was the apex of the Chosŏn system, but he did not have the centralized power of the Chinese emperor or the wealth and power of the Tokugawa shoguns.

On the other hand, the *yangban* elite, both officeholders and local elites, never gained autonomous political powers approximate to the daimyo within the Tokugawa system or the clear mandate of civil bureaucrats within the Chinese system. The system was a dynamic equilibrium that supported stability while checking the autonomous power of both king and *yangban.* This situation helped to perpetuate the Chosŏn system over centuries; it was marginally self-adjusting, but highly resistant to radical change and reform.

KOREA AND THE POLITICS OF IMPERIALISM

Interestingly, Korea was not "opened" by Western powers. It was its neighbor, Japan, that forced Korea into treaty arrangements in the changing international system after 1876. In fact, Korea's "response" to the changed international environment had begun in 1864. The ascension of a child monarch (Kojong, 1864–1907) led to a period of reforms within Korea guided by the monarch's father (the Taewŏngun) as informal regent. The Taewŏngun reforms attempted to redress the problem of military weakness in light of growing pressures on Korea to engage in trade with the West and, after 1868, to recognize the new Meiji emperor in Japan. They also attempted to redress the internal power balance within Korea that had shifted in the nineteenth century (through the domination of the throne by queen's clans) in favor of key bureaucratic factions and local aristocrats.

The Taewŏngun reforms exposed the weaknesses of the Chosŏn system in the new and more dangerous international situation. While initial attempts to strengthen military preparedness were popular, the aristocracy resisted other policies that sought to bring more resources under the control of the king and the central government. The failure of the Koreans to strengthen the power of the central state was in direct contrast to the successful Tongzhi [T'ung Chih] Restoration in China or the more dramatic centralization of power accomplished during the Meiji Restoration in Japan. In effect, the Taewŏngun restored a relative balance to the system, but much more would be demanded in the following decades.

The "opening" of Korea was forced by the Japanese, who were interested in destroying Korea's traditional relationship with China. The resulting 1876 Kanghwa Treaty marked the beginning of the end of Korea's long-standing reliance on its relationship with China as insurance against invasion. Within ten years, Korea was enmeshed in the unequal treaty system—a system that eroded its sovereignty, allowed the penetration of capitalism, and exposed its economic and military weakness in the region. There was recognition at the highest levels that new institutions, economic power, and technology were needed to survive in the changed circumstances of the late nineteenth century. Drastic changes within the political system, however, threatened the traditional prerogatives of the ruling elite.

Added to the inertia of the ruling elites and the weakness of the monarch, the fact that Korea's most dangerous enemy, Japan, was also its nearest model for change compromised radical reformers. In the 1880s advocates of the adoption of Western technology, ideas, and institutions in Korea were impeded by their early ties to Japanese influence. Conversely, the interests of conservatives in Korea were supported by Chinese interests. The ambiguous roles played by China and Japan within Korean politics in this period did much to dilute the impetus for reform and restructuring. Ultimately, the king maneuvered between conservative opponents of change and advocates of radical reform and relied on imperialist patrons to balance aggressive Japanese policies. This middle course prevented change, supported the inertia of conservative elites, and kept progressive forces out of politics in the last years of the dynasty.

MODERNIZATION AND NATIONALISM

The forces of economic and political change unleashed after the putative "opening" of Korea after 1876 also led to the closely linked movements of modernization and nationalism. The joining of Korea's economy to the world market began the process of destroying traditional handicraft industries, encouraged the shift of landed wealth into grain processing for the foreign market, and brought in foreign capital. The dislocations caused by the intrusion of capitalism into the traditional economy exacerbated tensions in the rural countryside in the late nineteenth century. Foreign economic interests and dynastic maladministration ultimately provoked widespread unrest that erupted in a peasant uprising in 1894 known as the Tonghak Rebellion. The rebellion was organized by the nativist Tonghak religion (a religious, and later political movement strikingly similar to the Taiping movement in China). The rebellion exhibited strong antiforeign sentiments along with a traditional set of demands for tax relief, removal of corrupt bureaucrats, etc. The rebellion remained loyal to the Chosŏn king, but it also showed a new consciousness of Korean identity vis-à-vis the outside world. This rebellion is usually used to date the beginnings of an incipient mass nationalism in Korea.

At the elite level, a nationalist program emerged in tandem with the progressive reform movement. Continuing from the 1880s, this movement ultimately produced the first modern nationalist leaders in Korea. Their program was unabashedly a reform program to Westernize Korea's antiquated politics, economics, and social institutions. Remaining loyal to the monarch, the early nationalists opposed the obdurate conservative elites who blocked any major reforms. Ultimately, the Japanese forced reforms upon the dynasty after their victory in the Sino-Japanese War (1895). This foreign intrusion delegitimated Korean progressivism and inhibited nationalist mobilization around the monarch or other symbols of the traditional system.

Ultimately, nationalism and modernizing reform efforts devolved to the private sector. The relatively early abolition of the civil service exams (1895), ten years before the similar reform in China, led to an expansion of new schools, an egress of students abroad (mostly to Japan), and the rise of a broad-based "new learning" movement in the civil sector. Unfortunately, the energy released by this movement was not mobilized in support of the government. However, it did provide the basis of a new nationalist intelligentsia that came of age during the period of Japanese colonial rule.

THE KOREAN EXPERIENCE UNDER JAPANESE COLONIAL RULE

The Chosŏn system was swept away by the annexation of Korea by the Japanese in 1910. Japan's occupation of Korea was unique in the history of world colonialism. As the only non-Western colonial power, Japan developed effective control policies based on a very close understanding of Korea's cultural and social system. Japan's proximity to its colony allowed it to ignore indigenous institutions and rule Korea by substituting a draconian state staffed by a large Japanese bureaucracy. The Japanese also brought large numbers of Koreans into the colonial state, state enterprises, and semigovernmental corporations. The Japanese state penetrated all aspects of Korean society, and its ethnically discriminatory policies, education, legal system, and political and cultural repression served as the major stimulant to the emergence of Korean nationalist consciousness.

Japanese rule stimulated Korean resistance in the form of expanded nationalist and social revolutionary movements. In exile and at home, Koreans organized to resist Japanese rule. Yet, Japanese military power and an adroit policy of divide-and-rule prevented Koreans from overthrowing the colonial state. The shift toward a "cultural policy" in the aftermath of nationwide protests of the March First movement (1919) (a movement in form and content that anticipated China's May 4th movement of the same year) led to a successful cooptation of the Korean middle class. In the 1920s and 1930s, the Japanese were able to win, at minimum, the passive acceptance of landlords, a nascent bourgeoisie, and many middle-class white-collar workers.

Hounded by the police and ideologically divided, radicals and moderate nationalists alike were unable to develop a mass base among the Korean peasantry, and, in the 1930s, the growing laboring class. Ultimately, Koreans' failure to overthrow their colonial masters had profound implications for legitimating a postliberation, unified Korean state after the Second World War. That so many intellectuals, entrepreneurs, and educated middle-class citizens collaborated or accommodated themselves to Japanese rule crippled the postwar social and political leadership. As late as the 1980s, oppositional forces in South Korea continued to criticize their government's historic ties to "tainted" classes of collaborators from before 1945.

In the cultural realm, the cultural assimilation policy (the forced adoption of Japanese names, forced Shinto worship, and required use of the Japanese language) during the war period (1937–45) left an indelible wound in the psyche of Korean society. Combined with labor mobilization, conscription into the imperial army, and the horrors of forced prostitution (the so-called comfort corps [kor. *wi'anbu,* jap. *ianfu*], an issue that exploded anew in 1990), the total mobilization left a bitter legacy after liberation. This legacy remains in both North and South Korea as an obstacle to smooth relations with Japan.

DIVISION AND CIVIL WAR

The continuing division of the Korean Peninsula stands as one of the few remaining monuments to the Cold War. Unfortunately, the linkage of the formal division to the emergence of the Cold War has also silenced the record with regard to the internal forces that led to the outbreak of the Korean War in 1950. While the joint occupation of the USSR and the United States stimulated a polarization of Korean politics in the period between 1945 and 1948, created the artificial boundaries of the present North-South divide, and mentored the development of client states, Cold War superpower struggle was not the sole determinant of the Korean War.

In 1945, Korean society was riddled with social and economic contradictions remaining from thirty-five years of Japanese rule and the traumatic war period. The depression of the early 1930s had accelerated rural tenancy and impoverished vast portions of the peasant population. Industrial expansion stimulated the beginning of labor migration from South to North, and hundreds of thousands of workers left Korea in the war period to work in Japan, Manchuria, and with the imperial forces overseas. The severing of the Korean economy from the Japanese empire in 1945 and the return flood of Korean workers further disrupted the Korean economy. Moreover, no one Korean group or leader could take credit for the fall of the Japanese colonial regime. After 1945 dozens of political leaders returned from exile and joined those in place in Korea to claim the leadership of an independent nation. It is clear that conditions for a civil struggle already existed and were made more volatile by the presence of two hostile occupying powers. It is important to stress that the Korean War was in fact a civil conflict compounded by superpower intervention.

DIVERGING ROADS TO SOCIAL AND ECONOMIC DEVELOPMENT

The Korean War froze the artificial division of Korea, and subsequent Korean history has been the story of two competing states, each justified in claiming status as the sole legitimate representative of the Korean nation.

THE DEMOCRATIC PEOPLE'S REPUBLIC OF KOREA (DPRK, NORTH KOREA)

After the civil war, the Democratic People's Republic of Korea, with Soviet assistance, rebuilt its economy and reorganized its polity more quickly than South Korea. Able to play the Soviet Union against the People's Republic of China, North Korea insinuated itself in the Socialist world system and achieved a rate of economic development that exceeded that of the South (up to the mid-1960s). This was also a period of political consolidation as the North Korean leader, Kim Il-sung, removed the last vestiges of political opposition (by 1956) and forged the basic shape of a mass society unified by one-party rule dominated by an ideology of political and cultural autonomy known as *chuche* (lit. self-reliance, autonomy). Over time, however, North Korea has struggled because of its highly insular foreign and economic policies. North Korea limited its development because of its adherence to *chuche* ideology in economic policy. By the 1970s, North Korea had reached the limits of growth sustainable by its own internal resources, and borrowing foreign capital and technology would contradict the essence of *chuche.* Overcoming this contradiction has become the central problem for the current regime.

After the mid-1970s North Korea watched its Chinese neighbor abandon its command economy in favor of market principles; in turn, the failure of the Soviet system further isolated the DPRK. With both China and the Russian Federation courting economic and political ties with the South, North Korea has been forced to confront the logic of its self-imposed isolation, no longer sustained by privileged economic and political relations with its socialist neighbors. Yet it is difficult to undo the thirty-year development of a cult of personality around Kim Il-sung as the wellspring of the North's unique ideology and socialist construction. For twenty years Kim Il-sung has been preparing a transition of power to his son, Kim Chong-il. There is some sentiment that the younger Kim is more cosmopolitan than his father, but he lacks clear support in all key sectors of the North Korean leadership.

In the 1990s, North Korea is caught between the desire to maintain its political and social system and the necessity of saving its failing economy. Joining the world system would require dropping its bellicose attitudes toward South Korea and the United States, allowing nuclear inspection, renouncing terrorism, and allowing foreign capital (and its attendant cultural influences) into the North. Whether or not they can maintain their adherence to *chuche* ideology and, in their minds, the unique qualities of their socialism in the face of the corrosive effects of such contact remains the central problem for North Koreans today.

THE REPUBLIC OF KOREA (ROK, SOUTH KOREA)

For its part, South Korea had tremendous difficulties after the war. It had trouble feeding its larger population, and it suffered the consequences of absorbing returning workers from throughout the empire after 1945 and refugees during the Korean War (1950–1953), together numbering in the millions. In contrast to the North, its infant'democratic institutions were unable to unify a deeply divided society. The early economic programs of the 1950s failed to created self-sustaining growth, and the South became deeply dependent on U.S. aid. In politics, authoritarian abuses belied the commitment to constitutional institutions. In the 1950s, the threat from the North was used repeatedly to justify draconian political and social policies. In the 1960s, social discipline for economic growth became an additional justification for authoritarianism.

The well-known economic "miracle" since the 1960s in South Korea set in motion forces that transformed the politics and society of South Korea. Coincidentally, authoritarian politics, an open world market, shrewd economic planning, talented entrepreneurs under government guidance, and the hard work of Korean labor came together to set the ROK economy on a path of economic growth that is the envy of the developing world. For twenty years, the ROK's GNP grew at a rate averaging close to 10 percent. Per capita income increased from roughly $80 in the 1960s to more than $3500 by the mid-1980s.

The transformation of material culture in the South spawned a demographic and social revolution as well. The growth of a new middle class, industrial labor, and continuing expansion of education brought new forces into the political sphere. The government could no longer maintain its monopoly on power through authoritarian abuses in the face of mounting demands for political, social, and economic equity. By the late 1980s, these new forces combined to force a new commitment to democratic pluralism in the form of government concessions to a new election law, free speech, and local political autonomy.

THE ISSUE OF REUNIFICATION

In spite of the difficult transition now underway in the political arena, South Korea has emerged in the 1990s as a strong economic and political actor in the world. In contrast, North Korea has been isolated by the collapse of world communism. Its estrangement from world finance and technology compounded the virtual collapse of its economic system. In response, North Korea's reevaluation of its situation has created the conditions for rapprochement on the peninsula. The once frozen divide between North and South Korea has begun to thaw.

It is no longer a question of whether reunification of the peninsula is possible; rather, it is now an issue of when and on whose
terms realignment will take place—a realignment that will decisively change the political shape of Northeast Asia in the future.
There will not be, however, a simple absorption of the North by
the South as in the reunification of Germany. Unlike Germany,
the Koreans fought a bitter civil war. The North will fight to protect its political system from the corrosive effects of participation
in the world system; the South will strive to minimize disruption
to its still fragile experiment in pluralist democracy. Sobered by
the dimensions of the problems facing a reunified Germany, the
South is now fearful, if anything, that the North will collapse
precipitately.

Korea remains for the foreseeable future a monument to the
Cold War of the post-World War II era. How reunification will
occur and at what speed will depend on the Koreans themselves
in tandem with the action of powerful interests surrounding the
peninsula. What has decisively changed since 1876, however, is
the political and economic strength of the two Koreas to control
and shape their own future.

NOTE

1. The *yangban* formed the top of the Korean social pyramid. These
were persons and families who inherited from their forebears their status
and prestige, usually land and wealth, and the opportunities for education, academic degrees, and public office. *Yangban* status was mostly
inherited, and it conferred eligibility for participation in the civil service
examinations to the exclusion of other status groups. Not all families
claiming *yangban* status were wealthy or current office holders. The
exams during the Chosŏn period legitimated power and provided opportunities for a slow turnover of different families vying for power within
the bureaucracy. Local elites were made up of families that traced their
status to former officeholding in the Koryŏ or Chosŏn dynasties. Over
time the numbers of people in Chosŏn society claiming *yangban* status
swelled. Therefore it is useful to distinguish between the politically powerful *yangban* of the central government (officeholders, around 1500
officials, and their extended families) and important, but less powerful,
local elites who did not currently hold office.

IV
Themes in Asian History

SOUTH ASIAN HISTORY: A CURSORY REVIEW

Ainslie T. Embree

INTRODUCTION

In 1813, as James Mill finished his great work on India, the first attempt in any language to give a comprehensive account of Indian history and culture, he wrote of the difficulties that confronted him as he struggled to make a coherent story from the confusing mass of materials that he had discovered. His conclusion was that there were only two possibilities for the historian: "Either he must resolve to observe minutely a part; or he must resolve to make a cursory review of the whole. Life is insufficient for more."[1]

Many teachers of Indian history will have somewhat the same response, and they may be inclined to Mill's first option of concentrating on some small fragment of the rich complexity of the Indian mosaic, on the ground that it is better to have firm control of a small area of history than to attempt to cover a vast range of material in a superficial manner. Without some knowledge of how the fragment fits into the whole, however, this method of concentrating on one's area of specialization will not lead toward an understanding of Indian civilization. One is driven, then, not just by the necessities of a curriculum requirement, but by the nature of the historical process, to the second option, a cursory review of Indian history. Such a review demands selection, that is, emphasizing some aspects of history while ignoring others, and, at the same time, identifying recurring patterns and themes. Properly speaking, one should use the term "South Asia" to take into account modern political divisions, but in referring to the period before 1947 it is simpler to use the older and more familiar designation for the subcontinent.

The difficulty, however, in making a cursory review of Indian history, is, as Mill pointed out, that so far from adding to understanding, it may be "effectual, not for removing error, and perfecting knowledge, but for strengthening all the prejudices, and confirming all the prepossessions or false notions, with which the observer set out." This is so because we tend to choose for emphasis those things which confirm our beliefs, while ignoring those which might suggest new ways of thinking.[2] And, of course, it is precisely in the hope of finding such new ways of thinking that we encourage the study of world history. Nonetheless, with the dangers inherent in writing a cursory review of Indian history in mind, I shall attempt one. I shall start by noting some of the themes and patterns that have been identified as giving coherence to the study of Indian history and civilization, and commenting briefly on their validity, and then look at the Indian historical experience in chronological sequence.

HISTORIOGRAPHY

At the outset, however, it is important to bear in mind that modern historical writing on India began in the nineteenth century, and that, whether it was done by foreigners or by Indians, it was a product of the new methods for using source material and reflected eighteenth- and nineteenth-century attitudes toward social change. This new historiography contrasts with the two very different historical traditions, one indigenous, the other borrowed from the Islamic tradition, that existed in India before the development of interpretations influenced by Western models.

In the indigenous, or Hindu, literary tradition, the writing of history, as understood in Western, Islamic, and Chinese cultures, had not evolved, despite the extraordinary richness of other literary genres. Indians had, of course, like all other peoples, reflected on their past and their social origins. These reflections had been embodied in literary texts that fall roughly into three categories, all of them of fundamental importance for an understanding of Indian social and religious life, but of less use in constructing a chronological framework or in tracing the development of social and economic forces. One of these is what is known, not very accurately, as epic literature; it is written in Sanskrit and includes the vast text of the *Mahābhārata*, composed over a period from perhaps 500 B.C.E. to 400 C.E., and the *Rāmāyaṇa*, a more integrated work, perhaps dating from 750 to 500 B.C.E. The stories of gods, kings, and heroes that fill these great works are "holy history," rooted in the actual geography of the Indian subcontinent. The second category, also in Sanskrit, is known as purana, a class of works concerned with the complex interweaving of relationships of the gods with each other and with humans. These comprise the myths and legends that color Indian life, but neither the events they narrate nor the time scale in which they are set are "historical." While scholars, both Western and Indian, tried to find a historical base in this material, they found it difficult to come to terms, in Lord Macaulay's oft-quoted words, with "a history, abounding in kings thirty feet high and reigns thirty thousand years long," that "would move laughter in girls at an English boarding school."[3] A third class of literature that bears more resemblance to conventional ideas of history is the bardic poetry, usually written in the regional languages, not in Sanskrit, which glorifies kings and warriors. It was such bardic literature that James Tod made use of in his reconstruction of the history of Rajasthan.[4]

The other great tradition of historical writing in South Asia that predated Western influence had its origin in the Islamic Middle East, specifically Persia. Almost from the beginning of the intrusion of invading forces into the subcontinent from the Middle East and later from central Asia, historians gave fairly detailed accounts of victories achieved and of the new dynasties that were established. This emphasis on success—or failure—is very often connected by the chroniclers with the extent of the leader's devotion to Islam, and the other side of this concern for Islamic triumph is the defeat of the people of India. The invaders, as one writer put it, "performed those wonderful exploits, by which the Hindus became like atoms of dust scattered in all directions, and like a tale of old in the mouths of the people."[5] ("Hindu" in this class of writings is more or less equivalent to the way "Indian" is used in modern writings. It denotes the people of the land, and is not particularly a religious referent.)

The third great historical tradition that has shaped our understanding of the Indian experience is, of course, that of nineteenth-century western Europe. While Western knowledge of all cultures is largely a product of Western scholarship, this is probably true to a greater extent in the case of India than of the other countries of Asia. This is due partly, as noted above, to the nature of historical writing in India, but mainly because of British political control throughout the nineteenth century and its impact on Indian intellectuals. Much of the best writing on Indian history in the nineteenth century was done by British administrators, who were aware that without knowledge of India's past, especially its structures of government, its languages, and its religion, it would be impossible to rule successfully. For knowledge of religion, they turned to the great tradition of Hindu learning embodied in the Sanskrit texts; but for government and politics they turned to the chronicles of their Islamic predecessors, particularly the Mughals. There were many different schools of thought among the British and other Western writers, but one can defend the generalization that almost all European writers, no matter how great their admiration might be for Indian literary and artistic achievements, assumed the superiority of the West in terms of ability to provide stable political institutions, efficient commercial practices, and what they called "practical morality."

THEMES

It is against this background that one can sort out the themes that have been used in nineteenth- and twentieth-century historical writings to give coherence to the political and social complexity of the history of the Indian subcontinent. The first of these is an emphasis on the continuity of Indian civilization in the geographical region that gave it birth. All of our themes must be hedged with qualifications, the chief of which must be that we are dealing with the history of a civilization, and that there is no political entity, no "India," to provide a continuity of focus. It is this qualification that, in effect, becomes a primary theme in examining the history of the Indian subcontinent. The obvious contrast is with China, which is a political entity, however shifting and broken, that can be traced from remote antiquity. On a different geographic and time scale, the same can be said for Japan and Korea in Asia, and for Britain, France, and even Germany and Italy in Europe.

What one finds instead in India is, quite literally, a subcontinent where through the centuries there are many political configurations, some of which, especially in south India, are of long duration, but none that can be called "India" in the political sense in which we can speak of China. Not until the early sixteenth century with the foundation of the Mughal Empire can one identify a political entity that is more or less continuous up to the present time. What one does find, without question, is a continuity in civilization and culture in the same geographical region over at least three thousand years. Of the world civilizations, only China has a similar historical experience, and it is this civilizational reality that must be constantly juxtaposed with the lack of enduring political entities.

It is a civilization where, for very long periods, there are mechanisms of social control within society that are stronger than the state, and an examination of these mechanisms constitutes a second theme of Indian history. They include kinship relationships, which are based upon family, tribe, region, class, and culture, all of which are often summed up by Western observers as "caste." In a very real sense, Indian history to be meaningful must be social history.

A third theme, the relationship of religion to society, is directly related to the second one, for Western observers were convinced that all the social structures of Indian life were inextricably bound up with religious beliefs. Here James Mill's reaction can be taken to be that of many outsiders when he spoke of the "manners" of India. By manners he meant the peculiar modes in which the ordinary business of life is carried on. Human beings everywhere are the same in that they eat, drink, work, and, in his words, "meet, converse, transact, and sport together." But how these things are done differ from culture to culture, and in India, he insisted, "so much of the entire business of life . . . consists in religious services, that the delineation of their religion is a delineation of the principal branch of their manners."[6] With elaborations, this idea receives powerful advocacy in the writings of the great Germans—Hegel, Marx, and Weber—as Harvey Goldman has shown in his analysis of their readings of Indian civilization.[7] Weber gave this view almost canonical status when he said that India had not experienced the same kind of economic transformation as had Europe because the social structure of Hinduism was "certainly not capable of giving birth to economic and technical revolutions from within itself, or even of facilitating the first germination of capitalism in its midst."[8]

Any discussion of the relation of social structure to religious beliefs and practices in India will lead of necessity to a consideration of outbreaks of violence between religious communities, specifically between Hindus and Muslims. It is important, however, to avoid reading into the past the tensions generated by the nationalist movements and those of independent India, and, above all, making an alleged primordial Hindu-Muslim antagonism an interpretive methodology.

Few knowledgeable observers would now accept all the implications of this older emphasis on the function of religion in Indian society, but if "civilization" or "culture" is substituted for "religion," the idea becomes more plausible. It is, in fact, quite close to the ideas being expounded with great vigor and great success in contemporary India by Hindu nationalists. They argue that what is of primary importance to modern India is not the apparatus of the Western state imposed by the British and their lackeys among the Westernized elites but Hindu civilization and culture.[9] Questions relating to the fundamental nature of Indian, or Hindu, civilization refer, admittedly, to a vague and amorphous concept, but it is, I think, a basic theme that must underlie any review of Indian history.

A fourth theme useful in surveying Indian history is the recurrent pattern of attempts by various powers to establish empires that encompass large areas of the subcontinent. Some of these powers are indigenous groups from within the territorial limits of Indian civilization; others are external bearers of cultures alien to India. Most of these imperial structures lasted less than two hundred years, although some of them, notably the Mauryas, the Guptas, the Delhi sultanate, Vijayanagar, the Mughals, and the British, had enduring social and economic consequences. Part of the pattern of empire building is the break-up of the imposed structure into what the geographer O.H.K. Spate has called "perennial nuclear regions," that is, areas of local political power that are absorbed into imperial structures but then reemerge with the decay of central authority.[10] These regions, definable in terms of language, culture, and economy, and often with quite distinct geographical boundaries, disappear and reappear on the political map of the subcontinent. Ancient names survive, for example, in the names of modern states and provinces, such as Punjab, Bengal, Gujarat, Kerala, Sind, and Tamil Nadu.

A fifth theme, and one that formerly gained more than its deserved share of attention, is the role of invaders. Many older histories used invasions as an organizing principle, beginning with the Aryans around 2000 B.C.E., and continuing with the Greeks under Alexander, the Scythians, the Huns, the Turks, and the British. This is partly because two of the invading groups, the Turks and the British, had long traditions of writing history, and they inevitably gave prominence to their own conquests. Equally inevitably, the conquered people read the record differently, with glorious conquests becoming brutal oppression. There is, however, another reason why foreign invasions have a special role in Indian history. Elsewhere, invaders were very frequently driven out, as happened to the Arabs in Spain; they were absorbed into the society, as happened in China; or they destroyed the existing societies, as in Latin America. In India, none of these patterns was followed in the case of the Muslims or the British.

In 1700, after five centuries of Muslim rule, India had a very large Muslim population, perhaps a fifth of the population; new styles of architecture were to be seen everywhere, and the Persian language and literature flourished. Nonetheless, the majority of the people were Hindu; Indian languages were dominant; and trade and commerce, as well as many levels of government, were largely in the hands of Hindus. The same was generally true during the period of British rule, except that only a very tiny proportion of the people adopted the religion of the conquerors. In terms of education, legal systems, economic change, and political forms, the British impact was very great, and yet at the end of a century and a half of British rule and five centuries of Muslim rule, an independent India emerged with a culture that was clearly continuous with its ancient origins. Unlike other invaders, the British did not assimilate with the local populations, and eventually, unlike all previous invaders, left India without leaving behind any settlers.

A sixth theme, and one of extraordinary difficulty to explore in brief compass, is the course of economic development. For the premodern period, the sources for sustained analysis are very meager, despite the fact that the agricultural productivity of the region sustained a population of probably one hundred million by the first century of the Common era. There were networks of internal and external trade, cities flourished, and rulers of even small principalities supported armies and made war. Early economic studies were usually concerned with explanations of the poverty of India, the lack of economic development, and comparisons, favorable or unfavorable, of economic conditions before and after the advent of the British. The most wide-ranging modern survey, *The Cambridge Economic History of India*, points out that current interests have shifted to an examination of "the structure and dynamics of economic life under a system of relations of production very different from those subsisting after the British conquest."[11]

A seventh theme, and one that dominated historical writing in India itself in the first half of the twentieth century, is the rise of a nationalist movement that culminated in the decomposition of the Indian Empire that the British had created and the emergence in 1947 of the two states of India and Pakistan, followed in 1971 by the secession of Bangladesh from Pakistan. This writing has come in for criticism in recent years on the ground that, whether it is the work of Western writers or of Indians, it expresses an "elitist" point of view. By this is meant that there has been a tendency among Western writers to interpret twentieth-century Indian history as the product of the policies, institutions, and culture of the British colonial rulers. From the Indian side, elitist writers have seen the developments of the twentieth century in terms of Indian elite personalities, such as Nehru, Gandhi, and Jinnah, or elite institutions such as the Indian National Congress or the Muslim League. In contrast, in the words of the manifesto of the group of historians known as "the subalterns," the stress should be on "the contribution made by the people on their own, independently of the elite, to the making and development of this nationalism."[12] This means an examination of the role of peasant uprisings and violence, in contrast to the conventional emphasis on the nonviolent movement associated with Mahatma Gandhi. Directly associated with such concerns are questions about the roles of women in Indian society, especially the formation of those roles through culture and political activism.

"Nationalism" is an inadequate word to describe the complex forces, some external, some internal, that were at work in the transformation of Indian society in the twentieth century. But alternatives such as "decolonization" are even more misleading if they do not acknowledge that the changes came essentially from within the fabric of Indian society. This means that the political forms that came into existence in 1947 are by no means the end of history for the peoples of the subcontinent. Radical revision is quite probable in the legal, administrative, economic, and political arrangements that are to a considerable degree the product of an imperial rule that was sometimes in alliance with, sometimes in opposition to, dynamic forces within the society.

PERIODIZATION

With these seven themes in mind, let us look at the chronological development of society on the subcontinent. As we do so, we are faced with one of the persistent problems of Indian historiography, the difficulty of finding a reasonably satisfactory method of periodization. The system widely used in the early histories written in the nineteenth century divided the Indian past into the Hindu period (from the earliest beginnings up to 1200 C.E.), the Muslim period (1200 to 1700), followed by the British period. There is now general agreement that these designations badly distort reality because they ignore continuities, imply radical cultural breaks that in fact did not occur, and overstress the role of both religion and foreign conquest. An alternative periodization of ancient, medieval, and modern is more neutral, avoiding the misleading emphasis of the older one, but it misrepresents historical developments by suggesting parallels with the West that do not exist. For our present purposes, it is probably most satisfactory simply to use dates, even though they are very inexact for the early periods, together with descriptive headings indicating the general characteristics of a period.

THE RISE OF CIVILIZATION: 3500 TO 600 B.C.E.

While evidence is continually accumulating of very ancient human habitation in South Asia, the oldest settled communities appear to have been in Baluchistan, in northwest Pakistan, in the first half of the fourth millennium B.C.E. Current archaeological discoveries suggest that from these early settlements came the impetus for developments that culminated in the great urban centers of Harappa and Mohenjodaro in what is known as the Indus Valley civilization in about 2300 B.C.E. The civilization covered a vast area in what is now Pakistan and western India, and there is widespread agreement that its culture did not disappear with the decay of the urban centers around 1750 B.C.E., but that it lived on in many aspects of later Indian civilization, especially in religion. It is here that the basic theme of the continuity of Indian history begins. As the archaeologists Bridget and Raymond Allchin concluded in their careful survey of the Indus civilization, there is much in the distinctive character of Indian culture which appears "to have been derived from this source, and which emphasize[s] the continuity which was already very old."[13]

The decay of the Indus civilization around 1750 B.C.E. was once attributed to the destructive activities of an invading people, but while this may have been a factor, archaeologists now tend to stress natural causes such as climatic changes, soil depletion, or great flooding from the Indus. What is certain is that the urban centers came to an end, not to be replaced for many centuries, and that a new people, known as the Aryans, made their appearance in India. The themes of continuity, invasion, and religion are strikingly exemplified by these people, for their religious ideas and the language in which they were expressed became dominant in later Indian culture.

The original homeland of the Aryans is not known with certainty, but they appear to have been a group of tribes from central Asia who spoke languages or dialects belonging to the Indo-European language family. Very little is known of their movements into

India, but some groups probably came into northwest India around 2000 B.C.E. and other groups six centuries later. While there are no material artifacts that can be definitely attributed to this period, the Aryans have left one of the world's most remarkable collections of literature, known as the Vedas, of which the oldest, the *Rig Veda*, was probably composed between 1300 and 1500 B.C.E. It is this literature that Hindus came to regard as sacred, and it is the storehouse that has supplied many of the great myths, the deities, and the rituals that are integral to Indian civilization. This literature reflects the dominant role of the priestly class, the Brahmans, and for this reason modern scholars refer to the religious ideology and practices that developed during this period as Brahmanism.

THE GROWTH OF INDIAN CIVILIZATION: 600 B.C.E.–300 C.E.

The period from about 600 B.C.E. to 300 C.E. was marked by developments which increasingly demarcated the boundaries of Indian civilization in cultural and political terms. In the realm of religious ideas, two great systems, Jainism and Buddhism, challenged the third, Brahmanism, which had become intellectually and culturally dominant by this time. All three share common presuppositions, such as belief in transmigration, but Buddhism specifically rejected Brahmanical dominance and Jainism espoused a nontheistic position while practicing a radical asceticism based on not causing injury to any living thing. Jainism, while it was never in any sense a majority religion, influenced both Brahmanism and Buddhism through its intellectual systems, and, in the social field, its adherents became leaders in trade and finance, possibly because of Jainism's strictures against any activity that involved violent action.

Buddhism, which was eventually to spread throughout Asia, is the first of the three great universal or missionary religions, the others being Christianity and Islam, that transcend cultural and geographic boundaries, seeking to include the entire human race. Although it died out in India, Buddhism had its origins in the life and teaching of Gautama Buddha, "the Enlightened One," who was born about 566 B.C.E., the son of a ruler whose kingdom was between what is now Nepal and Bihar. His teaching, summed up in a sermon preached to his followers at Sarnath, near Varanasi, included the four noble truths. These were that life is suffering; that the cause of suffering is desire; that it is possible to be free from suffering; and that there is a way or path to gain liberation. This teaching had a great appeal as a way of salvation to many individuals, but it also was very attractive to rulers as a way of uniting people in a new ideology and of transmitting ideas and values across cultural boundaries. It was perhaps for this reason that Ashoka, the great emperor of the Mauryan Dynasty in India, espoused it.

In the political sphere, the old tribal structure was replaced by numerous small kingdoms. Agriculture was the basis of social and economic life, but towns had come into existence, indicating the growth of trade and craft-based industries such as weaving and pottery. Trade routes linked the different regions of India, including the seacoasts. All of these changes must have been interrelated, with trade, for example, helping the spread of the new religious ideas, while increased wealth made possible the support of the power of kings.

The Mauryan Dynasty, with its capital at Pataliputra, near what is now Patna in the state of Bihar, achieved ascendancy over neighboring kings under Chandragupta, who came to power about 325 B.C.E. Under his grandson, Ashoka (c. 269–232 B.C.E.), Mauryan power made itself felt throughout much of the subcontinent. While Ashoka is well known in Buddhist legends, since he is supposed to have been converted to Buddhism, he was not known to objective history until his great edicts, carved on rocks and pillars, were deciphered in the early nineteenth century. Nonetheless, Ashoka has an important place in modern Indian history, as indicated by the fact that the symbol of the Mauryan Empire, the chakra, or Wheel of Righteous Law, appears on the national flag that India adopted when it became independent. A number of factors made Ashoka a peculiarly appropriate figure for a nation, new in its current status, but reaching back across a very long historical experience. The edicts are found throughout the subcontinent, thus speaking of the territorial unity of India under one sovereign, rather than of a region divided into many sovereignties. They also seem to stress religious tolerance, with the assertion that the king desires the "furtherance of the essential message of all sects." This message had crucial relevance at a time when India was being threatened by fratricidal strife between Hindus and Muslims. The edicts urge the abandonment not only of war but of the killing of animals for sport or food. This had special meaning in the light of the exaltation of nonviolence by Gandhi as the special mark of Indian culture. Ashoka's significance for contemporary India can be summed up in the words of a modern scholar who notes that the edicts seem to imply "a moral polity of active social concern, religious tolerance, ecological awareness, the observance of common ethical precepts, and the renunciation of war."[14]

By 187 B.C.E., the Mauryan Dynasty lost control of the territories it had subjugated, giving way to new kingdoms and empires. This was a pattern that was to be repeated many times in the history of the subcontinent, but there is no doubt of the continuity and vigor of Indian culture, despite political changes. In north India, in addition to local dynasties, there were a number of intrusions by foreign peoples, the most important of which were the Scythians, known in Indian history as the Sakas, who appear to have been nomads from central Asia. One of these groups, the Kushans, established a powerful kingdom that lasted from about 78 C.E. to 200 C.E., stretching from what is now Peshawar, in Pakistan, to Mathura, south of Delhi. The Kushans, who adopted Buddhism, helped its spread throughout central Asia. In the north, at Gandhara, there was strong Hellenistic and Roman influence on Buddhist art.

In south India, there was a gradual diffusion of Brahmanical religious influence, of which the Sanskrit language was an important vehicle, which enriched but did not overwhelm the existing cultures of the southern regions. An important literature developed in Tamil, expressive of philosophical and religious ideas which suggest the continuing vitality of a Dravidian, as distinct from the Indo-Aryan, literary and religious tradition. There was extensive trading with the Roman Empire, from the Indian side in textiles, precious stones, spices, and exotic animals, and from the Roman side in glass, pottery, gold, and silver. This is evidenced by hoards of Roman coins in south India and by many references in Latin literature. There was also trade with Southeast Asia, with what is now Cambodia, Bali, Java, and other areas.

300–1200 C.E.: POLITICAL AND CULTURAL DEFINITION OF THE INDIAN TRADITION

The changes and developments outlined in the previous section provided the basis for the definition of Indian civilization during the period from 300 to 1200 C.E. A time of creativity and vitality in social structure, political organization, literature, art, architecture, and religion, this period is often referred to as the Classic Age of Indian civilization.

In the North, the first two centuries of the period were dominated by the Gupta Dynasty. As was the case with the Mauryas, the Gupta conquests did not constitute a centrally administered empire, but an area where conquered rulers acknowledged Gupta overlordship while retaining their local power. The Guptas were weakened by internal struggles with their feudatories and by the invasion from the northwest by a people who seem to be the same as those known in European history as the Huns.

Following the decline of Gupta power, a number of strong rulers established themselves in the North, but by the tenth century a number of clans known as Rajputs enter the stage of Indian history. Their origins are uncertain, but they forged small kingdoms for themselves throughout north India, particularly in what is now Rajasthan. Styling themselves Kshatriyas, that is, members of the traditional class of warriors in the Brahmanical understanding of society, they became the guardians of Hindu religion and culture in succeeding centuries, and the upholders of a romantic code of chivalry.

In south India, old dynasties like the Pandyas and the Cholas declined, but new ones like the Pallavas claimed hegemony over large areas. These kingdoms were in no sense centralized states, but as was the case with their contemporaries in Europe, effective power was dispersed among chieftains, with the local populations being related economically and politically to these local lords rather than to the king. The rulers in India, unlike those in many ancient societies, were not regarded as "god-kings," even though they might acknowledge a particular deity as their overlord. As far as sacral status was concerned, the validation of their legitimacy came from the Brahmans, unlike in cultures grounded in monotheism, where rulers had a peculiar relation to an ultimate God. It is tempting to see in this understanding an explanation of the lack of emphasis on the state, the great Leviathan, which is so characteristic of European developments.

In both the North and the South, in this period there was a great flowering of the human spirit, with intense literary, philosophic, religious, and artistic creativity, making it comparable in many ways to the High Middle Ages in Europe a few centuries later. Examples of this creativity are easy to list: the poetry of Bhartrihari, the plays of Kālidāsa, the philosophy of Śankara, the paintings and sculptures at Ajanta and Ellora, the great temples at Mahabalipuram.

The exuberant creativity that had demonstrated itself in so many forms appears to have weakened in the eleventh and twelfth centuries. There is a tendency to attribute this change to the coming of a powerful new invader, the Turks, and, specifically, to their introduction of a new religion, Islam, that was hostile to many manifestations of the Indian spirit. While, as we will note in the next section, the new invaders and their religion undoubtedly had profound effects on Indian culture, it seems certain that some loss of vitality had preceded the Turkish conquests.

The invasion by the Turks, as well as political, religious, and economic forces within the various regions of India, worked to produce new social forms. We lack the sources for a careful analysis of these forces, but it is important to emphasize that virtually no aspect of Indian civilization disappeared as the result of the Turkic invasions and the coming of Islam. What happened in the Americas with the advent of the Europeans was not duplicated in India. Indian culture and civilization as it had developed over the course of the preceding centuries was able to withstand the Turks and the coming of Islam, just as at a later date it was able to withstand the pervasive power of Western imperialism.

1200–1750: RESTRUCTURING THE POLITICAL AND CULTURAL MAP

The entrance of the Turks into north India referred to in the section above was not the subcontinent's first encounter with followers of Islam. That had begun long before, when an Arab general from the eastern provinces of the Umayyad Empire conquered what is now Sind in Pakistan in 711–713. While this established a permanent Islamic presence, the conquest did not have much effect on the rest of India, for even if the Arab rulers had been able to meet the formidable challenge of the deserts to the east, they would have been prevented by strong Indian rulers from expanding their power.

The second and more fateful Islamic intrusion came not from the Arab heartland but from Turkic chieftains from central Asia who had long been active in the politics of Iran. One branch had established its base at Ghazna, in what is now Afghanistan, and from there conquered much of what is now Sind and Punjab in Pakistan. These Indian territories passed to another Turkic dynasty, the Ghurids, and it was their chieftain, Muhammad, who in 1192 defeated the ruler of Delhi. This date has been much dramatized in Indian history, but this was by no means the defeat by a foreign invader of the ruler of India, because no such ruler existed. It was the defeat of one local ruler, with territory around Lahore, of another local ruler, whose territory centered on Delhi. It is often asked why an alliance of Indian rulers, as the guardians

of Hinduism, did not repel the Islamic invader, and the best answer seems to be that the juxtaposition of Indian and foreigner,
Hindu and Islamic, reflects a modern way of thinking which was
not available in the twelfth century. The judgment of the Indian
historian, Romila Thapar, on these events in north India seems
incontrovertible: while it was accepted that conquerors would
rule, "the wider implications—such as the likelihood that the newcomers would alter and modify the pattern of Indian culture—was
not at first clearly realized."[15]

Using Delhi as their base, the Turks, under their commanders
who adopted the title of sultan, expanded their control during the
thirteenth century, first into Rajasthan to the southwest, down the
Ganges into Bengal, and then into central India. Not until the middle
of the fourteenth century, however, were they able to penetrate
deeply into the south. Although the period from 1200 to 1526 is
referred to as the Delhi sultanate, the Delhi sultan only briefly
exercised centralized control over the conquered territories. Almost
from the beginning, commanders of the armies exercised virtual
sovereignty in territories remote from Delhi, such as Bengal, Malwa,
Gujarat, and the Deccan.

The centers of power established by the sultan and his commanders were bases for armies of occupation, rather than states or provinces in the modern sense. When local Indian chieftains were
conquered, they were generally left in possession of their lands if
they agreed to pay tribute. The new rulers were essentially interested
in revenue, and this was the most expeditious way of getting it.

For much the same reason, the new rulers did not attempt any
widespread forcible conversion of the Hindu population to Islam. The
pious Muslim religious leaders argued that it was the duty of a
Muslim ruler to convert nonbelievers, but with few exceptions they
seem to have followed the commonsense policy of putting revenue
collection before the ideological demands of religion. The ruling
groups were aware of their limitations in a vast Hindu population;
conversion could be left to the persuasion of the professionally religious. And these, especially the Sufi missionaries, did convert millions of people over the course of the centuries. Many of the poor
and oppressed must have accepted Islam in the hope of improving
their economic and social conditions, even though there is little
evidence that this worked, while others probably accepted it to avoid
the jizya, the special tax imposed upon non-Muslims.

There was undoubtedly a growing impoverishment of the old Indian culture as the result of Turkish conquest. Indigenous forms
of art, such as sculpture, temple architecture, music, dance, and

Sanskrit learning, all of which depended upon the patronage of rulers, suffered greatly during the period, even though, as suggested above, a decline in vitality may have set in before the conquest. Over and against this loss must be set the introduction of new learning, new forms of art, and new architectural styles.

The Islamic Dynasty in India that is associated with the most brilliant cultural achievements, and the one that built up the greatest and most long-lasting empire, is that of the Mughals, who entered India in 1526. It is this dynasty that became known to the Western world, since its period of greatness coincided with the beginning of European expansion into Asia. When John Milton in the middle of the seventeenth century was searching for a metaphor for splendor, he found it, not in Europe, but in travelers' accounts of

> The wealth of Ormus and of Ind,
> Or where the gorgeous east with richest hand
> Show'rs on her kings Barbaric pearl and gold.[16]

What dazzled travelers was the lifestyle of the courts; the occasional glimpses we get of the lives of the peasants and the urban poor are remarkably similar to what one sees today in South Asia.

Through alliances and conquests the Mughals extended their control until during the reign of Aurangzeb (1658–1707) almost all of South Asia, including Afghanistan, was included in their empire. This expansion was followed by a decline in power during the next fifty years as imperial control was weakened by internal and external forces. Internally, in the pattern that can be seen many times in the history of the subcontinent, military commanders and governors asserted their independence of the center, with such important regions as Bengal in the east, Avadh in the Gangetic heartlands, and Hyderabad in the Deccan passing from imperial control.

The most formidable direct challenge to the Mughals came, however, from an indigenous group, the Marathas of western India. Although their chieftains had been feudatories of the Mughals, in the last half of the seventeenth century, under their leader Shivaji, they began open warfare against the imperial troops. In the eighteenth century their successes against the empire and other Indian rivals made them the strongest power in India. It seemed as if they would become successors to the Mughals, but they failed to create an administrative structure to hold their conquests together. In an attempt to overwhelm the empire, they were decisively defeated in 1761 in the Punjab, not by the Mughals but by Abdali, an Afghan chieftain who had gained control of the area some years before. While the Marathas had been defeated in their great bid for power, they remained a formidable military power, and it was they, not the Mughals, who were to prove the greatest obstacle to British conquest.

The Afghans who defeated the Marathas represented a combination of the internal and external enemies of the Mughals, for some were military commanders in the Mughal armies, while others were actual invaders, like Abdali, who had first invaded India in 1748 and had taken Delhi in 1757. Even before this the Persian ruler Nadir Shah had pillaged Delhi in 1739, so that by the 1760s, when the British began to establish territorial power in Bengal, what remained of the imperial institutions were little more than symbols.

For eighteenth- and nineteenth-century Western historians, a ready model for understanding the decay of Mughal power was at hand in that most evocative of European events, the decline and fall of Rome. The more perceptive British officials and administrators, most of whom had a strong historical sense, read in the decline of the Mughals lessons for what they should avoid, as did Indian nationalists when they began to write history. The internal forces that had weakened the Mughals spoke of the need for unity, whether imposed from without by the British or created from within by national sentiment. The external invasions reminded the British of the need for military security, while they reminded Indians of the internal weaknesses that had made them possible.

A common explanation of the Mughal decline, one that was much favored by early writers but is now given much less prominence, is dynastic weakness, that is, a succession of weak and ineffective rulers corrupted by the softness of court life. Another explanation, long popular with both foreign and Indian historians, was that the Emperor Aurangzeb, abandoning the tolerant practices of his predecessors, had aroused the antagonism of the Hindus by a fanatic attempt to impose Islam. In this argument Aurangzeb and Islam are counterpointed with Ashoka as the paladin of religious unity. Although there is little objective evidence to support this reading of history, it is of very great political importance for contemporary India.

Economic historians have given a more plausible interpretation by showing that the crushing burden of taxes on the peasants, made necessary to pay for war throughout the seventeenth century, led to the breakdown of the revenue system. As a corollary to expansion, the administrative mechanisms were not strong enough to control the vast territory that was included in the Mughal imperium. K.N. Chaudhuri, in a study of the economy of the Indian Ocean world up to 1750, stressed the great significance of cities for the Mughals, arguing that Mughal power to an extraordinary degree depended upon the control of the six primate cities: Lahore, Delhi, Agra, Patna, Burhanpur, and Ahmedabad. Their loss by the imperial authority demonstrates the close relations between "urban geography and the politics of decline."[17] Mughal decline must be related, however tentatively, to the worldwide changes which are referred to in another essay in this volume as "the encompassing of the world" by western European powers.[18] The crisis of the empire had occurred before the Western impact was really felt in India, but the strains that developed throughout the world altered old balances of external and internal trade as well as relations between the Asian countries. It should be noted that the arrival of the Portuguese in south India in 1497, succeeding where Columbus had failed in 1492, had minimal direct impact on India. In 1997, India will not celebrate Vasco da Gama's arrival as America did Columbus' in 1992.

The century of Mughal political decline in India was not characterized, as many Western writers have depicted it, as one of anarchy and chaos. Indian writers, some of whom were deeply involved in the Mughal power structure, were aware, however, of the changes in relationships—social, political, and economic—that were taking place. Culturally, the eighteenth century was one of great creativity, occasioned at least in part by the dispersal of political power to many new centers, such as Lucknow, Jaipur, Hyderabad, and Mysore, where the ruling elites became patrons of art, architecture, literature, and religion. Toward the end of this century of ferment and change, Europeans were also involved, although to a much lesser extent than has often been suggested. They do, however, provide the focus for the next period, when India became part of the world economic and political system in a way it had never been before.

1750–1947: THE INDIAN SUBCONTINENT BECOMES PART OF THE WORLD SYSTEM: THE ESTABLISHMENT AND DECOMPOSITION OF THE BRITISH IMPERIUM IN INDIA AND THE MAKING OF TWO NATION-STATES

"What has been the record of British rule in India?" Jawaharlal Nehru asked himself in jail in 1934, where he had been sent for his part in leading the nationalist movement. He concluded that it was a question to which no one could give an objective or dispassionate answer.[19] The cumbersome title of this subsection is an attempt to indicate the main themes of the history of the period from the decline of Mughal power in the middle of the eighteenth century to 1947, without claiming that it will be truly objective.

At the very beginning of British rule in Bengal, an official of the East India Company had given one answer to the question that Nehru was to ask two centuries later, and which was to be restated in many ways by many people, including Nehru himself. In 1769 Richard Becher, a servant of the East India Company in Bengal, reported as follows to his superiors in London:

> It must give pain to an Englishman to have reason to think that since the accession of the [East India] Company to the Diwani the condition of the people of this country has been worse than it was before. . . . This fine country, which flourished under the most despotic and arbitrary government, is verging towards its ruin.[20]

In contrast, at the beginning of the twentieth century, Sir Alfred Lyall, a very knowledgeable Government of India official, observing the beginning of the nationalist movement, remarked that no one could venture upon "any prognostic of the course which the subtle and searching mind of India will mark out for itself." After reviewing the record of British rule, however, he concluded that, "whatever may be the ultimate destiny of our Indian Empire, we shall have conferred upon the Indians great and permanent benefits, and we shall have left a good name for ourselves in history."[21] And it was not only self-congratulatory Westerners who thought that way. In 1871 Dadabhai Naoroji, the great Indian nationalist leader, could list what he regarded as the benefits of British rule: "Education, both male and female. . . . Peace and order. Freedom of speech and liberty of the press. . . . Equal justice between man and man. . . . Railways and irrigation."[22]

Most attempts to answer Nehru's question share a common error in that they attribute too much, for good or ill, to British rule. Three major misperceptions of Indian history are involved. One is the assumption that the changes we see in the nineteenth century actually took place then under the impact of British rule, whereas they may have started earlier. This misperception is due partly to the fact that we have much better sources for that century than we do for previous ones, and partly to the ethnocentric assumption, often quite unconscious, that since Westerners were in charge, they must have been the agents responsible for change. Many changes were already taking place before the British takeover because of the realignment of political power that followed the decay of the central authority of the Mughals. It is quite possible, for example, that Hindu elites might have given new directions to society in Bengal and Maharashtra as they gained economic and political power.

A second misperception comes from a failure to recognize the creativity and ferment inherent in Indian society. The intellectual vitality that characterized Bengal society in the nineteenth century, often referred to as "the Bengal renaissance," is usually linked with new ideas from the West, but in fact it can be seen as rooted in the culture itself. An obvious example is the condemnation of idol worship by various reformers in Bengal and elsewhere in the nineteenth century. This is usually seen as a direct reaction to Western criticism, but in fact one can find criticism of idolatry from within Hinduism long before the nineteenth century. This expresses itself in a different vocabulary of discourse because of contact with the West, but it is easy to find analogs in previous centuries.

A third misperception, and one that Nehru was fond of pointing out, is that India would not have had railways, telegraphs, and other products of industrialism except for British rule. These were, he insisted, the artifacts of a worldwide modernity that would have reached India without British conquest. They were, he said, "the veins and arteries through which the nation's blood should have coursed, increasing its trade, carrying its produce, and bringing new life and wealth to its millions." Instead, the very things that should have given India its place in the world, as they had Japan, were used to strengthen the imperial stranglehold and squeeze from India its life blood.[23]

In thinking about Indian history in the modern period, we must recognize that to a very great extent Indian civilization itself determined the nature of the Western impact. To see India as either the passive victim of Western imperialism or, on the other hand, as an unyielding opponent of the West is to misunderstand the dynamics of social change on the subcontinent. It is perfectly obvious that the impact of Western imperialism differed very greatly from one region to another, not only because different Western countries behaved differently but because the cultures on which they had an impact responded very differently. Indian civilization was not overwhelmed by the West as were, to take an extreme example, the fragile cultures of the native peoples of North America. India had highly evolved social, religious, economic, and political structures that could adjust themselves to the new pressures from without. India took what it wanted from the West and used it for its own purposes. Perhaps the best example of this is the astonishing demand among Indian elites for education through the medium of English. Almost from the very beginning there were those who saw that interaction with the modern West could lead to the restoration of India's greatness.

Perhaps, then, the most instructive way to look at Indian history in the modern period is to see the subcontinent, with its variety of political entities and cultures, becoming involved in a world system of economic, political, and cultural relationships. These three categories overlap, but they are distinct enough to provide a framework for analysis. And involvement is a better word than conquest to describe many of the relationships between India and the West in the century after Mughal decline. While there was, of course, actual military conquest by the British in large areas of India, and much warfare, the lasting consequences for India of its changed relationships with the rest of the world are to be found in the ways that Indian institutions of all kinds maintained their integrity while undergoing transformation.

The origins of India's linkage with the world system were economic, dictated by the European interest in Indian commodities such as spices, textiles, opium, and indigo, and also by the use of Indian ports as entrepots for goods from Southeast Asia. The Portuguese were the pioneers in establishing such linkages, after their voyage in 1497, with their creation of a number of forts on the west coast, including the great capital of their Asian sea-linked empire at Goa. They lost out, first to the Dutch, then to the English, in their attempts in the seventeenth century to control Asian trade with Europe. The Dutch switched their interests to Southeast Asia, and the rivalry for the Indian trade was left to the English and the French, with the English winning decisively over the French during the Seven Years' War (1756–1763).

Two central features of this stage of India's involvement with Europe must be kept in mind as one tries to understand its complexities and contradictions. One is that it was not the English government that was directly involved, but the East India Company, to which a charter of monopoly of the trade between England and India had been given in 1600 by Queen Elizabeth. The company has been succinctly described as a "constitutional anachronism . . . at once a manifestation of Western capitalism and overseas expansion," a business organization engaged in a large intercontinental trade but also the effective ruler of a vast territory in the Indian subcontinent.[24] The other important feature of this early involvement is that all through the seventeenth century and until the middle of the eighteenth, the European trading companies existed at the sufferance of the Indian powers, either the imperial authority or regional rulers. The Europeans were not invaders at first, but suppliants who were given permission to trade and build their establishments at obscure places that were of no importance to Indian rulers, such as the villages that became Calcutta, Madras, and Bombay. The activities of the European traders that loom so large in Western literature find no mention in contemporary Indian records. Their trade enriched local Indian merchants, as well as the Europeans, but it apparently was not seen as an important item in the imperial exchequer.

There is very wide disagreement among economic historians about the changes that took place in the Indian economy in the period of Western dominance. As indicated at the beginning of this section, a central charge of Indian nationalists was that the poverty of India was due to British rule, an interpretation that became widespread in anti-imperialist writing in the West. As one Marxist writer put it, "The British administration of India systematically destroyed all the fibers and foundations of Indian society through its fiscal, commercial, and economic policies."[25] The official British position, as enunciated in 1934, was equally unequivocal: "It can be claimed with certainty that in the period which has elapsed since 1858 when the Crown assumed supremacy . . . the material progress of India has been greater than it was ever within her power to achieve during any other period of her long and checkered history."[26] The truth is not to be found between these two extremes, but in a different interpretation that stresses the nature of the Indian, apart from government policies. As Morris D. Morris suggests in his essay in this volume, industrialization and economic modernization do not occur inevitably. There are certain necessary preconditions that were not present in India in the nineteenth century.[27] Most economic decisions were made by private parties, both Indian and foreign, who invested their money where it would bring the highest returns, which was generally in trade, not industry. Their primary interest was not in solving the problem of Indian poverty, and the government itself had a hands-off policy in regard to the economy. Nehru castigated the British for this, saying that their conception of ruling India was "to protect the State and leave the rest to others."[28] For most of the nineteenth century they would have agreed that the state should not interfere in the functioning of the market economy.

The second category of involvement, the political, was directly related to the economic one, for the East India Company had two major motivations for the takeover of the Mughal provinces of Bengal, which included what is now Bangladesh and the Indian states of West Bengal and Bihar. One was to gain control of the revenue administration so that it could use the surpluses in the public funds to buy goods for export; the other was to safeguard that trade from attacks by other Indian rulers. Later, questions of national prestige were important, as were the personal ambitions of governors and generals.

The emphasis, however, even in the early period of conquest, should not be on the foreign actors, for Indian rulers, traders, bureaucrats, and ordinary citizens were decisive at many points in transferring power to the British and in helping them to maintain their authority. At the same time, the conquest was not easy or sudden, and a number of Indian rulers fought very stubbornly, such as Haider Ali and Tipu Sultan, the rulers of Mysore, the Marathas in central and western India, and the Sikhs in the Punjab. The last major assault on British rule came in 1857, in the great uprising known to the British as "The Mutiny," and to later Indian nationalists as the "first war of independence." In addition, there were many local uprisings in rural areas against what was regarded as unfair and excessive taxation.

The most obvious result of the intrusion of British power in India was the political unification of the subcontinent under one political authority. As it became apparent in the 1930s that the British would have to share power with the Indians, a committee of the House of Commons discussing constitutional reform placed this fact high on the list of British achievements. The British, the report of the committee stated, had given India "that which throughout the centuries she had never possessed, a government whose authority is unquestioned in any part of the subcontinent, and, by having transformed India into a unitary state, had made possible the sense of nationality."[29] What this kind of understanding of Indian history ignores is the point made at the beginning of this essay, namely, that throughout history Indian rulers had striven with varying degrees of success to bring all the subcontinent under one authority, and the British were following, often quite consciously, this Indian pattern. When Lord Ellenborough was governor general (1842–1844), he declared that he "must act like Akbar," and that to have Delhi become "the ancient seat of empire, and to administer the government from it, has ever seemed to me to be a very great object."[30] It would be eighty years before Delhi would in fact become the seat of the unitary state which the British boasted of having created, and not long thereafter that the other continuous historical trend, of India dividing itself into constituent parts, reemerged. The emphasis on unified political control also ignores the fact that in large measure it was due to the accidents of history that this process of unification took place during the nineteenth century. All the advantages accrued to Britain from its possession of the mechanisms that made a unitary state possible: the railroad, the steamship, the telegraph, superior weapons.

As already noted, the British saw themselves as primarily the guardians of law and order, not the creators of a new society. Power was very narrowly concentrated in the hands of a small bureaucracy, virtually all of whose members were British, although the lower ranks were filled by Indians. Many Indians became rich and famous through trade and such new professions as the law, but they found no place in the political structure. The same was true of the army: of the total army of about 190,000, two-thirds were Indian, but all the officers were British. While British power depended upon this small army, it was a civilian despotism, not a military one.

Throughout the nineteenth century Indians had very little voice in how they were governed, but it was a despotism with a difference. The ultimate authority was the British Parliament, which, while certainly not the watchdog of Indian rights, was, as Indian nationalists were well aware, a court, along with British public opinion, to which appeal could be made. Furthermore, it was a despotism that ruled within the confines of the laws that it created, and there was a legal system that provided as fair a measure of protection as existed in many countries. The press was remarkably free, both in English and in the Indian languages, a condition that was of great importance for the nationalist movement.

The political condition of India by the end of the nineteenth century can be summarized by noting that it had the administrative infrastructure of a modern state before it became a nation. This illustrates the point made by Carl Friedrich when he wrote that "the building of the state comes first, and it is within the political framework of the state that the nation comes into being."[31] It was within this framework that Indian nationalism developed, but before turning for a brief glance at that phenomenon, it is necessary to look at cultural developments which undergird it.

Cultural developments, the third category of India's involvement with the West, are closely related to the economic and political changes that linked India to the world system in the nineteenth and twentieth centuries. While many regions of India shared in the changes, Calcutta, as the economic and political capital of India, best demonstrated how cultural confrontation and adaption took place. The second city in the British Empire, as Bengalis were fond of referring to it, Calcutta was the direct product of the great worldwide movements that produced its American contemporaries, Boston, Philadelphia, and New York. Nowhere does one see more clearly that Western culture was not something imposed upon a hostile population or upon one lacking its own high culture. Instead, what one sees in Calcutta is a lively, self-confident intelligentsia reaching out to extract from the West the knowledge that could benefit them. What they wanted from the West was defined by Ram Mohan Roy (1772–1833), the most famous of that group: "Mathematics, Natural Philosophy, Chemistry, Anatomy, and other useful sciences, which the natives of Europe have carried to a degree of perfection that has raised them above the inhabitants of the rest of the world."[32] Nothing is more erroneous than the idea that the Indians were obliged to learn English in order to supply themselves with clerks; on the contrary, the Bengal intelligentsia seized upon English with a passion as they looked at the economic and political changes taking place. A Bengali writer recently put it this way:

> This closeness to the seat of power gave the Bengalis, besides other advantages, a front seat before the window of the West. A civilization that had always excluded the foreigner from its soul despite dealing with him in material affairs, woke up to find its philosophical ideas challenging its own inward-looking spirituality.[33]

The Indian nationalist movement, which had its formal beginning with the establishment of the Indian National Congress in 1885, was the product of the interaction of the cultural, political, and economic forces of the nineteenth century with the complex factors of the Indian historical experience. The many centuries of Islamic rule, the imposing presence of British power, the diversity of languages and religions, the poverty and illiteracy of the masses over against a prosperous and sophisticated elite guaranteed a struggle for autonomy and independence that would be different from nationalist movements elsewhere. One of these differing characteristics was that the nationalist leaders were not nativists. None of them argued for a return to Indian patterns of government, but insisted that their goal was the attainment of representative, parliamentary government, on the British model, which would guarantee British freedoms to the people of India. Another characteristic was that the leaders were almost always men who had won distinction in the professions, and who were as respected by the British as they were by their own countrymen. And almost without exception they came from the traditional regional elites; there were few "new" men among them.

All of this meant that the nationalist movement did not call for social revolution or the transformation of society, but rather for a transfer of the control of the existing political and economic system from British to Indian hands. This was true even in the period after 1920 when Mahatma Gandhi dominated the Indian National Congress, for while he had a radical social vision, he argued that change was to come not through an attack on the existing system but through the transformation of the individual psyche. Gandhi's strategy of nonviolence was a potent weapon against the British, but his greatest contribution to the nationalist movement was to persuade Indians that his method of nonviolence was deeply rooted in Indian civilization, marking it off from the violent cultures of Islam and the West. He was able to make his ideas part of a coherent ideology formulated in the vocabulary of Indian religion, which made a very deep appeal to many levels of society. The point is often made that Gandhi appealed to the Indian masses, and this is of course true, but it was probably just as important that he was able to mobilize the professional classes, wealthy traders, women, and students. For the majority of the people of India, as for many foreigners, he had defined what it meant to be Indian.

Although the Indian National Congress was clearly the most articulate voice for Indian political aspirations, its stated goal of a democratically elected representative government was increasingly questioned throughout the twentieth century by Muslim leaders. What they began to formulate was, in effect, an alternative Indian nationalism that denied the vision of the Indian National Congress of a constitutional structure based on the Western model of majority rule by the political party that won an election. By the 1930s, Mohammed Ali Jinnah, as leader of the Muslim League, had begun to express what became known as "the two nation theory." India, according to that argument, was not, as the Congress claimed, a unitary state with a single national identity. It was, instead, two nations, one Hindu and the other Muslim. Jinnah desired independence from the British as fervently as did the Indian National Congress, but he argued that the unified India of which the Congress spoke was an artificial one, created and maintained by British bayonets. Hinduism and Islam were not religions in the Western sense; they were, he insisted,

different and distinct social orders . . . , two different civilizations which are based mainly on conflicting ideas and concepts.
. . . To yoke together two such nations under a single state, one
as a numerical minority and the other as a majority, must lead
to growing discontent and final destruction of any fabric that
may be so built up for the government of such a state.[34]

Jinnah's analysis, however logical it may sound in the light of the
later experience of such countries as the Soviet Union, was rejected
by the Congress, leading to the long and frustrating negotiations
between the Congress, the Muslim League, and the British. By the
end of the Second World War, however, two facts were inescapably
clear. One was that Britain, weakened by the war, would not attempt to maintain its power in India by force. The other was that
transferring power to a single national entity with a strong central
government, as the Congress demanded, presented insuperable difficulties in view of the Muslim League's position. With great reluctance, the British negotiators and the leadership of the Indian
National Congress agreed, as the only solution, to the partition of
the subcontinent between India, as the successor state of British
India, and the new state of Pakistan. The Muslim leaders were not
happy with the partition as it was worked out, for they got much
less territory than they had hoped for, and what they did get, West
Pakistan and East Pakistan, were separated by a thousand miles of
Indian territory. Nor was Pakistan by any means a home for all the
Muslims of the subcontinent: at the time of Partition, over fifty
million of them remained in India.

The coming of independence in 1947 to India and Pakistan, the
dislocation and human suffering occasioned by the movement of
over thirteen million refugees from one country to another, and the
efforts made in both countries to initiate schemes for social and
political reform, are indicative of the enormous changes that took
place. Nevertheless, as a perceptive historian of the period has put it,
the "institutions of government, the structure of society, and the
fundamental beliefs of most Indians did not change just because the
Union Jack was lowered and the last British troops marched to the
Gateway of India to board ship in Bombay harbour."[35]

POST-1947: TOWARD STABILITY

For both India and Pakistan, the tasks were as obvious as they
were formidable: creating stable political systems, formulating
economic policies, providing a measure of social justice for the

poverty-stricken masses, and defining relations with each other and with the other world powers, especially with the United States, the Soviet Union, and China. Not even a cursory review can be attempted here of the ways in which they attacked these problems, except to note the general framework of developments.

In India, under Jawaharlal Nehru, there was a commitment to national unity, parliamentary democracy, a socialist pattern of society, and a desire to play a significant role in foreign affairs. Of all these commitments, that to national unity was overriding. The memory of Partition was always at the forefront, but the long history of a unified state giving way to regional powers was always in the background. For this reason, with an awareness of the appeal that had been made to religious identity as a basis of nationality before Partition, there was great stress placed on the fact that India was a secular state, that is, one where all religions were free but without state sanction or support. Parliamentary democracy was maintained and personal freedoms guaranteed, except for the period from 1975 to 1977. During this period, Prime Minister Indira Gandhi suspended constitutional provisions and instituted authoritarian rule on the ground that abuse of freedom by her opponents threatened national unity.

As for the economy, Parliament had declared that India would follow a socialist pattern of society, both to provide social justice for the people and to strengthen the state. A series of five-year plans were instituted that created a mixed economy, with a public sector controlling large-scale industry deemed vital to the state, and a private sector meeting consumer needs. At the same time, a thoroughgoing, and largely successful, attempt was made to make India self-sufficient in food and other commodities.

In foreign affairs, Nehru formulated a policy of neutralism and nonalignment that was intended to keep India from entanglement in the quarrels of the great powers while at the same time permitting it to take an active role in the United Nations and other international bodies. In the period from 1947 to 1990, India was generally perceived by the outside world as following the Soviet Union rather than the United States, but the Indian explanation is that the Soviet Union consistently pursued polices that were in line with India's interests, while the United States did not. India's actions were in line, then, with its self-interest. This self-interest, as India perceived it, often involved relations with Pakistan, which were always strained, and on three occasions led to war between the two countries.

One of these wars involved the support India gave the secessionist movement that developed in East Pakistan in the 1960s when the political leaders of the region worked for independence from Pakistan. India's support guaranteed their success, and a new nation, Bangladesh, was created. This secession can be understood on two levels. On one, it is a continuation of the partition in 1947 of what Jinnah had referred to as the artificial state created by British bayonets in the nineteenth century. On the other, it is an expression of the power of ethnicity that has become so evident in the second half of the twentieth century.

The political and economic structures of the countries of South Asia have been greatly influenced by the links that were forged in the nineteenth century under the world order in which Great Britain played a dominant role. The readjustments and realignments that began around the time of the First World War were felt in South Asia, but not so profoundly as those that took place after the Second World War, including those of the 1990s. The countries of the region—India, Pakistan, Bangladesh, Nepal, and Sri Lanka—have a long-shared political and cultural history; they also have many shared, as well as conflicting, interests with each other and with the rest of the world. What Nehru said of India in 1947 is true of the whole of South Asia: at the dawn of history, India "started on her unending quest, and trackless centuries are filled with her striving and the grandeur of her success and her failures."[36]

NOTES

1. James Mill, *The History of British India* (London: Baldwin, Craddock, and Joy, 1826), 1:xiii.

2. Ibid., xiv.

3. Thomas Babington Macaulay, *Macaulay, Prose and Poetry*, ed. G.M. Trevelyan (Cambridge, MA: Harvard University Press, 1952), p. 723.

4. James Tod, *Annals and Antiquities of Rajasthan* (New Delhi: K.M.N. Publishers, 1971).

5. Al Biruni, *Alberuni's India*, trans. Edward Sachau, abr. ed. by Ainslie T. Embree (New York: Norton, 1971), p. 22.

6. Mill, *British India*, 1:376,b.

7. See his article, "Images of the Other: Asia in Nineteenth-Century Western Thought, Hegel, Marx, and Weber," in this volume.

8. H.H. Gerth and C. Wright Mills, eds., *From Max Weber* (New York: Oxford University Press, 1958), p. 413.

9. H.V. Seshadri, *Hindu Renaissance under Way* (Bangalore: Jagarana Prakashan, 1984).

10. O.H.K. Spate, *India and Pakistan: A General and Regional Geography* (London: Methuen, 1960), pp. 148–50.

11. Tapan Raychaudhuri and Irfan Habib, eds., *The Cambridge Eco-*

nomic History of India, vol. 1 (Cambridge: Cambridge University Press, 1982), p. xi.

12. Ranjit Guha, ed., *Subaltern Studies: Writings on South Asian History and Society* (Delhi: Oxford University Press, 1982), p. 3.

13. Bridget Allchin and Raymond Allchin, *The Rise of Civilization in India and Pakistan* (Cambridge: Cambridge University Press, 1982), p. 361.

14. John S. Strong, *The Legend of King Asoka* (Princeton: Princeton University Press, 1989), p. 4.

15. Romila Thapar, *A History of India* (Baltimore: Penguin, 1966), 1:266.

16. John Milton, *Paradise Lost*, book 2, lines 1–3, in *Paradise Lost and Paradise Regained*, ed. Christopher Ricks (New York: New American Library, 1968), p. 70.

17. K.N. Chaudhuri, *Asia Before Europe: Economy and Civilisation of the Indian Ocean from the Rise of Islam to 1750* (Cambridge: Cambridge University Press, 1990), p. 364.

18. Loyd E. Lee, "The Rise of an Interdependent World, 1500–1990," in this volume.

19. Jawaharlal Nehru, *Towards Freedom* (Boston: Beacon Press, 1958), p. 275.

20. In Ramsay Muir, ed., *The Making of British India* (Manchester: Manchester University Press, 1923), pp. 92–93.

21. Sir Alfred Lyall, *The Rise and Expansion of British Rule in India* (London: John Murray, 1907), p. 348.

22. Dadabhai Naoroji, *Essays, Speeches and Writings* (Bombay: Caxton, 1887), pp. 131–35.

23. Nehru, *Towards Freedom*, p. 277.

24. K.N. Chaudhuri, "East India Company," in *The Encyclopedia of Asian History*, Vol. 1 (New York: Scribners, 1988), p. 411.

25. Paul Baran, as quoted in Tony Smith, *The Patterns of Imperialism* (Cambridge: Cambridge University Press, 1981), p. 74.

26. *Joint Committee on Indian Constitutional Reform (Session 1933–34)*, 2 vols. (London: HMSO, 1934), 1:4.

27. Morris D. Morris, "An Approach to Modern Indian Economic History," in this volume.

28. Nehru, *Towards Freedom*, p. 277.

29. *Joint Committee*, 1:3,4

30. Quoted in Ainslie T. Embree, "The Diplomacy of Dependency," in Margaret Case and Gerald Barrier, eds., *Aspects of India* (New Delhi: Manohar, 1986), p. 147.

31. Quoted in Ainslie T. Embree, *India's Search for National Identity* (Delhi: Chanakya, 1988), p. 18.

32. Ram Mohan Roy, "Letter on Education," in *Sources of Indian Tradition*, vol. 2, ed. Stephen Hay (New York: Columbia University Press, 1988), p. 31.

33. Chidananda Das Gupta, *The Cinema of Satyajit Ray* (New Delhi: Vikas, 1980), p. 1.

34. Quoted in Hay, *Sources of Indian Tradition*, p. 230.

35. Judith Brown, *Modern India: The Origins of an Asian Democracy* (New York: Oxford University Press, 1985), p. 337.

36. Jawaharlal Nehru, *Independence and After (1946–1949)* (Delhi: B Publications Division, Government of India, 1949), p. 3.

SUGGESTED REFERENCES

The most useful source of information on books and articles on all aspects of South Asian civilization and culture is *South Asian Civilizations: A Bibliographic Synthesis,* edited by Maureen L.P. Patterson (Chicago: University of Chicago Press, 1981). For works published since 1980, the bibliographies published annually by the Association for Asian Studies can be consulted.

A *Historical Atlas of South Asia,* edited by Joseph E. Schwartzberg (Chicago: University of Chicago Press, 1978), is valuable not only for its many maps and charts of political, cultural, economic, and demographic developments, but also for its authoritative essays on many topics.

The volumes in the *New Cambridge History of India,* general editor Gordon Johnson (Cambridge: Cambridge University Press, 1987–), are short monographs based on recent scholarship, covering different periods of Indian history beginning with the sixteenth century. They include full bibliographies.

Sources of Indian Tradition (New York: Columbia University Press, 1989), 2 vols., edited by Ainslie T. Embree and Stephen Hay, includes selections of original sources from all periods on Indian intellectual history, with an emphasis on religion and politics.

The Cambridge Economic History of India (Cambridge: Cambridge University Press, 1982–1983) is in two volumes. Vol. I, edited by Tapan Raychaudhuri and Irfan Habib, covers the period from 1200 to 1750; vol. II is edited by Dharma Kumar and Megnad Desai and covers 1750 to 1970.

For subjects touched upon only in a tangential way in this essay, but which are of great importance to Indian civilization, see J.C. Harle, *The Art and Architecture of the Indian Subcontinent* (New York: Viking Penguin, 1986).

The Encyclopedia of Asian History (New York: Scribners, 1988) offers authoritative articles on most events and periods of Indian history.

There are a number of one-volume texts on India that teachers will find useful, but they are not as successful as those available for China and Japan. This is largely due to the point made in this essay, that South Asia lacks for very long periods any dominant political entity that can be used to focus a narrative history. The result is that one-volume histories tend to be so selective that many trends and developments are ignored or so crammed with facts, with so little interpretation, that they are not very readable. The following one-volume texts will, however, be useful:

Judith Brown. *Modern India: The Origins of an Asian Democracy*. New York: Oxford University Press, 1985.

Romila Thapar and Percival Spear. *A History of India*. 2 vols. Baltimore: Penguin, 1965–1966.

Stanley Wolpert. *A New History of India*. New York: Oxford University Press, 1988.

THEMES IN SOUTHEAST ASIAN HISTORY

David J. Steinberg

Teaching Southeast Asian history poses special problems for both the teacher and the student, not least because it seems so complex and so distant from any familiar frame of reference. Yet themes can be identified which apply equally to each of the countries and cultures of the region and also have a more universal, area-wide applicability.

In order to teach about Southeast Asia, it is necessary to find the signal and filter the static. But this is always the goal that the historian must strive to achieve. Henry Adams, the great American historian and observer, writing in his *Autobiography*, said "from cradle to grave this problem of running order through chaos, direction through space, discipline through freedom, unity through multiplicity, has always been and must always be the task of education." If history is not merely "one damn thing after another," the historian needs to determine the patterns and to explore the sequences.

The beautiful bas reliefs that surround the temples at Angkor celebrate the triumphs of famous Khmer kings. In them the historian can also find descriptions about the life and times of the people, even though those citizens were rarely considered as part of the artistic purpose of the friezes. Historians must halt history, like a strip of movie film, in order to examine it frame by frame. If the focus is not adjusted carefully, especially when the history is of a different culture and in an alien language, the players appear out of focus, moving across the stage of time as if they were cartoons of themselves.

EUROCENTRIC—ASIACENTRIC

The student must be transported into the world of Southeast Asian history, to the physical, architectural, and cultural geography of the past. Southeast Asian history has been partially obscured by the emphasis on the external stimuli, the foreigners on the stage, to the detriment of the study of indigenous institutions and people. At Cambridge University in England, the history tripos examination dealing with the Third World has been entitled, "The Expansion of Europe." If Southeast Asia is to be viewed from the deck of a Dutch East Indiaman or a Spanish galleon, then the view will be from the harbor across the port city to the distant mountains beyond. If the view is from the center of a teeming bazaar, then the European trading merchant ship standing at anchor in the harbor is far less important. If the view originates from the ornate court of a Muslim mosque, then one probably does not even know that there is a Dutch East Indiaman at anchor across the city in the bay.

In 1934 a young Dutch historian, Jacob Cornelius Van Leur, wrote an essay entitled "On the Study of Indonesian History" which revolutionized the understanding of Southeast Asia by identifying this Eurocentric bias. Van Leur argued that what was required was an Asiacentric approach, a spinning of the captain's spyglass so that what had once loomed as large appeared small. In the postwar era, when area studies were becoming the vogue in American universities, this Asiacentric notion gained wide currency. It remains the dominant approach today. Its value is its insistence that the central actors of the Southeast Asian drama are the Southeast Asians themselves. It has led naturally to the growing importance of regional and local history, as Southeast Asian and Western scholars have moved away from the capital city, from the trading emporium, from political and institutional history in favor of a closer examination of the social world beyond—the world of the peasant, of an ethnic or geographic minority, of those with a different lifestyle.

The risk of Asiacentric history is that it stresses polarities. An Asiacentric approach, like the Eurocentric approach that preceded it, operates implicitly on the Hegelian dialectic, in which the dispute is whether the thesis is the arrival of the Europeans or the existence of the indigenous Southeast Asian culture.

Southeast Asian history is rarely so schematic. Consider Malaysia. A group of sleepy sultanates stretching along the coast of Malaya were disturbed from their traditional pursuits by the arrival of explosive new forces and peoples. In 1819 Sir Stanford Raffles, wheeling and dealing for a British base in Southeast Asia, established a fort and emporium at a small island off the tip of Malaya called Singapore. The local sultan at Singapore, very little different from any of the other sultans ruling these *Negeri*, petty riverine ministates, inadvertently opened the Malay Peninsula not only to nineteenth-century British imperialism but also, and far more important, to the arrival of tens of thousands of Chinese who helped to build Singapore into one of the remarkable postindustrial centers of power in Asia today, often at the expense of the people and the countryside. The historian must focus on this Anglo-Chinese impact and recognize the Chinese-Malay tension as one of the central realities of modern Malaysia.

HISTORICAL MANIPULATIONS

On the small island of Mactan in the Philippines, there is a nineteenth-century Spanish monument glorifying God, Spain, the Queen Regent then in power, and Ferdinand Magellan, but making no reference to any local Filipino dimension. This monument would be all but forgotten except that the United States Navy paved over a good portion of Mactan Island during the Vietnam War to permit naval air transports to fly from the United States to Vietnam. At the foot of this Spanish monument, in 1941, just prior to the Second World War and thirty years before the Vietnam War, a historical marker entitled "Ferdinand Magellan's Death" was anchored into a stone. With dry historical prose it stated, "On this spot Ferdinand Magellan died on April 27, 1521, wounded in an encounter with the soldiers of Lapu Lapu, Chief of Mactan island. One of Magellan's ships, the Victoria, under the command of Juan Sebastian Elcano, sailed from Cebu on May 1, 1521 and anchored at San Lucar de Barrameda on September 6, 1522, thus completing the first circumnavigation of the earth." Ten years later, in 1951, the newly independent Republic of the Philippines erected a second marker, now entitled "Lapulapu." This new marker was affixed to the back of the stone against which the 1941 marker had been erected. That stone was turned so that the old marker was left in the shadows. The new marker read: "Here, on 27 April 1521, Lapulapu and his men repulsed the Spanish invaders, killing their leader Ferdinand Magellan. Thus, Lapulapu became the first Filipino to have repelled European aggression."

From the perspective of the expansion of Europe, the significant facts about this brief military encounter between the Europeans and those later called Filipinos was the ultimate circumnavigation of the globe, an extraordinary feat of early sailing prowess. From the nationalist perspective of the Philippine people, however, the way Filipinos have fought for their identity and independence assumed greater importance than any European activities. The Philippines was not "discovered" in 1521 when Magellan arrived; the Filipinos, the Chinese, the Indians, and many other Southeast Asians knew well where it was, what it was, and what one could get by going there to trade. The historian has to avoid portraying the Southeast Asians as people sitting in darkness, waiting for foreigners to arrive to turn on the lights for them.

THE "DEEP STRUCTURE" OF
SOUTHEAST ASIAN HISTORY

One of the most difficult tasks in teaching Southeast Asian history is to communicate its "deep structure," which underlies the complicated court rituals, ancient enmities, chance encounters, and foreign conquest.

The history of Southeast Asia includes the continuing process by which the indigenous peoples of the region have adapted and adopted the ideas, institutions, and value systems of people from elsewhere around the world. Southeast Asia has been and is still at a global crossroads. The tableaux of its historical past are vast. Southeast Asia has drawn from the great riches of India, including Hinduism and Buddhism. It has drawn from China, including Confucian and Neo-Confucian thought, Chinese art, cuisine, and customs. Islam, including traditional orthodoxy and Sufi mysticism, has converted tens of millions. Japan has played one of the catalytic roles in the twentieth century, a role which was partially destructive, partially beneficial. The West, including the United States, Latin America, Western Europe, and the Soviet Union, has had a profound impact.

Southeast Asia has had an opportunity to adopt from and to be enriched by other cultures. But the feast has also been a continuing source of Southeast Asian frustration, for the region's history is the struggle to pick and choose—to take that which the Southeast Asians want while discarding other institutions, ideas, and methods of accomplishing those ideas held dear by the country from which the institutions have come.

The deep structure of Southeast Asian history is the ongoing and continuous process of adaptation and adoption. The Eurocentric view—one shared by the Chinese and the Indians as well—is that the Southeast Asians were pawns, people of no real culture of their own who were overwhelmed by the Chinese, or Indian, or Western cultural influence. There is little autonomous Vietnamese identity in the word "Indochina." Many have assumed that the Southeast Asians were hapless people desperately in need of the blessings of civilization, whether from Tokyo, Peking, Calcutta, Mecca, or Paris. This condescension towards Southeast Asians has left a deep residue of hostility.

Southeast Asians are not merely cultural survivors able to absorb the external stimuli raining down upon them. The Southeast Asians have skillfully shown their ability to blend, to mix and match, to pick and choose. On the historical tapestry the woof is the continuum of cultural interaction and the warp, the specific events, problems, and interactions that have taken place at any given time. Thus in the period from the fifth to the tenth century C.E., for example, the continuity, the woof, was the Southeast Asian process of acculturation and accommodation, while the warp was the particular way in which the several Southeast Asian kingdoms integrated and domesticated the Hindu-Brahman religious, political, and cultural institutions. In the period from the end of the eighteenth century to the present, the continuity has been the Southeast Asian choices from among Western institutions and values, while the warp has been the interaction of issues like imperialism and nationalism, economic development, social change, and modernization.

The bedrock of modern history has been the need of people everywhere to readjust values and institutions to live in a scientific, materialist era. Southeast Asians like others have attempted to respond to the bewildering array of new forces, institutions, and ideas created by the scientific revolution, by the rise of the modern nation-state, and by the decline of traditional verities. One hundred years ago the Japanese, grappling with this problem of modernization, coined the phrase: "Eastern morals—Western science." This effort to sustain tradition while adjusting to modernity is at the core of much of modern history. While it is no less strenuous for the Southeast Asians than for other people across the globe, it is a task made familiar by prior efforts to acculturate Indian, Chinese, Islamic, and Christian influences.

HORIZONTAL SIMILARITIES AND DISSIMILARITIES

Is Southeast Asia a monolithic area? Is there a community of experience, similarity of culture, and worldview that joins each of the peoples in the region to the others?

Modern Southeast Asian history, while celebrating the distinctive character of each different country, has helped unify the region by creating a shared past, especially over the last century. Southeast Asia is subdivided into four traditional regions: a Roman Catholic Philippines; an Islamic Malay world including Indonesia, Malaysia, a small portion of the Philippines, and Thailand; a Theravada tier of mainland states, including Burma, Siam, Laos, and Cambodia; and a Sinitic (Chinese) Vietnam. These four regions have had a distinct historical past but a less distinct present.

There are Buddhist monks in Vietnam as well as in Cambodia, Thailand, and Burma. The monks in Vietnam, however, are not Theravada monks but rather Mahayana. They wear brown robes rather than saffron ones. Their variant of Buddhism comes via China and Japan, and their sense of self, their sense of faith, and their role in the society is very different from that of their counterparts in the Theravada states. These differences in Buddhist traditions are not of the relatively minor sort that separate a Methodist from a Presbyterian; they are much more the distinctions between the Greek Orthodox and the Southern Baptist traditions, or between Coptic Christians and the Roman Catholics.

The impact of Western science and rational materialism has blurred but not erased these distinctions. The political and economic expression of Western science and secular nationalism was imperialism. Its impact was very similar from one part of Southeast Asia to another, even though the American colonial pattern in the Philippines was distinct from the French one in Vietnam. The intensification of bureaucratic control, the establishment of a new and materialistically based elite structure, and the emergence of a primary city, the development of export economies, and the rise of national sentiment based on history, language, geography, and cultural identity were all phenomena of the impact of modernization.

The process of development in independent Siam, after 1939 known as Thailand, is akin to the same process in those parts of Southeast Asia conquered by European powers. The same intensification of bureaucratic structure, the development of a clear sense of national identity, the emergence of a cash economy, the pursuit of materialistic, industrial pursuits occurred in that country as in colonial Southeast Asia. There are variations, in part because of Thai social structure and in part because the Thai managed their own national evolution in a way that elsewhere was controlled by outsiders. However, the plural tensions of a changing society are understandable both to the Thai and to other peoples of Southeast Asia.

Southeast Asian countries have been struggling to build modern nation-states with a "plural society." Many years ago J.S. Furnivall coined this phrase to describe the lack of social consensus within Southeast Asia. The nationalist dream of a single folk, sharing a common set of priorities, must be juxtaposed against the fragmented historical reality. National integration is a goal which competes with the centripetal forces of diversity, difference, and distinction. Each Southeast Asian nation has an inherent tension; each is an unstable, plural society, torn between different religious groups, between rural and urban priorities, between uplander and lowlander, between rich and poor, between those of one ethnic, linguistic, or geographic region and those of another.

Yet each of the Southeast Asian nations is today grappling with a complex of common issues recurring elsewhere, and each must cross the same rugged terrain as it moves along its own road toward "development" and modernization.

PERIODIZATION

PREHISTORY

Southeast Asia does not have an ancient, recorded history. Unlike China, India, Greece, Rome, or Persia, Southeast Asia's antiquity is learned from anthropology and archeology. While it was one of the earliest inhabited places on the globe, like Japan, it did not have a written past until after the beginning of the contemporary era. As in Japan, there was a dramatic, rapid development of cultural and bureaucratic institutions because of the catalytic role played by another culture—in the case of Japan, China; in the case of Southeast Asia, the Hindu-Brahmin world of India. Again as in Japan, the earliest known written record of Southeast Asia appears in Chinese chronicles in which the Indianized state of Funan (the Southern Fu nation) is recorded as being below the Saigon delta.

THE EARLY STATES (THIRD–TWELFTH CENTURIES)

The importation of Indian institutions unleashed energy and creativity within Southeast Asia. In the straits of Malacca, a series of trading and religious empires developed, of which the most famous was Sri Vijaya, which emerged in the 670s on the Palembang River of southern Sumatra and survived for about seven centuries. On Java, a much more inward-looking and rice-oriented series of empires grew, the most famous of which was Majapahit (1293–1520). On the Southeast Asian mainland, the first major state was the kingdom of Chenla in what is now Cambodia, followed quickly thereafter by the emergence of two major epicenters of power, the kingdom of Champa and the even more important kingdom of the Khmer at Angkor. This kingdom of the Khmer, which rose to power in the early ninth century and reached its zenith with the erection of the great temples of Angkor Wat and Angkor Thom, was one of the world's greatest states at the time. Many other Indianized kingdoms emerged, including those of the Mon people in lower Burma and the Burman peoples in the middle zone of the Irrawaddy River. A relatively late participant in this Indianized period was an expanding Thai kingdom at Ayudhya, the ancient capital just north of Bangkok.

The Chinese ruled northern Vietnam until 939 C.E., when the Tang Dynasty acknowledged the long-sought independence of the Nam Viet people. The long era of Chinese colonial rule around the Red River delta near modern Hanoi was based on the Chinese desire to control the coastal trade that moved past Vietnam waters linking China to Southeast Asia, India, and Arabia. The Chinese altered Vietnamese culture profoundly, although the degree to which the Vietnamese were Sinicized remains disputed to this day. Chinese culture and language, institutions, and moral philosophy became official practice, although a strong Vietnamese sense of identity preserved the distinctive character of the people throughout.

THE UNIVERSAL RELIGIOUS IMPULSE (TWELFTH–FIFTEENTH CENTURIES)

The world of court domination and priestly control of these ancient kingdoms was broken by the spread of a series of universal religions, each of which offered a person the opportunity to relate directly to his creator bypassing the intermediaries of Mandarin or priestly Brahmin. The spread of the universal faiths of Theravada Buddhism, of Islam, and of Christianity dramatically altered the quality of life throughout Southeast Asia, overwhelming the court-centered, elitist institutions that preceded them. Exact chronological dating is impossible, but Theravada Buddhism, Islam, and Christianity all arrived between the twelfth and the fifteenth centuries.

Islam came through Indian traders and Sufi mystics, spreading simultaneously with the emergence of a global trade network that linked the Spice Islands east of Java with Constantinople and Alexandria. The Islamic tradition spread across Sumatra and Java, converting Hindu-Javanese kingdoms into sultanates. It reached across Borneo into the southern Philippines where by the 1580s it came into direct conflict with a proselytizing Christianity spreading in the other direction through Spanish power via the Philippines. When the Spanish settlers reached what later became the city of Manila in the late sixteenth century, they discovered a new Muslim sultanate recently established there.

The era of Spanish control over the Philippines, at least until the early nineteenth century, was similarly an era in which the Roman Catholic faith dominated the archipelago, shaping the institutional, cultural, and moral fabric. The local friar priest was the most important figure in the community, the arbiter of justice and the shaper of the social order. This cleric was also the voice and interpreter of the temporal power of Spain, identified by the isolated, weak figure of a governor general. The Philippines was, in effect, a colony of a colony, linked to Spain through Mexico. The priests represented the "civilizing" mission of a Spanish monarchy devoted more to the propagation of the faith than to the development of the economic potential of the colony.

TRADITIONAL STATECRAFT AND SELF-RULE (FOURTEENTH–EIGHTEENTH CENTURIES)

In the period from the fourteenth to the eighteenth century, there emerged a series of kingdoms and sultanates, which are now often characterized as "traditional." At one extreme of development were the sultanates of Java and the kingdoms of Burma and Siam. They were sophisticated, maintaining large armies, staffs of artisans, and court retinues. These kingdoms and sultanates were important centers of power not only within their region but for substantial distances beyond. They can quite properly be compared with many European states of the same period in terms of total wealth, and of institutional and cultural richness.

Operating at a less sophisticated level were a second, more dependent tier of upland principalities, smaller kingdoms and sultanates. These secondary- and tertiary-level societies, such as hinterland valleys of Laos, Cambodia, and Thailand, the smaller sultanates of Java or Sumatra, the Shan regions of upper Burma, and the remnants of Champa in the central highlands of Vietnam, created a complex mosaic of power politics as they interacted with each other and with the dominant major states. They had certain historical experiences in common, including endemic problems of dynastic succession in each of these states and the struggle to establish legitimacy. Because of both Hindu and Islamic institutions, most courts or sultanates had harems. Lesser states sent daughters as concubines. At least four queens were legitimate wives of the monarch. They rarely had children who were by sex or talent or age in the right sequence for succession. The oldest child might well not be from the oldest queen; the oldest son might be from a concubine; the most talented son might come from a lesser queen; or the most favored child might be a bastard. In other cases the most powerful maternal grandfather might be feared by the monarch or his family, or the discontented brothers and half-brothers of the monarch, who themselves had claims in an earlier era, might create alliances and conspiracies. Succession was never clear in either the Buddhist or Muslim worlds. This was a swashbuckling and bloody era, full of intrigue, conspiracy, and resort to force.

THE AGE OF MERCANTILISM AND EXPORT COLONIALISM (1600–1800)

From approximately 1600 to 1800, an era partially overlapping with that of the traditional states, Europeans and Chinese increasingly penetrated Southeast Asia to develop export marketplaces for highly prized Southeast Asian products. The most famous in the West was pepper, followed by other Southeast Asian luxury items such as vanilla, quinine, coffee, tea, cocoa, sugar, pearls, rubies, and many other export items. The Chinese were interested in these same exotica plus sharksfin, birdsnest, and various herbs for aphrodisiacs and medicinals. During this era, mercantile colonialism spread across Java from the great Dutch factory at Batavia. Trading became an important source of revenue for many of the traditional states which hitherto had been either self-sufficient or involved in commerce in less important ways. This mercantilist era, the development of plantations, and the creation of a cash economy all had important long-term consequences for the future of Southeast Asia. In this era of mercantilism, of company trading, of "country trade," of Muslim entrepreneurial activity, the traders, the foreigners, the Europeans and Chinese, Arabs, and Armenians, the people, both native and foreign, who were pushing for change, constituted but a small part of the total historical scene. Most critically, these people did not challenge the established Southeast Asian institutions and leaders. The Dutch, operating through the Dutch East India Company, "went" Javan. They lived with native women, operated as if they were part of the traditional environment, and accepted local institutions as a condition of survival and of the indigenous business scene. They were not there to change Southeast Asia, merely to profit from it and to survive in it.

THE IMPERIALIST IMPULSE (NINETEENTH CENTURY)

All of this changed dramatically at the end of the eighteenth century, when as a result of the Napoleonic Revolution and the emergence of the industrial revolution, the Europeans were no longer willing to accept the traditional environment of Southeast Asia or anywhere else. This new impulse to change, to alter the societies and to impose European institutions and ideas by force if necessary, represented a dramatic shift. It was the underpinning of imperialism, the divide between the colonial, mercantile era that preceded it and the period of rapid colonial conquest that followed.

Napoleon, having conquered Holland, abolished the Dutch East India Company as a bankrupt relic of an earlier era. He sent a close friend and Dutch colleague, Herman Daendels, to become governor general of the Dutch East Indies in 1808. Daendels was an authoritarian, perhaps even totalitarian governor. His goal in ruling the Dutch empire of the East was not merely to make it profitable again for Holland but also to impose on the natives the benefits of civilization as defined by the Europeans. His approach was rigid, his worldview narrow. He believed in discipline, hard work, and the incontestable superiority of a European vision.

Daendels did not succeed. It was impossible to succeed during that era, a period of mutual blockades in which nations as relatively rich as the United States were sucked into the conflict—the War of 1812—because of the interruption of trading patterns. The Indies had profited from export, but export was not possible in these conditions. Daendels' reforms failed. In 1811 a British expeditionary force from Calcutta conquered this Dutch colony of a Dutch appendage of a French emperor, establishing under the lieutenant-governorship of Sir Stamford Raffles, a new British outpost in Asia. Raffles was the foil for Daendels. He was a liberal of the classic nineteenth-century persuasion; he was an imperialist; he was imbued with the notions of enlightened self-interest of the late eighteenth century. Whereas Daendels was the authoritarian voice of the scientific revolution, Raffles was the voice of liberal democracy and parliamentary institutions. Raffles shared with Daendels, however, a vision: the notion that the Europeans were superior to the Asians, the belief that European institutions would by their innate quality and logical superiority help the Javanese out of their darkness. Although Raffles' reforms, diametrically distinct from those of Daendels, also failed for the same fundamental reasons (that during a global struggle between England and France economic dislocation aborted any chance of success politically), the Javanese world was fundamentally altered by these two men. After 1815 there was no return to the less threatening environment of the eighteenth century.

In 1824 the British and the Dutch divided the territory at the Straits of Malacca, dividing by fiat what is now Malaysia from what is now Indonesia. This nineteenth-century playing of global "Monopoly," in which vast pieces of real estate were bartered without any consideration for the people living within, was classic imperialism. Also, 1824 was the date of the first Anglo-Burman war. It was when the self-denial of a remarkable future monarch, King Mongkut, avoided a bloody succession dispute in Siam. From then, in every country but Siam, until the early twentieth century, imperialism flourished.

Europeans or other foreigners were not the sole source of momentum. In Siam the momentum for change was controlled by a remarkable father and son who reigned as King Mongkut and King Chulalongkorn in the nineteenth century. These two monarchs, working in concert with members of their own family and those of an equally important noble family, the Bunnag, reshaped the face of Siam, yielding their own absolute power as traditional *devaraja,* god-kings, and creating the structure and value system of a modern nation-state. Each was a remarkable figure. King Chulalongkorn came to the throne in 1868, the same year as his Japanese counterpart, the Emperor Meiji.

NATIONALISM (TWENTIETH CENTURY)

An antiforeign response emerged in virtually every country of Southeast Asia as soon as the Europeans or other foreigners attempted to interfere dramatically with the lifestyle, institutional framework, and elite structure of the country. Often this resistance took the form of prenationalist peasant rebellions. A modern ideology capable of combating the European value structure did not exist at first. Resistance was more a negative statement than a positive declaration of identity. The British called such peasant unrest, dacoity. Everywhere in Southeast Asia there was native resistance, sometimes well organized, often sporadic and chaotic. At times this resistance used traditional religion to rally individuals and groups. At other times it was purely secular.

From the mid-nineteenth century, intellectuals in Vietnam were grappling with the problems of cultural adjustment and foreign domination. Conversion to Catholicism by a large percentage of the Vietnamese population compounded the question of identity, the meaning of allegiance itself. Comparable movements existed at the elite level all across Southeast Asia.

The first major nationalist movement to develop was in the Philippines. Its growth from approximately 1872 to 1902 represented the coming of age of a modern technocratic oligarchy, the development of an infrastructure within an urban center, a matured hostility towards both Spanish and Roman Catholic institutions, and the emergence of a series of leaders, most especially the great novelist and poet José Rizal, capable of giving voice to the inchoate feelings of the people. This movement, which reached across the different classes of society, ultimately exploded into a rebellion against Spain in 1896, followed after the Spanish-American War of 1898 by a further rebellion against the newly imposed and far more powerful presence of the United States. Philippine nationalism took a particular form, in itself fascinating, and distinct from that which followed elsewhere in Southeast Asia. By 1904 the United States had coopted the newly emergent elite, creating a tacit collaboration with them through which the Americans gave power and status to the new oligarchy in return for allegiance and support. The American policy, based mainly on American ambivalence about imperialism itself, created a climate of mutual self-interest absent elsewhere in Southeast Asia. The British, the French, and the Dutch were not embarrassed by the word *imperialism*. Rudyard Kipling wrote his famous poem, "The White Man's Burden," addressed to the people of the United States. Kipling, and his contemporaries in Holland and in France, never doubted the wisdom of imperial conquest or the moral rightness of their actions. As a result, the nationalist movements in the other parts of Southeast Asia emerged far more combatively, compelled to resist and struggle more violently and, perhaps, more productively, than the movement that was forged by the Philippine-American compromise.

Nationalism developed across the twentieth century throughout Southeast Asia. In Indonesia it began as a religious movement, was briefly radicalized in the mid-1920s by a new Communist party, but was ultimately left in the hands of Sukarno and his associate, Mohammed Hatta, because the Communists tried prematurely to dominate the movement. In Vietnam, in contradistinction, it was the nationalist movement, the Viet Nam Quoc Dan Dong or VNQDD, which acted prematurely, leaving to Ho Chi Minh and the small Communist party of Indochina the opportunity to become paramount. In each case, local conditions helped shape the specific outcome of the nationalist struggle.

THE JAPANESE INTERREGNUM (1941–1945)

What is apparent with hindsight is that except in the Philippines and perhaps Burma, nationalism would not have succeeded in securing independence, and certainly not in the form in which it did succeed, had it not been for the conquest of Southeast Asia in 1941 by the Japanese Empire. The Japanese were the last imperialists, attempting to duplicate European success. In their effort to join the superpowers, the Japanese ironically destroyed the colonial order, the intellectual justification for imperialism, and the racist myth of white supremacy. Moreover, the Japanese conquest—known by Japan as the Greater East Asia Co-Prosperity Sphere—broke the traditional bonds governing Southeast Asian politics, releasing from jail many of the nationalists who had been incarcerated, arresting many of the evolutionary leaders (subsequently labeled as Uncle Toms), and creating a social, political, and economic situation of such disruptive force that a return to the status quo ante was impossible in the postwar era. The Japanese literally and figuratively unleashed the forces of national liberation. Like Humpty Dumpty after his fall, colonial Southeast Asia was never the same again.

SELF-RULE—ADAPTIVE NATIONALISM (1945–)

Few Europeans or Asians saw these consequences of the Second World War immediately. The French, in particular, believed that it was their destiny to return to Vietnam. It took the brutality and bankruptcy of a ten-year war in Vietnam to convince France that imperialism was no longer institutionally or philosophically valid. The Dutch struggled neither as long nor as hard, but started the postwar era convinced of their right and of the necessity to retain their empire in the Indies. The British electorate, having rejected Winston Churchill, supported rapid withdrawal from Burma, although Britain stayed longer in Malaysia and in Singapore.

Nationalism is a powerful engine defining the "we" and the "they" of society. It establishes cohesion but not necessarily direction. It defines the sense of collective self but not the ultimate objectives the nation-state must pursue. Each Southeast Asian nation went through bitter struggles as different groups competed for the right to steer the nationalist vehicle, to control the gear-shift of that powerful engine. Civil war, ideological struggle, and ethnic, religious, and geographic divisions all played an important part as elite groups contested with each other to determine which road the nation would follow, and to identify the ultimate destination—a secular utopia of the good life, of material well-being, long life, educational abundance, and social services for its citizens.

Nationalist leaders had many models to choose from: the Chinese, Indian, Russian, American, British, and prewar and postwar Japanese models. Throughout this modern period Southeast Asians had been grappling to adapt, just as they had during the Indian era a millennium before, so that those institutions from abroad that made indigenous sense would be established and those that did not could be abandoned.

HISTORICAL RAMIFICATIONS

How have the peoples of Southeast Asia accommodated to this plethora of primarily Western ideas, institutions, and values? It is relatively easy to describe the eclectic process by which some parts of the Western ideology or institutional structure are adopted while others are discarded. All of this has little meaning, however, without reference to the effect on individual lives. Every day in virtually every village and town of Southeast Asia, old values and new ones collide. In each case there are people who are defenders of the old order and others who challenge it. Often these controversies are subliminal, so that even the people themselves don't realize what is happening. The historical process does not occur only in the grand chambers of courts and palaces; it unfolds in all the dusty hamlets and rain-soaked towns. Every time there is a sick child in a peasant's hut, or a complication in the birth process, perhaps a breech delivery, the family must decide whether it is to the traditional native healer or to the public health nurse that it will turn. We in the West take for granted what the "correct," intelligent decision should be. We assume that the more the peasant knows, the more the peasant will want the public health nurse. This is not necessarily the case.

We may also take for granted that the lines on the map are somehow God-given, that the boundaries dividing nations are rational, and that the capital city is the one and only proper place for the capital. But, in Southeast Asia, as in many other places, the map is an arbitrary one, drawn a century ago by European imperialists for geopolitical considerations or with an ignorance that comes from a distance of 10,000 miles. Why should the division between Burma and Thailand or Malaysia and Indonesia remain constant? These were arbitrary lines, laid down in an arbitrary manner by arbitrary men. And yet, in the decades since independence, they have, in the main, been accepted by the Southeast Asians, even though linguistically, religiously, and ethnographically, they often offend the sensibilities of nearly everyone.

Why didn't the Southeast Asians move their capitals back to the traditional places where governance had once taken place? Why is the capital of Burma, recently renamed Myanmar, still Rangoon, though renamed Yangon, the nineteenth-century British export city, rather than Mandalay or its twin city, Ava, the preimperialist capital? At first blush, it would appear that for symbolic, nationalist purposes, the move back to a traditional seat of power would be one of the highest priorities of a newly independent nation. And yet Jakarta is the former Dutch capital, Batavia, and the ancient capital of Jogjakarta remains a city of only secondary importance.

This collision of values can perhaps most clearly be seen in the philosophy of the Southeast Asian elite leadership. The great leader of Burma at independence, Aung San, gave a speech just prior to his tragic assassination in 1947 in which he warned his people that he was "a great one for uttering the brutal truth, or the painful truth, as Thakin Nu calls it." Aung San, whose daughter, Aung San Suu Kyi, became the world-renowned leader of the "people power" resistance to the military in the late 1980s, noted that "independence is coming, but it is not going to bring a heaven on earth," warning the Burmese that "years of toil lie ahead of you, maybe twenty years, at the least, will pass before you see the fruits of your toil." Almost fifty years later Burma is still mired in appalling poverty.

Aung San spoke as a moralist, reflecting an internalized Puritan ethic, when he exhorted the Burmese to "work with perseverance, with unity and discipline, always conscious of your duties as citizens of a free country. Rights carry responsibilities; you cannot enjoy the rights without discharging the responsibilities." Students in the West will identify with these familiar and comforting words, which will make them sense instinctively that Aung San was a "good" leader. Indeed, he was that. He was a charismatic man of enormous potential, someone cut down in his life with tragic consequences for his nation. The issue here is not

Aung San's quality, but rather his internalized value system. The Burmese did not follow Aung San's advice, and the society has not "developed" in any way which Western students would view as positive. Per capita income is down, the standard of living is off; in a material sense, the nation is in a shambles. Was Aung San an Uncle Tom? To what extent were these work ethic values really his own or his nation's? So far, at least, his was a road not taken.

Elite alienation from the value system of the people in whose name the elite claims to rule is of primary importance. Twelve years before Aung San's death, the great Indonesian nationalist leader, Soetan Sjahrir, wrote a book, entitled in English *Out of Exile*, while he was rotting in a Dutch penal colony. At that time Sjahrir had no way of knowing that the Japanese interregnum would ever free him or permit Indonesia to reach independence. Rather, this extraordinarily honest statement explores his own sense of distance from the Javanese peasant.

Sjahrir asked, "Why am I vexed by the things that fill their lives, and to which they are so attached?" He wondered to what extent this sense of alienation from the peasantry is different from that of a Dutch intellectual and a Drents farmer, and he answered that "from the point of view of culture, they [the Indonesian intellectuals] are still unconscious, and are only beginning to seek a form and a unity." Sjahrir went on to note that "there has been no spiritual or cultural life, and no intellectual progress for centuries. There are the much-praised Eastern art forms but what are these except bare rudiments from a feudal culture then that cannot possibly provide a dynamic fulcrum for the people of the twentieth century?" Sjahrir speculated about the shadow puppets, the *wayang*, and he saw in them the parallel to the symbols of medieval Europe. Sjahrir posed the problem that his and his group's "inclination is no longer toward the mystical, but toward reality, clarity, and objectivity."

Sjahrir confronted candidly the fact that he was a modern, but not Western, man. But the great mass of Indonesian peasants were still premodern in their worldview, value system, and outlook. Sjahrir admitted, as few Southeast Asian intellectuals have, the contradiction he felt. He claimed to lead and to guide his people. He claimed to offer them a new and a better world. He rejected the values and the institutions that gave them cultural grace and psychological satisfaction. In effect, on behalf of the good of his people, he found himself advocating the destruction of that which they held dear. He wanted to replace that Eastern, less-materialistic environment with one of progress, science, and modernity.

The symbols of the past are, however, important sea anchors for people under rapid social change. Sukarno of Indonesia was a genius at refurbishing ancient symbols in a modern context. He understood that the mythical *garuda* bird, part dragon, part eagle, part lion, was an appropriate identity for the modern Indonesian airline. He understood that the people would take pride in glorifying the ancient Indonesian empire of Majapahit. He understood that by his own manner and actions, he could awaken an echo of myth and song, rekindling a belief in the nearly divine leader. Sukarno's claim to leadership was his modern sense of nationalism, his training as a civil engineer, and his capacity as an orator. He also understood, however, that he would be far more powerful if he could cloak himself in a mantle of ancient cloth, in the midst of symbols of traditional power.

Perhaps even more interesting has been the half-century career of Norodom Sihanouk of Cambodia, for Sihanouk was the king of Cambodia, the *devaraja* (the god-king). In his early years as Cambodia's ruler, he was surrounded with the ancient court panoply of multitiered umbrellas and traditional ritual. He abdicated his throne, appointing his parents as regents for his vacated monarchy, in order to free himself of that ancient symbolism and become prime minister of Cambodia instead. Jazz-loving, sports-car-driving, sophisticated in education and refined in culture, Sihanouk was a devoted and skillful nationalist. No one questioned who he was, and his legacy gave him an automatic claim to legitimacy of incalculable worth. Overthrown by the struggle between the United States and Vietnam, he again is the key player in the 1990s. Sihanouk has succeeded in achieving his national objectives by manipulating both the modern and the ancient, the alien and the domestic, to create a constantly shifting, skillfully elusive style of leadership.

In Siam King Chulalongkorn took advantage of the Buddhist modernization movement started by his father, Mongkut, to use creatively the traditional temple school as the vehicle by which to help modernize his nation. The Dhammayut sect of Buddhism was under royal patronage, and the selection of the chief abbot, like the choice of the Archbishop of Canterbury, was a carefully controlled decision of king and ministers. Because traditionally every child spent at least two years in a temple school learning to read and write, Chulalongkorn understood that he could package a new curriculum in old classrooms.

One of the things that makes the study of history fascinating is the search to understand why some things happen and others do not, why some movements succeed while others fail, why some values disappear while others triumph. It is not necessary to teach much about traditional Buddhist education or even much about the infrastructure of the hierarchy of the Dhammayut sect to convey the significance of what Mongkut and Chulalongkorn were able to do. And through that significance can come an appreciation of their talent, their creative capacity in the face of pressure, and their plain good sense.

The jeepney is the symbol of the Filipinos' journey into modernization. At the end of the Second World War, the drab, totally utilitarian army jeep was just about the only type of vehicle moving on the potholed roads of the Philippine archipelago. These mass-produced instruments of war were stripped down and rebuilt by the Filipinos, who converted them into minibuses holding between ten and fifteen passengers. They are still the mass transit system not only of Manila but also of the thousands of rural barrios. Decorated with tassels, bits of plastic stripping, foil, mirrors, and virtually anything else that could be attached to the chassis, individually the jeepneys are an artistic extension of their Filipino owners and collectively they are a vivid example of folk acculturation. Graced with religious iconography and prayers for divine protection (frequently needed when the brakes fail), named with elegance and occasional precision ("The Tondo Terror," "The Atom Bomb," or "Maria's Lover") and covered with devotionals to unknown maidens or to the Virgin Mary, these jeepneys bear noisy witness to the secular faith usually known as "development."

The jeepney with its Filipino driver can also serve as a paradigm of Western cultural bias. We often assume that there are universal truths governing, among other things, the way people drive and the way in which they perceive the space through which they move. Teodoro Valencia, a noted Manila columnist, commented many years ago that "Manila is the only modern city where it is prohibited to park on the side of the road but not in the middle of the busiest street to change a tire or repair a car." Visitors to the Philippines never cease to wonder at the way in which traffic moves or doesn't and at the way in which people ignore the "rules of the road." The newcomer to Manila is amazed when a jeepney driver, after sticking a finger out the side of his opensided jeepney, suddenly cuts across traffic as if there were no one else on the road. Similarly, it is a common sight to see a disabled jeepney sitting in the middle of an intersection because it has broken down. Although it may have a full complement of passengers, nobody attempts to push the jeepney to the side of the road in order to permit the free flow of traffic.

A shrewd anthropologist, Richard L. Stone, described this phenomenon as "the private, transitory possession (or ownership) of
public property." What Stone argued is that Filipinos see the space
over which they move in the same terms as they see stationary
space. The space on which one stands is one's own, even if it is in
what in the West would be called the "public domain." Thus, the
finger stuck out the side of a jeepney indicates a trajectory over
which the jeepney driver intends to move and a claim to that future
space into which he is turning. Thus as well, the driver whose
jeepney breaks down feels no sense of obligation to move his jeep
aside, because until he can get it moving again, that intersection
belongs to him. This is not simply the erratic attitude of those who
make their living by driving; otherwise the passengers in the broken
jeepney or in the many jeepneys backed up behind would apply,
through shouting, noise, or pushing, the necessary impetus to move
the jeepney and to assert the public's right to public space.

This mundane example offers insights into the larger concepts
of how Filipinos view private and public, how they perceive government position or the sanctity of personal property. The squat-
ter, and there are millions of them in Manila, who builds his
shanty out of corrugated tin and bamboo sees the land on which
he builds as his own. The sidewalk vendor or the beggar who
opens for business on a crowded street views that pavement as if
he owned the lease to the land.

Filipinos have often seen a career in the public sector less as a
sacred public trust than as a familial opportunity. The obligations
of kinship, the awareness of reciprocity in relationships, and the
high social value placed on wealth have encouraged nepotism as
well as other so-called anomalies. It is often impossible to distinguish the line between the bureaucrat and the politician, and the
politician and the technocrat. This interpenetration of functions
has altered a Western-imposed concept of a civil service. Since the
possession of office guarantees power, and therefore wealth, the
scramble to get elected or appointed can cheapen the political
process through fraud, murder, and bribery.

It is easy to label Southeast Asia "corrupt." It is also common to
look at institutional development, seeming abuses of power, or
other anomalies and dismiss them as clumsy greed. But to do
that is to ignore the dimension of Southeast Asian value systems,
to overlook the way in which the historical interaction between
Western and traditional institutions has occurred and continues
to occur in the societies of Southeast Asia today.

THE SINIC WORLD

Joshua A. Fogel

One of the questions those of us who work in Asian history often ask ourselves is: Is there such a thing as "Asia"? The word exists, although as a modern Western neologism; the concept exists, albeit with countless variations; and the space it occupies exists, though who belongs in it is far from an easy matter to resolve. The one truly unifying element is Buddhism, though even in this case we find rather different Buddhisms in India and China (as different as Judaism and Christianity), and "Asia Minor" has been immune to virtually any Buddhist influence. If we insist, as we should, that a cultural and geographical designation reflect the internal cultural and geographical conceptions as such, then "Asia" really does not work.

What does work is "East Asia," what we have designated here as the "Sinic world," the world that falls historically under Chinese cultural influence. From a contemporary geographic perspective, this unit comprises China, Japan, Korea, and Vietnam. At times, kingdoms and tribal federations in Inner Asia have also been part of this world. For the idea of a culturally conceived China-centered universe, we find support in all the major constituent nations of the region. We also find unifying belief systems, religions, languages, administrative structures, and the like. It works internally as well as externally.

The clearest and by far the oldest demonstration of the unity of the East Asian or Sinic cultural world is the Chinese language itself. The Chinese language developed over 3000 years ago, and when the nations on China's periphery began, at different points in time, to find the need for written languages of their own, they all gravitated to the adoption of Chinese. That would be perfectly natural if all the spoken languages of the region were of the same or related linguistic stock, as, say, is the case for the Latinate languages in Europe. In point of fact, Japanese and Korean, though syntactically very close to one another, could not be more linguistically and syntactically distant from Chinese. The adoption of Chinese thus provided a medium for literate discourse, but it also entailed the mastery of an exceeding difficult and altogether foreign tongue.

The very fact that the Koreans, a culturally advanced country in numerous ways, did not develop an alphabet of their own (hangul) until the fifteenth century, well over a millennium after adopting Chinese, speaks volumes about the honored place of the written Chinese language in their lives. The Japanese developed a syllabary alphabet (kana) as early as the ninth century. The Vietnamese created a native writing system *(nom)* based on Chinese for interspersing spoken elements into Chinese texts, as many other Inner Asian peoples had done with varying success, but this proved inefficacious; Vietnamese was eventually romanized by French missionaries in the seventeenth century, and it is this cumbersome transcription system (replete with complex diacriticals indicating tonal inflections) that remains to this day. Yet, even after the development of these native writing systems, the cultural elite in China's neighbors continued to use literary Chinese as a medium of discourse, of internal bureaucratic communication, and of literary composition right down into the early years of the twentieth century.

It also meant that the elite of all four nations in the Sinic world could communicate with each other. Koreans and Vietnamese, for example, separated by thousands of miles, might meet by chance while awaiting an audience with a Chinese official in Beijing or, centuries later, in a café in Paris while planning the overthrow of their respective governments, and they could communicate via the remarkable tool of the "brush conversation" in the ancient Chinese language. In this sense the Chinese language was really not "Chinese" pure and simple, but should be seen more as a regional East Asian lingua franca.

Language, of course, does not exist in a vacuum. It carries with it much of the cultural baggage that a people develops over time. Since many educated Koreans, Japanese, and Vietnamese felt similarly to Chinese literary culture as their counterparts in China, many of the great literary monuments of Chinese are best understood from a larger East Asian perspective.

For example, Confucianism was a system of intellectual and social thought developed in ancient China and rooted in the traditions of the mainland. Over time, however, Japanese, Korean, and

Vietnamese scholars contributed to the larger "Confucian" discourse in the form of commentaries and subcommentaries on the Confucian classical texts, and they invariably wrote them in literary Chinese. Some of these works even found their way into imperial Chinese compilations. Thus, Confucianism, while Chinese in origin, was not the sole ken of the Chinese; it was the common property of all East Asians.

Why did non-Chinese East Asians adopt cultural Chinese ways? What was in it for them? The attractions of Chinese institutions and systems of thought, like the attraction of the Chinese language itself, were both the result of their genuine utility for native development ("modernization") and the fact that there were no other choices. The Chinese model came, theoretically at least, as a well-integrated unity. One could not simply pick and choose this institution and that handful of Chinese characters in the initial stages. Ultimately, parts of the whole package found fertile ground in non-Chinese settings, and other parts found the terrain barren.

What was this Chinese model? It was an object lesson of sorts that taught that the well-ordered state required certain cultural and institutional trappings. These included Confucian ideas about the importance of specific family and political personal relationships; a national university system; an examination system; a unified currency; and well-administered land distribution and taxation systems. By the time the package was variously adopted in Japan, Korea, and Vietnam, it had already undergone centuries of development in China. Thus, the non-Chinese countries were getting finely tuned, well-tested institutions, but, by the same token, that did not mean that such institutions were well groomed for the character of their societies and political establishments. Several examples will help clarify this important point.

The creation of a National University dates to the former Han Dynasty (206 B.C.E.–8 C.E.) in China, the first long-lived regime to rule over a unified China, and it was tied into an examination system to select the best scholars in the land for advanced study and bureaucratic appointment. It was followed by similar institutions in subsequent eras. The Tang Dynasty (618–907), which had the most widespread impact on Korea, Japan, and Vietnam, developed an even more elaborate National University and considerably more extensive examination system. These institutions were dominated by China's distinctive aristocratic families, but, by the middle years of the Tang, China's ruling aristocratic structure was in decline and the essentially meritocratic nature of the examination system was coming to the fore. In the subsequent Song Era

(960–1279), these two developments were complete: China's aristocracy was effectively gone, and the basis for taking and passing every level of the examinations was merit and merit alone (with the still troubling proviso that only men could sit for the examinations). These men staffed the entire bureaucratic structure of the state (except for its pinnacle: the imperial institution).

How did the examination system and the university it supported fare in other East Asian societies? Japan, Korea, and Vietnam all vigorously adopted both institutions. The Korean state of Silla established a National University as early as the eighth century, based closely on the Tang model. As time passed, the Korean university and examination systems followed their own course, while the Korean aristocracy (yangban) was dissolved only under the Japanese Occupation authorities in the early twentieth century, a millennium after the similar dissolution of China's aristocracy. The Yi Dynasty (1392–1910) produced an elaborate examination system, but one had to be a member of the aristocracy (to be of certain specified surnames) to sit for the examinations.

In Japan, there was a slightly different twist. The national university and civil service examination systems were developed in the Nara and early Heian periods, at a time when few Japanese were equipped to teach at such an institution. Korean emigré scholars and Japanese scholars who had studied in China constituted the early staff. While the egalitarian underpinnings of these systems struck discordant notes with domestic Japanese society, the Japanese did not move over time to change radically the nature of the systems. In Japan, the examinations and the national university simply died out over time, as the more hierarchical nature of Japanese society and authority came to assert their predominance, just as military institutions came to play far greater social roles than in any other society in East Asia.

In Vietnam, a contemporary geographical designation that has been occupied by a number of states over time and has experienced few years of peace throughout its existence, there were several interesting changes. One of the remarkable characteristics of both the Chinese and Korean examination systems was a propensity to test for academic, scholastic knowledge, not for the practical affairs of government. In Vietnam there was a firm commitment by virtually every short- or long-lived regime to establish an examination and national university system. However, in the Tran Dynasty (1225–1400), for example, examinations were given in Confucianism, Daoism, and Buddhism, an anathematic development in China where the examinations were strictly Confucian.

Similarly, under the Nguyen family in the southern part of seventeenth-century Vietnam, we find a much more practically oriented examination system aimed at training men for administrative affairs, taxation matters, and ceremonial concerns. The Chinese model remained in form, but the content reflected domestic needs.

This rule about the adoption of Chinese institutions can be generalized further. Through many centuries the countries on China's periphery were often cut off from direct cultural exchanges, either because of wars, interdictions on contact, or disunion in China proper. These seeming impediments to the development of Chinese cultural forms in non-Chinese, East Asian settings did not, in fact, inhibit the growth of "Chinese" cultural institutions in Korea, Japan, or Vietnam, even in eras of intense animosity or prolonged warfare between the armies of China and her neighbors. Chinese culture was not seen as something that belonged solely to the Chinese, to be gloriously accepted in times of peace and friendship and rejected in times of discord or war. The Chinese themselves marketed it as universal, and their East Asian brethren understood it precisely in this manner. Thus, the Chinese language, Confucianism, the examination system, and the like were never seen as the private property of the Chinese. The fact that they were good for the Chinese meant that they would be good for others.

In the early years of the twentieth century, China found herself in a desperate situation, at the mercy of the imperialist powers of the West. The government sent thousands of students to Japan, where many of them rediscovered their own culture in a different form. It was revelatory to many of them, for they learned that, properly orchestrated, all of Chinese culture need not necessarily be blamed for China's contemporary ills. Japan, they learned, owed much of its strength at the time to qualities it had inherited centuries earlier from the Chinese. The last-ditch reform program instituted by the government of the Qing Dynasty on the eve of its demise (1901–10) was based substantially on the Japanese case, including the development of a Chinese national phonetic alphabet which was based on Japanese kana.

Cultural borrowings and a long-felt sense of respect for China did not mean that her younger neighbors would remain eternally at peace with her. China fought wars with or on the soil of all of her neighbors at some point in their histories; in the twentieth century alone, China fought a fifteen-year war with Japan (1931–45), invaded Vietnam (1979), and fought the United States in

Korea (1950–51). The Japanese have often been accused of using the slogan of "same culture, same race" as a pretext for imperialist encroachment throughout the mainland. By the same token, when China invaded Vietnam in 1979, the pretext was to "punish" the recalcitrant Vietnamese, to "teach them a lesson." The language suggests the lingering sense of a relationship between an older brother and a younger brother.

One final consideration is how this geographic, cultural sphere known as "East Asia," or the Sinic world, interacted with countries, peoples, or cultures that were not part of it. The traditional explanation usually given is that China (and often her culturally related neighbors as well) saw only themselves as civilized and everyone else as barbarian. This view of things distorts more than it explains. No period in Chinese history, for example, was as cosmopolitan and open to foreign contacts as the Tang Dynasty (618–907). In the seventh, eighth, and even ninth centuries, countless foreigners from all over the Sinic world and from West and central Asia as well came to trade, proselytize, study, and settle in China. Japanese and Koreans even studied and passed the Chinese civil service examinations. Countless religious systems prospered, from Zoroastrianism and Nestorian Christianity to the many sects of Buddhism. Unlike the Western world, where the crushing of religious heresy represented the assertion of the authority of the papacy or one Protestant sect, the state-sponsored anti-Buddhist edicts of the 840s were a purely economic means of returning thousands of clerics and religious properties to the state's tax rolls. Foreign religion was never seen as a threat to political authority.

Similarly, in early seventeenth-century Japan, the anti-Christian edicts and persecutions of the Tokugawa shogunate were not promulgated specifically to expunge heretical ideas from the sacred islands of Japan. Rather, Japanese converts to Christianity were seen as a threat backed up by the Portuguese (or Spanish), a political force with which the shogun did not wish to contend; and, in the final analysis, those Christians who suffered were overwhelmingly Japanese converts, not the Europeans.

Perhaps the most interesting and intriguing encounter between Europe and East Asia was the short-lived Jesuit-Chinese interaction of the late-sixteenth and early-seventeenth centuries. Unlike the later and much less successful missionaries in East Asia, the Jesuits, such as their most famous representative, Matteo Ricci (1562–1610), demonstrated a genuine respect for the host country. They learned Chinese exceedingly well, spent long periods of time in China, and earned the admiration of their elite Chinese acquaintances. They converted only a tiny number of Chinese, but they conveyed to Chinese intellectuals the highest accomplishments of European science, and in the areas of mathematics, astronomy, and calendrical science these achievements were an enormous boon to the level of Chinese science of the time.

When Westerners began trying to push open Chinese, Japanese, Korean, and even Vietnamese doors in the eighteenth, nineteenth, and early twentieth centuries—with the remarkably self-serving notion that open societies engaging in trade inhered in the natural order of things—East Asian countries tended to resist. The Westerners came to the hasty conclusion that these countries failed to understand trade and international relations. From there, it was only a small jump to the view of a hermetically sealed social order, fearful of external contact and set on keeping things just as they had always been. Views on the absence of history and change in China and elsewhere in East Asia can be found in the ideas of many European thinkers from the eighteenth and nineteenth centuries. That they were mistaken is both obvious and beside the point, for what they had done was to mistake their own distorted understanding of the present and immediate past for the whole story. Viewed from the macro-historical perspective adopted here, the idea of an insular East Asia is ludicrous. China was endlessly absorbing to her East Asian neighbors, and through most of her history to nations and cultures outside the Sinic sphere as well. Historically, the West entered the picture only toward the very end of the traditional order. Until that point East Asia was a dynamic and interactive world unto itself and unto others.

THEMES IN CHINESE HISTORY

Madeleine Zelin

NATIONAL IDENTITY AND CHINA'S CULTURAL TRADITION

China is one of the world's oldest continuous civilizations and the dominant cultural center of East Asia. With a flourishing philosophical, political, economic, artistic, and scientific tradition, it developed a strong identity as a universalistic civilization. For the last century and a half, China has been faced with the challenge of forging a new identity and of redefining its cultural values in a modern world.

China's natural geography played an important role in forging a continental empire. Civilization developed in China from earliest times in the valleys of three major rivers, the Huang He (Yellow River), the Yangzi (Yangtze) River and the Xi Jiang (West River). These river systems, running west to east, have shaped agricultural development and population growth throughout China's history. The Chinese coastline and the Grand Canal (first constructed in A.D. 605) were important for providing north-south communications, furthering unification of the country, and mitigating the regionalism fostered by the intersection of mountain chains.

Mountains and deserts in the west of China limited its contact with other major centers of civilization in the Middle East and South Asia. Elements of Chinese civilization—literary Chinese and its writing system, Confucian thought, and Buddhism (in forms developed and refined in China following its spread from India)—dominated the high culture of East Asia, creating a cultural sphere that encompassed what are today Japan, Korea, and Vietnam. The Chinese written language, which can be understood without reference to spoken language or pronunciation of characters, has also been an important element fostering China's cultural unity and the spread of her culture elsewhere in East Asia. Elements in early Chinese philosophical discourse which placed emphasis on the perfectibility of man and the power of the moral man to transform those around him also found expression in the Chinese understanding of their civilization as universal, not limited to one ethnic group or physical territory, but open to all who would be educated and assimilate to it. In this sense Chinese identity remained fluid and was able to absorb new blood as China's physical boundaries were extended, particularly during the eighth to the twelfth centuries, when China's economic and political center shifted south of the Yangzi River. This period, particularly during the Tang and the Song dynasties, saw the efflorescence of Chinese poetry, calligraphy, landscape painting, political thought, and historical writing. It was also a period of advance in astronomy, chemistry, and medicine and in agriculture and handicraft production that placed China far ahead of contemporary Western civilization in science and technology. Economic prosperity and commercial development continued from the Tang-Song to the Ming and early Qing periods. Marco Polo, travelling to China during the Yuan Dynasty, when the Mongols controlled China (1279–1368, between the Song and the Ming), commented with amazement on the contrast between its civilization and that of Venice, an advanced enclave in Europe at the time. His tales of Chinese cities were dismissed as fantasy by most Europeans.

The development of a strong, centralized bureaucratic state, beginning with the unification of China under the first emperor of the Qin, Shi Huangdi, in 221 B.C., also contributed to Chinese national identity. Consolidated under the Han (206 B.C.–A.D. 222), the empire was comparable in dates, size, and strength with the Roman Empire. The Roman and Chinese empires traded through intermediaries on an overland route through central Asia known as the "Silk Route." Even during frequent periods of political upheaval, a strong sense of the inevitable reunification of China prevailed. China's self-image as a cultural center of the world is manifest in the term used to describe China, "Zhongguo," which means Middle or Central Kingdom.

In the sixteenth century, the Chinese economy was still the most sophisticated and productive in the world, and the Chinese probably enjoyed a higher standard of living than any other people on earth. The Qing Dynasty continued this splendor. Contemporary Chinese called the eighteenth century, when all aspects of culture flourished, "unparalleled in history." Yet by the late eighteenth century this strong Chinese state contained some of the seeds of its own destruction, particularly in the pressure presented by an expanding population. Although China had already experienced two centuries of peaceful contact with the West, increasingly aggressive efforts to "open" China to Western trade and diplomacy threatened China's independence and jarred the Chinese view of themselves as a highly developed civilization. In the nineteenth century, Western military power was superior to that of the Chinese, and China was defeated in a series of military confrontations and forced to sign "unequal treaties" that opened Chinese ports (known as "treaty ports"), first to European and then to American and Japanese traders. The Chinese were further humiliated by having to relinquish legal jurisdiction over sections of these port cities and over foreigners residing in China. The Chinese were also forced under the treaties to allow Western Christian missionaries to proselytize in the interior of the country. Between the first major confrontation, the Opium War of 1839–42, and the early 1900s, the British, French, Germans, Americans, and Japanese competed for what are commonly called "spheres of influence" within China until it was at risk of being "carved up like a melon."

The Western notion of international relations among sovereign nation-states challenged Chinese identity as an advanced universal civilization with indistinct physical boundaries. Rather than absorb the newcomers, as it had in the past, the Chinese were forced for the first time to define national boundaries, who was and was not Chinese, and what role Chinese culture would play in a newly discovered multicultural universe. Much of the intellectual history of the late Qing and Republican periods (1912–1949) centers on the conflicting views within China of how to respond to this challenge. Antitraditionalists came to reject traditional claims of cultural superiority, dismissing Chinese culture as sick, corrupt, and detrimental to the development of a strong, modern China. Some antitraditionalists advocated wholesale Westernization. Protraditionalists rejected any import of Western culture and sought to strengthen the country through reform-within-tradition and cultural revival. A middle road was advocated by others, who promoted the idea of adopting Western technology in order to preserve the essence of Chinese civilization ("Western learning for application, Chinese learning for essence"). These competing approaches to the crisis of identity in China found their most dramatic expressions in the nineteen teens and twenties, during the so-called New Culture movement (also known as the May Fourth movement).

A combination of internal upheaval and foreign aggression led to the collapse of the Qing Dynasty in 1911. Among those who sought to replace imperial government with a republic were the forces under the nominal leadership of Sun Yat-sen. In 1912 they formed the Guomindang or Nationalist party to challenge the influence of military leaders in the formation of the new Chinese nation-state. The teens and twenties were a period in which competing regional centers of powers vied for control of the central state. This so-called warlord period came to an end when the country was partially reunited under the army of Chiang Kai-shek and the Nationalist party in 1928. However, in 1937 China was invaded by Japan and subsequently engulfed by the Second World War.

In the 1920s some Chinese found in Marxism an explanation for China's subjugation by the imperialist powers, a scientific method to achieve economic prosperity for all, and a means of defeating the imperialist powers through a revolution led by the working class. The Chinese Communist Party (CCP) was formed in 1921. After a brief period of cooperation with the Nationalist party, the CCP pursued a rural mobilization strategy. The Long March of 1935–36 brought the CCP into the remote mountainous area centered on Yan'an. Here the CCP gained strength by calling for resistance against the Japanese and experimenting with land reform and other policies to ease the plight of the peasants. After the Second World War ended with the defeat of Japan in 1945, a civil war continued between the Nationalists and the Communists over the right to lead China's political and economic development and reestablish China's position in the world. On October 1, 1949 the CCP, under the leadership of Mao Zedong, proclaimed the establishment of the People's Republic of China (PRC). The Nationalist government evacuated to the island of Taiwan, where it established the Republic of China.

The existence of two competing claimants to the legitimate government of China cast a shadow over the reestablishment of strong central government and unified rule over continental China. Remaining as well were issues of national identity and China's role in the international community. The new Chinese state was defined in terms of territorial boundaries. However, the establishment of "autonomous zones" for unassimilated ethnic groups and continued tensions over Chinese sovereignty in Tibet reflect the still unresolved question of who and what constitute

China. Mao Zedong's determination to adapt Marxism, a Western ideology, to the Chinese context was another expression of the continued Chinese discomfort over Western cultural imperialism.

The view that China's heritage itself was a major obstacle to economic development and social reform became a tenet of communist ideology that further complicated the quest for modern Chinese national identity. During the Cultural Revolution (1968–76) this was given cataclysmic expression in campaigns to burn old books, destroy cultural relics, and erase all traces of "Confucian thought." In the 1980s a reevaluation of China's cultural and historical traditions was embarked upon. However, an official ideology which continues to both condemn Western "spiritual pollution" and label many aspects of traditional and popular culture as "feudal remnants" greatly complicates this task. The economic reforms of the 1980s have led to disagreements among those who favor the "open-door" policy of contact and economic exchange and those who fear "bourgeois liberalization" of social and economic values. Just as in the 1800s, three positions can be discerned among Chinese leaders: (1) a "neotraditional" interpretation of Marxism that contains many traditional Chinese values (deference to seniors, paternalistic government, economic self-sufficiency, a Chinese-centered rather than a cosmopolitan culture); (2) complete Westernization, including the abandonment of socialism and Marxism, a position held by many younger people and reformers; (3) adoption of Western technology and managerial methods, while attempting to isolate these elements culturally. The idea of a "Chinese-style socialism" represents the desire to adopt all that is useful from the West while still retaining a distinctive, and indeed superior, Chinese cultural identity.

China's traditional self-image as a universalistic civilization and a world cultural center has made it difficult for it to forge an identity in a world of nation-states. Against this background, Chinese intellectuals and political leaders have debated the question of how China is to view itself: as a member of the socialist world, the Third World, or the Western-oriented international trading society that encompasses Europe, the Americas, Japan, and the rest of the Pacific Rim. China, with its large population and massive resource-rich territory, is potentially a great power. Within the United Nations, China is one of the five permanent members of the Security Council. For ideological as well as economic reasons, however, since the early 1960s the Chinese have preferred to align themselves rhetorically with the poorer countries of the Third World and to distance themselves from the two superpowers. By the late 1980s, China's relations with both the United States and the Soviet Union had substantially improved.

Within the Pacific region, China is potentially a major economic and political force. Its relations with Japan, Korea, and its Southeast Asian neighbors, Vietnam, Cambodia, Laos, Malaysia, Thailand, Indonesia, and the Philippines, will be determined by how they perceive this power will be used. By the late 1980s Japan had become China's primary trading partner and source of foreign investment. The Chinese remain sensitive to Japanese atrocities committed during World War II, but the two countries share a long history of cultural interchange and commonalities. After decades of strained relations, trade, cultural, and educational exchange between the United States and China are increasing. United States recognition of the People's Republic of China in 1979 did not mean an end to United States support for the Nationalist government on Taiwan, and the United States continues to insist that reunification with the mainland be achieved by peaceful means. Having experienced foreign encroachment and intrusion in their internal affairs from the mid-1800s to the mid-1900s, the Chinese remain sensitive to any perceived challenge to their national sovereignty and insist that this is an internal affair. During the 1990s informal contacts between Taiwan and the mainland have increased in the form of trade, Taiwanese investment and tourism in China, and cultural and intellectual exchanges.

AGRICULTURE AND POPULATION: THE AGRARIAN DILEMMA IN CHINA'S MODERNIZATION

China's economy has traditionally depended on wet-rice agriculture, a seasonally labor-intensive method of cultivation, with the farmer's family as the source of labor. A Chinese peasant could best raise his standard of living by having many children and buying more land with whatever extra income they could produce, a system that provided neither the incentive for modernization nor surplus for the state. Collectivized agriculture was introduced in the 1960s but proved to be unsatisfactory, and as part of the reforms of the 1980s, farming was once again contracted to individual families. While successful in raising output, it works against other goals, particularly population control.

China's economy depended traditionally on wet-rice agriculture, most particularly in southern and central China, where the climate and soil support two and sometimes three growing cycles a year. (Wheat is the staple crop in north China, but due to both the nature of the crop and the climate, the output per field is lower than that of rice.) In wet-rice agriculture, seeds are sown in small seedbeds. The seedlings are then transplanted one by one to prepared paddy fields. While the plants are maturing, they must be kept irrigated, but as the rice ripens, the fields are drained. The rice is then harvested and threshed by hand. Wet-rice agriculture is labor-intensive (as is the cultivation of silkworms and tea). Labor is particularly important when the fields are prepared and seedlings transplanted, and again when the rice is harvested. At these times, increasing the size of the labor force can significantly increase the productivity of each field. In some areas a farmer can increase productivity by double or triple cropping, a technique that requires even greater concentrations of labor, because the harvesting of one crop and the transplanting of the next crop occur virtually simultaneously. At other times during the winter or while the rice is maturing, the demand for labor is greatly diminished. Traditionally, Chinese farmers, with their families as their labor force, put everyone to work in the field when labor was needed. During slack periods, women and younger children could do other work for the family, including handicraft production.

Traditional agricultural methods and population growth were thus closely related. As output increased, population increased to the extent that it could be supported. As population increased, the added labor led to increased production. The more workers available to help in the field, the more rice one field could produce, and so it was to a family's advantage to have many sons (since daughters married out of the family, they generally were not considered assets). High infant mortality and the reliance of aged parents on their children for support reinforced the ideal of the large family. At the same time, the larger the family, the more rice the farm had to produce in order to feed them. Consequently, the best chance a Chinese peasant had to improve his life was to have a large family, intensify the family effort to cultivate rice, then use whatever extra income they were able to produce to buy more land until he owned just as much land as the whole family, working together, could farm at maximum productivity.

By the eighteenth century, population growth, fostered by a family and agricultural system that encouraged high rates of fertility, came to put pressure on China's political and productive resources. Having remained at 100 million through much of its history, under the peaceful Qing, the population doubled from

150 million in 1650 to 300 million by 1800 and reached 450 million by the late nineteenth century. (The population of the United States was 200 million in the 1980s.) The tradition of equal male inheritance meant that for most Chinese peasants, farm size was declining. Many families were only able to support themselves by diversifying their activities, hiring out labor, and engaging in commerce and handicraft production. While internal migration solved some of the problem of population pressure during the Ming and early Qing, there was little high-quality land available for this purpose by the late eighteenth century. The introduction of New World American crops through trade—especially sweet potatoes, peanuts, maize, and tobacco, which required different growing conditions from rice and wheat—encouraged migration to hilly and mountainous regions hitherto sparsely populated, but these too soon reached their productive capacity. The cost of this expansion in terms of deforestation, soil erosion, and flooding of China's major waterways put additional pressures on the resources of the Chinese state.

The traditional labor-intensive and highly productive agricultural system that prevailed throughout the Ming and Qing periods, while very sophisticated, provided neither incentives to modernize nor surpluses for the state, and eventually resulted in what has been called China's "high-level equilibrium trap" or "agricultural involution." A Chinese peasant had little capital to invest in machinery. His fields were small enough that his family could farm them effectively with manual labor and too small to make use of machinery profitable. Wealthy landlords who controlled properties large enough to make the use of modern agricultural technology feasible found it easier to rent to numerous small tenant farmers, from whom they collected an average of half the harvest in rent.

As early as the turn of the nineteenth century, observers of China's economy began to argue that industrialization was the key to solving the problem of agricultural involution and overpopulation in China. During the first half of the twentieth century, political fragmentation and war made any agricultural policy difficult to implement. Rural poverty was an important factor in the ability of the Chinese Communists to win popular support for its revolution. China's slow industrial development, and the large percentage of its population that resided in rural areas (80 percent in 1949), also account for the rural focus of China's socialist revolution despite Marx's emphasis on revolutionary leadership of the proletariat.

In order to achieve economic modernization, the government that came to power in 1949 had to find a way to squeeze the very small surplus out of the countryside and invest it in industry. At the same time, it sought to alleviate rural poverty by eliminating its source in the unequal distribution of land and encouraging the more efficient use of China's agricultural resources. Beginning in the mid-1950s, and reaching its height in 1958, the commune system of collectivized agriculture was implemented. Property was pooled to form large tracts of land that could be farmed more efficiently. Because of the state's concentration on industrial development, human labor, rather than state investment, became the key to agricultural improvement throughout the collective period. Large groups of peasants were also mobilized through the communes to engage in land reclamation and water control projects. They were rewarded for their communal labor by a system of work points, while the state exacted as much surplus as possible (largely in the form of quota sale of agricultural produce to the state at state prices) to invest in industrial development. Families were given only small plots for their personal farming, and markets for the sale of rural produce were limited mostly to the exchange of goods among local residents. While collective farming did allow the state to extract the maximum surplus from the countryside, excessive bureaucratic interference in production decisions and excessive procurement of agricultural surplus at times led to widespread famine, particularly during 1952–62 at the end of the Great Leap Forward. The commune system, ultimately judged inefficient and having major disincentive effects, was abandoned in the early 1980s.

By 1989, China, which occupies the third largest area in the world (surpassed only by the former Soviet Union and Canada), had the world's largest population, estimated at approximately 1.1 billion. With a population five times that of the United States, China has only half as much land suitable for farming. China today must feed approximately one-fifth of the human race on only 7 percent of the world's arable land. Population control did not play a part in national policy before the Communist period. Traditionally a large population was seen as a sign of good government and was encouraged by China's dynastic rulers. During much of the Maoist period, population control was deemphasized as well, as Mao came to believe that more hands meant more farmers and workers to produce wealth and defend China's sovereignty. Population control once again became a central element in China's economic development policies in the 1980s, in the recognition that continued growth could negate any gains made in this area and would impose impossible demands on the government's plans to provide adequate food, housing, education, and health care.

Population control cannot be divorced from agricultural policy. Under the agricultural reforms instituted in the 1980s, farming is now contracted to individual peasant families who are encouraged to increase output though market incentives. The simultaneous expansion of rural industry is designed to absorb agricultural labor, supply manufactured goods to improve agricultural production, and provide rural families with additional sources of income. Farmers are encouraged to contract to cultivate larger tracts of contiguous fields to improve efficiency. However, the return to family farming and the greater opportunities for the diversification of family labor has made it harder for the government to enforce China's "one-child policy" of population control in rural than in urban areas.[1]

FAMILY AND THE STATE: PATTERNS OF HIERARCHY AND PATERNALISM

Confucian philosophy, which holds that the correct ordering of hierarchical relationships within the family is key to the ordering of society in general, was reflected in all aspects of life. Modeled on the family, government was characterized by the rule of man, not of law; rule by moral example and rule by personal rather than official authority. These cultural patterns and assumptions continue to influence the political system and shape popular expectations of the role of government and of relationship in work units, schools, and other institutions.

Government and society in China were grounded in Confucian philosophy, which held that there was a basic order in the universe and a natural harmony linking man, nature, and the cosmos (heaven). It also held that man was by nature a social being, and that the natural order of the universe should be reflected in human relations. The family unit was seen as the primary social unit. Relationships within the family were fundamental to all others and made up three of the "five relationships" that were the models for all others: sovereign-subject, husband-wife, parent-child, elder brother-younger brother. In this hierarchy of social relations, each role had clearly defined duties. Reciprocity or mutual responsibility between subordinate and superior was fundamental to the Confucian concept of human relations. The virtue of filial piety, or devotion of the child to his parents, was the foundation for all others. When extended to all human beings, it nurtured the highest virtue, humaneness (ren), or the sense of relatedness to other persons.

In traditional China, therefore, the family, not the group or the individual, was central. The kinship network linked related families and also the living with the deceased through veneration of ancestors. The eldest male held supreme authority within the family. The status of females was unequal. Property was owned jointly by males and passed on to males equally. Emphasis was on the paternal line of ancestors. Great importance was placed on honoring these ancestors to ensure the continuity and prosperity of the family. Marriages were arranged by families.

Because of the strong sense of identification between an individual and his family and the idea of mutual responsibility, population registration, taxation, and self-policing were carried out for the government not by individuals but by families, grouped, for administrative efficiency, into larger units under the *baojia* system. Families and neighbors were responsible for mutual surveillance.

In traditional China it was assumed by adherents of all schools of thought that government would be monarchical and that the state had its model in the family. The ruler was understood to be at once the Son of Heaven and the father of the people, ruling under the Mandate of Heaven. Traditional thinkers, reflecting on the problem of government, were concerned primarily not with changing institutions and laws, but with ensuring the moral uprightness of the ruler and encouraging his appropriate conduct as a father figure. The magistrate, the chief official at the lowest level of government and the official closest to the people, was known as the "father-mother" official. Even today, under a radically different form of government, the Chinese term for the state is *guojia*, or "nation-family," suggesting the survival of the idea of this paternal relationship.

The notion of the role of the state as guarantor of the people's welfare developed very early, along with the monarchy and the bureaucratic state. It was also assumed that good government could bring about order, peace, and the good society. Tests of the good ruler were social stability, population growth (a reflection of ancient statecraft in which the good ruler was one who attracts people from other states), and ability to create conditions that fostered the people's welfare. The Mandate of Heaven was understood as granting the right to rule, with the corollary right of the people to rebel against a ruler who did not fulfill his duties to them. The state played an important role in water control, famine relief, and the maintenance of internal social stability and defense against external enemies. State granaries were important sources of grain in times of flood and drought and allowed the state to stabilize seasonal grain price fluctuations which affected the people's livelihood. Before the mid-Tang, Chinese rulers attempted to regulate commerce and the scope and location of markets. During the Song Dynasty the state attempted to take a more positive role in the promotion of agriculture and handicraft production. However, for the most part, the state's interference in the daily lives of the people was minimal. The traditional belief that low taxation was a sign of good government even limited the extractive demands of the state, although its inability to fund all of the tasks that it set for itself often meant that officials ended up extorting money from the people.

A complementary philosophical strain in Chinese thought was Legalism, first applied to government in the short-lived dynasty of the first emperor, Qin Shi Huangdi. Proponents of Legalism stressed an administrative approach to efficient and pragmatic government, universal and codified law rather than morality, and state power as an end in itself. As first applied, Legalism proved too harsh and disruptive, but for two millennia thereafter the Chinese state combined aspects of Legalist structure with the Confucian spirit, recognizing the effectiveness of a centralized bureaucratic state which could oversee massive public works, state monopolies, standardized weights and measures, and even script; attempt intellectual control; and enforce social order by suppressing revolt.

The family unit persists as the primary unit of social and economic organization in China today, despite periodic attempts by the government to incorporate family enterprise into larger socioeconomic units, such as communes. Even under the latter, work points were paid to the family and not the individual. Moreover, the state imposition of inherited class labels and urban or rural residence qualifications on all individuals according to the conditions of their families at the time of the revolution has reified the impact of family on one's life prospects. Recent economic reforms have actually reinforced the traditional importance of the family as an economic unit. Economic liberalization has brought a return to large expenditures for funerals and other family-centered ritual events. Marriage, while now often initiated by the couple, remains a family affair. Divorce is discouraged, and mediation to resolve marital discord is stressed.

The persistence of the ideal of state management of society

presents a potential obstacle to market-oriented reform. Government is still viewed as responsible for the people's welfare and for solving people's problems. Mao's concern with grain production and procurement, to ensure adequate supplies to feed the entire population, was in part responsible for economic dislocation and famines in the 1960s. (The requirement of regional grain self-sufficiency resulted in grain being grown in areas more suited to producing commercial crops, and many rural areas were forced by the state to remit grain to the state with little regard for their subsistence needs in an attempt to guarantee low-cost grain in urban areas.) Fears of grain shortages are still reflected in the state's determination to maintain grain quotas and in demands for rural self-sufficiency.

State control of industrial development and state regulation of prices are supported by the structure of the Chinese economy and political life and are difficult to change. State control of prices impeded free-market reform. Artificial prices are set for agricultural products to keep food prices in the cities low. This discourages farmers from growing more crops. It also helps create a dual economy, one in which goods are available cheaply in state stores and one in which farmers sell independently on the streets. At the same time, a reluctance to tax the rural populace leaves local government, as in the past, without adequate funding and is partly responsible for the rise in corruption today.

THE PERFECTIBILITY OF MAN AND
THE MORAL ROLE OF GOVERNMENT

The dominant strain of Confucian thought stressed the perfectibility of man, through self-cultivation, education, and the practice of ritual. One of the government's main aims was to educate and transform the people. The belief that the state is the moral guardian of the people and that men are perfectible is reflected in Chinese political institutions, historically in the merit bureaucracy and more recently in the style of Communist party leadership.

The dominant strain of Confucian thought stressed the perfectibility of man. Confucius (a philosopher who lived c. 551–479 B.C.) expressed a belief in the fundamental similarity of all persons and in the perfectibility and educability of each individual. Mencius and Xunzi, two of his prominent successors, held different views on human nature, Mencius arguing that it contained the seeds of goodness, and Xunzi that, in its uncultivated state, human nature tended to evil. Both, however, believed that human beings were perfectible through self-cultivation and the practice of ritual. From the eleventh century onwards, Neo-Confucian philosophers, engaged in the renewal and elaboration of Confucian thought, subscribed to the Mencian line, stressing the potential goodness of human nature and the importance of developing that goodness through education.

Belief in the innate goodness and perfectibility of man had strong implications for the development of the Chinese political system. The ruler's main function in the Confucian state was to educate and transform the people. This was ideally accomplished not by legal regulation and coercion, but by personal rule, moral example, and mediation in disputes by the emperor and his officials. Confucian political theory emphasized conflict resolution through mediation, rather than through the application of abstract rules to establish right and wrong in order to achieve social harmony.

The belief that the state was the moral guardian of the people was reflected in a number of institutions. Most important among these was the merit bureaucracy or civil service, in which all officials were to be selected for their moral qualities, qualities which would enable them not only to govern, but to set a moral example that would transform the people. The moral system elaborated in the Confucian classics became the basis for the education of all officials. From the Song Dynasty, examinations in these works became the main criteria for selection to serve in the bureaucracy. Official position and examination degree, not wealth, birth, or business acumen, came to be universally recognized marks of status. During the late nineteenth and early twentieth centuries the examination system came under attack by Chinese reformers who felt that its emphasis on moral qualities and literary skill, in contrast to technical and administrative expertise, was a major cause of China's weakness in the international arena. The examination system was eliminated in 1905.

Since 1949 the Chinese Communist Party, as a single party, has exercised authoritarian power, making policy and controlling all state functions. Party organizations exist in every social institution of any importance at all levels of society. Membership is selective and provides benefits in the form of access to scarce goods, housing, power, status, and information. The party has evolved from an organization of revolutionaries committed to an ideology to an organization of the privileged whose membership brings material gain, and whose proclaimed ideology justifies its monopoly of power.

From 1949 until his death in 1976, the personality and ideas of

Mao Zedong, chairman of the CCP, dominated Chinese political life. The Chinese belief in the perfectibility of man through education and the moral example of rulers was reflected in the CCP style of rule under Mao. Party members, steeped in ideology, were meant to lead by their personal commitment and moral example. Mass campaigns and the glorification of model citizens were frequently used to mold the populace to the party line. Mao's philosophy was particularly evident in the treatment of those who deviated from party policy. "Struggle" would be undertaken to reform and return the "deviant" to what was viewed as a useful role in society. Just as a criminal's level of remorse was viewed as an important factor in the traditional system of criminal justice in China, "rectification campaigns" and "criticism/self-criticism" meetings were used to convince people of the error of their ways in the PRC.

The Chinese belief in man's perfectibility through education can also be seen in Mao's belief that by participating in the revolutionary struggle, the peasantry could become the key element in the Chinese revolution. This contrasted with the orthodox Marxist view that urban workers, the proletariat, would act as the vanguard of the revolution, but was appropriate to China's situation as a predominantly rural society. In this educational process, Mao placed particular emphasis on the unity of theory and practice, disparaging those whose understanding of the world came only from books.

Also in contrast with orthodox Marxist theory was Mao's belief that man could overcome objective conditions and accomplish things by sheer force of will (often referred to as Maoist voluntarism), as depicted in the traditional Chinese fable of "The Foolish Old Man Who Moved the Mountain," which he cited. This led to a tension between being "red" (i.e., politically and, by extension, morally cultivated) and being "expert" (i.e., having scientific, technical, or intellectual expertise). This conflict became particularly acute during the "Great Leap Forward" (1958–60) and the "Cultural Revolution" (1968–76), when Mao encouraged "deprofessionalization and deurbanization" of industry and, in lieu of formal education, sent students to the countryside to live with and learn from the village population, who were idealized as the source of revolutionary zeal. Party members, whose qualifications were primarily political, had authority over experts, such as factory managers and school principals, reflecting again the Chinese notion that moral qualities, not technical expertise, ultimately benefit society.

THE RELATIONSHIP BETWEEN THE
INDIVIDUAL, SOCIETY, AND THE STATE

Although China has been ruled by strong central governments for much of the past two millennia, there has always been a tension between the loyalty owed the state and identification with family and local place. At the same time, the resources of the state have never been adequate to the task of direct management of society, leaving much room for elite activism at the local level. Under the PRC, direct state involvement in the everyday lives of the people has increased, but there is still much debate over the degree to which a "civil society" may have developed in China.

Neo-Confucian ideals held that (1) the educated individual had a responsibility to serve the state; (2) a morally upright official should courageously remonstrate with the ruler if his policies are damaging to the state; (3) the state could prosper only if the people prospered; and (4) any disruption to the economy or social order was probably due to corrupt political institutions. These ideas contributed to the longevity, strength, and adaptability of traditional Chinese political institutions. The best people were motivated to serve in government. While corruption was not uncommon, the ideal of public service and responsibility for the people's welfare remained strong. A powerful tradition of remonstrance and reform helped to ensure that the system adapted to change.

The relationship between the individual and the state was understood not in adversarial terms, as is characteristic of the modern West, but in consensual terms. This relationship was given its greatest expression in the Mandate of Heaven. Relations among people were also ideally based on the principle of harmony and conciliation. The state did not provide an elaborate system of civil law and encouraged mediation between aggrieved parties, often under the auspices of semiofficial or nonofficial local leaders. That such ideals did not always find expression in practice is evidenced by China's high rate of civil litigation and what scholars have now identified as a distinct body of customary practice governing the decisions of magistrates, who were the main source of local adjudication until the twentieth century. A Western-style civil code was promulgated during the Nationalist period, but largely abandoned in 1949.

Legal reform has played a part in the modernizing reforms in China since 1979. However, concepts such as "democracy" and "human rights" do not always take on the same meaning as in the

West. During the late nineteenth century, in trying to discover the
source of the strength and success of the West, the Chinese applied their own basic ideas to the interpretation of Western concepts. "Democracy" was understood as a highly developed form of
individual support for the state, and "human rights" were understood as the state's bestowing on every individual, and not just
officials, the responsibility to speak out on behalf of the welfare of
the people and to insist on the moral uprightness of the rulers. By
reinterpreting Western ideas in a Chinese context, the transitional
thinkers of the late 1800s and early 1900s left for later generations an unresolved tension between democracy and centralism.
Basically, this dilemma concerns whether popular political participation and other human rights are valuable only to the extent
that they help individuals to serve the state, or whether it is also
legitimate for the individual to exercise these rights for his own
benefit. Some Chinese argue that if the latter is not permitted, the
former cannot be achieved. The Chinese must address the question of how their understanding of democratic values and human
rights fits into the international dialogue. The official position in
China is that Western-style "bourgeois democracy" is delusory.
Only "socialist" democracy is authentic, in the sense that it is
founded on a true unity of interest among all citizens and between
citizens and the state. But there is a strong popular and reformist
view in the PRC today that the official version of democracy is
merely a rationalization for one-party rule or the dictatorship of a
strong personality, while the true Chinese democratic ideal of all
the citizens pulling together for the welfare of the entire nation
can only be achieved if the citizenry enjoys real freedoms, as in
the West.

The debate over democracy in China has led scholars to reex-
amine the extent to which the state has been able to control
society. The principles of benevolent rule, which required low taxation, combined with the weak extractive capacity of the premodern Chinese state to limit the growth of direct bureaucratic
rule in imperial times. As China's population grew, the size of its
government remained relatively stable. The burden of population
growth on the Chinese state was considerable. By the nineteenth
century district magistrates, at the lowest level of the Chinese
bureaucracy, were responsible for the welfare, control, and taxation of an average of 250,000 people. As a practical matter, many
aspects of societal management were left to local elites acting
independently and in cooperation with the bureaucracy. The diminishing ability of the Qing state to regulate society is reflected

in the numerous popular rebellions that erupted during the mid to late nineteenth century, the most famous being the Taiping Rebellion and the Boxer Rebellion. From late imperial times, a wide array of non-governmental associations existed, including lineage and merchant associations, native-place associations, academies, and religious associations, through which people provided for their own welfare and promoted their local interests. Some scholars have seen in the expanding range of activity among local elites and nongovernmental associations the foundations of a civil society. Others argue that despite this, the state never relinquished its control of the political discourse.

The situation in China today is quite different, particularly in urban areas. The individual's position within the group, whether family or work unit, remains important. In urban areas, most people are assigned to a work unit (factory, office, school) by the government. People rarely change work units, usually remaining in the same workplace for the rest of their lives. If a person does find another job, in most cases permission to change must be obtained from the old work unit. Work unit officials keep employee dossiers in which they record personal and political information, adding to them as they see necessary. If the individual is transferred, so is the dossier.

A work unit identity card is the basic form of adult identification, like a driver's license in the United States. It establishes the person's right to reside in the city of employment (one must be registered in order to establish legal residence in a Chinese city). The larger cities, where life is more comfortable, are generally closed to new permanent residents, although a work unit may arrange a transfer for a spouse or child to come to live in the city with one of its employees.

Work units provide most housing in China, which is very scarce in urban areas. As there is an average of 6 square yards of housing space per capita, the demand for a larger or better apartment is great. As of the late 1980s, a very small real estate market in apartments and houses was beginning in China, but urban housing remained primarily in government control, apportioned through work units. Young people usually cannot get married until they get an apartment. In order to get on the waiting list early, many register their marriage with the government but do not actually live together as husband and wife until they are assigned an apartment.

Work units also provide meal services, health care, and recreational programs; distribute certain kinds of consumer items or foods that are expensive or hard to buy; usually provide private bus transportation to and from work and sometimes maintain their own guest houses; and provide letters of introduction that enable the bearer to buy scarce airplane or train tickets in comfortable sections. Leaders in work units often get involved in the personal life of their employees: they provide advice on marriage partners (and in some cases strongly discourage or refuse to allow a marriage to be registered); counsel those seeking a divorce, and usually encourage them to try to work things out; mediate in cases of juvenile delinquency among young employees or older employees' children. Work units usually assume responsibility for ensuring that the children of employees find employment, often establishing a subsidiary unit such as a transportation service or a repair shop to provide employment.

Because the workplace provides so many important services, workers tend to stay in the same job, no matter how dissatisfied they are. As a result, work unit leaders have a great deal of power over them, an especially onerous situation during political campaigns prior to the 1980s, when the party dictated that its organizations in work units target people for political harassment. It has also led to serious problems of low morale and inefficiency. No matter how poor their performance, workers are almost never fired. Thus, to have a job is to possess an "iron rice bowl." Under the economic reforms of the 1980s, the government began experiments with the labor market and gave managers some rights to fire workers in an effort to raise productivity and crack the "iron rice bowl" mentality.

Since many desirable items and services are in scarce supply in China—access to better schools, consumer goods, housing, jobs, supplies or raw materials for business and factories—the cultivation of personal connections, or *guanxi* (kuan-hsi), reflecting the traditional Confucian emphasis on personal rule, continues to be important. The dependence of individuals on the state for most of the necessities of life has made true remonstrance very difficult. Much research has recently been devoted to the analysis of local cadres and their role as mediators between the state and society. Of particular interest has been the question of whether they represent the power of the state or whether, because they are often local people themselves and depend on local cooperation, they may be seen as standing for the interests of the locality vis-à-vis the state. As China's economic reforms progress, and the opportunity for economic activity outside the state plan expands, these questions may become less and less important to our understanding of modern China.

NOTES

This essay is an expansion of a previously published outline on "Central Themes for a Unit on China," coauthored by Andrew J. Nathan, Andrew Walder, Madeline Zelin, Irene Bloom, and Myron L. Cohen, edited by Roberta Martin, and published by the East Asian Curriculum Project at Columbia University.

1. For further discussion of the central themes in China's economic development, see the essay in this volume on "China's Economy in Comparative Perspective, 1500 Onward," by Madeline Zelin.

Themes in Asian History

CHINA IN THE CONTEXT OF WORLD HISTORY

Frederic Wakeman, Jr.

How does one distinguish between Western history and Chinese history? What is the single most determinate factor differentiating the two? The answer that Mark Elvin gave us in *The Pattern of the Chinese Past* was China's historical unity as a civilization. His explanation depended upon a kind of technological determinism, whereby military weapons and political tools decided the extent and duration of the empire. This interpretation works well enough for Han China (206 B.C.E. to 220 C.E.), if one thinks of it as roughly parallel to the Roman Empire, but it does not sufficiently explain the divergences between China and the West after the fourth century C.E. That is to say, by stressing technological factors above all, Elvin dismissed the ideological or normative notion of "unity" *(tongyi)*, which was such a powerful cultural notion in traditional China.

The idea of a *tianxia* (all-under-heaven), the Chinese ecumene or *tianchao* (heavenly dynasty), which was the empire at the heart of the traditional Chinese world order, may seem too simple an explanation for the emphasis on unity in Chinese civilization. But the idea at least provides a way to recognize the capacity of this multiethnic, multilinguistic entity to remain together and to reknit itself despite the same kinds of massive Euro-Asiatic migrations and barbarian invasions that sundered the unity of the Roman Empire in Europe and helped to lead to the fragmentation that characterized the Middle Ages.

The question then is: Why did the histories of China and Western Europe diverge from one another after the fall of the first great empires, the Han and the Roman? My answer is derived less from Mark Elvin than it is from the late Arthur Wright, who strongly emphasized cultural, religious, and ideological factors in order to explain why the Chinese empire was truly reunited in 589 C.E.

under the Sui Dynasty (589–618 C.E.), while the coronation of Charlemagne in 800 C.E. marked the creation of a Holy Roman Empire that represented only a fiction of unity. Europe subsequently experienced a long period of feudalism, whereas China returned, after 368 years of fragmentation, to that state of political unity which became identified with emperorship itself.

To be sure, the Sui Dynasty fell quickly—reminding contemporaries of the short-lived Qin Dynasty (255–206 B.C.E.), whose harsh rule enabled st ch massive public works as the Great Wall and Grand Canal but which in the end was only a predecessor to the Han. Like the Qin, the Sui was followed by a more irenic dynasty, the Tang (618–906 C.E.), which benefited from the centralizing measures of its predecessor and became another high point in Chinese history, its imperial expansion reaching across the inner Asian steppes, its paradigmatic high culture copied throughout East Asia, notably in the establishment of the ancient Japanese state, and its material contributions to world civilization large.

From the perspective of this recurrent unity, the thematic motif of Chinese history becomes not one of a fundamental break, or of a decline from classical grandeur to medieval institutions, followed by a renaissance associated with the rise of commerce and capitalism in the Song. Rather, it is a motif of return and recapitulation, of a repetitive restoration of the dynastic cycle, so that at this broad and figurative level Chinese history moves in whorls of reconstitution, rise, decline, fall, and then reconstitution anew.

This is very much a Chinese schoolroom view of Chinese history, but it continues to make considerable sense, if only because it became the dominant ideological motif of the traditional monarchy, especially after the Southern Song (1127–1279) succumbed to the barbarians and the Mongols ruled China under Kublai Khan and the Yuan Dynasty (1280–1367). Indeed, unity became a dominant motif at the very moment that the notion of unified imperial rule became problematical.

To Confucian historians then and later, the period of Mongol rule raised an important issue. Imperial governance originally meant unified rule by a virtuous emperor. In the ideal sense, unity and virtue went together. But did not the Yuan regnum suggest that one could unify China (in this case with Mongol ponies and Persian bureaucrats) without exemplary virtue? Could there, in other words, be unification without moral rule?

In the Confucian order of things, the two were supposed to go hand in hand. The ruler rules the ecumene and unifies the empire. When moral rule is combined with political and military unification, the emperor gains the realm, the "all-under-heaven." Yet it can be shown that there were periods of Chinese history, such as the seventeenth-century establishment of another foreign dynasty, the Qing, when unification carried its own justification with it, as if unity itself provided its own form of virtuous legitimation.

If unity was the great motif of imperial Chinese history, then how was it linked with the two other main themes of Chinese history: population growth and the rise of the gentry?

We might at least look for a moment at the rise of the city of Suzhou in the fourteenth to sixteenth centuries, when Suzhou became the largest city in the world in terms of population. One of the general factors behind that growth was the success of the Chinese in winning what the French historian Braudel called the "biological revolution" much sooner than the West did.

The conventional explanation for this, apart from a description of relatively minor technological innovations in agriculture, is that during the ninth to twelfth centuries China experienced a kind of "green revolution." The discovery of strains of rice in Southeast Asia, and mainly in the kingdom of Champa, led to their importation into China, where these new rice strains, grown in fairly disease-resistant form in the central and southern parts of the country, could yield two and even three crops per year. This new crop provided a caloric source that, until the transplantation of New World maize, or corn, was a markedly more efficient means of feeding a population than the wheats, barleys, and ryes of Europe. As a result, the population of China was able to quadruple in size between the fourteenth and eighteenth centuries.

That population growth in turn permitted urban conglomerations unprecedented in size, which accompanied the kind of exuberant commercialization that had astonished Marco Polo when he visited China in the late thirteenth century. Robert Hartwell, the economic historian, is fond of pointing out that if one looked at the level of coal and iron production in the early twelfth century in China, then it was not only comparable to, but greater than, coal and iron production in England on the eve of the Industrial Revolution. The reasons for the later decline of this proto-industrial production were manifold, but among the most important were the Jin and Mongol invasions (and the ensuing transformation of large parts of North China into feudal appanages) and the movement of capital away from Kaifeng (where the manufactories, which were mainly engaged in the manufacture of weapons, were largely located) to Hangzhou on the coast. The main point in this regard is, of course, comparative. We find levels of commercialization, manufacturing, and intraregional trade in China during the twelfth to eighteenth centuries that place the country at a level of economic development comparable to that of early modern Europe—and in some cases 400 years before Europe was reaching that point in its early modern development.

China's population growth rate was not constant, though economic historians such as Dwight Perkins try to show a steady incremental growth based upon a model of agricultural expansion created by increasing labor inputs rather than capital investments. This ever-rising growth in agricultural production was certainly true in a secular sense, but the rate of growth had its ups and downs, and during periods of climatic and ecological crisis, not to mention the accompanying human events in the form of peasant uprisings and wars, there were sharp declines in population.

One such period of decline was the "calamitous" fourteenth century, about which Barbara Tuchman wrote so evocatively in connection with Western Europe. The seventeenth century was another period of negative growth in both Europe and China. Climate had much to do with the latter crisis. During the period roughly from 1615 to 1675, the temperature of the globe declined by 2 or 3 degrees Celsius. During the low point in the 1630s, 1640s, and 1650s, this global cooling was accompanied by the signs of social catastrophe: famine, drought, flood, locust plagues, and, of course, epidemics of bubonic plague and smallpox. In China itself, the population may have declined by as much as 35 percent between 1610 and 1650. There also, the evidence of this climatic change is very vivid in the historical chronicles and records. Parts of the central Yangzi (Yangtze) River, which now entertains a mild climate, actually froze over. In the Northeast—or what Westerners and Japanese once called Manchuria—the harvest season declined by 20 to 30 days at the height of this crisis.

Meanwhile the Northeast, as well as most other parts of China, had been benefiting from the global trade expansion of the late sixteenth and early seventeenth centuries, fueled by silver bullion from the mines of the New World. Much of the silver produced by the mines of Peru and of Mexico was being shipped across the Pacific by Manila galleon to be exchanged in the Philippines for Chinese brocades that ended up gracing the altars of the New World's churches. As a result, upwards of 100,000 kilograms of silver a year poured into China, which remained the sink of precious metals for the entire world until about 1830, when the trade balance between China and the West began to shift. The seventeenth century also marked a momentary break in this influx of silver as climatic cooling took its toll. As trade declined, a severe economic depression set in throughout the Pacific economy.

This is one of the ways of accounting for the Manchus' expansion into the Korean peninsula, which was the first stage of their conquest of their neighbors, including China. That is, the Manchu population expanded in the late 1500s and early 1600s as trade in ginseng and sables with a prosperous China grew, but then this same population could not be fed by normal means in the 1620s as harvests began to diminish and trade fell. The invasion of Korea by the Manchus in 1629 was primarily to gain access to grain supplies, which the Koreans would not supply in sufficient quantities as simple tribute.

The Chinese thus simultaneously experienced the same global crisis as the West in the seventeenth century. What distinguished them was their different reaction to it. More quickly than any European country, China—under the leadership of the new Qing Dynasty founded by the Manchus—bounced back from the seventeenth-century crisis and resumed fairly rapid economic growth.

Like Europe, China underwent a particularly catastrophic set of peasant wars during this period. The Chinese peasant rebellions were perhaps not as ruinous as the peasant wars in Germany, but parts of the country—especially Northwest China—were overrun by peasant rebels. One of these rebel leaders, Li Zicheng, managed after repeated failures to gather an enormous conglomeration of refugees, discontented peasants, and bandit confederations in 1641. Reaching a crescendo of military development, Li Zicheng's rebels moved on the Ming capital of Beijing in 1644, precipitating the suicide of the Ming emperor and providing an opportunity for the rebel Li to occupy the Forbidden City and proclaim the "Shun" dynasty.

Li Zicheng, however, was unable to control his generals, who began to arrest and torture the upper classes of Beijing, trying to force them to reveal the location of the vast amounts of silver that they had hoarded away during this period of turmoil. Word of their suffering reached the Manchus outside the Great Wall in the Northeast. The Manchus were then ruled by a powerful regent, Dorgon, who had recently taken the seat behind the throne of the boy-emperor, Shunzhi. The Chinese collaborators in Dorgon's employ—men who had defected to the Manchus' side—persuaded the regent that this was a Heaven-sent opportunity for their soldiers to intervene as a "righteous army" in order to avenge the death of the last Ming emperor.

The problem was simply that the Manchu armies were used to raiding China for loot, slaves, or chattels. The Chinese collaborators serving the Manchus now told Dorgon that he would have to transform his men into a "righteous army" that would bring Confucian order back to the central plain of China. He would have to tell his Manchu tribal leaders and princes that they must instruct their own bannermen to change their tactics and enter China as "righteous troops." They were to be told that they were not to go in and treat the Chinese the same way they treated hares and foxes on the hunts. "Sheathe your swords and unstring your bows and treat these people as subjects." Women were not to be raped. Civilians were not to be cavalierly slaughtered. "If you don't comply," the Manchu bannermen were warned, "examples will be made of you." If you do comply, Dorgon's Chinese advisers added, then the all-under-heaven will be again unified and you will create a dynasty that will last for centuries.

In other words, the notion of restoration, recovery, and unification of proper dynastic rule led to a political-military invasion that succeeded not only in bringing China together once more into the most powerful empire of its history, which ruled from 1644 to 1912, but also brought about a successful recovery from the seventeenth-century climatic catastrophe earlier than England, France, Spain, or Germany.

The recovery began in a way that can readily be tabulated. Population growth resumed. Abandoned land was reclaimed. Sichuan, an area roughly the size of France in area and population, had been turned by a psychopathic rebel leader into a wasteland of ruined cities, covered with liana vines, through which roamed tigers and monkeys. The extent of such devastation was hard to imagine. Nonetheless, the Manchus soon brought order back to Sichuan, and successive waves of immigrants from other parts of China repopulated the province. At the institutional level, the Manchus combined a reconsolidation and strengthening of early Ming institutions with several unique inventions of their own (the banner system, the imperial household bureau, the royal bondservants, the secret palace memorial system) that restored a measure of centralized control over the provinces.

The recovery of the Manchus from the seventeenth-century crisis was accompanied by an imperial expansion against weaker neighbors, using military technology that was on a par with the West's as of about 1675. This expansion led the Qing Dynasty to enlarge the Chinese ecumene and spread as far as Ili in Xinjiang to the West, to come into contact with the expanding tsarist empire, to bring Tibet under Qing control, to render Korea a vassal state, to invade Annam, and so forth. The result by the late eighteenth century was the largest territorial empire in Chinese history, which created an appearance of military success that was not, however, won against states or peoples of truly equal or slightly superior strength. In other words, the Chinese imperial expansion of the eighteenth century occurred without necessitating any major changes in Chinese military technology or tax-collecting mechanisms. Here the comparison with the West is reversed, for Western nation-states, during that same period, were creating new fiscal mechanisms, new military techniques, and new kinds of weaponry in order to survive during an age of warfare among equals across the entire European continent.

Thus, when China encountered the West in the nineteenth century, it was still armed with the weapons of the seventeenth century. It had more or less stood still during the intervening eighteenth century while Western states became fundamentally "modern." China's recovery from the seventeenth-century crisis was thus in comparative global terms a temporary revival. The very obsession for unification that enabled China to recover quickly from the global catastrophe with traditional methods prevented the Chinese from recognizing their peril when they were forced to engage the West after Britain had colonized India, expanded the opium traffic, and begun to try to break down what Victorians took to be the Central Kingdom's barriers against free trade and expanded intercourse. The Qing rulers and their bureaucratic advisers also failed to recognize this peril in the nineteenth century for another reason, which was the nature of the Chinese ruling elite, the gentry.

The Chinese examination system is justly famous, and it inspired certain aspects of the English and French civil service. The exam system itself dated from Han times, but it did not become the sole major source of bureaucratic recruitment until the fifteenth century, when Ming emperors restricted the privileged right of the higher metropolitan gentry to recommend their heirs for office. After the Ming founder, Zhu Yuanzhang, abolished the prime ministership in 1381, he and his successors as emperor sought to destroy the independent basis of a bureaucratic elite by completely basing gentry status on the examination system. That is, one could only become and remain a member of the gentry by passing examinations that the throne held and controlled. By the late sixteenth century the main way to become an official was to spend one's lifetime learning the Confucian classics (according to interpretations defined by the throne), which meant memorizing texts of more than 900,000 characters altogether and then writing examination essays about them.

This was a staggering and stultifying task that did not necessarily recognize and award brilliance. The great polymath of the eighteenth century, Dai Zhen, failed to pass the metropolitan examination in 1743. In the last year of his life, when he was widely recognized as being one of the best scholars in the entire empire, he was finally given an honorary *jinshi* degree by way of compensation for his work on the emperor's encyclopedia projects.

There were three different levels to the examinations. The examiners were appointed by the Board of Rites, which also monitored the examinations. At the highest level, which was the palace examination, the emperor himself was supposed to sit and read the exams with five or six of his highest officials. The exams were numbered, but there were ways for the examiners to recognize the contestants by their calligraphy or handwriting. It was to the benefit of a high official to be the first to award the "primus" *(zhuangyuan)* degree to the best candidate, since that made the examiner a kind of surrogate teacher to a man who was bound to make a mark for himself at the highest levels of the government. This tells us a great deal about the importance of patron-client relations and factions in Chinese bureaucracy, as well as about the critical place of the Confucian canon in the legitimation of the mandarinate.

Japan was very different. Partly because the samurai were born to their position (instead of earning it by mastering a required body of texts), some of their rank proved more flexible when it came to dealing with a new kind of learning necessary to deal with the West after the Opium Wars of 1839–1842. The Chinese gentry, in contrast, had no choice but to focus on Confucian texts, since nothing else certified them for office. It took a full two-thirds of a century to change the educational system of China (by abolishing the old state examinations and starting new schools) in order to deal with the West. Late imperial China was lamentably slow to respond to that challenge—as many patriotic Chinese saw so painfully during the Battle of the Yalu River in 1894, when the Japanese utterly destroyed the Chinese fleet and left the country strategically bankrupt.

The examination system and the gentry it produced both came to an end with the fall of the Qing in the 1911 Revolution. But the theme of unity remained, as important a goal for the Nationalists, who failed to achieve it during the Republican period, as it was for the Communists who proclaimed China unified once more as the People's Republic in the 1949 Revolution. As before in Chinese history, however, unity alone is not sufficient to guarantee political and economic development. That is an ongoing story in the China of today.

Themes in Asian History

SOME MISCONCEPTIONS ABOUT CHINESE HISTORY

Cho-yun Hsu

Ever since the Europeans encountered Asia through trade, both China and the Chinese have been regarded as mysterious and unchanging. Although scholarship on China has made remarkable strides, some of the misconceptions developed during earlier periods linger on. The following are a few of the most common misconceptions about China to which many people cling.

China was a static, unchanging system until jarred by impact with the West.

In fact, China not only was a state, it was a cultural and economic system. Almost a world in its own right, China was comparable in size and complexity to the whole of Europe. The Chinese system underwent enormous change over the past two millennia, including several periods of major transformation. Chinese feudalism evolved into a multistate system during the period of Spring-and-Autumn and Warring States (from the eighth to the third century B.C.E.). China was subsequently unified as a universal empire, with an imperial-bureaucratic state that established its dynastic rule over the country in the Qin-Han periods (221 B.C.E.–220 C.E.). Between the third and the sixth centuries there was again prolonged disunity. China absorbed several waves of continental intruders, accepted a foreign religion (Buddhism), expanded southward, and consolidated hitherto underdeveloped regions. Both Confucianism and Taoism, which responded to the Buddhist challenge as well as to the distinctive conditions of the times, also experienced several stages of revision. Via contacts with other peoples in Asia, especially those in the Eurasian steppes, China repeatedly redefined its role in the world context. Beginning in the tenth century under the Song, China enjoyed sustained economic growth. Much of this economic development was correlated with China's participation in the emerging global economic sphere. During this time (from the tenth to the nineteenth century), Chinese society was gradually transformed. The changes in daily life, social structure, economic behavior, and worldview in this period were as thorough as those taking place in early modern Europe.

China is a vast land, yet it is often regarded as a single entity of great uniformity. In reality, there are distinctions between the core cultural centers and the periphery. Moreover, the centers have shifted from one region to another over the years. Examples include the shifts from Shaanxi to Henan, from the Yellow River valley to the Yangzi (Yangtze) River valley, from the interior to the coast. China has at times been a unified empire and at times an area divided into contending states. China's history is complicated and, like all histories, replete with change.

Social relations in traditional China were circumscribed by the five Confucian relationships.

This statement, while partly true, is overstated. It often implies that the five relationships were used to justify an authoritarian structure designed to control the individual. The five relationships, i.e., father-son, ruler-subject, husband-wife, superior-subordinate, and friendship, are in fact premised on the principle of reciprocity. Only caring parents have the right to expect their children to behave with filial piety, and only a benevolent ruler can ask for loyalty from his subjects. Only the loving spouse can enjoy the love of his or her partner. Faith and trust between the superior and the subordinate, and between friends, are mutual expectations.

These five categories of relationships are arranged in a concentric pattern in a grid of social space. This grid was gradually extended from the immediate to the extended family, to the community, to the state, to society as a whole, and finally to universal humanity, as a model for harmonious social and political relations. Friendship can be as significant as kinship. The so-called sworn brotherhood is a contractually reciprocal bond that ties friends together firmly, and can sometimes take priority over familial relations. In sum, the five Confucian relationships express the fundamental values of individual and social morality, which serve diverse purposes depending on the political and social context of the times.

Chinese science got off to a glorious start and then stagnated.

Implicit in this statement, which might be termed the Needham proposition after the great historian of Chinese science, Joseph Needham, is the assumption that the modern definition of science is a universal truth. In Chinese civilization, learning is an intellectual pursuit to enrich the spirit for the sake of one's life in society. Many of China's extraordinary inventions and discoveries, which Needham brings to our attention, are actually technological rather than "scientific" developments. It is not the pursuit of knowledge for its own sake that is important in the Chinese view, but knowledge that is related to societal and human concerns. Developing a device to save time, energy, or resources, i.e., a technological innovation, is concerned with its human benefit. Pursuit of sheer excellence, a Faustian mentality, is not endorsed in Chinese traditional society, not least because competition may harm social cohesiveness. Similarly, in a conflict between progress and stability, the Chinese may prefer the latter.

Since the fifteenth century the Europeans have outpaced the Chinese in science and technology. One might better ask, however, "What motivated and mobilized the Europeans to move forward in this area?" rather than simply assume that the Chinese suddenly lost the will to do so.

Chinese sea voyages might have resulted in the Chinese encircling and dominating the world, but they were stopped abruptly and China withdrew from the world.

This statement usually refers to the naval expeditions led by Zheng He [Cheng Ho] in the early fifteenth century. Zheng's seven voyages plowed the southern Pacific and Indian oceans as far as the East African coast and spread the influence of Ming China abroad. Indeed, it was a spectacular phenomenon for land-oriented China to turn its attention to the sea. It should be noted, however, that Ming China was the successor to the extraordinarily cosmopolitan Mongol Dynasty. China under the Mongols was reached by mariners of many nationalities on the seas that stretched between the Chinese coast and the Persian Gulf and Red Sea. Merchants routinely sailed back and forth along the maritime silk route, and many foreigners resided in Chinese coastal provinces. Under the Pax Mongolia, China was part of a network of international trade, and these activities continued in the early Ming Dynasty. Zheng He himself came from a Muslim background and was brought to the court from the southernmost province of Yunnan. The Chinese navy during the Ming period was created from the remnants of the Mongol navy. Thus overseas Ming activities should be regarded as a continuation of the Song-Mongol tradition rather than a sudden upsurge of Chinese interest in seafaring. The cessation of the voyages by the Ming government was due to a combination of barbarian border threats, court politics, and financial constraints, rather than a decision to withdraw from maritime contact.

The Chinese economy was basically a vast nationwide marketing system with a largely agricultural base. Overseas trade played a relatively insignificant role in the Chinese economy. Exchanges along the maritime silk route benefited the peoples along the route more than those at either end, i.e., China and Europe. Indeed, except for luxury items, China had little motivation to enter into foreign trade at all.

The situation was different in Europe, where after the fifteenth century there were strong motivations to engage in overseas trade and much to be gained from the riches of the East. The discoveries of new routes and new continents gave the European powers advantages over the Middle Eastern peoples along the old routes linking East and West. China eventually benefited from the influx of a large quantity of silver and its impact on manufacturing. The economic upsurge, especially in the coastal region, should be attributed to Ming China's new role in the emerging global market system. China faced no difficulties in overseas expansion as long as it manufactured silk, ceramics, and other profitable commodities.

Early Ming seafaring activities left imprints on Southeast Asia. It is an often ignored fact that emigrants from the southern coastal provinces of Fujian and Guangdong routinely settled in the numerous Pacific islands. Chinese organized overseas communities in present-day Indonesia, Philippines, and Malaysia, and on the Indochinese Peninsula. Long after the suspension of government-sponsored voyages like Zheng He's, Chinese merchants, as well as pirates, sailed and traded along these very busy waterways. Only the Europeans, with their government sponsorship and later their superior gunboats, forced the Chinese ships off the high seas. Chinese colonies, without any support from the Chinese government, had no choice but to surrender to European colonialism. Nevertheless, Chinese immigrants in South and Southeast Asia continued to regard themselves as the successors of Zheng He's expeditions. Their descendants still revere Zheng He as a kind of god, and towns, ports, hills, and anchorages throughout the Pacific islands bear his name.

China failed to modernize like the West and like Japan. The traditional system is responsible for what went wrong in China.

This is an issue that the Chinese have had to address ever

since their first confrontation with the Western powers in the mid-nineteenth century. A recent attempt to provide an explanation is the television documentary entitled "Lamentations of the Yellow River," which was widely seen in China in 1988. Of course, the validity of this statement depends on one's definition of the term "modern." Implicit in this statement is, once again, the assumption that all civilizations will take the same evolutionary route to a common destination.

The conventional culprit in China's failure to respond to the Western challenge in the nineteenth century has been Confucianism, which in its Chinese form is said to have inhibited the development of economic and technological change. In recent years, the rapid economic growth of Hong Kong, Korea, Singapore, and Taiwan has prompted a reexamination of the effect of Confucian ethics on the rapid development of capitalism and industrialization. It seems as if there has been a complete turnaround on this issue. Many who relate Confucian ethics to the rise of the newly industrialized countries of East Asia have, however, failed to note that the initial rise of capitalism may be associated with a certain set of conditions, while the rise of secondary capitalism takes place because of a different set of conditions. The pressure of a world economic system, which is built on the premise of capitalism, is crucial both as a stimulus and as a source of momentum for development.

The modernization of diverse cultures is a consequence of interaction among them and of their particular historical circumstance. The traditional systems of non-Western civilizations should therefore be examined to discern their respective indigenous conditions and decision-making patterns and the ways in which these factors determined the course of their modernization. In the case of China, the process of modernization can be said to have begun in the nineteenth century and extended across three revolutions into the late twentieth century.

PATTERNS OF THE PAST: THEMES IN JAPANESE HISTORY

Carol Gluck

By rights world history ought to encompass both the grand commonalities and the particular patterns of human experience. But this is a tall order for two reasons: First, because the main means of discerning common themes is comparison of different local variations, which tends to reduce entire cultures to schematic representations of singular entities, "India," "China," "the West," each with its own iconic characteristics enduring through world-historical time as if intact. Second, because the main materials for study are products of the strong modern traditions of national historywriting, which insist on the singularity of each nation, often reaching far back in time before "the nation" existed and enshrining national difference in a hallowed patriotic past. There is no easy escape from this double dilemma of historical caricature, which amounts to ethnocentrism from without—the way we see China—and from within—the way Chinese see China. But we can at least stress the point that the distinctive national themes are in fact particular patterns of grand commonalities in world history. And we can also show how the particularities operate as ideological values and mythic guides in the context of each national history. "Being Chinese," after all, was an operative notion in China's history for millennia, just as "being Indonesian" possessed signal importance in the twentieth-century history of Indonesia.

Such notions of national distinctiveness are not fabricated out of whole cloth but are themselves the outcome of history. In considering the central themes of any national (or regional) history, it is as if the nation first lives its past: in the United States, for example, the "peopling of America" in the colonial period. That, we might agree, is history. Then the nation tells stories about the experience, different stories at different times for different people: "a nation of immigrants," a "melting pot," a "destroyer of native cultures." These stories we identify as national myths or public memory. Then the nation relives these myths, for example, by striving to recreate them in the late twentieth century in a "multicultural, tossed-salad society" or an *"e pluribus unum* with renewed emphasis on the *unum."* At such moments both the history and the myth influence the society's definition of itself—what we think of as national identity. And these definitions are further reflected in the images that nations have of other nations: in the way, for example, that American diversity is reflected in media around the world, at times in rainbow images of healthy pluralism, at times in film footage of the L.A. riots. These images we know as the stereotypes that ricochet off contemporary issues and make nuanced international understanding difficult. From history to memory to identity to stereotype, and back again—in this way the patterns of the past continually affect the frameworks of the future.

Japan offers an instructive example of this interweaving of historical thematic and mythic stereotype. Here I focus on six broad themes that run through Japanese history. Each is often presented as distinctively Japanese, although all are better seen as variations on common world-historical patterns. Each has been woven into the fabric of Japanese memory and identity, and all march stereotypically through the international pageant of images of Japan. The themes are historical and mythic at the same time, and hence just as risky in the classroom as in the boardroom and the proverbial halls of power. While historically accurate in general terms, they can also be misleading. But like the other "cosmic generalities" we deploy in teaching world history, they offer summaries, if wielded with care, that help align the welter of local detail into patterns susceptible to translocal comparison.[1]

I. PATTERNS OF CULTURAL INTERACTION

All societies interact with others, but the major transformations in Japanese history were distinguished by a pattern of deliberate, massive, and aggressive cultural borrowing, followed by periods of gradual adaptation, or "Japanization," of foreign ways.

The so-called three great reforms in Japanese history once referred to the Taika Reform [literally, great change] of the seventh century, when ancient Japan transformed itself from tribal society to imperial state on the Chinese model; the Meiji Restoration [literally, renovation] of the nineteenth century, when modern Japan transformed itself from feudal shogunate to centralized nation-state along Western lines; and the Postwar Reforms, when postwar Japan transformed itself from imperial fascism to parliamentary democracy under American influence. This chronology of epochal change on foreign models appeared in the context of the initial postwar reforms after 1945. One might now amend it to the "three-and-a-half great reforms": the seventh and eighth-century borrowings by the ancient aristocracy from Tang China; the seventeenth-century borrowings by the Tokugawa shogunate from Song and Ming China; the nineteenth-century borrowings by the Meiji elite from the Euro-American West; and, for the half-great reform, the mid-twentieth century readjustment of those earlier Western borrowings in more expressly American form. The postwar reforms, in short, constituted a later phase of the longer modern transformation rather than a radical departure in a different historical direction. However one counts these transformations, all had in common an initial period of extreme openness to thought, practices, and institutions from "beyond the sea." Imported wholesale and with enthusiasm, it was as if the entire social world, from laws, customs, and institutions to religion, language, and art, had been reconceived in a new language, a new idiom of human experience. So the Sinification of the Nara period, the Neo-confucianization of the early Tokugawa, and the Euroamericanization of Meiji represented more than the selective or partial absorption of foreign ways of doing things. They represented instead an effort literally to re-think the realm. As ancient princes rethought Japan in Chinese shape, they adopted (often through Korea) the Chinese writing system, the institutions, codes, and capital city of the centralized imperial state, the ideology of imperial rule for their own son of Heaven (tennō), also systems of taxation, land distribution, and social stratification, Buddhist religion, architecture, and sculpture, even the national imperative to write their own history—to become, in short, "Japan" by adopting the ways of China. The effort was conscious and deliberate: "We propose at this present for the first time to regulate the myriad provinces. . . . The capital is for the first time to be regulated. . . . Let there now be provided for the first time registers of population. . . ."[2] In this litany of "first times" echoed the determination of "newness" that characterized each major era of cultural borrowing. The relation with power was equally characteristic, for it was the ruling elite that sought to launch the ship of state in a new direction with sails of a foreign cut unfurled against threats to their own newly established authority. So, too, the early Tokugawa shoguns and their attendant samurai elites worked to secure the new order with an eclectic rethinking of the realm in which Chinese neo-Confucianism (again with important Korean contributions) provided the main vocabulary of social, political, economic, philosophical, and moral speech and practice. The samurai, so recently warriors, were to become loyal civil servants of the moral exemplary sort; Buddhism lost its privileged link to medieval state power in favor of a new system of shogunal author-ity buttressed by assertions of moral rule; filial piety and the five Confucian relationships were commended as the basis for com-moner morality and obedience. Like their forbears a millennium earlier, seventeenth-century Japanese elites looked toward China with sincere and avid interest—indeed, they viewed neo-Confucian thought as the cultural vanguard of the age (and all the more important for Japan to preserve after the fall of the Ming to the "barbarians" in 1644)—but also with an astute eye toward its uses in stabilizing the new Tokugawa order.

The great borrowings also shared a third characteristic: they occurred first "on paper," pronounced from above by the state or the elite. The Meiji reforms set out to rethink—and remake—the realm as a modern nation-state openly modeled on the nine-teenth-century West. But as I have written in the chapter on modern Japan, paper reforms did not of themselves produce great transformations.[3] Such epochal change required a long historical process, first to take the measure of the foreign before the pro-nouncement of its adoption, and then afterward to weave the "newness" into the fabric of belief and practice that constitute social experience. And this process was never under the complete control of the state. Both the receptivity toward Chinese or West-ern ways and their subsequent adaptation always depended on the responses of Japanese society as much as on the dictates of the state. If filial piety had not worked for Tokugawa peasants, for example—if it had not served their economic and ancestral inter-ests—this much-expounded Confucian virtue would never have suffused folk morality the way it eventually did. And had it not fused into the compound slogan of "loyalty and filial piety (*chūkō*)—in that virtuous order—it would not have staked so per-suasive a claim on the Tokugawa samurai-turned-civil-servant. But because the slogan did make socio-moral sense in support of the samurai class, it not only established itself but it survived the

Tokugawa period, and the samurai class as well, to become a cardinal virtue in the ideology of the new Meiji state. This example points to the inevitable following phase of the process of transformation: the so-called Japanization, or indigenization, of the foreign borrowings. The adaptation took many forms. At times it was quite purposeful, as when the Confucian Mandate of Heaven failed to attach itself to the Japanese emperor, whose alleged descent from the Sun Goddess did not admit of any justification for dynastic change. Centuries later, paling at the prospect of open parliamentary contention of the British kind, the Meiji leaders consciously chose the Prussian bureaucratic model and then Japanized it for good measure with the "imperial line unbroken for ages eternal." But more often the adaptation proceeded in a slow and gradual "falling away" of the borrowed institutions rather than in a sudden turnabout against outlandish ways. The Chinese-style state bureaucracy (and examination system), for example, had little chance in the context of Japan's strong hereditary status hierarchy. Public tax-lands, though established in the Nara period, disappeared back into private family estates. Rather than falling away, some borrowings grew stronger as they indigenized, as Buddhism did, flourishing across the centuries. Too often the Japanization is presented as a simple reaction against the excesses of foreign borrowing instead of as a predictable reshaping of newly acquired goods. Like the boa constrictor that swallowed an elephant, the digestion of massive influence took time. And the historical result was neither foreign nor Japanese, but an amalgam of both.

Cultural interactions frequently produce such amalgams, which cannot be scientifically assayed to sift what is "Japanese" (or "Korean," or "Chinese") from what is not. The world-historical interest lies rather in the processes and the products of interaction. For once assimilated, the resulting patterns labeled Japanese (or Korean, or Chinese) can indeed be compared. In this regard, Japanese processes of cultural assimilation followed a pattern that tended to retain the old along with the new. Sometimes called an "easy eclecticism," this tendency to let inconsistencies lie characterized the early borrowings from China, including the adoption of Buddhism, against which the indigenous Shinto first defined itself. Their doctrinal differences notwithstanding, both religions survived, largely without resort to the holy wars that arose in other places. And as a contemporary example of ritual amplitude, it is often said that "Japanese today are born Shinto, die Buddhist, and celebrate *Kurisumasu*."

Three extremely brief but epochal texts—each enunciating a great reform based on foreign example—offer a glimpse of the syncretic style of Japanese borrowing.[4] The legendary "Seventeen-Article Constitution of Prince Shōtoku" (604) mixed Buddhist, Confucian, and local injunctions to provide laws "for the first time" for the emerging Yamato state. The Buddhist Article Two: "Sincerely reverence the three treasures" was followed by the Confucian Article Three: "When you receive the imperial commands, fail not scrupulously to obey them. The lord is Heaven, the vassal is Earth." And both were preceded by Article One: "Harmony is to be valued, and an avoidance of wanton opposition to be honored." Centuries later this phrase became the cornerstone of the invented "tradition" of harmony in modern Japan, but at the time it directly evoked the tribal struggle for power that accompanied the founding of the ancient imperial state. Indeed, the seventeen articles included the near and the foreign, the great and the small, the ideal and the practical: From "Good faith is the foundation of right" to "Let the ministers and the functionaries attend the court early in the morning, and retire late." But all stood in service of establishing a new state on the Chinese model.

A thousand years later, in 1615, the new Tokugawa shogunate promulgated the first of its "Laws Governing the Military Households." In another brief and general document of thirteen provisions, the shogunate mixed Confucian injunctions, feudal restrictions, and sumptuary regulations. Its main purport might be summarized in the one phrase, "Law is the basis of social order." For the "Laws" sought to secure the new shogunal order against recurrence of the civil wars that had preceded the Tokugawa victory in 1600. Henceforth, feudal lords (daimyō) were to pursue both "the arts of peace and war" and "select officials with a capacity for public administration." These Confucian maxims for governance stood alongside restrictions designed to prevent the lords from making war on the shogunate: no unauthorized castle repairs or marriage alliances, no factional conspiracies, no outsiders residing in a domain, no deviations from strictly regulated visits to the capital. And then, to keep society orderly, came the sumptuary regulations, so often issued because so often ignored throughout the Tokugawa period: restrictions on "type and quality of dress" and the blunt interdiction, "Persons without rank shall not ride in palanquins." The rest had to do with avoiding "drinking parties and wanton revelry" and, for the samurai, leading "a frugal and simple life." Here was the Tokugawa recipe for political peace and social order in a

Confucianized nutshell, an epitome of two-and-a-half centuries of stable shogunal rule.

And when that rule finally ended, the samurai leaders of the Meiji Restoration immediately pronounced, in the name of the emperor, "The Charter Oath" of 1868. Again this document enunciated the future in short, general, and capaciously ambiguous terms. Its five articles mixed Western and Confucian language, mentioning "the framing of a constitution and laws" together with "the establishment of the national weal on broad terms." It called for "deliberative assemblies," which could be, and were, variously interpreted as a hereditary council of feudal daimyō or a popularly elected parliament, two very different assemblies indeed. The pronouncement stated boldly that "evil customs of the past shall be broken off and everything based on the just laws of Nature," however they might be defined. And it conjoined the models of the modern West with the anciently indigenous emperor system: "Knowledge shall be sought throughout the world so as to strengthen the foundations of imperial rule." In effect, the Charter Oath allowed for both Euro-american civilization and Japanese institutional practices, without insisting on any logical alignment between one and the other.

Some have criticized this sort of eclecticism for failing to resolve apparent contradictions—such as instituting a Western-style parliament and an ancestral divine emperor side by side in the Meiji state—which left the way open for contrary actions encompassed by the same system—both democracy and autocracy under the Meiji constitution. Others prefer to cite the striking openness of the Japanese language to foreign words (once Chinese, now English) as a symbol of the hybridity of cultural adaptation in Japan. Still others point to the so-called bullet-train model of development, according to which new institutions were established alongside the old, just as the first postwar bullet-train tracks were laid parallel to the Meiji railway connecting Tokyo and Kyoto, which in turn followed the old Tōkaidō road from the shogunal era—and all the routes continued to operate, the new not instantly displacing the old. Among the metaphors for this historical process of borrowing-plus-adaptation, the pendulum image is perhaps the least apt, since the forces for Japanization almost never sought to drive out foreign ways, only to coopt and domesticate them.

The mythic version, however, told a different story. Ever since the high Heian period, when the court "Yamato-ized" the borrowed Chinese culture and institutions of the preceding period, Japan is said to have followed its phases of "openness" to foreign influence by periods of strong assertion of Japanese cultural difference. Never mind that the Heian courtiers continued to record state documents and compose poetry in Chinese; memory gives the pride of cultural place to Lady Murasaki's *The Tale of Genji*, written in "Yamato-language" and considered the great classic of "Japanese literature." Similarly, the story has it that the sinophilic Confucians of the Tokugawa period met their match in the nativists of the eighteenth century, who juxtaposed the logical Chinese mind, or heart (*karagokoro*) to the sensitive—and superior—Japanese mind (*wagokoro*). In fact, Confucian values continued to diffuse ever more widely and affected nativist thinkers as well as most everyone else. And after the headlong Euro-americanization of the early Meiji period, the "pendulum" is said to have again swung back toward "Japanization," with the Confucianization of moral instruction in the schools, Shinto-ization of imperial ceremony, and a "traditionalization" of women's roles as "good wives, wise mothers." But the pendulum did not swing anywhere near the Constitution, the Diet, the army and navy, steel and textile factories, trains, elementary schools, German medicine, the Western musical scale, and so many other products of the twin Westernizing slogans of "rich nation, strong army" (*fukoku kyōhei*) and "civilization and enlightenment" (*bunmei kaika*). The historical fact is that Japan retained much that it borrowed even as it massaged the borrowings into more familiar shapes.

What the myth reflects is the pattern of using the foreign to define what was Japanese. Perhaps because of the intensive borrowing, Japanese repeatedly sought to assert their national identity—to preserve their soul, their emperor, their women—by stressing cultural difference. Others in this volume have suggested that unity is a grand theme in Chinese history as continuity is in the history of India. In contrast, Japan was small and relatively easy to unify; it was isolated and not beset by radical rupture of its cultural continuity. But identity—identity was always an issue. That is why memory stresses the periods of Japanization and so often depicts the resulting amalgam as distinctively, even uniquely "Japanese." This national assertion has traveled the world in such stereotypes as the "imitative" Japanese (during the phases of openness) and the oddly, or even dangerously "different" Japanese (once indigenization has taken place). Both the national myths and the international stereotypes insist on the "differentness" of Japan, often prying Japanese history out of the world by rendering it incomparable.

In reality, these historical patterns of cultural interaction did not differ so greatly from similar episodes elsewhere. It is true that no foreign force invaded Japan (until 1945)—the divine winds *(kamikaze)* having blown the Mongols back in the early thirteenth century. Hence one extremely common medium of massive cultural influence was absent. Yet Japan after its early Sinification was linked to the Asian continent—not only to China, but by virtue of Buddhism also, distantly, to India—in a civilizational relationship not unlike the links between early Britain and Rome. Moreover, migrations from Korea had helped to form the early clan culture that later became the Japanese imperial state in a type of cultural diffusion found nearly everywhere in the world (That this Korean link—and perhaps even the Korean origin of the imperial house—seldom appears in the standard histories of Japan is due not to the facts of prehistory but to the myths of national identity.) It is also true that Japan had no continental borders of the sort that figured importantly in the cultural interfusions in Chinese and other Eurasian history. Japan, like England, was an isolated outpost at the edge of a great continent, but unlike England, experienced no Norman conquest to meld continental and island ways. And while ancient and medieval Japanese participated in a sea-based Asian economy, Japan did not become a crossroads of cultures like Southeast Asia, where influences from India commingled with those from continental China, or like the Ryūkyūan kingdom (present-day Okinawa), which was linked both to China and Southeast Asia by a thriving maritime trade. For much of its premodern history Japan was largely a one-way destination, a cultural borrower rather than a lender. But it was an avid and effective borrower, and its experiences may serve as a useful basis for comparison, precisely because the cultural interactions were so clearly delineated. For the study of world history, Japanese patterns of borrowing and adaptation provide an unusually clear case from which to draw insights that held true in many other places, including those in which the "borrowing" was more or less concealed by conquest, slow diffusion, or outright repudiation. No matter the tales that nations later told about the distinctive lineage of their particular national past, in world history, hybridity was everywhere the norm.

II. CONTINUITY WITHIN CHANGE

Japanese society accommodated aggressive pursuit of change within a framework of alleged continuity, a pattern which both disguised the initial impact of rapid change and tenaciously

preserved cultural forms, often by altering them to suit contemporary needs and then identifying the altered forms as timeless "tradition."

Change and continuity configure the interpretive template of every history; there is nothing distinctive in this pairing. The thematic point here relates rather to the way Japanese repeatedly used continuity in the service of change and change in the service of continuity. The concentrated instances of cultural borrowing probably exaggerated this juxtaposition, since people were quick to identify change with the new and the foreign, continuity with the familiar and the "Japanese." In a standard phrase, Japanese advocates for change are said to have "proposed new institutions in the name of old values."[5]

When Meiji leaders established the modern centralized state in 1868, to take a prime example, they did so in the name of the emperor, whose alleged descent from Sun Goddess offered the most ancient referent they could muster. By calling the event the "restoration of imperial rule," they suggested a righteous return to a situation that had earlier obtained. Going forward by going back—it may appear somewhat neo-classical or Golden-Age-ish, but such appearances mislead. First, in Japanese history "direct imperial rule" had long been the exception rather than the norm, so here the activists were asserting a pseudo-continuity. Second, the Meiji emperor would not rule directly but reign while others ruled in his name, so here those others, the samurai-bureaucrats, profited by "protecting" the imperial institution from change in its customary irrelevance to the actual practice of power. Third, those same bureaucrats then presided over the simultaneous transformation of the emperor into a modern constitutional monarch and a "manifest deity," thus conferring on him a symbolic and ideological relevance undreamt of by his august ancestors—a profound change indeed. The result was the modern emperor-system (*tennōsei*), which enshrined the imperial institution as the hallowed heart of tradition, the quintessence of Japaneseness, the "absent presence" in the physical center of Tokyo and the ideological center of national identity. Continuous with time immemorial but utterly changed in service of that continuity into a modern sovereign, who claimed absolute allegiance from his subjects because he was the literal "embodiment" of a "tradition," which itself was almost entirely reinvented in the Meiji period. Such were the twists and turns in the modern "imperial line unbroken."[6]

And this old-new-old-new imperial icon did not sink into insignificance when the emperor-system state was dismantled after the defeat in 1945. On the contrary, U.S. wartime planning called for retaining the imperial institution. The American planners believed that the Japanese people so deeply revered the emperor that any anti-imperial action would simply turn them against the Occupation and undermine its democratizing policies. Foregoing even the abdication of the wartime emperor, Hirohito, the Americans decided instead to democratize the office while he remained in it. In the 1947 Constitution they wrote that the emperor would henceforth be "the symbol of the state and of the unity of the people," in whom full sovereignty now resided. In the name of democracy the Occupation had, oddly enough, "restored" the emperor fully to the reign-but-not-rule practice of earlier times. The Occupation also drafted a "Declaration of Humanity," in which the emperor divested himself of his divinity, turning the once manifest deity into the mild-mannered monarch of postwar Japan. And this loss of sovereignty and divine ancestry notwithstanding, the imperial institution maintained its time-honored continuity yet again. After Hirohito died in 1989, the authorities conducted the enthronement ceremonies for his son, the new emperor, with all due respect to the sanctity of imperial "tradition." Few realized that this tradition was itself a rite of modernity, held for the first time in its present form when Hirohito was enthroned in 1928. Meanwhile the government was again celebrating the imperial institution as an expression of Japan's distinctive cultural identity, represented no longer by empire and war but by peace and prosperity. By dint of this national weave of change and continuity Japan ended the twentieth century a democracy with an emperor, perhaps the last emperor of any sort anywhere.

If at times new institutions were established "in the name of old values," at other times old names masked new realities. Think once more of the new Meiji state, which scarcely existed as such in the months immediately following the Restoration. Blandly called the "transition" between quasi-feudal shogunal rule and a centralized modern state, the years between 1868 and 1871 might better be described as stately administrative chaos. That, at least, is how things looked at the center, where the handful of mostly young samurai leaders groped toward consolidating their power by a process of trial and error. They had little choice, since they did not in fact control the realm, much of which remained in the hands of the daimyō who operated in their practiced feudal manner. The government had both to overcome the pro-Tokugawa forces and keep others from joining up with them. It first did this by including the feudal lords in the new central structure, which changed three times in the first eighteen months.

Then came something unprecedented, new in name and new in fact: the "return of the registers," by which the lords agreed to give up their proprietary feudal authority and "return" their lands to the state in 1869. Why the daimyō consented to this voluntary cession of their hereditary rights remains one of the striking puzzles of modern Japanese history. It becomes only somewhat less puzzling in the light of the fact that the lords were instantly renamed governors of their own territories. Perhaps the difference between feudal lord and governor sounded slight enough to the daimyō to warrant their collective cooperation, a cooperation they had become more accustomed to during the waning years of the shogunate. Immediately the government structure shifted again. This time the samurai reformers chose the oldest names they could find: they took the office titles from the eighth-century imperial state. Since no one understood them any more, "officials rushed out to secondhand bookstores to buy copies of the Taihō code (*Ryō no gige*) so they would know what the new office titles meant."[7] Not only that, but every officeholder was also assigned one of the nine ancient court ranks, an archaic system that had the strangely modern effect of leveling samurai, lord, and court noble and making them, depending on rank and office, subordinate to the largely low-ranking samurai leaders who were proceeding, slowly, to take over.

Only two years later, in 1871, these same leaders summarily announced (using the emperor as a shield) that the domains would henceforth become prefectures and that the feudal-lords-turned-governors would be replaced by government-appointed officials. And both lords and nobles lost their recently gained positions in the government. If indeed the lords had returned their registers in the expectation that they were experiencing the start of a shogunate by another name, they found themselves mistaken—as well as unemployed. And though the ancient titles and ranks lasted longer than the governorships of the feudal lords (that is, until the establishment of the cabinet system in 1885), the central authority behind the names had already shifted by 1871 to the young samurai, who began as imperial reformers and ended as the powerful bureaucrats known as the Meiji oligarchs. Their trial-and-error path toward centralization was probably unavoidable, considering their lack of military and political control over the nation. And the strategy of using the old to cloak the new helped both to conceal their own weakness as well as to consolidate their strength.

Others used the strategy to their own advantage. When, for example, the oligarchs demoted the Office for Shinto Affairs—which they had briefly elevated to serve its ancient purpose of sanctifying imperial rule—the Shinto establishment was not pleased at this sudden secularization of the state. The Shintoists crusaded for a return to public power, basing their claims on antiquity and continuity. They eventually succeeded, with the result that in the twentieth century new constitutional forms were infused with old theocratic elements, culminating in the national rites known as State Shinto.[8] State Shinto had never before existed—as a state cult it was new and indeed had to be defined as a non-religion in order to preserve the constitutional provision for freedom of religion. But Shinto was also old, as old as the "divine country," it was said, the very essence of identity and tradition. Thus by updating Shinto, by nationalizing it into an ideology of the modern state, its supporters preserved it. In 1891 when a new-style scientific historian wrote that Shinto was an "ancient form of nature worship," he lost his university position precisely because this ancient form was in the midst of refashioning itself as a modern national rite which claimed to be the repository of timeless tradition.

One consequence of this conscious interplay of old and new is the aura of tradition that lies so thickly over Japan's myths of its own past. History shows that Shinto and the emperor were modern reinventions of tradition, but myth insists that these traditions survived, unchanged, from the ancestral past, and that their survival represents Japan's cultural strength—its identity. In this sense the aura of tradition is false: the aspect in question is neither as old or as traditional as is alleged. And the same is true of far newer traditions, such as the so-called Japanese employment system, whose paternalistic practices are said to derive from village social relations of yore when they in fact arose from factory labor relations of the twentieth century.

Another consequence, paradoxically, is the cultural tenacity that derives from Japan's propensity to keep its traditions by changing them. The emperor is one powerful example, but the symbolic epitome of this continuity-by-change may well be Ise Shrine. The holiest precinct in the "divine land," the shrine of the Sun Goddess, progenitrix of the imperial family, the sacred building at Ise is torn down every twenty years and an exact replica, brand-new, is erected next to the old one. As a result of this constant razing and rebuilding, Ise Shrine today is a rare extant example of early wooden architecture, which nearly everywhere else fell eons ago to flame and ruin—and disappeared. The Parthenon exists because it is made of marble, a symbol of a civilization which meant its monuments to the gods to be everlasting. Ise Shrine exists because its wood and straw were replaced by new wood and straw, preserving the sacred site by holding it sacred in a different way. Not a monumental edifice but a flexible fabric, Japan's traditions endured because they so often swayed with the winds of change.

Somewhat different from consciously reinvented traditions like the emperor, Shinto, or the so-called traditional Japanese woman, this pattern of cultural preservation tended to happen "on the ground," in the social context of daily life.[9] To preserve the spirit changes were made in the form. Large festival floats could be pulled by masses of half-naked men or they could be motorized; seasonal cherry blossoms might be the palest clouds of the trees at Yoshino or gaudy pink plastic in the subterranean shopping malls of Tokyo. As long as the floats moved and the blossoms appeared in the proper month, the tradition held. When modern ethnographers bemoaned the changes in local festivals (matsuri)—which they did for most of the twentieth century—they meant the attenuation of rural community more than they did the dilution of ritual form. And when localities prided themselves on the age-old continuity of their traditional festivals, they did so knowing full well that these rites were undergoing constant and contentious change. Contrary to the impression given by the title of a documentary on national television—"The Major Role of 80-year-old Men: The People who have Sustained Kurokawa Noh for 500 Years"—the locality in question was messily embroiled at the time in replacing one hereditary family guild with another. It was also seeking simultaneously to benefit from urban tourism and still preserve its identity in the midst of the national "nostalgia boom" of the late 1980s. In the contemporary landscape of traditionalism, this rural area was "poised delicately between having a past—the basis of local concern—and being a past—the focus of metropolitan fascination."[10]

This metropolitan fascination was spurred on by mythic uses of tradition, which identified the countryside as the repository of Japaneseness. In the 1970s the national railways ad campaign urged people to get out and "Discover Japan," and in the 1980s government programs promoted "native-place making" (furusato-zukuri) to attract urban tourists to the "authentic" world of village Japan. The "politics of nostalgia" was premised on "a Japan that is kept on the verge of vanishing, stable yet endangered (and thus open for commodifiable desire.)"[11] The genuine Japanese country-side that was ever "on the verge of vanishing" was actually long gone, at least in its full-time rice-farming, *kami*-worshipping, *ie* (household)-system- sustaining incarnation of the Japanese earth and soul. But in the mirror of national identity, reflected in government policy as well as in the culture industry, the image of village Japan could still shimmer on, untouched by cities, semiconductors, or the Grateful Dead. In this case identity was enshrined as continuity and tradition evoked in defiance of change.

In other cases the lens of change served to magnify national distinctiveness. In contemporary political discourse it sometimes seemed as if lifetime employment, promotion by seniority, and enterprise unions grew out of the ground, the "natural" harvest of Japanese social soil, when they were instead grafts and hybrids of primarily postwar origin. In the recession of the first half of the 1990s, for example, the national media lamented the "end of lifetime employment," implying that corporate *risutora* (restructuring) marked the demise of the "Japanese"—not the postwar—way of employment. Of course it, too, was a *faux*-tradition to begin with. Not only was it of recent origin but only a limited percentage of fulltime male employees ever possessed a lifetime ticket. But raising "lifetime employment" as a banner of identity immediately placed corporate downsizing in a charged national context, which then determined the political debates about its consequences. The American counterpart was probably the much-evoked "death of the middle-class dream," which framed similar debates about economic change in the United States at roughly the same time. Both the "Japanese employment system" and the "middle-class dream" pertained to national identity, self-defined, the one presented as unchanging tradition, the other as the product of progress, but both depicted on the verge of vanishing.

Clearly this contemporary habit of playing off change and continuity in the name of national identity is not peculiar to Japan. It happens everywhere there is a nation-state or a subnationality, which is everywhere. But the combination of the historical pursuit of change with the mythic insistence on timeless tradition has rebounded as unrelenting stereotype in international views of Japan. Sometimes Japan appears to foreign observers to be a veritable machine of change, flinging itself headlong into the future, as it did during Meiji and again after the Second World War. Then, when it appears that everything did not change after all, international opinion is quick to conclude that nothing did: that Japan never changes, its traditions always stronger than its adaptations. Such views were common in the 1930s and again in the 1980s, when Japan threatened the world, once by military aggression, later by economic competition. Few prewar observers saw Japanese imperialism as a product of change; they said instead that feudal tradition had raised its martial head. And American and European competitors later condemned "Japanese capitalism" for refusing to abandon its "traditions" to fit the practices of the rest of the Western capitalist world. But like so many cross-national stereotypes, whether the ruggedly individualistic American or the stiff-upper-lipped Englishman, these cardboard images of traditional Japan were originally homegrown, the products of historical change frozen into national myth.

III. T E PRIMACY OF SOCIETY

Japan's insularity fostered a social closeness, which was reflected in the structures of family, community, and nation as well as in the centrality of social relations as the basis for thought and practice.

The importance accorded to the social order and the "human relations" (*ningen kankei*) that comprise it is a conspicuous theme in Japanese history. Like the other themes, its conspicuousness is relative, since society everywhere forms the basis of human experience. But in relative and comparative terms, society was often the primary principle, the value of first and last resort, in determining the decisions, actions, and patterns of Japanese behavior. If in premodern China, the state was the locus and guarantor of order, in Japan society more often played that role. If in modern France, politics supplied a code critical to reading the map of social power, in modern Japan social relations underlay political alignments that would be inexplicable by issues or doctrinal positions alone. To make sense of Japanese history, society is almost always the best place to start because social concerns drove so much of the action—not the logic of absolute power, the abstraction of philosophical principle, the authority of church or state, but the criss-crossing webs of social relations that held people up, tied them down, and wove the fabric of social order tightly about them.

Many trace the primacy of society to geography. A small country to begin with, Japan consists mostly of mountains, with only 16 percent of its land arable. Whatever one may think of topographical determinism as a historical principle, when combined with the communal imperatives of labor-intensive wet-rice agriculture, the result was that Japanese did indeed live and work very closely together. Within the villages they depended on one another for the labor to transplant, irrigate, and harvest the paddy fields. Because of the mountainous terrain, villages were often isolated from one another, intensifying local interdependence and sharpening the line between insiders and outsiders. For long periods in Japanese history (as in most premodern societies) the state did not much disrupt, or even penetrate, the localities. And the sea that is nearly everywhere visible from Japan's peaks had a similar impact upon the country as a whole: Japanese lived close together on their small islands, the line seeming salt-sea sharp between themselves and the outside world.

But ecology is not really destiny, and Japan's "socio-centrism" was as noticeable in the Heian court and the feudal domains as it was in the villages. The preeminence of the countryside in social explanation was itself a product of modern times, when the village became the favored trope for expressing the importance of communal ties and cooperative institutions in Japanese social organization. Generalized largely from Tokugawa examples, the archetypal image portrayed a village divided into households (*ie*), which were corporate family units collectively responsible for their members, with the village in turn assuming collective responsibility for its constituent households in everything from roof-thatching to tax-collecting. Like the nineteenth-century German distinction between community (*Gemeinschaft*) and society (*Gesellschaft*), the Meiji notion of the communitarian agricultural village took hold just as it appeared on the verge of vanishing, or more accurately, of being vanquished by modern mass society. Depending on one's view of modernity, the village was romanticized as a cooperative community or denounced as an oppressive hierarchy, but in both instances it was presented as Japan's indigenous social form.

Since the 1970s one iconoclastic medieval historian has sought to counter this received idea by studying the lives of "non-agriculturists" like the fishers and itinerant artisans who lived on the margins and in the spaces between the settled rice-growing communities that later prevailed as the political, economic, and ideological norm.[12] But his battle against what he calls the erroneous "common sense" of Japanese history is not yet won. The agricultural village, together with the household (*ie*), is insistently evoked as the model for Japanese social relations past and present. While the historian should approach such claims with caution, their prominence gives further proof of the centrality of the social in the grammar of Japanese experience. Examples of the way the village worked in history include the social ideology of "co-equality" and the rich associational tradition on the local level. Co-equality refers to the principle of even shares in—and even responsibility for—designated communal goods like access to water and common forestland or collective tasks like fire-fighting and performance of village rituals. In such matters fair share could override status, the well-off headman and the poor tenant each receiving his due in irrigation and each sending his sons to the young-men's association to do the cooperative village work. Tokugawa village rules prescribed all manner of collective action and interaction, from making up the taxes of those who could or did not pay to reporting and punishing crimes.

Prescribed community and considerable autonomy did not of course make all villagers either co-equal or serene. A tide of peasant protest rose from the seventeenth through the nineteenth century. At times whole villages communally contested the extractions of the feudal authorities, and, more frequently, groups contended within villages for redress, rebate, or reform of economic inequities. Such protest tended to be collective rather than individual, and it most often sought to restore the notional equilibrium within the social hierarchy rather than to overturn the hierarchy itself. At stake was the balance between the principle of co-equality and the practice of status distinction, a combination of horizontal and vertical relations that characterized not only the village but the larger Tokugawa order as well.

The Tokugawa status hierarchy itself reflected a penchant for social order—or orderliness—that reinforced the primacy of society in Japanese history. Standard Japanese renderings of the Tokugawa period (1600-1868) unfold under three banner labels: the feudal polity (the shogunal-domain system, *bakuhan taisei*), the seclusion policy (*sakoku*), and the status society (or status system, *mibunsei*). This last refers to the hereditary occupational hierarchy of samurai, peasants, artisans, and merchants, in that descending order of social prestige. The small samurai class, only some seven percent of the population, constituted the governing elite; the large peasantry (80 percent) came next, its second-to-samurai status assured by Confucian notions of the importance of agricultural producers in an agrarian economy; then the artisans, who made things, followed by the merchants, who in the same Confucian moral ranking, produced nothing but instead profited from the products of others. Historians rightly insist, as Henry Smith does in his chapter debunking the myths about early modern Japan, that these four estates never existed in the tidily uniform way evoked by the ideal scheme.[13] Nor, for example, in an age of increasingly widespread commercialization, did the merchants remain humbly at the bottom of the social barrel. But here the historical crux is less the social realities that violated the scheme than the social symbolics that supported it.

For no one in Tokugawa times remained in doubt as to his or her social place, which was inherited, not selected, and was also subject to a unrelenting array of moral injunctions and socio-economic proscriptions. As Saikaku relayed the wellworn social formula:

> Human beings by nature are all the same, whoever they may be, yet each reveals himself in his own way: the samurai by wearing a long sword, the Shinto priest by his court cap, the Buddhist priest by his black robes, the farmer by the mattock, the artisan by his adze, the merchant by his abacus.[14]

This vocational hierarchy—human beings "all the same" but stratified by their "own way"—remained in ideological place until the new Meiji government declared "the equality of the four peoples" after the Restoration.

Of its apparent longevity two points may be made. The first pertains to the transmigration of social value that over time invested each status with an enhanced definition of its particular worth. As the martial samurai of the Warring States era became the feudal bureaucrats of the long Pax Tokugawa, a "Way of the Warrior" (*bushidō*) evolved that prized learning and moral rule. These virtues suited samurai retainers who though they alone had the privilege of wearing swords were seldom permitted to use them. By analogy and extension, the lower orders developed validating "Ways" of their own. In the Way of the merchant, merchants appeared as "retainers of the town," their profit likened to the samurai's stipend, while the peasants fulfilled their Way by cultivating the "paddy fields of the realm." Loyalty for the samurai, honesty for the merchant, frugality for the peasant—to each a defining virtue, to all a definitive social place. In this manner Confucian values that had once belonged to the samurai came to permeate commoner morality as well. And the samurai concern for perpetuating the honor of the family name had stated parallels in the merchant's dedication to the family business and the peasant's devotion to his ancestral lands. Thus the hierarchy endured, even as each status asserted its identity and claimed social value commensurate with its indispensability to the whole.

A second noteworthy aspect of the Tokugawa status society was its persistence in the face of its own anachronism. Impoverished feudal lords in debt to wealthy merchants, low-ranking samurai unable to survive on their meager stipends, rich peasants wearing silk and drinking tea in violation of the rules of their estate—such topsy-turvy economic power belied the legislated social order. And there were other contraventions of the ideal scheme: the efflorescence of culture among the townsmen, the appearance of peasant-poets and technologists, the supposed oxymorons of illiterate samurai and merchant-philosophers. Yet it is the upside-down economic relation between the feudal elite, privileged but increasingly poor, and the merchants, lowly but increasingly rich, that poses the historical question: if the rich merchants had so much wealth and even power, why did they not demand a commensurate change in their allotted social status? And if the poorest peasants were so deeply immiserated, why did they not seek to unseat the rich landlords who were their proximate exploiters? In other words, why did the ideal scheme so long outlast the economic realities?

One answer lies in the elasticity of the supposedly rigid status lines. Merchants bought samurai status, country samurai worked the land, and entrepreneurial peasants engaged in trade. But another answer may well be a conception of social order that prompted commoners and samurai alike to maneuver within the framework rather than try to bring the whole structure down. While the shogunal state sought an orderly society with a place for everyone and everyone in place, the people agitated not to abolish their status but to be treated according to the dignity and worth their status deserved. In an 1855 uprising protesting intensified discriminatory measures against the outcaste class (*eta-hinin*), the *eta* called not for abolition of their class but for official recognition of their special occupational and taxpaying status. In this way the Tokugawa status system endured as a general template of social order even as it accommodated considerable change—and protest—in the economic and cultural contexts of daily life.

The primacy of society comprising coequality and status distinctions also operated in modern Japan. In the postwar period, for example, when Japan was "reborn" under the dual sign of peace and democracy, democracy came to be defined as much in social as in political terms. Rather than ballot-box representation, democracy came to mean coequal access to material and social goods. Fairness implied balanced allotment of salaries, benefits, and other pieces of the prosperity pie, with no big losers and no big winners either, at least in the ideal scheme of things. This notion of democracy undergirded the postwar conception of middle-class society that by the 1980s had some 98 percent of Japanese identifying themselves as middle-class. This idea was every bit as mythical—and every bit as tenacious—as the four-class schema of Tokugawa times. But, like its Tokugawa predecessor, it served as a template of social order, whose preservation had real economic and political consequences.[15]

At the same time, of course, status distinctions pervaded this great middle-ness, aligning people in multiple lattices of clearly delineated hierarchies. Thus, twentieth-century Japan was said to be an "education-credentialist society (*gakureki shakai*) in which the prestige of elite schooling counted more than the degree of achievement—the Tokyo University syndrome. Corporations were organized in a hierarchy of seniority; the master-disciple relationship operated not only in the traditional arts but also in the sciences and other enterprises; the father remained the now often pale but still patriarchal figure in the family. The collectivity provided the context for individual actions; collective responsibility and collective leadership were common. The Meiji oligarchy was a small group of elite bureaucrats who ran the government for decades; the *zaibatsu* oligopoly was a small group of powerful firms (Mitsubishi, Mitsui, and others) that represented the intensive concentration of capital in the prewar economy. The prefix *oligo-* conveys both the "groupness" and also the hierarchy of the few dominating the many. While these structural categories were never absolute, it is true that people often described themselves as enmeshed—both netted and supported—in a cross-hatch of social relations, both coequal and vertical, that they both identified with and helped to maintain.

The maintenance of social relations remained a priority. The preservation of the family, including the imperial one, had long been managed by the practice of adoption—the line assured not by blood but by adoptive continuity. The preservation of political lineage, once hereditary, retained that tendency: in the mid-1990s over one-fifth of the seats in the Lower House of the Diet were occupied by so-called hereditary representatives, related either by blood or loyalty to former members. So it was that social relations seemed often to outweigh political platform in determining electoral outcomes. In the business world the industrial groupings known as *keiretsu* linked large corporations and their subsidiaries not only by interlocking organizational structure but also by informal personal networks (*jinmyaku*). Much to the annoyance of foreign competitors, these networks were capable of prizing their relationship to the point of ignoring the outsiders' lower bids in favor of socio-centric corporate capitalism.

The primacy of society in history made its way into the heart of national identity in myth. In the modern period social closeness operated as the ideology of harmony (*wa*), which the state used to repress conflict between labor and management in the 1920s and families wielded to keep their relations in order. Touted as a defining element in Japaneseness, the value of social harmony was evoked to explain everything from "why Japanese are not litigious" to why individualism remained a dangerously "unJapanese" trait. Obviously, such social tales are not social truths: Japanese have a long and persistent history of taking to the law and filing suit, just as Japanese families, like Tolstoy's, are conflicted and unhappy in their own ways. A similar social myth surrounds Japan's much-brandished "homogeneity," which is neither true—ethnic minorities like the Ainu and the Koreans, social minorities like the *burakumin* (the former outcaste class), cultural minorities like the Okinawans, and others all gainsay the effort to efface them--nor even tried and true—the noisy assertion of a mono-ethnic Japan is largely a phenomenon of the postwar period. While these assertions are indeed false, they are also evidence of the primacy of society in national self-images.

And like each of these six historical themes, once translated into national myth, the social definition of "Japaneseness" also affected national policy. Discrimination against Koreans resident in Japan, some of them already in the fourth.generation, included the hated police fingerprinting as well as inferior opportunity of access to education, employment, and status. When "foreign workers" entered Japan in greater numbers in the late 1980s and 1990s, they found themselves treated with a fierce exclusivity that seemed almost consensual—as if their alienation were a foregone conclusion of Japanese homogeneity. Whether in refusing to accept a small number of boat people from Vietnam or ejecting a larger number of Iranian workers, over the years the argument remained that foreigners would not be able to "fit in" in Japanese society. The extrusion was not of course confined to foreign peoples, but was practiced against Japanese who were stigmatized by difference. Whether against victims "contaminated" by atomic radiation or industrial pollution or minorities tainted by historical association like the *burakumin,* inner discrimination marginalized those who did not "fit" the fiction of the harmonious homogeneous people known as "we Japanese."

Fictions like these have legs—they travel the world as national stereotypes. Hence the image of Japan as a group-oriented, regimented, consensus-driven society in which (in the inevitable media cliche) "the nail that sticks out is hammered down." Japan's social fictions have been so thoroughly absorbed into international characterizations that it requires great bursts of pedagogical energy to expose them. Two early lines of defense come to mind. First, to point out that the harmony-homogeneity constructs evolved precisely to disguise the conflict-diversity that affects Japanese society as it does all others. By confronting the mechanisms of marginalization of minorities, heterogeneity is revealed. By showing how the individual negotiates and manipulates his or her way through daily life in the social maze, the purported groupness fades in intensity. Fiction and film often serve this purpose well, since the protagonists of works as different as the eleventh-century *Tale of Genji*, the early twentieth-century novel *Kokoro*, and the late twentieth-century film *The Family Game* live their lives and make their choices as individuals, not social automatons.[16]

Second, to insist on the commonality of the Japanese emphasis on human relations with that of other societies. In one sense, of course, all societies share the structural stress on family, community, coequality and hierarchy; class and status distinctions are everywhere found; and patriarchy, it seems, knows no natural boundaries. The differences appear more in the weight or value accorded one or another of these elements in historical context. To contravene the conventional argument that the West prizes individualism and the United States its own "rugged" brand, historians have expended great efforts to show the limits of such generalizations. But in broad-brush terms, the distinction holds, and when Japanese society is compared to others not in the Euro-American ambit—whether China, Indonesia, Iran, or elsewhere—the primacy of society appears far less distinctive than when Japan is compared to the United States. In this instance world history has the virtue of liberating us from parochial contrasts into a wider world of comparative opportunities, which includes places were, as in Japan, social relations constitute not just the frame but the heart of the historical matter.

IV. INCLINATION TOWARD STABILITY

An inclination toward political and social stability—or a disinclination toward disorder—was reflected in the lastingness of political institutions that survived after power

had in fact devolved to other sectors as well as in the tendency toward evolutionary rather than revolutionary change.

Any understanding of Japanese history must confront the conspicuous durability—the lastingness—of institutional structures across time. These frameworks often endured long after they had ceased to make historical sense even in their own terms, as if suspended by habit or inertia in some suprasocial ether. The imperial institution is everyone's prime example, surviving from time primordial to prime time TV, its institutional continuity allegedly intact. But there are other less exalted but significant instances, including the Tokugawa shogunate and the postwar Liberal Democratic Party.

The premise of lastingness was the primacy of society. Because social relations were considered foundational, social stability was prized, giving rise to what I call a disinclination toward social disorder. Indeed, the different historical regimes devoted their initial efforts to securing the order, just as the early Tokugawa shoguns did when they tried to tie everything and everyone down in their pacified places. And when social change occurred—as it inevitably did—the later shoguns tried to "restore" everyone to that proper place, through prescription, regulation, and sometimes force. At times policy was preemptive: measures taken to head off conflict among feudal lords or commerce among peasants before it even arose. And as I have argued earlier, it was not only the state that showed a predilection for order. Villagers, merchants, samurai, peasants, and outcastes, too, preferred to improve their status rather than upturn the whole arrangement in a social revolution.

Political change often proceeded under the sign of a similar reluctance in regard to revolution. Not that Japan's history was pacific or lacked violence, warfare, or upheaval. From earliest times one tribe battled another: the gods of Izumo in the first written history, the eighth-century *Kojiki*, are said to represent the clan that lost out to the one whose god(dess) reigned at Ise, later to become the imperial clan. Ministers had their enemies murdered at the imperial court, and medieval samurai warred against one another, brothers included. From 1467 the country disintegrated into a century of civil war during the *Sengoku* (Warring States) era. Samurai violence in Kyoto in the 1860s and a rash of assassinations by the radical right in the 1930s made terrorism an agent of political change. This is not then a serene history of Heian courtiers in "bewitchingly baggy trousers," Zen-meditating medieval warriors, and scholarly literati minding the civil realm.

That being said, for very long periods political change occurred not against, but within, the existing institutional structures.

The classic example is the tendency toward devolution of power from the nominal ruler to the actual ruler. In the seventh and eighth centuries the emperors (six of them female) ruled directly over the newly established Chinese-style imperial state. In the mid-ninth century the Fujiwara family established itself as hereditary regents who ruled in the emperor's name. The rise of the warrior class and a great war between two rival clans in the twelfth century culminated in the founding of the Kamakura shogunate in 1185. Now the shogun in his Eastern capital of Kamakura ruled in the name of the emperor who continued to reign at the court in Kyoto. Then, from 1203 until the end of the Kamakura shogunate in 1333, the Hōjō family ruled as hereditary regents in the name of the shogun who ruled in the name of the emperor, who continued to reign in Kyoto. Throughout this period each office remained respectfully in place, while power was exercised by someone else. And the devolution had not ended yet. During the Ashikaga (Muromachi) shogunate (1338-1573), the shoguns again ruled in the name of the emperor, but by the time the Ōnin War began in 1467, the shogun had lost his power to the warring regional lords. Because these daimyō ruled their own domains and replaced—after the better part of a millennium—the centralized government of both emperor and shogun, John Whitney Hall claims that Japan was now becoming "completely feudal."[17] Yet, completely feudal or no, the daimyō did not disturb either the emperor or the shogun but left them both to reign in Kyoto, utterly powerless but still nominally in power.

In this way the legitimating name stayed but the actual power moved, maintaining a semblance of institutional continuity, even as the political reins changed hands. After the Warring States era, the country was unified in the form of the oxymoronic "centralized feudalism" associated with the new Tokugawa shogunate. From 1603 the Tokugawa shoguns ruled from Edo (Tokyo) in the name of the emperor at Kyoto, and for most of that time the imperial institution was stashed away as if in the cultural attic, its prestige as low as it had ever been. Gone perhaps but not abolished, so that when the shogunate itself finally fell in 1868—ending seven hundred years of one shogunal regime or another—there was the emperor ready to be ruled in the name of—this time by the oligarchs of the new Meiji state. And the end of the shogunate, too, saw this same process of devolution of power. For the shogun had gradually lost de facto power to the more dynamic of the feudal lords, just as the high ranking samurai-officials had lost power to the more dynamic lower samurai in several of the important domains. They called for the promotion of "men of merit" (like themselves) instead of the perpetuation of incompetence by hereditary office. But they did not call for the overthrow of the shogunate. That, as I have argued earlier, was a late and unintended consequence of Long End of the Tokugawa shogunate.[18]

The Tokugawa remained in power from 1600 to 1868, which was not especially long as kingdoms, dynasties, or shogunates went. What does seem long, however, is its ending, a period of several decades from roughly the 1820s through the 1860s (the beginning varies depending on the source), known to historians as the *Bakumatsu* (the end of the shogunate). The story of this period tells of the many factors that overlapped to overdetermine the ultimate end of shogunal rule, from the commercialization of the economy, the rise of lower ranking samurai as a "service intelligentsia," new religions and expanded literacy among commoners, famine and hardship among the peasantry, fiscal crisis and shogunal incompetence, the appearance of Commodore Perry and the gunboats of Western imperialism—and so on.[19] But even in the crisis atmosphere engendered by the Black Ships and the ensuing confusion in Edo and Kyoto, the shogunate took a very long time in ending. And the reason, I think, was the general viscosity of institutional change in Japanese history—the reluctance to bring the house, imperial or shogunal, crashing down on everyone's head. By the time the shogunal house did collapse, so much had changed that its demolition made astonishingly little noise.

The same might be said of the Long Reign of the Liberal Democratic Party (LDP), which like the Long End of the Shogunate appeared to last beyond its time. The LDP came to power in 1955—producing what in Japanese is called the "55 System"— and remained there, one-party dominant, until 1993. In fact, power moved among the different factions even while the party remained perpetually supreme, and when the party finally fell in 1993, the factions became parties jockeying for power along different alignments but in much the same way as earlier. When the LDP regained the premiership, if not the absolute majority, in 1996, the jockeying was by no means over. In short, political change occurred within the framework, without the framework itself being destroyed. This institutional tenacity characterized the Long Postwar as well, since the democratic system established

after 1945 remained the larger framework, which could accommodate change as long as it continued to serve as the perceived
guarantor of the social order.[20]

Historical change, then, was more often incremental than radical, but the larger lastingness had unceasing change within it.
The change was often evolutionary even when it had revolutionary
consequences, as was the case after the Meiji Restoration. Both
the preferred stability and the unceasing change were socially
based, and much was done to minimize conflict in the name of
avoiding social "chaos." The myth that grew from this historical
pattern of change emphasized stability sometimes to the point of
immobility, so that it frequently seemed to people that the institutional structures were immovable. The fixity of the gap between
the ruler and the ruled, for example, did not appear to many to be
bridgeable during the Tokugawa period. And in modern times
there was a similar cleft between the government, the "they," who
did as they pleased to the "us," who felt unable to influence the
structures of power. The politics of protest in modern Japan
sought to make a space for action apart from the state, lately
represented by such phenomena as the citizens' movements of the
1970s and the NGOs of the 1990s.

While national memory portrayed political structures as resistant to agents of change, it tended to render even small changes
in society as large threats to the social order. Through most of
modern Japanese history, youth and women served as the bell-
wethers of social change, or perhaps, as the canaries that succumbed early to the vapors of approaching social dangers. At the
beginning of the century critics complained of "idle youth" dreaming their social usefulness away in literature; at the end of the
century commentators heralded the "end of the Japanese work
ethic" in the teenyboppers mesmerized by L.L.Bean and *anime*. In
the 1920s young women in Tokyo were accused of being flippant
flappers bringing social morality into disarray; in the 1990s young
women in Tokyo were charged with refusing to bear enough children to prevent a demographic collapse. But in every case the
pace of change was greatly exaggerated for the sake of slowing
social alteration in its tracks. This repeated enunciation of social
crisis grew out of the disinclination toward disorder, so that it
revealed more about the value accorded to stability than about
the loss of stability itself.

Like the other myths spun from history, this relation of change
to unchange has become part of the image of Japan as seen from
afar. The political stability hardened into the "iron triangle" of the

bureaucracy, parties, and business that constituted "Japan, Inc." In the foreign media these structures seemed immutable, like a latter-day shogunate immune to the winds of political change. Blinded by the stereotype, outsiders frequently did not see the incremental changes occurring within the larger institutional continuities and therefore missed where most of history happens. And when it comes to society, foreign observers too often took the Japanese enunciation of social crisis at its word, thereby mistaking the canary for the country. The small signs that act as large warnings in Japan were taken literally by others. The result, at such times, was a dire portrait of a society coming entirely unglued, when the truth usually turned out to be quite the opposite.

Historical change everywhere is mostly incremental; rare is the radical shift, even rarer the revolution. And most people prefer order to chaos, stability to flux, so this, too, is nothing so particular. For world-historical comparison, the task is rather to assay the mix of factors that impels or inhibits change in different societies. Americans may want to "throw the bums out" every four years and cast their votes accordingly. Japanese may leave the bums in, thinking that one bum or another will not make much of a difference. In this respect it is the same world but two different ways of looking at it, which in themselves reveal the mechanisms that drive political change in the two democracies.

V. THE INWARD AND THE OUTWARD ECONOMY

Japan's size and lack of natural resources made the relation between the inward economy, which remained substantially agrarian well into the twentieth century, and the outward economy, which flourished at times and languished at others, a critical factor in the economic situation of the country.

In modern economic history, the "big story" tends to one version or another of the transformation across the centuries from a local agricultural economy to an economy commercialized by money and the market to an ineluctably global industrial capitalism--as if such things occurred in a straight, or even dialectical, line. For the modern period this story frequently becomes a tale of economic development, or underdevelopment, presented as another linear proposition. The teleology seems almost unavoidable. Perhaps the best one can do is avoid reducing the different economic trajectories to a single story derived from European models and to resist invidious comparisons based on civilizational determinism. Oddly enough, the economists, who pride themselves on their objectified variables and transnational theories (whether marxist or neo-classical) have sometimes been leapingly quick to resort to cultural reasoning when it comes to Asia and perhaps even more so in the case of Japan. And public commentators, both in Asia and the West, have generated a thriving cottage industry producing cultural explanations that find an all-too-ready market. Nonetheless, it should be possible to present Japanese economic history without recourse to such culturalist notions as "*ie*-society" or "Confucian capitalism."[21]

Of the many approaches available, I focus here on the relation between the internal and the external economy, not because it was peculiar to Japan, for it was not. Even in earlier times, few societies were entirely self-sufficient and impermeable to external economic exchange. And in the modern world, no society has escaped the penetration of capitalism and the market. Still, in Japan the inward-outward relationship often dominated conceptions of the economy, in part because of Japan's geographical boundedness and the consequently acute perception of the extra-economic dangers of commerce with the outside world. The early court and the later shogunates concerned themselves with the control of foreign trade, not only to secure its benefits but also to prevent its banes: from the "money sickness" spread by the import of Song coins in the twelfth century, through the depletion of silver and copper in the trade with China in the seventeenth century, to the imperialist threat carried in nineteenth-century Western demands to "open the country" to foreign trade. Again, such controls reflected no special Japanese pattern but rather the common sense and the common practice of governments around the world. With the inward-outward economy, as with the theme of cultural borrowing, the world-historical phenomenon is thoroughly general. It is the sharpness of its delineation that gives the pattern its perceived particularity.

In premodern history one needs a constantly doubled vision to keep in mind the role played by the external economy, even in periods when the country was allegedly "closed" to foreign intercourse, which in commercial fact it never truly was. When the Kamakura shogunate limited offical trade with Song China in the thirteenth century, private traders continued to cross the South China Sea. Even as the Mongols threatened to invade for the third time, the same shogunate continued a brisk trade with Yuan China; how else to finance the construction of grand shrines and temples? For four hundred years, from the thirteenth to the sixteenth centuries, coastal pirates (*wakō*) traded and looted their way through the waters between the Japanese islands, the Korean peninsula, and the south China seaboard. Through times of close economic and diplomatic ties and times when official relations were severed between the Japanese shogunate and the rulers of Koryŏ (Korea) and Ming China, the "Japanese" buccaneers (who included many Chinese and Koreans) continued their illicit trading and raiding. Indeed, efforts to remove this international menace stimulated new relations among Japan, China, and Korea. Meanwhile, the Chinese tribute system established what was in fact a trading regime, in which the tribute bearers brought luxury goods to the Ming court and received "gifts"—exports—in return. In this fifteenth-century context, the "king of Japan" (shogun) engaged in the tally trade with China, while trade, both official and private, flourished with Chŏson Korea. During the same period, the Ryūkūyan kingdom (present-day Okinawa) thrived as an entrepôt through which goods imported from the Philippines, Siam, Java and other Southeast Asian ports, as well as tribute gifts from China, were traded to Japan and Korea. This intra-Asian commerce not only constituted a dynamic regional trading system but also affected the domestic economies and politics of the individual countries. The rise and fall of dynasties, shogunates, and their wherewithal can be charted in the dispatch and withdrawal of the trading ships.[22]

And intra-Asian trade continued during the era of Tokugawa "seclusion," as Japanese bullion flowed out to pay for Chinese silk to dress the lords in. In an early example of import substitution, the shogunate first limited the export of metals and then supported agricultural programs for the domestic production of sugar, ginseng, and silk. Using Japanese thread, the famed Nishijin weavers of Kyoto prospered as never before, and by 1700, townsmen, too, were draping themselves in silken garments.[23] Thus the outward economy influenced developments in the Tokugawa inward economy with ultimately profound effect. Agricultural innovation and improvement contributed to increased productivity in the domestic economy, which later provided the financial basis for the infrastructures of Meiji modernity. And sericulture, once Japan was "opened" to the West, became the nation's single most important export, accounting for 45 percent of merchandise exports as late as the early 1920s. Considering the importance of exports in the high growth rates in late nineteenth- and early twentieth-century Japan, the Tokugawa development of domestic raw silk production had far-reaching consequences indeed. The point is always to keep the relation between the premodern inward and outward economies in dual focus, even when it seems as if the outside world lay beyond the commercial pale.

In modern history one needs the reverse: the focal length of the developmental lens must be adjusted to account for trajectories that did not depend on the so-called advent of the West, including commercialization of the economy and the emergence of "capitalism from within" during the Tokugawa period.[24] This is easier said than done, the more so because of the risk of retelling a single linear tale of development. Explorations of "indigenous" development too often suggest "preparation" for—or obstacles against—the moment of transition to capitalism, which appears Western in style as well as in provenance. As with feudalism, so, too, with capitalism: the comparative frame of reference is inevitably the West, with the result that the Japanese variant becomes either an analogue to or a deviation from the Western model. This comparative straitjacket confines Japanese and Western historians alike; it is an analytic commonality of the modern from which there is no easy escape.

But one can try to wriggle away from its most extreme forms, such as the search for a Japanese counterpart of the Protestant ethic to explain Japan's "industrious revolution" during the Tokugawa era.[25] And notions of deviance and backwardness can be avoided by defining capitalism in structurally broad but temporally indeterminate terms, as Marx did when he stressed a change in the organization of production. Think factories and wage labor: they emerged at different times and followed different patterns in different places but, like pornography, one knows industrial capitalism when one sees it. So did the factory workers when they lived it. The same is true of post-industrialism or late capitalism, a subsequent form of economic organization found in Japan and in the so-called advanced nations of the West. However singular the general condition, its particular stories are plural.

The inward-outward approach helps here as well. A wildly abbreviated tale of Japanese economic development since the seventeenth century would stress two aspects of the inward economy: the agricultural base and the commercial sectors. Paddy-field riziculture gradually enlarged the land under cultivation, increased yields with fertilizers, seed, and other agronomic improvements, and provided the tax base for the shogunal and Meiji governments. The distribution fell unevenly, so that rich peasants became landlords and poor peasants became tenants. Historians have argued long and hard over whether the Tokugawa peasant's life got better or worse, but the answer is surely: both better and worse, depending on the peasant, the region, the village, and the household. These peasants, who were at times moral, at times rational, worked hard, engaged increasingly in non-agricultural by-employment, and produced what Thomas Smith calls "pre-modern growth" in the countryside.[26] They also benefited from—and some say, caused, through fertility control and infanticide—an unusual demographic stability. Between the 1720s and the 1850s, Japan's population did not grow (this, without war or plague, if not without famine), producing a very different demographic regime from that of Europe or China. The early Meiji state was thus able to depend on a productive agrarian sector for food, land tax, and local entrepreneurship.

Peasant entrepreneurship contributed to the commercialization of the Tokugawa economy, which in its rural aspects included the expansion of cottage industry and the penetration of markets, money, and manufacturing throughout the countryside, although in a regionally uneven fashion. The merchants of the town, meanwhile, had prospered, as had the cities in which they did their business. Of the three great cities of Kyoto, Osaka and Edo, Osaka was styled as the "marketplace of the realm," where trade, industry, finance, and consumption burgeoned. In 1616 an Osaka man who renounced samurai rank and became a merchant declared his intentions with these words:

A great peace is at hand. The Shogun rules firmly and with justice at Edo. No more shall we have to live by the sword. I have seen that great profit can be made honorably. I shall brew saké and soy sauce, and we shall prosper.

And so they did. The man's name was Mitsui Takatoshi, the founder of what eventually became the Mitsui corporate empire.[27] The Sumitomo family, forebears of another future *zaibatsu*, operated the largest copper refinery in seventeenth-century Osaka, processing copper from mines all over the country. Equally or more important was the expansion of smaller scale business and light manufacturing in the towns and villages throughout the country. In addition to rural industries like saké brewing and soy sauce making, textile production expanded, especially in the areas around the heartland cities. Financial institutions such as banking, moneylending, and credit services developed not only in the cities but also in local areas. There commoners joined together in economic confraternities that provided "mutual assistance" to their members in the form of cooperative credit and insurance, exemplifying what Tetsuo Najita calls commoner practices of political economy or "country capitalism."[28]

Such developments in the inward economy were both advantaged and constrained by virtue of being closed off from expanding trade with the West. In the Tokugawa period the outward economy made its impact by absence, which only deepened the impression that when the West came, industrialization and capitalism came with it. Recent scholarship contests this notion of outside-in development at the same time that it resists the storyline of indigenous "preparation" for capitalism Western-style. David Howell's study of the Hokkaido fisheries, discussed in an earlier chapter, shows how "protoindustrial" links between commercialization and capitalism emerged before, and survived after, the Meiji state undertook its program of top-down economic modernization.[29] In fact, such analysis challenges the top-down model, making it clear that the processes and patterns of industrialization both preceded and exceeded the grasp of the state. There is no doubt that the "capitalist development state"—which Chalmers Johnson associates with the "soft authoritarianism" of Wilhelminian Germany, Meiji Japan, as well as with postwar Japan, South Korea, and Taiwan—sought to manage economic development through such means as industrial policy, protectionism, and control of labor unions.[30] But the economy seldom obeyed the dictates of the state in any docile or direct manner. Instead, economic processes operated in constant contestation between private business and public bureaucracy, elite politics and popular protest. And in the modern period, the relation between the inward and outward economy often proved more economically determining than did the manipulations of the state. For, as is it is so ubiquitously remarked, modern Japan's development soon came to depend on the world economy for markets, raw materials, and capital. In this respect the economic history of Japan since the 1880s is indeed the story of its integration into the capitalist world system, beginning at the periphery (in Wallersteinian terms) and moving by the 1980s to somewhere near the core (in G-7 or Asia/Pacific terms). And in this respect, Japan was like every other nation in the century of the global economic juggernaut, which intertwined the world in credit and debt, boom and bust, power and exploitation. Most Japanese argued, of course, that Japan was more so, more dependent and therefore more vulnerable than many of the great powers whose geopolitical club Meiji Japan had worked so hard to join.

At first Japan financed its modernization without borrowing, but at the beginning of World War I, 60 percent of the national debt was owed to foreign sources.[31] This changed with the war boom as exports to the West and to Asia brought in the foreign exchange necessary to pay for imports of raw materials and other goods. When the world went bust in the Depression, Japan lost its markets and its financial institutions failed. Recovery came by the mid-1930s as a result of another factor related to the outside world: military expenditure, which boosted heavy industry. This was the wartime phase of a sustained "technonationalism" that had linked security, technology, and the economy ever since the days of the 1870s slogan of "rich nation, strong army."[32] In time Japan's aggressive imperialist war against China and Asia ultimately did the economy, and the empire, in. But the structures of political economy that were put in place for wartime mobilization survived the surrender. The recently labeled "1940 system" gave production first priority, regulated competition, and enshrined corporate practices like indirect financing and the "Japanese" employment system. It was these historical products of wartime economic governance—not some cultural substratum—that laid the basis for postwar "high growth" in the inward economy.[33]

After 1945 the outward economy was at first managed largely by the United States, which arranged triangular trade among the U.S., Japan and Southeast Asia to close the "dollar gap," saw to it that Japan gained entry to the multilateral GATT, and jump-started Japanese prosperity with U.S. special procurements during the Korean War. By 1955 growth had begun again, closely linked as before with exports: at first textiles, succeeded by steel, ships, automobiles, televisions, electronics, semiconductors and the rest of the products that gained Japan both a substantial trade surplus and substantial "trade friction," especially with the United States. Domestic consumption rose, as did savings. In the early 1970s the trajectory of inward growth was interrupted by outward shocks: the oil and dollar shocks that once again revealed Japanese dependence on foreign raw materials, currency exchange rates, and export flows. The economy adjusted, then ballooned into the bubble economy of the 1980s, which burst in the 1990s primarily because of excesses in the inward economy such as grossly inflated land prices. Meanwhile the outward economy began to shift its emphasis away from North America toward Asia, as Japanese exports and foreign direct investment found increasing place in the dynamic East and Southeast Asian economies. While the vector of geo-economics shifted toward Asia, the structural dependence of the inner upon the outer economy did not much change.

This economic history is well enshrined in self-descriptive myth, the shortest version of which is the haiku-like lament: "Japan is a small island-country with no natural resources. O." Over the course of the twentieth century, Japanese got used to feeling vulnerable, and Japan's ascension to economic super-powerdom did little to shake their sense of vulnerability. Indeed, it was built into the woodwork of national identity, where it acted as fiber that strengthened pride and weakened confidence at one and the same time. Officials negotiated on the basis that Japan, unlike the United States, was wholly dependent on foreign oil; unlike Europe, had no organized regional economic context; unlike China, was small in size and shrinking in population, and so on. The favored metaphor for competitive foreign products was, inevitably, the "black ships," which likened satellite TV from Hong Kong or apples from Washington State to the menacing arrival of Commodore Perry. Every small step in deregulation or market opening was greeted like an alien wedge that would destroy the fragile economic ecology of the island-country.

Much of this mythology suited government policy, which sought to protect the inward economy from "shocks" from outside. But it also redounded to Japan's disfavor in international opinion. Foreign media presented a stereotype of a people who could pay forty dollars for a melon—to name a common example—and still claim the need for special economic dispensation in international trade. Rich countries, always the object of envy abroad, can expect little sympathy when they cry poor. And Japan's past military and present economic power both belied the national self-image of vulnerability. A counterpart perhaps was the international stereotype of an endlessly vast, endlessly rich, endlessly suburbed-and-lawned United States, which had some basis in history, more in myth, and no universal applicability in reality. The "small island-country with no natural resources" was also historically based, mythically enhanced, and not terribly relevant in the late twentieth-century world economy. But it did point to the abiding importance of the relationship between the inward and outward economy, which had for so long dominated the Japanese economic imagination.

VI. JAPAN AND THE WORLD

The world cut a double figure in Japanese history: it was a vital force in domestic development as well as the site of external relations. In international affairs, periods of reclusive with-

drawal alternated with times of active engagement, throughout which Japan searched for its "proper place" in relation to a changing world order.

In comparison to the usual nation-bound histories, world history has the advantage of a heightened awareness of the wider realm outside national borders. It pays greater heed to changes in the world—the Eurasian links in ancient and medieval times, the globe encompassed in the sixteenth century, the rise of Western imperialism, the twentieth-century global order—than the typical view of foreign relations seen from the vantage point of a single court or capital, whether Tokyo, Paris, or Washington. World history also inclines toward a narrative of globalization, telling, as it were, the story of itself: Over long historical time, "the world" expanded, as people discovered all that was out there, and then it shrank, as the parts became connected and the far was brought near. Too simple a story surely, since globalization, like industrialization, did not lead ever onward in the same direction: there were instances of de-globalization as there were of de-industrialization. But in modern times the world is more with us than ever it was before and its presence is therefore more insistent in nearly every national history.

Here then is another world-historical commonality, which nonetheless imprinted itself distinctively in the history of Japan. In a word, the "world-and-we" storyline had great presence in the Japanese past from the "beginning," a tale that usually opens with "whence came the Japanese people." As the themes of cultural borrowing and the inward/outward economy make clear, the relation to the outside world always figured prominently in the way change happened in Japan. The common image of engagement with, then withdrawal from external contact—the opening and closing of the country—evokes the periodic interruption of diplomatic relations. But what it really signifies is the abiding consistency of concern with the outside world. Else why make so much of this particular subplot in the larger narrative of national history? Indeed, it often seems as if people in Japan took an obsessive interest in the world, sometimes seeing it as the mirror reflecting their identity, sometimes as a lens through which to view their future. And when Japanese were not merely gazing at but also acting in the places outside their sea-girt borders, they faced some of the greatest challenges in their history. The course of Japan's relations with the modern world is a prime example. From the object of one imperialism to the subject of another, from international diplomacy to unilateral aggression and total war, from "escaping Asia" to plundering it, from attacking the U.S. to allying with it, from military muscle to economic clout—Japan's international relations were both more roiled and less "successful" than its domestic developments. At the end of the twentieth century, "Japan and the world" remained a major problem, the topic of constant debate and the occasion of national concern.

The importance of the world **within** domestic Japanese history must first be acknowledged: a pattern I think of as "bringing the outside in." In early times Japan fashioned itself on the model of China, and later generations seldom lost their honed comparative sense, which operated just as strongly during the so-called periods of cultural indigenization and diplomatic withdrawal as it did in times of flourishing external relations. Indeed, the world sometimes loomed larger in the gazing imagination when it was most absent in the environment of action. During the long Tokugawa isolation from all but the Dutch representatives of the mercantilist-imperialist "West," samurai intellectuals embarked with energy, industry, and some personal daring on a forbidden encounter with "barbarian books." From their Dutch learning (*rangaku*) came specific knowledge of Western medicine, astronomy, painting, social institutions and also the general, and liberating, perception that "the sun and moon shine on every place alike."[34]

Before Westerners themselves reappeared in Japanese waters in the early nineteenth century, "the West" was already established as an alternative metaphorical and methodological Other, through which to argue all matters from the celestial to the political. When Sakamoto Ryōma drafted his "Eight-point Program" in 1867—proposals that closely anticipated the Restoration reforms—he drew on ideas from Western sources that had become commonplace among activist samurai like himself.[35] (This is another brief text that lends itself to class discussion.) First they had confronted barbarian books, then the barbarians themselves. To defend Japan against the Western threat, the Restoration activists used Western ideas to transform the realm. In effect, the Meiji pursuit of "Euro-americanization" was a program of defensive modernization: bringing the civilizational outside in to keep the imperialistic outsiders out. The postwar reforms after 1945 also framed domestic change in conformance with the "standards of the world," as Americans of the time defined them. And these radical changes represented only the most dramatic instances of the ways in which Japanese of successive ages turned the external world to serve their internal purposes.

Over these ages the definition of the "world" changed for Japan as it did for other places And in interaction with the changing world, the nation that called itself "Japan" came into being. Japanese historians have recently reminded us that the unified nation-state of four main islands is a historical artifact of the modern period, not some natural production of the gods from time immemorial. To speak of "Japan" in ancient, medieval, and even Tokugawa times is to overlook changes both in the boundedness of national space and in the putative coherence of national identity within those boundaries. Ancient "Japan" of the archeological record means the people the Chinese called the Wa, who lived in the Western part of the archipelago. They interacted far more closely with the four early states in the Korean peninsula—which lay only 120 miles across the sea—than with other parts of what would later become the Japanese islands. The "world" consisted mostly of water between the peninsula and the islands, across which goods, arms, horses, and peoples moved. With historical Yamato and the founding of the Nara state in the eighth century, China became the cultural center of a Sinic "world" that dominated Japanese and East Asian relations for a millennium. The Buddhist cosmology identified three realms: our country (wagachō), China (Kara, a hybrid term for China and Korea), and beyond that, India (Tenjiku). But the "world" that counted was China, with Tenjiku less a geographical place than the mysterious distant land of the Buddha. And where would a name that means "rising sun" have come from if not from a consciousness of China, from whose continental point of vantage the sun would indeed appear to rise in the islands of the Eastern Seas?[36]

Once named, the country Nihon told its national history in terms of subjugation and expansion: the imperial court pacified the barbarians in the North and the medieval warriors moved "Japan" eastward to include the Kantō plain, where one day the city of Edo would rise. When it did, as seat of the Tokugawa shogunate from 1603, it became the center of a polity that clearly drew the physical borders of the country for the first time. It established these boundaries not by running a sharp line of sovereignty between the main islands and the outside world, but by subordinating peripheral peoples like the Ainu in the North (now Hokkaidō) and Ryūkyūans in the South (now Okinawa) as dependent upon, but ethnically outside, the entity called "Japan."[37] Not coincidently, this act of national delineation took place in a changing international context. The Europeans had come, the Japanese invasions of Korea had failed, the Ming had fallen to the

Manchu barbarians: Japan's world had altered yet again. Now it had "the West" in it. But this oft-told story also left things out. Because it was national history seen from the political center, it focused on the space of sovereignty, both inside Japan and out. Other "worlds" disappeared from view, whether the coastal connections of the marauding, trading *wakō* or the vast maritime routes that connected Southern Japan with Southeast Asia through Ryūkyūan commerce. Because of the long prominence of China, the story of international relations had what Japanese scholars now label a continental bias. The Japanese, they argue, had a seafaring past that was occluded by the national "Japan" articulated by the Tokugawa shogunate to enhance its legitimacy as its rulers. Using the new term "the Great Prince of Japan," the shogun conducted diplomatic relations with Korea—and only with Korea— thereby asserting the equality of the Japanese state in "the world" and at the same time limiting the scope of that world by the policies of seclusion.[38]

Shogunal policies notwithstanding, once the Portuguese, Spanish, English, and Dutch reached Japan, its imagined "world" would never be the same. The Portuguese landed at Tanegashima in 1543; Francis Xavier followed in 1549. And in an inversion of the mistake Columbus made in the Caribbean, Japanese identified the Iberians as "Men of Inde," assuming that the foreigners had come from the most distant place then known to Japan, which was India.[39] After the sixteenth century, Asian world maps suddenly had new continents on them, including those of the New World. Like mapmakers everywhere, Japanese cartographers sometimes moved Japan toward the center of their "maps of the myriad countries." But this cartographic bravado was not matched by confidence in Japan's place on the globe.

For in addition to continents, the world now contained Christianity, calls for commerce, and the specter of European imperial power, from which the shogunate shrank in its seclusion policies. Japan's "Christian Century" ended in 1540, when all Westerners but for a small Dutch trading post were driven from Japanese shores. In subsequent years scholars of Dutch learning avidly consumed knowledge about foreign countries, but they had almost no contact with foreigners themselves. That changed with the arrival of the black ships, not from the Eurasian direction but from America. By the end of the nineteenth century, Japan's world had developed a Pacific dimension, leading some to foresee a Japan no longer stranded on the Asian edge but in the center of transpacific trade routes. One Meiji commentator prophesied that the twentieth century would be the "Pacific Age"—perhaps the earliest sounding of what became a familiar theme some one hundred years later.[40]

As the "world" changed, so did conceptions of where Japan belonged in it. By the 1880s "Japan" had become Japan: a nation-state with fully outlined territorial borders that incorporated Hokkaidō and Okinawa and now declared the Ainu and Ryūkyūans to be "Japanese." Not all Japanese regions were equally "nationalized"; old regional differences persisted, and new ones arose.[41] But such unevennesses were seldom reflected in the way Meiji Japanese viewed the world from Tokyo. To them the globe was divided between East and West in the context of the Western imperialist order, and Japan faced a geopolitical either-or: either Japan could "escape from Asia" (in Fukuzawa Yukichi's famous and misused phrase) and join the ranks of the Western powers, or it could be the "leader of Asia" against the Western imperialists. Either way Asia would suffer Japan's imperialism; only the justification for it differed. Japan had taken the orientalist gaze that it had been subjected to by the West and transferred its oppression to Asia. If Japan had been defined as Europe's Other, then China became the Other's Other.[42] By the time of the Asia-Pacific War in the 1930s, racialized notions of Japan's "proper place" had expanded its imperial "leadership" to cover all of Asia and even beyond.[43] After the defeat in 1945, while the world expanded to thoroughly global proportions, it is fair to say that in Japan it also shrank. Tied to the United States and turned away from its wartime past, Japan operated in a transpacific, cold war world from which Asia seemed—in notional terms—almost to have disappeared. As the cold war waned and Asia's importance grew during the 1980s, Japan began to reimagine a world that had both Asia and itself in the same part of it. The task proved difficult, partly because of unconfronted memories of Japanese wartime actions and partly because of the either-or habit that made it seem—even in the 1990s—as if Japan's choice were either Asia or the West rather than both at the same time in a now inescapably global context.

And by this roundabout way I come to Japan's foreign relations proper. Why the detour? Because the importance of the world within Japan's domestic history as well as the changing conceptions of its "world" suggest a larger point about Japan's international relations and also about why the image of open country/closed country has remained so persistent. Briefly put, Japan generally had more success in bringing the outside in than it did in "taking the inside out"—or so at least it seemed. Time and again Japanese of the past found it easier to deal with foreign ways than with foreign peoples and more congenial to imagine the outside world than to take effective action in it.

Commonly given examples include Japan's repeated invasions of Korea. These began in ancient times, reached one crescendo with Hideyoshi's two routed attacks in the 1590s, and culminated in thirty-five years of hated colonial rule that ended only with the defeat in 1945. The two Meiji wars, the Sino-Japanese War of 1894-95 and the Russo-Japanese War of 1904-05, seemed glorious to many at the time, initiating as they did the Great Empire Japan and its acceptance into the ranks of the Western powers. But after Japan's Asian empire descended into the brutality of total war and then defeat, the modern imperialist enterprise seemed to most Japanese to have signified a catastrophic failure. Even those who found justification for the conflict did not deny the disastrousness of its outcome. Japan had apparently done better with adapting Western-style "civilization" than it had with Western-style imperialism. Once again, things had gone more creditably at home than abroad. Granted, the events of the twentieth century conditioned these negative views of Japan's international past. But this recent history sufficed to suggest to many that the theme of engagement and withdrawal, interaction and isolation, provided the key to understanding Japan's relation to the world, in both its good moments and its bad.

Hence the ubiquity of *sakoku*, the closed-off country, as a referent and metaphor in discussions of Japan's external relations. The term did not originate with the Tokugawa shogunate—to which redounds both credit and blame for closing off the country in the 1630s—but with a Westerner residing at Nagasaki in the 1690s. By the 1850s, *sakoku*, itself an artifact of linguistic borrowing, had established itself as a Japanese term. As seclusion was about to end, *sakoku* appeared in the debates over "opening the country," and it remained popular gospel ever after. In recent years scholars have expended great energy to show that Tokugawa Japan was never entirely closed to the world: it was closed to the West (except for the Dutch) but open to Asia.

The shoguns had not one "window to the world" at Nagasaki but "four gates" at the periphery: through the Satsuma domain to Ryūkyū, through the Tsushima domain to Korea, through the Matsumae domain to Ezochi (Ainu lands in Hokkaidō), and, of course, through Nagasaki to the Dutch traders. And more goods and people, including the Chinese merchants in Nagasaki, moved through those gates than the image of the "closed-off country" suggests. The correct term, we are told, is not *sakoku* but "maritime bans," which prohibited comings and goings by sea. These scholars further argue that the Tokugawa shogunate presided over a changed East Asian international order, which has the ungainly, but now accepted label of a "Japan-centered order of civilized and barbarian." This diplomatic regime amounted to a Japanese version of the Sinocentric order, in which the shogunal state became the independent center of a civilizational hierarchy recognized by Korea and Ryūkyū.[44]

Not surprisingly, this revisionist emphasis on Tokugawa relations with Asia took hold during the 1980s in the context of rethinking Japan's world with less West and more Asia in it. But the shogunate did not, after all, challenge the Chinese tributary system. Japan may have abstained from relations with the Qing, but Korea and Ryūkyū continued to send tribute missions to the Chinese court. And the Sinic order remained in place until it was challenged—and undone—by the European world order in the nineteenth century. Now a new hierarchy fell upon East Asia. Imperialism and international law, both from the West, demanded—often at the point of the gun—different definitions of sovereignty, protocols of diplomacy, and civilizational defenses. The modern international history of Japan and of East Asia revolved, for better and for worse, about the need to meet the demands of this new order imposed on the world by the West. For Japan, this meant forsaking seclusion and opening the country to the West, on the one hand, and abandoning diplomatic ritual for military imperialism in Asia, on the other. For those scholars engaged in resituating Japan in Asia, this history of war and empire had none of the appeal that the *sakoku* story offered. In recounting modern Japan's relations with Asia, the task was not revision but remembrance. And the public acknowledgment of Japanese wartime actions remained a vexing issue in Japanese-Asian relations at the end of the twentieth century. Japanese historians labored hard and with considerable success to bring the facts to light about the "comfort women," the Asian women dragooned into prostitution by the Japanese military; the biological experiments conducted on Chinese prisoners by the army's infamous Unit 731; the hideous brutality during the Rape of Nanking in 1937; and other heretofore hidden or unconfronted horrors of the wartime past. This important "memory work" had effect in the early 1990s, as these unsavory historical moments began to appear in textbooks and on television. Perhaps because there was still so much to do in the arena of memory, the history of the causes, contexts, and consequences of war and empire received less attention than one might expect.

We are left therefore with the earlier, somewhat unsatisfactory, stories that suspend modern Japan in larger international structures, which it reacted to but could not resist. Whether Japanese imperialism is presented as an inevitable consequence of capitalism, as a defense against the threat of Western imperialism, or as imitative of the imperialistic practices of the West—or as all three—Japan's imperial project seems somehow fated by external conditions. We know little about the social history of empire, either at home or in the colonies.[45] And policies taken toward Asia and the West often remain as if in separate worlds, so that the contextual interaction between Japan's multilateral diplomacy with the West and its unilateral actions in Asia is lost to sight. This global geometry is nowhere more important than in the years before World War II, when the actions of Japan, the United States, and other countries cannot be grasped in national or bilateral terms alone.[46] For a world war, at least, let the approach be world-historical. And the same holds for the aftermath of that war, from the advent of the nuclear age and the Cold War to the global linkages of geo-economics and geo-culture.

After 1945, announced as another "opening of the country," Japan in fact returned to a kind of seclusion, forgetting the empire and taking refuge from the world under protection of the United States. By the time the Cold War ended in 1989, Japan confronted the globe entire. The 1990s brought attempts to identify a new proper place in a new world order in which the East-West divide—whether European-Asian or communist-noncommunist—no longer obtained in the same way. Should Japan "escape from Europe" and "re-Asianize"? Should Japan remain the "number-one number-two superpower," following the lead of its ally, the United States? Or should Japan make the most of its half-century of postwar pacifism and become a "global civilian power"? Were these the only alternatives and must they be seen as alternatives, one excluding another? Questions such as these revealed the dilemma posed by Japan's international past. Always before Japan had fitted itself into an existing world order, first Chinese and then Western. Now Japan had to participate in constructing such an order in the context of an altered globe—a situation without precedent in its history. And Japan's modern experience of engagement with the world had brought some searingly painful outcomes—a history with as many bad precedents as good.

In the face of international uncertainties, it is perhaps no wonder that the *sakoku* metaphor appeared so frequently in speech
and comment in the 1990s. Some warned against the dangers of
isolation, others yearned for the days of sweet seclusion. But in
these inescapably globalized times, the closed-off country could be
no more than a mythic memory. And that is just what it was: the
transposition of Japan's relations with the world to the terrain of
national identity. The notion that Japan had repeatedly advanced
and retreated from the international arena had become linked to
the very idea of "Japaneseness." In retreat, the legend went,
Japan domesticated foreign ways and became most itself. In the
outburst of enthusiasm for Tokugawa times, conspicuous since
the 1980s, neo-nationalists referred to the "high civilization"
reached in Japan before—and without—the influence of the West.
This particular evocation of the splendors of national isolation
belonged to a genre of identity-talk called the "discourse on
Japaneseness" (*Nihonjinron*), and it had long depended on viewing
the image of Japan in the mirror of the foreign. Indeed, the world
in the mirror often proved more important in the formation of
Japanese national identity than the real world, which for long
stretches of time had in fact remained "beyond the sea." This
mythic "world-and-we" had its counterparts in many countries,
since national ideologies seem to require an Other in order to
operate. And while Japan suffered no shortage of Others with
which to feed its nationalism, *sakoku* was now a dead metaphor:
the closed-country option had been foreclosed by history.

But because Japanese so often evoked it, the seclusion idea
lived on in international images of Japan. From Kaempfer's day
forward, Europeans were fascinated by the notion of the
Tokugawa seclusion policy. During the Second World War, American propaganda blamed the closed-off country for the inability of
the Japanese people to resist the evil designs of their leaders. In
the Frank Capra film, "Know Your Enemy:Japan," the narrator
explains the graphic sequence in which the country is locked up,
key and all, as the action of Japanese warlords. "Frightened of
tolerance, brotherly love, and even equality," they threw out "the
West and its poisonous doctrines of peace," enabling Japan to
come back, two hundred years later, and practice "the old bushidō
double-cross."[47] Decades later, Japan was accused of locking away
its markets from world commerce, as it had done "before the arrival
of Commodore Perry."

The official Japanese rhetoric of "internationalization" in the
1980s and "international contribution" in the 1990s never took

hold abroad, and when Japan demurred at sending troops to participate in the Gulf War in 1991, Americans complained of Japan's irresponsible isolation from world crisis. To persuade the Japanese parliament to contribute another nine billion dollars to the war effort, the prime minister warned against the dire consequences if Japan were again isolated from international affairs. And his words did not conjure up *sakoku* but the diplomatic isolation from the West during the 1930s. Just as some Americans cautioned the U.S. against retreating again into isolation after the end of the Cold War, Japanese used their international past to make statements about their international future.

PATTERNS OF THE PAST, FRAMEWORKS OF THE FUTURE

The six themes outlined here are extremely general and in their generality, they say nothing entirely particular about Japanese history. But, considered together, they give a weighted sense of how the patterns of the Japanese past tended to arrange themselves and of how these arrangements became part of the way Japanese used history to cast national identity. Precisely because they are embedded in this way, these patterns are not likely to disappear, though they will not in the future—as they have never in the past—remain the same as the historical context changes around them.

A quick summary of present prospects suggests, first, that the pattern of cultural borrowing stands in a new moment. For the first time in Japanese history there is no model for domestic change "out there" in China or the West. Indeed, Japan itself is touted by some as a model for developing societies, which if those societies choose to make it so may be the case.[48] But because there are, as Japanese say, "no more models" at present, Japan is unlikely to experience another period of massive borrowing any time soon. Nor however will it cease being open to the steady stream of influences from abroad and their subsequent naturalization in Japanese social soil. This process is complemented by the growing trend of being borrowed from, in a global cultural exchange that is now very much a two-way street.

The theme of change-within-continuity remains in effect. Contemporary society is undergoing considerable change even as that change is couched in terms of continuity. Most of Japan is urban and exurban, concentrated in stunning megalopolitan density in the area around Tokyo, at the same time that the archipelago is "themed" with hometowns and newtowns that allegedly embody the rural values of community. People eat bread and revere rice, and the imperial institution faces no imminent danger of discontinuation. But traditions also change to suit the times. By labeling familial care for the aged a Japanese "tradition," some hope to solve the problem of eldercare that Japan's aging society will face in the next century. In these matters, it pays to attend to the change contained in the putative continuity.

The primacy of society still obtains, but Japan's practiced social coherence is sure to be strained by changes in both the "we" and the "they"—the Japanese and the "non-Japanese," as "they" are called in this context. Because the cohesiveness was gained at the expense of those Japanese who did not fit and in considerable isolation from non-Japanese outsiders, it faces two challenges. First, social strength based on "homogeneity" does not travel, and Japan's place in the global economy means living and working in other contexts, which does not come easily to Japanese untrained in cultural difference. Second, the number of outsiders living and working in Japan can only increase, and unless they are included in the social fabric, that fabric may be pulled taut. The same might be said for change within Japanese society—in the lives of women, or the structure of corporate organization, for example—although such internal social change is more readily, if not swiftly, accommodated than when "non-Japan" is involved.

The inclination toward stability, too, remains. The political system is likely to undergo incremental change until it looks different, but not dramatically so, than it did when the LDP fell in 1993. Deregulation and market-opening will proceed at a pace that seems glacial to Japan's trading partners and like quicksilver to Japanese. A single force large enough to unsettle these larger domestic structures is more likely to arise from outside—a crisis in the world economy or in regional security—than from within. Or, several serious shifts in socio-economic stratification might converge to produce significant structural change, though probably—in the light of the pattern of institutional viscosity—not a revolutionary collapse.

The inward economy will, if anything, depend even more on the outward economy than in the past. In the early 1990s Japanese talked bravely about a "borderless world" but felt vulnerable in their "island country." The parts of the global economy with which Japan intersects will both expand to include hitherto remote places in every continent and also shift away from the hitherto dominant, as exemplified in the increase in trade with Asia relative to trade with the United States. Here the imponderable is geo-politics, where a crisis could render the external economic regime dysfunctional, a prospect that only deepens Japanese feelings of vulnerability.

As for Japan in the world, it all seems to come down to this point. Japanese patterns of domestic change appear likely to continue in trajectories similar to the past, however different the specific historical content—unless, that is, they are unsettled from without. And Japan's past patterns of international relations do not offer a basis for the future comparable to its internal patterns. Japan's international posture is therefore more uncertain, and this, in an uncertain world. In respect to the "world-and-we" dilemma, the theme is not Japan's alone. After talking about globalization for a century or more, the world now has to learn how to do it. It will not be any easier for Japan than for the rest of us.

NOTES

1. For reference, see John Whitney Hall et al., eds., *The Cambridge History of Japan*, 6 vols. (New York: Cambridge University Press, 1989-93.)

2. From the "Reform Edicts" [Taika reform, 645], *Sources of Japanese Tradition*, ed., Ryusaku TSUNODA, W. Theodore de Bary, and Donald Keene (New York: Columbia University Press, 1964), vol. 1, p. 69-76.

3. See "Japan's Modernities" in this volume.

4. For these texts, which lend themselves to close reading in the classroom, see *Sources of Japanese Tradition*: "The Seventeen-Article Constitution of Prince Shōtoku," vol. 1, pp. 47-51; "Laws Governing the Military Households," vol. 1, pp.326-29; "The Charter Oath," vol 2., pp. 136-7.

5. E.g., Albert M. Craig, *Chōshū in the Meiji Restoration* (Cambridge: Harvard University Press, 1967), p.360.

6. See Takashi FUJITANI, *Splendid Monarchy: Power and Pageantry in Modern Japan* (Berkeley: University of California Press, 1996); Carol Gluck, *Japan's Modern Myths: Ideology in the Late Meiji Period* (Princeton: Princeton University Press, 1985).

7. Albert Craig, "The Central Government," in Marius B. Jansen and Gilbert Rozman, eds., *Japan in Transition: From Tokugawa to Meiji* (Princeton: Princeton University Press, 1986), p.51.

8. See Helen Hardacre, *Shintō and the State, 1868-1988* (Princeton: Princeton University Press, 1989).

9. For the "traditional" woman, see my essay on "Japan's Modernities" in this volume.

10. William Kelly, "Japanese No-Noh: The Crosstalk of Public Culture in a Rural Festivity," *Public Culture*, vol. 2, no. 2 (Spring 1990), pp. 65-81.

11. Marilyn Ivy, *Discourses of the Vanishing: Modernity, Phantasm, Japan* (Chicago: University of Chicago Press, 1995), p. 65.

12. None of AMINO Yoshihiko's major works has yet appeared in English, although translations are currently underway. In French, "Les Japonais et la mer," *Annales: Histoires, Sciences Sociales* (March-April 1995):235-58.

13. "Five Myths about Early Modern Japan" in this volume.

14. Ihara SAIKAKU, *Buke giri monogatari* [Tales of Samurai Duty], 1688; quoted in Donald Keene, *World within Walls* (New York: Holt, Rinehart and Winston, 1976), p. 193.

15. See Andrew Gordon, ed., *Postwar Japan as History* (Berkeley: University of California Press, 1993).

16. See Barbara Stoler Miller, ed., *Masterworks of Asian Literature in Comparative Perspective* (Armonk, NY: M.E. Sharpe, 1994).

17. John Whitney Hall, *Japan: From Prehistory to Modern Times* (New York: Dell, 1971), p. 128.

18. See "Japan's Modernities" in this volume.

19. E.g., E.H. Norman, *Origins of the Modern Japanese State* (New York: Pantheon Books, 1975); Harry D. Harootunian, *Toward Restoration: The Growth of Political Consciousness in Tokugawa Japan* (Berkeley: University of California Press, 1970); Thomas M. Huber, *The Revolutionary Origins of Modern Japan* (Stanford: Stanford University Press, 1981); George M. Wilson, *Patriots and Redeemers in Japan: Motives in the Meiji Restoration* (Chicago: University of Chicago Press, 1992); Marius B. Jansen, *Sakamoto Ryōma and the Meiji Restoration* (New York: Columbia University Press reprint, 1994); W.G. Beasley, *The Meiji Restoration* (Stanford: Stanford University Press, 1972).

20. For the Long Postwar, Carol Gluck, "The Past in the Present," in Gordon, ed., *Postwar Japan as History*, pp. 64-95.

21. Yasusuke MURAKAMI, "*Ie* Society as a Pattern of Civilization," *Journal of Japanese Studies* 10, no. 2 (Summer 1984), pp. 281-363. For scholarly perspectives on Confucian capitalism, Wei-ming TU, ed., *Confucian Traditions in East Asian Modernity: Moral Education and Economic Culture in Japan and the Four Mini-dragons* (Cambridge: Harvard University Press, 1996).

22. Shōji KAWAZOE, "Japan and East Asia," *The Cambridge History of Japan*, Vol. 3, *Medieval Japan* (New York: Cambridge University Press, 1990), pp. 396-446.

23. Marius B. Jansen, *China in the Tokugawa World* (Cambridge: Harvard University Press, 1992), pp. 25-41.

24. David L. Howell, *Capitalism from Within: Economy, Society, and the State in a Japanese Fishery* (Berkeley: University of California Press, 1995).

25. For the Protestant ethic, Robert Bellah, Tokugawa Religion:The Cultural Roots of Modern Japan (New York: Free Press reprint, 1985); for "industrious revolution," Akira HAYAMI, "A Great Transformation: Social and Economic Change in Sixteenth and Seventeenth Century Japan," *Bonner Zeitschrift für Japanologie*, vol. 8 (1986), pp. 3-13.

26. Thomas C. Smith, *Native Sources of Japanese Industrialization, 1750-1920* (Berkeley: University of California Press, 1988), pp. 15-49.

27. J. G. Roberts, *Mitsui: Three Centuries of Japanese Business* (New York: Weatherhill, 1973), p. 12 (the speech is family legend). For a substantial text conveying the merchant ethos, see the Mitsui house law of 1727: E. Sydney Crawcour, "Some Observations on Merchants: A Translation of MITSUI Takafusa's *Chōnin kōken roku,*" *Transactions of the Asiatic Society of Japan* 8, series 3 (1961), pp. 1-139.

28. Tetsuo NAJITA, "Political Economy in Thought and Practice among Commoners in Nineteenth-century Japan: Some Preliminary Comments," *The Japan Foundation Newsletter* 16, no. 3 (1988), pp. 13-18.

29. "Japan's Modernities (1850s-1990s)," above, pp. 561-593.

30. Chalmers Johnson, Japan, *Who Governs? The Rise of the Developmental State* (New York: W.W. Norton, 1995), pp. 38-50.

31. For a brief summary, see W.J. Macpherson, *The Economic Development of Japan 1868-1941* (Cambridge: Cambridge University Press, 1987.)

32. See Richard J. Samuels, *"Rich Nation, Strong Army": National Security and the Technological Transformation of Japan* (Ithaca: Cornell University Press, 1994).

33. NOGUCHI Yukio, *Senkyūhyaku-yonjūnen taisei: saraba "senji keizai"* [The 1940s system: farewell to the "wartime economy"] (Tokyo: Tōyō keizai shinpōsha, 1995]. Summaries should soon be forthcoming in English.

34. Donald Keene, *The Japanese Discovery of Europe 1720-1830* (Stanford: Stanford University Press, 1969), p.27.

35. See Marius B. Jansen, *Sakamoto Ryōma and the Meiji Restoration,* pp.295-96.

36. AMINO Yoshihiko, *Nihon no rekishi o yominaosu* (Tokyo: Chikuma shobō, 1991), pp. 200-202.

37. David L. Howell, "Ainu Ethnicity and the Boundaries of the Early Modern Japanese State," *Past and Present* 142 (February 1994), p. 71.

38. See Ronald P. Toby, *State and Diplomacy in Early Modern Japan: Asia in the Development of the Tokugawa Bakufu* (Stanford: Stanford University Press, 1991).

39. Ronald P. Toby, "The 'Indianness' of Iberia and Changing Japanese Iconographies of Other," in Stuart B. Schwartz, ed., *Implicit Understandings: Observing, Reporting, and Reflecting on the Encounters Between Europeans and Other Peoples in the Early Modern Era* (Cambridge: Cambridge University Press, 1994), pp. 327-28.

40. Pekka Korhonen, "The Pacific Age in World History," *Journal of World History* 7, no. 1 (Spring 1996), pp. 44-45.

41. See Kären Wigen, *The Making of a Japanese Periphery, 1750-1920* (Berkeley: University of California Press, 1995).

42. Stefan Tanaka, *Japan's Orient: Rendering Pasts into History* (Berkeley:University of California Press, 1993)

43. For "proper place," see John W. Dower, *War Without Mercy: Race and Power in the Pacific War* (New York:Pantheon Books, 1986).

44. See Toby, *State and Diplomacy in Early Modern Japan.* For *kaikin* (maritime bans) and *Nihongata ka-i chitsujo* (the Japan-centered civilizational order), see ARANO Yasunori, *Kinsei Nihon no higashi Ajia* (Tokyo: Tōkyō daigaku shuppankai, 1988).

45. For a valuable new view, see Louise Young, *Japan's Total Empire: Manchuria and the Culture of Wartime Imperialism* (Berkeley: University of California Press, 1997)

46. See also "Japan and America" in this volume.

47. Available on video, this 1945 propaganda film is useful in the classroom, the more so when paired with a Japanese counterpart like "Chocolate and Soldiers."

48. When it comes to world history, I regard the whole "model" business as having done enough harm already in its eurocentric and other forms and would not therefore encourage this line of thought.

THEMES IN KOREAN HISTORY

Michael Robinson

CULTURAL BORROWING AND CULTURAL TRANSMISSION

Koreans think of themselves as forming a distinct and separate people in East Asia. Archaeological and linguistic evidence supports this view because it links the earliest inhabitants of the Korean Peninsula to early Paleolithic migrations from central Asia (50,000–30,000 B.C.E.). The Korean language belongs to the Altaic language group, no more similar to Chinese than to English. In prehistorical and historical times, however, cultural borrowing and adaptation from China significantly shaped the subsequent development of Korean society. Situated on the Eurasian periphery with China in closest proximity, the Koreans were bound to be influenced by the older, more developed Chinese civilization. We must remember, however, that influence does not mean dominance. Over the centuries the Koreans have developed a habit of borrowing, synthesizing, and creating their own unique blend of culture that is an important part of the larger East Asian tradition we study today. Moreover, Korea's geographic placement within East Asia made it an important cultural bridge between China and Japan during key periods.

Early Chinese records mention the fierce Korean tribes to the northeast. It is clear that by the beginning of the common era, the area now occupied by North and South Korea and portions of Manchuria were under the influence of Chinese culture, political institutions, and technology. In fact, the early Han colonies in Korea (est. c. 108 B.C.E.) brought Koreans into direct contact with Chinese culture. In the following centuries separate Korean kingdoms (Koguryŏ, Paekche, and Silla) coalesced, and each kingdom developed a synthetic culture that blended indigenous and Chinese influences. Chinese models of kingship and the monarchical state influenced the process of state creation in Korea. In the period of the three kingdoms (300–660 C.E.), elites in the three Korean states used Chinese writing, adopted the Chinese designation of king *(wang)*, borrowed central bureaucratic structures, and patronized Buddhism and, in a lesser way, Confucian learning at their courts.

While many of the outward trappings of the three kingdoms would be familiar to any Chinese historian, their functions and meaning within the context of Korean society were profoundly influenced by earlier Korean patterns. For instance, the Silla state in the remote southeast corner of Korea made aristocratic status (status codified in their ancient bone-rank system) coincidental with rank in a Chinese-style bureaucratic system. Similarly, Korean acceptance of Buddhism brought with it iconographic, textual, and aesthetic influences from China. Yet, within a generation, the Koreans of the three kingdoms had begun to synthesize borrowings from China into their own religious and cultural heritage.

The case of Buddhism illustrates Korean cultural synthesis at its best. Early to receive Buddhism in East Asia, Koreans soon became important in the development of Buddhism in East Asia writ large. Numbers of monks from Korea made the trip to India to study the scriptures directly, important apocryphal texts are attributed to Korean Buddhist scholars (most notably Wŏnhyo, 617–689). And Koreans were most responsible for transmitting Buddhism to Japan in the period after the fourth century C.E. Indeed, Korean craftsmen, sculptors, and architects worked directly in Japan in the construction of Japanese temples.

It is important, therefore, to consider Korea's unique contributions to the larger East Asian civilization of which it was part. Influence from its larger neighbors helped to shape Korea's cultural identity; it also brought Korea into a wider flow of information and cultural formation. Thus the writings of Korean Buddhist scholars influenced Chinese and Japanese Buddhism. Sixteenth-century Korean Neo-Confucianists such as Yi I (Yulgok) and Yi Hwang (Toegye) influenced Neo-Confucians in China and Japan. Finally, Korean innovations in ceramic science, astronomy, printing, and naval architecture (ironclad ships) made their distinctive mark in East Asia.

Korea's culture and society owe much to the larger civilization of China. Its traditional elites used the Chinese language as the official court writing system until the late nineteenth century. Korea not only imported Buddhism and Confucianism, but also

Chinese medicine, cosmology, literary concepts, and political institutions. They then adapted them to the Korean situation. Over millennia, these borrowings became Korean in and of themselves. It becomes the task of the student of Korean society to recognize what is Korean about various institutions and ideas that at first glance might be considered copies of the Chinese tradition.

KOREA AND THE DYNAMIC EAST ASIAN STATE SYSTEM

The period between 300 and 700 C.E. was a period of cultural construction, warfare, and movement. It belies the later stereotype of Korea as the "hermit nation," a view rooted in nineteenth-century Western representations of the late Chosŏn period. In fact, Korea was always linked dynamically to the larger East Asian system. Between 300 and 700 the northernmost Korean state, Koguryŏ, expanded across the Yalu River and occupied larger areas of Manchuria, even the strategic Liaotung Peninsula. In times of Chinese contraction, the small states and tribes in the northeast were able to expand. At other times, Chinese political ascendancy pulled Korea into the larger cosmopolitan world of the empire. During the Tang Dynasty, Koreans participated in the cosmopolitan culture centered in the Chinese capital. Under the Mongols in the thirteenth century, Koreans of the Koryŏ Dynasty (918–1392) were again pulled into the Chinese orbit. As painful as such periods were for Koreans, they were also times when Korean arts, ceramics, and scholarship became known in the wider East Asian world.

It is important to remember, however, that for the most part Korea managed to maintain its political and cultural independence. The sobriquet of Korea as the "hermit nation" comes only from the last centuries before contact with the West. For most of its history Korea was in close contact with its East Asian neighbors. It managed its affairs with China on the basis of ritual subordination to the Chinese emperor; in return, the Chinese generally did not interfere in Korean affairs. Korea's relations with Japan were conducted on the basis of "neighborly" relations. For Japan, the major tension in the relationship was Korea's insistence on treating the Japanese as ritual inferiors just as the Koreans were treated by the Chinese. For Korea, with the exception of Hideyoshi's invasions of 1592 and 1597, its main problem with Japan was the suppression of Japanese pirates.

Korea was also invaded periodically by the Chinese. In periods of dynastic change expeditions were sent into Korea to enforce Korean recognition of the new regime. Except for the period of Mongol dominance (1230s to 1360s), however, the Koreans found ways to maintain the integrity of their state through diplomacy and scrupulous adherence to the ritual norms that governed its relations with China. It is commonplace to read of Korea as "oft conquered" or "subject to Chinese rule," but in reality the Koreans largely succeeded in guarding their independence. Again, it was the difficult years since the late nineteenth century that disrupted this historical pattern of autonomy. Korea's weakness in the face of Japanese and Western imperialism, Japanese colonization (1910–45), great power intervention after World War II, and political division too easily blind us to the longer earlier period of Korean autonomy. We forget that Korea's genius for diplomacy helped stabilize its borders and reduced the importance of its own military tradition, which was therefore weakened when its power was needed to confront nineteenth-century imperialist aggression. This aggression overwhelmed Korea's long tradition of independence and interdependence within East Asia, at least for the subsequent twentieth-century decades.

ARISTOCRATIC SOCIETY

A small, agrarian society, Korea developed a distinctive social system. From its earliest beginnings, Koreans worshiped ancestors. The family system changed and developed over the centuries as status distinctions, issues of lineal descent, and scrupulous attention to the memory of ancestors came to dominate a stable set of class relations by modern times.

At elite levels, traditional Korea was an aristocratic society. A small number of families dominated political and cultural leadership and perpetuated their power by inheritance of high status. Even in the ranked Chinese-style central bureaucratic state, social status determined bureaucratic rank in the system. While elites in the three kingdoms were often also warriors, by medieval times, "civilian" leaders began to gain dominance in the political system. By the time of the Chosŏn Dynasty (1392–1910), military elites assumed a secondary status to the families that dominated the bureaucracy and kingship.

Since the beginning of the Chosŏn period, hereditary elites developed sufficient power to balance the prestige and power of the monarchs. Thus, the Korean king never developed the transcendent aura of the Chinese emperor. Nor did the king ever successfully break the independent, landed power of aristocratic elites. Korea did not develop a decentralized feudal order, but neither did its state centralize power as in the Chinese case. During the Chosŏn period, Neo-Confucianism became state orthodoxy as a means of removing Buddhism from power and legitimating the new order. Over time, Neo-Confucian principles also became the main legitimating force for the maintenance of elite power in society. Elite families used ancestor ritual, marriage codes, status registers, exam passage, genealogies, and school degrees to maintain status. While the existence of a civil service examination system implied a certain possible social mobility, in fact, it was dominated by a restricted, circulating pool of lineages who successfully perpetuated their power in the Chosŏn system. Thus, Chinese institutions did not a little China make, but resonated with the needs and imperatives of preexisting Korean social patterns.

Below the elites, commoners tilled the land, and other low-status distinctions were maintained for slaves and low-status people. Over time, slavery as a separate category waned in importance, but even into the twentieth century, members of low-status families had difficulty escaping discrimination. By the nineteenth century, Korean society was organized as a small political elite group at the top and a larger number of local, landed-elite families in the hinterland, with the vast majority of the population made up of commoner peasants and other low-born people. While the Korean economy did begin to commercialize in the eighteenth century, merchant and artisan classes remained, unlike the situation in China and Japan, small and politically unimportant. While elite society was dominated by cosmopolitan East Asian institutions and culture, Korean folk culture shaped daily life for everyone. Confucian concepts and rituals seeped down to lower levels, but obeisance to local spirits, shamanic ritual, and village traditions were equally important.

IMPERIALISM, MODERNIZATION, AND NATIONALISM

The power, stability, and integrity of Korea's social and political arrangements in the late nineteenth century hampered its ability to maintain its political autonomy in the face of imperialism. While China's sheer size and complexity, indeed the inertial weight of its tradition, frustrated foreign aggression for decades, Korea, as a small and economically weak society, was vulnerable to absorption. Moreover, unlike in Japan, there was no powerful, progressive entrepreneurial class upon which to base revitalizing reforms. Once "opened" by Japanese pressure in 1876, Korea fell prey to new geopolitical arrangements in East Asia, the corrosive effects of the world market, and the destabilizing influences of new ideas and social norms.

There was a progressive impulse in late nineteenth century Korea. Traditional political elites frustrated this impulse to restructure Korean politics and develop economic and military strength because they viewed such change as challenging their traditional power in society. In addition, the most attractive model of change, Meiji Japan, was also the most serious political threat to the independence of the Korean kingdom. The early association in the 1880s of reform with Japanese influence strengthened the hand of conservatives who were bent on frustrating any reforms that undermined their political power, social preeminence, and economic privileges. To make matters worse, Chinese antagonism to Japanese interests in Korea supported reactionary forces within Korea.

In the end, the Korean state vacillated between imperialist patrons by attempting to play one against another. This only delayed the inevitable. By 1910, the Japanese were in a position to declare Korea a formal colony. The failure of the traditional regime in 1910 ended any attempt to build a positive nationalist movement around traditional symbols. The collapse of Chosŏn (1392–1910) discredited the royal house, the Chosŏn state, and its traditional elites. New groups needed to emerge to carry the fight for nationhood, and in the process Korean nationalism became a classic anticolonial struggle. While Japanese colonial repression became the wellspring for a broadened national consciousness, the policies of divide and conquer split Korea's progressive leadership class into antagonistic factions. With no central rallying point, the Korean nationalist movement ultimately evolved into a welter of different groups, divided by ideology, tactics, and their core conception of what precisely constituted the nation itself, each unable to attract a large enough constituency or develop enough power to unseat the Japanese.

Modernity was thus imposed upon Korea in colonial form, with all of its attendant distortions. Japanese economic policies supported a conservative landlord class in the colony, and its education system tutored a new literate class of bilingual intellectuals and bureaucrats. By the outbreak of war with China in 1937, Japanese colonial development had intensely mobilized Korean society. It created new urban spaces, began a migration from farm to factory, raised levels of literacy, and imposed aspects of Japanese culture on the entire population. Like other colonial regimes, it created enormous resentment within the Korean population while it bifurcated the political and cultural consciousness of Korea's articulate classes. Colonial authorities assiduously repressed leftist organizations of labor and tenants while allowing a certain cultural and political autonomy to more moderate forces within Korea. By 1945, the colonial experience had created enormous tensions and contradictions within Korean society. Its nationalist movement was seriously factionalized, rural poverty and high rates of tenancy pitted peasant against landlord, and a large portion of the middle class (and the tiny bourgeoisie) was compromised politically by their collaboration with the Japanese. More insidiously, the colonial creation of a modern, urban culture diluted nationalist identity and weakened anti-Japanese sentiment.

The defeat by the Allies in 1945, not Korean nationalists or social revolutionaries, compounded the difficulty. No one group could legitimately claim leadership of an independent Korea as victors over the hated Japanese overlords. To make matters worse, the joint occupation by the USSR and the United States began the unintended process of further polarizing the already complicated social and political situation. In 1945, Korean society began the arduous process of re-creating itself after a generation of colonial rule. Even with a unified and popular leadership this would have been a difficult task. In the case of liberated Korea, the situation was almost hopeless.

POLITICAL DIVISION, COLD WAR POLITICS, AND ECONOMIC DEVELOPMENT

Under joint occupation between 1945–48, a Korean solution to the problem of creating a unified independent state became increasingly difficult. The intrusion of great power politics onto the peninsula created a polarizing force that made political consensus building among Korean leaders impossible. By 1948, separate states, a socialist north and a democratic/capitalist south, emerged, mirroring the Cold War split between the U.S.S.R. and the United States. Korean moderates opposed to political division were swept aside in the scramble for patronage and the political recriminations of the immediate postliberation period. Ultimately, the Koreans found themselves in a brutal civil war that was exacerbated by the international involvement of Cold War superpowers. The Korean War (1950–53) froze the political division of the peninsula, and to this day the war remains the most important event in modern Korean history.

The reality of two Koreas, each claiming sole legitimate leadership of the Korean people, was supported by geopolitical power arrangements in the region until the fall of the Soviet Union in the late 1980s. Somewhat anachronistically, it continued to stand as the sole reminder of the post-World War II global order. The fact that, unlike the USSR or Eastern European socialist states, North Korea did not collapse is a testament to the bitter struggle for national development waged by both Koreas over the four decades since 1945.

North Korea's continuing existence was a reminder that indigenous forces in Korea's modern experience were also responsible for the political division. The Koreans, unlike the Germans, fought a bitter and catastrophic civil war; both North and South legitimated their existence with claims to leadership of the anticolonial struggle; and each state built a modern economy, social system, and political system out of the ashes of war. The division of Korea was not simply imposed by outside power. The tragedy is that outside power interests supported the continuation of this artificial division into the late twentieth century. This allowed each Korea to develop a separate political identity and begin a process of cultural divergence that would make reunification difficult.

The division also distorted economic and political development in the North and the South. The bitter legacy of war encouraged the maintenance of huge military forces in each state, and continuing appeals for discipline in the face of possible war legitimated authoritarianism on both sides of the demilitarized zone. Kim Il-sung in the North systematically eliminated rivals to his leadership and built a personality cult around himself and his family unrivaled in world history. Under the banner of *chuche* (self-reliance)—the single most important ideological tenet in the thought of the Great Leader—the North emerged as an isolated, almost hermetically sealed, maverick state. North Korea rebuilt its economy and cities in the 1950s and achieved dramatic growth in the 1960s. In subsequent decades, however, its increasing isolation blunted its economic growth and starved it for capital and new technology. After 1989 and the end of the Cold War, this situation became much worse. In the early 1990s, North Korea confronted its economic problems; yet mindful of the experience of the USSR and China, it was wary of "opening" for fear of losing control of its "unique" political and social system.

For its part, the distortions of national division supported the emergence of authoritarian politics in South Korea. U.S. interest in South Korea as a bulwark against communism supported the creation of authoritarian powers within the constitutional framework of the new republic. The twin pillars of national defense and economic growth justified continued abuses to the putative democratic institutions of the new republic. In spite of almost constant political instability, however, the South was able to achieve self-sustained economic growth in the 1960s. The so-called Miracle on the Han led to a social and economic revolution in the South. The forces unleashed by rapid economic development ultimately worked against the continuation of authoritarian practices.

In the late 1980s, South Korea shifted toward political reform and a movement to democratize politics. Increasing pluralism became the new trend in South Korean politics, but holdovers from the period of authoritarian rule such as the National Security Law, still remained. The economic and military balance that characterized the peninsular division from 1950 to the 1980s shifted. South Korea's increasingly powerful economy, its new relations with North Korea's former supporters, Russia and China, and the economic problems of the North made reunification seem possible. Reunification, however, was not likely to be on the model of East and West Germany. If anything, the South feared a precipitate political collapse in the North that would make the costs of an indigent Northern population and ruined economy impossible to shoulder. Moreover, the North remained unwilling to relinquish its socialist political and social system.

The situation in Korea is a lesson in both the forces that produced the Cold War era of the twentieth century and the problems that attend the creation of a new global order in the wake of its ending. How the division of Korea is resolved will tell us much about the new political and economic forces shaping the world at the turn of the twenty-first century.

ASIA AND LATIN AMERICA IN THE CONTEXT OF WORLD HISTORY

Theopolis Fair

The historical relationship between Asia and the Americas offers opportunities to incorporate the Americas into world history without making Latin America after 1492 appear as an appendage of Spain or, later, the United States.

PRE-COLUMBIAN CONTACT

The first contact of Asia with the Americas was the migration of the first known human inhabitants in the Western hemisphere, who crossed via a land bridge from Siberia in the millennia before the end of the last ice age (12,000 B.C.E.). In short, the first Americans were probably Asians. The physical type of their descendants, the Amerindians, is still considered by some anthropologists to be related to East Asians today.[1] Although discussions of native Americans usually begin with these Siberian roots, they seldom mention possible later contacts, which have been the subject of much investigation and speculation.

Nearly all scholars believe that the New World developed in situ, but this has not halted speculation, on the basis of evidence derived from plants that have no American origins and similarities of designs in pottery and architecture, that outside Asian influences may have interacted with the preeminent New World civilizations.[2] Although it is important to underscore that there is scant basis for such speculation, it may be of interest to recount some of the recurring hypotheses about possible pre-Columbian contact between Asia and the Americas. Some anthropologists postulate, for example, that Asians sailing across the Pacific Ocean may have contributed to the culture of Mesoamerican civilizations.[3] Several have argued that the pottery of Ecuador resembles that of early Japan, while others propose that the Asian source was southeastern Chinese; yet others contend that it was Malayan. The Valdivia ceramic complex in Ecuador has pottery designs that seem similar to the distinctive motifs of the Middle Jomon pottery produced in Japan around 3000 B.C.E.[4] It has been argued that the oceanic current which flows off Peru might have brought Japanese pottery to the west coast of South America. Some diffusionists assert that there may have been contact between Shang China, the Olmecs, and Chavín Peru; that metallurgy in Ecuador was influenced by Zhou China; and that red and black lacquer techniques used in Mesoamerica were similar to those used in China as early as the first century B.C.E.[5] Use of jade, similarity of designs in artifacts from China and Japan, sculpture, metallurgy, writing and artistic styles, common foods (including seaweed), and city planning have all been adduced to suggest Asian contacts with the Western Hemisphere in pre-Columbian times. However disputed these speculative assertions may be, their persistence itself is of interest.

Other areas of reputed contact with Mesoamerica are Malaysia, Borneo, India, and Indianized Southeast Asia. The Arawaks, Caribs, and interior tribes of Borneo show physical likeness and similar cultural patterns.[6] Teotihuacan, the pre-Aztec pyramidal complex outside Mexico City, suggests to some the influence of Hindu motifs. Chank shell appears in the art, at times with the rain god Tlaloc emerging from it. The chank was associated with the moon and fertility and used as a ceremonial horn. In India the chank horn also had associations with the moon, waters, and fertility and a god rising from it.[7] The great stone carvings of the Maya at the Museum of Natural History in New York do indeed bear a resemblance to the carvings of India and Southeast Asia. Even if direct influence cannot be proved, the similarity alone is worth noting in terms of common cultural motifs in different parts of the world.

As early as the late eighteenth century some argued that Asian peoples had island-hopped to the New World to create the Incan civilization. Attracted by the rising sun and carrying with them the names of the children of the sun for whom they searched, the explorer colonists are said to have landed on the coast of Peru at Arica. Francisco A. Loaysa, a Peruvian who lived in Japan from 1912 to 1922, concluded that Manco Capac, one of the legendary founders of the Incan civilization, was a Japanese colonist who deliberately followed the Black Current to America.[8] That current, just off Japan, runs thirty-five to forty miles a day and heads directly to Peru. Loaysa postulated that Manco Capac and his followers landed at Arica and trekked to Lake Titicaca, presenting philological and etymological arguments to prove his contentions, based on his knowledge of both Japanese and Quechua.[9]

None of this, of course, proves a pre-Columbian link between Asia and the Americas, but it does not disprove contact either. This is an area in which our imperfect knowledge and ongoing scholarly investigation (in Asia as well as the West) will likely continue to produce new evidence, speculation, and argument. At present, the most significant fact is the role played in the peopling of the Americas by the early migrations of Asians across the land bridge known as the Bering Straits.

COLONIAL CROP EXCHANGES

These civilizations, the Aztecs, Mayas, Incas, and others, were conquered by Spaniards in the sixteenth century who thought initially, like Columbus, that they were in Asia. Hence, names like Indian, which would refer to someone from the East Indies, and pepper, which is black pepper and not chili, are misnomers. Columbus never knew he had discovered a new hemisphere. The papal line of demarcation created by the Treaties of Alcoçovas and Tordesillas which divided the New World between Spain and Portugal prohibited Spain from trading with the East by sailing around Africa, but did not prevent it from commerce with Asia via the Americas.

The Moluccas had been Spain's first objective in the East Indies. After attempts to hold that area failed, China became Spain's main source of trade in Asia, but goods such as fine cottons and rugs also came from Mogul India. Acapulco, on the west coast of Mexico, and its excellent harbor became an entrepot of trade between the Spanish Empire and East Asia from 1565 until the last voyage in 1815.[10]

The Manila galleons, as the ships were called, sailed a dangerous route every year between Acapulco and Manila and brought back fortunes for Spain to Mexico and, ultimately, to the rest of Europe. These "China ships" carried gold and particularly silver to the East and returned with silks, spices, women's combs, Persian and Chinese rugs, fans, and sandalwood.[11] Peru was allowed to receive cargo and slaves for only a short period in the seventeenth century. The Lima census for 1613 made reference to "Indians of China of Manila," "Indians of Portuguese India," and "Indians of Japan."[12] Both Acapulco and Lima, via the prohibited but tolerated trade with Mexico, enjoyed the wealth, fame, and infamy created by the Asian trade in American silver.

The Japanese had a role in the early years of the Spanish-Asian trade, first with the merchant-adventurers of the latter part of the sixteenth century, then with the "vermilion-seal ships" which operated with license to trade for the Japanese government from 1592 until 1635. A Japanese diaspora developed, with the *Nihonmachi* (Japan town) in Manila numbering some 3,000 by the 1620s.[13] Japanese and some Chinese served on the crew of the galleon's ships.[14] Trade missions made their way to Mexico, and for a time Spain opened ports within Mexico and the Philippines to Japanese trade. From the Spanish fleets the Japanese bought Chinese silk, dye woods from Brazil, deerskins, wine, jars, honey, wax, and cloth in exchange for silver, salt meats, fish, and fruit. Between 1624 and 1639 the Japanese, rejecting both Christianity and trade, closed Japanese ports to ships from Manila and forbade foreigners from landing on Japanese soil under penalty of death.[15]

The China trade had other consequences. It served as an agent for carrying food crops, other cultigens, and animals from the Americas to Asia and vice versa. Old World animals proved more important to the Americas than plants. The horse, the donkey, and the mule, for instance, revolutionized transport in the Western hemisphere.[16] The reverse was true for the New World, which became the source of much of the world's food crops. Today at least three-fifths of the food crops cultivated around the world were grown in the Americas before 1492 by the American Indians,[17] including maize, white potatoes, sweet potatoes, manioc or cassava (tapioca), peanuts, chocolate (cacao), lima beans, cashews, peppers (chilies), varieties of squash (including zucchini), pumpkins, papaya, guava, pineapples, sunflower seeds, tepary beans, avocados, and tomatoes. Cultigens other than food crops included tobacco, cotton, coca leaves (cocaine when refined), quinoa, and rubber.[18] Many of these crops supported the growth and survival of Asian populations. Conversely, Asian crops such as rice and sugar cane came to America via Europe and transformed large parts of the Latin American economy, ecology, and diet.

This exchange of crops changed forever the two separate patterns of agricultural development that had existed in the Eastern and Western hemispheres before 1492 in which no crop of one hemisphere provided food for a significant segment of people in the other.[19] Profound changes occurred in Asia, as New World crops increased and improved food supplies for the subsequent three hundred years. These crops doubled, and even tripled, some food supplies in Asia.[20] Maize was, and remains, the wonder crop of American Indian civilization. It became as indispensable in China as it was in the Americas, because it provided sustenance for both man and beast. Like many other American Indian crops, maize has a different growing season from Asian crops and, therefore, did not compete with them for precious land.[21] Maize was easier to grow than rice and fit in with the Chinese multiple cropping system. Moreover, maize and some other crops grow in soil too poor to sustain certain Old World crops.[22] Furthermore, there are many varieties which grow in different climates—those too dry for rice and those too wet for wheat.[23]

Maize, sweet potatoes, and peanuts were very important to Chinese agricultural production. After corn was first introduced into Yunnan in the sixteenth century, it spread to other areas of South China; sweet potatoes became part of the poor man's diet in Fujian. After 1700 imperial edicts ordered peasants in northern China to cultivate sweet potatoes to prevent famine.[24] Although sweet potatoes were important only in certain areas of China until the late nineteenth century, today China is the world's largest producer, accounting for 80 percent of global production by the 1980s.[25]

Maize was valuable in another important way. It permitted the cultivation of idle, marginal land. This was particularly true in mountainous regions, where maize could give farmers provisions for six months. Corn and sweet potatoes were companion crops, the former growing on sunny hills and the latter on shady ones. Once the economic advantages of these crops were recognized by the peasants, they began to cultivate the mountainsides of China. As they did so, natives and migrants encroached on the traditional homeland of the Miao (also known as the Hmong) in western Hunan and provoked the Miao Rebellion at the end of the eighteenth century.[26] Nonetheless, these crops supported population growth in China in the eighteenth century.

Amerindian crops permitted greater land utilization and changed demographic patterns in densely populated south China. Maize, sweet potatoes, peanuts, and white potatoes provided the incentive and the means by which peasants could move inland and north as rice cultivation reached its saturation point around 1850.[27] The cultivation of New World crops on mountainsides also led to deforestation and changes in China's ecology that are at issue today.

Other New World crops were also important in China. Peanuts, although not as popular in the Chinese diet as in some parts of the Indian subcontinent and Indonesia, were growing in Shanghai within fifty years after the discovery of America.[28] East Asians depended on vegetables for most of their nourishment. Ninety-eight percent of Chinese calories are of vegetable origin, and a significant portion of that comes from American Indian crops.[29] Beans such as kidney, string, snap, frijole, butter, navy, French (haricot), Madagascar, Rangoon, and Burma, which are eaten in China, are all of American origin.[30] Pineapples, white potatoes, and chilies are popular in some regions—the chili pepper, in fact, transformed the cuisine of Sichuan.

These chili peppers came to be widely used in the cuisine of India as well as in Sichuan and other parts of China. Before 1492 black pepper was widely used, but native Americans used a totally unrelated plant of many colors, shapes and intensities—oranges, yellows, purples, greens, bells, milds, and varieties of hot peppers.[31] The cooks of the subcontinent adopted these American peppers and cayennes and incorporated them into their dishes.

Crops such as guava and pineapple were introduced into India in the 1500s, but were not widely used. By the end of the seventeenth century they reached Malaya, Java, and China.[32] It was not until the end of the eighteenth century that maize displaced millet in some regions, and by the end of the nineteenth century it was grown almost everywhere. Sweet potatoes are grown in poor soil areas, and the white potato is grown as a mountain or winter crop and supplements grain.[33] Furthermore, oil made from peanuts is very widely used in India, which is the world's largest producer.

Southeast Asians fuse Chinese and Indian cuisines, combining peanuts, chilies, tomatoes, and fruits. The powerful chili pepper *prik kee ne luang* is used by the Thais, while Hindu Balinese use a milder chili.[34] Bali also makes a peanut cookie *(rempeyeh)* and a liqueur from the New World passion fruit which is mixed with American avocados and rum, coffee, sugar, and milk to make a shake.[35] This is similar to the Brazilian drink *vitamina.* Around 1550 the pineapple reached India via Brazil and was cultivated in Malaya, Java, and China by the end of the seventeenth century.[36] Amerindian spices, so important in the south, have less importance in the cooler climates of northern China, Korea, Japan, and Mongolia.

Another American comestible crop grown in Asia, especially in Indonesia, is manioc (cassava or tapioca). Manioc, although without great nutritional value, grows in almost any tropical region. It withstands droughts and repels pests (one variety is poisonous until processed). Furthermore, it can be harvested anytime within a two-year period after ripening, thereby making it a useful food bank in times of famine.[37] Manioc arrived in the East Indies in the seventeenth century[38] and by 1900 Malaya alone had 65,000 acres in cultivation.[39] Today Indonesia is second only to Brazil in production.[40]

Other Western hemisphere plants were influential in Asia, including tobacco, quinine, and rubber. Spaniards found Indians using tobacco when they arrived in the Antilles, and they introduced the seeds into their own country in 1499. Tobacco was first smoked by Spanish royalty and then spread to other countries. It spread around the world faster than most stimulants, including two of its American counterparts, cocaine and peyote, but perhaps not as fast as a third one, chocolate.[41]

Rubber, yet another American crop, entered the world stage much later than most. Columbus encountered Indians using it on his second voyage, and Cortez noticed it in Mexico in 1521. Europeans were amazed to see bouncing balls used in games, one of which required the participants to place a ball through a circular hoop at both ends of a court by using elbows, knees, and shoulders. Rubber also had more practical uses. Amerindians used it to waterproof garments, fasten items, protect ropes, and make vessels for toting liquids. They did this by heating the sap and mixing it with sulphur in a process similar to vulcanization. The best plants grew in Brazil (*Hevea brasiliensis*), and that country had a monopoly on production until 1913, when Asian exports surpassed it.[42] The world was at the mercy of Amazon growers, who raised prices through the roof in the boom period from 1880 to 1910, which was created by the invention of the pneumatic tire and the bicycle and automobile craze that followed.

As early as the 1860s the British East India Company advocated transferring rubber plants to India. By June 1873 two thousand seeds were smuggled out of Brazil to be germinated at Kew and sent to Calcutta. Agents, including Henry Wickham, who is generally reputed to have stolen the first plants, were dispatched to collect seeds, which were sent to Calcutta and then to Ceylon, the proposed distribution center for India, Burma, and Assam.[43] The first recorded planting of rubber trees by commercial interests was in Malacca. Seeds were planted in Ceylon and Malaya, and Singapore became the rubber capital of the world before 1920. Malay workers did not want to work on these new plantations, and workers from India were imported for the arduous task.[44] In that way two American Indian crops, rubber and manioc, grew side by side on the Malay Peninsula by the twentieth century.

One can indeed argue that the influence of American Indian civilization has been understressed in Western and world history. The Indians did not conquer overseas worlds and were in fact subdued by Europeans, but their influence on human survival, especially in food crops, exceeded that of any other people.

ASIAN MIGRANTS IN LATIN AMERICA

Just as New World crops were scattered to Asia and all parts of the world by European trade and commerce, so were people brought to the Western hemisphere from Asia. Asians came to the Americas in the middle and late nineteenth century after the abolition of the slave trade and the end of slavery produced labor shortages and underpopulation. The continuation of the dispersal of world populations to the New World, which began in the sixteenth century with Europeans and Africans, was expanded to include Chinese, Japanese, East Indians, Indonesians (Javanese), Middle Easterners, and others in the late nineteenth and early twentieth centuries. Planters sought agricultural workers in Asia, while industrialization led capitalists to seek laborers in Europe and Asia to man their factories.

In the nineteenth century Chinese laborers were brought to Latin America to work in conditions barely distinguishable from slavery, especially in Cuba, Peru, and Mexico. The 800 Chinese brought from Amoy to Cuba in 1847 were the first.[45] Of the 132,435 Chinese brought to that island from Shanghai and Canton between 1853 and 1873, 13 percent died in transit. This was only ten years after a treaty between Spain and Qing China had been concluded to allow the traffic.[46] In 1877 Chinese represented 3 percent of the Cuban population, but, because of the high mortality, they constituted only about 1 percent in 1899. They worked cutting cane, laying rails, and harvesting beans. Disillusioned by treatment on the farms, many indentured servants escaped to the cities to become itinerant street vendors or returned to China.[47] The Chinese government protested the harsh treatment of coolies who had been inveigled into signing work contracts, and an investigative commission was established in 1874. The commissioners found that 80 percent of the Chinese brought from the Portuguese enclave of Macao to Cuba had been trapped and forced to sign contracts, which violated an agreement between China and Spain. The findings of the commission were purely academic, because on 27 March 1874, ten days after it arrived in Cuba and over a month before it reached a conclusion, Macao's governor closed the trade in this last port which permitted forcible detention.[48]

It was not Cuba, however, but Peru that was the destination of most Asians who came to Spanish America. President Ramón Castilla used the import of Chinese labor and guano revenues to abolish the African slave trade (1850) and emancipate the last 17,000 black slaves (1854), but not the Polynesians, who lived and died in inhuman conditions.[49] Coolies were needed to work in guano fields, build canals, create harbors, lay telegraph lines, and particularly construct railroads, as in the United States, because neither the black nor Quechua underclasses were available in sufficient numbers to complete those tasks. Diseases on the coast discouraged Indians from working there, and the end of the slave trade and miscegenation reduced the black population.[50] The elite preferred Europeans but could not get them, since crime and backwardness had dissuaded them from coming to Peru. Chinese contract laborers, mainly from Macao, were packed in sardine-like conditions into ships and sent overseas. Between 1849 and 1879 over 100,000 arrived in Peru, with 80,000 living there in 1875; 10 to 30 percent died on board "hell holes."[51] One ship lost 40 percent of those on board.[52]

Conditions in China, as well as opportunities abroad, contributed to the exodus of Chinese. The Taiping Rebellion (1850–64), a devastating civil war that killed twenty million, insurrection and conflicts in Guangdong and Guangxi, and other hardships caused 300,000 to leave for the Americas between 1850 and 1875.[53] Coolies were obligated to serve five years, remain where sent, and repay the advances given them. Some accepted these terms in the belief that the contractual agreements were lenient and that, once in America, there would be a chance to advance. Most, however, were taken against their will to Cuba and Peru.[54]

On arrival in Peru, coolies were given a suit, a pair of shoes, and a hat. They were then distributed to various parts of the country. Some were sent to guano fields, many to plantations, and others to lay railroads for the American capitalist Henry Meiggs. Meiggs' railroads, which united Lima and the port city of Callao, expanded the economic power of the capital, helped to increase the population of the metropolitan region, and fostered internal migration, used coolies from China and the United States.[55] Long gowns, queues, a strange language, and yellow skins made them a curious spectacle in a land of ponchos, double plaits, and white, brown, and black skins. Lima was quite a cosmopolitan city without its residents even knowing it. The Chinese were exploited by sugar plantation owners, harassed by freed Africans and cholos (mixed bloods), and denounced by self-serving politicians and journalists.[56] Chinese Peruvians were seen as being unable to integrate into the social order, but that was not the case. Since Chinese immigration was entirely male, intermarriage was common, and women found the Chinese to be good and reliable husbands. Immigrants excelled in commerce as purveyors in food markets and restaurants where they created *chifa*, a uniquely Peruvian Chinese cuisine. Selling at reasonable prices, they became grocers, tailors, bakers, butchers, and shoemakers in an area of Lima,[57] but by 1940, because of a high death rate, repatriation, acculturation, and miscegenation, only ten thousand ethnic Chinese remained.[58]

The Peruvian elite also sought laborers in Japan. The first eastward migration of Japanese overseas was to Hawaii in 1868, just after the Meiji Restoration. Unsettled conditions in Japan, economic difficulties in the countryside, and recruiting, profiteering companies encouraged migration. The Japanese government also supported contract labor and colonization schemes to reduce excess population. Emigration companies contracted for labor for the Americas and the rest of the world. Augusto B. Leguia, future president of Peru and owner of a sugar plantation, signed an agreement with one of those companies in 1898. That company, Morioka, was already supplying Brazil with immigrants, and between 1898 and 1923 four companies sent workers to Peru.[59] In April of 1899, 790 passengers arrived in Peru on the ship *Sakura Maru* from four Japanese prefectures—Niigata, Yamaguchi, Hiroshima, and Okayama. Over 17,000 legal and thousands more illegal workers entered Peru in the next twenty-three years. The 1940 census indicated that there were 17,598 native Japanese and 8,970 nisei in Peru.[60]

Immigrants worked on sugar plantations, but opportunities in towns and cities on the coast drew them into skilled labor and shopkeeping. Japanese became prominent as barbers, bakers, potters, carpenters, and plumbers, and produced 12 percent of Peruvian cotton. Ninety percent lived in metropolitan Lima-Callao and developed a virtual monopoly on vegetable supplies. Their success created hostility among Peruvians.[61]

When war broke out in Asia in 1937 (the second Sino-Japanese War) and in Europe in 1939, anti-Japanese sentiment was just under the surface and manifested itself in riots in Lima in 1940.[62] Chinese Peruvians, in order to protect themselves, wore signs which indicated their ethnicity. Moreover, the American government enlisted them to spy on the Japanese, though the Chinese were as much interested in the elimination of economic competition from the Japanese as in the allied cause.[63] Japanese newspapers, clubs, and schools were closed; Japanese were prohibited from owning guns, or telephones, traveling abroad, and having fishing and hunting permits. After the attack on Pearl Harbor, the situation worsened.

The United States feared subversion by Japanese populations in Latin America. It convened a meeting of Latin American ministers in Rio de Janeiro in 1942 to develop a propaganda strategy against Japan. More than 2000 Japanese were sent from twelve nations to be interned in the United States. Brazil, the American nation with the largest Japanese population, refused to comply. Peru supplied 1,024 persons, including 399 women and children, who were sent to Texas and New Mexico between April 1942 and July 1943.[64] In Central America, all or most of the small Japanese populations were arrested and sent to camps in the United States.[65] At the end of the war, the United States government declared Peruvian internees illegal aliens and, at the same time, ruled that they would not be able to return to Peru because of inter-American protocol. Postwar Japanese emigration remained scant, though in the late 1970s there were more than 50,000 Peruvians of Japanese descent, one of whom, Alberto Fujimori, became President of Peru in 1990.

Unlike Peru, Bolivia was not requested to intern its enemy aliens until 13 May 1944. Many went into hiding, and only 50 Germans and 28 Japanese were sent to Crystal City, Texas. Moreover, those who wished to return to Bolivia after the war were accommodated, and most returned to the rubber plantations in northeast Bolivia where they had once worked.[66] Some remained in the United States.

Immediately after the war, Bolivia's main goal was to become self-sufficient in food and fiber crops. Okinawans had constituted a large portion of the prewar immigration from Japan. With the financial aid of the United States, now in control of Okinawa, three Bolivian colonies of Okinawans were established forty miles from Santa Cruz by 1962. Over 172,000 applied to emigrate for the 50,000 hectares available, but those colonies contained only 3,000 Okinawans in 1962.[67]

Neither Bolivia nor Peru, however, received the bulk of East

Asian immigrants; that distinction belonged to their neighbor, Brazil. Several waves of Asians came in the nineteenth and twentieth centuries. After the transfer of the Portuguese court to Rio de Janeiro in 1808, following the Napoleonic invasion of Lisbon, Chinese workers were imported to plant tea in the botanical gardens. It was, however, the abolition of slavery in 1888 that was the impetus for large-scale Asian immigration in Brazil as it was in other Latin American countries. In 1892 the Brazilian government lifted its restriction on Asian immigrants, and the first large-scale emigration from Japan started after the turn of the century. Emigration corporations were established in Japan which sent Japanese between twelve and forty years old as contract laborers to Brazil. The first colony was settled in São Paulo, and between 1908 and 1924, 40,000 Japanese emigrated to Brazil. Emigration took off after the Exclusion Act of 1924 in the United States; 150,000 Japanese emigrated between 1925 and 1941.[68] Ten percent (over 200,000) of immigrants between 1889 and 1934 were Japanese, equaling the number of German immigrants. Encouraged by the Japanese government, they came from the main islands and Okinawa, many of them to work on coffee plantations around São Paulo.[69] The Japanese-Brazilians established themselves and became an important segment of the population and the largest community of Japanese origin outside Japan. In recent years, there has been a return immigration of these Brazilian Japanese to Japan as laborers, in numbers upwards of 100,000.

CONCLUSION

In summary, Asia and Latin America have influenced each other's histories for hundreds and perhaps thousands of years. The earliest migration of peoples from Asia to the Western hemisphere, the improbable but possible contacts in pre-Columbian times, the trade network created by European colonialism and imperialism, the exchange of New and Old World crops, and the transplanting of Chinese, Japanese, Javanese, Indians, and others in the nineteenth and twentieth centuries as workers in fields and factories are phenomena that connected the continents and revealed the historical interactions among societies active on the so-called periphery of world history. In recent years East Asian trade and investment have increased dramatically in Latin America, with the Japanese leading (e.g., Japan is now Chile's leading trade partner), followed by the Chinese in Peru and the Koreans in Chile. For their part, Latin Americans have begun to talk about their place on the "Pacific Rim," with Chile boasting that it will be a "fifth tiger," joining Taiwan, Korea, Hong Kong, and Singapore in economic growth. In the future, relations between Asia and Latin America are likely to be even more important than they have been in the past.

POPULATION STATISTICS FROM SELECTED AMERICAN NATIONS IN 1986

Country	Percentage of Asians		Dates
Surinam	37%	East Indian	June 1986
	15%	Javanese	
	2%	Chinese	
Guyana	51%	East Indian	July 1986
	1%	Chinese	
Trinidad	40%	East Indian	July 1986
	2%	Chinese	
Jamaica	3%	East Indian and Afro-East Indian	July 1986
St. Lucia	3%	East Indian	July 1986
Peru	1%	Chinese	July 1986
Cuba	1%	Chinese	July 1986
Brazil	1%	Japanese	July 1986

Note: Statistics from Central Intelligence Agency, *The World Fact Book* (Washington, D.C.: CIA, 1986).

NOTES

When I applied to participate in the Columbia-NEH Institute "Teaching Asia in Western and World History," the historical relationship between Asia and Latin America had never entered my mind. My university had just approved a new curriculum in which Global History Since 1500 was a required course, and, since Asia is my weakest field, I needed formal training in that area in order to teach that course. Furthermore, I had just begun research on a comparison of the attitudes of returned Spanish colonials from America with those of the British nabobs who returned to Britain. The Institute, therefore, seemed to me to be an excellent vehicle for developing some basic themes and bibliography to support both my teaching responsibilities and research interests. There was little presented in the papers and discussions that I could use in my Latin American course, although possible Chinese voyages to America and the Manila galleons were mentioned. I was, however, prodded into considering the relationship between Latin America and Asia, which turned out to be a fruitful topic.

1. J. Alden Mason, *The Ancient Civilizations of Peru* (Baltimore: Pelican Books, 1968), p. 212.
2. Betty Meggers, *Prehistoric America: An Ecological Perspective*, 2d ed. (New York: Aldine Publishing Co., 1972), p. 31.
3. Ibid., pp. 7–44.
4. Ibid., p. 35. On Jomon pottery, see also Betty J. Meggers and Clifford Evans, "A Transpacific Contact in 3000 B.C.," *Scientific American* 214 (January 1966): 1.
5. Stephen C. Jett, "Precolumbian Transoceanic Contacts," in *Ancient North Americans*, ed. Jesse D. Jennings (San Francisco: W.H. Freeman, 1983), pp. 557–604. For those interested in further reading, Stephen Jett lists the major scholars who advocate contact between Asia and the Americas in his notes.
6. Ibid., p. 569.
7. Ibid., pp. 594–95.
8. J.F. Normano and Antonello Gerbi, *The Japanese in Latin America* (New York: Institute of Pacific Relations, 1943), p. 63.
9. Kurt Severin, "The Japanese of Peru," *Travel*, LXXXII, February 1944, 4–9.
10. William Lytle Schurz, *The Manila Galleon* (New York: E.P. Dutton, 1939), pp. 27, 60.
11. Ibid., p. 33. See also the chapter by Wakeman, p. 7, and that by Rowe, p. 4, and note 8.
12. Henry E. Dobyns and Paul L. Doughty, *Peru, A Cultural History* (New York: Oxford, 1976), p. 118. The word Indians (*indios* in Spanish) means those from the Indies (Las Indias), the East Indies and the West Indies. To Spaniards both Americas were the West Indies, not just the islands in the Caribbean. There were, therefore, Indians of Peru (*indios del Peru*) and Indians of Japan (*indios del Japon*), as well as of China and of the Philippines.
13. Derek Masserella, *A World Elsewhere* (New Haven: Yale University Press, 1990), pp. 132–36.
14. James L. Tigner, "Japanese Immigration to Latin America, A Survey," *Journal of Interamerican Studies* 22 (1981): 458.
15. Schurz, *The Manila Galleon*, p. 120.
16. Alfred Crosby, *The Columbian Exchange* (Westport, CT: Greenwood Press, 1972), p. 109.
17. Jack Weatherford, *Indian Givers: How the Indians of the Americas Changed the World* (New York: Crown Publishers, 1988), p. 71.
18. Geoffrey Barraclough, ed., *The Times Concise Atlas of World History* (Maplewood, NJ: Hammond Inc., 1986), pp. 6–7.
19. Ibid., p. 169.
20. Crosby, *The Columbian Exchange*, pp. 107, 167.
21. Ibid., p. 176.
22. Ibid.
23. Weatherford, *Indian Givers*, p. 73; Crosby, *The Columbian Exchange*, p. 171.

24. Ping Ti Ho, *Studies on the Population of China, 1368–1953* (Cambridge, MA: Harvard University Press, 1959), p. 187.

25. Ho, *Population of China*, pp. 183–84; William H. McNeill, "American Food Crops in the Old World," in *Seeds of Change*, ed. Herman J. Viola and Carolyn Margolis (Washington, D.C.: Smithsonian Institution Press, 1991), p. 53.

26. Ho, *Population of China*, p. 146.

27. Ibid., p. 183.

28. Ibid.

29. Crosby, *The Columbian Exchange*, pp. 190–201.

30. Weatherford, *Indian Givers*, p. 72.

31. Ibid., p. 101.

32. Berthold Laufer, "The American Plant Migration," *Scientific Monthly*, March 1929, p. 151.

33. Crosby, *The Columbia Exchange*, p. 193.

34. Weatherford, *Indian Givers*, pp. 75–76.

35. Ibid., p. 104.

36. Laufer, "The American Plant Migration," p. 251.

37. Weatherford, *Indian Givers*, p. 74.

38. Crosby, *The Columbian Exchange*, p. 196.

39. J.H. Drabble, *Rubber in Malaya, 1876–1922* (Oxford: Oxford University Press, 1973), p. 14.

40. Crosby, *The Columbian Exchange*, p. 197.

41. Weatherford, *Indian Givers*, p. 211. Quinine comes from the bark of a Peruvian tree and is important in the prevention and treatment of malaria. It was widely used by the Incas and later by the Europeans in Asia.

42. Rollie E. Poppino, *Brazil, Land and People* (New York: Oxford University Press, 1968), p. 143.

43. Drabble, *Rubber in Malaya*, p. 2.

44. Ibid., p. 19.

45. Watt Stewart, *Chinese Bondage in Peru* (Durham, NC: Duke University Press, 1951), p. 17.

46. Nicolas Sanchez-Albornoz, *The Population of Latin America*, trans. W.A.R. Richardson (Berkeley: University of California Press, 1974), pp. 150–51.

47. Ibid., p. 150.

48. Stewart, *Chinese Bondage in Peru*, p. 37–47, 53.

49. Ibid., pp. 5–6, and Dobyns and Doughty, *Peru, A Cultural History*, p. 160.

50. Dobyns and Doughty, *Peru, A Cultural History*, p. 172.

51. J.K. Emmerson, *The Japanese Thread* (New York: Holt, Rinehart and Winston, 1978), p. 129.

52. Stewart, *Chinese Bondage in Peru*, p. 55.

53. Ibid., pp. 15–17.

54. Conrad Schirokauer, *A Brief History of Chinese and Japanese Civilization* (San Diego: Harcourt Brace Jovanovich, 1989), p. 396.

55. Dobyns and Doughty, *Peru, A Cultural History*, p. 193.

56. Emmerson, *The Japanese Thread*, p. 129.

57. Stewart, *Chinese Bondage in Peru*, pp. 224–27.

58. Emmerson, *The Japanese Thread*, p. 129.

59. C. Harvey Gardiner, *The Japanese in Peru, 1873–1973* (Albuquerque: University of New Mexico Press, 1975), pp. 23–33.

60. Emmerson, *The Japanese Thread*, p. 131.

61. Ibid., p. 139.

62. Carey McWilliams, *Prejudice: Japanese Americans, Symbol of Racial Intolerance* (Boston: Little, Brown, 1944), p. 149.

63. Emmerson, *The Japanese Thread*, pp. 135–42.

64. Ibid., p. 139.

65. McWilliams, *Prejudice: Japanese Americans*, p. 149.

66. James L. Tigner, "The Ryukyuans in Bolivia," *Hispanic American Historical Review* 43 (Fall 1963): 215.

67. James L. Tigner, "Japanese Settlements in Eastern Bolivia and Brazil," *Journal of Interamerican Studies and World Affairs* 24 (Fall 1982): 499.

68. McWilliams, *Prejudice: Japanese Americans*, p. 148; also, *Kodansha Encyclopedia of Japan*, vol. 1 (Tokyo: Kodansha, 1983), p. 69.

69. Poppino, *Brazil, Land and People*, pp. 191–92.

Themes in Asian History

JAPAN AND AMERICA: A TALE OF TWO CIVILIZATIONS

Carol Gluck

In the 1840s Japan and the United States each thought of the other as barbarians. And each of course defined civilization in terms of itself. Japan, like China, had long regarded the Christianizing, colonizing West as a threat to civilized East Asia. The United States considered Japan a heathen country whose refusal to trade threatened America's "mission of commerce to civilize the world." Neither knew very much about the other, for there had been no real contact between the ancient secluded island empire and the young expanding American nation.

The scene was set for what the Japanese call "the opening of the country," and with it, the official beginning of Japanese-American relations. Both occurred at the same time, in 1853, when Commodore Perry's black ships steamed into Tokyo Bay, demanding that Japan open its ports to foreign trade. Of the historical relationship between the two countries, three points may be made. First, the relationship is a long one. By the 1990s Japan and the United States had shared 150 years of mutual history. For Japan, this was the entire span of its relations with the modern world. For the U.S., it was more than two-thirds of its national history. Through cycles of admiration and resentment, amity and hostility, the histories of the two countries had grown increasingly intertwined and interdependent.

Second, the relationship had long been characterized by a disparity of power and of interest. From the first the United States wielded far greater military and economic power than Japan, which felt—and was made to feel—its inferior international status. And from the first the Japanese showed far greater interest in—and had a broader knowledge of—American culture, society, and politics than Americans did about Japanese affairs. But by the 1990s the disparity of power and interest had changed. Japan was more powerful in the world economy, and Americans were more interested in Japan than ever before. But neither country found it easy to adjust to the new situation after more than a century of international asymmetry in favor of the United States.

Third, changes in the relationship had always depended not only on changes within Japan and America but also on the world context. Although each country tended to think of the other primarily in bilateral terms, this transpacific tunnel-vision was misleading. From the mid-nineteenth to the late twentieth century, the Japanese-American relationship evolved in close dependence on its global context. In the half century after the end of the Second World War in 1945, Japan changed, America changed, and after 1989 the world changed as well. Japanese and Americans of the 1990s now faced the challenge of living intertwined and interdependent in a post-postwar world.

JAPAN AND THE WORLD, A DRAMA IN TWO ACTS

Viewed from the perspective of Japan, the long history of Japanese-American relations is like a drama in two acts. The first act began in 1853 with the opening of Japan to trade and ended in 1945 with the defeat in war. This period marked the first phase of Japan's relations with the modern world. Act One is divided into two scenes. During Scene One, here called "The Pursuit of Civilization," 1853-1912, Japan underwent the domestic transformation that is known as modernization, taking the Euro-American West as a model. In Scene Two, 1905-1945, Japan turned toward "The Pursuit of Power," seeking international parity with the Western powers through diplomacy, imperialism, and war. The domestic transformation largely succeeded, and Japan, it was said, joined the ranks of the "civilized nations." But in international relations Japan failed, first in its efforts to gain acceptance by the Western powers, then in the cataclysm of war and defeat.

In the second act, which began immediately in 1945, Japan conceived of itself as beginning again, both in domestic and international terms. From 1945 to the early 1970s, Japan undertook another thoroughgoing reform, this time with America as the guide and model. This was Act Two, Scene One, known to the Japanese as "Peace, Democracy, and Prosperity." Scene Two of the second act began in the seventies and has not ended yet. Entitled "Japan and the World," this period saw Japan re-emerge on the world stage, strong in its economy but uncertain of its international role. As before, Japan's domestic transformation had proceeded more smoothly than its entry into the international realm.

The world always figured importantly in the script of Japanese history. Every country deals with the world in its foreign policy, but Japan also brought the world deeply into its internal affairs, wholeheartedly adopting Western ways in order to be accepted as an equal by the West. And among the Western powers, the United States was long the country the Japanese had most closely to reckon with.

America, represented by Commodore Matthew Perry, had been present when the curtain rose in 1853, and America, in the form of a victorious army was there when the first act curtain fell on the surrender in 1945. In the person of General Douglas MacArthur, America ruled the occupation under which Japan embarked on its postwar new beginning. After independence in 1952, America became Japan's most important ally and remained Japan's largest trading partner. The U.S. relied on Japan to play its role in the Cold War by becoming economically strong and politically dependable. And when Japan's economic strength became truly formidable, it was the Americans who complained the loudest and made the greatest demands that Japan change its all-too-successful ways. No wonder the long drama of Japanese-American relations was marked by strong emotions on the part of both the players.

THE PURSUIT OF CIVILIZATION, 1853-1912

When Commodore Perry arrived in 1853, he intended to impress the Japanese with American military and technological superiority. He displayed steamships armed with cannon and presented the Japanese ruler with gifts of rifles, muskets, pistols, telegraph instruments and a working miniature locomotive, ("tender, passenger car, and rails complete"). In return the Japanese shogun gave the Commodore such ceremonial gifts as gold lacquered cases, lengths of silk pongee, flowered crepe, and other treasures of culture. The Americans paraded their frigates of war, the Japanese their sumō wrestlers. The disparity of power between the two countries was clear from the first.

The West posed a threat to Japan's national autonomy, as the Japanese well knew from the example of the British in China. In the mid-nineteenth-century world the Western presence in Asia meant imperialism. It proved significant for Japan that the United States, unlike Britain, was at the time neither a territorial imperialist nor a world power. Although America lay outside the mostly European-dominated "world order," it was nonetheless oriented primarily toward Europe, not Asia. The disparity of power between America and Japan was thus matched by a disparity of interest. America was suddenly of great importance to Japan, while for the United States Japan was little more than a coaling and trading station. Japan had time and space to react to the Perry shock.

Japan reacted to the Western threat, not by rejecting but by embracing the West. After the Meiji Restoration of 1868 Japan embarked on a massive program of political, social, and economic change. The Japanese sought "civilization," which they now identified with the West, often using the term Euro-Americanization to describe the changes necessary to catch up with the Western powers that threatened their nation. Japan's transformation was thus a "defensive modernization." For the sake of the nation, "we must rid ourself of Oriental traits," wrote one enthusiast, relegating Asia to the realm of the uncivilized. Then the Western powers would accept Japan as equals and revise the unequal treaties which had been the outcome of Perry's demand for trade. Without resorting to such extremes of self-abnegation, Japan proceeded to acquire the accoutrements of nineteenth-century civilization within three decades.

Americans in the 1890s praised this accomplishment, calling the Japanese "Asiatic Yankees" who, having wisely adopted American ways, had become promising "protégés" of the United States. But when Japanese goods began to sell in the American market, Americans labeled Japan an "unfair" rival in a "commercial war." When Japanese emigrants began to increase in number on the West coast, the Americans evoked "the sacred and ineradicable distinction of race" and called for the closing of their country to the "little brown men." And when the Japanese navy began to grow in size, the first spate of war scare literature prophesied a coming conflict between Japan and the United States.

These three phenomena, which were interrelated, appeared in the first decade of the twentieth century. Still, in 1912, when the Meiji emperor died and Japan proudly celebrated its achievements in civilization, America, along with the rest of the West, congratulated Japan on having sundered itself from the sleeping East and joined the company of civilized nations.

THE PURSUIT OF POWER, 1905-1945

Ever since the opening of the country, Japan had striven for parity in international relations. The quest for parity, in the form of revision of the unequal treaties, preoccupied Japan's foreign policy and drove its domestic modernization as well. It took forty years, from the 1850s, when the treaties were signed, until the 1890s, when the first of the treaties was finally revised, for the Japanese government to reach its goal of full autonomy as defined by nineteenth-century international law. For the next forty years Japan reached for parity of a different kind, seeking to gain "entry into the ranks of the powers" that dominated the twentieth-century world order. As the world order changed, so did the means Japan employed to acquire status within it.

Having learned the lessons of imperialism from the West, Japan began its own career as an imperialist by winning a war against China in 1894-05. But it was not until its victory over Russia in 1904-05 that Japanese began to speak of their country as a "great power." Americans, especially President Theodore Roosevelt, were also impressed by this victory of an Asian country over one of the West's five Great Powers. Some Japanese noted the irony that "Japan had been regarded as barbaric when peaceful, but now with victory in war, the foreigners call us civilized." Other Japanese twisted the rhetoric of civilization in a different direction. As the only civilized nation in Asia, Japan had a right, or a mission, to imperial control over Korea (and later over Manchuria and China), which lacked civilization of the latter-day sort. How quickly and strangely the barbarians and the civilized had changed rhetorical places.

Japan followed a policy epitomized by the phrase, "escape from Asia," which meant aligning with the supposedly civilized West and treating Asia as the West did. In addition to the practices of empire, Japan concluded diplomatic relations on the same escape-from-Asia principle, priding itself especially on the Anglo-Japanese alliance of 1902, which suggested that Japan had indeed arrived in the ranks of the powers.

But the impression proved false, most strikingly at the Paris Peace Conference in 1919 after the First World War. Nominally included among the victorious Big Powers, Japan nonetheless failed in its diplomatic goals, primarily because of the United States. On anti-imperialist grounds President Woodrow Wilson opposed Japan's territorial claims in China, despite the fact that the European powers had already recognized them. And Wilson thwarted Japanese efforts to include a racial equality clause in the preamble to the Covenant of the new League of Nations. "JAPAN DENIED RACE EQUALITY," proclaimed the headlines in San Francisco, while Tokyo papers chastised the conscience of the "so-called civilized world" of the Anglo-Saxons. Japan's first excursion into the world of multilateral diplomacy had miscarried, and it seemed to many Japanese that America—which, along with the newly created Soviet Union, was beginning its twentieth-century rise to world power—had been largely responsible for changing the rules of the international game.

In the 1920s Japan played according to the new rules, generally following America's lead in disarmament, multilateral diplomacy, and economic, rather than territorial, penetration in China. But racism rocked the Japanese-American relationship again in 1924, with the total exclusion of Japanese from immigration to the United States. This did not stop the Americanization of popular culture in Japan, as the jazz, talkies, and short skirts of the roaring twenties swept the youth of Tokyo. Yet, in Japanese-American relations the combination of racism and naval rivalry produced another crop of war scare literature on both sides of the Pacific.

In 1931 Japan changed tactics and embarked on a course of unilateral aggression in Manchuria in northeastern China. The military had long chafed at the constraints of escape-from-Asia diplomacy, and the civilian government now followed suit in affirming Japan's special rights on the Asian mainland. When first the United States and then the League of Nations condemned Japan's new puppet state in Manchuria, Japan withdrew from the League (which the U.S. had never joined), thus ending decades of escape-from-Asia foreign policy. In the 1930s Japan turned away from the West and justified its imperialist incursions by shifting the rhetoric of civilization and racism in a pan-Asian direction. Japan, as the most advanced Asian nation, now described itself as the "leader of Asia" against the forces of white western imperialism.

While Japan pursued power in Asia, relations with the United States were profoundly affected by the world context in two ways. First, against the background of a world depression, Japan and America, like so many other countries, turned to economic nationalism. The U.S. practiced protectionism against Japanese dumping, and Japan attempted to establish an independent bloc economy in Asia as an alternative to dependence on U.S. markets and raw materials. The tone of mutual economic hostility grew more and more strident.

Second, American foreign policy, though isolationist, was focused increasingly on the rise of Hitler and the menace of Nazi aggression. Americans called Japan "the Germany of Asia," but they were much more concerned about the real Germany and the threat it posed to Europe than they were about Asia. After Japan started an all-out war against China in 1937, American criticism was rhetorically strong but did not produce significant policy change. The U.S. only took a hard line against Japan in 1940-41, impelled then not by Asian concerns but by the European war, the fall of France, and Hitler's impending invasion of the Soviet Union.

On the eve of Pearl Harbor then, the two powers stood with their backs to the Pacific. Japan was fighting a seemingly unwinnable war in China, and America was anguished over what seemed to be the imminent "fall of Western civilization" to the Nazis. The disparity of power remained in American favor, but it seemed to Japan as if the isolationist U.S. might not be willing to use it. And the disparity of interest, while lessened by decades of Japanese-American relations, had not changed enough to make events in Asia anywhere near as important for Americans as was the fate of Europe.

Meanwhile the level of rhetorical hostility between Japan and the United States had risen, with an admixture of mutual racisms and resentments. Fighting against "encirclement" by the powers and for its imperial "self-preservation" and the "liberation of Asia," Japan attacked Pearl Harbor on December 7, 1941. America, which had refused to accede to Japan's demands in China, was at war immediately, not only against Japan in Asia but against Germany and Italy in Europe. The lines between barbarity and civilization were drawn yet again in a bloody global battle.

When the war was over, far from achieving parity in international relations, Japan had ravaged Asia and itself, ending in disgrace and defeat, after two atomic bombings and the acceptance of unconditional surrender on August 15, 1945. As for Japan and America, it was war that really brought the two countries face to face.

PEACE, DEMOCRACY, AND PROSPERITY, 1945-1970s

In 1945 Japanese were determined to begin again, to undo the forces that had led to war, and to build a new and peaceable Japan. The Americans were equally determined to remake Japan as a peaceful and democratic nation. That is one reason why the Japanese, having truly lost their sovereignty for the first time in their history, nonetheless welcomed General MacArthur's victorious forces as an "army of liberation." The disparity of power was greater than ever before, since Japan was under U.S. occupation, and MacArthur made it abundantly clear just who was in charge in Tokyo. As in the nineteenth century, Japan generally reacted to the foreign challenge by embracing foreign ways, and together the Japanese and Americans collaborated in a series of fundamental reforms that affected nearly every aspect of society.

Not all the reforms remained in the shape initially envisaged by the Americans or by the Japanese. The Americans shifted gears as the global context again intervened. The United States, now one of two superpowers in an emerging bipolar world, turned from structural reform to economic reconstruction in order to make Japan a strong ally in the Cold War in Asia. Japanese conservatives worked to moderate the more radical measures into forms they felt more comfortable with. But the principal reforms held, and the 1947 Constitution, which the Americans had drafted in less than a week, was transformed through five decades of constitutional practice into the fundamental basis of Japanese democracy. Known in Japan as the Peace Constitution, its Article Nine, the so-called No War Clause, remained in place. Japan's parliamentary democracy was one of the world's most stable, strikingly so, in that one party, the Liberal Democratic Party, remained in power from 1955 to 1993.

When the Occupation ended in 1952, Americans were well pleased, once again claiming Japan as a protégé. "Uncle Sam's pupil graduates," commented the American press. In "the American Century," which had been proclaimed by *Life* magazine in 1941, democracy was the highest goal, much as "civilization" had been in the nineteenth century. Building on earlier experiences with democracy in the 1880s and the 1920s, postwar Japanese enshrined democracy the way their forebears had once pursued civilization. Although Americans judged postwar Japan to be on the right road, they felt, as their forebears had, that Japan was still immature—a twelve-year old, said General MacArthur—in its development toward the ripeness represented by America. The close contact of occupation had not dissipated the condescension long displayed in American stereotypes of Japan.

Nor had the Occupation diminished the esteem of America in the minds of most Japanese, who were grateful to the blue-eyed shogun, as MacArthur was sometimes called, and glad to be associated with American society and culture. The association was also a matter of policy. By the terms of a Mutual Security Treaty signed at the same time as the Peace Treaty in 1951, Japan regained its independence and simultaneously became an ally of the United States, part of an economic and military "bulwark against communism in East Asia." American officials spoke of the alliance as a "Pacific partnership." The presence of U.S. military bases on Japanese soil, in some ways reminiscent of the unequal treaties, led critical Japanese in the 1950s to condemn the arrangement as "subordinate independence," and there were massive protests against the renewal of the Security Treaty in 1960. The treaty was nevertheless renewed, and as of the mid-nineties remained in force, receiving widespread support from Japanese on the occasion of its thirtieth anniversary in 1990.

By the 1960s postwar Japan had entered its "era of high growth." Its economy was growing at double-digit rates, the so-called income-doubling plan was creating a vast middle class, and people were enjoying a privacy and prosperity which would have been unthinkable in imperial Japan. The Tokyo Olympics of 1964 symbolized this prosperity and a new national confidence, as the nations of the world engaged in peaceful competition on Japanese soil. By 1968 Japan had the third highest GNP in the world, and its first Nobel Prize for literature. Japan, the Japanese felt, had indeed entered a new age.

Then, in the late 1960s, as Japanese products began to challenge sector after sector of the American market, the Japanese were again labeled "unfair" competitors and commercial rivals. In a series of binational trade wrangles, known in Japan as "economic frictions," the U.S. criticized Japan for unseemly success in a succession of industries, from textiles through steel, televisions, automobiles, and semiconductors. The Japanese, who had been told by the Americans to concentrate on economics and shun geopolitics of their own, now found themselves accused of too much peaceable commerce and urged by the United States to spend more on defense, the Peace Constitution written by the Americans notwithstanding. The escalation of hostile rhetoric continued until it acquired the name Japan-bashing in the mid-1980s. Each time the U.S. made demands, Japan reacted, but never rapidly or thoroughly enough to alleviate the friction.

By the end of the eighties, the Japanese had themselves taken to America-bashing, and there was talk on both sides of the Pacific of war—trade war. Still, President after President, and Prime Minister after Prime Minister, ceremonially reiterated the importance of the Japanese-American alliance, "the most important bilateral relationship in the world, bar none," according to the oft incanted phrase of Ambassador Mike Mansfield. Japan was peaceable, democratic, and prosperous at home, but abroad, it seemed, things were going less smoothly.

JAPAN IN THE WORLD, 1971-

For Japan the bilateral frictions with the United States were expressions of a larger issue: the role of Japan in the world. Postwar Japan had sought to "regain the trust of the world," as it was often said, by prospering peaceably and staying out of the international limelight, where it had failed so miserably in the prewar years. Japanese politicians called this "the separation of economics and politics," which had as one of its byproducts a low profile in foreign relations. For twenty-five years after the war, the low profile proved reasonably workable, while Japan followed the lead of its ally, the United States, which both set the framework of Japanese foreign policy and sheltered Japan from having to construct one of its own. Japanese and American leaders both felt more or less comfortable with this patron-client relationship. Discomfort began with the trade frictions, but the real pain occurred in the early 1970s. First the Nixon shocks of 1971 suddenly freed the dollar from a fixed relation to gold, which led to a sharp rise in the value of the yen, and at the same time, suddenly announced the normalization of U.S. relations with the People's Republic of China, a country of some importance to Japan. Yet the U.S. took both these initiatives without giving prior notice to its Pacific partner, Japan. Then the oil shock of 1973 showed the Japanese once again how dependent their economy was on volatile parts of the world for natural resources. Yet Japan had no developed Middle East policy of its own. These shocks signaled the end of the period of domestic reconstruction and the beginning of Japan's re-entry into the world order.

By the 1980s the world order itself was changing, as the bipolar world began to globalize into multipolar shape. Japan and Germany became major economic powers, newly industrializing economies (NIES) like Taiwan, Korea, and Singapore grew rapidly in Asia, the European Community drew closer together as it moved toward economic unity in 1992, the Third World grew more troubled and more needy, and the United States and the Soviet Union saw their power decrease in relative terms. Every June the seven advanced industrial countries, which included Japan, held an economic summit, the world's economic leadership concentrated in a very small portion of the more than 150 countries in the world.

As an economic superpower, Japan was being called upon to exert leadership and take international responsibility, most vocally by the United States. Japan faced a dual dilemma. First, for all its modern history, ever since Perry, Japan had practiced "reactive international relations," attempting to fit into an existing world order with an already defined agenda, whether it was the nineteenth-century world of the European powers and imperialism or the postwar world of American hegemony and the Cold War. Now, and especially since the end of the Cold War in 1989, as the world waited for the "new world order" that was as yet nowhere in sight, Japan had to help create that new order and set the international agenda.

Second, Japan had to resolve its old dilemma of where in the world it belongs. Once in centuries past, Japan was closed to the world, but isolation was no longer possible. Nor could Japan choose, as it did earlier in this century, either to escape from Asia or into it. By the same token Japan could no longer put all its international eggs into one American basket, as it had for decades after the Second World War. During those postwar decades when Japan faced the U.S. across the Pacific, it stood with its back toward Asia. Now it had to confront Asia, both its past actions and its future relations. And Japan had also to globalize, as it dealt with Eastern Europe, Africa, and the Middle East. For this task, too, it had little useful experience on which to draw. Meanwhile as Japan groped for an appropriate international role and a proper international place, other nations were increasingly critical of the single mindedness of Japanese economic behavior and resentful of Japanese economic success. Whatever problems Japan faced domestically, they paled before the tensions and difficulties of performing a new role in the center of the world stage. The drama of Japan in the world had not yet ended. The curtain was still up, and Japanese-American relations had its part to play.

JAPAN AND AMERICA AT 150 YEARS

By the 1990s the disparity of power and interest between the two players had shifted. Where Perry once dazzled Japanese with his locomotive, Americans marveled at the latest in Japan's consumer electronics. Where MacArthur introduced American educational institutions to Japan, Americans debated adopting aspects of Japanese schooling in the United States. The interchange was now in two directions, and both countries had gained from the two-way traffic: better to have both Coca Cola and sushi than only one or the other, and better to have the two strongest economies in the world friendly rather than hostile toward one another.

Just as Japan had to accept new responsibilities, so, too, did the United States have to adjust to a Japanese-American relationship of a less unequal kind. But historical habits die hard. Neither the U.S. nor Japan was quick to alter its practiced binational patterns in dealing with one another. Emotions often ran high, expressing heartiness and hostility in alternating extremes, as if the two countries had trouble subsiding into a relationship of modulated normalcy. After 150 years of mutual relations, it was not clear that either had learned that the only thing that ever separates the civilized from the barbarians is the ability to look inward and see that all of us are both—if we are not careful.

A CONCRETE PANOPLY OF INTERCULTURAL EXCHANGE: ASIA IN WORLD HISTORY

Lynda Norene Shaffer

INTRODUCTION

One of the most common themes in world history is the rise of one locality, northwestern Europe, to a position of global power. The story usually begins with an account of the revolutionary ocean voyages that Iberian royalty sponsored—across the Atlantic, around Africa, and ultimately around the world. These voyages are portrayed as unprecedented historical departures, and many of the developments associated with them are seen as the events that ultimately ushered in the modern world. And because the voyages were made by western Europeans, historians have been inclined to seek the causes for the voyages and the transition to modernity within the bounds of western Europe. So far, the explanations thus produced include everything from the uniqueness of its soil and seeds to the anxieties of its soul.

The purpose of this chapter is to suggest the inadequacy of such a narrow view of these events. From a global perspective, the voyages and many of the developments associated with them were not without their precedents. The western European episode was unique in that it linked the two hemispheres, but in most other respects it was just part of a larger process—the most recent act of a much longer drama. The stage upon which the preceding acts had been played was as large as the Eastern hemisphere, and the global scope of the western European developments was a momentous but incremental expansion of the hemispheric proportions already achieved.

Once one realizes its global nature, any understanding of modernization that is informed only by the history of the West or even by world history since 1492 seems partial. Thus it is also a purpose of this chapter to suggest that the search for the wellsprings of the modern world must cover much more than western Europe and must go back into history much further than the fifteenth century. Otherwise, the scholarly and pedagogical isolation of the Western developments deprives them of their context and precludes the possibility of finding their non-Western origins or causes.

This chapter thus provides a rough sketch of some portions of the earlier history of those developments often associated with the rise of the West—the development and dispersion of commercial crops such as sugar and cotton, the development of new overland and maritime trade routes, the trade in spices, the development and dispersion of a new mathematics and new technologies, and the development of new sources of bullion.[1] It traces some of the major thoroughfares along which material exchanges took place and some of the more important developments in that process that ultimately took place on the shores of the Atlantic.

THE BEGINNING IN INDIA

As historians, we know that marking the beginning of things is an arbitrary act, but perhaps the most logical starting point for an explication of the long process that eventually led to global empires and Western hegemony is India during the time of the Gupta Empire (320 to 535 C.E.). By 500 C.E. the improvement and commercialization of various crops, the pioneering of overseas trade routes, the development of a spice trade with maritime Southeast Asia, and the creation of the Indian numbers and a new mathematics had already occurred in India. Some of these developments, such as the mathematics, were still quite new in the sixth century C.E., but others were reaching their culminations after centuries in the making.

Indian civilization enjoyed tremendous prestige at this time, from Byzantium and Ethiopia in the West to Japan in the East. In some quarters its image remained untarnished until the ninth century, even though the Guptas fell in the sixth century and Harsha's restoration of imperial unity (r. 616–657) was only temporary. Indeed, Amr al-Jahiz [Dhahiz] of Basra (776–868/869), a man usually known for his sharp wit and sharper tongue, expressed unrestrained admiration for things Indian.

. . . As regards the Indians, they are among the leaders in astronomy, mathematics—in particular, they have Indian numerals—and medicine; they alone possess the secrets of the latter, and use them to practice some remarkable forms of treatment. They have the art of carving statues and painted figures. They possess the game of chess, which is the noblest of games and requires more judgment and intelligence than any other. They make Kedah swords, and excel in their use. They have splendid music. . . . They know a number of sprightly dances . . . , and are versed in magic and fumigation. . . . They possess a script capable of expressing the sounds of all languages, as well as many numerals. They have a great deal of poetry, many long treatises, and a deep understanding of philosophy and letters. . . . They are intelligent and courageous, and have more good qualities than the Chinese. Their sound judgment and sensible habits led them to invent pins, cork, toothpicks, the drape of clothes and the dyeing of hair. They are handsome, attractive and forebearing, their women are proverbial, and their country produces the matchless Indian aloes which are supplied to kings. They were the originators of the science of *fikir*, by which a poison can be counteracted after it has been used, and of astronomical reckoning, subsequently adopted by the rest of the world. When Adam descended from Paradise, it was to their land that he made his way.[2]

INDIAN COTTON

Some of these developments had begun not centuries, but millennia before. Farmers of the Indus River valley, for example, began growing domesticated cotton at some point between 2300 and 1760 B.C.E.[3] By the fourth century B.C.E. its cultivation had spread from India to the Persian Gulf island of BahrAin, but until the Gupta period, it appears that the Indians were the sole suppliers of their own domestic market and of an international market that included the shores of the Indian Ocean from East Africa to Sumatra, the South China Sea, and the eastern Mediterranean.

Cotton cultivation spread to the east during the Gupta period. Although there is one reference to a cotton plant on China's southern coast in the first century C.E., Chinese cotton production was not significant until the seventh century (the Tang Dynasty).[4] Indian indigo spread along with it, and it was this combination that would eventually produce the blue peasant garb for which China is well known. But cotton's significance was not limited to clothing. By the Song Dynasty (960–1279) China's ships were outfitted with canvas sails that were more energy-efficient than the woven mats that had previously been used.[5] India thus made a significant contribution to China's medieval maritime adventures.

The Arabs moved cotton cultivation westward from Mesopotamia to Spain and the Algarve (now southern Portugal) by the tenth century. Thus by 1000 C.E. India's own cottons were in competition with locally grown cotton throughout and even beyond its old markets, but this does not seem to have had a negative impact on Indian production and manufacture. It is quite possible that India's domestic and international markets expanded faster than local and foreign production.

Sometime after 1500 Mexican varieties of the cotton plant replaced the Indian varieties in most locations. Yet the dispersion of the Mexican plant to Eastern hemisphere fields did not undermine the market for Indian textiles. Indeed, "the ease with which [the Mexican plants] could displace [the Indian] may be explained by the tastes, agricultural skills, and industrial techniques which had been acquired in [the Eastern hemisphere] with [the Indian varieties] over a period of more than three millennia."[6] India's cotton textiles maintained their prestige and much of their share of the international market until the industrial revolution.

THE INDIAN DEVELOPMENT OF BORROWED FOOD CROPS

If there is a moral to this story, it might be that "today's most important lenders were yesterday's best borrowers." It is worth noting that even though the Indians played a singular role in the domestication and commercialization of cotton, with regard to staple food crops, the subcontinent was not an important cradle of domestication. Cultivation in the Indus River valley began early, some time in the third millennium B.C.E., but wheat and barley, the main crops of this region, had spread there from the Mesopotamian area. Since around 800 B.C.E., the staple crop of the Ganges River valley was rice, which by that time had been grown in various parts of Southeast Asia and southern China for more than two thousand years.

Rice spread from India to Mesopotamia sometime around the second century B.C.E., and by the sixth century C.E., it could be found in Ethiopia. After the Arab conquests it continued its spread westward into the world of the caliphates. Although it did not acquire the importance of wheat and sorghum in the Muslim areas overall, it took on great significance in certain strategic areas: in desert oases, in river marshes, and in places where rivers flooded the nearby plains naturally or artificially. In these locales it became the main source of food. It had become important in southern Spain by the tenth century, and its cultivation there was pushed unusually far north, all the way to Majorca.[7]

The Indians became remarkably adept at taking crops from Africa and Southeast Asia (both of which were important cradles of domestication), improving their varieties, and developing their commercial potential. In addition to rice, Southeast Asia supplied soybeans, pigs, chickens, bananas, coconuts, and cocayam. When maritime traffic on the Indian Ocean became significant (around the time of the Mauryan Empire [ca. 320–185 B.C.E.]), African domesticates, too, played a significant role in Indian agriculture. Sorghum, for example, now the world's fifth most important cereal food crop, was an East African domesticate. After the Indians acquired it, they developed the high-yielding and drought-resistant variety known as S. *durra*, and this variety then spread back to Africa and throughout Asia. Watermelons also were originally an African domesticate, but it was in India, around the Gupta period, that the large, sweet varieties were developed.[8]

THE CRYSTALLIZATION OF SUGAR

It was during the Gupta period that sugar, a product obtained from another of these overseas imports, developed into an international commodity. Sugar cane may have been domesticated in New Guinea. It was brought to the subcontinent more than a millennium B.C.E., but it was not until the Gupta period that someone in India discovered how to reduce the juice of the sugar cane into crystallized sugar[9] and thereby began an industry that has played a significant role in history for more than a millennium. The process of crystallization yielded the familiar granular stuff, which was much easier to store and ship, and soon thereafter sugar became an important commodity in India's domestic market, and an important export item. Sweets proliferated in India, but elsewhere sugar was used in small quantities. It generally was thought of as a spice and used in combination with other spices in order to season or preserve foods.

Sugar cane prefers plenty of water and tropical climes and, like cotton, generally will not grow (in the Northern hemisphere) north of the fortieth parallel. After the crystallization process spread to China, cane production and sugar manufacturing made a significant contribution to southern China's agricultural and commercial development. Sugar cane cultivation appears to have spread to Iraq (Mesopotamia) also around the time of the Guptas. It probably reached the Yemen and Ethiopia at about the same time.[10] After the seventh century Arab conquests, fields in the vicinity of Basra (at the top of the Persian Gulf, where the Tigris and Euphrates meet) became the most important sugar-producing area within the caliphates. In order to desalinate this land and expand production, the Arabs imported slaves from East Africa. Thus indirectly, if not directly, sugar cultivation in the Persian Gulf area was associated with African slavery.

Even though slave labor in the fields did not persist in the region, the East African population did. Indeed, some of their descendants are famous. Al-Jahiz, one of the most important writers in the history of Arabic literature[11] and the author of the tribute to the Indians quoted above, was a descendant of East African slaves.

It was the Arabs who were responsible for moving sugar cane cultivation and sugar manufacturing westward from Iraq, a movement much more difficult than the move eastward to China, since the western lands were comparatively arid and the Arabs had to adapt the plant to new conditions. By 1000 or so sugar cane was an important crop in the Yemen and various Arab oases, in irrigated areas of Syria, Lebanon, and Palestine, in Egypt, Cyprus, Crete, Sicily, the Maghreb, and Spain. Spain, during Muslim times, was a particularly hospitable environment for sugar production. Although Iberia's sugar industry withered after the Christian conquest, the orange and lemon orchards, which also came from India, survived into the modern period.

The Portuguese spread sugar from the Mediterranean isles to the Atlantic and the Western hemisphere, where sugar production in places such as Brazil and the Caribbean and its relationship to the Atlantic slave trade played so important a historical role.

INDIAN NUMERALS AND MATHEMATICS

Because India was the homeland of Buddhism, pilgrims came from afar to visit its holy places and its various institutions of learning, such as the monastery at Nalanda. The attraction of such institutions, which taught not only the sacred learning of Buddhism but also secular knowledge such as Indian mathematics, was in no way diminished by the fact that the Gupta kings were not Buddhists, but Hindus, and that by the fourth century C.E. Buddhism was no longer the vital force in Indian life that it had once been. The pilgrimage sites remained and the monasteries continued to flourish, and students came from all the Buddhist lands of Asia. A few even came from Iran, from beyond the bounds of Buddhism.

Among the treasures that visiting scholars found in India were its new numbers and the new astronomy and mathematics that these numbers made possible. Indeed, as early as 622 (the year that Muhammad and his followers migrated from Mecca to Medina, almost a century before the Muslims conquered the Indus Valley), the marvels of Indian mathematics were already known to Severuus Sebokht, a monk of the Syrian Christian Church.[12] He not only asserted that the Indians were far ahead of their Greek counterparts, but chided the Greeks for their ignorance of the Indians' work. The Indians, on the other hand, were familiar with the Greek tradition in mathematics as well as their own, which was of about equal vintage. They also were familiar with the Mesopotamian-Iranian tradition, and may have known something about the Chinese. But by the time of the Guptas, they had gone far beyond these classical traditions.

The secret to the Indian success was a unique combination of features possessed by their numerals, the very ones used today throughout the world: 1, 2, 3, 4, 5, 6, 7, 8, 9, and 0. Like some other peoples, they used a decimal system, that is, the base 10. Of more importance, they used a place-value system. (When we write the number 321, we are using the place-value system. That is, we understand that the first number on the right is in the "one's place," that the second number from the right is in the "ten's place" and really means 20, and that the third number from the right is in the "100's place" and really means 300.) The place-value system was not unique to India, but it was an important part of the mix. The unique part of the Indian system was the invention of the number zero, which occurred during the Gupta period. The exact date is not known, but Aryabhata, in a text dated 499 C.E. (the oldest surviving Indian mathematical treatise), is already quite familiar with its uses.

Why it was the Indians who first came up with the idea that "nothing" should be made into a special number and should have a digit to represent it like any other number is not discussed in the literature. But one cannot resist pointing out that it is entirely appropriate that it was in the homeland of the Buddhists that the number zero appeared. Buddhism teaches that salvation lies in an escape from human sufferings. The escape is achieved by extinguishing all desires for dubious goals and illusory pleasures, and the state of being that results from having achieved escape is called Nirvana (which has the idea of extinguished or gone). Emptiness was thus a goal in India, something to be achieved, and it was there that emptiness or nothingness became something, that is, a number.

The invention of the number zero was of great significance. It was the zero that made the place-value system superior to all other systems. The Indians were able thereafter to perform calculations more rapidly and accurately, and were able to see new mathematical relationships and perform much more complicated calculations.[13]

The Indian numerals spread to Southeast Asia and China in the middle centuries of the first millennium C.E. Although the Chinese did not adopt the Indian numerals for mathematical purposes until the modern period, by the Song Dynasty (960–1279) they had added a zero and reformed their own notation system so as to take advantage of the Indian discoveries. Al-Kharazmi (ca. 800–847) introduced Indian mathematics to the Arabic-reading world in his *Treatise on Calculation with the Hindu Numerals* (ca. 825). And by the eleventh century, Muslim scientists of many nationalities were making remarkable advances in algebra and trigonometry.[14]

The Indian numerals spread into the world of the Gothic scholars from Muslim Spain. At the end of the tenth century Gerbert of Aurillac (later Pope Sylvester XI; d. 1003), who had studied in Spain from 967 to 970, introduced them to Europe as the counters on an abacus.[15] The monks and their students were missing the zero, however, until the twelfth century, when al-Kharazmi's treatise on Indian numerals was translated into Latin (in Spain), perhaps by the English monk Adelard of Bath.[16] He brought his Latin translation of Euclid's *Elements* (itself translated from the Arabic) to Christian Europe from Cordova in 1120, and he is known to have translated al-Kharazmi's astronomical tables. Thereafter, al-Kharazmi's works became the prototypes of all medieval Arabic and Latin texts on the subject at least until the fifteenth century. In fact, it is from the title of one of his books that Latin picked up the word "algebra." And in Europe until the modern period the word *algorism*, a corruption of al-Kharazmi's name, meant doing mathematics with Indian numerals instead of doing calculations on an abacus.

For about a century this knowledge of Indian numerals and mathematics in Europe was shared by only a limited number of academics, but in 1202, with the publication of the *Liber Abaci* by Leonardo Fibonacci (also known as Leonardo of Pisa), the situation began to change. His explication of Indian numerals and their uses represents a second and independent introduction of the Indian mathematical tradition into Europe, for he had spent much of his childhood in Bejaia, Algeria, where his father served as the Pisan consul, and it was there that he had learned his mathematics from an Arab tutor. After explaining how the numbers worked, he went on to demonstrate their application to a number of practical commercial problems such as calculating interest and converting currencies. And in 1220, he published *Practica Geometriae*, an important work on Euclidean geometry.

By 1229 the Indian numbers must have been gaining currency in the markets of Italy, for in that year the Senate of Florence decided to ban their use and require that all numbers be written out in letters. Small differences in the way people wrote the numbers and the multiplicity of systems were causing too much confusion and error.[17] Nevertheless, in spite of the difficulties involved in switching over to the new system, the Indian numerals triumphed in the end, and the mathematics of the Renaissance, indeed, modern mathematics, was developed using them.

Suffice it to say that the significance of the Indian numbers was far-reaching. Georges Ifrah, a historian of numbers, claims that their invention had a significance in history comparable to the invention of writing in Mesopotamia.[18] This, of course, is debatable, but it would seem appropriate to begin a discussion of the astronomical and mathematical aspects of the scientific revolution with Aryabhata.

THE DEVELOPMENT OF NEW MARITIME SILK ROADS

INDIA'S SILK PORTS

China's silk industry dates back at least to the Shang Dynasty (ca. 1766–1122 B.C.E.), but the international trade in silk did not become significant until the second century B.C.E., when the earliest Silk Roads emerged. These were the famous overland routes that left Gansu in western China and proceeded to the Mediterranean by way of Iran or central Asia. By the turn of the first century B.C.E. there were equally, if not more, important routes that avoided Parthia and the steppes by transporting the silk, at least part way, by ship. These new routes also left from Gansu and crossed the deserts, but they went south through the mountains and made straight for the ports on India's northwest coast (in what is now Gujarat). Once on the coast, the lustrous cargo was loaded onto ships which took it to Red Sea ports whence it was taken overland to the Mediterranean (most often to Alexandria).[19] Indeed, from the latter part of the first century B.C.E. until the sixth century, for about six hundred years, Indian merchants and Indian Ocean ports played a central role in the silk trade.

By about 25 C.E. the entire length of one of the overland routes from China to India had fallen under the hegemony of a single power, the Kushanas, who developed and maintained these roads and ruled over them until 225 C.E. This dynasty, a contemporary of the Roman Empire, Parthia, and Han China, also played an important role in the cultural history of India and of Asia in general.

By the time of Kanishka (r. 78–96 C.E.), the most illustrious of the Kushana rulers, their power extended across northern India, to the heartland of Buddhism on the Ganges River, and after Kanishka's conversion to the faith, Buddhism spread throughout central Asia and eventually reached China. The Kushana realm thus became a major conduit linking India with the Greek-speaking communities left throughout the Iranian region by Alexander's conquests, and with central Asia and China.

The Kushanas also had an important maritime link with Ethiopia, which controlled much of the trade moving from the Indian Ocean to the Mediterranean via the Red Sea. Ethiopia had long been a major trading nexus, the place where overland routes delivering ivory and other African products met with the maritime routes of the Red Sea and the Indian Ocean. The Kingdom of Axum flourished there more or less at the same time as the various Indian Ocean Silk Roads, from the first to the sixth century C.E. One measure of the prestige garnered by Axum by the third century C.E. is the words of the Iranian prophet Mani (216–276), who referred to the kingdom in the "Kephalaia" as "one of the four greatest empires of the world."[20] The significance of Ethiopia's commercial connection with the Indian silk ports is apparent from the quantity of Kushana coins found there. These coins have been unearthed all the way from China to Ethiopia, but it was in the latter that the largest single cache was found.[21]

It was also during the first century C.E., as a result of this silk trade, that Mediterranean sailors discovered what local Indian Ocean sailors had known for some time—how to use the monsoons, the seasonal winds, to sail from the Red Sea to the East African coast or to India.

More than silk enriched the relationship between the Kushanas and Rome, which had expanded its power to Egypt and the Red

Sea at roughly the same time that the Kushanas had extended their power to India and the Indian Ocean. The two shared an animosity to Parthia and to the various Arab powers between the Indian Ocean and the Mediterranean. The significance of the relationship between the two was amply demonstrated by the warmth of the reception that the Emperor Trajan gave to a Kushana embassy of 99 C.E. Throughout their stay they received special treatment, including the privilege of senatorial seats in the arena.[22]

THE KRA PORTAGE AND FUNAN:
AN ALMOST-ALL-SEA ROUTE
BETWEEN INDIA AND CHINA

The demand for silk during the first century C.E. also stimulated the development of an almost-all-sea route from India to China. Ships from India sailed along the coast of the Bay of Bengal to the Kra (the place where the Malay Peninsula is most narrow) and unloaded their goods on its western shores. After the cargo was portaged across this strip of land, ships on the other side would carry it along the shores of the Gulf of Thailand until it reached the western side of the Mekong Delta.[23]

At the delta, one could find ships going to and coming from China. Most likely, these ships belonged to the Malay sailors, intrepid sea nomads who, as early as the second century B.C.E. sailed as far north as the China coast and who, at least by the first century B.C.E., could be found all the way from New Guinea to Madagascar. They were highly skilled navigators and pioneers of monsoon sailing.[24]

Funan, the first Southeast Asian kingdom to gain international fame, emerged in the first century C.E., at the place where the Mekong comes closest to the Gulf coast. Because the trip from India to Funan was made when the monsoon was blowing off the continent and the trip to China was made when the winds were blowing toward the continent, the travelers on this route usually had to lay over in Funan for several months waiting for the winds to shift.

Even Mediterranean merchants could be found in this Southeast Asian kingdom by the second century C.E. Indeed, two men claiming to be envoys from the Roman Emperor Marcus Aurelius showed up in Han China in 166 C.E. by this almost-all-sea route. (Most likely they were Greek merchants claiming official status in order to get access to the capital, which was then at Luoyang.) Funan was still prospering in the 240s according to the report of two Chinese visitors to the kingdom.[25]

The flourishing of the Kra portage and the Kingdom of Funan was in large part due to the reluctance of coastal sailors coming from India to go around the Malay Peninsula. This situation worked to the advantage of the Malay sailors, who not only bene- fited from carrying the traffic between Funan and China, but also found a new and lucrative market near their home ports. The lengthy stay of the international merchant community at Funan provided them with an opportunity to introduce Southeast Asian goods to the international market. It would appear that their most successful products in Funan's ports were aromatic woods and resins from islands now in Indonesia.[26]

MALAY SAILORS AND THE DEVELOPMENT OF AN ALL-SEA ROUTE FROM INDIA TO CHINA

After 226 and the growth of Sassanian power in Iran, there was a significant transition in trade patterns on the Indian Ocean. The Iranians began picking up silk at what is now Sri Lanka and taking it through the Persian Gulf and then overland to Mediterra- nean markets. Most likely it was the Malay sailors who were bringing the silk from China to Sri Lanka, not by using the Kra portage and clinging to the coast of the Bay of Bengal, but by plying their way through the Strait of Malacca or the Sunda Strait and riding the monsoons to Sri Lanka. In spite of the dangers, at some point in the fourth century the desire for profits had tri- umphed over the fear of maritime disaster, and merchants of many nationalities began to book passage on the Malay sailors' all-sea route through the straits. Presumably it was a faster and cheaper way to China.

Just how dangerous this new all-maritime route might be is clear from the Chinese Buddhist monk Fa Xian's account of his return voyage from India to China.[27] He had left his home monas- tery in Changan, China in 399 C.E., at the age of sixty-five, and gone to Gupta India by way of the trans-Karakoram mountain passes over which the silk destined for India's northwestern ports traveled. This overland route was also not without its dangers. It crossed formidable deserts, and some of the mountain passes were at an altitude of 18,000 feet. In 415, when Fa Xian was eighty years old and contemplating how he was going to return home from India, he dreaded the thought of once again crossing the Karakoram. In particular he could not imagine himself re- crossing the headwaters of the Indus River. At one point the river runs at the bottom of a 10,000-foot-deep chasm, and the bridge over it was no more than a web of rope that careened in the strong winds. Fa Xian had not forgotten that it had taken eighty paces to get over that bridge. Knowing what was behind, but not what was ahead, he chose to go home by the new all-sea route, and thus he discovered that the ways over the seas were just as terrifying as the ways overland.

Not long after leaving Sri Lanka his boat was battered by a storm and started to sink. Just in time it ran aground on an island, and the crew made repairs. But they were lost. Long overdue and with the rations long gone, they finally sailed into some port on or near the Java Sea. One would think that the mere fact that he was once again on land would have enamored Fa Xian with the place, but he does not seem to have liked it. Uncharacteristically he said little about it, except that Hinduism, not Buddhism, flourished there.

After the layover, Fa Xian boarded a boat for China. But it too was hit by a storm and blown far off its course. After seventy days there was still no sight of land, and so the sailors knew they had missed their targeted port and the continent as well. (The normal sailing time to Guangzhou was fifty days.) So they turned left (northwest), knowing that Asia was over there somewhere. Finally they ran aground on the Shandong Peninsula, 1000 miles north of their destination! When they beached they had no idea where they were, but Fa Xian knew he was home when he spotted a patch of Chinese vegetables.

Most of the passengers on these ships were not pious monks willing to risk their lives in order to study in the Buddhist homeland. From Fa Xian's account it appears that he was the only monk on board and that most of his fellow passengers were Hindu merchants.

DISPERSION OF SILK PRODUCTION

During the Han Dynasty the secrets of silk production had begun to spread, probably first to Korea. After the fall of the Han, Buddhist kingdoms in central Asia apparently mastered the art. Some sources say that the production process was known in Southeast Asia, India, and Iran soon thereafter, but it is difficult to distinguish in these materials the difference between the weaving or reweaving of imported silk yarns and the actual production of silk threads from worms. It is safe to say, however, that until the sixth century almost all the silk found on the international routes was Chinese in origin.

It is also well known that until the sixth century C.E. the peoples of the Mediterranean had no idea that silk was spun by a worm that feeds on mulberry leaves, even though there was already a sizable silk-weaving industry in eastern Byzantine lands. This was because the weavers used imported yarn or rewove imported textiles. The ability to produce raw silk did not reach the eastern Mediterranean until the sixth century, during Justinian's famous silk crisis. A war had broken out between Byzantium and Iran in 527, and by the 540s the amount of silk reaching Byzantine centers had fallen off dramatically. Among other things, the shortage of supplies left large numbers of weavers out of work.

Although a shortage of silk may not seem to be dire, Justinian treated the situation as a crisis. The peremptory measures that he then took (first trying to legislate the price and then confiscating the weaving establishments) are somewhat understandable if one realizes that the importance of imported silk and spice was not limited to the role they played in the Byzantine economy. Nor did they serve merely to please the empire's rich and powerful. Silk was political capital. The display of power through ceremonies of church and state required such imports, and so did much of Byzantine diplomacy. Silk shrouds and aromatic resins were used in a new Christian burial service, and both silk and pepper were used to reward, identify, and strengthen those frontier tribal leaders who allied with the empire. And when the alliances fell through, these imported "luxury" goods were used to bribe them. "Alaric, for example, exacted from Rome a ransom which included 4000 silken tunics and 3000 lb. of pepper, and Byzantine envoys had to soothe Attila's court with gifts of silk and Indian gems."[28]

In the end, according to a tradition repeated by Procopius, Justinian's silk crisis was solved by one of history's more remarkable acts of industrial espionage. In 551 Nestorian monks told Justinian the true story of silk production and suggested that they knew where to get some of the precious worms. By 553 they had successfully smuggled the worms from China to Byzantium in a bamboo cane.[29] There is some question about the date of this escapade and even about whether or not the monks did it, but by the middle of the sixth century the cultivation of mulberry trees and the production of silk were established in the Byzantine lands of the eastern Mediterranean. Thereafter, China was no longer the only significant producer. Silk textile manufacturing slowly spread to Italy, but it was not important there until the twelfth century.[30] The industry began to flourish under Roger II, the Norman ruler of Sicily, who took the matter of technology transfer firmly in hand when he sacked the Byzantine towns of Corinth and Thebes in 1147, took their silk producers prisoner, and moved them to Palermo.

SILK AND THE POST-1500 TRANS-PACIFIC TRADE

Chinese silk was also responsible in large part for the success of the first trans-Pacific trade route, the Acapulco-Manila run that developed after 1571. The Spaniards had seized the Philippines hoping for a share of the spice trade, but their spice business turned out to be unsuccessful. Instead, the Spaniards in Mexico (whence the Philippines was administered) sought their fortunes by trading American silver for Chinese silk, which could be gotten in Manila. (A Chinese merchant community had existed in Manila for centuries, and there was a somewhat newer and smaller community of Japanese merchants.) The Manila galleons (manufactured in the Philippines by Asian craftsmen) carried great quantities of silver west across the Pacific, and great quantities of silk sailed toward the east. Much of the silk was destined for Spanish markets and was portaged across Mexico to be loaded on Atlantic-crossing ships at Vera Cruz. C.G.F. Sinkins, in *The Traditional Trade of Asia,* has described the Chinese trade at Manila, indicating that it was much more than a trade in luxury goods.

> [Portuguese] Macao obtained great benefit from this new trade, but silk also reached Manila in Chinese junks, thirty to fifty of which arrived each year. They brought, in addition to silk and such other luxury wares as velvet, porcelain, jade, and bronze, local requirements for iron-ware, gunpowder, saltpetre, furniture, and many kinds of food.
>
> After paying modest harbour dues of 3 per cent, they took away bullion and such quantities of the Mexican dollar to Canton, Amoy, and Ningpo that it soon became the principal currency on the China coast [and remained the mainstay of Chinese currency until the 20th century, one might add]. In the peak year of 1597, Acapulco sent to Manila 12,000,000 pesos, a higher figure than the value of Spain's whole trans-Atlantic trade [for that year, presumably], but in more normal years the export was 3,000,000 to 5,000,000.[31]

According to Simkins, the Japanese were also involved in the Spanish trade, and would have like to have been more involved.

> . . . Japanese interest in trade was shown by an agreement in 1609, for friendly treatment of Spanish ships in return for aid in shipbuilding and mining; it was also shown by the arrival of two

Japanese ships in 1613 and 1616 at Acapulco where their welcome was not so friendly.[32]

Indeed, such new links between China and the Western hemisphere may have been an important factor in the social turmoil that brought down the Ming Dynasty (1368–1644). The inflow of large amounts of American and Japanese silver from 1570 until the 1630s had encouraged the further monetarization of China's economy, and the government began to insist that peasants pay their taxes in money instead of grain. Also because of the silver, the government had become accustomed to living beyond its means. (At its peak, during the early years of the seventeenth century, the inflow had been between 50,000 and 100,000 kilograms per year.) When the inflow of silver dropped precipitously in the 1630s, China's economy was thrown into turmoil. The government went bankrupt, and, unable to contend with either its internal or external enemies, it fell to the Manchus in 1644.[33]

Mesoamerican and Andean crops such as peanuts, corn, and sweet potatoes also made their way to China by a remarkably early date, within decades of the first voyage made by Columbus. Eventually, in part as a result of these crops, the acreage under cultivation in China doubled, and the empire's population tripled.[34] It may well be that their impact was greater in China than in Europe since both rice and wheat, the two main staples in China, are relatively particular about their growing conditions. Thus in the sixteenth century there was a considerable amount of waste land (dry hills, lofty mountains, and sandy loams) that was not used for farming. The Mexican and Peruvian crops, however, are amazingly hardy and productive even under adverse conditions, and they are ideal for Chinese latitudes, soil, and other growing conditions, and they, thus, filled up what until their introduction had been waste land.[35] [*For more on this topic see Theopolis Fair's chapter, "Asia and Latin America in the Context of World History."*]

THE DEVELOPMENT OF THE SPICE TRADE

PEPPER

Black pepper kernels, the kind that one can now buy in any grocery store, were once harvested for the international environment only in southern India. As early as Mauryan times (ca. 320–185 B.C.E.), when political and economic networks first linked the subcontinent's northern and southern parts, Indians in the north also began using quantities of pepper and other southern spices. Political integration, however, rarely equaled the economic, and the pepper coasts, in particular, maintained a tradition of independence throughout much of Indian history.

When the Mediterranean merchants of the first century C.E. figured out how to get to India by sea, they not only found silk in its northwestern ports, they also discovered the great pepper marts of southern India. Soon thereafter the Mediterranean demand for pepper outgrew the Indian-produced supply, and pepper grown in Sumatra then began showing up in India's southern ports in order to supply this market.[36]

In large part, it was this trade in spice rather than silk that, from the fourth to the sixth century, sustained the maritime trade route from India via the Red Sea to the Mediterranean. After the rise of the Sassanian Empire in the early part of the third century, the Iranians took over much of the silk trade, purchasing their cargoes in Sri Lanka and moving them through the Persian Gulf and then overland to the Mediterranean. As a result, the Red Sea trade experienced a noticeable slump. It was at this point in time that two newly Christianized powers—Byzantium and Axum— formed an alliance to revive this route, and although they did not succeed in recovering the silk trade, they did stimulate a thriving trade in spices.

Constantine pursued a comprehensive Red Sea policy and, according to one authority, "can be credited with reopening the world of the Southern Semites for Roman trade."[37] One of the crucial elements in the Byzantine success in redeveloping this route was the success of its alliance with the Ethiopian kingdom of Axum. King Ezana of Axum had converted to Christianity at about the same time that Constantine established his new Christian capital at Constantinople.

The Axumite Kingdom then dealt with their common concern regarding the power of the Sabaeans and the Himyarites, ancient Jewish communities in the Yemen. These communities had long been active in the Red Sea trade and seemed to have some connection with the Sassanians. At any rate, their trading position appeared to be waxing along with the fortunes of the new Iranian empire. Constantine thus sought an alliance with the Ethiopian king against them.

Although this Byzantine-Ethiopian alliance was unable to regain the silk trade that Iran now dominated, they did succeed in creating a successful Red Sea spice trade by establishing a profitable commercial relationship with merchants in the pepper ports of southern India and in Sri Lanka. Finds of Byzantine coins in southern India testify to the fact that this trade flourished from the time of Constantine I until the reign of Justin I (518–527). Although the Greeks did on occasion go as far as Sri Lanka, they were not found in significant numbers any further than Socotra (an island off the southern Arabian coast),[38] and most of these coins were taken to Indian by Ethiopian traders. Until the sixth century this African kingdom remained the predominant commercial power on the Red Sea and successfully skirted Iranian power in the Arabian Sea.[39]

A SIXTH-CENTURY CRISIS

The lucrative Red Sea spice route prospered until the middle of the sixth century, when troubles developed all along the maritime trade routes from China to the Mediterranean. Hephthalites (known as the White Huns) broke through the Iranian shield yet again in 520, and although the Guptas once more succeeded in repelling them, their power was weakened. Domestic problems also abounded, and by 535 their empire had faded away. The Southeast Asian empire of Funan also fell in the middle of the sixth century, and its territories were overrun by its northern neighbor, Chenla. There was also an outbreak of bubonic plague which entered the Mediterranean area in 541, apparently by the Red Sea route, and by 542 it had reached Constantinople. Plague and famine continued to devastate the eastern Mediterranean and Red Sea area for some 200 years. The last outbreak, in 747, left the city of Constantine "practically uninhabited."[40]

In the meantime Justinian was fighting two wars with Iran (ca. 527–532 and 540–562). No sooner had the second war ended than the Sassanians, in 570, sent an expedition across the Arabian Peninsula and destroyed the Ethiopian armies in the Yemen, and for the next sixty years, the Iranians occupied the area. In the early seventh century an Iranian army invaded Byzantium and managed to get all the way to Alexandria. It seemed that all was lost until Heraclius sailed in from Carthage to rescue the empire and roll back the enemy. In 629, after he had recovered Jerusalem, one of the first to send his congratulations was Harsha (r. 606–647),[41] an Indian prince who had managed to reconstruct an imperial umbrella over much of what had been the Gupta Empire. Indeed, in 629 Harsha might have thought that Heraclius would be able to replicate the successes of Constantine and Justinian, and re-create the alliance with Ethiopia that would guarantee the security of the Red Sea route.

The hot and cold wars between the Zoroastrians and the Christians came to an end only when Muhammad, a merchant of Mecca founded a new religion, and Muslim armies conquered all the overland routes between the Indian Ocean and the Mediterranean, both those focused on the Red Sea and those focused on the Persian Gulf. By the time most of the fighting was over and the eastern Mediterranean had begun to recover from its years of epidemic, famine, and war, the Abbasid Caliphate had established itself at Baghdad, and the Persian Gulf route was favored. The Red Sea would not regain its commercial importance for another three centuries, until the North African Fatimids conquered Egypt in the tenth century.

THE FINE SPICES

While Funan, India, the Red Sea area, and the Mediterranean were experiencing so much turmoil, the Chinese market for spices and other Southeast Asian products was growing. (The Chinese usually refer to this spice trade as the aromatics and medicine trade.) Furthermore, travel on the India-to-China route through the Strait of Malacca had become routine by the seventh century, and East Asia's Buddhist monks could expect to find a Buddhist rather than a Hindu realm to accommodate them during their stay in Southeast Asia. The first of the new Southeast Asian kingdoms to capture this trade (and the layover business) was Buddhist Srivijaya, which had its center in the vicinity of modern Palembang on the island of Sumatra, quite near the Strait of Malacca.[42]

It was also about this time that the trade in the "fine spices," cloves, nutmeg, and mace, assumed the same importance as the pepper trade. Small amounts of these spices had reached India and China in earlier centuries, but they did not become truly significant until around the seventh century. For centuries their importance continued to grow, and by the fifteenth and sixteenth centuries these spices would become what made the world go around, or at least, what made men go around the world.

Commercial qualities of the fine spices came only from the islands of Molucca, which are located some 2000 miles east of the Strait of Malacca. Clove trees grew on five small islands off the western coast of Halmahera (Ternate, Tidor, Motir, Makian, and Batjan). Nutmeg and mace, both of which come from the same tree, would not grow anywhere but in the Banda Islands, which appear on most maps as dots in the middle of the Banda Sea.

Palembang, Srivijaya's center near the Strait of Malacca, prospered as a depot for these fine spices, and for other Southeast
Asian products. From the late seventh until the eleventh century
the Moluccans delivered their spices to the Srivijayan port, where
international shippers congregated. A great many of the ships
coming into its ports were from the Arab Caliphate, plying their
way between China and the Persian Gulf. But Srivijaya's good
fortune came to an end early in the eleventh century, when it
suffered two blows: an invasion from the Chola Kingdom of southern India in 1025 and the development of a new commercial
center in East Java that managed to draw the international traffic
1000 miles east of the Strait.

TRANSITIONS IN SOUTHEAST ASIA AND
THE RECOVERY OF THE RED SEA ROUTE

The transporters of the Moluccan fine spices had always passed
near East Java, more or less the halfway mark, on their way to and
from Srivijaya's ports. But until about 900 C.E. the port area in
East Java (around present-day Surabaya) had not played an important role in international trade. But by 1037, Airlanga, one East
Java's most illustrious rulers, had dammed the Brantas and constructed a safe harbor.[43] Rice was now abundant at Surabaya, and
the people of the Moluccas began to devote almost all their efforts
to spice production. They then took their spices to East Java and
traded them for rice, and East Java became the international depot
for the rare Moluccan spices as well as for pepper. It was also at
this point that Chinese ships began for the first time to venture
south to the spice ports of Southeast Asia.

East Java's development was also contemporary with a weakening
of Baghdad's political and military position and the emergence of
strong regional powers within the caliphate. In the middle of the
tenth century the Fatimids of North Africa gained control of Egypt
(969–1171), established a rival caliph, and restored the Red Sea to
its former commercial importance. At roughly the same time the
Venetians managed to force important trading concessions from Byzantium, and the towns and cities of Western Europe's nascent
commercial revolution were growing. The Venetians and other Italian
city-states then became the suppliers of "sugar and spice and everything nice" to an expanding Western European market.

The thirteenth century brought further transformations that
served to strengthen the linkage between Southeast Asian and
western Mediterranean markets. In 1204 the Venetians and the

members of the Fourth Crusade occupied Constantinople. Venetians, Genoese, and Catalans thereafter competed for what had been the Byzantine position not only in the Mediterranean but in the Black Sea as well. Mongol armies conquered Kiev, Baghdad, and northern China. And Ghana's power was destroyed by the blacksmith king of Sosso.

In the midst of this disruption, the new Mamluk rulers of Egypt (1250–1517) managed to halt the Mongol advance and protect Egypt and the Red Sea route. They soon acquired the prestigious responsibility of protecting Mecca and Medina and organizing the grand pilgrimages. And Majapahit, the paramount power in East Java after the 1290s, managed to divert a Mongol invasion and destroy the Mongol troops after allying with them to wipe out local rivals. And an heir apparent of Mali, a former tributary state of Ghana's, revenged Ghana by defeating Sosso and creating an even grander empire.

Thus by 1300 conditions were ideal for the flow of spices from Southeast Asia to a rapidly developing western Europe. In fact, the expansion of western European demand had its greatest market impact on Southeast Asia not in the sixteenth century, when the Portuguese came by sea, but in the fourteenth and fifteenth centuries.[44] These were also the years when the Renaissance flourished in Italy (Dante, by the way, was listed as a spice dealer in Florence), when the most splendid mosques and palaces were built in Cairo,[45] and when much of maritime Southeast Asia became Muslim.

THE ESTABLISHMENT OF MALACCA

By 1400 the Majapahit government in East Java was in crisis. Business was good, and merchants in the ports on Java's northern coast began to feel that Majapahit's power over them was burdensome. Thereafter Majapahit became preoccupied with problems nearby. Although it was still capable of destroying those who attempted to establish rival kingdoms in the Strait of Malacca, it could not maintain constant vigilance over its large realm, which by that time stretched beyond the boundaries of contemporary Indonesia. At any rate it could not meet Chinese expectations with regard to security in the strait. The Ming Dynasty was annoyed by a Chinese pirate lair at Palembang, and the first of Zheng He's [Cheng Ho] expeditions (1405–1407) "cleaned up" this problem.[46] (Zheng arrested the pirate and took him back to China for prosecution.) Indeed, Zheng He's expeditions, on several occasions, engaged in what might be called gunboat diplomacy, all the way from the strait to Sri Lanka. He used his formidable naval power to overthrow those whom the Ming Dynasty thought of as illegitimate, and to install those upon whom the Chinese could depend to maintain stability in the region.

In 1406, while still on the first expedition, he played a crucial role in the establishment of the international port at Malacca. He lent the support of his fleet to a fledgling kingdom that had just been established in 1402 by a refugee prince from another part of the strait. The prince had already been wiped out by Majapahit in a previous attempt at another location, and Zheng He's umbrella of protection was an important factor in Malacca's survival during its early and most vulnerable years.[47]

Thereafter the Moluccan spice growers took ever larger quantities of their spices to the Strait of Malacca. Indeed, by the turn of the sixteenth century, the Banda Islanders were producing some 1200 metric tons of nutmeg and 100 metric tons of mace each year.[48] Tome Pires, an early sixteenth century observer, made a list of the merchants at Malacca that indicates that they came from sixty different places, including Byzantium, Ethiopia, and the East African ports of Kilwa and Malindi.[49]

One need not dwell upon the importance that the spice trade had for Western Europe from the late fifteenth to the late seventeenth centuries. It was the desire to find a westward all-sea route to the Spice Islands that inspired Isabella and Ferdinand to bankroll Columbus. As everyone knows, Columbus did not make it to the East Indies. Nevertheless, it is said that until his death, he insisted, and perhaps still believed, that the Caribbean islands he found were in Asia.

By 1492 the Portuguese had been trading on West Africa's southern coast for decades, and in 1488, due to a storm, Bartolomeu Dias had actually passed the Cape of Good Hope, without seeing it, and sailed into the Indian Ocean. It was on his way back to the Atlantic that he spotted what he called the Cape of Storms. But Dias' discovery was not followed up until after Columbus returned to Spain in March 1493 and made his claim to have found the Indies (which is to say the Spice Islands) by sailing west. The Portuguese decision to send a fleet around the Cape to the Indies was made in 1495, and under the command of Vasco da Gama, it sailed in 1497. Furthermore, Magellan's expedition of 1519–22, which included the first ship to sail all around the globe, was first and foremost an attempt to circumnavigate the still unappreciated Western hemisphere in order to get to the Spice Islands.[50]

Although historians often describe the circumnavigation of Africa as an end-run around the areas of Muslim control, the Iberian voyages were just as much an attempt to get around Venice and the Mediterranean trade routes which it controlled. Tome Pires was acutely aware of this, and when he wrote home about Malacca, his comment was none other than, "Whoever is lord of Malacca has his hands on the throat of Venice."[51]

But Malacca was not the throat. The Red Sea was, and the Portuguese could not throttle it for long. Although their naval battles in the Indian Ocean led to serious dislocations on the established maritime routes, by 1560 Venetian trade had made a complete recovery due to a "Red Sea Gap" maintained by the Ottomans. In 1513 a Muslim navy defeated Albuquerque in the crucial battle for Aden. By 1538 the Ottomans had firm control over the Red Sea and Aden, and by 1560 more spices were reaching Alexandria than Lisbon.[52]

THE DUTCH SEIZURE OF THE BANDA ISLANDS

It was not the Portuguese but the Dutch who did permanent damage to the business along many of the old spice routes. The Dutch began by demanding that the Banda Islanders provide them with a monopoly on all the spices that they produced, a demand that was rejected. The Banda Islanders had always asserted their autonomy, especially when it came to matters of trade and culture. Unlike the majority of their neighbors, including the clove producers on Ternate and Tidore, they had not become Muslims. Nor had they made any significant compromises with the Portuguese.

The Dutch found the islanders' independent attitude to be unacceptable, and in 1621 used their shipborne military capabilities to destroy them. The massacre was possible only because the islands were so small that they could be treated as immobile enemy ships. (On land, European military capabilities in Asia were not yet the equal of those of the local rulers.) Only a handful of the 15,000 Banda Islanders escaped. Many thousands were killed, and the rest were taken away to be sold as slaves.[53]

PATTERNS OF DISPERSION OF
SOUTHERN ASIAN THINGS

Judging from the selection of items discussed in this chapter, there seem to have been several episodes of dispersion with regard to Indian or Southeast Asian goods. In the earliest period one sees the dispersion first of cotton to Mesopotamia (around the fourth century B.C.E.) and then of rice and sugar. By the sixth century C.E. these items can be found all around the coastal areas of the western half of the Indian Ocean, at least as far as Ethiopia. The route from India to Mesopotamia had been an ancient maritime route, but the dispersion of Indian goods to Ethiopia would seem to reflect the new levels of interaction that grew from the Indian Ocean networks, particularly the route from India to the Red Sea, that flourished in the first six centuries C.E.

Another major episode of dispersion was the movement of such things as sugar, cotton, and mathematics from India to China, a process that probably began around the fourth century C.E. and reached its peak during the Tang Dynasty (618–906). When this movement began, China was not unified, and a number of Buddhist kingdoms ruled its various parts. Although merchants may have played some role in it, this dispersion seems to have been closely linked to the spread of Buddhism and Buddhist monasteries from India to China. Many of the products were agricultural, and monasteries, both in India and in China, maintained large agricultural establishments.

A third episode came as the result of the rise of Islam and the Arab conquests. After the Arab conquest of the Indus River valley between 708 and 715, Indian things begin to move westward. This process seems to culminate around the year 1000, by which time Muslim Spain was flourishing and attracting Christian monks, and by 1200 or so the Muslim version of what had been the Indian complex was beginning to have an impact on Italy.

Although Indian numerals and mathematics could and did spread into northwestern Europe, the important commercial crops such as cotton and sugar could not follow the roads north out of Spain and Italy. These lucrative crops would not grow in such cold climes, and it was only because these northerners, by the seventeenth century, possessed the West Indies that they were able to ensure their own supplies of sugar during the mercantilist age and of cotton during the early stages of the industrial revolution.

The spices, unlike sugar, cotton, rice, and silk, resisted all pre-1500 attempts to transplant them to new locations. In the pre-1500 period black pepper vines could not be found any further from India than Java. And prior to 1700, for commercial purposes, the fine spices were produced only in the Moluccas.

The Moluccans went to great lengths to prevent any sort of agricultural espionage, but their success may have been due to natural causes. The seeds are fragile and do not keep well, and the trees are exceedingly particular about their growing conditions. There was a common saying about these trees, "that nutmeg must be able to smell the sea, and cloves must see it."[54]

Because the spices would not move, everyone except the Moluccans had to content themselves with their transport and trade, rather than their production. Consequently, in order to avoid a long series of middlemen, one had to go directly to the Southeast Asian markets that distributed these spices. Otherwise, someone between Indonesia and the spices' ultimate destination was in a position to take part in at least a piece of that lucrative trade. As a result of the Mediterranean market, Indians, Ethiopians, Iranians, Arabs, the Fatimids, the Mamluks, the Ottomans, the Byzantines, and the Italians all did very well, at one time or another.

INDIANS, ARABS, AND BULLION SOURCES

GOLD SOURCES DEVELOPED BY INDIA

During Mauryan times, much of India's gold came from the north, from Siberia, and arrived in India by way of trade routes across the steppe and through the mountain passes. Shortly before the collapse of the Mauryans in 185 B.C.E., the Xiongnu [Hsiung-nu] (known in the West as the Hun) Empire arose on the steppe and the disturbances thus created appear to have deprived India of this source and encouraged maritime expeditions to Southeast Asia in search of an alternative supply. Thereafter, despite the dangers well recorded in the *Jataka* stories, Indian adventurers set sail for what they called the Land of Gold (Suvarnabhumi), that is, the Malay Peninsula and its environs.[55]

With the development of the Mediterranean market for silk and spice, both of which could be purchased in India, Roman bullion also began to augment the Indian supply. "Pliny, a well-informed advisor to Vepasian (C.E. 69–79), reckoned that each year Indian trade drained Rome of 12,500,000 denarii."[56] This supply, however, was abruptly curtailed when Vespasian prohibited the export of precious metals. This act of Roman protectionism has also been given as a reason for India's increasing exploitation of Southeast Asian sources of gold.[57] The Indian search for new sources of gold may also have contributed to the development of its production in southern Africa (in present-day Zimbabwe) in the sixth century C.E.[58] This African gold may have reached India by way of Ethiopia.

THE ARABS AND SILVER

After the Arabs had conquered the trade routes linking the Mediterranean and the Indian Ocean, they, too, expended considerable efforts developing new sources of bullion. They had conquered an Iranian sphere, whose currency had been silver, and a portion of the Byzantine realm, where the currency had been based on gold. Until about 725 both gold and silver currencies were used in the formerly Byzantine lands, but thereafter the silver became predominant.

During the same period in which silver was becoming the principal currency in the western part of the realm as well as the eastern part, and for more than a hundred years thereafter, from 650 until 850, its value, relative to gold, was declining. The main reason for this decline was that the Arabs had conquered what turned out to be two of the world's richest silver mining areas and had begun to mine and coin silver so enthusiastically that they caused what might be called a "silver glut." Near Tashkent (around the end of the eighth century) the Arabs reopened a silver mine that had been closed down before their arrival. In the early part of the ninth century they learned of a veritable Eastern hemisphere "Potosi," a silver mountain at Bajahir in the Hindu Kush (modern Afghanistan), and by 850 coins were being minted there as well.[59]

THE ARABS AND GOLD TO 1200

Around 850, the value of silver, relative to gold, stopped declining and began to go up, and by about 940 the gold-to-silver ratio had changed from one to seventeen to one to twelve. (Thus between 650 and 850 there had been a 70 percent rise and between 850 and 940 there had been a 50 percent decline in the value of gold. By 940 silver had almost, but not quite, regained its mid-seventh century value [one gram of gold to ten grams of silver].) The most likely reason for this is the large amount of gold that the Arabs introduced onto the hemisphere's trade routes in the eighth and ninth centuries. In other words, a "gold glut" had nearly erased the "silver glut."

Some of the gold that was causing this glut came from East Africa. By the eighth century, Arab traders were congregating in Kilwa, which was emerging as an important staging area for Zimbabwe's gold.[60] The Arabs were also able to acquire access to West African gold, which eventually would double the amount of gold in international circulation.⁶¹ When the Arabs conquered North Africa in the eighth century, they noticed that Berber tribesmen seemed to have an excellent source of gold. Investigation revealed that it arrived by camel along trans-Saharan routes that linked North Africa with the West African empire of Ghana.

Between 745 and 755 Abdul al Rahman, the Arab ruler of southern Morocco, immediately set about developing these routes across the Sahara. The international demand for gold stimulated the development of new West African gold fields, and by 1100 so much gold was flowing through Ghana that its price (relative to silver) on international markets dropped even further. Thereafter it fell throughout Europe, including England, and by the thirteenth century the gold glut had reached even China. Lopez, a Chinese scholar, found that "the gold to silver ratio in China fell from one to 12.1 in 1209 to one to 7.6 in 1282."⁶² Thus it appears that by the end of the thirteenth century the price of gold had fallen across the entire Eurasian continent.

Assuming that these fluctuations were due solely to supply, one could make the following generalizations. It appears that from 650 to 850 new sources of silver drove the value of gold (relative to silver) up 70 percent (even at a time when African gold had begun to increase the gold supply). However, after 850 the flow of gold was so great that its value (relative to silver) fell from 1 to 17 to 1 to 7.6 shortly before 1300. Thus in spite of the enormous proportions of the original silver glut, the subsequent gold glut reduced the value of gold by 24 percent, compared to what it had been shortly after the Arab Caliphate was established. Suffice it to say that the post-650 Arab contribution to the international bullion supply was certainly comparable to the post-1500 Spanish contribution.

THE POST-1200 PERIOD

In spite of the decline in the value of gold relative to silver, the flow of African gold onto international trade routes increased considerably in the post-1200 period, after the Mongol invasions, the coup that brought the Mamluks to power in Egypt, and the Mamluk defeat of the Mongols. The trans-Saharan trade routes had been slowly shifting eastward, and Morocco was no longer the main Mediterranean terminal for gold. By the time that Mali was established (ca. 1230), gold was reaching most of the ports on the Mediterranean's southern coast. This provided an opportunity for Venetian merchants who exchanged their timber and slaves and other northern products for gold. This gold then enabled them to go to Mamluk ports and purchase Asian and African imports, which they then sold in western European markets.

It was also after 1200 that there was a remarkable increase in the amount of gold coming out of East Africa.[63] Zimbabwe's political fortunes grew along with the flow of gold, and it reached the zenith of its power and glory during the centuries between 1200 and the arrival of the Portuguese on the East African coast. It is now accepted that the gold from East African ports amounted to "an annual average export of more than 1,000 kilograms for the peak periods during the fifteenth century."[64] (These estimates indicate that fifteenth-century gold exports from East Africa are roughly comparable with annual average exports of gold from British West Africa during the second half of the nineteenth century.)

One could thus see the fifteenth- and sixteenth-century Portuguese as followers in the footsteps (and the Indian Ocean wakes) of the Arabs. It is well known that the desire to find the source of West African gold was a significant factor in the Portuguese decision to explore the African coast and establish a maritime route to West Africa. Furthermore, once they had rounded the Cape, the gold that the Portuguese acquired in West and East Africa played an essential role in the early development of their trade in Indian Ocean and Pacific ports. Without it, they would have been unable to acquire the cargoes of spices and other Asian products that they carried back to Lisbon. Insofar as the Spaniards caused a silver glut using Western hemisphere sources, they, too, might be seen as successors to the Arabs.

THE TRANSFORMATION OF CHINA: THE FLOURISHING OF THE SOUTH

When Joseph Needham, in a 1964 article,[65] summarized the work he had done by that time on the history of Chinese science and technology, he listed forty-one items that originated in Asia and spread to Europe. Only six of the Chinese items will be discussed here (paper, the compass, the equine collar harness, porcelain, printing, and gunpowder). Of these six, only two, paper and the compass, were invented before or during the Han Dynasty (206 B.C.E. to 221 C.E.). The other four were invented only after the fall of the Han Dynasty and the establishment of Mahayana Buddhism in China.

Although the manufacturing and technological capabilities that the Chinese inherited from their Han Dynasty ancestors were considerable, many of the truly remarkable technological break-throughs came about only after several centuries of intensive interaction with central Asia, India, and Southeast Asia. The intensity and the duration of this borrowing were directly related to the growing importance of Buddhism in China after the fall of the Han, and particularly to the establishment of Buddhist monasteries, which prospered in China from at least the fourth century to the ninth century.

The Buddhist realm, at one time or another, included most of the lands and all of the roads from Pakistan to Japan. In the seventh century A.D., around the time that both printing and gunpowder were developed in China, Buddhist monasteries and the Buddhist worldview still flourished on the Indian subcontinent and in Sri Lanka, central Asia, China, and Korea, and were newly established in maritime Southeast Asia and Japan. The individuals living or staying at a Chinese monastery or temple at any given time often formed an international community whose impact on China's material and intellectual culture was profound.

The full measure of this interaction between what was already Chinese and what would become sinicized and the various transformations brought about by this interaction are not yet fully understood. Nevertheless, it is possible to say with some assurance that the material exchange that accompanied China's incorporation into the Buddhist realm had a greater impact on the south than on the north. Although Indian mathematics would seem to hold equal significance for the north and the south, many of the items coming from India and Southeast Asia, including a number of those that most changed China, were more appropriate for southern climes, and thereby played an important role in stimulating the transference of regional preeminence from the north to the south, a trend that did not abate until the fifteenth century. At the same time, this trend toward southern preeminence was reinforced periodically by steppe invasions that forced northern Chinese to take refuge in the south, thus increasing the demand for products that the new southern developments could supply.

The increasingly important role of the south is apparent in Chinese political history. When the Sui Dynasty (581–618 C.E.) reunited the empire for the first time since the third century, its capital was located at Changan, in the Wei River valley, where the capital of the Han had been. Nevertheless, it could not escape the north's new dependency on the southern rice bowls. Nor could it reproduce the south's new agricultural productivity in the north.

The Sui Dynasty could not rely on coastal shipping to move the rice north because of storms and pirates in coastal waters. The solution was the Grand Canal, which the Sui Dynasty constructed. The Tang Dynasty also established its capital at Changan, but it, too, was captivated by its exotic south. Indeed, the Grand Canal was its economic lifeline.[66] As mentioned earlier in the sections on Indian agriculture, cotton, indigo, and sugar were well established in China south of the Huai River by the time of the Tang Dynasty, and were already making a significant contribution to its agricultural and commercial development.

By the time of the An Lushan Rebellion (755), when the Tang Dynasty's power and prestige had begun to decline, the northern political reconsolidation also began to break down, and one can see the beginning of a momentous shift from north to south in the Chinese center of gravity. The founder of the Song Dynasty (960–1279) chose to put his capital at Kaifeng, which was then near the junction of the Yellow River and the Grand Canal. In 1127, when the Song Dynasty lost the Kaifeng area to a Jurchen people (invaders from the northeastern forests), the capital was moved to Hangzhou, south of the Yangzi (Yangtze) River. This was the first time that the imperial capital had been located in the south, in what was already the economic heartland of the empire, and the dynasty continued to flourish even without its northern rim.

CHAMPA RICE

In the early part of the Song Dynasty, when the capital was still at Kaifeng, a new variety of early-ripening rice was introduced into China from Champa, a kingdom then located near the Mekong River Delta in what is now Vietnam, and by 1012 it had been introduced to the lower Yangzi and Huai river regions.[67] The manner of its introduction was recorded by the Buddhist monk Shu Wenying.

> Emperor Cheng-tsung [Zhengzong] (998–1022), being deeply concerned with agriculture, came to know that the Champa rice was drought-resistant and that the green lentils of India were famous for their heavy yield and large seeds. Special envoys, bringing precious things, were dispatched [to these states], with a view to securing these varieties. . . . When [China's] first harvests were reaped in the autumn, [Zhengzong] called his intimate ministers to taste them and composed poems for Champa rice and Indian green lentils.[68]

Because this variety of rice was relatively more drought-resistant, it could be grown in places that older varieties had failed, especially on higher land and on terraces that climb hilly slopes, and it ripened even faster than the other early-ripening varieties already grown in China. This made double-cropping possible in more areas, and in some places, even triple cropping became possible.

Prior to the Song Dynasty, China's population had waxed and waned over the centuries, but, overall, it did not regain its Han Dynasty peak of 59.5 million in C.E.2 until the Tang Dynasty. However, between 754 (when the population was about 53 million) and the early twelfth century, the population in southern China tripled,[69] and the total population doubled, exceeding the 100,000,000 mark.[70] Much of this increase was due to the productivity of new varieties of rice, and, after about 1000 C.E., especially to Champa rice, which had made it possible to double the amount of rice acreage.[71] Indeed, the hardiness and the productivity of various varieties of rice were and are in large part responsible for the density of population in South, Southeast, and East Asia, which together now account for approximately 55 percent of the world population.

The growing importance of the south had tremendous social and political significance. In relative terms, it weakened the north, where privileged, non-tax-paying aristocrats and aristocratic institutions predominated, and lent new significance to the south, which had long been a frontier area. Below the Huai River, aristocratic roots were not well established. In the new southern society the tax-paying gentry and commercial communities were the important people, and thus this shift toward the south underlay a momentous social transformation that was consolidated during the Song Dynasty. Thereafter aristocracies in China became marginal, and the principal path to the highest offices in the land became the civil service examination system, which was open to 98 percent of the male population. The new importance of the south also encouraged China to face south toward the Southern Ocean (the South China Sea, the Indian Ocean, and parts between) for the first time, and Chinese maritime capabilities developed steadily from the twelfth century to the fifteenth.

THINGS CHINESE

PAPER

The invention of paper made from vegetable materials is often attributed to Cai Lun, who presented his product to an emperor of the Han Dynasty in 105 C.E. However, recent archaeological find-ings have pushed paper's existence back to the first century B.C.E.,[72] which suggests that Cai Lun's achievement lay in im-proving an already existing product. The early availability of paper in China encouraged the preservation and the development of China's great literary tradition, and one might add that it doubt-less contributed to the development of the imperial bureaucracy and other forms of paper-pushing during the Han. Shortly after 300 C.E. paper manufacturing spread to Korea and Vietnam, and subsequently from Korea to Japan.[73] East Asians still produce some of the world's finest papers, and many are the connoisseurs among them who can easily tell which is the up-side and which is the down side of a sheet.

Paper had spread to central Asia by the fourth or fifth century, but it did not reach the Indian subcontinent until the seventh century and did not become widespread there until the thirteenth century.[74] Apparently its initial impact on India was limited, per-haps because it was not much of an improvement over the tradi-tional writing material (made from palm leaves), and it was definitely more expensive.[75]

It is often said that after the Arab defeat of a Tang Dynasty army at Talas in central Asia in 751, the conquerors found Chi-nese papermakers among the many prisoners taken there. How-ever, given that papermaking was already known in various central Asian cities, an Arab tradition that suggests their intro-duction to paper in Samarkand in 704 is more likely. The paper-makers there (who may have been of Chinese ancestry) demonstrated the craft to the Arabs. Baghdad's first paper mill was set up in 795, and thereafter paper manufacturing spread throughout the Muslim lands.

> The advent of paper [in the Arab Caliphate], in the ninth century was a major factor in fostering cultural activities and the industry of book production, and the trade in books began. Samarkand long remained pre-eminent in this field. Paper, however, was made at Damascus, Tiberias, Syrian Tripoli, as well as in Baghdad. The Spanish town of Jativa, in Valencia, was known for its manufac-ture of thick, glossy paper. The early progress in writing material may be seen from these dates: from 719 to 815, the only writing materials seem to have been papyrus and parchment; between 816 and 912, paper is still rare; 913 to 1005 saw paper definitely replacing other and more expensive materials.[76]

Al Jahiz of Basra, the ninth-century admirer of things Indian quoted above, was one of the first to extol the virtues of paper. In a satirical piece he reproached a colleague for having led him astray by telling him that he should write on expensive parchment rather than cheap "China paper" or "Khurasan paper," because, regardless of its true quality, his work would appear more impressive and sell better in the market.

> . . . [Y]ou know very well that parchment is heavy and cumbersome, is useless if it gets damp, and swells in wet weather. . . . You know very well that on rainy days copyists do not write a single line or cut a single skin. Parchment has only to get moist, let alone left out in the rain or dipped in water, for it to bulge and stretch; and then it does not return to its original state, but dries noticeably shrunk and badly wrinkled. What is more, it smells worse, is more expensive, and lends itself more readily to fraud. . . . You are obliged to leave it to age in order to get rid of the smell and for the hair to fall out; it is full of lumps and flaws, more is wasted in scraps and clippings, it turns yellow sooner, and the writing very quickly disappears altogether. If a scholar wished to take with him enough parchment for his journey, a camel-load would not suffice, whereas the equivalent in [paper] could be carried with his provisions. . . .
>
> You did me a grave disservice when you made me take to using parchment instead of paper, and were the cause of my misfortune when you made me exchange light writing-books for volumes too heavy to hold, that crush people's chests, bow their backs and make them blind.[77]

Europe's first paper mill was built in Muslim Spain in 1150,[78] and Byzantium began to manufacture paper in the thirteenth century, after trading for two centuries in fine papers made in neighboring Muslim cities.[79] The common wisdom is that paper then spread to western Europe from Spain, but it might have come by way of Byzantium. The availability of paper, a cheap and satisfactory substitute for papyrus and parchment, is said to have stimulated intellectual activity in western Europe and, in the fifteenth century, to have contributed to the feasibility of a printing industry.

THE SOUTH-POINTING NEEDLE (OR THE COMPASS)

The Chinese knowledge of magnetism and the possible uses of a lodestone predate the Han Dynasty. A third century B.C.E. text states, "When the people of Zheng go out in search of jade, they carry a south-pointer with them so as not to lose their way in the mountains."[80] A true compass appeared in the Qin Dynasty (221–206 B.C.E.), when a lodestone carved in the shape of a ladle was placed upon a round bronze plate (representing heaven) that was embedded in the middle of a square plate (representing earth).

Thereafter the compass became ubiquitous in Chinese society as a tool for geomancers. Chinese geomancy *(fengshui)* is a massive body of lore, some of it technically quite sophisticated. It is principally concerned with where to locate ancestral graves and homes for the living so as to maximize the good fortunes of a family. The end results are usually aesthetically pleasing, energy-efficient, and structurally sound.

By the eleventh century C.E. two new, more sophisticated compasses were in use in China. One was a magnetized fish that floated at the center of a round bowl, and the other was a needle suspended from a silk thread. (The fish and the needle were examples of remanent magnetism. That is, they were magnetized not by being rubbed on a lodestone, but by being heated while held in a north-south position.)[81] The needle was so sensitive that Shen Kuo (eleventh century) was able to detect the declination between true north and magnetic north "400 years before this was discovered in the West."[82]

NEEDLE ROUTES

By the tenth century, armed with the compass, Chinese ships, for the first time, were willing to do something besides sail along the China coast. They ventured out onto what they called "needle routes," out onto the South China Sea and the Indian Ocean.[83] For the first time, they no longer waited for foreign mariners to come to their ports and began frequenting ports in the Philippines, Southeast Asia, Sri Lanka, and India. And by the fourteenth century there was already a Chinatown in East Java's principal port.[84] (One is tempted to point out here that, like Columbus, the Chinese set out for the Spice Islands, and that, unlike Columbus, they found them. Of course, they did not have to go around either Africa or the Western hemisphere to get there.)

These developments culminated in the first third of the fifteenth century with the voyages of Zheng He [Cheng Ho], the Ming Dynasty admiral who led Indian Ocean expeditions that went all the way to East Africa. After his death government-sponsored Indian Ocean voyages came to an end, but the economic and commercial importance of the south continued unabated.

The Arabs may have acquired the compass from the Chinese as early as the ninth century. In fact, some (non-Chinese) historians claim that the Arabs invented the instrument. (That is unlikely, although the Arabs may have used the Chinese compass for overseas navigation before the Chinese did.) During the Tang Dynasty there were large numbers of Muslim merchants in south China's ports, especially Guangzhou (Canton), and they could easily have seen a Chinese compass being used for geomantic purposes, and realized its possibilities for overseas navigation. In any case, the Arabs introduced the compass to Mediterranean sailors around 1250, and it obviously played an important role in the Iberian-sponsored voyages of the fifteenth century.

THE EQUINE COLLAR HARNESS

The problem with using horses to pull a plow (or anything else) without a Chinese equine collar harness is that horses (and donkeys, and so forth) do not have the protruding chest of an ox. When people first tried to strap a horse to some load, it was necessary to pass the strap across its neck, which interfered with its breathing and thus limited its ability to pull heavy loads.

The first solution to this problem was the breast-strap harness, which passes low around the horse's sternum but is held up by a strap over its back. It first appeared in China during the Shang (ca. 1766–1127 B.C.) and was widespread by the third century B.C. Eventually it made its way west, to the Germanic and Slavic-speaking regions, and to Ireland. Indeed, the oldest representation of a breast strap harness in Europe is on an eighth-century Irish monument.[85]

Some time around 500 A.D. the Chinese devised an improved harness, the equine collar harness, which has a hard, oval frame that goes over the horse's head and is cushioned at the point where it meets the sternum. (They may have derived the idea from a Bactrian camel harness.) The harness spread westward. Within a few centuries, it could be found in Spain and in Frankish miniature paintings of the tenth century.[86] This pattern suggests that it was the Arabs who brought it to Europe.

Needham suggests that this equine collar harness played a significant role in the agricultural revolution that began in Europe during the Carolingian period. The heavy plow, which was of great significance in this development, would not have been so useful if the Europeans had not had this Chinese collar harness with which to attach the heavy plow to a horse. Compared to an ox, a horse can produce 50 per cent more foot-pounds of energy per second (mainly because of its speed) and can work two hours longer per day because of its greater endurance.[87]

PORCELAIN

The Chinese have a long history of distinguished pottery manufacturing. Pottery first appeared in China sometime before 5000 B.C.E., and by 1000 B.C.E. the first glazes had been invented. A true porcelain emerged sometime between 200 and 400 C.E. Porcelain differs from other kinds of pottery in that it is much harder, a result achieved by using special clays, adding various substances to the clay, and firing at hotter temperatures. By the Sui Dynasty (581–618) porcelain manufacturing was an important industry. By the Tang (618–906) "china" had become an export product, and by the Song it could be found throughout most of the Eastern hemisphere. These dishes, like Hansel and Gretel, left behind them an easily followed trail of shards all the way from Japan to the eastern Mediterranean, Ethiopia, and East Africa, where they have proved useful in dating archaeological finds.

China has many famous porcelain manufacturing regions, but probably the most famous is Jingdezhen in Jiangxi, a complex of kilns established in the sixth century.[88] It has the advantage of a particular kind of clay now known as kaolin. During the Ming and Qing Dynasties it became the preeminent porcelain manufacturing center, with some 200 to 300 privately owned kilns employing thousands of workers.

True porcelain appeared in China at approximately the same time as the equine collar harness, but unlike the harness, it was not carried westward by the Arabs. Its manufacture spread to Korea and Japan, but until the early eighteenth century, true porcelain remained an East Asian monopoly. That the Arabs did not acquire the secret of its manufacture and move it westward was probably because its production had not spread from China to central Asia by the time of the Arab conquests.

It is not too surprising that the Arabs acquired such industrial secrets not in China, but in central Asian cities and villages that they had conquered. Conquest gives one the power to seize and relocate craftsmen and to force them to yield up their secrets. Foreign traders, on the other hand, regardless of how numerous they might be, do not necessarily have access to the industrial secrets of their hosts. Indeed, one suspects that foreign purchasers who delivered such Chinese goods as porcelain to markets throughout the hemisphere would have been the last people that the Chinese manufacturers would have let in on their secrets.

As soon as porcelain developed an international market during the Tang Dynasty, many peoples in the Middle East and North Africa attempted to copy the Chinese product, producing many beautiful varieties of "soft porcelain" (a technically inferior product) in the process. In the latter part of the sixteenth century western Europeans joined in the quest when the Italians made a serious, but unsuccessful, effort to copy the Chinese product. In the latter part of the seventeenth century, the Saint-Cloud factory near Paris began to manufacture a soft porcelain, and in Germany glass makers, attempting to capture the European porcelain market, added tin oxide to their wares, thus producing an opaque milk glass.[89]

But it was not until the Germans discerned the secret, in a conscious attempt at import substitution, that there was a true porcelain produced outside of East Asia. It was developed at Meissen in 1709 or 1710 by the alchemist Johann Bottger. The western European market for porcelain was expanding at the time due to the growing popularity of Chinese tea, and Augustus the Strong of Saxony had well nigh bankrupted his kingdom through to an insatiable desire for imported porcelain. Augustus showed his gratitude to Bottger by imprisoning him, thus ensuring that he could not reveal his methods to others. Apparently this tactic enjoyed some success, since Meissen managed to hoard the secret of true porcelain on the continent until 1760, when Frederick the Great looted the plant. And soon thereafter the potters of Maria Theresa of Austria were also manufacturing the real thing.[90]

It was also in the eighteenth century that the English, in an attempt to copy the Chinese product, began adding bone ash (a calcium phosphate made by roasting the bones of cattle and grinding them to a fine powder) and ground glass to their clay. But a true porcelain industry developed there only after 1738, when the Cherokee leader Oukanaekah (known to the English as The Little Carpenter) gave Andre Duche permission to export Cherokee "white clay," a mixture of petuntse and kaolin, to Georgia and England.[91] Subsequently "Josiah Spode the Second . . . added bone ash to the true, hard porcelain formula, and the resulting body, known as bone china, has since become the standard English porcelain."[92]

PRINTING

Printing was invented in China in the seventh century by Buddhist monks, and it appears to have emerged as the result of a curious overlapping of Chinese and Indian technological capabilities, local religious traditions, and Buddhist desires. The Mahayana Buddhists believed that a person could accumulate merit by painting a perfect image of the Buddha, or of the Buddhist *mandala* (a sort of spiritual world map), or by writing out a perfect copy of a sutra or a prayer. And the more merit that one accumulated, the better one's rebirth would be. They also believed that if one did not have the time or capability to reproduce such images oneself, one could acquire such merit by paying someone else to produce the image, or by purchasing an image already produced.

Furthermore, there was a tradition in the Himalayas and nearby areas that sanctioned the automation of religious acts. In Tibetan shamanism, fluttering flags have long been a form of prayer. It also became common practice in this region to use wind or water power to rotate prayer cylinders, in the belief that each time the wheel went around, the prayer was "said."[93] In order to accumulate merit one did not have to actually mouth a prayer or a sutra; one simply had to write it on something and then send some energy through it. The power of the wind or the water was sufficient to activate the power of the word.

When Buddhism came to China, the monks encountered both paper and the Chinese practice of seal carving. The Chinese carved their names or the names of offices on pieces of wood or ivory, and used these to stamp a wide variety of things, including official papers and paintings they did themselves or purchased. It may have been these seals and the availability of paper, possibly combined with Indian expertise in the dyeing of cotton textiles, that inspired the monks to carve images of the Buddha, sutras, or prayers onto a large wooden block, ink the block, place a piece of paper over it, and then brush the paper so that it picked up the ink from the raised portion of the block. At any rate, it was not long before the mass production of such images was underway.[94]

By the tenth century, the relevance of this new technology to texts was apparent, and the first emperor of the Song sponsored one of the more spectacular feats of publishing. In 971 he ordered the printing of the *Tripitaka*, the compilation of the Buddhist scriptures. It took the carvers of Chengdu, Sichuan twelve years to carve the 130,000 blocks, after which they were presented to the monasteries of the land and to neighboring states as well.

It was also during the Song, between 1041 and 1048, that movable type was invented by a craftsman named Bi Sheng. He carved characters onto small blocks of clay (one character to a block) and then fired them to make them hard. In order to make a page, he would take a platen (a shallow pan) and coat its bottom with a mixture of resin, wax, and paper ash. He then lined up all the characters he needed and pressed them into the wax mixture, which would hold them in place while the paper was placed over them and brushed. And by the end of the Song printers were experimenting with movable tin type as well.[95]

Nevertheless, movable type did not gain pride of place in Chinese printing until the nineteenth century. The aesthetic of Chinese writing did not lend itself to movable type, nor did the absence of an alphabet. There are tens of thousands of characters, and in the time it might take to search out enough for one page, one might as well carve the page onto a block.

The development of printing had a profound impact on China, an impact that was in some ways similar to the impact that printing had on Europe during and after the fifteenth century. Not long after the Buddhist scriptures were printed, so were the Confucian classics, and thereafter the humanist point of view of Neo-Confucianism gradually displaced the Buddhist worldview within the Chinese intellectual community. Furthermore, the availability of large quantities of inexpensive copies of this Neo-Confucian canon was a sine qua non for the institutionalization of the civil service examination system in the Song Dynasty, a system that rewarded merit and spelled the end of aristocratic dominance in China.

Printing spread rapidly from China to Korea and Japan, and Korean printers carried the technology of movable print much further than the Chinese had. On the other hand, printing does not seem to have been appreciated in the Muslim lands to China's west. Indeed, until recently it was thought that printing did not exist in the Middle East until 1729, when a printing press was established at Istanbul. The apparent rejection of the new technology has been attributed to Muslim restrictions on the reproduction of sacred texts and to resistance from scribes who felt that their livelihood was threatened by it.[96]

A 1987 article by Richard Bulliet, however, suggests that block printing was practiced in Egypt and presumably other places in the Middle East from the tenth century until the fourteenth century.[97] Apparently, it was perceived as a nefarious craft practiced by unscrupulous itinerant tinkers who mass-produced fake amulets and sold them to the gullible, those who were illiterate and were not aware of the difference between handwritten and printed letters. A real amulet, worn for the purpose of warding off evil, was a narrow strip of paper upon which the names of God and pieces of scripture had been hand-written. This strip was rolled up and placed within a metal cylinder that was worn on a chain around the neck in order to protect the wearer. A printed amulet, on the other hand, was considered to be an illicit faking of the scribe's genuine manual production. The Muslims did not share the Buddhist attitude toward the automation and mass production of religious acts and objects and considered such practices to be tantamount to fraud.

It would also appear that, as late as the thirteenth century, Muslims in the Middle East still harbored strong objections to the technology of printing, or at least to its applications. In his book *The Adventures of Ibn Battuta,* Ross Dunn describes the "astonishing transmigration of ideas and technologies" that occurred when Mongol conquerors ruled both China and Iran, as well as an unsuccessful introduction of Chinese printing.[98]

> . . . Ilkhanid culture [was] an eclectic synthesis of Persian, Arabic, Turkish, Chinese, and even Tibetan elements. Over the political bridge that Genghis threw across the Asian grassland-sea marched hundreds of Chinese engineers, scientists, doctors, artists, and propagators of Buddhism seeking service and opportunity in Persia. . . . Though direct communication between the two regions died down in the late thirteenth century when the Ilkhans converted to Islam and their diplomatic relations with the Peking Mongols deteriorated, Chinese cultural influences left enduring marks on Persian miniature painting, calligraphy, and textile and pottery design. In 1294 Gaykhatu Khan (1292–95) even introduced block printed paper money on Chinese inspiration, though Persians rejected this newfangled idea out of hand, resulting in a temporary collapse of the commercial economy.[99]

In the late fourteenth century, at the same time that Iranians were rejecting the notion of printing paper currency, the Italians began producing woodblock prints, and in Mainz by 1453–54 Gutenberg had printed the first Bible using movable type and a press. The significance of this development to the Renaissance and Reformation needs no reiteration here.

GUNPOWDER

The Taoist alchemists who discovered gunpowder were not looking for it. They were seeking a longevity pill that could reverse the degenerative effects of age upon the human body. In an attempt to understand and thereby manipulate the mysterious force that makes things live, and without which things die, they constructed models of the universe's processes, small-scale experiments designed to ferret out the secrets of the planet's energy flows. Han Dynasty emperors, in particular, were interested in their quest and supported their researches.

Like Columbus, what they found was not what they sought. In fact, it was almost the opposite. They produced a medicine made of sulphur (a remedy for skin diseases), saltpeter (potassium nitrate, a remedy for fevers), and charcoal and called it *huoyao* (literally firedrug) because it had a tendency to explode and set their labs on fire. The precise date of this Tang Dynasty discovery is not known, but since a detailed recipe for this immortality pill appeared in Sun Simiao's pharmacology text, it must have been before 800 C.E.[100] (The recipe included a warning about the fire hazard.) As late as the sixteenth century, gunpowder was still classified as a medicine since it was used to treat ringworm and other skin problems.

Gunpowder was also used for firecrackers and blasting, and (contrary to Western mythology) its military applications were realized quickly, probably before the Tang Dynasty fell in 906. A military encyclopedia compiled by Zeng Gongliang in 1044 devotes considerable attention to it, giving the recipe and describing its uses in grenades, bombs, and cannon.[101] The Chinese seem to have been most interested in its rocket-propelling capabilities and developed more than th'rty different kinds of fire-arrows designed to rain down on the enemy, explode, and catch everything around on fire. But they did not neglect cannon or other sorts of bombards. The earliest versions used bamboo barrels. The oldest extant bronze cannon, now in the Chinese History Museum, dates from 1332, but a recent discovery made by Robin Yates indicates that metal bombards were already in use by 1128.[102]

Although the Chinese had no desire to share gunpowder or the new military gadgets that went with it, they were unable to prevent its proliferation. They used gunpowder against the Jurchen invaders from the northeastern forests, to whom they lost northern China in 1127. The Jurchen set up the Jin [Chin] Dynasty in northern China, which lost to the Mongols in 1234, even though they had acquired gunpowder and used it against the new invaders. By 1258 the Mongols ruled much of the Eurasian continent from Korea to eastern Europe, and in the latter part of the century the Mongols in China used gunpowder against the Southern Song, the Japanese, and kingdoms in Southeast Asia.

Some authors state, sometimes tentatively, that Mongolian military campaigns spread gunpowder and cannon (the principal gunpowder application in the West) from China to Europe. But, so far there is no reliable report of the use of cannon and a true gunpowder anywhere west of China, by Mongols or anyone else, until 1326, when a cannon suddenly appears in Florence, Italy.[103]

The impact that gunpowder had on China has not yet been seriously investigated. It is obvious that it could not have had the same sort of impact that it had in Europe—the destruction of the fortifications surrounding feudal castles and the strengthening of the power of the emerging monarchies. At the time that gunpowder appeared in China, the Tang Dynasty already ruled over a united empire and the landscape was not dotted with feudal castles. Nevertheless, local aristocrats were a significant force during the Tang and had lost their importance by the time that the Song Dynasty was established. The question of whether or not the demise of their political and social significance was related in any way to gunpowder has rarely been raised, much less answered.

THE WESTWARD DISPERSION OF GUNPOWDER AND PRINTING

Like porcelain, neither gunpowder nor printing was spread to the West by the Arabs. This is not surprising, since these two revolutionary devices had not spread to central Asia by the time of the Arab conquests. In fact, they were invented only around the time of the Muslim expansion out of Arabia and did not reach the potential of their development within China until the eleventh or twelfth century. But unlike porcelain, which did not appear in the West until the eighteenth century, gunpowder and printing appeared in Italy in the fourteenth century, by a path most mysterious. Indeed, they appear to have gone from China to Italy in a single leap, at least a hundred years before the European maritime routes to Asia were established.

There does, however, appear to be a likely solution to this mystery which can be found in an article by Lynn White, Jr. which was published in the *American Historical Review* in 1960. The article does not concern gunpowder, printing, or even China. Rather, it is entitled "Tibet, India, and Malaya as Sources of Western Medieval Technology," and the author's purpose was to trace the international history of the concept of perpetual motion and the origins of such things as the vertical-axle windmill, the hot-air turbine, and the ball-and-chain governor. With regard to the last three, he concluded, "The appearance in Italy almost simultaneously of three items so closely related to Tibetan mechanized prayer . . . makes independent Italian invention improbable. But who were the carriers of such ideas?" He then proceeds to answer this question.

> The answer is to be found in the slave trade which built up a population of thousands of so-called Tartar slaves in every major Italian city of the period, and which reached its apogee in the middle of the fifteenth century. Canonical prohibitions against dealing in Christian flesh were fairly effective; with Saracenic ships in every Italian harbor, Islam seemed always close, and Muslim slaves were both surly and prone to escape. This meant that slaves from shamanistic and Buddhist areas of central Asia were the chief supply for the Italian market, and these the Genoese merchants secured in great numbers from slave raiders wholesaling in the Black Sea ports. The slaves were of both sexes, and the great majority ranged from eleven to twenty-five years of age at the time of sale; thus they brought with them detailed memories of their distant homelands. Lazari, who has studied most carefully the records of these unfortunates in Venice, assures us that the largest number came "from the regions bordering Tibet and China on the north." Thus we need not be astonished to find simple, but fundamental, Tibetan devices appearing in fifteenth-century Italy.[104]

One suspects that there may be sustained resistance to the notion that it was neither merchants nor soldiers, but slaves from China's Inner Asian frontier who made such a significant contribution to the rise of the West. Nevertheless, it is not impossible that these individuals were aware of many technologies new to Europe, including some that had originated in China. (One should add that, most likely, the slaves were not all Tibetans, but included a number of peoples who lived on the Inner Asian frontiers of China and shared the Lama Buddhist faith, which was based in Tibet. Thus they might have been Tibetan, Turkic, Mongolian, or even Manchu.) The *Tripitaka* was first printed in Sichuan, which shares a border with Tibet, and the stone sculpture of 1128 that depicts a metal cannon is also in Sichuan near the Tibetan border. Indeed, there are Tibetans who live within the contemporary borders of Sichuan. Tibet had close relations with the Tang Dynasty, and a Tibetan kingdom called Xi Xia [Hsi Hsia] ruled northwestern China (modern Gansu and its neighboring regions) from 1038 until 1227. There its people engaged in irrigated agriculture, pastoralism, and trade. Genghis Khan invaded Xi Xia in 1205, had defeated the Tibetans by 1209, and extinguished the kingdom in 1227.

Kublai Khan (r. 1260–1294), during his rule over China and theoretically over all lands ruled by the Mongols, even unto the Black Sea, converted from Mongolian shamanism to Tibetan Buddhism, and thereafter was often accused of favoring his co-religionists. During and after his reign many central Asians, including Tibetans, became enthusiastic participants in those things that were Chinese. Some even studied the classics and became officials in the government. There certainly were Tibetans who knew about printing and gunpowder. In fact, they may have known about such things before the Mongols came.

A 1964 article by Robert Lopez sheds more light on the Genoese connection with these enslaved peoples from China's Inner Asian frontier. He indicates that the Genoese were the first Europeans to open up trade with the western Mongolian states in Iran and southern Russia, and that they were the most numerous, if not the first, to extend that trade to "the eastern shores of China."[105]

Lopez seems to be unaware of White's identification of the slaves acquired in Black Sea ports as Tibetans or Lama Buddhists, but he does say that,

> In their [Black Sea] colonies the Genoese admitted to citizenship many Greeks, Armenians, Tatars, and other people of strange background and questionable beliefs. . . . They [the Genoese] wound up christening children of the best ancestry with such uncanny names as Saladin, Hethum, or Hulagu. . . .[106]

According to Lopez, after the expansion of the Ottoman Turks into the Black Sea region and the fall of Constantinople to them, the Genoese lost "their best trump card in the Levant," that is, their trade in Black Sea slaves and alum, and they thus turned to African slaves as a substitute. He also points out that although their rivals, the Venetians, were still able to obtain imported goods from Asia due to their commercial relationship with the Mamluks in Egypt, the Genoese were essentially cut off by the Ottomans from their source of Asian goods. This, he says, explains why at least one Genoese, Columbus, was so intent on finding another route to the Spice Islands.[107]

Given that the Buddhist slaves brought to Italy by the Genoese were a likely source of the Asian technologies, such as printing and gunpowder, that suddenly appear there after 1261, one wonders why they did not also bring with them East Asian methods of porcelain manufacture, and why the Europeans had to wait another four hundred years for its secret. One possible explanation might be that the right kind of clay did not exist along China's Inner Asian frontier and that the secrets of porcelain production were not known among this population even at this late date.

CONCLUSION

This paper has attempted to relate those western European developments usually associated with the rise of the West to their antecedents in other parts of the world. Perhaps the best way to recapitulate would be to focus upon the main thoroughfares along which this complex moved. By the time of the Guptas, processes set off by the emergence of great empires in the first millennium B.C.E. had reached a culmination in India. Thus a new road began with the emergence of Indian mathematics, the commercialization of sugar and cotton, and the development of new sources of bullion and new commercial routes. This new road took off from India along two separate paths. One lane, closely related to the expansion of Buddhism, led to China. Its arrival in China initiated a series of profound changes, and new technologies emerged there.

While China was in this state of ferment, a second lane took off from India to the West. This path was closely associated with the emergence of Islam and the Arab conquests. Within the lands of the Arab Caliphates, there was also much ferment, and what had been Indian and even some things Chinese spurred further development. By 1200 the Arabic way had reached the Italians, and soon thereafter the Mongol conquests created a lane that led from China to the Black Sea and ultimately to the Mediterranean. After 1261 and the arrival in Italy of peoples from the frontiers of China, many of the southern, central and East Asian developments that the Arabs had not acquired now spread to the West. After the Ottomans blocked the Genoese path to their source of Asian goods, the Iberians made their end run around Italy, around Africa, and around the globe. Ultimately the Iberian road reached into northwestern Europe, which, because of its northern latitude, could participate fully in the process only after it had acquired the West Indies.

Prior to the Iberian voyages, this process had already resulted in the commercial integration of the entire Eastern hemisphere. Judging from epidemic disease patterns thereafter, one can be fairly certain that in 1492 the only places not yet involved, one way or another, were the very tip of South Africa, Australia, the Pacific Islands, and the Western hemisphere.[108] And since it was the desire of the western Europeans to participate in this process in a way more beneficial to themselves that sent them sailing across the oceans, and since they would have had neither the desire nor the means to do so if the various lanes of this road had not left India and reached Italy in the manner that they did by the fourteenth century, it is exceedingly artificial to sever the final ocean-crossing episode from its larger global history.

NOTES

1. Space forces the omission of many important topics, e.g., the invention of the stirrup, as discussed in Lynn White's classic, *Medieval Technology and Social Change* (Oxford: Oxford University Press, 1962).

2. 'Amr ibn Bahr al-Jahiz, *The Life and Works of Jahiz: Translations of Selected Texts* (Berkeley: University of California Press, 1969), pp. 197–98.

3. Andrew M. Watson, *Agricultural Innovation in the Early Islamic World: The Diffusion of Crops and Farming Techniques, 700–1100* (Cambridge: Cambridge University Press, 1983), p. 32. The wild plant probably came from Africa, and there is some evidence for an independent domestication of cotton in West Africa in the first millennium B.C.E.

4. Ibid., pp. 35, 38.

5. Lo Jung-pang, "The Emergence of China as a Sea Power during the Late Sung and Early Yuan Dynasties," *Far Eastern Economic Review*, vol. 14, no. 4 (1955):8.

6. Ibid., p. 41.

7. Ibid., pp. 15–17.

8. Ibid., pp. 9–11, 58–59.

9. Watson, *Agricultural Innovation in the Early Islamic World*, pp. 24–25. See also Joseph E. Schwartzberg, *A Historical Atlas of South Asia* (Chicago: University of Chicago Press, 1978). The date 350 C.E. for the crystallization process appears in "A Chronology of South Asia," a pocket insert in the back of the book. Sidney Mintz, on p. 19 of *Sweetness and Power: The Place of Sugar in Modern History* (New York: Viking, 1985), suggests that crystallized sugar may have been produced in India as early as 400–350 B.C.E.

10. A.M.H. Sheriff, "The East African Coast and Its Role in Maritime Trade," in *UNESCO General History of Africa*, vol. II: *Ancient Civilizations of Africa*, ed. G. Mokhtar (Berkeley: University of California Press, 1981), p. 566.

11. Gaston Wiet et al., *History of Mankind: Cultural and Scientific Development*, vol. 3, *The Great Medieval Civilizations* (New York: Harper and Row, 1975), p. 720.

12. A.L. Basham, *The Wonder That Was India* (New York: Evergreen, 1959), frontmatter.

13. The Mayans invented the zero independently, at approximately the same time, and also used a place-value system. But they did not use the decimal system, and calculations with Mayan numbers were never easy.

14. R.M. Savory, *Introduction to Islamic Civilization* (Cambridge: Cambridge University Press, 1976), pp. 116–17.

15. Georges Ifrah, *From One to Zero: A Universal History of Numbers*, trans. from the French by Lowell Bair (New York: Viking Press, 1985), p. 476.

16. Ibid., p. 481.

17. See under "al Kharazmi," in *Encyclopedia of Islam* (Leiden: E.J. Brill; and London: Luzac and Co., 1960).

18. Much of the above is based on Ifrah, *From One to Zero*. Also see Donald Lach, "Mathematics and Astronomy," in *Asia in the Making of Europe*, Vol. II, Book 3: *Century of Wonder* (Chicago: University of Chicago Press, 1977), pp. 407–15. Lach lists those elements of Indian and Chinese mathematics that had been incorporated into European mathematics by the end of the sixteenth century.

19. Kenneth R. Hall, *Maritime Trade and State Development in Early Southeast Asian History* (Honolulu: University of Hawaii, 1985), pp. 29–31.

20. Y.M. Kobishanov, "Aksum: Political System, Economics and Culture, First to Fourth Century," in *General History of Africa*, vol. II, ed. G. Mokhtar, p. 383.

21. Liu Xinru, "Early Commercial and Cultural Exchanges Between India and China, First to Sixth Centuries A.D.," Ph.D. Dissertation, University of Pennsylvania, 1985 (UMI # 8603669), appendix.

22. Woodbridge Bingham, Hilary Conroy, and Frank W. Iklé. *A History of Asia*, Vol. I, *Foundations of Civilizations, from Antiquity to 1600*, 2d ed. (Boston: Allyn and Bacon, 1974), p. 169.

23. Hall, *Maritime Trade and State Development*, p. 30.

24. Keith Taylor, "Madagascar in the Ancient Malayo-Polynesian Myths," in Kenneth R. Hall and John K. Whitmore, *Explorations in Early Southeast Asian History: The Origins of Southeast Asian Statecraft* (Ann Arbor: University of Michigan Press, 1976), 25–60; O.W. Wolters, *Early Indonesian Commerce: A Study of the Origins of Srivijaya* (Ithaca, NY: Cornell University Press, 1967), pp. 153–54.

25. Hall, *Maritime Trade and State Development*, p. 48.

26. Wolters, *Early Indonesian Commerce*, pp. 95–127.

27. The following account of various episodes from Fa Xian's journey comes from H.A. Giles, (trans.), *The Travels of Fa-hsien (399–414 A.D.) or Record of the Buddhistic Kingdoms* (London: Routledge and Kegan Paul, 1923).

28. C.G.F. Simkins, *The Traditional Trade of Asia* (Oxford: Oxford University Press, 1968), p. 57.

29. Ibid., p. 87.

30. Ibid., p. 134.

31. Ibid., p. 188.

32. Ibid., p. 189.

33. William S. Atwell, "Some Observations on the 'Seventeenth-Century Crisis' in China and Japan," *Journal of Asian Studies* XLV, no. 2 (February 1986):229.

34. Frederic Wakeman, Jr., *The Fall of Imperial China* (New York: Free Press, 1975), p. 17.

35. Ho Ping-ti, *Studies of the Population of China, 1368–1953* (Cambridge, MA: Harvard University Press, 1959), p. 191.

36. Wolters, *Early Indonesian Commerce*, p. 66.

37. Ifran Shahid, *Byzantium and the Arabs in the Fourth Century* (Washington, DC: Dumbarton Oaks Research Library and Collection, 1984), p. 70.

38. Steven Runciman, *Byzantine Style and Civilization* (Middlesex, England: Penguin Books, 1975), p. 132.

39. William McNeill, *The Rise of the West* (Chicago: University of Chicago Press, 1963), p. 412.

40. Cyril A. Mango, *Byzantium: The Empire of New Rome* (New York: Charles Scribner's Sons, 1980), p. 68.

41. Maxine Rodinson, *Muhammad*, trans. Anne Carter (New York: Pantheon Books, 1980), p. 266.

42. Hall, *Maritime Trade and State Development*, p. 14.

43. Ibid., p. 129.

44. Ibid., p. 228–29.

45. Ross Dunn, *The Adventures of Ibn Battuta: A Muslim Traveler of the 14th Century* (London and Sydney: Croom Helm, 1986), p. 49.

46. Kenneth R. Hall, "Palembang," in Ainslie Embree, ed., *Encyclopedia of Asian History* (New York: Charles Scribner's Sons; London: Collier Macmillan Publishers, 1988), p. 201.

47. Kenneth R. Hall, "Trade and Statecraft in the Western Archipelago at the Dawn of the European Age," *Journal of the Malaysian Branch of the Royal Asiatic Society*, vol. LIV, part 1 (1981):31.

48. Philip D. Curtin, *Cross-Cultural Trade in World History* (Cambridge: Cambridge University Press, 1984), p. 130.

49. Citation of Pires in Curtin, *Cross-Cultural Trade in World History*, p. 130.

50. Simkins, *The Traditional Trade of Asia*, p. 187.

51. Cited in Walters, *Early Indonesian Commerce*, p. 31.

52. Simkins, *The Traditional Trade of Asia*, p. 182.

53. John Villiers, "Trade and Society in the Banda Islands in the Sixteenth Century," *Modern Asian Studies* 15, no. 4 (1981):749–50.

54. Henry N. Ridley, *Spices* (London: Macmillan Press, Ltd., 1912), p. 105.

55. Paul Wheatley, *The Golden Khersonese: Studies in the Historical Geography of the Malay Peninsula Before* A.D. 1500 (Westport, CT: Greenwood Press, 1973), p. 188.

56. Simkins, *The Traditional Trade of Asia*, p. 45.

57. Wheatley, *The Golden Khersonese*, p. 188.

58. The sixth century Byzantine geographer Cosmas Indicopleustes described Ethiopian merchants who went to some location inland from the East African coast to obtain gold. "Every other year they would sail far to the south, then march inland, and in return for various made-up articles they would come back laden with ingots of gold" (Runciman, *Byzantine Style and Civilization*, p. 132). The fact that the expeditions left every other year suggests that it took two years to get to their destination and return. If so, their destination at this early date may have been what is now Zimbabwe. The wind patterns are such that sailors who ride the monsoon as far as Kilwa can catch the return monsoon to the Red Sea within the same year. But if they go beyond Kilwa to the Zambezi River, from which they might go inland to Zimbabwe, they cannot return until

the following year. Regarding the monsoon and destinations see Sheriff, "The East Africa Coast and Its role in Maritime Trade," pp. 556–57.

Also see D.W. Phillipson, "The Beginnings of the Iron Age in Southern Africa," pp. 679–80, 688–90, and M. Posnansky, "The Societies of Africa South of the Sahara in the Early Iron Age," p. 726, both in *UNESCO General History of Africa*, Vol. II: *Ancient Civilizations of Africa*, ed. G Mokhtar (Berkeley, University of California Press, 1981). Phillipson indicates that there is evidence of exchange between Zimbabwe and the coast in this early period, and Posnansky refers to the work of archaeologist R.F.H. Summers, who believes that early prospecting and mining techniques in the southern part of Africa reveal Indian influence.

59. Struve Bolin, "Mohammed, Charlemagne, and Ruric," *Scandanavian Economic History Review* I (1953):21.

60. Sheriff, "The East African Coast and Its Role in Maritime Trade," p. 557, and Phillipson, "The Beginnings of the Iron Age in Southern Africa," pp. 686–89.

61. Anthony G. Hopkins, *An Economic History of West Africa* (New York: Columbia University Press, 1973), p. 82.

62. Robert S. Lopez, "Back to Gold, 1252," *Economic History Review* 9, no. 2 (1956):219–40.

63. D.T. Niane, "Relationships and Exchanges among the Different Regions," in *UNESCO General History of Africa*, vol. IV: *Africa from the Twelfth to the Sixteenth Century*, ed. D.T. Niane (Berkeley: University of California Press, 1984), p. 633.

64. Philip D. Curtin, "Africa in the Wider Monetary World, 1250–1850 A.D.," in *Precious Metals in the Later Medieval and Early Modern Worlds*, ed. John F. Richards (Durham, NC: Carolina Academic Press, 1983), p. 235, citing a discussion of the estimates in Magalhaes-Godinho, 1969.

65. Joseph Needham, "Science and China's Influence on the World," in *The Legacy of China*, ed. Raymond Dawson (Oxford: Oxford University Press, 1971), pp. 234–308.

66. Ho Ping-ti [He Bingdi], "Early-Ripening Rice in Chinese History," *Economic History Review* 9, no. 2 (1956):206.

67. Ibid., p. 204.

68. Ibid., p. 207.

69. Ibid., p. 206.

70. Ibid., p. 212.

71. Ibid., p. 201.

72. China Science and Technology Museum (CSTM), *China: 7000 Years of Discovery, China's Ancient Technology* (Beijing: China Reconstructs Magazine, 1983), p. 12.

73. Ibid., p. 8.

74. Ibid.

75. Gaston Wiet et al., *History of Mankind: Cultural and Scientific Development*, p. 385.

76. Ibid., p. 331.

77. al-Jahiz, *The Life and Works of Jahiz*, pp. 211–12.

78. CSTM, *China: 7000 Years of Discovery*, p. 8.

79. Tamara Abelson Talbot Rice, *Everyday Life in Byzantium* (London: B.T. Batsford, 1967), p. 194.

80. CSTM, *China: 7000 Years of Discovery*, p. 21.

81. Joseph Needham, "Science and China's Influence on the World," in *The Legacy of China*, ed. Raymond Dawson (Oxford: Oxford University Press, 1971), p. 253.

82. CSTM, *China: 7000 Years of Discovery*, p. 23.

83. Ibid.

84. Hall, *Maritime Trade and State Development*, p. 246.

85. Needham, "Science and China's Influence on the World," p. 271.

86. Ibid., p. 272.

87. Ibid., p. 273.

88. CSTM, *China: 7000 Years of Discovery*, p. 42.

89. *Encyclopedia Britannica Macropaedia* (Chicago: Encyclopedia Britannica, 1986), vol. 17, pp. 101–2.

90. *Colliers Encyclopedia* (New York: Macmillan Educational Co., 1987), vol. 5, p. 654.

91. Grace Steele Woodward, *The Cherokees* (Norman: University of Oklahoma Press, 1963), p. 69.

92. *Encyclopedia Britannica Macropaedia*, vol. 17, pp. 101–2.

93. Lynn White, Jr., *Medieval Technology and Social Change* (Oxford: Oxford University Press, 1962), p. 85.

94. Thomas Francis Carter, The Invention of Printing in China and Its Spread Westward (New York: Colujmbia University Press, 1955), 11–12, 37–39.

95. Ibid., pp. 212–17.

96. White, p. 85.

97. Richard Bulliet, "Medieval Arabic *Tarsh*: A Forgotten Chapter in the History of Printing," *American Oriental Society Journal* 107, no. 3 (1987):427.

98. Dunn, *The Adventures of Ibn Battuta*, p. 87.

99. Ibid., p. 88.

100. CSTM, *China: 7000 Years of Discovery*, p. 18.

101. China Science and Technology Palace Preparatory Committee and Ontario Science Center, *China: 7000 Years of Discovery* (Toronto: Ontario Science Center, 1982), p. 10.

102. In 1985, Robin Yates noticed a representation of a metal bombard in a high-relief sculpture in a Buddhist cave-temple in Dazu, Sichuan. An inscription indicates that the sculpture was completed in 1128. Yates kindly provided me with Lu Gwei-Djen, Joseph Needham, and Phan Chi-Hsing's unpublished manuscript, "The Oldest Representation of a Bombard," which describes his discovery. They are also the authors of Appendix A of Joseph Needham's *Science and Civilisation in China*, Vol. V, *Chemistry and Chemical Technology: Part 7, The Gunpowder Epic*, which also discusses this representation of a metal bombard (pp. 580–81).

103. James R. Partington, *A History of Greek Fire and Gunpowder* (Cambridge: W. Heffer and Sons, 1960), pp. 190–93.

104. Lynn White, Jr., "Tibet, India, and Malaya as Sources of Western Medieval Technology," *American Historical Review* 65, no. 3 (1960):520–21.

105. Robert S. Lopez, "Market Expansion: The Case of Genoa," *Journal of Economic History* 24, no. 4 (Summer 1964):449.

106. Ibid., p. 447.

107. Ibid., p. 458.

108. William McNeill, *Plagues and Peoples* (New York: Doubleday, 1976), p. 201. Remote parts of Siberia may also have been unusually vulnerable due to a lack of immunities to infectious diseases.

SELECTED REFERENCES

Abu-Lughod, Janet L. *Before European Hegemony*. Oxford: Oxford University Press, 1989.

Adelson, Howard L. *Medieval Commerce*. New York: Van Nostrand, 1962.

Anfray, F. "The Civilization of Aksum from the First to the Seventh Century." In *UNESCO General History of Africa*, vol. II: *Ancient Civilizations of Africa*, ed. by G. Mokhtar, pp. 381–400. UNESCO, 1981. Available from Berkeley: University of California Press.

Anon. *Periplus of the Erythraean Sea*. Trans. by Wilfred H. Schoff. New York: Longmans Green and Co., 1912. Also translated and commentary by G.W.B. Huntingford. London: Hakluyt Society, 1980. A third translation has recently been published: Casson, Lionel, Trans. and Ed. *The Periplus Maris Erythraei*. Princeton: Princeton University Press, 1989.

Atwell, William S. "Some Observations on the 'Seventeenth-Century Crisis' in China and Japan." *Journal of Asian Studies* 45, no. 2 (February 1986):223–44.

Bagchi, Prabodh Chandra. *India and China: A Thousand Years of Cultural Relations*. Westport, CT: Greenwood Press, 1975.

Basham, A.L. *The Wonder That Was India*. New York: Evergreen Press, 1959.

Beckwith, Christopher. *The Tibetan Empire in Central Asia*. Princeton: Princeton University Press, 1987. See the "Epilogue: Tibet and Early Medieval Eurasia Today," pp. 173–96.

Bingham, Woodbridge, Hilary Conroy, and Frank W. Iklé. *A History of Asia*. Vol. I, *Foundations of Civilizations, from Antiquity to 1600*. 2d ed. Boston: Allyn and Bacon, 1974.

Bolin, S. "Mohammed, Charlemagne, and Ruric." *Scandanavian Economic History Review* I:5–39.

Bulliet, Richard. *The Camel and the Wheel*. Cambridge, MA: Harvard University Press, 1975.

Bulliet, Richard. "Medieval Arabic *Tarsh*: A Forgotten Chapter in the History of Printing." *American Oriental Society Journal* 107, no. 3 (1987):427–38.

Carter, Thomas Francis. *The Invention of Printing in China and Its Spread Westward*. New York: Columbia University Press, 1955.

Chandra, Moti. *Trade and Trade Routes in Ancient India*. New Delhi: Abhinav Publications, 1977.

Chau Ju-Kua [Zhao Rugua]. *Chau Ju-Kua: His Work on the Chinese and Arab Trade in the Twelfth and Thirteenth Centuries, entitled Chu-fan Ch'i*. New York: Paragon Books Reprint Corporation, 1966. Translated and annotated by Friedrich H. Hirth and W.W. Rockhill. (Originally published in 1911.)

Chaudhuri, K.N. *Trade and Civilization in the Indian Ocean: An Economic History from the Rise of Islam to 1750*. Cambridge: Cambridge University Press, 1985.

China Science and Technology Museum. *China: 7000 Years of Discovery, China's Ancient Technology.* Beijing: China Reconstructs Magazine, 1983.

China Science and Technology Palace Preparatory Committee and Ontario Science Center. *China: 7000 Years of Discovery.* Ontario: Ontario Science Center, 1982.

Chittick, Neville. "East Africa and the Orient: Ports and Trade before the Arrival of the Portuguese." *Historical Relations Across the Indian Ocean: Reports and Papers of the Meeting of Experts.* Organized by UNESCO at Port Louis, Mauritius, July 15–19, 1974. UNESCO: Paris, 1981 (Studies and Documents Series, no. 3), pp. 13–22.

Chittick, Neville, and R.I. Rotberg, eds. *East Africa and the Orient: Cultural Synthesis in Pre-Colonial Times.* New York and London: Africana Publishing Co. (a division of Holmes and Meier Publishing, Inc.), 1975.

Chou Ta-kuan [Zhou Daguan]. *Notes on the Customs of Cambodia [1297].* Translated by J. Gelman d'Arcy Paul from French translation by Paul Pelliot. Bangkok: Social Sciences Associated Press, 1987.

Cosmas, Indicopleustes. *The Christian Topography of Cosmas, An Egyptian Monk.* Translated and edited by J.W. McCrindle. New York: B. Franklin Publishers, 1967. (Originally published 1897).

Crosby, Alfred. *The Columbian Exchange: Biological Consequences of 1492.* Westport, CT: Greenwood Press, 1972.

Crosby, Alfred. *Ecological Imperialism: The Biological Expansion of Europe, 900–1900.* Cambridge: Cambridge University Press, 1986.

Curtin, Philip D. "Africa in the Wider Monetary World, 1250–1850 A.D." In *Precious Metals in the Later Medieval and Early Modern Worlds,* ed. John F. Richards. Durham, NC: Carolina Academic Press, 1983.

Curtin, Philip D. *Cross-Cultural Trade in World History.* Cambridge: Cambridge University Press, 1984.

Dunn, Ross. *The Adventures of Ibn Battuta: A Muslim Traveler of the 14th Century.* London and Sydney: Croom Helm, 1986.

Encyclopedia of Asian History, ed. Ainslie T. Embree. New York: Charles Scribner's Sons; London: Collier Macmillan Publishers, 1988.

Encyclopedia Britannica. Chicago: Encyclopedia Britannica, Inc., 1972.

Encyclopedia Britannica Macropaedia. Chicago: Encyclopedia Britannica, Inc. 1986.

Encyclopedia of Islam, New Edition. Editorial Committee: H.A.R. Gibb, J.H. Kramers, E. Lévi-Provencal, and J. Schacht. Leiden: E.J. Brill; and London: Luzac and Co., 1960.

Fa Xian [Fa Hsien]. (See under translator, Giles.)

Filesi, Teobaldo. *China and Africa in the Middle Ages.* Translated by David L. Morisen. London: F. Cass, in association with the Central Asian Research Centre, 1972.

Garbe, Richard. *India and Christendom: The Historical Connections Between Their Religions.* Translated from the 1914 German edition by Lydia Gillingham Robinson. LaSalle, IL: The Open Court Publishing Co., 1959.

Gesick, Lorraine. "The 'Invisible Entrepreneurs': The Structural Study of Women in Southeast Asia." Paper presented at American Historical Association, December 27–30, 1987.

Giles, H.A., trans. *The Travels of Fa-hsien [Fa Xian] (399–414 A.D.), or*

Record of the Buddhistic Kingdoms. London: Routledge and Kegan Paul, 1923.

Gittinger, Mattiebelle. *Master Dyers to the World: Technique and Trade in Early Indian Dyed Cotton Textiles*. Washington, DC: The Textile Museum, 1982.

Gotein, S.D. *Letters of Medieval Jewish Traders*. Princeton: Princeton University Press, 1973.

Gotein, S.D. *A Mediterranean Society. The Jewish Communities of the Arab World as Portrayed in the Documents of the Cairo Geniza*. Vol. 1–3. Berkeley: University of California Press, 1967–71.

Grigg, D.B. *The Agricultural Systems of the World: An Evolutionary Approach*. Cambridge: Cambridge University Press, 1974.

Grigg, David. *The Dynamics of Agricultural Change*. New York: St. Martin's Press, 1982.

Grottanelli, Vinigi L. "Asiatic Influences on Somali Culture." *Ethnos* 4 (1947):153–81.

Hall, Kenneth R. *Maritime Trade and State Development in Early Southeast Asian History*. Honolulu: University of Hawaii, 1985.

Hall, Kenneth R. "Trade and Statecraft in the Western Archipelago at the Dawn of the European Age." *Journal of the Malaysian Branch of the Royal Asiatic Society* 54, part 1 (1981):21–46.

Hall, Kenneth R., and John K. Whitmore, eds. *Explorations in Early Southeast Asian History: The Origins of Southeast Asian Statecraft*. Ann Arbor: University of Michigan Press, 1976.

Headrick, Daniel. *Tools of Empire: Technology and European Imperialism in the 19th Century*. New York: Oxford University Press, 1981.

Headrick, Daniel. *The Tentacles of Progress: Technology Transfer in the Age of Imperialism*. Oxford: Oxford University Press, 1988.

Ho Ping-ti. "American Food Plants in China." *Plant Science Bulletin*, vol. 1, no. 1 (Jan. 1956): 1–3.

Ho Ping-ti. "Early-Ripening Rice in Chinese History." *Economic History Review* 9, no. 2 (1956):200–218.

Ho Ping-ti. "The Introduction of American Food Plants into China." *American Anthropologist* 57, no. 2, pt. 1, Memoir # 82 (April 1955):191–201.

Ho Ping-ti. *Studies on the Population of China, 1368–1953*. Cambridge, MA: Harvard University Press, 1959.

Hodges, Richard, and David Whitehouse. *Mohammed, Charlemagne and the Origins of Europe: Archeology and the Pirenne Thesis*. Ithaca, NY: Cornell University Press, 1983.

Hopkins, Anthony G. *An Economic History of West Africa*. New York: Columbia University Press, 1973.

Horton, Mark. "Asiatic Colonisation of the East African Coast: The Manda Evidence." *Journal of the Royal Asiatic Society of Britain and Ireland* 2 (1986):202–13.

Horton, Mark. "The Swahili Corridor." *Scientific American*, September 1987.

Hourani, George. *Arab Seafaring in the Indian Ocean in Ancient and Medieval Times*. Princeton: Princeton University Press, 1951.

Hu Shih. "The Indianization of China: A Case Study in Cultural Borrowing." In *Independence, Convergence, and Borrowing. Papers Presented at the Harvard Tercentenary Conference of Arts and Sciences (August 31–September 12, 1936)*. Cambridge, MA: Harvard University Press, 1937.

Hutterer, Karl L. *Economic Exchange and Social Interaction in Southeast Asia: Perspectives from Prehistory, History, and Ethnography.* Michigan Papers on South and Southeast Asia, no. 13. Ann Arbor: University of Michigan Press, 1977.

Ifrah, Georges. *From One to Zero: A Universal History of Numbers.* Translated from the French by Lowell Blair. New York: Viking Press, 1985.

al-Jahiz, 'Amr ibn Bahr. *The Life and Works of Jahiz: Translations of Selected Texts.* Translated from the original and edited by Charles Pelliat. Translated from the French by D.M. Hawke. Berkeley: University of California Press, 1969.

Kobishanov, Y.M., "Aksum: Political System, Economics and Culture, First to Fourth Century." In UNESCO *General History of Africa*, Vol. II: *Ancient Civilizations of Africa*, ed. G. Mokhtar, pp. 381–400. UNESCO, 1981. Available from Berkeley: University of California Press.

Lach, Donald. *Asia in the Making of Europe.* Vol. I, *Century of Discovery*, book 1 (1965) and book 2 (1965). Vol. II, *Century of Wonder*, book 1, "The Visual Arts" (1970); book 2, "The Literary Arts" (1977); and book 3, "The Scholarly Disciplines" (1977). With Edwin J. Van Kley. Vol. III, *A Century of Advance*, book 1, *Trade Missions Literature*; book 2, *South Asia*; book 3, *Southeast Asia*; book 4, *East Asia* (1993). Chicago: University of Chicago Press.

Levtzion, Nehemia. *Ancient Ghana and Mali.* London: Methuen and Co., 1973.

Lewicki, Tadeusz, and Marion Johnson. *West African Food in the Middle Ages.* Cambridge: Cambridge University Press, 1974.

Lewis, Archibald R., and Timothy Runyan. *European Naval and Maritime History, 300–1500.* Bloomington: Indiana University Press, 1985.

Liu Ruxin. "Early Commercial and Cultural Exchanges Between India and China, First to Sixth Centuries A.D." Ph.D. Dissertation, University of Pennsylvania, 1985 (UMI # 8603669). Now published as: *Ancient India and Ancient China: Trade and Religious Exchanges*, A.D. 1–600. Delhi: Oxford University Press, 1988.

Lo Jung-pang [Luo Rongbang]. "The Emergence of China as a Sea Power during the Late Sung and Early Yuan Dynasties." *Far Eastern Economic Review*, vol. 14, no. 4 (1955):489–503.

Lo Jung-pang [Luo Rongbang]. "Maritime Commerce and Its Relation to the Song Navy." *Journal of the Economic and Social History of the Orient* 1 (1969):57–101.

Lo Jung-pang [Luo Rongbang]. "The Termination of the Early Ming Naval Expeditions," in *Papers in Honor of Professor Woodbridge Bingham: a Festschrift for His Seventy-fifth Birthday*, ed. James B. Parsons, pp. 127–41. San Francisco: Chinese Materials Center, 1976.

Lopez, Robert S. "Back to Gold, 1252." *Economic History Review* 9, no. 2 (1956):219–40.

Lopez, Robert S. "Market Expansion: The Case of Genoa." *Journal of Economic History* 24, no. 4 (Summer 1964):445–69.

Ma Huan. *Ying Yai Sheng Lan, The Overall Survey of the Ocean's Shores [1443].* Translated into English by J.V.G. Mills. Cambridge: Cambridge University Press, 1970. Ma Huan accompanied the Ming Dynasty admiral Zheng He [Cheng Ho] on his second voyage.

Mahoney, Michael S. "Mathematics." In *Science in the Middle Ages*, ed.

David C. Lindberg, pp. 145–78. Chicago: University of Chicago Press, 1978.

McNeill, William. *Plagues and Peoples*. New York: Doubleday, 1976.

McNeill, William. *The Rise of the West*. Chicago: University of Chicago Press, 1963.

Mango, Cyril A. *Byzantium and Its Image: History and Culture of the Byzantine Empire and Its Heritage*. London: Variorum Reprints, 1984.

Mango, Cyril A. *Byzantium: The Empire of New Rome*. New York: Scribners, 1980.

Manguin, Pierre-Yves. "Shipshape Societies: Boat Symbolism and Early Political Systems in the Malay World." Paper presented at Symposium on Southeast Asia, Ninth to Fourteenth Centuries, 9–12 May 1984. Australian National University, Canberra, Australia. This paper has been included in Marr and Milner.

Marr, David G., and A.C. Milner. *Southeast Asia in the 9th to 14th Centuries*. Singapore: Institute of Southeast Asian Studies and Canberra: Research School of Pacific Studies, Australian National University, 1986.

Mathew, Gervase. "The East African Coast Until the Coming of the Portuguese." In *The History of East Africa*, edi. Roland Oliver and Gervase Mathew, vol. I. Oxford: Clarendon Press, 1963.

Mokhtar, G., ed. *UNESCO General History of Africa*, vol. II: *Ancient Civilizations of Africa*, UNESCO, 1981. Available from Berkeley: University of California Press.

Needham, Joseph. "Science and China's Influence on the World." In *The Legacy of China*, ed. Raymond Dawson. Oxford: Oxford University Press, 1964. Paperback, 1971, pp. 234–308.

Needham, Joseph. *Science and Civilisation in China*. Vols. I–VI. Cambridge: Cambridge University Press, 1954-ongoing.

Niane, D.T., ed. *UNESCO General History of Africa*, vol. IV: *Africa from the Twelfth to the Sixteenth Century*. Berkeley: University of California Press, 1984.

Niane, D.T., "Relationships and Exchanges among the Different Regions." In *UNESCO General History of Africa*, vol. IV: *Africa from the Twelfth to the Sixteenth Century*, ed. D.T. Niane, pp. 614–34. Berkeley: University of California Press, 1984.

Nurse, Derek, and Thomas Spear. *The Swahili: Reconstructing the History and Language of an African Society, 800–1500*. Philadelphia: University of Pennsylvania Press, 1985.

Parry, J.H. *The Establishment of the European Hegemony: 1415–1715*. New York and Evanston, IL: Harper Torchbooks, 1966.

Partington, James R. *A History of Greek Fire and Gunpowder*. Cambridge: W. Heffer and Sons, 1960.

Phillipson, D.W. "The Beginnings of the Iron Age in Southern Africa." In *UNESCO General History of Africa*, vol. II: *Ancient Civilizations of Africa*, ed. G. Mokhtar, pp. 671–92. Berkeley: University of California Press, 1981.

Pires, Tome. *Suma Oriental of Tome Pires and the Book of Francisco Rodriguez*. Translated by Armando Cortesao. Nendeln, Liechtenstein: Kraus Reprint, 1967. Reprint: Columbia, MO: South Asia Books, 1990.

Purseglove, J.W., E.G. Brown, C.L. Green, and S.R.J. Robbins. *Spices*. London: Longman, 1981.

Reid, Anthony. *The Lands Below the Winds. Southeast Asia in the Age of Commerce, 1450–1680*, vol. I. New Haven: Yale University Press, 1988.

Rice, Tamara Abelson Talbot. *Everyday Life in Byzantium*. London: B. T. Batsford, 1967.

Richards, D.S., ed. *Islam and the Trade of Asia*. Philadelphia: University of Pennsylvania Press, 1970.

Richards, J.F., ed. *Precious Metals in the Later Medieval and Early Modern Worlds*. Durham, NC: Carolina Academic Press, 1983.

Ridley, Henry N. *Spices*. London: Macmillan Press, Ltd., 1912.

Rodinson, Maxine. *Muhammad*. Translated by Anne Carter. New York: Pantheon Books, 1980.

Runciman, Steven. *Byzantine Style and Civilization*. Middlesex, England: Penguin Books, 1975.

Savory, R.M., ed. *Introduction to Islamic Civilization*. Cambridge: Cambridge University Press, 1976.

Schwartzberg, Joseph E. *A Historical Atlas of South Asia*. Chicago: University of Chicago Press, 1978.

Sedlar, Jean W. *India and the Greek World*. Totowa, NJ: Rowman and Littlfield, 1980.

Shahid, Irfan. *Rome and the Arabs: A Prolegomenon to the Study of Byzantium and the Arabs*. Washington, DC: Dumbarton Oaks Research Library and Collection, 1984.

Shahid, Irfan. *Byzantium and the Arabs in the Fourth Century*. Washington, DC: Dumbarton Oaks Research Library and Collection, 1984.

Sheriff, A.M.H., "The East African Coast and Its Role in Maritime Trade." In *UNESCO General History of Africa*, vol. II: *Ancient Civilizations of Africa*, ed. G. Mokhtar, pp. 551–67. Berkeley: University of California Press, 1981.

Simkins, C.G.F. *The Traditional Trade of Asia*. Oxford: Oxford University Press, 1968.

Sivin, Nathan. "Science and Medicine in China—The State of the Field." *Journal of Asian Studies*, vol. 47, no. 1 (February 1988):41–90. Superb bibliography.

Summers, Roger. "The Rhodesian Iron Age." In *Papers in African Prehistory*, ed. J.D. Fage and R.A. Oliver, pp. 157–72. Cambridge: Cambridge University Press, 1970.

Summers, Roger. "The Southern Rhodesian Iron Age." *Journal of African History* 2:1–13.

Summers, Roger. *Zimbabwe: A Rhodesian Mystery*. Johannesburg: Nelson, 1963.

Sutton, J.E.G. "East Africa before the Seventh Century." In *UNESCO General History of Africa*, vol. II: *Ancient Civilizations of Africa*, ed. G. Mokhtar, pp. 551–67. Berkeley: University of California Press, 1981.

Swetz, Frank J. *Capitalism and Arithmetic*. LaSalle, IL: Open Court Publishing Co., 1987.

Taylor, Keith. "Madagascar in the Ancient Malayo-Polynesian Myths," in *Explorations in Early Southeast Asian History: The Origins of Southeast Asian Statecraft*, ed. Kenneth R. Hall and John K. Whitmore, pp. 25–60. Ann Arbor: University of Michigan Press, 1976.

Teng Ssu-yu [Deng Siyu]. "Chinese Influence on the Western Examination System." *Harvard Journal of Asiatic Studies* 7 (1942):267–313.

Tibbetts, Gerard Randall. *Arab Navigation in the Indian Ocean Before the Coming of the Portuguese, being a translation of Kitab al Fawa'id fi u, sul al-ba, hr wa'l-qaw a'id.* London: Royal Asiatic Society of Great Britain and Ireland, 1981, c1971.

Villiers, John. "Trade and Society in the Banda Islands in the Sixteenth Century," *Modern Asian Studies* 15, no. 4 (1981):723–50.

Wakeman, Frederic Jr. *The Fall of Imperial China.* New York: Free Press, 1975.

Wang Gungwu. *The Nanhai Trade: A Study of the Early History of Chinese Trade in the South China Sea.* Kuala Lumpur, 1958.

Watson, Andrew M. *Agricultural Innovation in the Early Islamic World: The Diffusion of Crops and Farming Techniques, 700–1100.* Cambridge: Cambridge University Press, 1983.

Wernick, Robert. "Men Launched 1000 Ships in Search of the Dark Condiment." *Smithsonian* 14 (February 1984):128–48.

Wheatley, Paul. "Analecta Sino-Africana Recensa." In *East Africa and the Orient: Cultural Syntheses in Pre-Colonial Times,* ed. H. Neville Chittick and Robert I. Rotberg. New York and London: Africana Publishing Co. (a division of Holmes and Meier Publishers, Inc.), 1975.

Wheatley, Paul. *The Golden Khersonese: Studies in the Historical Geography of the Malay Peninsula Before* A.D. 1500. Westport, CT: Greenwood Press, 1973.

White, Lynn, Jr. *Medieval Technology and Social Change.* Oxford: Oxford University Press, 1962.

White, Lynn, Jr. "Tibet, India, and Malaya as Sources of Western Medieval Technology." *American Historical Review* 65, no. 3 (1960):515–26.

Wiet, Gaston, and Vadime Elisseeff, Philippe Wolff, and Jean Naudou, with contributions by Jean Devisse, Betty Meggers, and Roger Green. *History of Mankind: Cultural and Scientific Development,* vol. III: *The Great Medieval Civilizations.* Published for the International Commission for a History of the Scientific and Cultural Development of Mankind. New York: Harper and Row, 1975.

Wolters, O.W. *Early Indonesian Commerce: A Study of the Origins of Srivijaya.* Ithaca, NY: Cornell University Press, 1967.

Wolters, O.W. *The Fall of Srivijaya in Malay History.* Ithaca, NY: Cornell University Press, 1970.

Woodward, Grace Steele. *The Cherokees.* Norman: University of Oklahoma Press, 1963.

Wright, Henry T. "Early Seafarers of the Comoro Islands: The Dembeni Phase of the IXth-Xth Centuries A.D." *Azania* 19 (1984):13–59.

Zhau Rugua. [See Chau Ju-kua.]

Zhou Daguan. [See Chou Ta-Kuan.]

Postscript

Summaries of the Essays

I. ASIA IN WESTERN HISTORY

Introductions

"Asia in Western History"
by Ainslie T. Embree

The essays in this section look at the times and places where Asian civilizations interacted with the West in some significant fashion. The emphasis is on the context of Western history rather than that of the Asian civilizations. The points of intersection may be grouped under four headings: Asia in western thought, trade and commerce, imperial expansion, and war.

"The Shape of the World: Eurasia"
by Rhoads Murphey

The peoples of Europe and Asia developed early civilizations with distinctively different forms and styles located at opposite ends of the same Eurasian land mass, though not in total isolation from one another. Asia contains two of the world's major civilizations (India and China) and has always had between half and two-thirds of the world's population. From the earliest times, European contact with Asia has influenced and enriched the growth of Western civilization. Interest in the wealth of Asia, moreover, spurred the Age of Discovery and indeed the birth of modern Europe.

Period covered: The beginning of time to the early modern period in Europe.

"Brief Syllabus of Asia in Western History"
by Michael Marmé

Random coverage of Asia can destroy the "central narrative thread" of a Western history curriculum. The integrity of this curriculum can be preserved by systematically introducing significant Asian contributions to Europe and laying to rest harmful stereotypes of Asians. Highlighting Asian challenges to the West, moreover, debunks the myth of the inevitable course of European history.

Period covered: Eighth century to the present

"Asian Influences on the West"
by Cho-yun Hsu

Many are accustomed to thinking of the West and Asia as discrete civilizations only occasionally impinging upon one another. Yet Asian civilization has continually and variously influenced the course of Western civilization from the rise of pastoral societies to the present.

Period covered: 2000 B.C.E. to 2000 C.E.

Essays

"The Beginnings of Contact and Interdependence:
Western Asia and the West"
by Marc Van De Mieroop

Based on the modern geographic definition of Asia, contact between Asia and the Europe began in the area of the Aegean Sea among peoples occupying Anatolia, the Levant, and the Greek islands. Crucial instances of western Asian influence on early European cultural development can be solidly documented. These include the introduction of agriculture; the domestication of animals; the development of the alphabet and coinage; and the concept of monotheism. In turn, Europeans often remodeled Asian ideas which were then transmitted back to Asia.

Period covered: Fourteenth to first millennia B.C.E.

"Interfusion of Asian and Western Cultures:
Islamic Civilization and Europe to 1500"
by George Saliba

Major currents of classical Greek and early Roman intellectual and scientific thought were influenced by western Asian figures such as Posidonius of Aphamea (in modern Syria) and Galen of Pergamum (in modern Turkey). Later, the monotheistic traditions of ancient western Asian cultures resurfaced and took over the Greek, Roman, and western Asian worlds when the Byzantine Empire championed Christianity. The rise of Islam proved a synthesizing force which preserved, enriched, and transmitted the traditions of both Asia and Hellenistic Greece to the Western world. "Arabic" numerals were invented in India and incorporated into arithmetic by Islamic mathematicians. Translations of Islamic versions of ancient Greek texts long forgotten in the West, brought the classical tradition back to life in medieval Europe.

Period covered: Fourth century B.C.E. to sixteenth century C.E.

"The Mongols and the West"
by Morris Rossabi

Although contemporary accounts (written by the people they conquered) described them as brutal marauders, the Mongols played a crucial historical role by connecting Europe and East Asia, allowing Europeans to travel for the first time directly to China. The tales of immense Chinese wealth that people such as Marco Polo brought back to Europe contributed to the fascination with Asia which later inspired the European sea voyages of exploration. Islamic merchants, moreover, brought Chinese products and inventions safely through Mongol controlled territories to the Middle East and Europe.

Period covered: Thirteenth century C.E.

"Asia and the West in the New World Economy—
The Limited Thalassocracies: The Portuguese and the Dutch
in East Asia, 1498–1700"
by Derek S. Linton

Portuguese and Dutch trading activities in Asia during the sixteenth and seventeenth centuries ushered in not the beginning of Western domination but, instead, an "Age of Partnership." The Europeans required the cooperation of the local merchants and rulers to make their enterprises successful, while the large Asian empires could, if necessary, muster the military resources to resist the over-extended Europeans. The European drive to limit the importation of Asian porcelains and textiles to Europe played a role in the development of capitalism in the West. The desire for Asian products inspired the Europeans to seek new sources of wealth to finance the trade between Europe and Asia, which itself signaled the beginning of a world economy.

Period covered: 1498–1700.

"Asia and the West in the New World Order—
From Trading Companies to Free Trade Imperialism:
The British and Their Rivals in Asia, 1700–1850"
by Derek S. Linton

After the English East India Company replaced the Dutch, the British faced three increasingly serious problems—the outflow of bullion, the lack of a market in Asia for European manufactured goods, and competition from Indian textile manufacturers. Britain's attempt to solve these problems coincided with the decline of Asian powers like the Mughal Empire, the rise of European military superiority, and an era of European economic dynamism. The outcome was a new age of free trade imperialism in which the English East India Company was preeminent. Unequal exchange and colonial economic policies led to the deterioration of Asian economic and social structures. Instead of sending manufactured goods to Europe for bullion, Asians now exported raw materials and imported European finished goods. As a result, Indian textile manufacturing declined and Indians even imported cotton from Britain. In China, the trade in tea flourished in exchange for which the British sold Indian opium with the eventual result of imperialist incursion and war.

Period covered: 1700–1850.

Asia in Western Thought

"Some Suggested Readings"
by Leonard A. Gordon

An annotated list of Western texts in which Asia is mentioned or described.

Period covered: Fifth century B.C.E. to twentieth century C.E.

Asia in Western Thought

"Asia in the Enlightenment and Early British Imperial Views"
by Leonard A. Gordon

Age-old European stereotypes of Asia were dismantled as travelers, missionaries, and traders brought to Europe new information about Asia. Enlightenment thinkers such as Montesquieu and Voltaire wrote of Asia as a measure both for criticizing and commending Europe. British Orientalists and Utilitarians like John Mill held mixed views on India: Some sympathetic, some hostile, and some providing valuable contributions to knowledge of Indian languages and traditions.

Period covered: Fifteenth to twentieth centuries.

Asia in Western Thought

"Images of the Other: Asia in Nineteenth-Century Western Thought—Hegel, Marx, and Weber"
by Harvey Goldman

Hegel, Marx, and Weber, arguably the three greatest minds of nineteenth-century Europe, wrote extensively on Asia. Hegel endeavored to integrate Asia (the "East") as one stage in his schema of the linear development of the human spirit. Marx interpreted the "Asiatic mode of production" according to his theory of social and economic development and analyzed the effects of European imperialism on Asia. Weber judged Asia according to his idea of the "Occidental personality" and sought explanations for the absence of "the spirit of capitalism." All three thinkers studied Asia but then imposed meaning on it rather than engaging in the "equal and open encounter" with the patterns of Asian civilization.

Period covered: Nineteenth century.

"The Rise and Fall of Western Empire in Asia: 1500–1975"
by Edward Malefakis

European empires in Asia differed from those in the Americas and Africa, both in their chronologies and their substance. In South America and Africa the original takeovers occurred in two decades or so; in Asia the same process unfolded over three centuries. It began in 1498 with Vasco da Gama's voyages but Europeans established first territorial control and then hegemony only in the nineteenth century. Even then, Asia's large size and diversity ensured that the European empires there remained far more heterogenous and incomplete than in the other two continents.

Period covered: Sixteenth to twentieth centuries.

"Asia and the West in the Twentieth-Century World Order"
by Marilyn B. Young

The end of the Cold War and the receding of European hegemony in Asia allow shifting historical perspectives on twentieth-century history. Such global issues as modernization, imperialism, nationalism, and revolution are dramatically illustrated by the example of China. A review of modern Asian history offers the reassessments of regionalism and global integration in the present.

Period covered: Twentieth century.

II. ASIA IN WORLD HISTORY

Introduction

"Asia in World History"
by Carol Gluck

Recent scholarly and curricular activity has multiplied the "ways to world history," which now include ramified variants of the older civilizational and the newer transnational approaches, all concerned to treat the world's past without undue Westcentrism. Remaining "pedagogical potholes" include the lust for coverage, the difficulty of selecting topics, the distortions of the linear grand narratives, the anachronisms of national history, and the demands of historical correctness. A macro-narrative derived from the essays in this book might divide the subject of "Asia in world history" into three periods: The Beginning, or The Invention of Everything; The Middle, or the Afro-Eurasian Era; and The Modern, or The Invention of Everything Else. A micro-world history might work outward from particular places or themes and "world-ize" them both by keeping the global context always in mind and by stressing the world-historical commonalities embodied in the diversity of cultural patterns.

Essays

"The Neolithic Transition: Hunting-Gathering to Sedentary Village Farming and Pastoralism"
by Walter A. Fairservis

The transition from hunting-gathering societies to sedentary village farming and pastoralism—the neolithic revolution—appears to have taken place first in western Asia. There, from 10,000 to 5500 B.C.E., the diversity of human groups and ecological settings fostered experimentation with domestication of animals and plants and a growing complexity of language. While there is evidence of the gradual diffusion of these developments both west and eastward, there is also evidence of indigenous experimentation with cultivation in India (6000 B.C.E.), China (fifth millennium), and Southeast Asia.

Period covered: Neolithic era (10,000–4000 B.C.E.).

"Primary Civilization in Asia"
by Walter A. Fairservis

Primary civilizations are defined here as indigenous—i.e., relatively uninfluenced by the contacts or conquests that characterize secondary civilizations. Of the four primary civilizations, the earliest was the Sumerian, which originated in the large agricultural communities of the Tigris River plain in southern Mesopotamia, late in the fourth millennium B.C.E. Almost at the same time, Egyptian civilization emerged from among the small neolithic settlements in the Nile River valley. A thousand years later, around

2300 B.C.E., Harrapan civilization appeared in the Indus Valley. Chinese civilization developed out of the neolithic farm cultures of the Yellow River valley, and encompassed three successive dynasties: the Xia (ca. 2200–1750 B.C.E.), the Shang (ca. 1750–1100 B.C.E.), and the Zhou (ca. 1100–256 B.C.E.). A civilization is defined here in terms of possessing a written language complex enough to represent abstract ideas, literary reflections, and other symbolic expressions of the human condition.

Period covered: fourth to first millennia B.C.E.

"The Origins of Civilization in China"
by Cho-yun Hsu

Late neolithic China encompassed five major clusters located across the area that is now China. Their interactions produced a cultural homogeneity, a "Chinese-ness" in very early times. The Xia and Shang states were pivotally located to take advantage of the flow of culture and resources. Shang inscriptions testify to a sophisticated writing system; a calendar of festivals, ceremonies, and sacrifices; and diverging views of the relationship of man to the gods. In the transition from Shang to Zhou, a new belief in the Mandate of Heaven appears and with it the concept of moral accountability. The rationalist and universalist principles inherent in the Shang-Zhou transition prepared the ground for the later emergence of Confucianism, Taoism and Mohism.

Period covered: 3000 B.C.E. to 1200 B.C.E.

"Some Contrasts and Comparisons of Zhou China and Ancient Greece"
by Cho-yun Hsu

The Zhou conquest, in China, of its more sophisticated neighbor, the Shang state, resembles the Dorian conquest of the more advanced Minoan and Mycenaean worlds. Yet the political entity created by the Zhou retained central authority, while the Hellenic world divided into small city-states, with the result that China maintained a unitary hierarchical state and the Greek polis moved toward democracy.

Plato and Confucius, are often cited as pivotal thinkers in the creation of Western and Eastern civilizations. Just as Plato proposed a philosopher-king whose active rule fostered a society of pure reason, Confucius' envisaged a sage-king who served as an exemplar and reigned rather than ruled over a society where humaneness and reciprocity prevailed.

Period covered: 1500 B.C.E. to 327 B.C.E.

"The Spread of Power: Empires East and West"
by Richard A. Billows

An empire is an institutionalized system allowing one elite to exploit formerly autonomous regions in exchange for protection and access to a "universal" ideal. In the four regions of Asia— western Asia, the Indian subcontinent, the steppes of northern Asia, and China—the empires of western Asia and China stand out. The Persian Empire enhanced and protected the security and prosperity of its peoples until it fell to the superior military technology of the Greeks. Later imperial presences in western Asia included Rome and Byzantium, associated with the spread of Christianity in the West. On the Indian subcontinent, the Mauryan Empire reached its height in the mid-third century B.C.E. and encouraged the spread of Buddhism. The nomadic cultures of northern Asia, for geographic and climatic reasons, did not settle in one place long enough for a similar empire to develop. The Chinese empire, in contrast, stands out for its long cultural and ethnic continuity. Though the first Chinese imperial dynasty, the Qin, was short lived (221–210 B.C.E.), the Han and successive dynasties kept China unified despite occasional disruptions. (See "Empire in East Asia" by Cho-yun Hsu for more on the Chinese empire.)

Ancient empires showed that a supranational state could offer a degree of stability among peoples of different regions that might not exist among separate autonomous entities.

Period covered: Sixth century B.C.E. to sixth century C.E.

"Empire in East Asia"
by Cho-yun Hsu

The feudal Western Zhou state (twelfth to eighth century B.C.E.) was the prototype for the later Chinese imperial system. The Han Empire (205 B.C.E.-C.E. 220) gave the Chinese their national identity as a people. Its administrative bureaucracy was recruited from all regions of the empire; an agricultural economy thrived in a vast network of exchange and fostered expansion southward; Confucianism became the universal ideology.

The empire defended itself militarily against encroaching nomadic groups from the North and expanded economically to the South. A succession of nomadic empires in the Eurasian steppes, most notably the Mongols, did not survive the period of their rapid expansion. Among the Chinese and nomadic empires there was occasional hybridization that sometimes led to Sinicization, as it did in the case of the Manchus (Qing dynasty, 1644–1911).

The imperial extension of Chinese power through a central bureaucracy and state ideology differed from the diffusing pattern of citizenship of Imperial Rome, and more resembled the centralized Byzantine empire.

Period covered: Twelfth century B.C.E. to twentieth century C.E.

Systematizing the Transcendental

"The Emergence of Religions and World Views"
by Peter J. Awn

A survey of emerging religious world-views in Asia begins with Mesopotamian gods of the third millennium B.C.E. and traces the shift from a pantheon—henotheism—to one transcendent deity—monotheism—as Hebrew texts incorporated and transformed the Mesopotamian heritage. An analogous transition occurred in the Greek world, where the pantheon of the *Iliad* and the *Odyssey* was replaced in the writings of Plato and Aristotle by concepts of an originating principle or a supreme reality. The three Semitic religions (Judaism, Christianity, and Islam) shared both monotheism and the emphasis on revelations with Zoroastrianism in Persia.

On the Indian subcontinent, the Sanskrit Vedas emerge in the second millennium B.C.E. with a world view focused on an eternality of time, an immutable soul, and cycles of existence. In the mid-sixth century B.C.E., Shakyamuni Buddha countered the Vedic view with one of detachment moving toward enlightenment, Nirvana. The Buddhist message spread from—and ultimately out of—India to China, Korea, Japan, and Southeast Asia.

Each of these Asian world views of the fourth to the first millennium remain active as religions on the modern world.

Period covered: Third millennium B.C.E. to first millennium C.E.

Systematizing the Transcendental

"The *Analects* of Confucius, Then and Now"
by Irene T. Bloom

The *Analects* of Confucius may not strike the first-time reader as a classic of world thought. Confucius' cast of mind was deeply practical and human centered, concerned less with transcendence than with "the ultimacy of the ordinary." The place to start is with the personality of Confucius as revealed by this record of conversations between Confucius and others. The focus is on interpersonal relationships and the personal cultivation of rulers, ministers, and subjects within these relationships. Where the conversations contained in the Indian Upanishads concern the metaphysical nature of reality, Confucius deflects such issues to questions of virtue and ethical action.

Confucius' three main concepts—filial devotion, humaneness, and respect for rites—are both ideas and practices. Confucius makes no distinction between "secular" and "sacred." Heaven is a natural order that produces human and social virtue, and the sage recognizes and promotes that order. The concept of transcendence in the Confucian view is not Other to this world, but instead resides in the sense of wholeness of things within this world.

Period covered: Sixth century B.C.E. and the present.

Systematizing the Transcendental

"Religions and World Views in Asian and World History"
by Julia Ching and Willard G. Oxtoby

Several major religious traditions have functioned over great spans of space and time as world views. How do history and religion interact? Karl Jaspers once postulated an axial age, with 500 B.C.E. as the axis, as a turning point in world religious and philosophical history. (Jaspers mentions Confucius and Laozi in China; Buddha and the Upanishads in India; Zarathustra in Persia; Elijah, Isaiah, Jeremiah, and Deutero-Isaiah in Israel; and Parmenides, Heraclitus, and Plato in Greece.)

Other questions include: Why did Christianity eventually define Western civilization while Buddhism, despite its spread through China, Japan, and Southeast Asia, did not similarly define Asian civilization? How do we explain Islam's uneven spread over vast regions in Asia? Why has China not influenced India as India influenced China through Buddhism?

In the modern world, the strength of religion has survived Communist ideology in the former Soviet republics of Asia. What will be the case in China?

Period covered: Eighth century B.C.E. to 1990s

"The Era of Asian Discovery:
Trade and the Contact of Cultures"
by Richard W. Bulliet

World historians give a special place to movement and trade among civilizations as causes of externally generated change. The period between the third and thirteenth centuries C.E. saw unprecedented material and cultural exchange across Eurasia, which is often obscured by the focus on the subsequent age of European exploration.

Four factors facilitated this extraordinary era of cultural contact: First, the movement of people resulting from great political upheavals; second, organized land (the Silk Road) and coastal sea trade dependent on an elaborate infrastructure developed over a long period of time; third, increased urbanism due, on the one hand, to economic and demographic growth in China and, on the other, to migration of converts to Islam to Islamic garrison centers in the Iranian plateau and central Asia; fourth, a remarkable expansion of religions in Asia made possible by the first three factors. Europe, isolated at the western end of the Eurasian land mass, had little contact with this ferment during this millennium of exchange.

This Era of Asian Discovery refers less to new lands, explorers, and conquerors than to the contact with new material, technological, religious, and philosophical traditions.

Period covered: Third to thirteenth centuries C.E.

"China, 300–1200"
by Michael Marmé

Historians should exaggerate neither the ease of cultural contact nor enthusiasm for it. Arab trade along the South China coast during the Sui, Tang, and Song dynasties and Chinese overseas trading were restricted and controlled by imperial administrations seeking to supplement the existing tribute system. There was a constant need for defense against the so-called barbarian regimes that had taken control of North China after the mid-eighth century. Even the barriers to Chinese appropriation of Buddhism were formidable.

The great revolt of the high Tang's most powerful general, An Lushan (755) led to profound military, economic, political and social changes. In the course of the Song dynasty (960–1279), a medieval economic revolution brought about a preindustrial peasant-based society, the very strengths of which may have prevented its further evolution to an industrial or capitalist order.

Period covered: 300 C.E. to 1,200 C.E.

"Song China, 960–1279"
by Robert Hymes

All historians of China recognize that Chinese society was changed under the Song (960–1279) in ways that are still important today to China and also to Western views of China. During the Tang (618–107) Chinese ate wheat and drank wine; the subsequently typical "Chinese" customs of rice eating and tea drinking began only in the Song. The population "explosions" which are now so commonly associated with China also characterized the Song; the Confucianism which came to serve as government orthodoxy was a Song reformulation; the binding of women's feet was a Song practice as well.

The Song can arguably be considered the height of Chinese wealth and economic power in relation to the rest of the world of that time. However, recent research has made clear that it is too simple to look upon the Song in terms of historical achievements both uniquely promising and also as promise unfulfilled. Still, we may say that if the penetrating, bureaucratizing, standardizing, and homogenizing state is a major feature of "modernity," and if state power has played an important role in processes of industrialization, then in the political sphere the Song may indeed mark the beginnings of a specifically Chinese direction of change toward the modern.

Period covered: Tenth to thirteenth centuries, C.E.

"Japan, 550–838"
by H. Paul Varley

From the mid-sixth to the mid-ninth centuries, Japan borrowed massively but selectively from China and Korea. The construction of a centralized, bureaucratic state modeled on that of China provided the focus of that borrowing, although the Confucian concepts that underlay this model were modified by the hereditary structures of indigenous society. Buddhism was the most powerful force in Japan's early cultural borrowing but did not become dominant until only several centuries later and never fully replace the indigenous beliefs (Shinto). Japan also borrowed the Chinese writing system and adapted it to express Japanese, a language of different antecedents. This first period of cultural borrowing from China ended with the demise of the Tang dynasty. Chinese influence on Japanese literature, for example, waned in the late ninth century as the *waka* poetry written in Japanese became the "queen of the arts."

Period covered: Seventh to tenth centuries C.E.

"India, 100 B.C.E.–1500"
by Hermann H. Kulke and Dietmar Rothermund

Trade between India and Rome expanded during the reign of Augustus (30 B.C.E. to 14 C.E.) but declined in third and fourth centuries C.E. The quest for Roman gold was the driving force on

India's side. The transmission of Indian culture to central Asia, China, Japan, and Southeast Asia constituted one of the great cultural movements in world history. Historians have formulated several theories, some of them now discredited, attributing the transmission of Indian culture to Southeast Asia to colonizing warriors, traders, or Brahman missionaries. Buddhist monks must be added to this list. On their side, the Southeast Asian kingdoms were not passive recipients but actively sought Indian trade and culture. Indian historians have long debated which region of India was most important, with the consensus that South India had the greatest influence in Southeast Asia. Islam had an important impact on India and on Indian contact with Southeast Asia up until the mid fifteenth century.

Period covered: 100 B.C.E. to 1500 C.E.

"Separate Spheres and New Links: A New Stage in World History, 1000–1500" by Peter N. Stearns

In teaching and conceptualizing this five-hundred-year span of world history, the dual challenge is to make it more than a grab bag of facts and yet maintain a geographical balance

In this period Asia is a more appropriate starting point than the West. China, India, and Western Asia were the flourishing commercial centers of what was then the developed world. Such phenomena as the innovative uses of Confucianism in Song China or the challenge of Islam in India give insight into the relation between change and continuity during this dynamic time.

Moving from Asia to the world, we see the emergence of three major civilizational zones: The first combined well-established traditions with ongoing innovations—in Asia and Byzantium; the second developed in adjacent areas, using techniques and ideas borrowed from more powerful centers—as was the case in Japan and Southeast Asia; and the third evolved separately from the first two in the Americas and the more distant centers of Africa. Northern Europe remained relatively separate during the earlier medieval age. In all cases, however, a grasp of the emergence of world networks is vital in describing both the links and the separations that characterized this period.

Period covered: Eleventh to fifteenth century C.E.

"The Case of China, 1000–1500" by Michael Marmé

While no place in Europe even approached the flourishing the Song Empire and its many achievements, Song China was nonetheless threatened by northern nomadic kingdoms and riven by internal dissension. The defeat of the Song by the Mongols in the twelfth century was not, however, the unmitigated disaster it has sometimes been portrayed to be. Under the Yuan dynasty, the Mongols established an Asian world network, albeit a short-lived one which did not bring great benefits to China. When the Mongols fell in the fourteenth century, the weakened state of Chinese institutions opened the way for the founder of the Ming dynasty to remold society. In so doing, he completed the shift from an aristocratic to a meritocractic society while creating a gap between the emperor and the bureaucracy. The Ming can truly be called the Middle Kingdom, whose achievements in many cases outshone even those of the Song. The static vision of the founder, however, proved ill-suited to deal with the economic expansion, population growth and migrations that occurred later in the dynasty.

Period covered: Eleventh to fifteenth centuries C.E.

"The Case of Japan, 1000–1500"
by H. Paul Varley

The eleventh century represents the culmination of ancient court life and culture and the beginnings of the greater participation by the warrior class in national affairs. By the end of the twelfth century the warriors became the ruling class of medieval Japan. From the twelfth through the late sixteenth centuries the principal features of Japanese state and society bore a striking resemblance to those of feudal Europe. The medieval age in Japan was the great era of religious awakening as embodied in the salvationist sect of Buddhism. At the end of the fifteenth century, the Ōnin War plunged Japan into a century of civil disorder known as the era of the Warring States. By 1500, however, a new class of feudal lord had begun to emerge, from whose ranks emerged the leaders of national unification in the late sixteenth century.

Period covered: Eleventh to fifteenth centuries, C.E.

"The Rise of an Interdependent World, 1500–1900"
by Loyd E. Lee

Western European circumnavigation of the globe in the sixteenth century signified the emergence of an interdependent world and the origins of a distinctively modern civilization. Subsequent world history can be divided into three distinct periods: The first, from 1500–1750, was one of European expansion in Asia and Asian linkage to the early modern world; in the second, from 1750 to 1914, Europe was transformed through, nationalism, imperialism, and revolution while Asia combined indigenous trend and outside challenges in the process of modernization; and the third, from 1919 to the present, was a time of reshaping the globe, as European empires dissolved and Asia developed economic and political power in the changing globe. Two analytical approaches, modernization theory and comparative history, if used carefully, help to make sense of this interdependent world.

Period covered: 1500–1900 C.E.

"The Expansion of Europe, 1450–1700"
by John W. Cell

The Western dominance of the world which ended in the middle of the twentieth century, deviated from the norm of international anarchy and thus needs explanation. One way to pose the problem is to ask why China did not expand its overseas trade and exploration as Europe did? Both ends of Eurasia possessed the technological and organizational capacity to expand, but China was an empire focused on defending its borders and maintaining internal stability while Europe, with no central political authority, was in the throes of a fierce competition of nascent small national states. Portugal began its seaborne search for empire, and the other European powers followed. An examination of economic, political, social, and ideological factors in early modern Europe (1450-1700) indicates that Europe was in the early stages on the path toward a world hegemony which would lead to actual dominance after the eighteenth century.

Period covered: Fifteenth to the seventeenth century C.E.

"Japan and the West, 1543–1640"
by Michael Cooper

When Europeans first arrived in Japan (1543) no centralized authority existed to forbid their entry. As long as feudal domains were at war with one another, the presence of the "southern barbarians" (Europeans) continued. If the ruler of one domain rejected them they could simply move to another. These lords frequently had financial problems, and which impelled them to deal with European traders in order to raise capital. The first Catholic missionaries came to Japan in 1549, aided in their proselytizing by the decline of Buddhism and general social instability. But the Tokugawa shogunate, which emerged to rule a unified country at the beginning of the seventeenth century, viewed the Christian presence with suspicion and in 1614 issued a decree expelling missionaries from Japan. By 1640, Portuguese and

Spanish traders had been banished or executed for their role in aiding Japanese Christians, and only a small Dutch factory was allowed to remain near Nagasaki.

Period covered: 1543–1640 C.E.

"Europe and the World in an Expanding World Economy, 1700–1850" *by John W. Cell*

During the last half of the eighteenth century, by developing industrial techniques and modes of economic organization, and, more importantly, by peripheralizing and exploiting the rest of the world, Europeans constructed the framework of the modern world-system. Actually, three more or less distinct though intersecting world economies (the North Atlantic, the South Atlantic, and the Indian Ocean) existed in the eighteenth and early nineteenth centuries. By the early nineteenth century, one can divide the world into core, semi-peripheral, and peripheral economic zones. Comparisons with Asian and other European countries help to explain the industrial revolution and the role England that came to play in the world economy. The industrial revolution in Europe should be understood as more than technological innovations: There were sweeping alterations in financial and managerial organization and in attitudes, which brought great benefits but exacted costs as well. Industrialization, together with changes in social and political organization, effected a systematic transformation in Europe and opened up a widening gap between Europe and peripheral areas in the world capitalist system. But Europeans did not, however, exercise effective dominance over large parts of the world until after 1850.

Period covered: 1700–1850 C.E.

"China and the World, 1500–1800" *by William T. Rowe*

China's history during the first phase of Western expansion constituted part of an increasingly interconnected world history. While overseas trade accounted for a fraction of China's overall economy, it played a significant role in exchanges with Southeast Asia, Western Europe, and Spanish America. Silk, then cotton, and finally tea were the primary Chinese exports. New world crops imported to China provided a hedge against famine for a swelling population. Although political turmoil led to the dynastic transition from Ming to Qing in the mid-sixteenth century, China under the new Manchu rule remained a centralized bureaucratic empire. It is misleading to characterize this preeminent universal empire as immobile or xenophobic, since China's integration into the world continued even as the balance of global power shifted to England during the late seventeenth century.

Period covered: 1500–1800 C.E.

"China's Economy in Comparative Perspective, 1500 Onward"
by Madeleine Zelin

While China undoubtedly experienced a commercial revolution beginning in the 16th century, it was slow to develop an indigenous industrial economy. Some of the reasons for this became evident when one compares China and Japan in terms of their political and economic structures and the role of their governments in the industrialization process. Among other considerations are, ironically, that China was trapped by the very success of its pre-twentieth century small peasant economy. In the late twentieth century, many questions remain concerning China's economy and its future as a communist state.

Period covered: 1500 C.E. onward.

"An Approach to Modern Indian Economic History"
by Morris David Morris

The rapid growth of the Indian cotton textile industry demonstrates that India's poverty and lack of modern economic growth can be attributed neither, as Marx suggested, to India's social structure, culture, and values nor, as a more recent interpretation proposes, to British imperialism. Indian entrepreneurs did not repeat this success in other sectors of the economy because, counter to these assumptions of these two common interpretations, industrialization is not inevitable. Certain preconditions must be met before modern large-scale economic organization can emerge across the board, including political stability, predictability, and flexibility; increasing capital accumulation to finance larger investment expenditures; increasing agricultural productivity; a labor force that is both geographically and occupationally mobile; and expanding market demand. Policies to establish these preconditions would have demanded systematic public development and mobilization of national energies, which lay beyond the capacity of the imperialist system.

Period covered: nineteenth and twentieth centuries C.E.

Modern Asia, 1600–1990

"Tokugawa Japan, 1600–1867"
by William B. Hauser

The Japan of 1850 differed dramatically from the Japan of 1600. Although largely isolated from the West until the mid-nineteenth century, Japan during the Tokugawa period experienced thoroughgoing social, economic, and cultural changes that became the ground for full-scale industrialization and political centralization after the Meiji Restoration of 1868.

Period covered: 1600–1867 C.E.

"Five Myths About Early Modern Japan, 1600–1867"
by Henry D. Smith, II

Five myths—Japan is a small country; Tokugawa Japan was a feudal society; the shogunal regime was a police state; Tokugawa society was divided into four separate classes; Tokugawa Japan isolated itself from the rest of the world for over two centuries— myths that are persistent and in some cases even pernicious, continue to distort our view of early modern Japan.

Period covered: 1600–1867 C.E.

"State and Society During the Qing Dynasty, 1644–1911"
by Myron L. Cohen

The social system of traditional China during the Qing dynasty was highly integrated and thus lends itself to the holistic approach of anthropology. One measure of this integration was homogeneity in language: 70 percent of the Qing population spoke various dialects of Mandarin. The homogeneity of the Han Chinese with respect to social organization was even more pronounced than its linguistic manifestations. That a small centralized bureaucracy managed to run the entire country is also of major importance for understanding China's social system. Other factors contributed as well. Rural-urban differences in Qing China, for example, were quantitative rather than qualitative, because in both contexts the same basic principles of social organization obtained. Religious institutions, practices, and beliefs also helped to provide coherence.

Period covered: mid-seventeenth to early twentieth centuries, C.E.

"Japan's Modernities, 1850s–1990s"
by Carol Gluck

If one avoids the perils of frontal comparison (especially that between Japan and China) and considers instead the relation between context and conjuncture in modern Japanese history, then Japan becomes another world-historical instance of modernity that displays both commonalities and its own particular figurations. The processes of becoming modern may be divided into four periods, also shared with other places: the "national modern" (1850s-1900s), which followed "the long restoration" and reshaped everything, from politics to gender, under the sign of the nation-state; modernity and the social (1900s-1940s) saw the social consequences of rapid change and the growth of urban mass society, both then caught up in the rise of fascism, imperialism, and total war; late modernity (1940s-1980s), when the postwar reforms sought to forsake a bad past and remake Japan on the premises of peace, democracy, and the "standard-of-living modern"; postmodern times (with a question mark, 1980s-90s), when Japan faced, finally, the end of its "long postwar" and, together with the rest of the world, the challenge of an as yet unclear future.

Period covered: 1850s-1990s, C.E.

"Modern China, 1840–1990"
by Madeleine Zelin

China's political and social development since the mid-nineteenth century can best be studied through an approach to a long period of modernization that focuses on problems common to many societies. A number of serious domestic challenges, combined with the advent of Western imperialism, to precipitate China's long process of industrialization and modern political change.

Period covered: 1840–1900 C.E.

"Modern India, 1885–1990"
by David Lelyveld

An overarching problem in modern South Asian history has been the effort to fit a complex civilization into the conventional template of the nation-state. The objective of the nationalist movement at the end of British rule was to establish social order. Clustering loyalties around concepts such as religious community, caste and tribe, and language and region impeded India's integration as a fully mobilized nation-state. Negotiating cultural self-definition and making the parts into a unified whole were often more important than securing national power or wealth. The price for such "galactic pluralism" was the limitation of the ability of the central government to protect the weak.

Period covered: 1885–1990

"Modern Korea, 1860–1990"
by Michael E. Robinson

Modern Korean history can be understood by examining three periods—the Chosŏn dynasty (1392–1910), the period of Japanese colonial rule (1910–1945), and the period of division (1945–present). The strengths of the Chosŏn dynasty belie the stereotypical views of Korea as isolated, stagnant, and weak. Chosŏn rule brought a remarkable degree of political and social stability to Korea. During the colonial period, Japan "opened" Korea to the modern era in an attempt to destroy Korea's traditional relationship with China. Japanese control was based on a close understanding of Korean culture but left a bitter legacy. The stark differences between North and South Korea as well as speculation over the prospect of unification are central themes in Korean history in the post-war period.
Period covered: 1860–1990.

III. THEMES IN ASIAN HISTORY

"South Asian History: A Cursory Review"
by Ainslie T. Embree

Seven themes or assertions, if used carefully, can give meaning and coherence to the political and social complexity of South Asian history. The first emphasizes the continuity of Indian civilization in the geographical region that gave it birth. The second posits that in South Asian civilization mechanisms of social control within society are stronger than the state. A third stresses the influence of culture on social structure. The fourth involves the recurrent attempts to establish empires in large areas of the subcontinent. The fifth highlights the role of invaders in South Asian history. The sixth concerns economic development and the seventh the rise of nationalist movements.
Period covered: Entire history.

"Themes in Southeast Asian History"
by David J. Steinberg

Despite the great diversity of Southeast Asia, certain historical themes apply to each of the countries and cultures of the region. Among these themes, perhaps the most important is the continuing process by which the indigenous peoples of the region adapted and adopted the ideas, institutions, and value systems of peoples from elsewhere around the world. It must be emphasized, however, that the Southeast Asians were not mere passive borrowers but actively chose and modified foreign ways according to their own needs. Another important theme is the inherent tension found in each Southeast Asian nation that arise from ethnic, religious, linguistic, social, and economic differences.

Period covered: Entire history.

"The Sinic World"
by Joshua A. Fogel

China, Japan, Korea and Vietnam constitute a "Sinic World" which has developed historically under Chinese cultural influence. This world shared unifying belief systems, religions, language, and administrative structures. Sinic culture was not viewed as the private property of the Chinese but as a universal commodity that was preserved within these countries on China's periphery despite long centuries when they were cut off from direct cultural contact with China.

Period covered: Entire history.

"Themes in Chinese History"
by Madeleine Zelin

A number of central themes can provide a framework to encompass the vast complexity of Chinese history: National identity and China's cultural tradition; agriculture and population; the agrarian dilemma in China's modernization; family and the state; patterns of hierarchy and paternalism; the perfectibility of man and the moral role of government; the relationship between the individual, society and the state; and economic development.

Period covered: Entire history.

"China in the Context of World History"
by Frederic Wakeman, Jr.

The durability of the notion of unity under empire best distinguishes Chinese history from that of the West. In fact, it was this notion which influenced China's response to the seventeenth-century worldwide crisis and determined China's fate in the nineteenth-century encounter with the West. While Europe settled into a system of competitive nation-states, China by the mid-seventeenth century had already been reconstituted into a unified empire.

Period covered: 206 B.C.E. to present

"Some Misconceptions About Chinese History"
by Cho-yun Hsu

Common misconceptions about Chinese history, still surprisingly widely held, include the views that China was a static, unchanging system until jarred by impact with the West; that traditional Chinese society can be summarized by the five Confucian relationships; that Chinese science got off to a glorious start and then stagnated; that Chinese sea voyages might have led to Chinese domination of the world, but were abruptly halted; that China's traditional system is responsible for its failure to modernize as did the West and Japan.

Period covered: Entire history.

"Patterns of the Past:
Themes in Japanese History"
by Carol Gluck

Six themes, each a variation of a common world-historical pattern, run through Japanese history, first as history, then as memory and identity, and further as stereotypes in the international images of Japan. First, a pattern of massive and enthusiastic cultural borrowing followed by gradual Japanization; second, aggressive pursuit of change within a framework of alleged continuity and tenaciously preserved and reinvented "tradition"; third, the primacy of society, in which insularity fostered social closeness and the centrality of social relations impelled both thought and practice; fourth, an inclination toward political and social stability, or a disinclination toward disorder, reflected in the lastingness of institutional arrangements and a tendency toward evolutionary rather than revolutionary change; fifth, the critical importance of the relationship between the inward and the outward economy in a country small in size and poor in resources; sixth, the role of the world, both as a force in domestic developments as well as the site of external relations in which Japan sought its "proper place" in the existing, and changing, world order.

"Themes in Korean History"
by Michael E. Robinson

Cultural borrowing and adaptation from China significantly shaped the development of Korean society. Yet Koreans are justified in thinking of themselves as a distinct and separate people in East Asia. Chinese influence did not mean dominance, and Koreans developed a habit of borrowing, synthesizing, and creating

their own blend of culture. Moreover, Korea's geographic placement within East Asia frequently made it an important cultural
bridge between China and Japan.
    Period covered: Entire history.

"Asia and Latin America in the Context of World History"
by Theopolis Fair

The historical relationship between Asia and the Americas offers
opportunities to incorporate the Americas into world history without making Latin America after 1492 appear as an appendage of
Spain, or later, the United States. Indeed, Asia and Latin America
have influenced each other's histories for hundreds, perhaps
thousands, of years. The earliest migration of peoples from Asia to
the Western Hemisphere, the improbable but not impossible contacts in pre-Columbian times, the trade network created by European colonialism and imperialism, the exchange of New and Old
World crops, and the migrating of Asians into Latin America—all
connected the two continents, revealing the historical interactions
among societies that belonged to the so-called periphery of world
history.
    Total coverage.

"Japan and America: A Tale of Two Civilizations"
by Carol Gluck

The United States and Japan share 150 years of mutual history,
characterized, until recently, by a great disparity of power, with
America dominant, and of interest, with Japan far more interested
in the United States than vice versa. The relationship evolved
always in close dependence on changes in the larger world context. Its history appears here as a drama in two acts, their titles
taken from Japanese history, their action from the relations between the United States and Japan. Act One, 1853-1945, has two
scenes, The Pursuit of Civilization and The Pursuit of Power; Act
Two, 1945-present, begins with Peace, Democracy, and Prosperity
and ends with Japan and the World, the curtain still up on the
lighted stage of late twentieth-century international relations.

"A Concrete Panoply of Intercultural Exchange: Asia in World History"
by Lynda Norene Shaffer

The rise of northwestern Europe to a position of global power is a
common theme in world history but it gives a narrow view of what

is only the most recent act in a much longer drama. Any understanding of global empires and Western hegemony must begin with consideration of the Gupta Empire (320–535 C.E.) in India and include a look at maritime silk roads, the spice trade, the patterns of dispersion of Southern Asian things, the transformation of China under the Song, and the impact in the world of Chinese inventions and innovations.

Period covered: 320 C.E. on.

Historical Timelines

INDIAN HISTORY

Dates	Periods	Events
B.C.E. 3000		
	PREHISTORY	
2300	**Indus River Civilization (ca. 2300–1750)**	Development of urban grain-growing civilization on the Indus River; two main cities are Harappa and Mohenjo Daro; undeciphered proto-Dravidian script; destroyed by environmental pressures, migrations.
1750	**Aryan Migration (ca. 1750–1000)**	Migration into Northwest of India of nomadic herding tribes from Iranian plateau; Indo-European language development; oral religious traditions preserved in *Vedas*, oldest of which, the *Rig Veda*, predates migration.
1000	**Brahmanism (ca. 900)**	Early Hinduism characterized by sacrificial rituals, belief in karma and reincarnation, and division of society into four classes (*varnas*).
500	*Buddhism*	
	Jainism	
326	**Invasion of Alexander the Great**	
	Mauryan Empire (324–200)	Domination of North India by Chandragupta, extended to South by grandson, Ashoka.
250	**Development/Diffusion of Sanskrit Culture**	Major texts of Hindu tradition take shape: *Mahābhārata, Rāmāyaṇa,* codification of laws, grammar, science, arts; gods Shiva, Vishnu are major figures; spread of Sanskritic culture to South India.
200	**Invasions of North India**	Invasians by Central Asian tribes: Bactrian Greeks; Sakas; Kushans (establish dynasty ca. 78–200 C.E.).
C.E. 300	**CLASSICAL HINDU CULTURES**	Classical Hindu tradition expressed in poetry, drama (Kalidasa); art, temple architecture; philosophy (Vedanta); and new forms of devotional (*bhakti*) worship.
320	**Gupta Dynasty (320–550)**	Guptas dominate North India at beginning of "classical" period.

Dates	Periods	Events
455	**Invasions of Huns** (ca. 455–528)	Successive invasions of Huns; other Central Asian tribes destroy Gupta empire.
650	**Rajput Dynasties**	Warlike clans appear in Rajasthan.
	South Indian Dynasties (ca. 650–1336)	Pallava dynasty dominates the south; continuing conflict with Cholas, Cheras, Pandyas.
711	**Arabs Take Sind (711)**	
1000	**Raids of Mahmud of Ghazni (997-1027)**	
	MUSLIM DOMINANCE	Invasions of Muslims from Central Asia lead to political dominance of Muslims in North India and introduction of Persian culture and Islamic religion into South Asia.
1192	**Delhi Sultanate** (1192–1526)	Turko-Afghan chieftains establish sultanate at Delhi; dominate North India.
	Vijayangar (1336–1646)	Rise of Hindu kingdom in South India; independent of Muslim rulers until destruction of capital city in 1565.
	Portugese traders in India (1498)	
1526	**Mughal Empire** (1526–1858)	Mughal Empire unifies North and parts of South India under its rule; amalgam of Persian and Indian culture created in its courts and territories.
	European traders in India	Establishment of trading outposts in India: Dutch (1609); English (1612); French (1674).
1700	**Rise of Regional Powers**	Weakening of Mughal authority frees local Muslim rulers; rise of indigenous regional powers: Sikhs (Punjab), Rajputs (Rajasthan), and Marathas (West India).
1757	**Battle of Plassey**	Victory over Nawab of Bengal gives East India company control of Bengal and begins expansion of British power in India.
1800	**BRITISH RULE**	Political dominance of Britain introduces Western culture, language, methods of government, and technology into urban administrative centers.

Dates	Periods	Events
1947	**MODERN SOUTH ASIA** **India (1947)** **Pakistan (1947)**	Independence from British rule; partition of British India into modern countries of India and Pakistan (East and West).
1971	**Bangladesh (1971)**	War between East and West Pakistan results in separation of Pakistan into two states: Pakistan and Bangladesh.

Prepared by Judith Walsh, associate professor, Comparative Humanities Program, State University of New York, Old Westbury.

CHINESE HISTORY

Dates	Periods	Events
B.C.E. 5000		Neolithic cultures
3000	**XIA/HSIA DYNASTY (ca. 2200–1750)**	
1800	**SHANG DYNASTY (ca. 1750–1100)**	One of the Three Dynasties, or San Dai (Xia, Shang, and Zhou), thought to mark the beginning of Chinese civilization; characterized by its writing system, practice of divination, walled cities, bronze technology, and use of horse-drawn chariots.
1200	**ZHOU/CHOU DYNASTY** **Western Zhou (ca. 1100–771)** **Eastern Zhou (771–256)**	A hierarchical political and social system with the Zhou royal house at its apex; power was bestowed upon aristocratic families as lords of their domains or principalities. Although often compared to European "feudalism," what actually gave the system cohesion was a hierarchical order of ancestral cults. The system eventually broke down into a competition for power between rival semi-autonomous states in what became known as the Spring and Autumn period (722–481) and the Warring States period (403–221). It was during these tumultuous times that Confucius (551–479) lived.
600		
	QIN/CH'IN DYNASTY (221–206)	Created a unitary state by imposing a centralized administration and by standardizing the writing script, weights, and measures. Known for its harsh methods of rule, including the suppression of dissenting thought.
C.E.	**HAN DYNASTY** **Western Han (202 B.C.E.–9 C.E.)** **Eastern Han (25 C.E.–220 C.E.)**	Modified and consolidated the foundation of the imperial order. Confucianism was established as orthodoxy and open civil service examinations were introduced. Han power reached Korea and Vietnam. *Records of the Historian*, which became the model for subsequent official histories, was completed.

Dates	Periods	Events
	PERIOD OF DISUNITY (220–581)	The empire was fragmented. The North was dominated by invaders from the borderland and the steppes. The South was ruled by successive "Chinese" dynasties. Buddhism spread.
600	**SUI DYNASTY (581–618)**	China is reunified.
	TANG/T'ANG DYNASTY (618–906)	A time of cosmopolitanism and cultural flowering occurred. This period was the height of Buddhist influence in China until its repression around 845. Active territorial expansion occurred until defeat by the Arabs at Talas in 751.
1200	**SONG/SUNG DYNASTY Northern Song (960–1126)** **Southern Song (1127–1279)**	An era of significant economic and social changes: the monetization of the economy; growth in commerce and maritime trade; urban expansion and technological innovations. The examination system for bureaucratic recruitment of neo-Confucianism was to provide the intellectual underpinning for the political and social order of the late imperial period.
	YUAN DYNASTY (1271–1368)	Founded by the Mongols as part of their conquest of much of the world. Beijing was made the capital. Dramas, such as the famous *Story of the Western Wing*, flourished.
	MING DYNASTY (1368–1644)	The first Ming emperor, Hongwu, laid the basis of an authoritarian political culture. Despite early expansion, it was an inward-looking state with an emphasis on its agrarian base. Gradual burgeoning of the commercial sector; important changes in the economy and social relations in the latter part of the dynasty; also a vibrant literary scene as represented by publication of the novel *Journey to the West*.
1800	**QING/CH'ING (1644–1912)**	A Manchu dynasty. Continued the economic developments of the late Ming, leading to prosperity but also complacency and a dramatic increase in population. The acclaimed novel *Dream of the Red Chamber* was written in this period. Strains on the polity were intensified by a rapid incorporation of substantial new territories. Its authoritarian structure was subsequently unable to meet the military and cultural challenge of an expansive West.
1900		

Dates	Periods	Events
	REPUBLIC (1912–1949)	Weak central government following the collapse of the dynastic system in 1911–12; Western influence was shown by the promotion of "science" and "democracy" during the New Culture Movement. The attempt of the Nationalist government (est. 1928) to bring the entire country under its control was thwarted by both domestic revolts and the Japanese occupation (1937–45). The Nationalists fled to Taiwan after defeat by the Communists.
	PEOPLE'S REPUBLIC (1949–)	Communist government. The drive for remaking society ended in disasters such as the Great Leap Forward and the Cultural Revolution. Economic reform and political retrenchment since around 1978.

Prepared by Michael Tsin, assistant professor of Chinese history, Department of East Asian Languages and Cultures, Columbia University.

JAPANESE HISTORY

Dates	Periods	Events
B.C.E.		
c.4000	**JŌMON CULTURE**	Prehistoric culture characterized by hand-made pottery with rope pattern design.
500		
	YAYOI CULTURE (ca. 300)	More advanced agricultural society, using metals and wheel-turned pottery.
C.E.		
200		
	Tomb Period (ca. 300)	Great earthen grave mounds and their funery objects, such as clay *haniwa*—terra-cotta figurines of people and animals, models of buildings and boats—attest to emergence of powerful clan rulers. Among these was the Yamato clan, whose rulers began the imperial dynasty that has continued to the
400		present.
	Introduction of Buddhism (552)	
600	**Taika Reform (645)**	Reorganization and reform based largely on learning imported from China: Buddhism, writing system, bureaucratic organization, legal theories.
	NARA (710–784)	Establishment of first permanent capital at Nara; emergence of Japanese patterns of administration and institutions. Beginning of classical period.
800	**HEIAN (794–1185) (Late Heian: FUJIWARA)**	Great flowering of classical Japanese culture in new capital of Heian-kyō (Kyoto). Court aristocracy, especially women, produced a great body of literature—poetry, diaries, the novel *The Tale of Genji*—and made refined aesthetic
1000		sensibility their society's hallmark.
1200	**KAMAKURA (1185–1333)**	Beginning of military rule, as samurai (warriors) replaced nobles as actual rulers of Japan. Imperial court remained in Kyoto but shogun's governing organization was based in Kamakura, which is south of modern Tokyo.
	Kemmu Restoration (1333–1336)	

Dates	Periods	Events
1400	**ASHIKAGA (1336–1573) (MUROMACHI)**	New warrior government in Kyoto retained marginal control of the country, but from its base in Kyoto's Muromachi district became patron of newly flourishing artistic tradition, influenced by Zen Buddhist culture as well as samurai and court society.
	Country at War	Warring factions engaged in lengthy, destructive civil wars.
	Unification (1568–1598)	
1600	**TOKUGAWA (EDO) (1600–1867)**	Country unified under military government which maintained 250 years of secluded peace, leading to development of vibrant urban "middle-class" culture with innovations in economic organization, literature, and the arts.
1800		
1900	**MEIJI RESTORATION (1868) Meiji Period (1868–1912) Taishō (1912–1926) Shōwa (1926–1989)**	Emergence, through Western stimulus, into modern international world marked by dramatic alterations in institutions, traditional social organization, and culture.
	CONTEMPORARY JAPAN 1945–PRESENT Heisei (1989–)	Japan as a world power in the twentieth century.

Prepared by Amy Vladeck Heinrich, director, C.V. Starr East Asian Library, Columbia University.

KOREAN HISTORY

Dates	Periods
B.C.E.	
ca. 300	**OLD CHOSŎN (ca.300–37 B.C.E.)** **HAN TRIBES (ca. 300–42 B.C.E.)**
100	**CHINESE HAN COLONIES** **(108 B.C.E.–313 C.E.)**
	KOGURYŎ (37 B.C.E.–668 C.E.) ⎫ ⎧ Sometimes called the **PAEKCHE (18 B.C.E.–663 C.E.)** ⎬ ⎨ Three Kingdoms **SILLA (57 B.C.E.–668C.E.)** ⎭ ⎩
C.E.	
	KAYA (47 C.E.–562)
100	
600	
	UNIFIED SILLA (668–935)
900	**KORYŎ (918–1259)**
1300	**MONGOL DOMINATION (1231–1336)**
1400	**CHOSŎN (1392–1910)**
1900	**JAPANESE COLONIAL RULE (1910–1945)**
1940	**REPUBLIC OF KOREA (SOUTH KOREA)** **(1948–)** **DEMOCRATIC PEOPLE'S REPUBLIC** **(NORTH KOREA)(1949–)**

SOUTHEAST ASIAN CHRONOLOGY

	ROME and INDIA	BURMA'S MONS, PYU	MALAY ISTHMUS
0	Heavy trade, Mediterranean eastward	Mon contacts with south India and Telingana; Thaton as capital	
	Vespasian halts export of bullion		
	Indian trade shift to Southeast Asia	Use of Meklong River portage route	
			Portages: Takuapa to Chaiya Trang to Ligor Kedah to Patani
	Roman missions cross Southeast Asia en route to China by sea		
		Pyu Śrikshetra	
200	Pallavan influence	Overland trade with China	
			Origins of states: Tun-sun Kolo P'an P'an
		Cultural borrowing from India	
	Gupta influence, peak of Indian culture		Increased Indianization
400		Appearance of:	Funan control includes the isthmian region and shores of Gulf of Siam
		Vishnu cult Buddhism Divine kingship	
		Mon influence to Haripunjaya and Lavo	
	Impact of Chola Tamil influence		
	Decline of Gupta Influence	Pyu control of Arakan and Irrawaddy Valley	
500			
	Pallavan (Telegu) influence from India's Deccan		
			Emergence of independent: Dvaravati Tambralinga
600			Lankasuka
	Pala rule in north India; Nalanda	Rising Mon power in Lower Burma	

FUNAN to CHENLA	CHAMPA and VIETNAM	MALACCA STRAITS	JAVA and INDIES	
Mythical Kaundinya I	Vietnam under Han China control			0
Port of Go Oc Eo in lower Mekong delta		Pirate-infested and little used		
	Champa founded (K'iu-lien)			
				200
Fan Shih-man			Poss-ŭ China trade	
		Kedah port		
Fan Hsun				
	Fan Yi	Palembang on lower Sumatra	Taruma in West Java	
Chu Chan-t'an	Fan Fo Bhadravarman		Purnavarman in West Java	
				400
	Fan dynasty rulers, seven of them			
Kaundinya II		Fa-Hsien's journey via Java or Borneo		
Jayavarman				
			Indianization of Java	
				5)0
	Rudravarman I	Predominance of Kedah-Lankasuka state		
	Sambhuvarman			
Chenla's Bhavavarman I				
Funan collapses				600
Chenla's		Palembang and Malayu trade	T'ang China encourages trade revival	
Isanavarman I				
	Bhadresvaravarman			
Jayavarman I		Śrivijayan Empire I-ching's visits	Simo, central Javan ruler	

	INDIA and WEST	PYU, MONS, BURMANS	CAMBODIA
700	Pala (Nalanda) influence in north India		Land Chenla in upper Mekong Valley
		Arakan state	
		Nan Chao Shans press from Yunnan	Multiple states in Water Chenla
		Śrikshetra falls	
800			Jayavarman II (from Java?)
	Development of Arab-Persian trade to China	Fall of Pyu capital Halingyi to Nan Chao Shans	
			Devaraja cult established
		Burman intrusion at Kyaukse granary	
			Impact of Nalanda culture
		Burman expansion to Minbu and Shwebo granaries	
			Yasovarman I
900		Mon rule in Lower Burma from Thaton	Yasoharapura founded (Angkor site)
	Negapatam shrine in south India for Indies pilgrims	Burmans found Pagan capital	Rajendravarman II Jayavarman V
			Banteay Srei Phnom Bakeng Champa wars Sujita at Lavo
1000	Islam reaches northwest India	Mon Confederacy of Ramanyadesa, disrupted	Suryavarman I from isthmus and Lavo
	Tamil Cholas take Ceylon and attack Śrivijaya		Khmer monuments: Takeo
		Emergence of Pagan dynasty	Phimenakas Baphoun
		Aniruddha	
		Close Ceylon connections	Rebellions and popular unrest
	Revival of Negapatam shrine	Thiluin Man and the Ananda temple	
		Myazedi inscription in Pyu, Mon, Burmese	
1100	Gujerati cloth to Java for spices	Cansu I and the Thatpyinnu temple	Suryavarman II Angkor Wat

ŚRIVIJAYA	JAVA and INDIES	CHAMPA and NAM VIET	CHINA	
Trading empire Buddhist center	Sanjaya and the Śailendras	Vikrantavarman I and II of Champa	T'ang dynasty Encouragement of seaborne trade	700
	Forays against Champa			
		Nam Viet under T'ang rule		
		Indravarman I		
	Kedu Valley monuments Borobudur Chandi Mendut Chandi Pawan			800
			Persian and Arab traders in South China	
Śailendra rule from Java	Śaivite kingdom of Mataram		Persians sack Canton	
		Indravarman II of Champapura		
Modulation to Śiva cult				
Decline of China trade			Decline and collapse of T'ang rule	900
	Sindok, ruler of east Java	Independence of Nam Viet from China		
		Temporary vogue of Buddhism and Javan art and religion		
	The Prabanan shrines		Emergence of Sungs	
Revival of China trade; Sungs	Dharmavamsa vs. Śrivijayan trade policies	Feuding along the Annam coast	Canton trading agency established	
Javanese attacks are defeated			Śrivijayan and Javan embassies	
Loss of north isthmus to Cambodia	Downfall of Mataram by Śrivijaya			1000
Chola attacks from south India	Emergence of Airlangga's Kediri	Annamese capture of Cham Vijaya	Active promotion of Southeast Asian trade	
Revival of empire at Jambi	Development of Molucca-Indian spice trade via the Sunda Straits			
Decline of Śrivijayan political influence		Khmer capture of Vijaya	Decline of Sung trade with Southeast Asia	1100

	BURMA	SIAM	CAMBODIA
1150	"War" with Ceylon		Angkor destroyed by Chams
	Cansu II and the Gawdawpawlin		Jayavarman VII avenges the Cham attack
		Thai-Shan intrusions southward from China	
	Sulamani pagoda		Annexation of Champa for a time
1200	Natonmya's Htilominlo temple		Angkor Thom and Bayon
		Sukhotai founded	
	Mongol threats and invasion	Fall of Nan Chao	
			Loss of Menam Valley and isthmus to Siamese
	Fall of Pagan; Wareru over Mons; Shan brothers' rule	Rama Khamheng founds	
1300	at Kyaukse	state of Siam	Indravarman III
	Ava founded	Ayuthia founded by Rama T'ibodi	Thai invasion to Tonle Sap and
	Kings Binnyu to Razarit at Pegu		Angkor area
		Siamese attack Khmers	
1400	Independence of Arakan		
		Boromoraja Destruction of Angkor	Angkor area abandoned
		Boromo Trailok	Lovek as capital
	Mohnyin Shan tribes harass Ava	Thai suzerainty over Malay states	
1500			
	Mohnyin Shans destroy Ava		
	Toungoo dynasty		
	Tabinshweti		
	Bayinnaung		
	Capture of Pegu	Burmese invasions	Temporary return to Angkor
	Attacks on Siam and Laos	Ayuthia recovers Angkor	Escapades of Veloso and Ruiz

MALAYA-SUMATRA	VIETNAM-CHAMPA	INDONESIA-PHILIPPINES	CHINA	
	Chams destroy Angkor			1150
Decline of Śrivijaya				
	Jayavarman VII takes vengeance on Champa		Sung decline	
		Collapse of Kediri		
	Champa annexed to Cambodia temporarily		Mongols dominate North China borders	1200
Disintegration of Śrivijaya		Emergence of Senghasari in east Java	Mongol conquest of Nan Chao and Hanoi	
Jambi's leadership	Kublai's army captures Hanoi	Kertanagara's rule Mongol invasion of Java	Conquest of Sungs by Kublai	
Visit of Polo and the Mongol fleet	Defeat of repeated Mongol invasions	Majapahit displaces Senghasari	Mongol attacks on Southeast Asia	
			Decline of Mongol influence in Southeast Asia	1300
Muslim entry into ports of Sumatra: Pasai, Pedir, Kampar, Acheh	Vietnamese press southward at expense of Champa	Gaja Mada era Majapahit pressure on: Bali, Madura, Sunda	Mings replace the Mongols	
Founding of Malacca Paramesvara Chinese fleet visits		Rising power and trade of north Javanese port cities	Cheng-ho's seven voyages to Southeast Asia and Indian Ocean	1400
Kedah and Patani turn Muslim	Final collapse of Cham Vijaya Chams try to turn Muslim to get aid	Javanese commercial connections with Malacca trade in cloth and spices	Mings lose interest in Southeast Asia	
Tun Ali of Malacca				
Tun Perak				
Tun Mutahir		Decline of Majapahit		1500
Portuguese capture Malacca			Mings rebuff the Portuguese contacts	
		Javanese attack Portuguese Malacca		
Attacks by: Acheh Javanese Johore	Vietnamese invade the Mekong delta			
		Spanish at Manila	Macao to Portugal	
Portuguese peace with Acheh		Interior Mataram dominates Java		

	INDIA	BURMA	SIAM-CAMBODIA	VIETNAM
1600	Portuguese in Macao, Ceylon, Bengal islands	De Brito episode	Dutch-Chinese trading predominance	Prolonged feuding, Trinh versus Nguyen
	Shah Jahan and the Taj Mahal	Burman Ava versus Mon Pegu		Alexander of Rhodes and French mission
	European trade dominance; Dutch take Ceylon	Revival of Pegu	Cambodian vassalage to both Siam and Vietnam	Feuding finally ends
			French missions Phaulkon affair	Shares vassalage over Cambodia
	British at Madras and Bombay		Isolationist policy	Ming refugees to Mekong delta
1700	Collapse of Mogul power in India			
	French take Madras temporarily	Mons overrun Ava	Siamese control over Laos areas	
	Robert Clive versus French and Bengal	Alaungpaya and the Konbaung dynasty	Burman wars and destruction of Ayuthia	Pierre Poivre episode
	Licensed "country" vessels in China and Southeast Asian trade	Siam invasions Ayuthia destroyed		Tay-son rebellion
		Chinese invasion repelled		Pigneau de Behaine and Nguyen Anh
	Hastings to Cornwallis to Wellesley	Conquest of Arakan	The Chakri dynasty: Rama I	
1800		Symes's missions Bodawpaya to Bagyidaw	Rama II	Emperor Gia Long
	Bentinck		Crawfurd mission	French influence declines under Minh Mang
		First British war Loss of Arakan and Tenasserim	Rama III	
	Dalhousie	Second British war Loss of Lower Burma	Burney mission; American treaty	Thieu Tri to Tu Duc
			Rama IV (Mongkut); Bowring treaty	French at Tourane and Saigon
	Sepoy Rebellion End of Company rule	Mindon	French assume suzerainty over Cambodia	Rule of the admirals
		Lower Burma as India province	Rama V (Chulalongkorn)	
	Opening of Suez Canal trade	Rapid agricultural development	Modernization with foreign advisors	Lagrée and Garnier
		China trade issue; Thibaw and third war		Tongking control
			Loss of Mekong areas to France	Pavie and Laos de Lanessan
	Indian Empire includes Burma kingdom	Annexation and pacification		Doumer's role
		Economic development		

MALAYA	NETHERLANDS INDIES	PHILIPPINES	CHINA-JAPAN	
Portuguese Malacca declines in favor of Acheh, Siam, and Dutch traders	Dutch end Portuguese spice monopoly	Spanish at Ternate	Tokugawa rule	1600
	Batavia founded, defended against Mataram Java	Periodic Dutch attacks on Manila	Decline of Mings	
Dutch capture Malacca and Portuguese Ceylon	Dutch control of Sunda area of Java	Missionary failure in China and Japan	Manchu dynasty	
Dutch neglect Malacca trade	Conquest of Java, Macassar, Moluccas	Importance of clergy in local government and land-holding	Chinese intervention in Burma	
Sultanates are vassal to Siam	Pattern of Asian trade develops	The galleon trade	Emperor K'ang Hsi	
	The coffee-tribute system Strife with Java Chinese		Rites controversy	1700
			Missionaries expelled from China	
		British capture Manila	The Co-hong trade system at Canton	
British acquire Penang Island base	Bankruptcy of Dutch Company	Charles III and reforms	Growth of opium trade from India	
American participation in Southeast Asia, China, India trade	Involvement in the American war	Tobacco-culture monopoly	MacCartney mission to China	
	End of the Dutch Company	Severance of connections with New Spain		1800
British occupy Malacca and straits	Daendels in Java		Amherst mission	
Raffles founds Singapore	Raffles in Java	Direct ties to Spain		
The Straits Settlements	Dutch recover Indies except the Malay Peninsula	Anticlerical nationalism	Opium War; opening of Chinese ports	
Clearing piracy from the straits	Culture system of production	Colorum and Katipunan rebellions	Opening of Japan	
	British Sarawak, Brunei, North Borneo	Manila bankrupted	Arrow war	
Chinese-Malay feuding	Max Havelaar Liberal policy introduced	José Rizal	Meiji restoration	
		Aguinaldo		
British intervention in tin-area sultanates	Dutch war with Acheh for a quarter century	United States defeat of Spain	Sino-Japanese War Japan in Formosa	
Federation of Malaya formed	Inception of the Ethical policy	Annexation of islands		

	INDIA	BURMA	SIAM	FRENCH INDOCHINA
1900	Congress Party development Minto-Morley Reforms	The YMBA Burma Research Society	Loss to France of: Laos and Mekong enclaves Battambang Siemreap Surrender of Malay suzerainty claims	Economic development on mercantilist lines French take from Siam: Mekong enclaves Battambang Siemreap
	Cooperation in World War I Montagu-Chelmsford reforms Amritsar	Governor Harcourt Butler Governor Craddock's reform plans	Sides with Allies in World War I Dilettante Rama VI	French bureaucracy Chambers of commerce and agriculture Lack of self-government concessions
1920	Dyarchy reforms	Dyarchy application		
	Gandhian boycott Simon Commission report Roundtable conferences	National schools strike The GCBA and boycott of dyarchy Saya San rebellion London conferences	Sayre and recovery of treaty equality Rama VII's reforms alienate many The 1932 coup	Heavy French franc investments Suppression of nationalism Communist influence Nguyen Ai-Quoc Trotskyites
	Constitution of 1935 Congress Party governments	Constitution of 1935 University strike Governments under: Dr. Ba Maw U Pu U Saw	Pibun's orientation toward Japan Recovery of French annexations with	Recovery from depression Vichy acceptance of Japan's demands French suppress anti-
1940	Congress boycott of war	Thakins and the Freedom Bloc	Japan's aid, plus Malay and Shan States	Japanese nationalism
	Japanese invasion Partition of India, Pakistan End of British raj	Collaboration with the Japanese The AFPFL moves against Japanese AFPFL collaboration with Mountbatten Aung San to Nu Independent Burma	Japanese occupation Free Thai movement; Pridi for Pibun Pibun returns to power SEATO affiliation	American and KMT aid to Ho Chi Minh Viet Minh versus Dong Ming Hoi Ho versus France Bao Dai fiasco Dien Bien Phu

MALAYA	NETHERLANDS INDIES	PHILIPPINES	CHINA-JAPAN	
Unfederated states; cancelation of Siamese suzerainty	Ethical policy introduced	Suppression of Filipino resistance		1900
Start of rubber plantations	Plantation development in: Rubber Tobacco Oil extraction	Taft's commissionership	Russo-Japanese War	
Tin-mining expansion	Copra	Elections and the Legislature	Fall of Manchu dynasty	
		Osmeña's leadership		
Labor recruitment, Indians and Chinese	Darul Islam	Harrison's role	Japan's twenty-one demands	
	Volksraad reform	The Jones Act		
	End of Ethical policy emphasis	Decline of administrative standards	Japanese commercial and political predominance	
Rapid economic expansion	Administration reform pattern	Wood-Forbes report	Washington Conference	1920
Increased control of Federated States	Outer Island development emphasis	Wood versus Quezon	Period of party governments in Japan	
	Communist infiltration of Darul Islam	Stimson for Wood		
Depression problems	Sukarno and the PNI Depression doldrums Dutch suppression of nationalism	Depression opposition to Philippines trade privileges	Manchurian incident Lytton Commission report	
	Economic recovery	Hare-Hawes-Cutting Act to Tydings-McDuffie Act	Japan military attacks China KMT resistance	
Ending of Indian labor recruitment		Philippines Commonwealth	Japan's emphasis shifts to Southeast Asia	
Conquest by Japan	Japanese pressure Japanese occupation	Occupation of Indochina Conquest by Japan Hukbalahap rebels	Japan's conquest of Southeast Asia	1940
Alternative postwar plans	Sukarno and Hatta collaboration Two Dutch police actions	American reconquest Independence: Roxas Quirino Magsaysay	"Greater East Asia Co-Prosperity Sphere" Defeat of Japan	
Malayan independence and Federation	Merdeka for Indonesia		Communist victory in China	
Malaysian Federation to include British Borneo			China's Southeast Asia pressure on Nanyang Chinese	

EAST ASIA IN THE NATIONAL STANDARDS FOR WORLD HISTORY

*Carol Gluck**

The National Standards for History consist of a set of voluntary guidelines intended as a curricular compendium—not a single suggested syllabus—for teaching history in the schools. The product of several years of work by literally thousands of scholars and teachers, the Standards represent one version of the state of the historical field in the United States in the mid-1990s.[1] Their initial publication in late 1994 unleashed what came to be called "a firestorm of controversy," bringing unexpected national attention and public condemnation. Conservative critics accused the Standards of having "hijacked history," and in early 1995, the Senate passed, 99 to 1, a nonbinding resolution against the Standards.[2] The sudden flammability of the controversy derived largely from the politics of the mid-term congressional election of November 1994, with the result that polemical heat overwhelmed historical light and polarized, rather than galvanized, the forces interested in improving historyteaching in the schools.

As a participant, together with Ainslie Embree, Richard Bulliet, and many others, in the drafting of the World History standards, I was struck by the admirable but unwieldy (and ultimately impossible) notion of trying to write history by democratic consensus.[3] Since national history is always an incendiary subject, the strong reaction to the U.S. History Standards should probably have come as no surprise, especially at a time of the so-called culture wars over issues of canon, identity, and education. Critics denounced the American materials as suffering from a surfeit of social history and an insufficiency of patriotism. Although most of the attention concentrated, predictably, on the U.S. Standards, some criticism spilled over to World History as well, primarily for neglecting the contributions of Western civilization to "the increase in freedom and prosperity around the world." Lynne Cheney agreed but also declared that "there is too much that is too old." And the president of the American Federation of Teachers called the Standards "a travesty" that represented Europeans, Americans, and "white people" as "evil and oppressive, while Genghis Khan is a nice sweet guy just bringing his

*With special thanks to Irene Bloom and Madeleine Zelin for their contributions on China

culture to other places."[4] While this was unfair both to the Standards and to the Mongols, it played better on talk radio and in op-ed columns than it did in the classroom.

To respond to the criticism and retrieve the original objective, the Standards were revised according to the recommendations of a newly formed "independent" panel and published in 1996, trimmed in content and expressed in more general language.[5] The "teaching activities" — the concrete suggestions of sources, examples, and assignments that had accompanied each standard—were omitted from the revision since it was their specificity that had occasioned the loudest denunciations. The omission, while understandable in light of the admitted unevenness of the examples, left the Standards denuded of some of their richest material—the harvest of years of classroom experience in schools and colleges around the country. But once the controversy faded, teachers and writers began to put the Standards to their proper test by using them to develop new curricula and textbooks for U.S. and World History.[6]

There was certainly much work to be done, particularly in World History. Early in the collective drafting process, it had become clear that while the U.S. History Standards could draw on mountains of narrative material and oceans of curricular experience, World History was nearly a start-from-scratch operation. It required three almost entirely reconsidered iterations just to produce the periodization and the macro-historical framework. Even then the threshold of historiographical agreement was but barely crossed. The task of deciding what to include proved even more difficult. In some of the discussions, we historians seemed like figures in a global allegory, each representing "our" area and acting as advocates for its inclusion in every period. As a result, even the three years of World History instruction between the fifth and the twelfth grades optimistically called for by the Standards would not be enough to contain the material without losing one's pedagogical sanity. "A jungle of runaway inclusiveness," reported the *Wall Street Journal*, a steadfast foe of the Standards, though in this instance at least the judgment was not undeserved.[7]

This outcome had little to do with politics; the problem arose from the nature of world history itself. Some of us felt, quite simply, inadequate to the task. The field was just now unfolding in its late-twentieth-century form, and we lacked cumulative wisdom in managing the subject in the classroom in a comprehensive yet coherent way. Few of the participants in the drafting were satisfied with the Standards—the generous embrace of coverage and the inevitable regional excisions made them seem too much and too little at the same time. But the experience of thinking through the world's past proved exhilarating, and the Standards—as they stand—mark only a small step in a long process that is underway in many forms in many places.

What follows here is a crib-sheet of material on East Asia—in fact, almost entirely China and Japan—prepared for the use of the committee charged with the second iteration of the framework for the World History Standards.[8] The idea was to provide the historical topics to fit the Standards, to help to integrate, or "infiltrate," Asia into the world history curriculum. The idea did not work, both because the drafting process shifted direction, ramifying as it went, and also because the Standards grew ever more general, even abstract, in tone. But the history did not change and East Asia still needs to be integrated into any World History course worthy of the name. In the hope that the crib-sheet might be useful toward this end, it is here arranged under the Standards as they appeared in the 1996 revision. If nothing else, the exercise reveals yet again the difficulty of remaining true both to the world and to its parts in the context of a grand macro-narrative.

NOTES

1. The initial version of the World History Standards: National *Standards for World History: Exploring Paths to the Present* (Los Angeles: National Center for History in the Schools, 1994).

2. "An Update on National History Standards," *OAH Newsletter* (February 1995) and *AHA Perspectives* (March 1995), p. 17.

3. See my "Let the Debate Continue," *The New York Times* (November 19, 1994), p. 23.

4. "Freedom and prosperity," from a draft of the Senate resolution, but not included in final text, which in any case was later dropped from the bill; Lynne Cheney, quoted in "World History Teaching Standards Draw Critics," *The Washington Post,* (November 11, 1994); Albert Shanker, quoted in *The Wall Street Journal* (November 11, 1994).

5. The Council for Basic Education appointed two independent panels, one for U.S. history, one for world history. For the revised version: *National Standards for History,* Basic Edition (Los Angeles: National Center for History in the Schools, 1996) [1100 Glendon Avenue, Suite 927, Box 951588, Los Angeles, CA 90095-1588; Fax: (310) 794-6740].

6. E.g., Henry Kiernan, "Asia and the Voluntary World History Standards: A Teacher's Perspective," *Education About Asia* 1, no. 2 (Fall, 1996): 12-14. Kiernan participated in nearly every phase of the drafting of the World History Standards.

7. *The Wall Street Journal* (December 30, 1994).

8. A collective effort on the part of historians associated with The East Asian Curriculum Project at the East Asian Institute, Columbia University. Irene Bloom and Madeleine Zelin supplied the materials on China. The lack of Korea and Vietnam is unfortunate here as it is in the Standards themselves. The ad hoc World History Committee was chaired by Michael Winston and included nine teachers and scholars.

EAST ASIA IN THE NATIONAL STANDARDS FOR WORLD HISTORY

Note: In the Standards, world history is divided into nine chronological periods; within each era only those Standards relevant to East Asia are included here. The crib-sheet follows the final revised version entitled *National Standards for History*, published in 1996 by the National Center for History in the Schools at UCLA.

Era 1: The Beginnings of Human Society
Era 2: Early Civilizations and the Emergence of Pastoral Peoples, 4000-1000 B.C.E.
Era 3: Classical Traditions, Major Religions, and Giant Empires, 1000 B.C.E.-300 C.E.
Era 4: Expanding Zones of Exchange and Encounter, 300-1000 C.E.
Era 5: Intensified Hemispheric Interactions, 1000-1500 C.E.
Era 6: The Emergence of the First Global Age, 1450-1770
Era 7: An Age of Revolutions, 1750-1914
Era 8: A Half-Century of Crisis and Achievement, 1900-1945
Era 9: The Twentieth Century Since 1945: Promises and Paradoxes

ERA 1: THE BEGINNINGS OF HUMAN SOCIETY

STANDARD 2: *The processes that led to the emergence of agricultural societies around the world.*

STANDARD 2B: *The student understands how agricultural societies developed around the world.*

The Neolithic Revolution in China

Agriculture

Domestication of millet (not wheat) in Wei & Yellow River Valley in North China [ca. 4000 B.C.E.] in the Yangshao & Lungshan settlements. Also, rice in the south, showing how agriculture arose in different ways with different crops in different ecologies. Examples of "independent origins," including maize in Mesoamerica.

Villages

Pit-dwellings in clearings in river valleys; walls suggesting tribal warfare; divination using bones & perhaps ancestor worship;

burial of dead with food. The first legendary Chinese dynasty, the Xia [ca. 2200-1760 B.C.E.], may have been late Neolithic or early Bronze Age, but the important point is to acknowledge the long overlap between Neolithic communities and later complex settlements: the Neolithic in short, did not disappear with the "rise of civilization."

Stone Tools

Pottery already in tripod shapes characteristic of Chinese civilization, e.g., bronze tripods of the Shang and later. To wit: the various early civilizations grew out of, but did not wholly replace, their Neolithic predecessors.

Archeological Site

Banpo village in North China, now a museum, example of Neolithic remains [cf. Lascaux].

ERA 2: EARLY CIVILIZATIONS AND THE EMERGENCE OF PASTORAL PEOPLES (4000-1000 B.C.E.)

STANDARD 2: *How agrarian societies spread and new states emerged in the third and second millennium* B.C.E.

STANDARD 2A: *The student understands how civilization emerged in northern China in the second millennium* B.C.E.

Shang Dynasty [Eighteenth Century-1050 B.C.E.]

The earliest Chinese civilization(Bronze Age). Lateness of Shang civilization compared with Mesopotamian, Egyptian, Indian civilization, partly due to China's geographical isolation (mountains and deserts as "barriers in depth"). How city-states arose in Neolithic areas of North China; the capital at An-yang (the Shang capital moved, so that, more like the Indus valley, and less like Egypt and Mesopotamia, there was no monumental capital architecture).

How was the Shang Comparable to Early Civilizations Elsewhere, and What Enduring Features of Chinese Civilization Appeared in the Shang?

The Emergence of the State

State based on family organization, political and religious authority inseparable in the ruler. Shang kings ruling their cities and others, commanding armies that went to war with chariots and foot soldiers against tribes and other cities.

Development of a Rigid Social Hierarchy

A ruling class of aristocrats who lived within the city served by an agricultural peasantry living outside in pit-dwellings; as ultimate example of stratification, the human sacrifice that buried slaves, prisoners of war, wives, and servants along with the king.

Religion and Cosmology

Belief in a deity *di*—sometimes called the high god *Shangdi*—establishing the close relation between religion and cosmology that continued in Chinese civilization; divination (on oracle bones to secure the mediation of the ancestral spirits between the human world and the god, *di*); ancestor veneration and importance of kinship relations, another enduring aspect of Chinese society and religion.

Writing

Evolution of earlier signs into the pictographs and ideographs of Chinese language, on bamboo and oracle bones. Compare with hieroglyphics, etc. Although language existed in all societies, the invention of writing systems did not; the adoption of one culture's writing system by another helps to explain patterns of cultural dominance. E.g., the adoption of Chinese writing system by Korea and Japan, whose languages belonged to a different linguistic family, helped to make Sinic civilization dominant in East Asia. Hence, the importance of the Chinese written language as a sinicizing lingua franca.

Bronze Culture

Designs based on earlier Neolithic pottery combined with advanced technology to produce the beautiful Shang bronzes.

Non-urban

The city-states of the Shang existed in the midst of large numbers of **small Neolithic settlements**, with which the Shang interacted but did not overwhelm. As elsewhere, the majority of Chinese continued to live non-urban lives in agricultural villages.

Sources

Divination records on **oracle bones** are the remaining written records of Shang China; inscribed **bronzes** show ceremonial and military life; later Chinese **myths** incorporated stories of the Shang; **archaeological** remains of the capitals, burial sites, etc.

Reference

David Keightley, "Early Civilizations in China: Reflections on How It Became Chinese," in Paul Ropp, ed., *The Heritage of China* (University of California Press, 1990), pp. 15-54.

STANDARD 4: *Major trends in Eurasia and Africa from 4000 to 1000* B.C.E.

STANDARD 4A: *The student understands major trends in Eurasia and Africa from 4000 to 1000* B.C.E.

What Does it Mean to Be Civilized?

What common features do "civilized" societies have in common (e.g., relatively inegalitarian social structures, formation of social hierarchies, urban concentrations, writing)?

What were the first urban civilizations and where did they arise (Mesopotamia, Egypt, Indus Valley, Yellow River (China), Mesoamerica (Olmec)?

How did scale, centralization, and degree of interactions contribute to the development of these civilizations (e.g., division of labor, social and gender hierarchy, exchange, irrigation systems, military and political organization, religions, developed writing systems)?

ERA 3: CLASSICAL TRADITIONS, MAJOR RELIGIONS, AND GIANT EMPIRE 1000 B.C.E.-300 C.E.

STANDARD 3: *How major religions and large scale empire arose in the Mediterranean basin, China, and India, 500* B.C.E.-300 C.E.

STANDARD 3C: *The student understands how China became unified under the early imperial dynasties.*

How were the feudal states of classical Chinese civilization transformed into a unified imperial empire?

The Zhou Dynasty

[1050-256 B.C.E.] ruled by a king, who enfeoffed subordinate lords in a feudal kingdom in which real (and later fictive) kinship ties were crucial. Having conquered the Shang, the Zhou kings based their political legitimacy on **the Mandate of Heaven**, a principle of rightful government that linked politics with the cosmos and endured until the end of the last dynasty in 1911. The Zhou dynasty established the common symbolic universe of politics, society, and ideas that constituted classical Chinese civilization. Its values later spread through the communicability of the written language to different peoples and in different dialects.

Unity and Empire

Out of the disunity of the Warring States period [401-256 B.C.E.] at the end of the Zhou came the **idealization of unity**, perhaps the most fundamental theme in Chinese history, the idea of a **universal empire** ["All under Heaven"]. Confucius and others of the "hundred flowers" of philosophical schools invoked the Chinese past as a Golden Age of **good government of virtuous men**, thereby re-conceiving rulership in moral terms, another abiding characteristic of political thought in China.

The Qin dynasty

[221-207 B.C.E.] unified the realm under the rule of a single **emperor**, and the **Han dynasty** [206 B.C.E.-220 C.E.], which transformed the feudal states into a single **imperial bureaucratic state**, together established the classical **Chinese empire** on a scale of power and organization comparable with Rome during the same period.

The Empire

The assertion of the **emperor** as the "son of heaven"; the development of an efficient **bureaucracy** (with statuses and salaries) which replaced the feudal hierarchy (the beginnings of what later became the civil service examination system); **centralized** administration based on law, including taxation, establishment of an imperial university, large mobile armies of **expansion** and **conquest** (campaigns in Central Asia, Anna, & Korea, which became a colony of the Han in first century B.C.E.), elaborate **defense** systems (the Great Wall); **standardization** of measurement, currency, writing system, ideas (state-sponsored Confucianism from 131 B.C.E., burning of the books). The Han offers an early example of the **dynastic cycle**, from the rise of the virtuous ruler to breakdown and eventual collapse of the dynasty, a pattern believed to be repeated over and over again across Chinese history. The reasons for rise and fall of the Qin and Han dynasties included both domestic decline and barbarian invasions.

Population

By the time of the first empire in the third century B.C.E., China had the largest population in the world, a fact that remains true to this day.

How Did the Family Become the Principle of Society, Economics, and Government in China?

The Family

Socially, as elsewhere, the family was the basic social unit and kinship ties formed the basis of social and political relations. Economically, the family was the unit of economic production, as society came to depend on independent rural farming and a peasantry increasingly of freeholders. [Slavery, in comparison with other ancient civilizations such as Greece and Rome, was numerically insignificant in Chinese history.] Under the Han empire, familial relations became more hierarchical, and gender inequality was more pronounced than in the Zhou. [Compare Confucius' *Analects* from the Zhou with the *Classic of Filial Piety* from the Han.]

In Politics

The family became the **fundamental metaphor of all relationships**, so that the relation between the ruler and his subjects was cast in terms of **filial piety** (in comparison to the loyalty between ruled and ruler in Western political thought). Morally, family relationships provided the model for individual and social virtues alike.

Insider/Outsider

The enduring distinction between the Chinese [**civilization**] and the threats from outside [**barbarian**] was made early in regard to the steppes people who challenged the literate and sedentary Chinese throughout their history, most often nomadic tribal peoples on China's vast land borders, whom China continually fought, often subdued, and sometimes were subdued by, only to civilize the barbarians by **sinicizing** them (and making them Chinese). [Some were the same tribes that approached Europe from the East, e.g., the "Huns" who were known to Han Chinese as the Hsiong Nu.]

How Did Ancient Empires Establish and Expand Their Economic Base?

State Revenues

Taxation; state intervention in the economy; monopolies of salt, iron, liquor; state monopolies remained the source of government revenues in China.

Growth in commerce and trade

Roads, canals, markets, often intertwined with issues of military expansion; an East Asian trading sphere in the Former Han [second-first century B.C.E.] comparable to that of the Roman empire; Silk Road linking Han capital of Chang-an and Rome (camel caravans), but in economic terms this was a luxury trade; growth of large landowners in the countryside, later to become a powerful landed aristocracy, resulting in de-centralization after the fall of the Han. An abiding theme is the cycles of prosperity and the flux between central state control and newly rising local power.

Welfare

"Ever-normal granaries" storing crops against times of scarcity; Confucians were anti-militarist and concerned with economic subsistence for all, emphasized agriculture rather than commerce and favored minimal role of the state. [See "Debates on Salt and Iron," in *Sources of Chinese Tradition*, I, 220-23]

Sources

The famous **tomb** of the first Qin emperor, the unifier, at Sian with the army of life-size terra cotta soldiers; the early importance of **written history** in China. (First history from documents by

Sima Qian in first century B.C.E. [*Records of the Grand Historian of China*]; also, the beginning of dynastic history [Pan Ku]—the **history-mindedness** of Chinese civilization); definition of what it means to be Chinese [Han] in this period by language and common culture; the earliest "history" of Japan occurs in Chinese dynastic histories; before the Japanese had acquired writing, Chinese recorded their observations of the then tribal society on the Japanese islands.

How and Why Did Religious Systems Arise and Spread?

In China, in the chaos of the Warring States period, an intensified quest for reordering the cosmos produced vigorous contention and mutual interaction among various schools of thought, called the "Hundred Schools." These included Confucianism, Taoism, Legalism, Mohism, and yin-yang cosmology.

How is Religion Defined in Different Places?

Religion in China

No anthropomorphically conceived deity; rather a concept of a **beneficent Heaven**, or Nature [*tian*]; the Chinese concept of Heaven has religious, cosmological, and naturalistic implications. **Mandate of Heaven** (*tian-ming*): the idea that rulers are sanctioned by Heaven as long as they are virtuous and rule for the sake of the people; this idea was originally employed to justify Zhou conquest of the Shang but became a potent idea in moral thought down to the present.

No clear division between **secular and sacred** realms: e.g., concept of *tian* as Heaven **or** Nature, and as a source of order in universe; **ritual** as transcending spheres of "secular" and "sacred" [see Herbert Fingarette, *Confucius: The Secular as Sacred* (Harper Torchbooks, 1972) The ultimacy of ordinary life. The **this-worldliness** of Confucianism [see *Analects* of Confucius, 11:11]

How Did Different Ideas of Good Government, Justice, and Individual Morality Develop?

The Nature of Civilization

How do Chinese understand the nature of civilization (*wen*)? Association of *wen* with *literacy* and respect for the written language; the idea of civilization as a *process* of civilizing. While Chinese society, like many traditional societies, remained inegalitarian, there was a persistent tendency in various schools of thought to address the **problem of inequality.** [See below, e.g., Confucian views on equality in human nature and education, the examination system as a meritocratic institution, land reform in Tang, etc.]

How is **the universe** defined in Chinese terms? What are the characteristic views of the natural world?

Confucianism

The Dao as a human way; the human conceived in terms of the universe and the universe in terms of the human; interrelatedness of the human and the universe.

Daoism

The Dao as the way of nature; human values to derive from perceptions of natural processes; the idea of non-striving (*wu-wei*), no unnatural action.

Yin-yang Cosmology

The idea of two complementary—not antagonistic—principles, associated with darkness/light; cold/heat; female/male, etc.; "the most ultimate principles of which the ancient Chinese could conceive." [See Joseph Needham, *Science and Civilisation in China*, vol. 2 (Cambridge University Press, 1956), p. 232.]

What Are Some Distinctively Confucian Ideas?

The Individual

Human beings essentially alike by nature [Analects of Confucius 17:2]; the **"noble person,"** or gentleman (*junzi*) redefined by Confucius as noble by character rather than birth; different views of human nature in early period, but eventual dominance of the strongly optimistic view of Mencius [fourth century B.C.E.] that **human nature** as intrinsically good [Mencius 2A:6 and 6A:6]; perfectibility of the self through cultivation; importance of learning and of education; **benevolence**, or humaneness (ren), as a social virtue, related to reciprocity; its expression in human interaction. There is no idea of original sin, no idea of afterlife or reincarnation ["one person; one lifetime"], no mind-body dualism or dichotomy of reason and emotion.

Society

Centrality of the **family** as center of loyalty and devotion; idea of filial piety; idea of **continuity** between individual, family, state, and the universe; cultivation on the part of the individual influences all spheres (See the "Great Learning" in *Sources of Chinese Tradition*)—Importance of **rule by virtuous men** [a government of good men rather than of good laws]; assumption that society would be patriarchal and that the state would be monarchical [no reflection (as in Plato or Aristotle) on alternative forms of government apart from monarchy]; preference for **ritual over law** (and voluntarism over coercion) as a means of social control.

Evolution of Confucian Thought

Over time Confucianism interacted with Mohism's utilitarian orientation and the idea of "universal love"; Taoism's concern with nature rather than human nature; Legalism's statist orientation, emphasis on penal law, techniques of rule (some Legalist elements incorporated into Confucian value system during and after the Han).

Sources

Chinese bronzes, tomb art, literary classics
—How is a "sacred text" or a **"classic"** to be defined? "Sacred texts," "scriptures," and "classics" differ in different cultures. China has no revealed texts: no distinction between "revealed" and "remembered" as in Brahmanical tradition, no idea of a revealed text as in Judeao-Christian Bible [another example of the human-centered posture of the Confucian tradition.] Characteristics of Chinese "classics": unlike Greek or Latin classics (The term "classics" from Latin classicus—"classy"), Chinese word for classics [jing] means the warp and woof in weaving, suggesting their human production.)

History as literature

Why is the writing of history central in Chinese culture? Civilization conceived as an ongoing process, contributions to which must be recorded; idea of the past as a means of ordering the present, the "mirror" of humankind, in which people could see the fortunes and misfortunes of the past and relate them to their own present; humanism as the guiding principle of the historian, reflected in the centrality of biographies in the work of Sima Qian.

ERA 4: EXPANDING ZONES of EXCHANGE and ENCOUNTER (300-1000 C.E.)

STANDARD 3: *Major developments in East Asia and Southeast Asia in the era of the Tang Dynasty, 600-900* C.E.

Eurasia: Interactions within East and Southeast Asia

How Did Interactions within East Asia Expand the Sphere of Sinic Civilization and Affect the Early History of Korea, Japan, and Southeast Asia?

Korea, Vietnam, and Japan adopted and adapted the ways of China, which was the developed high civilization in East Asia, becoming part of the Sinic sphere and developing their indigenous national histories at the same time. This is "civilization by diffusion" and underlines the importance of **cultural borrowing** in Japanese and Korean history.

The Spread of Buddhism

From India to China [first century B.C.E.]; spread to all China by fifth century C.E., to Korea in fourth century, to Japan via Korea in sixth century, and by another route to Southeast Asia. Buddhism was extremely significant in the transmission of culture, whether writing, art, ritual, or philosophy, to the other developed societies. Although Buddhism disappeared in India about 1000 C.E., absorbed by Hinduism, it remains vital in East and Southeast Asia to this day.

The Chinese Writing System

Korea, Vietnam, and Japan adopted Chinese characters to write their indigenous languages, which are unrelated linguistically to Chinese. This marked the beginning of their written history, literature, and, paradoxically, their distinctive national traditions.

Chinese ideas and institutions of the State

Bureaucracy and **Confucian** precepts of government by virtuous men infused the emerging polities of Korea and Japan.

Direct Relations

Japan sent official embassies to China, students from Korea and Japan studied in China, Buddhist monks came from China. To wit: this is aggressive cultural borrowing, not happenstance diffusion. Trade and tributary system within East Asia.

STANDARD 3A: *The student understands China's sustained political and cultural expansion in the Tang period.*

Heights of Chinese Development Reached in the Tang and Song [907-1129 C.E.]

Unity Regained

Three centuries of disunity followed the fall of the Han, the longest inter-dynastic interregnum in Chinese history. China reunified under the Sui dynasty [589-618 C.E.] and reached new heights of state unity and development under the Tang [618-907 C.E.] and the Song [907-1179] dynasties. The trend thereafter was toward ever longer dynastic periods and ever shorter periods of transition or interregnum. This period brought the medieval height and the subsequent enduring form of China's **universal empire**.

The Flowering of Tang China [618-907]

Strengthening the State

Return to the **examination system**, state schools; role of the aristocracy, a legacy of the long period of disunity, now within the new dynastic polity as local elite and source of state officials; **economic reforms**: land and tax reforms as attempts to move toward greater equality in landholding based on the old "equal-field system," but gradual re-concentration of landholding among the wealthy; agricultural growth.

Expansion and Sinicization of the Empire

Conquest of the Turks [who, stopped by the Tang in the seventh century, later moved south and west into Islamic lands and India], control of Tibet, northern Korea and Vietnam, Southeast Asia. Empire extended from Korea to the borders of Persia (late seventh century); massive migrations to the South and the sinicization of South China, making rice the major crop and enlarging the empire to include South China [Yangzi (Yangtse) valley].

Cosmopolitan Culture

China open to the world—silk road, travelers, luxury goods, and religion [including Nestorian Christianity and Islam]; influence beyond Chinese borders, including the flowering-by-borrowing in early Japan; technological advance; invention of printing and golden age of Chinese literature, some of the most famous poetry reflecting sympathy for the common people [Li Bo and Du Fu].

STANDARD 3B: *The student understands developments in Japan, Korea, and Southeast Asia in an era of Chinese ascendancy.*

Interactions within East Asia

The case of Japan, from beginnings through 1156 C.E.; an island country in a regional Asian setting. As a peripheral civilization, Japan was to India via Korea and China what ancient Britain was to Rome via Northern Europe.

Early Japan

Indigenous Develoment

Stone age Jōmon period [ca. 8000-300 B.C.E.] followed by a simultaneous Neolithic/Bronze/Iron revolution, probably from across the straits from Korea, in the Yayoi period [ca. 300 B.C.E.-300 C.E.], associated with wet rice agriculture [originally from southern China and Southeast Asia] and scattered tribal settlements characteristic of Neolithic villages. During the age of the Kofun, or tombs, [ca. 300-600 C.E.], the Yamato clan came to dominate, its kings, kinship groups, gods and nature beliefs [later called Shint)], and contacts with the Korean kingdom of Paekche, forming the foundation for the first Japanese imperial state, which emerged after the borrowings from China during the seventh century.

The Imperial State of the Nara [680-794 C.E.] and Heian [794-1156] Periods

Rule centered on the emperor, a central Confucian bureaucratic state modeled on Tang China, flourishing Buddhist institutions, and evolution of aristocratic court culture in the capital of Heian, present Kyoto [including the masterpiece and world's "first novel," *The Tale of Genji*, whose author belonged to the female cultural elite at court].

Patterns of Adaptation and Blending

Whereby the Chinese borrowings were molded, or abandoned, to suit the Japanese case: e.g., the emperor, one lineage descended from the Sun Goddess [no Mandate of Heaven]; preference for heredity and status hierarchy over equalizing principles like merit in the bureaucracy and the "equal-field system"; the deep impact of Buddhism without antagonism toward it as a foreign religion; the eclectic blending of beliefs, art, political forms. Significant, too, is the subsequent **continuity** of these early forms even as the historical content changed: e.g., despite the devolution of political power to aristocratic families, regents, and later shoguns, the emperor was never dislodged from the supreme position, although power was wielded in his name by others from the ninth through the twentieth centuries.

Patterns of Contact and Withdrawal

After the period of aggressive borrowing, embassies to China were ended in the ninth century, and for three centuries Japan assimilated foreign ways in the relative absence of foreign contact.

STANDARD 7: *The student understands major global trends from 300 to 1000* C.E.

How Did Movements of People, Ideas, Things, and Diseases Affect the Different Parts of the Vast EURASIAN CONTINENT?

Trade

Silk, tea, & spices, etc., primarily continental trade across the Silk Route [efflorescence in the Tang, with Arabs and Persians in the cities of China]; maritime trade via India to Southeast Asia & China [Chinese shipping in the Song, Indian ocean trade].

Ideas

Not only religions but Indian mathematics [the number zero], etc.

Crops and Bullion

In several directions.

Things

From China, paper [second century C.E., not in Europe until twelfth century], the magnetic "compass," iron-casting [fourth century B.C.E.] porcelain, printing [ninth century C.E.], gunpowder [ninth or tenth century]; the improved horse harness moved West, following the Arab conquests [invented after Buddhism entered China, bringing interactions with other parts of the Eurasian exchange]. These things and others [stirrups, etc.] may stand for the importance of Chinese inventions to later developments in Europe [quote Francis Bacon on the consequences for the scientific revolution of discoveries, "of which the origins, though recent, is obscure and inglorious: namely, printing, gunpowder, and the magnet . . . " from *The Scientific Revolution*, no mention of China]

Germs

Plague and smallpox from Europe causing epidemics in China.

Conquests and Migrations

Conquests of the steppe peoples ["barbarian" invasions of China and Europe, fourth-fifth century], periodic threats thereafter [culminating in Mongol conquest of China in thirteenth century]; but also conquests by the Tang Chinese of scores of Asian peoples who then recognized Chinese overlordship by the seventh century; the Tang were halted by the Arabs in Central Asia in mid-eighth century; massive migrations of Chinese into the Yangzi valley and South China; Annam [Vietnam] under Tang rule.

ERA 5: INTENSIFIED HEMISPHERIC INTERACTIONS, 1000-1500 CE

STANDARD 1: *The maturing of an interregional system of communication, trade, and cultural exchange in an area of Chinese economic power and Islamic expansion.*

STANDARD 1A: *The student understands China's extensive urbanization and commercial expansion between the tenth and thirteenth centuries.*

The thesis that **Song** had attained "modernity" in a unified empire, the power, government, and culture of which was not seen elsewhere for centuries before or after. In this period, China was, by most standards, the most developed state and society in the world. [Compare Europe in disunity, since seventh century]

Buddhism

It had flourished during the centuries of disunity, but lost momentum by the time of the Song. It was as if Buddhist salvation had been an attractive alternative during the period of chaos. In the Song there was a Confucian renaissance, partly animated by the long interaction with Buddhism, which resulted in a creative synthesis that prevailed as the dominant thought of the subsequent seven centuries of Chinese history.

The glories of Song China [907-1129]

Dominance of the State over Society

The state extended its control over government through a state-defined literati, or gentry, elite selected through the now thoroughly institutionalized examination system [replacing the Tang aristocracy]; control over culture through a new neo-Confucian orthodoxy [and suppression of local beliefs as heterodox], control over private practices through standardization of domestic rituals, especially marriages and funerals.

To wit: The strong state associated with much of Chinese history reaches one of its summits in the Song, but through a shift toward merit and gentry bureaucracy, not aristocracy or imperial autocracy.

Economic Prosperity

The agricultural and commercial revolutions, with such developments as double-cropping of rice in the South, spread of markets and commerce, state promotion of overseas trade, paper money, land as a marketable commodity, the growth of cities [by 1100, five cities of more than one million people], and a technological revolution that included the invention of movable type, gunpowder, rudder and magnetic compass, etc.

Social Status and Mobility

Development of the family as a corporate group and main economic actor, succession to property by equal division among brothers and status based on wealth [which fostered mobility in both directions]; exam system conferred status by achievement instead of by birth [and also fostered mobility]; increasing restrictions on women symbolized by the spread of footbinding and cloistering of women in the household [linked to the neo-Confucian conception of the social order.]

A Neo-Confucian Philosophical Synthesis

Confucian response to Buddhism and Taoism and re-commitment to Confucian social activism; formation of an intellectual tradition, including neo-Confucian commentaries on the classics, which later became the canon that formed the content of the exam system; metaphysical synthesis of Zhu Xi [twelfth century], dividing the universe into principle [*li*] and material force [*chi*], used to comprehend both nature and human nature; extension of the neo-Confucian world view to Korea, Japan, and Vietnam, especially the idea of the scholar-official, good rule through learning and virtue.

The Prematurely "Modern" Song

The commercial revolution, status by achievement not heredity [exam system], rise of cities, social mobility, technology, etc. suggest a high degree of "development" and pose the question: What happened after the Song to explain why this development did not continue? The flourishing of the Tang and Song also underlines the fact that for centuries, Asia was the "center" and Europe the "periphery" of world civilization.

STANDARD 1B: *The student understands developments in Japanese and Southeast Asian civilization.*

Medieval Japan [1185-1600]

Rise of a warrior class (samurai) and development of **feudalism** in landholding, warfare, and decentralized government by the military houses [the Kamakura (1185-1333) and Ashikaga (1336-1467) shogunates, followed by the Warring States period of civil war (1467-1600)]. Similarities and differences between European and Japanese feudalism. Under feudalism, primogeniture prevailed [and remained], and with increasing warfare, the status of women fell [and remained low]. Cultural dynamism: warriors and Zen Buddhism, popular salvationist Buddhism, Song-influenced brush painting, Noh drama. [for teaching activity: the warrior tales and their heroes, Yoshitsune, etc.]

Unification [1575-1600]

Conquest by three powerful feudal lords, each one in turn victorious over all others, until the establishment of the Tokugawa shogunate in 1600, which both unified and pacified the realm, which remained so for the ensuing 268 years.

Korea

From aristocratic to military rule [Koryŏ, twelfth-fourteenth centuries] Compare medieval pattern with Japan and also differences of Korea's international context.

STANDARD 3: *The rise of the Mongol empire and its consequences for Eurasian peoples, 1200-1350.*

Globalization through Land Contact: The Case of China

What Was the Significance of China's Universal Empire in an Age of Global Contact?

The Yuan [Mongol] dynasty [1279-1368]

Conquest of China by a "barbarian" people from its continental borders.

Significance for Eurasia

A universal empire in a geographical sense, the Mongols linked Eurasia from China to the borders of Western Europe, facilitating a period of intense continental contact [the Pax Mongolica, silk route, Marco Polo, pasta] between the West and their integrated empire of agrarian China and pastoral Central Asia.

Significance for China

Initial tension between Mongol and Chinese notions of state and society gave way to the sinicization of the Mongol rulers, who ended up running a Chinese-style dynasty, examination system and all. This is the universal empire in a cultural sense, acting as a solvent for ethnically and politically alien peoples, a role it had always played on the borders of China but now played in the Chinese court.

Significance for Future Ages of Global Contact

China's long history of global interaction had consisted of **sinicization** (civilization) of barbarian peoples on its land borders; **tributary relations**, whereby surrounding countries paid tribute to China; and **cultural influence**, which was voluntarily sought by countries like Japan. The idea of China as the "central kingdom" had seemed to be borne out by history. Compare the later situation when China was faced with the intrusion of the West, unlikely to be sinicized and unsusceptible to the dynamic of the universal empire.

Significance for East Asian International Relations

Mongols turned back by divine winds [kamikaze] in late thirteenth century, sparing Japan from external invasion. Trade and piracy by Japan in Asian seas [fifteenth-sixteenth century], official "red-seal trade" with China [late sixteenth-early seventeenth century]; Hideyoshi's abortive invasions of Korea [late sixteenth century]. For Japan, a period of contact and openness to Asia. Compare with Korea, e.g., the proximity of China and the Mongols to Korea. As with Japan, the point is to show both Korean developments and the context of the East Asian regional order.

ERA 6: THE EMERGENCE OF THE FIRST
GLOBAL AGE, 1450-1770

STANDARD 1: *How the transoceanic interlinking of all major regions of the world from 1450-1600 led to global transformations.*

STANDARD 1B: *The student understands the encounters between Europeans and peoples of Sub-Saharan Africa, Asia, and the America's in the late and early 16th centuries.*

STANDARD 3: *How large territorial empires dominated much of Eurasia between the sixteenth and eighteenth centuries.*

China

The Ming Dynasty [1368-1644]

Re-establishment of a native Chinese dynasty, which continued the strengthening of the centralized state, rule by virtue and meritocracy; a **paternalistic state** in which the state was to assure peace and prosperity as father to the people [compare European absolutism]. Coincidence of political, intellectual, and economic (landlord) elite in one class, the gentry.

Expansion of the Private Economy

Little state regulation of markets or trade combined with low taxation to foster growth of family industry and market networks; growth of private trade with Southeast Asia [after cessation of the state-sponsored voyages of Zheng He in the fifteenth century, trade did not cease but moved instead to private hands.] Emergence of the **entrepreneurial family**, with land, labor, and services regarded as saleable commodities, regulated among families by contracts, with private property vested collectively in the family, not in the individual. Equal succession among brothers worked against concentration of wealth and in favor of dominance of small family farms. Important to note the long tradition of family entrepreneurship in China.]

The Jesuits in China [late sixteenth-early seventeenth centuries]

Matteo Ricci and others who enjoyed favor at court for their knowledge of European science; the "rites controversy," which revolved around whether Christian converts could also practice ancestor worship and later led to the banning of Christianity.

The **Chinese maritime expeditions** [fifteenth century]: The impressive armadas of Zheng He that crossed the Indian Ocean to East Africa and then were ended for reasons of barbarian border threats, court politics, and financial policy. [While the Portuguese and others were drawn to the "fabled" riches and spices of the East, there was little to attract the Central Kingdom in the other direction. China's so-called withdrawal from global exploration misreads the nature of the fifteenth-sixteenth century world as the Chinese perceived it.]

Globalization by Maritime Contact: The Case of Japan

Portuguese and Spanish arrive in Japan

Earlier, Japan known in the West through Marco Polo, who reported hearsay about "Zipangu," [Columbus had Marco Polo's book with him when he thought he had found Japan in the Caribbean]. Portuguese [the Southern Barbarians] landed off Japan in 1543, introducing the musket, trading, and proselytizing. Francis Xavier and others converted whole feudal domains to Catholicism [late sixteenth century]. As unification proceeded, the unifiers were first suspicious of the danger of colonialism, as in the Philippines, and then of the threat to the new stability of the realm posed by foreign traders and missionaries. The result was the expulsion of Westerners and the suppression of Christianity in the early seventeenth century. Although relations with East Asia continued, by 1640 Japan was in **"seclusion"** from relations with the West, except for Dutch merchants at Nagasaki, a phase of withdrawal from the world that continued until the mid-nineteenth century.

Factors within Japan, especially unification and the reestablishment of peace and order, determined Japanese cessation of intercourse with the West during the first global age.

STANDARD 5: *Transformations in Asian societies in the era of European expansion.*

STANDARD 5A: *The student understands the development of European maritime power in Asia.*

STANDARD 5B: *The student understands the transformations in India, China, and Japan in an era of expanding European commercial power.*

STANDARD 5C: *The student understands major cultural trends in Asia between the sixteenth and eighteenth centuries.*

The main point here is to underline the changes and developments that occurred elsewhere in the world **before** the direct challenge of the modern West precipitated modernization in the nineteenth century.

The Case of Tokugawa Japan [1600-1868]

Understanding the developments that some call "proto-modern" but that all agree were decisive in the ways in which Japan eventually responded to the Western challenge and embarked on the course of its modernization.

The Tokugawa State of "Centralized Feudalism"

Central shogunate and independent domains; peace and domestic stability for more than two centuries; growth of national infrastructure [roads, communication, markets, etc]; development of elite class of samurai-turned-civil bureaucrats; and a reconception of government, morality, and world-view in terms of neo-Confucianism borrowed from Song and Ming China, supplemented by imperial and "nativist" thought insisting on a Japanese national identity in contrast to China. Some call this the incipient "nation-state" dynamicentury [For teaching activity: the story of the 47 *ronin*, samurai retainers torn between the law and loyalty to their lord.]

Commercialization, Economic Growth, and Demographic Stability

Rise in agricultural production [technological improvements], commercial growth in rural industries, trade in an increasingly national market, stable population which relieved burden on agricultural economy. Some call eighteenth-nineteenth century Japan "proto-industrial," but commercialization is not tantamount to capitalism and no industrial revolution occurred.

Changes in Social Relations

The putative status hierarchy of four estates [samurai, peasant, artisan, and merchant, in order of Confucian views of descending social value] altered over time, so that merit came to vie with heredity in samurai status, merchants rose in wealth and power, rich peasants became entrepreneurs. There are social developments "in the direction of change."

Intellectual Trends

Commoner education and rising literacy, Neo-Confucian reinterpretations of political economy, incorporating a money economy; nativist configurations of national identity; "Dutch Learning" introducing Western science, thought, and art into the "closed" country, well in advance of the appearance of the "real West" in Japanese waters in the nineteenth century.

The Case of Qing China [1644–1911]

The Qing State

Another foreign dynasty, founded by the Manchus after their conquest of the Ming, brought a sinicized Manchu court ruling in the Chinese style and, once again, a strengthened state and the peace and prosperity of the "High Qing," [roughly the eighteenth century]

Economic Growth

Diversification of the economy, increased production of cash crops and handicrafts; extension of internal frontiers and highlands, partly as a result of introduction of New World crops like maize, sweet potato, and peanuts; infusion of silver from foreign trade; flourishing internal trade and markets.

Social Change

Dramatic population growth, a result of peace and prosperity; increased power of the local elite, or gentry; movement of elite to towns and cities; White Lotus rebellions and ethnic risings on the borders; spread of literacy.

Qing Culture

Confucian rejection of speculation and turn toward "evidential research," which meant close textual examination of the classics; the masterpiece of Qing fiction, *The Dream of the Red Chamber*, portrays family structure, women, religion, and sexuality in an almost "realistic" style.

Global Connections

Links to the world economy, especially the inflow of New World silver and trade with Europe of tea, porcelain, cotton, and silk; regulation of foreign merchants within China; the famous Macartney mission [1793] and the emperor's reply to the British request for trade [we have not "the slightest need of your country's manufactures"].

The Case of Yi Dynasty Korea [1392-1910]

The Korean mission of a Confucianized, Sinic state [Yamgban society and bureaucracy, rise of practical learning, etc.]; compare to China and Japan, much as France, Germany, etc., are compared within Europe.

The Case of Annam (Vietnam)

Like Korea, a variant of a Chinese-influenced state, tributary to China, but insistently independent (since 935 CE).

ERA 7: AN AGE OF REVOLUTIONS, 1750-1914

STANDARD 3: *The transformation of Eurasian Societies in an era of global trade and rising European power, 1750-1870.*

STANDARD 3D: *The student understands how China's Qing dynasty responded to economic and political crises in the late eighteenth and nineteenth centuries.*

The Case of China: What Were the Characteristics and Course of China's "Long Modernization?"

Prologue

China's path toward the modern began with the technological and commercial revolution of the Song (960-1279) and extends even to the late twentieth century. It combined territorial expansion, perfection of the bureaucratic institutions of universal empire, adjustment to foreign incursion the absorption of non-Chinese ethnic groups, and growth of the commercial economy without industrialization. Among its social manifestations were the spread of literacy, elimination of most hereditary status classifications, movement of elites to towns and cities, and relatively small differentials in wealth among classes.

The Nineteenth Century

Combination of **domestic problems** and **imperialism** precipitated the long modernization.

Internal Developments

Acceleration of **population growth** during the High Qing resulted in strains on government, pressure on the land, and the closing of the internal frontier; **rebellion and social unrest** increased, culminating in the epochal Taiping Rebellion [1850-64], during which at one point the rebels controlled one third of China.

External Pressures

Western imperialism in the form of the opium trade, defeat at the hands of the barbarians [the British] in the Opium Wars, unequal treaties, and finally, treaty ports and spheres of influence. **Economic impact** included introduction of new technologies and communications, lack of impetus to China's industrial development (classical colonial economic relationship without political colonization), opium and finished goods exported to China while Westerners and Japanese purchased agricultural products; Western-dominated treaty ports became main centers of modern production and services, even for Chinese, who invested their capital there to avoid the insecurity caused by unrest elsewhere. **Political impact** contributed to decline of the Qing, the last imperial dynasty: defeats by barbarians lowered Qing prestige in Chinese eyes; unequal treaties and indemnities diminished government resources for defense and economic development. **Intellectual impact**: introduction of Western political ideas such as those of the nation-state and constitutional monarchy undermined the premises of dynastic rule and the concept of the central kingdom.

The Search for Modernity

The resulting political and cultural crisis generated **three quests** in the Chinese search for modernity:

1. The quest for a **new national identity**: Efforts to combine Western technology with Chinese essence, or to practice a kind of Confucian reformism within the dynastic framework; concept of the nation-state and national identity resulting in the end of the belief in dynasty and universal empire [late 19th and early twentieth century]; **what is China**?—geographic versus cultural identity.

2. The quest for a **new political forms**: Decline of dynastic power and the rise of regional power; constitutionalism and the challenge to the Confucian consensus; **how to reconfigure the state**.

3. The quest for **economic modernization**: central and regional government efforts to encourage **industrialization**; vitality of the domestic market economy as an impediment to urban-based industrialization.

STANDARD 3E: *The student understands how Japan was transformed from feudal shogunate to modern nation-state in the nineteenth century.*

The Case of Japan: What Was the Nature and Course of Japan's Rapid Nineteenth-century Modernization?

Tokugawa preconditions combined with the challenge of the West to provoke a **defensive modernization**. After the fall of the Tokugawa shogunate and the establishment of a **centralized modern state** under the emperor in the Meiji Restoration of 1868, Japan pursued modernization as "westernization," [to become like the West in order to be accepted by the West] in a series of fundamental reforms that included everything from compulsory education to a constitution. **Social changes** included the abolition of the four hereditary statuses, education of girls as well as boys, and rendering farmers title to their land, to be taxed in cash, not kind. [teaching activity: Fukuzawa Yukichi, a hero of modernizing Meiji: "Heaven creates no man above or below another man."] Under the slogan "rich country, strong army," the nation pursued **economic growth** through industrialization, and **military strength** through a conscript army. **Ideology** for the subject of the new Meiji state stressed imperial loyalty and national identity. **International status** was sought through revision of the unequal treaties and in wars against China [1894-5] and Russia [1904-5]. Japan, the first modernized country in Asia, was also the first Western-style Asian imperialist.

Japan had followed its familiar pattern of aggressive **borrowing**, this time from the West, and transformed its domestic political, social, and economic arrangements into modern forms within a few decades. The so-called late-developing countries, of which Japan was an early example, felt that they had **little choice** in the direction or timing of their modernization, which was achieved at no small human and social cost. Although modernity eventually became a global phenomenon, many societies experienced it either as West-led or West-dominated in its initial phases, sometimes giving rise later to reactions against both the West and (Western-style) modernity at one and the same time.

STANDARD 5: *Patterns of global change in the era of Western military and economic dominance, 1800-1914.*

STANDARD 5C: *The student understands the causes of European, American, and Japanese imperial expansion.*

STANDARD 5D: *The student understands transformations in South, Southeast, and East Asia in the era of the "new imperialism."*

How Did the Presence of the West and Western Imperialism Differ within the Countries of East Asia and from Elsewhere in the World in the Nineteenth Century?

China, Japan, Korean, and Vietnam

Begin with the differences in the four countries "on the eve of the Western intrusion." Then compare the different character of each intrusion.

China and Britain

Opium trade and Opium Wars, defeat, and unequal treaties (1842 & 1858), while threats from within (Taiping rebellion) and a continued commitment to the Chinese imperial system set the scene for China's interactions with the West's "new imperialism."

Japan and the United States

The United States "opened" Japan to trade (1853), value as a coaling station [i.e., not as valuable as China, United States not the same kind of imperial power as Britain, plus the lessons Japan learned from the negative example of Opium Wars], unequal treaties but no defeat (1858), set the scene for Japan's "defensive moderniza-tion" to meet the external threat of the West by Westernizing, repeat-ing Japan's recurrent pattern of cultural borrowing.

Korea and China and Japan

Japan "opened" Korea (1876) to trade via its own unequal treaty, which both asserted Korea's sovereignty vis a vis China and opened Korea to the West (unequal treaty with United States, 1882), setting the scene for Korea's enlightenment & reform move-ments and for contention between Japan and China over develop-ments in Korea. In the case of Korea, it was not the West but Japan which acted the role of imperialist-plus-challenge to mod-ernization, a role associated with Euro-america elsewhere. This imperialism resulted in Japan's annexation of Korea in 1910 and the ensuing 35 years of harsh colonial rule.

Vietnam and France and China

French seizure of Vietnam resulted in war with China on behalf of its tributary state, which resulted in French victory (1885) and protectorate over an area called French Indochina, setting the scene both for rising Chinese nationalism and the long Vietnam-ese struggle for independence.

The Intersection

Four national histories and intra-East Asian regional relations intersect with the international relations of Western imperialism with consequences for the domestic modernization and interna-tional status of each country, a story that plays out over the course of a century, from the mid-nineteenth-century incursions through modernization, national independence, and international status in the mid to late twentieth century.

This is East Asia's **long modernization**," of which the imperialist incursions of the nineteenth were an impelling but in no way determining factor of the process or the outcome in the four coun-tries of the Sinic world.

STANDARD 6: *The student understands major global trends from 1750-1914.*

Migrations and POPULATION Change: East Asia

Compare nineteenth-century China and Japan in terms of population growth and stability and note how the differences affected economic modernization: China, in population growth, Japan in demographic stability.

Reform and Revolution: MODERNIZATION in East Asia

What Were the Different Characteristics and Different Chronologies of the Process of Political, Economic, and Social Modernization in East Asia?

Assume that the **empirical definition of "modernization"** usually includes industrialization and economic development, forms of leveling of traditional social hierarchies, mechanisms for inclusion of larger numbers of people in political participation, formation of an independent nation-state with an ideology of national identity, and integration of the autonomous state into the international order.

The main point is the different patterns and chronologies in the different countries [and the same may be said of other parts of the world, where such modernity occurred in different patterns at different times, roughly a nineteenth-twentieth-century process, but not to be compared in strictly chronological terms.] In East Asia, this means characterizing **Japan's rapid modernization** [1830s-1890s] in terms of domestic social, economic, and political preconditions, challenging but non-invasive external pressures, historical patterns of cultural borrowing, evolutionary rather than revolutionary change, etc. **China's long modernization** [1840s-1970s] proceeded across two centuries and a series of rebellions, reforms, and three revolutions [1911, 1928, 1949] on the basis of different and more difficult preconditions, subject first to Western then to Japanese imperialism, through anti-Japanese war, civil war, and cold war, and following its own historical patterns toward new political forms and economic development. In both **Korea and Vietnam**, modernization was vexed by a context of colonial domination, nationalist movements for independence, world war and cold war that divided both countries, with different timing and outcomes.

IDEOLOGIES of East Asia

How Were Traditional Ideologies Such as Confucianism, Familism, or Nativism Transformed in Combination with New Ideas of Democracy, Marxism, Nationalism, and the Like?

Here **nationalism** and **Marxism** are the two critical topics, plus the point that Western ideas did not displace traditional ideas but transformed and were transformed by them.

[The common case is that of Confucianism, which is said to have been an obstacle to modernization in nineteenth-century China, to have been jettisoned, then retrieved during modernization in nineteenth-century Japan, and to account for the rapid economic rise of Korea, Singapore, and Taiwan in the contemporary period. Clearly there are as many Confucianisms as there are nationalisms, and none of them can be assigned such simple causal efficacy.]

ERA 8: A HALF-CENTURY OF CRISIS AND ACHIEVEMENT, 1900-1945

STANDARD 1: *Reform, revolution and social change in the world economy of the early twentieth century.*

STANDARD 1A: *The student understands the world industrial economy emerging in the early twentieth century.*

Japan

Characteristics of Japan's industrialization, including the importance of the agricultural base, both for capital and the source of foreign exchange (silk); role of the state and of private entrepreneurship; fiscal strains, including the deflation of the 1880s, with positive effects on economy growth and negative social impact on the countryside; wars against China and Russia and their economic consequences, including foreign debt, heavy industry, and the beginnings of modern industrial relations; high GNP growth on a semi-industrialized base, with cottage industry still more important than heavy industry until the First World War.

STANDARD 1B: *The student understands the causes and consequences of important resistance and revolutionary movements of the early twentieth century.*

China

The Chinese revolution of 1911, here compared to Russia in 1905, the Young Turks, the Mexican Revolution, which has the advantage of chronological synchronicity, but needs to be balanced by linking the 1911 revolution in China to earlier and later efforts at political reform and also perhaps by allusion to developments in East Asia, e.g., the Meiji Restoration.

STANDARD 2: *The causes and global consequences of World War I.*

STANDARD 2A: *The student understands the causes of World War. I.*

How Did the "World Wars" Affect Asia?

European colonies involved in India and Southeast Asia; consequences of World War I for China and Japan; rise of Asian nationalism in the wake of World War I, including China's May 4th and Korea's March 1st movements, Vietnamese and Indian nationalism]; Japanese aggressive war in China [1937-45] and its impact on Chinese civil war and communist victory; global alliances of wartime convenience in World War II [Japan, Germany, and Italy; United States, the USSR, China]; the end of Western territorial imperialism in Southeast Asia as the ironic outcome of Japan's wartime empire; postwar settlements and their effects on Asia, decolonization & cold war divisions. The **globalization of total war**.

STANDARD 3: *The search for peace and stability in the 1920s and 1930s.*

STANDARD 3A: *The student understands postwar efforts to achieve lasting peace and social and economic recovery.*

Japan at Versailles

Japan's experience as "one of the Powers," including territorial settlements, the Shandong question, the racial equality clause; charges of diplomatic failure at home; importance of "Washington Conference System" in Japan's cooperation with European and American-led multilateral diplomacy.

STANDARD 3B: *The student understands economic, social, and political transformations in Africa, Asia, and Latin America in the 1920s and 1930s.*

STANDARD 3E: *The student understands the causes and global consequences of Great Depression.*

Imperialism and fascism in Japan

Aggression in Manchuria, 1931, followed by establishment of puppet state and Japan's withdrawal from the League of Nations, signals the beginning of the "fifteen-year war." The end of multilateral diplomacy as Japan decided to "go it alone" as territorial imperialist in Asia; instigation of all-out war against China in 1937, with atrocities such as the Rape of Nanking and without victory—1937 as the beginning of World War II in Asia. In domestic politics, 1932, the end of party governments and the beginning of the power of the military in politics, but with cooperation of the civilian leaders. As in other countries, the deep depression of the early 30s prompted protectionist economic policies; in Japan, as in Germany [but unlike the United States] military spending sparked recovery by the mid-30s.

Nationalism vs. Communism in China

Nationalist revolution of 1928, followed by struggle between the nationalists and the communists; two versions of possible solutions to political reorganization and economic development; Japanese invasion and war; role of the "war of resistance against the Japanese" [World War II] in domestic politics, e.g., united front, peasant mobilization, etc.

STANDARD 4: *The causes and global consequences of World War II.*

STANDARD 4A: *The student understands the causes of World War II.*

STANDARD 4B: *The student understands the global scope, outcome, and human costs of the war.*

Geometry of Global War

Importance of the international context in nearly every aspect of the war, e.g., Japan attacked Pearl Harbor as part of a strategy to win the war in China; the United States got tough on Japan in 1941 because of Germany's impending invasion of the Soviet Union; Nationalists in China sought support from the United States on grounds of anti-communist struggle, etc. Importance of regional developments, including the anti-colonial movements galvanized further by Japan's war [Subhas Bose in India] or wartime occupation [Indonesia, Philippines]; communist movements that prevailed in postwar China, North Vietnam, North Korea. Importance of the domestic conditions in each country, including economic crisis, political instability, and social conditions.

STANDARD 5: *Major global trends from 1900 to the end of World War II.*

See below, Era 9, Standard 6.

ERA 9: THE TWENTIETH CENTURY SINCE 1945: PROMISES and PARADOXES

STANDARD 1: *How post-World War II reconstruction occurred, new international power relations took shape, and colonial empires broke up.*

STANDARD 1B: *The student understands why global power shifts took place and the Cold War broke out in the aftermath of World War II.*

Cold War in Asia

Consequences of the cold war in the division of Korea and Vietnam, the alliance of United States and Japan, U.S. recognition of Taiwan and nonrecognization of the PRC; integration of Southeast Asia into the economic system of "containment at the rim"; proxy hot wars in Korea and Vietnam, which Japan's economy profited from. Again, international, regional, and domestic factors are interrelated and ought not to be treated separately.

STANDARD 2: *The search for community, stability, and peace in an inter-dependent world.*

STANDARD 2A: *The student understands how population explosing and environmental change have altered conditions around the world.*

Population dilemmas

In India and China: efforts at population control, e.g., China's one-child policy.

Ecological challenge

In every country: pollution within Japan (Minamata, etc.), destruction by Japan of rainforests of Southeast Asia; the challenge posed to China by industrial and automobile pollution, etc. National, regional, and international responses and non-responses.

STANDARD 2B: *The student understands how increasing economic interdependence has transformed human society.*

How Has Asia's Part in the Global Economy Changed over the Twentieth Century?

Shifts from colonial economies to offshore manufacturing to entrepreneurial state-led capitalism in Southeast Asia, etc; shifts from industrial development based on exports of primary products [e.g., imperial Japan and silk] to industrial and post-industrial economies based on exports of high tech products [e.g., Japan, Korea, Taiwan in electronics]; technology transfer and economic development; rise of Japan as a world economic power; the economic development of the Newly Industrialized Economies (NIES); the economic development of China, including expanded international trade and investment; Asia and multilateral institutions of international political economy, including World Trade Organization (WTO). Post-industrial developments: Japan as an information society, "computopia," etc.; importance of intra-Asian media structures.

All of these phenomena were entirely intertwined with, and dependent upon, world markets, capital, and mechanisms of the world economy, supporting the truism that in the twentieth-century economic development was impossible in isolation from the international economy. Also, the importance, as before in history, of intra-Asian regional economy, with inequities of economic power within the region and within a country, as in China.

STANDARD 2C: *The student understands how liberal democracy, market economies, and human rights movements have reshaped political and social life.*

Democracy in Asia

Comparison of the different definitions and practices of democracy and changes in them: Japan, Korea, Taiwan, China, post-reversion

Hong Kong. Is "democracy" singular? How do different countries around the world define democracy at the end of the twentieth century?

Market Economies in Asia

Similar comparisons and similar questions. Is there such a thing as Confucian capitalism? Do all "market economies" look alike? What definition is being used?

Human rights

Domestic issues: Constitutional and political changes extending suffrage and participation; legal guarantees of civil rights for minority groups, for women, i.e., part of the long modernization process; social changes in gender roles occurring as a result of women in the workplace, smaller families, etc.; ethnic and regional rights, e.g. Tibet.

International issues: The application of international law and human rights and its effects [e.g., China]; new economic migrants [foreign workers, etc.] creating new minorities and posing new problems to countries that have not defined themselves as "immigrant societies" [e.g., Japan].
The question of "Asian values" and international human rights.

STANDARD 2D: *The student understands major sources of tension and conflict in the contemporary world and efforts that have been made to address them.*

Asia

Regional issues, including North Korea and Korean unification; postwar regional security and nuclear issues; the place of China in Asia; redefinitions of "Asia," including Asian multilateral institutions and their relation to the world order. Domestic forces of destabilization and international pressures.

STANDARD 2F: *The student understands worldwide cultural trends of the second half of the twentieth century.*

Asia and World Culture

Particularizing forces: cultural nationalism in Japan, Korea, etc. Ethnic nationalisms in China and elsewhere. Is there such a thing as an "Asian" consciousness and identity?

Globalizing forces: Communications [viewers in Japan watching "Little House in the Prairie" and viewers in Southeast Asia watching the Japanese program "Oshin," fax machines all manufactured in East Asia, satellite television connecting intraAsia and the world; internationalized popular culture, two-way cultural interchange; the notion of an "Asian-Pacific century."

STANDARD 3: *Major global trends since World War II.*

Note: The Standards separate the twentieth century into two halves, which makes sense in terms of the importance of 1945; yet, in the longer view of the twentieth century and, especially in view of "major global trends," it often seems historically more appropriate to treat the "long twentieth century" together, as the following examples suggest:

How Were War, Revolution, and National Liberation Intertwined in Asia?

The long struggle of countries like Vietnam and Indonesia for national liberation, in the context of Western and Japanese imperialism, from the 1910s through the 1970s, and how the world wars, democracy [the West/United States] and communism [USSR/China] figured in the struggle. [Soekarno/Ho Chi Minh]

Pursuing political change through **social revolution** in China, continuing the century-long process of regaining political unity, establishing a modern national state, and promoting economic momentum, by transforming the Marxist idea of a proletariat revolution into the Maoist organization of a peasant revolution [1949], and the rocky road that followed, from the Cultural Revolution [1965-76] through Tiananmen [1989] and into the post-Deng era.

Processes of **decolonization** and nation-making in India, Philippines, Burma, Indonesia, Vietnam, etc, another long process. For Korea, decolonization after a half-century of Japanese rule but within U.S. or USSR dominated cold war framework.

Both **Korea** and **Vietnam** share the contexts and challenges of world war, cold war, hot wars, decolonization, nation-building, economic development [capitalist/socialist], democratization, etc., with other nations around the world. The reemerging East/Southeast Asian regional alignments should also be noted, a regional configuration of the past being reconfigured in the present.

In nearly every country in Asia the post World War II period saw the struggle for independence succeed eventually and the ensuing battle for economic development, increased political participation (democracy), and international stature continue to this day.

The Case of Japan and the World in the Twentieth Century

What Did Japan Have in Common with Other Nations in the Twentieth Century?

The main point is the **international history** of the twentieth century, which consists both of globalized international relations and commonalities within the histories of different nations.

Examples: challenges to expanding democracy [from popular rights movement in the 1880s, through Taishō democracy in the 1920s, to occupation reforms and postwar democracy]; adjusting political economy to a state/private sector mix typical of industrialized states [1920s-1960s];transition from light to heavy industry to postindustrial sectors, often in conjunction with armament and war [e.g., 30s, Korean war]; economic dislocations as a result of external developments [the Depression as a negative, the post World War II boom as a positive factor]; unstable fears on left and right, difficulty of holding to the center, with fascism as one result [1920s/30s]; militarism and war as "solutions" to domestic and international dilemmas [1931-45]; postwar reforms under the occupation as another instance of aggressive change on the part of Japan, simultaneously continuing past Japanese trends and borrowing from America; incorporation into the cold war framework through the U.S.-Japan alliance; postwar commitment to peace [atomic bomb, peace constitution] and shift of emphasis from the state and public duty to private lives and livelihood [consumer society, prosperity]; change in women's roles from cooption by the state as "good wives, wise mothers" to middle-class family managers, "education mamas," and self-improving individuals, etc.

Whatever the themes evoked in the twentieth-century section, Japan may best be compared in the first instance with the industrialized nations of the West, rather than with China, whose history in this period belongs more to the still unfolding story of long modernization than does Japan's.

How Did China in the Twentieth-century Continue the Three Quests Begun but Not Resolved in the Nineteenth-century Phase of its Long Modernization?

1. The quest for **national identity**: what does it mean to be Chinese in the modern world? Early twentieth-century elite rejec-

tion of traditional Chinese culture and of wholesale westernization exemplified the cultural dilemma. This resulted in repeated **cultural revolutions** [May 4th movement in 1919 and after, Guomindang New Life movement in the 1930s, Communist Party's New Socialist Man of the 1950s, the Great Proletarian Cultural Revolution in the 1960s, and the anti-spiritual pollution campaigns of the 1980s.] The same anti-traditionalism also intensified the gap between elites and the populace, especially in the People's Republic of China.

2. The quest for **new political forms**: Three major revolutions in the twentieth century, each with its own goals, but each with the overarching objective of creating a political form that could both foster economic development and national strength in a world context.

a. **Republican revolution** (1911): Expansion of the arena of political participation and overthrow of dynastic rule (the fall of the Qing), under the leadership of Sun Yat-sen, followed by a period of rampant warlordism and disunity. b. **Nationalist revolution** (1928): National political unification under Chiang Kaishek and the Guomindang, followed by civil war between the nationalists and the communists. c. **Communist revolution** (1949): Economic and social justice and the redistribution of political power, under the leadership of Mao Zedong, followed by strong party leadership without mass political participation.

3. The quest for **economic modernization**: Continued development of the commercial economy with modest industrialization and increasing integration with the world economy through 1949; Nationalists' attraction to national socialism and bureaucratic capitalism (1928-49); Communists' state controlled industrial development, agricultural collectivization, and curtailment of the private market economy; post-1979 de-collectivization of agriculture, legalization of private entrepreneurship, and the private market economy.

The Case of China and the World in the Twentieth Century

The growth of a **large overseas Chinese community** from the nineteenth century on (United States, the Caribbean, Great Britain, Southeast Asia). Importance of the Chinese diaspora as migrants and sojourners, as entrepreneurs and social networks.

The **shift in international frameworks** from Western spheres of influence and the Open Door [late nineteenth-early twentieth centuries] to Japanese imperialism and war in Manchuria and

China [1931-45] to the Cold War, the Soviet Union and the Sino-Soviet split of 1961, border tensions, and the move toward rapprochement in the 1980s.

The United States and Japan as China's main **trading partners** in post-1979 China: Hong Kong after 1997; Taiwan, and the People's Republic of China (PRC). The emergence of the **greater Chinese cultural and economic zone** (Taiwan, Hong Kong, and PRC since the 80s).

Chinese Links to Contemporary Issues

The entrepreneurial family and the economic miracle in Taiwan, Hong Kong, and the PRC; the international media connection—fax, phone, computers, satellite, music linking China to the rest of the world despite government efforts at cultural control; population growth and the quest for economic development. Link to issues of global ecological concern such as deforestation, use of fossil fuels, trade-offs between the environment and growth in lesser developed countries like China; the re-emergence of a market economy and concerns over the intensification of class and regional inequalities that accompany capitalism (e.g., advanced development in coastal vs inland China); the question of China's political future in the face of growing economic liberalization and a generational transition in the ruling elite. The question of democracy in Taiwan and the PRC.

Suggested Resources for MAPS to be used in conjuction with Asia In Western and World History A Guide for Teaching

The three volumes listed here contain maps that relate to the historical eras and events discussed in *Asia in Western and World History*. The *Hammond Concise Atlas of World History* is an excellent resource widely available in paperback. The other two volumes, *The Earth and its Peoples: A Global History* and *The Heritage of World Civilizations*, are world history textbooks available only in hardcover from their respective publishers.

HISTORICAL ATLAS

(AWH): *Hammond Concise Atlas of World History*
5th Edition, 1998. Geoffrey Barraclough, editor
(Hammond Incorporated, Maplewood, NJ, 07040–1396)
ISBN 0–8437–1121–3
www.hammondmap.com

Many of the maps and information contained in *Hammond Concise Atlas of World History* overlap with the material discussed in the chapters of *Asia in Western and World History*. When specific references in a given chapter are not coincidental with the annotations on the map listed under that chapter, the map may still be a useful indicator of geographical or political contours or boundaries.

WORLD HISTORY TEXTBOOKS

The two textbooks listed here are recommended for their excellent coverage of Asian history within world history. The maps in these textbooks, while perhaps less detailed than those in *Hammond Concise Atlas of World History*, provide additional perspectives that complement the essays in *Asia in Western and World History*.

(EP): *The Earth and its Peoples: A Global History*
Richard W. Bulliet et al, editors
(Boston: Houghton Mifflin Company, 1997)
ISBN 0–395–52757–0
http://www.hmco.com/college/history/world/bulliet/index.htm

(HWC): *The Heritage of World Civilizations*
Albert M. Craig et al, editors
(Upper Saddle River, NJ: Prentice Hall, 1997)
ISBN 0–13–010137–0
http://www.prenhall.com/books/hss_013262494x.html

The chapter titles below are from *Asia in Western and World History*. The source book for each map is indicated with the initials, shown above in parenthesis, of the book title.

I. ASIA IN WESTERN HISTORY

Introductions

The Shape of the World: Eurasia

[*The maps listed for this essay were selected because they show the Eurasian continent*]

Asian Influences on the West

Essays

**The Beginnings of Contact and Interdependence:
Western Asia and the West**

Interfusion of Asian and Western Cultures: Islamic Civilization and Europe to 1500

The Mongols and the West

Asia and the West in the New World Economy— The Limited Thalassocracies: The Portuguese and the Dutch in Asia, 1498–1700

European expansion overseas, 1493–1713, *pp. 66–67*
  Map 2: Commercial expansion to the East, 1600–1700
South-East Asia, 1511–1826, *pp. 70–71*

EP Map 21.2 European colonization in the Indian Ocean to 1750, *p. 618*
   Map 17–3 European exploration, 1420–1542, *p. 494*

HWC Map 17–1 European voyages of discovery and the colonial claims of Spain and Portugal in the fifteenth and sixteenth centuries, *p. 451*

Asia and the West in the New World Order—From Trading Companies to Free Trade Imperialism: The British and Their Rivals in Asia, 1700–1850

AWH East Asia, 1511–1826, *pp. 70–71*
   European imperialism, *pp. 100–1*

EP Map 26.3 European possessions in the Indian Ocean and South Pacific, 1870, *p. 754*

The Rise and Fall of Western Empire in Asia: 1500–1975

AWH European expansion overseas, 1493–1713, pp. 66–67
    Map 2: Commercial expansion to the East, 1600–1700
   South-East Asia, 1511–1826, *pp. 70–71*
   India under British rule, *pp. 104–5*
   Modern Japan, 1868–1941, *pp. 126–27*
   Retreat from empire after 1947, *pp. 138–39*
   Asia and Africa after independence, *pp. 140–41*
     Map 1: Post-independence wars and revolutions

Asia and the West in the Twentieth-Century World Order

II. ASIA IN WORLD HISTORY

Essays

The Neolithic Transition: Hunting-Gathering to Sedentary Village Farming and Pastoralism

Map 2: Palestine at the time of David, c. 980 B.C.

Map 5: The Persian Empire, 550–331 BC

The Greek world, 497–185, *pp. 22–23*

The world religions c. 500 B.C.–A.D. 500, *pp. 26–27*

Map 1: The diffusion of religions

India and China: The first empires, *pp. 28–29*

Christianity and Judaism, c. 600–1500, *pp. 38–39*

Map 1: Christianity in Asia

The Islamic world, 632–1517, *pp. 40–41*

EP   Map 8.1 Asian trade and communication routes, *p. 222 [for Buddhism]*

Map 10.1 Early expansion of Muslim rule, *p. 441*

Map 35.1 World religions, *p. 1022 [in 1990s]*

HWC Map 5–7 The spread of Christianity, *p. 171*

Map 7–3 The spread of Buddhism and Chinese states in 500 C.E., *p. 215*

Map 14–1 The Islamic heartlands, 1000–1500, *p. 376*

The Era of Asian Discovery: Trade and the Contact of Cultures

China, 300–1200

Japan, 550–838

India, 100 B.C.E–1500 A.D.

AWH Trading links of the ancient world, *pp. 24–25*

Map 1: Eurasian trade routes, c. AD 200

The world religions c. 500 B.C.–A.D. 500, *pp. 26–27*

The barbarian invasions, *pp. 32–22*

Map 1: Barbarian invasions of the ancient world

The Islamic world, 632–1517, *pp. 40–41*

China and its neighbours, 618–1644, *pp. 50–51*

Separate Spheres and New Links: A New State in World History, 1000–1500
The Case of China, 1000–1500
The Case of Japan, 1000–1500

The Expansion of Europe, 1450–1700

Japan and the West, 1543–1640

Europe and the World in and Expanding World Economy, 1700–1850
China and the World, 1500–1800
China's Economy in Comparative Perspective, 1500 Onward
An Approach to Modern Indian Economic History

III. MODERN ASIA, 1600–1990

Tokugawa Japan, 1600–1867
Five Myths about Early Modern Japan

AWH China and its neighbours, 618–1644, *pp. 50–51*
     Map 3: Civil war in Japan, 1467–1590 [*shows Japan just prior to unification under the Tokugawa*]

EP   Map 27.4 Japan in the 1800s, *p. 787*

HWC Map 20–3 Tokugawa Japan and the Korean Peninsula, *p. 564*

State and Society During the Qing Dynasty, 1644–1911

AWH China under the Ch'ing Dynasty, 1644–1911, *pp. 106–107*

EP   Map 22.1 Romanov-Qing rivalries, 1650–1750, *p. 634*

HWC Map 20–2 The Ch'ing Empire at its peak, *p. 554*

Japan's Modernities, 1850s–1990s

AWH Modern Japan, 1868–1941, *pp. 126–27*

EP   Map 28.3 Expansion and modernization of
     Japan, 1868–1914, *p. 821*

HWC Map 33–3 Formation of the Japanese Empire,
     p. 916

Modern China, 1840–1990

AWH The Chinese Revolution, 1911–1949, *pp. 122–23*

EP   Map 32.1 The Chinese Communist movement
         and the war with Japan, *p. 923*
     Map 34.2 World population density, *p. 990*

HWC Map 33–2 The Northern expeditions of the
     Kuomintang, *p. 904*

Modern India, 1885–1990

AWH India under British rule, 1805–1947, *pp. 104–5*
     Retreat from empire after 1947, *pp. 138–39*
         Map 1: Decolonisation, 1947–1990
EP   Map 33.1 Decolonization, *p. 948*

HWC Map 27–4 Asia 1880–1914, *p. 762*
     Map 38–1 Contemporary Asia, *p. 1037*

Modern Korea, 1860–1990

AWH China under the Ch'ing Dynasty, 1644–1911,
         pp. 106–7
     Map 1: Imperial expansion, 1644–1760
     Map 4: The dismemberment of the Chinese
         Empire, 1842–1911

Index

Abbasid Caliphate, 828

Acapulco, 784, 824

Achaemenid Persia, 236, 273

Acheh, 63, 68

Adams, Henry, 663

Aden, 68, 832

Adyar River, battle of, 93

Aegean, culture mix of, 31; early agriculture in, 32; Mycenean and Minoan civilizations in, 34, 258; Western civilization roots in, 7

Aeneid (Virgil), 268

Afghanistan, Indian army in, 180; Islam in, 315; stirrup technology in, 319; urbanization in, 324

Africa, civilization spread in, 373; Indian army in, 180; Islam in, 372; Marxism in, 20; Portuguese trade and, 66, 433; slave trade from, 174, 433, 435; Western empires in, 172, 424; in world history study, xvi. *See also* East Africa; North Africa; South Africa; West Africa Age of Discovery, empires created during, 18; interdependence from, 397-99; Marco Polo as catalyst to, 8, 58-61; Mongol catalyst of, 56, 62; trade impact of, 65. *See also* Portuguese trade; *specific explorer; specific trading company*

Agriculture, Asian technology and, 30n. 2; in Bengal, India, 96-97; camel breeding and, 321-23; Champa rice and, 839-40; Columbian Exchange concept and, 435, 784-89, 795n. 12, 796n. 41, 825; cotton cultivation and, 812-13, 833, 855n. 3; domestication of animals and cereals and, 32-33, 217, 220-25, 230-31, 316, 813-14; in early Western Asia, 32-34; of Han Dynasty, 281-82; irrigation techniques and, 33-34; Japanese equal-field system of, 352-53, 355, 356; migration of people and, 230-31, 316, 320; plow technology and, 226, 233, 316; slash-and-burn agriculture and, 230, 231; sugar crystallization and, 814-15, 855n. 9; in Tokugawa Japan, 481-83, 508, 511, 752, 753-54; wet-rice cultivation and, 333-34,

Agriculture *(continued)*
337, 383, 695-96. *See also* Neolithic transition period; Nomadic migration; Pleistocene period; *specific country, civilization, period*

Aguinaldo, Emilio, 407

Ahura Mazda, Zoroastrian god of truth, 37, 271, 288-89, 290

Al-Jahiz, Amr ibn Bahr, 812, 815

Al-Khwarizmi, 48, 817

Albuquerque, Alfonso de, 67-68, 370, 832

Alexander the Great, Arrian on, 118; death of, 40, 41; "empire" components of, 267, 268, 311, 819; in India, 9, 15, 130, 275, 636; Persian Empire and, 271-72, 311

Alexandria, Hellenistic influence on, 40; Iranians in, 827; scientific figures in, 42, 50; trading center of, 671

Algeria, 29

Ali, Haider, 653

Almagest (Ptolemy), 50

Alphabet, Aramaic, 34; in early Western Asia, 32-34; Greek developments in, 35-36; Hebrew, 34, 36; Japanese, 684; Korean, 684; Phoenician, 34-36; proto-Canaanite script and, 35

Amboina, 75, 173

Ammonius Saccas, 41

Amoy, 106, 594

Amsterdam, 77

An Lushan Rebellion, 839

Analects (Confucius), "analects" definition and, 297; conversations contained in, 297; *junzi* (noble person) of, 301, 307n. 11; on learning, 298-99; on the living vs. the dead focus, 299-300; Mandate of Heaven in, 304-06, 317-18nn. 20, 23, 33; philosophical vs. religious classification of, 295-96, 300-301, 304-06, 307-08nn. 20, 23, 33; practicality of, 296, 297-98, 306, 308n. 33; on *ren* (humaneness), 302-03; Upanishads compared to, 295, 298, 300, 307n. 9; on *xiao* (filial devotion), 301-02

Enlightenment *(continued)*
nationalist movement and, 142; Indian impact on, 4; Orientalists vs. Westernizing reform writers of, 127; process of knowing and, 128-30; suggested readings on, 120-22. *See also specific writers*

Erastosthenes, 42

Erlitou culture (China), 246, 253

Essai sur les moeurs (Voltaire), 134

Estado da India, 68-69, 70

Ethiopia, gold trade and, 834, 857-58n. 58; India silk ports and, 819, 826; Indian army in, 180; Ottoman Turks in, 400; sugar cultivation in, 815

Euclid, 42, 817

Euphrates River. *See* Tigris and Euphrates River

Eurasia, 867; cross-Eurasian connections of, 8-9; as half the world, 13; independence of cultural spheres of, 9-11; labor divisions in, 458-59; landmass of, 7-8; territory of, xvi; in Western development, 11-13; in world history, 210. *See also* Europe: *specific time periods*; Neolithic transition period; Nomadic migration; *specific nations*

Eurocentricity, vs. Asiacentricity, xv-xvi, 664-65, 666-67

Europe: 1450-1700, age of discovery and, 397-98; expansion in Asia of, 398, 399-400, 424-35; Asian developments and, 400-402; Asia in modern world history and, 402; American contacts of, 433-35; economic system of, 430-31; labor force of, 434-35; nation-states development and, 431-32; social and ideological system of, 432-33; world division of labor and, 431. *See also* Western empires in Asia

Europe: 1700-1850, Asian trade imbalance and, 84-86, 374-75, 455; European migration and, 450; the Indian Ocean region and, 454-63; joint-stock company and, 446-48, 464n. 5; the North Atlantic region and, 448-50; overview of, 445-48; Portuguese trade and, 446; the South Atlantic region and, 450-54; trade and war strategy and, 448, 456; world economy of, 446-48, 458

Europe: 1750-1919, 1800s imperialism and, 5; economic transformation of, 398,

Europe: 1750-1919 *(continued)*
403-05; Asian developments and, 398-99, 405-11; democratic revolutions and, 404-05; Industrial Revolution and, 403-04

Europe: 1919-1992, global reshaping and, 399, 411-13; eclipse of, 413-15; Asian world reconstruction and, 399, 415-22

Evangelical Enlightenment writers (Westernizing), 122-23, 127, 128-29, 139-41

Exploration. *See* Age of Discovery

Extraterritoriality (China), 597

Ezana, king of Axum, 826

Fa Xian, 326, 821-22

Familial clans, 227, 776-77

Fascism, in Japan, 421, 563-64, 575-76, 577, 580-81

Fatimids, of North Africa, 828, 829, 833

Ferdinand, king of Spain, 5

Fertile Crescent. *See* Sumerian civilization

Feudalism, Crusades and, 17; in High Middle Ages, 374; in Japan, 356, 373, 391-92, 399, 475, 516-17, 740, 747; samurai of, 356

Fibonacci, Leonardo, 817

Finegan, Jack, 311

Fishing industry, 439

Five Dynasties (China), 337

Foochow, port of, 106

Formosa, 183, 574

Forster, E. M., 126

Foucault, Michel, 128

Four modernizations (China), 420

Four Noble Truths, of Buddhism, 291, 640-41

France, in Cambodia, 178; Dordogne caves in, 218; Dutch trade competition with, 73; Enlightenment writers from, 130-35; Indies trading company from, 92-93; in Indochina, 178, 407, 418; industrialization in, 459-60; Japanese ideology and citizenship compared to, 565; in Laos, 178; Meiji Restoration vs. French Revolution and, 566-67; Montesquieu on, 131-32; Napoleon III in, 177; Napoleonic Wars and, 97, 99, 101, 110, 176; nation-state system of, 431, 436n. 13, 569, 570; naval activities of, 108; North American trade of, 174;

Greece *(continued)*
287; India trade with, 9; legacy of movement and, 40; medicine and pharmacology of, 42; Mesopotamian impact on, 42-44; Montesquieu on, 121; nationalism in, 185; Neoplatonism of, 41-42; Pythagoras of, 309, 310; scientific traditions of, 42-44; secondary civilization of, 236; Stoic philosophy in, 41, 42; Sumerian roots of, 241; Turkish conflict with, 1 85; Western Asian role in, 15. *See also* Greco-Macedonian Empire; Greek civilization; Hellenistic Age

Greek civilization, Dorians, Ionians and, 260, 261; from Minoan culture, 258-59; Persian Empire and, 270-71; Platonic philosophy in, 263-64; states and nations formed in, 260-61, 262; Zhou Dynasty compared to, 257-64. *See also* Hellenistic Age

Guangzhou, English and French in, 177-78, 597; port of, 594, 597, 844

Gujarat, Delhi sultanate and, 645; English East India Company in, 94; Portuguese trade and, 67, 71, 87; trading port of, 370, 636

Gulf of Suez, 9

Gunpowder, 12, 17, 84, 336, 383, 429, 849-54, 859n. 102

Guomindang Party (China), Chiang Kai-shek and, 419, 601-02, 693; economic development and, 604; New Life Movement of, 579; Sun Yat-sen and, 419, 601, 693

Gupta Dynasty (India), 10, 276, 636, 643; crops cultivated in, 812-13, 814; cultural advancements of, 811-12; fall of, 318, 827; mathematic concepts of, 816, 838; in Southeast Asia, 367

Gutenberg, 849

Halhed, Nathaniel Brassey, 137, 141

Han Dynasty (China), 277; administrative bureaucracy of, 281, 691, 727; agricultural economy of, 281-82; civil service exam in, 716; decline of, 10-11, 318; expansion of, 282; gunpowder technology of, 849; Korea influenced by, 773; National University system of, 685; paper technology of, 11, 48, 318, 378, 380, 837, 840-42; Roman Empire

Han Dynasty (China) *(continued)*
and, 10, 691, 710; silk trade during, 321, 330, 691, 822. *See also* Qin-Han Dynasty

Hangzhou, 60, 384

Hapsburg empire, 400-401, 431

Harappan civilization, artifacts of, 243-44; in Baluchistan, 639; decline of, 244-45; "Indianized" culture of, 244, 245; language, writing system of, 245; Mohenjo-Daro urban site of, 243; Neolithic village farming roots of, 244; primary civilization of, 236; society of, 244-45, 250; technology of, 237, 244

Harsha, Indian prince, 827

Hastings, Warren, 135-36, 137

Hatta, Mohammed, 676

Hebrews, alphabet of, 34, 36; Hindu laws compared to, 137; Mesopotamian sources for, 287; Persian empire and, 270-71; Second Isaiah and, 309-10

Hegel, Georg Wilhelm Friedrich, Asian impact on, 4; Marx vs., 156-57, 160; on Oriental "spiritual" context, 146, 147, 149-56, 635, 664; on trade with India, 357-58; writings of, 124, 664

Heian (Kyoto), Japan, 354, 355

Heian period (Japan), 354-56, 390, 391-92, 686, 729-30, 739

Hellenistic Age, Asian influence on, 41-42; Byzantine Empire and, 41, 47-54; Christianity in, 44-46; in Indus Valley, 424; Islam and, 47-54; Neoplatonism of, 41-42; Persia impact on, 15; scientific traditions of, 42-44, 49-50; Stoic philosophy of, 41

Henan, 245, 246, 719

Henry the Navigator, 12, 66

Hephthalites, 16, 827

Heraclitus, 827

Herder, Johann Gottfried von, writings of, 123

Herodotus, on China, 9-10; Europe and Asia distinction of, 31; on Persian culture, 271; on Persian, Greek conflict, 6, 15, 147-48; writings of, 118, 128

Heterodoxy, in Qing Dynasty, 555-60

High Middle Ages, 17, 374

Hindu Kush Mountains, 268, 269, 276

Hinduism, *Analects* compared to, 297; *Bhagavad Gītā* and, 136, 137, 291;

Xanadu, 59

Xavier, Francis, 458, 761

Xenophon, 271

Xerxes, king of Greece, 271

Xi Jiang river valley, 690

Xi-xia kingdom (China), 333

Xia Dynasty (China), 245, 246; Neolithic period of, 252-53; Zhou Dynasty and, 257

Xiamen, 594

Xiangyang, battle of, 58

Xiao (filial devotion), 301-02

Xinjiang, 594, 595

Xiongnu tribal confederation, 23-24, 55, 277, 278, 282, 283, 319, 834

Xuanzang, 326

Xunzi, 702

Yangban of Korean society, 619, 627n. 1

Yangshao culture, 230-32

Yangtze River. See Yangzi River

Yangzhou, 58

Yangzi River, agriculture and, 278-79, 690, 713; early civilization on, 277, 278, 690; Grand Canal and, 257, 690; Neolithic period in, 252; population migration and, 337, 719; in Qing Dynasty, 595; urbanization along, 402

Yates, Robin, 850, 859n. 102

Yellow River valley. See Huang He River

Yelü Tashi, 57

Yemen, Byzantine-Ethiopian alliance against, 826; Ottoman Turks in, 400; sugar cultivation in, 815

Yi Dynasty (Korea), 618, 686

Yi Hwang, 774

Yi I, 774

Yi Jing, 153, 248

Yongle, emperor of Ming China, 387

Yongzheng emperor (China), 595

Yoshimune, shogun, 521

Yoshino Sakuzō, 577

Yuan Dynasty, inflation during, 339; Japanese trade in, 751; Mongol conquest during, 385, 691, 711

Yuan Shikai, 409

Yue Zhi tribal confederation, 277, 278

Zagros Mountains, agricultural development in, 32, 33; animal and cereal domestication in, 222-23; hunting-gathering lifestyle in, 219; Silk Road through, 320; Sumerian roots in, 240

Zaibatsu (Japan), 743, 754

Zen Buddhism, 394

Zeno of Citium, 41

Zhang Qian, 278, 387

Zhang Zhidong, 603

Zheng He, 386, 389n. 2, 402, 427, 428, 720-21, 830-31, 843

Zhou Dynasty (China), 245, 247-48, 249; ancient Greece compared to, 257-64; Confucius philosophy in, 248, 256, 262-64; Eastern Zhou Dynasty and, 281; Hua-Xia nation of, 260; Jiang people and, 258, 259; Mandate of Heaven concept in, 248, 255, 280-81, 308n. 23; religion roots in, 256; rise of, 257-58, 259; Shang Dynasty and, 255-56, 257, 259-60, 262; states and nations formed in, 259-60, 261-62; Western Zhou Dynasty and, 280-81

Zhou Enlai, 399

Zhu Jiang. See Pearl River

Zhu Xi, Neo-Confucianism of, 310, 348, 377, 384, 385, 386, 388

Zhu Yuanzhang, 386, 716

Zhuang Zi, 248

Zimbabwe, gold from, 834, 835, 837, 857-58n. 58; rise of, 373, 378

Zipangu. See Japan

Zoroaster, Zoroastrianism, 37, 154; Christianity and, 828; covenant myth of, 289; dualism in, 288-89, 290; in East Asia, 688; Manichaeism from, 327; in Persian Empire, 271, 309, 310, 311; Sanskrit Vedas and, 289-90; Semitic religion roots in, 288-91; Zoroaster's life, 288

Contributors

Peter J. Awn is professor of Islamic religion and comparative religion at Columbia University. His book, *Satan's Tragedy and Redemption: Iblis in Sufi Psychology* (1983), a study of the devil in Islamic mysticism (Sufism), was the recipient of a book award from the American Council of Learned Societies. Professor Awn has received numerous grants and conducted research in many parts of the Islamic world. He writes on medieval and modern Islam and Islam's interaction with the Christian West.

Richard A. Billows is associate professor of history at Columbia University and chair of the graduate program in classical studies. His research interests span classical Greece, the Hellenistic world, and republican Rome; and he has written two books on the Macedonian empire in western Asia of the late fourth to early first centuries B.C.E.: *Antigonos the One-Eyed and the Creation of the Hellenistic State* (1990), and *Kings and Colonists: Aspects of Macedonian Imperialism* (forthcoming).

Irene T. Bloom is chair of the department of Asian and Middle Eastern Cultures, Barnard College; Wm. Theodore and Fanny Brett de Bary and the Class of 1941 Collegiate Associate Professor to Asian Humanities, Columbia University; and program director of the Columbia University Committee on Asia and the Middle East. She is co-editor, with Wm. Theodore de Bary, of *Approaches to the Asian Classics* (1990) and has written and edited books and articles in the area of Chinese and comparative philosophy.

Richard W. Bulliet is professor of history at Columbia University and director of its Middle East Institute. He has written on Islamic social history—*Islam: The View from the Edge* (1994)— and history of technology—*The Camel and the Wheel* (1990)—and has participated in a number of projects in world history.

John W. Cell is professor of history at Duke University. His books include *British Colonial Administration in the Mid-nineteenth Century* (1970); *The Highest Stage of White Supremacy: The Origins of Segregation in South Africa and the American South* (1982); and *Hailey: A Study in British Imperialism, 1872–1969* (1992). He has taught both Western civilization and world history for many years.

Julia Ching, a specialist in Chinese philosophy and religion, teaches at the University of Toronto. She is a fellow of the Royal Society of Canada and author of *Christianity and Chinese Religions* (1989).

Myron L. Cohen is professor of anthropology at Columbia University where he is also affiliated with the East Asian Institute. He has done fieldwork in north, east, and west China, and in Taiwan. Professor Cohen is the editor of *Asia: Case Studies in the Social Sciences* (1992), a companion volume to this one. In addition, he is author of *House United, House Divided: The Chinese Family in Taiwan* (1976) and articles on Chinese family organization, kinship and community relations, religion, social change, and national identity.

Michael Cooper was editor of *Monumenta Nipponica*, Sophia University, Tokyo, 1971–97. He is the author or editor of *They Came to Japan* (1965, 1981); *Rodrigues the Interpreter* (1974); and *This Island of Japon* (1973).

Ainslie T. Embree is Professor Emeritus of History at Columbia University and former chairman of the department of history. He was associate dean and acting dean of the School of Public and International Affairs. He taught history in India from 1948 to 1958 and at Duke University from 1969 to 1972. He was cultural counsellor at the American Embassy in Delhi, 1978–1980. He was president at the American Institute of Indian Studies and of the Association for Asian Studies. His books include *India's Search for Identity* (1988); *Imagining India* (1989); and *Utopias in Conflict* (1990). He edited *Pakistan's Western Borderlands* (1977); *Encyclopedia of Asian History* (1988); and *Sources of Indian Tradition* (1988).

Theopolis Fair is department chair and associate professor of history at La Salle University. He is author of articles on returned colonials in Spain (indianos) and in Great Britain (nabobs).

The late **Walter A. Fairservis** was professor emeritus of anthropology at Vassar College where he was chairman of the department of anthropology for many years and also established a department of Japanese studies. His publications include *The Origins of Oriental Civilization* (1959); *The Roots of Ancient India* (1975); *The Threshold of Civilization: An Experiment in Prehistory* (1975); and *Asia, Traditions and Treasures* (1981).

Joshua A. Fogel is professor of history at the University of California, Santa Barbara. He is the author of *Politics and Sinology: The Case of Naitō Konan* (1984); *Ai Ssu-ch'i's Contribution to the Development of Chinese Marxism* (1987); and *Nakae Ushikichi in China: The Mourning of Spirit* (1989). He is translator of nine volumes and is presently completing a manuscript entitled "The Literature of Travel in the Japanese Rediscovery of China, 1862–1945." He is also editor of the journal *Sino-Japanese Studies*.

Carol Gluck is George Sansom Professor of Japanese History at Columbia University. She is author of *Japan's Modern Myths: Ideology in the Late Meiji Period* (1985) and co-editor of *Showa: The Japan of Hirohito* (1992).

Harvey Goldman is professor of sociology at the University of California, San Diego. He is the author of two books on German social thought and culture, *Max Weber and Thomas Mann: Calling and the Shaping of Self* (1988) and *Politics, Death, and the Devil: Self and Power in Max Weber and Thomas Mann* (1992).

Leonard A. Gordon is professor of history at Brooklyn College and at the Graduate Center of the City University of New York. He is the author of *Bengal: The Nationalist Movement, 1876–1940* (1974), awarded the Watumull Prize by the American Historical Association, 1974, and of *Brothers against the Raj: A Biography of Indian Nationalists Sarat and Subhas Chandra Bose* (1990). A senior research associate of the Southern Asian Institute, Columbia University, he is also director of the Taraknath Das Foundation.

William B. Hauser is professor of history at the University of Rochester. His publications include *Economic Institutional Change in Tokugawa Japan: Osaka and the Kinai Cotton Trade* (1974) and *The Bakufu in Japanese History* (1985), edited with Jeffrey P. Mass, as well as articles on Tokugawa social and economic history and on Japanese film images of the Pacific War.

Cho-yun Hsu is University Professor of History at the University of Pittsburgh. His publications include *Ancient China in Transition* (1965); *Bibliographic Notes on Studies of Early China* (1982); *Western Chou Civilization* (with Kathryn M. Linduff) (1988); *Han Agriculture: The Formation of Early Chinese Agrarian Economy, 206 B.C. - A.D. 220* (1980).

Robert Hymes, professor of Chinese history at Columbia University, specializes in the social and cultural history of China's middle period. He is the author of *Statesmen and Gentlemen: The Local Elite of Fu-chou, Chiang-hsi, in Northern and Southern Sung* (1986) and coeditor with Conrad Schirokauer of *Ordering the World: Approaches to State and Society in Sung Dynasty China* (1993). He has worked on marriage and lineage organization, on the social place of physicians, on ideas of commerce and political economy, and is currently completing a book on local Taoist saints' cults, exorcist sects, and competing models of human-divine relations in Chinese religion.

Hermann Kulke is professor of history at the Südasien-Institut, Heidelberg. His publications include *History of India*, with Dietmar Rothermund (1986); *Katakarajavamsavali: A Traditional History of Orissa with Special Reference to Jagannatha Temple* (1987); co-editor, with Gunther D. Sontheimer, *Hinduism Reconsidered* (1989).

Loyd E. Lee is professor of history at the State University of New York, the College at New Paltz. He has published in nineteenth century German history and is the author of *The War Years: A Global History of the Second World War* (1989) and editor of *World War II: Crucible of the Contemporary World, Commentary and Readings* (1991).

David Lelyveld is the author of *Aligarh's First Generation: Muslim Solidarity in British India* (1978) and articles in *Modern Asian Studies, Comparative Studies in Society and History*, and other journals. He was the South Asia editor of *The Encyclopedia of Asian History* (1988) and is currently the South Asian section editor of the American Historical Association's *Guide to Historical Literature*. He has taught at Columbia University, the University of Washington, and the University of Minnesota. His current research deals with problems of language standardization and ethnic conflict in modern South Asia.

Derek S. Linton is associate professor of history at Hobart and William Smith College where he teaches European and world history. He is the author of *Who Has the Youth, Has the Future: The Campaign to Save Young Workers in Imperial Germany* (1991) and a number of articles which have appeared in the *Journal of Interdisciplinary History, European History Quarterly* and *History of Education* among others. He is presently writing a book on public health, bacteriology and the diffusion of hygienic practices in Imperial Germany.

Edward Malefakis, who also previously taught at Northwestern University and the University of Michigan, has been professor of modern European history at Columbia University since 1975. Author of *Agrarian Reform and Peasant Revolution in Spain* (1970) and of numerous articles, editor of *Indalecio Prieto* (1975) and *La Guerra de Espana* (1986), he is presently working on a comparative history of Southern Europe since 1800. Also interested in non-European affairs, he has intermittently taught courses in world history since 1972.

Michael Marmé is assistant professor of history at the College at Lincoln Center, Fordham University. Specializing in the social and economic history of imperial China, he is author of "Heaven on Earth: Suzhou, 1127–1550" in L. C. Johnson, ed., *The City in Late Imperial Jiangnan* (1993) and of *Where the Goods of All the Provinces Converge: Suzhou in Early and Mid-Ming* (forthcoming).

Morris David Morris is Professor Emeritus of Sociology at Brown University and Professor Emeritus of Economics at the University of Washington. His publications include *The Emergence of an Industrial Labor Force in India: A Study of the Bombay Cotton Mills, 1854–1947* (1965) and, with Michelle B. McAlpin, *Measuring the Condition of India's Poor* (1982).

Rhoads Murphey is professor emeritus of history at the University of Michigan where he is also director of the Center for South and Southeast Asia. He is a past president of the Association for Asian Studies, has done extensive fieldwork in South and East Asia, and was a recent visiting scholar at Oxford University. His many publications include *China Meets the West: The Treaty Ports* (1975); *The Outsiders: Westerners in India and China* (1977); and *A History of Asia* (1992).

Willard G. Oxtoby, professor in the study of religion at the University of Toronto, is a specialist of the Middle East before Islam. He has served (1991–93) as president of the American Society for the Study of Religion, and is completing two volumes on world religions for Oxford University Press.

Michael E. Robinson is professor of history at Indiana University where he teaches courses on Korean history and civilization. He is author of *Cultural Nationalism in Colonial Korea* (1988) and co-author of a commonly used text on Korean history, *Korea Old and New: A History* (1990). He is currently researching the origins of popular culture in Korea during the inter-war period.

Morris Rossabi is professor of Chinese and Central Asian history at the City University of New York. He is the author of *Khublai Khan* (1988), *Voyager for Xanadu* (1992), and of chapters in three volumes of the *Cambridge History of China* as well as other works.

Dietmar Rothermund, professor of history and head of the department of history, Sudasien-Institute, Heidelberg, is author of *The German Intellectual Quest for India* (1986); *An Economic History of India: From the Precolonial Period to 1986* (1988); *Emporia Commodities and Entrepreneurs in Asian Maritime Trade, c. 1400–1750* (1991). He has also co-authored works with Hermann Kulke, listed above.

William T. Rowe is professor of history at the Johns Hopkins University. His publications include *Hankow: Commerce and Society in a Chinese City, 1796–1889* (1984), *Hankow: Conflict and Community in a Chinese City, 1796–1895* (1989), and several articles on the thought and policy of the eighteenth-century Chinese official Chen Hongmou.

George Saliba is professor of Arabic and Islamic science at Columbia University. He has published several books and scores of articles dealing with Arabic science and technology and Arabic history. His most recent book, *A History of Arabic Astronomy: Planetary Theories During the Golden Years of Islam* (1993) is a survey of the Arabic planetary theories that were developed in Islamic lands between the eleventh and fifteenth centuries which were critical of the Greek astronomical tradition.

Lynda Norene Shaffer is associate professor of history at Tufts University where she teachers Chinese history. Since 1982, she has also taught courses in world history and Native American history. Her publications include *Mao and the Workers: The Hunan Labor Movement, 1920–23* (1982) and *Native Americans Before 1492: Moundbuilding Centers of the Eastern Woodlands* (1992).

Henry D. Smith, II is professor of Japanese history at Columbia University and specializes in the history of visual and urban culture in modern Japan. He is author of *Hiroshige, One Hundred Famous Views of Edo* (1986), *Kiyochika: Artist of Meiji Japan* (1988), and the editor of *Learning from SHOGUN: Japanese History and Western Fantasy* (1980).

Peter N. Stearns is Heinz Professor of History and Dean, College of Humanities and Social Sciences, at Carnegie Mellon University. He has written widely on issues in social and in world history, including the co-authored text, *World Civilizations: The Global Experience* (1992). He has served in a number of world history panels and policy groups, including co-chairmanship of the College Board's Pacesetter world history project, and he regularly teaches a freshman world history course.

David J. Steinberg is president of Long Island University. He is editor and a co-author of *In search of Southeast Asia* (1987). His book, *Philippine Collaboration in World War II*, won the University of Michigan Press Award in 1969. The third edition of *The Philippines: A Singular and a Plural Place* (1993) is an extended essay on his central historical area of interest.

Marc Van De Mieroop, associate professor in the departments of the Middle East languages and cultures and of history at Columbia University, studies the social and economic history of the Ancient Near East. His latest book is *Society and Enterprise in Old Babylonian Ur* (1992).

H. Paul Varley is professor of history at the University of Hawaii. His books include *Japanese Culture* (Third Edition 1984) and *Tea in Japan, Essays on the History of Chanoyu* (1989, coedited with Kumakura Isao). His most recent book is *Warriors of Japan, As Portrayed in the War Tales* (1994).

Frederic Wakeman, Jr. is the Haas Professor of Asian Studies and director of the Institute of East Asian Studies at the University of California, Berkeley. His publications include *Strangers at the Gate* (1966), *The Fall of Imperial China* (1975), and *The Great Enterprise* (1985). During 1986–1989 he served as president of the Social Science Research Council, and in 1992 he was president of the American Historical Association.

Marilyn B. Young received her Ph.D from Harvard University and is a professor of history at New York University. Her books include *The Rhetoric of Empire: American China Policy 1895–1901* (1969) and *Transforming Russia and China: Revolutionary Struggle in the Twentieth Century*, with William Rosenberg (1982). Her most recent publication is *The Vietnam Wars: 1945–1990* (1991).

Madeleine Zelin is professor of history and East Asian languages and cultures at Columbia University and director of the East Asian Institute. Her book, *The Magistrate's Tael* (1984) was the recipient of the Lilienthal Prize. In recent years Professor Zelin has written numerous articles on Chinese economic development, business history and civil law. She has also translated Mao Dun's novel, *Rainbow* (1992).